Strategic Management in the Global Economy

Third Edition

Heidi Vernon-Wortzel

Northeastern University

Lawrence H. Wortzel

Boston University

JOHN WILEY & SONS, INC.

New York   Chichester   Brisbane   Toronto   Sing.

Lawrence H. Wortzel died in February 1996, shortly after this book was completed. He will be remembered for his deep devotion to family, students, and colleagues, his prodigious intellect, his amazingly eclectic range of interests, and for his uniquely clever sense of humor.

ACQUISITIONS EDITOR: Ellen Ford
DESIGNER: Harry Nolan
MARKETING MANAGER: Leslie Hines
PRODUCTION EDITOR: Melanie Henick
MANUFACTURING OPERATIONS DIRECTOR: Susan Stetzer
ASSISTANT MANUFACTURING MANAGER: Mark Cirillo
COVER PHOTOGRAPH: David Rigg/Tony Stone Images
ILLUSTRATION COORDINATOR: Anna Melhorn

This book was set in Times Roman by Achorn Graphics and
printed and bound by Donnelley/Crawfordsville. The cover was printed by Lehigh Press.

Library of Congress Cataloging in Publication Data:

Strategic management in the global economy / [compiled] by Heidi
  Vernon-Wortzel, Lawrence H. Wortzel. — 3rd ed.
      p. cm.
    Rev. ed. of: Global strategic management. c1990.
    Includes bibliographical references.
    ISBN 0-471-15873-9 (pbk. : alk. paper)
    1. International business enterprises—Management.
  2. International business enterprises—Planning. 3. Strategic
  planning. 4. International economic relations. I. Vernon-Wortzel,
  Heidi, 1938– II. Wortzel, Lawrence H. III. Global strategic
  management.
  HD62.4.V483 1997
  658.4'012—dc20   96-8695
                                                        CIP

Printed in the United States of America

10 9 8 7 6 5 4 3 2 1

PREFACE

Managers no longer think the boundaries of their business world begin and end in their own home country. Whether based in New York, Washington, D.C., Sao Paolo, Paris, or Tokyo, over the last decade managers have become increasingly sophisticated in assessing worldwide opportunities and threats. Foreign competition inside home markets has steadily increased as has foreign investment through mergers, joint ventures, and greenfield startups.

Observing the U.S. situation, Robert B. Reich predicted that by the year 2010 a majority of Americans would be working directly or indirectly for global entities that have no particular nationality. The issue of nationality continues to be less and less important. Companies of all nationalities serve global customers. In the mid-1990s, Unilever PLC, the Anglo-Dutch consumer products giant, sold its ice cream, detergent, and beauty aids all over the industrialized world and did extremely well in developing countries such as Brazil, China, and India. Moet Hennessy Louis Vuitton, the French champagne, perfume, and luggage company, recorded huge profits from its exports. Asian consumers snapped up the company's expensive luxury products. Samsung, the South Korean conglomerate, became a highly significant force in the global market for microprocessor chips.

Reflecting this global view, Coca Cola Company was the first major U.S. business to eliminate the concept of ''domestic'' and ''international.'' In January 1996, Coke announced a basic shift in its world view by downgrading its U.S. business to just one of six international business units in the company's geographical regions. As an analyst noted, Coke could now adopt the song ''We Are the World'' as its corporate motto.[1]

American managers, like their European and Japanese counterparts, have become more and more sophisticated in searching for, identifying, and capitalizing on overseas ventures. Restrictive national legislation at home and abroad is diminishing. National borders and protectionist legislation provide few barriers to investments, mergers, acquisitions, and takeovers.

Companies are looking to global markets and even undertaking dramatic reorganization to become globally more competitive. U.S. telecommunications giant AT&T, for example, announced its plan to split into three parts: a communications services company; a computer company; and a communications equipment company. To be sure, there were domestically competitive reasons for this dramatic move but increasing the

---

[1] Glenn Collins, ''Coke Drops 'Domestic' and Goes One World,'' *New York Times,* January 13, 1996, p. 35.

company's global competitiveness was a key factor in the split-up. The new entities would allow AT&T to offer products to the entire global communications industry. Under the new structure AT&T proposed to build and launch a multibillion-dollar global satellite network. This move would take the Internet into outer space. AT&T's traditional use of fiber optics, undersea cable, copper wires, and land-based communication switches would be augmented by a network of satellites relying on spacecraft positioned around the earth. Each of the 12 satellites would have a data-carrying capacity of 1 billion bits of information per second and could serve 10 million customers worldwide.

U.S. firms and foreign subsidiaries based in the United States are recognized global opportunities and experiencing substantial growth. In 1994, these companies increased their combined overseas shipments 8 percent to $151 billion. The largest portion of exports, about 55 percent, went to the industrialized markets in Europe, Canada, and Japan. Other Asian markets are booming as consumer demand increases for a wide variety of products and services. DRI/McGraw-Hill forecasts that Asia's market for imports will reach $564 billion in 1995 and growth will average 12 percent annually over the next five years.[2]

Asia continues to make substantial progress in slashing tariffs, deregulating financial sectors, and opening former monopolies to foreign and local investors. The members of the Association of South East Asia Nations (ASEAN) are making progress toward a common market of 420 million people. Indonesia, Singapore, Thailand, the Philippines, Malaysia, Vietnam, and Brunei have already agreed to push for the year 2003 as their deadline for slashing tariffs on manufactured goods to no more than 5 percent.

The 18 members of Asia-Pacific Economic Cooperation (APEC) include the world's three largest national economies: the United States, Japan, and China. Talks among members have resulted in a commitment to substantial trade facilitation and liberalization. Although members have different political and ideological agendas, plans to implement liberalization measures will begin in January 1997. No doubt problems and difficulties will occur, but most observers think there is good reason to believe that Asian regional trade organizations will be successful.

Asian businesses, taking advantage of the new environment, are becoming global players. Many Japanese companies and some Korean companies are already industrial giants. The new Asian entrants into the global marketplace are overseas Chinese conglomerates. Many are forming strategic alliances with global companies to gain access to higher levels of technology and expertise. In the near future, these traditional family-run companies will need huge numbers of professional managers who can straddle the Asian and Western cultures. Many of the new managers will be U.S.-educated family members who know the value of professionalizing management, sticking with core businesses, and remaining entrepreneurial.

European companies will take advantage of continued European integration and incorporation of new members into the European Union (EU). The move toward a single currency, while still difficult and moving forward in fits and starts, should be resolved by the year 2000. Eastern European integration is likely to continue as free market principles are pursued.

---

[2] James Aley, ''New Life for the U.S. Export Boom,'' *Fortune,* November 13, 1995, p. 73.

European officials are taking aggressive steps to forge new alliances. In November 1995, they approved initial work leading to a new Trans-Atlantic Free Trade Agreement with the United States. The EU already provides more than half of all foreign direct investment in the United States, while more than 40 percent of U.S. overseas investment is in Europe.[3] Europeans are looking to develop new global markets wherever opportunities occur.

The Mexican monetary crisis and peso devaluation put a temporary damper on enthusiasm for NAFTA. But by 1996, U.S. companies found that they had suffered very little, if at all. Most companies managed to find other markets for products that would have been sold in Mexico. A few companies were even able to take advantage of the weak peso that made their products cheaper abroad. Before the devaluation, Eastman Kodak had exported nearly two-thirds of the film, floppy disks, cameras, and camera parts it made in Guadalajara. After the devaluation, Kodak increased exports to 85 percent. Compaq Computer offset a decline in Mexican sales with gains in other Latin American markets.[4]

Almost no one feels that NAFTA has lived up to the expectations of its most vocal supporters. Although tariffs between the United States and Mexico have been slashed, large numbers of jobs in the United States and Mexico have not materialized. However, Mexico has accelerated the sale of government-owned railroads, airports, and the oil monopoly. Mexico has also liberalized its foreign investment law so that U.S. companies are now major players in banking, telecommunications, and other important parts of the economy.[5]

New Latin American players have emerged. Brazil, Argentina, Uruguay, and Paraguay together account for 70 percent of South America's total gross domestic product. Their new trade agreement, Mercosur, is working toward eliminating most tariffs. The European Union, hoping to offset sluggish demand at home, is pressing for a free trade agreement with Mercosur by 2005. Chile, whose incorporation into NAFTA is still pending, signed a separate free trade agreement with Mexico and is wooing Japanese investors. Some observers worry that U.S. businesses will lose opportunities in an environment where others are taking a more active role.

The challenges for global managers are immense as the next millenium approaches. The development of the World Trade Organization and the reduction of trade barriers creates a new trade environment for everyone. Advances in telecommunication and global information integration offer unlimited and currently unforeseeable opportunities. Mergers and acquisitions across national boundaries reduce national cultures and identities. New global competitors merge as former competitors decline.

In the last edition of this book we focused on U.S. corporations and competitiveness. We noted that global corporate restructuring and a ferociously competitive international environment made it imperative that managers develop new skills and new global per-

---

[3] Kyle Pope and Robert S. Greenberger, "Europe Seeks Trade Pact with U.S. Similar to Nafta," *Wall Street Journal,* November 27, 1995, p. A14.

[4] "Many U.S. Companies in Mexico Escape Serious Damage from Economic Woes," *The Wall Street Journal,* September 22, 1995, p. A10.

[5] Anthony DePalma, "For Mexico, Nafta's Promise of Jobs Is Still Just a Promise," *New York Times,* October 10, 1995, p. A1.

spectives. We observed that the business functions—marketing, production, finance, and R&D—would be more complex to manage and more difficult to control.

Today's global managers are concerned with *multiculturalism.* The notion is that as the world's centers of economic activity are becoming more dispersed, global companies should choose board members and senior managers who broaden their perspective. Multiculturalism includes more than awareness of other cultures. It incorporates global standards of diversity, ethics, environmentalism, and quality. It requires global managers to acquire new perspectives and skills.

We have changed the title of this edition of the book to reflect its global orientation. We have tried to eliminate ethnocentricity in the readings and introductory essays. Although the two previous editions have had some carryover in readings, we decided to keep only three selections from the previous edition. We have responded to the comments of faculty and students who told us what was valuable and what we could do better. The readings in this edition are very current. They reflect our commitment to application and to helping students develop real global management skills for the remaining years of this century.

We designed this book to give upper-level undergraduates and M.B.A. students a firm grasp of issues central to the management of global corporations and new ventures. Instructors will find they can use these readings in lieu of a textbook or in combination with internationally focused cases. We are grateful to our editors Petra Sellers and Ellen Ford, production editor Melanie Henick, illustration coordinator Anna Melhorn, marketing manager Leslie Hines, and to colleagues who reviewed the previous edition and this manuscript and who provided valuable comments in the development of the third edition. These include: Douglas Ross, Towson State University, Bruce McKern, Carnegie Mellon University, Len Trevino, University of Miami, Charles Toftoy, George Washington University, Elizabeth Rozell, Missouri Southern State University, Mingfang Li, California State University Northridge, and Stanley Slater, University of Colorado.

CONTENTS

GLOBAL FIRMS AND THE GLOBAL ENVIRONMENT

Multinational and global firms have been part of the world economic landscape for some years. They have been increasing in numbers, in diversity of industry, and in countries of origin. Foreign, multinational, and global corporations affect the prospects of domestic firms and industries and, increasingly, the prospects of nation-states. Events and competitors in the Taiwanese personal computer industry, the Italian pasta industry, and the Brazilian shoe industry can have a significant impact on the fortunes of those countries and their counterpart industries in many other countries. In this section of the book, we will look at the history and growth of multinationals and their relations with governments.

READING SELECTIONS

Raymond Vernon (who prefers to use *multinational* rather than *global* in labeling these firms) points out that in the 1950s they were primarily of American origin. By the mid-1990s every industrialized country and many industrializing countries as well had spawned their own multinationals. Multinationals had become dominant in many industries.

In his article, Vernon traces the history of the multinationals, identifying key changes in their behavior as they have grown and matured. Vernon's analysis compares and contrasts American, European, and Japanese firms on several dimensions, for example: the headquarters–subsidiary relationship typical of firms from each of the three countries; their growth paths, such as the extent to which growth came from mergers versus the establishment of greenfield subsidiaries; and the motivations for expanding outside their home countries.

Vernon observes that the characteristics of product markets have become more important in shaping these firms' behavior, while national origin has become a less powerful factor. He notes the differences evident in firms of various national origins in their earlier years as multinationals. These differences seem to diminish in importance as firms gain experience in the global market. We might well ask whether competing in the same markets makes disparate firms more alike. Is the world economy a melting pot in which national origin is a matter of diminishing importance in understanding a firm's behavior? Or, on the contrary, will a firm's national origin continue to influence its behavior?

Vernon identifies key factors that should affect the future of the multinationals. He notes that, whether through alliances or through their own networks, multinationals will continue to grow in importance. He is especially interested in the responses national governments can make to firms that are attuned primarily to market opportunities and that are less concerned about the national interests of the countries in which they operate. The power of national governments to control multinational firms, he believes, has been declining.

Henry Wai-Chung Yeung introduces us to some important new players in the global environment: transnational firms from Asian developing countries. He argues that the usual label for these firms, *Third-world multinationals,* is ideologically biased. Yeung prefers to call these new players *transnational corporations* (TNCs). TNCs, Yeung points out, are a very diverse group, encompassing both public and private-sector firms. They are becoming the largest foreign investors in other developing countries.

Yeung goes on to analyze TNCs on several important dimensions, *inter alia,* market entry form and ownership patterns, parent–subsidiary relationships, capital and funding sources, choice of technology, methods of production and marketing, foreign trade orientation, and locational choice. It would be a worthwhile exercise for readers to compare the developing countries' TNCs on as many dimensions as possible with the multinationals from the United States, Europe, and Japan as analyzed in Vernon's article.

Yeung also points out the important role of Asian national governments in influencing the behavior of their firms. In both South Korea and Taiwan, the government targeted specific ''strategic'' industries for development, designing and implementing policies aimed at enhancing their development as global competitors rather than domestic industries. The article concludes with some speculation about the future of these developing-country TNCs. It is interesting to compare Yeung's and Vernon's predictions to try and develop some sense of how an increasingly diverse group of multinational firms will fare into the next century.

Morss and Stopford each examine the role of nation states in a new environment populated by myriad multinational firms, international organizations, and special-interest groups that transcend national borders. Morss sees a trend from collaboration between national entities within national borders to a variety of collaborative arrangements that transcend borders. He presents several examples of such collaborations and concludes that firms are losing their national identities and nation states are losing their ability to control world events. He argues that the power lost by nation states will be taken up by international organizations that are increasingly independent of the countries that may have spawned them. Special-interest groups, he also argues, will exert their influence globally rather than nationally.

Stopford believes partnerships between nations and firms are possible, with potential benefits to both sides. He notes the increasing economic interdependence among nation-states resulting from foreign direct investment. He sees a world in which three forces determine how the benefits of economic activity are allocated: firms competing for a share of the global market; governments competing for the perceived benefits that firms' activities can bring to their nations; and bargaining between firms and national governments. In Stopford's world, the nation-state is very much alive and, together with its business firms, can forge policies that are of benefit to both.

As readers study subsequent sections on corporate strategies and national government strategies, they should keep in mind the analyses presented in these four articles. Readers should develop an understanding of the content of business and government strategies. They should build, at the same time, an understanding of the areas in which there may be opportunities for confluence and where conflicts are likely to arise.

1

WHERE ARE THE MULTINATIONALS HEADED?

RAYMOND VERNON

Four decades ago, the multinational enterprise was widely regarded as a peculiarly American form of business organization, a manifestation of the existence of a pax Americana. Today, every industrialized country provides a base for a considerable number of multinationals, which collectively are becoming the dominant form of organization responsible for the international exchange of goods and services. Indeed, by the end of the 1980s, even the larger firms in some of the rapidly industrializing countries of Asia and Latin America had joined the trend (UN Commission on Transnational Corporations 1990; Lall 1991).

For scholars who want to understand the factors affecting international trade in goods and services, these changes are of consummate importance. In the past, whenever the international behavior of multinationals appeared at odds with a world regulated by comparative advantage and capital market theory, the deviation could be treated as idiosyncratic, the basis for a footnote in passing. But today, with multi-

nationals dominating the international traffic in goods and services, the question of what determines their behavior takes on considerable significance.

I cannot pretend to provide a definitive answer to this central question in the pages that follow; that is a labor which will take many minds over an extended period of time. But I have two goals in mind which contribute to that central task. The first is to persuade the reader that explanations of the behavior of multinational enterprise which draw on the national origins of the enterprise as a major explanatory variable are rapidly losing their value, to be replaced by an increased emphasis on the characteristics of the product markets in which the enterprises participate. The second is to plant a few ideas regarding the motivations and responses of the multinational enterprise that I believe must figure in any rounded explanation of the behavior of these enterprises in the various product markets they face.

U.S. FIRMS ASCENDANT

The sudden growth of U.S.-based multinational networks after World War II was in fact some time in the making. Many decades earlier, the first signs that

The author is indebted to Ernest Chung and Subramanian Rangan for their research support in preparing this paper and to Richard Caves and Lawrence H. Wortzel for their incisive comments on an earlier draft.

large enterprises might find themselves pushed to develop a multinational structure were already beginning to appear. Setting the stage for the development of these multinational networks were the dramatic improvements in the technologies of transportation and communication, coupled with the vastly increased opportunities for scale economies in industrial production. Operating with high fixed costs and low variable costs, a new crop of industrial giants felt especially vulnerable to the risks of price competition. And by the beginning of the twentieth century, these risks were beginning to be realized; the country's industrial leaders, including firms in machinery, metalworking, and chemicals, were coming into bruising contact not only with rivals from the United States but also with some from Europe.

Facing what they perceived to be dangerous and destructive competition, the leaders in many U.S. industries went on the defensive. By the beginning of the century, many of the new industries of the country had organized themselves in restrictive market-sharing arrangements and were reaching out to their European competitors to join agreements that were global in scope.

From the first, however, it was apparent that these restrictive arrangements were fragile responses to the threat of competition, especially for firms based in the United States (Hexner 1945; Stocking and Watkins 1946; 1948). The diversity and scope of the U.S. economy, coupled with a hostile legal environment, made it difficult for U.S. leaders to stifle the appearance of new firms inside the country; those same factors put a brake on the leaders' engaging in overt collusion with European rivals. Nevertheless, global market-sharing agreements persisted at times, especially when patents and trademarks provided a fig leaf for the participants. By and large, though, the role of U.S. firms in these restrictive arrangements was cautious and restrained.

While participating in the international division of markets in a number of products before World War II, many large firms also established the first of their subsidiaries in foreign locations during that period. Commonly, however, large firms used these subsidiaries to implement their restrictive agreements with other firms, as in the case of the Du Pont–ICI subsid-

iaries located in Latin America. Often, too, firms established such subsidiaries as cautionary moves against the possibility that competitors might be in a position to cut them off from raw materials in times of shortage or from markets in times of glut. U.S. firms that were engaged in extracting and processing raw materials, for instance, typically developed vertically integrated structures that covered the chain from wellhead or mine shaft to the final distribution of processed products; and because other leading firms shared the same fear, partnerships among rivals commonly appeared at various points in these vertical chains, in the form of jointly owned oil fields, mines, and processing facilities. Meanwhile, other U.S. firms, such as General Motors, Ford, and General Electric, established subsidiaries in Europe, to serve as bridgeheads in the event of warfare among industry leaders. Such bridgeheads, consistent with their function, were usually allowed to operate with considerable independence and autonomy (Chandler 1990, 38–45, 205–33; Wilkins and Hill 1964, 360–79; Wilkins 1970, 93–96).

For a decade or two after World War II, the defensive responses of U.S.-based firms to their perceived risks in world markets were a little less in evidence. The reasons were too obvious to require much comment. The proverbial "animal spirits" of U.S. business were already at an elevated level as a result of the technological lead and financial advantages that U.S. firms enjoyed over their European rivals. Dramatic advances in communication and transportation were enlarging the stage on which those spirits could be released. The real cost of those services was rapidly declining; and with the introduction of containerized freight, airborne deliveries, and the telex, the range of those services was widening. These improvements expanded the business horizons of U.S.-based firms, allowing them to incorporate more distant locations in the marketing of their products and the sourcing of their needed inputs.

The first reaction of most U.S. firms to their expanding product markets was to meet demands by increasing exports from the home base. But, as numerous case studies attest, the establishment of local producing subsidiaries soon followed. Almost all of the first wave of manufacturing subsidiaries established in foreign countries after World War II were dedicated principally to serving the local markets in which they were placed.[1] As a consequence, about four-fifths of the sales of such subsidiaries during the 1960s were directed to local markets (Lipsey and Kravis 1982, 3).

The motives of the firms in serving local markets through producing subsidiaries rather than through exports were usually complex. In some cases, for instance, the establishment of a producing subsidiary was simply perceived as a more efficient means for serving the foreign market, a consequence of the fact that sales in the market had achieved a level sufficient to exploit the existing economies of scale in production. But other factors contributed to the scope and timing of these decisions as well. There were indications, for instance, that the decisions taken to establish subsidiaries abroad, whether for the marketing of products or for the production of required materials and components, were often reactive measures, stimulated by and intended as a hedge against some perceived threat. Once a U.S. firm lost its unique technological or marketing lead, as seemed inevitable in most products over the course of time, governments might be tempted to restrict imports in order to encourage domestic production. In that case, the foreign subsidiary served to protect existing market access.

But even without the threat of action by governments, U.S.-based firms frequently faced threats posed by rivals in the product markets in which they operated. And some rich anecdotal evidence strongly suggests that foreign subsidiaries were often created as a hedge against such threats.

That hypothesis may help to explain why, in the first few decades after World War II, U.S.-based firms were engaged in follow-the-leader behavior in the establishment of new producing subsidiaries abroad. Once a U.S.-based firm in an oligopolistically structured industry set up a producing subsidiary in a given country, the propensity of other U.S.-

based firms in the oligopoly to establish a subsidiary in the same country was visibly heightened (Knickerbocker 1973, 22–27; Yu and Ito 1988, 449–60). Such a pattern, of course, does not conclusively demonstrate that the follower is responding defensively to the behavior of the leader. Alternative hypotheses also need to be entertained, such as the possibility that both follower and leader were responding to a common outside stimulus or that the follower was responding in the belief that the leader had done a rational analysis equally applicable to both their situations.

However, stimulated by my reading of various individual cases, I am strongly inclined to attribute such follow-the-leader behavior in many cases to the follower's desire to hedge a threat posed by the leader. Although the follower may be unsure whether the leader has properly analyzed the costs and benefits of its move in establishing a foreign subsidiary, the follower is understandably fearful of allowing a rival to enjoy the benefits of undisturbed exploitation of its foreign opportunities. As long as the number of rival producers in the market is small, therefore, following the leader often seems to entail smaller downside risks than failing to follow. Failing to follow a leader that was right in making its move would give that leader an unrivaled opportunity to increase its competitive strength, whether by increasing its marketing opportunities or by reducing its production costs; if the leader was wrong, the follower's risks from committing the same error would be limited by the leader's having shared in it.

If the hedging of a threat was sometimes necessary for the growth of U.S.-based multinational enterprises, however, it was certainly not sufficient for such growth. Still to be explained was why in so many cases U.S.-based firms chose to establish producing subsidiaries rather than to exploit their strengths through licensing or other contractual arrangements with a local firm. In some cases, the high transaction costs associated with searching out and dealing with local firms may provide an adequate explanation. But here too, I am inclined to put heavy weight on explanations that see the establishment of a subsidiary in part as a hedge against various risks. Whenever licensing agreements are negotiated, both

---

[1] Even as late as 1975, about two-thirds of the manufacturing subsidiaries of U.S.-based firms were engaged almost exclusively in serving their local markets (Curhan, Davidson, and Suri, 1977, 393).

parties face the uncertainties generated by asymmetrical information; the licensee is uncertain of the value of the information it is to receive, while the licenser is uncertain of the use to which the licensee proposes to put the information. Moreover, enforcing the provisions of any licensing agreement carries both parties into areas of major uncertainty, based partly on the difficulties of monitoring the agreement and partly on the difficulties of enforcing its provisions.

In any event, the late 1960s registered a high watermark in the spread of the multinational networks of U.S.-based industrial enterprises, as the number of foreign affiliates added annually to such networks reached an all-time high (UN Commission on Transnational Corporations 1978, 223). For at least a decade thereafter, the number of foreign affiliates added annually was much reduced. Without firm-by-firm data of the kind compiled by the Harvard Multinational Enterprise Project for the period up to 1975, it is hard to know more precisely what was going on at the firm level during the succeeding years. But the rate of growth of these networks appeared to pick up again in the late 1980s.

The high rate of growth in recent years, however, appears to be based on somewhat different factors from those that prevailed in earlier decades. Anecdotal evidence indicates that U.S.-based firms continue to use their multinational networks to transfer newly generated products and processes from the United States to other countries. But with the U.S. lead greatly diminished in the generation of new products and processes, it is doubtful that the transmission of new products and processes from U.S. parents to foreign subsidiaries plays as important a role in the business of U.S.-based enterprises as it did some decades ago. Indeed, by the 1990s, the ostensible purpose of some U.S.-based firms in establishing foreign subsidiaries in Japan was not to diffuse existing skills but to acquire new skills for their multinational network in the hope that their Japanese experience would strengthen their competitive capabilities in markets all over the world.[2] With Japanese

and European firms acquiring subsidiaries in the United States at the same time for the same purpose, it was apparent that the distinctive characteristics of U.S.-based multinational networks were beginning to fade.

Another factor that began to change the behavior of U.S.-based enterprises was the increasing familiarity of their managers with the problems of operating in foreign environments. At least until the 1970s, in their decisions when and where to establish subsidiaries in foreign countries, U.S.-based firms had been giving a heavy preference to the familiar. Careful analyses of the geographical sequence by which these firms established manufacturing facilities abroad demonstrated a historically heavy preference for setting up the first foreign production unit in Canada, with the United Kingdom taking second place and Mexico third.[3] By the 1960s, U.S.-based firms were bypassing Canada for Europe and Latin America as the first point of foreign manufacture; by the 1970s, although Europe and Latin America continued to provide the principal first-production sites, Asian sites were beginning to turn up with increasing frequency[4] (Vernon and Davidson 1979, 52, 134–35).

The role played by experience during these early postwar decades could be seen even more directly by trends in the reaction times of U.S.-based firms in setting up foreign production facilities. Where new products were involved, U.S.-based firms character-

---

[2] See ''American Business Starts a Counterattack in Japan,'' *New York Times,* Feb. 24 (1992, p. 1). A survey conducted by Japan's Ministry for International Trade and Industry in January 1990 reports that 38 percent of the foreign direct investors in Japan responding to the survey listed ''engineering skill is high'' as a reason for their investment, while 18 percent listed ''collection of technical information and market information.'' Reproduced in *Nippon* 1991 (1992, 109).

[3] The generalizations are based on an unpublished study of the manufacturing subsidiaries of 180 U.S.-based multinational enterprises as of 1964. The 180 firms, whose multinational networks are covered in the computerized files of the Harvard Multinational Enterprise Project, were all large U.S.-based firms with substantial foreign manufacturing facilities (Vaupel 1971).

[4] The study is based on the same multinational enterprises as those in Vaupel (1971). Conclusions in the two paragraphs following are based on data in the same study.

istically set up their first production sites within the United States. Eventually, however, they set up production sites abroad as well; as these firms gained experience with producing in a given country, the time interval involved in setting up production facilities in the country for new products showed a marked decline. Moreover, as the number of foreign production sites in any product increased, the time interval in setting up another facility in a foreign country also declined. By the 1970s, therefore, U.S.-based firms were beginning to show less hesitation in setting up production subsidiaries abroad for their new products and were scanning a rapidly widening circle of countries for their production sites.

The pattern toward which U.S.-owned multinational networks seem to be moving, therefore, is one in which the parent firm in the United States is prepared to survey different geographic locations on their respective merits, with a much reduced presumption in favor of a U.S. location. Instead, when assigning tasks to the various units of their multinational networks, U.S. business managers are increasingly likely to discount the distinction between home-based and foreign facilities, except as government restraints compel them to recognize that factor. This does not mean that the role played by geography is altogether obliterated. U.S.-based firms, for instance, continue to rely on Latin America more than on Asia to provide their low-cost labor needs, while the reverse is true for Japanese firms.[5] But the sense of uncertainty associated with producing outside the home economy has substantially declined, and the preference for nearby production locations such as those in Latin America over more remote locations such as those in Asia has declined as well.

For enterprises operating in oligopolistic markets, however, a major source of uncertainty remains. Even when such enterprises are fully familiar with the foreign environments in which they are obliged to operate, they are still exposed to the predatory and preemptive tactics of their rivals in the oligopoly. The reasoning that led the international oil and minerals firms to develop vertically integrated structures before World War II, therefore, can be glimpsed in more recent decades in the behavior of U.S.-based firms operating in oligopolistic markets. For instance, U.S.-based oil companies, having been separated from some of their captive crude oil supplies by the nationalizations in the 1970s, remain unwilling to rely upon the open market for the bulk of such supplies despite the existence of a large public market for the product. Facing the latent threat posed by the vertical integration of the Saudi and Venezuelan state-owned oil companies, U.S.-based firms are repairing and strengthening their upstream links.[6]

Such cautionary behavior is not confined to the raw materials industries. Similar behavior is apparent among U.S. firms in the electronics industry: under pressure to reduce the costs of labor-intensive components, firms such as IBM and Texas Instruments have chosen to manufacture a considerable part of their needs within their own multinational networks rather than to rely upon independent suppliers. A major factor in that decision, according to many observers, has been the fear that predatory rivals might withhold the most advanced versions of those components from competitors while incorporating them in their own products. (U.S. Congress 1991, 97–100; Schwartz 1992, esp. 149; Teece 1987, 65–95.)

For some U.S.-based enterprises, it was only a small step from using their foreign subsidiaries as feeders for manufacturing facilities in the United States to using those facilities to fill requirements arising anywhere in the network; by the 1980s, it had become apparent that this process was well advanced (Lipsey 1988). Of course, in practically every multinational network, the parent unit in the United States typically continued to occupy a unique position: characteristically, the parent's U.S. sales still ac-

---

[5] United Nations data affirm the preferences of U.S.-based and Japan-based firms for direct investment in nearby locations during the years 1971 to 1986, as well as the tendency of these geographical preferences to decline over time (UN Centre on Transnational Corporations 1988, 518–20, table A.5).

[6] For an account of the downstream movements of the various state-owned oil companies, and of new upstream ties forged by Gulf Oil, Sun Oil, Citgo, and Texaco, see *Business Week* 1988.

counted for the bulk of network sales, its U.S. facilities were responsible for the most important research and development work in the network, and its U.S. offices still coordinated some of the network's functions that might benefit from a centralized approach, such as the finance function. But the direction was clear. Although the centralized functions of the network would presumably remain in the United States indefinitely, the historical and institutional forces that resisted the geographical diffusion of other functions to locations outside the United States were growing weaker.

A more novel trend, however, has been the growing propensity of U.S.-based firms to enter into alliances of one kind or another with multinational networks based in other countries—typically, in other highly industrialized countries. Such alliances, for instance, sometimes take the form of a joint subsidiary established to perform a specified function or of an exchange of licenses in a specified field. At times, the arrangements link suppliers to their customers; at other times, the parties involved in such limited linkages appear to be direct rivals. A considerable literature is already developing regarding the operation of these alliances (Contractor and Lorange 1988; Gomes-Casseres 1989; Lewis 1990; Lynch 1989; Parkhe 1991). Although the definitions are muddy and the data far from complete, such alliances seem to be concentrated in industries in which barriers to entry are high and technological change is rapid and costly.

Part of the motivation for these alliances is apparent: an effort of each of the participating firms to reduce the risks associated with lumpy commitments to new research and development projects and to ensure that they are abreast of their competitors in their research resources. The alliances, therefore, are not much different in function from the jointly owned mines and oil fields that rival refiners and marketers shared in decades gone by, such as ARAMCO in Saudia Arabia, Southern Peru Copper in Peru, and HALCO in Guinea. Moreover, with common interests linking rivals to their suppliers and to one another in these new alliances, the likelihood that any one of the rivals might steal a technological lead on the others is obviously reduced. As with the partners

in the raw material subsidiaries, therefore, there may well be a sense among some of the partners in the new alliances that their ties with rivals and suppliers could be used to reduce the harshness of future competition among them.

In one respect, however, many of the new alliances differ from those in the raw material industries. In industries with rapidly changing technologies and swiftly changing markets, the interests of the participants in any given alliance are likely to be relatively unstable; such firms will be constantly withdrawing and regrouping in order to satisfy their rapidly shifting strategic needs. Nevertheless, the possibility remains very real that these arrangements will serve at times to take the edge off the competition in some product markets.

For all the evidence that defensive motivations have been dominating the behavior of U.S.-based enterprises, there are various signs that the animal spirits of some U.S. managers can still be roused. One sign of such spirits is the global spread of U.S.-based firms in various service industries, including fast foods, advertising services, and management consulting. Some of these service-oriented firms developed multinational networks simply by following their multinational clients abroad in an effort to maintain an existing relationship; others, relying on a technological or managerial capability that their foreign rivals had not yet matched, bravely set out to master new environments without any apparent defensive motivation. Such initiatives, it appears, depend on the extent to which enterprises feel protected by some unique firm capability, such as a technological or managerial lead, or a patent or trademark.[7] But whether such situations are common or not in the future, defensive responses can be counted on to compel many large firms in the United States to maintain and extend their multinational networks.

---

[7] The reader will recognize this theme as a major element in John H. Dunning's ''eclectic theory.'' For his view of U.S. foreign direct investment trends in relation to the theory, see Dunning (1985, 66–70).

EMERGENCE OF THE EUROPEANS

European industry often enjoys a reputation among Americans for sophistication and urbanity that equips them especially for the role of global entrepreneurs. But their performance as a group after World War II presents a very mixed picture.

In the decades just prior to World War II, the principal strategy of the leading European firms was to protect their home markets from competition, not to seek out new foreign markets. When they established subsidiaries in foreign countries, they tended to concentrate on countries to which their home governments had close political ties (Franko 1976, 81). And their typical reaction to the threat of international competition in those decades was to develop market-sharing arrangements along national lines.

In the immediate postwar period, European firms continued to cling to their home markets. Absorbed in the rebuilding of their home economies and saddled with the need to catch up technologically, they had little slack to devote to the establishment of new foreign facilities. True, enterprises headquartered in some of the smaller countries that possessed a technological edge, such as the pharmaceutical companies of Switzerland and the Netherlands and the machinery firms of Sweden, often felt compelled to set up subsidiaries outside their home countries in order to exploit their technological lead and to finance their ongoing innovational efforts; and the subsidiaries they set up in foreign countries typically operated with greater autonomy in foreign locations than did subsidiaries of some of their U.S. rivals. Moreover, manufacturing firms headquartered in the larger European countries were not altogether averse to establishing producing subsidiaries in areas over which their home governments still exercised strong political or economic influence. Between 1945 and 1965, for instance, British parents established about four hundred manufacturing subsidiaries in Australia, Canada, and New Zealand. (Harvard Multinational Enterprise Project data banks).

The disposition of European firms to identify closely with their home governments has some of its roots in history. Until recently, many were family-owned enterprises, with a long history of dominance in some given city or region. Some were so-called national champions, accustomed to especially favorable treatment by their governments in the provision of capital and the purchase of output (Michalet 1974, 105–25). The idea of maintaining close ties to their home government when operating abroad therefore represented an easy extension of their relationship at home.

After 1960, the emergence of a common market on the European continent began to affect the strategies of European firms. At first, however, these developments did little to encourage European firms to set up subsidiaries in other countries within the area. For one thing, the promise of a duty-free market among members of the European Community actually served to eliminate one of the motivations for creating such subsidiaries, namely the threat that frontiers might be closed to foreign goods. And with land distances relatively small and national markets relatively limited in size, the economic reasons for establishing such subsidiaries often did not appear compelling.

On the other hand, by the 1960s, U.S.-based companies were beginning to set up their subsidiaries in Europe in large numbers. Data from the Harvard Multinational Enterprise Project show that whereas, in the fifteen years between 1945 and 1959, U.S. parents had established some three hundred manufacturing subsidiaries in Europe, between 1960 and 1975 these parents established nearly two thousand manufacturing subsidiaries in Europe. Typically, the first landing of the U.S. invaders was in the United Kingdom, despite that country's delay in entering the European Community; but the U.S.-based firms were not long in establishing subsidiaries on the continent as well.

One might have expected the appearance of these subsidiaries to stimulate moves to renew the restrictive market-sharing agreements of the prewar period, but the environment following the end of World War II was much less conducive to such agreements. For one thing, rapidly expanding markets and swiftly changing technologies generated an environment that made agreements difficult. In addition, although enforcement of U.S. antitrust laws had grown lax in the postwar period, the European Community itself had adopted and was occasionally enforcing some exemplary measures aimed at preventing enterprises from dividing up the European market (Goyder 1988, esp. 71–133).

Eventually, however, most large European firms were led through the same defensive cycle that some U.S.-based firms had already experienced. Having reestablished export markets for their manufactured goods in many areas, including the Middle East and Latin America, they faced the same kind of threat that had moved their U.S. counterparts to set up producing subsidiaries abroad, namely the fear of losing a market through import restrictions. By 1970, manufacturing firms based in Europe were adding affiliates to their multinational networks in numbers over twice as high as those recorded by their U.S. counterparts (Harvard Multinational Enterprise Project data).

Moved largely by defensive considerations, European firms were adding rapidly to their holdings in the United States. There they showed a strong preference for investing in existing firms rather than in wholly new undertakings, and a strong disposition to team up with a U.S. firm in the process.[8] Such entries, some European managers supposed, would give them exposure to the latest industrial technologies and marketing strategies, thus strengthening their ability to resist the U.S. onslaught in their home markets and in third countries.

By the end of the 1960s, however, the Europeans had begun to have less reason to fear the dominance of U.S.-based firms. The differences in technological achievement between U.S. firms and European firms had obviously shrunk, and access to capital no longer favored the Americans. Not surprisingly, then, some of the motivations that lay behind the expansion of the European networks grew more nearly akin to that of the Americans—that is, largely defensive moves aimed at protecting a foreign market from import re-

strictions or copycat responses to the initiatives of rivals in setting up a subsidiary abroad (Flowers 1976).[9] In an apparent response to such stimuli, the number of European-owned subsidiaries appearing in various parts of the world increased rapidly (Harvard Multinational Enterprise Project data).

These new transborder relations have not wholly obliterated the distinctive national traits that have characterized European firms. German enterprises, for instance, continue to huddle in the shelter of their big banks, French companies in the protective cover of their national ministries. Moreover, despite the existence of the European Community, European firms continue to owe their existence to their respective national enabling statutes, which reflect wide differences in philosophical values and political balance. The United Kingdom, for instance, cannot agree with its continental partners on such fundamental issues as the responsibilities of the corporation to its labor force; whereas the British tend to see corporate managers primarily as the agents of their stockholders, continental governments generally take the view that labor has a quasi-proprietary stake in the enterprise that employs it, which stake managers are obliged to recognize. Differences such as these have served to block projects for the creation of a European company under the European Community's aegis.

Nevertheless, cross-border mergers are growing in number in Europe. In 1987, among the large industrial enterprises based in the community, only 75 cases were recorded in which a firm based in one EC country gained control of a firm based in another, but by 1990 the number had risen to 257 (European Commission 1991, 228). Indeed, in this universe of large industrial firms, the number of such transborder acquisitions in 1990 for the first time exceeded the number of like acquisitions involving firms in a single member country.

In part, the trend toward cross-border mergers is

---

[8] In the period from 1960 to 1970, about 80 percent of the manufacturing subsidiaries established by European parents in the United States were through acquisition or mergers with U.S. firms. The comparable figure for manufacturing subsidiaries of U.S. parents in Europe for the same period was 67 percent (Harvard Multinational Enterprise Project data).

[9] The assumption that the spread of European networks was due in part to follow-the-leader behavior, at least until the 1970s, is fortified by some unpublished studies undertaken by Fred Knickerbocker (1973), whose analysis of the behavior of U.S.-based manufacturing subsidiaries is cited elsewhere in this chapter.

a consequence of the many liberalizing measures that the member countries of the European Community have taken with regard to capital flows. In addition, however, there appears to be a visible weakening of the family conglomerate, a distinctly national form of big business. In Italy, for instance, where that kind of structure has been particularly prominent in the private sector, the country's leading family conglomerates have fallen on especially hard times.[10]

The disposition of many firms to cling to the shreds of their national identity will lead many of them to hesitate over transborder mergers and consolidations in which they are not the surviving entity or, when they finally succumb to the pressures for merger, to insist on retaining a minority interest in the subsidiary that has been joined to the network of the foreign-based firm. That same disposition suggests why European firms appear to give a heavier preference to consortia and alliances as a way of combining their strengths with a foreign firm than U.S.-based competitors would do. But, because I see such arrangements as fragile over time, I see transborder mergers as the preferred vehicle in spite of the obstacles. Such mergers may still generate resistance and hostility in some countries.[11] A few decades from now, however, the national differences in Europe's business communities are likely to prove no more important than the differences between Texas-based enterprises and Massachusetts-based enterprises in the United States.

In explaining the growth of the networks of firms based in Europe, then, I return to some of the same themes that were stressed in the case of U.S.-based firms. The summary of the factors that have pushed U.S.-based enterprises to develop and expand their multinational networks in the past decades stressed the continuous improvements in the technology of communication and transportation as the powerful exogenous factor; the decisions of the U.S.-based firms to expand their enterprises were seen in large part as a response aimed at reducing the uncertainties and countering the threats that accompanied such developments. I feel sure that these generalizations will carry the observer a considerable distance in understanding the behavior of Europe-based firms as well.[12] Over time, the differences that heretofore have distinguished U.S.-based from Europe-based multinational networks are likely to diminish as the conditions of their founding and early growth begin to lose their original importance.

LATECOMER JAPAN

Studying the factors behind the growth of multinational enterprises based in Japan, a phenomenon of the past two or three decades, will bring us back to the same defensive motivations, including the need of Japanese enterprises to protect their interests against the hostile acts of foreign governments and business competitors, and their desire to build up competitive strengths by exposing themselves to the most challenging technological and marketing environments.

Indeed, the defensive motivations that commonly lie behind the creation and spread of multinational enterprises are likely to act even more powerfully on the Japanese than on their U.S.-based and Europe-based competitors. To see why, it helps to review briefly the evolution of Japan's industrial structure (see, e.g., Wilkins 1990, 585–629).

From the earliest years of the Meiji restoration in the last decades of the nineteenth century, the industrial structure of Japan exhibited some distinctive national characteristics. Dominating the core of Japan's modern economy were half a dozen conglomerate organizations, each with its own captive bank, trading company, and portfolio of manufacturing and service enterprises. The conglomerate structure, well developed before World War II, was modified only a little by Japan's loss of its foreign territories and by the ensuing occupation. Japanese firms lost their

---

[10] For an account of the troubles of the Agnelli and Pirelli family conglomerates, see *Financial Times* (1992a).

[11] For a rich account of such hostilities in France's reactions to the Agnelli family's efforts to acquire control over Perrier, see *Financial Times* (1992c).

[12] A study of European banking confirms the existence of each of the major tendencies identified above. See Campayne (1992).

investments in the territories its armies had occupied, but these investments had largely been controlled by the so-called new zaibatsu, companies that depended for their existence on Japan's foreign conquests and that had very little stake in the home economy itself.

In Japan proper, the holding companies that sat at the apex of each conglomerate were liquidated during the occupation. But the member firms of the conglomerates maintained their old ties by cross-holdings of stock and by shared memories of past loyalties. And in the 1960s and 1970s, as foreign enterprises began to show some interest in acquiring control over Japanese firms, member firms within each conglomerate systematically built up their cross-holdings even further as a means of repelling foreign boarders (Ito 1992, 191).

From the early emergence of these conglomerate organizations, a fierce rivalry existed among them— but a rivalry based much more on comparative rates of growth and market shares that on nominal profits. Within each conglomerate, the financing of the contest was left to the conglomerate's captive bank rather than to public capital markets. But the general scope and direction of the lending by these banks to their affiliates were largely determined by continuous consultation with key government agencies, especially the Ministry of Finance, the Bank of Japan, and the Ministry for International Trade and Industry (MITI).

By the 1980s, however, it was becoming apparent that major changes were taking place in the conglomerate structures. Perhaps the most obvious change was the dramatic shift in the financing practices of the industrial firms. As the rate of growth of the Japanese economy slowed up a little in the 1980s and as the need to finance capacity expansion grew less urgent, Japanese firms found that internally generated cash was going a much longer way toward meeting their capital needs.

At the same time, under pressure from foreign sources and from Japan's own financial intermediaries, the Ministry of Finance was gradually relaxing its tight controls over the development of internal capital markets, thereby providing Japanese companies for the first time with a real option for raising their capital needs through the sale of securities in public markets.

Concurrently, Japanese firms were being granted permission to raise capital in foreign currencies by selling their securities abroad or borrowing from foreign banks. Japanese banks, trading houses, and other service facilities, therefore, were strongly represented in the outflow of direct investment from Japan to major foreign markets.[13] And because Japanese manufacturing firms were always a little uncomfortable when dealing with foreigners as service suppliers, the existence of those service facilities in foreign markets eased the way for the manufacturers to establish their foreign subsidiaries outside of Japan (Gittelman and Dunning 1992, 237–67).

In accounting for the changes in the character of the multinational networks based in Japan, however, one must place particularly heavy emphasis on the increasing technological capabilities of these enterprises. In the very first stages of the development of multinational networks by Japan-based firms, in the 1960s and 1970s, some scholars entertained the hypothesis that these firms would develop a pattern of foreign direct investment quite different from that pioneered by U.S.-based and Europe-based firms (Kojima 1978, 85–87). At that stage, Japan's penetration of foreign markets for manufactured goods was most in evidence in South and Southeast Asia and was heavily concentrated in relatively simple items such as batteries, noodles, radios, and other consumer goods—items in which Japan's comparative advantage was already fading. Given the unsophisticated nature of the products and the lack of a need for after-sales services, Japanese producers usually used their affiliated trading companies as their agents in these foreign markets; indeed, in many cases, the Japanese producers were not large enough even to consider marketing their own products abroad and so had no choice but to rely on trading companies.

In these cases, when the risk that the government might impose restrictions became palpable, the trad-

---

[13] In the 1980s, the relative importance of services in the outflow of foreign direct investment from Japan was substantially higher than for FDI outflow from the United States, the United Kingdom, West Germany, or France (UN Centre on Transnational Corporations 1991, 16, table 6).

ing company typically took the lead in establishing a local production facility, often through a three-way partnership that combined the trading company with a local distributor and with the erstwhile Japanese exporter (Yoshino 1976, 95–126). From this early pattern, it appeared that the Japan-based multinational enterprise might root itself much more deeply in its foreign markets than did the U.S.-based and Europe-based companies, with results that might prove more benign from the viewpoint of the host country.

By the 1980s, however, the patterns of foreign direct investment by Japanese firms were converging toward the norms recorded by their U.S. and European rivals (Encarnation 1992, 9–35). As with U.S.- and Europe-based firms, the object of Japanese firms in establishing a producing subsidiary in a foreign country was commonly to protect a market in a relatively differentiated product that originally had been developed through exports from Japan.

Compared with U.S.-based or Europe-based firms, however, the stake of Japanese firms in the export markets of other industrialized countries soon grew very large.[14] The spectacular growth of Japanese exports to the markets of such countries exposed Japanese firms once more to threats of restrictive action on a major scale. At this advanced stage, however, the markets to be protected were considerably different in character from those that the first generation of Japan-based multinationals had developed. One difference was in the identity of the markets under siege, now located mainly in the United States and Europe. Another was the nature of the products involved; these were relatively sophisticated products, such as automobiles, camcorders, and computer-controlled machine tools. And a third was the channels of distribution involved; such sophisticated products were usually marketed through channels under the direct control of the manufacturers rather than through trading companies.

The networks that Japan-based firms created in response to the new threats came closer to emulating those of the U.S.-based and Europe-based firms with multinational networks. Moreover, as with their European rivals, many of the foreign acquisitions by Japan-based firms were explained by a desire to acquire advanced technological skills; this motive was especially apparent in the acquisition of various medium-sized high-tech firms in the United States (Kester 1991; Kogut and Chang 1991).

Although the multinational networks that Japan-based firms produced in this second generation bore a much greater resemblance to the networks of their counterparts from other advanced industrialized countries, some characteristic differences remained. One such characteristic was the high propensity of Japan-based multinationals to control their producing subsidiaries tightly from Japan. Symptomatic of that fact was the near-universal use of Japanese personnel to head their foreign subsidiaries.[15] A striking illustration of the same desire for control was the limited leeway allowed subsidiaries in the acquisition of capital equipment. Australian subsidiaries of Japanese firms, for instance, possessed far less leeway in the selection of new machinery than did the subsidiaries of U.S.-based or Europe-based firms (Kreinin 1988). Some signs existed in the 1990s that a few Japanese firms were breaking away from their traditional controls and giving their foreign subsidiaries greater leeway, but the illustrations were still exceptional (*Economist* 1992).

The early reluctance of Japan-based firms to develop a multinational network and the tendency of the foreign subsidiaries of such firms to rely upon their established sources in Japan have been attributed to a number of different factors. They have been variously explained as a consequence of the relative inexperience of Japanese firms with the novel problems of producing abroad, as a result of the heavy reliance on the consensual process in firm decision making, or as a consequence of the extensive use of

---

[14] Data on the identities of the world's leading multinationals in the latter 1980s, with partial statistics on their respective stakes in foreign markets gleaned primarily from annual reports, appear in UN Commission on Transnational Corporations (1978, 287–316).

[15] For instance, a study of the U.S. subsidiaries of Japanese electronics firms reports that only 2 percent of Japanese electronics firms in the United States had U.S. chief executive officers (U.S. Congress 1991, 99).

just-in-time producing processes, which demand the closest coordination between the firms and their suppliers (Kester 1991, 109). Introducing strangers into the system, according to the argument, entails major modifications in firm practices that cannot be achieved overnight.

Nevertheless, by the end of the 1980s, Japan-based firms were expanding their multinational networks at an unprecedented rate. What is more, their manufacturing affiliates in the United States and Europe were drawing a considerable fraction of their inputs from sources located in the host country (Gittelman and Dunning 1992, 40). Moreover, it appeared that some of the very factors that had slowed the growth of Japan-based multinational networks in the past could be expected to reinforce the expansion rather than to slow it down. For example, the desire of Japanese firms to rely on Japanese sources means that the foreign subsidiaries of major Japanese firms are pulling large numbers of satellite suppliers with them into foreign locations. While this has not been an unknown phenomenon in the establishment of the multinational networks of firms based in the United States, it appears to be an especially powerful force in the case of Japan-based firms (Wilkins 1990, 612–16).[16] Moreover, if one pair of authoritative observers is to be believed, Japanese firms already are being drawn into Europe by the conviction that they must assimilate some distinctive regional emphases if they are to be successful in major industries, such as automobiles and electronic equipment (Gittelman and Dunning 1992). Finally, given the intense rivalry of Japanese firms, with their stress on market share, it is not unreasonable to expect a pattern of copycat behavior even stronger than that observed with respect to firms based in other countries.

Whether the Japanese government will seek at some point to restrain the overseas movement of its firms through administrative guidance is unclear; but even if it makes such an attempt, there is no certainty that the attempt would prove effective. The growing financial independence of Japanese firms means that the Ministry of Finance and MITI have lost one of their principal sources of coercion. The Japanese firms' commitment of a large proportion of their assets to foreign locations means that they will be exposed to stimuli not strikingly different from those affecting their U.S. and European rivals. Developments such as these promise to contribute to the movement of Japan-based multinationals toward the norms typical of multinationals based in other countries (Lipsey 1991, 87).

PATTERNS OF THE FUTURE

In the future as in the past, some powerful exogenous factors will influence the spread of multinational enterprises, including changes in the technologies of transportation, communication, and production. But it is not easy to project the consequences of such changes. For instance, if just-in-time manufacturing takes on added strength, the clustering tendency of related enterprises should grow stronger; but if flexible manufacturing processes gain in strength, smaller and more self-contained plans could dominate, reducing the tendency toward clusters (Auty 1992; Dunning 1992, esp. 158–62). Despite uncertainties of this sort, however, I anticipate that multinational networks and transborder alliances, already a major factor in international economic flows, will grow in importance.

THE RESPONSE OF GOVERNMENTS

How governments will respond to that situation is a little uncertain. Although globalization and convergence may prove to be major trends defining the behavior of multinational enterprises in the future, it is implausible to assume that national governments will stand aside and allow such behavior to develop as it may. With jobs, taxes, payment balances, and technological achievement seemingly at stake, governments are bound to act in an effort to defend national interests and respond to national pressures. Their efforts, involving carrots in some cases and

[16] A hint of the strong tendency of Japanese firms to buy from enterprises with which they have close links appears also in Gittelman and Dunning (1992). See also *Financial Times* (1992a), an account of Nissan's impact on northeast England.

sticks in others, will continue to pose threats and offer opportunities to the multinationals.

Some governmental responses will take the form of restrictions, unilaterally adopted, aimed at holding inbound and outbound foreign investment in check. But from all the signs, political leaders in the major industrialized countries seem aware that national autarky is not an available option unless a country is prepared to absorb some overwhelming costs. That recognition explains why so many countries now eye the possibility of developing regional blocs—areas large enough to satisfy the modern requirements of scale and scope, and small enough to promise member countries that they will exert some influence in shaping their joint economic policies.

There is surface plausibility to the idea that such blocs may figure importantly in the future, a plausibility reflected in the preeminence of Japanese interests in South and Southeast Asia, European interests in Africa, Eastern Europe, and the Middle East, and U.S. interests in Latin America. But it is easy to misinterpret the significance of those concentrations. As already suggested, they may reflect little more than the myopic learning process of business managers, and increasing experience may push them toward scanning over a wider geographical range.

In any case, when seen through the eyes of the managers of multinational enterprises based in the industrialized areas, the managers' principal stake by far lies in other industrialized areas, not in the hinterlands of their respective ''regions.'' That has been the case for decades, and it has shown no signs of changing in recent years. To be sure, such enterprises will not hesitate to use the influence of their respective governments to promote their interests in these regions. But from the viewpoint of the firms, such efforts will be a sideshow compared to their respective stakes in other industrialized economies.

At the same time, the influence that individual governments are in a position to exert over their respective multinational enterprises appears rapidly on the decline. Although governments have been known to remain blind to the obvious for remarkably prolonged periods of time, that ineluctable fact should eventually lead them to limit their unilateral efforts at control. Where control of some sort still seems necessary or desirable, the option remaining will be to pursue mutually agreed-upon measures with other countries. In the decades ahead, the United States, Europe, and Japan are sure to find themselves addressing the feasibility and desirability of international agreements that define more fully the rights and obligations of mulinational enterprises. Although most other countries may be slower to address the issue, a few such as Singapore and Mexico along with the non-European members of the Organization for Economic Cooperation and Development (OECD) are likely to be involved as well. Already some of the elements of an international system are in place with respect to a few functional fields, such as the levying of corporate income taxes. It does not stretch the imagination very much to picture international agreements on such subjects as the competition of governments for foreign direct investment, the threats to market competition posed by restrictive business practices and mergers, the rights and obligations of multinational enterprises in national political processes, and other issues relating to the multinational enterprise.

THE DEVELOPMENT OF THEORY

In the past, as multinational networks appeared and grew, some researchers concerned with understanding the causes of their behavior found it useful, even indispensable, to distinguish such enterprises according to their national base. If I am right in seeing strong tendencies toward national convergence, distinctions based on the national origin of the network are likely to lose their analytic and descriptive value, and distinctions on other dimensions are likely to grow in importance. Even more than in the past, distinctions based on the characteristics of the product market and the production process are likely to prove particularly fruitful.

As I observed earlier, many multinational enterprises created global networks in response to perceived threats and operated under circumstances in which ignorance and uncertainty were endemic. For the most part, the enterprises operated in product markets with significant barriers to entry, including static and dynamic scale economies, patents and trademarks. With the passage of time, however, a considerable proportion of these multinational enterprises overcame their sense of acute uncertainty in foreign markets, especially as the products and their related technologies grew more stable and standardized.

These tendencies often reduced barriers to entry, increased the number of participants, and elevated the role of price competition. In the production and sale of metals and petroleum, for instance, the number of sellers on world markets inexorably increased, and the role of competitive pricing grew. In big-ticket consumer electronics, an intensification of competitive pricing among multinational enterprises also has become commonplace, despite the persistent efforts of sellers to differentiate their products. In such cases, their is considerable utility in models that cast the participants as fully informed actors operating in a market in which their choices are known, under conditions in which some scale economies exist (Helpman and Krugman 1985, 225–59; Grossman and Helpman 1991, 197–200). I see no reason why models based on these assumptions should not generate useful first approximations to the behavior of multinational enterprises in a considerable number of industries.

Other models may also have something to contribute, such as those that view multinational networks as the consequence of decisions by firms to internalize certain types of transactions. The international market for the sale of technology and management skills, for instance, is a grossly inefficient market from the viewpoint of both buyer and seller (Teece 1986; Galbraith and Kay 1986). Internalization can be viewed as a response to those inefficiencies, in a setting in which the enterprises are otherwise fully aware of the set of choices they confront and of the facts bearing on those choices (Casson 1987, 1–49; Williamson 1971).

Models based on the internalization hypothesis therefore fit comfortably into the structure of the models described earlier, which are based essentially on a neoclassical framework driven by costs and prices. But they have tended to crowd out the analysis of other motivations that seem at least as important in explaining the behavior of the managers of such enterprises. For instance, various measures taken by the firm to create a multinational network may be driven by another motive, namely a desire to avoid being exposed to the predatory behavior of rivals, including the risk that such rivals might cut off needed supplies or deny access to a distribution system during some future contingency.

That possibility pushes the modeler in a very different direction in attempting to explain the behavior of multinational enterprises. Such enterprises continue to figure prominently in many product markets that have not yet attained a stable middle age. In such markets, the number of producers is often sharply limited, products and related services are often highly differentiated, technologies are in flux, and price differences are not the critical factor in competition. Moreover, externalities of various kinds commonly play a dominant role in locational decisions, as when enterprises try to draw on various national environments to produce the stimuli they think will improve their competitive strengths. Firms engaged in producing microprocessors, aircraft engines, and wonder drugs, for instance, are strongly influenced by one or another of these factors.

Needless to say, where the number of rivals in a market is low, that fact fundamentally conditions the strategies of the participants. Some of them may long for the security of a market-sharing arrangement and may even take some tentative steps in that direction, such as entering into partnerships with some of their rivals. But developing an effective market-sharing arrangement is usually difficult and dangerous.

In any event, when a limited number of participants are involved in a product market, theorists must entertain the possibility that the firms that are engaged in such markets see any given transaction as only one move in a campaign stretching across time. In each transaction, the principal objective of the firm is to strengthen its position in relation to its rivals or to neutralize the efforts of its rivals to steal a march; with that objective paramount, share of market becomes a critical measure of success. In such circumstances, invading a rival's principal market may prove a useful defensive strategy, aimed at reducing the rival's propensity for warfare elsewhere. And, given the imperfect knowledge under which each firm is assumed to operate, a policy of following a rival into new areas of supply and new markets may be seen as a prudent response to the rival's initiatives.[17]

Of course, by shedding many of the assumptions underlying the neoclassical model, models built on such behavioral assumptions relinquish the support provided by a comprehensive body of well-explored theory. Instead, the analyst is thrown into a world of uncertain outcomes, explored so far largely by game theorists, specialists in signaling theory, and others outside the neoclassical mainstream. It is hardly surprising, therefore, that most of the scholars who have sought to model the behavior of the multinational enterprise have avoided the implications of high uncertainty and limited numbers, preferring instead to concentrate on hypotheses that require less radical departures from neoclassical assumptions.

Nevertheless, any serious effort to project the behavior of multinational enterprises in the future will have to recognize that the players in many major product and service markets will see themselves as engaged in a campaign against specific adversaries in a global market, with individual decisions being shaped in light of that perception. At different times and places, there will be efforts to call a truce, efforts to weaken specific adversaries, and efforts to counter the aggressive behavior of others. The behavior that emerges will not be easily explained in terms of models that satisfy neoclassical conditions. Therein lies a major challenge for those who are attempting to cast light on the behavior of multinational enterprises through systematic modeling.

REFERENCES

Auty, Richard M. 1992. *Changing competitiveness of newly industrialized countries in heavy and chemical industry: Effects of the product cycle and technological change.* Amsterdam: University of Amsterdam.

---

[17] Casson (1987, 53–83) and Bower (1992) omit any reference to such possibilities. See also Graham and Krugman (1989), where such possibilities are presented not in the theory section of the report but in an annex entitled ''Industrial Organization Explanations of Foreign Direct Investment.''

Bower, Anthony G. 1992. Predicting locational decisions of multinational corporations. N-3440-CUSTR. Santa Monica, Calif.: Rand Corporation.

Business Week. 1988. Why kings of crude want to be pump boys. 21 March, pp. 110–12.

Campayne, Paul. 1992. Cross investment in the European banking sector. In *Multinational investment in modern Europe: Strategic interaction in the integrated community,* ed. J. Cantwell. London: Edward Elgar.

Casson, Mark. 1987. *The firm and the market: Studies on multinational enterprise and the scope of the firm.* Cambridge, Mass.: MIT Press.

Chandler, Alfred D. 1990. *Scale and scope: The dynamics of industrial capitalism.* Cambridge: Belknap Press.

Contractor, F.J., and Peter Lorange, eds. 1988. *Cooperative strategies in international business.* Lexington, Mass.: Lexington Books.

Curhan, Joan P., William H. Davidson, and Rajan Suri. 1977. *Tracing the multinationals: A sourcebook on U.S.-based enterprise.* Cambridge, Mass.: Ballinger Publishing.

Dunning, John H. 1992. The competitive advantage of countries and the activities of transnational corporations. *Transnational Corporations* 1, no. 1 (February): 135–69.

———, ed. 1985. *Multinational enterprises, economic structure and international competitiveness.* New York: John Wiley and Sons.

Economist. 1992. Japan's less-than-invincible computer makers. 11 January, pp. 59–60.

Encarnation, Dennis J. 1992. *Rivals beyond trade: America versus Japan in global competition.* Ithaca, N.Y.: Cornell University Press.

European Commission. 1991. *20th report on competition policy.* Brussels: European Commission.

Financial Times. 1992a. Leaders that have lost their way. 21 January, p. 18.

———. 1992b. Benefits beyond the automotive sector. 18 February, p. 28.

———. 1992c. Dynastic hopes fall flat in France. 25 March, p. 14.

Flowers, E.B. 1976. Oligopolistic reactions in European and Canadian direct investment in the United States. *Journal of International Business Studies* 7 (3): 43–55.

Franko, Lawrence G. 1976. *The European multinationals.* New York: Harper and Row.

Galbraith, Craig S., and Neil M. Kay. 1986. Towards a theory of multinational enterprise. *Journal of Economic Behavior and Organization* 7 no. 1 (March): 3–19.

Gittelman, Michelle, and John H. Dunning. 1992. Japanese multinationals in Europe and the United States: Some comparisons and contrasts. In *Multinationals in the new Europe and global trade,* ed. Michael W. Klein and Paul J.J. Welfens. Berlin: Springer-Verlag.

Gomes-Casseres, Benjamin. 1989. Joint ventures in the face of global competition. *Sloan Management Review* 30, no. 3 (Spring): 17–26.

Goyder, D.G. 1988. *EEC competition law.* New York: Clarendon Press.

Graham, Edward M., and Paul R. Krugman. 1989. *Foreign direct investment in the United States.* Washington, D.C.: Institute for International Economics.

Grossman, Gene, and Elhanan Helpman. 1991. *Innovation and growth in the global economy.* Cambridge, Mass.: MIT Press.

Helpman, Elhanan, and Paul R. Krugaman. 1985. *Market structure and foreign trade.* Cambridge, Mass.: MIT Press.

Hexner, Ervin P. 1945. *International cartels.* Chapel Hill: University of North Carolina Press.

Ito, Takatoshi. 1992. *The Japanese economy.* Cambridge, Mass.: MIT Press.

Kester, W.C. 1991. *Japanese takeovers: The global quest for corporate control.* Boston: Harvard Business School Press.

Knickerbocker, Frederick T. 1973. *Oligopolistic reaction and multinational enterprise.* Boston: Harvard University, Graduate School of Business Administration, Division of Research.

Kogut, Bruce, and Sea Gin Chang. 1991. Technological capabilities and Japanese foreign direct investment in the United States. *Review of Economics and Statistics* 73, no. 3 (August): 401–13.

Kojima, Kiyoshi. 1978. *Direct foreign investment: A Japanese model of multinational business operations.* London: Croom Helm.

Kreinin, Mordechai E. 1988. How closed is Japan's market? Additional evidence. *World Economy* 11, no. 4 (December): 529–42.

Lall, Sanjaya. 1991. Direct investment in South-East Asia by the NIEs: Trends and prospects. *Banca Nazionale del Lavoro Quarterly Review* 179: 463–80.

Lewis, Jordan D. 1990. *Partnerships for profit: Structuring and managing strategic alliances.* New York: Free Press.

Lipsey, Robert E. 1988. Changing patterns of international investment in and by the United States. In *The United States in the world economy,* ed. Martin Feldstein, 475–545. Chicago: University of Chicago Press.

———. 1991. Foreign direct investment in the United States and U.S. trade. *Annals of the American Academy of Political and Social Science* (July): 76–90.

Lipsey, Robert E., and Irving B. Kravis. 1982. U.S.-owned affiliates and host-country exports. NBER Working Paper no. 1037. Cambridge, Mass.: National Bureau of Economic Research.

Lynch, Robert Porter. 1989. *The practical guide to joint venture and corporate alliances.* New York: John Wiley and Sons.

Michalet, Charles-Albert. 1974. France. In *Big business and the states,* ed. Raymond Vernon. Cambridge, Mass.: Harvard University Press.

New York Times. 1992. American business starts a counterattack in Japan. 24 February.

Nippon 1991: Business facts and figures. 1992. New York: JETRO.

Parkhe, Arvinde. 1991. Interfirm diversity, organizational learning, and longevity in global strategic alliances. *Journal of International Business Studies* (4): 579–601.

Schwartz, Jacob T. 1992. America's economic-technological agenda for the 1990s. *Daedalus* 121, no. 1 (Winter): 139–65.

Stocking, George W., and Myron W. Watkins. 1946. *Cartels in action: Case studies in international business diplomacy.* New York: 20th Century Fund.

———. 1948. *Cartels or competition?* New York: 20th Century Fund.

Teece, David J. 1986. Transaction cost economics and the multinational enterprise. *Journal of Economic Behavior and Organization* 7 no. 1 (March): 21–45.

———. 1987. Capturing value from technological innovations: Integration, strategic partnering and licensing decisions. In *Technology and global industry: Companies and nations in the world economy,* ed. Bruce R. Guild and Harvey Brooks. Washington, D.C.: National Academy Press.

UN Centre on Transnational Corporations. 1988. *Transnational corporations in world development: Trends and prospects.* New York: United Nations.

———. 1991. *World investment report 1991: The triad in foreign direct investment.* New York: United Nations.

UN Commission on Transnational Corporations. 1978. *Transnational corporations in world development: A re-examination.* New York, E/C. 10/38, based on data from the Harvard Multinational Enterprise Project.

———. 1990. *Non-conventional transnational corporations.* New York: United Nations.

U.S. Congress, Office of Technology Assessment. 1991. *Competing economies: America, Europe and the Pacific Rim.* OTA-ITE-498. Washington, D.C.: U.S. Government Printing Office.

Vaupel, James W. 1971. Study of manufacturing subsidiaries of 180 U.S.-based multinational enterprises as of 1964. Paper presented at June conference, Turin, Italy.

Vernon, Raymond, and W.H. Davidson. 1979. *Foreign production of technology-intensive products by U.S.-based multinational enterprises.* Report to the National Science Foundation, no. PB 80 148638.

Wilkins, Mira. 1970. *The emergence of multinational enterprise.* Cambridge, Mass.: Harvard University Press.

———. 1990. Japanese multinationals in the United States: Continuity and change, 1879–1990. *Business History Review* 64 (Winter): 585–629.

Wilkins, Mira, and Frank Ernest Hill. 1964. *American business abroad: Ford on six continents.* Detroit: Wayne State University Press.

Williamson, Oliver E. 1971. The vertical integration of production: Market failure considerations. *American Economic Review* 61 (May): 112–23.

Yoshino, Michael Y. 1976. *Japan's multinational enterprises.* Cambridge, Mass.: Harvard University Press.

Yu, C.J., and K. Ito. 1988. Oligopolistic reaction and foreign direct investment. *Journal of International Business Studies* 19 (3): 449–60.

COMMENT   Richard E. Caves

Raymond Vernon writes about the changing activity patterns of multinational enterprises from a long and intense involvement with the subject. His observations cover important trends or attributes in three areas of their operations: (1) multinationals based in different countries become more similar over time, just as U.S.-based leviathans grow less dominant and the national sources of multinationals more diffuse; (2) public policies remain important constraints and threats affecting multinationals' decisions; (3) foreign investment is influenced importantly by strategic considerations such as denying tactical advantage to oligopolistic rivals. I shall comment on each of these areas.

That the activities of multinationals based in different countries grow more homogeneous is clearly correct and rests on a number of underlying trends. As noted by Vernon, one of these is that, among different countries' largest firms, institutional differences that differentially affect their potential performance (such as predominant family ownership) are dying out. This is true for the simple Darwinian reason that inefficient institutions tend not to survive forever, although institutional differences can coexist that do not differentially affect firms' performance as foreign investors.

A second source of reduced difference lies in increasingly similar comparative-advantage patterns, broadly defined, of the major industrial countries. With labor-intensive manufacturing gravitated to the newly industrializing countries, the developed nations that are the principal homes of multinational firms exhibit increasingly similar patterns of comparative advantage in trade. This similarity is evidenced by the large increase in intraindustry trade among the OECD countries that has occurred since World War II. This increased similarity in comparative-advantage patterns translates (it can be argued) into increased similarity in nations' patterns of foreign investment.

A third factor, harder to pin down, is greater homogeneity of both tastes and technology among the industrial countries. *Homogenization* is perhaps not quite the right word: the operative force is awareness of differences in consumption sets and ways of doing things that translates into selective adoption of foreign ways and things, driven by greatly reduced costs of international communication and travel. For potential multinational firms, this trend lowers many components of the fixed cost of adaptation to a foreign environment. This trend is especially evident in the development of Japan's multinational firms. Japanese foreign investment in the United States during the 1970s and 1980s was driven by its complementarity with Japanese exporting activities and Japan's growing research capability, as one would expect. In the 1980s, it also came to be positively related to industries' advertising intensities, as Japanese firms demonstrated the capability to steer around the national style differences that seem to prevail in most advertising-intensive products (Drake and Caves 1992).

Regarding countries' interventions in multinationals' activities, Vernon argues in essence that the trend is more of the same. Significant amounts of foreign investment take place, he feels, to avert profit losses caused by the importing country's restrictions on the foreign firm's exports. Governments are certainly growing no less solicitous about preserving substantial (if limited and inexplicit) property rights of workers in their jobs. Because domestic firms' property rights in their rents are much less secure, foreign investment that threatens only investors' rents is viable where exports that threaten both investors' rents and employees' job opportunities are not. (The glorious confusion surrounding this public policy preference is illustrated by the debate in the United States over what is a foreign automobile.)

Although I basically agree with Vernon's *plus ça change . . .* judgment, I suggest that invasive public policies have been somewhat muted by the increased symmetry of the industrial countries' positions as sources and hosts of foreign direct investment. Xenophobic reactions to foreigners, as suppliers of imports, investors, owners of property, and so on, can be taken for granted. Those familiar with other countries' complaints about U.S. multinationals two and three decades ago can only regard with bemusement the rise of exactly the same complaints about foreign multinationals in the United States during the past decade. Nonetheless, when xenophobia clamors for translation into public policy, the interests of multinationals based in the afflicted country demand to be weighed in the balance. The result, I suggest, is an important damper on restrictive policies analogous to the one on trade policies that Milner (1988) documented, which was due to increasing symmetries of trade positions. Independently, the developing countries have chosen less restrictive policies since the 1960s, part of their more general recognition of the productivity-raising effects of market-based incentive structures. That a code of conduct toward multinational enterprises was even on the table for discussion in the Uruguay Round under the General Agreement on Tariffs and Trade testifies to the increased similarity of nations' policy preferences; a quarter-century ago, broad international agreement on the treatment of multinationals would have been inconceivable.

Statistical research has shown that much of the variance in the activity levels of multinational enterprises can be explained by transaction cost factors that call for internalization within the enterprise to avert what would otherwise be contractual failures in arm's-length transactions. This explanation for multinationals and their activity levels is nonstrategic in the sense that expansion abroad by one firm does not directly affect the payout in reduced transaction costs to a parallel expansion by its market rival. Vernon urges, however, that a large amount of foreign investment is strategic and influenced specifically by oligopolistic interaction of competing firms. (I am not sure how he would define *large:* the criterion might be the proportion of foreign investment decisions ranked in some upper tier by dollar amount.) In view of the great interest that industrial economics has recently taken in game theory and strategic interactions, this position merits close examination.

Vernon starts by noting the familiar evidence of the extent of international collusion and market-sharing agreements in important industries between World Wars I and II. It might be attractive for researchers to revisit this evidence in light of modern game theory, in order to characterize more precisely what processes were at work. The role of foreign investment in this process has always, to me, seemed problematic, because the division of markets involves a pledge to forgo investing in some nations. If the deployment of subsidiaries as threats or hostages was indeed involved, the evidence would make excellent grist for modern students of industrial organization who are oriented toward game theory.

The pattern that Vernon finds prevalent, however, is the one discerned by Knickerbocker (1973): parallel and imitative foreign investments by competing firms in a U.S. oligopoly in the same host country markets and period of time. The mechanism seems to be the following. The oligopolists are few enough that they can sustain a price exceeding marginal cost in any market where they operate, and scale economies are (implicitly) not sufficiently large to inflict substantial losses if all firms invest in a given foreign market and period of time. A firm that does not join the investment race suffers a certain loss of profits on its exports to that market (local production is assumed to convey a substantial marketing advantage); that firm also takes the risk that, by virtue of experience in the foreign market, a rival might acquire some new competitive asset that could be used to improve its competitive position in the home market.

This model seems coherent in identifying imitative foreign investments as a prisoners' dilemma game; it conveys the interesting implications that the direct profits of foreign investments could be negative and that such unprofitable rounds of advantage-seeking investments could continue until the oligopoly's core excess profits were eliminated. Knickerbocker claimed to confirm the model empirically by showing that imitative foreign investment bouts occur more commonly in U.S. industries that are concentrated and therefore prone to the recognition of oligopolistic interdependence.

The theoretical coherence and empirical validity of this model strike me as issues that remain important. One reason why they deserve attention is the apparent prevalence in recent years of races among large international firms to undertake mergers that cross national borders but stay largely within a narrowly defined product or service market. Such international horizontal mergers, creating or extending multinational enterprises, seem to have occurred in pharmaceuticals, branded food products, major home appliances, and the entertainment (motion pictures, recordings) and publishing industries, among others.

These mergers pose an interesting problem for industrial economics, because they contain elements not fully explained either by the Knickerbocker-type model summarized previously or by the models of horizontal mergers that are standard in the literature of industrial organization. The latter models focus on the incentives that might exist for mergers between direct competitors in a homogeneous market, while the nonnourishing conclusion that the incentive is pervasive if the firms are price competitors (Bertrand behavior) and almost nonexistent if they are quantity competitors (Cournot). None of these industrial-organization models explain merger waves or races, nor do they explain why (as apparently happens) the short-run supply strategy of the acquired firm or business is often left independent of the acquirer's supply decisions. Knickerbocker's model is also insufficient to explain the absence of coordinated policies.

I have argued (Caves 1991) that an explanation might lie in extension of the theory of real options, constructed along the following lines. Consider an international horizontal merger in an industry whose national product markets are independent for purposes of short-run price or quantity competition but potentially interdependent in the application of innovations, design changes, or other such investment-type forms of nonprice competition. Assume that Nature periodically reveals new opportunities for such investments; assume also that the speed with which a firm can seize an opportunity depends on its having in place an appropriate coalition of resources. Assume finally that an international horizontal merger extends this coalition of resources and therefore increases the number of possible opportunities that the firm can seize. The international horizontal merger then becomes analogous to the purchase of a portfolio of real options.

The value of such an acquisition does not depend on any immediate redeployment of the assets of the acquired unit, so that apparently passive acquisitions can be explained. Furthermore, one firm's improvement of its response capability is adverse to the expected profits of its competitor; possibly (though not necessarily), the competitor's best reply is to make a similar acquisition in order to shrink or nullify the rival's conditional advantage. The occurrence of waves of similar acquisitions can thus be explained. The normative implication is not that horizontal mergers point toward monopolistic restriction of output but that they represent strategic rent-seeking in oligopolistic markets.

My effort to test this model in a way similar to Knickerbocker's yielded negative results, perhaps because it was not targeted closely enough on those internationally concentrated industries for which the model is a priori plausible. Nonetheless, the approach does seem useful for extending Vernon's (and Knickerbocker's) insight concerning strategic foreign investments with the theory of horizontal mergers in industries that give scope for strategic behavior.

REFERENCES

Caves, Richard E. 1991. Corporate mergers in international economic integration. *European financial integration,* ed. Alberton Giovannini and Colin Mayer, 136–60. Cambridge: Cambridge University Press.

Drake, Tracey A., and Richard E. Caves. 1992. Changing determinants of Japanese foreign investment in the United States. *Journal of the Japanese and International Economies* 6 (September): 228–46.

Knickerbocker, Frederick T. 1973. *Oligopolistic reaction and multinational enterprise.* Boston: Harvard Business School, Division of Research.

Milner, Helen V. 1988. *Resisting protectionism: Global industries and the politics of international trade.* Princeton, N.J.: Princeton University Press.

DISCUSSION SUMMARY

Robert Feenstra questioned *Raymond Vernon*'s conclusion that the patterns of foreign direct investment now coming from the industrialized Asian economies would be increasingly harmonized with the former patterns from the United States. He noted that the trade patterns from the Asian countries show marked differences from those of the United States and Europe, partly in response to the differences in market structure of the countries. In addition, the market structures of the Asian countries are not explained well by the transactions cost theories developed in a U.S. contest. On this basis, *Feenstra* suggested there should be some interesting differences in the patterns of direct investment from the Asian and western economies, rather than harmonization. *Donald Lessard* and *Kenneth Froot* questioned why firms might follow each other in establishing production facilities in a foreign market. There was some agreement that this action depended on an "option value" from establishing overseas facilities or merging with foreign firms. *Edward Graham* described a model of this type, with two countries (A and B) and two firms (1 and 2), both of which are initially located only in country B. If firm 1 moves into country A, then firm 2 might choose to follow because it believes A has some superior information about market conditions there: the "option value" reflects the possibility that demand might be especially high or costs low in that country.

There was some discussion of the model described by *Graham,* with *Feenstra* asking whether firm 2 would have entered country A in any case and *Froot*

arguing that there must be some initial distortion present for this "leader-follower" behavior to occur. *Lael Brainard* noted that there was not a good model of this behavior in the industrial organization literature, but she suggested two approaches that might help. First, there has been increased attention recently to locational choices within a country (such as the agglomeration of firms), and these factors might help to explain locational choices across borders. Second, it has been empirically established that transportation costs and distance are important determinants of trade patterns, and we might expect them to also be determinants of foreign investment.

In response to the last point, *Peter Petri* argued that "distance" can reflect many different factors, so we should be wary about its interpretation. *Richard Caves* suggested that cement production, a good example of an industry in which transportation costs are obviously important, was now experiencing some international mergers, so a case study might be useful. *William Zeile* noted that the latest data on foreign investment in the United States would be available from the Bureau of Economic Analysis, U.S. Department of Commerce in July 1992 and would include information on the cement industry.

2

TRANSNATIONAL CORPORATIONS FROM ASIAN DEVELOPING COUNTRIES: THEIR CHARACTERISTICS AND COMPETITIVE EDGE

HENRY WAI-CHUNG YEUNG*

ABSTRACT   Since the late 1970s, there has been a proliferation of empirical studies of transnational corporations (TNCs) from Asian developing countries. Drawing on this body of empirical literature and original research into Hong Kong firms and their ASEAN operations, this paper provides a succinct and thematic assessment of the various characteristics and competitive advantages of Asian developing country transnationals in terms of size of investment, main actors, form of market entry and ownership pattern, parent-subsidiary relationship, capital and source of funding, choice of technology and capital-labor intensity, method of production and marketing, foreign trade orientation, pattern of competition

* School of Geography, University of Manchester

and collaboration, locational choice, and the influence of the state. It is noted that TNCs from Asian developing countries are becoming a serious force in the capitalist global economy. They are even more significant in host developing economies. An assessment of the future of these emerging transnationals is discussed in the concluding section.

INTRODUCTION

The past two decades have witnessed not only a rapid proliferation and internationalization of indigenous firms from Asian developing countries, but also an ever-increasing importance of these transnational corporations (TNCs) in the global marketplace. By now, major TNCs from Asian developing countries, such as Gold-Star, Hyundai and Samsung from South Korea, Acer and Tatung from Taiwan and many other service TNCs, have become household names among the Pacific Asians. These gigantic TNCs from within the developing world are particularly important as engines of growth and transformation in many developing regions because "they are becoming a significant mechanism for the transfer of capital, technology, management and other assets within and between developing and developed countries" (Linge, 1984: 193). They also possess distinctive characteristics in their ownership patterns, investment strategies, and sectoral composition that sometimes differ from their counterparts from developed countries (Agmon and Kindleberger, 1977; Kumar and McLeod, 1981; Chen, 1983a; 1990; Lall, 1983a; Wells, 1983; Khan, 1986a; Fujita, 1990; Tolentino, 1993; Ulgado et al., 1994). As their domestic economies grow together with the "global shift" (Dicken, 1992), however, there is a strong tendency

I am extremely grateful to Professor Peter Dicken for reading successive drafts related to this paper. An anonymous referee has also provided very detailed and thoughtful comments and suggestions which are much appreciated. Financial support from the National University of Singapore and Developing Areas Research Group of the Institute of British Geographers are acknowledged. I also benefitted enormously when I was Visiting Associate at the Institute of Southeast Asian Studies, Singapore (from October 1993 to August 1994) and Visiting Scholar at the Centre of Asian Studies, University of Hong Kong (from December 1993 to May 1994). All errors and/or misinterpretations are, however, my sole responsibility.

for these developing country TNCs to evolve further and possibly to become less distinctive as a group. Rather, the distinction between developed and developing country TNCs is increasingly blurred over time.

By now, there exists a substantial body of empirical literature on this emerging phenomenon of Asian TNCs.[1] These studies, however, are rarely embedded in a comparative approach and remain rather idiosyncratic in their empirical and substantive focus (Yeung, 1994a). We do not know much, for example, of the nature and organization of Asian TNCs as a whole. It is the objective of this paper to examine what Heenan and Keegan (1979) refer to as this "apparent contradiction" of multinationalism from the Asian developing world on the basis of their characteristics and competitive edge. It should be recognized that Asian TNCs are far from homogeneous in their organizational forms and investment strategies (cf. Buckley and Mirza, 1988). Having said that, this paper intends to draw some common threads from the previous literature in order to arrive at a clearer picture of TNCs from Asian developing countries. Whenever possible, this paper brings in some recent evidence to update trends of the 1970s and 1980s. Because of limited space, this paper does not purport to provide a comprehensive explanation of the transnational operations of Asian TNCs (cf. Yeung, 1994a).

Three methodological notes are necessary here. First, the term "Third World multinationals" has gained such a wide currency in the literature that almost every empirical study adopts it uncritically (Yeung, 1994a). This study intends to dispute the usage of this term because it is biased ideologically and misleading empirically. The term is also fraught with definition problems. Instead, this paper proposes a relatively unbiased term hereafter known as "developing country transnationals." Developing country TNCs are defined as "domestic enterprises headquartered in developing countries which control assets and/or exert influence in the decision-making process of one or more cross-border subsidiaries and/or affiliates" (Yeung, 1994a: 298). Second, this paper relies substantially upon a diverse range of existing empirical studies of and scattered secondary information on Asian TNCs. The paper is also based on original research in which the author conducted corporate interviews with top executives from more than 110 Hong Kong TNCs and some 60 of their transnational operations in the ASEAN region.[2] Third, this paper excludes those studies of foreign direct investment (FDI) *per se* (e.g., Lee, 1990; Shin and Eugene, 1990; Lall, 1991; Thee, 1991; 1992; 1993). This is deemed necessary because these FDI studies are largely macro-economic and concerned with financial flows from developing countries; they offer relatively little substantive on the organizational forms and geographical spread of transnational operations from developing country enterprises.

EMERGING TRANSNATIONAL CORPORATIONS FROM ASIAN DEVELOPING COUNTRIES

TNCs from Asian developing countries have proliferated on a regional scale since the early 1970s. By the early 1980s, these TNCs spanned across at least thirty countries worldwide. Asian developing country TNCs originated primarily from the Newly Industrialized Economies (NIEs) such as Hong Kong, Singapore, South Korea and Taiwan, with the exception of Indian transnationals. Most of these "unconventional" TNCs (Giddy and Young, 1982) are found in the primary and manufacturing sectors, whereas relatively few of them are engaged in service industries. Table 1 presents the geographical distribution of outward FDI stock from nine Asian developing countries up to 1988. As shown in the total FDI stock, Hong Kong, with more than U.S. $13,952 million, has been the leading investor from Asian developing countries (Yeung, 1994b; also Ramstetter, 1993), followed by Singapore (U.S.

$1,407 million), South Korea (U.S. $1,119 million) and Taiwan (U.S. $704 million). Up to the early 1980s, Hong Kong had an overseas direct equity stock of between U.S. $1.5 to U.S. $2 billion mainly in manufacturing. Of this, it is estimated that at least some U.S. $600–700 million came from indigenous Chinese firms (R. Lall, 1986: 3). In 1982, the value of Singapore's FDI within Asia was U.S. $469 million, out of which U.S. $309 million went to Malaysia (Lim and Teoh, 1986: 342). By the end of 1990, overseas direct investment by Singapore companies had soared to S $7.5 billion or U.S. $5 billion. Almost 90 percent of this huge outward investment was made in the Asian region (Régnier, 1993: 309). By the late 1980s, South Korea and Taiwan became another two fierce "tigers" in the family of Asian developing country TNCs (Shin, 1989; Chang, 1990; Lee and Plummer, 1992; Chiu and Chung, 1993; Poon, 1993; Lee, 1994; Li, 1994). Even TNCs from the Peoples' Republic of China (P.R.C.) and Indonesia have experienced a boom since the late 1980s (Gang, 1992; Tseng, 1992; Lecraw, 1993). What then are the distinguishing characteristics and competitive edge of these TNCs?

SIZE OF INVESTMENTS

Any casual statement on the size of investment by Asian developing country TNCs can be extremely misleading. Not only are these generalizations built on shaky empirical data, but they are also constantly subject to change. What appears on excessively large direct investment in the early 1980s may quickly become insignificant in the early 1990s in an era of intensified globalization of economic activities. In view of these potential but real methodological problems, this paper elaborates on the *relative* size of Asian developing country TNCs on the basis of multiple indicators: (1) total stock; (2) firm asset and employment size; (3) percentage share of inward investment stock in developing countries; (4) sectoral distribution; and (5) number of foreign subsidiaries.

Tolentino (1993: 24-5) estimated that in 1960 the stock of foreign direct investment originating from developing countries amounted to U.S. $540 million

TABLE 1. Geographical Distribution of Outward Foreign Direct Investment from Developing Asian Countries, 1988*

Country	China[1]	Hong Kong[2]	India[3]	Pakistan[4]	Philippines[5]	Singapore[6]	South Korea[7]	Taiwan[8]	Thailand[9]
DEVELOPED COUNTRIES	1155.5 (66.7)	1704.9 (12.2)	5.87 (7.72)	12.95 (5.67)	5.37 (13.60)	322.39 (22.91)	620.84 (55.47)	501.31 (71.25)	50.93 (24.00)
NORTH AMERICA	255.6 (14.8)	1389.3 (9.9)	1.06 (1.39)	0.13 (0.06)	5.37 (13.60)	40.13 (2.85)	490.56 (43.83)	425.65 (60.50)	48.96 (23.07)
USA	238.5 (13.8)	939.7 (6.7)	1.06 (1.39)	0.13 (0.06)	5.37 (13.60)	31.17 (2.21)	398.26 (35.58)	425.65 (60.50)	48.96 (23.07)
Canada	17.1 (1.0)	449.6 (3.2)	—	—	—	8.96 (0.64)	92.30 (8.25)	—	—
WESTERN EUROPE	112.1 (6.5)	—	4.62 (6.08)	12.26 (5.37)	—	175.33 (12.46)	41.07 (3.67)	—	0.55 (0.26)
Austria	—	—	—	—	—	—	—	—	—
Belgium and Luxembourg	0.9 (0.1)	—	—	—	—	58.64 (4.17)	2.17 (0.19)	—	—
Denmark	—	—	—	—	—	—	—	—	0.10 (0.05)
France	27.3 (1.6)	—	0.01 (0.01)	—	—	—	3.25 (0.29)	—	0.01 (0.01)
Germany	25.1 (1.4)	—	0.42 (0.55)	0.57 (0.25)	—	0.30 (0.02)	12.20 (1.10)	—	0.02 (0.01)
Greece	—	—	0.17 (0.22)	—	—	—	—	—	—
Ireland	—	—	—	—	—	—	4.50 (0.40)	—	—
Italy	7.2 (0.4)	—	—	—	—	2.15 (0.15)	0.23 (0.02)	—	—
Netherlands	5.6 (0.3)	—	—	—	—	82.76 (5.88)	0.34 (0.03)	—	0.15 (0.07)
Norway	1.9 (0.1)	—	—	—	—	—	—	—	—
Portugal	—	—	—	—	—	—	0.27 (0.02)	—	—
Spain	16.6 (1.0)	—	—	—	—	—	0.25 (0.02)	—	—
Sweden	—	—	—	—	—	—	—	—	—
Switzerland	10.6 (0.6)	—	0.01 (0.01)	—	—	7.16 (0.51)	—	—	—
United Kingdom and Northern Ireland	7.3 (0.4)	—	4.01 (5.29)	11.03 (4.83)	—	24.32 (1.73)	17.86 (1.60)	—	0.27 (0.13)
Other European countries	9.5 (0.5)	—	—	0.65 (0.28)	—	—	—	—	—
AUSTRALASIA	802.6 (46.3)	—	0.19 (0.25)	—	—	97.13 (6.90)	58.90 (5.27)	—	0.19 (0.09)
Australia	759.5 (43.9)	—	0.19 (0.25)	—	—	92.18 (6.56)	58.84 (5.26)	—	0.19 (0.09)
New Zealand	7.1 (0.4)	—	—	—	—	4.95 (0.35)	0.06 (0.01)	—	—
OTHER DEVELOPED COUNTRIES	21.3 (1.2)	315.6 (2.3)	—	0.57 (0.25)	—	9.80 (0.69)	30.31 (2.70)	75.66 (10.75)	1.23 (0.58)
Japan	21.3 (1.2)	315.6 (2.3)	—	—	—	5.55 (0.39)	29.71 (2.65)	—	1.08 (0.51)
Turkey	—	—	—	—	—	—	0.60 (0.05)	—	0.15 (0.07)
Israel	—	—	—	—	—	4.25 (0.30)	—	—	—
DEVELOPING COUNTRIES	574.5 (33.2)	12246.9 (87.8)	69.74 (91.78)	215.42 (94.33)	34.10 (86.40)	1084.71 (77.09)	498.32 (44.53)	202.27 (28.75)	161.23 (76.00)
AFRICA	94.4 (5.5)	—	27.88 (36.68)	88.33 (38.68)	15.02 (38.05)	74.66 (5.31)	12.79 (1.14)	—	0.43 (0.20)
Algeria	1.0 (0.1)	—	—	—	—	—	—	—	—
Cameroon	1.6 (0.1)	—	—	—	—	—	1.28 (0.11)	—	—
Ivory Coast	—	—	—	—	—	—	0.40 (0.03)	—	—
Egypt	5.9 (0.3)	—	0.90 (1.18)	—	—	—	0.26 (0.02)	—	—
Gabon	4.1 (0.2)	—	—	—	—	—	—	—	—
Ghana	—	—	—	—	—	—	—	—	—
Kenya	—	—	8.90 (11.71)	—	—	—	—	—	—
Liberia	4.4 (0.2)	—	—	10.00 (4.38)	15.02 (38.05)	73.91 (5.26)	0.01 (0.01)	—	0.43 (0.20)
Mauritius	19.1 (1.1)	—	0.07 (0.09)	—	—	0.15 (0.01)	—	—	—
Morocco	0.2 (0.1)	—	—	—	—	—	0.21 (0.02)	—	—
Nigeria	8.7 (0.5)	—	6.37 (8.38)	0.56 (0.25)	—	—	1.36 (0.12)	—	—
Senegal	0.1 (0.1)	—	9.41 (12.39)	—	—	—	0.43 (0.04)	—	—
Seychelles	—	—	2.04 (2.68)	—	—	—	—	—	—
Sudan	—	—	—	77.77 (34.05)	—	—	—	—	—
Uganda	—	—	0.19 (0.25)	—	—	—	—	—	—
Other	49.4 (2.9)	—	—	—	—	0.60 (0.04)	8.84 (0.79)	—	—
EAST, SOUTH and SOUTHEAST ASIA	378.8 (21.9)	12246.9 (87.8)	38.25 (50.34)	11.06 (4.84)	10.46 (26.50)	899.32 (63.91)	254.41 (22.74)	171.75 (24.41)	159.48 (75.17)
Bangladesh	6.8 (0.4)	—	1.61 (2.12)	—	—	0.05 (0.01)	0.57 (0.05)	—	0.04 (0.02)
Brunei Darusalam	—	—	—	—	5.63 (14.26)	27.37 (1.95)	0.01 (0.01)	—	0.21 (0.10)
Ceylon	—	—	—	—	—	—	—	—	—
China	—	8236.8 (59.0)	—	—	—	45.63 (3.24)	—	—	1.48 (0.70)
Hong Kong	274.2 (15.8)	—	0.03 (0.04)	1.00 (0.44)	4.83 (12.24)	268.95 (19.11)	15.45 (1.38)	—	105.04 (49.50)
India	—	—	—	—	—	0.50 (0.04)	0.14 (0.01)	—	—
Indonesia	—	1867.5 (13.4)	10.42 (13.71)	—	—	33.78 (2.40)	188.74 (16.87)	40.20 (5.71)	20.29 (9.56)
Malaysia	1.2 (0.1)	421.7 (3.0)	6.62 (8.71)	4.51 (1.97)	—	477.41 (33.93)	29.02 (2.59)	19.27 (2.74)	0.18 (0.08)
Pakistan	8.9 (0.5)	14.4 (0.1)	—	—	—	—	—	—	—

TABLE 1 (Cont'd).   Geographical Distribution of Outward Foreign Direct Investment from Developing Asian Countries, 1988*

Country	China[1]	Hong Kong[2]	India[3]	Pakistan[4]	Philippines[5]	Singapore[6]	South Korea[7]	Taiwan[8]	Thailand[9]
Philippines	12.7 (0.7)	175.6 (1.3)	0.24 (0.32)	—	—	6.40 (0.45)	3.05 (0.27)	52.86 (7.52)	0.01 (0.01)
Singapore	19.4 (1.1)	—	3.40 (4.47)	5.20 (2.28)	—	—	4.74 (0.42)	20.72 (2.94)	31.97 (15.07)
South Korea	—	100.9 (0.7)	—	—	—	1.10 (0.08)	—	—	—
Sri Lanka	2.5 (0.1)	161.9 (1.2)	4.17 (5.49)	0.35 (0.15)	—	10.31 (0.73)	2.51 (0.22)	—	0.06 (0.03)
Taiwan	—	990.6 (7.1)	8.16 (10.74)	—	—	11.56 (0.82)	—	—	0.16 (0.08)
Thailand	51.7 (3.0)	277.5 (2.0)	—	—	—	16.26 (1.16)	10.15 (0.91)	38.70 (5.50)	—
Other	1.5 (0.1)	—	3.60 (4.74)	—	—	—	0.03 (0.01)	—	0.04 (0.02)
WESTERN ASIA and MIDDLE EAST	19.2 (1.1)	—	1.82 (2.40)	106.47 (46.62)	—	3.50 (0.25)	175.74 (15.70)	—	0.31 (0.15)
Bahrain, Oman, United Arab Emirates	—	—	1.09 (1.44)	13.36 (5.85)	—	—	135.99 (12.15)	—	—
Iran	—	—	—	1.99 (0.87)	—	—	0.26 (0.02)	—	—
Iraq	—	—	—	—	—	—	—	—	0.04 (0.02)
Lebanon	—	—	—	2.34 (1.02)	—	—	—	—	—
Qatar	—	—	—	—	—	—	0.20 (0.02)	—	—
Saudi Arabia	0.2 (0.1)	—	0.42 (0.55)	88.78 (38.88)	—	3.50 (0.25)	39.29 (3.51)	—	0.19 (0.09)
Jordan	—	—	0.31 (0.41)	—	—	—	—	—	—
Other	19.0 (1.0)	—	—	—	—	—	—	—	0.08 (0.04)
EUROPE	6.5 (0.4)	—	1.97 (2.59)	—	—	—	—	—	—
Hungary	—	—	0.03 (0.04)	—	—	—	—	—	—
Malta	6.5 (0.4)	—	0.01 (0.01)	—	—	—	—	—	—
USSR	—	—	0.35 (0.46)	—	—	—	—	—	—
Yugoslavia	—	—	1.58 (2.08)	—	—	—	—	—	—
LATIN AMERICA	60.9 (3.5)	—	0.05 (0.07)	0.17 (0.07)	8.60 (21.80)	81.76 (5.81)	25.98 (2.32)	—	1.01 (0.48)
Argentina	—	—	—	—	—	—	4.31 (0.40)	—	—
Bermuda	—	—	—	—	0.01 (0.03)	—	1.00 (0.09)	—	—
Brazil	44.2 (2.6)	—	—	—	—	—	1.61 (0.14)	—	—
Cayman Islands	—	—	—	—	—	—	0.50 (0.04)	—	—
Chile	2.7 (0.2)	—	—	—	—	—	3.95 (0.35)	—	—
Costa Rica	—	—	—	—	—	—	3.02 (0.27)	—	—
Dominican Republic	—	—	—	—	—	—	0.82 (0.07)	—	—
Jamaica	—	—	—	—	—	—	2.15 (0.19)	—	—
Mexico	0.5 (0.1)	—	—	—	—	4.55 (0.32)	—	—	—
Netherlands Antilles	—	—	—	—	—	5.20 (0.37)	—	—	—
Panama	0.6 (0.1)	—	0.05 (0.07)	—	7.81 (19.79)	0.05 (0.01)	7.20 (0.64)	—	0.80 (0.38)
Other	13.0 (0.8)	—	—	0.17 (0.07)	0.78 (1.98)	71.96 (5.11)	1.42 (0.13)	—	0.21 (0.10)
OCEANIA	14.7 (0.8)	—	0.15 (0.20)	—	—	6.25 (0.44)	29.40 (2.63)	—	—
Fiji	2.9 (0.2)	—	0.10 (0.13)	—	—	—	0.75 (0.07)	—	—
Papua New Guinea	1.7 (0.1)	—	—	—	—	6.25 (0.44)	19.50 (1.74)	—	—
Tonga	—	—	0.05 (0.07)	—	—	—	—	—	—
Other	10.1 (0.6)	—	—	—	—	—	9.15 (0.82)	—	—
OTHER UNALLOCATED DEVELOPING COUNTRIES	1.5 (0.1)	—	—	9.39 (4.11)	0.02 (0.05)	19.22 (1.37)	—	30.52 (4.34)	—
TOTAL	1731.5 (100)	13951.8 (100)	75.99 (100)	228.37 (100)	39.47 (100)	1407.10 (100)	1119.16 (100)	703.58 (100)	212.16 (100)

Sources: Tolentino (1993), *Technological Innovation and Third World Multinationals*, London: Routledge, Tables 10.1–10.8.

UNCTC (1992), *World Investment Directory 1992: Volume 1, Asia and the Pacific*, New York: United Nations, various country tables.

*All data are in US$millions unless otherwise specified. All percentages are in parentheses.

[1]Data are based on cumulative approved outflows from 1979–1987 in millions of yuan.

[2]Data have been obtained on the basis of inward stock attributed to Hong Kong up to 1987 in the various host countries.

[3]Data represents the value of Indian investments in joint ventures abroad in production or under implementation as at the end of calendar year.

[4]Data obtained on the basis of cumulative ouflows since 1972.

[5]Data represent cumulative outflows of registered investments with the Central Bank of the Philippines since 1980.

[6]Data represent domestic investors' ordinary paid-up shares in overseas subsidiaries and associated enterprises as at end of year and the net amounts due to overseas branches up to 1987.

[7]Data represent cumulative flows of realized investment abroad since 1968.

[8]Data represent cumulative approved outflows since 1959.

[9]Data represent cumulative flows of investment abroad since 1978.

(0.8 percent of total global FDI stock). But by 1975, this estimate had risen sharply to around U.S. $3,304 million, representing 1.2 percent of the world's FDI stock and an annual average growth rate of 13 percent since 1960. By 1992, developing country FDI stock had increased almost twenty-fold to U.S. $62,418 million (3.2 percent of global FDI stock), experiencing an annual average growth of 23 percent from the 1975 figure. This rate was double that of developed countries (12 percent) (UNCTAD, 1994: Annex Table 4). A tentative conclusion from these figures is that despite its small volume, FDI from developing countries has been accelerating at a very rapid rate since the late 1970s and early 1980s.

Asian developing country TNCs may be small in total capital assets and employment size by world standards, but they may be very large locally and sectorally. For examples, fourteen of the world's five hundred largest industrial companies and thirty-five of the world's five hundred largest banks were from Asian developing countries in 1987. In 1986, the top thirteen largest financial companies from developing countries were Asian (Buckley and Mirza, 1988: 52 and Table 5). In terms of international employment size, small enterprises (up to two hundred workers) constitute a large number of all overseas subsidiaries. These subsidiaries are by no means small in developing countries since most domestic enterprises are small and medium enterprises (SMEs) with employment size of less than a few hundred employees.

If the FDI stock from Asian developing countries is measured in relation to its percentage share in host developing countries, it may be an important source of foreign investment. UNCTC (1989: 3) estimates that in China and Malaysia, half of inward FDI is from other developing countries. Table 2 shows the geographical origins of cumulative foreign investment in the ASEAN-5 countries up to 1994. Hong Kong and Taiwan have been respectively the second and third largest investors in Indonesia up to June 1994, only next to Japan (Yeung, 1994b). Between 1967 and 1993, Japan and Hong Kong were the top-two largest investors in Indonesia, measured in terms of cumulative FDI stock. The total FDI stock from Hong Kong to Indonesia amounted to U.S. $1,061 million (10.3 percent) in 1980 and soared to U.S.

$2,316 million (7.1 percent) in 1988 (UNCTC, 1992: 149) and U.S. $6,116 million (8.1 percent) by June 1994. In Malaysia, Singapore has always been one of the largest investors in the manufacturing sector. Up to the late 1970s, Singapore was consistently the second largest foreign investor in Malaysia, with investments spread across a number of industries (Lall, 1979; 1980b; 1982). In the manufacturing sector of Malaysia, Singapore was even ranked as the largest investor in the early 1980s (Lim and Teoh, 1986: 344). By the late 1980s, both Taiwan (measured by FDI flows in 1990) and South Korea (measured by total FDI stock in 1987) became the top developing country investors in Malaysia (UNCTC, 1992: 161-5). From the early 1980s to the late 1980s, intra-regional FDIs from East Asian NIEs amounted to more than two-thirds of Japanese FDI. On a per capita basis, the NIEs were investing at a rate of 33 percent faster than the Japanese (Guisinger, 1991: 36). In Indonesia and Malaysia, for example in Table 2, the NIEs provided the largest portion of total foreign investment up to June 1994 and December 1992 respectively.

In terms of sectoral distribution, foreign investment and TNCs from Asian developing countries occupy an even more pronounced position, corresponding to their national competitive advantages (see Porter, 1990; cf. Dunning, 1993a; 1993b; Redding, 1994). Widely-cited examples are Hong Kong in the textile and garment industries and financial and business services, Singapore in airlines and transportation, South Korea in construction, automobiles, footwear, and electronics and Taiwan in the electronics and shipping industries. Another indicator of the size of developing country TNCs is the number of subsidiaries abroad. Chen (1981; 1983a) and Wells (1983: 9) suggest that only 6 out of 963 TNCs from developing countries would qualify if the Harvard definition of a "multinational corporation"—controlling more than six subsidiaries abroad—is applied: two from India, two from Hong Kong, one from Colombia and one from Mexico. If the UNCTC's (1978) less restrictive definition of TNCs (i.e., controlling one or more subsidiaries abroad) is adopted, there were more than 500 TNCs with over 3,000 foreign affiliates from Asian developing countries alone by

TABLE 2. Geographical Origins of Cumulative Foreign Investment in ASEAN-5 Countries

Country	Indonesia[1] in US$million	Indonesia Percentage	Malaysia[2] in RM$million	Malaysia Percentage	Philippines[3] in US$million	Philippines Percentage	Singapore[4] in S$million	Singapore Percentage	Thailand[5] in Bt$million	Thailand Percentage
DEVELOPED COUNTRIES	30974.1	41.3	6445.7	59.9	3208.3	86.9	45095.0	71.7	60691.0	56.7
NORTH AMERICA	3808.2	5.1	492.2	4.6	1898.6	51.5	11108.4	17.7	7620.0	7.1
USA	3692.8	4.9	476.3	4.4	1845.8	50.0	11108.4	17.7	7620.0	7.1
Canada	115.4	0.2	15.9	0.1	52.8	1.4	—	—	—	—
AUSTRALASIA	1564.8	2.1	244.7	2.3	68.3	1.9	3122.8	5.0	486.0	0.5
Australia	1541.6	2.1	238.3	2.2	68.3	1.9	3122.8	5.0	486.0	0.5
New Zealand	23.2	0.0	6.4	0.1	—	—	—	—	—	—
EUROPE	10665.7	14.2	1892.0	17.6	551.9	15.0	18414.7	29.3	7138.0	6.7
Austria	9.7	0.0	—	—	27.5	0.7	—	—	—	—
Belgium	292.8	0.4	1.3	0.0	—	—	—	—	—	—
Denmark	105.7	0.1	145.6	1.4	19.4	0.5	—	—	—	—
Finland	62.0	0.1	0.7	0.0	—	—	—	—	—	—
France	464.6	0.6	16.0	0.1	44.2	1.2	—	—	—	—
Germany	1961.3	2.6	258.1	2.4	38.5	1.0	1008.1	1.6	955.0	0.9
Ireland	11.0	0.0	—	—	—	—	—	—	—	—
Italy	24.5	0.0	15.5	0.1	—	—	—	—	—	—
Luxembourg	817.6	1.1	15.6	0.1	14.8	0.4	—	—	—	—
Netherlands	2636.6	3.5	301.5	2.8	155.1	4.2	4623.2	7.3	1652.0	1.5
Norway	241.1	0.3	9.1	0.1	—	—	—	—	—	—
Spain	59.8	0.1	—	—	—	—	—	—	—	—
Sweden	54.5	0.1	12.3	0.1	38.6	1.0	—	—	—	—
Switzerland	595.4	0.8	155.0	1.4	84.0	2.3	2537.6	4.0	—	—
United Kingdom	3329.1	4.4	961.3	8.9	129.8	3.5	8238.1	13.1	4531.0	4.2
Other	—	—	—	—	—	—	770.0	1.2	—	—
JAPAN	14935.4	19.9	3816.8	35.5	689.5	18.7	12449.1	19.8	45447.0	42.5
DEVELOPING COUNTRIES	24536.7	32.7	4220.3	39.2	401.2	10.9	8986.5	14.3	26461.0	24.7
AFRICA	434.2	0.6	13.5	0.1	—	—	—	—	—	—
Cyprus	—	—	2.0	0.0	—	—	—	—	—	—
Liberia	430.2	0.6	11.5	0.1	—	—	—	—	—	—
Nigeria	3.0	0.0	—	—	—	—	—	—	—	—
Ghana	1.0	0.0	—	—	—	—	—	—	—	—
ASIAN NIES	22562.6	30.1	3779.4	35.1	347.9	9.4	4472.1	7.1	24829.0	23.2
Hong Kong	6116.4	8.1	411.8	3.8	233.0	6.3	4187.4	6.7	11939.0	11.2
Singapore	4314.3	5.7	2368.3	22.0	30.0	0.8	—	—	2530.0	2.4
South Korea	3634.9	4.8	85.5	0.8	51.6	1.4	—	—	—	—
Taiwan	8497.0	11.3	913.8	8.5	33.3	0.9	284.7	0.5	10360.0	9.7
OTHER ASIAN COUNTRIES	867.3	1.2	166.8	1.5	11.4	0.3	4514.4	7.2	1632.0	1.5
Brunei Darusalam	170.0	0.2	1.0	0.0	—	—	—	—	—	—
Ceylon	1.5	0.0	—	—	—	—	—	—	—	—
China	147.4	0.2	6.3	0.1	—	—	—	—	—	—
India	217.8	0.3	21.9	0.2	—	—	—	—	527.0	0.5
Indonesia	—	—	58.9	0.5	—	—	—	—	—	—
Malaysia	184.7	0.2	—	—	11.4	0.3	—	—	1105.0	1.0
Pakistan	1.0	0.0	3.6	0.0	—	—	—	—	—	—
Papua New Guinea	0.0	0.0	—	—	—	—	—	—	—	—
Philippines	44.8	0.1	29.1	0.3	—	—	—	—	—	—
Sri Lanka	—	—	0.3	0.0	—	—	—	—	—	—
Thailand	100.1	0.1	45.7	0.4	—	—	—	—	—	—
LATIN AMERICA	670.6	0.9	218.0	2.0	41.9	1.1	—	—	—	—
Bahamas	86.5	0.1	—	—	8.5	0.2	—	—	—	—
Bermuda	56.2	0.1	88.6	0.8	9.9	0.3	—	—	—	—
Panama	527.9	0.7	129.4	1.2	23.5	0.6	—	—	—	—

TABLE 2 (Cont'd). Geographical Origins of Cumulative Foreign Investment in ASEAN-5 Countries

Country	Indonesia[1] in US$million	Indonesia Percentage	Malaysia[2] in RM$million	Malaysia Percentage	Philippines[3] in US$million	Philippines Percentage	Singapore[4] in S$million	Singapore Percentage	Thailand[5] in Bt$million	Thailand Percentage
MIDDLE EAST	2.0	0.0	42.6	0.4	—	—	—	—	—	—
Arab countries	—	—	41.8	0.4	—	—	—	—	—	—
Saudi Arabia	—	—	0.8	0.0	—	—	—	—	—	—
Yemen Arab Republic	1.0	0.0	—	—	—	—	—	—	—	—
Jordan	1.0	0.0	—	—	—	—	—	—	—	—
OTHER OR UNKNOWN	19516.6	26.0	99.5	0.9	80.6	2.2	8829.2	14.0	19859.0	18.6
TOTAL	75048.8	100.0	10765.5	100.0	3689.9	100.0	62910.5	100.0	107011.0	100.0

Notes:

[1] For Indonesia, data refer to cumulative FDI approvals in all sectors up to 15 June 1994 by the BKPM.

1. Excluding oil, banking, non-banking financial institution, insurance and leasing.
2. Investment figures are number of new project and change of status.
3. Investment value is total investment value of new project and expansion and change of status.
4. Investment value without number of project is expansion.

Source: Unpublished database generated by the Investment Coordinating Board (BKPM), 15 June 1994.

[2] For Malaysia, data refer to paid-up capital in approved FDI projects in the manufacturing sector as at 31 December 1992, except hotel and tourist projects.

Source: Unpublished data supplied by the Malaysian Industrial Development Authority (MIDA), 13 July 1994.

[3] For the Philippines, data refer to cumulative foreign equity investment stock from 1965–1991.

Source: Central Bank of the Philippines (various years), *Annual Statistics,* Manila: CBP, 1990, 1991 and data supplied by Eric Ramstetter, December 1993.

[4] For Singapore, data refer to cumulative foreign equity investment in 1981–1991.

Source: Department of Statistics (1994), *Yearbook of Statistics, Singapore 1993,* Singapore: DOS, Table 4.1.

[5] For Thailand, data refer to cumulative registered capital of firms granted Board of Investment promotion certificates from 1960–April 1994.

Source: Board of Investment (September 1993), *Key Investment Indicators in Thailand,* Bangkok: BOI, Table 10. Board of Investment (1994), unpublished data files, 14 May 1994.

the late 1980s (UNCTC, 1989: 3). By 1994, Hong Kong TNCs, coupled with the upsurge of direct investment in the Pearl River Delta in the P.R.C., control at least several thousand overseas subsidiaries and/or affiliates (Yeung, 1994b). In the ASEAN region alone, Hong Kong TNCs have established more than 1,000 operations in sectors ranging from resource-based and primary industries to manufacturing and service-oriented industries. In short, the above statistical indicators show that the transnational operations of TNCs from Asian developing countries are still in their embryonic stage if compared to the standard of developed country TNCs. If we measure in relative terms, however, Asian developing country TNCs do stand up as significant economic players in many developing economies.

MAIN ACTORS

If the above statistics about TNCs from Asian developing countries are accepted *prima facie,* who then

are the main players in this diverse group of transnationals? Monkiewicz (1986) suggests three types of actors from developing countries in general: (1) governments (inter-governmental agreements); (2) public sector companies and (3) private enterprises. More than half of these actors from developing countries belong to private sector initiatives. Out of 580 subsidiaries identified in the early 1980s, 87 (15 percent) were inter-governmental agreements. These agreements are an especially prominent form of transnational operations from Latin America (Diaz-Alejardro, 1977; White, 1981) and the Middle East (Nugent, 1986). In the ASEAN region, intergovernment agreements are also a major form of intra-regional economic cooperation through which ASEAN countries come together to exploit their comparative advantages in mutually beneficial ways (Pangestu et al., 1992; Tan et al., 1992). The development of the Singapore-Johor-Batam growth triangle, for example, should be viewed in this perspective, i.e., the concern of Singapore, Malaysia, and Indonesia with internationalizing their own domestic economies (Toh and Low, 1993; Thant et al., 1994).

Another 118 subsidiaries (20.3 percent) identified by Monkiewicz (1986) were the result of overseas expansion by public sector companies. Examples of such public sector companies from Asia are Pertamina (Indonesia), Sime Darby and Petronas (Malaysia), Keppel Group and Sembawan Group and Singapore Airlines (Singapore) and Chinese Petroleum (Taiwan). The remaining 375 (64.7 percent) foreign subsidiaries belonged to the overseas expansion of private enterprises. These private enterprises can be further divided into at least three groups: (1) colonial trading and services companies, e.g., Haw Par Group, Hong Kong Land, Hong Kong and Shanghai Bank, Jardine Matheson, Jardine Fleming and Inchcape Berhad; (2) indigenous trading, manufacturing and service conglomerates such as Liem Group (Indonesia), Hong Kong Chiap Hua (1937), Hopewell and Sun Hung Kai (Hong Kong), Kuok Brothers (Malaysia), San Miguel Brewery (The Philippines), Creative Technologies and Jack Chia-MPH (Singapore), Hyundai, Goldstar and Samsung (South Korea) and Acer and Tatung (Taiwan); and (3) national banks from most developing countries.

FORMS OF MARKET ENTRY AND OWNERSHIP PATTERNS

The literature on developing country transnationals has shown consistently that the joint-venture with minority equity share is the most preferred mode of market entry. To cite an instance, out of 602 manufacturing subsidiaries in Wells' (1983: 108) well-known study, only 57 were wholly-owned by parent firms from developing countries. In a study of Korean FDI in Singapore, the Koreans wholly owned only 161 out of their 243 subsidiaries, of which 134 were in the trading sector (Khan, 1986b: 6). This strong preference for joint-ventures contrasts sharply with developed country TNCs which typically prefer wholly-owned subsidiaries. For example, IBM and Coca Cola have been well known for their insistence on wholly-owned operations to the extent that they withdrew from India to protest pressure for equity-share from the host government. In fact, U.S.-based TNCs owned almost 66 percent of their manufacturing subsidiaries abroad in the mid-1980s.

One of the most accepted reasons for such a discrepancy is that developing country TNCs do not have the equivalent level of proprietary technology and firm-specific know-how that must be internalized through majority ownership (Buckley and Casson, 1976; Dunning, 1981; 1988; 1993b; Cantwell, 1989; 1993; Tolentino, 1993). Whether this internalization logic is correct remains a myth rather than a reality.

In fact, not all TNCs from Asian developing countries like to engage in joint-ventures. Even if joint-ventures are preferred, these specific contractual relationships may be young and subject to change over time. For example, Vernon (1977: 27) reports that in a survey of Indian joint-ventures abroad at the start of 1976, of 65 projects abroad, nearly half were less than two years old, and 63 more such investments were in process at that time. In order to provide a more permanent basis of transnational operations, many TNCs from Asian developing countries may still employ the conventional forms of market entry such as vertical integration. For example, Euh and Min (1986), in their survey of fifty Korean firms in 1984, found 62 percent of firms were wholly-owned subsidiaries abroad, 18 percent were joint-ventures with majority holdings and only 20 percent were joint-ventures with minority holdings. This finding contrasts sharply with Indian TNCs which are largely engaged in joint-ventures abroad.

We also observe changing forms of Taiwanese investment in the P.R.C. Sole proprietorships have become more popular in recent years because of the accumulation of past experience and increasing management flexibility. Even in joint ventures, Taiwanese investors usually take up a relatively higher proportion of shares. Taiwanese investors vary in size, from large enterprises to small and medium-sized firms. The amount and scale of investment have also been increasing. Using Xiamen as an example, which has seen the greatest growth in Taiwanese investment, the average amount of each Taiwanese investment project was U.S. $1 million in 1988. This rose to U.S. $3.7 million in 1989. Some investment projects even involved more than several billion and undertakings have gradually moved from short-term to long-term investments (Wei, 1993: 167).

Other studies of developing country TNCs also discovered an extensive use of vertical integration among natural resource TNCs. Examples of such studies are Argentine manufacturing and petroleum transnationals (Katz and Kosacoff, 1983), Brazilian iron and aluminum companies (C. Wells, 1988), Hong Kong's furniture companies (Wells, 1978), and service transnationals from Hong Kong in ASEAN (Yeung, 1995). In my study of Hong Kong firms and their ASEAN operations, more than half of 110 parent Hong Kong transnationals preferred to set up wholly-owned subsidiaries and/or affiliates in the ASEAN region (see Yeung, 1995). Joint ventures and partnerships, nevertheless, are more common in Indonesia, Malaysia and Thailand than in Singapore. Executives typically explain that choice of operational form depends very much on the host country regulations. In the former three countries, many sectors and industries are either closed to foreign companies or some local equity participation is required. It suffices therefore to argue that there is a complex bundle of social and political rationale behind most of these overseas ventures by TNCs from Asian developing countries.

PARENT-SUBSIDIARY RELATIONSHIPS

In the empirical literature on developing country TNCs, the relationship between parent companies from developing countries and their foreign subsidiaries is found to be different from developed country TNCs. The kind of parent-subsidiary relationship in the forms of increasing global integration and centralized coordination over time, typically observed in developed country TNCs is insignificant among Asian developing country TNCs. Instead, after an initial supply of core technology and management from the parent company in developing countries, foreign subsidiaries of Asian developing country TNCs are usually given more autonomy as time passes by. Euh and Min (1986) observed, for example, that among Korean manufacturing TNCs, only 50 percent of the parent firms had control over the long term planning.

More than a decade ago, Wells (1984: 141) correctly pointed out that "the parents of multinationals from developing countries are likely to make a major contribution to the subsidiary in the form of technology at the outset, but that they are unlikely to have the kind of continuing impact that has characterized some U.S.-based multinationals." The parent-subsidiary relationship in developing country TNCs has been characterized as loose, fluid, and informal. Unlike the stable relationship between parent companies and foreign subsidiaries in many developed country TNCs, this informal relationship among developing country TNCs is always in a constant flux and transformation.

CAPITAL AND SOURCE OF FUNDING

In most Asian developing countries, there is either foreign exchange control or a conservative banking system. A well-developed local capital market is virtually non-existent except in certain more advanced developing countries such as Hong Kong and Singapore. Limited access to capital and finance presents a critical barrier to many foreign investment projects by Asian developing country TNCs (e.g., India). Alternative ways of financing transnational operations in many Asian developing countries depend upon three factors: (1) the size of the project; (2) the nature of the project, and (3) the availability of wealthy local partners. Empirical studies have shown that most foreign ventures are financed by home country sources; capital is paid either in cash or bank guarantee. In the case of South Korean TNCs (Euh and Min, 1986), manufacturing firms tend to use internal capital funds from the parent companies, whereas capital for mining firms is supplied by borrowing from Korean EXIM Bank. In the case of Singaporean TNCs (Pang and Komaran, 1985), if the project is small in capital input, it is most likely financed through the company's internal reserve. Conversely, if the project involves heavy capital outlay, the firm may resort to bank loans and guarantees. In the case of Hong

Kong firms, most tend to fund their projects from internal reserves. Local banks play only minor roles in the transnationalization processes of Hong Kong firms. My interviews with over 110 Hong Kong TNCs also suggest a similar finding (see Low et al., 1995).

The nature of transnational ventures also matters in the choice of capital sourcing. If the project involves no equity holdings, the TNC does not need to invest capital. Instead, other inputs into the non-equity contractual arrangement are required, such as machinery and technological and managerial expertise. In conjunction with these non-equity forms of transnational operations, empirical studies have found occasional partnerships of Asian developing country TNCs with local capital. This is especially the case for Indian TNCs which favor minority-equity joint ventures with local partners. Indian transnationals prefer to export their technological and managerial expertise rather than their scarce domestic capital. Their reluctance to invest capital abroad is a direct consequence of the strict foreign exchange controls imposed by the Indian government. A viable alternative is to rely upon host country capital. The availability of rich local partners becomes an important location-specific advantage to many Indian TNCs. In the case of TNCs from the P.R.C., access to host country financial and capital markets plays an important role in the decision to operate in that country. For example, Hong Kong has traditionally been performing the role as a financial intermediary for those PRC TNCs and venture capitalists who are desperate for funds (Tseng, 1992; Chen and Wong, 1994). There are now thousands of P.R.C. enterprises operating in Hong Kong and more than twenty of them are listed in the Hong Kong Stock Exchange. These enterprises are mostly state-owned or recently privatized trading and manufacturing companies.

CHOICE OF TECHNOLOGY AND EXPERTISE AND CAPITAL-LABOR INTENSITY

Technology transfer among Asian developing countries has been a subject of considerable debate and research. Empirical studies of different countries have been completed, e.g. India (Lall, 1982; 1984b; 1985), Hong Kong (Chen, 1983a; 1983b; 1984), Singapore (Hill and Pang, 1991), South Korea (Westphal et al., 1984; Shin, 1989; Lee and Plummer, 1992; Lee, 1994) and Taiwan (Amsden, 1984; Chang, 1990; Lee, 1994). These studies have shown that FDI by domestic enterprises is one special way for Asian developing countries to export their industrial technology, based on the concept of "revealed comparative advantage" (Lall, 1980a; 1982; 1984a; Lee and Plummer, 1992). This "revealed comparative advantage" varies from country to country in the Asian developing world. Developing countries not only reveal markedly different "stocks" of total technological capability, but they also specialize in different industries and modes of technology export. In non-industrial sector, South Korea dominates by virtue of its success in the Middle East construction boom. By 1988, highly competitive technological capabilities of seven Korean construction firms, for example, have enabled them to capture more share (U.S. $5.4 billion) in the Middle East construction boom, against their world-class competitors from ten French firms (U.S. $5.3 billion) and twelve German firms (U.S. $2.7 billion) (Fujita, 1990: 44). India comes next, though very far behind South Korea, with Brazil very near to India. Direct investment in non-industrial activities is largely limited to Hong Kong, Singaporean, and South Korean TNCs. In the industrial sector, the picture is more mixed. India seems to predominate in project exports and Hong Kong, Singapore, South Korea, and Taiwan in direct investments, with a roughly similar showing by India, Singapore, South Korea, and Taiwan in disembodied technical and consultant service exports.

Empirical studies argue that this "revealed comparative advantage" of each Asian developing country and its TNCs is manifested in three ways: (1) low cost of skilled manpower; (2) appropriate technology and (3) the "unpackaged" nature of technology sales. First, developing country transnationals can compete successfully with giant TNCs from developed countries because of their lower cost of skilled labor. For example, Kumar (1982: 406) noticed in the early 1980s that it cost a U.S. firm about U.S. $100,000 to keep a middle level executive in Malaysia for a year, while the corresponding cost for an Indian firm was about U.S. $20,000. Other costs in the form of fringe benefits, bonuses, and subsidies were significantly lower among developing country TNCs. Wells (1978) also found among Hong Kong manufacturing multinationals that the salary structure of expatriate managers and technical specialists was more dependent upon variable bonuses and less on fixed salary. In this way, the company could maintain a lower cost structure to compete successfully with local and developed country firms. Even in the 1990s, the salaries payable to senior executives among developing country TNCs are still considerably lower than those paid to foreign expatriates from the Triad (i.e., North America, Western Europe, and Japan).

In the manufacturing sector, the lower labor cost structure of many developing country TNCs implies that a more labor-intensive production process is preferred (Wells, 1982). Highly labor-intensive production is also employed to relieve financial constraints, to reduce import of capital-intensive inputs, and to circumvent foreign exchange control. This labor-intensive production process can be observed in many industries in which developing country transnationals have a significant stake. Examples are construction, electronics, footwear, textiles, and toys in manufacturing industries; and banking, financial, securities trading, and shipping in service industries.

Second, the use of ''appropriate technology'' in the transnational operations of many Asian developing country enterprises enables them to compete with local and foreign firms by occupying a special *niche* market. The literature shows that this ''appropriate technology'' is embodied in the form of locally-adapted technology and machinery.[3] The general trend for many Asian developing country TNCs is to learn more sophisticated process and product technology from licensing and from joint-venture relationships with large TNCs from developed countries that reciprocally need a local partner to penetrate protected markets in some Asian developing countries. This sophisticated technology is then modified and adapted to local market and factor conditions. For example, Acma Electrical Industries, a Singaporean refrigerator manufacturer, originally acquired the technology from Sanyo and Frigidaire on the basis of a licensing agreement to manufacture refrigerators and air-conditioners. Subsequently, the company established a small research and development unit beginning with one full-time engineer assisted by personnel from other departments. By 1982, this department had expanded into a laboratory employing twenty-four Singaporean engineers, more than half with Ph.D.s. The company now designs its own products and components including moulds, dyes, cabinets and cooling systems although it continues to import the compressor. A large part of the R & D department's activities is geared toward making necessary changes in their products to suit the requirements of their clients (Lim and Teoh, 1986).

It should be noted that modification is mainly based on product technology and less on process technology. The typical method of modifying product technology is known as descaling. Descaling refers to the down-scaling of the size of production technology so that a smaller scale of operations can be maintained at the same level of technology. The reason for descaling is that small home and host markets in developing countries do not enable economies of scale required to maximize the potential of borrowed technology. Economies of scope are more important considerations in the context of limited markets in developing countries. The reliance upon borrowed technology from developed countries by developing country transnationals can be shown with reference to their low level of research and development (R & D) expenditure. Data from the Harvard Multinational Enterprise Project shows that in the 1970s about 58 percent of the subsidiaries of firms from developing countries were in industries characterized by low R & D expenditures. Such industries accounted for only 30 percent of subsidiaries of American TNCs and about 36 percent of subsidiaries from other developed countries. Only 26 percent of the subsidiaries of developing country TNCs were in high R & D industries, whereas the equivalent figures were 55 percent and 52 percent for the subsidiaries of U.S. and other developed country TNCs respectively (Wells, 1983; 1986).

Through descaling, many developing country TNCs are able to convert proprietary technology from developed country TNCs to their own firm-specific advantage. The first effect of this descaling is the smaller-scale of operations and a flexible technology for customized production. The outcome of these modifications should be a reduction in over-capacity in production facilities. Empirical studies have confirmed this estimated higher capacity utilization (48 percent) in developing country TNCs, compared to only about 26 percent in TNCs from developed countries (Wells, 1983: 22). Another consequence of descaling is a higher degree of integration of operations by developing country TNCs with local technological base. Thailand is a good example in which developing country TNCs are able to operate their descaled technology in parallel with local technology.

In the 1990s, many giant TNCs from the NIEs have developed firm-specific technological capabilities to compete successfully with TNCs from the Triad regions. Two examples are Acer from Taiwan and Hyundai from South Korea. In 1986, Acer launched the world's second 32-bit personal computer, ahead of IBM (Compaq was first). By the end of the 1980s, Acer was shipping over 3 percent of the total world market for IBM-compatible personal computers and about 6 percent of the market for the more powerful machines based on Intel's 386 microprocessor. This is only one of several achievements which place Acer only a few months to a year behind the state-of-the-art technologies. In 1988, Acer and Mitac (the second main computer firm in Taiwan) signed cooperative agreements with IBM to license IBM's personal computer patents on a running royalties basis. In return, IBM receives an initial fee plus the right to license Acer and Mitac patents on the same reciprocal basis (Wade, 1990: 106–7). Acer has also formed alliances with Texas Instruments, with Daimler-Benz's microelectronics subsidiary and with Smith Corona. Recently, Stanley Shih, the founder of Acer, branched out to promote the quality and image of Acer. He wants Acer to be the "Sony of Taiwan." To this end he has founded a Brand International Promotion Association in Taipei.

Another successful story is Hyundai, a major Korean automobile producer (Wade, 1990: 310–2). By 1986, the Hyundai Excel had become by far the best-selling new car import in American history, following an earlier success in the Canadian market. In 1988, Hyundai produced 650,000 automobiles, half as many as Fiat and Renault, of which 63 percent

were exported. In response to the growing potential and capability of the Korean automobile industry and to catch up with GM's existing joint venture with Daewoo, Ford and Chrysler rushed to establish joint ventures with Korean partners. But Ford's proposal to Hyundai was rejected and finally the former jointed up with Kia, with the help of its Japanese equity partner, Mazda. By the late 1980s, Hyundai had already set up several plants in Canada and R & D offices in the United States.

Third, the transfer of technology from developing country TNCs is usually in an "unpackaged" form. Since small-scale operations, relatively simple techniques and customized flexible products characterize the technological choice of TNCs from developing countries, the transfer of this technology can be achieved without the massive package typically found among green-field or turnkey projects from developed country TNCs. A recipient country therefore does not have to import a whole series of "redundant" technologies in order to satisfy the package-deal. It benefits not only from a saving in unnecessary parts, but also from a customized product technology.

METHODS OF PRODUCTION AND MARKETING

TNCs from Asian developing countries are characterized in the literature as specialists in the production of "old" and mature products using batch-production methods. These products are meant specifically for local markets. In tropical countries, some developing country TNCs modify their product technology to produce so-called "tropical products." For example, sun-fast dyes developed for tropical markets by Indian firms (Khan, 1986b). Other products are tailored to lower-income segments of the developing country markets. It should be noted, nevertheless, that many TNCs from developing countries may produce relatively high value-added products for North American and European markets. Well-known examples by now would be Acer computers, Hyundai cars, Samsung memory chips and many other O.E.M. (Original Equipment Manufacturing) products, not to mention leading service TNCs from Hong Kong and Singapore in banking and finance and business services. This high value-added aspect of developing country TNCs is often overlooked in the literature.

The literature demonstrates that the specialization on mature and low-tech products by many developing country TNCs implies a lack of product differentiation and other elements of non-price competition such as brand names, continuous interaction with customers, design exchange, tailoring of products, technological linkages, and extensive after-sales services. These attributes of marketing are particularly lacking among Indian multinationals (Lall, 1983a; 1985; cf. R. Lall, 1986). Developing country TNCs also spend little on marketing and advertisements (with the exception of some large service TNCs such as airline and shipping companies). There is thus a high reliance on third party distributors for marketing. In recent years, many of the largest TNCs from Asian NIEs have established their own marketing channels in North America and Western Europe to gain direct market access. The more successful ones also market their products under their own brand names. As will be shown later, this heightened concern with marketing activities has prompted further investment from Asian TNCs to developed countries. It also changes our perceptions of TNCs from Asian developing countries.

In order to gain a competitive advantage in some narrow, but accessible, niche markets, many developing country TNCs have to rely upon lower price as the basic tool of marketing and competition. This low-price marketing strategy further reinforces the earlier discussed phenomenon of exploiting lower costs of production in developing countries. The fundamental marketing strategy is based upon a ''survival-first principle'' rather than that of competing for global markets among TNCs from developed countries. Taiwan's indirect investment in the P.R.C., for example, is a typical reflection of this ''survival-first'' strategy (Chiu and Chung, 1993).

FOREIGN TRADE ORIENTATION

The transnational operations of Asian developing country enterprises can either be import-substituting or export-promoting. In some cases, these operations are catered for local markets. To cite an example, some Chinese investors in the noodle business from Hong Kong set up their foreign operations in Southeast Asia to supply ethnic food products to local markets—the Chinese communities in the region. In other cases, however, enterprises from developing countries invest in other host countries in order to export to a third country. Hong Kong textile and garment investment in Southeast Asia and the Pearl River Delta in China is best known for its circumvention of voluntary quotas and trade restrictions imposed by developed countries from North America and Europe (Leung, 1993; Chen and Wong, 1994; Yeung, 1994b). These textile and garment industries typically invest in developing countries so as to export to the third-party country in North America and/or Europe. The anticipated end of the Multi-Fiber Agreement (MFA) and increasing regional trade liberalization in the next few years will necessarily bring some changes to these investment patterns. For example, the end of textile and garment quotas means that most of these Hong Kong firms can now invest as much as they wish in a single country to supply to a third country because quota availability no longer poses a locational constraint. Attractive host country conditions (e.g., lower production costs) will probably become critical to investment decisions. Overseas ventures by these manufacturing TNCs from Asian developing countries will also be likely to increase in view of high costs in home countries.

The relative share of these two counterveiling orientations (i.e., investment for local market and investment for export) in the transnational operations of developing country TNCs is hard to assess. Some empirical evidence is in favor of the latter—many developing country TNCs invest abroad to export to a third country. For example, Svetlicic (1986: 78) shows that third markets tend to absorb the largest share of the foreign sales of developing country TNCs. Local markets account for 25 percent of sales while exports account for over 40 percent. This export-orientation can be attributed to several reasons: first, a great proportion of these exports comes from ''quota jump'' investments typically made by TNCs from NIEs, particularly Hong Kong. Second,

TNCs from developing countries tend to invest in industries and sectors which are more export-oriented (e.g., the manufacture of mature products and service industries). For example, in study of Taiwanese indirect investment in the P.R.C., Chiu and Chung (1993) found that Mainland investment has a much higher export propensity than Taiwanese FDI elsewhere (e.g., in ASEAN countries). They attributed this phenomenon to three reasons: (1) the P.R.C. adopts a conservative policy towards FDI, prompting the so-called ''two ends out'' policy (i.e., imported materials and exported products); (2) there is a lack of local support and linkages and (3) the predominance of small and medium Taiwanese companies in the P.R.C. means that large production support systems are absent. A caveat here is that this evidence is inconclusive and further research is needed.

On the other hand, imports among developing country TNCs are attributed to machinery and inputs of production. Private subsidiaries usually import much more machinery from home countries (80 percent) than public firms. Hong Kong TNCs (Wells, 1978; 1983; Chen, 1983a) and Korean TNCs (Han and Brewer, 1987), for example, carry with them machinery and technology from parent companies in their transnational operations. Public sector TNCs from developing countries import machinery largely from developed countries (almost twice as much as private firms). Private subsidiaries, however, do not rely on local machinery at all while public enterprises do (Svetlicic, 1986: 78). In terms of production inputs, TNCs from developing countries import less than their counterparts from developed countries. Wells (1983: 40) observes that factories in Thailand belonging to parents from other developing countries import only 39 percent of their raw materials, whereas subsidiaries of TNCs from developed countries import 76 percent. Even domestic Thai enterprises import more (65 percent) than those subsidiaries from other developing countries.

PATTERNS OF COMPETITION AND COLLABORATION

The patterns of competition and collaboration among Asian developing country TNCs are sometimes dif-

ferent from their counterparts from developed countries. Wells (1986) argues that both competition and collaboration *with* developed country TNCs are observed in the transnational operations of developing country TNCs. If there is any competition with existing TNCs from developed countries, it is mainly at the ''tail'' of the product life cycle, i.e., mature products. Price competition becomes the single most important weapon in competing for the market in these standardized products. Conversely, it is possible for Asian developing country TNCs to collaborate with TNCs from developed countries in order to gain access to the latter's technology, marketing skills and distribution networks through (1) joint ventures (most common); (2) informal production links; (3) vertical integration by large TNCs; and (4) non-equity participation (e.g., technology licensing). Some observers go so far as to suggest that TNCs from developed countries should be more engaged in joint ventures with their competitors from the developing world, given a high degree of complementarity of their firm-specific assets in certain industries and/or market segments (Connolly, 1984).

The pattern of competition and collaboration *among* developing country TNCs is also interesting. Asian developing country TNCs do not normally compete with each other, except in low-end products and services. They tend to occupy rather different segments of an industry or a market, reflecting the competitive advantage and historical trajectories of their home countries (Porter, 1990). In most cases, firms from developing countries tend to complement each other. Empirical studies have shown that firms from many NIEs are *not* in direct competition with one another. Examples cited are Hong Kong and Singaporean firms (Pang and Komaran, 1985) and South Korean and Taiwanese firms (Levy, 1988; Levy and Kuo, 1991; Li, 1994). When comparing South Korean and Taiwanese firms in the manufacture of footwear, production of keyboards and assembly of personal computers, the former group of firms tend to specialize in high volume, high productivity manufacturing of standardized products, whereas the latter group is better at smaller niche markets that demand greater flexibility, customization of products and rapid response. A conclusive assessment can only be arrived with more future research.

LOCATIONAL CHOICE

The locational choice of transnational operations from Asian developing countries can be conveniently analyzed according to two major groups of destinations: (1) investment in developing countries and (2) investment in developed countries. Up to now, the majority of foreign investments by Asian developing country TNCs has been confined to their fellow developing countries. This locational pattern contrasts significantly with developed country TNCs which tend to make a global presence in the Triad regions (Ohmae, 1985). Another interesting observation about the geography of developing country TNCs is their *intra-regional* focus. Transnational operations from developing countries are intra-regional to such an extent that "the Asian countries invest in Asia and the Latin Americans in Latin America" (O'Brien, 1980: 304). Although this statement is rather crude and out-dated, it does contain some elements of truth. Fujita (1990: 43) has reminded us, however, that "[i]n any case, as the overall level of developing-country FDI is relatively small, one large investment can influence the pattern of geographical as well as sectoral distribution."

As evident in Tables 1 and 2, within the Asia-Pacific region, most investments from the four NIEs (Hong Kong, South Korea, Singapore, and Taiwan) and India go to the P.R.C. and Southeast Asia.[4] For example, from the early to mid-1980s, there were slightly more than 1,000 subsidiaries and affiliates of intra-regionally-based TNCs in the Asian region, with a total foreign direct capital stock of at least U.S. $7 billion. About 93 percent of this intra-regional FDI in Asia (U.S. $6.5 billion) originated in six home countries: Hong Kong, Singapore, Taiwan, South Korea, Malaysia, and India (ESCAP/UNCTC, 1988; Yeung, 1994b). Tolentino (1993: 337) reports that in 1988, almost 92 percent of Indian outward direct investment in joint ventures was directed toward developing countries, particularly East, South and Southeast Asian and African countries, especially those with substantial ethnic Indian communities, such as Malaysia, Indonesia, Thailand, Sri Lanka, Nigeria, Kenya, and Senegal.

At a sub-national level, most developing country TNCs agglomerate heavily in the principal cities of host countries. This spatial bias is explained by the access to information, communication and transportation, access to banking and financial services, and political stability associated with these so-called "primate cities." Investment incentives provided by host governments may sometimes be inherently spatially biased toward large capital cities. In Indonesia, for example, two-thirds of the investors from developing countries have their plants located in Jakarta, compared to less than half of those from developed countries (Wells, 1981; Lecraw, 1992). There are only a handful of natural resources-based manufacturing firms—all from developed countries—planning to locate in the outer islands of Indonesia: Sumatra, Sulawesi, Kalimantan and East Java (Forbes, 1986).

Investments in developed countries by developing country TNCs tend to be highly place-specific. For example, San Miguel Corporation from the Philippines, established in 1890, expanded into the United States with the acquisition of George Muehleback Brewery Company in Kansas City as early as 1937. This initial U.S. investment was followed in 1939 by an acquisition of another brewery in San Antonio, Texas. These ventures were, however, divested in the late 1950s due to severe competition posed by the emergence of larger national breweries in the U.S. market (Tolentino, 1993: 241). In order to understand the geography of Asian TNCs in developed countries, their investment purposes must be comprehended beforehand. These purposes are sometimes no different from that of developed country TNCs (Sanyal and Torkornoo, 1988). TNCs from developing countries invest in their developed counterparts (1) to integrate forward into the production chain; (2) to gain marketing experience; (3) to enable technology transfer; (4) to reduce transport costs; and (5) to overcome rising protectionism.

Given the overall small volume of these investments compared to those in developing countries, a clear spatial organization is not easy to map out. Suffice to say that most locations are in North America, Western Europe and Australia. Table 1 shows that the P.R.C., South Korea and Taiwan invested more than half of their FDI stock by 1988 in developed countries. Whereas the United States was a favorite choice for the South Koreans and Taiwanese, the Chinese had particular interest in Australia. Within these large geographical continents, operations are concentrated largely in services and high technology sectors which are bounded in specific territorial complexes. To cite a few illustrations, Hong Kong and Singaporean bankers and financial companies have established offices in London and New York, while Korean and Philippine construction firms are involved in contracts as far away as the Middle East and Latin America (Lecraw, 1988). As for service investments, around 16 percent (A$865 million) of total investment in Australia in 1983 was made by Southeast Asian investors. Some A$469 of this A$865 was in real estate, accounting for 45 percent of spending in that particular sector (Forbes, 1986: 110). Large property development TNCs from Hong Kong are particularly keen in the Canadian property market (Olds, 1995).

Some high technology industries from Asian countries are also spatially reproduced in various Sunbelts of the U.S. (Sanyal and Torkornoo, 1988) and European countries, in particular the United Kingdom (*The Wall Street Journal,* 26 October 1994). For example, Hyundai, a South Korean automobile manufacturer, has invested in the Silicon Valley of California for research and development, pilot production, transfer of technology and marketing (Linge, 1984: 185; also Lee, 1994). Recently, its electronics division in the United States has agreed to buy AT & T Corp's NCR Microelectronics Production division for more than U.S. $300 million (*The Wall Street Journal,* 11 November 1994). By 1988, only 23 percent of Korean FDI had been directed to Asian Pacific countries, compared to a much higher proportion in 1978. Similarly, by 1988, only 29 percent of Taiwanese FDI was directed to developing countries whereas in the 1960s and 1970s, more than 50 percent of Taiwan's outward direct investment had been poured into Indonesia, Malaysia, Singapore, Thailand, and the Philippines (Tolentino, 1993: 340–41). For example, Acer started in 1976 with eleven employees and capital of $25,000. As Taiwan's flagship computer manufacturer, it opened a branch in Silicon Valley in 1984 to perform a key role in its R & D activities; it also has licensing agreements and joint ventures with a number of Japanese and American companies

(Chang, 1990: 13). In 1990, Acer paid U.S. $94 million for Altos, a Silicon Valley firm, to improve its distribution in America (*The Economist,* 16 November 1991).

THE INFLUENCE OF THE STATE

The state exerts potent influence in nearly all developing countries, particularly when it is pursuing either an import-substitution or export-promotion policy. The state serves *both* as a constraint and an enabling mechanism to the transnational operations of developing country TNCs.[5] In some instances, government restrictions are critical in guiding the nature of foreign operations by domestic enterprises. For example, the restrictive policies of the Indian government result in a strong preference for equity participation among Indian TNCs. Viewed in the context of these restrictions, FDI from India can be considered as "a disguised form of capital flight from India" (R. Lall, 1986: 89). Although these regulations have been particularly liberalized over time, the basic rationale and FDI pattern remain largely unaltered.

The role of the state also works the other way around: the state as a promoter of foreign investment. The case of South Korean construction firms is illuminating because of their success in capturing a large share of the global market. The South Korean government has designated the construction industry as a "strategic industry" (Ghymn, 1980; Westphal et al., 1984; Han and Brewer, 1987; Enderwick, 1991). Recent years have also observed the rise of some Philippine construction TNCs in the Middle East market prompted by the vigorous promotion of the export of Filipino manpower in the government's 1974 labor policy (Tolentino, 1993). The *raison d'être* of these construction TNCs from Asian developing countries rests on the need to nurture some "national champions" to compete in the world market against giant TNCs from developed countries. The South Korean government typically grants special financial and tax incentives for domestic construction firms. Special industrial training is also provided by government agencies in former military bases.

The information industry from Taiwan, as another

example, has been classified as a ''strategic industry'' since a series of institutional changes during the late 1970s and early 1980s (Chang, 1990). In May 1979 (during the second oil crisis), the Executive Yuan passed the ''Science and Technology Development Program'' in which the information industry was identified as a ''strategic industry.'' Two months later, the Institute for Information Industry (I.I.I.) was established to help government formulate short- and long-term development plans for the information industry. In 1980, the Executive Yuan approved as official policy the ''Ten Year Development Plan for the Information Industry, 1980–1990'' which was prepared by the Council for Economic Planning and Development (CEPD). By the late 1980s, several computer and electronics companies (e.g., Acer and Tatung) emerged from Taiwan's drive towards international recognition of its information industry—a reflection of the effectiveness of the official ten year plan.

CONCLUSION: THE FUTURE OF ASIAN DEVELOPING COUNTRY TRANSNATIONAL CORPORATIONS

Transnational corporations from Asian developing countries are a complex manifestation of the capitalist beast. The transnational operations of domestic business organizations from these Asian developing countries are probably as diverse as their intercountry differences. This phenomenon is not surprising given the great diversity of their historical backgrounds, cultural and social specificity, and political-economy systems. TNCs from the Asian developing world, though small in their direct investments relative to developed country TNCs, do compete successfully in the regional and global marketplace; they also play an active role in many host developing countries. Table 3 presents a summary of various characteristics and competitive edge of Asian developing country TNCs discussed in this paper. This paper contests that these attributes by no means claim universality and are certainly subject to dynamic changes in the global capitalist space-

economy. In the context of the emergence of the Asia-Pacific region as the world's largest market by the year 2020, we should not be surprised that many ''stereotypes'' of TNCs from Asian developing countries may disappear rapidly and the reality may be constituted by mosaics of TNCs operating on different platforms and corporate strategies (Yeung, 1994a). Meanwhile, empirical evidence increasingly suggests that catch-phrases such as ''Third World multinationals'' or ''unconventional multinationals'' have failed to depict a true picture of the reality of TNCs from Asian developing countries. We should no longer conceptualize these emerging TNCs as *deviant* from ''mainstream'' developed country TNCs. This paper has shown that despite great diversity among different TNCs, the boundary between developed and developing country TNCs is blurred by developments in both home countries and the global economy. Perhaps, future researchers should abandon this arbitrary distinction, particularly in the conceptual realm.

After moving a long way from the characteristics and competitive edge of Asian developing country TNCs, it is time to consider the future of these transnationals. It should be noted that predictions offered in the literature are speculative rather than definitive. The literature has provided no conclusive evidence in this respect. Two possible scenarios can be reconstructed in speculating the future of Asian developing country transnationals. The first scenario is that they will continue to flourish in their current *niche* markets. The second scenario is a more pessimistic one—it imagines that these TNCs will be slowly swallowed by the vigorous and unstable vortex of intra-regional and global competition. Some business scholars also argue that the basis of competition for developing country TNCs, the ''revealed comparative advantage,'' is not sustainable in the long run. This revealed comparative advantage tends to be location-specific in developing countries. It offers, however, limited prospects for building global business due to five potential changes: (1) growing Japanese FDI in low-cost locations; (2) continued domestic pressure to increase wages and re-value currencies; (3) increasing unwillingness of TNCs from developed countries to cede the bottom end of

TABLE 3. Characteristics of Transnational Corporations from Asian Developing Countries: A Summary Table

Key Themes	Transnational Corporations from Developing Countries
1. Size of investment	• total stock: very small; 2–3% of total world FDI stock • firm assets: small globally but large locally • employment size: largely SMEs but some global firms • percentage share in host countries: substantial in many developing countries • sectoral distribution: labour-intensive manufacturing and service industries; some in capital-intensive industries • number of foreign subsidiaries: still small
2. Main actors	• private firms: more than 50% of the total • government-directed or quasi-government firms: significant among NIEs except Hong Kong
3. Forms of market entry and owner-ship patterns	• minority equity joint ventures preferred • more wholly-owned firms among NIE TNCs • technological licensing common in some sectors
4. Parent-subsidiary relationships	• loose, fluid and informal • substantial autonomy to local executives and/or partners
5. Capital and source of funding	• home sources of capital: capital and financial markets • local partners: usually in minority equity joint ventures
6. Choice of technology and capital-labour intensity	• low cost of skilled manpower • appropriate technology: descaling of product technology • localized technological innovation • ''unpackaged'' nature of technology sales
7. Methods of production and marketing	• production of mature and ''old'' products • appropriate products for local consumption • high reliance on third party distributors
8. Foreign trade orientation	• largely export-promoting to third countries • some for host country markets • import of machinery and inputs of production
9. Patterns of competition and collaboration	• price competition at the ''tail'' of the product life cycle • few direct competition among developing country TNCs • cooperation with global TNCs to gain access to marketing, technological and managerial expertise
10. Locational choice	• intra-regional in focus: neighboring countries • some FDI in developed countries: particularly NIE TNCs
11. Influence of the state	• FDI restrictions in some countries, e.g. India • active promotion in NIEs: concept of ''strategic industries'' and/or ''national champions''

the *niche* market to those from developing countries; (4) the entry of new TNCs from developing countries; and (5) rising barriers in the world trading environment (Vernon-Wortzel and Wortzel, 1988).

In the changing global capitalist world, speculations are bound to outdate themselves. From the "snap-shot" discussions of this paper, it seems that Asian developing country TNCs are likely to thrive on the basis of their competitive advantages accumulated over the past two to three decades. In fact, there is a tendency toward greater regionalizations; more domestic firms are joining the "bandwagon" of internationalization (e.g., the recent upsurge of Singaporean investment in the P.R.C.). This optimism is largely derived from three trends: First, the future of the Asia-Pacific as a growth region has already been predicted. Indigenous TNCs grown from the region are likely to benefit substantially from increasing intra-regional trade and investment. Second, these Asian TNCs are beginning to gain competitive advantage over their counterparts from the Triad as both human resources at home are developed and the international transfer of expertise speeds up. A third trend is the continuing active support of home country governments in the transnational operations of domestic firms (Wade, 1990), e.g., the Singapore government's recent aggressive promotion of the regionalization of Singaporean firms (Régnier, 1993).

Another implication of this paper regards future research into the international business of Asian developing countries (Yeung, 1994a: 312–3). The pressing need now is not merely to collect more empirical information on TNCs from Asian developing countries; more original effort should be put on deconstructing Western-centric economic models of TNCs and building a theoretical framework that allows a historically- and culturally-sensitive explanation of TNCs from *any* country. To cite a concrete case, Chinese business in Asia is largely embedded in business networks which rely substantially on pre-existing social relations in terms of family business, ethnic ties, trust mechanism and institutional bondage. At the aggregate level, one may explain the transnational operations of TNCs from Asian developing countries *vis-à-vis* location-specific advantages such as lower labor costs and availability of domestic markets. If detailed micro-level explanations are sought, however, one must acknowledge the immense power and capability embodied in complex Chinese business networks throughout the Asia-Pacific rim. Many Hong Kong and Singaporean TNCs, through their interlocking network relations with China and Southeast Asia, are able to set up competitive operations in the respective countries. Not surprisingly, Hong Hong champions as the largest investor in China, whereas Singapore emerges as one of the leading investors in Malaysia and Thailand.[6] It was estimated that by June 1991, up to U.S. $16 billion of investment in the Guangdong Province, the P.R.C. (four-fifths of the total FDI in Guangdong) came from Hong Kong (*The Economist,* 16 November 1991). By September 1992, the total contracted FDI in China was U.S. $78.6 billion of which just over U.S. $25 billion had been realized. Some U.S. $66.8 billion might have come from Hong Kong companies and their local partners in China (*Financial Times,* 4 May 1993). Many transnational operations by Asian developing country TNCs are not only established through family business networks, but also succeed within the family chain through generations. In conclusion, much more theoretical work needs to be done before any serious explanation of the behavior of the emerging and important TNCs from Asian developing countries is warranted.

NOTES

1. Japan is effectively excluded from the discussion of "Asian TNCs" hereafter in this paper which is concerned only with Asian developing countries.

2. ASEAN refers to the Association of Southeast Asian Nations that comprises Brunei, Indonesia, Malaysia, the Philippines, Singapore and Thailand. For the purpose of this paper, Brunei is excluded because of the lack of data and the limited foreign investment in that country.

3. In the service sector, this "appropriate technology" is expressed in the form of localized expertise and knowledge. Very often, local connections and networks of business relationships are crucial to successful business contracts. In my studies of Hong Kong financial, insurance, shipping, and freight-forwarding companies operating in the ASEAN region, top executives often cite their expertise with the local and regional market and extensive

contacts and connections as their essential competitive advantage over established developed country TNCs or local companies.

4. Recently, India has received large inflows of FDI from Asian developing countries, following the nation's growing liberalization of markets.

5. Aggarwal and Agmon (1990) foster a dynamic model of comparative advantage to explain the changing relationship between the state and domestic TNCs in the Asian NIEs. The model remains, however, an idealized postulate rather than an empirically grounded explanation (cf. Yeung, 1994a).

6. The two major financial centers in the Asia-Pacific region have also performed the function of international investment intermediaries from which foreign owned TNCs in these two city-states invest and control their subsidiaries and/or affiliates in nearby countries. For example, the share of overseas investments by wholly-foreign owned firms in Singapore's total outward FDI grew from 17–25 percent in 1981–1988 to 45 percent in 1989 (see Low et al., 1995).

REFERENCES

Raj Aggarwal and Tamir Agmon. 1990. "The international success of developing country firms: role of government-directed comparative advantage." *Management International Review.* 30. 163–80.

Tamir Agmon and Charles P. Kindleberger. eds. 1977. *Multinationals from Small Countries.* Cambridge. MA: The MIT Press.

Alice H. Amsden. 1984. Taiwan. *World Development.* 12. 491–503.

Board of Investment. 1993. *Key Investment Indicators in Thailand.* Bangkok: Board of Investment.

Peter J. Buckley and Mark C. Casson. 1976. *The Future of the Multinational Enterprise.* London: Macmillan.

Peter J. Buckley and Hafiz Mirza. 1988. "The strategy of Pacific Asian multinationals." *The Pacific Review.* 1. 50–62.

John Cantwell. 1989. *Technological Innovation and Multinational Corporations.* Oxford: Basil Blackwell.

——— 1993. "Technological competence and evolving patterns of international production." In *The Growth of Global Business.* Howard Cox, Jeremy Clegg and Grazia Ietto-Gillies eds. London: Routledge. 19–37.

Central Bank of the Philippines. various years. *Annual Statistics.* Manila: Central Bank of the Philippines.

Tung-lung Chang. 1990. *The Competitive Strategies of Firms in Their Internationalization Process: The Case of Taiwanese Firms in the Information Industry.* Unpublished Ph.D. Thesis. George Washington University. Ann Arbor, Michigan: University Microfilms International.

Edward K.Y. Chen. 1981. "Hong Kong multinationals in Asia: characteristics and objectives." In *Multinationals from Developing Countries.* Krishna Kumar and Maxwell G. McLeod. eds. Lexington. MA: D.C. Heath. 79–99.

——— 1983a. *Multinational Corporations, Technology and Employment.* London: Macmillan.

——— 1983b. "Multinationals from Hong Kong." In *The New Multinationals: The Spread of Third World Enterprises.* Chichester: Wiley. 88–136.

——— 1984. "Hong Kong." *World Development.* 12. 481–90.

——— ed. 1990. *Foreign Direct Investment in Asia.* Tokyo: Asian Productivity Organization.

——— and Teresa Y.C. Wong. 1994. *Economic Synergy—A Study of Two-Way Foreign Direct Investment Flow Between Hong Kong and Mainland China.* Mimeo. Hong Kong: Centre of Asian Studies. University of Hong Kong.

Lee-in Chen Chiu and Chin Chung. 1993. "An assessment of Taiwan's indirect investment towards mainland China." *Asian Economic Journal.* 7. 41–70.

Seamus G. Connolly. 1984. "Joint ventures with Third World multinationals: a new form of entry to international markets." *Columbia Journal of World Business.* 19. 18–22.

Carlos F. Diaz-Alejardro. 1977. "Foreign direct investment by Latin Americans." In *Multinationals from Small Countries.* Tamir Agmon & Charles P. Kindleberger. eds. Cambridge, MA: The M.I.T. Press. 167–95.

Peter Dicken. 1992. *Global Shift: The Internationalization of Economic Activity.* Second Edition. London: Paul Chapman.

John H. Dunning. *International Production and the Multinational Enterprise.* London: Allen & Unwin.

——— *Explaining International Production.* London: Unwin Hyman.

——— 1993a. "Internationalizing Porter's Diamond." *Management International Review.* 33(2). 7–15.

——— 1993b. *The Globalization of Business.* London: Routledge.

Peter Enderwick. 1991. "Service sector multinationals and developing countries." In *Multinational Enterprises in Less Developed Countries.* Peter J. Buckley & Jeremy Clegg. eds. London: Macmillan. 292–309.

ESCAP/UNCTC. 1988. *Transnational Corporations From Developing Asian Economies.* Bangkok: ESCAP/UNCTC.

Yoon-dae Euh and Sang H. Min. 1986. "Foreign direct investment from developing countries: The case of Korean firms." *The Developing Economies.* 24. 149–68.

Dean Forbes. 1986. "Spatial aspects of Third World multinational corporations' direct investment in Indonesia." In *Multinationals and the Restructuring of the World Economy: The Geography of Multinationals.* Michael Taylor and Nigel Thrift. eds. London: Croom Helm. 105–41.

Masataka Fujita. 1990. "TNCs from developing countries." *The CTC Reporter.* 30. 42–5.

Ye Gang. 1992. "Chinese transnational corporations." *Transnational Corporations.* 1. 125–33.

Kyung-il Ghymn. 1980. "Multinational enterprises from the Third World." *Journal of International Business Studies.* 11. 118–22.

Ian H. Giddy and Stephen Young. 1982. "Conventional theory and unconventional multinationals: Do new forms of multinational enterprise require new theories?" *New Theories of the*

Multinational Enterprise. In Alan M. Rugman. ed. London: Croom Helm. 55–78.

Stephen Guisinger. 1991. "Foreign direct investment flows in East and Southeast Asia: Policy issues." *ASEAN Economic Bulletin.* 8. 29–46.

Min C. Han and Thomas L. Brewer 1987. "Foreign direct investments by Korean firms: An analysis with FDI theories." *Asia-Pacific Journal of Management.* 4. 90–102.

David A. Heenan and Warren J. Keegan. 1979. "The rise of third world multinationals." *Harvard Business Review.* 101–9.

Hal Hill and Eng-fong Pang. 1991. "Technology exports from a small, very open NIC: the case of Singapore." *World Development.* 19. 553–68.

Jorge Katz and Bernardo Kasacoff. 1983. "Multinationals from Argentina." In *The New Multinationals: The Spread of Third World Enterprises.* Chichester: Wiley. 137–219.

Khushi M. Khan. ed. 1986a. *Multinationals of the South: New Actors in the International Economy.* London: Frances Pinter Publishers.

———— 1986b. "Multinationals from the South: emergence, patterns and issues." In *Multinationals of the South: New Actors in the International Economy.* Khushi M. Khan. ed. London: Frances Pinter Publishers. 1–14.

Krishna Kumar. 1982. "Third World multinationals: A growing force in international relations." *International Studies Quarterly.* 26. 397–424.

———— and Maxwell G. McLeod. eds. 1981. *Multinationals from Developing Countries.* Lexington: D.C. Heath.

Sanjaya Lall. 1979. "Multinationals and market structure in an open developing economy: the case of Malaysia." *Weltwirtschaftliches Archiv.* 115. 325–50.

———— 1980a. "Developing countries as exporters of industrial technology." *Research Policy.* 9. 24–52.

———— 1980b. *The Multinational Corporation: Nine Essays.* London: Macmillan.

———— 1982. *Developing Countries as Exporters of Technology: A First Look at the Indian Experience.* London: Macmillan.

———— 1983a. "The rise of multinationals from the Third World." *Third World Quarterly.* 5. 618–26.

———— 1983b. *The New Multinationals: The Spread of Third World Enterprises.* Chichester: Wiley.

———— 1984a. "Exports of technology by newly industrialized countries: an overview." *World Development.* 12. 471–80.

———— 1984b. "India." *World Development.* 12. 535–65.

———— 1985. "India." In *Multinational Enterprises, Economic Structure and International Competitiveness.* John H. Dunning. ed. Chichester: Wiley. 309–35.

———— 1991. "Direct investment in South-East Asia by the NIEs: trends and prospects." *Banca Nazionale del Lavore Quarterly Review.* 179. 463–80.

Rajiv B. Lall. 1986. *Multinationals from the Third World: Indian Firms Investing Abroad.* Delhi: Oxford University Press.

Donald J. Lecraw. 1988. "Third World multinationals in the service industries." In *Multinational Service Firms.* Peter Enderwick. ed. London: Routledge. 200–12.

———— 1992. "Third World MNEs once again: the case of Indonesia." In *Multinational Enterprises in the World Economy: Essays in Honour of John Dunning.* Peter J. Buckley & Mark Casson. eds. Aldershot: Edward Elgar. 115–33.

———— 1993. "Outward direct investment by Indonesian firms: motivation and effects." *Journal of International Business Studies.* 24. 589–600.

Chung H. Lee. 1994. "Korea's direct foreign investment in Southeast Asia." *ASEAN Economic Bulletin.* 10. 280–96.

Kuen Lee and Michael G. Plummer. 1992. "Competitive advantages, two-way foreign investment, and capital accumulation in Korea." *Asian Economic Journal.* 6. 93–114.

Tsao Yuan Lee. 1990. "NIC investment in ASEAN: the pattern in the Eighties." In *Foreign Direct Investment in ASEAN.* Soon Lee Ying. ed. Kuala Lumpur: Malaysian Economic Association. 112–35.

Chin-kin Leung. 1993. "Personal contacts, subcontracting linkages, and development in the Hong Kong-Zhujiang Delta region." *Annals of the Association of American Geographers.* 83. 272–302.

Brian Levy. 1988. "Korea and Taiwanese firms as international competitors: the challenges ahead." *Columbia Journal of World Business.* 23. 43–51.

Brian Levy and Wen-jeng Kuo. 1991. "The strategic orientations of firms and the performance of Korea and Taiwan in frontier industries: lessons from comparative case studies of keyboard and personal computer assembly." *World Development.* 19. 363–74.

Peter Ping Li. 1994. "Strategy profiles of indigenous MNEs from the NIEs: the case of South Korea and Taiwan." *The International Executive.* 36. 147–70.

Mah-hui Lim and Kit-fong Teoh. 1986. "Singapore corporations go transnational." *Journal of South East Asian Studies.* 17. 336–65.

Geoffrey J.R. Linge. 1984. "Developing-country multinationals: a review of the literature." *Pacific Viewpoint.* 25. 173–95.

Linda Low, Eric D. Ramstetter, and Henry Wai-chung Yeung. 1995. *Accounting for Outward Direct Investment from Hong Kong and Singapore: Who Controls What?* Paper Presented at the Annual Conference of the National Bureau of Economic Research. Chicago. 19–20 May 1995.

Jan Monkiewicz. 1986. "Multinational enterprises of developing countries: some emerging characteristics." *Management International Review.* 26. 67–79.

Jeffrey B. Nugent. 1986. "Arab multinationals: problems, potential and policies." In *Multinationals of the South: New Actors in the International Economy.* Khushi M. Khan. ed. London: Frances Pinter Publishers. 165–83.

Peter O'Brien. 1980. "The new multinationals: developing country firms in international markets." *Futures.* 12. 303–16.

Kenichi Ohmae. 1985. *Triad Power: The Coming Shape of Global Competition.* New York: The Free Press.

Kris Olds. 1995. *World Property Markets and the Global Culture Economy: Tales from Vancouver and Shanghai via Mammon's Temple.* Paper Presented at the Institute of British Geographers'

Annual Conference. University of Northumbria at Newcastle. 3–6 January 1995. Copy available from author.

Eng-fong Pang, and Rajah V. Komaran. 1985. ''Singapore multinationals.'' *Columbia Journal of World Business*. 20. 35–43.

Mari Pangestu, Hadi Soesastro and Mubarig Ahmad. 1992. ''A new look at intra-ASEAN economic co-operation.'' *ASEAN Economic Bulletin*. 8. 333–52.

June M. L. Poon. 1993. ''Korean subsidiary companies in Malaysia: management practices and investment motives.'' *Malaysian Management Review*. 28. 9–16.

Michael Porter. 1990. *The Competitive Advantage of Nations*. London: Macmillan.

Eric D. Ramstetter. 1993. ''Asian multinationals in the world economy.'' *International Economic Insights*. 4. 19–22.

Gordon S. Redding. 1994. ''Competitive advantage in the context of Hong Kong.'' *Journal of Far Eastern Business*. 1(1). 71–89.

Philippe Régnier. 1993. ''Spreading Singapore's wings worldwide: a review of traditional and new investment strategies.'' *The Pacific Review*. 6. 305–12.

Rajib N. Sanyal, and Hope K. Torkornoo. 1988. ''Emerging Davids in the land of the Goliaths? A survey of direct foreign manufacturing investment in the USA from developing countries.'' *The Proceedings of the Symposium on Business in Southeast Asia: Issues in Research & Teaching*. Centre for South and Southeast Asian Studies. University of Michigan.

Mann-Soo Shin. 1989. *The Internationalization of Korean Firms and its Impact on Managerial Sophistication*. Unpublished Ph.D. Thesis. University of Illinois at Urbana-Champaign. Ann Arbor, Michigan: University Microfilms International.

Woong-shik Shin and Eugene J. Oh. 1990. ''Recent developments in Korea's foreign investment.'' *Journal of World Trade Law*. 26. 31–56.

Singapore Department of Statistics. 1994. *Yearbook of Statistics, Singapore 1993*. Singapore: Department of Statistics.

Marjan Svetlicic. 1986. ''Multinational production joint ventures of developing countries, their economic development and specific features.'' In *Multinationals of the South: New Actors in the International Economy*. Khushi M. Khan. ed. London: Frances Pinter Publishers. 67–87.

Hong Yam Tan, Mun Heng Toh and Linda Low. 1992. ''ASEAN and Pacific economic co-operation.'' *ASEAN Economic Bulletin*. 8. 309–32.

Mayo Thant, Min Tang and Hiroshi Kakazu. eds. 1994. *Growth Triangles in Asia: A New Approach to Regional Economic Co-operation*. Hong Kong: Oxford University Press.

The Wall Street Journal. 26 October 1994. ''Asian tigers are on the prowl in Europe.''

——— 11 November 1994. ''Korean concern agrees to buy AT & T division.''

Kian Wie Thee. 1991. ''The surge of Asian NIC investment into Indonesia.'' *Bulletin of Indonesian Economic Studies*. 27. 55–88.

——— 1992. ''The investment surge from the Asian newly-industrialising countries into Indonesia.'' *Asian Economic Journal*. 6(3). 231–64.

——— 1993. ''Foreign investment and the ASEAN economies, with special reference to Indonesia.'' *The Indonesian Quarterly*. 21(4). 434–50.

Mun Heng Toh and Linda Low. eds. 1993. *Regional Cooperation and Growth Triangles in ASEAN*. Singapore: Times Academic Press.

Paz Estrella E. Tolentino. 1993. *Technological Innovation and Third World Multinationals*. London: Routledge.

Choo Sin Tseng. 1992. ''Entrepreneurship and outward foreign direct investment by PRC multinationals.'' *Proceedings of the ENDEC World Conference on Entrepreneurship*. August 11–14, 1992. Marina Mandarin. Singapore. 447–58.

F.M. Ulgado, C. Yu and A.R. Negandhi. 1994. ''Multinational enterprises from Asian developing countries: management and organizational characteristics.'' *International Business Review*. 3(2). 123–133.

UNCTAD. 1994. *World Investment Report 1994: Transnational Corporations, Employment and the Workplace*. New York: United Nations.

UNCTC. 1978. *Transnational Corporations in World Development: A Re-examination*. New York: United Nations.

——— 1989. ''Asia largest investor among developing regions.'' *Transnationals*. 1. 3.

——— 1992. *World Investment Directory 1992: Foreign Direct Investment, Legal Framework and Corporate Data. Volume 1: Asia and the Pacific*. New York: United Nations.

Raymond Vernon. 1977. *Storm Over the Multinationals*. Cambridge, MA: Harvard University Press.

Heidi Vernon-Wortzel and Lawrence H. Wortzel. 1988. ''Globalizing strategies for multinationals from developing countries.'' *Columbia Journal of World Business*. 23. 27–35.

Robert Wade. 1990. *Governing the Market: Economic Theory and the Role of Government in East Asian Industrialization*. Princeton: Princeton University Press.

Yan-sheng Wei. 1993. ''The development and prospect of economic relations among Mainland China, Hong Kong and Taiwan.'' In *Politics of Economic Cooperation in the Asia-Pacific Region*. Kuang-Sheng Liao ed. Hong Kong: The Chinese University of Hong Kong. 161–89.

Christopher Wells. 1988. ''Brazilian multinationals.'' *Columbia Journal of World Business*. 23. 13–23.

Louis T. Jr. Wells. 1978. ''Foreign investment from the Third World: the experience of Chinese firms from Hong Kong.'' *Columbia Journal of World Business*. 13. 39–49.

——— 1981. ''Foreign investors from the Third World.'' In *Multinationals from Developing Countries*. Krishna Kumar and Maxwell G. McLeod. eds. Lexington, MA: D.C. Heath. 23–36.

——— 1982. *Technology and Third World Multinationals*. Working Paper No. 19. Multinational Enterprise Programme. Geneva: International Labour Office.

——— 1983. *Third World Multinationals: The Rise of Foreign*

Investment from Developing Countries. Cambridge, MA: The M.I.T. Press.

———— 1984. ''Multinationals from Asian developing countries.'' In *International Business Strategies in the Asia-Pacific Region: Environmental Changes and Corporate Response.* Richard W. Moxon. Thomas W. Roehl and J. Frederick Truitt. eds. Greenwich, CT.: JAI Press. 127–43.

———— 1986. ''New and old multinationals: competitors or partners.'' In *Multinationals of the South: New Actors in the International Economy.* Khushi M. Khan. ed. London: Frances Pinter Publishers. 196–210.

Larry E. Westphal, W. Rhee Yung, Kim Linsu and Alice H. Amsden. 1984. ''Republic of Korea.'' *World Development.* 12. 505–33.

Eduardo White. 1981. ''The international projection of firms from Latin American countries.'' In *Multinationals from Developing Countries.* Krishna Kumar and Maxwell G. McLeod. eds. Lexington, MA: D.C. Heath. 155–86.

Henry Wai-chung Yeung. 1994a. ''Third World multinationals revisited: a research critique and future agenda.'' *Third World Quarterly.* 15. 297–317.

———— 1994b. ''Hong Kong firms in the ASEAN region: transnational corporations and foreign direct investment.'' *Environment and Planning A.* 26. 1931–1956.

———— 1995. *Business Networks and Transnational Operations: A Study of Hong Kong Firms in the ASEAN Region.* Paper Presented at the Institute of British Geographers' Annual Conference. University of Northumbria at Newcastle. 3–6 January 1995. Copy available from author.

3

THE NEW GLOBAL PLAYERS: HOW THEY COMPETE AND COLLABORATE

ELLIOTT R. MORSS

Boston University, Boston, Massachusetts

ABSTRACT   The era in which nations ruled the world is over. With the information revolution and the demise of the United States as the dominant world power, three groups have joined nations as important global players: transnational corporations, international organizations, and special interest groups.

Global players can be expected to collaborate in different ways on a wide range of issues. Some collaborations will benefit the global citizenry while others will be detrimental. Policy analysis is needed, but the field of international relations, with its focus on nations, does not provide a sufficiently broad conceptual framework for the needed analytical work.

INTRODUCTION

In the last two years, growing attention has been given to ''global'' issues. This is seen in the media, in professional journals, and in conferences for businessmen, academics, and government officials. There are several reasons for this upsurge. The most obvious is the large number of important changes in the world order, dominated by the decline in the East-West struggle—a ''cold'' war which had probably involved the use of more resources than were devoted to both world wars. Another reason is the

I want to thank Arthur Clarke, Neva Goodwin and Paul Streeten for the time they took reviewing drafts of this paper with me.

growing realization that the benefits and costs resulting from actions of individual nations affect other nations. Factors that have governed the behavior of Western nations for more than 40 years are also coming into question. For example, consider the following list of assumptions, agreements, and beliefs.

—The agreement between the Soviet Union and the Allied powers at the end of WWII to control the actions of Germany and Japan;

—Satisfaction with the international organizations established at the end of WWII;

—Acceptance of dictatorships and significant human rights violations;

—"North," "South," "East," and "West" as meaningful categories for groupings of nations;

—The belief that communism constitutes a viable political system;

—The belief that population growth in developing countries will not pose serious threats to the well-being of Western nations;

—The belief that military actions are more threatening to the well-being of nations than economic, environmental or migratory activities.

The above list represents some of the most important assumptions, agreements, and beliefs affecting world happenings that have held sway for nearly one-half century. Note that each item on this list applies to nations and their relations with each other. This is quite understandable: nations and groups of nations have been seen as the important players on the world scene.

The purpose of this essay is to elaborate on the emergence of important new players on the global scene—players that are not nations. It also describes the new and changing nature of interactions among players.

GENERAL STATEMENT

Nations, while continuing as important gobal players, must increasingly deal with an emerging set of entities which have power, either singly or as blocs, that is significant relative to the power of nations.

The newly important entities include large corporations that have lost their national identities, international organizations, and special interest groups. Consequently, international relations is no longer adequate as a discipline to study important global developments inasmuch as "international" means "between nations."[1] It is not particularly useful to describe the activities of the new entities as international inasmuch as they think and behave in a transnational or global fashion.

In part because of changing players, the nature of interactions, particularly in the economic realm, is also changing. For example, through global mergers, buy-outs, and agreements to collaborate, extremely large, transnational firms[2] and groupings thereof are emerging. These firms and groupings will be larger, wield more market power, be more mobile, and be less dependent on the policies of particular national governments than has been true in the past. However, these firms and groupings will be constrained in how they use their new power by global regulatory bodies and by the emergence of special interest groups aligned with various causes.

Just how all of this will affect the nature of interactions is far from clear. Competition among producers, as traditionally defined by economists and the courts, will probably be less important, but new forms of competition will emerge. Despite what traditional economists believe, the net effect of these changes will not necessarily be a reduction in global welfare. For example, countries might band together in trading blocs to attract the new transnational firms to produce within their borders. Economists have traditionally argued against the formation of such blocs, fearing they will impose protective tariffs, thereby reducing competition. However, it is possible that increased competition within a bloc resulting from the elimination of trade barriers among blocs could more than offset the loss of competition resulting from bloc activities with the rest of the world.

PAST FORMS OF COMPETITION AND COLLABORATION

In the past, nations have collaborated with their "own" business entities to enhance their respective interests: major European commodity and trading companies worked closely with "their" governments in the acquisition and development of colonies; during the World Wars, many companies converted to wartime production at the request of "their" governments (e.g., Pan American World Airways built overseas airports and General Motors converted to the production of military vehicles); since 1946, C. Wright Mills and President Eisenhower wrote and spoke, respectively, about the "military-industrial complex." Less noted but equally impressive in terms of results has been the relationship between the US government and its farming sector. Much attention has recently been focused on the close and effective linkages between the governments of Asian Rim nations and "their" producing entities. It is highly significant to note that most of the past government/business coalitions were intracountry, based upon joint perceptions of national economic, political, and security interests.

Following WWII, a large portion of the world's international organizational infrastructure came into being when the United States was established to replace the League of Nations. The principal organs of the United Nations, as stated in its charter, are the General Assembly, the Security Council, the Economic and Social Council, the Trusteeship Council, the International Court of Justice, and the Secretariat. Sixteen specialized agencies were formed.

Some of the specialized agencies developed affiliates. For example, the Bank for International Settlements and the International Finance Corporation (IFC) are affiliates of the World Bank. Other international organizations with looser connections to the United Nations also exist. Examples include various regional development banks such as the Inter-American Development Bank and the Asian Development Bank.

These international organizations were the result of multinational agreements. But the primary funder in almost all cases was the United States. With few notable exceptions, they took their policy direction from the United States.

In a strictly literal sense, a special interest group focuses on some particular subject, e.g., a historical society or a group of antique car lovers. In colloquial use, the phrase has taken on a more particular meaning: ". . . a person or group having an interest in a particular part of the economy and receiving or seeking special advantages therein often to the detriment of the general public" (*Webster's New Collegiate Dictionary*, 1981, p. 1107). For purposes of this paper, a special interest group will be defined as one that acts to convince others as to the correctness of its view, regardless of whether it is self-serving.

Defined in this manner, it is obvious that special interest groups have been around since the beginning of society. Until recently they focused most of their energies on influencing rulers and citizens at the national and subnational levels in their "home" countries.[3] These groups have commonly focused on obtaining a bigger slice of the economic pie for those they represent through tax breaks and government support; national religious movements are also a common manifestation. Recently, new groups have emerged claiming to represent the public interest on specific issues, e.g., the environment, minority rights, nuclear proliferation, disarmament, poverty, and consumer rights.[4]

THE NEW GLOBAL PLAYERS

The transportation and communication revolutions have dramatically broadened international contacts and have facilitated the emergence of the new global players. One of the most significant features of these new players is their loss of national identity and interest.

Firms are losing their national identities, both in terms of employees and their willingness to cooperate with the initiatives of their "home" country governments. US (and soon Japanese) companies can no longer be counted on to promote US (Japanese) national interests.[5]

As capital markets continue to expand globally, it will be increasingly difficult to determine a company's national identity. The elimination of international capital restrictions and the growth of equity markets means a firm's ownership can be purchased by anyone through a wired purchase order. Just as the elimination of restrictions on people's movements among nations reduces the significance of individuals' national identities, the elimination of restrictions on capital flows among nations reduces the significance of the national identities of publicly traded companies.[6]

International organizations, formerly captives of the countries that created them, are increasingly developing lives of their own. In large part, this results from the maturation and growing decision-making role of each organization's bureaucracy; this is fostered by the broadening of each organization's financial support base as U.S. support relatively declines.

Special interest groups are increasingly focusing their energies on global issues. Human rights, environment and disarmament are areas where they have been particularly important. Unlike many of their predecessors which often acknowledged representing monied minorities, these new groups claim to represent either the ''dispossessed'' or the entire human race.

The attention given in the above paragraphs to the new global players is not meant to suggest that nations do not continue to be important on the world scene; rather, it means that nations, which in the past dominated world activities, will in the future have to share power with the new global players. This power sharing will take various forms, examples of which are presented below:

—The U.S. Department of Defense provides a low-interest loan to Turkey to purchase Northrup fighter jets; Northrup in turn agrees to market Turkish agricultural products to the Soviet Union.

—ENI, the quasi-governmental Italian oil conglomerate, agrees to buy only as much oil from the Soviet Union as ENI can sell engineering and construction services to the Soviet Union.

—Bristol-Myers and Squibb, two of the world's largest drug companies (one originally British, the other US) agree to merge, citing economies in research and marketing.

—Japanese car makers, both independently and in partnership with U.S. firms, start building automobiles in the United States and announce plans to export more cars from the United States than from Japan by the early 1990s;

Honda, already the fourth largest US producer, announces plans to export 50,000 cars to Japan by 1991; Toyota makes a $850 million investment in the United Kingdom.

—Philips Electronics, a Dutch company with the world's largest marketing network, enters into an agreement with Japanese companies whereby the latter would establish a joint research center in the Netherlands; in return, the Japanese companies will be allowed to use the Philips marketing outlets to sell their products.

—Lockheed and Aerospatiale, a French plane producer, agree to produce and sell commercial planes in competition with Boeing and the European consortium.

—In the United States, the enforcement of antitrust laws is put on hold, allowing the formation of various company consortia, e.g., Sematech.

—A conservative U.S. government relies primarily on Amnesty International for data on human rights violations and thereby is forced to be extremely critical of the government of Chile.

The activities cited above reflect patterns of behavior not easily explained by existing economic or political theory. However, upon closer examination, it appears that these activities are consistent with certain global changes. These changes are listed below:

—The new global players (private and quasigovernmental enterprises, international organizations, and special interest groups) are shedding their national identities; indeed, it is largely because of this that they are becoming important global players.

—National borders are becoming less important; we see waves of nearly uncontrollable population movements; borders have no effect on the spread of certain pollutants; new information technologies make it extremely difficult to control cross-border information and capital flows.

—A massive collaboration movement that involves all the global players is underway.

Each of these happenings is discussed in greater detail below.

THE SHEDDING OF NATIONAL IDENTITIES

For more than a decade, firms that operate in more than one country have recognized the importance of shedding their identification with their country of origin. In Japan, IBM wants to be known as a Japanese company; in the United States, Honda and other auto makers with Japanese origins want to be credited for introducing management and productive practices that increase the efficiency of US workers. Shedding a national identity presents a formidable public relations challenge: on the one hand, the foreign company must integratiate itself to a new country; on the other, it must attempt to minimize the negative fall-out in its country of origin (Stokes, 1989).

Of course, this is far more than a public relations problem. Transnational firms are bound to pressure national governments quite differently than firms having all their production activities in one country. For example, the concerns of transnational companies that produce within the European Common Market will be quite different from the concerns of businesses hoping to export into the Common Market.

Interesting frictions have also developed as international organizations attempt to chart their courses independently of their primary benefactors. The United States remains the primary benefactor of virtually all UN organizations, but as its relative share of financial support for their operations declines, its influence will decline as well. While the charters of many UN organizations allow major powers to exercise vetoes to block actions, the United States has usually been in a position of *de facto* control. This is all changing, and the international organizations with the shrewdest leaders will play the major powers against one another, thereby increasing the control they exercise over their own operations.

Special interest groups are encountering their own problems as they switch from national to global areas of concern. For example, US environmental groups have traditionally mobilized US public opinion as a means of influencing US government policies at all levels. They now recognize the importance of actions in other parts of the world as threats to the environment, and they are in the process of developing new methods to influence actions elsewhere.[7]

THE DIMINISHING IMPORTANCE OF NATIONAL BORDERS

In the past, nations have been able to exercise considerable control over what crosses their borders. The information revolution has dramatically reduced nations' abilities to control their borders.

Recently, Chinese students in the West used facsimile machines to provide information to students throughout China on political developments in Beijing and international reactions to them. This information was transferred over telephone lines, and the Chinese rulers were not ready to cut off telephone links to the West to keep it from entering the country.[8]

New information technologies allow private businesses to enter into new kinds of contractually binding agreements with others. The most important type of agreement involves wiring money: financial institutions can instantly transfer control over any amount of money to anywhere in the world.

The combination of natural forces and human-made pollution has also provided stark illustrations of how little control countries have over their borders. Wind-blown radioactive particles have no respect for national borders; the same can be said for pollutants transported by rivers or oceans.

The flow of people from Eastern to Western Europe in 1989, the movements of refugees, and the number of illegal Mexican immigrants working in the United States, all testify to the difficulty of controlling the movement of people across national borders. To the consternation of state and local officials in both Mexico and the United States, border towns from each country have started holding joint town meetings (Pierce, 1989).

THE GLOBAL COLLABORATION MOVEMENT

Nations, corporations, international organizations, and special interest groups are increasingly entering into agreements to work together.[9] Agreements occur within each group (e.g., agreements among nations) and between groups (e.g., agreements between nations and corporations). Some of the more recent global agreements will be considered in the following paragraphs.

Collaborations in the corporate world have been numerous and striking: most prominent have been those in the automotive, financial, airline, aircraft construction, military, chemical, and drug industries. Various reasons for these collaborations have been cited, including economies of scale related to regulatory approval, production, marketing, distribution, technology acquisition, and technology development; border hopping, i.e., setting up production facilities within a country so as to avoid import duties; public relations; and enhancing the possibilities to think and act globally.[10]

In recent years there has been increased interest and activity among nations regarding the establishment of trading blocks.[11] The United States and Canada have recently entered into an agreement to eliminate trade barriers between them; the European Common Market appears to be moving toward greater integration; and various efforts to establish trading blocs involving Asian nations are being considered. Publicly, the countries promoting these blocs have pointed to the increased efficiency among members of the blocs resulting from the increased competition that will occur when trade barriers are eliminated. At the same time, firms and nations that are not bloc members fear that the blocs will erect higher external trade barriers than now exist. These fears lead firms to establish production activities within the bloc to insure continued market access.

Finally, special interest groups have also developed impressive global networks and are proving capable of effectively collaborating and coordinating their efforts on various issues of common concern.

In addition to the numerous intragroup agreements to work together, there have also been a large number of intergroup agreements. For example, a corporation may agree to locate production facilities or a research center in a country in return for assurances it will have market access and the right to remit profits in hard currencies. Or consider another example: the World Bank assures a coalition of environmental groups that it will put more resources into environmental projects. Of course, nations regularly enter into a wide variety of agreements with international organizations.

POLICY ASSESSMENT OF THE COLLABORATION MOVEMENT

Collaboration between companies and nations could lead to a diminution of competition and a consequent loss in global welfare. It is therefore worth asking what is causing the collaborations to occur. As noted above, there are many reasons for collaborations, but an important one that has not received the attention it deserves is the states' fear of unemployment.

One effect of the fear of unemployment is seen when national governments, concerned that their workers will not be fully employed, attempt to insure that most of the domestic market demand will be filled by local producers (employers). Consequently, they impose tariffs to keep out imports and to induce transnational companies to locate production facilities within their borders. This smaller a country's domestic market, the smaller will be the market-access inducement a country can offer to a global firm.

Countries join trading blocks, *inter alia,* to increase the significance of the market-access inducement. By the same token, some firms collaborate in order to get inside tariff barriers.

What would happen if national governments did not fear unemployment? What if they believed their citizenry would be fully employed by producing for the domestic market and exporting? In such circumstances, they would not need to protect their domestic markets from imports and they would have no reason to use market access as an incentive to attract transnational firms.

The importance of full employment was recognized at the Bretton Woods meeting following WWII.

The second element in the strategic vision at Bretton Woods was full employment. . . . Full employment was valued partly because of its importance in sustaining an adequate overall level of demand, but the

*Bretton Woods delegations also believed that poli-
cies promoting full employment in the major industrial countries would make trade liberalization possible. As the Treasury of the United Kingdom noted
in its 1943 proposal for an International Clearing
Union, "If active employment and ample purchasing
power can be sustained in the main centres of world
trade, the problem of surplus and unwanted exports
will largely disappear" (Mead, 1989).*

Fortunately, a concern for the level of global aggregate demand and unemployment has not totally
vanished in today's world. Bradford (1988) has developed a model that allows us to study the interrelationships among imports, exports, and the actions of
nations to restrict trade. His model consists of a
world with 12 trading blocs. The willingness of the
blocs to allow imports depends on their ability to
export: the less the trading blocs are able to export,
the more protectionist they will be. Since one bloc's
exports are other bloc's imports, the model is interactive.

Bradford uses the model to simulate two scenarios: in the first, world export and gross domestic
product (GDP) outcomes are based on "a current
policy course for the world economy"; in the second, world export and GDP outcomes are based on
a level of global aggregate demand that allows blocs
to realize their export targets. He finds that under
current policies, global aggregate demand (world
GDP) would have to be $1.6 trillion[12] more than it
is projected to be under "the current policy course"
for blocs to achieve their export targets. This difference is roughly equivalent to the combined 1985
gross domestic products of Brazil and Japan. The difference in global exports between the two seasons is
about $860 billion,[13] or more than three times the
1985 level of US exports.

Putting the findings somewhat more generally,
Bradford concludes that a huge increase in global
aggregate demand is needed if "the problem of surplus and unwanted exports" is to be avoided. Failing
to alleviate this problem will spur the formation of
trading blocs and other protectionist measures,
which will in turn accelerate the collaboration of

large multinational business concerns, nations, and
trading blocs.

LOOKING INTO THE FUTURE

There are many important implications of the emergence of new global players and new modes of interaction that remain to be explored. As a step in this
direction, we will consider the motivations of the
global players and speculate about their future actions.

Streeten frequently asserts that, throughout history, the primary motivations of nations have been
fear, greed, and prestige. But times might be changing! In the past, the actions of nations have primarily
been determined by their leaders. These leaders saw
the accumulation of wealth and power through military conquest as primary goals; they assumed that
the role of their citizens (or subjects) should be to
help them attain these goals.

There is reason to question whether today's leaders can get away with behaving as past leaders did.
In the first place, military technology has advanced
to the point that all-out war would clearly be cata-
strophic for both sides. Second, the information revolution has kindled a desire on the part of nearly all
the world's citizens for their governments to pursue
policies that reflect citizens' wants. In order to remain popular, national politicians will increasingly
have to concern themselves with how to improve the
quality of life of their citizens. Since economic well-
being is an important dimension of the quality of life,
leaders will have to be concerned with their country's employment level and competitive position in
the world economy.

While there is reason to believe that the deleterious effects of the actions and policies of nations will
be somewhat muted in the future, it remains true that
three "evil" global industries (military armaments,
terrorism, and hazardous drugs) derive most of their
support from nations. Since the end of WWII,
there have been more than 350 "low-intensity"
conflicts,[14] and at the beginning of 1990, 26 of
these conflicts continue with unceasing support from
the global military industry. Most terrorist acts are

Table 1. Frequency Distribution of Firms and Countries, 1988

No. of Firms	Sales or GDP	No. of Countries
0	$119 billion–$5 trillion	14
105	$10–119 billion	43
620	$1–9 billion	52

Sources: World Bank (1988) and Business Week (1988).

intended to focus attention on the actions or policies of nations. A new, highly sophisticated industry that supplies terrorist devices has emerged. Finally, the large profits made in the hazardous drug industry result directly from restrictions on the sale of drugs in Western nations and ineffective policing in the countries in which they are produced.

Considerable work has gone into understanding the motivations of transnational companies, and this has already been summarized in the collaboration section above.[15] In passing, it is worth mentioning the resources controlled by companies relative to those of nations. A rough sense of magnitudes can be gained by looking at the gross national products (GNPs) of nations against the gross sales of the largest companies. This information is presented in Table 1.

The left-hand column indicates the number of firms with sales of more than $119 billion, $10 billion, and $1 billion. The right-hand column indicates the number of countries with GNPs in excess of those amounts. The table indicates the considerable economic power of firms relative to nations.

Given the growing importance of international organizations and special interest groups as global players, there is a need for more attention to be given to their motivations and behavior. However, the empirical work that has been done on these groups[16] suggests that as they mature, they will assume well-documented bureaucratic characteristics.[17] That is, their original mission will be redefined to suit their bureaucratic imperatives. The other possibility is that they may become ''cause zealots'' and could be viewed as a greater or lesser threat to the global order. The only apparent way to keep these organizations from becoming self-serving is to keep them accountable, either through market competition or the political process.

FUTURE COLLABORATIONS

The purpose of this section is to imagine what types of collaboration can be expected in the future. This should then inform the subsequent discussion of policy implications.

As regards nations, military blocs will give way to economic trading blocs as a primary form of collaboration. Debtor nations can be expected to share information among themselves on matters pertaining to debt reduction. Countries that are leaders in technology development can be expected to press for international sanctions against countries that allow the pirating of international property. On this point, one can expect high-tech companies to locate in nations willing and able to impose penalties on others when piracy does occur.

One can also anticipate that population pressures will lead to certain groupings among nations. Labor-abundant developing countries are eager for their citizens to find employment elsewhere; Western nations are likely to become increasingly concerned about population pressures resulting from immigration relative to their need for low-cost labor.

Small nations are more likely to join in trading blocks than large nations. A small nation alone cannot offer much of a market-access inducement to transnational businesses.

Nations concerned about pollution and environmental degradation are likely to work together just as countries are concerned about economic growth are likely to act as a bloc to oppose global environmental regulations.[18]

As has been discussed earlier, there are numerous reasons for companies to collaborate. We are likely to see more transnational collaboration than has been true in the past. While the media are full of reports of trading bloc activity, little attention has focused on the new partnerships designed to neutralize the deleterious effects of these blocs on firms' future profitability.

Increasingly, international organizations are recognizing the importance of working together to achieve their ends. Collaboration among them can increase the pressure they can apply to individual countries to achieve various objectives. For example, major donor organizations (both international and bilateral) are coordinating their efforts so that significant aid monies are withheld until countries agree to major policy reforms.

While the above paragraphs have only discussed possible intragroup agreements in the future, it is as easy to imagine the attractiveness of intergroup agreements as well. Already, we are seeing more agreements between transnational companies and governments. For example, the US government recently set aside antitrust regulations to allow large US transnationals to engage in joint technology research. Environmental groups, having successfully pressured international donors into making more resources available for the environment, can be expected to receive contracts from these donors to determine how these resources should be used.

POLICY IMPLICATIONS

When social scientists get to that part of a book, paper, or memo that deals with policy implications, their primary audience is normally a group of government policy makers whose actions are constrained in various ways. Indeed, the normal challenge to the social scientist interested in policy is to come up with recommendations that policy makers with limited options can implement that will have positive outcomes. This paper is examining a set of issues from a global perspective, and there is no natural audience of government policy makers for the discussion of policy implications that follows. This is somewhat troubling, for there are clearly important issues for global policy makers to consider. But perhaps this is using too limited a definition of policy makers. Perhaps it is more accurate to say that in the absence of global government, the policy makers become the global players: the leaders of nations, transnational corporations, international organiza-

tions, and special interest groups operating in the global arena.

Charting the nature and magnitude of the coming alliances is an important and difficult task. Undoubtedly, the alliances will result in citizen benefits as well as costs. Consider an example from the economic realm: some agreements will further consolidate market power, raising the question of whether a global antitrust enforcer is needed; in contrast, other agreements will allow business to achieve economies of scale and avoid government regulations that are costly to consumers.

Consider the policy implications of globalization for a particular country. For example, to the US government, what should ''promoting US business'' mean? If it is agreed that the US government should pursue policies that increase the competitiveness of US business, how does one define a US company (Reich, 1990)? Putting it somewhat differently, if the US government does decide to offer incentives in the form of government subsidies, tax breaks, and/or regulatory changes, what companies should be offered these incentives? In the automobile industry, for example, should government incentives be offered only to the traditional US auto makers, or should Honda, Nissan, Toyota and other companies with production facilities in the United States also be included? Or, to take another example, should US government-sponsored consortia such as Sematech include or exclude foreign firms?

Various definitions for determining which firms are ''US companies'' have been offered, including the locus of incorporation: the locus of corporate headquarters; the nationality of a majority of senior executives and/or board members; the nationality of the largest group of employees; and the nationality of the largest group of equity holders. None of these legalistic definitions seems satisfactory, at least not before undertaking a comprehensive review of the changing global economic setting and US interests.[19] For example, few would argue the notion that US citizens will benefit from government policies that generate full employment and productivity increases. But what if, in contrast to the past, the most likely agents for US employment gains and productivity increases in the future are ''foreign'' transnationals? Should the various US government supports be limited to ''US'' firms? Should future antitrust waivers be limited to groups that include the technology leaders, without regard to country of origin?

For policy purposes, it might be useful to adopt a new set of definitions. For example, a national firm conducts all its activities within one country; a multinational firm operates in more than one country but has a primary allegiance to one country; a transnational firm operates in more than one country with a weak or nonexistent primary allegiance. Using these definitions, one would say there are numerous transnational firms with European or US origins while most Japanese firms remain in the multinational mold.

Let us consider another area for policy concern.[20] In past decades when nations were the only effective global players, there was general agreement that it would be desirable to have a forum in which they exchanged views. This led to the formation of the League of Nations and more recently, the United Nations. With few exceptions, the policies and actions of UN organizations are determined by boards that consist exclusively of member nations' representatives.

If one accepts the major argument of this paper—that new global players are emerging—it is important to ask whether the UN structure is adequate to insure that the views of these new players are heard and given the attention they deserve. The new players are definitely making their views known, but they remain outsiders: there are no official forums for them to publicly present and debate their views.

In this context, it is worth remembering that the League of Nations and the United Nations were not created out of a respect for the wisdom of national leaders; rather, they were created in hopes that forcing a public debate among national leaders would reduce the danger of global warfare. As the threat of global warfare subsides, it is being replaced by issues which are of great interest to the new global players.

Is there a need for new public and private forums for the new global players, or could the United Nations be reformulated in a manner which would give the new players roles commensurate with their global power? It is highly questionable whether the United Nations can serve as a satisfactory home for the new global players: it is, after all, the United Nations with its own patterns and traditions that necessarily reflect the interests of its members. An alternative would be to establish four new organizations—United Firms, United Special Interest Groups, United International Organizations, and the Organization of Global Players—where the three new ''United'' groups and the United Nations could discuss matters of common interest. While this structure has the merit of formally recognizing the new global players, it sounds a bit unwieldy. An obvious alternative would be to have one new entity in which all of the new global players are represented.

Whatever the structure, the method of finance is important. In recognition of its purpose, it should be financed by the citizens of the world and not the global players.[21]

SUMMARY

This paper has argued that the era in which nations are the dominant global players is ending. Largely as a result of the information revolution and the demise of the United States as the dominant world power, new global players have emerged. This paper focused on three emerging players: transnational corporations, international organizations, and special interest groups. While nations have lost power in relative terms, they remain significant global players.

Global players can be expected to collaborate in different ways on a wide range of issues. Some collaborations can be expected to benefit the global citizenry while others will be detrimental. Policy analysis is needed, but the field of international relations, with its focus on nations, does not provide an adequate conceptual framework for the needed analytical work.

NOTES

1. In this essay, the term(s) nation(s) and state(s) are used interchangeably; the term nation-state(s) is avoided on grounds of redundancy.

2. ''Transnational'' is defined later in this paper to describe firms that have a weak or nonexistent primary country allegiance.

3. Important exceptions to this generalization include a few religious and political movements, e.g., the Crusades, later Christian missionary activities, the German Fascist Party, and the International Communist Party.

4. One might wonder why I choose to use a phrase that colloquially has pejorative connotations to describe these latter groups. There are two reasons: first, I cannot think of a phrase that in its literal meaning describes these groups as well; second, history tells us there is reason to view critically groups that claim to speak for humanity (see Hoffer, 1951).

5. This is more apparent among US and European companies, but there is increasing evidence that Asian companies are freeing themselves from the tight alliances with their ''home'' governments. For example, it is quite clear that the Japanese government is not pleased with the extent to which Japanese car makers are setting up overseas production facilities.

6. For this point as applied to individuals, see Weiner (1989).

7. For example, they have pressured the World Bank and other donor agencies to be more concerned about environmental issues in their programs; in the United States, the Coolidge Center for Environmental Leadership offers environmental seminars for foreign graduate students; efforts are also going into developing transnational networks of locally based interest groups.

8. Effective use of the fax was halted when the Chinese military took charge of most of the fax machines on university campuses.

9. In the following section, the term ''collaboration'' can mean anything from an agreement to work together to an actual merger of two or more entities. In all cases, these actions are likely to reduce competition as the term is traditionally defined.

10. For more on the reasons for these agreements, see Mody (1988) and Mowery (1989).

11. In one sense, trading blocs can be seen as the reaction of nations to the emergence of new global players.

12. In 1980 dollars.

13. In 1980 dollars.

14. Military conflicts across national borders.

15. See also Porter (1986).

16. On international organizations, see Morss and Honadle (1984) and Moseley (1987). On special interest groups, see Harrell-Bond (1986).

17. See Weber (1947) and Downs (1967).

18. Systematic policy analysis is needed. For example, it has been widely assumed that on environmental issues, the interests of developed nations conflict with those of developing nations. But consider the following: ''If China, by burning its huge coal reserves, causes the world to warm and the sea to rise, then Africans will starve and Bangladeshis drown long before the rich countries suffer'' (*Economist*, 1989), p. 13.

19. Earlier in this paper, it was suggested that ''national,'' ''multinational,'' and ''transnational'' might serve as useful categories for analyzing firm behavior. There is, however, no direct link between these categories and the firms that should be favored by the policies of national governments.

20. I am indebted to Neva Goodwin for many of the points raised in this section.

21. There is an ambiguity over who finances the United Nations. One could argue it is supported by its members, i.e., nations. On the other hand, nations could be seen as proxies for citizens.

REFERENCES

Bradford, Colin I., ''A strategic perspective on trade regimes and trade theory.'' (Discussion Draft, Washington, DC: World Bank, November 2, 1988).

Business Week, ''The global 1000'' (July 18, 1988).

Downs, Anthony, *Inside Bureaucracy* (Boston: Little, Brown and Company, 1967).

Economist (July 15, 1989), p. 13.

Harrell-Bond, Barbara, *Imposing Aid: Emergency Assistance to Refugees* (London: Oxford University Press, 1986).

Hoffer, Eric, *The True Believers: Thoughts on the Nature of Mass Movements* (New York: Harper & Row, 1951).

Mead, Walter R., ''The United States and the world economy, part II,'' *World Policy Journal,* Vol. 6, No. 3 (Summer 1989), p. 393.

Mody, Ashoka, ''Changing firm boundaries: Analysis of technology-sharing alliances,'' draft (Washington, DC: World Bank, August 1988).

Morss, Elliott R., and George H. Honadle, ''Differing agendas,'' in E. Morss and D. Gow (Eds.), *Implementing Rural Development Projects: Lessons from AID and World Bank Experiences* (Boulder, CO: Westview Press, 1984).

Moseley, Paul, ''Conditionality as bargaining process: Structural adjustment lending, 1980–86,'' Essays in International Finance No. 168 (Princeton, NJ: Princeton University, Department of Economics, October 1987).

Mowery, David C., ''International collaborative ventures and commercialization,'' Paper prepared for the Conference on Economic Growth and the Commercialization of New Technologies sponsored by the Technology and Economic Growth program of the Center for Economic Policy Research (Stanford University: September 11–12, 1989).

Pierce, Neil, ''Cross border happenings,'' *National Journal* (June 3, 1989), pp. 1337–1342.

Porter, Michael E. (Ed.), *Competition in Global Industries* (Cambridge, MA: Harvard Business School Press, 1986).

Reich, Robert B., ''Who is us?'' *Harvard Business Review,* Vol. 90, No. 1 (January–February 1990), pp. 53–64.

Stokes, Bruce, ''Multiple alliances,'' *National Journal* (November 11, 1989), pp. 2754–2758.

Weber, Max, *The Theory of Social and Economic Organization* (Glencoe, IL: The Free Press, 1947).

Webster's New Collegiate Dictionary (Springfield, MA: G. & C. Merriam, 1981).

Weiner, Myron, ''International population movements: Implications for foreign policies and migration policies,'' Paper pre-

pared for The United States-French Immigration Policies Conference (L'Abbaye de Royaumont: October 1989).

World Bank, *World Development Report 1988* (New York: Oxford University Press, 1988).

4

THE GROWING INTERDEPENDENCE BETWEEN TRANSNATIONAL CORPORATIONS AND GOVERNMENTS*

JOHN M. STOPFORD**

ABSTRACT   The rapid growth of foreign direct investment has brought the transnational corporation centre-stage in the international political economy. Foreign direct investment has significantly increased the economic interdependence of nations and has made key factors of production more mobile. These developments challenge the traditional assumption of comparative advantage. Rather than concentrating on natural endowments, attention needs to be focused on *created assets*. This article, using the concept of ''triangular diplomacy'', argues that a greater degree of partnership in wealth creation between transnational corporations and nations is possible, provided that both parties understand each other's requirements more fully. In particular, the article argues the need to consider policy and policy coordination in terms of a positive-sum game, not the zero-sum game that has dominated so much Western thinking.

The optimism that greeted the fall of the Berlin Wall has proved to be short-lived. The hope was for an acceleration of progress towards a liberalized world economy, in which the beneficial impetus to world growth from intensifying global competition could be given free rein. Instead, the removal of the common threat of communism has had the perverse effect of releasing pent-up economic rivalry in the form of increasingly bitter trade fights. The long de-

* An earlier version of this article was presented at a symposium in Stuttgart, Germany, sponsored by the Carnegie-Bosch Institute, April 1993. The author acknowledges with gratitude the support of that Institute.

** Professor, London Business School, London, United Kingdom, and Stockholm School of Economics, Stockholm, Sweden.

lay in completing the Uruguay Round of Multilateral Trade Negotiations, combined with symptoms of a world of adversarial trade blocs, suggest a new mood of national self-interest.

Trade frictions are caused in part by the fact that the pace of building an increasingly interdependent world economy through investments is continuing at an unprecedented rate. Mobile investments and intensifying global competition affect the source and nature of the associated trade flows. How to capture more of the benefits within a country has become a pressing issue for governments. What national policies can induce firms—both domestic and foreign—to invest for production and exports and thereby increase national wealth? Within the past two years, this question has emerged centrally in the political debate in Sweden, the United Kingdom, the United States and, more recently, Germany. There, the Solidarity Pact talks among politicians, trade unions and industry have been aimed at ensuring the competitiveness of Germany as an investment location in the 1990s. Regional issues are taking a back seat in the national debates. The same debates have taken place in many developing countries, as a prelude to adopting far-reaching policies of liberalization and privatization.

Yet, governments' responses to international economic developments are inherently ambiguous. They want the benefits of foreign direct investment (FDI) and are increasingly prone to intervene to increase their share, but fear the consequences when other nations do the same. They also fear possible losses of national sovereignty. For example, some policy makers in the United Kingdom see no inconsistency in simultaneously espousing the cause of market forces and opposing European integration on issues that threatened the country's ability to determine its own future. Those fears are most acute in high-technology industries, such as aircraft, semiconductors, supercomputers, high-definition television and the like, regarded by many as crucial for their national security and for the strength of their national industries.[1] How governments resolve the dilemmas bred of ambiguity is a matter that no transnational corporation (TNC) can afford to ignore.

This article argues that managers need to look beyond their products and markets when calculating their global strategies. They need to develop a greater understanding of the forces driving change in the "global political economy" if they are to be spared surprise. What game is really being played, under whose rules? The answers involve more than the effect of domestic political influences on individual project negotiations. The rules of the game are, in effect, determined by the outcomes of a three-way tug of war: domestic political imperatives pull one way; international economic imperatives can pull in another; and firms' global competitive imperatives

can add a third dimension. Conventional perspectives and calculations do not readily capture the dynamic interactions at work and may blind many to the reality of new sources of risk.

In particular, risks are created as two quite different perspectives about how to build competitiveness come increasingly into conflict. Though rather oversimplified, firms can be regarded as being engaged in a race to create and accumulate new resources that change the structures of competition and fuel further interdependence across borders. This dynamic perspective on a positive-sum game of wealth creation is shared by many governments in Asia. By contrast, governments of countries in Europe and North America can be regarded as espousing more static policies to promote and protect indigenous firms. Their actions can directly affect the location of production and thus the welfare of nations in a "beggar-thy-neighbour" zero-sum game.

To make the case, the evidence on growing economic interdependence and the central role of TNCs in that process is summarized first. Then, some of the political and policy issues are explored that are involved in the building of a simple model of triangular diplomacy that illustrates the form of interactions affecting both States and firms. Because government calculations are often made on the basis of static and increasingly out-dated notions of the Ricardo/Heckscher-Ohlin theory of comparative advantage, some attention to theory will help explain why frictions in policy choice are likely to continue.[2] The aim is to illuminate the sources of friction and risk and to suggest that firms should raise their voice in influencing the policy debates.

GROWING ECONOMIC INTERDEPENDENCE

Is the world moving toward the "ideal" state of a global economy in which growth is fuelled by close economic interdependence among the leading nations in trade, investment and cooperative commer-

---

[1] An eloquent statement of the threat to one nation from other governments' interventions in high-technology industries is provided in Tyson (1992).

[2] For an excellent summary of the theory and economists' subsequent modifications, see Findlay (1991).

cial relations, combined with relatively little restriction on cross-border transactions or discrimination against foreign-owned entities? There are two parts to this depiction of an ideal: economic interdependence, as well as harmonization of policy among leading nations. If one looks only at the first part, the evidence might be used as support for K. Ohmae's (1990) claim that strategy should be based on the presumption of a ''borderless world'' and that governments' powers to dictate terms to the market are in terminal decline.[3] Discussion of the second part provides an alternative conclusion, but that is deferred until after considering why Ohmae and others are making the claims they do.

Growing economic interdependence can be seen in the evidence that world trade has been growing faster than world GDP. Even more impressively, FDI has been growing four times faster than trade since 1982, despite a downturn during the recent recession. Deregulation of capital markets has fuelled an equal boom in cross-border financial flows. Daily transactions across the foreign-exchange markets now routinely exceed $900 billion, a figure that dwarfs national accounts of annual current account deficits or surpluses.

Central to this growth has been the role of TNCs in reshaping the world economy (Caves, 1982; Dunning, 1993). Their expansion has four notable features, some of which are indicated in Table 1:

● First is the growth of output of TNCs. At some point during the 1970s, the output from assets located in one country, but owned and controlled in another, exceeded the volume of world trade for the first time. That output is highly concentrated: just 420 of the largest of the 37,000 or so parent TNCs account for over half of the total output.[4] The implications for governments are far-reaching, for it is much harder to control foreign investors within a coun-

try than to control trade flows at the border. And controlling large firms and harnessing their resources effectively demands particular skills and resources that few nations possess in large quantities.

● A second feature is the growing share of TNCs in exports, both from their home countries and from many of their host countries. Transnational corporations manage about three quarters of world trade in manufactured goods, over a third of which is inter-affiliate trade. For example, United States-owned affiliates abroad now sell more than twice what the whole of the United States exports. Leading the impetus for the North American Free Trade Agreement (NAFTA), Mexican-based affiliates of United States firms already account for over 40 percent of Mexico's trade with the United States, its largest trading partner (UNTCMD, 1992).

● A third indicator of the significance of TNCs relates to technology. Transnational corporations are the primary source of privately funded research and development and dominate the international trade in technology payments that is estimated to exceed $30 billion a year. The vast bulk of this trade is in the form of transfers among affiliates in the same group. Understanding the decisions of TNCs about where to locate their innovation effort deserves more attention than has been given so far.[5]

● A fourth indicator of the importance of TNCs is the growth of both strategic alliances among these firms and of other non-equity forms of collaboration with local firms. Alliances can change the structures of competition and challenge the powers of national and regional competition regulations: the economic unit of competition can become wider than that defined by the legal boundaries of a single firm. Moreover, the constantly evolving bargains within an alliance underscore the dynamism of the race to acquire resources. As one study concluded, ''companies that are confident about their ability to learn may even prefer some ambiguity in the alliance's legal structure. Ambiguity creates more potential to acquire skills and technologies'' (Hamel, Doz and Prahalad, 1989, p. 139).

The growth of local, contract-based collaboration has far-reaching, often subtle implications for the transfer of technology and other resources. For example, General Motors' policies of collaboration with local parts suppliers in Brazil have required hundreds of engineers to spend long periods in Brazil

---

[3] This sense that economic determinism was eroding Government power was foreshadowed by Raymond Vernon (1971) in his classic treatise, *Sovereignty at Bay,* though he later modified his position.

[4] For details, see Stopford (1992). John H. Dunning (1993) has challenged the UNTCMD (1992) estimate of 37,000 parent TNCs and proposed a lower, but still substantial, population estimate.

[5] One exception is Cantwell (1993).

Table 1. Foreign Direct Investment and Selected Economic Indicators, 1981–1991 (Billions of Dollars and Percentage)

Indicator	Value, 1991 (Billion dollars, current prices)	Annual growth 1981–1985 (Percent)	Annual growth 1986–1990 (Percent)	Annual growth 1990–1991 (Percent)
FDI outflows	180	4	24	−23
FDI stock	1900	5	11	11
Foreign sales of TNCs	5500[a]	2[b]	15	n.a.
GDP at factor cost	22300[b]	2	9	−6[c]
Gross domestic investment	5100[b]	1	10	n.a.
Exports	3800	2	10	4

Source: UNCTAD, DTCI (1993).
[a]For 1990.
[b]For 1982–85.
[c]Estimate.

and to incur costs that far exceed the formal value of their assets there. Yet, neither alliances nor contracts are well recorded in the official statistics of FDI. In other words, the official indicators of the reach of TNCs are understated and ignore many other, hidden aspects of growing and deepening economic interdependence.

Firms' motivations to pursue growth vary considerably, but can be grouped in three, well-known basic categories. One is market-seeking growth to gain greater returns on the resources, technical or managerial, already developed. Another is resource-seeking, to gain access to natural resources or the human and technical resources in other countries. The third—efficiency-seeking—is growing fastest at present, as firms seek new ways to link together previously separate operations so as to both lower total system costs and increase their abilities to respond to changes in demand anywhere in the world. In some cases, all three motivations guide policy choices simultaneously in different parts of a single enterprise.

These motivations have taken various forms that have reflected the delicate balance that needs to be struck between gaining scale efficiencies from global integration on the one hand and maintaining responsiveness to local differences on the other. As C.A. Bartlett and S. Ghoshal (1989) demonstrated, firms are attempting to create a variable geometry of organization that is both appropriate to their strategies

and capable of being managed effectively.[6] For the purposes of this argument, one can depict the evolution of the strategies of many TNCs as a combination of market and resource-seeking policies occurring within regions where there are efficiencies to be gained by specialization of production and trade in products. Simultaneously, they are building world-scale efficiencies in functions such as technology and information systems, and their trade across regional boundaries is growing in the intangibles of knowledge and finance.

The effect of these developments is to transform some firms' structures in the way depicted in figure 1. The implication is that at least some TNCs have already developed their strategies in ways that provide them options for responding to possible trade wars among the trade blocs of NAFTA, the European Union and in East Asia. The implication is also that they are becoming much harder to control within any one nation.

GOVERNMENT RESPONSES

Given that investment is one of the keys to economic growth, governments are motivated to seek as many

[6] For equivalent evidence that few TNCs have become global in all functions, see Morrison *et al.* (1991).

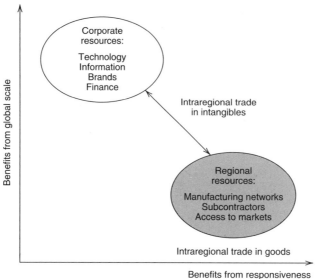

Figure 1. The Differentiated Global Network.

sources of new investment as possible. Small wonder that so many have been putting out the welcome mat to TNCs and fattening the incentive packages on offers to bias firms' location decisions. Within Europe, there are constant contests both among nations and among regions within nations to attract mobile wealth-creating capital. More generally there has been a general liberalization of investment policy in many, especially developing, countries. And the pace of liberalization has accelerated. Of 82 policy changes adopted by 35 countries during 1991, 80 reduced restrictions on foreign investors. Furthermore, 64 bilateral investment treaties for the promotion and protection of FDI were signed during the first 18 months of the 1990s, compared with 199 such treaties signed during the 1980s (UNTCMD, 1992, p. 3). Privatization and deregulation of communications, as well as of financial markets, have also helped extend the sense of greater mobility of critical resources.

One needs, however, to put the investment contribution of TNCs into context. Inward FDI—a form of transfer of world savings—is only a marginal proportion of total national capital formation. There is, of course, wide variation in this figure. Some of the poorer nations, especially in Africa, attract virtually no foreign capital. At the other end of the scale, Singapore relied on TNCs for over 35 percent of its capital formation during the period 1986–1989 (UNTCMD, 1992). In the same period, that figure was over 12 percent for the United Kingdom and 7 percent for the United States. In almost all countries, these shares have risen significantly above the levels obtained in the early 1970s (UNTCMD, 1992). Though relatively small in value, the composition of inward FDI can be crucial. The United Kingdom, for example, relies on TNCs for infusions of new technologies in industries such as electronics (including consumer electronics) and automobiles.

Enhancing the investment function by promoting inward FDI is, however, a double-edged sword. It can create growth and add needed skills, but it can also hinder growth.[7] Moreover, there are growing concerns about trade consequences. Many foreign affiliates import much more than local firms. For example, in the United States, they import twice as

---

[7] Some data from developing countries indicate that as much as 30 percent of foreigners' investment projects can inhibit growth. See Encarnation and Wells (1986).

much per worker in the same industry, thus partially or wholly offsetting export gains (Krugman, 1990, p. 127). Such evidence has led to calls to revise the generally liberal trade policy of the United States and has added to the sense of ambiguity in the general policy response.

There are added concerns that inward FDI can create strategic vulnerability. One example is the European debate about the growth of alliances in politically salient industries such as electronics. As one Olivetti executive put it,

"In the 1990s, competition will no longer be between individual companies but between new, complex corporate groupings. A company's competitive position no longer (solely) depends on its internal capabilities; it also depends on the type of relationships it has been able to establish with other firms and the scope of those relationships" (Financial Times, 29 May 1990).

The electronics industry in Europe is not, therefore, the same as the European electronics industry. Calculations of an appropriate response have sparked a prolonged debate. Some argue that Europe should focus on creating conditions that enhance its value-adding capability regardless of ownership. Others disagree and argue that ownership matters, because it shapes future prospects in any one region: firms give preference to the home territory, making the burden of adjustment to adverse trading conditions fall at the periphery of the system.

Similar fears of dependency and vulnerability have been voiced in the United States, coupled with a more general concern that the United States is losing out in the race to accumulate resources (Reich, 1991; Thurow, 1992). Government persistence in supporting local, high-technology players in Japan, Europe and some developing countries like the Republic of Korea, Taiwan Province of China and Brazil has sparked serious trade frictions with the United States. The reasons are not hard to find. These are industries in which the returns from technical advance create beneficial spill-over effects in related industries and create new barriers to entry that can protect first movers. These are also industries in

which a nation's competitive position is clearly not determined by factor endowments. Instead, the competitive position is created by the strategic interactions among domestic firms and their home governments and among domestic and foreign firms and governments.

Oligopolistic competition and these strategic interactions have effectively replaced the invisible hand of market forces and "violate the assumptions of free trade theory and the static economic concepts that are the traditional basis for US trade policy" (Tyson, 1992, p. 3). The growing relationship between trade and FDI has provoked a fierce debate among economists about the welfare effects of free trade. Some analyses have suggested that free trade is not automatically the best policy for high-technology industries.[8] National intervention can promote local welfare when it provides spillover effects to local related industries and trade barriers can be used to shift oligopolistic rents from foreign to domestic locations of production.

Even though proponents of such arguments have themselves shown that governments are poor at picking winners and that the unilateral gains from interventionist support of automobiles, semiconductors and commercial airlines have been meagre (for example, Baldwin, 1988), the arguments can carry great political weight in domestic policy debates. There are clear signs that the current administration in the United States is responding to them and starting to put in place more directly interventionist policies that might provoke retaliation elsewhere. Moreover, there is a real danger that these responses will extend to other industries, as in the current disputes over countervailing duties, tax policies for foreigners, and the rules for public procurement.

Further distortions and impediments to trade are created by national differences in the rules governing competition, even in those high-technology industries characterized by an international dispersion of manufacturing and a separation of the location of research from manufacture (Yoffie, 1991). Such im-

---

[8] For a summary of recent developments in strategic trade theory, see Baldwin (1985), Krugman (1987) and Ernst and O'Connor (1992).

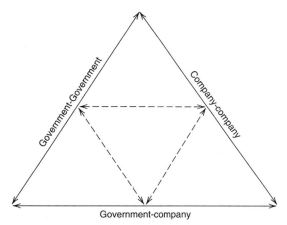

Figure 2. Triangular Diplomacy.
Source: Stopford and Strange (1991).

pediments are so deeply embedded in national structures that attempts to negotiate their removal meet stubborn resistance, as the faltering progress of the United States-Japan Structural Impediments Initiative talks indicates. Japan has acceded to *gaiatsu* (pressure from abroad) on those agenda items, such as infrastructure spending, where self-interest matched foreign desires. But where Japan sees no national gain—for example, loosening *keiretsu* trading relationships and ending exclusionary business practices—it has dragged its feet.

TRIANGULAR DIPLOMACY

The competing national and international forces can be represented in a simple model of triangular diplomacy (Figure 2). One side of the triangle represents competition among firms for shares of the global market-place. Another represents the agenda of bargaining between firms and governments. The third represents competition among governments, in terms of trade policy, the web of bilateral and multilateral treaties and domestic policies that have international repercussions. As diplomacy shifts from competition for power from more territory toward a competition for wealth as a means to gain power, TNCs have a more direct influence on the conduct of intergovernmental relations. Connecting all the three sides of

the triangle are interlocking bargains that together shape the operating rules of the game.[9]

The impact on individual States depends on the relative importance of international and purely national transactions, the types of goods and assets traded and the forms of agreement created to support a state's objectives. The great variation of national size and resources, the state of development and so on, suggest that the outcomes are likely to vary enormously. Growing interdependence does not mean a convergence of outcomes—but diversity. This adds pressure on managers to understand the fine grain of the interplay of forces in each region and to ensure that their options for response are indeed as flexible as some now claim them to be.

Triangular diplomacy can be seen at work among the East Asian economies. Led by Japanese firms, East Asian economies are becoming more interconnected, even without a formal trade pact. The Asian regional developments are clearly being influenced by the extent to which Japan can export its ideological preference for lending the invisible hand a bit of administrative guidance to other, similarly inclined, neighbours.

Japanese firms enjoy access to official support from at least two sources. One is the Japanese International Development Organisation, set up in 1989 by the Keidanren (an association of large Japanese employers), with about one fifth of its capital supplied by the government. This agency provides financial assistance for investment in developing countries, especially in Asia. The other source is the Japanese aid programme that concentrates on infrastructure projects and provides over half of all aid to the Association of South East Asian Nations and to China. Though official policy is that there are no ties between the public and the private purse, critics point to outcomes that seem more than coincidental. For example, Japanese firms won over a third of the aid contracts in the year up to 31 March 1992. The link between public and private capital is well illustrated by China's Liaoning Province, where Japanese investment was modest until 1988, when $145 mil-

[9] For a full exploration of the model, see Stopford and Strange (1991).

lion was pledged to finance a dam. ''This spurred a flood of private cash. The biggest project was a $155 million cement plant . . . and . . . half of the foreign investment in Liaoning now comes from Japan'' (*The Economist*, 24 April 1993, p. 80).

The possibility of ties is also suggested by apparent biases in the direction of Japan's outward FDI in Asia that cannot be wholly explained by market forces alone. Matsushita, for example, now relies on Asia for 59 percent of all its overseas production, up sharply from the beginning of the 1990s. Already one tenth of Matsushita's Asian production is exported to Japan, and that proportion is growing. The simultaneous drives for both market-seeking and efficiency-seeking investments seem enhanced by tacit government support. The resulting advantages in such products as air-conditioners and compressors, as well as in consumer electronics, will increasingly affect trade elsewhere in the world.

The export of administrative guidance could have repercussions far beyond the region, with serious consequences for Western investors. Consider, for example, the impact on world financial markets as Asia continues to grow at much faster rates than elsewhere. Asia commanded 14 percent of central bank reserves in the early 1980s, a share that has now risen to 43 percent. One forecast is that the growing interconnections in the region could boost the emerging Asian bond market to the scale of the Eurodollar market. The most favourable terms exist for Asian countries and for Western countries operating in those countries. Capital availability for the United States and others could become increasingly dependent on Asian sources, and on Asian terms.[10] The implications for corporate strategy are clear and at odds with much recent corporate behaviour, for many United States firms have reduced, relatively or absolutely, their investments in the region since 1985.

A further manifestation of triangular diplomacy is that, when governments clash in one industry, the repercussions can be felt in others. One example can

serve to make the point. While the fourth round of negotiating the terms and conditions of the Multi-Fibre Arrangement was taking place, the United Kingdom unilaterally reduced its import quota for Indonesian T-shirts. Looking for retaliation against ''perfidious Albion,'' Indonesia embargoed a chemical project that was being built locally by a United Kingdom firm. A value of 100 million pounds of assets were put at risk because of a conflict over less than 5 million pounds of annual trade. Who in the plant construction business would routinely track developments in the textile trade? Yet, a close understanding of all the principal influences on a Government might have given better advance intelligence of looming problems and, perhaps, might have suggested some measures to protect the project.

RICARDO REVISITED

One symptom of a government clinging to Ricardian notions of comparative advantage is when it measures national competitiveness primarily in terms of trade performance, as shown in the balance of payments (particularly the current account), and the presumed effect on the exchange rate. For long, in many Western countries, trade and money have been considered central. Where TNC behaviour and influence on trade performance appeared at odds with received wisdom, they were dismissed as a curiosity worth at best a footnote. Those footnotes, however, are now appearing in the main text. Ricardian notions cannot explain why Sony (Japan) exports televisions from the United Kingdom while national producers have all but disappeared, or why Malaysia is one of the world's largest exporters of semiconductors.

The problem is that the central tenet of the theory—the immobility of assets across borders—no longer holds true. Not only does capital move in the place of goods, but also other factors of production, especially the created, intangible assets of technology and organizational skill, are increasingly mobile within firms. The growth of intra-industry trade and investment reflects such mobility. Moreover, it is increasingly apparent that costs at the level of the firm

---

[10] Data and forecast provided by Ken Courtis, Senior Economist, Deutsche Bank Capital Markets Asia, at a Business Week conference, Palm Beach, April 1993.

are not the same as those for the nation and that foreign investors can enjoy new advantages as they transfer their systems of production across borders. The lean production systems of the Japanese automobile producers give their transplant assembly operations an edge over local firms and allow for greater exporting opportunity, even though they have the same costs of labour, transport and other infrastructure factors.[11]

These increasingly important manifestations of a new order are drawing attention to the need to distinguish productive assets that are created from those that are natural endowments.[12] Created assets are primarily in the form of human capital—the stock of knowledge, technological and organizational capacity, infrastructure and governing policies. Endowments, primarily land, mineral resources and labour, remain immobile, but are of decreasing importance in determining outcomes. Richly endowed countries like the former Soviet Union or Zaire can remain relatively poor if they fail to enhance their human capital as fast as their competitors. In other words, policy makers need to concern themselves with the inputs to future competitiveness, not just react to outcomes after the event.

Some policy makers have well understood the new realities. The Governor of the Central Bank of the Republic of Korea once said: "Don't listen to 'comparative advantage' advice. Whenever we wanted to do anything the advocates of comparative advantage said 'we don't have comparative advantage.' In fact, we did everything we wanted, but whatever we did we did well" (Alagh, 1989, quoted in Wade, 1992, p. 270). The Republic of Korea's growing ability to create new resources and transform its competitiveness was not recognized by the World Bank's first mission there in the early 1960s. Holding conventional views of the static nature of

resources, that mission dismissed projections of rapid growth as ludicrously optimistic because performance had been so poor in the 1950s. Much the same could be said for the post-war development of Japan. The state, it would seem, can have a positive role in influencing market forces in ways that help its constituent firms to grasp the lightning rod of innovation. That is precisely what the present debate is now about in the United States and Europe.

Consider the issue of labour. It used to be thought that the possession of a large pool of low-cost labour conferred an advantage on a nation. Today, direct labour costs are becoming a relatively minor part of the total costs of production in many industries. In electronics, they can be as low as 3 percent and, according to a recent IFC study, even in standardized automobile components (coil springs, piston rings and valves) companies report that direct labour costs are only 10–15 percent of total manufacturing costs and falling (Miller, 1993). Similarly, indirect labour costs are falling as a proportion of total costs. The old argument is losing its power and the issue is focused on the possession of trained labour and how skills in one country can be transferred to another by firms, rather than by national educational policies. For example, General Motors and Ford have trained the local work-force as part of their successful transfer of advanced engine manufacturing to Mexico.

The same issues affect the shifts of location of TNCs among developed countries. There is much evidence that, within Europe, inward investors are avoiding locations of relatively low skill and eschewing the cash advantages of investment incentives. Instead, they are preferring locations where they can have ready access to a pool of highly trained labour, even though the short-term costs may be higher. The argument is that the ability of the work-force to upgrade itself to satisfy the demands of next-generation products will determine by how much total long-run costs can be lowered to enhance the durability of the firm's competitiveness.

Increasingly, national competitiveness is coming to depend on the abilities of people and firms to innovate—to create new products and services, to lower the real costs of supply by increasing productivity and to build relationships with customers at home

---

[11] For a careful exploration of the new economics of automobile production across borders, see Womack, Jones and Roos (1990).

[12] Economic growth theory has been emphasizing the growth-enhancing role of technology and human capital accumulation, as well as the possibilities of increasing returns to scale at the aggregate level. See, for example, Romer (1987), Helpman (1992) and Dennison (1985).

and abroad—and of society to organize its affairs effectively. The innovative assets are a central part of the created assets of a State. They are intangible and primarily the property of firms, especially in those industries in which the costs of research exceed the capacity of individuals or, in some cases, even governments, to fund. This means that firms, not the state, have the right, within the constraints of the law, to exploit these assets wherever and however they choose. Rising scale for innovation means that TNCs will provide increasingly the well-spring for progress, the outcome of which is measured in terms of trade flows, income levels and income differentials.

It is perhaps curious that Michael Porter (1990) ignored many of these developments in his recent, influential book. He gave little weight to the role of TNCs or multilateral agencies and ignored the effects of inter-state bargaining. He seemed to regard domestic resource creation as the dominant determinant of competitiveness, considering global influences as little more than interesting additions to his domestic ''diamond'' of factors. Indeed, recent analysis has demonstrated that Porter's implied policy prescriptions are muddled and sometimes inappropriate (e.g., Cartwright, 1993). Part of the difficulty is that Porter, like many government officials, assumed that firms are conditioned by local factors before they go abroad. He undervalued the intangible advantages TNCs possess in terms of their ability to lower the transaction costs of the global market and thus work toward integrating country-specific factors as they transform their internal resources.

Moreover, the imperatives of competition now mean that competitors in a global industry resemble one another more closely. Previous notions of fundamental differences in terms of enterprises' national origin—United States firms behave differently from Japanese ones, and so on—have to be revised (Vernon, 1992). The implication is that a more productive way to address the issues may be to start from a clearer depiction of the forces in the international political economy and then work backward to consider how specific national conditions fit into the whole and are shaped by the changing motivations of the key investors. Only then might one be able to see and understand the causes of the diversity of the outcomes.

POLICY CO-ORDINATION

The globalization of markets does not mean that governments lose control of their economic destinies. But to retain control, they must revise their approaches to capture the benefits from new, innovative sources of advantage within their own borders. A central issue is the extent of coordination—perhaps even, on occasion, integration—of policy, both domestically across ministerial departments and across national borders. Even though the domestic organization, both private and public, controls most of the ingredients needed to foster greater created sources of advantage, no state today can be wholly self-sufficient in commanding all the resources it needs. Transnational corporations provide complementary, but not substitutive, resources that can accelerate progress. Their extending reach means that their influence on national and international policy is moving away from the periphery of special-interest pleading toward a more central position on the stage.

There are many obstacles to be overcome before effective policy coordination can be achieved. Not only must policy makers shift from a static, defensive posture and come to grips with the global dynamics, but they must also have to understand more fully how the interplay of regulatory and competitive forces impacts on industries in different ways. A general policy that makes economic sense for one industry may be disastrous for another. Furthermore, short-run domestic political agendas can deny them the commitment to build for longer run strength. One recent study concluded that ''the competitiveness of a country rests both on the ability of its firms to organize and utilize their own assets efficiently and also on the ability of government to ensure that the markets in which firms compete are the least distorted. In order to achieve these objectives, governments need to restructure their own internal systems of management so as to gain the maximum benefits from an integrated system of governance'' (Dunning, 1992, pp. 44). At the very least, this requires harmonization of a diverse agenda ranging from tax and competition policy to common environmental standards.

It is seldom clear what is the optimum degree of domestic policy coordination, let alone what defines the best constituent policies. The difficulty is that the calculus of optimality is in constant flux, not just because of competition, but also because states keep changing their expectations. "A state has objectives that are multiple . . . It wants to be efficient and competitive and to preserve social peace and the cohesion of the state with society. It wants autonomy and the freedom to choose its own path to economic development and access to advanced technology and overseas markets" (Stopford and Strange, 1991, p. 135). Success in managing these domestic dilemmas may be a necessary condition for progress, but is not a sufficient condition for managing the wider web of relationships in the international economy.

The domestic uncertainties are multiplied across borders, raising the important question of whether it is either beneficial or, indeed, possible to achieve international policy coordination. The case for coordination rests on the fact that national policies affect others, both at the macro level of, say, currency intervention and at the micro level of industry policy. The case is also based on the premise that coordination increases the chances that governments will achieve individual and collective economic goals. The case against coordination rests on the fact that uncertainties and shocks are so severe as to wipe out any possible gains.[13]

A recent study reviewed all such arguments and, on the basis of some carefully crafted simulations for the United States economy, concluded that some forms of coordination were possible and, despite obvious risks, were more desirable than independent approaches (Ghosh and Masson, 1993). The authors argued that uncertainty provides an incentive to cooperate and that coordination is beneficial, provided

that policy makers' perceptions of how the economy works is not unduly flawed and is revised to take account of experience. They went further to argue that coordination in the form of simple, non-activist policies that are cautious and respond only imperfectly to macroeconomic developments may be better than attempts to find and agree on fully optimal policies. They also addressed the familiar argument that the greatest gains are likely to arise from information sharing among the major industrial nations. They showed that information sharing alone, free of any policy commitment, can be valueless and may even lower welfare: the temptation to mislead can make information about policy intentions less credible. Given the arguments earlier in this article, caution and simplicity seem essential ingredients of fruitful attempts to achieve some gains from the uncertainties bred of the rapid changes in the rules that shape the form of the deepening economic interdependence of nations.

TRANSNATIONAL CORPORATIONS AS DIPLOMATS?

If TNCs are truly moving more centre-stage in affecting the emerging rules, then the question naturally arises as to whether their influence is helpful to the cause of policy coordination or a hinderance. The corollary is to ask how the managers of these enterprises are responding to their new responsibilities and whether they may be expected to change their behaviour in ways that might add impulses for further change in the underlying relationships.

Relationships between states and TNCs are necessarily based on bargaining, for there are mutual hostages to be exchanged. But when the rules are in flux, one must ask such questions of managers as "Can they afford to wait for governments to sort out new rules, domestically and internationally?" or "Should they actively intervene in the debates?" The available evidence suggests that the answers are diverging according to the position of individual firms, but in roughly predictable ways. The difficulty for governments, though, is that these responses are

---

[13] Coordination can range from formal, institutionalized rules for an international monetary system to ad hoc bilateral agreements. For an extensive review of possibilities, see Horne and Masson (1988).

often hard to decode, for firms hold quite different attitudes as to the nature and extent of their engagement in the public debate. Some seem unwilling to engage in the debate at all, fearful of attracting criticism that they are intervening in politics. Others openly espouse the cause of greater liberalization of the rules for managing cross-border transactions of all kinds. Yet others are busily lobbying governments for greater degrees of protection.

If one looks behind the façade of these debating positions one can discern that much of the response has to do with the economics of the business involved. Those United States managers whose international business is primarily through FDI have tended to greet the debate with a big yawn (Wells, 1992). The same has been true for many Europeans in the same sorts of industries. Both appear to consider that their configuration of invested assets gives them adequate insurance against continuing trade frictions. Those whose international business is primarily through trade take the opposite view. They are deeply concerned to have some voice in the debate, for they have more at stake.

There is, however, an added consideration affecting the response: the competitive strength of the business. Those who are relatively weak are more prone to invoke the support of home or regional governments.[14] Consider, for example, the European automobile industry. Some executives, like M. Calvet of Peugeot (France), argue passionately that a liberalization of investment and trade restrictions should be delayed for as long as possible for fear of destroying the existing European producers. There is an alignment of interests between the government of France and French producers for deep integration of local policy, but also for protectionism at the borders to impede international integration. That sense of alignment is not, however, shared by the United Kingdom, which has argued equally strongly that a liberalization and integration of markets is essential if the United Kingdom is to retain its share of world automobile production. For them, the local presence of United States and Japanese producers is vital in the aftermath of the failure of British Leyland (now the Rover Group).[15]

The weakness of the European electronics industry creates a similar diversity of views and introduces dilemmas that seem incapable of solution by rationality alone. None of the obvious options is wholly satisfactory. Further protection shows no sign of arresting the decline and would merely maintain higher prices. Besides, the consequential inward FDI flows would threaten the incumbents more directly. The dilemma of existing protection is illustrated by Regulation No. 288/89 [OJL 33, of 4 February 1989] that requires the diffusion process for semiconductor manufacturing to be located in a member state to guarantee free circulation within the European Community. Many think that this restriction will create inefficiency and hurt local buyers. Selective encouragement for some segments does not appear to have helped in the past, because of technical changes that have eroded the protectability of the segment boundaries. Moreover, mergers to gain greater scale do not provide a clear solution. Rather than encouraging any Europe-wide administrative guidance, the dilemmas mean that it is a case of *sauve qui peut.*

The sense of dilemma can cause leading industrialists to make inconsistent statements. For example, one top official in Philips, the troubled leader at the centre of the storm, reaffirmed his support for free trade, but then went on to argue for policies that would oblige governments to buy European (Van der Klught, 1986). Moreover, Philips successfully argued for European price protection for video tape recorders to maintain inefficient local production. The extra margins awarded to the Japanese had the

---

[14] For a fuller exploration of the combined effects, see Stopford (1992), from which some of the general arguments presented here are drawn. See also Milner (1988) for an exploration of TNC influence on the politics of international trade.

[15] The sale of 80 percent of Rover to BMW, its German competitor, in early 1994 has upset the arrangements with Honda (Japan) and has created another round in the endless speculation about whether the consolidation of the world automobile industry will proceed along continental lines, heavily influenced by government support policies, or whether a few individual firms will transcend continental borders to build a truly global oligopoly. Speculation about such structural dynamics is beyond the scope of this article.

perverse effect of adding to their cash-low capability to fund the development of next-generation products faster than the protected Europeans could achieve.

To whom then should governments listen? The evidence from many industries indicates there is a growing divergence in positions taken by leading TNCs from the European Union in responding to shifts in global competition and regionalization. There is a dilemma in the sense that industry's voice in the debate is likely to be one-sided. Weak firms are much more vociferous in lobbying both their national governments and the European Community than are most of the strong players. Strong leaders in investment-intensive industries have been relatively silent, reflecting perhaps their confidence and sense of indifference to changes in trade policy. Few have gone as far as British Petroleum, which stated in 1990 that ''as an international company, BP's commercial success is crucially dependent on . . . the maintenance and enhancement of the GATT-based multilateral trading system''.

If firms fail to rise to the challenge of acting more as diplomats and continue to act on the basis of short-run perceptions of shareholder requirements, they may provoke policy responses that are the opposite of longer-run shareholder interests. The short-termism debate, especially as it affects the workings of the capital markets, cannot be excluded from the debate. But the issue of time perspective in managing adjustments in a turbulent global economy introduces further dilemmas for states and firms alike. Though TNCs (and, indeed, the official position of the European Union) may, in general, resist protectionism, there are so many special cases of weakness, especially in trade-oriented industries, that the fears of a ''Fortress Europe'' developing selectively may prove to be justified. Precisely the same effect could develop within NAFTA and across East Asia.

IS PARTNERSHIP POSSIBLE?

All of the foregoing suggests at least two alternative scenarios for future development. The optimistic scenario is that the silent majority of strong TNCs will have a crucial and more overt role in nudging governments toward adopting policies that reflect more appropriately the present competitive realities. Should that happen, one might see faster progress toward the twin ideal of a liberalized global economy with growing economic interdependence, matched by moves to erode, or even eliminate, domestic distortions to the terms and conditions of operating across borders in developing and developed countries alike. One recent forecast of possibilities in this scenario is for a fourfold real increase in FDI flows by the year 2020, with the fastest growth occurring in developing countries, where the marginal returns to fresh capital transfers are likely to be greatest (Julius, 1993). As DeAnne Julius (1993, p. 7) argued, ''to bring about such a scenario requires long-term commitment. Companies must commit their [resources] to develop distant markets. Governments must commit to continuing the politically difficult process of economic liberalisation . . . If such commitments can be made and kept, then together we can reap the growth potential from building an increasingly integrated world community.''

The pessimistic scenario is that weaker Western firms will continue to be tempted to bargain for political solutions for their troubles. The effect might be to add further muddle to an already confused set of signals to governments at regional and national levels. If, simultaneously, governments preserve outdated notions of static comparative advantage, it is unlikely that North America and Europe will pay sufficient attention to building jointly the created assets needed for future competitiveness.

Of the many possible shocks that could move the world toward this pessimistic scenario, the impact of FDI and further economic interdependence on welfare—both within and across countries—stands out as a cause of dangerous instability. Transnational corporations are not the benign engines of growth the United Nations is now suggesting (UNTCMD, 1992). The growing concentration of investment flows within the Triad markets of the United States, Europe and Japan—for quite understandable competitive reasons—affects the international division of labour and makes it more difficult for latecomer countries to break into the charmed circle of development. The expected rapid growth of population in poor countries is storing up trouble for the next generation. Already, the phenomenon of economic refugees is causing trouble on some frontiers, and could add further pressures for states to strengthen their policies of national self-interest. Even within countries, the wealth effects of inward FDI are skewed in their distribution. Wholly market-based competition does not necessarily promote social justice.

It is perhaps the sheer pace of change that makes it so hard for many states to develop the administrative capacity needed to manage the multiple dimensions of the task simultaneously. How to train officials to comprehend the new realities adequately and to abandon old shibboleths? How to build internal resources as fast as competing states? How to harness TNC skills and resources in durable bargains? Very few nations have the political will to build indigenous resources ahead of demand, as the Republic of Korea has done in its long sustained policies of education, technology enhancement and institution building. Yet even the Republic of Korea is finding that, to maintain its momentum of growth, it has to change and accord foreigners a greater role than hitherto.

To support the development of such national capacity for intelligent bargaining and to provide some form of insurance against welfare and other shocks, the global economy needs a stronger international polity to foster greater clarity, consistency and credibility in policy development. Progress will only be made possible by strong states that understand the new competitive realities and that are prepared to develop the needed new resources. Markets alone are unlikely to assist that process.

The real gains from policy coordination are unlikely to be reaped until there is a stronger basis for partnership between governments and firms, regardless of nationality of origin. Both need to adjust their behaviour to understand the other side better. Because they cannot make forecasts to choose among the possible scenarios—that would defeat the purpose of making scenarios—managers, thus, need to pay increased attention to the mentalities of governments, to be alert to indicators of their emerging policy responses in a post-Ricardian world and to calculate how action in other industries may affect them

for good or ill. To maintain a narrow perspective on one's own products, markets and proximate competitors is to take undue risks. Firms cannot afford to ignore their diplomatic role in influencing how Governments determine effective policies that will influence the attractiveness of any one location for investment. Failure to confront the tensions and frictions of conflicting perspectives will serve to worsen the fears of trade wars and impede the recovery of the global economy.

REFERENCES

Alagh, Yoginder (1989). "The NIEs and the developing Asian and Pacific region: a view from South Asia," *Asian Development Review,* 7, 2, pp. 113–127.

Baldwin, Robert E. (1992). "Are economists' traditional trade policy views still valid?" *Journal of Economic Literature,* 30 (June), pp. 804–829.

———, ed. (1988). *Trade Policy Issues and Empirical Analysis* (Chicago: Chicago University Press).

Bartlett, C.A. and S. Ghoshal (1989). *Managing Across Borders* (Boston, Mass.: Harvard Business School Press).

Cantwell, John, ed. (1993). *Transnational Corporations and Innovatory Activities: United Nations Library on Transnational Corporations* (London: Routlege).

Cartwright, Wayne R. (1993). "Multiple linked diamonds: New Zealand's experience," *Management International Review,* Special issue, 33, pp. 55–70.

Caves, Richard E. (1982). *Multinational Enterprises and Economic Analysis* (Cambridge, Mass.: Cambridge University Press).

Dennison, Edward F. (1985). *Trends in American Economic Growth 1929–1982* (Washington, D.C.: The Brookings Institution).

Dunning, John H. (1993). *Multinational Enterprises and the Global Economy* (Reading, Mass., Addison Wesley).

——— (1992). "The global economy, domestic governance, strategies and transnational corporations: interactions and implications," *Transnational Corporations,* 1, 3 (December), pp. 7–45.

Encarnation, D.J. and L.T. Wells, Jr. (1986). "Evaluating foreign investment," in T.H. Moran, ed., Investing in Development: New Roles for Private Capital? (Oxford: Transaction Books), pp. 61–86.

Ernst, Dieter and David O'Connor (1992). *Competing in the Electronics Industry: The Experience of Newly Industrialising Countries* (London: Routledge).

Findlay, Ronald (1991). "Comparative advantage," in Eatwell, John, Milgate, Murray and Peter Newman, eds., *The New Palgrave: The World of Economics* (London: Macmillan), pp. 99–107.

Ghosh, Atish R. and Paul R. Masson (1993). *Economic Cooperation in an Uncertain World* (Oxford: Basil Blackwell).

Hamel, G., Y.L. Doz and C.K. Prahalad (1989). ''Collaborate with your competitors—and win,'' *Harvard Business Review,* 67 (January-February), pp. 133–139.

Helpman, Elhanan (1992). ''Endogenous macroeconomic growth theory,'' *European Economic Review,* 36 (April), pp. 237–267.

—— and Paul R. Krugman (1985). *Market Structure and Foreign Trade: Increasing Returns, Imperfect Competition and the International Economy* (Cambridge, Mass.: MIT Press).

Horne, Jocelyn and Paul R. Masson (1988). ''Scope and limits of international cooperation and policy coordination,'' IMF *Staff Papers,* 35, 2 (June), pp. 259–296.

Julius, DeAnne (1993). ''Liberalisation, foreign investment and economic growth,'' Shell Selected Paper, March, mimeo.

Krugman, Paul R. (1987). ''Is free trade passé?'' *Journal of Economic Perspectives,* 1 (Fall), pp. 131–144.

—— (1990). *The Age of Diminished Expectations* (Cambridge, Mass.: MIT Press).

Miller, Robert R. (1993). ''Determinants of US manufacturing investment abroad,'' *Finance and Development,* 30, 1 (March 1993), pp. 16–18.

Milner, Helen V. (1988). *Resisting Protectionism* (Princeton, N.J.: Princeton University Press).

Morrison, A.J. *et al.* (1991). ''Globalization and regionalization: which way for the multinational?'' *Organizational Dynamics,* 19, 3 (Winter), pp. 17–29.

Ohmae, K. (1990). *The Borderless World* (New York: Harper Business).

Porter, Michael (1990). *The Competitive Advantage of Nations* (London: Macmillan).

Reich, Robert (1991). *The Work of Nations* (New York: Knopf).

Romer, Paul R. (1987). ''Crazy explanations for the productivity slowdown,'' in NBER *Macroeconomic Annual* (Cambridge, Mass.: National Bureau of Economic Research).

Stopford, John M. (1992). *Directory of Multinationals* (London: Macmillan).

—— (1992), ''Offensive and defensive responses by European multinationals to a world of trade blocs'' OECD Development Centre Technical Paper No. 64 (Paris: OECD).

—— and Susan Strange (1991). *Rival States, Rival Firms* (Cambridge: Cambridge University Press).

Thurow, Lester (1992). *Head to Head: The Coming Economic Battle Among Japan, Europe and America* (New York: William Morrow).

Tyson, Laura (1992). *Who's Bashing Whom? Trade Conflict in High-Technology Industries* (Washington, D.C.: Institute for International Economics).

United Nations, Transnational Corporations and Management Division (1992). *World Investment Report 1992: Transnational Corporations as Engines of Growth* (New York: United Nations), United Nations publication, Sales No. E.92.II.A.19.

UNCTAD, Division on Transnational Corporations and Investment (1993). *World Investment Report 1993: Transnational Corporations and Integrated International Production* (New York: United Nations), United Nations publication, Sales No. E.93.II.A.14.

Van der Klught, C.J. (1986). ''Japan's global challenge in electronics—the Philips' response,'' *European Management Journal* 4, 1, pp. 4–9.

Vernon, Raymond (1971). *Sovereignty at Bay* (New York: Basic Books).

—— (1992). ''Transnational corporations: where they are coming from, where are they headed,'' *Transnational Corporations,* 1, 2 (August), pp. 7–35.

Wade, Robert (1992). ''East Asia's economic success: conflicting perspectives, partial insights, shaky evidence,'' *World Politics,* 44 (January), pp. 270–320.

Wells, Louis T., Jr. (1992). ''Conflict or indifference: US multinationals in a world of regional trading blocs,'' OECD Development Centre Technical Paper No. 57 (Paris: OECD).

Womack, J.P., D.T. Jones and D. Roos (1990). *The Machine that Changed the World* (New York: Rawson Associates).

Yoffie, David B. (1991). ''Technology challenges to trade policy.'' Paper presented at the National Academy of Engineering Symposium on ''Linking trade and technology-policies: an international comparison,'' Washington, D.C., June 1991.

SECTION 2

THE GLOBALIZATION PROCESS

How do firms become international? multinational? global? Is it the result of a carefully planned and orchestrated process? Is it sequential? Or do firms just grow international aimlessly and uncontrollably? Understanding the answers to these questions should help managers anticipate some of the competitive situations they are likely to face. Managers will be better able to plan their own firm's moves in the global economy. This section presents a firm- and industry-level perspective of the process by which firms become international.

In studying the articles in this section, readers should keep in mind that we now manage in a global economy that already has a large "installed base" of multinational and global firms. This means that far fewer firms have the luxury of setting a slow pace toward internationalization. The firm with a new product or a new idea must move much more quickly than was the case just ten or fifteen years ago. The articles in this section explore the history of internationalization and the new imperatives brought about by an environment crowded with competitors.

READING SELECTIONS

Leif Melin presents a comprehensive review and synthesis of studies and perspectives on the internationalization process. With a strategic focus he views internationalization as a key component of the firm's strategy process. He presents three alternative models that purport to explain the internationalization process. Melin then analyzes the strengths and weaknesses of each explanation.

Stage models help explain the past behavior of multinational firms. These models describe firms as passing through several sequential stages beginning with exporting and progressing to foreign direct investment. Concomitantly, firms expand both the number of countries in which they operate and the depth of their involvement in each country. Stage models do a better job of explaining a firm's behavior at early rather than late stages of internationalization.

Structure-follows-strategy models see internationalization as a process of diversification that leads to a new organizational structure that, in turn, favors further diversification. These models do not take into account the learning and political processes that take place in the firm as it proceeds down the internationalization path.

Management process models are, in essence, an extension of the structure-strategy model. Melin's criticism of them is that they are atheoretical and do not relate to what we already know about management. Unaccounted for in all three models is the large role acquisitions have played in the internationalization process.

Campbell and Verbeke report on the globalization processes of service multinationals. Service firms, while an increasingly important sector of the world market, have been too little studied. In their article, Campbell and Verbeke show how the unique characteristics of services affect the internationalization processes of service firms. The authors identify, for example, networking flexibility as a critical component of success in the global services market. Networking flexibility is especially critical in service categories where firms must modify their offerings to accommodate the idiosyncracies of customers in different markets.

Ayal and Izraeli offer a framework for dealing with another critical problem, internationalizing firms with high-technology products. Because of the characteristics of most high-technology products, including short life cycles and fast imitation, marketers of such products operate in a highly turbulent environment. These firms must expand internationally very quickly even if they are young and comparatively small. If they do not expand, they risk losing the market opportunity even at home. The authors attack two of the central problems these firms face: what markets to enter and in what order to enter them.

Oviatt and McDougall then generalize about the early internationalization problem, positing a theory of international *new* ventures. They point out that much-improved communications, technology, international transportation systems, and homogenization of markets make entry into a foreign market feasible almost ''at birth.'' These same factors encourage competitors to enter new markets early. Innovation breeds imitation at a faster and faster rate. They propose and explain the conditions under which they believe a new venture can be successful in the global market. The import of their theory is that a firm should plan its international strategy from the firm's very inception and organize to carry it out at the appropriate time.

5

INTERNATIONALIZATION AS A STRATEGY PROCESS

LEIF MELIN

Department of Management and Economics, Linköping University, Linköping, Sweden

ABSTRACT   This paper critically reviews the field of international business research. The field is characterized by considerable intellectual diversity, where theoretical focus is blurred by the multidisciplinary nature of the field. The review focuses on three themes that help shed light on internationalization as a strategy process; stage models of internationalization, studies of the link between strategy and structure in MNCs, and studies of administrative processes in MNCs and recent organizational models for MNCs. Sequential stages models are too deterministic and stress only early stages of internationalization. Conceptual contributions from research on structures following strategies have a very static character. Research on management processes in MNCs have a questionable empirical base and normative bent. Three key themes for future research on internationalization as a process are suggested. These themes, dealing with major omissions and weaknesses identified in the review, are: the study of acquisition processes and internationalization, the study of dynamic processes in MNCs, and the study of internationalization processes in their outer contexts.

INTRODUCTION

The corpus of international business research produced over the last three decades reveals a field characterized by considerable intellectual diversity drawing on a wide span of disciplines. The purpose of the paper is to review that corpus and explore the meaning of internationalization as a process. Key themes for future research on internationalization as a strategy process are suggested. Our review is based on an extensive reading of works categorized as international business research. The review task includes an ambition to discover and analyze certain underlying assumptions concerning theoretical and methodological issues.

A brief characterization of the broad field of international business will help to clarify the choice of subfields and themes in this review. As Toyne (1989) stated, there seems to be a lack of consensus about the conceptual domain of international business. Theoretical focus is blurred by the multidisciplinary nature of the field. Compare, for instance the content of articles published in a single volume of the *Journal of International Business Studies* (JIBS, 1991):

analysis of information content in multinational advertisements; theories underlying Japanese lifetime employment; measurement of performance in international joint ventures; nontariff barriers for foreign investments; and factors related to expatriate and spouse repatriation adjustment. This not only demonstrates diversity but indicates a natural lack of a common theoretical base. To more systematically illustrate the broad scope of research on international business, we have categorized all articles published in the last three full volumes of JIBS (1989–91). Here are the seven *most frequent* areas of international business published in the three volumes of JIBS (with a total of 76 articles):

—Finance and banking (9 articles)

—Cross-cultural aspects (8 articles)

—International joint ventures (7 articles)

—Human resources (including expatriates) (6 articles)

—Foreign direct investments (5 articles)

—Coordination and control in MNCs (5 articles)

—Host government relationships (3 articles)

These seven areas represent alternative theoretical frameworks of international business research, each with fundamental differences. In addition, few empirical studies reported in these volumes were founded on longitudinal studies and/or dynamic theory, i.e., the process dimension of internationalization was weakly represented. Most articles were based on cross-sectional methods and static models. International business research as a whole does not

Thanks are due to Andrew Pettigrew for numerous suggestions and to my colleagues in the Strategic Change Research Group at Linköping University for all their support. In addition I would like to thank the Axel and Margaret Ax:son Johnson Foundation for funding the research on which this article is based.
Key words: Internationalization, strategy process, multinational corporation, stage models, global integration, local responsiveness, acquisition, differentiation, longitudinal approach.

Activities \ Organizational Boundaries	Within organizations —across borders	Between organizations —across borders
Entry modes	A • Internationalization stage models	B
Transactions	C • Internalization; transaction costs • Intraorganizational trade; transfer prices .	D • International trade • International marketing • Foreign direct investments • International business networks • Transfer of technology
Coordination mechanisms	E • Global strategies • Structural forms • Formal control systems • Informal/social integration and coordination	F • Alliances and joint ventures • Host government relationship

Figure 1. The field of international business—activities across borders.

have the preponderance of U.S. researchers found in many other subfields of management research. This may help to explain the greater methodological diversity to be found in the field of international business.

The field of international business has its roots in international economics, including a number of theories on international trade, such as the comparative advantage of nations. However, from the 1960s onward we find other research themes. In Figure 1, most major key themes in international business research are cataloged (exceptions include the international finance and banking theme). These key themes are structured along two lines: the type of activity in focus and whether the activities are intraorganizational or interorganizational. Figure 1 illustrates that the research on international business deals with organizational activities across borders. A large proportion of the work focuses on the intraorganizational activities of large firms, with the obvious intent to explain and characterize the structural form of the typical multinational corporation (MNC). In fact, research on strategy, structure and administrative processes in MNCs forms the basis for a named subfield, international management (IM).

Since a brief paper cannot fairly review the whole

field of international business and management, we will limit our discussion to three themes (boxes A, B and E in Figure 1) that help shed light on internationalization as a strategy process:

—stage models of internationalization

—studies of the link between strategy and structure in MNCs

—studies of administrative processes in MNCs and recent organizational models for MNCs.

We restrict ourselves to research themes that either address the process dimension of the international enterprise's formation and continuance (Toyne, 1989) or are kindred to this dimension. Consequently, themes rooted in economics (such as the eclectic theory with the internalization theory, Dunning, 1981; Buckley, 1988) are excluded because of their static view of the multinational enterprise. Content-oriented research on international strategy is ruled out for the same reason. Our focus on the firm level automatically excludes such themes as the competitiveness of nations (Porter, 1990).

The paper has five sections. In the first section the significance and certain methodological consequences of internationalization as a strategy process is discussed. The three following sections contain a review of major contributions and the underlying assumptions and weaknesses of the three selected themes of internationalization: stage models, strategy-structure relationships, and management processes in MNCs. The concluding section suggests three key themes and questions for future research.

INTERNATIONALIZATION AS A STRATEGY PROCESS

Strategy making is about changing perspectives and/ or positions (Mintzberg, 1987). Internationalization—the process of increasing involvement in international operations across borders (Welch and Luostarinen, 1988)—comprise both changed perspectives and changed positions. Thus internationalization is a major dimension of the ongoing strategy process of most business firms. The strategy process determines the ongoing development and change in the international firm in terms of scope, business idea, action orientation, organizing principles, nature of managerial work, dominating values and converging norms. The internationalization dimension is related to all these aspects of the strategy process. As is shown in this paper, structural theory on MNCs has advanced much further than dynamic theory on internationalization as a strategy process. In a survey of academic researchers in strategic management, Lyles (1990) argued that the internationalization theme regarding global competition was viewed as the coming decade's most important area of strategic management research (see also Bettis, 1991). This notwithstanding, the research in strategic management currently pays little attention, says Lyles, to internationalization. Furthermore, the strategic management field is still dominated by cross-sectional research that 'proceeds from a distance, with a remote researcher gathering data from organizations he knows almost nothing about' (Miller and Friesen, 1982: 1014). At the same time, there seems to be increasing consensus among researchers that longi-

tudinal research would enable a better understanding of organizations. According to Huff and Reger (1987: 227) . . . there is danger in believing that statistically rigorous, narrowly focused studies are superior to the rich, complicated understanding that results from careful understanding of a few organizations.

In sum, there remains a considerable need for research that is responsive to the longitudinal character of internationalization as a development process through time (Welch and Luostarinen, 1988). However, different meanings of development processes can be identified, depending on the methodological approach used to reveal the process. In fact, the longitudinal approach incorporates at least four different approaches (graphically illustrated in Figure 2):

—In type A, process is a time-series of detached critical *events,* or *states,* e.g., structural or economic. Most management studies that include the time dimension in their explanatory models seem to use this approach, analyzing situations disjoint in time. Typical are the large number of studies of the correspondence between strategy, structure, and performance. Recent illustrations include a study by Gomez-Mejia (1992) who related corporate performance during a 5-year period to changed strategies, and a study by Habib and Victor (1991) where the fit between strategy and structure in MNCs was related to performance of the two following years. We see that the process dimension is weakly developed in this type of longitudinal approach.

—In type B, process is relatively short *episodes.* The approach here may be to study a single episode such as an acquisition from the preacquisition phase to the postacquisition phase (Haspeslagh and Jemison, 1991), or to study several episodes in sequence or in parallel. The time period for an episode may vary from a few weeks to a few years.

—In type C, process is lengthy *epochs.* An epoch may be the strategic development of a company under an influential CEO. A series of epochs may be long periods of evolutionary change disrupted by shorter episodes of revolutionary change. An epoch may be from 2 to 20 years. Illustrative examples of epoch-oriented studies are found in Pettigrew (1985a) and Pettigrew and Whipp (1991).

—In type D, process is seen as *biographic history.* Here the biography of a firm captures the whole development

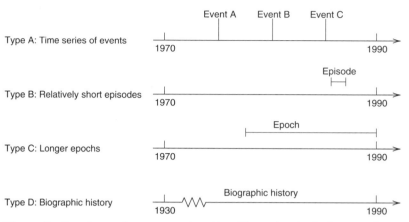

Figure 2. Four types of process captured by different longitudinal approaches.

from the time of its founding to the present time, (see for example the classic case studies of Chandler, 1962). The time period may vary considerably but for large MNCs it will extend over several decades.

We use this process typology to characterize the process studies covered by our review and to determine the types of process studies that might be desirable in future research on internationalization. A broad reading of empirical studies in the field indicates that longitudinal studies of internationalization processes representing types C and D are very infrequent. Models and methods in the IM field are overly static. This is a weakness since the IM field, like the (overlapping) field of strategic-management focuses 'on managerial problems, for which timing, sequence and change are key elements' (Hambrick, 1990: 244).

Descriptions of internationalization processes, as of other strategy processes, include information about change. The degree of change may differ from a state of more or less *status quo* to radical transformation. Between these extremes, we find three kinds of change: expanded reproduction, incremental change and evolutionary transition (Wilson, 1992). Change must always be understood within a process context. Change concerns the dynamics in development over time (Pettigrew, 1985b). Change is implicitly related to content, in other words, some particular thing becomes different. When we study

longitudinal processes such as the internationalization process of a firm, we must also focus on content. The dichotomy of process vs. content in strategy research has been misleading and should be avoided in international management research.

INTERNATIONALIZATION AS A SEQUENCE OF STAGES

Significant models in the field of international business describe the internationalization process as a gradual development taking place in distinct stages and over a relatively long period of time. Two often cited models will be discussed here, the *product (life) cycle model* (Vernon 1966) and the (Uppsala) *internationalization process model* (Johanson and Vahlne, 1977). Both models still exert considerable influence on the field and the internationalization process model in particular attracts many followers. Their longitudinal character satisfies one criterion of internationalization as a process. Their shortcomings include certain problems inherent to stage models labelled by Stubbart (1992) as the 'deceptive allure of developmental models'.

The *product cycle model* developed by Vernon (1966) is an attempt to bridge a country-based perspective of international trade theory with an individual firm's perspective of international investment theory. Vernon wished to remedy a lack of realism found in the dominating comparative-costs-advantage theory by emphasizing the role of product innovation, the effects of scale economies and the role of uncertainty in influencing trade patterns across national borders (Vernon 1966: 190). He identified several stages in the life cycle of a product, each of which has different implications for the internationalization of the innovative company and the product itself. The introduction stage is domestic, having its orientation in the country where the product was developed. Export to other industrial countries may support the emerging goal of achieving economies of scale in production. In the growth stage, export activities increase and foreign direct investments in manufacturing plants are made in countries with an expanding demand for the product. In the maturity stage, when major markets are saturated and the product standardized, the manufacture is relocated to countries with low labor costs. Finally, in the stage of decline, manufacture, and in some cases also the demand, definitely leaves the industrial country which was home to the original innovation (Vernon, 1966; McKiernan, 1992).

Although the product cycle model takes the company level into account, it has its main focus on the country level. Its main contribution is the developmental view on relocalization of production activities; such change is related to various national characteristics such as technological know-how, demand and labor costs. A general conclusion is that increasing product maturity makes it less critical to have a short distance between the production facilities and the corporate centers for decision-making and product development. However, the descriptive value of this stage model is weak for products with short life cycles, a circumstance which applies to more and more products (McKiernan, 1992). The applicability of this model is also limited if new products are developed in companies that already have considerable operations in foreign countries (see Vernon, 1979). Furthermore, as we will see below, new localization patterns emerge in MNCs as new organizational forms are introduced, implying a new way of thinking about where to establish product development centers and manufacturing units.

The second stage model of importance is the *internationalization process model* (Johanson and Vahlne, 1977). This process, whereby a firm gradually increases its international involvement, is described as being sequential from the initial export activities to the setting up of foreign production units (Johanson and Wiedersheim-Paul, 1975). Each firm goes through a number of logical steps of international behavior, based on 'its gradual acquisition, integration and use of knowledge about foreign markets and operations, and on its successively increasing commitment to foreign markets' (Johanson and Vahlne, 1977). The focus is on market knowledge and market commitment (through engaged resources). The learning through development of experiential knowledge about foreign markets is necessary in order to overcome the 'psychic distance' to these markets, i.e., differences between any two countries in terms of language, culture, education level, business practice and legislation. According to Johanson and Vahlne (1990), the firm enters new markets with successively greater psychic distance. This perceived distance is expected to disturb the flow of information between the firm and the foreign market. Therefore firms start their internationalization on markets with the lowest perceived market uncertainty, in other words, markets that they can rather easily understand, often in neighboring countries.

Similar models which build on the behavioral theory of the firm (Cyert and March, 1963, later applied to international investments by Aharoni, 1966) have been introduced by Bilkey (1978) and Cavusgil (1980). The internationalization process model contributes an alternative and significant view on internationalization as compared to the dominating theory on foreign investments, the 'eclectic paradigm' (Dunning, 1980, 1988). The eclectic paradigm argues that three distinct sets of advantages explain the involvement of firms in foreign production; these are ownership-specific advantages, internalization advantages (further emphasized by Buckley, 1988 and Rugman, 1980), and localization advantages. The eclectic paradigm is based on economic theory and has transaction costs and factor costs as its main explanatory variables together with the assumption of rational decision-making in international firms which make foreign direct investments. However it explains the existence of the multinational enterprise rather than the process of internationalization even if the ambition is to make the internalization theory more dynamic and more behavioral in its orientation (Buckley, 1990; 1991). The internationalization process model on the other hand explains internationalization as one distinct pattern of growth. It is based on behavioral theories, with assumptions about lack of information and the importance of perceived risk and uncertainty (Cavusgil, 1980). Within this view, the internationalization process is not seen as a sequence of deliberately planned steps founded on rational analysis. Instead the incremental nature of successive learning through stages of increasing commitment to foreign markets is the main characteristic of the internationalization process, which according to Johanson and Vahlne (1990) will proceed along the presented stages regardless of whether strategic decisions in this direction are made or not. This process model matches two of the four types of processes in Figure 2, the episodical and the epochal, since the internationalization stage can be seen as a sequential chain of episodes or epochs.

The internationalization process model has a number of shortcomings which have been accepted by Johanson and Vahlne (1990). It is too deterministic; its significance is limited to the early stages of internationalization; and as the world becomes more homogeneous, the explanatory value of psychic distance tends to decrease. The deterministic, sequential nature of this process model excludes other options of strategic choices, e.g., to initiate local production in a foreign country without having gone through the steps of exporting or having local sales subsidiaries. Leapfrogging of intermediate stages is in fact quite common (Hedlund and Kverneland, 1984; Björkman, 1989; McKiernan, 1992). The internationalization model is based on empirical research about Swedish firms, but has gained strong support in several other studies (Bilkey, 1978; Cavusgil, 1980; Denis and Depelteau, 1985; Johanson and Nonaka, 1983), showing that this model's validity is not limited to small countries which are highly dependent on export. However, most empirical support comes

from studies on the early stages of internationalization represented by the model. The model tells us little about the internationalization process taking place in experienced companies which have learned through decades of international activities. Furthermore the internationalization process model does not pay enough attention to the acquisition choice as a route to internationalization, a shortcoming shared with the mainstream of foreign direct investment theory (Forsgren, 1990).

In more general terms, both stage models discussed in this section suffer from distinct limitations. The focus of stage models is on the nature, sequence and order of activities (Van de Ven, 1992). According to Van de Ven (p. 172) these stage models represent a unitary progression, which means a sequence of the form $U \rightarrow V \rightarrow W$ where U, V and W represent qualitatively different stages that must occur in an ordered progression. Each stage of development is seen as 'a necessary precursor of succeeding stages' (Van de Ven, 1992; 177). The implication is that stage models describe developmental history as the result of predetermined factors and preprogrammed forces. But the consequences of unforeseen environmental interactions are hardly predetermined (Stubbart, 1992). Furthermore, stage models downplay the possibility for managers to make voluntary strategic choices. According to Stubbart (1992), another problem related to stage models is their disregard of individual differences. Variations and differences are not made a part of the pattern of sequential stages.

STRATEGY, STRUCTURE AND CONTROL IN THE MULTINATIONAL CORPORATION

During the last two decades a large share of the research in the field of international management has been devoted to structural aspects of MNCs. During the 1970s, interest mainly focused on structural forms and formal control mechanisms, but during the 1980s emphasis shifted toward less formal ways of coordinating the MNCs. In an exhaustive literature survey, Martinez and Jarillo (1989) identify 82 empirical studies published between 1964 and 1988 on coordination mechanisms in MNCs. A notable share of these—about 25 percent—have their roots in two business schools, the Harvard Business School and the Stockholm School of Economics. Earlier contributions from two distinguished Harvard scholars, Alfred Chandler and Joe Bower, have been especially influential in this part of the IM field. In fact, the influence of these two scholars has generated two rather distinct schools of thought. The text below is organized in line with this evolution. The first part deals with studies following Chandler's (1962) work on strategy and structure, and the second part reviews the so-called process school of international management, based on Bower's (1970) work on strategy process.

THE STRUCTURE OF MNCs FOLLOWS STRATEGY (RESEARCH FOLLOWING CHANDLER)

The origin of this stream of research is made clear in the first paragraph of an *Administrative Science Quarterly* article by Fouraker and Stopford:

One of the landmark studies in the field of business administration is Strategy and Structure *by A.D. Chandler, Jr. A central proposition in Chandler's book is that the strategy of diversification led to organizational problems and eventually to the emergence of a new corporate structure . . . International business activity is a form of diversification. . . . In some sense, this development may be considered a replication against which Chandler's thesis may be tested. . . . the new diversification should lead to new problems of organization and, finally, to different structural accommodations (1968: 47–48).*

The early research on internationalization strategy and organizational structure starts with the assumption that structure follows strategy. Not surprisingly, this assumption is given strong support in the first major study, where Stopford and Wells found that managers in multinational enterprises 'following similar strategies in quite different industries have developed similar organizational structures (1972:

5). Stopford and Wells studied epochs of internationalization (i.e., process type B in Figure 2) in order to identify the structural state of 187 large U.S. manufacturing firms, all internationally dispersed and each having manufacturing facilities in at least six foreign countries. An initial phase of international structure with relatively autonomous subsidiaries was followed by a second phase in which the MNCs organized an international business division intended to increase control and coordination of the expanding international activities. This division covered all foreign activities of the firm and became its locus of international expertise (Stopford and Wells, 1972: 21 and Åman, forthcoming). The international division grew and as the ratio of foreign sales to total sales continued to increase, top managers recognized that the enterprise needed a global perspective. The presence of an autonomous international division actually served to constrain the integration process since only the general manager of the international division had responsibility that transcended national boundaries. The predominant international division was superseded by two new types of global structures: worldwide product division and geographic area division for all products. Worldwide product division was the choice of firms with high product diversity, in which each domestic product division was assigned responsibility for the worldwide activities of its particular line of products. Area divisions emerged in firms with greater geographic diversity. Each such area division was made responsible for one geographic region of the world market. In some cases a combination of these two types of global structures was found, where some product lines were managed on a worldwide basis and others through area divisions (Stopford and Wells, 1972: 26–53). However, in the beginning of the 1980s, the international division structure still seemed to be the most frequent in MNCs based in the United States (Daniels, Pitts and Tretter, 1985).

In a parallel study, Franko (1976) compared the 85 largest industrial firms of the western part of continental Europe, focusing on (in his terminology) their international networks. The organizational structure of 70 of these firms was analyzed in greater detail. A biographic approach was used to identify epochs of dominating structural forms (see Figure 2). In contrast to multinational enterprises based in the United States, 26 of the European MNCs retained the parent-subsidiary form, with direct ties between the corporate head office and each autonomous subsidiary. The route to global structure differed from that found in the U.S. firms studied by Stopford and Wells. Most European multinationals did not choose the international division as an intermediate form, but went directly from the parent-subsidiary structure to a worldwide product structure (24 enterprises did so). As 84 percent of the European enterprises in Franko's study were diversified outside the home country, one would expect that an even greater number of product division structures would have been introduced. Franko's conclusion is that 'in continental Europe, structure did not follow strategy until there was a (new) change in the competitive environment' (Franko, 1976: 204). Scandinavian MNCs show a similar pattern to the European firms studied by Franco. The Scandinavian firms retained the parent-subsidiary structure until the 1970s at which time most big firms went directly to the global product division structure without ever having introduced the international division (Hedlund, 1984; Hedlund and Åman, 1984; Åman, forthcoming).

Also Stopford and Wells (1972) softened their conclusion on the strategy-structure fit despite their empirical evidence. They emphasized that the relationship between strategy and organization 'is clearly not the simple one in which strategy is determined first and then a structure established to implement it' (p. 6). However, for Stopford and Wells, strategy → structure was still the natural sequence, a statement later questioned by several authors (e.g., Hall and Saias, 1980; Peters, 1984; and Melin, 1989).

The studies of Stopford and Wells (1972) and Franko (1976) represent a landmark in international management research. These studies give a valuable understanding of the historic development of international strategies and structures for multinational enterprises. However, their major findings have to do with *which* strategies and structures actually emerged. Their contribution is far more modest

when they attempt to deal with *why* strategies and structures are changed. The process dimension of *how* they changed is almost completely absent. Although these studies take a longitudinal approach, they can hardly claim to capture the essence of internationalization as a process. Rather they present steady states of structural forms and fail to describe the processes of formation and implementation related to these structures. In addition, they emphasize mainly formal aspects of structure.

Notably, both studies contain early observations about a new structural form for the MNC, the global matrix. Stopford and Wells (1972) called this the 'grid structure' which apparently opened their eyes for a necessary shift from the formal view on structure to a stronger emphasis on informal and fluid aspects of structure. They made several significant observations about the grid structure: *Boundaries* between divisions and departments become increasingly *blurred* in a global grid structure. Emphasis shifts from hierarchical to *contractual* management. Grid structures can function as systems of *creative conflicts*. In a grid structure, 'the creation among the managers of a sense of cooperation and shared values is one way of combating the control problem' (op. cit., p. 173). Unfortunately, these significant and quite novel observations did not stake a direction to subsequent research in international management during the 1970s. Another important discussion often ignored by (U.S.) researchers in both strategic management and international management is the skepticism expressed by Stopford and Wells about the possibility of drawing linear conclusions on the relationship between strategy–structure and performance. These authors conclude that it is very difficult to make any satisfactory analysis that relates structure to performance. The reason given is that 'performance is an amalgam of many factors . . . , even if one could decide how best to measure performance, one could never be sure that the results were influenced by the choice of structure' (Stopford and Wells, 1972: 79). From their noteworthy findings that some multinational enterprises with mismatched strategies and structures grew faster and showed a greater foreign profit than others with matched strategies and structures, Stopford and Wells allege that the success of an enterprise relies more on managerial skills and abilities than on the structural form within which these managers work.

Several IM researchers later studied the strategy and structure relationship in MNCs, among others Davidson and Haspeslagh (1982) and Egelhoff (1988). Furthermore, Björkman (1990) put forth an alternative explanation for changed structures in MNCs. He regards the changed structure as being the result of mimetic behavior rather than of the influence exerted by a company's individual strategy. A new structural form becomes the fashion, or norm, and is imitated by several followers (DiMaggio and Powell, 1983).

RESEARCH ON INFORMAL COORDINATION MECHANISMS IN MNCs

In addition to the focus on structure of the MNC, there are two other coordination dimensions which received attention from several IM researchers (Martinez and Jarillo, 1989). One dimension concerns the degree of centralization of decision-making and bureaucratic control mechanisms (e.g., Brooke and Remmers, 1970; and Schollhammer, 1971). The other dimension is the less formal and more elusive mechanisms of control and coordination. Wiechmann (1974) found, that formal and informal integrative devices were closely interrelated in multinational enterprises. Notably, one of the devices was corporate acculturation. This relates to findings regarding the Japanese type of MNC ('type Z') that maintained control through a process of acculturation and socialization of employees (Ouchi and Johnson, 1978). In subsequent studies, the cultural control mechanisms were given extended meaning by Jaeger and Baliga (1985). In the same vein, Edström and Galbraith (1977) presented arguments for transfer of managers in multinational organizations as a deliberate means to develop control through a socializing process and the creation of a verbal information network. The objective seemed to be to create a somewhat uniform corporate culture that transcended national boundaries (see also Jaeger, 1983), today a questionable proposition. That notwithstanding, Edström and Galbraith (1977: 248) wanted their

article to be understood as a call for further research. However, the internationalization theme on which they focused (as did Ouchi and others) has not yet become a major stream in international management research, even if the 'process school' (see below) shows interest in informal management systems. Martinez and Jarillo (1989) suggest that the informal and social mode of control has emerged in MNCs as a necessary result of the increased integration and dispersion of these firms' operations to several units in many countries. However, a recent study of Swedish MNCs (Rolander, Zander, and Hedlund, 1989) draws a different picture. This study claims that these firms instead introduce more formal mechanisms of control. One explanation of this divergency may be that Swedish MNCs made early use of social control mechanisms and only recently have adjusted to the combined mode of formal and informal control. If so, these different pictures instead illustrate a converging movement regarding control mechanisms throughout the entire MNC population.

THE 'PROCESS SCHOOL' OF MNCs

The emergence of a process perspective in policy research (Bower, 1970) has resulted in a large body of empirical research dealing with managerial issues of MNCs. The doctoral dissertations of Prahalad, Doz and Bartlett (all at Harvard Business School between 1975 and 1979) seem to have laid the foundation for a visible stream of research in international management. Researchers in this stream are referred to as 'belonging to the process school' of the diversified multinational corporation (DMNC) (Bartlett and Ghoshal, 1991; Doz and Prahalad, 1991). Today this school holds paradigmatic qualities, according to Doz and Prahalad (1991: 145): 'The development of a ''process school'' of research on the DMNC over the past 15 years has led to the emergence of a new paradigm.'

This new so-called paradigm represents knowledge on DMNC management, which emphasizes the global integration/local responsiveness framework. The basic unit of analysis is considered to be the individual manager. Most scholars within this paradigm, it is claimed, have 'put managerial relevance before theoretical elegance,' 'have underexploited the theories available to them' and 'often been engrossed in the complexity of what they studied, and failed to develop, or borrow, a sufficiently powerful conceptual framework' (op. cit., p. 161). According to Doz and Prahalad, the result has been a missing link between the DMNC phenomenon and available organization theory. However, this is not regarded as being a problem since the emerging paradigm constitutes a theory on its own:

Taken together the work of Prahalad, Doz, Bartlett, Ghoshal, Hedlund, Hamel, and others following the same research approach provides us with a rich organization theory of the DMNC and with detailed understanding of managerial tasks of DMNCs (Doz and Prahalad, 1991: 158).

According to Doz and Prahalad, this organization theory contains mid-range constructs and provides a set of such integrative constructs for observation, analysis and understanding, as well as for normative assessment of DMNC managers. The main conceptual contributions from this new paradigm, are briefly presented below, but it must first be emphasized that it is quite unusual for a rather small group of researchers to appoint themselves as constituting a new paradigm. Does not a new paradigm emerge in a rather less deliberate way, as a result of an institutionalization process drawing on ideas and debates from several related fields?

Doz and Prahalad (1984) want to supplement the multinational management literature, which in their opinion is too 'architectural' in its search for the right structure. Their own contribution builds on the identification of the constant balancing of MNC managers between (a) the economic imperative, i.e., the impact of global competition that pressures the MNC to transcend the boundaries of national markets, develop a global strategy and rationalize global operations through central control and coordination and (b) the political imperative, i.e., the adjustments made necessary by host government demands, which work to give greater autonomy to the local subsidiary, and through diversity among na-

tional markets, regarding customer needs, distribution channels etc., that call for increased local responsiveness (Doz, 1980; Doz, Bartlett, and Prahalad, 1981; Prahalad and Doz, 1981a; Doz and Prahalad, 1984). No specific structure provides the solution to this dilemma. Direct substantive control is not possible. The alternative for top management is to create an *organizational* context as a more subtle strategic control mechanism. The design of this organizational context has been in focus in most of the work presented jointly by Doz and Prahalad (1981, 1984, 1987; and Prahalad and Doz 1981a, 1981b and 1987). Their framework for strategic control in multinational companies can be depicted as a matrix of (a) subprocesses of change and (b) a collection of management tools. To be more precise, the subprocesses of change have three dimensions: cognitive perspective, strategic priorities and power allocation. The management tools are of three kinds. Data management tools provide data for critical decisions. Managers' management tools express the rules of the game that shape executive perception and expectations. Conflict resolution tools are used to create decision structures for careful trade-off between priorities of global integration and national responsiveness.

Alongside this framework, Doz argues that the diversified multinational company should strive for *multifocal strategies*. This means that 'responsiveness and integration needs are weighted one against the other separately for each decision, with no *a priori* assumption of dominance of one over the other' (1986: 214). The multifocal MNC will trade-off the costs and benefits regarding national responsiveness and multinational integration in a flexible manner. The key organizational capability of the multifocal strategy firm is the capability to 'shift the locus and logic of decision from a national concern to a global view, and vice versa, from decision to decision' (1986: 214). Doz believes that a matrix structure that assigns equal power to executives with differing responsibilities would lead to corporate paralysis. Instead, conflicting views should be confronted, which leaves the relative power of various executives unspecified. The ideal situation for Doz is constant tension between defenders of national responsiveness and managers supporting multinational integration, and this is something quite apart from balance and power symmetry.

Bartlett and Ghoshal (1987, 1989) focus their interest on how large crossborder enterprises organize their activities. The studies of these authors emphasize the functioning and capabilities of the MNC, not its structural form. Important elements are informal mechanisms of coordination, including normative values, and modes and patterns of internal communication. Bartlett and Ghoshal's work represents a surprisingly strong belief in the environment-strategy-structure paradigm which they claim 'provides a powerful way to understand differences in corporate performance' (1987: 53). They mean, however, that as the global industrial world becomes more complex, the unidimensional concepts of strategic fit should be replaced by a more dynamic view. The main driving forces for changes in MNCs, according to Bartlett and Ghoshal, are environmental. But Bartlett (1986) also calls attention to the administrative heritage, i.e., the history and background of the firm. The basic assumption in the research of Bartlett and Ghoshal concerning large MNCs is that environmental forces shape the strategic profile of a business, while a company's administrative heritage molds its organizational form and capabilities.

In an empirical project, Bartlett and Ghoshal found three clearly distinguishable organizational models among nine multinational companies (three each from Japan, Europe and the U.S.). Each model is 'characterized by distinct structural configurations, administrative processes and management mentalities' (1989: 49). The importance of a company's administrative history is evident in these organization models, as each of them is related to specific dependence on their respective European, Japanese or U.S. cultural background. The *multinational organization model* fits the management norms of many European companies that grew internationally during the prewar period. Bartlett and Ghoshal label this model 'a *decentralized federation* of assets and responsibilities' (1989: 49) which allow foreign units to respond to local differences. The *international organization model*— which suited the management norms of many U.S.

firms, especially during the 1950s and 1960s—is a *coordinated federation,* where the parent company transfers knowledge and expertise to foreign markets which lay open to exploitation. The subsidiaries are more dependent on the parent company, compared with the multinational model, while the international model requires more formal systems for control of subsidiaries. The *global organization model* fits the managerial norms of many Japanese firms, which reached global competitive positions during the 1970s and early 1980s. It is characterized as a *centralized hub,* where most assets and decisions are centralized. Foreign operations are used as delivery pipelines to what is regarded as a unified global market. The subsidiaries are highly dependent on the parent company and are tightly controlled. This empirically founded typology gives an important understanding of three distinct forms of MNCs and supplements the old, but still valid, conceptions of the global enterprise presented by Perlmutter (1969); the ethnocentric, the polycentric, and the geocentric types. However, the framework by Bartlett and Ghoshal lacks process dimensions, such as the dynamic transition from one form to another, and characteristics of the strategy process within each model.

According to Bartlett and Ghoshal all three MNC models have problems in today's complex global environments, because they cannot meet the demand to simultaneously achieve national responsiveness, global efficient integration, and an ability to develop and transfer knowledge worldwide. Bartlett and Ghoshal have constructed a solution to this demand, the *transnational organization model,* which is not derived from empirical evidence as are the other three models. Instead the transnational solution—the configuration of tomorrow's competitive MNC—is a more speculative suggestion impelled by the studies of these two scholars. They found that several of the nine MNCs in their study increasingly converged to the structural form of a differentiated network (Ghoshal and Bartlett, 1990). In the transnational company, efficiency is a means to achieve global competitiveness, while local responsiveness is a means to achieve increased flexibility, and company-wide organizational learning is a means to develop innovations vital to corporate survival. The transnational firm should function as an *integrated network*. The subsidiaries should have differentiated and specialized roles and they should participate in a worldwide sharing and development of knowledge. This type of organization is not easy to manage. The threat of internal fragmentation and dissipation is obvious, because of the strong degree of dispersion. Furthermore, the interdependence may counteract the need for flexibility, since the complexity can obstruct the necessary learning capability. However, according to Bartlett and Ghoshal, these problems can be resolved by top management if they succeed in legitimizing diverse perspectives, developing multiple coordination and innovation processes, and building shared vision and individual commitment.

Hedlund (1986) has developed a similar, speculative model for the modern multinational company, the *heterarchy*. He sees the unidimensionality within the traditional structure-follows-strategy view as being too narrow and believes that multinationals must transform their hierarchical form to something more flexible if they are to survive (Hedlund and Rolander, 1990). Some of the main characteristics of the heterarchial MNC are: many centers, in which traditional headquarter functions are dispersed; strategic roles for foreign subsidiaries; flexibility in governance modes; global integration by normative mechanisms, such as shared culture and ethics; a holographic organization, where each part of the company shares information about the whole and has access to detailed information; strategic action, based on heuristic search orientation and exploitation of current potential (Hedlund and Rolander, 1990: 25–27).

To complete the picture of the 'process school' in international management, the new concepts for understanding strategic capabilities of MNCs (introduced by Hamel and Prahalad) should also be presented. These concepts emphasize the role of *strategic intent* in strategic development processes (Hamel and Prahalad, 1989); the importance of developing *core competencies* in diversified MNCs in order to reach global competitiveness (Prahalad and Hamel, 1990); and the role of *resource leverage* and the importance of *aspirations* outstripping resources for proactive strategy making (Hamel and Prahalad, 1992). The concepts introduced by Hamel and Prahalad are intuitively quite reasonable, but when considered more carefully, they are vague and lack descriptive precision.

The configurations suggested by the 'process school' are complex and require an extremely skillful and powerful top management team that can orchestrate all internal forces in a large worldwide corporation. The attitudes of the members of the 'process school' range from critique of the possibility to find the *right* structural form, to the suggesting of ways to find the *right* balance and compromises between all interests and units and thus simultaneously achieve global efficiency, local responsiveness, flexibility and learning. The ambition to capture the complexity in large, global business firms is desirable (see Melin, 1987 and 1989). However, the strong belief—expressed by Bartlett and Ghoshal, 1989, and by Doz and Prahalad, 1984—in a new type of fit, much more dynamic than the old structure-follows-strategy-follows-environment is based on an extended use of cultural control. A rather monolithic culture seems to be necessary to unite the dispersed MNCs. This implies a view on culture as a variable that can be controlled from the top of the organization and based on an underlying assumption that manipulation of cultural dimensions will lead to intended changes in the mind sets of organization members. These assumptions are questioned by many students of organizational culture (e.g., Smircich, 1983; Alvesson and Berg, 1992).

In a critical review of 'Managing the Global Firm' (with Bartlett, Doz and Hedlund, as editors, 1990), Forsgren (1992) identifies two main problems in the models of transnational, heterarchic and multifocal firms:

First, the need and possibilities of integration is strongly overemphasized compared to differentiation. There is a tendency for integration (especially in combination with the word 'global') to be understood as a more progressive device than differentiation. There is an apparent risk that this tendency will lead to a neglect of the limitations and costs of inte-

gration. Second, even though several authors maintain that the global firm is moving away from a hierarchy towards a multi-center structure, there seems to be little doubt about the headquarter's possibility to design the structure and systems in such a way that a beneficial integration is created ... The problem is primarily presented as analytical and a question of design, rather than a political problem (Forsgren, 1992: 479–480).

The power dimension is of utmost importance in theory-building about multinational enterprises, as shown by Larsson (1985) in his political analysis of foreign acquisitions made by several Swedish multinational firms. A valid description concerning the dynamics of MNCs must contain more of the power struggle of individuals and groups on different levels that actually characterizes these large organizations. We need to better understand how and why MNCs are able to perform comparatively well despite the counteractive forces and inertia that are embedded in the culture of these mature organizations.

The 'process school' has further weaknesses. The researchers found within this school have mainly used a clinical (or phenomenological) research method which, however, is seldom explained in detail. The reader does not get much help when the bridge between empirical work and conceptual development is described as 'intensive research suggests' or 'detailed analysis was performed' (Doz and Prahalad, 1984: 59–60). There are exceptions, of course, like the methodology appendix in Bartlett and Ghoshal (1989). The conceptual language emanating from this school is built up from empirical research, and with the expressed ambition of putting managerial relevance before theoretical elegance. Organization and strategic management theory have been avoided (with a few exceptions) in the interpretation and concept generating phases of research. The developed framework on managing MNCs has seldom been related to prevailing concepts describing similar phenomena in other contexts than that of the international firm. The striving for managerial relevance has also led to a normative bias. The normative bent seems to be increasing with an increased degree of speculation in conceptual frameworks

without empirical support. This is the case with the models for the emerging new MNC: the multifocal strategy, the heterarchy, and the transnational solution (Hagström, 1991).

The 'process school' emphasizes the dynamic dimension of strategy and structure. But, apart from the change process study (by Doz and Prahalad, 1987) of the transition in sixteen MNCs from local to cross-national orientation, *the process orientation* is in fact rather *restricted*. Doz and Prahalad developed in their study a four-stage process model of strategic redirection—incubation, variety generation, power shift, and refocusing (Doz and Prahalad, 1987: 67–74). The empirical focus in the 'process school' is on global MNCs, but their conceptual contributions are expressed in rather general terms, and should be seen as belonging to the fields of organization theory and strategic management rather than constituting an isolated IM theory.

This notwithstanding, the research group representing the 'process school' of international management has increased the knowledge in this field in several aspects. The researchers have identified new organizational patterns of MNCs. They have contributed a richer conceptual characterization of the global multinational firm with its coordination mechanisms and strategic logic in use in complex MNCs. They have articulated the strong need for more multidimensional approaches in (international) management research. Furthermore, the empirical research is based on access to several top managers in global MNCs, a fresh contrast to much of the U.S.-based strategy research with its very weak empirical connection to strategists in action.

KEY THEMES FOR FUTURE RESEARCH ON INTERNATIONALIZATION PROCESSES

Three major themes in the field of international management have been reviewed. The first theme, regarding stage models of internationalization, reflects the conventional mode of internationalization that goes from export activities to foreign direct investment. The sequential stage model is too deterministic and stresses only early stages of internationalization. This model should be supplemented with research on new patterns of internationalization of the 1980s and 1990s, covering also the process whereby internationally mature firms further increase their degree of internationalization. The second theme, research on structures following strategies in MNCs, describes the historical development of structural forms of MNCs such as the parent-subsidiary structure, the international division and the worldwide product division. Major weaknesses within this theme are its attachment to the linear thinking evident in strategy–structure-fit arguments, and the static character of their conceptual contributions, in spite of the apparent longitudinal nature of their research approach. The role of learning and political processes in the internationalization of the firm is not accounted for at all. The third theme focuses on the management of DMNCs and constitutes the so-called process school in international management. This school of thought contributes a rich set of new and thought-provoking concepts which both describe and prescribe management processes in MNCs. Major weaknesses of this school are its questionable empirical base, and weak relationship with existing management theory and its overprescriptive nature. Furthermore, despite the label of the school, the process orientation in the theoretical body of the school is undeveloped.

This concluding section suggests three key themes for future research: the study of acquisition processes and internationalization, the study of dynamic processes in MNCs, and the study of internationalization processes in their outer contexts. Each theme will be operationalized through a number of questions pertinent to research. These themes deal with major omissions and weaknesses identified in the review of the field. Research on these themes should produce additive knowledge on internationalization as a strategy process. This knowledge should be of a descriptive nature, based on the belief that the purpose of (international) management research is to develop new models and frameworks that will help us understand how organizations work rather than how organizations should work (see Daft and Buenger, 1990).

THE ACQUISITION THEME: RESEARCH ON THE DOMINANT MODE OF INTERNATIONALIZATION

Acquisitions have been a predominant feature of internationalization during the last decade according to recent empirical evidences (McKiernan, 1992). Between 1983 and 1988, acquisitions worldwide rose by more than 20 percent annually. This implies a far-reaching concentration process with a remarkable increase in foreign ownership on many markets. In this situation, research in international business is really lagging behind. Conventional theories on internationalization, including foreign direct investment theory have paid little attention to acquisition as a major route to internationalization (Forsgren, 1989; 1990). The significant role of acquisitions as a major mode of internationalization demands comprehensive research efforts. In general, process theory on acquisitions is still weakly developed (Trautwein, 1990). We need descriptions and conceptualizations on crossborder acquisitions in order to develop our understanding of the processes and mechanisms of internationalization. Some key research questions on international acquisition processes are suggested below:

What are the typical patterns shown by cross-border acquisition processes, in terms of their different strategic and organizational characteristics? What driving forces impel these acquisition processes? What strategic logic is embraced in cross-border acquisitions? The strategic logic may express not only rational formulas, but even institutionalized myths and subjective rationales. An illustration is the announcement of the late eighties about E.C.-92 which led non-E.C. companies to escalate acquisitions in the Common Market. Research about these acquisition processes might reveal not only cases of purposeful strategic intent to use acquisition as a means of securing a competitive European position, but even cases which were a sudden reaction to the then-prevalent E.C. hysteria and which illuminates mimetic or legitimating strategic behavior (see Hellgren and Melin, 1991). Such reactive ways of acting show that managers may be more concerned with jumping on the acquisition bandwagon than with corporate profit (see Daft and Buenger, 1990).

What characterizes the strategic choices in international acquisition processes? One such strategic choice concerns the selection of a foreign market to be entered by taking over some other firm which may be a rational choice of a specific country or a more inherent consequence of a company being available for acquisition (Lindell and Melin, 1991). Another strategic choice is between foreign acquisitions and organic growth through foreign greenfield investments (Hennart and Park, 1992). An acquisition does not increase the overall manufacturing capacity and is therefore a suitable action in a mature and declining industry. In such industries, crossborder acquisitions as a means of global restructuring will increase the degree of internationalization and at the same time reduce the population of firms.

In which phases of a firm's internationalization are acquisitions to be found? Regarding newcomers on international markets, recent studies show that these home-country-based firms may go international directly through acquisition of a foreign competitor (Sharma, 1991; Luostarinen, 1991), contrary to the prediction of the sequential stage model. Forsgren claims that 'the less internationalized the firm, the higher its acquisition propensity' (1990: 262). These new observations should be followed by more empirical studies in order to develop descriptive models of internationalization phases, where the acquisition mode is included and where the order of phases is not sequentially predetermined.

In conclusion, an empirical focus on acquisition processes creates good opportunities to better understand acculturation processes as one important dimension of internationalization. Acculturation is an ongoing process in all international firms with crossborder operations. But the acculturation process should be more evident and visible when two different cultures meet in the integration process that follows every crossborder acquisition.

THE PROCESS THEME: A PROCESS PERSPECTIVE ON MNCs

The IM field has been dominated by studies on structure, control and coordination of MNCs. The research is characterized by cross-sectional approaches, or at least findings expressed in terms of structural constructs. The process perspective is (with few exceptions) absent in analyses and theory generation. Knowledge about structural forms of international business is unusually well-developed, while the knowledge about the transition of these structures is certainly insufficient. Five clusters of research questions covering different aspects of a process perspective on MNCs are suggested:

A common assumption in the IM field is that structures change as a result of strategic adaptation to a changing environment. As discussed earlier, this linear view should be questioned: What internal forces impel change in MNCs, regarding strategies, organizational forms and coordination mechanisms? How do internal and external forces interplay in the strategic processes of MNCs? How and why do control and coordination mechanisms change over time and how do these changes interplay with strategic actions? These questions imply a need for research on strategic and structural change in MNCs based on a more reciprocal, dynamic and complex view than the model of environment–strategy–structure fit (Pettigrew, 1987; Melin, 1985; 1989; Hedlund and Rolander, 1990).

Several researchers in the IM field, from Stopford and Wells and onward, have identified distinct structural forms of MNCs. In accordance with Child (1972), in his early critique of the contingency school, we argue that research on MNCs should be more concerned with processes over time and should regard structures as rather temporary manifestations of such processes. What characterizes the continuous change of these temporary MNC structures? If more stable structures are to be revealed, what determines the steady state of each form and the transformation from one identified form to the following? According to Åman (forthcoming), who has studied the transition from a traditional parent-subsidiary structure to an across-the-border type of MNC, this transition is a long-term evolutionary process with several 'in between' phases.

The research on coordinating mechanisms in MNCs describes the development in these organizations towards global integration, even if local responsiveness is part of the game (see Ghoshal and

Nohria, 1989). This research describes a rather homogeneous and well-united international organization. However, a dispersed organization such as the MNC is a plurality of systems, where intended actions of powerful members as well as unintended consequences of the social action structure play important roles (Brown, 1992). Besides coordination, another inherent but less controllable mechanism continuously affects the function of the MNC: the differentiation mechanism. How do differentiation processes influence the management of MNCs? Which differentiation mechanisms are found in political and cultural processes in MNCs? Research on differentiation processes should pay attention to political and cultural forces that do not originate from the MNC headquarters. These forces may have their origins not only inside various units of the dispersed MNC but also outside, in the local environments of these units.

The focus on heterogeneity and diversity raises further questions on power processes and fluid boundaries of MNCs: Will MNCs remain hierarchical or will they grow into a multicenter form, in other words, have several power centers (characterized by Forsgren, 1992 as internationalization of the second degree; see also Hedlund, 1986)? This multicenter model is based on the observation that different units of the MNC are integrated in different local business networks (Forsgren, 1990; Forsgren and Johanson, 1992). How does the power distribution in these networks influence the strategic freedom of action for the MNC headquarters? How do units in the internal network of the MNC become integrated in these external business networks (see Ghoshal and Bartlett, 1990; Kogut, 1989)? What characterizes the interplay regarding exchange processes and political processes between these two types of networks?

The need for more research on long-term internationalization processes of MNCs should also be noticed. Prevailing knowledge on internationalization as a process focuses on firms in the early phases of internationalization. But most MNCs are internationally very experienced: What characterizes ongoing globalizing processes of mature MNCs? What new patterns of phases and modes of internationalization can be found in these processes (see Bouchikhi and

Kimberly, 1992)? A research effort taking this perspective is a comparative project of internationalization patterns and organizational capabilities in British and Swedish firms (see Macdonald *et al.,* 1991, and Gustavsson *et al.,* 1992). To allow the illumination of the full internationalization process of a firm and to uncover developmental trajectories of this process, we need comprehensive studies that capture long epochs and even biographic histories (see Figure 2) of the whole development of the firm. Such an approach should increase our understanding of internationalization as a 'fundamental engine of organizational development' (Kimberly and Bouchikhi, 1991: 25).

THE CONTEXT THEME: UNDERSTANDING THE EMBEDDEDNESS OF INTERNATIONALIZATION IN OUTER CONTEXTS

This third theme stresses the importance of relating the internationalization process of the firm to its surrounding context, which the reviewed research fails to do. Two suggested subthemes focus on internationalization embedded in two outer contexts; the institutional and social context and the sectoral context.

The first subtheme concerns the embeddedness of internationalization processes in its social and political outer context. Internationalization inherently means that the international firm acts in a number of different social and cultural contexts, often country-based. Hofstede (1983, 1991) has shown the diversity in cross-cultural patterns. Whitley (1992) has shown the diversity in the institutionalized structure of business systems in different countries. What characterizes the link between the internationalization process of an individual firm and this institutional, social and cultural diversity? How does the MNC that pursues a rather uniform and integrated global strategy maneuver such diverse institutional environments? Mutabazi (1992) argues, for example, that all attempts to reach cultural uniformity in MNCs are doomed to failure. According to Jones (1991: 13), mainstream theories of the MNC are unable to access the institutional and social environment 'due to their undersocialized construction,' which underlines the need for new research efforts on this subtheme.

When studying internationalization within a strategy process framework, it is crucial to focus on 'organizations in their sectors' (Child, 1988). The second subtheme, contrasting the first, emphasizes the embeddedness of internationalization processes in the context of industrial sectors crossing borders. Most industrial sectors of today are international and characterized by global competition where rivals within one sector compete against one another on a worldwide basis (Porter, 1986). Furthermore, most international sectors are interlaced through widespread collaborative arrangements between competitors in different overlapping constellations. The global auto industry is a good illustration. The internationalization process of MNCs, or rather of strategic business units within MNCs must be understood in a dynamic and global sector perspective, where collaborative forces with 'win–win' relationships and competitive forces of zero-sum character act simultaneously across borders (Hellgren and Melin, 1991).

In addition to the three suggested research themes, future research on international management should also take into consideration that all organizational processes are engrained by subjective sensemaking (Gioia and Chittipeddi, 1991). As the MNC acts in the perhaps most complex and turbulent of all environments, the management process through creation and transfer of meaning should here be especially critical (cp Salzer, 1992). In order to capture the essence of symbolic interaction and sensemaking processes we need radically different research methodologies that have been used in the field of internationalization, such as an ethnographic and interpretive field work approach (cp Botti, 1992).

I will end with some final concluding points. The research themes suggested above illustrate the need for a better connection between international management and theoretically more mature subdisciplines of management. This call for a closer theoretical relationship with organization and (strategic) management theory raises a question not only about the boundaries but also about the autonomy of the field of international management. The boundaries

between organization theory, strategic management and international management are fluid and blurred. This review points toward a conclusion that the internationalization dimension should be regarded as an empirical focus and not form the basis for a theoretical field of management on its own. The general issues of business strategy, organizational structures, and coordination mechanisms that have been the core of international management should hardly be divided into one subtheory for international firms and another for noninternational firms. But this is what IM researchers have tended to do, often not relating their results and conceptual models to existing theories. On the other hand, the multinational enterprise represents one category of organizations to which scholars of organization theory should devote more interest and research efforts. Students of organizations are served an important challenge by this type of large and dispersed organization, with an inherent mosaic of cultures, unclear and ambiguous boundaries (within the intraorganizational network and also in relation to its outer context), a complex power structure, and multiple organizational identities.

In conclusion, studies of internationalization as a strategy process must capture the development and dynamics over time, the driving forces of the process, and the content of the process. Internationalization processes are characterized by a high degree of complexity, variability and heterogeneity, which taken together require holistic research and truly longitudinal approaches.

REFERENCES

Aharoni, Y. (1966). *The Foreign Investment Decision Process.* Division of Research, Harvard University, Boston, MA.

Alvesson, M. and P.O. Berg (1992). *Corporate Culture and Organizational Symbolism.* Walter de Gruyter, Berlin.

Åman, P. *The Emergence of a Cross-border Firm. The Transformation of Alfa Laval* AB. IIB, Stockholm School of Economics, forthcoming.

Bartlett, C. (1986). 'Building and managing the transnational: The new organizational challenge'. In M. Porter (ed.), *Competition in Global Industries.* Harvard Business School Press, Boston, MA, pp. 367–401.

Bartlett, C., Y. Doz and G. Hedlund (eds.) (1990). *Managing the Global Firm*. Routledge, London.

Bartlett, C. and S. Ghoshal (Fall 1987). 'Managing across borders: New organizational responses.' *Sloan Management Review*, pp. 43–53.

Bartlett, C. and S. Ghoshal (1987). *Managing Across Borders. The Transnational Solution*. Harvard Business School Press, Boston, MA.

Bartlett, C. and S. Ghoshal (Summer 1991). 'Global strategic management: Impact on the new frontiers of strategy research,' *Strategic Management Journal*, **12**, pp. 5–16.

Bettis, R. (1991). 'Strategic management and the straightjacket: An editorial essay,' *Organization Science*, **2**(3), pp. 315–319.

Bilkey, W.J. (1978). 'An attempted integration of the literature on the export behavior of firms,' *Journal of International Business Studies*, pp. 33–46.

Björkman, I. (1989). 'Foreign direct investments. An empirical analysis of decision making in seven Finnish firms.' Doctoral dissertation, No 42, The Swedish School of Economics and Business Administration, Helsinki.

Björkman, I. (1990). 'Foreign direct investments: An organizational learning perspective.' Working paper, The Swedish School of Economics and Business Administration, Helsinki.

Botti, H. (1992). 'The internationalization paradox in Parodi: A research tale,' *Scandinavian Journal of Management*, **8**(2), pp. 85–112.

Bouchikhi, H. and J. Kimberly (1992). 'Large French firms' FDI in the USA: Radical and incremental processes associated with two management configurations.' In Proceedings from the first International Federation of Scholarly Associations of Management Conference, Tokyo, pp. 448–451.

Bower, J.L. (1970). *Managing the Resource Allocation Process: A Study of Corporate Planning and Investment*. Harvard University Press, Boston, MA.

Brooke, M.S. and H.L. Remmers (1970). *The Strategy of Multinational Enterprise*. American Elsevier, New York.

Brown, R. (1992). *Understanding Industrial Organizations: Theoretical Perspectives in Industrial Sociology*. Routledge, London.

Buckley, P.J. (1988). 'The limits of explanation: Testing the internalization theory of the multinational enterprise,' *Journal of International Business Studies*, **19**(2), pp. 181–184.

Buckley, P.J. (1990). 'Problems and developments in the core theory of international business,' *Journal of International Business*, **21**(4), pp. 657–665.

Buckley, P.J. (1991). 'The analysis of international corporate strategy: An integrated framework and research agenda.' In H. Vestergaard (ed.), *An Enlarged Europe in the Global Economy*, (Proceedings of the 17th annual EIBA conference). The Copenhagen Business School, Vol. 1, pp. 541–575.

Burns, T. and G.M. Stalker (1961). *The Management of Innovation*. Tavistock, London.

Cavusgil, T. (November 1980). 'On the internationalization process of firms,' *European Research*, pp. 273–281.

Chandler, A.D. (1962). *Strategy and Structure*. MIT Press, Cambridge, MA.

Child, J. (1972). 'Organization structure and strategies of control: A replication of the Aston study,' *Administrative Science Quarterly*, **17**, pp. 163–177.

Child, J. (1988). 'On organizations in their sectors,' *Organization Studies*, **9**, pp. 13–19.

Cyert, R. and J. March (1963). *A Behavioral Theory of the Firm*. Prentice Hall, Englewood Cliffs, NJ.

Daft, R. and V. Buenger (1990). 'Hitching a ride on a fast train to nowhere: The past and future of strategic management research.' In J. Fredrickson (ed.). *Perspectives on Strategic Management*, Harper Business, New York, pp. 81–103.

Daniels, J.D., R.A. Pitts and M.J. Tretter (1985). 'Organizing for dual strategies of product diversity and international expansion.' *Strategic Management Journal*, **6**, pp. 223–237.

Davidson, W.H. and P. Haspeslagh (1982). 'Shaping a global product organization,' *Harvard Business Review*, **60**(4), pp. 125–132.

Denis, J.E. and D. Depelteau (1985). 'Market knowledge, diversification and export expansion.' *Journal of International Business Studies*, **16**, pp. 77–89.

DiMaggio, P. and W. Powell (1983). 'The iron cage revisited: Institutional isomorphism and collective rationality in organizational fields,' *American Sociological Review*, **48**, pp. 147–160.

Doz, Y. (Winter 1980). 'Strategic management in multinational companies.' *Sloan Management Review*, **21**, pp. 27–46.

Doz, Y. (1986). *Strategic Management in Multinational Companies*. Pergamon Press, Oxford.

Doz, Y., C. Bartlett and C.K. Prahalad (Spring 1981). 'Global competitive pressures vs. host country demands: Managing tensions in multinational corporations,' *California Management Review*, **23**, pp. 63–74.

Doz, Y. and C.K. Prahalad (1981). 'Headquarter influence and strategic control in MNCs,' *Sloan Management Review*, **23**(1), pp. 15–29.

Doz, Y. and C.K. Prahalad (Fall 1984). 'Patterns of strategic control within multinational corporations,' *Journal of International Business Studies*, **15**, pp. 55–72.

Doz, Y. and C.K. Prahalad (1987). 'A Process model of strategic redirection in large complex firms: The case of multinational corporations.' In A. Pettigrew (ed.), *The Management of Strategic Change*. Basil Blackwell, Oxford, pp. 63–83.

Doz, Y. and C.K. Prahalad (Summer 1991). 'Managing DMNCs: A search for a new paradigm,' *Strategic Management Journal*, **12**, pp. 145–164.

Dunning, J.H. (Spring/Summer 1980). 'Toward an eclectic theory of international production: Some empirical tests,' *Journal of International Business Studies*, **11**, pp. 9–30.

Dunning, J.H. (1981). *The Eclectic theory of the MNC*. Allen & Unwin, London.

Dunning, J.H. (1988). 'The eclectic paradigm of international production: A restatement and some possible extensions.' Journal of International Business Studies, **19**, pp. 1–31.

Edström, A. and J.R. Galbraith (June 1977). 'Transfer of managers as a coordination and control strategy in multinational organizations.' *Administrative Science Quarterly,* **22,** pp. 248–263.

Egelhoff, W.G. (1988). 'Strategy and structure in multinational corporations: A revision of the Stopford and Wells model.' *Strategic Management Journal,* **9**(1), pp. 1–14.

Forsgren, M. (1989). *Managing the Internationalisation Process: The Swedish Case.* Routledge, London.

Forsgren, M. (1990). 'Managing the international multi-centre firm,' *European Management Journal,* **8**(2), pp. 261–267.

Forsgren, M. (1992). 'Book review: C.A. Bartlett, Y. Doz and G. Hedlund (eds.): Managing the global firm.' *Organization Studies,* pp. 477–480.

Forsgren, M., U. Holm and J. Johanson (1992). 'Internationalization of the second degree: The emergence of European-based centres in Swedish firms.' *Europe and the Multinationals.* Edward Elgar, Aldershof, pp. 235–253.

Forsgren, M. and J. Johanson (eds.) (1992). *Managing Networks in International Business.* Gordon and Breach, Philadelphia.

Fouraker, L.E. and J.M. Stopford (1968). 'Organization structure and multinational strategy,' *Administrative Science Quarterly,* **13**(1), pp. 47–64.

Franko, L.G. (1976). *The European Multinationals: A Renewed Challenge to American and British Big Business.* Greylock, Stamford, CT.

Ghoshal, S. and C. Bartlett (1990). 'The multinational corporation as an interorganizational network.' *Academy of Management Review,* **15**(4), pp. 603–625.

Ghoshal, S. and N. Nohria (1989). 'Internal differentiation within multinational corporations,' *Strategic Management Journal,* **10**(4), pp. 323–337.

Gioia, D.A. and K. Chittipeddi (1991). 'Sensemaking and sensegiving in strategic change initiation,' *Strategic Management Journal,* **12,** pp. 433–448.

Gomez-Mejia, L. (1992). 'Structure and process of diversification, compensation strategy, and firm performance,' *Strategic Management Journal,* **13**(5), pp. 381–397.

Gastavsson, P., L. Melin, S. Macdonald and A. Pettigrew (1992). 'Global uniformity versus glocalising through learning.' Paper presented at the annual Strategic Management Society Conference, London.

Habib, M. and B. Victor (1991). 'Strategy, structure, and performance of U.S. manufacturing and service MNCs: A comparative analysis.' *Strategic Management Journal,* **12**(8), pp. 589–606.

Hagström, P. (1991). The 'wired' MNC. The role of information systems for structural change in complex organizations. Doctoral dissertation, Stockholm School of Economics.

Hall, D. and M. Saias (1980). 'Strategy follows structure!' *Strategic Management Journal,* **1,** pp. 149–163.

Hambrick, D. (1990). 'The adolescence of strategic management, 1980–1985: Critical perceptions and reality.' In J. Frederickson (ed.), *Perspectives on Strategic Management.* Harper Business, New York, pp. 237–253.

Hamel, G. and C.K. Prahalad (1989). 'Strategic intent,' *Harvard Business Review,* **89**(3), pp. 63–76.

Hamel, G. and C.K. Prahalad (1992). Presentations at the annual Strategic Management Society Conference, London.

Haspeslagh, P. and D. Jemison (1991). *Managing Acquisitions: Creating Value through Corporate Renewal.* The Free Press, New York.

Hedlund, G. (1984). 'Organization in-between: The evolution of the mother-daughter structure of managing foreign subsidiaries in Swedish MNCs.' *Journal of International Business Studies,* **15**(2), pp. 109–123.

Hedlund, G. (Spring 1986). 'The hypermodern MNC: A heterarchy?' *Human Resource Management,* pp. 9–35.

Hedlund, G. and Å. Kverneland (1984). *Investing in Japan—Experience of Swedish Firms.* IBB, Stockholm School of Economics, Stockholm.

Hedlund, G. and D. Rolander (1990). 'Action in heterarchies: New approaches to managing the MNC.' In C. Bartlett, Y. Doz and G. Hedlund (eds.), *Managing the Global Firm.* Routledge, London, pp. 15–46.

Hedlund, G. and P. Åman (1984). *Managing Relationships with Foreign Subsidiaries.* Sveriges Mekanförbund, Stockholm.

Hellgren, B. and L. Melin (1991). 'Corporate strategies in Nordic firms facing Europe—Acquisitions and other collaborative strategies.' In L.G. Mattsson and B. Stymne (eds.), *Corporate and Industry Strategies for Europe.* Elsevier, Amsterdam, pp. 327–351.

Hennart, J.F. and Y.R. Park (1992). 'Greenfield vs acquisition: The strategy of Japanese investors in the United States.' Paper presented at the annual meeting of the Academy of Management, Las Vegas, NV.

Hofstede, G. (1983). 'National culture in four dimensions,' *International Studies of Management and Organizations,* **13,** pp. 97–118.

Hofstede, G. (1991). *Cultures and Organizations. Software of the Mind.* McGraw-Hill, London.

Huff, T. and R. Reger (1987). 'A review of strategic process,' *Journal of Management,* **13**(2), pp. 211–236.

Jaeger, A.M. (Fall 1983). 'The transfer of organizational culture overseas: An approach to control in the multinational corporation.' *Journal of International Business Studies,* pp. 91–114.

Jaeger, A.M. and B.R. Baliga (1985). 'Control systems and strategic adaptation: Lessons from the Japanese experience,' *Strategic Management Journal,* **6,** pp. 115–134.

Johanson, J. and J. Vahlne (Spring–Summer 1977). 'The internationalisation process of the firm: a model of knowledge development on increasing foreign commitments,' *Journal of International Business Studies,* pp. 23–32.

Johanson, J. and J.E. Vahlne (1990). 'The mechanism of internationalisation,' *International Marketing Review,* **7**(4), pp. 11–24.

Johanson, J. and F. Wiedersheim-Paul (October 1975). 'The internationalisation of the firm: Four Swedish case studies,' *Journal of Management Studies,* pp. 305–322.

Johanson, J.U. and F. Nonaka (1983). 'Japanese export marketing: Structures, strategies, counterstrategies,' *International Marketing Review,* **1**, pp. 12–25.

Jones, M. (1992). 'Mainstream and radical theories of the multinational enterprise: Towards a synthesis.' Paper presented at the annual meeting of the Academy of Management, Las Vegas, NV.

Kimberly, J. and H. Bouchikhi (1991). 'The engines of organizational development and change: How the past shapes the present and constrains the future.' Working paper, Wharton School, Philadelphia, PA.

Kogut, B. (1989). 'A note on global strategies,' *Strategic Management Journal,* **10**(4), pp. 383–389.

Larsson, A. (1985). Structure and change: Power in transnational corporations.' Doctoral dissertation. Acta Universitatis Upsaliensis, Uppsala.

Lindell, M. and L. Melin (1991). 'Acquisition and realization of vision: Diversification through strategic bridging.' Paper presented at the annual Strategic Management Society Conference, Toronto.

Luostarinen, R. (1991). 'Development of strategic thinking in international business.' In J. Näsi, *Arenas of Strategic Thinking.* Foundation for Economic Education, Helsinki.

Lyles, M. (1990). 'A research agenda for strategic management in the 1990s,' *Journal of Management Studies,* **27**(4), pp. 363–375.

Macdonald, S., A. Pettigrew, P. Gustavsson and L. Melin (1991). 'The learning process behind the European activities.' In H. Vestergard (ed.), *An Enlarged Europe in the Global Economy,* (Proceedings of the 17th annual EIBA conference). The Copenhagen Business School, **1**, pp. 1–30.

Martinez, J.I. and J.C. Jarillo (Fall 1989). 'The evolution of research on coordination mechanisms in multinational corporations,' *Journal of International Business Studies,* **20**(3), pp. 489–514.

McKiernan, P. (1992). *Strategies of Growth: Maturity, Recovery and Internationalization.* Routledge, London.

Melin, L. (1985). 'Strategies in managing turnaround: The Scandinavian TV industry,' *Long Range Planning,* **18**(1), pp. 80–86.

Melin, L. (1987). 'Commentary on chapter 4: Understanding strategic change.' In A. Pettigrew (ed.), *Management of Strategic Change.* Basil Blackwell, Oxford, pp. 154–165.

Melin, L. (1989). 'The field-of-force metaphor.' In T. Cavusgil (ed.), *Advances in International Marketing,* Vol. 3, JAI Press, Greenwich, CT, pp. 161–179.

Miller, D. and P.H. Friesen (1982). 'The longitudinal analysis of organizations: A methodological perspective,' *Management Science,* **28**(9), pp. 1013–1034.

Mintzberg, H. (Fall 1987). 'The strategy concept I: Five PS for strategy.' *California Management Review,* **30**, pp. 11–23.

Mutabazi, E. (January 1992). 'What are the best methods for dealing with the intercultural aspect of management?' In Group ESC Newsletter, Lyon, No 8.

Ouchi, W.G. and J.B. Johnson (June 1978). 'Types of organizational control and their relationships to emotional well being,' *Administrative Science Quarterly,* **23**, pp. 293–317.

Perlmutter, H.V. (1969). 'The tortuous evolution of the multinational corporation,' *Columbia Journal of World Business,* pp. 9–18.

Peters, T. (Spring 1984). 'Strategy follows structure: Developing distinctive skills,' *California Management Review,* **26**(3), pp. 111–125.

Pettigrew, A.M. (1985a). *The Awakening Giant: Continuity and Change in ICI.* Basil Blackwell, Oxford.

Pettigrew, A.M. (1985b). 'Examining change in the long-term content of culture and politics.' In J. Pennings (ed.), *Organizational Strategy and Change.* Jossey-Bass, San Francisco, CA, pp. 269–318.

Pettigrew, A.M. (1987). 'Context and action in the transformation of the firm,' *Journal of Management Studies,* **24**(6), pp. 649–670.

Pettigrew, A. and R. Whipp (1991). *Managing Change for Competitive Success.* Blackwell, Oxford.

Porter, M.E. (1986). *Competition in Global Industries.* Harvard Business School Press, Boston, MA.

Porter, M.E. (1990). *The Competitive Advantage of Nations.* Macmillan, London.

Prahalad, C.K. and Y. Doz (1981a). 'Strategic control—the dilemma in headquarters–subsidiary relationship.' In L. Otterbeck (ed.), *The Management of Headquarters—Subsidiary Relationships in MNCs.* Gower, London, pp. 187–203.

Prahalad, C.K. and Y. Doz (1981b). 'An approach to strategic control in MNCs,' *Sloan Management Review,* **22**(4), pp. 5–13.

Prahalad, C.K. and Y. Doz (1987). *The Multinational Mission,* Free Press, New York.

Prahalad, C.K. and G. Hamel (May–June 1990). 'Core competence of the corporation,' *Harvard Business Review,* pp. 79–91.

Rolander, M., U. Zander and G. Hedlund (1989). 'Managerial control systems in Swedish MNCs—Divisionalization and formalization processes in the 1980s.' In R. Luostarinen (ed.), *Dynamics of International Business,* Proceedings of the 15th annual EIBA conference, Helsinki, pp. 1005–1029.

Rugman, A. (1980). 'A new theory of the multinational enterprise: Internationalization versus internalization,' *Columbia Journal of World Business,* **15**, pp. 23–29.

Salzer, M. (1992). 'Scandinavian management across borders?' Paper presented at the Scandinavian Management Workshop, Gothenburg.

Schollhammer, H. (September 1971). 'Organization structures in multinational corporations,' *Academy of Management Journal,* pp. 345–365.

Sharma, D. (1991). *International Operations of Professional Firms.* Chartwell-Bratt, Lund.

Smircich, L. (1983). 'Concepts of culture and organizational analysis,' *Administrative Science Quarterly,* **28**, pp. 339–358.

Stopford, J.M. and L.T. Wells, Jr. (1972). *Managing the Multinational Enterprise.* Basic Books, New York.

Stubbart, C. (1992). 'The deceptive allure of developmental models of strategic processes.' Paper presented at the annual Strategic Management Society Conference, London.

Toyne, B. (1989). 'International exchange: A foundation for theory building in international business.' *Journal of International Business Studies,* **20,** pp. 1–17.

Trautwein, F. (1990). 'Merger motives and merger prescriptions,' *Strategic Management Journal,* **11,** pp. 283–295.

Van de Ven, A. (Summer 1992). 'Suggestions for studying strategy process: A research note,' *Strategic Management Journal,* **13,** pp. 169–188.

Vernon, R. (May 1966). 'International investment and international trade in the product cycle,' *Quarterly Journal of Economics,* pp. 190–207.

Vernon, R. (1979). 'The product cycle hypothesis in a new international environment,' *Oxford Bulletin of Economics and Statistics,* **41**(4), pp. 255–267.

Welch, L.S. and R. Luostarinen (1988). 'Internationalization: Evolution of a concept.' *Journal of General Management,* **14**(2), pp. 34–55.

Whitley, R. (ed.) (1992). *European Business Systems: Firms and Markets in their National Contexts.* Sage, London.

Wiechmann, U. (Winter 1974). 'Integrating multinational marketing activities,' *Columbia Journal of World Business,* pp. 7–16.

Wilson, D. (1992). *A Strategy of Change: Concepts and Controversies in the Management of Change.* Routledge, London.

6

THE GLOBALIZATION OF SERVICE MULTINATIONALS

ALEXANDRA J. CAMPBELL* AND ALAIN VERBEKE**

The challenge of strengthening and exploiting cross-border synergies within multinational corporations (MNCs) has recently emerged as one of the major issues in global strategic management. The fundamental challenge of balancing local demands while maintaining a global vision has been the topic of several influential works about the design of MNCs.[1] The central theme of these frameworks is how multinational managers can design an organizational structure that allows firms to cope with the twin pressures of central co-ordination of activities across borders and autonomous subsidiary responsiveness to local market demands. This involves developing multiple strategic capabilities which allow MNCs to capitalize on the key advantages of national responsiveness, scale economies and scope economies.

Most frameworks used to aid managerial decision-making in multinationals are largely based upon data collected in the manufacturing sector. This article examines how far these frameworks apply to the service sector. Based upon the analysis of nine case studies of multinational service firms, we conclude that 'transnationalism' may require different strategic capabilities in the service sector from those in manufacturing.

Without exception, analytical frameworks used to guide multinational managerial decision-making have been based upon an analysis of data collected in the manufacturing sector. Much of the recent restructuring occurring in manufacturing MNCs such as downsizing, a renewed focus on core businesses and a growing disenchantment with conglomerate operations are consistent with the normative pre-

The authors are grateful for the helpful suggestions of Alan Middleton and for the research assistance of Karl Moore.

* Alexandra Campbell is Assistant Professor of Marketing at York University, Canada.

** Alain Verbeke is Research Director of the Center for Strategic Management at the University of Brussels and author of *Global Competition: Beyond the Three Generics,* JAI Press, Greenwich, Conn. (1993).

scriptions of these frameworks. However, in contrast to these trends, the service sector has been characterized by a different pattern of organizational restructuring. This pattern includes continuing internationalization and increasing firm size and scope.[2] This suggests that the key challenges facing service MNCs may be quite different from those facing manufacturing MNCs. The differences between the inherent characteristics of services vs manufactured goods suggests that there may also be critical differences in the principles which guide the strategic management of service MNCs.[3] Many of the traditional rules of business strategy shaped in the manufacturing environment may not be relevent to services.

Trade in international services represents an increasingly important share of world exports due to service trade liberalization, technological change and socioeconomic trends.[4] Competition in the service sector is intensifying and globalizing which has prompted a fundamental restructuring of many service industries. This restructuring means there is a greater need for managers in service MNCs to think strategically and develop effective competitive strategies to create and sustain competitive advantages worldwide. But currently, there are few tools available for managers of service MNCs to guide their strategic thinking.

In this article, we examine how the unique characteristics of services affect the strategic capabilities necessary to deal with the competitive challenges facing service MNCs. Based upon an analysis of nine service MNCs, we argue that service MNCs build upon different core competencies as compared to manufacturing MNCs. The nine service MNCs in our research sample operate in four major service sectors: financial services (Citicorp Banking and American Express); management consulting (McKinsey, Towers Perrin, Arthur Andersen and Ernst and Young); hotels (Four Seasons and Sheraton Hotels); and data processing (National Data Corporation). While the types of services rendered are very different in each of these four sectors, the common element is that in each sector the core competence of the firm lies in the management of its human capital. These firms were the subject of case studies

which consisted of in-depth interviews with managers and the analysis of publicly available information.

Classification schemes for services are logically based upon the characteristics which distinguish service experiences from physical goods and which have an impact on the marketing strategies of the firm. As a starting point, we examine how the inherent characteristics of services affect a service MNC's bases of competitive advantage.

'TRANSNATIONAL' SERVICES

Services deliver a bundle of benefits to the customer through the experience that is created for that customer. The service literature has consistently identified five characteristics which differentiate services from physical goods marketing: intangibility; inseparability of production and consumption; heterogeneity; variability; and regulation.[5] While all five characteristics influence the strategic options available to service MNCs, we restrict our discussion to those service characteristics which directly affect internal organizational design issues (service intangibility, inseparability and heterogeneity).

In contrast, analytical frameworks used to analyse the manufacturing sector have identified three strategic capabilities as critical to so called 'transnational' management processes, namely, economies of scale, economies of scope and national responsiveness. Economies of scale arise from heavy investment in specialized assets and are based upon global efficiencies associated with integrating activities across different markets or organizational sub-units. Scope economies arise from a firm's ability to share knowledge and learning across different sub-units within the organization. In a transnational management context, the primary source of scope economies is the diffusion of innovation across subsidiaries within the organization. Finally, national responsiveness refers to a firm's ability to respond in flexible manner to competitive changes in individual local markets. The truly transnational company is then seen as the firm able to develop these three capabilities simultaneously.[6] The implications of service intangibility, inseparability and heterogeneity for transnationalism in the service sector are examined in turn.

THE 'INTANGIBILITY' OF SERVICES

Since services are performances rather than objects, they cannot be seen or touched in the same manner as goods. Intangibility increases the purchase risk, thereby increasing the importance for customers to acquire relevant information with which purchasing uncertainty can be reduced. Intangibility creates difficulties in the achievement of differentiation since customers do not always understand what information is being conveyed by different competitors. As a result, successful service companies focus on creating, in the minds of customers, tangible elements of an otherwise intangible experience. For example, firms may standardize tangible elements like the interior (American Express) or exterior (McDonalds) of buildings. Since services themselves are difficult to standardize, any economies of scale which do exist tend to occur in marketing (through branding or investment in corporate image) rather than in production.

The difficulties in establishing a well-defined service concept increases the importance of national responsiveness and economies of scope. The former allows firms to personalize their service offerings in local markets. The latter allows service products in industries such as banking, accounting and insurance to share common characteristics across borders (e.g. through the effective use of the information processing capabilities offered by computer systems). In this context, the ongoing ability to rapidly adapt and transfer information and service innovations to international markets is a key requirement for a service firm's competitive success.

'INSEPARABILITY' OF PRODUCTION AND CONSUMPTION

Inseparability means that production and consumption of services often occur simultaneously so that services must be produced when they are required. Since services are consumed as they are created, there is a high level of buyer-seller interaction. The major implication of inseparability for transnational management is the importance of national responsiveness in order to tailor offerings to suit local market preferences and culture.

Inseparability encourages a focus strategy in which a company develops expertise in meeting the needs of specific segments. There is more opportunity to customize services to the individual customer than in manufacturing and unlike manufacturing, service industries tend to be fragmented with firms specializing in particular market segments. The extent of national responsiveness required to meet the needs of these market segments depends on the degree to which the segment needs are homogeneous across national borders. While some market needs are global, thus allowing economies of scope, in many cases a central aspect of the service delivered is an intimate knowledge of the local economy. In industries such as management consulting, the firm is expected to have an understanding of the trends and issues facing firms and industries in the country in which it is based.

'HETEROGENEITY' OF SERVICES

Services have the potential for considerable variability in their performance or delivery due to the labour-intensity of most services production. Because services are people-centred, the marked differences between individuals result in an equivalent heterogeneity in service production. This characteristic has two main strategic implications. The first is that it increases the importance of quality control, particularly in the case of branded services. Firms meet this challenge by either attempting to reduce the human element in service production (by substituting capital for labour, for example, as in the case of Automatic Teller Machines within the banking industry) or through extensive employee training in which service operations are broken down into minute and discrete stages.[7]

The second implication of service heterogeneity is that it increases the difficulty of achieving success with new products. The variability of individual performance means that past performance may not be a valid indicator of future success. Thus, the ability to obtain scope economies by adapting and transferring innovations to international markets is a key requirement for global competitive success. An important question for service MNCs then, is whether knowledge should be created in the home country and transferred from it or whether know-how should be developed and diffused from various geographical sources.

IMPACT OF SERVICE CHARACTERISTICS

The inherent characteristics of services present unique problems and opportunities for the effective management of the strategic capabilities of service MNCs. Service MNCs do not appear to use the three transnational capabilities (economies of scale, scope and national responsiveness) in the same way as do manufacturing firms. For service firms, scale economies occur primarily in the marketing area and are thus typically far less important than for manufacturing firms. This does not mean that scale economies are trivial. American Express is one example where extensive international coverage provides a barrier to entry and backs up the competitive claim of prompt credit card replacement service for travellers regardless of the country in which they travel. However, scale economies appear to be of less strategic importance than national responsiveness and scope economies.

In service MNCs, national responsiveness and the centralization of innovation (leading to scope economies) may not represent discrete options, in contrast to the situation described by strategic planning models based on manufacturing firms. Service inseparability implies that decisions about the management of innovation influence a firm's ability to be nationally responsive and vice versa. Since most service innovations are immediately experienced by customers, there is a close link between a firm's upstream activities such as innovation and its downstream activities such as marketing. These activities are more closely related in service firms than in manufacturing and often cannot be separated. Hence, it seems likely that centralized innovation in the home country and high national responsiveness cannot be achieved simultaneously, even with sophisticated telecommuni-

cation systems. When innovation is centralized in the home country, the lack of possibilities for subsidiaries to innovate in host countries automatically reduces the firm's opportunities to be nationally responsive in marketing. A similar logic may apply to the relationship between decentralized innovation and high national responsiveness. When innovation is decentralized and subsidiaries *are* allowed to innovate in host countries, the firm's level of national responsiveness at the downstream level of activities is automatically increased.

The analysis of the business strategies of the nine service firms in our research sample tends to support this reasoning. Firms were either very nationally responsive (whereby subsidiaries abroad were allowed to engage in decentralized innovation), or they tended to focus on centralized innovation which reduced the potential of subsidiaries to be nationally responsive. In our sample, firms which emphasize national responsiveness are organized as MNCs consisting of multiple national subsidiaries that are only loosely connected across national boundaries (Ernst & Young, McKinsey, Citicorp and Towers Perrin). The competitive position of these firms is based on a strategy of high national responsiveness and decentralized transfer of organizational learning across national borders. The parent companies manage a portfolio of multiple national entities, each characterized by a strong local presence, which market tailored products. Organizational characteristics important to the success of this strategy are extensive teamwork and a strong common corporate culture to allow the diffusion of organizational learning.

In contrast, firms that emphasize the centralization of innovation mostly have their subsidiaries operate according to guidelines and directions from the parent companies (American Express, Arthur Andersen, Four Seasons, Sheraton Hotels and National Data Corporation). Quality control and service consistency are paramount and any new knowledge and expertise is generally first developed in the parent companies and only then transferred to overseas subsidiaries.

The strategies currently being pursued by these nine service MNCs demonstrate the limitations of current frameworks in helping managers to deal with the strategic issues currently facing service MNCs. Not only are scale economies of less strategic importance to service MNCs, service inseparability suggests that national responsiveness and scope economies actually reflect only one strategic capability. Service firms leverage their core competencies either through centralized innovation (and low national responsiveness) or through high national responsiveness (and decentralized innovation).

An additional strategic capability which may be particularly important to service multinationals is suggested by service intangibility. Service intangibility means that the customer often finds it difficult to isolate service quality from the quality of the service provider. Since a firm's reputation is critical to a customer's purchasing decision, it is important that the firm appear 'legitimate' in the eyes of its customers. Institutional theory[8] deals with how firms respond to environmental pressures to justify their activities or outputs. These environmental pressures encourage similarity (or isomorphism) among firms within a given business environment. According to institutional theory, one important way in which firms can respond to pressures for similarity and enhance their legitimacy is by building relationships with other firms in their business environment. This network of relationships becomes strategic when it is composed of relationships which have an important impact on the firm.[9] Potentially, strategic networks may include relationships with competitors, suppliers, customers or firms in related industries.

There are a number of strategies open to firms to improve their perceived legitimacy. These include demonstrating or improving the firm's reputation, image, prestige, or congruence with prevailing norms in its institutional environment. Although empirical studies that relate legitimacy specifically to external relationship formation are scarce, there is some evidence which indicates that new organizations are able to increase their legitimacy as a function of their ability to invoke affiliations with known organizations.[10]

In view of the significant problems posed by service intangibility, we think that a strategic capability critical to multinational service firms is networking flexibility. Networking flexibility refers to the extent to which a multinational service firm is able to adapt its behaviour and organizational structures to conform to pressures for similarity in various global market places. It represents the ability within sub-units of the firm to develop networks of relationships with external parties in order to improve the firm's 'legitimacy' and thus the service experience of customers. The concept of networking flexibility reflects a company's strength in imitating organizational structures and patterns of behaviour which appear legitimate to customers. It thus reflects a firm's ability to develop networks of relationships at various levels, including the local, sub-national, national, regional trading bloc and even global level.

NETWORKING FLEXIBILITY

In order to assess the relevance of networking flexibility for service multinationals, the nine firms in our research sample were represented in a matrix (Figure 1) which reflects two strategic capabilities. The first is networking flexibility (horizontal axis) and the second is a firm's emphasis on either national responsiveness or centralized innovation (vertical axis). On the basis of the two axes in Figure 1, four cases can be distinguished.

In the first quadrant of Figure 1, a firm's strategic posture emphasizes centralized innovation and high networking flexibility. Firms in this quadrant are organized as consortia in which sub-units have different operating forms which parallel those found in firms with whom they have close business relationships. Since national responsiveness is low, this strategic posture is most likely when firms are serving multiple market segments which cross national borders. Serving multiple market segments compounds the difficulties that service firms face in achieving differentiation and brand identification. This may explain why none of the firms in our study conforms exactly to this picture. However, there is some indication that service MNCs are beginning to move towards the concept of consortia operations. In developing its AMRIS computer system, American Airlines is now beginning to share reservation and capacity management systems with hotel and car

		NETWORKING CAPABILITY	
		High	Low
USE OF CORE COMPETENCIES IN THE FIRM	Centralized Innovation	Sheraton Hotels 1	American Express Four Seasons Hotel Arthur Andersen National Data Corp. 3
	High national responsiveness	2 McKinsey Towers Perrin Ernst and Young	4 Citicorp

Figure 1. The Impact of Networking Flexibility on Multinational Service Firms.

rental companies. This may result in a loose consideration of separately owned firms that operate together through close working relationships.[11]

In our sample, the firm closest to this organizational form is Sheraton Hotels, due to the diversity of its service offerings. Sheraton has three classes of hotel types: Sheraton Hotels, Inns and Suites. Although all three hotel classes focus on the business traveller, each hotel grouping has a distinct positioning which requires different external linkages. Sheraton Inns pursue the midscale traveller, Sheraton Hotels concentrates on the leisure and convention guest and Sheraton Suites caters to the upscale traveller. Currently, the different hotel groupings do not have distinct organizational structures. The parent company's knowledge and capabilities are developed by the senior management team and local operations are strictly controlled through the Sheraton Guest Satisfaction Standards Program which ensures the consistency of service levels across all units of the firm. Service is not completely standardized, however, since the hotel general managers do operate independently and have some flexibility to develop working relationships with different local firms. Thus, it is possible that over time, Sheraton's different hotel groupings may evolve into distinct organizational structures.

In quadrant 2, firms are highly nationally responsive and simultaneously respond effectively to the pressure of conforming to the organizational structures of firms in different relevant environments. Three of the four consulting firms in our sample fit into this category (McKinsey, Towers Perrin and Ernst and Young). All three firms are highly nationally responsive to their customers but simultaneously use project teams in which specialists can originate from any country. These project teams with experts considered credible by the customer reflect the capability of networking flexibility. At both McKinsey and Ernst and Young, innovations developed at one location are shared through informal communication linkages throughout the organization. However, Towers Perrin illustrates the potential pitfalls of this position. Towers Perrin has grown through acquisitions to become a conglomerate of very different consulting groups, each with its own corporate culture and organizational structure. Since Towers Perrin is completely decentralized, informal communication between sub-units occurs only randomly. As a result, knowledge acquired by one subsidiary is rarely transferred to other sub-units within the organization.

Networking flexibility does not need to occur at the expense of effective knowledge transfer within the organization. At McKinsey for example, subsidiaries are decentralized and employees are driven by their own operating principles. Yet, McKinsey has been successful at developing common resource centres such as the one in Brussels to deal with pan-European issues in a way that is perceived legitimate to pan-European firms. This allows different subsidiaries to pool knowledge and share innovations without imposing a rigid organizational structure. In addition, employees who share common interests at McKinsey are also encouraged to participate in Competence Arenas on general topics which include improving the firm's knowledge base and its legitimacy *vis-à-vis* customers with needs in specific competence areas.

In the third quadrant (American Express, Four Seasons, Arthur Andersen and National Data Corporation) firms have low networking flexibility and build their competitiveness predominantly from centralized innovation. These firms have pursued a focus strategy specializing in narrow global market segments so there is less need for national responsiveness. In contrast to Sheraton Hotels, Four Seasons has a low product diversity (hotels and resorts) targeted at only one market segment (upscale international business travellers) which does not require the firms to pursue legitimacy *vis-à-vis* various customer segments. American Express has pursued a focus strategy and expanded its product offerings to a customer base characterized by above-average incomes, frequent travel and complex financial requirements.[12] National Data Corporation's (NDC) expertise is in the area of electronic data processing which is quite standardized across all countries.

Subsidiaries in these companies have limited freedom to modify core products and any new knowledge and expertise is first developed in (or transmitted to) the parent company and only then transferred to other overseas subsidiaries. Different organizational mechanisms are used to ensure the smooth and timely flow of information across different sub-units. National Data Corporation, for example, has applied much of its proficiency in data communications to its intra-company communication systems. All communications are wholly controlled by the corporate head office and innovations are rapidly transferred to NDC's entire network of branches. Both Arthur Andersen and American Express have centralized training facilities where employees are taught new techniques or innovations. In both companies, common training means that the processes for most activities are standardized resulting in a 'by the book' approach to service delivery across the entire customer base.

Firms in this quadrant may be experiencing an increase in strategic vulnerability due to their lack of networking flexibility. One example of a firm in this position could be American Express. American Express is currently under severe pressure from its competitors and needs to increase 'switching costs' for its customers in its established markets such as North America and Europe. Whereas successful rivals such as Visa and Mastercard benefit from their relationships with the banks, American Express has not yet developed strategic affiliations with these financial institutions in different markets. This encourages inter-product competition in which American Express and other financial institutions compete for similar business but where American Express is often perceived as less credible, especially by lower and middle income customers given its lack of linkages with, for example, local banks.

Finally, in quadrant four, a firm has a strategic posture emphasizing national responsiveness but has low networking flexibility. An example of a firm with an administrative heritage in this quadrant is Citicorp. Citicorp considers itself to be a 'geographically organized bank' although this position may be transitional since Citicorp's worldwide strategy is currently undergoing some changes. Historically, Citicorp's administrative structure has been characterized by decentralization in which branches were both geographically and administratively isolated. This resulted in high national responsiveness since branches had the autonomy to develop their own strategies according to the needs of the local marketplace. In order to increase internal knowledge transfer, new business methods are transmitted through a group of individuals called the International Staff. This group is split up and placed in different countries for periods of 6 months to 3 years, and then rotated to other countries.

Recently, however, on-line computer systems have transcended the physical barriers of geographic isolation for individual branches. In response to declining profits, the firm is in the process of reorganizing subsidiaries into interdependent activity centres. This has already occurred for Citicorp's JENA (Japan–Europe–North America) corporate bank subsidiary. The purpose of this reorganization is to foster a common vision and values within the organization. In addition, Citicorp is now attempting to institute strict financial and information control systems. However, the domination of the corporate banking approach may also reduce Citicorp's ability to engage in modes of behaviour perceived as legitimate in other areas of banking. One example of this occurred in the bank's British subsidiary. The customers of this particular branch used to buy gilts (a low-margin type of British government security) as part of their product portfolio along with other more profitable products. In 1980, an American manager discontinued the British branch's sale of gilts due to its low profit margins. Gilts were perceived by customers of the UK subsidiary as an essential part of their product portfolio. The decision to discontinue this product line has affected Citicorp's credibility with investors at the British subsidiary, many of whom now perceive the company to be obsessed with the bottom line at the expense of customer service.[13] Networking flexibility reflects the extent to which a subsidiary's network of relationships (which may be quite different from the network of the firm's head office) is recognized and allowed to exist. The gilt decision by head office indicates low networking flexibility since Citicorp failed to realize that the British subsidiary had its own network of customer relationships. The customer network of the UK subsidiary was completely ignored given that it differed from the corporate customer network of Citicorp's head office.

The above analysis suggests that a 'transnational solution' may be even more complex for service MNCs than for MNCs in the manufacturing sector. Global competitiveness in the service sector implies the choice between national responsiveness (and decentralized innovation) and centralized innovation. This first capability should then be complemented by high networking flexibility in order to improve the firm's legitimacy and thus the service experience of customers.

It should be emphasized that our positioning of particular firms in the four quadrants reflects primarily the researchers' judgement rather than the perceptions of the firms' managers who were interviewed. While this judgement appears to be corroborated by the internal organizational structures currently in place within these firms, further research regarding these relationships is needed. In this research, we ex-amined the importance of networking flexibility to firms in four different service sectors. Although we have offered some speculation about the possible threats and opportunities for firms operating in each quadrant, it is not yet clear how a lack of networking flexibility may affect relative performance outcomes such as market share, profitability or firm size.

CONCLUSIONS

Although the data collected in this study provide a preliminary basis for understanding how service MNCs can leverage their strategic capabilities, the logical implications developed in our discussion of service 'intangibility', 'inseparability' and 'heterogeneity' suggest that service MNCs face quite different strategic challenges from manufacturing MNCs. Specifically, our results suggest that 'national responsiveness' and 'economies of scope' are of critical strategic importance to service MNCs. However, high national responsiveness can only be successful when combined with decentralized innovation. In contrast, economies of scope resulting from centralized innovation severely limit a firm's potential to respond to the requirements of different countries. This view is in sharp contrast with Bartlett and Ghoshal's transnational solution for manufacturing firms which suggest that national responsiveness can and should be combined with any form of learning and scope economies.

Our analysis suggests that a 'transnational solution' for service MNCs may require development through two stages. First, firms need to develop a strategic capability which allows either national responsiveness or centralized innovation. Second, given the administrative structure resulting from the first choice, firms need to develop networking flexibility. To achieve networking flexibility requires the ability to initiate relationships with outside suppliers or related organizations at any geographical level (local, regional or global) deemed appropriate in order to enhance the firm's perceived legitimacy in the view of customers.

REFERENCES

1. Two particularly influential books which deal with organizational design issues facing manufacturing MNCs are: C.K. Prahalad and Y.L. Doz, *The Multinational Mission: Balancing Local Demands and Global Vision,* The Free Press, New York, (1987); and C.A. Bartlett and S. Ghoshal, *Managing Across Borders: The Transnational Solution,* Harvard Business School, Boston, Massachusetts (1989). In both books the authors suggest that successful MNCs possess multiple strategic capabilities which allow them to create cross-border synergies. Prahalad and Doz deal with how managers in MNCs can deal with conflicting pressures for local responsiveness and global integration while Bartlett and Ghoshal propose a new organizational model for the 'transnational corporation' which combines the key advantages of nationally responsive firms, global companies that build upon scale economies, and firms that rely primarily upon sharing know-how across borders.

2. P. Enderwick, The Scale and Scope of Service Sector Multinationals in Peter J. Buckley and Mark Casson (eds), *Multinational Enterprises in the World Economy: Essays in Honour of John Dunning,* pp. 134–152, Edward Elgar Publishing, Vermont (1992).

3. I. Wilson, Competitive Strategies for Service Businesses, *Long Range Planning,* **21** (6), 10–12 (1988).

4. E. Trondsen and R. Edfelt, New Opportunities in Global Services, *Long Range Planning,* **20** (5), 53–60 (1987).

5. J.E.G. Bateson, *Managing Services Marketing: Text and Readings,* Dryden HBJ, Toronto (1992); J.E.G. Bateson, Why We Need Service Marketing, in O.C. Ferrell, S.W. Brown and C.W. Lamb Jr. (eds), *Conceptual and Theoretical Developments in Marketing,* pp. 131–146, American Marketing Association, Chicago (1992); J.H. Dunning, *Transnational Corporations and the Growth of Services: Some Conceptual and Theoretical Issues.* UNCTC Current Studies Series A No. 9, United Nations, New York (1989); P. Enderwick (ed), *Multinational Service Firms,* Routledge, London (1989); D.F. Channon, *Global Banking Strategy,* John Wiley, Chichester (1988); J. Nusbaumer, *Services in the Global Market,* Kluwer, Boston, Mass (1987).

6. C.A. Bartlett and S. Ghoshal, op. cit. (1987).

7. P. Enderwick, op. cit.

8. Institutional theory proposes that there are two related ways in which firms can increase their perceived legitimacy. The first is by emulating the types of organizational structures found in their relevant environments. Firms are perceived legitimate when they appear to be in agreement with the prevailing norms, rules, beliefs or expectations of external constituents. Firm behaviour aimed at creating a greater degree of similarity between the focal firm and other firms in its industry acts as a powerful signalling device to external firms. For a description of the theoretical bases of institutional theory see: P.J. DiMaggio, Interest and agency in institutional theory, in L.G. Zucker (ed), *Institutional patterns and organizations,* pp. 3–21, Ballinger, Cambridge, MA (1988); P.J. DiMaggio and W.W. Powell, The iron cage revisited: Institutional isomorphism and collective rationality in organizational fields, *American Sociological Review,* **48,** 147–160 (1983); M.L. Fennell, C.O. Ross and R.B. Warnecke, Organizational environment and network structure, in S.B. Barcharach (ed), *Research in the sociology of organizations,* pp. 311–34, JAI Press, Greenwich, CT (1987).

9. C. Snodgrass, Use of Networks in Cross Border Competition, *Long Range Planning,* **26** (2), 41–50 (1993).

10. See, W. Wiewel and A. Hunter, The interorganizational network as a resource: A comparative case study on organizational genesis, *Administrative Science Quarterly,* **30,** 482–496 (1985); J. Byrne, The McKinsey Mystique, *Business Week,* Sept. 20, 66–74 (1993); and J. Huey, How McKinsey Does It, *Fortune,* Nov. 1, 56–68 (1993).

11. P. Enderwick, op. cit.

12. J.L. Heskett (1986) *Managing in the Service Economy,* Harvard Business School Press, Boston, Mass.

13. Can Citicorp get its Act together in Europe?, *Institutional Investor,* p. 159 (1988).

7

INTERNATIONAL MARKET EXPANSION OF HIGH-TECHNOLOGY FIRMS

IGAL AYAL AND DOVE IZRAELI

INTRODUCTION

A high-technology firm planning its international market expansion strategy faces a series of strategic issues and decision problems. The main strategy components requiring problem elaboration, analysis, and decisions are:

1. General mode and rate of expansion.
2. International market selection and entry priorities.
3. Structural aspects, including global structure and specific market presence options.

This paper will present a conceptual framework for the analysis of such issues. Clearly, the extent and importance of the problems involved are such that many papers and entire monographs have been written on each of them. Thus our treatment here will be limited to highlighting the conceptual framework, focusing mainly on the third set of issues above. We will assume that the firm has defined its business using the conventional marketing policy dimensions of: (a) technologies; (b) served markets and segments; (c) customer functions and benefits; (d) stage in the value-added system (Day, 1984). The firm is now planning growth on the second dimension, through international expansion. Some adaptations of its position on the other dimensions may be required in the context of market expansion strategy, but major changes in these dimensions (with the possible exception of the stage in the value-added system) are not contemplated as part of the present strategic analysis.

CHARACTERISTICS OF HIGH-TECHNOLOGY MARKET ENVIRONMENTS

The nature of ''high technology'' and the characteristics of high-technology firms have been dealt with extensively in the other papers in this volume. Certain common characteristics have to be specified here, as basic assumptions for the analysis.

SHORT LIFE CYCLES

The life cycles of hi-tech products are short, and may well be getting shorter. This is inherent in the definition of ''high technology,'' placing it at the leading edge of technological change. The typical life cycle for a hi-tech chemical product is on the order of between 7 and 10 years; an electronic product 4 to 7 years; and a software product about 3 years (Ayal & Raban, 1990). Thus the strategic window for the firm is narrow, and expansion must be relatively rapid, otherwise valuable comparative advantage will be lost. This is certainly true in the context of expansion in order to reap the economic benefits of a single new product. The time pressure is somewhat less but still evident when the product is to be used as a stepping stone for the introduction of other products in the future.

SIMILARITY OF CUSTOMER FUNCTIONS

A good salesman has frequently been defined as someone who can sell refrigerators in the Arctic

Circle—as devices for keeping food relatively warm. In hi-tech products, such extensions of customer functions and benefits are far more difficult. Hi-tech products tend to be industrial (or "business-to-business"), and their target customers tend to have similar needs and to expect similar benefits from the products.

RAPID COMMUNICATION GRAPEVINES

High-technology customers tend to be well-informed, and more cosmopolitan in their outlook. They are likely to monitor technological and market developments, be in touch with each other, read professional literature, attend international trade-fairs and exhibitions, and so forth. Thus there are rapid intramarket and intermarket communications, narrowing the strategic window on the one hand and facilitating rapid expansion on the other.

NEED FOR HIGH R&D EXPENDITURES

Branches of industry are usually defined as high-technology on the basis of high (i.e., over 5%) expenditures on R&D relative to sales, and/or on the basis of high skill ratio (proportion of scientific and technical employees in the labor force). In any case, high R&D intensity tends, in general, to drive return on investment down (see Buzzell & Gale, 1987). Thus speed and efficiency in international market expansion may well be crucial for firm survival and success.

TURBULENT ENVIRONMENT

Short life cycles and rapidly evolving technologies make for turbulent operating environments. Competition may well come from totally different technological quarters (thus the existence of many *potential* competitors). In addition, the customer facing a turbulent technological environment (and usually expecting that larger benefits will be available for a far lower price within a matter of months), may well postpone a purchase. Considerable sales and service efforts are needed before, during, and after a sale.

NEEDS FOR MULTIPLE FLOWS OF INFORMATION

Hi-tech marketing requires managing multiple flows of information (Ayal & Izraeli, 1990). Information regarding new applications, technical changes and improvements must flow from producer to market. Information regarding customer requirements and operational problems must flow quickly and reliably from market to producer. Information regarding use opportunities, new applications, and use results must flow from one market to the others. Thus a high-capacity integrative device (global structure) is necessary.

RELATIVELY LOW INTERNATIONAL BARRIERS

Tariff barriers to international trade are on a long-term decline trend. Nontariff barriers (other than true public protection measures) are erected and dismantled as a function of international market conditions, local conditions, and various political pressures. High-tech products, however, being mostly industrial, tend to be perceived as enhancing the international competitive position of the importing industry. Thus both types of barriers tend to be lower than in the case of medium-tech and low-tech products, a fact which facilitates international market expansion.

In summary, seven "universal" characteristics of hi-tech operating environments have been described above. Five of them require and/or facilitate rapid international market expansion, while two—i.e., turbulent environments and the need for high-capacity information channels—place considerable demands on the resulting structure. We will now proceed to the elaboration and analysis of strategic issues in international market expansion.

EXPANSION MODE AND RATE

The general expansion mode and rate issue has been described by Ayal and Zif (1979) as a two-dimensional construct, comprised of concentration versus diversification strategy both on markets and on segments. This classification, when the dimensions are treated as dichotomies (rather than the more accurate multichotomous "gradations"), leads to four illustrative strategies.

1. *Segment Concentration and Market Concentration.* The firm (e.g., a medical electronics manufacturer) focuses its efforts on one, or at most, a few user segments in all its geographical markets. For example, it develops a specialized product for dental surgeons with specific qualifications, practice size, type of clientele, and resources. It also expands its operations one market at a time, with a relatively high level of involvement (e.g., sets up a sales subsidiary or a joint venture) in each market.
2. *Segment Concentration and Market Diversification.* The firm still focuses on its selected segment(s), but expands into many markets almost simultaneously, with a relatively low involvement level in each market. For example, it uses international exhibitions, trade fairs, and direct mailing lists to rapidly develop an extensive international network of agents, letting each agent or distributor "do whatever he/she can."
3. *Segment Diversification and Market Concentration.* The firm, for example, a pharmaceutical manufacturer, tries to cater to the needs of many different segments at the same time (e.g., various categories of medical practitioners, private clinics, hospitals of various sizes). It expands its geographical coverage gradually, due to different and expensive drug registration requirements and procedures.
4. *Segment Diversification and Market Diversification.* The firm (e.g., a software producer with a new electronic spreadsheet) attempts to capitalize on a technological advantage which has broad-spectrum usefulness in a less tightly regulated field, by expanding rapidly into many markets and multiple user segments.

For most hi-tech firms, this discussion of similarity of customer functions means that segment diversification can usually be attained only with multiple products. The strategic issue of expansion on the product dimension (customer functions/benefits) is beyond the scope of the present discussion. Thus we will assume that segment concentration is selected. Regarding the market concentration/diversification issue, a theoretical analysis by Ayal and Zif (1979) identified 10 product/market factors which affect op-

timal strategy choice. In the case of hi-tech products, 5 of the 10 usually favor diversification: sales stability in each market is low (turbulent environment); competitive lead times are short; spillover effects are high (rapid communications grapevines); economies of scale in distribution are relatively low (high value/weight ratio and concentrated buyers); and the extent of constraints (tariff and nontariff barriers) is relatively low. Five other factors, on the other hand, favor concentration: an S-shaped sales response curve (buyers have to be educated and change their habits and/or systems); a high growth rate in each market; high needs for product adaptation (applications engineering); high needs for communication adaptation; and high program control requirements (particularly product service and technical support).

Thus, the issue of expansion mode and rate poses a dilemma for the internationally expanding high-technology firm: rapid expansion is both extremely desirable and practically difficult. Innovative solutions are called for. A conventional one is licensing (Contractor, 1981; McDonald & Leahy, 1985). One little-used alternative (in the context of hi-tech products) has been proposed by Ayal and Izraeli (1990)—"comprehensive" franchising.

INTERNATIONAL MARKET SELECTION, AND ENTRY ORDER

International market selection issues are extensively dealt with in any standard international marketing and/or international business textbook (e.g., see Keegan, 1989; Toyne & Walters, 1989). In principle, the "stationary" market entry and development issue should be seen as an investment problem, weighing expected return against risk. One appealing approach when a concentration strategy is selected, is to adapt the General Electric/Shell Chemical directional policy matrix approach to the classification of *markets* (rather than SBU's or products) on the general dimensions of market attractiveness and comparative advantage (see methodology and illustrative applications in Ayal, Peer, & Zif [1987]; Harrell & Kiefer [1981]). This method can be used with macroeconomic measures, as a screening device identifying the "interesting" country subset. Finally, the problem of order of entry has to be analyzed in a *dynamic* context. A possible approach is to classify the selected subset into relatively homogenous clusters (e.g., see Doyle & Gidengil, 1978; Sethy 1971). This way, experience from entering one cluster member can be employed when entering the other member countries. Market potential, competitive conditions, spillover effects and firm experience will be the most important determinants of entry order. A detailed exposition, however, is well beyond the scope of this paper.

STRUCTURAL ASPECTS

The structural aspects of international market expansion have to be analyzed on several different levels: (1) mode of entry; (2) level of structure; (3) level of firm dominance; (4) global network structure. Following are some pertinent considerations in each one of these areas.

MODE OF ENTRY

This issue conventionally involves, first and foremost, decisions on the locus of production (see Davidson, 1982; Davidson & Haspeslagh, 1982). At the highest level, full production will take place in the target country. A lower level of commitment of production resources and know-how will involve partial production, or only assembly in the target country. At the lowest level will be exports to the target countries (combined perhaps with local packaging). Since cases of multiple loci of full production for hi-tech products (apart from extensive licensing arrangements) are extremely rare in international marketing, we will assume that export, local assembly, or at most partial production (of uncritical components), is involved.

An interesting example is international market expansion of "off the shelf" software packages. For many of these, master tapes are exported to most target countries, and the programs are reproduced on disks (frequently, manuals are also translated if necessary, and printed) locally. On the face of it, the actual product sold to the customer is produced locally, but since the skill element is contained in the master tapes, we can treat it as a case of local assembly, akin to local bottling of Coca-Cola without access to the "secret formula."

A second question regarding the mode of entry is the level of commitment and investment on the marketing side. This question will be discussed in the following sections in the context of two separate but interrelated issues: (1) level of structure, and (2) level of firm dominance in the marketing channel.

LEVEL OF STRUCTURE

Ayal and Izraeli (1990) analyzed channel structure options in the context of international market expansion for new hi-tech products. A transactional cost analysis framework, as applied to marketing channel design (Izraeli, 1972, 1982; Williamson, 1981) was utilized to identify the characteristics of a channel system which would be more likely to cope successfully with the contradictory pressures for concentration and diversification, discussed above. Various types of marketing channel institutions were ordered on a continuum of levels of structure, from the lowest structure level ("market") of independents, through technology licensing, "loose" franchise, "comprehensive" franchise and joint venturing, to the highest structure level ("hierarchy") which is a wholly-owned channel system. The analysis highlights 13 channel performance characteristics which are affected by the level of structure. Characteristics that are optimized by high structure include:

1. specialization and technical ability of channel members;
2. standardization of approach and public image;
3. speed of two-way information flow, and accuracy of transmission;
4. minimization of variable costs per transaction (or per another unit of channel output);
5. economies of scale; and
6. protection from involuntary (on the part of the manufacturer) channel "rupture."

Characteristics which tend to be optimized by low channel structure include:

1. ratio of channel market coverage to resources invested by the firm in setting up the channel;
2. channel set-up speed;
3. the ratio of transaction outputs to fixed costs;
4. channel member initiative;
5. channel flexibility, and ability to deal with environmental change;
6. local name and reputation; and
7. host-country cooperation.

Illustrative examples presented in the paper show how comprehensive franchising or ''market'' licensing may, under certain conditions, be better compromises between ''low'' and ''high'' structures than the conventionally accepted solutions of technology licensing or joint venturing.

LEVEL OF FIRM DOMINANCE

Various aspects of power and coordination in the marketing channel are well covered in the literature. (See an extensive review in Stern & El-Ansari [1988].) Our purpose here is to analyze the power issue, as it relates to structure problems and to the mode of entry decisions made specifically by an internationally expanding hi-tech firm. Both the context of international expansion and the characteristics of high technology environments make this a special case, requiring nonstandard treatment.

The level of firm dominance in the marketing channel system, is clearly a function of structure level: higher structure level is synonymous with higher control, and *ceteris paribus* implies higher dominance of the initiating firm in the channel. Still, given a specific structure level, the level of firm dominance will be an increasing function of the needs for inputs from local (or ''subglobal'') channel partners. Table 1 lists three sets of factors affecting these needs, and the direction of their effects.

Most of the factors in Table 1, as well as the direction of their influence, are self-explanatory. Thus, larger firms with better established global names and more experience clearly require less support from local market-channel elements, while a higher risk perception by customers requires stronger local support and reassurance. Advantages in basic technology or production processes (quality and cost) are internal to the firm, and can easily be manifested to the potential customer. An advantage in customized applications, on the other hand, lies on the interface between the firm and the customer, and thus a strong local presence is needed for its fruition. As for the third set of factors, higher intermarket variability in functional needs of customers and in physical use conditions leads to higher product adaptation requirements (see Keegan, 1969). Higher variability in cultural and educational backgrounds would lead to higher communication adaptation requirements. Higher variability in potential customer ''economics'' could lead to both, as well as to pricing policy adaptation requirements. Clearly, any increase in local adaptation requirements means higher needs for local channel member inputs.

It should be noted that a high level of needed inputs from local channel partners can be partially countered by adopting a market and/or segment concentration strategy. Furthermore, higher needs for inputs may or may not lead to adopting a lower structure, but they will *generally* lead to lower firm dominance in the channel, and to getting a lower share of the proceeds.

Finally, high levels on the three intermarket factors, as well as high variability among markets in the eight product/market factors would tend to require higher flexibility and multiplicity of substructures in the global network employed by the firm. This is the subject of the next section.

GLOBAL NETWORK STRUCTURE

Izraeli (1972) analyzed the division of labor in marketing channels as involving two interrelated processes: differentiation among tasks for greater efficiency of each and of the whole, and integration to achieve a unified effort. The appropriate mechanisms for both are affected by two determinants of structure: environmental stability and the nature of interdependence among channel units.

The degree of certainty and stability of the environment is positively related to the level of structure

Table 1. Factors Affecting Level of Needs for Inputs from Local Channel "Partners"

Factors	Direction of Effect on Needs
"Firm" Factors	
A. Overall size and accessible resources of firm	Negative
B. International experience of firm (extent, length, similarity to the specific market)	Negative
C. Global reputation and image of firm	Negative
D. Ability of management to take risks and apply long-term view ("investment" approach to market development)	Negative
E. Type of technology advantage over major global competitors:	
1. Advantages mainly in basic technology	Negative
2. Advantages mainly in production process and costs	Negative
3. Advantages mainly in tailor made or customized applications	Positive
Product/Market Factors (in each market)	
A. Total market size and spread	Positive
B. Typical size of purchase by end-customers	Positive
C. Risk perceived by potential customer	Positive
D. Certainty and stability of the market environment	Negative
E. Difficulty and operational complexity of adoption by customers	Positive
F. Size and visibility of advantage to buyer	Negative
G. Global similarity of needs and use conditions, as perceived by potential customer ("global" vs. "local" orientation of potential customers)	Negative
H. Needs for local product service, customer service, and technical support	Positive
Intermarket Factors	
A. Variability among markets in functional needs and physical conditions of use	Positive
B. Variability in cultural and educational background of potential customers	Positive
C. Variability in potential customer "economics"—ability and willingness to pay	Positive

in organizations (Burns & Stalker, 1961). A multiplicity of operating environments for each subsystem, however, may require a multiplicity of different structures (Lawrence & Lorsch, 1967).

Interdependence among organizational units has been classified by Thompson (1967) into three types:

1. *Pooled*—each unit renders a discrete contribution, and is supported by the whole, but no direct interaction is required.

2. *Sequential*—asymmetrical interdependence, where the order of interdependence can be specified.

3. *Reciprocal*—outputs of each unit are inputs for the others, and thus each unit is "penetrated" by the others.

Extending Thompson's work to marketing channels, it can be stated that reciprocal interdependence would lead to lower structure, pooled to higher. Dealing specifically with the design of the global channel network for an expanding high-technology firm, certainty and stability of the environments frequently change and vary among markets, and so does the nature of interdependence: Relationships between channel members in large developed countries and the firm's home office, as well as *among* channel systems in developed countries, are likely to be reciprocal (transfer of experience, new applications, competitive and technological intelligence). With less developed and/or smaller markets, they would tend to be sequential. All members of the channel system are likely to have at least some level of pooled interdependence with all or most others—at least regarding their reputation and consequently in relation to some task performance.

The probable need for a multiplicity of channel structures leads to "messy" design problems. These can be alleviated, however, with the aid of the modern concept of network organizations and networking (see Lipnack & Stamps, 1986; Hine, 1977). Thorelli (1984) discussed networks as providing a range of alternatives between "market" arrangements and hierarchical channel structures. The present authors' treatment of franchising is clearly one such network option. According to Thorelli, "In its strategic planning the company should not only keep one or even several theories of the firm in mind, it should also think in network terms to open new perspectives of structure, strategy, and performance . . . *the network may be viewed* . . . as an instrument for reaching new clientels and/or additional countries." If we accept this approach, we realize that the high technology firm seeking international market expansion should not be limited to seeking a single, "optimal" channel structure. Various structures may well be employed in different countries, e.g., a wholly owned subsidiary in one major market; joint ventures in two or three other key markets; technological licensing in some markets where the barriers to entry are relatively high and protection of proprietary knowledge can be enforced; possibly comprehensive franchising in other markets where the firm has a name to be reckoned with and qualified franchisees can be found; and more "independent" partners in smaller, less interesting markets. All of

these can be integrated under the network concept, provided that one applies a holistic view and is successful in developing a bond of shared values among participants.

Both interorganizational and intraorganizational networking are becoming more prevalent among business corporations in recent years (Wilson & Dobrzynski 1986). According to Robert K. Mueller, former Chairman of Arthur D. Little Inc., networking is even more prevalent among hi-tech firms with global and post-industrial tendencies:

in order to successfully manage innovation in our complex, diversified, interdependent environment, from within and outside our corporation, we need to create ten (or more) networks to solve our problems. . . . Managers can balance the bias toward systems and control with appreciation and sponsoring of networks and networking (Mueller, 1986, pp. 104–105).

In conclusion, we have utilized a combination of two different approaches—transactional cost analysis and networking—to develop a conceptual framework for the international market expansion problems of hi-tech firms. As Johanson and Mattson (1987) have written:

The merits of the transaction-cost approach are related to its ability to explain the existence of different governance structures or institutional forms in different situations. It seems to have a quite wide area of applicability. With its focus on conditions for stable equilibrium, it tends, however, to be deterministic, making it less suitable for strategy analysis. In contrast, the network approach stresses the action possibilities of the firm. In particular, it is a useful tool in analyzing approaches to, and strategies in, different markets (p. 47).

REFERENCES

Ayal, I., & Izraeli, D. (1990). International market expansion for new high tech products through franchising. *Journal of High Technology Management Research, 1*(2), 167–179.

Ayal, I., Peer, A., & Zif, J. (1987). Selecting industries for export growth: A directional policy matrix approach. *Journal of Macromarketing, 7*(1), 22–33.

Ayal, I., & Raban, J. (1990). Developing hi-tech industrial products for world markets. *IEEE Transactions on Engineering Management, 37*(3), 177–184.

Ayal, I., & Zif, J. (1979). Market expansion strategies in multinational marketing. *Journal of Marketing, 43*, 84–94.

Burns, T., & Stalker, G.M. (1961). *The management of innovation.* London: Tavistock.

Buzzell, R.D., & Gale, B.T. (1987). *The PIMS principle.* New York: Free Press.

Contractor, F.J. (1981). The role of licensing in international strategy. *Columbia Journal of World Business, 16*(4), 73–83.

Davidson, W.H. (1982). *Global Strategic Management.* New York: Wiley.

Davidson, W.H., & Haspeslagh, P. (1982, July–August). Shaping a global product organization. *Harvard Business Review, 60*(4), 125–132.

Day, G.S. (1984). *Strategic market planning: The pursuit of competitive advantage.* St. Paul, MN: West.

Doyle, P., & Gidengil, Z.B. (1978). Defining international opportunities through Wishart's mode analysis. *Journal of the Operational Research Society, 29*, 147–157.

Harrell, G.D., & Kiefer, R.O. (1981, Winter). Multinational strategic market portfolio. *MSU Business Topics,* 5–15.

Hine, V. (1977). The basic paradigm of a future socio-cultural system. *World Issues Magazine,* 19–22.

Izraeli, D. (1972). *Franchising and the total distribution system.* London: Longman.

Izraeli, D. (1982). *Criteria for optimal channel structure.* Paper presented at TCA Conference, Northwestern University.

Johanson, J., & Mattsson, L.G. (1987). Interorganizational relations in industrial systems: A network approach compared with the transaction-cost approach. *International Studies of Management and Organization, 1,* 39–48.

Keegan, W.J. (1969, January). Multinational product planning: Strategic alternatives. *Journal of Marketing, 33,* 58–62.

Keegan, W.J. (1989). *Global marketing management* (4th ed.). Englewood Cliffs, NJ: Prentice Hall.

Lawrence, P.R., & Lorsch, J.W. (1967). Differentiation and integration in complex organizations. *Administrative Science Quarterly, 12,* 1–47.

Lipnack, J., & Stamps, J. (1986). *Networking.* New York: Routledge & Kegan Paul.

McDonald, D.W., & Leahy, H.S. (1985). Licensing has a role in technology strategic planning. *Research Management, 28*(1), 35–40.

Mueller, R.K. (1986). *Corporate networking.* New York: The Free Press.

Sethy, S.P. (1971). Comparative cluster analysis for world markets. *Journal of Marketing Research, 8*(3), 348–354.

Stern, L.W., & El-Ansary, A.I. (1988). *Marketing channels* (2nd ed.). Englewood Cliffs, NJ: Prentice Hall.

Thompson, J.D. (1967). *Organizations in Action.* New York: McGraw Hill.

Thorelli, H.B. (1986). Networks between markets and hierarchies. *Strategic Management Journal, 7*(1), 37–51.

Toyne, B., & Walters, P.G.P. (1989). *Global marketing management: A strategic perspective.* Needham, MA: Allyn and Bacon.

Williamson, O.E. (1981). The economics of organization: The transaction cost approach. *American Journal of Sociology, 87*(3), 548–577.

Wilson, J.W., & Dobrzynski, J.H. (1986, March 3). And now the post-industrial corporation. Special Report, *Business Week,* 60–63.

8

TOWARD A THEORY OF INTERNATIONAL NEW VENTURES

BENJAMIN M. OVIATT*
Georgia State University

PATRICIA PHILLIPS MCDOUGALL**
Georgia Institute of Technology

ABSTRACT   The formation of organizations that are international from inception—international new ventures—is an increasingly important phenomenon that is incongruent with traditionally expected characteristics of multinational enterprises. A framework is presented that explains the phenomenon by integrating international business, entrepreneurship, and strategic management theory. That framework describes four necessary and sufficient elements for the existence of international new ventures: (1) organizational formation through internalization of some transactions, (2) strong reliance on alternative governance structures to access resources, (3) establishment of foreign location advantages, and (4) control over unique resources.

INTRODUCTION

The study of the multinational enterprise (MNE) has focused on large, mature corporations. Historically, many MNEs developed from large, mature, domestic

This article was awarded first prize in the 1993 *Competition for the Best Paper on Entrepreneurship and Innovation* sponsored by New York University's Center for Entrepreneurial Studies. The authors gratefully acknowledge financial support for this research from the Bernard B. & Eugenia A. Ramsey Chair of Private Enterprise at Georgia State University and from the Society of International Business Fellows, based in Atlanta, Georgia.

Received: June 1992; Revised: December 1992, April & August 1993; Accepted: August 1993.
* Benjamin M. Oviatt is Assistant Professor of Management at Georgia State University. He received his Ph.D. in strategic management from the University of South Carolina. His research focuses on strategic management, organizational turnaround, and international new ventures.
** Patricia Phillips McDougall is Associate Professor of Strategic Management at Georgia Institute of Technology. She received her Ph.D. in strategic management from the University of South Carolina. Her research focuses primarily on new and young firms, with a special emphasis on strategies and internationalization.

firms [Chandler 1986], and they commanded attention because they wielded significant economic power, especially after World War II [Buckley & Casson 1976; Dunning 1981; Hennart 1982]. However, recent technological innovation and the presence of increasing numbers of people with international business experience have established new foundations for MNEs. An internationally experienced person who can attract a moderate amount of capital can conduct business anywhere in the time it takes to press the buttons of a telephone, and, when required, he or she can travel virtually anywhere on the globe in no more than a day. Such facile use of low-cost communication technology and transportation means that the ability to discover and take advantage of business opportunities in multiple countries is not the preserve of large, mature corporations. New ventures with limited resources may also compete successfully in the international arena.

Since the late 1980s, the popular business press has been reporting, as a new and growing phenomenon, the establishment of new ventures that are international from inception [Brokaw 1990; *The Economist* 1992, 1993b; Gupta 1989; Mamis 1989]. These start-ups often raise capital, manufacture, and sell products on several continents, particularly in advanced technology industries where many established competitors are already global.

LASA Industries, Inc., which sold an unusually efficient microprocessor prototyping technology, is representative of these international new ventures formed within the past decade. As detailed by Jolly, Alahuhta and Jeannet [1992], LASA's strategy was international in multiple respects. Its founders were American, Swiss, and French. Its funding was European. The operational headquarters and R&D were located in the United States, while marketing was managed from France and finance from Switzerland. Manufacturing was centered in Scotland to take advantage of attractive regional grants, and initial sales were in France and the United States.

IXI Limited, a British venture that became a leading supplier of desktop windowing computer software for UNIX operating systems, violated the usual expectation that firms begin with sales in their home country and later sell to foreign countries. Ray Anderson, the venture's founder and chairman, had previously worked for a British computer company that failed. Through Anderson's work in that company's Boston and Canadian operations he became aware of the needs of the North American market. While discussing the failure of his former company Anderson said,

. . . it did not succeed because we tried to sell the product by starting up in England and then selling in the U.S., and by that time it was too late. We should have developed our products first of all for the U.S. market and then sold it back into England. [Anderson 1992]

When Anderson started IXI, his stated strategy was to target the United States first, Japan second, and then move back into the United Kingdom. Funding for the venture was from the United Kingdom, Germany, Austria and Japan. Foreign subsidiaries were set up in the United States and Japan. Only after establishing itself in both those countries did IXI turn its attention to its home country, and then to mainland Europe. In an interview four years after the product's introduction, Anderson estimated 60% of IXI's revenues came from the United States, 20% from the United Kingdom, 10% from Japan, and 10% from other countries.

Actually, international new ventures have existed for centuries. The famous East India Company was chartered in London in 1600 [Wilkins 1970]. In early 19th century America, the unprecedented value of cotton exports gave birth to specialized cotton traders [Chandler 1977]. The Ford Motor Company also seems to have been an international new venture at its founding in 1903 [Wilkins & Hill 1964]. However, the focus of interest has been on MNEs that developed over time from large, mature, integrated enterprises [Chandler 1986], and we believe that has obscured the existence of international new ventures.

As a result, scholars of organization science have ignored international new ventures until very recently. Figure 1 depicts our sense of the domain of scholarly literature on organizations. A substantial body of research has been published on established firms, both domestic and international, and on domestic new ventures. However, there is much less work in the quadrant of international new ventures. Entrepreneurship research on international issues has largely concerned itself with (1) the impact of public policies on small-firm exporting (e.g., Rossman [1984]), (2) entrepreneurs and entrepreneurial activities in various countries (e.g., Ohe, Honjo, Oliva, Considine & MacMillan [1991]; Westhead [1990]), and (3) comparisons between small-firm exporters and non-exporters (e.g., Kedia & Chhokar [1985]).

The age of an organization when it internationalizes has been considered infrequently. Vozikis and Mescon [1985] did show that exporters that were start-ups reported more problems with export operations than did mature small exporters. More often, reports of new ventures that were international at or near inception have been regarded as exceptional (e.g., Welch & Loustarinen [1988]). In addition, the age of small exporters has frequently been viewed as an unimportant demographic characteristic (e.g., Malekzadeh & Nahavandi [1985], or a side issue (e.g., Cooper & Kleinschmidt [1985]).

However, since 1989, reports based on case studies of international new ventures have begun to ap-

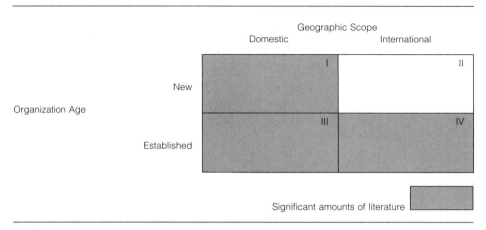

Figure 1. The Domain of Academic Literature on Organizations[1]
[1]adapted from the presentation of Candida Brush in McDougall, Oviatt & Brush [1991]

pear from scholars of entrepreneurship. Some have shown that such ventures form because internationally experienced and alert entrepreneurs are able to link resources from multiple countries to meet the demand of markets that are inherently international [Coviello & Munro 1992; Hoy, Pivoda & Mackrle 1992; McDougall & Oviatt 1991; Oviatt, McDougall, Simon & Shrader 1994; Ray 1989]. Other case studies have shown that the success of international new ventures seems to depend on having an international vision of the firm from inception, an innovative product or service marketed through a strong network, and a tightly managed organization focused on international sales growth [Ganitsky 1989; Jolly et al. 1992; McDougall, Shane & Oviatt 1994].

Collectively, these case studies indicate that international new ventures are an important phenomenon. They have identified the formation of international new ventures in more than ten countries in all parts of the world, suggesting that global forces may be promoting their development. In addition, the studies show that interest in the topic is recent and has emerged independently and nearly simultaneously from several groups of scholars. Finally, while many of the ventures studied were in high-tech businesses, services and even aquaculture were represented, suggesting that international new ventures may appear in a wide range of industries.

Additional indicators of the emergence of international new ventures have also appeared. Brush's [1992] study of small, internationalized, U.S. manufacturers found 17 firms—13% of her random nationwide sample—were internationalized during their first year of operation. Ernst and Young's survey of 303 firms in the North American electronics industry [Burrill & Almassy 1993] showed that in 1987 53% of the firms in the industry were operating domestically. In 1992, only 17% were domestic, and by 1997 only 9% were expected to be. A third of the firms surveyed were still in development with less than $5 million in revenue.

The fact that the business press believes the emerging phenomenon of international new ventures is important and that some academics working independently around the world have described similar organizations indicates a need for systematic research on these infrequently studied new ventures. However, the overall purpose of this paper is not to add to the growing descriptions of particular international new ventures. Rather, it is to define and describe the phenomenon and to present a framework explaining how international new ventures fit within the theory of the MNE. We hope that a well-delineated, theoretical framework will unify, stimulate and guide research in the area.

The next section provides a formal definition of

international new ventures. Following that, certain problems are considered regarding the application of standard MNE concepts to international new ventures. Next, a theoretical framework explaining international new ventures is presented. It integrates accepted MNE theory with recent developments in entrepreneurship and strategic management research. Finally, four types of international new ventures are described in terms of our international new venture framework, the number of value chain activities they coordinate [Porter 1985], and the number of countries in which they operate.

A DEFINITION OF INTERNATIONAL NEW VENTURES

We define an *international new venture as a business organization that, from inception, seeks to derive significant competitive advantage from the use of resources and the sale of outputs in multiple countries.* The distinguishing feature of these start-ups is that their origins are international, as demonstrated by observable and significant commitments of resources (e.g., material, people, financing, time) in more than one nation. The focus here is on the age of firms when they become international, not on their size. In contrast to organizations that evolve gradually from domestic firms to MNEs, these new ventures begin with a proactive international strategy. However, they do not necessarily own foreign assets; in other words, foreign direct investment is not a requirement. Strategic alliances may be arranged for the use of foreign resources such as manufacturing capacity or marketing. Thus, consistent with Buckley and Casson's [1976] definition of the multinational enterprise, the definition of the international new venture is concerned with value added, not assets owned [Casson 1982].

The fact that international new ventures are international from inception implies that some decision must inevitably be made about when inception occurs. Much has been written in the entrepreneurship literature concerning the point at which a new venture is considered to exist as an organization (e.g.,

Katz & Gartner [1988]). However, Vesper argued that there can be no ultimate resolution, because the emergence of a venture is "spread over time in which its existence becomes progressively more established" [1990, p. 97]. Thus, empirical studies of international new ventures must resolve a definitional ambiguity. We believe researchers should rely on observable resource commitments to establish a point of venture inception. For new ventures that have no sales because their product or service is under development, there must be a demonstrated commitment to sell the output in multiple countries upon completion of development.

PROBLEMS IN THE APPLICATION OF MNE THEORY TO INTERNATIONAL NEW VENTURES

Stage theories of the MNE and the common emphasis on organizational scale as an important competitive advantage in the international arena are inappropriate explanations of multinational business activity for new ventures that are instantly international.

THE STAGE THEORY OF MNE EVOLUTION

MNEs are believed by many people to evolve only after a period of domestic maturation and home market saturation [Caves 1982; Porter 1990]. Empirical researchers have in the past found that large, mature MNEs and small exporters go through distinct stages in the development of their international business. They begin perhaps with an unsolicited foreign order, proceed sometimes through exporting and the development of an international division, and occasionally advance to the establishment of a fully integrated, global enterprise [Aharoni 1966; Bilkey & Tesar 1977; Czinkota & Johnston 1981; Stopford & Wells 1972].

This staged development of firm internationalization is described as an incremental, risk-averse and reluctant adjustment to changes in a firm or its environment [Johanson & Vahlne 1977, 1990]. The process preserves routines that bind organizational coalitions, and recognizes the difficulty of gaining knowledge about foreign markets. Differences in language and culture and, in the past, the slow speed of communication and transportation channels between countries have inhibited the gathering of information about foreign markets and have increased the perceived risks of foreign operation.

With a logical explanatory theory and repeated empirical confirmation, stage models of MNE development have been transformed from descriptive models, and "were soon applied prescriptively by consultants, academics, and managers alike" [Bartlett & Ghoshal 1991, p. 31]. In addition, Caves indicated that international firms must experience an extended evolutionary process when he directly contrasted MNEs with "newly organized firms" [1982, p. 96]. However, recent studies have found contradictions. For example, Welch and Luostarinen [1988] discussed reports of small English firms, Australian start-ups, and established Swedish firms that skipped important stages and were involved with unexpected speed in direct foreign investments. In addition, Sullivan and Bauerschmidt [1990] found that a firm's stage of international involvement was an unexpectedly poor predictor of European managers' knowledge and beliefs. Finally, Turnbull [1987] presents a strong conceptual and empirical criticism of the stages theory of internationalization.

Johanson and Vahlne [1990] dismissed these concerns as merely indicative of the need for adjustment to their model of firm internationalization. We believe, however, that the emergence of international new ventures presents a unique challenge to stage theory. It purportedly best applies to the early stages of internationalization with only three exceptions [Johanson & Vahlne 1990]. First, firms with large resources are expected to take large steps toward internationalization. Second, when foreign market conditions are stable and homogeneous, learning about them is easier. Third, when firms have considerable experience with markets that are similar to a newly targeted foreign market, previous experience may be generalizable to the new arena. Yet none of the exceptions seem to apply to international new ventures. Resources are constrained by their young age and usually by small size. Their markets are among the most volatile (indeed, several of the inter-

national new ventures we have studied appear to contribute to industry volatility). Finally, new ventures, by definition, have little or no experience in any market. Therefore, according to Johanson and Vahlne's [1990] own standards, stage theory needs more than a minor adjustment.

SCALE AND THE MNE

In addition to the belief that firms must go through stages of evolution before venturing into foreign lands, large size is often thought to be a requirement for multinationality. The first modern MNEs evolved in the 1880s and 1890s and were large, mature, integrated companies [Chandler 1986]. They and their descendants have reaped substantial economies of scale in R&D, production, marketing, and other areas. An additional advantage of large, vertically integrated or diversified MNEs has been their ability to efficiently manage international communication and transportation and the exchange of production and market information among many countries [Stopford & Wells 1972]. In addition, their market power in oligopolistic industries has been highlighted as a source of MNE advantage [Dunning 1981; Glickman & Woodward 1989; Porter 1990].

Yet, if large size were a requirement for multinationality, international new ventures would seldom form because they are almost always small organizations. One key to understanding how they can exist is to recognize that large size may be both a cause and an effect of multinational competitive advantage. In some industries, such as pharmaceuticals, the sales volume generated by multinational operation makes feasible a large-scale R&D effort. In turn, R&D produces differentiated products, such as patented drugs, that provide competitive advantages over purely domestic firms in many countries. Thus, despite the fact that size is the main firm-specific variable that has explained multinationality [Glickman & Woodward 1989], large MNE size may be a concomitant, not a cause, of other more elemental sources of competitive advantage [Casson 1987; Caves 1982]. Those more elemental sources of advantage make international new ventures possible.

THE CHANGING INTERNATIONAL ENVIRONMENT

Although large size continues to be an important source of advantage for some MNEs, changing economic, technological, and social conditions have in recent years highlighted additional sources. Dramatic increases in the speed, quality, and efficiency of international communication and transportation have reduced the transaction costs of multinational interchange [Porter 1990]. Furthermore, the increasing homogenization of many markets in distant countries has made the conduct of international business easier to understand for everyone [Hedlund & Kverneland 1985]. The upshot is that increasing numbers of business executives and entrepreneurs have been exposed to international business. International financing opportunities are increasingly available [Patricof 1989; Valeriano 1991]. And human capital is more internationally mobile [Johnston 1991; Reich 1991].

With such conditions, markets now link countries more efficiently than in the past, and the hierarchies of large, established firms no longer have the competitive advantage they once enjoyed in international communication and trade [*The Economist* 1993a]. Internationally sustainable advantage is increasingly recognized to depend on the possession of unique assets [Barney 1991; Caves 1982; Hamel & Prahalad 1990; Stalk, Evans & Shulman 1992].

A priori, valuable unique assets should permit organizations with more constrained resources, such as new ventures, to enter the international arena. In addition, improved international communication and transportation along with the homogenization of markets in many countries should, a priori, simplify and shorten the process of firm internationalization. Thus, firms may skip stages of international development that have been observed in the past, or internationalization may not occur in stages at all.

We believe that is precisely what has been observed recently by a number of business journalists and business academicians—firms not following the theories of incremental firm internationalization. However, that does not mean that established theories are wrong; they still apply to some firms and industries. Yet it does mean that the established theories are less applicable in an expanding number of situations where technology, specific industry environments, and firm capabilities have changed as we have described.

NECESSARY AND SUFFICIENT ELEMENTS FOR SUSTAINABLE INTERNATIONAL NEW VENTURES

With many markets internationalizing, fewer new ventures can escape confrontations with foreign competition, and more entrepreneurs are adopting a multinational viewpoint [Drucker 1991; Ohmae 1990; Porter 1986, 1990]. Thus, the stage theory of firm internationalization is increasingly incongruent with recent developments, and large scale has become only one among many ways to compete internationally. As a result, a new framework is needed to lead both theoretical development and empirical investigation toward greater understanding of international new ventures.

The foundation of the theoretical framework that we propose is traditional in its reliance on transaction cost analysis, market imperfections, and the international internalization of essential transactions to explain the existence of the MNE. However, the framework also incorporates recently developed ideas from entrepreneurship scholars about how ventures gain influence over vital resources without owning them and from strategic management scholars about how competitive advantage is developed and sustained. Together, all these elements describe the international new venture as a special kind of MNE.

Essentially, the theoretical framework is an elaboration of Figure 1 (shown earlier), which classifies four types of organizations by age and geographic scope. Figure 2 depicts the framework. The boxes show sets of economic transactions that are of particular interest in this paper. The arrows represent elements that distinguish a subset from a larger set of transactions.

The framework begins with the box at the upper left, which is the set of all types of *Economic Transactions*. Four necessary and sufficient elements, which are enumerated within the large arrows, pro-

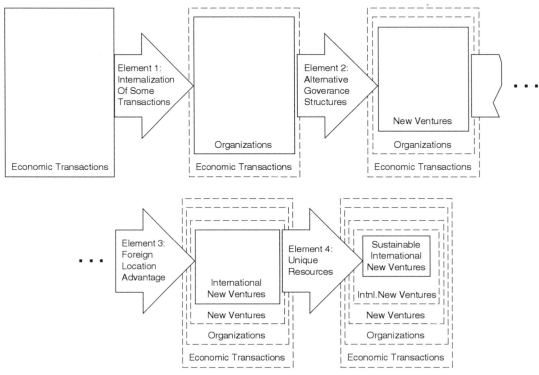

Figure 2. Necessary and Sufficient Elements for Sustainable International New Ventures.

gressively distinguish subsets of transactions. "Element 1: Internalization of Some Transactions" distinguishes transactions that take place in *Organizations* from those that are governed by markets. From the set of all *Organizations,* strong reliance on "Element 2: Alternative Governance Structures" separates the subset of transactions associated with *New Ventures* from those in established firms. Next, "Element 3: Foreign Location Advantage" distinguishes the subset of transactions constituting *International New Ventures* from those that constitute domestic new ventures. Finally, "Element 4: Unique Resources" differentiates the subset of *Sustainable International New Ventures* from those likely to be short-lived. The dashed concentric boxes highlight the fact that the interior boxes depict the progressively more narrow subsets, and the shading shows the path of our narrowing interests. The effects of the four elements are fully described in the sections below.

ELEMENT 1: INTERNALIZATION OF SOME TRANSACTIONS

The internalization element is most basic and is clearly part of traditional MNE theory. Organizations form where economic transactions are inefficiently governed by market prices [Coase 1937; Williamson 1985]; in other words, where market imperfections exist. It is the defining element of all organizations, whether new or established, domestic or multinational. When the transaction costs of constructing and executing a contract and monitoring the performance of the contracting parties are at their lowest in an organization, its hierarchical authority (not market prices or a hybrid contract) will be the governance mechanism chosen, and the transaction is said to have been internalized within an organization [Buckley & Casson 1976; Dunning 1981, 1988].

It should be noted that the internalization element of MNE theory is often used to explain foreign direct investment; that is, ownership of assets located in foreign countries. Indeed, Hymer's [1960] seminal work on the internalization of international transactions was among the first theoretical presentations to distinguish between passive portfolio investment and foreign direct investment, and it focused on explaining the latter. Nevertheless, *ownership* of foreign assets is not a defining characteristic of either MNEs or international new ventures [Casson 1982]. Of course, an organization must own some assets, else it will have nothing of value to exchange in an economic transaction.

ELEMENT 2: ALTERNATIVE GOVERNANCE STRUCTURES

Poverty of resources and power may not be a defining characteristic of the new venture, but it is a nearly universal association [Stinchcombe 1965; Vesper 1990]. Thus, new ventures commonly lack sufficient resources to control many assets through ownership. The result is that new ventures tend to internalize, or own, a smaller percentage of the resources essential to their survival than do mature organizations. Entrepreneurs must rely on alternative modes of controlling many vital assets [Vesper 1990], and that fact distinguishes new ventures from other organizations.

Williamson [1991] noted that under conditions of moderate asset specificity and low to moderate disturbance frequency, hybrid structures, such as licensing, and franchising, are often useful alternatives to both internal control and market control over the exchange of resources. Hybrid partners share complementary assets to their mutual benefit. However, due to the potential for opportunism, as evidenced by the elaborate contracts that usually structure the relationships between the parties and the frequent reports of hybrid failure [Kanter 1989; Porter & Fuller 1986], new ventures risk expropriation by their hybrid partners of the valuable assets that they do own [Teece 1987]. Large Japanese firms, for example, have sometimes appeared to form predatory alliances with American high-technology start-ups.

An even more powerful resource-conserving alternative to internalization for new ventures is the net-

work structure [Aldrich & Zimmer 1986; Larson 1992]. Networks depend on the social (i.e., informal) control of behavior through trust and moral obligation, not formal contracts. Cooperation dominates opportunism because business and personal reputations are at stake that may greatly affect economic rent in and beyond a spot transaction. Larson's [1992] rich description of the gains in resources and knowledge of four entrepreneurial organizations in seven intimate network alliances is impressive. Yet risks were also clear. Two of the seven relationships failed after many years of successful operation, leaving both partners with weaknesses. Nevertheless, even after failure, proprietary knowledge was protected and trust was maintained.

In summary, a major feature that distinguishes new ventures from established organizations is the minimal use of internalization and the greater use of alternative transaction governance structures. Due to their poverty of resources and power, new ventures may even use such structures when the risk of asset expropriation by hybrid partners is high.

ELEMENT 3: FOREIGN LOCATION ADVANTAGE

The location advantage element of the framework distinguishes international from domestic organizations. Essentially, firms are international because they find advantage in transferring some moveable resources (e.g., raw material, knowledge, intermediate products) across a national border to be combined with an immobile, or less mobile, resource or opportunity (e.g., raw material, a market) [Dunning 1988].

However, a firm conducting transactions in a foreign country has certain disadvantages vis-à-vis indigenous firms, such as governmentally instituted barriers to trade and an incomplete understanding of laws, language, and business practices in foreign countries. As noted earlier, MNEs have often relied on the advantages of scale to overcome such obstacles. But international new ventures must usually rely on other resources.

Private knowledge is the most obvious alternative, and it has some interesting properties [Buckley & Casson 1976; Caves 1982; Rugman 1982]. The property that provides location advantage for modern

MNEs, including international new ventures, is the great mobility of knowledge once it is produced. With modern communication infrastructures, valuable knowledge can be reproduced and can travel literally with the speed of light at minimal marginal cost. For example, software often requires years of development, but once written, it may be copied and used ad infinitum with insignificant additional costs. Knowledge can then be combined with less mobile resources in multiple countries (e.g., factories where the software is needed). Thus, private knowledge may create differentiation or cost advantages for MNEs and international new ventures that overcome the advantages of indigenous firms in many countries simultaneously.

That appears to be why knowledge-intensive industries have been globalizing at such a rapid pace [Reich 1991], and why a new venture with valuable knowledge is propelled to instant rather than evolutionary internationalization. When a firm introduces valuable innovative goods or services it signals at least the existence, if not the essence, of its special knowledge to outsiders.

Competitors, therefore, will try to uncover the secret or to produce equifinal alternative knowledge, and the recent increased efficiency of international markets speeds the whole competitive process. New ventures confronted with such circumstances must be international from inception or be at a disadvantage to other organizations that are international already. Thus, the prevalence of international new ventures is predicted to accompany the increasing efficiency of international markets.

ELEMENT 4: UNIQUE RESOURCES

The first three elements define the necessary conditions for the existence of an international new venture: Internalization of some transactions, extensive use of alternative transaction governance structures, and some advantage over indigenous firms in foreign locations. However, these are not sufficient conditions for sustainable competitive advantage.

Sustainable competitive advantage for any firm requires that its resources be unique [Barney 1991]. Unfortunately, for the knowledge-based international new venture, knowledge is at least to some degree a public good. Its easy dissemination threatens a firm's rent-earning opportunity because knowledge may not remain unique for long. Thus, the ability to reproduce and move knowledge at nearly zero marginal cost, is a simultaneously beneficial (as noted in Element 3) and troublesome property. The international new venture must limit the use of its knowledge by outsiders in many countries for it to have commercial value. In general, the use of such knowledge may be limited by four conditions.

First, if knowledge can be kept proprietary by direct means, such as patents, copyrights, or trade secrets, then the possessor of internalized valuable and rare knowledge may be able to prevent imitation and slow the development of substitutes. Yet patents and copyrights are ignored in some countries. Even where they are respected, release of patented knowledge into a market may advance competitors' production of alternative or even improved technology. Thus, knowledge that has potential commercial value is often best protected with secrecy.

Imperfect imitability is the second condition that may keep expropriable knowledge proprietary [Barney 1991; Schoemaker 1990]. A unique organizational history, socially complex knowledge, and ambiguous causal relationships between knowledge and the competitive advantage it provides may all prevent imitation by competitors. New ventures often claim their unique management style and organizational culture provide advantages, perhaps because they embody all three characteristics of imperfect imitability. However, it should be noted that these same characteristics that block competitors' imitations may constrain the spread of such intangible assets as management style into multiple national cultures within the same organization. Yet where it can be accomplished, the inimitability of an international new venture is further reinforced.

Licensing is the third way outside use of a venture's knowledge may be limited. When knowledge is expected to retain its value for a lengthy period, a limit pricing strategy (i.e., low license fees) may be used to discourage competitors or to influence the rate and direction of knowledge dissemination. When demand is strong for expropriable knowledge, but its valuable life is believed to be short (e.g., some personal computer innovations), high fees may be used to extract maximum rents over a short period.

The fact that new ventures frequently use network governance structures (as discussed under Element 2) is the fourth condition that may limit the expropriation of venture knowledge. Although alliances with complementary organizations, such as manufacturers and downstream channels, risk expropriation [Teece 1987], the network structure itself tends to control the risk. The relationships inherent in a network can have high personal and economic value because network members usually share rents and the relationships contrast so starkly with the usual background of economic opportunism [Larson 1992]. Thus, venture network members are at least somewhat inhibited from usurping the venture's knowledge. For such relationships to exist in new ventures that cross national borders, logic suggests that founding teams must usually include internationally experienced business persons of various national origins.

TYPES OF INTERNATIONAL NEW VENTURES

The previous section described basic elements for all sustainable international new ventures, but the published papers that describe actual cases indicate that these elements manifest themselves in a variety of ways. Some ventures actively coordinate the transformation of resources from many parts of the world into outputs that are sold wherever they are most highly valued [McDougall & Oviatt 1991]. Other international new ventures are primarily exporters that add value by moving outputs from where they are to locations where they are needed [Ray 1989]. In the sections that follow, different types of international new ventures will be identified, some published examples will be considered briefly, and the variety of ways that the necessary and sufficient elements are manifested will be described.

Figure 3 shows that different types of international new ventures may be distinguished by the number of value chain activities that are coordinated and by the number of countries entered. The figure identifies particular types of firms at the extremes of the two continua, but mixed types certainly appear in between, and over time new ventures may change type by coordinating additional or fewer activities and by operating in additional or fewer countries. Although the figure uses Porter's [1985] value chain and is similar to Porter's [1986] depiction of international strategy for established MNEs, Figure 3 focuses on international new ventures only. In addition, the horizontal dimension of Figure 3 simply concerns the number of countries in which any value chain activities occur. Porter's diagram focuses on the degree of dispersion among activities when sales are assumed to be in many countries.

NEW INTERNATIONAL MARKET MAKERS (FIGURE 3, QUADRANTS I AND II)

New International Market Makers are an age-old type of firm. Importers and exporters profit by moving goods from nations where they are to nations where they are demanded. The most important value chain activities and, therefore, the ones most likely to be internalized are the systems and knowledge of inbound and outbound logistics. Transactions involving other activities tend to be governed by alternative structures. Direct investment in any country is typically kept at a minimum. The location advantage of such new ventures lies in their ability to discover imbalances of resources between countries and in creating markets where none existed. Sustained competitive advantage depends on (1) unusual abilities to spot and act on (sometimes by charging high fees) emerging opportunities before increased competition reduces profits in markets they had previously established, (2) knowledge of markets and suppliers, and (3) the ability to attract and maintain a loyal network of business associates. New International Market Makers may be either Export/Import Start-ups or Multinational Traders. Export/Import Start-ups focus on serving a few nations with which the entrepreneur is familiar. Multinational Traders serve an array of countries and are constantly scan-

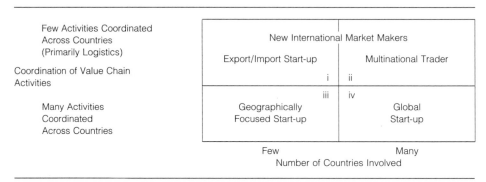

Figure 3. Types of International New Ventures.

ning for trading opportunities where their networks are established or where they can quickly be set up.

GEOGRAPHICALLY FOCUSED START-UPS (FIGURE 3, QUADRANT III)

Geographically Focused Start-ups derive advantages by serving well the specialized needs of a particular region of the world through the use of foreign resources. They differ from the Multinational Trader in that they are geographically restricted to the location of the specialized need, and more than just the activities of inbound and outbound logistics are coordinated. They differ from the Export/Import Start-up only in the latter respect. In other words, competitive advantage is found in the coordination of multiple value chain activities, such as technological development, human resources, and production. Successful coordination may be inimitable because it is socially complex or involves tacit knowledge. That advantage may be further protected by a close and exclusive network of alliances in the geographical area served.

For example, in recent years, numerous entrepreneurs have established firms to profit from the transfer of Western management and economic know-how to formerly communist countries. *Profit* magazine was formed by two former editors of *Soldier of Fortune* magazine who were familiar with Eastern Europe [McDougall & Oviatt 1991]. It published practical advice for Eastern European entrepreneurs, and it was written by or about successful entrepreneurs in the United States who came from Eastern Europe. The first issue of the magazine was printed in the Czech Republic with English and Czech translations on facing pages and was distributed by a Czech entrepreneur who shared the profits. Additional versions were planned for other European countries emerging from centrally planned to market-driven economies. However, there was no strategy to move beyond that geographic region because their competitive advantage was in their unique knowledge of the Eastern European culture and their ability to establish a network there.

GLOBAL START-UPS (FIGURE 3, QUADRANT IV)

The phrase ''Global Start-up'' is used because it is a common term of trade [Mamis 1989]. It is the most radical manifestation of the international new venture because it derives significant competitive advantage from extensive coordination among multiple organizational activities, the locations of which are geographically unlimited. Such firms not only respond to globalizing markets, but also proactively act on opportunities to acquire resources and sell outputs wherever in the world they have the greatest value.

Global Start-ups may be the most difficult international new ventures to develop because they require skills at both geographic and activity coordination. However, once successfully established, they appear to have the most sustainable competitive advantages due to a combination of historically unique, causally ambiguous, and socially complex inimitability with close network alliances in multiple countries. One global start-up we studied identified its "proprietary network" as its essential competitive advantage.

Another example was Momenta Corporation of Mountain View, California [Bhide 1991; McDougall & Oviatt 1991], a start-up in the emerging pen-based computer market. Its founders were from Cuba, Iran, Tanzania, and the United States. From its beginning in 1989, the founders wanted the venture to be global in its acquisition of inputs and in its target market. A global market would permit rapid growth and was believed to be necessary because potential competitors were global. Input acquisition was global because all the highest value (i.e., high quality to cost ratio) factors of production were not to be found in any single country. Thus, software design was conducted in the United States, hardware design in Germany, manufacturing in the Pacific Rim, and funding was received from Taiwan, Singapore, Europe, and the United States.

CONCLUSION

This article has identified, defined and described the emerging phenomenon of international new ventures, and has shown that some current theories of the MNE do not explain it well. Most important, it has integrated the traditional MNE concepts of internalization and location advantage with recent entrepreneurship research on alternative governance structures and with developments in strategic management on the requirements for sustainable competitive advantage. The result is a rich yet parsimonious theoretical framework that explains the existence of international new ventures, and appears useful in describing their distinct types.

Our framework describes sustainable international new ventures as controlling assets, especially unique knowledge, that create value in more than one country. Their internationality occurs at inception largely because competitive forces preclude a successful domestic focus. Their emphasis on controlling rather than owning assets is due to resource scarcity that is common among new organizations.

The framework indicates that empirical investigators interested in international new ventures will find larger sample sizes in industries where international competition for unique knowledge is a dominant characteristic. The framework also identifies ways of protecting rents derived from such knowledge (i.e., direct patent protection, uncertain imitability, license fees, and network alliances), but empirical research is needed to understand the differential success of these mechanisms more completely.

This article is partially a response to Casson's [1985] call to include the role of the entrepreneur in explaining the dynamics of the MNE. The defensive role of network formation and, thus, the importance of social interaction by entrepreneurs is highlighted. Although networks certainly provide vital information, their function as a defense against the expropriation of tenuously defended valuable and rare knowledge needs more attention. How unusual are the intimate alliances that Larson [1992] describes, and what social and economic processes and conditions promote network building across national borders? Although entrepreneurship scholars have examined some of these issues within various countries (e.g., Aldrich, Birley, Dubini, Greve, Johannisson, Reese & Sakano [1991]), we are unaware of investigations that explicitly include a sample of international new ventures.

Considering a wider arena, it may be recognized that our emphasis on the importance of alternative governance structures for new ventures is consistent with the advice of some scholars that all organizations may find advantages in outsourcing [Quinn, Doorley & Paquette 1990] and impartitioning [Barreyre 1988]. The primary advantages are (1) increased concentration of limited resources on the primary internal sources of competitive advantage and (2) the cost, quality and flexibility benefits that may be derived from using outside experts to supply all peripheral resources. However, the risks of dissipating competitive advantages, losing opportunities for learning, and becoming a "hollow corporation" are significant [Teece 1987]. The existence of international new ventures that must outsource many inputs provides a natural laboratory from which to gain insight into the results of this trade-off.

REFERENCES

Aharoni, Yair. 1966. *The foreign investment decision process.* Boston: Division of Research, Graduate School of Business Administration, Harvard University.

Aldrich, Howard & Catherine Zimmer. 1986. Entrepreneurship through social networks. In Donald L. Sexton & Raymond W. Smilor, editors, *The art and science of entrepreneurship.* Cambridge, MA: Ballinger.

Aldrich, Howard E., Sue Birley, Paola Dubini, Arent Greve, Bengt Johannisson, Pat R. Reese & Tomoaki Sakano. 1991. The generic entrepreneur? Insights from a multinational research project. Paper presented at the Babson Entrepreneurship Research Conference, Pittsburgh.

Anderson, Ray. 1992. Personal interview, June 23.

Barney, Jay. 1991. Firm resources and sustained competitive advantage. *Journal of Management,* 17: 99–120.

Barreyre, P.Y. 1988. The concept of 'impartition' policies: A different approach to vertical integration strategies. *Strategic Management Journal,* 9: 507–20.

Bartlett, Christopher A. & Sumantra Ghoshal. 1991. *Managing across borders.* Boston: Harvard Business School Press.

Bhide, Amar. 1991. Momenta Corporation (A) and (B). Case numbers N9-392-013 and N9-392-014. Boston: Harvard Business School, Harvard College.

Bilkey, Warren J. & George Tesar. 1977. The export behavior of smaller sized Wisconsin manufacturing firms. *Journal of International Business Studies,* 3(Spring/Summer): 93–98.

Brokaw, Leslie. 1990. Foreign affairs. *Inc.,* November: 92–104.

Brush, Candida G. 1992. *Factors motivating small companies to internationalize: The effect of firm age.* Unpublished dissertation. Boston University.

Buckley, Peter J. & Mark Casson. 1976. *The future of the multinational enterprise.* New York: Holmes & Meier.

Burrill, G. Steven & Stephen E. Almassy. 1993. *Electronics '93 the new global reality: Ernst & Young's fourth annual report on the electronics industry.* San Francisco: Ernst & Young.

Casson, Mark. 1982. Transaction costs and the theory of the multinational enterprise. In Alan M. Rugman, editor, *New theories of the multinational enterprise.* New York: St. Martin's Press.

———. 1987. *The firm and the market.* Cambridge, MA: The MIT Press.

———. 1985. Entrepreneurship and the dynamics of foreign direct investment. In Peter J. Buckley & Mark Casson, *The economic theory of the multinational enterprise.* New York: St. Martin's Press.

Caves, Richard E. 1982. *Multinational enterprise and economic analysis.* Cambridge, MA: Cambridge University Press.

Chandler, Alfred D., Jr. 1977. *The visible hand.* Cambridge, MA: The Belknap Press.

———. 1986. The evolution of modern global competition. In Michael E. Porter, editor, *Competition in global industries,* 405–48. Boston: Harvard Business School Press.

Coase, Ronald H. 1937. The nature of the firm. *Economica N. S.,* 4: 386–405.

Cooper, Robert G. & Elko J. Kleinschmidt. 1985. The impact of export strategy on export sales performance. *Journal of International Business Studies,* 15: 37–55.

Coviello, Nicole & Hugh Munro. 1992. Internationalizing the entrepreneurial technology-intensive firm: Growth through linkage development. Paper presented at the Babson Entrepreneurship Research Conference, INSEAD, France.

Czinkota, Michael R. & Wesley J. Johnston. 1981. Segmenting U.S. firms for export development. *Journal of Business Research,* 9: 353–65.

Drucker, Peter F. 1991 (second edition). The changed world economy. In Heidi Vernon-Wortzel & Lawrence H. Wortzel, editors, *Global strategic management.* New York: Wiley.

Dunning, John H. 1981. *International production and the multinational enterprise.* London: George Allen & Unwin.

———. 1988. The eclectic paradigm of international production: A restatement and some possible extensions. *Journal of International Business Studies,* 19: 1–31.

The Economist. 1992. Go west, young firm. May 9: 88–89.

———. 1993a. The fall of big business. April 17: 13–14.

———. 1993b. America's little fellows surge ahead. July 3: 59–60.

Ganitsky, Joseph. 1989. Strategies for innate and adoptive exporters: Lessons from Israel's case. *International Marketing Review,* 6(5): 50–65.

Glickman, Norman J. & Douglas P. Woodward. 1989. *The new competitors.* New York: Basic Books.

Gupta, Udayan. 1989. Small firms aren't waiting to grow up to go global. *The Wall Street Journal,* December 5: B2.

Hamel, Gary & C.K. Prahalad. 1990. The core competence of the corporation. *Harvard Business Review,* 68(3): 79–91.

Hedlund, Gunnar & Adne Kverneland. 1985. Are strategies for foreign markets changing? The case of Swedish investment in Japan. *International Studies of Management and Organization,* 15(2): 41–59.

Hennart, Jean-Francois. 1982. *A theory of multinational enterprise.* Ann Arbor: The University of Michigan Press.

Hoy, Frank, Miroslav Pivoda & Svatopluk Mackrle. 1992. A virus theory of organizational transformation. Paper presented at Babson Entrepreneurship Research Conference, INSEAD, Fontainebleau, France.

Hymer, Stephen H. 1960. *The international operations of national firms: A study of direct foreign investment.* Cambridge, MA: The MIT Press (published in 1976).

Johanson, Jan & Jan-Erik Vahlne. 1977. The internationalization process of the firm—A model of knowledge development and increasing foreign market commitment. *Journal of International Business Studies,* 8(1): 23–32.

———. 1990. The mechanism of internationalization. *International Marketing Review,* 7(4): 11–24.

Johnston, William B. 1991. Global work force 2000: The new world labor market. *Harvard Business Review,* 69(2): 115–127.

Jolly, Vijay K., Matti Alahuhta & Jean-Pierre Jeannet. 1992. Challenging the incumbents: How high technology start-ups compete globally. *Journal of Strategic Change,* 1: 71–82.

Kanter, Rosabeth M. 1989. Becoming PALs: Pooling, allying, and linking across companies. *Academy of Management Executive,* 3: 183–93.

Katz, Jerome & William B. Gartner. 1988. Properties of emerging organizations. *Academy of Management Review,* 13: 429–41.

Kedia, Ben L. & Jagdeep Chhokar. 1985. The impact of managerial attitudes on export behavior. *American Journal of Small Business,* Fall: 7–17.

Larson, Andrea. 1992. Network dyads in entrepreneurial settings: A study of the governance of exchange relationships. *Administrative Science Quarterly,* 37: 76–104.

Malekzadeh, Ali R. & Afsaneh Nahavandi. 1985. Small business exporting: Misconceptions are abundant. *American Journal of Small Business,* 9(4): 7–14.

Mamis, Robert A. 1989. Global start-up. *Inc.,* August: 38–47.

McDougall, Patricia P. & Benjamin M. Oviatt. 1991. Global start-ups: New ventures without geographic limits. *The Entrepreneurship Forum,* Winter: 1–5.

——— & Candida Brush. 1991. A symposium on global start-ups: Entrepreneurial firms that are born international. Presentation at the annual Academy of Management meeting, August, Miami.

McDougall, Patricia P., Scott Shane & Benjamin M. Oviatt. 1994. Explaining the formation of international new ventures: The limits of theories from international business research. *Journal of Business Venturing,* forthcoming.

Ohe, Takeru, Shuji Honjo, Mark Oliva & Ian C. MacMillan. 1991. Entrepreneurs in Japan and Silicon Valley: A study of perceived differences. *Journal of Business Venturing,* 6: 135–44.

Ohmae, Kenichi. 1990. *The borderless world.* New York: HarperBusiness.

Oviatt, Benjamin M., Patricia P. McDougall, Mark Simon & Rodney C. Shrader. 1994. Heartware International Corporation: A medical equipment company ''born international.'' *Entrepreneurship Theory and Practice,* forthcoming.

Patricof, Alan. 1989. The internationalization of venture capital. *Journal of Business Venturing,* 4: 227–30.

Porter, Michael E. 1985. *Competitive advantage.* New York: The Free Press.

———. 1986. Competition in global industries: A conceptual framework. In Michael E. Porter, editor, *Competition in global industries.* Boston: Harvard Business School Press.

———. 1990. *The competitive advantage of nations.* New York: The Free Press.

——— & Mark B. Fuller. 1986. Coalitions and global strategy. In Michael E. Porter, editor, *Competition in global industries.* Boston: Harvard Business School Press.

Quinn, James B., Thomas L. Doorley & Penny C. Paquette. 1990. Technology in services: Rethinking strategic focus. *Sloan Management Review.*

Ray, Dennis M. 1989. Entrepreneurial companies 'born' international: Four case studies. Paper presented at Babson Entrepreneurship Research Conference on Entrepreneurship, St. Louis.

Reich, Robert B. 1991. *The work of nations.* New York: Alfred A. Knopf.

Rossman, Marlene L. 1984. Export trading company legislation: U.S. response to Japanese foreign market penetration. *Journal of Small Business Management,* October: 62–66.

Rugman, Alan M. 1982. Internalization and non-equity forms of international involvement. In Alan M. Rugman, editor, *New theories of the multinational enterprise.* New York: St. Martin's Press.

Schoemaker, Paul J.H. 1990. Strategy, complexity, and economic rent. *Management Science,* 10: 1178–92.

Stalk, George, Philip Evans & Lawrence E. Shulman. 1992. Competing on capabilities: The new rules of corporate strategy. *Harvard Business Review,* 70(2): 57–69.

Stinchcombe, Arthur L. 1965. Social structure and organizations. In James G. March, editor, *Handbook of organizations,* 142–93. Chicago: Rand McNally.

Stopford, John M. & Louis T. Wells. 1972. *Managing the multinational enterprise.* New York: Basic Books.

Sullivan, Daniel & Alan Bauerschmidt. 1990. Incremental internationalization: A test of Johanson and Vahlne's thesis. *Management International Review,* 30(1): 19–30.

Teece, David J. 1987. Profiting from technological innovation: Implications for integration, collaboration, licensing, and public policy. In David J. Teece, editor, *The competitive challenge.* Cambridge, MA: Ballinger.

Turnbull, P.W. 1987. A challenge to the stages theory of the internationalization process. In Philip J. Rosson & Stanley D. Reid, editors, *Managing export entry and expansion.* New York: Praeger.

Valeriano, Lourdes L. 1991. Other Asians follow Japanese as investors in U.S. firms. *Wall Street Journal,* January 7: B2.

Vesper, Karl H. 1990 (revised edition). *New venture strategies.* Englewood Cliffs, NJ: Prentice Hall.

Vozikis, George S. & Timothy S. Mescon. 1985. Small exporters and stages of development: An empirical study. *American Journal of Small Business,* 9: 49–64.

Welch, Lawrence S. & Reijo Luostarinen. 1988. Internationalization: Evolution of a concept. *Journal of General Management,* 14(2): 34–55.

Westhead, Paul. 1990. A typology of new manufacturing firm founders in Wales: Performance measures and public policy implications. *Journal of Business Venturing,* 5: 103–22.

Wilkins, Mira. 1970. *The emergence of multinational enterprise.* Cambridge, MA: Harvard University Press.

——— & F.E. Hill. 1964. *American business abroad: Ford on six continents.* Detroit: Wayne State University Press.

Williamson, Oliver E. 1991. Comparative economic organization: The analysis of discrete structural alternatives. *Administrative Science Quarterly,* 36: 269–96.

———. 1985. *The economic institutions of capitalism.* New York: The Free Press.

SECTION 3A

COMPETITIVE ANALYSIS AND STRATEGIC PLANNING: THE CORPORATE VIEW

No business, whether domestic or global, will prosper unless it can identify opportunities to develop a competitive advantage and then capitalize on those opportunities. The tasks of competitive analysis and strategic planning are central to building a competitive advantage. Competitive analysis and strategic planning are complex exercises for businesses that are purely domestic. Where the scope of the business is international or global, the complexities multiply.

As the geographic scope of business broadens, business strategists must contend with a considerably wider variety of competitors, consumers, and business environments. The multinational or global firm must compete not only against domestic firms in each country in which it markets, but also worldwide against other multinational and global firms. Domestic firms as well must take into account foreign competitors as they plan. In many countries, domestic firms' toughest competitors are not other domestics, but multinationals and global firms headquartered elsewhere.

The core problem of strategic planning, specifying the products with which the business will compete and the markets in which it will compete with those products, is common to both the smallest domestic and the largest global business. But this problem is considerably more difficult for the multinational or global firm to handle.

To market automobiles in any one country, for example, General Motors must identify consumer segments and then design and position specific cars for each segment in which it wants to compete. It must go through a similar segmentation and positioning exercise for each country in which it wants to market. Then it must develop a product line that takes into account manufacturing and shipping economics as well as consumer desires. In sum, it must undertake those activities that give it the maximum competitive advantage in each country.

A product line consideration specific to multinational and global firms is whether they should standardize their products worldwide or customize them for individual countries or even regions. The advantage of one strategy over the other has been the subject of much debate. For the firm's standpoint, the advantages of standardization are clear: The result is a much simpler, more easily managed business that may be

125

able to offer lower prices than competitors offering customized products. Consumers, on the other hand, may be willing to pay somewhat more for a customized product they believe will fit their needs more precisely.

In many industries, choosing the right production location(s) is also critical to maintaining a competitive advantage. This is true for domestic firms and even more so for multinational and global firms. With so many potential sites around the world, the choices are not easy because the many issues involved are complex and the advantages of one site over another can rapidly shift.

READING SELECTIONS

Michael Porter's now classic article builds his discussion of strategy around the value chain. He views strategy as a process of deciding on the firm's *configuration*, for example, deciding where to undertake various value chain activities, and its *coordination* mechanisms, how it will coordinate similar activities around the globe. He goes on to discuss the advantages of concentrated versus dispersed configurations and of tight versus loose coordination. Porter argues that successful global strategies require an increasing degree of both dispersion and coordination. It is worth noting that implicit in Porter's argument is that where the firm locates activities is an important determinant of competitive advantage.

Karin Fladmoe-Linquist and Stephen Tallman discuss resource-based strategies in the context of competitive advantage among multinationals. Like Porter, they believe that configuration affects competitive advantage. They argue that understanding a competitor firm's country of origin adds to a manager's ability to predict that firm's competitive strength and behavior. Their discussion posits why firms with different countries of origin may seem to be pursuing different strategies and sets the stage for the reading in the next section.

The reader might want to analyze the Fladmoe-Linquist and Tallman discussion in two contexts. The first context is to connect it to the reasoning presented in the articles of Section 1. Readers should also analyze it in connection with the readings on R&D innovation and technology management in Section 8 readings. Articles in the first section of this book argue, after all, that country-of-origin is becoming less important in distinguishing among mature multinationals. A question very much worth pondering is if resource-based competitive advantages are important, do they come from the luck of being born in the right place, or from deliberately selecting a configuration that assigns activities to the optimum location wherever that may be?

Michael Hitt et al. cite several examples as they make a case for the importance of understanding one's multinational competitors' strategic intent. While they focus principally on joint ventures and other alliances, the examples apply to nonventuring, nonaligned competitors as well. It has been argued that strategic intent, though an intriguing concept, is difficult to measure. Perhaps not. If resources are an important determinant of competitive advantage, then a competitor's configuration should be at least a rough approximator of that competitor's strategic intent.

Inga S. Baird, Marjorie Lyles, and J.B. Orris present the results of a study conducted among a very much neglected class of international players, small businesses. They compare their results with strategies adopted by larger firms. They find that small firms' international strength is in the uniqueness of a product or process. Environmental change stimulates entry into the international market.

9

CHANGING PATTERNS
OF INTERNATIONAL COMPETITION

MICHAEL E. PORTER

When examining the environmental changes facing firms today, it is a rare observer who will conclude that international competition is not high on the list. The growing importance of international competition is well recognized both in the business and academic communities, for reasons that are fairly obvious when one looks at just about any data set that exists on international trade or investment. Exhibit 1, for example, compares world trade and world GNP. Something interesting started happening around the mid-1950s, when the growth in world trade began to significantly exceed the growth in world GNP. Foreign direct investment by firms in developing countries began to grow rapidly a few years later, about 1963.[1] This period marked the beginning of a fundamental change in the international competitive environment that by now has come to be widely recognized. It is a trend that is causing sleepless nights for many business managers.

There is a substantial literature on international competition, because the subject is far from a new one. A large body of literature has investigated the many implications of the Heckscher-Ohlin model and other models of international trade which are

rooted in the principle of comparative advantage.[2] The unit of analysis in this literature is the country. There is also considerable literature on the multinational firm, reflecting the growing importance of the multinational since the turn of the century. In examining the reasons for the multinational, I think it is fair to characterize this literature as resting heavily on the multinational's ability to exploit intangible assets.[3] The work of Hymer and Caves among others has stressed the role of the multinational in transferring know-how and expertise gained in one country market to others at low cost, and thereby offsetting the unavoidable extra costs of doing business in a foreign country. A more recent stream of literature extends this by emphasizing how the multinational firm internalizes transactions to circumvent imperfections in various intermediate markets, most importantly the market for knowledge.

There is also a related literature on the problems of entry into foreign markets and the life cycle of how a firm competes abroad, beginning with export or licensing and ultimately moving to the establishment of foreign subsidiaries. Vernon's product cycle of international trade combines a view of how products mature with the evolution in a firm's international activities to predict the patterns of trade and investment in developed and developing countries.[4] Finally, many of the functional fields in business

Source: California Management Review Vol. 28, no. 2 (Winter 1986), pp. 9–40. © 1986, The Regents of the University of California.

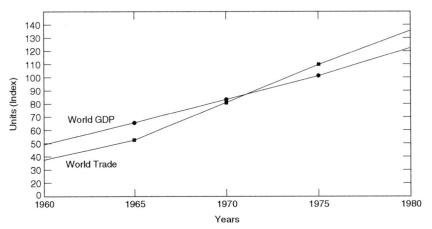

Exhibit 1. Growth of World Trade
Source: United Nations, *Statistical Yearbooks*

administration research have their branch of literature about international issues—for example, international marketing, international finance. This literature concentrates, by and large, on the problems of doing business in a foreign country.

As rich as it is, however, I think it is fair to characterize the literature on international competition as being limited when it comes to the choice of a firm's international strategy. Though the literature provides some guidance for considering incremental investment decisions to enter a new country, it provides at best a partial view of how to characterize a firm's overall international strategy and how such strategy should be selected. Put another way, the literature focuses more on the problem of becoming a multinational than on strategies for established multinationals. Although the distinction between domestic firms and multinationals is seminal in a literature focused on the problems of doing business abroad, the fact that a firm is multinational says little if anything about its international strategy except that it operates in several countries.

Broadly stated, my research has been seeking to answer the question: what does international competition mean for competitive strategy? In particular, what are the distinctive questions for competitive strategy that are raised by international as opposed to domestic competition? Many of the strategy issues

for a company competing internationally are very much the same as for one competing domestically. A firm must still analyze its industry structure and competitors, understand its buyer and the sources of buyer value, diagnose its relative cost position, and seek to establish a sustainable competitive advantage within some competitive scope, whether it be across-the-board or in an industry segment. These are subjects I have written about extensively.[5] But there are some questions for strategy that are peculiar to international competition, and that add to rather than replace those listed earlier. These questions all revolve, in one way or another, around how a firm's activities in one country affect or are affected by what is going on in other countries—the connectedness among country competition. It is this connectedness that is the focus of this article and of a broader stream of research recently conducted under the auspices of the Harvard Business School.[6]

PATTERNS OF INTERNATIONAL COMPETITION

The appropriate unit of analysis in setting international strategy is the industry, because the industry is the arena in which competitive advantage is won or lost. The starting point for understanding international competition is the observation that its pattern differs markedly from industry to industry. At one end of the spectrum are industries that I call *multidomestic,* in which competition in each country (or small group of countries) is essentially independent of competition in other countries. A multidomestic industry is one that is present in many countries (e.g., there is a consumer banking industry in Sri Lanka, one in France, and one in the U.S.), but in which competition occurs on a country-by-country basis. In a multidomestic industry, a multinational firm may enjoy a competitive advantage from the one-time transfer of know-how from its home base to foreign countries. However, the firm modifies and adapts its intangible assets to employ them in each country and the outcome is determined by conditions in each country. The competitive advantages of the firm, then, are largely specific to each country. The international industry becomes a collection of essentially domestic industries—hence the term "multidomestic." Industries where competition has traditionally exhibited this pattern include retailing, consumer packaged goods, distribution, insurance, consumer finance, and caustic chemicals.

At the other end of the spectrum are what I term *global* industries. The term global—like the word "strategy"—has become overused and perhaps under-understood. The definition of a global industry employed here is an industry in which a firm's competitive position in one country is significantly influenced by its position in other countries.[7] Therefore, the international industry is not merely a collection of domestic industries but a series of linked domestic industries in which the rivals compete against each other on a truly worldwide basis. Industries exhibiting the global pattern today include commercial aircraft, TV sets, semiconductors, copiers, automobiles, and watches.

The implications for strategy of the distinction between multidomestic and global industries are quite profound. In a multidomestic industry, a firm can and should manage its international activities like a portfolio. Its subsidiaries or other operations around the world should each control all the important activities necessary to do business in the industry and should

enjoy a high degree of autonomy. The firm's strategy in a country should be determined largely by the circumstances in that country; the firm's international strategy is then what I term a "country-centered strategy."

In a multidomestic industry, competing internationally is discretionary. A firm can choose to remain domestic or can expand internationally if it has some advantage that allows it to overcome the extra costs of entering and competing in foreign markets. The important competitors in multidomestic industries will either be domestic companies or multinationals with stand-alone operations abroad—this is the situation in each of the multidomestic industries listed earlier. In a multidomestic industry, then, international strategy collapses to a series of domestic strategies. The issues that are uniquely international revolve around how to do business abroad, how to select good countries in which to compete (or assess country risk), and mechanisms to achieve the one-time transfer of know-how. These are questions that are relatively well developed in the literature.

In a global industry, however, managing international activities like a portfolio will undermine the possibility of achieving competitive advantage. In a global industry, a firm must in some way integrate its activities on a worldwide basis to capture the linkages among countries. This will require more than transferring intangible assets among countries, though it will include it. A firm may choose to compete with a country-centered strategy, focusing on specific market segments or countries when it can carve out a niche by responding to whatever local country differences are present. However, it does so at some considerable risk from competitors with global strategies. All the important competitors in the global industries listed earlier compete worldwide with coordinated strategies.

In international competition, a firm always has to perform some functions in each of the countries in which it competes. Even though a global competitor must view its international activities as an overall system, it has still to maintain some country perspective. It is the balancing of these two perspectives that becomes one of the essential questions in global strategy.[8]

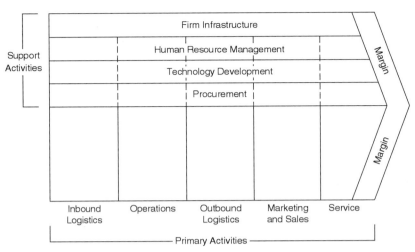

Figure 1. The Value Chain

CAUSES OF GLOBALIZATION

If we accept the distinction between multidomestic and global industries as an important taxonomy of patterns of international competition, a number of crucial questions arise. When does an industry globalize? What exactly do we mean by a global strategy, and is there more than one kind? What determines the type of international strategy to select in a particular industry?

An industry is global if there is some competitive advantage to integrating activities on a worldwide basis. To make this statement operational, however, we must be very precise about what we mean by "activities" and also what we mean by "integrating." To diagnose the sources of competitive advantage in any context, whether it be domestic or international, it is necessary to adopt a disaggregated view of the firm. In my newest book, *Competitive Advantage,* I have developed a framework for doing so, called the value chain.[9] Every firm is a collection of discrete activities performed to do business that occur within the scope of the firm—I call them value activities. The activities performed by a firm include such things as salespeople selling the product, service technicians performing repairs, scientists in the laboratory designing process techniques, and accountants keeping the books. Such activities are technologically and in most cases physically distinct. It is only at the level of discrete activities, rather than

the firm as a whole, that competitive advantage can be truly understood.

A firm may possess two types of competitive advantage: low relative cost or differentiation—its ability to perform the activities in its value chain either at lower cost or in a unique way relative to its competitors. The ultimate value a firm creates is what buyers are willing to pay for what the firm provides, which includes the physical product as well as any ancillary services or benefits. Profit results if the value created through performing the required activities exceeds the collective cost of performing them. Competitive advantage is a function of either providing comparable buyer value to competitors but performing activities efficiently (low cost), or of performing activities at comparable cost but in unique ways that create greater buyer value than competitors and, hence, command a premium price (differentiation).

The value chain, shown in Figure 1, provides a systematic means of displaying and categorizing activities. The activities performed by a firm in any industry can be grouped into the nine generic categories shown. The labels may differ based on industry convention, but every firm performs these basic categories of activities in some way or another. Within each category of activities, a firm typically performs a number of discrete activities which are particular to the industry and to the firm's strategy. In service, for example, firms typically perform such discrete activities as installation, repair, parts distribution, and upgrading.

The generic categories of activities can be grouped into two broad types. Along the bottom are what I call *primary* activities, which are those involved in the physical creation of the product or service, its delivery and marketing to the buyer, and its support after sale. Across the top are what I call *support* activities, which provide inputs or infrastructure that allow the primary activities to take place on an ongoing basis.

Procurement is the obtaining of purchased inputs, whether they be raw materials, purchased services, machinery, or so on. Procurement stretches across the entire value chain because it supports every activity—every activity uses purchased inputs of some kind. There are typically many different discrete procurement activities within a firm, often performed by different people. Technology development encompasses the activities involved in designing the product as well as in creating and improving the way the various activities in the value chain are performed. We tend to think of technology in terms of the product or manufacturing process. In fact, every activity a firm performs involves a technology or technologies which may be mundane or sophisticated, and a firm has a stock of know-how about how to perform each activity. Technology development typically involves a variety of different discrete activities, some performed outside the R&D department.

Human resource management is the recruiting, training, and development of personnel. Every activity involves human resources, and thus human resource management activities cut across the entire chain. Finally, firm infrastructure includes activities such as general management, accounting, legal, finance, strategic planning, and all the other activities decoupled from specific primary or support activities but that are essential to enable the entire chain's operation.

Activities in a firm's value chain are not independent, but are connected through what I call linkages. The way one activity is performed frequently affects the cost of effectiveness of other activities. If more is spent on the purchase of a raw material, for example, a firm may lower its cost of fabrication or assembly. There are many linkages that connect activities,

not only within the firm but also with the activities of its suppliers, channels, and ultimately its buyers. The firm's value chain resides in a larger stream of activities that I term the value system. Suppliers have value chains that provide the purchased inputs to the firm's chain; channels have value chains through which the firm's product or service passes; buyers have value chains in which the firm's product or service is employed. The connections among activities in this vertical system also become essential to competitive advantage.

A final important building block in value chain theory, necessary for our purposes here, is the notion of *competitive scope.* Competitive scope is the breadth of activities the firm employs together in competing in an industry. There are four basic dimensions of competitive scope:

- *segment* scope, or the range of segments the firm serves (e.g., product varieties, customer types);
- *industry* scope, or the range of industries the firm competes in with a coordinated strategy;
- *vertical* scope, or what activities are performed by the firm versus suppliers and channels; and
- *geographic* scope, or the geographic regions the firm operates in with a coordinated strategy.

Competitive scope is vital to competitive advantage because it shapes the configuration of the value chain, how activities are performed, and whether activities are shared among units. International strategy is an issue of geographic scope, and can be analyzed quite similarly to the question of whether and how a firm should compete locally, regionally, or nationally within a country. In the international context, government tends to have a greater involvement in competition and there are more significant variations among geographic regions in buyer needs, although these differences are matters of degree.

INTERNATIONAL CONFIGURATION AND COORDINATION OF ACTIVITIES

A firm that competes internationally must decide how to spread the activities in the value chain among countries. A distinction immediately arises between

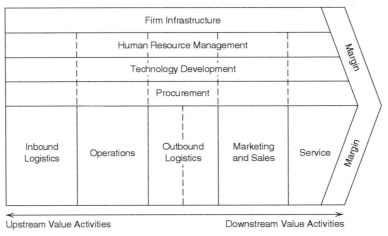

Figure 2. Upstream and Downstream Activities

the activities labeled downstream on Figure 2, and those labeled upstream activities and support activities. The location of downstream activities, those more related to the buyer, is usually tied to where the buyer is located. If a firm is going to sell in Japan, for example, it usually must provide service in Japan and it must have salespeople stationed in Japan. In some industries it is possible to have a single sales force that travels to the buyer's country and back again; some other specific downstream activities such as the production of advertising copy can also sometimes be done centrally. More typically, however, the firm must locate the capability to perform downstream activities in each of the countries in which it operates. Upstream activities and support activities, conversely, can at least conceptually be decoupled from where the buyer is located.

This distinction carries some interesting implications. The first is that downstream activities create competitive advantages that are largely country-specific: a firm's reputation, brand name, and service network in a country grow out of a firm's activities in that country and create entry/mobility barriers largely in that country alone. Competitive advantage in upstream and support activities often grows more out of the entire system of countries in which a firm competes than from its position in any one country, however.

A second implication is that in industries where downstream activities or buyer-tied activities are vi-

tal to competitive advantage, there tends to be a more multidomestic pattern of international competition. In industries where upstream and support activities (such as technology development and operations) are crucial to competitive advantage, global competition is more common. In global competition, the location and scale of these potentially footloose activities is optimized from a worldwide perspective.[10]

The distinctive issues in international, as contrasted to domestic, strategy can be summarized in two key dimensions of how a firm competes internationally. The first is what I term the *configuration* of a firm's activities worldwide, or where in the world each activity in the value chain is performed, including in how many places. The second dimension is what I term *coordination,* which refers to how like activities performed in different countries are coordinated with each other. If, for example, there are three plants—one in Germany, one in Japan, and one in the U.S.—how do the activities in those plants relate to each other?

A firm faces an array of options in both configuration and coordination for each activity. Configuration options range from concentrated (performing an activity in one location and serving the world from it—for example, one R&D lab, one large plant) to dispersed (performing every activity in each country). In the latter case, each country would have a complete value chain. Coordination options range from none to very high. For example, if a firm pro-

Value Activity	Configuration Issues	Coordination Issues
Operations	• Location of production facilities for components and end products	• Networking of international plants • Transferring process technology and production know-how among plants
Marketing and Sales	• Product line selection • Country (market) selection	• Commonality of brand name worldwide • Coordination of sales to multinational accounts • Similarity of channels and product positioning worldwide • Coordination of pricing in different countries
Service	• Location of service organization	• Similarity of service standards and procedures worldwide
Technology Development	• Number and location of R&D centers	• Interchange among dispersed R&D centers • Developing products responsive to market needs in many countries • Sequence of product introductions around the world
Procurement	• Location of the purchasing function	• Managing suppliers located in different countries • Transferring market knowledge • Coordinating purchases of common items

Figure 3. Configuration and Coordination Issues by Category of Activity

duces its product in three plants, it could, at one extreme, allow each plant to operate with full autonomy—for example, different product standards and features, different steps in the production process, different raw materials, different part numbers. At the other extreme, the plants could be tightly coordinated by employing the same information system, the same production process, the same parts, and so forth. Options for coordination in an activity are typically more numerous than the configuration options because there are many possible levels of coordination and many different facets of the way the activity is performed.

Figure 3 lists some of the configuration issues and coordination issues for several important categories of value activities. In technology development, for example, the configuration issue is where R&D is performed: one location? two locations? and in what countries? The coordination issues have to do with such things as the extent of interchange among R&D centers and the location and sequence of product introduction around the world. There are config-

uration issues and coordination issues for every activity.

Figure 4 is a way of summarizing these basic choices in international strategy on a single diagram, with coordination of activities on the vertical axis and configuration of activities on the horizontal axis. The firm has to make a set of choices for each activity. If a firm employs a very dispersed configuration—placing an entire value chain in every country (or small group of contiguous countries) in which it operates, coordinating little or not at all among them—then the firm is competing with a country-centered strategy. The domestic firm that only operates in one country is the extreme case of a firm with a country-centered strategy. As we move from the lower left-hand corner of the diagram up or to the right, we have strategies that are increasingly global.

Figure 5 illustrates some of the possible variations in international strategy. The purest global strategy is to concentrate as many activities as possible in one country, serve the world from this home base, and tightly coordinate those activities that must inher-

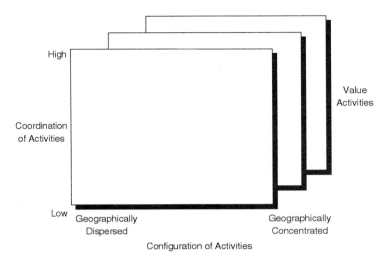

Figure 4. The Dimensions of International Strategy

ently be performed near the buyer. This is the pattern adopted by many Japanese firms in the 1960s and 1970s, such as Toyota. However, Figures 4 and 5 make it clear that there is no such thing as one global strategy. There are many different kinds of global strategies, depending on a firm's choices about configuration and coordination throughout the value chain. In copiers, for example, Xerox has until recently concentrated R&D in the U.S. but dispersed other activities, in some cases using joint-venture partners to perform them. On dispersed activities, however, coordination has been quite high. The Xerox brand, marketing approach, and servicing procedures have been quite standardized worldwide. Canon, on the other hand, has had a much more concentrated configuration of activities and somewhat less coordination of dispersed activities. The vast majority of support activities and manufacturing of copiers have been performed in Japan. Aside from using the Canon brand, however, local marketing

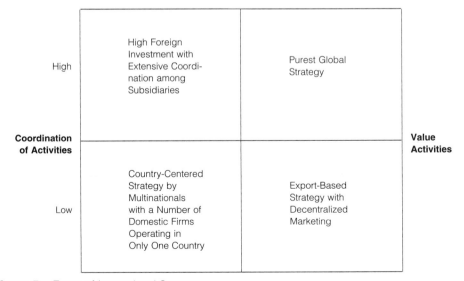

Figure 5. Types of International Strategy

subsidiaries have been given quite a bit of latitude in each region of the world.

A global strategy can now be defined more precisely as one in which a firm seeks to gain competitive advantage from its international presence through either concentrating configuration, coordination among dispersed activities, or both. Measuring the presence of a global industry empirically must reflect both dimensions and not just one. Market presence in many countries and some export and import of components and end products are characteristic of most global industries. High levels of foreign investment or the mere presence of multinational firms are not reliable measures, however, because firms may be managing foreign units like a portfolio.

CONFIGURATION/COORDINATION AND COMPETITIVE ADVANTAGE

Understanding the competitive advantages of a global strategy and, in turn, the causes of industry globalization requires specifying the conditions in which concentrating activities globally and coordinating dispersed activities leads to either cost advantage or differentiation. In each case, there are structural characteristics of an industry that work for and against globalization.

The factors that favor concentrating an activity in one or a few locations to serve the world are as follows:

- economies of scale in the activity;
- a proprietary learning curve in the activity;
- comparative advantage in where the activity is performed; and
- coordination advantages of co-locating linked activities such as R&D and production.

The first two factors relate to *how many* sites an activity is performed at, while the last two relate to *where* these sites are. Comparative advantage can apply to any activity, not just production. For example, there may be some locations in the world that are better places than others to do research on medical technology or to perform software development. Government can promote the concentration of activities by providing subsidies or other incentives to use a particular country as an export base, in effect altering comparative advantage—a role many governments are playing today.

There are also structural characteristics that favor dispersion of an activity to many countries, which represent concentration costs. Local product needs may differ, nullifying the advantages of scale or learning from one-site operation of an activity. Locating a range of activities in a country may facilitate marketing in that country by signaling commitment to local buyers and/or providing greater responsiveness. Transport, communication, and storage costs may make it inefficient to concentrate the activity in one location. Government is also frequently a powerful force for dispersing activities. Governments typically want firms to locate the entire value chain in their country, because this creates benefits and spillovers to the country that often go beyond local content. Dispersion is also encouraged by the risks of performing an activity in one place: exchange-rate risks, political risks, and so on. The balance between the advantages of concentrating and dispersing an activity normally differ for each activity (and industry). The best configuration for R&D is different from that for component fabrication, and this is different from that for assembly, installation, advertising, and procurement.[11]

The desirability of coordinating like activities that are dispersed involves a similar balance of structural factors. Coordination potentially allows the sharing of know-how among dispersed activities. If a firm learns how to operate the production process better in Germany, transferring that learning may make the process run better in plants in the United States and Japan. Differing countries, with their inevitably differing conditions, provide a fertile basis for comparison as well as opportunities for arbitraging knowledge, obtained in different places about different aspects of the business. Coordination among dispersed activities also potentially improves the ability to reap economies of scale in activities if subtasks are allocated among locations to allow some specialization—for example, each R&D center has a different area of focus. While there is a fine line between such forms of coordination and what I have termed configuration, it does illustrate how the way a network of foreign locations is managed can have a great influence on the ability to reap the benefits of any given configuration of activities. Viewed another way, close coordination is frequently a partial offset to dispersing an activity.

Coordination may also allow a firm to respond to shifting comparative advantage, where shifts in exchange rates and factor costs are hard to forecast. Incrementally increasing the production volume at the location currently enjoying favorable exchange rates, for example, can lower overall costs. Coordination can reinforce a firm's brand reputation with buyers (and hence lead to differentiation) through ensuring a consistent image and approach to doing business on a worldwide basis. This is particularly likely if buyers are mobile or information about the industry flows freely around the world. Coordination may also differentiate the firm with multinational buyers if it allows the firm to serve them anywhere and in a consistent way. Coordination (and a global approach to configuration) enhances leverage with local governments if the firm is able to grow or shrink activities in one country at the expense of others. Finally, coordination yields flexibility in responding to competitors, by allowing the firm to differentially respond across countries and to respond in one country to a challenge in another.

Coordination of dispersed activities usually involves costs that differ by form of coordination and industry. Local conditions may vary in ways that may make a common approach across countries suboptimal. If every plant in the world is required to use the same raw material, for example, the firm pays a penalty in countries where the raw material is expensive relative to satisfactory substitutes. Business practices, marketing systems, raw material sources, local infrastructures, and a variety of other factors may differ across countries as well, often in ways that may mitigate the advantages of a common approach or of the sharing of learning. Governments may restrain the flow of information required for coordination or may impose other barriers to it. The transaction costs of coordination, which have recently received increased attention in domestic

competition, are vitally important in international strategy.[12] International coordination involves long distances, language problems, and cultural barriers to communication. In some industries, these factors may mean that coordination is not optimal. They also suggest that forms of coordination which involve relatively infrequent decisions will enjoy advantages over forms of coordination involving on-going interchange.

There are also substantial organizational difficulties involved in achieving cooperation among subsidiaries, which are due to the difficulty in aligning subsidiary managers' interests with those of the firm as a whole. The Germans do not necessarily want to tell the Americans about their latest breakthroughs on the production line because it may make it harder for them to outdo the Americans in the annual comparison of operating efficiency among plants. These vexing organizational problems mean that country subsidiaries often view each other more as competitors than collaborators.[13] As with configuration, a firm must make an activity-by-activity choice about where there is net competitive advantage from coordinating in various ways.

Coordination in some activities may be necessary to reap the advantages of configuration in others. The use of common raw materials in each plant, for example, allows worldwide purchasing. Moreover, tailoring some activities to countries may allow concentration and standardization of other activities. For example, tailored marketing in each country may allow the same product to be positioned differently and hence sold successfully in many countries, unlocking possibilities for reaping economies of scale in production and R&D. Thus coordination and configuration interact.

CONFIGURATION/COORDINATION AND THE PATTERN OF INTERNATIONAL COMPETITION

When benefits of configuring and/or coordinating globally exceed the costs, an industry will globalize in a way that reflects the net benefits by value activity. The activities in which global competitors gain competitive advantage will differ correspondingly. Configuration/coordination determines the ongoing competitive advantages of a global strategy which are additive to competitive advantages a firm derives/possesses from its domestic market positions. An initial transfer of knowledge from the home base to subsidiaries is one, but by no means the most important, advantage of a global competitor.[14]

An industry such as commercial aircraft represents an extreme case of a global industry (in the upper right-hand corner of Figure 4). The three major competitors in this industry—Boeing, McDonnell Douglas, and Airbus—all have global strategies. In activities important to cost and differentiation in the industry, there are compelling net advantages to concentrating most activities and coordinating the dispersed activities extensively.[15] In R&D, there is a large fixed cost of developing an aircraft model ($1 billion or more) which requires worldwide sales to amortize. There are significant economies of scale in production, a steep learning curve in assembly (the learning curve was born out of research in this industry), and apparently significant advantages of locating R&D and production together. Sales of commercial aircraft are infrequent (via a highly skilled sales force), so that even the sales force can be partially concentrated in the home country and travel to buyers.

The costs of a concentrated configuration are relatively low in commercial aircraft. Product needs are homogeneous, and there are the low transport costs of delivering the product to the buyer. Finally, worldwide coordination of the one dispersed activity, service, is very important—obviously standardized parts and repair advice have to be available wherever the plane lands.

As in every industry, there are structural features which work against a global strategy in commercial aircraft. These are all related to government, a not atypical circumstance. Government has a particular interest in commercial aircraft because of its large trade potential, the technological sophistication of the industry, its spillover effects to other industries, and its implications for national defense. Government also has an unusual degree of leverage in the industry: in many instances, it is the buyer. Many airlines are government owned, and a government official or appointee is head of the airline.

The competitive advantages of a global strategy are so great that all the successful aircraft producers have sought to achieve and preserve them. In addition, the power of government to intervene has been mitigated by the fact that there are few viable worldwide competitors and that there are the enormous barriers to entry created in part by the advantages of a global strategy. The result has been that firms have sought to assuage government through procurement. Boeing, for example, is very careful about where it buys components. In countries that are large potential customers, Boeing seeks to develop suppliers. This requires a great deal of extra effort by Boeing both to transfer technology and to work with suppliers to assure that they meet its standards. Boeing realizes that this is preferable to compromising the competitive advantage of its strongly integrated worldwide strategy. It is willing to employ one value activity (procurement) where the advantages of concentration are modest to help preserve the benefits of concentration in other activities. Recently, commercial aircraft competitors have entered into joint ventures and other coalition arrangements with foreign suppliers to achieve the same effect, as well as to spread the risk of huge development costs.

The extent and location of advantages from a global strategy vary among industries. In some industries, the competitive advantage from a global strategy comes in technology development, although firms gain little advantage in the primary activities so that these are dispersed around the world to minimize concentration costs. In other industries such as cameras or videocassette recorders, a firm cannot succeed without concentrating production to achieve economies of scale, but instead it gives subsidiaries much local autonomy in sales and marketing. In some industries, there is no net advantage to a global strategy and country-centered strategies dominate— the industry is multidomestic.

Segments or stages of an industry frequently vary in their pattern of globalization. In aluminum, the upstream (alumina and ingot) stages of the industry are global businesses. The downstream stage, semi-fabrication, is a group of multidomestic businesses because product needs vary by country, transport costs are high, and intensive local customer service is required. Scale economies in the value chain are modest. In lubricants, automotive oil tends to be a country-centered business while marine motor oil is a global business. In automotive oil, countries have varying driving standards, weather conditions, and local laws. Production involves blending various kinds of crude oils and additives, and is subject to few economies of scale but high shipping costs. Country-centered competitors such as Castrol and Quaker State are leaders in most countries. In the marine segment, conversely, ships move freely around the world and require the same oil everywhere. Successful competitors are global.

The ultimate leaders in global industries are often first movers—the first firms to perceive the possibilities for a global strategy. Boeing was the first global competitor in aircraft, for example, as was Honda in motorcycles, and Becton Dickinson in disposable syringes. First, movers gain scale and learning advantages which are difficult to overcome. First mover effects are particularly important in global industries because of the association between globalization and economies of scale and learning achieved through worldwide configuration/coordination. Global leadership shifts if industry structural change provides opportunities for leapfrogging to new products or new technologies that nullify past leaders' scale and learning—again, the first mover to the new generation/technology often wins.

Global leaders often begin with some advantage at home, whether it be low labor cost or a product or marketing advantage. They use this as a lever to enter foreign markets. Once there, however, the global competitor converts the initial home advantage into competitive advantages that grow out of its overall worldwide system, such as production scale or ability to amortize R&D costs. While the initial advantage may have been hard to sustain, the global strategy creates new advantages which can be much more durable.

International strategy has often been characterized as a choice between worldwide standardization and local tailoring, or as the tension between the economic imperative (large-scale efficient facilities) and the political imperative (local content, local production). It should be clear from the discussion so far that neither characterization captures the richness of a firm's international strategy choices. A firm's choice of international strategy involves a search for

competitive advantage from configuration/coordination throughout the value chain. A firm may standardize (concentrate) some activities and tailor (disperse) others. It may also be able to standardize and tailor at the same time through the coordination of dispersed activities, or use local tailoring of some activities (e.g., different product positioning in each country) to allow standardization of others (e.g., production). Similarly, the economic imperative is not always for a global strategy—in some industries a country-centered strategy is the economic imperative. Conversely, the political imperative is to concentrate activities in some industries where governments provide strong export incentives and locational subsidies.

GLOBAL STRATEGY VS. COMPARATIVE ADVANTAGE

Given the importance of trade theory to the study of international competition, it is useful to pause and reflect on the relationship of the framework I have presented to the notion of comparative advantage. Is there a difference? The traditional concept of comparative advantage is that factor-cost or factor-quality differences among countries lead to production of products in countries with an advantage which export them elsewhere in the world. Competitive advantage in this view, then, grows out of *where* a firm performs activities. The location of activities is clearly one source of potential advantage in a global firm. The global competitor can locate activities wherever comparative advantage lies, decoupling comparative advantage from its home base or country of ownership.

Indeed, the framework presented here suggests that the comparative advantage story is richer than typically told, because it not only involves production activities (the usual focus of discussions) but also applies to other activities in the value chain such as R&D, processing orders, or designing advertisements. Comparative advantage is specific to the *activity* and not the location of the value chain as a whole.[16] One of the potent advantages of the global firm is that it can spread activities among locations to reflect different preferred locations for different activities, something a domestic or country-centered competitor does not do. Thus components can be made in Taiwan, software written in India and basic R&D performed in Silicon Valley, for example. This international specialization of activities within the firm is made possible by the growing ability to coordinate and configure globally.

At the same time as our framework suggests a richer view of comparative advantage, however, it also suggests that many forms of competitive advantage for the global competitor derive less from *where* the firm performs activities than from *how* it performs them on a worldwide basis; economies of scale, proprietary learning, and differentiation with multinational buyers are not tied to countries but to the configuration and coordination of the firm's worldwide system. Traditional sources of comparative advantage can be very elusive and slippery sources of competitive advantage for an international competitor today, because comparative advantage frequently shifts. A country with the lowest labor cost is overtaken within a few years by some other country—facilities located in the first country then face a disadvantage. Moreover, falling direct labor as a percentage of total costs, increasing global markets for raw materials and other inputs, and freer flowing technology have diminished the role of traditional sources of comparative advantage.

My research on a broad cross-section of industries suggests that the achievement of sustainable world market leadership follows a more complex pattern than the exploitation of comparative advantage per se. A competitor often starts with a comparative advantage-related edge that provides the basis for penetrating foreign markets, but this edge is rapidly translated into a broader array of advantages that arise from a global approach to configuration and coordination as described earlier. Japanese firms, for example, have done a masterful job of converting temporary labor-cost advantages into durable systemwide advantages due to scale and proprietary know-how. Ultimately, the systemwide advantages are further reinforced with country-specific advantages such as brand identity as well as distribution channel access. Many Japanese firms were fortunate enough to make their transitions from country-based

comparative advantage to global competitive advantage at a time when nobody paid much attention to them and there was a buoyant world economy. European and American competitors were willing to cede market share in "less desirable" segments such as the low end of the producer line, or so they thought. The Japanese translated these beachheads into world leadership by broadening their lines and reaping advantages in scale and proprietary technology. The Koreans and Taiwanese, the latest low labor cost entrants to a number of industries, may have a hard time replicating Japan's success, given slower growth, standardized products, and now alert competitors.

GLOBAL PLATFORMS

The interaction of the home-country conditions and competitive advantages from a global strategy that transcend the country suggest a more complex role of the country in firm success than implied by the theory of comparative advantage. To understand this more complex role of the country, I define the concept of a *global platform*. A country is a desirable global platform in an industry if it provides an environment yielding firms domiciled in that country an advantage in competing globally in that particular industry.[17] An essential element of this definition is that it hinges on success *outside* the country, and not merely country conditions which allow firms to successfully master domestic competition. In global competition, a country must be viewed as a platform and not as the place where all a firm's activities are performed.

There are two determinants of a good global platform in an industry, which I have explored in more detail elsewhere.[18] The first is comparative advantage, or the factor endowment of the country as a site to perform particular activities in the industry. Today, simple factors such as low-cost unskilled labor and natural resources are increasingly less important to global competition compared to complex factors such as skilled scientific and technical personnel and advanced infrastructure. Direct labor is a minor proportion of cost in many manufactured goods and automation of non-production activities is shrinking it further, while markets for resources are increasingly global, and technology has widened the number of sources of many resources. A country's factor endowment is partly exogenous and partly the result of attention and investment in the country.

The second determinant of the attractiveness of a country as a global platform in an industry are the characteristics of a country's demand. A country's demand conditions include the size and timing of its demand in an industry, factors recognized as important by authors such as Linder and Vernon.[19] They also conclude the sophistication and power of buyers and channels and the product features and attributes demanded. Local demand conditions provide two potentially powerful sources of competitive advantages to a global competitor based in that country. The first is *first-mover advantages* in perceiving and implementing the appropriate global strategy. Pressing local needs, particularly peculiar ones, lead firms to embark early to solve local problems and gain proprietary know-how. This is then translated into scale and learning advantages as firms move early to compete globally. The other potential benefit of local demand conditions is a baseload of demand for product varieties that will be sought after in international markets. These two roles of the country in the success of a global firm reflect the interaction between conditions of local supply, the composition and timing of country demand, and economies of scale and learning in shaping international success.

The two determinants interact in important and sometimes counterintuitive ways. Local demand and needs frequently influence private and social investment in endogenous factors of production. A nation with oceans as borders and dependence on sea trade, for example, is more prone to have universities and scientific centers dedicated to oceanographic education and research. Similarly, factor endowment seems to influence local demand. The per capita consumption of wine is highest in wine-growing regions, for example.

Comparative disadvantage in some factors of production can be an advantage in global competition when combined with pressing local demand. Poor growing conditions have led Israeli farmers to innovate in irrigation and cultivation techniques, for example. The shrinking role in competition of simple factors of production relative to complex factors such as technical personnel seem to be enhancing the frequency and importance of such circumstances. What is important today is unleashing innovation in the proper direction, instead of passive exploitation of static cost advantages in a country which can shift rapidly and be overcome. International success today is a dynamic process resulting from continued development of products and processes. The forces which guide firms to undertake such activity thus become central to international competition.

A good example of the interplay among these factors is the television set industry. In the U.S., early demand was in large-screen console sets because television sets were initially luxury items kept in the living room. As buyers began to purchase second and third sets, sets became smaller and more portable. They were used increasingly in the bedroom, the kitchen, the car, and elsewhere. As the television set industry matured, table model and portable sets became the universal product variety. Japanese firms, because of the small size of Japanese homes, cut their teeth on small sets. They dedicated most of their R&D to developing small picture tubes and to making sets more compact. In the process of naturally serving the needs of their home market, then, Japanese firms gained early experience and scale in segments of the industry that came to dominate world demand. U.S. firms, conversely, cut their teeth on large-screen console sets with fine furniture cabinets. As the industry matured, the experience base of U.S. firms was in a segment that was small and isolated to a few countries, notably the U.S. Japanese firms were able to penetrate world markets in a segment that was both uninteresting to foreign firms and in which they had initial scale, learning, and labor cost advantages. Ultimately the low-cost advantage disappeared as production was automated, but global scale and learning economies took over as the Japanese advanced product and process technology at a rapid pace.

The two broad determinants of a good global platform rest on the interaction between country characteristics and firms' strategies. The literature on comparative advantage, through focusing on country factor endowments, ignoring the demand side, and suppressing the individual firm, is most appropriate in industries where there are few economies of scale, little proprietary technology or technological change, or few possibilities for product differentiation.[20] While these industry characteristics are those of many traditionally traded goods, they describe few of today's important global industries.

THE EVOLUTION OF INTERNATIONAL COMPETITION

Having established a framework for understanding the globalization of industries, we are now in a position to view the phenomenon in historical perspective. If one goes back far enough, relatively few industries were global. Around 1880, most industries were local or regional in scope.[21] The reasons are rather self-evident in the context of our framework. There were few economies of scale in production until fuel-powered machines and assembly-line techniques emerged. There were heterogeneous product needs among regions within countries, much less among countries. There were few if any national media—the *Saturday Evening Post* was the first important national magazine in the U.S. and developed in the teens and twenties. Communication between regions was difficult before the telegraph and telephone, and transportation was slow until the railroad system became well developed.

These structural conditions created little impetus for the widespread globalization of industry. Those industries that were global reflected classic comparative advantage considerations—goods were simply unavailable in some countries (who then imported them from others) or differences in the availability of land, resources, or skilled labor made some countries desirable suppliers to others. Export of local production was the form of global strategy adapted. There was little role or need for widespread government barriers to international trade during this period, although trade barriers were quite high in some countries for some commodities.

Around the 1880s, however, were the beginnings of what today has blossomed into the globalization of many industries. The first wave of modern global competitors grew up in the late 1800s and early 1900s. Many industries went from local (or regional) to national in scope, and some began globalizing. Firms such as Ford, Singer, Gillette, National Cash Register, Otis, and Western Electric had commanding world market shares by the teens, and operated with integrated worldwide strategies. Early global competitors were principally American and European companies.

Driving this first wave of modern globalization were rising production scale economies due to advancements in technology that outpaced the growth of the world economy. Product needs also became more homogenized in different countries as knowledge and industrialization diffused. Transport improved, first through the railroad and steamships and later in trucking. Communication became easier with the telegraph, then the telephone. At the same time, trade barriers were either modest or overwhelmed by the advantages of the new large-scale firms.

The burst of globalization soon slowed, however. Most of the few industries that were global moved increasingly towards a multidomestic pattern—multinationals remained, but between the 1920s and 1950 they often evolved towards federations of autonomous subsidiaries. The principal reason was a strong wave of nationalism and resulting high tariff barriers, partly caused by the world economic crisis and world wars. Another barrier to global strategies, chronicled by Chandler,[22] was a growing web of cartels and other interfirm contractual agreements. These limited the geographic spread of firms.

The early global competitors began rapidly dispersing their value chains. The situation of Ford Motor Company was no exception. While in 1925 Ford had almost no production outside the U.S., by World War II its overseas production had risen sharply. Firms that became multinationals during the interwar period tended to adopt country-centered strategies. European multinationals, operating in a setting where there were many sovereign countries within a relatively small geographical area, were quick to establish self-contained and quite autonomous subsidiaries in many countries. A more tolerant regulatory environment also encouraged European firms to form cartels and other cooperative agreements among themselves, which limited their foreign market entry.

Between the 1950s and the late 1970s, however, there was a strong reversal of the interwar trends. As Exhibit 1 illustrated, there have been very strong underlying forces driving the globalization of industries. The important reasons can be understood using the configuration/coordination dichotomy. The competitive advantage of competing worldwide from concentrated activities rose sharply, while concentration costs fell. There was a renewed rise in scale economies in many activities due to advancing technology. The minimum efficient scale of an auto assembly plant more than tripled between 1960 and 1975, for example, while the average cost of developing a new drug more than quadrupled.[23] The pace of technological change has increased, creating more incentive to amortize R&D costs against worldwide sales.

Product needs have continued to homogenize among countries, as income differences have narrowed, information and communication has flowed more freely around the world, and travel has increased.[24] Growing similarities in business practices and marketing systems (e.g., chain stores) in different countries have also been a facilitating factor in homogenizing needs. Within countries there has been a parallel trend towards greater market segmentation, which some observers see as contradictory to the view that product needs in different countries are becoming similar. However, segments today seem based less on country differences and more on buyer differences that transcend country boundaries, such as demographic, user industry, or income groups. Many firms successfully employ global focus strategies in which they serve a narrow segment of an industry worldwide, as do Daimler-Benz and Rolex.

Another driver of post–World War II globalization has been a sharp reduction in the real costs of transportation. This has occurred through innovations in transportation technology including increasingly large bulk carriers, container ships, and larger, more efficient aircraft. At the same time, government impediments to global configuration/coordination have been falling in the postwar period. Tariff barriers have gone down, international cartels and patent-sharing agreements have disappeared, and regional economic pacts such as the European Community have emerged to facilitate trade and investment, albeit imperfectly.

The ability to coordinate globally has also risen markedly in the postwar period. Perhaps the most striking reason is falling communication costs (in voice and data) and reduced travel time for individuals. The ability to coordinate activities in different countries has also been facilitated by growing similarities among countries in marketing systems, business practices, and infrastructure—country after country has developed supermarkets and mass distributors, television advertising, and so on. Greater international mobility of buyers and information has raised the payout to coordinating how a firm does business around the world. The increasing number of firms who are multinational has created growing possibilities for differentiation by suppliers who are global.

The forces underlying globalization have been self-reinforcing. The globalization of firms' strategies has contributed to the homogenization of buyer needs and business practices. Early global competitors must frequently stimulate the demand for uniform global varieties; for example, as Becton Dickinson did in disposable syringes and Honda did in motorcycles. Similarly, globalization of industries begets globalization of supplier industries—the increasing globalization of automotive component suppliers is a good example. Pioneering global competitors also stimulate the development and growth of international telecommunication infrastructure as well as the creation of global advertising media—for example, *The Economist* and *The Wall Street Journal*.

STRATEGIC IMPLICATIONS OF GLOBALIZATION

When the pattern of international competition shifts from multidomestic to global, there are many implications for the strategy of international firms. While a full treatment is beyond the scope of this paper, I will sketch some of the implications here.[25]

At the broadest level, globalization casts new light on many issues that have long been of interest to students of international business. In areas such as international finance, marketing, and business-government relations, the emphasis in the literature has been on the unique problems of adapting to local conditions and ways of doing business in a foreign country in a foreign currency. In a global industry, these concerns must be supplemented with an over-riding focus on the ways and means of international configuration and coordination. In government relations, for example, the focus must shift from stand-alone negotiations with host countries (appropriate in multidomestic competition) to a recognition that negotiations in one country will both affect other countries and be shaped by possibilities for performing activities in other countries. In finance, measuring the performance of subsidiaries must be modified to reflect the contribution of one subsidiary to another's cost position or differentiation in a global strategy, instead of viewing each subsidiary as a stand-alone unit. In battling with global competitors, it may be appropriate in some countries to accept low profits indefinitely—in multidomestic competition this would be unjustified.[26] In global industries, the overall system matters as much or more than the country.

Of the many other implications of globalization for the firm, there are two of such significance that they deserve some treatment here. The first is the role of *coalitions* in global strategy. A coalition is a long-term agreement linking firms but falling short of merger. I use the term coalition to encompass a whole variety of arrangements that include joint ventures, licenses, supply agreements, and many other kinds of interfirm relationships. Such interfirm agreements have been receiving more attention in the academic literature, although each form of agreement has been looked at separately and the focus has been largely domestic.[27] International coalitions, linking firms in the same industry based in different countries, have become an even more important part of international strategy in the past decade.

International coalitions are a way of configuring activities in the value chain on a worldwide basis jointly with a partner. International coalitions are proliferating rapidly and are present in many industries.[28] There is a particularly high incidence in automobiles, aircraft, aircraft engines, robotics, consumer electronics, semiconductors and pharmaceuticals. While international coalitions have long been present, their character has been changing. Historically, a firm from a developed country formed a coalition with a firm in a lesser-developed country to perform marketing activities in that country. Today, we observe more and more coalitions in which two firms from developed countries are teaming up to serve the world, as well as coalitions that extend beyond marketing activities to encompass activities throughout the value chain.[29] Production and R&D coalitions are very common, for example.

Coalitions are a natural consequence of globalization and the need for an integrated worldwide strategy. The same forces that lead to globalization will prompt the formation of coalitions as firms confront the barriers to establishing a global strategy of their own. The difficulties of gaining access to foreign markets and in surmounting scale and learning thresholds in production, technology development, and other activities have led many firms to team up with others. In many industries, coalitions can be a transitional state in the adjustment of firms to globalization, reflecting the need of firms to catch up in technology, cure short-term imbalances between their global production networks and exchange rates, and accelerate the process of foreign market entry. Many coalitions are likely to persist in some form, however.

There are benefits and costs of coalitions as well as difficult implementation problems in making them succeed (which I have discussed elsewhere). How to choose and manage coalitions is among the most interesting questions in international strategy today. When one speaks to managers about coalitions, almost all have tales of disaster which vividly illustrate that coalitions often do not succeed. Also, there is the added burden of coordinating global strategy with a coalition partner because the partner often wants to do things its own way. Yet, in the face of copious corporate experience that coalitions do not work and a growing economics literature on transaction costs and contractual failures, we see a proliferation of coalitions today of the most difficult kind—those between companies in different countries.[30] There is a great need for researching in both the academic community and in the corporate world about coalitions and how to manage them. They are increasingly being forced on firms today by new competitive circumstances.

A second area where globalization carries particular importance is in *organizational* structure. The need to configure and coordinate globally in complex ways creates some obvious organizational challenges.[31] Any organization structure for competing internationally has to balance two dimensions; there has to be a *country* dimension (because some activities are inherently performed in the country) and there has to be a *global* dimension (because the advantages of global configuration/coordination must be achieved). In a global industry, the ultimate authority must represent the global dimension if a global strategy is to prevail. However, within any international firm, once it disperses any activities there are tremendous pressures to disperse more. Moreover, forces are unleashed which lead subsidiaries to seek growing autonomy. Local country managers will have a natural tendency to emphasize how different their country is and the consequent need for local tailoring and control over more activities in the value chain. Country managers will be loath to give up control over activities or how they are performed to outside forces. They will also frequently paint an ominous picture of host government concerns about local content and requirements for local presence. Corporate incentive systems frequently encourage such behavior by linking incentives narrowly to subsidiary results.

In successful global competitors, an environment is created in which the local managers seek to exploit similarities across countries rather than emphasize differences. They view the firms's global presence as an advantage to be tapped for their local gain. Adept global competitors often go to great lengths to devise ways of circumventing or adapting to local differences while preserving the advantages of the similarities. A good example is Canon's personal copier. In Japan, the typical paper size is bigger than American legal size and the standard European size. Canon's personal copier will not handle this size—a Japanese company introduced a product that did not meet its home market needs in the world's largest market for small copiers! Canon gathered its marketing managers from around the world and cataloged market needs in each country. They found that capacity to copy the large Japanese paper was only needed in Japan. In consultation with design and manufacturing engineers, it was determined that building this feature into the personal copier would significantly increase its complexity and cost. The decision was made to omit the feature because the price elasticity of demand for the personal copier was judged to be high. But this was not the end of the deliberations. Canon's management then set out to find a way to make the personal copier saleable in Japan. The answer that emerged was to add another feature to the copier—the ability to copy business cards—which both added little cost and was particularly valuable in Japan. This case illustrates the principle of looking for the similarities in needs among countries and in finding ways of creating similarities, not emphasizing the differences.

Such a change in orientation is something that typically occurs only grudgingly in a multinational company, particularly if it has historically operated in a country-centered mode (as has been the case with early U.S. and European multinationals). Achieving such a reorientation requires first that managers recognize that competitive success demands exploiting the advantages of a global strategy. Regular contact and discussion among subsidiary managers seems to be a prerequisite, as are information systems that allow operations in different countries to be compared.[32] This can be followed by programs for exchanging information and sharing know-how and then by more complex forms of coordination. Ultimately, the reconfiguring of activities globally may then be accepted, even though subsidiaries may have to give up control over some activities in the process.

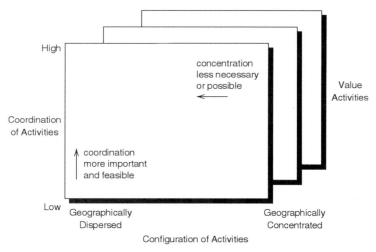

Figure 6. Future Trends in International Competition

THE FUTURE OF INTERNATIONAL COMPETITION

Since the late 1970s, there have been some gradual but significant changes in the pattern of international competition which carry important implications for international strategy. Our framework provides a template with which we can examine these changes and probe their significance. The factors shaping the global configuration of activities by firms are developing in ways which contrast with the trends of the previous thirty years. Homogenization of product needs among countries appears to be continuing, though segmentation within countries is as well. As a result, consumer packaged goods are becoming increasingly prone toward globalization, though they have long been characterized by multidomestic competition. There are also signs of globalization in some service industries as the introduction of information technology creates scale economies in support activities and facilitates coordination in primary activities. Global service firms are reaping advantages in hardware and software development as well as procurement.

In many industries, however, limits have been reached in the scale economies that have been driving the concentration of activities. These limits grow out of classic diseconomies of scale that arise in very large facilities, as well as out of new, more flexible technology in manufacturing and other activities that is often not as scale sensitive as previous methods. At the same time, though, flexible manufacturing allows the production of multiple varieties (to serve different countries) in a single plant. This may encourage new movement towards globalization in industries in which product differences among countries have remained significant and have blocked globalization in the past.

There also appear to be some limits to further decline in transport costs, as innovations such as containerization, bulk ships, and larger aircraft have run their course. However, a parallel trend toward smaller, lighter products and components may keep some downward pressure on transport costs. The biggest change in the benefits and costs of concentrated configuration has been the sharp rise in protectionism in recent years and the resulting rise in nontariff barriers, harkening back to the 1920s. As a group, these factors point to less need and less opportunity for highly concentrated configurations of activities.

When we examine the coordination dimension, the picture looks starkly different. Communication and coordination costs are dropping sharply, driven by breathtaking advances in information systems and telecommunication technology. We have just seen the beginning of developments in this area, which are spreading throughout the value chain.[33] Boeing, for example, is employing computer-aided design technology to jointly design components on-line with foreign suppliers. Engineers in different countries are communicating via computer screens. Marketing systems and business practices continue to homogenize, facilitating the coordination of activities in different countries. The mobility of buyers and information is also growing rapidly, greasing the international spread of brand reputations and enhancing the importance of consistency in the way activities are performed worldwide. Increasing numbers of multinational and global firms are begetting globalization by their suppliers. There is also a sharp rise in the computerization of manufacturing as well as other activities throughout the value chain, which greatly facilitates coordination among dispersed sites.

The imperative of global strategy is shifting, then, in ways that will require a rebalancing of configuration and coordination. Concentrating activities is less necessary in economic terms, and less possible as governments force more dispersion. At the same time, the ability to coordinate globally throughout the value chain is increasing dramatically through modern technology. The need to coordinate is also rising to offset greater dispersion and to respond to buyer needs.

Thus, today's game of global strategy seems increasingly to be a game of coordination—getting more and more dispersed production facilities, R&D laboratories, and marketing activities to truly work together. Yet, widespread coordination is the exception rather than the rule today in many multinationals, as I have noted. The imperative for coordination raises many questions for organizational structure, and is complicated even more when the firm has built its global system using coalitions with independent firms.

Japan has clearly been the winner in the postwar globalization of competition. Japan's firms not only had an initial labor cost advantage but the orientation and skills to translate this into more durable competitive advantages such as scale and proprietary tech-

nology. The Japanese context also offered an excellent platform for globalization in many industries, given postwar environmental and technological trends. With home market conditions favoring compactness, a lead in coping with high energy costs, and a national conviction to raise quality, Japan has proved a fertile incubator of global leaders. Japanese multinationals had the advantage of embarking on international strategies in the 1950s and 1960s when the imperatives for a global approach to strategy were beginning to accelerate, but without the legacy of past international investments and modes of behavior.[34] Japanese firms also had an orientation towards highly concentrated activities that fit the strategic imperative of the time. Most European and American multinationals, conversely, were well established internationally before the war. They had legacies of local subsidiary autonomy that reflected the interwar environment. As Japanese firms spread internationally, they dispersed activities only grudgingly and engaged in extensive global coordination. European and country-centered American companies struggled to rationalize overly dispersed configurations of activities and to boost the level of global coordination among foreign units. They found their decentralized organization structures—so fashionable in the 1960s and 1970s—to be a hindrance to doing so.

As today's international firms contemplate the future, Japanese firms are rapidly dispersing activities, due largely to protectionist pressures but also because of the changing economic factors I have described. They will have to learn the lessons of managing overseas activities that many European and American firms learned long ago. However, Japanese firms enjoy an organization style that is supportive of coordination and a strong commitment to introducing new technologies such as information systems that facilitate it. European firms must still overcome their country-centered heritage. Many still do not compete with truly global strategies and lack modern technology. Moreover, the large number of coalitions formed by European firms must overcome the barriers to coordination if they are not to prove ultimately limiting. The European advantage may well be in exploiting an acute and well-developed sensitivity to local market conditions as well as a superior ability to work with host governments. By using modern flexible manufacturing technology and computerizing elsewhere in the value chain, European firms may be able to serve global segments and better differentiate products.

Many American firms tend to fall somewhere in between the European and Japanese situations. Their awareness of international competition has risen dramatically in recent years, and efforts at creating global strategies are more widespread. The American challenge is to catch the Japanese in a variety of technologies, as well as to learn how to gain the benefits of coordinating among dispersed units instead of becoming trapped by the myths of decentralization. The changing pattern of international competition is creating an environment in which no competitor can afford to allow country parochialism to impede its ability to turn a worldwide position into a competitive edge.

NOTES

1. United Nations Center on Transnational Corporations, *Salient Features and Trends in Foreign Direct Investment* (New York: United Nations, 1984).

2. For a survey, see R.E. Caves and Ronald W. Jones. *World Trade and Payments,* 4th ed. (Boston: Little, Brown, 1985).

3. There are many books on the theory and management of the multinational, which are too numerous to cite here. For an excellent survey of the literature, see R.E. Caves, *Multinational Enterprise and Economic Analysis* (Cambridge: Cambridge University Press, 1982).

4. Raymond Vernon, "International Investment and International Trade in the Product Cycle," *Quarterly Journal of Economics,* Vol. 80 (May 1966): 190–207. Vernon himself, among others, has raised questions about how general the product cycle pattern is today.

5. Michael E. Porter, *Competitive Strategy: Techniques for Analyzing Industries and Competitors* (New York: The Free Press, 1980); Michael E. Porter, "Beyond Comparative Advantage," working paper, Harvard Graduate School of Business Administration, August 1985.

6. For a description of this research, see Michael E. Porter, ed., *Competition in Global Industries* (Boston: Harvard Business School Press, forthcoming).

7. The distinction between multidomestic and global competition and some of its strategic implications were described in T.

Hout, Michael E. Porter, and E. Rudden, "How Global Companies Win Out," *Harvard Business Review* (September–October 1982): 98–108.

8. Howard V. Perlmutter, "The Tortuous Evolution of the Multinational Corporation," *Columbia Journal of World Business* (January–February 1969): 9–18. Perlmutter's concept of ethnocentric, polycentric, and geocentric multinationals takes the *firm* not the industry as the unit of analysis and is decoupled from industry structure. It focuses on management attitudes, the nationality of executives, and other aspects of organization. Perlmutter presents ethnocentric, polycentric, and geocentric as stages of an organization's development as a multinational, with geocentric as the goal. A later paper (Yoram Wind, Susan P. Douglas, and Howard V. Perlmutter, "Guidelines for Developing International Marketing Strategies," *Journal of Marketing,* Vol. 37 (April 1973): 14–23) tempers this conclusion based on the fact that some companies may not have the required sophistication in marketing to attempt a geocentric strategy. Products embedded in the life style or culture of a country are also identified as less susceptible to geocentrism. The Perlmutter et al. view does not link management orientation to industry structure and strategy. International strategy should grow out of the net competitive advantage in a global industry of different types of worldwide coordination. In some industries, a country-centered strategy, roughly analogous to Perlmutter's polycentric idea, may be the best strategy irrespective of company size and international experience. Conversely, a global strategy may be imperative given the competitive advantage that accrues from it. Industry and strategy should define the organization approach, not vice versa.

9. Michael E. Porter, *Competitive Advantage: Creating and Sustaining Superior Performance* (New York: The Free Press, 1985).

10. Buzzell (Robert D. Buzzell), "Can You Standardize Multinational Marketing," *Harvard Business Review* (November–December 1980): 102–113; Pryor (Millard H. Pryor, "Planning in a World-Wide Business," *Harvard Business Review,* Vol. 23 (January–February 1965); and Wind, Douglas, and Perlmutter, "Guidelines," point out that national differences are in most cases more critical with respect to marketing than with production and finance. This generalization reflects the fact that marketing activities are often inherently country-based. However, this generalization is not reliable because in many industries, production and other activities are widely dispersed.

11. A number of authors have framed the globalization of industries in terms of the balance between imperatives for global integration and imperatives for national responsiveness, a useful distinction. See C.K. Prahalad, "The Strategic Process in a Multinational Corporation," unpublished DBA dissertation, Harvard Graduate School of Business Administration, 1975; Yves Doz, "National Policies and Multinational Management," an unpublished DBA dissertation, Harvard Graduate School of Business Administration, 1976; and Christopher A. Bartlett, "Multinational Structural Evolution: The Changing Decision Environment in the International Division," unpublished DBA dis-

sertation, Harvard Graduate School of Business Administration, 1979. I link the distinction here to where and how a firm performs the activities in the value chain internationally.

12. See, for example, Oliver Williamson, *Markets and Hierarchies* (New York: The Free Press, 1975). For an international application, see Mark C. Casson, "Transaction Costs and the Theory of the Multinational Enterprise," in Alan Rugman, ed., *New Theories of the Multinational Enterprise* (London: Croom Helm, 1982); David J. Teece, "Transaction Cost Economics and the Multinational Enterprise: An Assessment," *Journal of Economic Behavior and Organization* (1986).

13. The difficulties in coordinating are internationally parallel to those in coordinating across business units competing in different industries with the diversified firm. See Michael E. Porter, *Competitive Advantage: Creating and Sustaining Superior Performance* (New York: The Free Press, 1985), Chapter 11.

14. Empirical research has found a strong correlation between R&D and advertising intensity and the extent of foreign direct investment (for a survey, see Caves, *Multinational Enterprise*). Both these factors have a place in our model of the determinants of globalization, but for quite different reasons. R&D intensity suggests scale advantages for the global competitor in developing products or processes that are manufactured abroad either due to low production scale economies or government pressures, or which require investments in service infrastructure. Advertising intensity, however, is much closer to the classic transfer of marketing knowledge to foreign subsidiaries. High advertising industries are also frequently those where local tastes differ and manufacturing scale economies are modest, both reasons to disperse many activities.

15. For an interesting description of the industry, see the paper by Michael Yoshino in Porter, ed., *Competition in Global Industries.*

16. It has been recognized that comparative advantage in different stages in a vertically integrated industry sector such as aluminum can reside in different countries. Bauxite mining will take place in resource-rich countries, for example, while smelting will take place in countries with low electrical power cost. See Caves and Jones, *World Trade and Payments*. The argument here extends this thinking *within* the value chain of any stage and suggests that the optimal location for performing individual activities may vary as well.

17. The firm need not necessarily be owned by investors in the country, but the country is its home base for competing in a particular country.

18. See Porter, *Competitive Advantage.*

19. See S. Linder, *An Essay on Trade and Transformation* (New York: John Wiley, 1961); Vernon, "International Investment"; W. Gruber, D. Mehta, and R. Vernon, "R&D Factor in International Trade and International Investment of United States Industries," *Journal of Political Economics,* 76/1 (1967): 20–37.

20. Where it does recognize scale economies, trade theory views them narrowly as arising from production in one country.

21. See Alfred Chandler in Porter, ed., *Competition in Global Industries,* for a penetrating history of the origins of the large industrial firm and its expansion abroad, which is consistent with the discussion here.

22. Ibid.

23. For data on auto assembly, see "Note on the World Auto Industry in Transition," Harvard Business School Case Services (#9-382-122).

24. For a supporting view, see Theodore Levitt, "The Globalization of Markets," *Harvard Business Review* (May–June 1983): 92–102.

25. The implications of the shift from multidomestic to global competition were the theme of a series of papers on each functional area of the firm prepared for the Harvard Business School Colloquium on Competition in Global Industries. See Porter, ed., *Competition in Global Industries.*

26. For a discussion, see Hout, Porter, and Rudden, "How Global Companies Win Out." For a recent treatment, see Gary Hamel and C.K. Prahalad, "Do You Really Have a Global Strategy?" *Harvard Business Review* (July–August 1985): 139–148.

27. David J. Teece, "Firm Boundaries, Technological Innovation, and Strategic Planning," in L.G. Thomas, ed., *Economics of Strategic Planning* (Lexington, Mass.: Lexington Books, 1985).

28. For a treatment of coalitions from this perspective, see Porter, Fuller, and Rawlinson, in Porter, ed., *Competition in Global Industries.*

29. Hladik's recent study of international joint ventures provides supporting evidence. See K. Hladik, "International Joint Ventures: An Empirical Investigation into the Characteristics of Recent U.S.-Foreign Joint Venture Partnerships," unpublished doctoral dissertation, Business Economics Program, Harvard University, 1984.

30. For the seminal work on contractual failures, see Williamson, *Markets and Hierarchies.*

31. For a thorough and sophisticated treatment, see Christopher A. Bartlett's paper in Porter, ed., *Competition in Global Industries.*

32. For a good discussion of the mechanisms for facilitating international coordination in operations and technology development, see M.T. Flaherty in Porter, ed., *Competition in Global Industries.* Flaherty stresses the importance of information systems and the many dimensions that valuable coordination can take.

33. For a discussion, see Michael E. Porter and Victor Millar, "How Information Gives You Competitive Advantage," *Harvard Business Review* (July–August 1985): 149–160.

34. Prewar international sales enjoyed by Japanese firms were handled largely through trading companies. See Chandler, in Porter, ed., *Competition in Global Industries.*

10

RESOURCE-BASED STRATEGY AND COMPETITIVE ADVANTAGE AMONG MULTINATIONALS

KARIN FLADMOE-LINDQUIST AND STEPHEN TALLMAN

ABSTRACT   Several empirically based models of the multinational firm focus on the importance of home country derived resources in providing competitive advantage. This paper demonstrates that the resource-based model of strategy provides a theoretically sound justification for these models. The unique aspect of home country resources in the multinational firm provides illuminating evidence for the resource-based model.

INTRODUCTION

Why do multinational firms act differently from one another? Why do multinationals not choose similar governance and control structures? These questions have been at issue in multinational studies for years. Today, as business firms face increasingly global markets and competition, these questions have moved into the mainstream of all business disciplines; but none more than business strategy. As strategists begin to look seriously at international business studies, they might expect to find a unified body of evidence that can be placed in their increasingly rigorous models to define the conditions that affect international strategy. However, from a strategic management perspective, multinational studies appear to be fragmented, based on empirical observations of individual phenomena, and without a unifying theory of the strategic system of the global firm. Strategy, structure, assets, country, industry—all are addressed at some point in the many empirical studies and conceptual models of the multinational or of foreign direct investment, but nowhere are these issues pulled together under a single theory.

The consequence of this fragmentation is a continuing tension between the basic theories of multinational strategy. Models of strategic behavior, or oligopoly power, derive from industrial organization economics. These models suggest that large multinational firms behave in a manner consistent with the structural form of the industry to which they are affiliated. Multinationals seek to extend their oligopolistic advantages from imperfect home markets to foreign markets using foreign direct investment to limit competition. Success is the result of industry structure and strategic conduct. In contrast to the oligopoly models of the multinational, internalization models look to transaction costs economics to explain why some multinationals might choose internal governance structures while others export or license similar products to the same markets. While they preserve economic efficiency, internalization models focus strictly on structural issues in relation to performance, with little concern for other competitive strategies. Those who study multinationals from these two perspectives seem perpetually in conflict, insisting on the noncompatibility of their views of the world (Buckley, 1988; Dunning, 1988a). International business studies need a theory of multinational firm strategy in which competitive advantage and strategic success are not inherently at odds with governance efficiency and structural integrity.

We would like to thank Allen Morrison, Jim Robins, and Bruce Kogut for their comments and useful suggestions on earlier drafts of this paper and Jane Dutton, our editor, for a thorough job that has strengthened this paper substantially.

The objective of this paper is to demonstrate that resource-based strategy (Barney, 1991; Conner, 1991) may provide such a theory, compatible with but moving beyond existing concepts of multinational firms operating in worldwide markets. Resource-based theory focuses on unique firm-specific resources (FSRs), rather than industry structure, and addresses both competitive advantage and the strategies intended to exploit such advantage (Tallman, 1992). Governance structural efficiency, the key to transaction cost economics models of the multinational, is also compatible with resource-based models. Conner (1991) shows that resource-based strategy is compatible with and more general than either of these economic theories which underly most modelling of multinational firms.

Resource-based strategy theory suggests that the complex organizational systems that are the bases for strategic advantage derive from the unique historical backgrounds of individual firms. However, the actual origins of such resources remain unclear. This paper suggests that a key source of these unique resources for multinational firms is home country competitive context. This position is based on previous research in international business regarding differences in home country national institutions. Therefore, this paper makes two primary contributions: (1) the development of a resource-based explanation for the strategies and structures of multinational firms, and (2) a discussion of the origins and strategic effects of FSRs in multinationals.

Much of the early work on multinationals was based on studies of American and British firms and assumed a general homogeneity of strategy and structure across all such firms. More recently, substantial evidence indicates that firms from different countries in the same industry use different strategies and organizational structures to exploit unique sources of competitive advantage (Bartlett & Ghoshal, 1989; Dunning, 1981). Recent works by Porter (1990) and Kogut (1991b) suggest that low rates of diffusion of technological and organizational innovations across borders result from unique home country national institutions and encourage nationally delineated strategic groups within global industries. Research in comparative management shows

that cultural differences between home countries (Hofstede, 1980; Boyacigiller & Adler, 1991) produce substantive differences in style and concerns among managers from different countries. Such studies imply that institutional differences among countries may well generate differences in firm-level resources among the firms native to these countries. When the unique firm-level resources that derive from home country conditions can provide sustained competitive advantage, they appear to be much the same as the FSRs that are described by resource-based strategy.

In an initial effort to demonstrate the power of resource-based strategy as a model of multinational firm strategy, we focus on the following research questions: (1) can certain multinational firm specific resources be identified that generate unique strategies and sustained competitive advantage, and; (2) can these FSRs be identified with the national origins of the firms? This paper develops a model of the effect of home country–based firm specific resources on sustained competitive advantage and firm strategy, and suggests a set of researchable propositions to investigate this relationship.

The next section of the paper provides an overview of the resource-based strategy framework. This is followed by a description of several current models of the multinational firm and global strategy that rely on firm-specific resources to function. In the third section, we present a resource-based model of multinational firm strategy along with a more detailed discussion regarding the different resources and a set of propositions that could be the basis for confirmatory empirical research. Finally, we discuss the implications of a resource-based perspective for multinational research and business.

RESOURCE-BASED STRATEGY

The resource-based model of business strategy focuses on how sustained competitive advantage is generated by the unique bundle of resources that are at the core of the firm (Barney, 1991; Conner, 1991; Dierickx & Cool, 1989; Grant, 1991; Mahoney & Pandian, 1992; Wernerfelt, 1984). Resource-based strategy relates sustainable competitive advantage to complex organizational systems, described as rent-producing resources or core competencies, developed over time within specific firms. These competencies, or firm-specific resources (FSRs), are unique to the firm, and therefore a source of differentiation. Fundamentally, the resource-based model argues that heterogeneous firms result from a unique mixture of physical, human and intangible resources (Mahoney & Pandian, 1992).

Barney (1991) proposes that sustained competitive advantage derives from the possession of resources that are: (1) valuable; (2) rare; (3) imperfectly imitable; and (4) imperfectly substitutable. Valuable resources should be able to provide excess profits or quasi-rents to the firm. Rare resources are possessed by no more than a few firms in an industry. Uncertain imitability is necessary to protect sustainable competitive advantage and preserve the value of assets. It is primarily a result of: (a) firm-specific historical factors; (b) causal ambiguity; and/or (c) social complexity. Finally, imperfect substitutability of resources also is key to sustaining competitive advantage.

Only some attributes of a firm qualify as rent-producing resources. Other attributes of the firm may be needed to conduct business, but cannot provide competitive advantage, usually due to their common availability or ease of substitution. Barney contends that rent-yielding resources are specific to the organization; noting, however, that while only a few firms possess a particular resource, it can still be a source of advantage. Industry-specific resources cannot be unique to one (or a few) firms, they must be common to all in the industry; thus, their potential value is competed away.

Barney (1991, p. 101) suggests three types of rent-yielding FSRs: physical capital, human capital, and organizational capital. He contends that physical resources (e.g., physical technology, plants and equipment, geographic location, and raw materials access) seldom generate sustainable advantage because these resources are relatively easy to copy or work around. Grant (1991) provides a broader set of resource categories that adds financial (internal), technological, and reputational resources to the above categoriza-

tion. Of these resources, the most likely sources of true sustainable advantage are the "invisible assets" (Itami, 1987) or "core competencies" (Prahalad & Hamel, 1990) of human (e.g., training, experience, and relationships) and organizational skills (e.g., formal reporting structures, control and coordination systems, and informal relationships). These FSRs are organizationally embedded, socially complex, and difficult to identify specifically, thus difficult to copy.

Resource-based strategy theorists do not specify the sources of these resources, other than to say that they are based on firm history (Barney, 1991; Dierickx & Cool, 1989). In an earlier article, however, Barney (1986) proposes that these resources result from imperfect information in the markets for resources. Some firms may be luckier or better informed in being able to acquire future rent-yielding resources below their true, but unrecognized, market value. Lippman and Rumelt (1982) describe a random draw from a set of strategic possibilities, and presumably also a concurrent draw from a set of resources. Dierickx and Cool (1989) propose that most critical resources develop within the firm and are so unique as to preclude a legitimate market for such resources. Barney (1991) supports this concept with his discussion of a historical basis for firm specific rent-yielding resources. The reasons why such resources develop in one (or a few) firms and not others remain unclear in the strategy literature, however.

Conner (1991) makes a strong case for resource-based strategy as a general theory of the firm. She argues that the resource-based framework incorporates key parts of "Bain-type" industrial organization economics, the basis for the IO stream of work on multinationals and foreign direct investment, in that both theories anticipate persistent profits for certain firms within constraints defined by the environment. However, resource-based models, unlike IO economics, do not require collusive behavior and look beyond industry structure to the internal organization of firms and the activities of their managers as vital to competitive advantage (Conner, 1991, p. 133).

Conner also demonstrates that the resource-based model fits with transaction cost economics, which is the basis for the internalization models of the multinational firm. Both theories are concerned with asset (resource) specificity. However, the resource-based model focuses on both protecting unique resources and applying these FSRs to gain strategic advantage while transaction cost economics concentrates strictly on the avoidance of opportunism and efficient asset governance. In addition, transaction cost models assume the same economic activities can be performed (at different costs) via markets or hierarchies while resource-based strategy treats the organization as a unique bundle of assets that will not function in the same way in an alternate relationship (Conner, 1991, p. 142). If the resource-based theory is, as Conner argues, a more general theory than the oligopoly and transaction cost concepts currently applied to studies of the multinational, then a model of international competitive advantage based on resource-based theory should be considered complementary to and more general than the current models of the multinational firm.

HOME COUNTRY IDENTITY AND MULTINATIONAL STRATEGY

This section addresses the existing literature of the multinational firm. It has two key purposes. First, the two major theoretical models of the multinational are described more fully and are compared to a resource-based model. These models are shown to be similar to the more general models which Conner (1991) argues are compatible with the resource-based theory of the firm. Therefore, a parallel argument for multinational firms is advanced in the following section. Second, the role of home country or nation of origin in generating unique resources and sustainable competitive advantages for multinational firms is examined through a discussion of several empirically based models of the multinational firm. The potential for identifying home country resources with sustained competitive advantage in multinationals is the focus of the resource-based model of multinational firm strategy proposed here.

THE THEORIES

The two major theoretical perspectives on multinationals in the international business literature are based on IO economics and transaction cost economics, respectively. The earliest formulation of an explicit link between strategy and structure for multinational firms is found in Hymer's original work (Hymer, 1960). As extended by Kindleberger (1969) and Caves (1971), this model suggests that oligopolistic firms in concentrated industries will use foreign direct investment (hierarchical governance) to extend their market power to international markets. As a reflection of the IO economics model of strategy on which they are based, these models assume that the conduct of such firms is determined by the structure of the industries in which they are competitors. High performance is linked to the market power of oligopolistic multinationals in competition with weaker host country firms. Power is assumed to come from size (Hymer, 1960) or product differentiation skills (Caves, 1971). This approach is closely analogous to the business strategy models of Bain (1956), Porter (1980), and Caves and Porter (1977). The key feature of these models is the linkage of oligopolistic industry with the potential for high performance.

The internalization model of the multinational developed as an efficient market alternative to oligopoly power models (Buckley, 1988) and derives from early work in transaction costs economics (McManus, 1972). Currently the most widely accepted model of the multinational firm, internalization focuses on efficient structures for controlling intermediate goods and assets. This research stream originates from the question of why firms develop multinational organization structures (McManus, 1972; Buckley & Casson, 1976; Hennart, 1982), but has been extended to examine the strategies of multinational corporations through the use of transactions cost frameworks (Teece, 1986; Casson, 1987). A critical limitation of this model in explaining strategic decisions derives from its strict focus on ''the internalization of markets to . . . model the growth of the firm'' (Buckley, 1988, p. 182) rather than addressing competitive advantage in these markets. As a result, internalization models provide little explanation of the original purposes of managers in devising the strategies which these efficient governance structures support (Borys & Jemison, 1989).

Oligopoly power and strategic behavior in inefficient markets generally conflict with structural efficiency and cost minimization objectives (Calvert, 1981). However, if resource-based theory is compatible with both theories as Conner (1991) suggests, then competitive advantage (established at the firm rather than industry level) and governance cost minimization (placed in a strategic context) can be integrated. Resource-based strategy therefore may provide a unifying theory of multinational firm strategy. It also appears to be capable of providing a theoretical basis for several broad but atheoretical empirical studies that exist in the literature of the multinational which are examined next.

THE EMPIRICALLY BASED MODELS AND HOME COUNTRY ADVANTAGE

Of the established empirically based models of the multinational firm, the Eclectic Model of the multinational firm presents a paradigm that combines competitive advantage, internalization imperatives, and locational economics (Dunning, 1981, 1988a, 1988b). In this widely referenced model, firms possess three key sets of ''advantages'' [Dunning's (1988a) term] relating to their potential for becoming multinationals: (1) ownership advantages; (2) internalization advantages; and (3) location advantages. Ownership advantages are factors unique to the nature or nationality of the ownership of the firm and are referred to as the ''why of multinational activity'' (Dunning, 1988b). Dunning suggests (1988a, pp. 2–3) that ownership factors relate to the multinational's ability to compete in foreign markets and that these advantages derive from unique country, industry, and firm specific variables. Ownership advantages are similar conceptually to FSRs, in that they are the unique internal factors that generate the firm's competitive advantage in the marketplace.

Internalization advantages determine whether the firm will organize efficiently through markets or through internal (hierarchical) means and address the ''how of involvement'' (Dunning, 1988b). This question is formulated as the fundamental choice between a wholly-owned subsidiary or a market based (licensing or export) strategy. Locational advantages affect the choice of foreign country for multinational operations and are referred to as the ''where of production'' (Dunning, 1988b) for multinational operations. Specific types of locational advantages include the host country economic system and governmental policies (Dunning, 1988b).

The purpose of the Eclectic Model is to explain international production in general (Dunning, 1988b) rather than how critical resources generate competitive advantage. However, Dunning does suggest that different resources are critical in different industries, and that for any given industry, firms from one home country will have somewhat different ownership advantages than firms from other home countries (1988a, pp. 5–6). Clegg (1987) tests Dunning's assertions in a study of firms from several industrial countries and provides support for the idea that country differences affect multinational strategy and structure. He observes that the patterns of export and investment by firms in the same industries from different countries are quite different. For instance, American research intensive firms use more direct investment than less technology-intensive American firms, while research intensity in firms from the other countries is more likely to increase exports from the home country but does not correlate with increased direct investment.

Bartlett and Ghoshal (1989) examine alternative strategies and structures through case analysis of several MNEs of different national origin and industry affiliation. They propose a ''transnational'' model in which the administrative heritage, or historical development of strategies, structures, and control systems, of the firm affects its strategic and structural options. The characteristics of its industry determine whether a particular firm's combination will be successful. Their recommended transnational form combines global efficiency, local responsiveness, and world-wide technology sharing, but in a manner unique to each firm and its asset base. Bartlett and Ghoshal explicitly associate much of the administrative heritage of the multinational firm with country of origin. They further suggest that this parochial background must be updated through international experience to derive the organizational assets and competencies needed to compete globally.

A new framework with which to examine the international strategies of multinational firms has been developed by Porter (1990). Porter builds a model in which the international success of nations is based on the competitive abilities of their home-based multinational firms. The ability of companies to compete in global industries is associated with four attributes of the home nation competitive environment that promote or impede creation of international competitive advantage (1990, p. 71). Porter's "competitive diamond" combines the traditional factors of production (i.e., resources, labor, and capital) with non-traditional factors (i.e., human factors, knowledge, and financial infrastructure) in one dimension. The other dimensions of the model are domestic competition, home market demand conditions, and home country support industries. Porter considers all four home country–related factors to be vital to encouraging innovation and competitive advantage in the international marketplace and to maintaining competitive advantage among native firms. He demonstrates empirically, through extensive use of case analysis, that such an advantage can be sustained and is not subject to erosion by competitive imitation. As a result, firm specific sources of competitive advantage—critical resources—can be identified with home country conditions, and can be sustained as unique even as firms from other countries attempt to copy them in global industries.

In this section, we have summarized the two most used theoretical approaches to the multinational firm and to global strategy. We have also covered several empirical models that describe the role of home country characteristics in determining competitive advantage and strategic success among multinational firms. In the following section, we develop a resource-based model of multinational firm strategy that is compatible with the theories and models described here. We then use the observed and inferred effects of home country on FSRs to develop a set of propositions.

MULTINATIONAL STRATEGY: A RESOURCE-BASED MODEL

This section has two major parts. First, we present our general resource-based model of multinational strategy. This model connects firm-level resource development with multinational strategy and competitive advantage in worldwide markets. Second, specific associations of defined home country characteristics with identifiable types of FSRs and particular strategic choices of multinational firms are developed in the next section as specific researchable propositions. Barney's (1991) typology of resources is the basis for our discussion of FSRs, with additions specific to the international environment.

A THEORY-BASED MODEL

The model is derived from the resource-based model of firm strategy and of sustained competitive advantage described above. Figure 1 provides a graphic conceptualization of the basic model. Our discussion and propositions focus on the two center boxes labelled "FSRs" and "Strategic Choices" and the relationship between them.

The ultimate basis for competitive advantage in resource-based theory is the combination of unique resources bundled in a firm. Sources of FSRs were discussed earlier in this paper, but resource-based models are not totally in agreement on this issue. In this model, we suggest five major types of FSRs for the multinational firm: physical, human, and organizational, and also financial and political resources. We believe the first three categories capture the general discussion of resources in the literature (Barney, 1991; Dierickx & Cool, 1989; Grant, 1991; Mahoney & Pandian, 1992). The remaining resource types are important additions to the group and extend the model from a domestic formulation to one that is more specific to international business.

Our model in Figure 1 suggests three primary sources of FSRs in multinational firms. First, the foci of most resource-based models (Dierickx & Cool, 1989), are purely idiosyncratic firm endowments, such as firm-specific organizational routines, skills, and values. These resources (e.g., "the Hewlett-

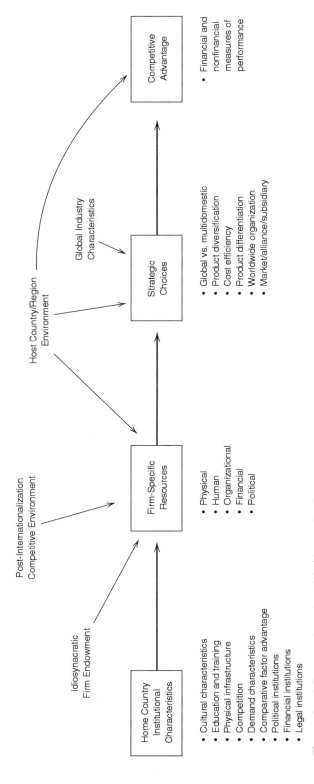

Figure 1. A Resource-based model of international strategy.

Packard Way'') are incorporated (through luck or unique insight) into the firm at formation or develop internally through interactions among the various parts of the firm, or what Bartlett and Ghoshal (1989) call the firm's administrative heritage. These organizational processes are viewed as the major source of truly unique resources and the key to most competitive advantage (Dierickx & Cool, 1989; Grant, 1991). However, purely idiosyncratic resources are difficult to relate to performance as we cannot differentiate among their effects.

Firms also develop FSRs as they absorb assets from the environment in response to competition. Therefore, multinational firms faced with pressures from global competitors and exposed to international markets for resources may well develop FSRs unique to their particular experiences as global companies, such as particular skills in managing subsidiaries (Buckley, 1988). This second source of potential competencies generally applies to the firms in a worldwide industry, and does not allow us to differentiate firms clearly.

Finally, we suggest that firm-specific resources can arise due to the firm's interactions with external inputs or pressures from social, financial and political institutions in their home countries. There is growing evidence that most firms seem to retain their identities as parts of the social and business structure of their home countries long after they have become multinationals. This research stream indicates that certain FSRs of multinational firms are artifacts of early organizational responses to their home country conditions (Collis, 1991; Dunning, 1988a; Kogut, 1991b; Porter, 1990). For example, the decision making style of large Japanese firms results partly from the shared educational and employment history of many of the executives. These home country derived FSRs are the focus of the model in this paper. Such resources can be expected to be held by only a few firms in a worldwide industry, but are not totally idiosyncratic to one firm, and therefore are amenable to study using statistical techniques.

Porter (1990) provides extensive empirical evidence that competitive advantage is developed by firms competing and cooperating within a national industry as a group and is carried over into global competition. These firms have skills and assets unlike those of multinational firms from other countries. In resource-based terms, home country origin affects the distribution of FSRs among multinational firms of different national affiliations within an industry. Such factors as differences in culture, differences in education and training of the workforce, and differences in the physical infrastructures of countries have major effects on the types of FSRs developed in multinational firms from different nations. Porter (1990) also emphasizes the impact of different levels of competition, demand characteristics, and industry structure on the firms from a country. Differences in the political, legal, and financial institutions of nations also will affect the development of specific competencies and assets among their firms (Dunning, 1988b).

In explaining how such differences can lead to sustainable advantage, Kogut (1991b) shows that cultural and political barriers to the transmission of technical and especially organizational knowledge slow international dissemination of "invisible assets" and thus create competitive advantage. Under these conditions, competitive advantage could reside within a small group of firms from one nation in one industry for a considerable length of time, as observed by Porter (1990). Within the resource-based literature, Barney (1991) proposes that a few firms in an industry can possess common FSRs and still accrue quasi-rents, so long as the level of imitation and substitution is not excessive. It appears that the observations of Porter (1990) and the models of Dunning (1988a) and Kogut (1991b) fit with Barney's concept of a small group of firms holding similar sources of competitive advantage. Furthermore, home country based assets and competencies fulfill Barney's (1991) four stated requirements for sustainable advantage—value, rarity, inimitability, and nonsubstitutability. In a resource-based model, firms with such differentiated resource bases should employ different multinational strategies and demonstrate different competitive advantages (Collis, 1991).

In the general model illustrated in Figure 1, most of the home country related resources of firms should fit into Barney's typology of physical, human, and organizational resources. Locating advantage with hard assets such as capital goods or intellectual property, the learned skills of workers and managers, or with the organizational structures and systems designed to perpetuate competencies with proven track records seems general enough to be considered directly applicable to multinationals.

Extension of the resource-based framework to the multinational enterprise requires additions to the original conceptualization of rent-yielding FSRs, however. Since the resource-based framework is essentially domestic in nature as currently conceptualized, it does not consider the impact of institutions that are homogeneous within countries but often very different across national boundaries. Two additional areas of critical home nation based resources that are important for multinational firms are external financial and political institutions. Financial and political assets and capabilities that can generate profits develop in the context of specific home country institutions, but become embedded in firms from these countries, much as other FSRs.

As shown in Figure 1, competitive advantage based on home country conditions arises in a firm via the development of a resource base and the application of this base through strategic and structural decisions. We do not expect a simple and direct relationship of home country with firm performance or a direct relationship of FSRs with performance. As described by Conner (1991), resource-based models provide considerable leeway for managerial decision making, with little of the deterministic approach of most economic models remaining. Available FSRs will be considered, whether explicitly or implicitly, in making key strategic decisions in any multinational. Resource-based strategy theory states that the main source of uncertain imitability of FSRs is the causal ambiguity of competitive advantage (Reed & DeFillipi, 1990). Therefore, Tallman (1992) suggests that strategies will be chosen to exploit FSRs with rent yielding capacities proven under previous strategies. The characteristics of the worldwide industry, which may be somewhat different from those of the home country domestic industry, also will influence strategic decisions, and may limit which FSRs can be applied internationally. Also, host coun-

try environmental conditions may limit the potential for applying some FSRs that might be valuable in other contexts, thus further restricting strategic choices. Tallman (1992) suggests, for instance, that capital constraints might force a firm to joint venture for a marketing subsidiary, even though whole ownership might be preferred to exploit a brand image properly. As the model in Figure 1 shows, the path from unique resource through appropriate strategy to sustained competitive advantage is somewhat more complicated for a multinational firm than for a domestic firm.

The second part of our model concerns the set of strategic choices that comprise multinational strategy (see Figure 1). These choices include alternatives for diversification across product lines and across geographical markets and national boundaries. Determination of the degree of global integration among subsidiaries and product divisions is another key decision of the multinational firm (Porter, 1986). The relative emphasis on global cost efficiency and/or local market responsiveness and/or product differentiation that determines what FSRs will be emphasized also is a critical strategic decision for the multinational firm (Bartlett & Ghoshal, 1989). Other issues such as product market selection, timing of multinational expansion, geographic scope of expansion, human resource development and direction, use of mergers and acquisitions as opposed to greenfield investment, and participation in strategic alliances are also of strategic significance. For instance, a firm that finds itself with available financial and managerial resources and a need for rapid expansion may consider acquisitions to speed entry into new markets. A multinational with a core competence in research and development may pursue product differentiation through product technology as its key global strategy. Another firm in another industry may seek its rents market by market by heavily modifying its products to match local preferences.

The choice of governance arrangements and transaction cost efficiency also may be affected by FSRs as firms attempt to choose control and operating structures for their multinational strategy (Dunning, 1988a; Bartlett & Ghoshal, 1989). Differentiated resource structures, combined with different strategic outlooks for different multinationals and host country conditions, can be expected to generate a variety of structural solutions. These solutions run from markets through cooperative ventures to hierarchies for a single firm, under conditions where simple transaction cost models might imply uniform responses (Ghoshal & Nohria, 1989). The various strategic choices will be affected differently by each of the five resource areas, however. For example, a firm with a single unique product technology (physical resource) may wish to use alliances and acquisitions to buy into distribution channels, while a firm with a complex and productive R&D organization may need to use internally developed (greenfield), wholly-owned subsidiaries to transmit this skill abroad. Conner's discussion of the importance of resource bundling (1991, p. 142) to competitive advantage is specifically relevant to the choice of entry structure for a foreign market, and may be at odds with concerns for opportunistic behavior.

Strategic management models such as resource-based strategy focus on performance differences across firms as indicative of resource advantages. The models of the multinational described previously also predict performance effects from the ownership of unique resources. Performance effects imply the existence of or lack of competitive advantage, but are influenced also by strategic decisions and by the conditions in the host market (Tallman, 1992). Performance involves the entire resource base of the firm, including both home-country based and truly idiosyncratic FSRs. This is a complex relationship, but the results reported by Porter (1990) imply that some part of performance can be tied to resources derived from home country affiliation.

We do not address the specific effects of resources on performance in any detail in this paper, due to spacial limitations. We focus the rest of the discussion on the relationship of specific home country characteristics to the strategic decisions of multinational firms. This relationship is expected to be generated through the FSRs derived from different country related effects and applied to the choice of strategies.

FIRM-SPECIFIC RESOURCES AND PROPOSITIONS

This section discusses the concept of firm-specific resources in greater detail and develops six propositions from our resource-based model of multinational strategy (see Figure 1 and the preceding discussion). A general proposition considers the potential effect of the total bundle of FSRs on the strategic choices of the multinational firm. The five categories of home-country based critical FSRs are then considered separately to develop theoretical propositions regarding a resource-based model of multinational strategy. We provide both theoretical and anecdotal support for the propositions in this section.

Porter (1990), Dunning (1988a), and Bartlett and Ghoshal (1989) all have suggested possible characteristics of home country industries which might affect the development of FSRs among national firms. National political, cultural, legal, and educational institutions affect the way business is conducted in a country, to include business-government relations, labor relations, and social relationships. Financial and economic institutions affect the availability and cost of capital and the financial structures of firms, in such areas as defining permissible levels of debt load. The physical infrastructure of the country determines, to some extent, what businesses will develop in a country and whether firms can compete in the global environment. For instance, a country with few good roads is not likely to develop a global level automobile industry. Finally, political institutions and policies control the level of competition and cooperative activity, and can influence the abilities of firms to compete in more or less competitive markets. Tight anti-trust policies in the United States are often blamed for slowing the commercial development of new technologies through industry consortia, for instance.

The general dependent variable for each proposition is the strategy of the multinational firm. Specific strategic choices, however, vary by resource type. The concept of strategic choice encompasses a broad range of international options that include the structure, contractual alternatives (i.e., strategic alliances and joint ventures), entry patterns, use of expatriates, scale and scope of expansion and timing of expansion. While much international research limits itself to the choice of market entry structure, the set of strategic choices facing a multinational is much more extensive than a simple binary choice on one option.

Firm-specific Resources In the proposed framework, multinationals make strategic choices based on their ability to exploit FSRs in international environments. Firm-specific resources must fulfill the requirements of value, rarity, inimitability, and non-substitutability and are operationalized at the level of the firm. The FSRs of a multinational firm that are based on home country institutions and conditions fit into one of the five resource categories of physical, human, and organizational factors and external financial and political institutions. The greater the variation among countries regarding these assets, the more likely that the pattern of multinational strategic choices will vary among firms from different countries within the same industry. The general proposition considers the five resources as a group because strategic decisions are rarely made with only one resource in mind. For example, organizational resources of high complexity and implicit nature are considered the most likely source of sustainable advantage (Barney, 1991). However, the political, cultural, geographical, and institutional boundaries between countries make the other four categories of FSRs more likely to generate sustainable advantage for multinational firms than for firms operating in a purely domestic market.

It is likely that even between firms from one country there will be variations on these dimensions. However, we suggest that a significant portion of the variation in strategic choices in a group of multinational firms will be attributable to the institutional environment in their separate home countries. These national institutions include the educational, social, political and economic systems and are responsible for creating the network of human and organizational resources that are among the core resources affecting competitive advantage of a firm. Furthermore, the political and financial institutions of a na-

tion can allow or restrict the possible options available for multinational strategy. Multinationals that are from the same countries have developed under similar institutional circumstances and should therefore possess similar bundles of resources and should exhibit more similarity in their patterns of strategic choices than should firms from different home environments.

Proposition 1: The greater the differences in national institutions between home countries, the greater should be the differences in resource bundles and patterns of strategic choice among multinational firms in one industry from these countries.

Physical Resources Physical resources are the first country-based, firm specific resource type that we examine. Such resources include plants and equipment, geographic location, access to raw materials and the physical technology used by the firm (Barney, 1991). Dependence on physical resource factors such as raw materials has historically been a catalyst that affects the strategic choices of multinational firms. For example, firms in extractive industries such as mining are dependent on the natural location of the raw materials. The less adequate home country raw material supplies are for economic scale production, the sooner firms become multinationals and expand internationally, often through wholly-owned subsidiaries. Mining firms such as Kennecott Copper pursued international expansion early in their corporate histories to find and develop additional sources of ore as domestic sources ran out or became too expensive to pursue. During the high-point of international expansion, extractive firms used wholly-owned subsidiaries because of the heavy investments needed to develop the resource and the desire to protect it from sales to competitors. However, this pattern of ownership in the extractive industries has changed dramatically due to host country government takeovers during the 1960s and 1970s (Kobrin, 1988). Today, extractive multinationals use either licensing arrangements or joint ventures with host country governments.

Unlike mining companies that internationalized in

response to a **shortage** of physical resources, firms with key physical technologies have an **abundance** of physical resources with further potential for market scope economies that encourages international expansion. However, the underlying structure of technology can be very different among nations. For example, the technical format used by European video cassette recorders is PAL format and is completely unreadable by the American and Japanese NTSC standard machines. These differences make any video-based technology incompatible between the United States and Europe, so that a simple, direct application of technical advances in one region to the others is not possible.

As a result of such differences, physical technological resources such as patents or proprietary designs are more difficult to diffuse across national and cultural borders than within a national industry (Kogut, 1991b; Kobrin, 1991) and are greatly affected by differences in supporting industries and demand patterns (Porter, 1990). Therefore, physical resources are more likely to yield sustainable advantage internationally than in a purely domestic context. Porter's (1990) discussion of the printing press industry in Germany demonstrates this difficulty. The technologies of American and German printing presses were incompatible and required significant changes to be applied by competitors from other countries. Each industry has developed on its own without being able to integrate the advances of the other, and foreign markets are served by exports or greenfield, wholly owned subsidiaries.

Sharing of technologies, even if desired, is difficult and suggests that strategies that rely on shared resources, such as mergers, acquisitions, or joint ventures, will not be used. Much of the rationale for such strategies is based on the possible synergies, often technological, that may be achieved by combining the resources of two or more firms. If such synergies are technically incompatible, the incentives to use such arrangements are limited. Therefore, the greater the dependence on home country specific technologies, the more likely that firms will either rely on market (export or licensing) arrangements or expand through wholly-owned greenfield ventures. Export arrangements allow firms to avoid substantial technological

makeovers, licenses place development burdens on the licensee, and the wholly-owned greenfield operations permit firms to internally transfer technology that has already been tested.

Proposition 2: The greater their dependence on unique home country physical technologies, the more likely MNEs are to engage in international expansion through the use of markets or wholly-owned greenfield subsidiaries, and the less likely they are to use mergers, acquisitions, and joint ventures.

Human Resources A multinational firm's human resource system is influenced by the diverse cultures, traditions, and educational systems of its home country and, as a result, will likely generate different configurations of human resources (Boyacigiller & Adler, 1991). These resources include training, experience, technical skills, relationships among managers, and insight of employees (Barney, 1991). The bundle of strategic choices that are most affected by these resources include the use of expatriate managers and technicians, management control systems, and use of strategic alliances. These choices rely on the background, education, and managerial relationships that are key to the human resource category. For example, the choice to use expatriate managers is often based on the nonavailability of "adequately" trained host-country managers (Boyacigiller, 1991). Such training includes an understanding of home-country business procedures, such as accounting standards and financial measures, cultural standards, social patterns, and the like. An absence of host-country managerial staff that understand home-country standards encourages MNEs to use expatriate staff rather than host-country nationals. This reduces the need to train host country nationals and facilitates internal corporate communication.

These specific strategic choices are important because their usage affects the actual implementation of corporate strategy and policy. Research in international business on headquarter-subsidiary relationships suggests that maximum control of local operations is gained by using senior staff that are both home-country and home-office trained (Dowling & Schuler, 1990). Such control is considered central to ensuring consistency with the philosophy of the parent company and is important to MNEs attempting either an integrated global or transnational strategy (Dowling & Schuler, 1990). Clearly, if the local subsidiary is operating as an independent unit with little relationship to the headquarters unit, such control becomes less important.

This pattern of expatriate usage is observable in the international expansion of Japanese multinationals. Through the wide use of greenfield subsidiaries with expatriate Japanese managers, these corporations attempt to replicate the set of relationships among managers that they believe is critical to effective and efficient decision making (Bartlett & Ghoshal, 1989). These relationships develop from the early training and education of Japanese managers, who grow up in a homogeneous culture, attend university together, are hired at the same time into the same firm or into linked firms, and undergo similar training and work experiences. These social and educational relationships then create the relationship base-line that the Japanese believe is an integral part of their business relationships, decision-making processes, and competitive advantage. By comparison, American managers come from a more heterogeneous and diverse culture, are educated in a variety of institutions, come from many parts of the United States, and often move among the major corporations at regular intervals. The set of relationships that Japanese executives develop are simply not imitable in the American environment. As a result, American MNEs may place more importance on technical, managerial skills that are acquired in MBA programs. In a sense, the MBA education provides the "common thread" that provides the shared experience for American managers. As a result, it is less important for an American multinational to replicate a critical set of social relationships, and foreign nationals are used widely if they have the proper MBA technical skills.

This pattern of strategic choices would be consistent with evidence that multinationals tend to expand initially to countries that are more similar culturally to their homes (Dowling & Schuler, 1990). For American firms, Canada and Western Europe often are the earliest target countries for international expansion due to the similarity of language and cultural heritage. As international expansion continues, the cultural diversity of the countries in which MNEs operate increases as managers become more comfortable with working in countries with substantially different languages and heritages, such as Thailand or Saudi Arabia.

Consequently, we suggest that the **abundance** of similarly trained and educated personnel in host countries influences the choice of ownership and control structures. The concept of "similarly trained and educated" managers varies from country to country. For American MNEs, the criterion may be MBA-based managerial competence, a Japanese MNE may use social networks as the important measure, and a German MNE may consider a technical background in engineering the key factor. Whatever the key criterion, the greater the availability of managers that are "similarly trained and educated" in important concerns, the more likely that a multinational will use local managers and ownership arrangements that involve shared control. Alternatively, if most host country managers have a fundamentally different type of training or education on a key issue, the MNE will perceive a **lack** of managers with home-country compatible training. These MNEs will be more inclined to use expatriates and wholly-owned subsidiaries in the international operations to maintain integration and cohesiveness of corporate strategic direction.

Proposition 3:   The greater the importance of a common home culture or training among managers for successfully implementing a corporate strategy, the more likely MNEs are to use wholly owned subsidiaries and expatriate managers.

Organizational Resources   The third category of firm specific resources is organizational resources. These resources develop from diverse legal, political, and cultural traditions and create different administrative heritages among firms from different nations (Bartlett & Ghoshal, 1989; Collis, 1991; Porter, 1990). Barney (1991) suggests that organizational resources include a firm's reporting structure, formal and informal planning systems, controlling and coordinating systems, and informal relations among groups within a firm and among different firms. Organizational resources involve firm-specific routines, defined by Nelson and Winter as "regular and predictable behavioral patterns of firms" (1982, p. 14), rather than specific product skills or knowledge.

The historical development of different routines and systems in firms of different nationalities is important in understanding why firm specific "invisible" resources vary across firms (Bartlett & Ghoshal, 1989; Collis, 1991). Even within a culturally similar setting, such resources are generally difficult to substitute for or to imitate due to the socially complex nature of their development. At the international level, given widely varying firm cultures, organizational resources become particularly insulated (Bartlett & Ghoshal, 1989; Kogut, 1991b; Porter, 1990). Consequently, these resources are considered to be a major source of sustainable competitive advantage (Dierickx & Cool, 1989). Organizational resources affect the strategic choices concerning the product market and the ability to coordinate globally dispersed operations (Porter, 1986) and use of alliance arrangements. Flaherty (1986) uses the cases of several firms in the chemicals and heavy equipment industries to describe global coordination of manufacturing operations. She concludes that such firms develop routines for coordination which vary from firm to firm. Information sharing may involve worldwide vendor information, controlling for globally interchangeable parts, to coordinating manufacturing processes. Without these well-established organizational routines, these firms would not be able to maintain global strategies. Such firms may be considered to have **extensive** organizational resources that facilitate their multinational strategies.

Not all firms have the ability or the organizational mechanisms, such as information systems, management development, organizational cultures, or structural forms to manage a world-wide network of subsidiary units or strategic alliances that result from global expansion. These firms would be better served by using strategies such as exporting or multidomestic expansion, because these approaches require less coordination and integration among operating units (Porter, 1986). These firms may be considered to be **limited** in their organizational resources.

Hamel and Prahalad (1985) contend that limitations on organizational integration derived from fragmented home market conditions have seriously hurt the development of global strategies among large European multinationals. Bartlett and Ghoshal (1989) also describe European administrative heritages as fragmented. These authors contend that the politically and economically fragmented markets in Western Europe led these firms to focus on highly independent national subsidiaries that do not require centralized coordination by headquarters. This independence and the considerable power of country managers have made transnational coordination and control extremely difficult, placing European multinationals at a disadvantage compared to American and Japanese firms because of the growing need to develop more integrated global and transnational strategies. Indeed, the opportunity for firms to learn how to operate in a large unified market was a major issue in the Europe 1992 initiative in the European Community ("After 1992," 1992). In this way, a firm's organizational resources will vary as a result of its national heritage and experience and affect its choice of internalization and of global integration.

Proposition 4: The more extensive their experience in integrating organizational resources, the more likely multinationals will use transnational and global strategies.

Financial Resources Another major difference among countries is the structure of their financial institutions and the accessibility of capital to home-country firms. As a result, we have added the dimension of financial resources to the resource-based model of the multinational firm. The financial resources addressed derive from such institutions as domestic capital markets that vary in size, sophistication and structure (Porter, 1990). Although MNEs have access to global markets, they obtain much of their financing from home-based multinational banks and design their financial structures to the standards of the home market where their ownership is concentrated.

For example, there is substantial variation among multinationals of different countries regarding the amount of debt that they are allowed to carry. Traditionally, Japanese and German firms have carried much higher debt levels than comparable American multinationals (Daniels & Radebaugh, 1992). In addition, the degree of financial dependency on domestic sources varies across countries. Japanese firms rely heavily on domestic markets due to special relationships with the financial community, such as interlocking directorates, significant commercial bank ownership positions, and keiretsu network arrangements. These financial institutions and banking relationships allow the long term strategic horizons of Japanese multinationals and have been seen as a key to their competitive advantage. Long-term government funding is important for multinationals from countries such as Korea in specific industries (e.g., automobiles). The Korean government uses the chaebol structure (large conglomerate groups) to facilitate funding global competition in selected industries. In these cases, **ample** financial resources from a protected home financial market (Daniels & Radebaugh, 1992) become a source of competitive advantage when firms can use capital intensive structures, such as wholly-owned subsidiaries, without facing pressures for early returns on investment.

Alternatively, national capital markets with excessively short-range orientations or with expectations of lower debt ratios may limit international expansion of their native firms through wholly-owned subsidiaries. These markets may not be willing to allow multinationals to bear the financial risk of extremely capital intensive expansion methods, such as wholly-owned subsidiaries. In this situation, an **absence** of financing would limit the strategic choices of multinational firms, and firms might use alternate approaches to reduce their required capital investments. These approaches include joint ventures, licensing, franchising, and strategic alliances and typically rely on outside sources of funding. This arrangement allows the financial risk to be shared among several investors, rather than placing the entire burden on the MNE.

Proposition 5: Multinationals will more likely establish "greenfield" and wholly-owned subsidiaries in foreign markets, the more protected and managed by the government are their home-country financial markets.

Political Resources Home country political institutions provide the fifth major resource that affects the strategic choices and competitive advantage of multinational firms. Generally, these institutions include government ownership or part ownership of the multinational firm, trade and protectionism policies, and intergovernmental relations. Openness of competition at home, a key dimension of Porter's (1990) model, is a political institution which will affect resource development in local business firms. Government regulations concerning market activity, such as antitrust laws, significantly affect the degree of competition among firms. The intense competition of multiple competitors in Japan compared with the stagnation of government supported or owned national champions in Europe provides an example of how national policies influence global competition (Adams & Brock, 1989). The roles of political actors, such as the Ministry of International Trade and Industry (MITI), in influencing business to focus on new technologies of national significance has been widely described as critical to the rapid development of Japanese multinationals.

MNE strategic choices also may be affected by the overall political climate of the home country and by intergovernment relations between the home country and a potential host country (Tallman, 1988). Specific examples include restrictions on market access by U.S. firms to the Warsaw pact countries during the Cold War and the use of commercial activity as an international political weapon, such as the U.S. ban on pipeline sales by Dresser's French subsidiary to the USSR in response to the invasion of Afghanistan. Firms from some countries such as Canada may be seen as more politically neutral and preferred, whereas American firms have been viewed as agents of the American government and its policies. The McDonald's Restaurant in Moscow is technically a joint-venture between a Russian firm and McDonald's Canada, partly for this reason.

These political resources have a direct effect on the strategic choices of multinational firms. The choices of product market location, scope of expansion, level of host-country investment, and governance structure alternatives are affected most. These alternatives depend on governmental policies concerning trade and commerce. For example, the earlier ban by the Mexican government on foreign wholly-owned subsidiaries forced the use of joint venture arrangements by Mexican and American firms.

These political resources may be viewed as **facilitating** or **impeding** international competition. Multinationals from countries with facilitating policies may be considered to have an abundance of supportive political resources. For example, the set of American policies that permits the free movement of currencies is considered a facilitating policy. Many countries, such as Brazil, have very restrictive currency policies that indirectly and directly hinder the ability of multinationals to move goods and services and to repatriate profits and licensing fees. Under these conditions, international business becomes difficult to conduct and firms may consider transferring entire sets of operations to other countries whenever possible.

Firms that are severely impeded may be viewed as operating in a politically resource poor environment. Previously, Mexico, in an effort to encourage the development of domestic businesses, made the importation of certain goods and services very difficult. On the surface, this would seem to facilitate the international competitiveness of Mexican industry. However, the problems of importing critical parts coupled with severe limitations on licensing and strategic alliances along with currency restrictions only served to limit the development of internationally competitive firms. Recently, many of these restrictions have been either dropped or modified by the administration of President Salinas de Gotari. Since home country political efforts tend to focus on build-

ing the home economy, supportive governments will encourage exports, foreign investment in assembly and marketing that keeps high value-added activities at home, and repatriation of profits.

Proposition 6: The greater the abundance of supportive home country political resources, the more likely multinationals are to increase their global expansion efforts through exports, investment for market expansion, and low value-added foreign operations.

DISCUSSION

Application of resource based theory to multinational strategy provides an explanation of why multinational firms from different countries have not converged to a universal set of strategies and structures. Instead, we observe that they are able to sustain competitive advantage over time, using a variety of strategic choices based on significantly different resource pools. One key reason for this resource variation is that multinationals retain assets and skills developed in the unique institutional environments of their home countries prior to their going international (Kogut, 1991b; Porter, 1990). These variations in FSRs lead to patterns of strategic choice that are more similar among multinationals that share a common national heritage than among multinationals in the same industry but with different home countries. Conceptually, Dunning (1988a, 1988b) contends that home country conditions applied within a given industry are a major source of critical resources and competitive advantage. The importance of home country derived FSRs is also shown in Bartlett and Ghoshal's (1989) discussion of administrative heritage as the source of unique organizational capabilities and the basis for successful strategy-structure configurations. Porter (1990) proposes that the industry context in any home country hones the competitive skills of firms from that country in a specific way, creating sustainable international strategic advantages.

As an example of national influences on competitive advantage, the strong scientific culture of Germany has facilitated the development of firms in those industries that have strong technological components. The German educational system involves an extensive network of institutes, apprenticeships, technical universities and schools that train and educate large numbers of individuals to perform technically oriented jobs. The availability of well trained staff as a core human resource would encourage German industry to continue to expand its competitive advantage in technically complex areas such as optics, medical and precision instruments, and pharmaceuticals.

A second important aspect of our framework is the treatment of strategic choices as an interactive set that includes structure, product market, human resources, geographic scope, and control issues. The choice of a joint venture in one country over a wholly-owned subsidiary in another may be affected by both the political and financial resources of the firm and ultimately determined by the human resources available to work with the joint venture arrangement. To illustrate this point, imagine an American MNE interested in developing either a joint venture in China as a global export platform (physical resource) and for access to a potentially large market or a wholly-owned subsidiary in England, a major market for the final product. The intergovernmental relationships (political resources) between the United States and China are more changeable than those between the United States and England. Furthermore, the instability of the Chinese business climate may cause home-country financial institutions (financial resources) to be hesitant about backing a Chinese investment project, even one that involves shared financial resources. Finally, the managerial training in China may not be adequate and expatriate assignments would be needed. However, no one in the firm speaks Chinese or is familiar with the Chinese culture (human resources). As a result of the interaction of the firm's political, financial, and human resources, the final strategic choice is a wholly-owned manufacturing and marketing subsidiary (strategy and structure) in England although the long-term strategic potential of a physical resource in China may be greater.

The above example demonstrates that examining just one strategic choice, such as the use of joint ventures, would be as unrealistic as examining the impact of one resource alone on the strategic choices of the multinational firm. We believe it is important to begin to look at both the full set of resources and the full set of strategic choices. Multinational firms should not make strategic choices based on isolated factors. Rather, the resources and strategic choices are a dynamic set of conditions and alternatives that affect each other in the decision-making process.

CONCLUSION

This paper shows how analysis of home country institutional differences and their impact on the competitive advantage of multinationals in different industries provides insights on international competition and brings a new, general theory of competitive strategy to bear on multinational issues. Resource-based analysis is a general theory of strategy and the firm (Conner, 1991) that provides a theoretical framework which can be used to integrate the previous work on MNE strategy and structure by Dunning (1981), Teece (1986), Porter (1990), and Kogut (1991b). The framework also expands the general theory of the multinational (Buckley & Casson, 1976; Hennart, 1982; McManus, 1972) beyond the focus on governance structure to explain why and how firms become multinationals and compete in international markets.

This paper also adds to the theoretical development of resource-based analysis by extending it to the multinational enterprise. Only by observing common inputs and common, but not identical, outputs, can we test the theory empirically. By examining the impact of home country conditions on the FSRs and strategies of a small subset of international firms in an industry and comparing these firms to firms from other countries, we expect to learn more about the origins and impacts of rent-yielding resources.

The next phase of our research is to define the resource items empirically. The precise resources in each category must be operationalized to be tested. For example, if informal relationships are important organizational resources, informal structures must be defined and explored. Human resources might be operationalized as a specific type of training and education such as a general business education, a general college/liberal arts education, or a specific technical education. Financial resources would likely include measures of capital availability, and financial institutional requirements on debt and expected performance measures. Political resources would include measures of currency controls, structural controls and intergovernmental relationships.

A possible extension of our framework from a conceptual perspective may integrate the concept of forming strategic alliances as taking options on specific markets (Kogut, 1991a). Traditionally, strategic alliances are treated as less attractive, but sometimes required, alternatives to wholly-owned subsidiaries. The options approach treats strategic alliances as limited investments which create platforms for potential future growth, either within-country or across-country. Considering alliances as options on organizational resources which are "bought" at prices below their ultimate market value reflects a logic similar to Barney's (1986) discussion of strategic factor markets. However, strategic alliances are only one of a large set of organizational resources in a resource-based model of the multinational. Most resources which are internalized or developed by the firm before it experiences its full market potential can be seen as options on future strategies. FSRs obtained in the home country, before the firm could invest in international exploitation, seem particularly suited to this analysis. An options approach to resources or competencies would reinforce the concept of an interactive set of resources and choices discussed above by treating the entire bundle of choices as a platform for future growth.

This paper is intended to show that strategic management and international (multinational, global, transnational, etc.) strategy can both be strengthened if they are brought together. We have shown that the conceptual basis for one set of models is improved at the same time that the potential for empirical testing of the other set of theories is expanded, and finally, that new directions in strategic thinking can be broadened by attention to solid theory and to extensive empirical research.

REFERENCES

Adams, W., & Brock, J.W. (1989). *Dangerous pursuits.* London: Pantheon Books.

After 1992. (1992, September 26). *The Economist,* pp. 77–78.

Bain, J.S. (1956). *Barriers to new competition.* Cambridge, MA: Harvard University Press.

Barney, J. (1991). Firm resources and sustained competitive advantage. *Journal of Management, 17*(1), 99–120.

Barney, J. (1986). Strategic factor markets: Expectations, luck, and business strategy. *Management Science, 32*(10), 1231–1241.

Bartlett, C.A., & Ghoshal, S. (1989). *Managing across borders: The transnational solution.* Boston: Harvard Business School Press.

Borys, B., & Jemison, D.B. (1989). Hybrid arrangements as strategic alliances: Theoretical issues in organizational combinations. *Academy of Management Review, 14,* 234–249.

Boyacigiller, N. (1991). The international assignment reconsidered. In M. Mendenhall & G. Oddou (Eds.), *International human resource management* (pp. 148–155). Boston: PWS-Kent Publishing.

Boyacigiller, N., & Adler, N.J. (1991). The parochial dinosaur: Organizational science in a global context. *Academy of Management Review, 16*(2), 262–290.

Buckley, P.J. (1988). The limits of explanation: Testing the internalization theory of the multinational enterprise. *Journal of International Business Studies, 19*(2), 181–194.

Buckley, P.J., & Casson, M. (1976). *The future of the multinational enterprise.* London: Macmillan.

Calvet, A.L. (1981, Spring/Summer). A synthesis of foreign direct investment theories and theories of the multinational firm. *Journal of International Business Studies,* pp. 43–59.

Casson, M. (1987). *The firm and the market.* Oxford: Basil Blackwell.

Caves, R.E. (1971). International corporations: The industrial economics of foreign investment. *Economica, 38,* 1–27.

Caves, R.E., & Porter, M.E. (1977). From entry barriers to mobility barriers: conjectural decisions and contrived deterrence to new competition. *Quarterly Journal of Economics,* pp. 241–261.

Clegg, J. (1987). *Multinational enterprise and world competition.* New York: St. Martin's Press.

Collis, D.J. (1991). A resource-based analysis of global competition: The case of the bearings industry. *Strategic Management Journal, 12*(SI), 49–68.

Conner, K. (1991). A historical comparison of resource-based theory and five schools of thought within industrial organization economics: Do we have a new theory of the firm? *Journal of Management, 17*(1), 121–154.

Daniels, J.D., & Radebaugh, L.H. (1992). *International business:*

Environments and operations (6th ed.). Reading, MA: Addison-Wesley.

Dierickx, I., & Cool, K. (1989). Asset stock accumulation and sustainability of competitive advantage. *Management Science, 35*(12), 1504–1514.

Dowling, P.J., & Schuler, R.S. (1990). *International dimensions of human resource management.* Boston: PWS-Kent.

Dunning, J. (1988a). The eclectic paradigm of international production: A restatement and some possible extensions. *Journal of International Business Studies, 19*(1), 1–32.

Dunning, J. (1988b). *Explaining international production.* London: Unwin Hyman Publishers.

Dunning, J. (1981). *International production and the multinational enterprise.* London: George Allen and Unwin.

Flaherty, M.T. (1986). Coordinating international manufacturing and technology. In M.E. Porter (Ed.), *Competition in global industries* (pp. 83–109). Boston: Harvard Business School Press.

Ghoshal, S., & Nohria, N. (1989). Internal differentiation within multinational corporations. *Strategic Management Journal, 10,* 323–337.

Grant, R.M. (1991). The resource-based theory of competitive advantage: Implications for strategy formulation. *California Management Review, 33*(3), 114–135.

Hamel, G., & Prahalad, C.K. (1985, July/August). Do you really have a global strategy? *Harvard Business Review,* pp. 139–148.

Hennart, J.-F. (1982). *A theory of the multinational enterprise.* Ann Arbor: The University of Michigan Press.

Hofstede, G. (1980). *Culture's consequence.* Beverly Hills, CA: Sage.

Hymer, S. (1960). *The international operations of national firms: A study of direct foreign investment.* Unpublished Ph.D. dissertation, MIT.

Itami, H. (1987). *Mobilizing invisible assets.* Cambridge, MA: Harvard University Press.

Kindleberger, C.P. (1969). *American business abroad: Six lectures on direct investment.* New Haven, CT: Yale University Press.

Kobrin, S.J. (1991). An empirical analysis of the determinants of global integration. *Strategic Management Journal, 12*(SI), 17–31.

Kobrin, S.J. (1988). Trends in ownership of American manufacturing subsidiaries in developing countries: an inter-industry analysis. *Management International Review,* Special Issue, 73–84.

Kogut, B. (1991a). Joint ventures and the option to expand and acquire. *Management Science, 37*(1), 19–33.

Kogut, B. (1991b). Country capabilities and the permeability of borders. *Strategic Management Journal, 12*(SI), 33–47.

Lippman, S.A., & Rumelt, R.P. (1982). Uncertain imitability: An analysis of interfirm differences in efficiency under competition. *Bell Journal of Economics, 13,* 418–438.

Mahoney, J.T., & Pandian, J.R. (1992). The resource-based view within the conversation of strategic management. *Strategic Management Journal, 13*(5), 363–380.

McManus, J. (1972). The theory of the international firm. In G. Paquet (Ed.), *The multinational firm and the nation state.* Don Mills, Ontario: Collier Macmillan, Canada.

Nelson, R.R., & Winter, S.G. (1982). *The evolutionary theory of economic change.* Cambridge, MA: Harvard University Press.

Porter, M.E. (1990). *The competitive advantage of nations.* New York: The Free Press.

Porter, M.E. (1986). Competition in global industries: a conceptual framework. In M.E. Porter (Ed.), *Global competitive strategy* (pp. 15–60). Boston: Harvard Business School Press.

Porter, M.E. (1980). *Competitive strategy: Techniques for analyzing industries and competitors.* New York: The Free Press.

Prahalad, C.K., & Hamel, G. (1990, May/June). The core competence of the corporation. *Harvard Business Review,* pp. 70–91.

Reed, R., & DeFillippi, R.J. (1990, January). Causal ambiguity, barriers to imitation, and sustainable competitive advantage. *Academy of Management Review, 15*(1), 88–102.

Tallman, S. (1992). A strategic management perspective on host country structure of multinational enterprises. *Journal of Management, 18*(3), 455–471.

Tallman, S. (1988). Home country political risk and foreign direct investment in the United States. *Journal of International Business Studies, 19*(2), 219–234.

Teece, D. (1986). Transactions cost economics and the multinational enterprise. *Journal of Economic Behavior and Organization, 7,* 1–45.

Wernerfelt, B. (1984). A resource-based view of the firm. *Strategic Management Journal, 5,* 171–180.

11

UNDERSTANDING STRATEGIC INTENT IN THE GLOBAL MARKETPLACE

MICHAEL A. HITT, BEVERLY B. TYLER, CAMILLA HARDEE, AND DAEWOO PARK

ABSTRACT In this article we underscore how important it is for corporate players in the world's competitive arena to understand the strategic orientation and intent of competitors, partners, and one's own often nationally diverse management team. We offer several examples to illustrate what it takes to succeed in this arena, and include some advice for companies interested in revising their perceptual maps. Such revisions have become imperative as competition in global industries intensifies, as more companies learn to manage across borders, and as the economies of nation states become interlinked.

"When you understand your competitors and yourself, you will always win."

Sun Tzu
The Art of War

Although Sun Tzu was referring to enemies in battle, the ancient military strategist could have just as easily been analyzing Japan's success in U.S. markets. Indeed, Japan's global competitiveness has been attributed to its visceral understanding of customers, suppliers, partners, regulators, influence peddlers, and competitors.[1] A case in point is Komatsu Limited, now the world's second-largest earth moving equipment company. In the 1950s, protected from outside competition by the Japanese Ministry of International Trade and Investment (MITI), there was little incentive for Komatsu to augment its product line or to improve product quality. In the early 1960s, however, the MITI believed that Japan did not have a competitive advantage in the earth moving equipment industry and opened it to foreign capital investments to protect the emerging Japanese auto and electronics industries. When Caterpillar Tractor Co., the world's largest earth moving equipment company, proposed a Mitsubishi-Caterpillar joint venture, Komatsu's president, Yashinari Kawai, pressured the MITI to delay the project two years. The company's survival depended on his ability to quickly take advantage of the Japanese govern-

ment's policies requiring that foreign companies help Japanese companies in return for access to Japan's markets. Thus, Komatsu entered into licensing arrangements with three U.S. companies: International Harvester, Bucyrus-Erie, and Cummins Engine.

Kawai understood Komatsu's customers and employees as well. He realized that Japanese companies would prefer quality products, and Komatsu's current products did not meet international standards. He knew as well that, as third world countries began to industrialize, price would become more important in the marketplace, a plus for his firm because Japanese employees were willing to work for lower wages than U.S. employees. He also knew how to use the turbulence and crisis within the company to encourage employee participation and commitment, focused on the desire to "Maru C" (surround Caterpillar).

Komatsu understood the motives and intentions of its government, customers, competitors, partners and employees. The Japanese government wanted industries that would compete in world markets, customers wanted quality products and services at a reasonable price, employees desired job security, participative leadership, and a sense of achievement, and competitors and partners wanted access to the Japanese markets. By understanding the orientations of each of these players, Komatsu was able to position itself so that it could become a world-class player.[2]

UNDERSTANDING COMPETITORS

Relying too heavily on a static analysis of one's competitors generally does not provide insight into their direction or speed[3] and provides little basis for understanding a competitor's strategic intent or basic orientation for developing competitive positions.[4]

Komatsu decided to compete with Caterpillar on its home soil in Japan, and in the U.S. Komatsu carefully studied and understood Caterpillar's strategic orientation and intent.[5] Its move into the U.S. market was deliberate, with careful attention paid to its competitors and customers. Understanding Caterpillar's competitive strengths, including its dealer network, quality products, and product support, Komatsu began to imitate Caterpillar by building its dealer network and studying customer concerns. Komatsu built a plant in Chattanooga, Tennessee, to begin manufacturing some of the large equipment sold in the U.S. because of the strong sense of protectionism in the U.S. and pressure to buy U.S. made goods. Concurrently, changes in the value of the dollar and the yen made it more cost effective to build in the U.S. instead of shipping products from Japan.

Samsung, a South Korean firm, has also shown an uncanny ability to understand the strategic intent and orientation of its competitors. It became the leading manufacturer of memory chips by matching its Japanese competitors on quality and delivery and besting them on price. Samsung executives suggest that they have learned from their competitors' successes and shortcomings. For example, they avoided the shortsightedness of U.S. manufacturers who significantly reduced their capital expenditures for production equipment during cyclical downturns and had inadequate capacity when the demand for chips increased.[6]

These two examples illustrate the importance of understanding competitors. In this era of rapid globalization, no company can afford to limit its competitor analysis to the past or current experiences. Rather, companies must seek information regarding competitor's government support (e.g., tariffs, subsidies), potential options for action and reaction (e.g., plant locations, technological capabilities, tacit skills) and probable partnerships (e.g., licensing agreements, joint ventures, technological alliances). In short, they must develop adequate information to predict competitors' strategic orientation and intent.

UNDERSTANDING PARTNERS

Cooperative strategies are becoming common in domestic and international markets. For example, large and small corporations have joined with startups to develop leading-edge technology, and U.S. companies have aligned with foreign concerns to penetrate international markets. General Electric Co. boasts of over 100 such partnerships, IBM has joined in over 400 strategic alliances, and AT&T has had partners in the Netherlands, Italy, Spain, South Korea, Taiwan, and Japan since 1980. *Fortune* reports that "alliances are so central to Corning's strategy that the corporation now defines itself as a 'network of organizations'."[7] However, several of these partnerships have not been successful. Executives sometimes conclude deals without adequate consideration of the potential consequences and find that their partner's management style, motivations, or commitment conflict with their own. Two of the primary reasons these relationships go astray are: failure to agree in advance on how to run the business, and inflexible contractual agreements that cannot be changed as the business evolves. Other problems arise from the tendency of partners to think their own technology is best, lack of trust between the partners, and the desire to control rather than collaborate.[8]

Painful Lessons Careful planning, negotiation, and contracting are necessary to avoid such problems in cooperative partnerships. Many U.S. companies still remember the painful lessons learned in the 1970s and 1980s, when they were deceived by partners who obtained technology and market knowledge only to use it to compete against them. Even contracted sales restrictions can be annulled through government intervention. A case in point was Komatsu's decision in the early 1980s to become a full-line supplier of earth moving equipment. This required a reevaluation of its licensing relationships with technology suppliers Bucyrus-Erie and International Harvester. Komatsu appealed to Japan's fair trade commission to support objections to contractual terms restricting the export of two new products using Bucyrus-Erie technology. The commission agreed that the terms constituted a restrictive business practice that impaired competition and allowed Komatsu to buy its way out of the contract. Soon thereafter, it also bought out its obligations to International Harvester. A Komatsu senior manager said ''Komatsu had digested its licensed technology and had established its own technology. Therefore, we just got out of the various licensing agreements.''[9]

While Komatsu has been successful in dealing with its competitors and some partners, some of its partnership arrangements have soured. For example, in its desire to ''Maru C'' it developed a joint venture with U.S.-based Dresser Industries. The intent was to form a joint venture with equal ownership, based on the principles of shared and equal management. Products were to be supplied by Komatsu and Dresser plants in North and South America. The deal was expected to help Komatsu gain a greater foothold in the North and South American markets. Dresser was mired in a downturn in its industry and had excess production capacity. While Komatsu wanted to increase its production in the U.S., Dresser needed to upgrade its plant and equipment. Komatsu injected $200 million and provided production engineers to help in modernizing seven Dresser production facilities. Originally, Komatsu was supposed to shift 60 percent of its production for the U.S. market to the joint venture plants. The two firms were supposed to merge their manufacturing, engineering and finance operations. The Komatsu and Dresser product lines were intended to remain distinct and sold through their separate dealership networks. They ended up competing, however, and numerous clashes erupted between the approaches used by Japanese and American executives in the joint venture. Dresser executives felt excluded from Komatsu decision making. One manager suggested that top Japa-

nese executives often made crucial decisions during Friday evening sessions (held in Japanese) and he learned about the decisions from Japanese subordinates on Monday morning. Some executives charged that Komatsu made the joint venture pay up to 15 percent above market value for its goods. But, Dresser executives refused to provide product information to their Komatsu counterparts because they were afraid of losing sales. As a result of the problems, Dresser hired an industrial consultant to teach its employees how to deal with the Japanese. Furthermore, it sent employees to Japan to learn more about the Japanese culture and work habits. To date, this joint venture has lost market share, but may still pay dividends.[10]

Communication Gaps Often, alliances become troubled because the partners do not clearly understand each other's intent—their strategy, goals and purposes—because they are unable to communicate clearly with managers from a different culture. Such communication gaps often lead to an atmosphere of frustration and mistrust. This problem is exemplified by the partnership of GM and Daewoo, a Korean firm. In 1984, GM and Daewoo signed an agreement to invest $199 million each in a factory to produce the Pontiac LeMans subcompact car. The automobile would utilize GM's German-based technology responsible for the Opel Kadett. The Daewoo Group didn't have the engineering expertise to design or manufacture a LeMans-class car, and GM's U.S. manufacturing operations couldn't produce the LeMans profitably in the numbers needed. Therefore, this partnership looked like a match made in heaven. Not only did GM's European affiliate, Opel, provide the car design, but Opel engineers also set up Daewoo's assembly line plant to manufacture the Pontiac LeMans.

The venture went beyond joint manufacturing of the LeMans in Korea. The two firms also opened three auto parts ventures to make steering gears, axles, brakes, radiators, and air conditioning components. Also, GM took responsibility for the North American marketing of the Daewoo manufactured Pontiac LeMans automobile. Daewoo was hoping to take advantage of GM's engineering, financing and marketing strengths to gain market share from one of its chief Korean competitors, Hyundai.

Unfortunately, multiple problems began to develop. Sales of the LeMans fell dramatically short of projected targets. While Daewoo blamed GM for failing to promote the car, GM blamed Daewoo for quality and supply problems. The GM management expert sent to Korea to correct the problems stated that the Koreans had neither the manufacturing heritage nor an adequate understanding of the auto industry. While Daewoo had the capacity to produce up to 278,000 cars per year, annual combined sales in the U.S. and Korean markets reached only 100,000. Daewoo felt that the LeMans was not a priority product for GM. Furthermore, Daewoo wanted to invest aggressively to take advantage of Korea's booming domestic auto market which was growing at an average of 60 percent per year. However, GM was not interested in additional investments to take advantage of this market. As a result, Daewoo sought help from other firms, including Japan's Suzuki Motor Company, to develop an automobile that would sell well in the Korean market.

Sales of the LeMans continued to decline to slightly over 39,000 autos in the U.S. in 1990. There were numerous management clashes and operational disputes between the two firms. Daewoo wanted to make decisions and move quickly, and GM's methodical approach prolonged decision making and created conflict. Neither party fully understood the other's strategic goals nor its strengths and weaknesses. Thus, what was now an obvious mismatch in strategic orientation and intent had not even been considered as a possibility by either party prior to forming the venture.[11] As a consequence, GM and Daewoo went through a bitter divorce. Each company acknowledged that both underestimated obstacles faced by their venture, including different cultures, languages and business aspirations. One executive noted that the two partners never learned to walk together before trying to run together. These partners did not understand one another before or during the venture and therefore the venture failed.[12]

Even though many cooperative partnerships have proven unsuccessful, the number of such partnerships, including equity ownership, licensing agreements, joint ventures, strategic alliances, and other types of contractual agreements, has increased exponentially over the past decade. As industries globalize, industry players, large and small, are creating strategic alliances in order to survive the competitive shakeout. The desire for lower sourcing costs served as one of the earliest motivations for cooperative relationships. A number of U.S. firms moved manufacturing facilities to foreign locations, often in Asia or Latin America, in an effort to save on labor costs. In so doing, several have formed joint ventures, such as General Motors and Daewoo, or have purchased equity positions, such as Ford's 25 percent position in Mazda, 10 percent position in Kia Motors of Korea and 75 percent position in Aston Martin Lagonda.[13] However, this strategy must be implemented carefully. The negative experiences of companies such as General Motors with Daewoo serve as reminders of the obstacles to success.[14]

UNDERSTANDING A NATIONALLY DIVERSE MANAGEMENT TEAM

Michael Porter argues that "Firms can no longer view the domestic and foreign spheres as separate and different but must see the whole—how to conceive and implement overall strategies for competing globally."[15] It has become increasingly evident that the old ways of competing internationally have become obsolete. Currently, firms are confronted with a bewildering array of competitive and management problems in implementing their own intrafirm agreements.[16] Kenichi Ohmae describes the borderless world with an interlinked economy, toward which he believes we are moving. He believes that on a competitive map—as compared to a political map—showing the actual flows of financial and industrial activity, boundaries between countries have largely disappeared. In this world, *global citizenship* is no longer only a phrase but a reality.[17]

Perhaps equally as critical as understanding one's competitors and partners is a firm's understanding of the strategic orientations of its nationally diverse

Table 1. Top Five Criteria Used in Strategic Acquisition Decisions

U.S. Executives	Korean Executives
1. Projected Demand for Target Firm's Product(s)	1. Attractiveness of Target Firm's Industry(ies)
2. Discounted Cash Flow	2. Sales Revenue
3. Return on Investment	3. Market Share
4. Attractiveness of Target Firm's Industry(ies)	4. Manufacturing Capabilities
5. Management Talent/Expected Synergy	5. R&D Capabilities

management team. Many multinational firms are evolving into almost stateless corporations, whereby executives come from multiple countries with diverse cultures, and decisions are made without regard to national boundaries. In these firms, differences in managers' strategic orientations should be understood, appreciated and utilized to the advantage of the firm.[18]

It is imperative that firms with international operations understand their own managers' strategic orientations and intent. If a firm has operations in Korea, for example, it is important to understand the potential strategic actions that might be undertaken by top managers of that unit. This is particularly important in multinational companies because of the need to provide autonomy to these national units so that they can be responsive to the local markets and compete effectively. It is also critical to coordinate among the separate units in order to build cost advantages through centralized global operations. Coordination requires effective communication and integration that can only be achieved if management understands how various managers think, what they value and how they are likely to respond. To illustrate this point, when we examined how top U.S. and Korean executives evaluate an acquisition decision,[19] we found significant variation in the decision criteria.

As shown in Table 1, U.S. executives considered projected demand for the target firm's product to be the most important criterion, followed by cash flow, return on investment, attractiveness of the industry in which the firm operated, management talent, and the expected synergy between the two firms. On the

other hand, the Korean executives regarded attractiveness of the target firm's industry as the most important criterion, followed by the target firm's sales revenue, market share, and capabilities in manufacturing and research and development. Among the top criteria for each group of executives, only industry attractiveness was common to both.

While decisions of executives from both the U.S. and Korea were determined primarily by the objective criteria on which each target firm was evaluated, U.S. executives' decisions varied more by individual than those of their Korean counterparts. The Koreans' strategic decision criteria reflected the more homogenizing influences present in the Korean culture. The Korean cultural heritage fosters a form of management Chandler called "group capitalism."[20]

In addition, while U.S. executives placed heavy weight on financial criteria, the Koreans focused more on current market position and capabilities. By and large, U.S. executives focus on financial criteria, such as cash flow and return on investment (ROI), because of emphasis on maximizing shareholder wealth. On the other hand, Korean executives pursue ROI for the purpose of market expansion and growth. U.S. firms are financed largely through the capital market, whereas Korean firms are often financed through government-guided bank loans. U.S. executives often feel pressure to meet stockholder demands for high dividends, and thus may focus more on profitability than potential growth opportunities. In contrast, Korean executives are less sensitive to short-term profitability and more sensitive to long-term growth strategies.[21]

REVISING PERCEPTUAL MAPS

Firms moving into global markets will have to revise their perceptual maps of competitors and markets. Undoubtedly, movement from a domestic to a global market opens a new arena for competition. Furthermore, the markets and network of competitors are clearly more complex. Thus, while it becomes even more important to understand the strategic orientation and intent of your competitors, partners and nationally diverse management team, it also becomes more difficult to do so.[22]

While there are several ways that firms might attempt to examine their competitors, potential partners and their own managers, we recommend the following actions:

To Understand Your Competitors

- Go beyond standard static analyses of competitors.

- Examine their national history (e.g., dominant religion, government-business relationships, level of economic development, etc.).

- Analyze their managerial values, goals and strategy.

- Profile their strategic orientations and predict their strategic intent.

To Understand Your Potential Partners

- Analyze their corporate culture, structure and operating systems to combine with information on top executives' strategic orientation.

- Analyze how the specific alliance fits into the partner's overall strategy.

- Analyze partner's costs and benefits from the alliance, both tangible and intangible.

- Predict partner's strategic intent for the alliance.

To Understand Diverse Members of Your Management Team

- Examine the culture of their country of origin and its other relevant characteristics.

- Analyze the types and amount of experience they have achieved.

- Analyze their previous major strategic decisions.

- Use this information to profile their strategic orientation.

NOTES

1. F.S. Worthy, "Keys to Japanese Success in Asia," *Fortune,* October 7, 1991, 157–169.

2. C.A. Bartlett and U.S. Rangan, *Komatsu Limited,* Harvard Business School, case #9-385-277, 1985; Bartlett, *Komatsu Limited,* Harvard Business School, teaching note #5-388-130, 1988; U.S. Rangan and C.A. Bartlett, *Caterpillar Tractor Co.,* Harvard Business School, case #9-385-276, 1985.

3. G. Hamel and C.K. Prahalad, "Strategic Intent," *Harvard Business Review,* May-June 1989, 63–76.

4. Hamel and Prahalad, *op. cit.;* D. Park and M.A. Hitt, "Executive Effects on Strategic Decision Models: Examination of Strategic Intent," paper presented at the Strategic Management Society, Toronto, Canada, October, 1991.

5. B. Kelly, "Komatsu in a Catfight," *Sales and Market Management,* April 1986, 50–53.

6. L. Nakarmi and N. Gross, "Masters of the Clean Room: How Samsung Upstaged Japan to Become Number One in ORAMS," *Business Week,* September 27, 1993, 107–108.

7. J.B. Levine and A. Byrne, "Corporate Odd Couples," *Business Week,* July 21, 1986, 100–104; S. Sherman, "Are Strategic Alliances Working?" *Fortune,* September 21, 1992, 76–78.

8. Bartlett and Rangan, *Komatsu Limited, op. cit.;* Levine and Byrne, *op. cit;* Sherman, *op. cit.*

9. Bartlett and Rangan, *Komatsu Limited, op. cit.*

10. J. Mullich, "Heavy Equipment Venture Packs Powerful Punch," *Business Marketing,* March 1993, 10; K. Kelly, "A Dream Marriage Turns Nightmarish," *Business Week,* April 29, 1991, 94–95; W.G. Krizan and N. Usui, "Dresser, Komatsu Strike Deal," *ENR,* February 11, 1988, 7; "Dresser, Komatsu Form North American Joint Venture," *Engineering and Mining Journal,* October 1988, 53.

11. L. Nakarmi, L. Armstrong and J.B. Treece, "Is the GM-Daewoo Deal Running on Empty?" *Business Week,* September 12, 1988, 55; J.B. Treece, "Why GM and Daewoo Wound Up on the Road to Nowhere," *Business Week,* September 23, 1991, 55; P.A. Eisenstein, "Inchon Landing," *Chilton's Automotive Industries,* February 1990, 116–118.

12. D. Darlin and J.B. White, "Failed Marriage: GM Venture in Korea Nears End, Betraying Firm's Fond Hopes," *The Wall Street Journal,* January 16, 1992, A-1, A-12.

13. Park and Hitt, *op. cit.;* K. Kell, O. Port, J. Treece, G. DeGeorge, and Z. Schiller, "Learning from Japan," *Business Week,* January 27, 1992, 52–60.

14. Strategic alliances can be successful. For example, Corning obtained more than half of its $133.3 million in net income in 1985 from nearly two dozen alliances. Corning executives argue that the company's success with corporate linkups comes from working with a long-term perspective. They seek lifetime associa-

tions because of the enormous energy it takes to make a partnership work. Corning works hard to avoid the pitfalls of many U.S. companies that are trying to gain the upper hand. Above all, Corning wants to establish a feeling of mutuality and trust. To do this it seeks partners with compatible values, presses for 50-50 ownership, installs good managers, and sets the venture apart from both parents. See endnote 6, *op. cit.*

15. M.E. Porter, *Competition in Global Industries* (Boston, MA: Harvard Business School Press, 1986).

16. Porter, *op. cit.,* 1–2.

17. K. Ohmae, *The Borderless World* (New York, NY: Harper Perennial, 1991).

18. W.J. Holstein, S. Reed, J. Kapstein, T. Vogel and J. Weber, ''The Stateless Corporation,'' *Business Week,* May 14, 1990, 98–105.

19. A detailed discussion may be found in M.A. Hitt, B. Tyler and D. Park, ''A Cross-Cultural Examination of Strategic Decision Models: Comparison of Korean and U.S. Executives,'' *Proceedings of Academy of Management,* August 1990, 111–115.

20. C.A. Bartlett and S. Ghoshal, *Managing Across Borders: The Transnational Solution* (Boston, MA: Harvard Business School Press, 1991).

21. K.H. Chung and H.C. Lee, ''National Differences in Managerial Practices,'' in K.H. Chung and H.C. Lee (eds.) *Korean Managerial Dynamics* (New York, NY: Praeger, 1989), 163–180.

22. W. Boeker, ''Strategic Changes: The Effects of Founding and History,'' *Academy of Management Journal,* 32, 1989, 489–515; J. Leontiades, ''Going Global: Global Strategies versus National Strategies,'' *Long Range Planning, 19,* 1986, 96–104.

ABOUT THE AUTHORS

Michael A. Hitt holds the Paul M. and Rosalie Robertson Chair in Business Administration at Texas A&M University. He received his Ph.D. from the University of Colorado and previously served on the faculty at Oklahoma State University and University of Texas at Arlington. He is the author or coauthor of several books, book chapters and numerous articles in such journals as the *Academy of Management Journal, Strategic Management Journal, Journal of Applied Psychology, Organization Science,* and *Academy of Management Executive.* He is the former editor of the *Academy of Management Journal* and is Vice President and Program Chair of the Academy of Management. He is coauthor of a new book entitled *Downscoping: How to Tame the Diversified Firm* (Oxford University Press).

Beverly B. Tyler is an assistant professor of strategic management in the School of Business at Indiana University, Bloomington. Her research, teaching and consulting activities focus on corporate strategic cognitive and decision processes as they relate to innovation and change, cooperation and global integration. Her work has been published in the *Strategic Management Journal, Research in Personnel* and *Human Resources Management,* and the *High Technology Management Research Series.*

Camilla A. Hardee is vice president of marketing for Woodbine Development Corporation, a real estate company associated with Hunt Oil Company of Dallas. Prior to joining Woodbine in 1991, she was manager of corporate communications for Hunt Oil, where she had worked since 1980. A *magna cum laude* graduate of Trinity University, San Antonio, she earned a bachelor's degree in journalism and worked for several years as a reporter and editor for *Dallas/Fort Worth Business Journal, Arlington Citizen-Journal,* the *Jackson* (Tenn.) *Sun* and *North San Antonio Times.* She later earned an MBA with a marketing emphasis from the University of Texas at Arlington.

Daewoo Park (Ph.D., Texas A&M University, Organizational Behavior) is an assistant professor of organizational behavior and strategy at Xavier University, Cincinnati, Ohio. His primary research interests are in the application of macro organizational psychological theories to the implementation of organizational innovation and globalization. For his research and teaching, he has worked with many corporate executives of *Fortune 500* companies (e.g., Procter & Gamble, Cincinnati Milacron, General Electric) and Japanese companies (e.g., Andrew Jergens, Toyota).

12

THE CHOICE OF INTERNATIONAL STRATEGIES BY SMALL BUSINESSES

INGA S. BAIRD,[1] MARJORIE A. LYLES,[2] AND J.B. ORRIS[3]

As business and industries globalize, the development and performance of a small firm may be tied to its strategic options, particularly those exercised in the international arena. The international strategies of multinational corporations such as global coordination, national responsiveness, formation of cooperative alliances, and developing global-scale efficiencies and learning capabilities (Bartlett and Ghoshal 1987) have received considerable research attention. However, beyond exporting (Czinkota and Johnston 1983, Namiki 1988), the international strategic options of small firms have not been studied in depth. Small firm characteristics such as limited financial and managerial resources, personalized objectives of owner/managers, and informal centralized planning and control systems (Cavusgil 1984, Roth 1992) indicate that global strategies and structures of small firms may differ from those of larger firms.

This study examines small firms' strategies and organizational responses to increasing global competition. The objectives of the study are as follows: (1) to examine the international strategies of small firms, (2) to assess the relationship between an international strategy and firm performance and (3) to evaluate the attributes associated with adoption of an international strategy.

THEORETICAL DEVELOPMENT

GLOBAL STRATEGY: A BRIEF REVIEW

Studies show that there are three strategic orientations for large multinationals: (1) world-wide integration strategies where economies of scale and lower costs are achieved through global volume; (2) national responsiveness strategies where products are tailored to local needs; and (3) administrative strategies that use learning capabilities to manage across various industry structures (Ghoshal 1987, Hamel and Prahalad 1985). These studies emphasize the development of the multinational corporation (MNC) into an organization that gains efficiencies from all of its operations and applies learning capabilities across all of its subsidiaries.

Global strategies of MNCs are affected by the ability to achieve a competitive advantage. Ghoshal (1987) states that multinationals can achieve competitive advantage through national differences, scale economies, or scope economies. Size is the common denominator of these bases of competitive advantage. However, Morrison and Roth (1992), in their study of business-level strategies in global manufacturing industries, did not find size advantages used to achieve a global integration-low cost strategy. Only domestic product niche, exporting high-quality offerings, international product innovation, and quasi-global combination strategies were revealed.

[1] Dr. Baird is an associate professor in the Department of Management at Ball State University. Her research interests are in risk, diversification, and cooperative strategies.
[2] Dr. Lyles is an associate professor of strategic management at the Indiana University School of Business. Her research interests are in the areas of the globalization of strategies, organizational learning, and international joint ventures.
[3] Dr. Orris is professor of business administration at Butler University in Indianapolis. His research interests include statistical software development and neural networks.

GLOBAL STRATEGIES FOR SMALL BUSINESSES

Nature of Small Businesses Small businesses are defined as firms with fewer than 500 employees but with sales greater than $500,000. Much of the research on the strategic management of small firms has dealt with the formality of strategic planning (Robinson and Pearce 1983) rather than the content of the strategies or reasons for their adoption. However, strategic choices of small firms and the factors that influence these choices are being identified (Lyles, Baird, Kuratko, and Orris 1993).

Discussion of small business international strategies involves recognizing that research on MNCs is not directly transferable to small firms. Shuman and Seeger (1986, 8) state that ''Smaller businesses are not smaller versions of big businesses . . . smaller businesses deal with unique size-related issues as well, and they behave differently in their analysis of, and interaction with, their environment.'' Ballantine, Cleveland, and Koeller (1992) find that within the same industry, there are important differences between the asset development, advertising, and foreign expansion strategies that work well for small and large firms.

Strategic Options of Small Businesses The question of which strategic options result in optimal small firm performance has been addressed but not resolved. Cooper (1979) proposes that growth-minded small businesses should choose a niche strategy, concentrating on where they have competitive advantages because they can innovate and change products quickly. Dilts and Prough (1989) and Chaganti, Chaganti, and Mahajan (1989) suggest that small firms can grow through a concentration strategy aimed at improving performance in their current products and markets, broad product-line development, or new market development including international expansion. O'Neill and Duker (1986) find that successful small business options may involve avoidance of debt and fixed asset investment while differentiating on quality in current markets.

International Strategic Options of Small Firms Namiki (1988) identifies the following effective export strategies for small firms: competitive pricing and brand identification, manufacturing capabilities for specialty products, technological superiority, and customer service. Sriram and Sapienza (1991) find that customization of products and direct distribution are associated with higher market share. However, managerial, production capacity, and information system limitations may lead to unfamiliarity with export trading companies' services, poor foreign communication skills and personal contacts, joint venture limitations, and problems in transaction-creation activities (DeNoble, Castaldi, and Moliver 1989). Also, small businesses' tendency to react to the environment, rather than predicting or controlling it, may make them hesitant to actively seek out foreign customers.

The strategic options available to the small business can be followed by acting independently (competitive strategies) or by acting cooperatively with other firms (cooperative strategies). D'Souza and McDougall (1989) suggest that cooperative strategies are not frequently adopted by small firms. However, Shan (1990), Brown (1991), and Van Horn (1990) propose that for small firms, cooperative arrangements are a good mode of commercializing products in foreign markets and overcoming resource scarcity.

RESEARCH QUESTIONS

Previous research on small and large firms indicates that industry and firm characteristics influence the adoption and effectiveness of particular international strategies. The relationship between these variables and the international strategy and effectiveness of the small firm is the focus of this study. The model presented in Figure 1 summarizes these variables.

Characteristics of the firm are the first set of variables that may influence a firm's international strategy. A more adequate resource base may enable larger and older small firms to develop an international orientation. Also, manufacturing firms with a tangible product may be more likely to internationalize, using a product differentiation strategy to provide the mechanism for foreign market entry. Parents may be very important as a means of protecting their

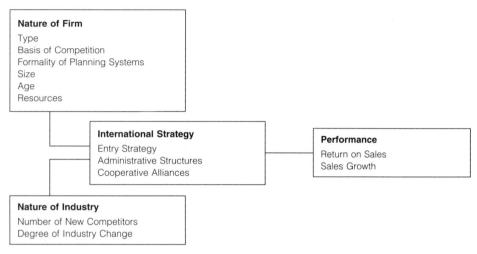

Figure 1. Conceptual Model of Factors Influencing International Strategy for Small Businesses

position. Less important methods of competing would be differentiation based on service, image, or price since the small firm may not have the size to support these strategies in international markets.

Research Question 1: *Are small firms with an international strategy different in size, age, or type from firms with little emphasis on international strategy?*

Research Question 2: *Are small firms with an international strategy more likely to be manufacturing firms, to have a patent, and to compete on the basis of product differentiation than firms with little emphasis on international strategy?*

Environmental characteristics are the second set of variables dealt with in the model that may affect adoption of an international strategy. An increasing number of domestic competitors and a rapidly changing industry may be associated with movement into global markets. The existence of a formal planning system that monitors and helps formulate responses that environmental changes may enhance adoption of an international strategy.

Research Question 3: *Does a relationship exist between perception of rapid environmental change and developing an international strategy?*

Research Question 4: *Are small firms with international strategies more likely to have formal planning systems than firms with little emphasis on international strategy?*

The literature suggests that as firms become more international, they develop better control and monitoring systems to manage the more complex activities and operations. Small firms with international strategies may demonstrate changes in their internal systems toward more formality.

Research Question 5: *Does a relationship exist between small firms developing international strategies and internal administrative changes?*

Some empirical support exists for suggesting that firm performance will be related to the firm's international orientation (Roth 1992).

Research Question 6: *Does a relationship exist between small firms developing international strategies and their performance?*

METHODOLOGY

SAMPLE

The purpose of this study is to examine whether there are systematically different patterns of international strategies as firms contend with largely similar environmental constraints. Therefore, in order to control for the mediating effects of external factors such as taxes, labor costs, etc., the sample was restricted to a single geographic setting. The firms were all subject to the same non-industry-specific government programs aimed at increasing the international involvement of small firms. For small businesses in particular, these effects are important and can affect performance. Therefore, some researchers suggest finding a regionally restricted setting to study small firms (Robinson and Pearce 1988).

Since the purpose of this exploratory study involved identifying common international strategies across industries, the sample was not restricted to one particular industry. McDougall and Robinson (1990), Roth (1992), and Carter et al. (1994) suggest that this is necessary to allow a broader interpretation of results and identification of basic archetypes.

Robinson and Pearce (1988) state that although differences among industries may affect strategies, it is not always possible or desirable to collect data from enough firms in a single industry within the requisite geographic area to do necessary statistical tests. Therefore, in order to obtain an adequate sample size for statistical tests and to provide a basis for broad interpretation of the results, a multi-industry sample was selected. The mean values of descriptive and strategy items were compared across broad industry groups, and no significant differences were found. Industry effects on performance were controlled by standardizing the returns based on industry means.

Variables controlled through sample selection were age, size in employees, and size in sales. To be included, firms had to be at least 4 years old, have 500 or fewer employees, and gross sales greater than $500,000. The sample of 160 Indiana firms ranged in size from 5 to 500 employees with a mean of 66. Thirty percent had more than 50 employees. Mean sales were $7.5 million. The range extended from $500,000 to $65 million, with 76 percent of the firms having 1988 sales of $10 million or below. The firms averaged 30 years old. Firm types consisted of 26 service, 18 construction, 51 retailing, 54 manufacturing, and 11 other/agriculture firms. The sample does not exhibit any size or type bias when compared with the typical distribution of the state's small businesses.

Owners/managers of businesses within the region chosen for the study were contacted and interviewed by students who followed a structured interview format. The students received training in interviewing. The owners were advised that the research was part of an on-going university effort to study small businesses, asked to participate, and an interview time was established. Few of the owners contacted refused to be interviewed. Nonparticipants said they were too busy, that they never give out information, or that they merely were not interested in participating. The basic characteristics of the firms that refused were not different from the responding firms. There was no indication of a nonresponse bias.

SURVEY INSTRUMENT

The survey included four sections dealing with firm characteristics, perceived environmental changes, organizational changes, and strategic responses in terms of strategies, bases for competition and planning. The survey was pretested to guard against any problems with interpretation.

Firm Characteristics Variables included firm age, size in employees, type (a dummy variable where 1 = manufacturing and 0 = nonmanufacturing), and size in gross sales. Financial data including sales, growth in sales, and net income were requested. Sixty firms supplied information on net income. These businesses were compared to the other firms on company characteristics and showed no significant differences.

Environmental Changes Questions addressed the number of new product introductions, industry return on sales, and entrance of new competitors into the market. Lists of elements of the general and industry environments (regulation, demand, product and process technology, suppliers, competition, and growth rate) were presented and respondents were asked to identify those changes that had been most important over the past three years. Industry change and environmental change variables are totals of changes indicated in each category. This conforms with the method for looking at environmental dynamism and change proposed by Miller and Friesen (1980).

Internal Changes Respondents were also asked to indicate the major internal changes made during this time period in systems, structure, new product development, production technology, product line, and strategy. These responses were summed to calculate the number of systems changes, structure changes, process changes, and strategy changes. Degree of planning formality was determined by utilizing the scale developed by Robinson and Pearce (1983).

Strategic Orientation Respondents were asked to indicate on a scale of 1 to 5 the extent to which they relied on nine strategies to ensure the continued success of their firms. These strategies included competitive and cooperative strategies in the domestic and international arenas. The five bases of competition (image, service, price, technology, and quality) were adopted without change from widely used descriptive schemes of competitive advantage. Shortell and Zajac (1990) have demonstrated convergent validity between perceptual and archival measures of strategic orientations.

ANALYSIS

The analysis utilized statistical methods that reveal the underlying dimensions of the firms' international strategies. Principal components factor analysis was used to identify these dimensions. The use of factor analysis on scale data is supported by Kachigan (1982). Reliability coefficients were calculated. In analyzing performance, stepwise regression was used to test which of the independent variables, including the international strategy factors, had the greatest explanatory power. A significance level of .10 was specified as the criterion for variables to enter the equation.

RESULTS

An examination of the means, standard deviations, and correlations shows that firms indicated an aver-

age of 20 new competitors had entered their markets. The bases of competition were image, service, and quality with less emphasis placed on price or innovation. Few had patents. The majority (100) did no formal planning. Between 1985 and 1988 compound sales growth was 6 percent per year. Mean return on sales (ROS) for the 60 firms that gave that data was 9.2 percent.

STRATEGIES

To determine the strategic orientations, a principal components factor analysis was performed to obtain the best linear combinations of the nine strategy items (Table 1). Three factors with eigenvalues approximating one or greater were extracted and rotated with varimax factor rotation. Varimax rotation was selected to minimize the number of variables that had high loadings on a factor and to enhance the interpretation of the factors. Alpha coefficients are presented in table 1.

The first factor constitutes the international strategy since exporting, foreign equity investment, and foreign alliances to develop new products and enter new markets load on this factor. It accounts for 37.8 percent of the variance. The next factor represents domestic alliance formation. Using domestic alliances to enter new markets and develop new products and domestic equity investment load on this factor. The final factor has an eigenvalue of only .945 but is retained because it represents a domestic solo strategy that is important and comprehensible. Entering new markets and developing new products by itself load on this factor. The three factors explain 62.3 percent of the variance.

CLASSIFICATION INTO INTERNATIONAL VERSUS NON-INTERNATIONAL FIRMS

The sample was split into quartiles based on factor scores on the international strategy. Students' *t*-tests were performed comparing the highest and lowest quartile firms (Table 2). Firms with an international strategy were significantly larger than noninternationally oriented firms and were more likely to be manufacturing enterprises, making more changes to

Table 1. Factor Analysis Results on Strategies*

Item	Factor 1 International	Factor 2 Domestic Alliances	Factor 3 Domestic Solo
Develop New Products-Foreign Alliances	.773		
Exporting	.761		
Foreign Equity Investment	.759		
Enter New Markets-Foreign Alliances	.648	.452	
Enter New Markets-Domestic Alliances		.810	
Domestic Equity Investment		.644	
Develop New Products-Domestic Alliances		.578	.417
Enter New Markets by Self			.791
Develop New Products by Self			.660
Eigenvalue	3.402	1.343	0.945
% Variance Accounted for	37.8	14.9	10.5
Cumulative Variance	37.8	52.7	63.2
Cronbach's Alpha	.79	.58	.47

*Only factor loadings greater than .40 shown.

Table 2. Comparisons of International and Non-International Firms

Variable	Non-International Mean	s.d.	International Mean	s.d.	t
Age	31.80	28.98	31.83	26.04	0.01
New Competition	17.61	82.81	12.82	31.78	0.32
Size	47.12	71.59	96.31	39.07	−2.70*
Type	0.01	0.02	0.36	0.49	5.80*
Alliance Strategy	0.84	0.95	0.07	1.25	3.16*
Solo Strategy	0.26	0.88	0.40	1.03	0.83
Planning	1.45	0.71	1.60	0.63	0.98
New Products	5.25	7.34	8.69	10.94	−1.55
Image Competition	4.12	1.31	3.38	1.50	2.40*
Service Competition	4.21	1.03	4.05	1.08	0.75
Price Competition	3.29	1.37	2.95	1.32	1.14
Technological Competition	2.64	1.58	2.71	1.44	−0.19
Quality Competition	4.07	1.15	3.61	1.49	1.57
Environmental Change	2.12	0.97	2.48	1.45	−1.33
Industry Change	2.38	1.43	3.19	2.16	−2.09*
System Change	1.57	1.21	1.69	1.35	−0.41
Structural Change	2.55	2.23	3.02	2.41	−0.94
Process Change	0.45	0.63	0.86	0.78	−2.61*
Growth	1.88	5.36	0.76	1.86	1.12

*Significance level of at least .05.

Table 3. Regression Results: Antecedents and Effects of International Strategy

Variables	International Strategy			
	Beta	Chg. R^2	t-value	Sig. t
Type	−.396	.157	−4.298	.000
Industry Changes	.209	.042	2.288	.024
Planning Formality	.177	.031	1.989	.049
Patent	.152		1.510	.133
Overall R^2	.231			
Adjusted R^2	.208			
Overall F	9.73*			
df	3,97			

Variables	Return on Sales			
	Beta	Chg. R^2	t-value	Sig. t
International Strategy	.398	.200	2.650	.014
Solo Domestic Strategy	−.441	.105	−2.864	.008
Age	.295	.086	1.994	.056
Quality Competitive Advantage	.262	.063	1.741	.094
Overall R^2	.453			
Adjusted R^2	.370			
Overall F	5.399*			
df	4,26			

Variables	Growth in Sales			
	Beta	Chg. R^2	t-value	Sig. t
New Competitors	.284	.125	2.725	.008
Patent	.286	.030	2.565	.012
International Strategy	−.228	.036	−2.043	.044
Age	−.183	.031	−1.710	.084
Overall R^2	.222			
Adjusted R^2	.182			
Overall F	5.503*			
df	4,97			

*$p < .01$

their production processes. They did not make significantly more internal adjustments. The international firms were unlikely to engage in domestic alliances or compete based on image. More industry changes were perceived by the internationally active firms.

ANTECEDENTS OF AN INTERNATIONAL STRATEGY

To determine variables associated with adoption of the international strategy, a stepwise multiple regression was performed with factor scores on the international strategy as the dependent variable (Table 3). Type of firm, number of industry changes, and planning formality entered the equation. Manufacturing firms were associated with adoption of an international strategy. A higher number of perceived environmental changes was positively related to an international strategy. Small firms with more formal planning were more likely to adopt an international strategy. Possession of a patent entered the regression next but was only close to significance. The overall equation explains 23 percent of the variance and is significant at the .001 level.

PERFORMANCE OF BUSINESSES PURSUING AN INTERNATIONAL STRATEGY

Two stepwise multiple regressions were performed with return on sales and growth in sales as the dependent variables. The generic strategies, firm characteristics, environmental change, planning formality, and the bases of competitive advantage were the independent variables.

The variables that entered the stepwise regression on ROS included solo domestic strategy, age, international strategy, and quality as a competitive advantage. International strategy was positively associated with ROS, and explained 20 percent of the variance. Utilizing the solo domestic strategy had a negative relationship to ROS. Development of new products and entry into new markets by firms acting alone was associated with lower returns. Older firms in the sample had a higher ROS. Firms that compete based on quality were likely to have high ROS. R^2 was .45.

A very different picture emerged when growth in sales was examined. Growth in sales was positively and significantly associated with a high number of new competitors entering the market and possession of a U.S. patent. Negative relationships occurred between growth in sales and age and international strategy. Overall R^2 was .22.

DISCUSSION

THE NATURE OF INTERNATIONAL SMALL FIRMS

The first and second research questions addressed whether a firm that develops an international strategy is different in terms of size, age, type, patent possession, or basis of competition from firms without an international strategy. The results indicated that international firms are larger and tend to be manufacturing firms. International small businesses tend to build their strategy on a patent or manufacturing capability and process changes. As expected, the international strategy was not related to competing on service or image.

An international strategy for these firms means a combination of exporting, alliances, and foreign investment. Further work on global integration versus national responsiveness strategies for small firms is needed. A quasi-global strategy (Morrison and Roth 1992) may be useful for small businesses.

ANTECEDENTS OF INTERNATIONAL STRATEGY ADOPTION

The third research question considered the relationship between environmental changes and the choice of an international strategy. The results indicated that industry change in regulation, demand, product and process technology, suppliers, competition, and growth rate are salient to the internationally oriented firms. In regard to research question 4, it was found that firms that are internationally oriented tend to have formal planning systems.

ADMINISTRATIVE STRUCTURES

The fifth research question addressed the basic concept that as large firms move towards globalization, internal administrative changes also occur. This study found that international small businesses develop some organizational capabilities and resources different from the domestic-oriented firms. Greater formality of the planning systems and capabilities for new product development emerged for the international firms. However, these results confirm Roth's (1992) statement that the international configuration of small firms is often not fully developed. Additional research is needed to refine understanding of this configuration. Studying other dimensions, such as organizational structure, ownership structure, or specific activities, may be useful.

PERFORMANCE OF INTERNATIONALLY ORIENTED SMALL FIRMS

The last research question considered whether an international strategy is related to performance. Two elements of performance—profitability and growth—showed opposite relationships to the international strategy. The international strategy is positively related to return on sales but negatively related to growth. Older firms seem to be increasing their ROS by taking their current products into foreign markets either on their own or through foreign alliances. This strategy is more profitable than the domestic solo strategy. A topic that warrants more work is the relationship between international strategy and growth in sales. It may be useful to separate the effects of industry life cycle stage and international strategy on growth in sales.

The normal provisos relation to cross-sectional data apply to this study. Significant relationships shown by this sample do not imply causality. The sample characteristics could limit the generalizability of the results.

A factor not addressed here is the influence of top managers on the decision and choice of international strategy. Studies suggest that management attitudes are important to successful exporting (Czinkota and Johnston 1983; Dichtl, Koeglmayr, and Mueller 1990). Future research should address the management's enthusiasm to explore types of international opportunities, including joint venturing. A related topic is whether owner/founders have different attitudes than professional managers toward the choice of international strategy.

The choice of strategies is another area for further work. Alliances are an important option for small firms moving abroad. They are a means of overcoming the condition of ''resource poverty,'' but may also pose a threat, particularly for firms competing based on new product development. Future research should address how small firms can protect themselves from loss of technological advantage (or bleedthrough) in their cooperative relationships (Lyles 1990).

CONCLUSIONS

This study presents a classification of three strategies that are useful for understanding the internationalization of small businesses. The results demonstrate that small firms that are internationally oriented view exporting, foreign alliances, and foreign equity investments as a single international strategy. Entry options of MNCs, such as wholly owned subsidiaries or establishing large scale manufacturing operations in host countries, appear to be less appropriate options for small firms. Instead they choose global strategy options that fit their scope of operations. The distinctive challenge for the international strategy of a small firm is to overcome the conditions unique to small companies and develop international strategies such as exporting or joint ventures (Baird, Lyles, and Orris 1993) that are effective in their situations.

REFERENCES

Ballantine, J.W., F.W. Cleveland, and C.T. Koeller (1992), ''Characterizing Profitable and Unprofitable Strategies in Small and Large Businesses,'' *Journal of Small Business Management* 30 (April), 13–24.

Baird, I.S., M.A. Lyles, and J.B. Orris (1993), ''Alliances and Networks: Cooperative Strategies for Small Businesses,'' *Mid-American Journal of Business* 8 (April), 17–24.

Bartlett, C.A., and S. Ghoshal (1987), ''Managing Across Borders: New Strategic Requirements,'' *Sloan Management Review* 28 (Summer), 7–17.

Brown, D. (1991), ''Strategies for Europe's New Market,'' *Small Business Reports* (January), 36–42.

Carter, N.M., T.M. Stearns, P.D. Reynolds, and B.A. Miller (1994), ''New Venture Strategies: A Multi-Industry Comparison,'' *Strategic Management Journal* 15 (January), 21–42.

Cavusgil, S.T. (1984), ''Organizational Characteristics Associated with Export Activity,'' *Journal of Management Studies* 21 (January), 3–21.

Chaganti, R., R. Chaganti, and V. Mahajan (1989), ''Profitable Small Business Strategies Under Different Types of Competition,'' *Entrepreneurship Theory and Practice* 13 (Spring), 21–35.

Cooper, A.C. (1979), ''Strategic Management: New Ventures and Small Business,'' in *Strategic Management: A New View of Business Policy and Planning,* ed. D.E. Schendel and C.W. Hofer, Boston: Little, Brown & Co., 316–332.

Czinkota, M.R., and W.J. Johnston (1983), ''Exporting: Does Sales Volume Make a Difference?'' *Journal of International Business Studies* 14 (Spring), 147–153.

DeNoble, A.F., R.M. Castaldi, and D.M. Moliver (1989), ''Export Intermediaries: Small Business Perceptions of Services and Performance,'' *Journal of Small Business Management* 27 (April), 33–41.

Dichtl, E., H. Koeglmayr, and S. Mueller (1990), ''International Orientation as a Precondition for Export Success,'' *Journal of International Business Studies* 21 (First Quarter), 23–40.

Dilts, J.C., and G.E. Prough (1989), ''Strategic Options for Environmental Management: A Comparative Study of Small versus Large Enterprises,'' *Journal of Small Business Management* 27 (July), 31–38.

D'Souza, D.E., and P.P. McDougall (1989), ''Third World Joint Venturing: A Strategic Option for the Smaller Firm,'' *Entrepreneurship Theory and Practice* 13 (Summer), 19–33.

Ghoshal, S. (1987), "Global Strategy: An Organizing Framework," *Strategic Management Journal* 8 (September), 425–440.

Hamel, G., and C.K. Prahalad (1985), "Do You Really Have a Global Strategy?" *Harvard Business Review* 63 (July–August), 139–148.

Hamel, G., Y.L. Doz, and C.K. Prahalad (1989), "Collaborate with Your Competitors—and Win," *Harvard Business Review* 67 (February), 133–138.

Kachigan, S.K. (1982), *Multivariate Statistical Analysis.* New York: Radius Press.

Lyles, M.A. (1990), "Technology Protection and International Joint Ventures," in *Proceedings of the Second International Conference on Managing the High Technology Firm,* ed. L.R. Gomes-Mejia and M.W. Lawless, Boulder, Colo.

Lyles, M.A., I.S. Baird, D.F. Kuratko, and J.B. Orris (1993), "The Impact of Formalized Planning on Strategic Choice in Small Businesses," *Journal of Small Business Management* 31 (April), 38–50.

McDougall, P., and R.B. Robinson, Jr. (1990), "New Venture Strategies: An Empirical Identification of Eight 'Archetypes' of Competitive Strategies for Entry," *Strategic Management Journal* 11 (October), 447–467.

Miller, D., and P. Friesen (1980), "Momentum and Revolution in Organization Adaptation," *Academy of Management Journal* 23 (December), 591–614.

Morrison, A.J., and K. Roth (1992), "A Taxonomy of Business-Level Strategies in Global Industries," *Strategic Management Journal* 13 (September), 339–418.

Namiki, N. (1988), "Export Strategy for Small Business," *Journal of Small Business Management* 26 (April), 32–37.

O'Neill, H.M., and J. Duker (1986), "Survival and Failure in Small Business," *Journal of Small Business Management* 24 (January), 30–37.

Robinson, R.B., and J.A. Pearce (1983), "The Impact of Formalized Strategic Planning on Financial Performance in Small Organizations," *Strategic Management Journal* 4 (July–September), 197–207.

Roth, K. (1992), "International Configuration and Coordination Archetypes for Medium-Sized Firms in Global Industries," *Journal of International Business Studies* 23 (Third Quarter), 533–549.

Shan, W. (1990), "An Empirical Analysis of Organizational Strategies by Entrepreneurial High-Technology Firms," *Strategic Management Journal* 11 (February), 129–139.

Shortell, S.M., and E.J. Zajac (1990), "Perceptual and Archival Measures of Miles and Snow's Strategic Types: A Comprehensive Assessment of Reliability and Validity," *Academy of Management Journal* 33 (December), 817–832.

Shuman, J.C., and J.A. Seeger (1986), "The Theory and Practice of Strategic Management in Smaller Rapid Growth Firms," *American Journal of Small Business* 11 (Summer), 7–18.

Sriram, V., and H.J. Sapienza (1991), "An Empirical Investigation of the Role of Marketing for Small Exporters," *Journal of Small Business Management* 29 (October), 33–43.

Van Horn, M. (1990), "Market-Entry Approaches for the Pacific Rim," *Journal of Business Strategy* 11 (March/April), 14–19.

COMPETITIVE ANALYSIS AND STRATEGIC PLANNING: THE COUNTRY VIEW

Just as firms must develop a competitive advantage to be successful in the global economy, many believe countries must do the same. Most, if not all countries are actively pursuing goals variously stated as economic development, improving their citizens' standard of living, or improving their quality of life. Reaching these goals requires that the country's citizens have access to good-paying jobs and that the government have access to tax revenues generated by well-paid workers and profitable businesses. Thus, encouraging an active, profitable business sector is a virtual requirement for a country's development.

In a global economy where international trade and foreign direct investment are not only possible but facilitated, nations see themselves competing with each other to ensure they receive their fair share of the good jobs and the corporate profits. Governments, then, become very concerned with instituting policies and taking actions that facilitate the growth and profitability of the firms operating within their borders. They also become concerned with attracting and nurturing high-value-added industries, since these are the industries that provide the highest potential incomes for their workers.

Over the last several years, scholars have begun to study quite intensively the factors that lead to country competitive advantage. More recently, they have begun to speculate about the effects of country strategies on multinational firm strategies and about the effect on the world economy resulting from countries competing for advantage in markets that are finite in size.

In this section of the book, we will cover both the key concepts of country competitive analysis and its effects on multinational firms and the global economy. The reader should study this material in more than one context. Clearly, the insights in this section are useful to the government policy maker. They are also useful to managers seeking to identify where future competitors may arise. The *Diamond model,* as presented by Porter and extended by Dunning, is also a potentially very useful tool in identifying manufacturing and R&D locations.

READING SELECTIONS

John Dunning presents a thoughtful extension and elaboration of Michael E. Porter's Diamond model. Porter in his article viewed the quest for country comparative advantage as a phenomenon influenced primarily by domestic firms and domestic activities. He asserts that national prosperity comes from a nation's industries' ability to innovate and upgrade. Dunning observes the importance of the international environment in developing a country's competitive strategy. He notes that multinational firms that operate within a particular country influence the Diamond as do the foreign activities of the country's domestic firms. The influence of products and services not yet available in a particular country can also affect demand in that country.

Thomas Murtha and Stefanie Lenway develop a framework that integrates country and multinational firm competitive strategies. They first focus on how the political institutions in countries of different characteristics can affect the strategies of the multinationals that do business within their borders. They then look at the implications of their analysis for multinational firms' strategy formulation. They conclude that governments and businesses work together most effectively when they adjust to the uniqueness of the situation in which they find themselves.

Brahm raises serious questions about the consequences of policies governments may institute to gain competitive advantage. He looks specifically at high-tech industries, and argues that the effect of many nations simultaneously encouraging the development of the same industry is creating destructive competition. Brahm identifies a list of specific targeting techniques and discusses their effects on industry development. His article offers useful insights for firms as well as governments; analyzing the actions governments are taking should help a firm identify the competitive situation it is likely to face.

13

THE COMPETITIVE ADVANTAGE OF COUNTRIES AND MNE ACTIVITY

JOHN H. DUNNING

INTRODUCTION

The dynamic interplay between the competitive advantages of countries and those enterprises of a particular nationality is a subject commanding the increasing attention by students of the MNE. Indeed, it has been suggested that a fuller understanding of the nature, content and determinants of this interaction, as it affects the globalization of production and markets, may provide the basis for one of the next advances in the theory of foreign value-added activity[1] (Dunning, 1990).

Since the mid-1970s, the focus of scholars interested in explaining the existence and growth of the MNE has been directed to identifying and evaluating the relative costs and benefits of organizing the cross-border transactions of intermediate products by hierarchies or markets. In the early 1990s, however, renewed attention[2] is being given to explaining the origin and composition of the resources and capabilities[3] of corporations to engage in production outside their national boundaries and to the determinants of their success in managing and organizing the international portfolio of resources rather than ownership or control. Faced with the same economic conditions and prospects, why are some firms significant global players and others are not? Why is the share of international direct investment accounted for by Japanese companies rising so rapidly? Why is Europe claiming a larger share of US based MNE activity than it used to? What explains the rapid growth of the participation of foreign owned firms in the United States? What determines which developing countries will emerge as important international investors? Why do firms conclude strategic alliances with some firms, but avoid them with others? Why is foreign direct investment (FDI) in services rising more rapidly than that in goods?

These are just some of the questions now demanding answers by MNE researchers. What is their response? Well, one response by the scholar of the MNE, *qua MNE,*[4] is that only part of the explanation for the growth of foreign owned production may have to do with the increasing propensity of firms to internalize their cross-border transactions. For example, a particular competitive advantage which may help to explain the capability of a firm to supply a particular market, or set of markets, is not, in itself, a sufficient reason for that firm to create, or add value to, that advantage from a foreign located facility.

Take, for example, a pharmaceutical patent as a competitive advantage of a UK MNE. The *origin* of that advantage is likely to be determined by a combination of factors, including the amount of resources the company allocates to innovatory activities, the quality and motivation of R&D personnel, the organization and technical efficiency of the R&D department, and the successful commercialization of that R&D. The *outcome* of that advantage is that it may enable the UK firm to increase its penetration of the world drug market. Is the possession of this advantage an explanation for any increase in foreign production, which might directly arise from such an advantage; or, is it simply to be taken as an exogenous variable which may or may not lead to such production?

Supposing, next, it can be shown that it pays the UK firm to produce the new pharmaceutical product for worldwide distribution from its German plant rather than to export it from its UK plant. Is this an explanation of international production; or is it rather an explanation of the location of economic activity, *given* its ownership? Or, is the explanation of MNE activity concerned only with the circumstances in which a firm engages in foreign value-added activity rather than the next best option open to it, *given* its resources and capabilities and the locational opportunities open to it?

If this latter is thought to be the main focus of interest, then Michael Porter's book *The Competitive Advantage of Nations* will be of limited appeal.[5] If, however, it is perceived that, for example, part of Japanese direct investment in the US car industry is due to the success of Japanese owned firms in producing highly saleable motor vehicles, irrespective of the mode by which this advantage is exploited, and that the reasons for such a success are, themselves, part of the explanation for their foreign activities, then much of the Porter monograph is highly relevant to the student of the MNE.

Our own view is that Michael Porter has rendered a very considerable service in identifying many of the explanatory variables which help us better appreciate some *country specific* explanations of the changing pattern of international production by MNEs. In particular, his extensive field research has advanced our knowledge of why corporations domiciled in some countries have been successful in penetrating foreign markets in some product areas but not in others; and also why some countries have been able to attract inbound MNE activity in some value-added activities but not in others. The book also offers a penetrating insight as to why, in some countries and sectors, the activities of MNEs help stimulate the technological and organizational efficiency of local firms, and why, in other cases, they inhibit it. More generally, many of the ideas and concepts articulated by Porter help enrich our understanding of the dynamic interplay between the strategy of MNEs and the competitive advantages of countries in which they operate.

THE 'DIAMOND' OF COMPETITIVE ADVANTAGE

By now, most readers of this volume will be familiar with the main analytical tools used by Porter in his latest book, viz. the diamond of competitive advantage. By competitive advantage, Porter means the ability of a country—or more specifically indigenous firms of a country—to use its location-bound resources in a way which will enable it (them) to be competitive in international markets. Porter likens the determinants of this ability to a diamond which comprises a set of attributes which 'shape the environment in which local firms compete, and which promote or impede the creation of competitive market' (Porter, 1990: 71). He goes on to argue that the diamond is a naturally reinforcing system, with each of its determinants being contingent on the state of the other (ibid.: 72).

According to Porter, the strength, composition and sustainability of a nation's competitive advantage will be demonstrated by the value of its national product[6] and/or the rate of growth of that product, *relative to that of its leading competitors.* The extent to which a country is successful in achieving this goal then depends on the kind of goods and services produced by its enterprises, and the efficiency at which they are supplied. This, in turn, Porter suggests, rests on the extent and quality of, and the interaction between, four sets of attributes:

1. The quantity and quality of demand for goods and services by its domestic consumers.
2. The level and composition of its natural resources and created factor capabilities.[7]
3. The domestic rivalry of wealth producing agencies, i.e., the nature and extent of interfirm competition.
4. The extent to which its firms are able to benefit from agglomerative or external economies by being spatially grouped in clusters of related activities.

Surrounding and influencing these variables are two others, viz. the role of government and chance. Excluding the MBA component (to be discussed later), Figure 1 sets out Porter's depiction of the 'structure' of the diamond.

The main objective of Porter's work is twofold. First, it is to show that these facets of the diamond, and the way in which they interact, will vary between countries. Second, it is to suggest that the principal ways in which countries may improve their competitiveness are to upgrade the quantity or quality of their resources and capabilities and/or to utilize their existing resources and capabilities more efficiently.

Much of Michael Porter's treatise, which extends to over 800 pages, is directed to providing the reader with examples of the ways in which the various facets of the diamond are systemically interrelated. Indeed, one of the author's main contentions is that the efficiency at which the facets of the diamond are coordinated with each other is an important competitive advantage in its own right. To this extent, there is, in Porter's mind, a parallel between the efficiency of the governance of resources and competencies by firms, and that by the governments of countries.

In one sense, there is nothing original in Porter's analysis. Throughout history, a succession of scholars have attempted to identify and evaluate the supply and demand conditions necessary for a country to be competitive in world markets. Indeed, most have been more comprehensive than Porter, who identifies only four sources of competitive advantage and pays little or no attention to such variables as investment and entrepreneurship.[8] The scholars include those who focus on the so called ESP paradigm, which suggests that the economic prosperity of a country rests on its environment (factor endowments) and markets (E), its economic system (S) and the economic and social policies pursued by its Government (P).[9] Most of Porter's analysis can be subsumed under one or other of these headings.

However, what Porter does do, and, we think, does very successfully, is first to set out a paradigm within which the determinants of national competitiveness may be identified, and the way in which they interrelate with each other, and second to offer some hypotheses as to why the significance of these pa-

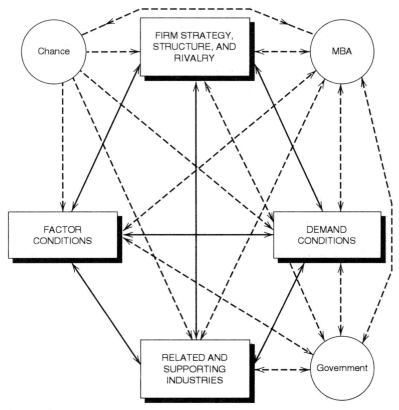

Figure 1. The Porter diamond: the complete system

rameters may vary between countries and sectors. The monograph contains eight country case studies[10] and four industry case studies—each of which is addressed to these issues.

The Competitive Advantage of Nations is full of short case studies, persuasive illustrations and intriguing anecdotes of why the structure of competitive advantage, e.g., as between industrial sectors, differs between countries, although Porter makes no attempt to substantiate his propositions by any formal econometric (or for that matter any other) testing! Indeed, on several occasions, the reader feels that the author comes near to rationalizing his arguments, and that, had he chosen to do so, he could have provided illustrations which point to the opposite of the conclusions he draws.

One of the most interesting chapters of the book concerns the role of governments. Porter prefers to consider government not as an attribute of the diamond, but as a fashioner of its structure and efficiency. This makes sense! Although, as producers and consumers, governments may directly affect the supply and demand of both immobile and mobile resources and capabilities affecting competitiveness, they alone have the ultimate responsibility for shaping the framework, or system, under which these resources and capabilities are organized. They set the 'rules of the game' and set the signals, which trigger a response by firms, which determine whether national competitiveness is advanced or not. Moreover, in a variety of ways, they affect the ability and motivation of a nation's citizens and firms, for example to save, to be entrepreneurial, to work efficiently, to accept new ideas and attitudes and to upgrade human and technological capacity. By affecting exchange rates, by participating (or not) in supra-national trading schemes, and by their policies and regulations towards FDI, they may influence the extent to which, and the form in which, a country is involved in international commerce.

It is not the purpose of this chapter to give a detailed critique of Porter's work, but rather to examine its relevance to our understanding of international business activity. In several places, the author addresses himself to the ways in which outward and inward direct investment by MNEs may affect both their own competitiveness and that of the countries in which they operate. In general, however, he seems to believe that the main thrust to improving national competitiveness must come from a better use of indigenous resources and capabilities by domestic corporations. Indeed, Porter frequently cautions governments from relying too much on the affiliates of foreign MNEs to fulfil this task.

While, in principle, we would not wish to take issue with Porter on this point, the fact that between 30 per cent and 40 per cent of the sales of the leading industrial MNEs are now produced outside their national boundaries, and that the value of these sales now considerably exceeds that of international trade, suggests to us that more explicit attention should be given to the ways in which the transnationalization of business activity could affect the nature and character of the diamond of competitive advantage of the countries involved. Certainly, there is ample evidence that the technological and organizational assets of MNEs are influenced by the configuration of the diamonds of the foreign countries in which they produce, and that this, in turn, may impinge upon the competitiveness of the resources and capabilities of their home countries.[11]

Indeed, we would submit that in the global economy of the 1990s, it is entirely appropriate to consider a country's involvement in foreign trade and commerce as a separate exogenous variable affecting the facets of the diamond in the same way in which Porter treats the role of government. However, for the purpose of this chapter, we shall consider only the foreign production of domestic owned firms and the domestic production of foreign based MNEs as they affect the shape of particular national diamonds.

THE ACTIVITIES OF MNEs AS AN ADDITIONAL EXOGENOUS VARIABLE AFFECTING THE DIAMOND

Let us then treat the foreign business activities of MNEs, i.e., the foreign output of domestic MNEs and the domestic output of foreign non-resident owned companies, as an exogenous factor, along with chance and government, affecting the diamond of competitive advantage. Figure 1 introduces this new component, i.e. multinational business activity (MBA) into the Porter schema. How might this affect the strength and composition of a nation's competitive advantage?

First, let us briefly remind ourselves of the distinctive features of MNEs, i.e., those which might be attributed specifically to their transnationality. Consider, for example, some of the unique characteristics of *inward* direct investment. First, it is likely to provide a different package of resources and capabilities (e.g., finance capital, technology, management skills, etc.) than that provided by domestic investors. This is partly because these are being imported from a country which has a different combination of competitive advantages, and partly because some of these assets, at least, are likely to be specific to the firm which owns them. Japanese owned subsidiaries in the UK, for example, draw upon a different set of resources and capabilities (or the same resources and capabilities at different prices) than do UK owned firms. Put another way, the sourcing and marketing opportunities and the production and organizational capabilities of the two groups of firms are likely to be different.

Second, the use made of these assets is likely to be different, partly because the firm is foreign owned, and partly because of the distinctive characteristics of multinationality *per se,* for example, those to do with the international arbitraging of resources and capabilities and the spreading of risks of environmental volatility (Kogut, 1985). *Inter alia,* this suggests that decisions taken by the local subsidiary of an MNE might be different than if it were domestically owned, and that a decision on local resource allocation by a uninational firm might be different than if that firm operated a global network of subsidiaries.

It is the balance between the asset transfer and the control of the use of these assets that is the essence of the uniqueness of MNE activity; although, depending upon the macro-economic situation in the home and host country and the assumptions made about government macro-organizational policies, it is possible that inward investment might also affect the *level* of economic activity.

Consider next some unique features of *outward* direct investment. There are at least three distinguishing attributes of MNEs compared with uninational (or international trading) firms. The first is the additional options to the former in the geographical configuration of their value-added activities. Second, MNEs have more opportunity to diversify their assets and economic activity to reduce exchange and other risks of producing in different countries. Third, MNEs find it easier to gain access to foreign resources, markets, economic systems, business relationships, infrastructure and forms of competition. Indeed (borrowing from Porter's terminology), an important competitive advantage of MNEs is their unique ability to draw upon and make use of different national diamonds of competitive advantage.

Given these (and other) distinguishing characteristics of cross-border business activity, how might it affect the competitiveness of countries? The answer will mainly rest on the values of three contextual variables. The first relates to the *nature* of the MNE activity. Here, the relevant questions include: Is it market seeking, resource seeking, efficiency seeking (e.g., cost reducing) or strategic asset seeking in its intent? Is it primarily to protect or exploit an existing competitive advantage or to acquire a new advantage? Is the investment a greenfield investment or an acquisition of existing assets? Is it a 100 percent subsidiary or a joint venture? Is it an initial or sequential investment? Is it a stand alone or an integrated investment?

The second group of variables relate to the content and structure of the *existing* competitive advantages of a country. Is domestic rivalry, prior to outward or inward investment, weak or strong? Are its factor endowments plentiful or not? Are domestic consumers demanding more differentiated products or not?

What role do governments play in upgrading or standardizing product quality? And so on.

The third main variable, which affects and is affected by the second, are the economic signals provided by governments. To what extent, and in what way, might (or do) governments, directly or indirectly, influence both the competitiveness of the resources and capabilities within their jurisdiction, and the actions of their own, and/or foreign, MNEs?

Clearly, the significance of each of these three variables will depend on (home and host) *country* (or region), *firm* and *activity* specific circumstances; and while, at any given moment of time, they might be independent of each other, over time they are closely interlinked. For example, FDI may both impact on the technological capabilities of rival domestic firms and be affected by them. However, for the purpose of our analysis, it may be appropriate to consider the impact of a change of inward or outward investment on *the existing competitive advantages of firms and industries.*

We would make one other general point. In most analyses of the impact of MBA on national competitiveness, inward and outward direct investment are considered independently of each other. Although each kind of investment has its distinctive consequences, there is some merit in considering these as opposite sides of the same coin. This is especially so when looking at the macro-organizational dynamics of competitiveness. Though there is no necessary connection between a change in inward investment and the propensity of domestic firms to engage in outward investment (i.e., it may affect only domestic resource allocation), in practice, in a world in which four-fifths of MNE activity is within the advanced industrial countries, and is primarily intra-industry in character, the volume and structure of outward and inward direct investment are likely to be closely interwoven, and governed by broadly similar factors.

The evidence suggests, however, that the relationship between the two is not straightforward (Dunning, 1985). Indeed, a fascinating topic for additional research (and one not really tackled at all by Porter) is the identification of the circumstances in which changes in the level and/or structure of outward and inward MBA move in similar directions (i.e., are

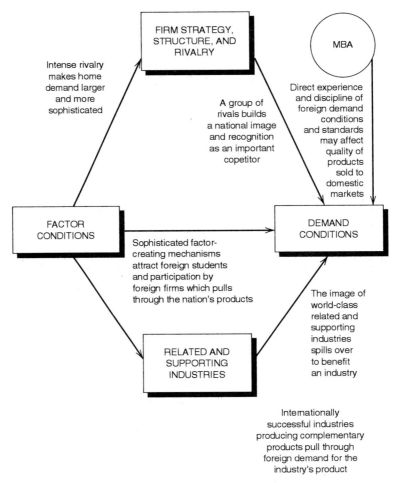

Figure 2. Influences on home demand conditions

complementary to each other), and those in which they move in opposite directions (i.e., are substitutable for each other).[12]

For the purpose of this chapter, however, we will try and analyze some of the implications of a spontaneous or induced change in outward and inward MNE activity on each of the four facets of the diamond of competitive advantage, both directly and indirectly through their repercussions on the actions of government. Again, we shall concentrate on just one or two aspects of each of the four facets. We would also reiterate that the facets are closely interlinked and that the more one takes a dynamic perspective of the impact of MNE activity, the less useful it is to consider each competitive-related variable separately.

THE CONDITIONS OF DEMAND

Porter argues that the *structure* of domestic demand may affect the competitiveness of firms in the international market by providing an impetus for domestic firms to produce high quality, well designed, reliable and differentiated goods, relative to those supplied by their foreign competitors. Assuming that such an emphasis on product consistency or differentiation, rather than on a cost-reducing strategy, is the most effective strategy for firms to pursue,[13] to what extent is MNE activity likely to affect, or be affected by, such demand conditions?

Consider first the likely interaction between local patterns of demand and *inward* investment. Here the impact of such investment is likely to depend on the pattern and quality of the existing demand, and how it compares with that of the investing nation and that of other countries in which the MNE produces. It is also likely to depend on the product strategy of the investing firms and the extent to which they perceive product quality and reliability, themselves, to be critical competitive advantages. Another relevant variable is the extent to which a country's citizens have been previously exposed to the products of the investing company (e.g., through exports), and/or how far the products have been produced for export markets by indigenous companies. Much will also rest on whether the FDI takes the form of an acquisition of, or merger with, an existing firm, or a greenfield venture. Finally, over time, the affect on demand quality will rest on the impact of FDI on other facets of the diamond, e.g., domestic rivalry and indigenous technological capability.

It is possible to conceive of a number of possible scenarios. Take, for example, the case of a foreign chocolate producer which acquires a domestic firm in the same line of business, with the aim of gaining access to the local market. Assume, next, that the acquired firm produces high quality chocolate, but that the acquiring firm's competitive advantage lies in producing standardized low cost chocolate. Assume, too, that the acquiring firm has chocolate producing facilities elsewhere in the world, and that it does not intend exporting from the country of the acquired firm. Then, in such cases—unless the acquiring firm simply adds to the product range of the acquired firm—there could be a *lowering* of the standards of demand by the citizens of the host country.[14]

Consider next a scenario in which an investing firm perceives its main competitive advantage to be consistency of the quality of its color television sets. Assume that some impact on domestic consumer demand (via informing consumers about defect-free products and raising their purchasing standards) may have been made by the exports of the investing country, but that the presence of local production facili-

ties increases this awareness. Then, given the other facets of the diamond, the upgrading of consumer expectations might force other firms to improve the quality, or lower the costs, of their products, which might, in turn, advance their competitiveness. This, in fact, is what appears to have happened as a result of Japanese direct investment in the European and US motor vehicles and consumer electronics industries.

Earlier, we suggested that the impact of inward investment on the diamond of competitive advantage may depend on the purposes of that investment. As far as the impact on *domestic* demand is concerned, this is clearly most likely to be felt where the intention of the investment is to service the domestic, and sometimes adjacent, markets, i.e. import substituting investment; although, whether or not this is the case depends, in part at least, on the extent to which the host government may influence the conditions of demand.[15]

Indirectly, demand conditions in the home country, including the influence of the host government over them (e.g., via the level and structure of direct and indirect taxation, their control over the quality of public goods and services, the harmonization and upgrading of technical standards, such as in the procurement of telecommunication systems, and the imposition of rigorous safety, health and environmental regulations) may influence the extent to which foreign firms are willing to invest in the host country, and hence their contribution to other parts of the diamond.

Consider next the way in which foreign activities of domestic MNEs affect, or may be affected by, the structure and content of domestic demand. Take the case of foreign investment by a company from a country in which either intermediate or final product consumers are relatively unsophisticated (perhaps because they are protected from foreign competition) operating in a country in which consumers are highly demanding. Assume, for the moment, that such an investment is possible because the investing companies have some kind of technological or marketing advantage over competitive firms in the recipient country. Then, insofar as consumer expectations and requirements in the foreign market affect the compa-

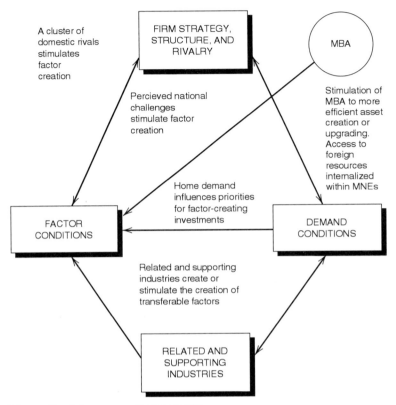

Figure 3. Influences on factor creation

rability, quality or cost of the product supplied to that market they may, in turn, influence the kinds of products sold in the domestic market. Alternatively, 'easy pickings' in an important foreign market could make a firm less aware of, or less willing to cater to, the more stringent demands of domestic consumers and, indeed, even lower the product quality and reliability of its locally produced output.

On the other hand, the ability of a firm to become an outward investor, may be influenced by the extent to which domestic consumers have forced indigenous firms to provide more differentiated or higher quality products than those normally accepted by foreign consumers. A classic case is that of Japanese outward investment in the motor vehicles and consumer electronics sectors;[16] while, similarly, Japanese component suppliers faced with the rigorous demands of their industrial customers in these same

sectors are in a better position to supply the latter's competition in the international market.

So much for extremes and generalities. To what extent can one identify the conditions necessary for MNE activity to act as a vehicle for upgrading consumer demand?[17] We would suggest that the answer is comparatively simple. Consider first the demand conditions of the home country of the inward investor, or the host country of the outward investor, and compare these with those of the countries in which the inward or outward MNE already produces. Second, consider whether or not such knowledge about these conditions, and/or the impetus to create them, could be, or are, being achieved at lower cost, through alternative means. Third, consider whether or not consumers are likely to embrace such conditions. How sensitive are they, for example, to foreign purchasing customs and standards? Fourth, consider the *power* of consumers to influence the quality of products supplied by competitive firms. For example, how significant are they in relation to the purchases of similar products?

Finally, consumer awareness, or pressure for quality improvement, is not always a necessary (and rarely is it a sufficient) condition for the upgrading of consumer demand. Nor is it necessarily desirable if it results in a reduction of economic welfare in other directions.[18] One of the best examples which comes to mind is the quality of in-flight facilities provided by international airlines. Customers, irrespective of their nationality, applaud the quality of food and in-flight service offered by such airlines as Singapore, Thai, Cathay Pacific and Swiss Air, and almost unanimously believe that the caliber of the equivalent amenities provided by many US airlines is inferior. Why, then, it might be asked, don't US air travelers insist upon higher quality from their own airlines?

The answer seems to be twofold. First, the US airlines tend to compete on the basis of (indirect) price reductions, e.g., through generous frequent flyer mileage programs, which may appeal even to the most discerning business traveler. Second, there is no competition from the best foreign airlines on *domestic* US routes, which still account for the majority of business by US airlines. Thus, whether inward or outward investment raises quality standards very much depends on variables apart from consumer reaction *per se,* although it would be difficult to deny that such foreign investment offers options to consumers which might otherwise not be available.[19]

THE LEVEL AND STRUCTURE OF NATURAL ENDOWMENTS AND CREATED CAPABILITIES

Traditionally, the main benefit of inward direct investment has been perceived as the resources and competences it provides—at lower real cost than by the next best alternative modality—and its distinctive impact on the productivity of indigenous resources. This may be achieved in two main ways. First, by the redirection of intermediate products (both along and between value added chains) to where they can be more productively employed. Second, by improving the quality of existing assets and capabilities, or by putting them to more effective use. This latter objective may be accomplished through the injection of more dynamic and successful entrepreneurship and/or by the provision of superior technology and organizational skills. At the same time, inward direct investment has been criticized on the grounds that it may lead to a lowering of the value of indigenous resources and capabilities, e.g. by means of a socially unacceptable rate of depletion of natural resources, or by the repatriation of assets, e.g. R&D facilities, which a foreign firm might have acquired from a domestic firm at a socially unacceptable price.

Outward direct investment may also be viewed in two ways. On the one hand, it may extend the traditional boundaries of the assets owned by the investing companies, and, by opening up new markets, or protecting existing markets, enable domestic resources and capabilities to be used more efficiently. On the other hand, it may transfer such resources and capabilities, notably finance capital and technology, which might have been deployed more productively in the domestic market.

Again, the balance of these costs and benefits, and the interaction between them, will depend on the motives for, and types of, MNE activity; the existing level, pattern and productivity of indigenous resources; and the economic environment in which the investment is made.[20] It will also rest on the alternatives to acquiring resources by FDI.[21] For example, throughout most of the post-war period, Japan has managed to obtain many of the benefits which inward investment might have provided by way of non-equity transfers of technology and human skills (including the conclusion of strategic alliances with foreign firms) and by importing knowledge intensive products. Smaller European countries like The Netherlands, Switzerland and Sweden could not have improved or retained their competitive positions without their companies producing much of their output outside their home countries. By contrast, some commentators (Gilpin, 1975, 1987) have argued that, by exporting advanced technology through outward direct investment, the US has eroded its competitive position, and reduced the capability of its own companies to maintain their innovating capabilities *vis-à-vis* their European and Japanese counterparts.[22]

The distinctive impact of MNEs on the international allocation of natural resources and created capabilities depends not only on ability and desire of such companies to internally transfer such assets between countries but also on the control exerted over the deployment of these and other intermediate products under their control. This is mainly reflected in the type of economic activity undertaken, which, in turn, will affect the kind and productivity of resources used, and the ability of the economy to adapt to changes in world supply and demand conditions. Moreover, insofar as foreign firms may effect both the sourcing of inputs and the destination of outputs, they may also have consequences for the stability of domestic resource deployment.

In examining the specific impact of FDI, it is important to distinguish between short and long run consequences. It is quite possible that in the short run, by producing more efficiently than its indigenous competitors, over a limited range of the value-added chain, a foreign firm may increase domestic output. However, if, in so doing, it competes out of existence a domestic firm that, taking the value added chain as a whole, has a higher domestic value added per resource used, this may lead to a less efficient use of resources and capabilities in the long run.

Such a consequence, however, might be acceptable to the host country if the actions of the foreign firm were in response to competitive market signals and the resources released could be redeployed more productively elsewhere in the economy. To this extent, it is important not to take a partial approach in examining the consequences of FDI. Let us give two examples. Take first a situation in which outward investment is directed either to activities which require resources and capabilities in which the investing country is comparatively disadvantaged, or is losing its comparative advantage, or where the purpose of the investment is to acquire resources and capabilities, which will add to the competitiveness of the existing assets of the investing company. Suppose, next, that, due to appropriate structural adjustment policies and the willingness of firms to reallocate resources, the resources released were taken over by foreign investors, who, by combining these with other foreign assets, e.g. entrepreneurship, technology, organizational capability, were able to use them more productively. Then, in such a case, MBA is likely both to increase and upgrade indigenous competences.

Consider now a second example. Assume that a foreign firm responds to import controls imposed by the host government, or takes defensive oligopolist reaction to produce goods which require resources, valued at international market prices, in which the home country has a comparative advantage. Suppose, too, that, to avoid unwelcome industrial or penal fiscal policies pursued by their own government, domestic firms choose to increase their foreign, rather than their home, investments. Then, in such cases, although overseas production might be a second or third best solution, the first best solution, in terms of domestic factor endowments, might be for the government to modify its macro-economic policies so that the prices of domestic inputs and outputs more accurately reflect their true opportunity cost.

Finally, the net effect on factor endowments and created capabilities of MNE activity is likely to rest on the price paid for the inward investment and the gains accruing from outward investment to the investing country. For example, a takeover of a domestic firm might reduce the competitiveness of the resources used by the acquired firm (although it may help to improve the competitiveness of those used by the acquiring firm). However, from the perspective of the host country, the takeover would be undesirable only if the agreed price was insufficient to compensate for these (possible) adverse effects. Here the distinction between the social and private price of an acquisition is of critical importance (Dunning and Steuer, 1969).

Similarly, the returns from outward investment should include not only the foreign income earned by the affiliate, but all the other benefits existing from its presence, e.g. the feedback of technological or managerial know-how and the increased market it makes possible for domestic resources. Various studies have shown that, in some sectors, and by some countries, MBA has made a significant contribution to the restructuring and upgrading of domestic resources.[23] Indeed, the foreign activities of Japa-

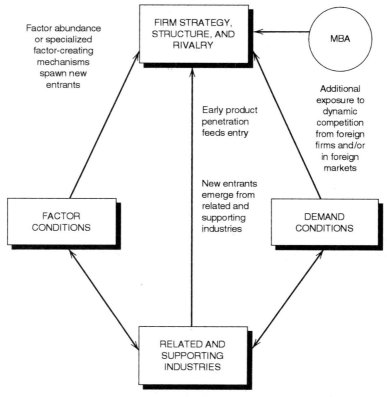

Figure 4.   Influences on domestic rivalry

nese MNCs have played an integral part in the restructuring and upgrading of the Japanese economy since the mid-1960s (Ozawa, 1989).

DOMESTIC RIVALRY

Porter also argues that the extent and degree of competition between domestic rivals is an important variable affecting national competitiveness. In particular, he points to the larger number of firms competing with each other in Japan than in the US as a factor making for the higher industrial competitiveness of the former country.

The optimum structure of a market for competitive and innovatory stimulus has always been a matter for debate. Certainly, it would be erroneous to argue that a greater population of firms necessarily means more *effective* competition. The Canadian experience—and that of other countries with small markets—completely belies this. However, there can be little doubt that the number and type of competitors is an important variable affecting the strategic conduct of firms, and that some forms of market structure are more conducive to the promotion of short or long term competitiveness than others. Lawrence (1987), for example, views an optimum market structure as one which allows neither cut-throat or destructive competition on the one hand nor lethargy on the other, on the part of the constituent firms.[24]

The literature also suggests that MNEs are likely to impact on domestic market structure both by the resources, capabilities and/or markets they can provide and by the control exerted over these assets, and any others germane to their jurisdiction. In turn, these effects may impinge on the behavior of their competitors and the structure of the industry in which they operate.

Again, it may be helpful to illustrate from two extreme scenarios. The first is where a foreign firm takes over an existing producer and uses its global power to drive out local competitors. Furthermore, assume that this power is being used not to advance efficiency, but to promote a monopoly position. In such a case, it is likely that domestic rivalry will be adversely affected by such investment—although whether or not this lowers overall economic competitiveness will depend upon the other consequences of the takeover. The second scenario is where a foreign firm injects a new element of competition into a market supplied by a local monopolist, or where, as a result of an acquisition, it revitalizes an industry which might otherwise have perished because of insufficient or inappropriate competition.

A major drawback of most attempts to identify the optimum market structure of firms is that they tend to limit their attention to domestic or national markets. In a world in which the bulk of activity in many sectors is dominated by MNEs, this is unacceptable. Competition between the major pharmaceutical, consumer electronics, banking, oil, tire and motor vehicle companies is not mainly played out in national, but in world, markets. Michael Porter cites the greater number of Japanese firms in several industries as an illustration of competitive rivalry. Yet, at the time of Porter's research, the Japanese market was largely closed to foreign competition. Not only this: until recently, the majority of the output of Japanese companies was sold to domestic consumers.

The situation is very different in the case of some smaller advanced industrialized or industrializing countries, which are also well up in the competitiveness league table, notably Switzerland, Sweden, The Netherlands, Singapore and Hong Kong. We think it unlikely that the Chief Executives of Nestlé, Philips or SKF would accept that the competition they encounter is any the less intense than that faced by their Japanese or US equivalents. The difference is that the former is almost exclusively provided by foreign competitors. What is more important is that, as markets become globalized, and cross-border trading barriers are relaxed, the international dimension of interfirm rivalry is likely to increase.

Indeed, it is possible to go further and argue that a persuasive case can be made out that, in the right circumstances, rivalry by foreign firms might offer greater benefits than that between domestic firms. At the same time, domestic firms, which also produce outside their national boundaries, are, for the most part, likely to face tougher competition than those which supply only domestic markets—particularly where the latter markets are protected.

Our conclusion is, then, that there are consequences on domestic rivalry which are distinctive to MBA. We accept that, *a priori,* it may be difficult to predict whether or not, in the long run, these are likely to be beneficial or not. But, it is possible to argue that both inward and outward direct investment do have the potential for increasing healthy domestic rivalry, and hence improving this particular facet of the diamond of competitive advantage. Whether the potential is translated into reality depends on the existing domestic and international market structure, the type and form of FDI and its impact on the market structure,[25] and the role played by national governments in setting the appropriate signals for rivalry.

AGGLOMERATIVE ECONOMIES AND THE CLUSTERING OF RELATED INDUSTRIES

The presence of economies external to the firm but internal to a network or cluster of firms located in a particular geographical area is a familiar competitive advantage articulated by economists since the time of Alfred Marshall. The fact that clusters of related activities do exist and confer considerable benefits to the participating firms has been spelled out in various regional studies, notably those on the City of London (Dunning and Morgan, 1971), California's Silicon Valley (Scott and Angel, 1987), the location of government research establishments in south east England (Hall *et al.,* 1987), the Greater Grenoble area in France (Boisgontier and de Bernardy, 1986), several districts in Northern Italy (Malerba, 1990) and the Ibaragi Prefecture in Japan.[26] Moreover, these studies suggest that the need for firms to draw on resources and capabilities, which have to be geographically concentrated to be efficiently supplied, is increasing.

The advantages of clusters, as described by Porter, is that firms benefit from a shared culture and learning experience, supply capabilities and local infra-

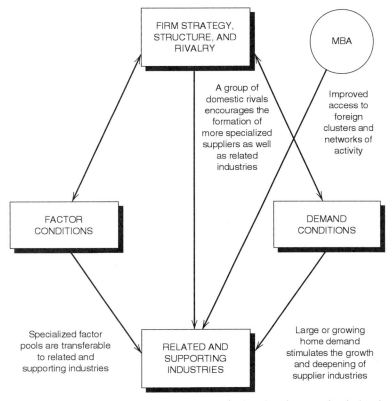

Figure 5. Influences on the development of related and supporting industries.

structure, which gives them a competitive edge in both domestic and international markets.

Geographical clusters or networks of economic activity may take various forms. They may be between firms producing different products across value-added chains, or between firms producing similar products at different stages of the same chain. The related presence is assumed to benefit all firms within the cluster and, hence, protect or advance competitiveness.

In his book, Porter does not attempt to measure the significance of clusters as a facet of the diamond, nor whether or not this particular advantage has become more important with the passage of time. Nor does he give much attention to the conditions which make for successful clusters. Clearly, not all firms need to be part of a network of vertical or horizontal linkages. Moreover, not all linkages need to be in the same or similar locations.

Let us now consider the extent to which efficient clustering is likely to be affected by the MBA in either home or host countries. In what way does it respond to, or affect, the propensity of firms to cluster differently than that conducted by non-MNEs?

Perhaps the first point worth making is that the MNE (and, more especially, the large diversified MNE) is *par excellence* a network of interrelated activities. Indeed, one of its strengths derives from the external economies associated with particular types of activities, which it, as a coordinator of these activities, can capture. Corporate integration makes possible the economies of common governance. Sometimes, these economies are best exploited in the same location, and sometimes in different locations.

At the same time, there is some suggestion that MNEs may create their own clusters of foreign based activity. Indeed, Knickerbocker observed this as a phenomenon of MNE activity two decades ago

(Knickerbocker, 1973), while, in the 1980s and 1990s, there is ample evidence that Japanese motor vehicle consumer electronics, rubber tire and chemical firms are pursuing a 'follow my leader' strategy in investing in Europe and the US. More than this, the presence of such firms is encouraging investment by Japanese component suppliers and subcontractors, and new intra-industry value chain networks are being established.

However, the data are inconclusive on the geographical distribution of these activities. Currently, 75 percent of output of color television sets of Japanese affiliates produced in the UK are from factories located in South Wales. The Midlothian industrial conurbation in Scotland attracts two-thirds of all foreign owned firms producing semi-conductors in the UK. More than one-half of Japanese direct investment in German manufacturing industry is sited in the Dusseldorf area. And, there are suggestions that north-east England may become an important new center for the production of motor vehicles and their components. At the same time, the Japanese investors were not initially attracted by a strong cluster of existing activities; indeed, they have helped create their own clusters.

But, there are other examples which point to the contrary conclusion. The examples of clustering centers cited earlier in this chapter have all attracted foreign based companies which have generally reinforced the value of existing agglomerations of activity. On the other hand, outward investment might be expected to lead to a reduction in the intensity of domestic galaxies. An exception, perhaps, is in R&D and other high value activities of MNEs which tend to be concentrated in their home countries. The critical issue is to identify the optimum grouping of firms to gain the maximum external net economies at the lowest cost; for after a point, diseconomies of agglomeration arise. Such evidence as we have on the effect of foreign firms on clustering does not permit us to come to any generalized conclusion.

Again, however, it is not difficult to point to cases where foreign owned firms might enhance or inhibit particular types of clusters. For example, if such firms replace domestic firms and transfer their R&D activities to their home countries, this could reduce the agglomerative economies of R&D. If, on the other hand, affiliates upgraded factor endowments and the quality of output by increasing the demand for the products of the host country, this could lead to an increase in new kinds of clustering economies. Much would seem to depend upon the type of activities in which a foreign affiliate engages (cf. domestic firms) and the extent to which it buys from local suppliers or sells to local consumers.

The effect of outward investment on the domestic networking of activities is equally ambiguous. There is some suggestion that the Continental European investment of UK motor vehicle component firms was prompted by the better agglomerative economies offered by concentrations of industrial activity in the Ruhr Valley and in Belgium, and that this investment decreased the viability of the corresponding clusters in the UK (Cowling, 1986). At the same time, the competitiveness of the investing firms may well be improved by their investments in foreign clusters, and this may have other beneficial effects on the home economy.

MNEs, GOVERNMENTS AND COMPETITIVENESS

Although Porter addresses a whole chapter to the role of governments as a shaper and monitor of economic activity, he has very little to say about the extent and way to which government policy is, itself, influenced by global economic forces, and, in particular, to those which are the result of the internationalization of production.

The interaction between MNEs, governments and competitiveness is a complex subject which is only now being addressed seriously by scholars.[27] Yet it is known to be extremely important, particularly in some developing and smaller developed economies. For the purpose of this chapter, however, we will confine our remarks to just two issues which we believe need to be incorporated into any analysis of the competitive advantages of nation states.

First, one of the distinguishing features of MNEs is their ability to shift value-added activities across national borders more easily than can uninational firms; indeed, this is a *sine qua non* for their existence. In the past, the spatial strategies of MNEs have been primarily based on the size of domestic markets and the relative competitiveness of national resources. In today's global economy, where international sourcing and markets are as, if not more, important as their domestic equivalents, the configuration of MNE activity (particularly within the Triad) is less dependent upon the availability and cost of unimproved natural resources, and more on the knowledge base and infrastructure facilities of economies in which they are producing or contemplating producing.

At the same time, governments can and do strongly influence the extent, quality and cost of these factors by their education, science and technology, industrial, trade, environmental, transport and communications and fiscal policies. Indeed, in a variety of ways, nation states are increasingly competing for resources and capabilities offered by MNEs.[28] The combination of the footloose nature of much modern industry (especially within integrated regions such as the EC) and the increasing significance of government influence on the transaction costs of such activity—and especially of high value activities in which MNEs tend to have a competitive advantage—is something which deserves the attention of scholars.

Second, MNEs can, themselves, influence government behavior, including that which directly impinges on the diamond of competitive advantage. In most industrial economies, MNEs are accounting for an increasing proportion of value-added activity. Egged on by the recent wave of cross-border acquisitions and mergers (A&Ms), such activity is also being concentrated in the largest 'x' percent of firms. In their emphasis on wealth creating activities and competitiveness, governments are being forced to acknowledge the views of the leading wealth creators.

At the same time, such firms do not always (or solely) have their home country's interests at heart, as an increasing proportion of their sales and profits are earned outside their national boundaries (Dunning, 1993). So, governments may be prompted to take action which may affect the competitiveness of their location bound assets in a variety of ways, as described by Porter. In some instances, this can lead to more competitiveness and a synergy of goals between the long run interests of corporations and those of nation states; a good example is the initiative taken by some leading European MNEs to push forward the completion of the EC's internal market program. In others, the interest of MNEs may be best served (or perceived to be best served) by urging governments to adopt policies which, far from promoting dynamic competitiveness, may inhibit it by giving shelter to inefficient or non-innovatory firms.[29]

There can be little doubt that policy rivalry between nation states is a feature of the late twentieth century, and is likely to continue to be so for the foreseeable future. Up to now, most attention has been paid to the merits and demerits of strategic trade policy.[30] However, the real issue is one of competitive strategy, which embraces not only the facets of the diamond identified by Porter, but also the ability of firms to reallocate and upgrade their human and physical capabilities to the changing needs of the marketplace at minimum adjustment cost. In each of these areas, as Porter acknowledges, governments have a critical role to play both in setting the framework within which market forces and/or hierarchies can operate, and in counteracting any efforts, either by the participants of the market, or by other governments, to rig the workings of market to their own benefit.

However, in analyzing the behavior of particular national governments, an understanding both of the international forces affecting that behavior, and of the likely consequences of their actions on the goals of other governments is essential. In their role as instruments of the globalization of economic activity and as links between the strategic policies of the governments of the countries in which they operate, MNEs are likely to have a distinctive impact on the shaping of a whole range of government related actions which, directly or indirectly, affect the shape and quality of national diamonds of competitive advantage.

CONCLUSIONS

In answer to the question, 'Is foreign inward and outward direct investment likely to affect the diamond of competitive advantage?' our answer must surely be 'yes.' Multinationality does confer its own unique characteristics and bring about a distinctive impact on resource allocation and usage. Similarly, the evidence set out in this chapter suggests that the significance of this impact, particularly in the sectors in which the industrialized nations are seeking to promote their competitive advantages, is sufficiently noteworthy for the transnational business variable to be considered as a separate factor affecting the configuration of these advantages.

In answer to the question, 'Will foreign inward and outward investment improve the competitive advantage of host or home countries?'—the answer that is all too frequently (but justifiably) given by economists is 'it all depends.' The most (but this should not be belittled) an economist can do is first to set out the conditions under which, and the ways in which, domestic or foreign MNEs are likely to benefit national competitiveness (either in an industry or an economy) in the short and/or long run, and second to indicate what might be done (and at what cost) to optimize the impact of outward and inward investment (and associated activities, e.g. strategic alliances) on that competitiveness.

The interaction between the globalization of economic activity and national competitiveness provides a rich agenda for the scholar of the MNE. This chapter has sought to identify the ways in which national diamonds of competitive advantages are linked to each other by the operation of transnational enterprises. While Michael Porter provides a useful paradigm in identifying the main determinants of national competitiveness, his lack of attention to the ways in which such competitiveness may be affected by the ownership structure of firms and the way

cross-border markets are organized weakens both the content and force of his thesis. But, the good news is that Porter has left the IB scholar plenty of interesting research to do![31]

NOTES

1. Defined as production financed by foreign direct investment or controlled by foreign owned multinational firms.
2. We say renewed attention as some of the earlier explanations of the foreign value-added activity of firms focused largely on their ability to engage in such activities (e.g., Vernon, 1966; Caves, 1971).
3. Amit and Schoemaker (1990) distinguish between resources and capabilities in the following way.

Resources consist of proprietary know-how (e.g., patents and trade secrets), financial or physical assets (e.g., property, plant and equipment), human capital, government licenses, etc. Capabilities, in contrast, are tangible or intangible (invisible) assets that are firm-specific and are created over time through complex interactions among the firm's resources. They can be thought of as 'intermediate goods' generated by the firm to provide enhanced productivity of its resources as well as flexibility and protection for its final product or service. Capabilities are based on developing, carrying, and exchanging information through the firm's human capital.

4. For a distinction between the theory of the MNE and the theory of MNE activity see Dunning, 1992.
5. At least as an explanation of the growth of the MNE.
6. More particularly that part which enters into international transactions.
7. *Natural* factor endowments are defined as the stock of unimproved resources and the uneducated labor force of a country. *Created* factor endowments or capabilities are the difference between these and the actual wealth creating assets of a community. These include not only the *ability* to create wealth, but also its *willingness* to do so.
8. Even though Porter's approach is essentially Schumpeterian.
9. For an elaboration of the ESP paradigm see, for example, Koopmans and Montias, 1971.
10. Seven from developed and one from a relatively advanced developing country (Korea). It is interesting to speculate on the relevance of Porter's analysis and conclusions to the great majority of developing economies. For a recent analysis of the interactions between the international competitiveness of developing country firms and government policies, see Agarwal and Agmon, 1990.
11. To give one (admittedly a rather extreme) example, 95 per cent of the sale of Nestlé is accounted for by their foreign subsidiaries. It follows that the diamond(s) of competitive advantage of foreign countries within which Nestlé operates may be more

important to determining the contribution of Nestlé to the Swiss GNP than the equivalent diamond within which Nestlé operates in Switzerland. The point is further explored in an MNE detailed study of the competitive advantages of Sweden (Solvell, Porter and Zander, 1991).

12. To give an illustration, first at an industry level, inward investment in the UK motor industry might rise (fall) with outward investment, or inward investment might rise (fall) as outward investment falls (rises). Second, at a meso-level, inward investment in the UK industry might rise (fall) with outward investment in *other* sectors, or the total outward investment might fall (rise) in sympathy with outward investment. The net effect on competitiveness of all these movements is highly ambiguous and dependent upon the precise configuration of the components of the UK's diamond of competitive advantage.

13. Although the two are not necessarily exclusive alternatives.

14. This is not to say that the investment may not be beneficial as it could stimulate domestic rivalry and raise efficiency in the production of low cost chocolates!

15. Either directly or by affecting the demand of consumers. In India, for example, the priority of the Indian government has been to encourage self-sufficiency of output rather than raise the quality of domestic demand.

16. We accept that part of the stimulus to foreign demand may come from exports.

17. Rather than indirectly by domestic rivalry or innovation.

18. For example, by driving out competition and making possible monopoly pricing.

19. Similarly, if the US airways were open to foreign competition, almost certainly the quality of air travel would improve.

20. For further details, see Dunning 1993.

21. For example, is it prompted by market distortions, or a response to market forces? Is it part of a defensive oligopolistic reaction or a result of the increased efficiency of cross-border hierarchies?

22. A somewhat more sophisticated argument is that, rather than investing overseas to protect or advance their competition in high technology products, it might have more productivity in the long run if the US firms had devoted more resources to product innovation or improving production efficiency in their domestic plants.

23. See especially those contained in Dunning, 1985 and Reddaway, Potter and Taylor, 1968.

24. To quote from Lawrence: 'An industry needs to experience rigorous competition if it is to be economically strong. Either too little or too much competitive pressure can lead an industry to a predictably weak economic performance characterized by its becoming inefficient and/or non-innovative' (Lawrence, 1987: 102).

25. For example, it is possible to envisage multinationalization leading to international cartelization, or helping to inject competition into markets dominated by a single or few producers.

26. Where a new science city at Tsukube already has the reputation as a world-class center for R&D (*Japan Update,* 1990).

27. For an analysis of this interaction, see Chapters 12 and 13 and Behrman and Grosse, 1990.

28. Witness, for example, the strenuous efforts by state legislatures in the US to attract inward direct investment. On the interaction between the strategy of resource usage by governments and MNEs, see an interesting paper by Stopford (1990).

29. For an analysis of the interaction between the politically oriented strategies of firms and the likely response of governments, see Rugman and Verbeke (1990).

30. See Stegemann (1989) for a review of the literature on this subject.

31. Some further thoughts on the appropriateness of Porter's focus on a country's 'domestic' diamond of competitive advantage are contained in a special issue of Management International Review, edited by Alan Rugman, in the Spring of 1993.

REFERENCES

Agarwal, R. and Agmon, T. (1990) 'The international success of developing country firms role of government-directed comparative advantage,' *Management International Review 30.*

Amit, R. and Schoemaker, P.J. (1990) *Key Success Factors: Their Foundation and Application,* Evanston, Ill.: Northwestern University Working Paper.

Aydalot, P. and Keeble D. (eds) (1988) *High Technology and Industry and Innovatory Environment: The European Experience,* London: Routledge.

Behrman, J. and Grosse, R. (1990) *International Business and Governments,* Columbia: University of Carolina Press.

Botsgontler, P. and de Bernardy, M. (1986) *Les Enterprises de 'micro' et la Technopole,* Grenoble CEPS: Université des Grenobles.

Buckley, P. and Casson, M. (1985) *The Economic Theory of the Multinational Enterprise,* London and Basingstoke: Macmillan.

Caves, R.E. (1971) 'International corporations: the industrial economics of foreign investment,' *Economics 38:* 1–27.

Cowling, K. (1986) 'The internationalization of production and deindustrialization' in Amin, A. and Goddard, J. (eds) *Technological Change, Industrial Restructuring and Regional Development,* London: Allen and Unwin.

Dunning, J.H. (ed.) (1985) *Multinational Enterprises, Economic Structure and International Competitiveness,* Chichester: John Wiley.

Dunning, J.H. (1990) *The Globalization of Firms and the Competitiveness of Countries: Some Implications for the Theory of International Production,* Lund: Institute of Economic Research, Lund University.

Dunning, J.H. (1991a) 'Governments, economic organization and international competitiveness' in Mattson, L.G. and Stymne, B. (eds) *Corporate and Industry Strategies for Europe,* Amsterdam: Elsevier Science Publishers, B.V.

Dunning, J.H. (1991b) 'Governments and multinational enterprises: from confrontation to cooperation?,' *Millenium (Journal of International Studies)* 20: 225–243.

Dunning, J.H. (1992) 'The theory of transnational corporations' in UNCTC Library on Transnational Corporations, London and New York: Routledge.

Dunning, J.H. (1993) *Multinational Enterprise and the Global Economy,* Wokingham, Berks: Addison-Wesley.

Dunning, J.H. and Morgan, B.V. (1971) *An Economic Study of the City of London,* London: Allen and Unwin.

Dunning, J.H. and Steuer, M. (1969) 'The effects of US direct investment on British technology,' *Moorgate and Wall Street,* Autumn: 1–30.

Gilpin, R. (1975) *US Power and the Multinational Corporation,* London: Macmillan.

Gilpin, R. (1987) 'Trade investment and technology policy,' in Giersch, H. (ed.) *Emerging Technologies: Consequences for Economic Growth, Structural Change and Employment,* Tübingen: J.C.B. Mohr.

Hall, P., Breheny, M., McQuaid, D. and Hart, D. (1987) *Western Sunrise,* London: Allen and Unwin.

Japan Update (1990) 'Direct investment in Japan: new developments,' *Japan Update,* Winter: 12–15.

Julius DeAnne (1989) *Global Companies and Public Policies: The Challenge of the New Economic Linkages,* London: Chatham House.

Knickerbocker, F.T. (1973) *Oligopolistic Reaction and the Multinational Enterprise,* Cambridge, Mass.: MIT Press.

Kogut, B. (1985) 'Designing global strategies: profiting from operational flexibility,' *Sloan Management Review 26,* Fall: 27–38.

Koopmans, K. and Montias, J.M. (1971) 'On the description and comparison of economic systems' in Eckstein, A. (ed.) *Comparison of Economic Systems,* California: University of California Press.

Lawrence, P.R. (1987) 'Competition: a renewed focus for industrial policy,' in Teece, D.J. (ed.) *The Competition Challenge,* Cambridge, Mass.: Ballinger.

Lipsey, R. and Dobson, W. (1987) *Shaping Comparative Advantages,* Ontario: Prentice Hall for C.D. Howe Institute.

Malerba, F. (1990) 'The Italian system of innovation,' Paper presented at the Workshop on The Organization of International Competitiveness, Brussels, May–June 1990.

Ozawa, T. (1989) *Japan's Strategic Policy Towards Outward Direct Investment,* Fort Collins: Colorado State University (mimeo).

Porter, M.E. (1990) *The Competitive Advantage of Nations,* New York: Free Press.

Reddaway, W.B., Potter, S.T. and Taylor, C.T. (1968) *The Effects of UK Direct Investment Overseas,* Cambridge: Cambridge University Press.

Rugman, A. and Verbeke, A. (1990) *Global Corporate Strategy and Trade Policy,* London and New York: Routledge.

Safarlan, A.E. (1989) 'Firm and government strategies in the context of economic integration,' Paper presented to a round-table on *Multinational Firms and European Integration,* Geneva, May 1989.

Scott, A.J. and Angel, D.P. (1987) 'The US semi-conductor industry: a locational analysis,' *Environment and Planning A 19:* 875–912.

Solvell, O., Porter, M.E. and Zender, I. (1991) *Advantage Sweden,* Stockholm: Norstedts.

Stegemann, K. (1989) 'Policy rivalry among industrial states: what we can learn from models of strategic trade policy?,' *International Organization 43,* Winter: 73–100.

Stopford, J. (1990) 'Global strategic change and resource usage,' Paper presented at International Symposium on *MNEs and 21st Century Scenarios,* organized for the studies of Multinational Enterprise, Tokyo.

Vernon, R. (1966) 'International investment and international trade in the product cycle,' *Quarterly Journal of Economics 80:* 190–207.

14

COUNTRY CAPABILITIES AND THE STRATEGIC STATE: HOW NATIONAL POLITICAL INSTITUTIONS AFFECT MULTINATIONAL CORPORATIONS' STRATEGIES

THOMAS P. MURTHA

School of Business Administration, University of Michigan, Ann Arbor, Michigan, U.S.A.

STEFANIE ANN LENWAY

Carlson School of Management, University of Minnesota, Minneapolis, Minnesota, U.S.A.

ABSTRACT   This article presents a framework for the analysis of how MNCs' strategies interact with states' industrial strategies. It first shows how national institutional arrangements can systematically contribute to state strategic capabilities that form a basis of competitive advantage. It then examines conditions under which these arrangements and capabilities affect, or fail to affect, the international strategies and organization structures of home firms, incoming foreign direct investors, and home firms' international customers, collaborators and competitors.

Can governments make strategic choices that affect firms' international strategies? The answer depends, in part, on governments' abilities to implement industrial strategies. In order to implement an industrial strategy, a government must have capabilities to integrate and motivate the complex organizational structure of its country's political and economic institutions to take concerted action (Katzenstein, 1977; Hall, 1986). These capabilities vary across countries, as do the strategies, if any, that governments can implement (Reich, 1989; Murtha, 1991). Some governments appear capable of causing firms to change their strategies and organization structures in ways that genuinely increase their international competitiveness. Others appear capable only to forbid firms, particularly home firms' competitors, from making investments or taking other steps their managers might choose (Encarnation, 1989). In still other cases, the effects of government strategies are illusory and potentially misleading. Firms may behave much as they would have done without the government's intervention. Yet their competitors may respond less vigorously than they would have in the absence of the government's involvement, if they give the strategies more credibility than they deserve (see Murtha, 1991).

This article provides a framework to take account of how governments' organizational capabilities and countries' political institutional structures affect multinational corporations' (MNCs') international strategies and organization structures. We offer two reasons why this framework adds a relevant set of new elements to contemporary business strategy paradigms.

First, recent academic interest in the contributions of country capabilities to home firm competitiveness (e.g., Porter, 1990; Kogut, 1991; Shan and Hamilton, 1991; Fladmoe-Lindquist and Tallman, 1994) has

The authors gratefully acknowledge helpful comments and encouragement from John R. Freeman, Gary Hamel, Robert T. Kudrle, C.K. Prahalad, Peter Smith Ring, Michael P. Ryan, Karen Schnatterly, Edward Snyder, the anonymous referees, and participants in the *SMJ* Special Issue Conference held September 16–17, 1993, at the School of Business Administration, University of Michigan, Ann Arbor, Michigan.
Key words: Industrial policy, multinational corporate strategy, state strategic capabilities

not, as yet, encompassed firm/state strategic interaction. Porter, in particular, has ascribed a peripheral, unsystematic role to government policy in creating country advantage. We parsimoniously show how government organization and national political economic institutional arrangements can systematically contribute to (or detract from) country capabilities that form the basis of firms' competitive advantages. Our framework shows how, why and under what conditions government officials' strategic choices affect managers' strategic choices. In particular, we show how public and private choices interact to influence whether and where MNCs invest in firm-specific intangible assets and when and where they commit capital to product-specific production assets that preempt competitors.

Second, strategy researchers have focused on conflict models of international firm/state interaction, in which changing preferences and relative bargaining power allow host governments to shift policies toward MNCs over time, usually to the detriment of the firms' interests (Vernon, 1971; Fagre and Wells, 1982; Lecraw, 1984; Kobrin, 1987; Kim, 1988; Gomes-Casseres, 1990). Successful industrial strategy implementation, however, relies on collaborative interaction between businesses and governments (Lodge, 1990). Furthermore, formal economic models of effective industrial strategy implementation rely on the assumption that government policies represent credible commitments (e.g., Spencer and Brander, 1983; Krugman, 1984; Brander and Spencer, 1985). Governments that enter credible commitments bind themselves to nonreversible courses of action (see Schelling, 1960) that beneficiary firms, their competitors and their customers can rely upon as strategic planning assumptions (see Murtha, 1993). Our framework models mechanisms by which political institutions, government organization and enterprise ownership interact to shape industrial policy preferences, the specificity of resulting policy choices, and their consistency of implementation over time.

Our argument relies on classical conceptions of state and society that distinguish between organization structures that embody national governance capabilities, and groups of decision makers who govern (see Weber, 1978). We refer to the former as 'the state' and to the latter as 'government.' States, as institutions, embody national values and legal orders that tend to persist in time (Benjamin and Duvall, 1985; Goldstein and Lenway, 1989: 306). Governments, on the other hand, usually come and go with relatively little impact on governance institutions (Skocpol, 1979). Consequently, governments' abilities to implement and maintain consistent industrial strategies are largely predetermined by state organizational structures, national political institutions, and society's expectations regarding the appropriate economic role of the public sector.[1]

Although state organizational structures and national political institutions remain relatively stable within countries over time, countries exhibit variation among themselves on these factors. These cross national variations affect international industry structures, MNCs' organizational forms and their capabilities to operate as networks of interdependent affiliates. Consequently, in our view, these variations matter as much for international industry and competitive analysis as they matter to firm/state relations.

POLITICAL INSTITUTIONS AND STRATEGIC INTERACTION BETWEEN STATES AND MNCs

Figure 1 presents a model of governments' strategic capabilities, defined as capabilities to formulate and implement industrial strategies that affect MNCs' strategies. Several of the concepts that comprise this definition require clarification for the sake of our discussion. We define industrial strategies as government plans to allocate resources with intent to meet

---

[1] Chandler's (1962) thesis held that for firms, structure follows strategy. It is now well accepted that although firm structure constrains strategy, it also embodies critical resources that enable firms to compete. Consequently, strategy follows structure, as well (Bower and Doz, 1979; Burgelman, 1983; Bartlett and Ghoshal, 1989). We argue here that governments enjoy relatively less flexibility than do management groups to alter organizational structure.

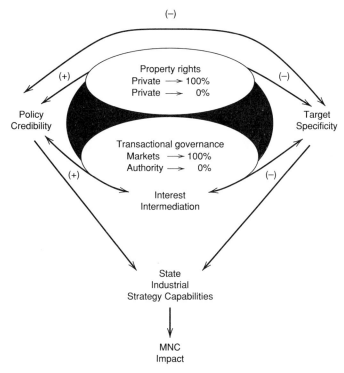

Figure 1. How National Political Institutions Affect Multinational Corporations' Strategies

long-term national economic objectives, including growth and international competitiveness. Our idea of strategy for governments, as for corporations, envisions a coherent pattern linking organizational policies and objectives. Strategic capabilities enable governments to infuse the elements of national economic policy with this programmatic coherence, which requires policy consistency across bureaucratic subunits and over time.[2]

We say that an industrial strategy affects an MNC's strategy when it causes the firm to take actions that depart from its previously established strategic criteria. Many government policies that may seem to meet such a condition really do not. For example, governments often use financial incentives to influence MNCs' facilities location plans. Evidence suggests, however, that MNCs' managers generally

discount such offers, out of concern that governments will take advantage of sovereign prerogatives to change policies in midstream (Grosse, 1989; Murtha, 1993; Robinson, 1983).[3] Where these concerns

[2] Many authors have discussed consistency, coherence and intention as elements of a corporate strategy concept, including notable statements by Andrews (1980) and Hamel and Prahalad (1989).

[3] Survey evidence has suggested that unless managers regard government policies as nonreversible commitments, these policies rarely induce MNCs to take strategic actions that they would not have taken anyway (Robinson, 1983; Murtha, 1993). As the president of a pharmaceutical firm's international division told Kobrin (1982: 121), 'We are willing to cope with harsh rules or even bad regulations, so long as we know what the rules are and that they won't be changed.' Many managers have reported that unless they can calculate the bottom line impact of government policies with certainty, they discount them 100 percent in project assessments (see especially Robinson, 1983). In the case of incentives, this has the effect of applying preordained strategic criteria. Excessive restrictions result in 'no go' decisions or scale-back of ongoing operations, as do uncertain restrictive environments. Of course, managers can miscalculate, and MNCs' affiliates, once set up, may experience policy surprises. But it seems appropriate to assume that no manager knowingly strikes an obsolescing bargain (see also Grosse, 1989).

exist, the relative generosity of governments' incentives may cause an MNC to prefer one location among several that intrinsically fit within its strategic guidelines. But the incentives will not alter the fundamental strategic criteria driving the MNC's decision process. The new location can retain its strategic viability and role with or without the government's help.

If, on the other hand, incentives cause an MNC to expand capacity and export from its home country when it had been considering more cost-competitive production sites abroad, this represents a departure from the firm's strategic criteria. If the MNC's expansion also intimidates international rivals into ceding market share, this meets the conditions that formal strategic trade models specify for an export subsidy program that enhances national welfare (see, for example, Spencer and Brander, 1983; Krugman, 1984; Brander and Spencer, 1985). Both outcomes critically depend on managers' perceptions that all elements of the government will consistently pursue the same policy over time. Strategic capabilities, as we define them, form the basis for policy consistency.

We regard strategic capabilities as properties of state organizations placed at the disposals of national governments. We derive these capabilities as functions of national institutional arrangements that vary relatively widely across countries, but relatively little over time. These institutional arrangements concern property rights allocations between countries' public and private sectors, and interorganizational transactions allocations between authoritative planning and market institutions of governance. In this section, we discuss these concepts that underlie the strategic capabilities model and the relationships that we propose exist among them.

THE BASIS OF GOVERNMENTS' STRATEGIC CAPABILITIES: AUTHORITY, MARKETS AND PROPERTY RIGHTS

States, by definition, make the laws within the territories under their control. They also incorporate the institutions that defend and enforce these laws, including the courts, police and armed forces. While these attributes of sovereignty form the basis of gov-

ernments' powers to command or forbid activities, governments need additional capabilities to take strategic economic actions that require business cooperation. As Lindblom pointed out, governments can not 'command business to perform. They must induce, rather than command' (1977: 173). In our view, governments' industrial strategy implementation capabilities largely rest on the specificity and credibility of the economic policy instruments that state organizations make available.

Target specificity describes the degree to which a state can disaggregate and isolate component activities of the national economy as objects of policy intervention. Policy instruments range in specificity from macroeconomic tools of monetary and fiscal policy that affect entire economies (not very specific) to microeconomic tools such as loans or subsidies that may target a particular transaction among firms (very specific). Instruments that can target sectors, industries or firms fall in the range between these limiting types. As the target specificity of a state's policy instruments increases, so does its government's capability to single out industries and firms, with their customers for benefits such as export subsidies or investment incentives. Governments' capabilities to discriminate in their policies between foreign and domestic firms also increase.

Policy credibility refers to governments' capabilities to commit themselves, in others' eyes, to consistent courses of action over time. In formal models of strategic trade policy (e.g., Spencer and Brander, 1983; Krugman, 1984; Brander and Spencer, 1985) firms faced with a government-subsidized competitor cede market share, because their managers assume that the subsidies represent a nonreversible, credible commitment that, by definition, can not change over time (see Schelling, 1960).[4] On this assumption, retaliation is hopeless because the subsi-

[4] We use the term 'credible commitment' in the formal sense as originated by Schelling (1960). In this sense, credible commitments, as well as credible threats, represent self-evidently nonreversible actions that one or more adversaries take in strategic interactions, in hope of limiting the range of probable responses that they rationally need anticipate from each other. The example is often given of a neighborhood bully who ties one hand behind his back, to convince other children to allow him into their games.

dized firm will outlast its competitors in an ensuing market glut. The targeted firm reaps profits and learning economies that exceed the government resources invested in the scheme.

We do not treat policy credibility as an assumption about states, but rather as a phenomenon that varies across countries, depends on public/private sector interaction and can be empirically evaluated. States inherently lack the credibility that formal strategic trade models attribute to them (Murtha, 1991).[5] By definition of sovereignty, no higher authorities exist that can bind states to implement their announced policies (Yarbrough and Yarbrough, 1987; Grandy, 1989). Empirically, the credibility of states' industrial policies significantly varies depending on two factors: (1) their reputations among managers for implementing economic policies consistently over time, and (2) targeted firms' strategic choices, given state capabilities (Murtha, 1991; 1993).

Institutional arrangements: Property rights and transactional governance. Variations across states in policy credibility and instrument target specificity result from the interaction of national institutional arrangements along two dimensions. First, countries vary in their assignments of property rights in productive assets between their public and private sectors. That is, countries differ in the economic activities that they assign to private and state ownership, and in the relative sizes of these sectors (Aharoni, 1986; Freeman, 1989). Second, countries vary in the relative influence of authoritative planning vs. market governance of transactions in domestic resource allocation. In specifying this variable, we do not mean to compare prospective efficiencies of markets vs. firm hierarchies for governing individual transac-

tions (e.g., Williamson, 1985). Rather, we concern ourselves with empirically given differences among countries in the degree to which they rely on markets vs. public planning to govern transactions among existing organizations.[6]

Referring to Figure 1, we expect policy credibility to increase as the relative influence of authority diminishes in transactional governance and as the public sector declines in its proportion of property rights assignments. These expectations follow, in part, from the properties of sovereignty. When public authority replaces markets, transactions become subject to public policy contingencies. Politics can cause public policies and their targets to change without notice. Firms that have benefited from targeting have no recourse to higher authority in the event of such disruptions. Empirical evidence suggests that the potential for disruptions increases as the number of public interventions increases, contributing to a deterioration in states' reputations for policy consistency and an increase in managers' perceptions of uncertainty regarding customers, partners and competitors (Murtha, 1993). Government ownership detracts from credibility, because it makes states parties to contracts, raising the possibility that a firm will invoke sovereign prerogatives in a contractual dis-

---

[5] The models also sidestep the efficiency issue of whether governments can more wisely choose promising firms or industries than can managers and/or markets. We do not deal with this issue here for two reasons. First, many other researchers have addressed it while few have discussed the issues of state organizational capabilities and credibility that underlie implementation. Second, if a government targets a market competitor using, for example, an export subsidy, other firms will experience a competitive impact at least in the short run, whether or not the subsidy passes a test of efficiency. Even a relatively brief price war may shake out marginal competitors.

[6] History and ideology embodied in state institutions partly explain cross-national variation in the mix between markets and public planning in domestic resource allocation. Lodge (1990), for example, associates ideology with the level of business/government collaboration in economic strategy. Individualist ideologies emphasize individual rights over community interests and tend to create adversarial business/ government relationships that constrain states' abilities to devise internally consistent industrial strategies. Communitarian ideologies, in contrast, foster cooperative business government relations. Others, such as Gerschenkron, have offered more historical explanations. Gerschenkron (1962) argued that through history individual countries' industrialization processes have seemed to demand increasingly large investments to achieve international parity and to create plants large enough to compete on the basis of scale efficiencies. Consequently, while entrepreneurs led the process in the earliest countries to industrialize, only banks and finally states could marshal the resources in countries that started later (Gerschenkron, 1962). States differentiated their organizations to develop economic capabilities that met their particular historical contingencies.

pute.[7] Public property rights are never well-defined, most notably in regard to the key underlying characteristic of excludability.[8] Consequently, government ownership makes firms more susceptible to citizens' demands that they place social and political goals, such as employment, ahead of efficiency and profit.

We expect target specificity to decrease as markets gain influence in transactional governance and the private sector increases its proportion of property rights assignments. We associate high specificity with authority, rather than markets, because authority corresponds in our taxonomy either to states' capabilities to autonomously plan economic activities, or to institutional arrangements that facilitate public/private sector economic coordination for industrial strategy implementation. We associate high specificity with public ownership of productive assets, because state ownership facilitates state intervention in managerial decision making.

Target specificity, policy credibility, bounded rationality and uncertainty. By implication of their proposed relationships with property rights and transactional governance, target specificity and policy credibility are negatively correlated. We also posit a direct negative causal relationship between target specificity and policy credibility. As the specificity of policy instruments increases, we argue, increasing information processing requirements gradually overwhelm governments' abilities to use them. As policy instruments decrease in specificity, governments rely to a greater extent on the information processing capacities of markets. For example, policies that broadly target basic research rely on market forces to determine which of many possible product applications will succeed. Policies that target a particular technology or product, however, amount to a bet unless a government can control or perfectly

anticipate all economic factors that pertain to its success. Under the circumstances, firms can anticipate considerable policy inconsistency associated with errors and false starts. Firms will avoid nonreversible commitments that reduce their flexibility to change courses.

INDUSTRIAL STRATEGY FORMULATION: INTERMEDIATING THE INTERESTS OF PROPERTY RIGHTS HOLDERS

National institutional arrangements for any given country imply a system of political economic interest intermediation. We define interest intermediation system as the policy network that governs communications, advocacy, decision- and burden-sharing among property rights holders in a country. Katzenstein (1977; 1985; 1994) uses the term policy network to refer to the set of interest group organization structures that exist in a country, including the relationships that link the public and private sectors. In the next subsection, we define a taxonomy of national systems of interest intermediation. In the following subsection, we compare some aspects of interest intermediation in capitalist countries.

Political economic interest intermediation. In Figure 2, we define a two-dimensional interest intermediation space, with property rights on the horizontal axis, and transactional governance on the vertical. Any number of empirical measures might serve, if they could be obtained, to represent variation on these axes. For the sake of exposition, we consider property rights as the proportional allocation of real assets between private and state ownership. Moving from left to right on the graph, economies range between 100 percent state and 100 percent private ownership. We define transactional governance as the proportion of interorganizational transactions governed by the price mechanism, relative to the proportion of transactions governed by plan. Moving from south to north on the graph, economies range between 100 percent planning and 100 percent market transactions.

In theory, every country occupies a unique location in the space of Figure 2. Regions of the space, however, connote shared tendencies that fit within

---

[7] For example, Petroleos Mexicanos (Pemex), the Mexican state-owned oil company, has invoked the U.S. Foreign Sovereign Immunities act, which shields foreign governments from a wide variety of suits in U.S. courts, in a variety of business disputes with U.S. citizens (*The Wall Street Journal,* September 27, 1993).

[8] We are grateful to Ted Snyder for emphasizing the importance of this issue.

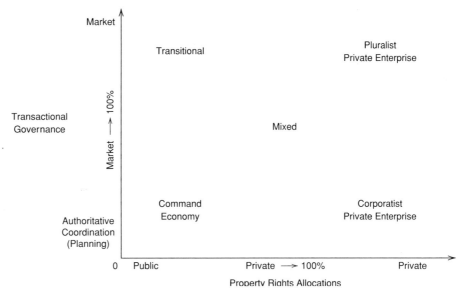

Figure 2. Systems of Public/Private Political Economic Interest Intermediation

generally accepted taxonomies of interest intermediation systems. Command economies (lower left) assign ownership rights in all productive assets to the state. State planning dictates transactions among enterprises (as well as labor) by fiat. In transitional economies (upper left) the state predominates in property rights allocations, but prices govern transactions. Within capitalism (right hand side), the major distinction separates pluralist (upper right) and corporatist (lower right) systems. Pure pluralist, private enterprise economies assign all property rights to the private sector and let unregulated markets govern enterprise and labor transactions. In corporatist, private enterprise economies authoritative coordination mechanisms, such as industry associations and national labor unions collaborate with government to play important roles in governing transactions.

In examining the map with its classifications, it is important to note that, in reality, no pure forms exist of the alternative political economies shown.[9] Most

countries' political economic systems exhibit hybrid tendencies, mixing public and private enterprise ownership and striking some balance between authoritative planning and market governance of resource allocation. The mixed category that occupies the middle of the map reflects this. Table 1 draws from a number of comparative political economic studies to provide examples of country classifications.

Corporatist vs. Pluralist Interest Intermediation in Capitalist Economies   The academic industrial strategy debate construes international competition not only as rivalry among firms, but as rivalry among states that have adopted different forms of capitalism (see Stopford and Strange, 1991; Hart, 1992). The differences rest on how policy networks institutionalize and formalize interest recon-

---

[9] No pure examples exist, even of these capitalist and socialist extremes, although the historic Soviet Union and the United States offer the closest examples. Both have employed some mix of private and public enterprise. In the former Soviet Union, politically dangerous resistance from the peasants

together with massive inefficiencies in food production resulted in the distribution of private plots to collective farm members. The produce from these private plots could be sold in peasant markets (Lindblom, 1977: 282–283). In the United States, the Amtrak passenger rail system, and the National Aeronautics and Space Administration (NASA) exemplify state-owned enterprises (SOEs).

Table 1. Illustrative Taxonomy of Countries by Interest Intermediation System

Transitional	Pluralist
Transitional economies in Central Europe:[1]	U.S. (4.4)[2]
Poland [58]	U.K. (17)[3]
Hungary [60]	India (33.8)[4]
Slovakia [80]	Canada (11)[6]
The Czech Republic [85]	Italy (19.5)[6]
Command	**Corporatist**
People's Republic of China	Brazil (22.8)[5]
Cuba	Argentina (19.6)[5]
	Japan (11.4)[5]
	Korea (22.8)[5]
	Taiwan (32.4)[5]
	Tanzania (30.3)[4]
	Netherlands (14)[6]
	West Germany (12)[6]
	Austria (31.3)[7]

Notes on figures and sources: Square brackets enclose public enterprise as a percentage share of GDP. Parentheses enclose public enterprise as a percentage share in gross fixed capital formation. Classification sources: Britain, Italy, Austria (Freeman, 1989); Japan, U.S., West Germany, Netherlands (Wilensky, 1987); Japan, Korea, Taiwan (Wade, 1990); Tanzania (Nyang'oro, 1989); Argentina, Brazil (Hagopian, 1993); Poland, Hungary, Slovakia, and the Czech Republic (*The Economist*, 3/13/93); India, Canada, PRC, and Cuba (authors' judgements).

[1] Figures as of 1992 (*The Economist*, 3/13/93: 10).

[2] Figures as of 1978 (Short, 1983 as quoted in Wade, 1990: 177).

[3] Figures as of 1981 (Short, 1983 as quoted in Wade, 1990: 177).

[4] Figures as of 1977 (Short, 1983 as quoted in Wade, 1990: 177).

[5] Figures as of 1980 (Short, 1983 as quoted in Wade, 1990: 177).

[6] Figures as of 1973 (Freeman, 1989: 11).

[7] This number reflects the production of state enterprises as a percent of the Austrian economy in 1976 (Freeman, 1989: 174–175).

ciliation among public and private property rights holders. In pluralism relatively decentralized, fragmented interest groups gain recognition from grass roots constituencies. State institutions tend to be relatively decentralized, weak, and subject to capture by constituencies. In contrast, the two most important attributes of corporatism include: (1) formal state recognition of encompassing interest groups as collaborators in government decision making, and (2) either authoritarianism or multiparty parliamentary democracy.

Pluralism unambiguously classifies only one case: the United States. The U.S. constitution reserves all powers to the nation's constituent states except for those explicitly granted to the federal government. Federal powers are divided among legislative, executive and judicial branches. The resulting decentralized system presents many obstacles to national industrial strategy formulation and to developing a consensus for implementation. Narrow interest groups face incentives to seek measures that focus large resources on themselves, rather than create encompassing benefits that they must share with others. The exchanges of favors that typically reconcile competing interests do not add up to a coherent economic strategy. Instead they may create patchworks of political expediencies that reduce economic efficiency and market flexibility (see Olson, 1982).

In typical corporatist arrangements, labor and business interact with government through officially recognized peak associations to agree on economic and social policies.[10] Before the 1980s in Sweden and the Netherlands, for example, annual tripartite agreements among such associations and the governments set wages and prices (Katzenstein, 1985: 49–50). Most corporatist arrangements, however, are more focused and less formal. Sometimes they are also less inclusive. In Japan, for example, the Ministry of International Trade and Industry (MITI) and the association of business enterprises (*Keidanren*) work together to address issues at economy, sector, industry, and product market levels (Hart, 1992). The resulting MITI 'visions' have no formal legal standing. Labor has little voice in the deliberations. Particularly in small countries such as Austria and Switzerland, key government and business decisions frequently involve many of the same people (Katzenstein, 1985). Elite members' careers often cross between business and government, reinforcing for-

[10] Peak associations are federations of blue and white collar unions and employers' associations that generally include sizable proportions of countries' labor forces and business communities.

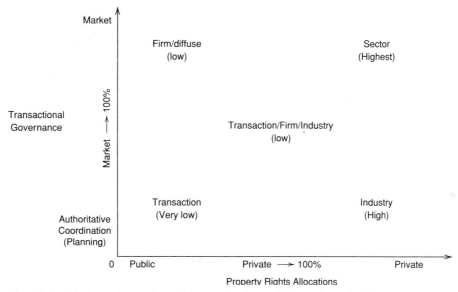

Figure 3. Maximum Target Specificity and Credibility (in Parentheses) of Most Accessible Economic Policy Instruments for Various Interest Intermediation Systems

mal consensus-building processes with informal social and professional ties.

THE IMPLICATIONS OF TRANSACTIONAL GOVERNANCE, PROPERTY RIGHTS ALLOCATIONS AND INTEREST INTERMEDIATION FOR STRATEGY FORMULATION

Within the interest intermediation systems defined in Figure 2, Figure 3 indicates the target specificity of the most politically feasible policy instruments for states and the relative credibility associated with these instruments. The specificity levels reflect maximums. We assume that if instruments are feasible at a given level of specificity, then less-specific instruments are also feasible and equally credible. More specific instruments are neither as feasible nor as credible.[11] In increasing order of specificity, the targets we consider are the national economy, sectors, industries, firms, and transactions. We regard sectors as aggregations of firms in a set of industries defined by ownership class (e.g., state-owned, public, private) or market category (e.g., consumer products, defense, high technology); or by value chain activities cutting across organizations (e.g., the manufacturing sector; the basic research sector).[12]

credibility. This holds as an implication of the direct negative relationship between target specificity and credibility specified in Figure 1. Furthermore, a government that uses less politically feasible instruments departs from its path of least political resistance and enters an arena of choice in which it has less experience and competence. We expect industrial strategies to display central tendencies, therefore, toward politically feasible instruments. Political feasibility does not imply that particular instruments create efficient economic results for countries, firms or the world economy. Misapplication, abuse, interest group capture, mistaken targeting and bungling can bring about economically undesirable outcomes.

[11] We acknowledge that governments may, at times, employ more specific instruments than seem politically feasible. The use of more specific instruments, however, carries a price in

[12] We consider the definitions of the terms defining other specificity categories as self-evident.

Target Specificity   States in command economies (lower left) determine prices and quantities for all domestic transactions, and own most means of production. This implies target specificity at the transaction level of analysis. States in transitional economies (upper left) own most means of production but, in principle, let markets determine prices and quantities. We expect these institutional arrangements to permit target specificity at the firm level of analysis. Capitalist economies with corporatist interest intermediation range from high to intermediate in the role of authority relative to markets in transactional governance and have norms and institutions that foster coordination between public and private decisionmakers. Some corporatist economies have sizable state enterprise sectors. But, since the states never own all enterprises, we expect target specificity to range from firm to industry levels as property rights vary from mixed toward private. Pluralist capitalist economies range from high to very high in market orientation toward transactional governance. Although large state enterprise sectors have existed at times in pluralist countries, orientation toward private enterprise ownership and distrust of state leadership in industrial development (see Vogel, 1978) reduce target specificity. Consequently, we expect pluralism to generally associate with sector target specificity.

Policy Credibility   The Figure 1 framework suggests that states should enjoy the comparatively highest policy credibility in pluralist, private enterprise economies, where markets govern most interorganizational transactions and private property rights dominate. States in command economies should exhibit the lowest credibility, because they invert these relationships. We argue below that the credibility differences between all of the categories of states hinge more heavily on property rights allocations than on the transactional governance dimension. Consequently, we anticipate that in economies where private property and authoritative planning coexist (lower right), corporatist states will exhibit a considerably higher degree of credibility than states in transitional economies that combine markets with predominantly public ownership of productive enter-

prises (upper left). States in mixed economies must also overcome impairments to credibility that vary depending on how well the public/private sector boundary is specified.

We argue that property rights have a greater impact on credibility than transactional governance, because market mechanisms operate imperfectly when the title to resulting surpluses remains unclear or subject to political dispute. Public property rights, by nature, always exhibit this impairment. As long as property rights remain vested in the state, governments can abrogate exchange agreements on the basis of sovereign privilege. Credibility does not very rapidly improve (and may even deteriorate) as economies move toward modes of property holding that mix public and private ownership. The power of private and public property rights holders is asymmetrical in any dispute involving both, while the relevance and efficacy of court jurisdiction remains ambiguous. This retards the development of a reputable court system. Song (1990) suggests that in China, the devolution of property rights in the absence of courts, a viable contracting tradition, and a working tax system has caused government and producers to rely on traditional means that she characterizes as 'industrial feudalism,' to guarantee exchange relationships. These means include hierarchic claims and privileges, corruption, regional relationships and intense monitoring.

Many corporatist systems that combine private property rights with relatively pervasive economic planning have strong traditions of voluntary coordination and mutual adjustment between government and business. Murtha (1991) offered evidence to suggest that corporatist formulas that combine public resources and authoritative coordination with private firm strategic choices may prove very credible with customers and competitors in domestic and international markets. Mixing state and private ownership may compromise coordination, however, if state enterprises use sovereign privilege to support capricious or opportunistic behavior toward private actors (e.g. *The Wall Street Journal,* September 27, 1993). Mixed economies operate least effectively under pluralism (Freeman, 1989). The decentralization and interest group permeability of pluralist bureaucracies subjects the enterprises to a fragmented set of cross-cutting political demands, replacing managerial direction with political expediency. In the 1980s, for example, many Indian state-owned enterprises operated without CEOs for prolonged periods. As the public commercial sector and its oversight bureaucracy expanded, private business opportunities and the scope for market choices atrophied (Prahalad, 1993).

THE IMPLICATIONS OF TARGET SPECIFICITY AND POLICY CREDIBILITY FOR INDUSTRIAL STRATEGY IMPLEMENTATION

Policy credibility and target specificity work together to determine states' industrial strategy implementation capabilities. Policy specificity increases states' capabilities because it permits discrimination between domestic- and foreign-owned firms and among all local firms. One way to understand the role of credibility is to consider the impact of its absence. Governments implement industrial strategies to influence the strategies of home firms, incoming foreign direct investors and home firms' international customers, collaborators and competitors. Home firms choose whether and how to comply with governments' influence attempts. If they comply, customers, collaborators and competitors choose how to respond.

The credibility of governments' strategies must enter these calculations, because compliance imposes costs and may require investments that can turn into losses. When home firms comply with government designs they trap themselves, with their competitors, in repeated plays of prisoners' dilemma. In the immediate term retaliation will create losses for both the home firms and their foreign competitors. The home firms must count on their governments to make good any losses they incur each period. But governments can not be held to such promises. Since the size of the losses depends on the competitors' reactions, a government could front a home firm an amount to cover the worst case scenario. But the worst case scenario—massive retaliation—is a violation of the model's assumption that foreign competitors will back down.

Clearly, home firms face a political calculation of how long the subsidies will last. Given the result of the calculation, a firm has two options. It may use the money in a way that maintains flexibility and gains short term profits. It may, for example, temporarily run its plants at capacity or outsource production to rent an increased market share. Alternatively, it can make strategic choices that create credible threats to its competitors, such as investing in inflexible assets to permanently expand production. In the former case, a government's strategy has no impact on the home firm's strategy. In the latter, the opposite holds.

Competitors increase their losses, if they behave as strategic trade models predict and do nothing or retreat. Rational, financially viable competitors will retaliate, whether or not the state is credible, and whether or not their own governments support them. Countries are better off in any round if they cooperate (Brander, 1986), refrain from subsidies, and their companies likewise cooperate in a stable oligopoly. Eventually, such an outcome can be expected to emerge (Axelrod, 1984).[13] But when it does, credibility will again play a critical role, as incentives always exist in an oligopoly for individual companies to cheat for short-term gain.

States also implement industrial strategies to elicit cooperation between domestic and foreign firms. From this perspective, targeting represents an inducement to home firms, incoming investors, and home firms' international customers and collaborators. But accepting inducements implies adjustments to the firms' international strategies. Firms, for example, may add capacity, replace traditional sources of supply with subsidized sources in other countries, produce at home rather than elsewhere, or take a partner rather than retain sole ownership. These adjustments impose real costs as well as opportunity costs. They also affect MNCs' international network configurations, creating internal and external dependencies that potentially let one country's indus-

---

[13] Axelrod ran two open-invitation, round-robin prisoner's dilemma tournaments, and reported on the outcomes in his 1984 book. In both tournaments, tit-for-tat strategies that accommodated long periods of cooperation dominated.

trial strategy changes send rippling effects through firms' international systems.

If governments are not credible, home firms, their customers and collaborators, and incoming foreign direct investors may prefer to accept inducements only when compliance fits their preexisting strategies. This leaves them no worse off when governments change plans. Industrial strategy has little effect on firms in such cases. But firms have a financial interest in finding ways to accept government offers, even when states lack credibility. Empirical evidence suggests that home firms may invest governments' resources in transaction specific assets, to demonstrate that they will sustain their strategies even if their subsidies end (Murtha, 1991).

INTEREST INTERMEDIATION, STATE INDUSTRIAL STRATEGY IMPLEMENTATION CAPABILITIES AND MNCs' STRATEGIES AND ORGANIZATION STRUCTURES

In this section we discuss the implications of the Figure 1 framework for MNCs' strategies as home government targets, as incoming foreign direct inves-

tors, and as targeted firms' customers, collaborators and competitors.

Command and Transitional Economies Command economies rely on very specific policy instruments that subject firms to authority at every point of interaction with their environments. Furthermore, states own all firms. Even if command economies could achieve internationally competitive efficiencies, they would suffer from an uneasy institutional interface with international markets. Command economies are not known as incubators of MNCs. Institutional arrangements within command economies tend to pull home firms toward international strategies of exporting to unaffiliated parties, generally through centralized state trading agencies (see Figure 4). Consequently, the likelihood that any industrial strategies would be sustained depends entirely on the state. Our framework suggests that competitors or customers should regard the credibility of targeting policies as low. The public policy contingencies that attend transactions subject all economic relationships to the risk that *ex post* recontracting demands will emerge for political reasons, or because an excess of targets over instruments has over-

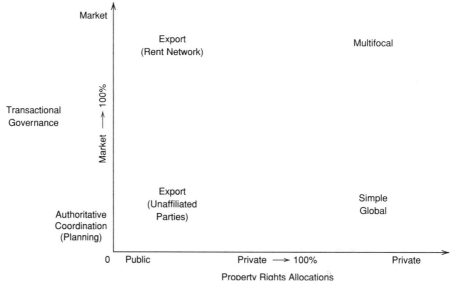

Figure 4. Gravitational Tendencies that Home-State Strategic Capabilities Bring to Bear on MNCs' Strategies

whelmed a state's planning machinery (see Tinbergen, 1952).[14] Enterprise strategies that adjust for or circumvent planning also detract from credibility because they involve corrupt practices such as black marketeering for inputs in short supply.[15]

When command economies implement strategies to attract MNCs, they adopt elements of transitional or mixed economies. As hosts, these states have often reconciled outside interests with local institutional arrangements by requiring that states hold ownership shares in affiliates. Once affiliates are established, controlled access to labor, inputs, local markets and hard currency for imports plus the myriad of permissions required to operate greatly complicate managements' tasks (Grub, 1991; Pearson, 1991). As command economies make the transition toward markets, institutional compatibility with the international economy may improve. But as home countries for MNCs, transitional economies continue to suffer from an historic failure to build up the firm-specific advantages that drive foreign direct investment and make it profitable. Buckley and Casson (1976), Rugman (1981), Hennart (1982) and Teece (1986) discuss theoretical factors underlying foreign direct investment. The most critical factors historically absent in command and transitional economies have to do with failures to define and clearly assign title to returns from innovation. In the short run, incoming MNCs may substitute for the underdeveloped organizational resources in these economies, to use Bruce Kogut's phrase (1983: 51), by renting their networks to them (see Figure 4).

Command economies have historically associated with single party states and authoritarianism. Empirically, single party longevity in executive power significantly associates in MNCs' managers' minds with policy consistency (Murtha, 1993). As command economies introduce elements of markets or private property, credibility may deteriorate. First, states continue to control most enterprises, which impairs many contracts MNCs' affiliates might enter. Second, where the changes associate with democratization, MNCs' managers may treat them as evidence of instability until new institutional arrangements take shape. In the early 1990s, for example, few MNCs took strong steps to build their presences in Central Europe, where most former communist countries undertook a transition to democracy (*Economist,* March 13, 1993). But China, which introduced economic reforms while adhering to authoritarianism, enjoyed double digit economic growth and a surge of foreign direct investment (*Economist,* August 14, 1993). Third, the breakdown of central planning may leave behind fragmented bureaucratic and regional fiefdoms (Song, 1990). These may pursue mutually inconsistent policies toward MNCs, and significantly delay market entry permissions or other initiatives.

Institutional change takes place slowly (Skocpol, 1979). MNCs' managers will ask whether expected long-term gains from transitional economies necessitate market presences during the transition. Governments may overcome some strategic disabilities from their lack of credibility by not using their most specific policy instruments. They can also build reputations for policy consistency by running disciplined macroeconomic programs that keep inflation low.

MNCs will prefer flexible strategies that do not depend on government inducements for commercial success. Consequently, governments in transitional economies gain the greatest leverage by concentrating any inducements they can afford on industries and sectors that reflect comparative advantage. In other words, the greatest gains to the local economy will come from offering incentives to MNCs to pursue options that they would find attractive anyway. In these circumstances the government's credibility or lack of it will not matter.

Why pay MNCs to do things that they might be willing to do 'for free?' First, such payments may be necessary to compete with other developing countries that typically make such offers (see Moran,

---

[14] Tinbergen (1952) demonstrated that the simultaneous achievement of any number of policy tasks requires an equal number of instruments.

[15] The transactional inefficiency associated with such activities stands aside from the production inefficiencies that emerge from perverse incentives set up by planning. Berliner (1957) described the case of the Soviet shoe factory that faced production targets set by weight. The factory installed very thick soles on each individual shoe.

1992). Second, the expenditures may represent an efficient policy response to a lack of information among MNCs about local production possibilities.

Pluralist and Corporatist Capitalism Industrial strategies under capitalism depend on the availability of policy instruments for reallocating resources from declining firms and industries to new firms or industries. In order to credibly target a narrow subset of firms or industries, countries need mechanisms to compensate and share benefits with nontargeted industries. High target specificity and policy credibility provides governments with the capability to make these distinctions. Governments may use this capability to limit managerial discretion in local affiliates of foreign enterprises, as well as to exclude them from the benefits conferred by industrial strategy. If foreign firms share the benefits, this speeds the international diffusion of competitive advantages that the strategies foster.

Discrimination figures heavily in our judgements of capitalist states' strategic capabilities and their effects on MNCs. Although states in pluralist, private enterprise economies enjoy high policy credibility, their policy instruments are relatively nondiscriminatory.[16] Some analysts, for example, have construed U.S. industrial strategy as a set of sectoral policies to fund basic research under military and university auspices (Hart, 1992; Wilensky and Turner, 1987). Commercial applications emerge from the private sector, so that markets rather than the government choose. Non-U.S. firms, however, often first recognize promising applications of U.S. research. Any MNC can establish R&D facilities to employ U.S.-trained researchers anywhere in the world.

Corporatist private enterprise systems can support industries while excluding foreign firms. Many studies have suggested that the Japanese state has targeted industries by protecting them, financially assisting them, and helping them to coordinate their competitive behavior in overseas markets (e.g., Encarnation and Mason, 1990; Johnson, 1982). If in-

coming MNCs could get the same treatment, such programs would have less impact on Japan's competitiveness. But MITI proscribed foreign investment in Japan until the early 1960s, gradually moving toward complete capital liberalization by 1980. MITI granted only a few exceptions (IBM and Texas Instruments, for example), on condition that the entering investors license their technology to Japanese competitors in the same industries (Encarnation, 1992).

MNCs have leveraged their positions in state-targeted industries in discriminatory countries by taking equity positions in local firms. Equity ownership in corporatist economies, however, does not necessarily confer proportionate influence in corporate governance. Boards of directors may include key participants in the national strategic consensus, in some instances diluting foreigners' representation. European corporations, for example, have historically provided labor and banks with significant board representation (Hall, 1986).

Corporatist political arrangements can act as two-edged swords affecting home firms' and industries' international competitiveness. Government subsidies can diminish local firms' credibility as competitors and suppliers. If targeted local firms make inflexible investments to offset such perceptions, they tie up capital so that it can not be easily redeployed for new strategies when market opportunities change (Murtha, 1991). Consensual interest intermediation structures may also pressure private firms to share the social burden of economic adjustment. The lifetime employment norm in Japan's largest enterprises implicitly acknowledged such an obligation (Dore, 1986; Abegglen and Stalk, 1985). Under cost and political pressure to establish production centers abroad, however, Japanese firms struggled to disestablish this norm in the early 1990s (*Economist,* September 18, 1993).

Mixed systems of property rights complicate the analysis. State ownership raises the maximum specificity of policy instruments to the firm level in both corporatist and pluralist capitalist economies. But it also diminishes policy credibility. State ownership can compromise firms' international competitiveness, even if the firms officially operate on profit-maximizing criteria. As public sector organizations,

---

[16] Market philosophy as well as technical capabilities favor the principle of nondiscrimination in the industrialized capitalist economies, which include most pluralist private enterprise economies. The principle is a mutually-agreed norm among OECD countries.

these firms face political obstacles, such as demands that they sustain employment rather than respond to changing competitive conditions.

Trends toward internationalized production systems contravene gravitational tendencies in corporatist political institutions that pull home firms toward simple global strategies (see Figure 4). As described in Porter's (1986) taxonomy of international strategies, simple global strategies centralize most value chain activities in home countries and treat the world as a unified market that can be served through national market and sales affiliates.

Pluralist systems of interest intermediation create diffuse, relatively nonbinding pressures on home-based MNCs' international strategies. Aside from national security contingencies (see Lenway and Crawford, 1986), host country institutions' demands for responsiveness may exert more compelling gravitational pulls. We expect MNCs based in pluralist countries to balance global efficiency with historic tendencies toward nationally responsive strategies. In terms of the strategic taxonomy of Prahalad and Doz (1987), these countries' firms may display distinctive competence in multifocal strategy implementation, which can decentralize and network production, information and decision-making authority across multiple countries.

CONCLUSION

In this article, we have presented a framework that shows implications of variations in states' strategic capabilities for the strategies of home firms, their customers, collaborators and competitors, and for incoming direct investors. In command and transitional economies, state ownership creates ambiguous property rights regimes that retard the development of firm-specific advantages that drive outward direct investment. Their competitive advantages are primarily cost-based. Incoming investors must generally share ownership with governments or other local partners. Their strategies tap the local resources that create international cost advantages, provide conduits of intrafirm exports, and make bets on future market development.

In the 1990s, many developing and former Communist countries have struggled to build international economic capabilities by redefining the critical institutional dimensions of their domestic political economies. Other countries are seeking to better understand and use the capabilities already at their disposals. Our framework depicts transitions from planned to market economies as comprising two distinct reform processes: privatization of productive enterprises and replacement of planning with market resource allocation. Where property rights reform has lagged market development, traditional hierarchic relations and corruption have continued to play heavy roles in transactional governance (Song, 1990; Prahalad, 1993). Our framework suggests that this happens because continued state equity participation in significant numbers of enterprises compromises the authority of courts in contractual enforcement. These difficulties reduce the credibility of a government's liberalization policies and send a negative signal to MNCs (Prahalad, 1993).

History offers one remedy. In the long run, states can build reputations through consistent policy implementation. But the long run will consist of many short runs in which governments, which may face elections, have responsibility for the reputation-building process. In the early stages of a transition, our framework suggests that governments should give precedence to establishing private property rights over creating markets. Markets operate imperfectly when many contracts are unenforceable and the titles to profit streams remain ambiguous. In targeting strategies, governments improve their chances of sustaining financial commitments if they address relatively few firms or industries. But directing policy to a small number of very narrow targets also means increasing the gamble that any policy will produce a viable competitor. Targeting at a more diffuse, sectoral level increases the role of markets in selecting domestic winners and losers, and decreases chances of creating distortions. Building credibility in specific industries without betting the treasury on long odds may mean making a few very visible commitments to incoming MNCs with proven international track records.

In both corporatist and pluralist capitalist economies, private property rights regimes foster development of firm-specific advantages that drive firms to compete in international markets by investing abroad. Corporatism may limit home firms' international strategic flexibility, however, when the public and private sectors coordinate to sustain employment and economic growth. Incoming foreign direct investors join the national strategic consensus when they can. Where they can not join, they must often cope with discrimination. Firms from pluralist economies enjoy greater strategic discretion, and may be inherently more decentralized and flexible. But this flexibility may render their strategies more susceptible to other states' influence. Most incoming investors enjoy similar flexibility and share many benefits of local industrial assistance programs with their domestic competitors.

We argue that for both transitional and capitalist states, policy credibility plays the critical role in determining whether either home or host governments' strategies really influence MNCs' strategies or only appear to do so. In home as well as host countries, governments often target MNCs with inducements that appeal to competitive self-interest. MNCs will always accept inducements, provided governments' proposals fit within ranges of activities that the firms would pursue on their own, given their corporate strategies. But this article concerns the conditions that underlie MNC/government interactions that result in jointly determined strategic paths. MNCs will not enter into processes of mutual strategic adaptation with governments unless they have assurances that the governments can and will pursue consistent policies over time.

Governments can pursue credible strategies provided they formulate them to fit within their states' capabilities. As these capabilities vary across countries along with national political institutional arrangements, so also do the politically feasible strategies that governments can implement. Our framework suggests that in given countries, governments and MNCs can achieve more by understanding and acting upon each others' unique capabilities than they can by replicating other countries' strategies. Public officials should recognize that industrial strategies have the highest probabilities of success when they maximize the scope for market mechanisms to select winners and losers. Managers should

recognize that governments have a higher probability of sustaining policies when they are targeted at politically feasible levels of specificity. The existence of specific policy instruments does not require that governments use them. Less specific policies always operate with greater credibility. At the same time, they increase the scope for market mechanisms to mature and impose discipline on how firms use the resources that states can provide.

REFERENCES

Abegglen, J.C. and G. Stalk, Jr. (1985). *Kaisha: The Japanese Corporation.* Basic Books, New York.

Aharoni, Y. (1986). *The Evolution and Management of State-Owned Enterprises.* Ballinger Press, Cambridge, MA.

Andrews, K. (1980). *The Concept of Strategy.* Irwin, Homewood, IL.

Axelrod, R. (1984). *The Evolution of Cooperation.* Basic Books, New York.

Bartlett, C.A. and S. Ghoshal (1989). *Managing across Borders: The Transnational Solution.* Harvard Business School Press, Boston, MA.

Benjamin, R. and R. Duvall (1985). 'The capitalist state in context.' In R. Benjamin and S. Elkins (eds.), *The Democratic State.* University of Kansas Press, Lawrence, KA, pp. 1–57.

Berliner, Joseph S. (1957). *Factory and Manager in the USSR.* Harvard University Press, Cambridge, MA.

Boddewyn, J. (1988). 'Political aspects of MNE theory,' *Journal of International Business Studies,* **19**(3), pp. 341–365.

Bower, J.L. and Y. Doz (1979). 'Strategy formulation: A social and political process.' In D. Schendel and C.W. Hofer (eds.), *Strategic Management: A New View of Business Policy and Planning.* Little, Brown, Boston, MA, pp. 152–166.

Brander, J.A. and B.J. Spencer (1985). 'Export subsidies and international market share rivalry,' *Journal of International Economics,* **50,** pp. 707–722.

Brander, J.A. (1986). 'Rationales for strategic trade and industrial policy.' In P. Krugman (ed.), *Strategic Trade Policy and the New International Economics.* MIT Press, Cambridge, MA, pp. 23–46.

Buckley, P.J. and M. Casson (1976). *The Future of the Multinational Enterprise.* Macmillan, London.

Burgelman, R.A. (1983). 'A model of the interaction of strategic behavior, corporate context, and the concept of strategy.' *Academy of Management Review,* **28,** pp. 223–244.

Chandler, A.D. (1962). *Strategy and Structure: Chapters in the History of the American Industrial Enterprise.* M.I.T. Press, Cambridge, MA.

Dore, R. (1986). *Flexible Rigidities.* Stanford University Press, Stanford, CA.

The Economist (August 14, 1993). 'China's perpetual revolution,' pp. 29–30.

The Economist (September 18, 1993). 'Japanese industry: Losing its way,' pp. 78–79.

The Economist (March 13, 1993). 'A survey of Eastern Europe,' special insert.

Encarnation, D.J. (1989). *Dislodging Multinationals: India's Strategy in Comparative Perspective*. Cornell University Press, Ithaca, NY.

Encarnation, D.J. and M. Mason (1990). 'Neither MITI nor America: The political economy of capital liberalization in Japan,' *International Organization, 44,* pp. 25–54.

Encarnation, D.J. (1992). *Rivals Beyond Trade: America Versus Japan in Global Competition*. Cornell University Press, Ithaca, NY.

Fagre, N. and L.T. Wells (1982). 'Bargaining power of multinationals and host governments,' *Journal of International Business Studies, 13*(2), pp. 9–23.

Fladmoe-Lindquist, K. and S. Tallman (1994). 'Resource-based strategy and competitive advantage among multinationals.' In P. Shrivastava, A. Huff, and J. Dutton (eds.), *Advances in Strategic Management,* Vol. 10. JAI Press, Greenwich, CT (forthcoming).

Freeman, J.R. (1989). *Democracy and Markets: The Politics of Mixed Economies*. Cornell University Press, Ithaca, NY.

Gerschenkron, A. (1962). *Economic Backwardness in Historical Perspective: A Book of Essays*. Belknap Press of Harvard University Press, Cambridge, MA.

Goldstein, J. and S.A. Lenway (1989). 'Interests or institutions: An inquiry into-congressional-ITC relations,' *International Studies Quarterly, 33*(3), pp. 303–328.

Gomes-Casseres, B. (1990). Firm ownership preferences and host government restrictions: An integrated approach,' *Journal of International Business Studies, 21*(1), pp. 1–22.

Grandy, C. (1989). 'Can government be trusted to keep its part of a social contract?' *Journal of Law, Economics and Organization, 5,* pp. 249–269.

Grosse, R. (1989). *Multinationals in Latin America*. Routledge, New York.

Grub, P.D. (1991). *Foreign Direct Investment in China*. Quorum Books, New York.

Hagopian, F. (1993). 'After regime change: Authoritarian legacies, political representation and the democratic future of South America,' *World Politics, 45*(3), pp. 464–500.

Hall, P. (1986). *Governing the Economy: The Politics of State Intervention in Britain and France*. Oxford University Press, New York.

Hamel, G. and C.K. Prahalad (1989). 'Strategic intent?' *Harvard Business Review,* May–June, pp. 63–76.

Hart, J.A. (1992). *Rival Capitalists: International Competitiveness in the United States, Japan, and Western Europe*. Cornell University Press, Ithaca, NY.

Hennart, J-F. (1982). *A Theory of the Multinational Corporation*. University of Michigan Press, Ann Arbor, MI.

Johnson, C. (1982). *MITI and the Japanese Miracle: The Growth of Industrial Policy 1927–1975*. Stanford University Press, Stanford, CA.

Katzenstein, P. (ed.) (1977). *Between Power and Plenty: Foreign Economic Policies of Advanced Industrial States*. University of Wisconsin Press, Madison, WI.

Katzenstein, P. (1994). *Corporatism and Change: Austria, Switzerland and the Politics of Industry*. Cornell University Press, Ithaca, NY.

Katzenstein, P. (1985). *Small States in World Markets*. Cornell University Press, Ithaca, NY.

Kim, W.C. (1988). 'The effects of competition and corporate political responsiveness on multinational bargaining power,' *Strategic Management Journal, 9*(3), pp. 289–295.

Kobrin, S.J. (1982). *Managing Political Risk Assessment: Strategic Response to Environmental Change*. University of California Press, Berkeley, CA.

Kobrin, S.J. (1987). 'Testing the bargaining hypothesis in the manufacturing sector in developing countries,' *International Organization, 41*(4), pp. 609–638.

Kogut, B. (1983). 'Foreign direct investment as a sequential process.' In C.P. Kindleberger and D.B. Audretsch (eds.), *The Multinational Corporation in the 1980s*. MIT Press, Cambridge, MA, pp. 39–56.

Kogut, B. (1991). 'Country capabilities and the permeability of borders,' *Strategic Management Journal*. Summer Special Issue, **12,** pp. 33–48.

Krugman, P.R. (1984). 'Import protection as export promotion: International competition in the presence of oligopoly and economies of scale.' In H. Kierzkowski (ed.), *Monopolistic Competition and International Trade*. Clarendon Press, Oxford, pp. 180–193.

Lecraw, D. (1984). 'Bargaining power, ownership and profitability of transnational corporations in developing countries.' *Journal of International Business Studies, 15*(1), pp. 27–43.

Lenway, S.A. and B. Crawford (1986). 'When business becomes politics: Uncertainty and risk in east–west trade.' In J.E. Post (ed.), *Research in Corporate Social Performance and Policy*. JAI Press, Greenwich, CT, pp. 29–53.

Lindblom, C. (1977). *Politics and Markets: The World's Political and Economic Systems*. Basic Books, New York.

Lodge, G. (1990). 'Roles and relationships of business and governments.' In G. Lodge (ed.), *Comparative Business-Government Relations*. Prentice-Hall, Englewood Cliffs, NJ, pp. 1–40.

Moran, T.H. (1992). 'Strategic trade theory and the use of performance requirements to negotiate with multinational corporations in the third world: Exploring a 'new' political economy of north–south relations in trade and foreign investment,' *The International Trade Journal, 8*(1), pp. 45–84.

Murtha, T.P. (1991). 'Surviving industrial trageting: State credibility and public policy contingencies in multinational subcontracting,' *Journal of Law, Economics and Organization, 7*(1), pp. 117–143.

Murtha, T.P. (1993). 'Credible enticements: Can host governments tailor multinational firms' organizations to suit national objectives?' *Journal of Economic Behavior and Organization,* **20,** pp. 171–186.

Nyang'oro, J.E. (1989). 'State corporatism in Tanzania.' In J.E. Nyang'oro and T.M. Pshaw (eds.), *Corporatism in Africa: Comparative Analysis and Practice.* Westview Press, Boulder, CO, pp. 67–82.

Olson, M. (1982). *The Rise and Decline of Nations: Economic Growth, Stagflation, and Social Rigidities.* Harvard University Press, Cambridge, MA.

Pearson, M.M. (1991). *Joint Ventures in the People's Republic of China: The Control of Foreign Direct Investment under Socialism.* Princeton University Press, Princeton, NJ.

Porter, M. (1986). 'Competition in global industries: A conceptual framework.' In M. Porter (ed.), *Competition in Global Industries.* Harvard Business School Press, Boston, MA, pp. 15–60.

Porter, M. (1990). *The Competitive Advantage of Nations.* Free Press, NY.

Prahalad, C.K. and Y.L. Doz (1987). *The Multinational Mission: Balancing Local Demands and Global Vision.* Free Press, New York.

Prahalad, C.K. (1993). 'Globalization: Pitfalls, Pain and Potential.' Rajiv Gandhi Institute for Contemporary Studies, Paper no. 2.

Reich, S. (1989). 'Regulating foreign investment: Europe and the U.S.,' *International Organization,* **43**(4), pp. 543–584.

Robinson, R.D. (1983). *Performance Requirements for International Business: U.S. Management Response.* Praeger, New York.

Rugman, A. M. (1981). *Inside the Multinationals.* Columbia University Press, New York.

Schelling, T. (1960). *The Strategy of Conflict.* Harvard University Press, Boston, MA.

Shan, W. and W. Hamilton (1991). 'Country-specific advantage and international cooperation,' *Strategic Management Journal,* **12**(6), pp. 419–432.

Short, R. (1983). 'The role of public enterprises: An international statistical comparison.' Department Memorandum Series 83/84, International Monetary Fund, Washington, DC.

Skocpol, T. (1979). *States and Social Revolutions.* Cambridge University Press, New York.

Song, Z.Z. (1990). 'Institutional factors underlying the issues in Sino-foreign joint ventures in China: An extension of transaction cost economics to underdeveloped hybrid markets,' Unpublished Ph.D. Dissertation, University of Michigan.

Spencer, B.J. and J.A. Brander (1983). 'International R&D rivalry and industrial strategy,' *Review of Economic Studies,* **50,** pp. 707–722.

Stopford, J. and S. Strange (1992). *Rival States, Rival Firms: Competition for World Market Shares.* Cambridge University Press, New York.

Teece, D.J. (1986). 'Transactions cost economics and the multinational enterprise: An assessment,' *Journal of Economic Behavior and Organization,* **7,** pp. 21–45.

Tinbergen, J. (1952). *On the Theory of Economic Policy.* North Holland, Amsterdam.

Vernon, R. (1971). *Sovereignty at Bay: The Multinational Spread of U.S. Enterprises.* Basic Books, New York.

Vogel, D. 1978. 'Why businessmen distrust their state: The political consciousness of American corporate executives,' *British Journal of Political Science,* **8,** pp. 45–78.

Wade, R. (1990). *Governing the Market: Economic Theory and the Role of Government in East Asian Industrialization.* Princeton University Press, Princeton, NJ.

The Wall Street Journal (September 27, 1993). 'Commercial risk: In Mexico a dispute over a business deal may land you in jail,' p. 1.

Weber, M. (1978). *Economy and Society,* Vol. 2. University of California Press, Berkeley, CA.

Wilensky, H.L. and L. Turner (1987). *Democratic Corporatism and Policy Linkages: The Interdependence of Industrial, Labor–Market, Incomes and Social Policies in Eight Countries.* Institute of International Studies, University of California, Berkeley, CA.

Williamson, O.E. (1985). *The Economic Institutions of Capitalism.* Free Press, New York.

Yarbrough, B.V. and R.M. Yarbrough (1987). 'Institutions for the governance of opportunism in international trade,' *Journal of Law, Economics and Organization,* **3,** pp. 129–139.

15

NATIONAL TARGETING POLICIES, HIGH-TECHNOLOGY INDUSTRIES, AND EXCESSIVE COMPETITION

RICHARD BRAHM

Graduate School of Management, University of California, Irvine, California, U.S.A.

ABSTRACT   This paper explores some fundamental changes in market dynamics that are unfolding in the new competitive landscape as a result of aggressive industrial intervention by nation-states. The thesis is that national targeting policies are likely, under identifiable conditions, to cause rivalry in high-technology industries to become excessively competitive, strictly defined in terms of producer welfare. The paper analyzes why this is likely to occur in high-technology sectors rather than in other types of industries, and how excessive competition is likely to be manifested in specific dimensions of competitive rivalry. The paper also discusses research opportunities for further development of a theory of the political economy of excessive competition and for strategy scholars to make new contributions to trade policy debates.

Competition today is more intense than it's ever been. A major reason is that we have substantial world-wide excess capacity. We estimate that in a normal situation—without a U.S. recession—there's a world excess capacity of about 8.4 million units, and about 6 million are directed at the U.S. market. For example, a North American customer now has the opportunity to choose among 650 different car and truck models compared with about 530 ten years ago. As a result we have heavy competition for market share, and that's causing very costly marketing programs, and putting severe pressure on margins for everyone. That situation will intensify in Europe. (Quotation of Harold A. Poling, Chairman, CEO,

Ford Motor Company [Kahalas and Suchon, 1992: 72])

. . . defensive [industrial] targeting to meet foreign policies will often be a way of ensuring that investment is funneled into areas with excess capacity and depressed rates of return. (Krugman, 1987: 276)

How do the aggregate strategic targeting actions of national governments affect the nature and intensity of rivalry in contemporary international high-technology industries? I examine this question here, using the term 'targeting' broadly to refer to 'the whole spectrum of policies by which a government may promote particular industries' (Krugman, 1984a: 77).[1] For two reasons, the question is important to

I would like to thank Harry Bowen in particular, and also Paul Feldstein, Richard McKenzie, Tom Buchmueller, Stephanie Lenway, Tom Murtha, Rebecca Henderson, Lee Hanson, Ian Taplin, Joanne Oxley, Special Issue Editors Mike Hitt and Rich Bettis, and three anonymous *Strategic Management Journal* reviewers for their encouragement and suggestions. Key words: excessive competition, industrial policy, high technology

[1] Many usages and definitions of 'targeting' exist in the industrial policy, development economics and trade literatures. My definition is deliberately vague about whether or not the underlying government motive is intendedly consistent with economic rationality, since I wish to include policies motivated by either political or economic rationales in the analysis. For a more restricted usage that implicitly emphasizes intervention as an intendedly welfare-enhancing response to

gaining an accurate understanding of changing competitive dynamics in many parts of the new competitive landscape. First, the continuing trend toward economic globalization increases the impact of the national economic policies of any one country on economic outcomes in all others (Dicken, 1992; O'Brien, 1992). Second, nation-states (hereafter 'states') have become increasingly active in their attempts to intervene in international high-technology industries to foster improved outcomes for domestic firms operating within them (Lee and Reid, 1991; Ostry, 1990). Understanding how national targeting policies affect the dynamics of high-technology rivalry therefore promises new insights into the changing nature of contemporary industrial competition and new questions for future strategic management research.

'New' strategic trade theories and a considerable amount of mainstream international economics and strategy literature frequently represent high-technology industries as less than perfectly competitive as a result of various kinds of entry barriers and characteristics conducive to potential monopoly profits, or 'rents' (Caves, 1989; Krugman, 1989; Scherer, 1992; Tyson, 1993). The view developed in this paper is quite different: I contend that many of these industries are probably *excessively* competitive, at root because of the manner in which simultaneous targeting of them by too many states interacts with certain of their endogenous structural characteristics. The thesis of the paper is that states' targeting actions in aggregate tend to promote over-investment in many international high-technology industries, thereby initiating a dynamic process of reactions by both firms and states that, under identifiable conditions, is likely to cause these industries to become excessively competitive.

In contrast to the traditional economic literature on 'cut-throat' competition, as explained further in the next section, *excessive competition* in this paper

refers to a dynamic industry equilibrium characterized by subnormal average economic returns and many or all of the following features: severe price and cost competition; high average rates of structural excess capacity; and, most importantly, over-accelerated innovation and investment races in both process and product technology. This paper explores the interrelationships between these dimensions of excessive competition and state targeting policies, working toward a theory of the political economy of excessive competition in international high-technology markets.

In this paper, the term 'excessive competition' is defined in terms of producer welfare (i.e., producers' economic returns). Competition is 'excessive' when rivalry in an industry results in a sustained average rate-of-return below the competitive rate (i.e., a dynamic equilibrium in which unit costs exceed price). This definition of excessive competition does not necessitate any particular conclusion, either pro or con, about the effect of national targeting policies on net social welfare (producer plus consumer surplus). Normally competition that is excessive in terms of producer welfare would also be suboptimal in terms of social welfare because of the opportunity costs associated with producers' over-investment in the industry. However, if positive externalities exist (i.e., if benefits are not fully appropriated by producers), the social value of the increased investment may exceed the subsequent private loss incurred by producers. Theoretically, therefore, it is possible for competition to be excessive in terms of producer welfare, independent of net social welfare. Normally, however, a long-run equilibrium involving subnormal economic returns could not be sustained since adjustment (e.g., exit) would occur until economic returns once again became competitive. As this paper attempts to show, state targeting of high-technology industries may, under certain conditions, present an important exception to this fundamental 'normal' rule.

The paper begins with a brief review of background literature, then pursues the core arguments in three sections. The first summarizes the literature on high-technology targeting policies and presents an explanation for why these policies are likely to produce persistent over-investment in the targeted

---

market failures, see Krugman (1987: 266). For additional discussions of targeting see, for example Anchordoguy (1988); Dixit and Grossman (1984); Flamm (1987); General Accounting Office (1985); Hufbauer and Shelton Erb (1984: 107–110); and U.S. International Trade Commission (1983; 1984; 1985).

industries. It includes a brief discussion of inefficiencies in the market mechanisms by which states are disciplined for uneconomical targeting policies. The next section analyzes the probable competitive effects of cumulative national targeting policies, exploring relationships between targeting, over-investment, and several dimensions of excessive competition. It includes a brief analysis of some market failures in high-technology industries that are likely to induce managers to pursue excessively competitive responses to other nations' targeting policies. The final section discusses research implications for further development of a theory of the political economy of excessive competition.

BACKGROUND LITERATURE

COMPETITION IN INTERNATIONAL HIGH-TECHNOLOGY INDUSTRIES

Most commentators on contemporary international competition agree that one outcome of recent trends toward economic 'globalization' has been the escalation of industrial rivalry especially in technology-intensive sectors. The managerial literature on international high-technology competition is thoroughly imbued with this theme. Perhaps nowhere is this better articulated than in D'Aveni's recent work on 'hypercompetition':

Hypercompetition results from the dynamics of strategic maneuvering among global and innovative combatants. It is a condition of rapidly escalating competition . . . In other words, environments escalate toward higher and higher levels of uncertainty, dynamism, heterogeneity of the players, and hostility. (1994: xiii–xiv)

On the other hand, the international business and trade literatures based upon industrial organization (IO) economics generally portray the picture somewhat differently. International high-technology industries are typically characterized by structural mobility barriers such as irreversible commitments and product differentiation; static and dynamic economies of scale, scope, and learning that create increas-

ing returns to scale; and path dependencies and R&D races with high uncertainty and potential first mover benefits (Arthur, 1990; Heiduk and Yamamura, 1990; Helpman and Krugman, 1985; Porter, 1990; Richardson, 1989; Scherer, 1991). These structural characteristics are viewed as creating imperfectly competitive markets in which supernormal profits, or rents, may be possible, and in which time becomes a fundamental dimension of competition (Schumpeter, 1942; Stalk, 1988).

Thus, while the managerial literature on international high-technology industries stresses their growing competitiveness, the IO economics-based literatures routinely emphasize departures from perfect competition arising from these industries' structural characteristics. That many high technology industries might in fact be excessively competitive in terms of producer welfare despite these characteristics, as is argued in this paper, has received very little attention.[2] On the other hand, there is a long-standing literature on excessive competition in the traditional economics literature that is related to, yet quite different from, the concept of excessive competition adopted in this paper.

TRADITIONAL ECONOMICS LITERATURE ON EXCESSIVE COMPETITION

In the traditional economics literature, excessive competition—usually described in the Western economic literature as either 'cut-throat', 'ruinous,' or 'destructive' competition (Bell, 1918; Reynolds, 1940)—refers to a market characterized by sustained price competition beyond perfectly competitive levels, i.e., where price falls below firms' average unit costs (see Scherer and Ross, 1990: 294–306, for an excellent review of much of this literature). Conventional economic analysis recognizes two theoretical settings when an industry with substantial excess capacity and a 'proportionately large investment in fixed and specialized plant' (Jones, 1920: 473) may drive competitors to engage in cut-throat price competition. One is when the industry faces a declining

---

[2] For an exception, see Bower (1986: Chapter 3) for an interesting discussion of destructive competition in capital-intensive manufacturing industries.

demand curve and high exit barriers; a second is during the recession stage of an industry with sharp cyclical downturns and an oligopoly of evenly matched firms (Scherer and Ross, 1990: 294). Regarding the first situation, Scherer and Ross note that:

. . . competition is likely to drive prices down to levels that yield investors much less than a normal return on their capital. When firms' cost structures include a high proportion of fixed costs, this profitless existence can continue for years or even . . . for decades, since producers find it preferable to continue operation and cover at least their (relatively modest) variable costs than to shut down and have their investments wiped out completely. (1990: 294).

Firms in the second situation, Scherer and Ross remark, may

. . . engage in especially bitter competition during recessions. Each company may strive to increase capacity utilization and cover overhead costs by price shading, and none will cease operations, relaxing the pressure of its supply on price, until all are near the brink of collapse. (1990: 296)

However, the authors add that, should this occur:

One thing is indisputable. When all-out competition does break out during business slumps, driving price below the unit costs of efficient producers, prices must rise above full cost during booms if average profits over the complete business cycle are to attract a continuing supply of investment. (1990: 298)

Scherer and Ross's summary serves as a good departure point for clarifying how the use and analysis of the term *excessive competition* in this paper compares to conventional economic analyses. Three important points in common, to be developed further below, are the notions that an excessively competitive industry is characterized by abnormally high excess capacity, high sunk costs, and sustained subnormal profits. Several points of difference also exist.

First, in this paper the cause of an industry's excessive competition is not viewed as residing solely in the endogenous structure of the market itself, but rather in the interaction between the exogenous actions of states and the endogenous characteristics of high-technology markets. Second, the primary focus on excessive competition in this paper is not on static fixed costs and price competition, as in the traditional economics literature, but instead on technological uncertainty and over-investment in dynamic, future-oriented competition, as will be developed below. Third, while the traditional literature focuses either on declining industries or on cut-throat pricing during the declining demand phase of a cyclical industry, this paper focuses either upon industries that are still growing or upon aggregate, excessively competitive outcomes for the *combined* growth and decline phases of cyclical demand industries. Fourth, an essential feature of traditional concepts of excessively competitive industries is the idea that their low profitability will deter reinvestment. The argument here is nearly opposite. Industrial targeting of high-technology industries frequently causes reinvestment levels, principally in capital equipment and R&D, to rise. Finally, as explained in the introduction, excessive competition is viewed here solely in terms of producer welfare, independent of net social welfare. The traditional literature generally assumed these to be identical.[3]

INDUSTRIAL TARGETING AND OVER-INVESTMENT

A prerequisite to this paper's theory of the political economy of excessive competition is to establish the

---

[3] I should also note here that the rapidly developing literature on the timing of innovation and R&D races also explicitly addresses questions of excessive competition, but does so from the perspective of losses to social welfare, or to producers' jointly optimal outcome, but assuming that producers' private returns remain competitive or positive. (See Baldwin and Scott, 1987, and Reinganum, 1989, for what Cockburn and Henderson describe as 'excellent surveys of a voluminous though disappointingly inconclusive literature' (1994).) My paper shifts the perspective to producer returns and allows for the possibility that they can fall into a dynamic equilibrium of negative returns, independent of net gains or losses in social welfare.

Figure 1. Types of State Targeting Policies*
*It should be noted that these lists are far from exhaustive. Although many of the mechanisms serve dual roles, I have classified them according to their primary usage except for government procurement, which is frequently used either to protect or promote. (For a discussion of when protective mechanisms can also function as industrial promotion, see Krugman, 1984b).

plausibility of the ideas that state targeting of high-technology industries frequently does happen; that states frequently target the same high-technology industries; and that governments' motives for their targeting actions often involve objectives inconsistent with seeking producer rents directly in the targeted sector. I address these issues next.

INDUSTRIAL TARGETING
AND SECTOR-SPECIFIC INDUSTRIAL POLICIES

A wide variety of sector-specific trade and industrial policy mechanisms are used to implement targeting objectives. Figure 1 contains a representative summary of these, classifying them into four categories according to the goal of the targeting policy (industry promotion or protection) and the nature of the intervention in achieving its goal (direct or indirect).

Direct promotion policies include a wide variety of domestic subsidies, export subsidies, industry-specific tax reductions, preferential capital costs and terms for foreign exchange, and specific industry-restructuring policies. *Indirect promotion* policies include government procurement of an industry's output; foreign aid tied to purchasing requirements

from domestic producers; foreign policy sales linkages for specific industries; subsidy spillovers from one sector to a targeted one; and deliberately weak protection for foreign intellectual property rights. *Direct protection* policies include tariffs and exercise taxes, quotas, voluntary export restraints (VERs), local content requirements, rules of origin; antidumping laws, countervailing duties, and industry-specific licensing restrictions. Frequently used *indirect protection* policies include government procurement (from uncompetitive mature firms), competition policy, foreign ownership limits, technical standards and testing restrictions, and health and safety regulations. (For more detailed explanations of each of these types of policy mechanisms, see Jones, 1988; or Ohlin, 1978.)

There should be little doubt that national targeting of 'strategic' high-technology industries does quite frequently occur, although the forms, mechanisms, and motives vary considerably across nations and industries. Laura Tyson's analysis of international competition in high-technology industries is representative of a large literature regarding the pervasiveness of national targeting and sector-specific trade and industrial policies in high-technology:

Subsidies and promotional targeting by governments are the rule rather than the exception in high-technology industries in most countries . . . Moreover, even though overall subsidies have been cut in the advanced industrial countries, the decline has been concentrated in agriculture and in sunset industries such as steel and shipbuilding. There has been no such tendency in the high-technology realm. (1993: 280)

The U.S. government, for example, has considered industrial targeting pervasive and threatening enough that various branches have commissioned numerous studies of it (e.g., U.S. International Trade Commission, 1983, 1984, 1985; General Accounting Office, 1985). Similarly, the OECD has been publishing for a number of years an annual review of industrial policy in OECD countries, which provides ample evidence of widespread high-technology targeting throughout most OECD member countries (OECD, 1993). Thus, there is a large body of evidence which indicates that national industrial targeting of high-technology industries is quite common, and that states frequently target the same high-technology industries.[4] For example, either several or many countries have targeted each of the following industries for national development toward sales in international markets: automobiles (Dyer, Salter, and Webber, 1987; Mutoh, 1988), chemicals (Martinelli, 1991), commercial aircraft (Baldwin and Krugman, 1987; Moxon *et al.*, 1985); color television (Millstein, 1983), computers (Anchordoguy, 1988; Flamm, 1987), high-definition television (Tyson, 1993), machine tools (Collis, 1988), semiconductors (Borrus, 1982; Howell *et al.*, 1988), telecommunications equipment (Tyson, 1993). Recognition of the pervasiveness of high-technology targeting leads to the next stage of the argument: how do tar-

geting practices affect the amount of investment in the targeted industries?

GOVERNMENT MOTIVES FOR INDUSTRIAL TARGETING POLICIES

I contend that high-technology targeting policies in aggregate tend to induce over-investment in the targeted industries, both because governments' motives for targeting industries differ from the logic of private sector investment and because market mechanisms are inefficient at disciplining governments which use economic incentives to induce investment into domestic industries that would not otherwise be profitable. Differences between government targeting motives and private investment motives are not hard to find. As Stiglitz has noted, 'Many of the organizations which play an important role in resource allocation [in modern economies], including governmental organizations, are not profit-maximizers' (1991: 15). There are two principal classes of motives why states target high-technology industries: political and economic. Each of these categories can be further subdivided into two groups of intended beneficiaries: producers and society (see Figure 2).

Political motives for high-technology targeting depart from the assumption of intended economic rationality (Hindley, 1984). As is well known, politicians' incentive structures, at least in democracies, are quite different from private investors, emphasizing votes or currying favor with powerful special interest groups. On one hand, politicians may act to favor certain *producer* groups which seek to extract economic support for their industries in exchange for political support or contributions, even when such government expenditures suboptimize social welfare (Bartlett, 1984; Destler, 1986; Schultze, 1983). Examples include protecting uncompetitive producers, promoting growth industries in the absence of comparative advantage, and counterbalancing foreign targeting policies (Krugman, 1987). On the other hand, political rationales for targeting policies may be intended to benefit *society* beyond narrow producer groups. Examples include: providing national defense, even when the same goods could be ob-

---

[4] For additional empirical studies on targeting and sector-specific government policies in specific countries and regions, see, for example, Adams (1989); de Carmoy (1978); Delorme (1989); Graham (1992); Graham and Seldon (1991); Johnson (1982); Johnson *et al.* (1989); Komiya *et al.* (1988); Patrick (1986); Rushing and Brown (1986); Salvatore (1991); Wade (1990); and Warnecke (1978).

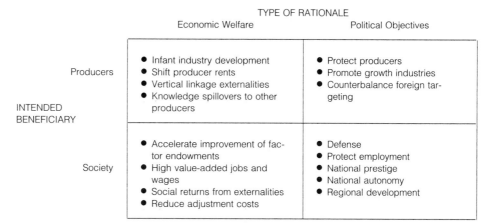

Figure 2. Rationales for Industrial Targeting

tained more economically in international markets (Prestowitz, 1989: 1–58; Seabury, 1984; Srinivasan, 1987); generating or protecting employment (despite intervention costs in excess of net employment benefits); increasing national prestige or autonomy; and enhancing equity considerations, such as income redistribution (Graham, 1992; Krugman, 1987; Shull and Cohen, 1986). All of these political rationales for targeted intervention distort investment patterns, inducing more domestic investment into the targeted sector than the market would provide on its own— otherwise there would be no need for the interventions.

Unlike political rationales, economic motives for high-technology targeting are designed to improve net domestic economic welfare. A number of targeting rationales can be welfare enhancing for *societal* groups other than producers, at least theoretically (lower left quadrant of Figure 2). These motives address certain kinds of externalities and market failures, and may warrant state targeting of an industry regardless of the direct economic attractiveness of the sector. Examples include: to accelerate improvements of factor endowments, thereby promoting improved terms of trade (Anchordoguy, 1988); to sustain or create high value-added jobs (see Tyson, 1993, for pros; and Krugman, 1987, for cons); to obtain social returns from positive externalities (e.g., consumer welfare gains from subsidized investment in 'leaky' technologies with low appro-

priability (Ostry, 1990: 59)); or, less importantly for high-technology sectors, to reduce adjustment costs, typically in declining sectors (Harrison, 1992; Pinder, 1982).

A second group of potentially welfare-enhancing economic rationales are intended to serve *producers'* interests (upper left quadrant of Figure 2). However, only two of these—supporting an infant industry with potential comparative advantage and shifting producer rents—provide rationales for targeting a specific industry consistent with private investor interests in the direct profitability of that industry. The economic logic of the infant industry argument is based on the joint conditions that the nation has a potential comparative advantage in the industry, and that there is some form of failure in capital markets which prevents private investment from investing in the industry at a welfare-maximizing level (this rationale has a long history extending back at least to Freidrich List's work in the 1830s and 1840s). On the other hand, the most common theoretical rationale for targeting an industry in search of producer rents occurs in the trade literature. It refers to government intervention in an imperfectly competitive international industry in order to 'shift rents' from foreign producers to domestic ones in excess of the cost of the intervention itself (Brander and Spencer, 1985; Spencer and Brander, 1983). The other rationales listed, including addressing vertical linkage-externalities in strategic intermediate industries (e.g., semiconductor production equipment—Borrus, 1988; Howell *et al.*, 1988) and knowledge spillovers to other producers (e.g., Borrus, 1988; Tyson, 1993), actually involve targeting investment into one industry in order to generate producer benefits *in other, related but different sectors*. In these latter types, the targeting policy is not driven by the direct economic attractiveness of the targeted industry itself, and may in fact reduce the industry's attractiveness by promoting more competition.

To sum up: it seems clear that government targeting often does follow logics quite different from the logic of private capital investment, providing economic incentives to induce investment into domestic industries that would not otherwise be profitable. As a result, it seems quite possible that targeting actions may frequently result in periods when aggregate investment exceeds perfect competition equilibrium levels in the targeted industries. The next question is, do market clearing mechanisms work well enough to ensure that these periods of over-investment are short lived?

MARKET CLEARING MECHANISMS AND THE LONGEVITY OF TARGETING-INDUCED OVER-INVESTMENT

Because of differences between market mechanisms for private vs. government investment policy, the answer may in fact be no (for a review of economic theories of how markets clear, see Carlton, 1989). The market pricing mechanism usually works well at clearing uneconomical private investment. Normally investments that produce poor returns will be visible enough that rent-seeking investors will reallocate the resources involved fairly expeditiously to more profitable uses. However, the penalties that markets impose on governments for uneconomical targeting policies are likely to be neither clear nor timely, nor effective at motivating the government officials who make the policies. There are three interrelated, primary market mechanisms by which states are penalized for uneconomical targeting policies (or rewarded for social welfare–enhancing ones); inflation rates, nominal interest rates, and exchange rates.

Some or all of these will move in an unfavorable direction when a state's aggregate fiscal situation shows clear indications of deteriorating.

It seems fairly obvious, however, that none of these mechanisms is very responsive to the costs/benefits of a state's individual targeting actions. Frequently there are long time delays before the long-term welfare effects of a targeting policy can be determined (witness the debates over European states' aid for Airbus Industrie, which for years generated negative returns despite market share growth). This is especially true when outcomes are dependent upon the uncertain responses of other firms and other states, or when a state's targeting objectives are based largely on expected spillover benefits outside the targeted industry (see Grossman, 1986; or Krugman, 1987; for representative cautionary comments). Additionally, the effects of a targeting policy, even when known, tend to be dominated by the aggregation of the myriad government policies containing fiscal ramifications. In terms of impact on either inflation, interest rates, or exchange rates, the effects of targeting an industry probably are so small that they are negligible, or at least ineffective as a sanction.[5] Finally, states have 'deep pockets'—many can carry the costs of some uneconomical targeting policies for prolonged periods of time with little appreciable difficulty. As Jones notes:

In general, once a government embarks upon the path of industrial policy, powerful institutional forces are established to sustain it. If the policy fails to achieve its designated goals, such forces will—far from abandoning it—practically guarantee its renewal, implying ever-increasing government involvement, expense, and potential for international dispute. (1988: Chapter 18, 11).

It appears, therefore, that the mechanisms for penalizing states' targeting actions in high-technology

---

[5] Other difficulties include agency problems relating to who makes the government policy decision vs. who gets penalized; the diffusion of costs among all citizens; and the limitations of voting as a corrective mechanism, especially in weak democratic countries.

industries are relatively ineffective, at least over the short to medium term, and that as a result state-induced over-investment frequently will not clear efficiently from these markets. This invites the question, how does sustained over-investment impact the nature of rivalry specifically within international high-technology industries?

THE DYNAMICS OF EXCESSIVE COMPETITION

STRUCTURAL OVER-INVESTMENT AND EXCESSIVE COMPETITION

Within the conventional economic framework of profit-maximizing firms and efficient markets, over-investment in production will persist only if it is subsidized such that the marginal private rate-of-return (i.e., a representative firm's profit margin inclusive of subsidies) is equal to or greater than marginal costs. If, following the introduction of economic assistance from targeting policies (for convenience, referred to as 'subsidies'), all firms in the industry possess essentially the same net cost structure inclusive of subsidies, then total industry output could remain in an equilibrium of overproduction (Houck, 1986: Chapter 10).[6] There are two situations in which this could occur. One is if all producers receive a per unit subsidy at least equal to the marginal decline in price. A second is if only the less efficient producers receive the new subsidies in an imperfectly competitive industry that previously had been generating rents to the more efficient producers. The second situation requires that the marginal drop in price does not exceed either the per unit subsidy received by the less efficient subsidized firms or the per unit surplus profit previously earned by the unsubsidized, more efficient firms. In either of these situations, producers could lower price to enable them to sell the excess output and still earn a competitive private return on investment. Under these conditions—even with over-investment and overproduction—no incentive would exist for a set of producers to initiate greater competition, so there should be no expectation of excessive competition. Approximations of these scenarios seem to occur in at least some global agricultural markets (Hufbauer and Shelton Erb, 1984).

The expected outcome may change, however, when the subsidies induce a substantial expansion of output such that the increase, if sustained, would force a drop in price below some relatively large existing firms' long-run marginal costs (i.e., the least efficient among the non-subsidized large incumbents; for convenience referred to simply as 'incumbents'). As expanding industry output forces price below this point, incumbents face a difficult decision. In the short run, either they must: (a) obtain compensating assistance from their own government(s); (b) reduce their own output and concede market share gains to the expanding, subsidized firms (for convenience, referred to as 'challengers'); or (c) engage in destructive price competition.

If the disadvantaged incumbents are able to obtain compensating assistance from their own government, then they can protect their profit margins and the situation essentially returns to the first scenario described above. The industry is likely to become over-subsidized; overproduction will ensue; and all subsidizing countries will suffer a welfare loss unless net positive externalities are generated (Grossman and Richardson, 1985; Grossman, 1986; Krugman, 1987). If the offsetting government assistance reestablishes parity in net cost structures, again there should be no expectation of excessive competition. These remarks can be summarized to identify explicitly some preconditions for over-investment to cause excessive competition:

Preconditions: Necessary preconditions for national targeting policies to cause an international

---

[6] Even if firms' net cost structures were heterogeneous, an overproduction equilibrium could still be possible as long as no producers' marginal costs exceeded their marginal private returns (i.e., inclusive of subsidies). An example could be when relatively inefficient firms are able nonetheless to make at least normal profits by residing within the umbrella of a price leader in an oligopolistic industry in which the leader is earning rents.

market dynamic to become excessively competitive include:

i. National targeting policies provide sufficient economic benefits to domestic producers in the targeted industry that these 'challengers' expand production for the world market beyond a level that can sustain normal economic returns for at least some relatively large incumbents in that industry;

ii. These disadvantaged incumbents are unable to obtain compensating assistance from their own governments.

When disadvantaged incumbents are unable to obtain offsetting government relief, they must choose between the second two response options identified above. In high-technology industries, which typically are characterized by economies of scale and learning curve effects, subsidized challengers who are expanding will gain a reduction in net costs as a direct result of the subsidy, and a secondary efficiency gain from the increasing returns to scale as they expand output (Brander, 1986; Spencer and Brander, 1983). As a result, the profit-maximizing option for the incumbents typically would appear to be to adopt an 'accommodating' (Dixit, 1988) or 'submissive' (Scherer, 1991) response. Many of the strategic trade literature arguments for government intervention rely on this analysis of incumbents' 'response function' as negative:

When a government pursues a policy of profit capture, it makes a strategic irreversible commitment that alters the domestic firm's behavior in a credible way. The foreign firm then responds by changing its behavior. An export subsidy, for example, lowers the private marginal cost of the domestic firm, which leads it to act more aggressively in output competition. The foreign firm's best response in any particular conflict is usually an accommodating output reduction. In this way, the outcome is altered in the domestic firm's favor. (Dixit, 1988: 154)

Accommodation enables incumbents to avoid a destructive output/price war with challengers, settling instead for an adjusted industry equilibrium with reduced output and market share. The incumbents presume that their collective output reductions will allow price to float back up to levels allowing them to earn normal profits (Brander, 1986: 28). On the other hand, in high-technology industries, accommodation may be the first step down a very slippery slope. For firms like American television manufacturers, short-term cost-saving measures and flight from head-on competition were steps toward elimination as significant contenders in the suddenly more competitive industry following Japanese targeting policies of the 1950s and 1960s (Choate, 1990: Chapter 6; Prestowitz, 1989: 349–358).

Based on widespread accounts of the dangers of such short-term strategic thinking, it seems reasonable to question the long-term implications of the accommodation response in high-technology industries, and to inquire when incumbents might choose aggressive retaliation instead. This possibility is well recognized by both advocates and critics of strategic trade theory. They routinely acknowledge that incumbents' 'response function' is not well understood and may, when positive, induce an 'aggressive' rather than a submissive reaction to foreign targeting policies (Dixit, 1988; Grossman, 1986; Krugman, 1987; Spencer and Brander, 1983). Yet this issue is very under-researched, particularly by management scholars, who can apply theories of organization action that are more subtle and realistic than the comparatively simplistic, black-box profit-maximizing representations typically utilized by trade economists.

In essence, the question being asked here is, *given that governments are inducing over-investment in a sector, why don't disadvantaged firms reduce their commitment or exit?* Clearly this issue warrants substantial further theoretical and empirical research. In this paper, I have space only for a brief sketch of a number of alternative theoretical rationales which are intended to show the plausibility of the idea that firms are sometimes likely to choose to respond aggressively to challengers' gains, since this idea is central to explaining how targeting can initiate excessive competition. Earlier the paper showed that there are many political and economic explanations for why *governments* target industries even though domestic firms are likely to require subsidies in order to earn a normal private rate of profitability. Here we look for equally compelling reasons why *firms* might aggressively defend their positions in an industry even when doing so might worsen their current economic performance and contribute to poor average returns.

Four characteristics of competition in high-technology industries seem especially relevant. First, as technology-intensive industries evolve, capital intensity generally rises and capital investments, once made, tend to be largely irreversible (Abernathy and Utterback, 1978; Dixit and Pindyck, 1994). This means that high-technology firms' assets often are highly immobile. Second, many high-technology industries are characterized by dynamic increasing returns to scale. This points to the importance of forward pricing and output competition, and to the likelihood that changes in market share can produce long-lived effects (Arthur, 1989; Ross, 1986). Third, innovation races are central determinants of competitive advantage (Utterback, 1994). Being an early mover frequently provides market power and opportunities to capture rents (Lieberman and Montgomery, 1988; Wheelwright and Clark, 1992). Finally, competition in high-technology industries is inherently uncertain, particularly on time-based technological dimensions of competition, such as who will win the innovation races; how long until superior or substitute products become available; and how future technological developments will alter current technological interdependencies (Clark, 1988; Pindyck, 1991). The inherent uncertainty of these features means that investment in capital assets and innovation capabilities is always a gamble; that outcomes are always imperfectly predictable; and that luck and surprises are real (Barney, 1986).

These features of high-technology competition help to explain why firms might consider it optimal to respond aggressively to government-assisted foreign challengers—and why firms' aggressive responses might contribute to a vicious cycle of below-average industry performance. First, disadvantaged incumbents cannot costlessly shift assets out of the industry; doing so, in fact, is likely to prove quite expensive. Compounding this problem are the disincentives to surrender market share in industries with

dynamic returns to scale: giving ground today may send a signal that invites further expansion by challengers tomorrow, and also may worsen the firm's relative cost position as the challengers make more rapid progress down the learning curve. Third, although incumbents may find themselves losing competitiveness to subsidized challengers, they will know that winning the next round of innovation competition could change relative cost positions dramatically and reestablish their basis for profitability. This knowledge may induce them to increase their commitments to efficiency improvement and innovation, even if doing so damages their economic performance in the current period. When growth prospects for the industry are healthy, the risks posed by these increased investments are likely to appear more acceptable. On the other hand, when an incumbent is highly diversified and has only a relatively small portion of its assets invested in the targeted industry, an aggressive response may impose opportunity costs greater than the losses that would accompany a passive response. In such cases, the firm would be likely to react passively, conceding market share losses in the targeted sector and shifting some of its resources to other growth sectors in which it expects to generate better economic returns.

Finally, a firm always possesses asymmetric information about what it can achieve relative to its competitors' capabilities. Particularly if the newly disadvantaged incumbent has been a leader in the past, it is likely to believe that it possesses the basic capabilities to regain competitive advantage. Managerial hubris, analogous to Roll's hypothesis about executives' acquisition activities (1986), may play a role in this decision process as firms over-estimate what they can achieve relative to their competitors' capabilities. The disadvantaged firm is also likely to believe that its core business represents its best chance at regaining profitability, assuming industry growth prospects are still good. In technology-intensive industries, human capital becomes highly immobile, along with plant and equipment, because of the specialization of knowledge and because of its social, organizational character. As a result, selecting the optimal response to challengers' gains may take the form of choices between the lesser of evils, rather than choosing the optimal investment level where marginal costs equal expected marginal gains. Incumbents may conclude that accommodation is likely to be costly and to lead to further long-term erosion of their competitiveness, providing no acceptably safe 'fall back' position where profitability can be restored. If so, the choice of an aggressive response may become optimal, and the firm may be willing to accept a higher risk of failure than it would have under less threatening circumstances.

The explanations offered so far retain the assumption that firms intend to maximize profits. Each also stresses the impact of high-technology market imperfections on incumbents' optimal response choice. However, other explanations of aggressive retaliation could be constructed from theories that abandon profit-maximizing assumptions. Examples might include: agency problems arising from executives' incentives to try to retain size and share even at the loss of profitability; escalating commitment processes, such as those reported by Staw (1976); bounded rationality, satisficing, and other related organizational processes described in the behavioral theory of the firm (Cyert and March, 1963; March and Simon, 1958); or personal level decision-making explanations, such as Tversky and Kahneman's work on biases and heuristics used in decision-making under uncertainty (1974).

This brief overview indicates that there are many potential theoretical explanations why incumbents in high-technology industries might react aggressively to foreign challengers' incursions into their markets. While further research on this topic clearly is needed, my main point here is that when aggressive reactions do occur, the industry is well on its way to becoming excessively competitive. This outcome is likely not only because the escalating competition generally is reinforced by some governments' sustained targeting policies, as indicated above; but equally because in high-technology industries firms are likely to continue to compete aggressively as long as the competitiveness gap between themselves and their competitors does not widen too far (Aoki, 1991; Lippman and McCardle, 1987).

In the next section, I explain how excessive competition is likely to be manifested in high-technology industries. First, however, I summarize the preceding

remarks about how targeting can initiate excessive competition in a high-technology industry:

Characteristic 1A—Given the preconditions for excessive competition identified above, disadvantaged incumbents may perceive an aggressive reaction to be their optimal response to subsidized challengers' expansions.

i. Because of some combination of high-technology industry characteristics, including sunk costs, increasing returns dynamics, optimism about winning innovation contests, and uncertainty about future outcomes, incumbents can perceive an aggressive reaction to be optimal even though the average rate of return in the industry is below the normal rate for capital.

Characteristic 1B—When aggregate targeting policies induce over-investment in a high-technology industry and when disadvantaged incumbents react aggressively to challengers' gains, a dynamic process of excessive competition is initiated.

Characteristic 1C—When national targeting policies continue to sustain over-investment in the industry despite incumbents' aggressive reactions, it perpetuates the excessively competitive industry dynamic.

MANIFESTATIONS OF EXCESSIVE COMPETITION

Severe Price Competition   Given the conditions identified above, including aggressive responses by large incumbents, the impact on the market is likely to be severe price competition.[7] In their attempts to retain market share, aggressive incumbents will maintain or even expand their own levels of output. At least in the short run, then, incumbents' aggres-

---

[7] I assume that the incumbents are not able to solve their overproduction problems by developing effective collusive agreements with the challengers who are pursuing market share gains. This assumption seems reasonable for most plausible high-technology circumstances, given states' and challengers' long-term designs on incumbents' market shares, as well as the absence of reliable institutional mechanisms for stabilizing international collusive agreements.

sive reactions establish the conditions for a bitter market share war. This judgment is echoed in Itoh's comment:

. . . the presence of a computer, semiconductor, air-craft, or other high technology industry in a given country may make a big difference in its national income. Therefore, each of the advanced countries will attempt to foster these industries in its own country. And once an industry becomes a target of policy-making, a scramble for market share is likely to ensue. (1990: 96)

One manifestation of such market share wars, stimulated by overproduction, is severe price discounting. Intense market share rivalry will squeeze profit margins; when the rivalry is severe enough to keep price below unit costs, it will drive an industry's average rate-of-return below the normal rate for capital. The impact of price pressure on profitability will be worsened by firms' corresponding need to undertake highly competitive reinvestment programs simultaneously (see Characteristic 5, below). Reinvestment costs in pursuit of future gains depress firms' margins in the current period. If reinvestment costs are driven up by challengers' rising competitiveness, they exacerbate the effects of price competition. Thus:

Characteristic 2—In international high-technology industries, targeting policies may create excessive price competition and, in conjunction with increasingly competitive reinvestment pressures, force the average rate-of-return for the world industry below the normal rate for capital. This is likely when:

i. The preconditions for excessive competition identified above are met and incumbents decide to react aggressively to challengers' gains; and

ii. Incumbents have deep pockets, or can cross-subsidize from successful diversification, such that they can sustain a price war if they choose to do so.

Structural Excess Capacity   As noted above, high-technology manufacturing industries tend to become capital intensive over time. Capital intensity arises from economies of scale, especially in R&D, distribution, and production, typically with substan-

tial asset specificity and irreversible costs (Tyson, 1993). As a result, industry capacity adjustment tends to be 'lumpy' (i.e., new capacity enters in large increments). Examples include automobiles, telecommunications equipment, wide-body commercial aircraft, jet engines, and semiconductor wafer manufacturing, where a new minimum efficient scale plant costs tens or even hundreds of million dollars.

In these types of industries, as in others, the conventional short-term mechanism for obtaining relief from the severe price competition described above is to reduce output in order to allow prices to rise. However, when capacity is lumpy and its cost largely irreversible, output can be reduced incrementally but capacity cannot. Firms that reduce output may therefore continue to maintain underutilized capacity for substantial amounts of time, especially when industry growth projections provide hope that the excess capacity can be profitably reutilized in the future. But when, for the types of reasons reviewed earlier in the paper, states regularly renew and prolong their targeting policies, in effect they continue to reintroduce overinvestment such that the tendency toward excess capacity in the targeted industry may become structural.

As is well recognized, few scenarios are as threatening to a capital-intensive industry's profitability as prolonged reductions in firms' capacity utilization ratios, since the proportionally higher fixed costs drive up unit costs at the same time that firms come under tremendous pressure to reduce prices. This places firms in the dilemma described earlier. If they maintain output to retain share, their profitability is eroded from ensuing pressures on price. If they reduce output to retain profit margins, their market share gets eroded; their capacity utilization rate is likely to fall; their cost structure rises; and their long-term viability in the industry is threatened. When over-investment is severe in high-technology industries with the types of characteristics described above, firms are likely to try to balance the alternatives of destructive price competition and excess capacity, but will probably end up with comparatively poor performance on each. Thus:

Characteristic 3—In international high-technology industries where the preconditions for excessive competition are met, targeting policies are likely to produce a chronically high level of average excess capacity despite continued long-term industry growth. This propensity will be positively associated with:

i. The relative magnitude of over-investment in global production capacity;

ii. The size of firms' irreversible commitments to production;

iii. Expectations of future growth in demand for generations of the product that can be produced with current production assets (e.g. longer product lifecycles or higher percentage of reusable process technology).

Severe Cost Competition Pressures on both price competition and capacity utilization rates are exacerbated by more dynamic dimensions of competition in high-technology industries. In the long term, there are two principal options for incumbents to re-establish a competitive position that has been threatened by state supported challengers: (1) cut operating cost structures; or (2) accelerate product innovation so as to move to a new cost curve, potentially creating first mover advantages along the way.

When targeting leads to increased rivalry in an industry, incumbents face mounting pressures to slash their production cost structures—*faster than they otherwise would have done in the absence of states' targeting policies.* It is the acceleration of the rate of cost-cutting that is at issue here, since virtually any pattern of competition includes some dimension of cost reduction over time. But when incumbents react aggressively to challengers, they are forced to accelerate the projected path of efficiency improvement, and thereby intensify the pattern of rivalry even as they seek to adjust to it.[8]

---

[8] One prominent potential objection to this line of reasoning warrants scrutiny. From the point of view of economic theory, if the incumbents are all assumed to be profit maximizers, they should already have been on a path to minimize costs. What is the origin of their new cost-cutting capability following challengers' incursions into their markets? I am indebted to my colleagues, Paul Feldstein and Tom Buchmueller, for bringing this issue to my attention and helping me to try to address it. I have space here only to list a few possible explanations.

One possible means of cost-cutting that may not have been

Since firms operate with imperfect information, it is probable that incumbents will be able to locate additional sources of cost reductions as challengers' gains force them to expand their search costs and discover potential efficiency gains that previously were either unrecognized or unnecessarily risky. Examples might include relocating production offshore; reorganizing work to achieve administrative efficiencies; cooperating with former competitors, suppliers, or customers in order to gain economies of scale, scope, and speed; outsourcing; or other out-

---

available to incumbents prior to enactment of foreign targeting policies is to use foreign challengers' expansions as a bargaining tool to extract wage concessions from labor or price concessions from suppliers. If the industry had been imperfectly competitive prior to foreign targeting policies, labor and/or suppliers may have been sharing rents with producers, depending on their relative sources of bargaining power (Porter, 1980). But when incumbent producers' profits have been reduced to losses, they can credibly force labor to choose between surrendering these rents or accepting fewer jobs. A similar argument could be constructed to explain producers' ability to force suppliers to accept lower prices (or higher quality standards) for their goods.

This line of analysis can be extended further by focusing on labor's and suppliers' own sunk costs in industry or firm-specific assets, which typically are substantial in high-technology industries. For example, following foreign challengers' expansions, domestic laborers are likely to accept wage reductions even greater than the rent elimination just described if their skills and knowledge are significantly less valuable in other labor markets. Otherwise they would risk bearing the adjustment costs of finding new employment at a lower point on a wage curve in a new industry. If the threat of employment loss is not credible until after the challengers' successful expansion, this could explain why incumbents previously were unable to exploit labor's immobility. The same basic logic again extends to suppliers to the extent that their assets are specific to uses for the incumbent producers. Moreover, while these remarks are focused on prices, essentially the same analysis could be applied to productivity improvements within a cost structure. For example, following challengers' gains in competitiveness and market share, unionized work rules that had previously reduced labor productivity might be subject to renegotiation, or suppliers might be held to higher quality standards for the same price. This later analysis revolving around labor or suppliers sunk costs raises the possibility that excessive competition can produce deleterious social externalities in addition to the sub-normal profit problem faced by producers.

comes produced by accelerated organizational learning. While each of these types of change has been a prominent feature of best managerial practice for at least the past decade, escalating competition should cause their impact on cost structures to be relatively larger in targeted, excessively competitive high-technology industries, because firms will be compelled to implement them more aggressively.

Severe cost competition is also a spur for innovation in process and product technology, and for the increased investments that these innovations may require. I extend the analysis to dynamic innovation and investment races next, but first summarize some conclusions about cost competition when targeting has caused producer rivalry to become excessive:

Characteristic 4—As targeting policies create the preconditions for excessive competition in an international high-technology industry, unaided incumbent firms will experience rising pressure to reduce costs:

i. Cost reduction pressures will increase as the gains in competitiveness achieved by subsidized challengers erode incumbents' profitability and market shares;

ii. The rate of change in labor intensity will fall faster for incumbents than for the average of all other domestic producers in similar industrial sectors (e.g., service vs. manufacturing), controlling for capital intensity in the initial period of comparison;

iii. The ratio between suppliers' profit margins and their productivity gains for goods sold to incumbents will rise more slowly than for other domestic industrial suppliers, although the difference in these rates will be moderated by suppliers' bargaining power relative to the incumbents in the target industry.

Accelerated Innovation and Investment Races

Portfolio pruning, layoffs, wage reductions, supplier price cuts, offshore relocation of operations, and similar tactics help reduce costs and improve competitiveness in the short run. In high-technology industries, however, more dynamic sources of competitive advantage are also needed. Because of the importance in high-technology industries of learning curve effects (Arrow, 1962), first mover advantages (Lieberman and Montgomery, 1988), irreversible

commitments (Pindyck, 1991), and path dependencies (Arthur, 1989), time is a crucial dimension of rivalry and creating competitive advantage (Reinganum, 1989; Stalk, 1988).

The importance of timing issues in high-technology competition is manifested not only in product innovation races (Utterback, 1994), but also in decisions about the optimal timing of investments in new plant and equipment (Dixit and Pindyck, 1994). Innovations in the next generation of a product can shift a firm's relative cost structure and restore its competitiveness, especially if the firm can gain early mover advantages and sustain them by leading the way down the learning curve (Ross, 1986). Similarly, new process technology also can be a potent source of productivity improvement that generates potential positive feedback effects by jump-starting the firm down a superior learning curve (Arthur, 1990). Frequently, however, the efficiency gains can only be achieved at a higher level of minimum efficient scale (Lieberman, 1987; Scherer and Ross, 1990: 119)—adding to market share competition and excess capacity pressures.

Thus, excessive competition forces firms to lower prices, raise quality, and reduce costs in order to maintain market share in a current period of time, even though these efforts are destructive to average current profitability in the industry. Equally or more important, excessive competition simultaneously compels firms that are committed to remaining among the industry's viable long-term competitors to accelerate their rate of investments in product innovation and capital equipment modernization (i.e., increase the relative amount of expenditure per unit of time). This is particularly true for incumbents who decide to respond aggressively to state-supported challengers, since the incumbents' prior path of expected dynamic efficiency improvement will no longer be optimal following challengers' gains (Scherer, 1991). Incumbents will weigh the probability of succeeding in recreating competitive advantage through aggressive reactions in highly uncertain innovation and capital improvement races, against the near certainty of long-term competitive decay through any alternative, submissive course of response. They will also compare the probable benefits of success with the costs of achieving it. As long as the expected value of an aggressive response outweighs the probable benefits of trying to use the same resources to develop an alternative line of business (including the probable long-term losses of the adjustment costs produced by a submissive response), it is likely that the incumbents will choose the aggressive path and increase their rates of investment in product and process technology innovation and improvement.

In fact, it is this tendency for positive change in incumbents' apparently optimal investment behavior that is the essential feature at the heart of excessive competition in high-technology industries. The decision to accelerate investment in pursuit of future competitiveness, despite subnormal profitability in the current period, is the private, complementary market mechanism that reinforces the political mechanism of state targeting-induced over-investment. Because of it, aggressive incumbents in an excessively competitive industry respond to challengers' gains with a further acceleration of rivalry and investment. Meanwhile, state targeting policies may be designed with the intent of producing essentially this same effect among domestic challengers in order to facilitate their evolution toward world class competitiveness (Johnson, 1982; O'Brien, 1989; Pinder, 1982). When the incumbents and their state-supported challengers each respond aggressively to each others' moves and gains, the dynamics of accelerated innovation and investment races ensue and all firms in the industry are likely to find themselves locked into intensifying investment and R&D races.

Consequently, state targeting of high-technology industry, followed by incumbents' aggressive responses based upon expectations of future payoffs, induces over-investment in product innovation and modernization of capital structures in the current period and, along with vigorous price and market share competition, destroys the current, average profitability of the industry. Industry leadership may be 'churned' as various firms temporarily succeed in leapfrogging their competitors. But as long as nations continue to target the industry aggressively and induce domestic over-investment, the profitable future can be indefinitely postponed for most firms in the industry.

On the other hand, while this analysis supports the proposition that an excessive rate of competition in a high-technology industry can be sustained in dynamic equilibrium for an indefinite period of time (Aoki, 1991), it does not imply that once excessive competition has commenced it necessarily must continue indefinitely. It is always possible that some firms' accelerated investments in innovation and capital improvements will succeed in transforming the nature of the competitive contest to their sustained advantage (Jelinek and Schoonhoven, 1993: Chapter 1). This will occur when the early mover or efficiency gains that some firms achieve become so large that at least some major competitors concede that the probability of closing the competitiveness gap appears too remote to justify the risks of continued aggression. This concession may be made either by firms, or by the states that are supporting some of the firms.

For example, during the past decade an intense rivalry has occurred among both firms and states for leadership in the emerging global high-definition television industry. In the past couple of years, however, European states have had to acknowledge that their targeting policies, which were intended to create a European technology standard favoring European producers, had been so unsuccessful that the policies had to be abandoned. So it certainly is possible for a state to abandon a targeting policy that has become exorbitantly expensive and obviously futile. An analogous calculation can also occur at the level of the firm. For example, many American firms were forced to abandon the semiconductor memory industry in the early and mid-1980s because they could not keep pace with the accelerated improvements of government-assisted Japanese rivals (Borrus, 1988).

Thus, the keys to sustaining a dynamic equilibrium of excessive competition are that: (a) nations continue to induce over-investment in the industry; (b) international institutional mechanisms are incapable of stabilizing any collusive reductions of rivalry; (c) incumbent firms respond aggressively to challengers' gains; and (d) no single firm or group of firms gets so far ahead in the investment race that they succeed in driving out competitors who collectively account for a substantial percentage of market share in the industry. The following interrelated sets of characteristics of excessively competitive innovation and investment dynamics sum up this section:

Characteristic 5—As sequential state targeting actions induce over-investment in an international high-technology industry where preconditions for excessive competition are met:

  i. Unaided incumbent firms will increase their rate of investment in new product and process innovation;
  ii. Unaided incumbent firms will increase their rate of investment in plant and equipment relative to sales revenues;
  iii. The average useful lifespan of plant and equipment will decline;
  iv. The length of time during which followers can profitably introduce imitations of an innovator's new product in that industry will diminish.

In concluding this section, three points bear emphasis. First, targeting induced over-investment in technology-intensive industries sets off a complicated chain of events. When preconditions for the development of excessive competition are met and incumbents react aggressively, the ensuing dynamic may include not only increased price, market share, and cost competition but, more importantly, accelerated innovation and investment competition in new products, plant, and equipment beyond rates that can sustain average industry profits at normal levels in any given current period. Second, because government rationales for targeting an industry are different from, and frequently inconsistent with, the private sector profit motive, ongoing government targeting policies can function as a mechanism that continually reinforces over-investment and excessive competition in a targeted industry. Third, while the resulting dynamic may be excessively competitive in terms of producer welfare, it does not necessarily result in a social welfare loss. Aggregate producer losses plus the total costs of direct and indirect sub-

sidies may be more than offset by the combination of large gains in consumer welfare via outward shifts in the product demand curve, and positive spillover gains that cannot be fully appropriated by firms producing them.

CONCLUSION

This paper argues that state targeting policies can and do reach a collective level where they promote over-investment in global industries viewed as strategic by many nations. When these industries are scale sensitive and technologically intensive, the impact on rivalry may be to produce a dynamic that is excessively competitive. This occurs for three primary reasons. First, state industrial targeting frequently is driven by motives other than the direct profitability of a targeted sector, such that levels of investment exceed perfectly competitive amounts. Second, market clearing mechanisms at the global level are inefficient, allowing structural over-investment to persist for considerable time lags because states' unprofitable investment policies are not penalized by clear and proximate financial sanctions, and because other policy objectives may outweigh even those costs which are imposed. Third, incumbent firms may not be willing to cede market share and reduce capacity and output corresponding to the expansions induced by states' targeting actions, preferring instead to cut costs and/or accelerate innovation so as to regain competitiveness and retain market share. When this occurs, the industry shifts into a self-reinforcing mode of competition that can quickly erode even a normal rate of return—i.e., a mode that is excessively competitive. When governments continue their targeting policies despite incumbents' aggressive reactions, excessive competition can be sustained for an indeterminate period of time.

My analysis of excessive competition accepts standard contemporary economic descriptions of international high-technology industry characteristics: structural mobility barriers such as irreversible commitments and product differentiation; static and dynamic economies of scale, scope, and learning that create increasing returns to scale; and path dependencies and R&D races with potential first mover benefits. Along with many others, I also emphasize the inherent role of states as strategic actors within these industries. But I depart from most contemporary work by emphasizing as well the diversity of motives for states' investment-inducing trade and industrial policies; the relative inefficiency of existing market mechanisms for clearing over-investment; and the roles of time dependency and uncertainty in encouraging incumbent firms to respond aggressively to state-sponsored challengers. Thus, my interpretation of contemporary global high-technology competition is primarily not a market story about imperfect competition and rents, as is assumed in most contemporary economic models, but rather a political economy story about the causes of excessive competition and its consequences.

A central purpose of this paper is to draw attention to the importance of pursuing this research, and to the opportunity for strategic management scholars to make significant contributions both to improved understanding of international high-technology competition and to the debates on trade policy issues that rely on this knowledge in order to draw appropriate conclusions. Studying when and why firms respond to targeting with aggressive, vs. accommodating, reactions seems to raise especially promising issues that seem central to understanding how competition in an industry is affected by targeting induced over-investment.

Nonetheless these issues remain sorely underresearched. This is no doubt true at least in part because trade theorists generally have not been very interested in or very well equipped for addressing firm-level dynamics of competitive behavior. As Scherer notes: 'Even in their "new" versions, the theories of international trade and comparative advantage paint with broad brush strokes. They are more "macro" than "micro" (1992: 174): Strategic management scholars, on the other hand, have traditionally stayed away from research topics that require expertise (and interest) in trade theory. However, with a much richer set of theoretical repertoires to draw upon from their knowledge of strategic man-

agement and organization theories, strategy scholars should also be able to generate more penetrating insights into competitive dynamics following various kinds of government intervention in high-technology industries.

By pursuing these kinds of research, strategy researchers should be able to generate not only new theory, but also new insights to help influence policy debates, as has been called for by leading strategy researchers such as Bettis (1991) and Hambrick (1993). The new competitive landscape, defined in part by the expanded impact of the state in international high-technology markets (Boddewyn and Brewer, 1994; Dicken, 1994; Lenway and Murtha, 1994; Tyson, 1993), invites us to cross this divide, and to focus upon how actions at the level of both the state and the firm jointly shape the dynamics of technology-intensive international industries. In the absence of much more research on the political economy of competition in high-technology industries, our understanding of technological transformation and the new competitive landscape would seem destined to remain fundamentally incomplete. These issues should provide a wealth of new and illuminating questions for applied research and policy analysis.

REFERENCES

Abernathy, W.J. and J.M. Utterback (1978). 'Patterns of industrial innovation,' *Technology Review,* **80**, pp. 40–47.

Adams, W.J. (1989). *Restructuring the French Economy: Government and the Rise of Market Competition since World War II.* The Brookings Institution, Washington, DC.

Anchordoguy, M. (1988). 'Mastering the market: Japanese government targeting of the computer industry,' *International Organization,* **42**, pp. 509–543.

Aoki, R. (1991). 'R&D competition for product innovation: An endless race,' *American Economic Review,* **81**, pp. 252–256.

Arrow, K.J. (1962). 'The economic implications of learning by doing,' *Review of Economic Studies,* **29**, pp. 155–173.

Arthur, W.B. (1989). 'Competing technologies, increasing returns, and lock-in by historical events,' *Economic Journal,* **99**, pp. 116–131.

Arthur, W.B. (February 1990). 'Positive feedbacks in the economy,' *Scientific American,* pp. 92–99.

Baldwin, R. and P.R. Krugman (1987). 'Industrial policy and international competition in wide-bodied jet aircraft.' In R.E. Baldwin (ed.), *Trade Policy Issues and Empirical Analysis.* University of Chicago Press, Chicago, IL, pp. 45–71.

Baldwin, R. and J.T. Scott (1987). *Market Structure and Technological Change.* Harwood Academic Publishers, Chur, Switzerland.

Barney, J.B. (1986). 'Strategic factor markets: Expectations, luck, and business strategy,' *Management Science,* **32,** pp. 1231–1241.

Bartlett, B. (1984). 'Trade policy and the dangers of protectionism.' In C. Johnson (ed.), *The Industrial Policy Debate.* Institute for Contemporary Studies, San Francisco, CA, pp. 159–172.

Bell, S. (1918). 'Fixed costs and market price,' *Quarterly Journal of Economics,* **32,** pp. 507–524.

Bettis, R.A. (1991). 'Strategic management and the straightjacket: An editorial essay,' *Organization Science,* **2,** pp. 315–319.

Boddewyn, J.J. and T.L. Brewer (1994). 'International-business political behavior: New theoretical directions,' *Academy of Management Review,* **19**(1), pp. 119–143.

Borrus, M.G. (1982). *International Competition in Advanced Industrial Sectors: Trade and Development in the Semiconductor Industry: A Study Prepared for the Use of the Joint Economic Committee, Congress of the United States.* U.S. Government Printing Office, Washington, DC.

Borrus, M.G. (1988). *Competing for Control: America's Stake in Microelectronics.* Ballinger, Cambridge, MA.

Bower, J.L. (1986). *When Markets Quake: The Management Challenge of Restructuring Industry.* Harvard Business School Press, Boston, MA.

Brander, J.A. (1986). 'Rationales for strategic trade and industrial policy.' In P.R. Krugman (ed.), *Strategic Trade Policy and the New International Economics.* MIT Press, Cambridge, MA, pp. 23–46.

Brander, J.A. and B.J. Spencer (1985). 'Export subsidies and international market share rivalry,' *Journal of International Economics,* **16,** pp. 83–100.

Carlton, D.W. (1989). 'The theory and the facts of how markets clear: Is industrial organization valuable for understanding macroeconomics?' In R. Schmalensee and R. Willig (eds.), *Handbook of Industrial Organization,* Vol. 1. Elsevier, New York, pp. 909–946.

Caves, R.E. (1989). 'International differences in industrial organization.' In R. Schmalensee and R. Willig (eds.), *Handbook of Industrial Organization,* Vol. 2. Elsevier, New York, pp. 1225–1250.

Choate, P. (1990). *Agents of Influence.* Alfred A. Knopf, New York.

Clark, K.B. (1988). 'Managing technology in international competition: The case of product development in response to foreign entry.' In A.M. Spence and H.A. Hazard (eds.), *International Competitiveness.* Ballinger, Cambridge, MA, pp. 27–74.

Cockburn, I. and R. Henderson (1994). 'Racing to invest? The dynamics of competition in ethical drug discovery,' *Journal of Economics and Management Strategy,* **3**(3), pp. 481–519.

Collis, D.J. (1988). 'The machine tool industry and industrial policy, 1955–82.' In A.M. Spence and H.A. Hazard (eds.), *International Competitiveness.* Ballinger, Cambridge, MA, pp. 75–114.

Cyert, R.M. and J.G. March (1963). *A Behavioral Theory of the Firm.* Prentice-Hall, Englewood Cliffs, NJ.

D'Aveni, R.A. (1994). *Hypercompetition.* Free Press, New York.

de Carmoy, G. (1978). 'Subsidy policies in Britain, France and West Germany: An Overview.' In S.J. Warnecke (ed.), *International Trade and Industrial Policies.* Holmes & Meier, New York, pp. 35–57.

Delorme, R. (1989). 'Economic intervention in the history of the French and other European states: A comparative study.' In M.S. Alam (ed.), *Governments and Markets in Economic Development Strategies.* Praeger, New York, pp. 23–49.

Destler, I.M. (1986). *American Trade Politics: System under Stress.* Institute for International Economics, Washington, DC.

Dicken, P. (1992). *Global Shift: The Internationalization of Economic Activity* (2nd ed.). Guilford Press, New York.

Dicken, P. (1994). 'Global–local tensions: Firms and states in the global space-economy.' In P. Shrivastava, A.S. Huff and J.E. Dutton (eds.), *Advances in Strategic Management,* Vol. 10B. JAI Press, Greenwich, CT, pp. 217–247.

Dixit, A. (1988). 'International R&D competition and policy.' In A.M. Spence and H.A. Hazard (eds.), *International Competitiveness.* Ballinger, Cambridge, MA, pp. 149–171.

Dixit, A. and G. Grossman (1984). 'Targeted export promotion with several oligopolistic industries.' National Bureau of Economic Research Working Paper No. 1344. National Bureau of Economic Research, Cambridge, MA.

Dixit, A.K. and R.S. Pindyck (1994). *Investment Under Uncertainty.* Princeton University Press, Princeton, NJ.

Dyer, D., M.S. Salter and A.M. Webber (1987). *Changing Alliances.* Harvard Business School Press, Boston, MA.

Flamm, K. (1987). *Targeting the Computer: Government Support and International Competition.* Brookings Institution, Washington, DC.

General Accounting Office (1985). *Foreign Industrial Targeting: U.S. Trade Law Remedies.* GAO/NSIAD-85-77. General Accounting Office, Washington, DC.

Graham, A. and A. Seldon (1991). *Government and Economies in the Postwar World.* Routledge, New York.

Graham, O.L., Jr. (1992). *Losing Time: The Industrial Policy Debate.* Harvard University Press, Cambridge, MA.

Grossman, G.M. (1986). 'Strategic export promotion: A critique.' In P.R. Krugman (ed.), *Strategic Trade Policy and the New International Economics.* MIT Press, Cambridge, MA, pp. 47–68.

Grossman, G.M. and J.D. Richardson (April 1985). 'Strategic trade policy: A survey of issues and early analysis.' *Special Papers in International Economics,* **15.** International Finance Section, Department of Economics, Princeton University.

Hambrick, D. (August 1993). 'Presidential address.' Fifty Third Annual Meeting of the Academy of Management, Atlanta, GA.

Harrison, B. (1992). 'Where private investment fails,' *American Prospect,* **11,** pp. 106–114.

Heiduk, G. and K. Yamamura (eds.) (1990). *Technological Com-*

petition and Interdependence. University of Washington Press, Seattle, WA.

Helpman, E. and P.R. Krugman (1985). *Market Structure and Foreign Trade: Increasing Returns, Imperfect Competition, and the International Economy.* MIT Press, Cambridge, MA.

Hindley, B. (1984). 'Subsidies, politics and economics.' In D. Wallace, Jr., F.J. Loftus and V.Z. Krikorian, (eds.), *Interface Three: Legal Treatment of Domestic Subsidies,* International Law Institute, Washington, DC, pp. 29–34.

Houck, J.P. (1986). *Elements of Agricultural Trade Policies.* Macmillan, New York.

Howell, T.R., W.A. Noellert, J.H. MacLaughlin and A.W. Wolff (1988). *The Microelectronics Race: The Impact of Government Policy on International Competition.* Westview Press, Boulder, CO.

Hufbauer, G.C. and J. Shelton Erb (1984). *Subsidies in International Trade.* Institute for International Economics, Washington, DC.

Itoh, M. (1990). 'The impact of industrial structure and industrial policy on international trade.' In G. Heiduk and K. Yamamura (eds.), *Technological Competition and Interdependence.* University of Washington Press, Seattle, WA, pp. 87–106.

Jelinek, M. and C. Bird Schoonhoven (1993). *The Innovation Marathon.* Jossey-Bass, San Francisco, CA.

Johnson, C. (1982). *MITI and the Japanese Miracle.* Stanford University Press, Stanford, CA.

Johnson, C., L. Tyson and J. Zysman (1989). *Politics and Productivity: How Japan's Development Strategy Works.* Harper Business, New York.

Jones, E. (1920). 'Is competition in industry ruinous?' *Quarterly Journal of Economics,* **34,** pp. 473–519.

Jones, K. (1988). 'Subsidies, industrial policy, and international trade.' In I. Walter and T. Murray (eds.), *Handbook of International Business* (2nd ed.). Wiley, New York, Ch. 18.

Kahalas, H. and K. Suchon (1992). 'Stepping up to global competition: An interview with Ford CEO Harold A. Poling,' *Academy of Management Executive,* **6**(2), pp. 71–82.

Komiya, R., M. Okuno and K. Suzumura (eds.) (1988). *Industrial Policy of Japan.* Academic Press, San Diego, CA.

Krugman, P.R (1984a). 'The U.S. response to foreign industrial targeting.' *Brookings Papers on Economic Activity, 1.* Brookings Institution, Washington, DC, pp. 77–131.

Krugman, P.R. (1984b). 'Import protection as export promotion: International competition in the presence of oligopolies and economies of scale.' In H. Kierzkowski (ed.), *Monopolistic Competition and International Trade.* Oxford University Press, Oxford, pp. 180–193.

Krugman, P.R. (1987). 'Targeted industrial policies: Theory and evidence.' In D. Salvatore (ed.), *The New Protectionist Threat to World Welfare.* North-Holland, New York, pp. 266–296.

Krugman, P.R. (1989). 'Industrial organization and international trade.' In R. Schmalensee and R. Willig (eds.), *Handbook of Industrial Organization,* Vol. 2. Elsevier, New York, pp. 1179–1223.

Krugman, P.R. (1990). *Rethinking International Trade.* MIT Press, Cambridge, MA.

Lee, T.H. and P.R. Reid (eds.) (1991). *National Interests in an Age of Global Technology.* National Academy Press, Washington, DC.

Lenway, S.A. and T. Murtha (1994). 'The state as strategist in international business research.' *Journal of International Business Strategy.* 25(3), pp. 513–535.

Lieberman, M.B. (1987). 'Market growth, economies of scale, and plant size in the chemical processing industries,' *Journal of Industrial Economics,* **36,** pp. 175–191.

Lieberman, M.B. and D.B. Montgomery (1988). 'First mover advantages,' *Strategic Management Journal,* Summer Special Issue, **9,** pp. 41–58.

Lippman, S.A. and K.F. McCardle (1987). 'Dropout behavior in R&D races with learning,' *RAND Journal of Economics,* **18**(2), pp. 287–295.

March, J.G. and H.A. Simon (1958). *Organizations.* Wiley, New York.

Martinelli, A. (ed.) (1991). *International Markets and Global Firms: A Comparative Study of Organized Business in the Chemical Industry.* SAGE, London.

Millstein, J.E. (1983). 'Decline in an expanding industry: Japanese competition in color television.' In J. Zysman and L. Tyson (eds.), *American Industry in International Competition.* Cornell University Press, Ithaca, NY, pp. 106–141.

Moxon, R.W., T.W. Roehl, J.R. Truitt and J.M. Geringer (1985). *Emerging Sources of Foreign Competition in the Commercial Aircraft Manufacturing Industry.* U.S. Department of Transportation, Washington, DC.

Mutoh, H. (1988). 'The automobile industry.' In R. Komiya, M. Okuno and K. Suzumura (eds.), *Industrial Policy of Japan.* Academic Press, San Diego, CA, pp. 307–365.

O'Brien, P.A. (1989). 'The development of the Japanese steel industry,' Harvard Business School Case, 9-387-118. Harvard Business School, Boston, MA.

O'Brien, R. (1992). *Global Financial Integration: The End of Geography.* Council on Foreign Relations Press, New York.

OECD (1993). *Industrial Policy in OECD Countries: Annual Review:* OECD, Paris.

Ohlin, G. (1978). 'Subsidies and other industrial aids.' In S.J. Warnecke (ed.), *International Trade and Industrial Policies.* Holmes & Meier, New York, pp. 21–34.

Ostry, S. (1990). *Governments and Corporations in a Shrinking World.* Council on Foreign Relations Press, New York.

Patrick, H. (ed.) (1986). *Japan's High Technology Industries: Lessons and Limitations of Industrial Policy.* University of Washington Press, Seattle, WA.

Pinder, J. (1982). 'Causes and kinds of industrial policy.' In J. Pinder (ed.), *National Industrial Strategies and the World Economy.* Allanheld, Osmun & Co., London, pp. 41–52.

Pindyck, R.S. (1991). 'Irreversibility, uncertainty, and investment,' *Journal of Economic Literature,* **29,** pp. 1110–1148.

Porter, M.E. (1980). *Competitive Strategy.* Free Press, New York.

Porter, M.E. (1990). *The Competitive Advantage of Nations.* Free Press, New York.

Prestowitz, C.V. (1989). *Trading Places.* Basic Books, New York.

Reinganum, J.F. (1989). 'The timing of innovation: Research, development and diffusion.' In R. Schmalensee and R. Willig (eds.), *Handbook of Industrial Organization,* Vol. 1. North-Holland, Amsterdam, pp. 849–908.

Reynolds, L.G. (1940). 'Cutthroat competition,' *American Economic Review,* **30,** pp. 736–747.

Richardson, J.D. (1989). 'Empirical research on trade liberalization with imperfect competition,' *OECD Economic Studies,* No. 12.

Roll. R. (1986). 'The hubris hypothesis of corporate takeovers,' *Journal of Business,* **59**(2), Part I, pp. 197–216.

Ross, D.R. (1986). 'Learning to dominate,' *Journal of Industrial Economics,* **34,** pp. 337–353.

Rushing, F.W. and C.G. Brown (1986). *National Policies for Developing High Technology Industries.* Westview Press, Boulder, CO.

Salvatore, D. (ed.) (1991). *National Economic Policies.* Greenwood Press, Westport, CT.

Scherer, F.M. (1991). 'International R&D races: Theory and evidence.' In L.G. Mattson and B. Stymme (eds.), *Corporate and Industry Strategies for Europe.* Elsevier, Amsterdam, pp. 117–137.

Scherer, F.M. (1992). *International High-Technology Competition.* Harvard University Press, Cambridge, MA.

Scherer, F.M. and D. Ross (1990). *Industrial Market Structure and Economic Performance* (3rd ed.), Houghton Mifflin, Boston, MA.

Schultze, C.L. (Fall 1983). 'Industrial policy: A dissent,' *Brookings Review,* pp. 3–12.

Schumpeter, J.A. (1942). *Capitalism, Socialism and Democracy.* Harper & Brothers, New York.

Seabury, P. (1984). 'Industrial policy and national defense.' In C. Johnson (ed.), *The Industrial Policy Debate.* Institute for Contemporary Studies, San Francisco, CA, pp. 195–216.

Shull, S.A. and J.E. Cohen (eds.) (1986). *Economics and Politics of Industrial Policy.* Westview Press, Boulder, CO.

Spencer, B.J. and J.A. Brander (1983). 'International R&D rivalry and industrial strategy,' *Review of Economic Studies,* **50,** pp. 707–722.

Srinivasan, T.N. (1987). 'The national defense argument for government intervention in foreign trade.' In R.M. Stern (ed.), *U.S. Trade Policies in a Changing World Economy.* MIT Press, Cambridge, MA, pp. 337–363.

Stalk, G. (1988). 'Time—the next source of competitive advantage,' *Harvard Business Review,* **66**(4), pp. 41–51.

Staw, B. (1976). 'Knee-deep in the big muddy: A study of escalating commitment to a chosen course of action,' *Organizational Behavior and Human Performance,* **16**(1), pp. 27–44.

Stiglitz, J.E. (1991). 'Symposium on organizations and economics,' *Journal of Economic Perspectives,* **5**(2), pp. 15–24.

Tversky, A. and D. Kahneman (1974). 'Judgment under uncertainty: Heuristics and biases,' *Science,* **185,** pp. 1124–1131.

Tyson, L.D. (1993). *Who's Bashing Whom?* Institute for International Economics, Washington, DC.

U.S. International Trade Commission (1983). *Foreign Industrial Targeting and Its Effect on U.S. Industries, Phase I: Japan.* USITC Publication 1437. U.S. International Trade Commission, Washington, DC.

U.S. International Trade Commission (1984). *Foreign Industrial Targeting and Its Effect on U.S. Industries, Phase II: The European Community and Member States.* USITC Publication 1517. U.S. International Trade Commission, Washington, DC.

U.S. International Trade Commission (1985). *Foreign Industrial Targeting and Its Effect on U.S. Industries, Phase III: Brazil, Canada, the Republic of Korea, Mexico, Taiwan.* USITC Publication 1632. U.S. International Trade Commission, Washington, DC.

Utterback, J.M. (1994). *Mastering the Dynamics of Innovation.* Harvard Business School Press, Boston, MA.

Wade, R. (1990). *Governing the Market.* Princeton University Press, Princeton, NJ.

Warnecke, S.J. (ed.) (1978). *International Trade and Industrial Policies.* Holmes & Meier, New York.

Wheelwright, S.C. and K.B. Clark (1992). *Revolutionizing Product Development.* Free Press, New York.

SECTION 4

STRATEGIC ALLIANCES

It seems that virtually every internationally involved firm is either forming, participating in, or disentangling from one or more strategic alliances. Correctly managed strategic alliances, with the right partners in well-chosen situations, can lead to competitive advantage. They can also lead to disaster because they are much more difficult to maintain than to enter. There are in fact few, if any, decisions firms make that are as promising yet as fraught with risk as the decision to strategically ally. In this section we explore two critical aspects of strategic alliances: when to engage in them and how to sustain them.

READING SELECTIONS

David Lei describes the motivation for forming alliances as a mutual need to learn and acquire technologies, products, skills, and knowledge not available to competitors. It is important to note his use of the word *mutual;* an alliance endures only as long as *both* partners reap some unique rewards from it. He points out that alliances can work to protect an existing advantage as well as to create a new one.

Lei goes on to present several examples of alliances predicated on different needs, exploring the costs and benefits associated with each. He points out the risks inherent in the sharing of technology, products, skills, and knowledge as well as the benefits that can accrue from so doing. There is often a thin line between maintaining a partnership and sharing too much, a situation that raises the danger of creating a competitor.

Stephen Tallman and Oded Shenkar frame their discussion around cooperative ventures. They present and discuss a decision tree that helps managers determine when a cooperative venture might be appropriate and how to choose the right form of such a venture. They offer propositions, however, that they believe will describe how firms actually behave and the conditions under which they will actually form different types of ventures.

In studying the propositions, it is worthwhile to ask both whether firms are likely to behave as the propositions suggest, and, even more importantly, whether they *should* act as the propositions suggest. Are the actions Tallman and Shenkar posit the optimum strategies under the conditions they describe? A satisfactory cooperative venture requires two satisfied partners. Each participant, therefore, must believe the same tree path to be the best one.

Ranjay Gulati, Tarun Khanna, and Nitin Nohria examine the roles of commitment and process in sustaining an alliance. They emphasize that both partners must perceive they are benefiting from the venture for it to be successful. They also emphasize and explain why unilateral actions are important to the success of a venture. Managerial process is also significant and must adapt to the inevitable changes in conditions that occur during the course of an alliance.

Arvind Parkhe highlights the importance of choosing the right partner. He notes that partnerships are often created to take advantage of interdependencies between the partners. It is likely, however, that interdependent partners may have dissimilar characteristics. Unresolved or poorly managed differences in partner characteristics, in turn, may have a negative effect on the longevity and effectiveness of that partnership.

With this formulation in mind Parkhe goes on to develop a typology of interfirm diversity as it applies to strategic alliances and to examine the effects of these diversity dimensions on the performance of an alliance. Using a model of organizational learning, he explores how firms can manage their alliances to reduce the effects of diversity. Parkhe's formulation poses an interesting question common to many aspects of organizational behavior and organization culture. How much of the success of an alliance is due to choosing the right partner and how much to postalliance learning?

16

A MANAGERIAL DECISION MODEL OF INTERNATIONAL COOPERATIVE VENTURE FORMATION

STEPHEN B. TALLMAN*
University of Utah

ODED SHENKAR**
Tel-Aviv University and University of Hawaii at Manoa

ABSTRACT   This paper develops a model of international cooperative venture formation that is centered on the decisionmaking process of MNE executives. Central issues for managerial decisions are developed from the organizational studies literature. A framework delineating the sequence and criteria

* Stephen B. Tallman (Ph.D., UCLA) is an Associate Professor of Management at the David Eccles School of Business of the University of Utah, Salt Lake City, Utah 84112. His primary research interests are business strategy, global strategic management, and international business alliances.
** Oded Shenkar (Ph.D., Columbia University) is with the Faculty of Management at Tel-Aviv University, Tel-Aviv 69978, Israel; and the College of Business Administration, University of Hawaii at Manoa, Honolulu, Hawaii 96822. His research interests are in international and comparative management.

used in the decision to form international cooperative ventures is developed from these defined issues and from existing models. Propositions pertaining to the venture formation decision process are outlined.

People (i.e., individuals) have goals; collectivities of people do not.

(Cyert and March 1963)

INTRODUCTION

International cooperative ventures are a rapidly proliferating variety of foreign direct investment [Beamish 1988; Contractor and Lorange 1988].[1] As with most foreign direct investment models, cooperative venture formation is typically explained in terms of the market imperfections concepts of industrial organization economics models [Stopford and Wells 1972; Harrigan 1984; Beamish 1985] or the transaction cost economics approach of internalization models [Beamish and Banks 1987; Hennart 1988; Buckley and Casson 1988]. These economics-based models have had success in providing rationales for the existence of joint operations. However, such models do not provide a sufficient explanation of the original decision by multinational enterprise (MNE) managers to establish an international cooperative venture (ICV), nor do they adequately address the contractual joint ventures that comprise a majority of ICVs [Contractor and Lorange 1988]. While the number of studies of equity joint ventures is growing rapidly, only a small number of studies address contractual ventures; most authors take an economic perspective that focuses on ownership issues and treat all non-equity ventures as simple market transactions.

Economic models also do not explain the myriad of interpersonal and organizational factors affecting the formation and stability of ICVs [Sherman 1992].

The authors would like to thank Dr. Nakiye Boyacigiller for her encouragement on this project and the editor of *JIBS* and three anonymous reviewers for their insightful comments which undoubtedly improved this article. Naturally, the ideas and opinions expressed remain our responsibility.

To follow on a popular analogy of viewing ICVs as marriages, the decision to form an ICV, as well as the selection of cooperative strategies, organizational forms and partners, is not strictly economic, but also a social, psychological and emotional phenomenon. Thus, what is nominally a legally contracted economic partnership is in fact a relationship involving many considerations, only a few of which are economic in nature. It is no coincidence that ICVs are frequently described using such terms as "trust," "shared visions," and "understanding." Notice, for instance, how Dow executives recount their venture with personal care:

We eventually had a contract with many details on paper, but our alliance was really formed by the shared vision and understandings we developed before then . . . Our informal understanding was a central feature of the alliance. Building the management commitment and people commitment is what it's all about. Dow would not have proceeded without this.

(*quoted in* Lewis 1990, p. 104)

Jemison and Sitkin [1986] suggest that full comprehension of acquisitions requires knowledge of strategic and organizational fits and a process perspective on acquisition strategies. In a similar manner, this article develops a model of ICV formation that focuses on the managerial processes leading to the ICV formation decision. It provides a framework of reference within which a variety of theories—economic, organizational, sociological and psychological—are applied to ICV formation. As such, the article takes a phenomenological perspective, appealing to theory to aid in understanding an event that is often observed but inadequately explained. It goes beyond the economic imperatives of most current models to address strategic and organizational factors in cooperative venture formation. The purpose of the article is to suggest that the observer of ICV initiations can focus on the phenomenon and use different theoretical constructs to provide perspective and further an inductive process of model development. More knowledge of the managerial activity may accrue to this approach than to the deductive process of selecting a single theory and using ICV formation as a test of that theory. This approach is in keeping with the comments of Parkhe [1993], who recommends that international joint venture research should still be in the "test of realism" phase, not having matured to the level of positivist theory testing.

The article begins with a brief description of current economics-based models of the ICV. This is followed by the identification of several key considerations derived from the strategic management, organizational theory, and decisionmaking literatures which are relevant to the ICV decision. A managerial decision framework is presented to explain how managers choose to use ICVs in international markets as well as why and when they are likely to select equity joint ventures (EJV) versus contractual joint ventures (CJV). Researchable propositions follow the sequence of the decisionmaking process.

CURRENT MODELS OF INTERNATIONAL COOPERATIVE VENTURES

Oligopoly Models Early studies of ICVs focused on MNE-local shared equity joint ventures and were conducted within the industrial organization or oligopoly power model of competition [e.g., Franko 1971; Stopford and Wells 1972]. These studies generally view the EJV as the result of bargaining between an MNE and the local government. Motivated by strategic attempts to deter competitive market entry and improve oligopoly profit potential, MNEs establish EJVs in less developed countries in order to extend their home country market power into a new location at lower cost and with less interference than a wholly owned subsidiary (WOS) would generate [Harrigan 1984; Kogut 1988]. In the oligopoly model, EJV formation is the result of industry structure, competition based on market share, and exoge-

nous forces such as government policy. When those exogenous forces make sole ownership impossible (for instance, when host government regulations require a local equity position), or strategic maneuvering requires cooperation rather than confrontation on unfavorable terms, EJVs are accepted as second best, temporary solutions, to be used until the venture can be converted to a WOS, or a host market presence is no longer necessary. The local party typically offers a short-term solution to market-specific difficulties in the host nation and the EJV serves to control potential competition in the host market [Beamish 1985]. More recently, the oligopoly model has come to see ICVs involving multinationals as a way of extending collusive control of an industry internationally in order to reduce competition and increase profitability.

Internalization Models In keeping with the general literature of multinationals, most recent work on ICVs has worked in the internalization paradigm [Buckley and Casson 1976]. Internalization models focus on imperfect markets for intermediate goods, particularly knowledge skills, rather than oligopoly power in final goods markets [Kogut 1988]. These models emphasize minimizing the sum of transaction and governance costs to explain the structural forms of foreign direct investment [Teece 1986; Buckley 1988]. Hladik [1985], for instance, has shown that while early ICVs established by U.S. MNEs fit the oligopoly model, more recent ventures tend to be independent of the MNE's home country market power.

As in the oligopoly model, the internalization approach focuses on EJVs while treating non-equity cooperative ventures as purely market transactions. EJVs are treated as quasi-hierarchical modified forms of contractual governance structures, with partial equity positions taken to minimize the opportunistic behavior embedded in competitive market activity at a lower resource cost than whole ownership. Thus, Buckley and Casson [1988] suggest that EJVs provide a compromise contractual arrangement that reduces the impact of mistrust when the costs of co-ownership are lower than whole ownership. In other words, the residual profits of EJVs are held mutually hostage to desired behavior by the partners, hence reducing transaction costs [Kogut 1988; Hennart 1988]. In keeping with the internalization concept, Beamish and Banks [1987] state that only by reducing the expected costs of transactions—due to opportunism, bounded rationality, uncertainty, and small numbers conditions—can EJVs be justified on other than political grounds. The transaction cost school does address ICVs between MNEs as well as MNE-local ventures, but continues to focus on equity forms of cooperation as a means of ensuring trustworthiness under conditions where complete hierarchical merger is not desirable. As derivatives of structural economics, transaction cost models treat EJVs as situated at a midpoint between market and hierarchy, hybrids with intermediate degrees of the same transactional characteristics attributable to markets and hierarchies [Williamson 1991].

Most importantly, the transaction costs approach does not go beyond oligopoly models in highlighting the *process* leading to ICV formation. Borys and Jemison, in their model of hybrid organizations, state that "transaction cost analysis offers a rigorous post hoc discussion of the criteria for (venture) boundary definition; yet, it has little to say about how to identify important factors ex ante or about organizational dysfunctions associated with (organizational issues)" [1989, p. 240]. Yet, as Sherman notes, "the difficulty (with ICVs) lies not only in the management of the business but also in fuzzy areas, such as the personal relationships of managers from divergent corporate cultures. When conflicts erupt, they are typically much harder to resolve than in conventional companies . . ." [Sherman 1992, p. 78]. Parkhe [1991] draws a distinction between "Type I" resource diversity that generates alliances in a search for synergy and "Type II" organization cultural diversity that tends to disrupt alliances.

Horaguchi and Toyne [1990] argue that transaction cost minimization cannot explain the creation of a new market, and as a whole it assumes a reactive rather than a proactive approach on the part of the investing firm. Indeed, even the less deterministic economic theories, such as evolutionary economics [Nelson and Winter 1982], fail to provide a realistic account of managerial behavior, e.g., the preference

for "satisficing" solutions [Simon 1945]. Donaldson [1990] and Hirsch, Friedman, and Koza [1990] note that economic models essentially allow for merely one type of individual activity—that of opportunistic agents seeking their net advantage, while failing to acknowledge other bases for managerial action.

As the following pages suggest, a proactive approach towards the study of the ICV decision can be derived from organization theory concepts, providing an essential value-added input to the current economic models. By expanding the conceptual basis for the study of ICVs, it becomes possible to address their unique formation process beyond simple economic hybridization [Larson 1992].

UNDERSTANDING THE DYNAMICS OF ICV FORMATION: TOWARDS A MANAGERIAL DECISIONMAKING MODEL

The ICV decision is a multistep, complex process. This process is guided by a variety of non-economic issues, and by a quasi-rational assessment of economic costs and benefits that also are filtered through behavioral processes of perception and interpretation. The decision process is not limited to dealings with other firms. Rather, it also involves *intra*-organizational decision-making dynamics negotiated among the coalitions of the firm [Simon 1945; Cyert and March 1963]. It is a process that pits one organization unit against the other in an intense bargaining game [Allison 1971]. The process also involves isomorphic development of organizational forms unrelated to transactional efficiency [Meyer and Rowan 1978]. These and other considerations stemming from organization theory and strategic management are described below.

ORGANIZATIONAL ISSUES IN THE ICV FORMATION DECISION

An organizational analysis assuming managerial choice requires the fulfillment of a number of rules or conditions, going appreciably beyond the economic issues of market power or transaction costs, in the ICV formation process.

Managerial Discretion ICVs are the result of managerial decision processes, influenced by expectations of economic performance as well as by the dynamics of internal and external organizational demands. While economic expectations are certainly part of the decision to undertake an ICV, the actual economic costs and benefits of the venture are typically recognized only after the ICV is in active operation. Transaction costs are incurred as soon as an exchange is begun, but the bulk of the costs and all of the benefits occur during operation, and can only be estimated during ICV formation. Deterministic models imply that companies making decisions regarding the formation of ICVs operate as unitary, single-minded, rational actors [Allison 1971]. The managerial decision approach proposed here asserts that economic and noneconomic factors are assessed and given priorities in the parent firms by human actors with limited information processing capabilities and a tendency toward ''satisficing'' decisions [Simon 1945; Cyert and March 1963]. These actors have variable degrees of access to relevant information by virtue of their divisional, functional and interpersonal affiliations, as well as variable perceptions regarding the accrued benefits and costs to themselves and to their firm should an IJV be formed. The role of individual discretion is particularly important given the centrality of ''champions'' in the ICV formation process. Since many ICVs are the result of aggressive promotion by champions (whose motives will be explored later), individual judgment tends to weigh more than it would in other decision circumstances.

The Limits of Environmental Determinism
One organization theory model explicitly addressing interfirm cooperation is resource dependence [Pfeffer and Salancik 1978], which attributes organizational processes to the dependencies of organizations on their environments for vital resources. It has been applied to the study of domestic JVs, showing their formation to be related to reducing potential uncertainties among interdependent firms [Pfeffer and

Nowak 1976; Berg, Duncan and Friedman 1982]. While its economic counterpart—transaction costs—treats organizational responses as economically efficient, the resource dependence approach suggests that strategic purposes lie behind such adjustments.

However, while allowing for meaningful organizational discretion in enacting the environment and negotiating the organization's position in it, the resource dependence perspective still treats these negotiations as purely rational responses to exogenous dependencies [Romanelli and Tushman 1986]. The same is true for Borys and Jemison's [1989] model of hybrid organizations, which combines Williamson's [1975] model of transaction costs and resource dependence effectively with other theories of the organization but retains the deterministic outlook of its parent models. Although not applied to firms in an international setting, the hybrid model's inherently deterministic outlook would suggest that while the MNE may consider various investment forms, the formation of an ICV is still ultimately determined by a strict accounting of costs, dependencies, or other contextual factors.

From a strategic management perspective, the multinational firm (or any firm, for that matter) develops strategies that do not merely represent anticompetitive maneuverings, but are rather intended to protect and exploit competitive advantages based on the unique resources or competencies of the firm. Tallman [1992] suggests that entry strategies and structures are the result of managers attempting to reduce uncertainty and improve performance in host markets. Constrained by the idiosyncratic resources of the firm and its worldwide strategy, these managers are also subject to a variety of subjective concerns related to their inherent bounded rationality. In such circumstances, the economic rationality of cost minimization and profit maximization plays a role in providing feedback to an ongoing decision process, but is difficult to estimate in the initial entry process.

The ICV Decision as an Internal Bargaining Game Simon [1945] and Cyert and March [1963] show that managerial limitations result in coalition building and a negotiated internal organizational environment. Organizational issues, both inside and outside the firm, become political power concerns when managers are active participants in strategic and organizational processes, with the negotiated aspect of internal decisions also reflecting the difficulty of finding an optimal outcome in an uncertain environment. The balance of risk and return represented by an ICV may thus be the result of a political process in the parent firm [Bower and Doz 1979]. As Aharoni [1966] notes, a firm's commitment to the establishment of an ICV as well as to its continued existence has much to do with the initial and ongoing status of ICV proponents in the parent firm and with the internal political power of their coalition. For instance, Lewis [1990, p. 3] notes that senior executives at both General Electric and SNECMA "had to use their authority to overcome internal resistance" to the proposed CFM International EJV, by executives who, in the case of SNECMA, questioned GE's lack of market experience, and, in the case of GE, feared the creation of a new competitor. In SNECMA's case, its president had to "retire or fire" individuals who opposed the alliance [Lewis 1990, p. 185]. When such extreme steps are not taken, the choice of an ICV, and the particular ICV form, may provide a compromise solution between conservative supporters of a limited market commitment and aggressive supporters of a WOS.

The ICV Decision as a Reflection of Corporate Culture and Structure   From the MNE's point of view, corporate culture can be used as a means for 'behavioral control' [Schneider 1988]. In other words, a strong corporate culture can serve to lower the cost of transactions as the subsidiary becomes more similar to the parent firm [Casson 1990]. Some corporate cultures may be more amenable to IJV formation than others. For example, Corning Glass Works' preference for IJVs has been explained in terms of its "unpretentious—almost humble corporate culture." Corning's management offers that looking for partners with similar culture is the secret of their IJV's success [Goldenberg 1988].

Litwak and Hylton [1962] discuss the relative similarity in organizational structures as a predictor of the types of organizational linkages that are likely to emerge between given organizations. Differences in organizational structure, they point out, can be as much a basis for conflict as incompatible objectives. Lane and Beamish [1990] make the same point with explicit reference to ICVs. Companies with global structures may have different decision procedures on ICVs than companies with an international division. In the former case, a decision may be based more on technical and product criteria; in the latter case, on country-specific information.

ICV Decisions as Institutionalized Responses
Institutional models [Meyer and Rowan 1978; DiMaggio and Powell 1983] also address organizational issues under uncertainty. These models suggest that isomorphism, or the use of institutionalized standard responses, is an expected outcome of uncertainty. Managers respond to environmental pressures by following standard organizational procedures, whether explicit or implicit, to reduce their perceived uncertainty. To draw on Cyert and March's [1963] "attention flows" concept, as well as Aharoni's [1966] findings on the foreign investment decision process, it is possible that the sequence of decisionmaking will also become institutionalized, e.g., acceptable equity positions will be determined prior to partner selection. Thus, decisions become a matter of organizational inertia, artifacts of a previous context [Romanelli and Tushman 1986].

ICVs as Solutions to Partial Interdependencies in an External Bargaining Relationship
MacMillan [1979] describes negotiated interorganizational relationships as an expected consequence of interdependencies under uncertainty. These interorganizational relations are effectively portrayed by Litwak and Rothman ([1970]; see also Litwak and Hylton [1962]), who identify six variables affecting the formality of organizational linkages: the interdependence among organizations, the extent to which organizations are aware of that interdependence, the number of organizations or linkages involved in a relationship, the uniformity of transacted events, the resources devoted to maintaining interorganizational linkages, and the structure of the organizations involved in a relationship. The model emphasizes that, at any given time, organizational members are aware of only some of the organization's interdependencies

and act only on those of which they are aware, precluding purely ''rational'' response. Therefore, choices are the products of a managerial decision, rather than being driven by invisible forces of technology, transaction economics, or resource dependence.

ICVs can be seen as solutions to states of ''partial interdependence'' [Litwak and Hylton 1962; Litwak and Rothman 1970], that is, instances where organizational decisionmakers conclude that *some* of the firm's objectives will be better served by cooperative arrangements than by other options, which range from ''go-it-alone'' to a full-fledged merger. Parameters for such decisions include the *perceived* value of the potential partner's resources for one's firm, the substitutability of those resources, their vitality and scarcity [Pfeffer and Salancik 1978], and (from an economic perspective), the *relative* cost of the transaction vis-à-vis that of alternative options [Buckley and Casson 1988].

In MacMillan's [1979] model, ICVs make sense in symbiotic relationships (vertical relations), when the two parent MNEs have only partial interests in common. In such a case, organizational capital can be acquired, and performance can be better assessed than in a market relationship [Balakrishnan and Koza 1993]. In commensal, or horizontal, relationships, ICVs are established to reduce competitive interaction [Pfeffer and Nowak 1976] or other dependencies (e.g., Harrigan [1988]; Kogut and Singh [1988]).

National Cultural Differences Differences in the national cultures of the partners in an ICV are widely seen as affecting managers in making the formation decision, but the actuality is less well defined. Brown, Rugman and Verbeke [1989] propose that ambient culture can be regarded as a country-specific advantage. In an attempt to incorporate culture into the economic explanations of IJV formation, they present a matrix of cultural and economic 'compatibility' to explain IJV failure. Woodcock and Geringer [1991] suggest that cultural 'divergence' is likely to increase the probability of contractual inefficiency by one or more of the principals as it becomes more difficult to monitor agents' behavior, making some ownership necessary. Anderson and

Gatignon [1986] acknowledge that the transaction cost based entry mode literature presents conflicting views regarding the impact of sociocultural distance. One view is that when the distance is high, firms that want to impose their mode of operation in the host country will acquire transaction-specific assets and therefore are better off seeking control of the affiliate. The other view is that when the cultural distance increases, firms adjust to local methods while relinquishing control. Anderson and Gatignon explain that both views are compatible with the transaction costs approach, and that the choice of either alternative depends on ''the gains from doing business in unconventional foreign ways for a given culture'' [1986, p. 18]. However, the gains mentioned are unclear. For example, how would one measure the gain (loss) from imposing U.S. organizational practices in Japan?

The ''cultural distance'' approach represents an oversimplistic perception of culture as a unitary coherent construct while in reality culture is a multidimensional variable. For instance, Shenkar and Zeira [1992] find that while cultural distances on power distance and masculinity (see Hofstede [1984]) increase the role ambiguity of CEOs of EJVs, individualism and uncertainty avoidance distances actually *reduce* such ambiguity. When cultural differences are properly constructed, the universality of existing models of ICVs can be challenged. Similarly, Dore [1986] suggests that transaction cost theory is not universally applicable but that in Japan, for example, norms of reciprocity alter the risks of opportunism.

ICVs as Product of Bargaining among Key Stakeholders ICVs are formed following intense bargaining among prospective partners as well as other stakeholders in the environment of the foreign, and especially host, country. As Ghoshal and Bartlett [1990] point out, such stakeholders as customers, suppliers, and regulators are part of an external network with whom various organizational units interact. By virtue of the dependencies they create, such entities affect the parameters within which IJV formation decisions are made without necessarily participating directly in the bargaining process. It is important to realize that the impact of stakeholders on the IJV decision is more complex than the bargaining school assumes (e.g., Gomes-Casseres [1990]). Not only do such stakeholders include non-government entities, but their impact is also influenced by a multitude of factors. Lorange and Roos [1990] define "stakeholder strength" in terms of whether the IJV would have been pursued in a different form without its support, identifying significant differences in how Swedish and Norwegian firms reacted to such differences. Koh and Venkatraman [1991] examine the role of shareholders as significant stakeholders, showing that IJV formation tends to increase market value.

A Decision Tree Analysis of ICV Formation

A number of key considerations relevant to the ICV formation decision have been discussed. In this section, a decision tree framework is proposed to illustrate what we perceive to be a realistic, albeit stylized, portrayal of the ICV formation decisionmaking process incorporating these issues (see Figure 1). The framework focuses on the initial market entry decision, whether into a national market or a global product market. While the same basic decision process would be expected in subsequent restructurings, the complete organizing cycle would involve various feedback mechanisms and interactive decisions that would complicate the essential message delivered here. Therefore, the model focuses on how economic, organizational, and behavioral considerations influence managers to choose cooperation and then to select one general cooperative form—shared equity or contractual—over the other *at initial entry*. The extent to which the decision process described here is actually followed in all its detail will obviously vary. Large firms with ICV experience, such as Dow Chemical, follow "each branch, to the smallest leaf, to see where it leads" (*cited in* Lewis 1990, p. 129). In other firms, the process may be less robust and more intuitive, but the model is still generally applicable.

The model presented here focuses on the decisionmaking process leading to the establishment of various types of ICVs. We do not discuss performance, survival and stability of such ventures, except to acknowledge that the perceived prospects for success—whether based on past experience or not—are likely to influence formation. In addition to portraying what we believe is a realistic sequence of the decision process leading to ICV formation, we seek to predict when an ICV is likely to be used and in what form. In making such predictions, we incorporate economic variables derived from existing theories, as well as behavioral, organizational and strategic variables emanating from the considerations described earlier.

As can be seen in Figure 1, the decision to use an ICV is structured as a multistage process. In any particular case, the actual decision process may well have both simultaneous and sequential aspects, but a stepwise approach improves clarity and will be followed. In the first stage, a variety of considerations lead to a choice among pure market transaction, cooperative, and single-owner hierarchical control structures in a particular market. For instance, Ford "generally compares alliance opportunities with internal possibilities," while Corning decides "whether it can be in the business on its own . . . or whether it can do better with a partner" [Lewis 1990, p. 288, 28]. If cooperation is chosen, for reasons outlined below, decisionmakers are faced with a second basic decision, whether to use contractual or shared equity forms of cooperation. If an extended contractual relationship is selected, then one or more of a variety of contracts can be used. If a shared EJV is selected, the partners must then negotiate their relative degrees of control over managerial decisions [Gatignon and Anderson 1988; Yan and Gray 1992].

During the process of structural decisionmaking, firms also scan the environment for potential partners. Such scanning can be broad, encompassing all major players in a particular market, as with Corning, or keyed initially towards a targeted partner, as in the ICV between Apple Computer and Northern Telecom [Lewis 1990]. As earlier suggested, previous cycles are important. For example, firms with partners already in place may seek to upgrade their level of involvement without scanning a full range of potential partners, choosing a satisficing rather than an optimizing solution. The scanning process itself may be routinized also. For example, Corning "often uses third parties to learn how a potential ally

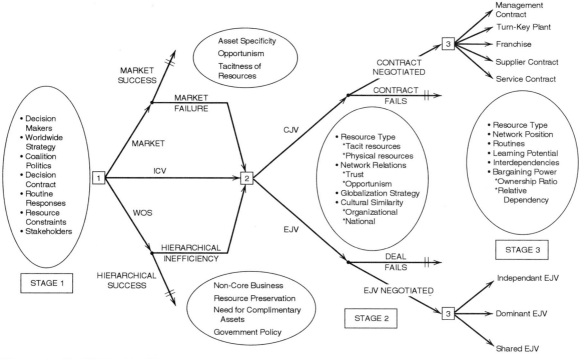

Figure 1. The ICV Decision Tree
Note: The selection of actual partners will be made between Stage 1 and Stage 2, in order to choose ICV type based on known resources.

conducts itself as a partner'' [Lewis 1990, p. 221]. Our model addresses two key decision steps in the selection of venture structure, ICV vs. market vs. WOS; and contractual JV vs. shared EJV [Contractor and Lorange 1988], without dwelling on partner-specific adjustments. Recognize, however, that the specific capabilities of targetted or committed partners will interact with more abstract considerations in actual venture structure decisions.

STAGE 1: TO COOPERATE OR NOT TO COOPERATE?

The initial decision for a new international market entry permits a choice among pure market transactions (exports or one-time licensing), ICVs, and WOSs. A specific objective here is to highlight the contention that a cooperative form may be the preferred, ''first-best'' solution of MNE managers contemplating entrance into a new market. The is-

sues addressed in the previous section influence this decision, as follows.

The Decisionmakers Assuming that managers are subject to bounded rationality and are affected by their own past experiences and learned responses, we expect managers in the respective partner firms to input their personal value systems, stereotypes, and interests into this decision process. Thus, managers with personal interests or relationships in a particular country or in a particular foreign firm are likely to be influenced in their choice of location and entry form. In making the decision, managers will also be influenced by their anticipated reward in regard to venture formation and failure, as well as the value they attach to that reward. Fornell, Lorange and Roos [1990] emphasize the importance of internal push by champions or sponsoring managers to the formation of cooperative ventures. Beamish [1988] notes that the reward systems in MNEs encourage executives to "show results" for their trips by returning with signed contracts, not for opting out of a risky ICV, while Lane and Beamish [1990] describe how an MBO process pushed an executive to support the formation of an ICV. While agency theory recognizes individual reward as a key consideration, we clearly go beyond that in assuming that executives may opt for foreign direct investment in countries in which they have inherent interest (and where the value of their country-specific expertise will be enhanced). In the case of Beijing Jeep, the key American Motors executive had a personal interest in China that led him to champion the joint venture [Mann 1990].

Proposition 1:	The greater the economic uncertainty of a potential international transaction, the more likely an ICV will be used in a target market where key managers have a personal interest.

Worldwide Strategy   From a resource-based strategy perspective, firms pursue market entry only if their particular competencies are perceived to yield competitive advantage in a given market. However, application of firm-specific resources typically involves the use of complementary assets such as distribution networks, production facilities, laborers, and market knowledge, which represent a major variable for MNEs considering an ICV. Even an experienced firm may find that its location-sensitive assets are inappropriate to a new country or region [Tallman 1992]. Unless the firm wishes to risk failure during an adjustment period, use of a local partner to provide location-specific complementary assets is to be expected. Thus, even as WOSs become legal in markets such as China or Russia, most foreign investors continue to seek local partners. However, because competitive advantage accrues to the core competencies that the MNE brings to the new market, the managers of the multinational also seek to control the ICV in such a way as to fit their overall strategic position. Global firms which must closely control the interactions of their subsidiaries to exploit global resource bases are most likely to find partners to be strategic encumbrances.

Proposition 2:	ICVs with local partners are more likely to be formed by MNEs with multidomestic strategies and independent subsidiaries than by global multinationals with interdependent subsidiaries.

Coalition Politics   When the internal negotiations surrounding the MNE entry decision are intense, an ICV may be used as a hedge against failure. A cooperative venture requires commitment of fewer resources, hence a lower opportunity cost, and implies a limited commitment to the project. MNEs also attempt to capitalize their contribution of intangible assets to ICVs, particularly in areas seen as high risk, such as China. The low commitment of the firm also implies a need to continually reaffirm the value of the venture. Thus, Tod Clare, vice president for international operations and the "champion" of Beijing Jeep at American Motors, said, "the importance of the opportunity must be demonstrated again and again, since many people at a company have not traveled outside the United States" [Goldenberg 1988, p. 34].

Proposition 3:	The choice of an ICV is more likely than whole ownership when top management of the MNE is divided on issues of internationalization or of entry into particular markets.

Organizational Decision Context   The choice of structural form for an investment will be influenced by the organizational "identities" of the partners which provide internal contexts for decisionmaking. Thus, the corporate culture of some firms seems to entail a perception of the corporation as a loose network with an increased willingness to undertake boundary obscuring activities such as alliances. For instance, Corning defines itself as a network of organizations, and an executive suggests that only an organizational commitment to long-term relationships can justify the huge investment in time and energy needed to make cooperative ventures work [Sherman 1992]. Less mechanistic, more decentralized structures are more amenable to ICV formation. Thus the more decentralized structure of

General Electric in the 1980s is acknowledged to be vital to the formation of its venture with Huntsman Chemical; the same is true for Ford's domestic venture with Excel [Lewis 1990].

> Proposition 4: ICVs are more likely to be formed among loosely coupled, decentralized MNEs.

Routine Responses Companies tend to find routine ways to do things such as choosing an entry form [Nelson and Winter 1982]. Franko suggests that cooperative organizational forms are related to "corporate tolerance for joint ventures" [1971, p. 204] (see also Bivens and Lovell [1966]). Beamish [1988] notes that in many companies, attitudes towards IJVs have become institutionalized [Meyer and Rowan 1978] or, in the words of Nelson and Winter [1982], their use has become an organizational routine, whether explicit or not. Writes Lewis [1990, p. xii]:

Successful companies that shared their experiences . . . have had few guidelines for strategic alliances . . . That they have not translated their mastery into formal guidelines is probably because, having learned by doing, they absorbed key lessons implicitly.

An example of routine responses is British Aerospace's recent announcement that "all its future aircraft development programs would involve joint venture arrangements with international partners" [Fullick 1991, p. A7B]. When this is the case, the decision is no longer whether or not to establish an ICV, and the ICV is no longer measured against other entry mode options. Rather, the decision is limited to partner selection, specific ICV form, ownership stake and location.

> Proposition 5: Firms with ICVs in place will tend to use ICVs in new markets more often, and firms in industries with a large proportion of ICVs will use cooperative forms of investment more than firms in general.

Perceived Resource Constraints We have already suggested that certain conditions within an MNE may make its managers more receptive to the use of cooperative forms. However, since cooperation requires a partner, we must also address external considerations. Partial interdependencies, of which parents are explicitly aware, represent a recognition on the part of a parent firm that it has limited but critical interests in the other's competencies, suggesting not only the use of ICVs, but also the choice of specific partners. Awareness of the interdependencies appears to be a key factor. Hladik [1988] suggests that the recognition of resource dependencies influences the decision to conduct R&D operations in EJVs. While transaction cost economics also predicts the formation of ICVs when only some organizational assets are of interest, the full costs of a transaction are known only after the fact. Gomes-Casseres [1989] finds that U.S. MNEs are less likely to establish IJVs in their core business than in domains in which they have had less experience, and therefore have greater dependence on the partner.

> Proposition 6: MNEs in the same industry will form ICVs in markets perceived to be secondary as a way to reduce competitive interactions when the parents compete in primary markets.

Participating Stakeholders Although forming an ICV involves bargaining between the principals to the deal, other stakeholders in the venture will have an impact on the process and the outcome. For instance, the government of the People's Republic of China allows the formation of WOS, but frequently creates incentives for a foreign firm to form an ICV (such as permitting it to sell in the domestic market), thus altering the relative value of an ICV without changing the transaction costs (a similar condition is argued in Kogut [1988]). Thus, when an external stakeholder has considerable power, the outcomes of the bargaining may be bounded from the start.

> Proposition 7: MNEs are more likely to use ICVs in centrally planned or hybrid economies

when the government indicates a preference for cooperation, even if a WOS is permitted.

The seven propositions outlined above are intended to indicate specific conditions under which an MNE is likely to prefer an ICV form in international markets as its first choice. Figure 1, while illustrating the ICV decisionmaking process in the proposed model, also delineates boundaries of the ICV decision from the oligopoly and internalization perspectives in which it is seen as a second-best alternative. Internalization economics suggest an ICV when opportunism and asset specificity cause market failure, but resource constraints or governance costs make a WOS seem excessive. The market power approach suggests an EJV as the second-best choice, selected when exogenous factors, such as government policy, rule out the preferred WOS or when financial and managerial resources must be conserved. Internalization models suggest that non-core businesses or needs for complementary assets will push firms toward EJVs rather than full hierarchical relationships with subsidiaries. These positions are argued at great length in the literature [Kogut 1988; Madhok 1991], and will not be pursued here. However, note that even if cooperation is seen as the result of market or hierarchical failure, noneconomic pressures still affect the selection of an ICV form in Stage 2.

STAGE 2: CONTRACT OR EQUITY?

Once a cooperative venture is proposed, managers must choose between shared equity forms (EJVs) and extended contractual relationships of various types. This is a key distinction, in that a contractual relationship is specified as to duration and purpose, while an EJV is more likely to be open-ended in both senses. This generality holds, although contractual relationships can be, and often are, renewed indefinitely and some shared equity ventures have a set duration (which may be extended by mutual agreement). While a given contract will specify payment terms, and an EJV is proclaimed to be an efficient hostage to mutual residual payments, the two forms

are often mixed such that the reality of economic relations is hardly clear. Perhaps the only absolute distinction between the two forms of ICV is that an EJV involves creation of a new organizational entity with shared ownership and separate management while contractual joint ventures (CJVs) provide defined relationships without a separate organizational life.

Resource Considerations By the time the choice between an EJV and a CJV is made, the potential partner, or a short list of prospects, should have been identified. The resources on which the venture is dependent are then identified in terms of their "tacitness," or organizational embeddedness. As Kogut [1988] suggests, tacit resources do not cause market failure, but do make knowledge transmission difficult unless organizational forms are shared. Organizational learning models [Fiol and Lyles 1985] suggest that tacit resources will greatly encourage a formal merging of organizational strategies, structures, and cultures in an equity venture in order to transmit both the skills and their milieu.

An ICV formed to improve market access to a foreign country is likely to be an MNE-local firm EJV in which the MNE provides the product and the local firm provides local expertise that is primarily tacit knowledge [Kogut 1988]. Such a venture is formed with the understanding that it will have a short life, unless mandated by the local government, as rapid learning on the part of both partners will make the ICV redundant by eliminating perceived dependencies [Beamish 1985].

An ICV formed to share complementary technical knowledge is likely to take place between two MNEs with equivalent levels of sophistication, both seeking equal access to the other's new technology, and may well take the form of cross-licensing, as technical knowledge is usually codifiable [Osborn and Baughn 1990]. Stuckey [1983] finds that both vertically and horizontally integrated aluminum firms established EJVs because of a perception that managerial and technical know-how was not easily transmitted (see also Beamish and Banks [1987]), while Osborn and Baughn [1990] find that the formation of EJVs was more likely when organizationally embedded knowledge was involved than in cases of transferable technology, despite the focus of transaction cost theorists on the opportunism risks to explicitly identifiable high technology. This suggests that EJVs are selected when the perceived dependencies are focused on the organization rather than the technology.

> Proposition 8: EJVs are more likely to be formed than CJVs when the partners are sharing organizational skills rather than specific technologies.

Trust Formation Trust between partners has been frequently highlighted as the essence of successful ICVs (e.g., Sherman [1992]). Most discussions of cooperative ventures as network organizations, as opposed to simple hybrids, revolve around social control processes involving ''reciprocity norms, personal relationships, reputation, and trust'' [Larson 1992, p. 76]. For instance, Jarillo [1988] describes clan mechanisms of control based on trust developed over an extended reciprocal relationship. Dwyer, Schurr and Oh [1987] show that, from a social exchange perspective [Emerson 1976], trust makes working out all contingencies in formal contract form unnecessary. While network models do not require a priori faith in a partner, the trust developed over a period of time is seen as a viable alternative in time-extensive contractual relationships to the need for mutual hostages in the face of possible opportunism characteristic of an EJV. Anderson and Weitz state that ''Stability of relationships [in a distribution channel] can be maintained without creating special relationships . . . by cultivating trust'' [1989, p. 322]. Thus, unless the parents are comfortable with a situation of ''shared opportunism'' [Lewis 1990, p. 121], contractual relations will be preferred due to personal trust or higher tolerance for ambiguity.

> Proposition 9: Extended relationships between partners resulting from perceived fair dealing will generate trust and result in greater use of long-term CJVs.

International Strategy and Structure The strategies and structures of the venture partners will be significant to the choice of cooperative form. Specifically, firms that operate with multidomestic strategies and are structured with essentially independent national subsidiaries are more likely to employ EJVs if they take a partner. The independence of the subsidiary permits both parents to focus on local market performance and makes alignment of ownership interests likely. The likelihood of a long-term relationship and the consequent need for flexibility make an equity venture attractive as well. On the other hand, a globally oriented MNE desiring a subsidiary that will be part of a worldwide integrated network may be more satisfied with a contractual alliance. If the MNE is concerned with overall network performance while the local partner is interested in returns on a single venture, the inherent incompatibility of interests makes long-term shared ownership problematic. However, with an explicit role in the network, with agreed objectives and payments, partners may be able to work together for different purposes.

> Proposition 10: CJVs are more likely to be selected by MNEs with global strategies and structures, while EJVs are more likely to be selected by MNEs with a multidomestic strategy.

Organizational Cultures The limited and defined interactions of a contractual relationship may reduce the strains of constantly evolving shared ownership. Therefore, firms with very different organizational cultures may prefer contractual relationships. While complementarities in hard skills and assets are widely considered to be at the root of most joint ventures [Contractor and Lorange 1988], dissimilarities in culture or style may create strains and speed failure when two firms are meshed in an EJV [Parkhe 1991]. Organizational culture is a multidimensional construct, similar to national culture, according to Sackmann [1992]. Different aspects of firm culture may be more or less central, more or less difficult to transmit, and more or less critical to operations. In a two-stage process, great differences in organizational operating style or culture may make meshing the organizations in an EJV difficult and failure-prone. However, the strictly defined terms of a contractual relationship may make such organizational factors less intrusive on the joint activities.

Proposition 11: Firms with similar organizational cultural aspects are more likely to choose EJVs over CJVs and vice versa.

National Cultural Similarities   While organizational culture has a direct impact on the operation of MNEs, differences in national culture between prospective partners raise the uncertainty of decisionmakers. Kogut and Singh [1988] find that cultural distance increases the likelihood of joint venturing over whole ownership. Erramilli [1991] shows that cultural distance and experience interact to effect ownership in a nonlinear function. As suggested above, however, aggregate measures of cultural differences are unlikely to be accurate, so specific constructs must be developed. Shane [1993], for instance, proposes that people in collectivist societies tend to be less opportunistic and therefore managers in such societies will see lower costs in any given transaction.

Proposition 12: EJVs are more likely to be used than CJVs when the parent firms are from more individualistic national cultures than if the parents are from collectivist cultures.

We also suggest that an EJV is more likely when the dominant parent comes from a high power distance environment while the other comes from a low power distance environment or when the dominant parent has low uncertainty avoidance while the less dominant parent has high uncertainty avoidance and hence is willing to perform operational, "programmed" tasks.

Proposition 13: Complementarity of power needs or uncertainty avoidance in parent firms' national cultures should favor the use of EJVs over CJVs.

STAGE 3: SPECIFYING THE TERMS OF THE RELATIONSHIP

The decision about ICV type eventually will proceed to a specific definition of the relationships between the partners and with the venture organization in which the type of contractual venture is decided or, in an equity deal, in which the control relationships between the partners are settled. Full discussion of the details of this decision stage are beyond the scope of this paper. However, compatible models for this decision are available. Contractor and Lorange [1988] discuss the possible contractual cooperative forms and the costs and benefits of these over whole ownership from strategic and economic perspectives. Yan and Gray [1992] and Blodgett [1991] describe bargaining models in which overall and specific control responsibilities are negotiated between partners. Interestingly, ownership is formally modelled as only one input to the bargaining, although a significant one. Bargaining over equal, majority, or independent status for an equity venture is based largely on a set of concerns similar to those described above. For example, it may become formal or informal company policy not to accept a minority stake in an EJV, or not to accept a state-owned partner, regardless of what "rational" economic analysis would suggest. Alternatively, the organizational embeddedness of resources critical to a contractual venture may well determine the type of contract to be executed. The managerial issues which we use to depict the Stage 1 and 2 decisions would appear to be equally relevant to the final negotiation of control and responsibility between partners.

SUMMARY

The decision to form an ICV appears to be a managerial and organizational process, in which economic factors play a vital, if nonexclusive and indirect, role. Some of these factors come into play subsequent to the failure of another mode of control and as feedback to managers evaluating a cooperative venture once it has already been in operation. Obviously, performance expectations are an important component in the ICV decision process, although, as other authors have suggested, economic measures of performance are not always an important consideration [Kogut and Singh 1988; Hladik 1988]. Even when superior economic performance is the purpose of the ICV, economic success can be measured only after competition develops. Managers make decisions based on incomplete, perceptual visions of economic and noneconomic relationships. Environmental (usually economic) factors probably do drive out highly ineffective structural forms of ICV, even though the equilibrium conditions favored in economic models are never attained in real systems. Hence, managers should anticipate the high levels of failure associated with ICVs [Beamish 1985], given their complex cost structures and complicated reasons for initiation.

The complex, intuitive framework that we have proposed reflects many of the same concerns about current economics-based research into ICVs that are expressed by Parkhe [1993]. Parkhe suggests that positivist, single-theory-oriented conceptual and empirical models will not illuminate critical concerns about international joint ventures. His key research questions revolve around the choice of organizational structure, the design of alliance structures, and the evolution of collaborative ventures. He specifically questions the realism of strict assumptions of opportunistic behavior. Parkhe proceeds to a discourse on methods of scientific inquiry. We have focused on detailed examination of and specific explanations for managerial behavior rather than typologies of investigation. However, it does seem that our phenomenological, realism-oriented approach provides certain specific suggestions about answers to Parkhe's questions that he does not find in traditional modelling.

Many issues of venture formation and activity have not been treated fully in the present paper. Future studies should focus more on the variety of ICVs (e.g., Osborn and Baughn [1990]), and examine contractual relationships in common with equity forms of cooperation. Most importantly, the full range of motivations for embarking on a cooperative venture must be considered across functional and regional lines, with a special emphasis on hitherto neglected cognitive processes. Studies may be initially limited

to certain venture types or to MNE-local firm ventures and then generalized across other ICV options. We have, perhaps, reached the point in the study of ICVs at which simplifying models must make way for models with mixed motives, multiple alternatives, and imprecise outcomes.

NOTE

1. International cooperative ventures are broadly defined here as any formal, cooperative activities between separately constituted, legally autonomous, business organizations across national boundaries. This definition of ICVs is considerably more limited than that of ''strategic alliances'' (e.g., Contractor and Lorange [1988]) in that it does not include activities that are either limited to specific product technology (e.g., licensing, joint R&D) or impinge on the legal autonomy of the participating parties (e.g., cross share-holding).

REFERENCES

Aharoni, Yair. 1966. *The foreign investment decision process.* Boston, MA: Harvard University Press.

Allison, Graham T. 1971. *Essence of decision: Explaining the Cuban missile crisis.* Boston: Little, Brown.

Anderson, Erin & Hubert Gatignon. 1986. Modes of foreign entry: A transaction cost analysis and propositions. *Journal of International Business Studies,* Fall: 1–26.

Anderson, Erin & B. Weitz. 1989. Determinants of continuity in conventional industrial channel dyads. *Marketing Science,* 8: 310–23.

Balakrishnan, Srinivasan Balak & Mitchell P. Koza. 1993. Information asymmetry, adverse selection, and joint ventures: Theory and evidence. *Journal of Economic Behavior and Organization,* 20: 99–117.

Beamish, Paul W. 1985. The characteristics of joint ventures in developed and developing countries. *Columbia Journal of World Business,* Fall: 13–19.

———. 1988. *Multinational joint ventures in developing countries.* London: Routledge.

——— & John C. Banks. 1987. Equity joint ventures and the theory of the multinational enterprise. *Journal of International Business Studies,* 19: 1–16.

Berg, Sanford V., Jerome Duncan & Philip Friedman. 1982. *Joint venture strategies and corporate innovation.* Cambridge, MA: Oelgeschlager, Gunn & Hain, Publishers.

Bivens, Karen K. & Enid B. Lovell. 1966. *Joint ventures with foreign partners, international survey of business opinion and experience.* New York: National Industrial Conference Board.

Blodgett, Linda L. 1991. Toward a resource-based theory of bargaining power in international joint ventures. *Journal of Global Marketing,* 5(1–2): 63–78.

Borys, Bryan & David B. Jemison. 1989. Hybrid arrangements as strategic alliances: Theoretical issues in organizational combinations. *Academy of Management Review,* 14: 234–49.

Bower, Joseph L. & Yves Doz. 1979. Strategy formulation: A social and political process. In D. Schendel & C.W. Hofer, editors, *Strategic management,* 152–66. Boston: Little, Brown.

Brown, Lee T., Alan M. Rugman & Alain Verbeke. 1989. Japanese joint ventures with western multinationals: Synthesizing the economic and cultural explanations of failure. *Asia Pacific Journal of Management,* 6(2): 225–42.

Buckley, Peter J. 1988. The limits of explanation: Testing the internalization theory of the multinational enterprise. *Journal of International Business Studies,* 19(2): 181–94.

——— & Mark Casson. 1976. *The future of the multinational enterprise.* London: Macmillan.

———. 1988. A theory of cooperation in international business. In Farok Contractor & Peter Lorange, editors, *Cooperative strategies in international business,* 31–54. Lexington, MA: Lexington Books.

Casson, Mark. 1990. Entrepreneurship and business culture. Paper presented at the Academy of International Business Meetings.

Contractor, Farok J. & Peter Lorange. 1988. Why should firms cooperate? The strategy and economics basis for cooperative ventures. In Farok Contractor & Peter Lorange, editors, *Cooperative strategies in international business,* 3–30. Lexington, MA: Lexington Books.

Cyert, Richard M. & James G. March. 1963. *A behavioral theory of the firm.* Englewood Cliffs, NJ: Prentice-Hall.

DiMaggio, Paul J. & Walter W. Powell. 1983. The iron cage revisited: Institutional isomorphism and collective rationality in organizational fields. *American Sociological Review,* 48(2): 147–60.

Donaldson, Lex. 1990. The ethereal hand: Organizational economics and management theory. *Academy of Management Review,* 15(3): 369–81.

Dore, Ronald P. 1986. *Structural adjustments in Japan, 1970–1982.* Geneva, Switzerland: International Labor Office.

Dwyer, F. Robert, Paul H. Schurr & Sejo Oh. 1987. Developing buyer-seller relationships. *Journal of Marketing,* 51(2): 11–27.

Emerson, Robert M. 1976. Social exchange theory. *Annual Review of Sociology,* Vol. 2. Annual Reviews, Inc.

Erramilli, M. Krishna. 1991. The experience factor in foreign market entry behavior of service firms. *Journal of International Business Studies,* 22(3): 479–501.

Fiol, C. Marlene & Marjorie A. Lyles. 1985. Organizational learning. *Academy of Management Review,* 10(4): 803–13.

Fornell, Claes, Peter Lorange & J. Roos. 1990. The cooperative venture formation process: A latent variable structural modeling approach. *Management Science,* 36(10): 1246–55.

Franko, Lawrence G. 1971. *Joint venture survival in multinational corporations.* New York: Praeger Publishers, Inc.

Fullick, N. 1991. British aerospace, Japanese, discuss jet joint venture. *The Wall Street Journal,* December 2: A7B.

Gatignon, Hubert & Erin Anderson. 1988. The multinational corporation's degree of control over foreign subsidiaries: An empirical test of a transaction cost explanation. *Journal of Law, Economics, and Organization,* 4(2): 305–36.

Ghoshal, Sumantra & Christopher Bartlett. 1990. The multinational corporation as an interorganizational network. *Academy of Management Review,* 15(4): 603–26.

Goldenberg, Susan. 1988. *Hands across the ocean: Managing joint ventures.* Boston: Harvard Business School Press.

Gomes-Casseres, Benjamin. 1989. Joint ventures in the face of global competition. *Sloan Management Review,* Spring: 17–25.

———. 1990. Firm ownership preferences and host government restitutions: An integrated approach. *Journal of International Business Studies,* 21: 1–22.

Harrigan, Kathryn R. 1984. Joint ventures and global strategies. *Columbia Journal of World Business,* Summer: 7–13.

———. 1988. Strategic alliances and partner asymmetries. In Farok Contractor & Peter Lorange, editors, *Cooperative strategies in international business,* 205–26. Lexington, MA: Lexington Books.

Hennart, Jean-François. 1988. A transaction costs theory of equity joint ventures. *Strategic Management Journal,* 9: 361–74.

Hirsch, Paul M., Ray Friedman & Mitchell P. Koza. 1990. Collaboration or paradigm shift?: Caveat emptor and the risk of romance with economic models for strategy and policy research. *Organization Science,* 1(1): 87–97.

Hladik, Karen J. 1985. *International joint ventures.* Lexington, MA: Lexington Books.

———. 1988. R&D and international joint ventures. In Farok Contractor & Peter Lorange, editors, *Cooperative strategies in international business,* 187–204. Lexington, MA: Lexington Books.

Hofstede, Geert. 1984. *Culture's consequences.* Beverly Hills: Sage Publications.

Horaguchi, Haruo & Brian Toyne. 1990. Setting the record straight: Hymer, internalization theory and transaction cost economics. *Journal of International Business Studies,* 21(3): 487–94.

Jarillo, Jose-Carlos. 1988. On strategic networks. *Strategic Management Journal,* 9: 31–41.

Jemison, David B. & Sim B. Sitkin. 1986. Corporate acquisitions: A process perspective. *Academy of Management Review,* 11(1): 145–63.

Killing, J. Peter. 1983. *Strategies for joint venture success.* New York: Praeger Press.

Kogut, Bruce. 1988. Joint ventures: Theoretical and empirical perspectives. *Strategic Management Journal,* 9: 319–32.

——— & Harbin Singh. 1988. Entering the United States by joint venture: Competitive rivalry and industry structure. In Farok Contractor & Peter Lorange, editors, *Cooperative strategies in international business,* 241–51. Lexington, MA: Lexington Books.

Koh, Jeongsuk & N. Venkatraman. 1991. Joint venture formations and stock market reactions: An assessment in the information technology sector. *Academy of Management Journal,* 34(4): 869–92.

Lane, Henry W. & Paul W. Beamish. 1991. Cross-cultural cooperative behavior in joint ventures in LDCs. *Management International Review,* 31 (Special Issue): 87–102.

Larson, Andrea. 1992. Network dyads in entrepreneurial settings: A study of the governance of exchange relationships. *Administrative Science Quarterly,* 37: 76–104.

Lewis, Jordan D. 1990. *Partnerships for profit: Structuring and managing strategic alliances.* New York: The Free Press.

Litwak, Eugene & Lydia F. Hylton. 1962. Interorganizational analysis: An hypothesis on co-ordinating agencies. *Administrative Science Quarterly,* 6: 395–420.

Litwak, Eugene & Jack Rothman. 1970. Towards the theory and practice of coordination between formal organizations. In William R. Rosengren & Mark Lefton, editors, *Organizations and clients: Essays in the sociology of service,* 137–86. Columbus, OH: Merrill.

Lorange, Peter & Johan Roos. 1990. Formation of cooperative ventures: Competence mix of the management teams. *Management International Review,* 30: 9–86.

MacMillan, Ian C. 1979. Commentary [on Bower & Doz]. In D. Schendel & C.W. Hofer, editors, *Strategic management,* 166–72. Boston: Little, Brown.

Madhok, Anoop. 1991. Joint venture formation: A review and comparison of the internalization and competitive strategy perspectives. Paper presented at the Academy of International Business Conference.

Mann, Jim. 1990. *Beijing jeep.* New York: Touchstone.

Meyer, John W. & Brian Rowan. 1978. The structure of educational organizations. In J.W. Meyer & Associates, editors, *Environments and organizations,* 78–109. San Francisco: Jossey-Bass.

Nelson, Richard R. & Sidney G. Winter. 1982. *An evolutionary theory of economic change.* Cambridge, MA: Belknap Press of Harvard University Press.

Osborn, Richard N. & C. Christopher Baughn. 1990. Forms of interorganizational governance for multinational alliances. *Academy of Management Journal,* 33(3): 503–19.

Parkhe, Arvind. 1993. ''Messy'' research, methodological predispositions, and theory development in international joint ventures. *Academy of Management Review,* 18(2): 227–68.

———. 1991. Interfirm diversity, organizational learning, and longevity in global strategic alliances. *Journal of International Business Studies,* 22(4): 579–602.

Pfeffer, Jeffrey & Phillip Nowak. 1976. Joint ventures and interorganizational interdependence. *Administrative Science Quarterly,* 21: 398–418.

Pfeffer, Jeffrey & Gerald R. Salancik. 1978. *The external control of organizations: A resource dependence perspective.* New York: Harper & Row.

Romanelli, Elaine & Michael L. Tushman. 1986. Inertia, environments, and strategic choice: A quasi-experimental design for comparative-longitudinal research. *Management Science,* 32(5): 608–21.

Sackmann, Sonja A. 1992. Culture and subcultures: An analysis of organizational knowledge. *Administrative Science Quarterly,* 37: 140–61.

Schneider, Susan C. 1988. National vs. corporate culture, implications for human resource management. *Human Resource Management,* 27(2): 231–45.

Shane, Scott. 1993. The effect of cultural differences and the perception of transaction costs on national differences in the preference for international joint ventures. *Asia-Pacific Journal of Management,* 10(1): 57–69.

Shenkar, Oded & Yoram Zeira. 1992. Role conflict and role ambiguity of chief executive officers in international joint ventures. *Journal of International Business Studies,* 23(1): 55–76.

Sherman, S. 1992. Are strategic alliances working? *Fortune,* September 21: 77–78.

Simon, Herbert. 1945. *Administrative behavior.* New York: The Free Press.

Stopford, John M. & Lewis T. Wells. 1972. *Managing the multinational enterprise.* New York: Basic Books, Inc.

Stuckey, John A. 1983. *Vertical integration and joint ventures in the aluminum industry.* Cambridge, MA: Harvard University Press.

Tallman, Stephen. 1992. A strategic management perspective on the host country structures of MNEs. *Journal of Management,* 18(3): 455–71.

Teece, David. 1986. Transactions cost economics and the multinational enterprise. *Journal of Economic Behavior and Organization,* 7: 21–45.

Williamson, Oliver E. 1975. *Markets and hierarchies.* New York: Free Press.

———. 1991. Comparative economic organization: The analysis of discrete structural alternatives. *Administrative Science Quarterly,* 36: 269–96.

Woodcock, C. Patrick & J. Michael Geringer. 1991. An exploratory study of agency costs related to the control structure of multi-partner, international joint ventures. *Academy of Management Proceedings,* 115–19.

Yan, Aimin & Barbara Gray. 1992. A bargaining power approach to management control in international joint ventures: A multi-case study of U.S.-Chinese manufacturing joint ventures. Paper presented to the Academy of Management.

17

OFFENSIVE AND DEFENSIVE USES OF ALLIANCES

DAVID LEI

ABSTRACT   This paper focuses on the relationship between learning, skill acquisition, and strategic alliances to build competitive advantage. In particular, we focus on how senior management can structure their alliances as learning platforms to assimilate new technologies and skills to revitalize their core operations and to find new uses for existing skills. Firms that enter strategic alliances without recognizing how knowledge and skills form the basis for future competitive advantage are likely to lose not only their technologies and skills, but also their ability to shape future products in that industry. Co-operation or interaction with an alliance partner to enter new markets or to develop new products also leads to competition in learning new skills and insights from one another.

One must not enter into alliance with other state sovereigns before he is well acquainted with their designs.
(Sun Tzu, circa 500 BC)

This article focuses on how senior management can better understand the complex relationship between learning, skill acquisition, and strategic alliances to build competitive advantage. As costs and risks of new product and process development skyrocket over time, strategic alliances between companies will become more prevalent, especially those across national borders and cultures. At the same time, however, building and sustaining competitive advantage mandate a new strategic paradigm that fosters learning and assimilating new sources of knowledge, skills, and core competencies that will become the basis of future products and industries.[1] Strategic alliances can help firms to transform their operations and to gain access to new and multiple sources of technologies, markets, and insights that would be extremely difficult for the firm to learn solely on its own. Although alliances can supplement the firm's own internal development and learning efforts, working within a strategic alliance presents a di-

Support for this research was provided by the Corrigan junior faculty grant at Southern Methodist University.

lemma in which co-operation with a partner often means competing to learn and absorb new skills and ideas from each other. While many companies have begun to revitalize their value-adding activities through a combination of strategic alliances and internal efforts, firms that excessively rely on strategic alliances to build competitive advantage without considering the dangers of long-term dependence on a partner may find that their ability to learn new skills will deteriorate over time.[2]

Strategic alliances may be thought of as coalignments between two or more firms in which the partners hope to learn and acquire from each other technologies, products, skills, and knowledge that are not available to other competitors. However, accurate assessment of the benefits and costs of entering a strategic alliance demands a comprehensive understanding of not only how changing technologies and new skills contribute to building competitive advantage, but also how the partner's rate of learning and strategic intent influence the evolution of the alliance. The first part of this article examines how firms can use strategic alliances to supplement their efforts to learn and apply new skills, technologies, or processes to redefine their core competences and to enter new markets or industries. Sweeping changes in industry structure and converging technologies make strategic alliances a potentially useful mechanism to help firms adapt competence-shaping technologies to realign firm capabilities. Secondly, we examine some of the potential hidden dangers and costs of entering into strategic alliances, particularly given the growing production and technological-based interrelationships that exist across different product/markets.[3] Alliances predicated upon a technology-sharing or joint development effort can often result in firms' simultaneously co-operating and competing with one another in many markets if they are not careful. Knowledge flows between companies can turn out to be serious skill drains. Third, we examine some steps that firms can take to enhance, protect, and refine their underlying skill sets and competences when entering into alliances with prospective partners. We also focus on how individual firms can structure their array of alliances to indirectly attack and defend their market and technological positions from other competitors. Defensive strategy and steps to discern partner's intentions are elaborated that could enable management to identify both their own strategic vulnerabilities and the strategic intent of their simultaneous partner–collaborator in building competitive advantage.

ALLIANCES, CORPORATE TRANSFORMATION AND CHANGING TECHNOLOGIES

Table 1 provides a partial list of the growing number of alliances currently underway in the semiconductor industry, where exponentially rising costs of developing new generations of memory chips, chipmaking equipment, and microprocessors have hastened many U.S. firms to collaborate with one or more alliance partners to compete in this fast-

Table 1. Strategic Alliances in the Semiconductor Industry

U.S. Firm	Partner	Technology
AT & T	NEC	Custom-designed chips
	Mitsubishi	Manufacturing and design skills
Advanced Micro Devices	Sony	Microprocessors
	Fujitsu	Flash memory chips
Intel	NMB Semiconductor	DRAM Technology
	Samsung	DRAM Technology
	Sharp	Flash memory chips
Texas Instruments	Hitachi	16-megabit chips
	Kobe Steel	Logic semiconductors
	Sharp	DRAM Technology
	Canon	DRAM Technology
Motorola	Hitachi	Specialized logic chips
	Toshiba	Advanced microprocessors
LSI Logic	Kawasaki Steel	Application specific (ASIC)
	Mitsubishi	chips and HDTV chips
MIPS	Digital Equipment	RISC Technology
	NEC	
	Kubota	
	Siemens	
Sun Microsystems	Fujitsu	RISC Technology
	Texas Instruments	
	N.V. Philips	
	Cypress Semiconductor	
	Bipolar Integrated	

changing industry. A similar pattern of rapid alliance formation has occurred also in such other industries as automobiles, power-generating equipment, steel, carbon fibres, computers and composite materials, where the investment expenditures for R&D and advanced manufacturing processes are often beyond the resource scope of any one firm. Within the semiconductor industry alone, the estimated costs for developing each successive generation of new memory chip are thought to exceed $1bn for a product whose life cycle is rapidly shrinking with every new generation. The evolution of memory chips and related devices to incorporate vastly smaller (sub-micron) circuits and less power-consuming features entails learning and applying the latest know-how, design technologies and processes that are often beyond the capability and experience of any single firm. While the pace of technological evolution in this industry has accelerated markedly in the last decade, the required mastery of even more sophisticated (and oftentimes untested) manufacturing processes has accentuated the risks of failure. Because the development and manufacturing effort required for ever-denser chips demands not only specialized knowledge but a critical mass of expertise working together in ultra-modern facilities, these alliances are likely to proliferate and involve even more partners in the future.

While co-operation among firms in a given industry can help the alliance partners master new technologies, it is becoming increasingly clear that firms can utilize these collaborative mechanisms as platforms to redefine their own sources of competitive advantage. In many cases, the U.S. semiconductor firm looks to a partner for both financing as well as expertise in applying new manufacturing skills acquired from other industries. Merging U.S. design skills with sophisticated Japanese manufacturing prowess helps accelerate time-to-market. Many Japanese firms seek alliances with U.S. firms both to learn technologies as well as to rationalize their manufacturing capacity. Notable entrants on Table 1 include Kubota, a leading maker of agricultural and tool implements, as well as Kobe Steel and Kawasaki Steel. In these cases, the new Japanese participants view an alliance with U.S. semiconductor firms as a lim-

ited form of both market-based diversification and experimental centres of learning.

COMPETENCE-CHANGING TECHNOLOGIES

Many observers have noted that changes in product and process technologies have begun to blur and alter traditional industry structures. Within the computer and telecommunication industries, for example, the advent of fibre optics, wireless communications, faster microprocessors and new transmission materials have redefined the conventional notions of how computers and communications can interact to create new digital-based systems.[4] In this context, one firm that has confronted the impact of revolutionary, competence-changing technologies is AT&T, which has utilized a combination of strategic alliances and internal development efforts to adjust to a radically new competitive and technological environment. The focus of telephone operations and transmission technology has shifted from relying upon sequential mechanical switches, copper or metal alloy-based wires and large numbers of semi-skilled personnel to microwave transmission, digital switching and signalling, and sophisticated software to carry out vastly more complex, faster and flexible operations, based on voice data, and video. All of these advances require manufacturing skills and expertise that traditionally have been beyond the scope of AT&T's knowledge base and operations, even though the firm's Bell Labs unit invented the transistor in the 1950s. Industrywide, the introduction of cheaper, on-site computing power as well as newer types of transmission platforms has redefined the essence of telecommunications from being 'ground-wired', centralized, mechanical operations to that of 'wireless' (or 'softwired'), decentralized, networked systems where information and data are available freely and accessible in many forms.

Table 2 shows how AT&T has been using a wide array of strategic alliances with different types of companies to realign its technological focus. Two separate agreements signed with NEC of Japan give the firm access to new semiconductor and chipmaking technologies whose manufacturing experi-

Table 2. AT&T's Alliance Strategy

Partner	Technology	Intent
NEC	Customized chips and Computer-design tools	Learn new core technologies from NEC, increase sales position in Japan
	Mobile phones	Penetrate cellular phone markets; compatible standards
Mitsubishi	SRAM and gallium-arsenide chips	Increase sales in Japan; learn new semiconductor technologies
Italtel	Telecommunications	Expand beachhead in Europe
N.V. Philips	Circuitboards	Market and technology access; venture purchased in 1990
Lucky-Gold Star	Fibre optics, telecommunications, circuits	Entry into Asian markets; technology sharing agreement
Telefonica	Telecommunications and integrated circuits	Expand production and marketing beachhead in Europe
Zenith	High-Definition television	Apply and learn digital compression technology to set new broadcast standards in U.S. and global markets
Intel	Personal computer networks and integrated circuits	Share manufacturing technology and capacity. Develop UNIX computer operating system for local area networks
Hoya	Photomasks and semiconductor equipment	Develop ion-beam masks and mask design software in Japan and U.S.
Mannesmann	Microwave radio gear and cellular phone technology	Serve as OEM supplier to German firm
Go Corp.	Pen-based computers and wireless networks	Set industry standards for telecommunications power and range
Olivetti	Personal computers	Failed in 1988
Eo Corp.	Personal communicator devices	Create new hand-held computers
Matsushita & NEC & Toshiba	Microprocessors	Encourage new technology standards for Hobbit-based systems
McCaw Cellular	Cellular telephones	Secure downstream market in U.S.

ence can help the firm learn how to better integrate computers with communications. In addition, another joint development deal with NEC in mobile cellular telephones helps AT&T not only to penetrate the Japanese market, but also to test new products and to help set a likely converging global industry standard. AT&T's deal with Mitsubishi gives it access to gallium-arsenide chips as well as new memory chips that will be important in speeding up processing time in both computers and other uses. An agreement with semiconductor and equipment maker Hoya of Japan is designed to assist AT&T build the necessary competences and skills to make semicon-

ductors on its own, while another venture with Gold Star of Korea gives the U.S. giant access to both the Korean market and a co-production agreement for integrated circuits. Within Europe, AT&T's progression has been even more remarkable. An early deal with Italy's computer giant Olivetti that stumbled because of cultural differences gave AT&T considerable experience in learning how to deal with both state-controlled and high-profile European companies that are themselves looking to invest in new technologies. One venture reached with Spain's Telefonica in 1985 helps AT&T gain a production and marketing beachhead in Southern Europe, while another exclusive deal with Italtel ensures AT&T a steady flow of business in upgrading the Italian phone system. More recently, a deal signed with Germany's Mannesmann gives AT&T a near-exclusive OEM agreement whereby the German company will sell the U.S. firm's mobile cellular phone gear and other equipment under its own label. In the U.S., partnerships with Sun Microsystems, Go Corporation and Intel are designed to let AT&T co-develop both hardware and software necessary for new forms of wireless and network-based communications. Finally, AT&T's joint venture with Zenith Electronics to co-develop the next generation of high-definition television (HDTV) technology stands out not only because it has the potential to set future industry and technological standards, but also because it provides a platform for both companies to learn and apply largely untested digital technologies to a growing market with little risk of failure in other markets.

Thus, a broad array of strategic alliances can be effectively used to help transform a company's focus and create a new set of core competences that are markedly different from before.[5] This combination of multiple global alliances and internal development efforts has given AT&T access to new technologies and new markets to better position the firm in both the computer and communications industries. Other firms in different industries that have formed broad alliances in the hope of redefining their core operations and technologies include General Motors (partners include Toyota, Isuzu, Suzuki, Hitachi, Fanuc and Calsonic Harrison), Olivetti (partners include Canon, Hitachi and Eastman Kodak), N.V. Philips (partners include Siemens, SGS-Thomson, Eastman Kodak, Matsushita and Kyocera) and Samsung of Korea (alliances incude Motorola, Intel and General Electric).

LEARNING AND APPLYING NEW TECHNOLOGIES

AT&T's alliance strategy is largely based on the company's need to rapidly learn and assimilate new technologies essential to compete in a radically changed environment. In another vein, firms may also employ strategic alliances to deepen their knowledge and experience base by extending their existing and budding core competences and skills into new or unrelated areas. One such firm that has engaged in long-term strategic alliances with numerous partners in seemingly unrelated industries is that of Corning Incorporated. Corning's joint venture strategy is based on using its highly refined skills and knowledge to enter new markets and to further advance its competences in developing new glass and ceramic materials. Table 3 presents some of the more well-known alliances

Table 3. Corning's Major Alliances

Venture	Partner	Technology
Pittsburgh-Corning	PPG Industries	Shared production
Owens-Corning	Owens-Illinois	Auto, industrial fibreglass
Dow Corning	Dow Chemical	Silicone technology
Iwaki Glass	Asahi Glass	Glass bulbs
Samsung-Corning	Samsung	TV tubes
Siecor	Siemens	Fibre optics production
Genencor	Genentech and Eastman Kodak	Industrial enzymes
Ciba Corning	Ciba-Geigy	Medical diagnostics Sold in 1989
Corning-Asahi	Asahi Glass	Colour TV tubes
NGK-Corning	NGK Insulators	Ceramics for catalytic converters
Corning-Vitro	Vitro	Household glassware

that Corning has implemented over its long history, with partners ranging from traditional glass manufacturers (PPG, Iwaki, Asahi, Vitro) to producers of enzymes and ceramics technologies (Genentech, Eastman Kodak, NGK Insulators), to high-technology electronics firms (Siemens and Samsung). The rationale of Corning's many alliances may be inferred from the company's continuous investment and experimentation with new forms of glass moulding and enzyme processes that are important to shaping different types of hard and brittle materials. Skills, technologies and competences acquired from working with glass-like materials are also applicable to similar materials such as fibres and ceramics, an area of growing importance to the automobile and semiconductor packaging industries. Complementing this materials-based competence is Corning's heavy investment in advanced laboratories that supplement enzyme and other chemical research. Early alliances with Dow Chemical and PPG were based on rationalizing and sharing manufacturing capacity for existing glass-making technologies. Ventures signed with Samsung of Korea and Asahi of Japan were designed to penetrate the fast-growing consumer electronics markets in the Far East. A co-production deal with Siemens helps both firms overcome the enormous costs of producing fragile fibre-optic glass materials needed for communications, while the arrangements with NGK Insulators, Genentech and Eastman Kodak are based on Corning's long experience with catalysts and enzymes that have important applications to material science research. An earlier 50–50 venture with Ciba-Geigy in medical diagnostics was sold to the Swiss parent in October 1989 when Corning's management concluded that the diagnostic technology required for the venture's success was more medical-based than materials-based. The two companies, however, remain on very friendly terms. Consequently, even though Corning appears to have engaged in a series of unrelated alliances with firms from numerous industries, these complementary partnerships are still based on expanding, experimenting and extending Corning's deep and rich experience with glass, ceramic and enzyme/laboratory technologies into new promising arenas.

ALLIANCES, SKILLS AND RISKS OF CO-OPERATION

In the wake of fierce global competition, rapidly changing technology and fragmented markets, the only sustainable competitive advantage left for firms is their ability to learn and generate new sources of knowledge. Continuous innovation demands a corporate memory and an organizational capability to develop, apply, and embed knowledge from whatever source it is acquired. Entering into an alliance can pose a considerable strategic risk for those firms that are unaware of how skills and ideas acquired from working with one set of technologies may be applicable elsewhere in unanticipated ways. This consideration is particularly important as numerous production and technological-based interrelationships have begun to blur once-distinct industry boundaries and lessen the rigidity of sharing manufacturing processes. Although many alliances are originally designed to share costs, reduce risks, gain economies of scale or access to new markets, the potential and unintended costs of technology or skill loss could significantly outweigh these benefits. The sharing of costs and risks usually requires both partners to share their knowledge and technological skills concerning the immediate product or manufacturing process under development. The central nexus of this problem is that the skills acquired from working with one set of products, designs or manufacturing processes often cannot be confined to a narrow product/market scope. The cumulative learning and experience a partner gains from working with another firm's products, designs, or insights can potentially be applied to a broader range of different industries and products that are beyond the scope of the current alliance. For example, alliances based on joint development and/or production of imaging technologies in photocopiers involve skills that are directly applicable to such related products and industries as medical systems, consumer electronics, flat panel displays and even high-definition television (HDTV). In another industry, the wide incorporation and use of carbon fibres and hybrid composites in the aerospace industry has led to more efficient process technologies that allow such materials to be used in sporting equipment (e.g., gold clubs and fishing rods) to electrical insulators, and even automobile engine components. In both cases, an alliance originally defined along one specific product class may represent an indirect offensive by the alliance partner to learn not only that particular technology, but also the related skills and derivative applications that emanate from a far deeper core competence. Alliances designed around a specific product or technology contain the real possibility that the partner may absorb the underlying skill base whose application goes far beyond the original product. In particular, alliances based on outsourcing or long-term supply agreements effectively give the alliance partner a platform by which to experiment, test and build its indigenous skills using the other firm's products and markets. The alliance partner, however, gains not only the knowledge that is embodied in the product and the generic technology, but also an opportunity to ingrain and embed its own manufacturing and design-related skills learned from working and improving the original product or technology. In effect, the partner gets 'to practice' skill improvement and learning with little risk to itself.[6] The numerous U.S. alliances with Japanese partners in the power-equipment (e.g., Westinghouse–Mitsubishi), office equipment (e.g., Kodak–Canon) and consumer electronics industries (e.g., General Electric–Samsung) have followed this pattern, whereby the Japanese or other Asian partners have far outlearned their U.S. counterparts in developing and applying new technologies to other uses. Consequently, alliances envisioned upon developing and producing a broad-based, generic technology are difficult to manage because the skills involved are applicable to any set of products that share similar technical features or processes. The firm's entire array of skills, technologies and competences are potentially open to absorption by the partner, especially if the alliance partner's original intent was to 'deskill' the firm.[7] Because highly interweaved and shared manufacturing skills or experience can provide the platform for entering many new markets, technology sharing alliances can potentially undermine a firm's internal development efforts and leave the firm weakened if it is not careful. In effect, excessively

close cooperation or interaction with another firm may result in the unintended creation of another competitor.

MANAGING ALLIANCES TO RENEW COMPETITIVE ADVANTAGE

Many of the risks associated with alliances—poor compatibility with partner, knowledge and technology loss, skill deterioration—result when managers rush into alliances and view them as a complete substitute for internal development efforts to improve product performance. Carefully conceived and organized alliances can help firms learn much from their partners, as Japanese firms have done from their American and European counterparts in a host of different industries. Western firms, with few exceptions, have been unable to utilize alliances to learn new skills as effectively as their Japanese partners. One critical reason is that senior management often fails to realize that collaboration and competition can go hand-in-hand when working with the partner.[8] Excessive dependence on alliances to outsource difficult or time-consuming problems with manufacturing or engineering takes away opportunities for the firm to experiment and to learn new skills and technologies; in turn, the firm's knowledge and skill base can degenerate over time. Alliances can help renew competitive advantage when they are implemented in conjunction with other firm-based learning and development efforts. Close interaction with partners in one particular business does not necessarily preclude their attempting to enter similar or related businesses not covered by the formal agreement.

UNDERSTAND THE FIRM'S CORE COMPETENCE AND SKILLS

Perhaps the single most important step that managers must take to better understand how alliances relate to building competitive advantage is to define and understand their own core competences and skills. Many studies have shown that all too many firms in the West underestimate the importance of nurturing their own set of distinctive skills and competences to build future products. Prahalad and Hamel's seminal work on core competence notes that firms should view themselves as a portfolio of competences as opposed to a set of products and individual businesses. Each product actually reflects and embodies a series of deeply embedded, value-adding set of skills whose application can be fully deciphered by an alliance partner only through close day-to-day contact and direct viewing.

In many industries ranging from machine tools to plastics to jet aircraft, skills such as design, manufacturing, and marketing have become so tightly interwoven that learning, skill refinement, and product commercialization occur in a nearly 'seamless' value chain in which it is almost impossible to determine at what point one activity commences and another ends. Skills learned by using CAD/CAM systems, flexible manufacturing systems, and close integration of research with engineering are among the most important sources of renewable and sustainable competitive advantage. Japanese firms, in particular, are highly cognizant of the relationship between skill nurturing and control of the value-adding process. On the other hand, firms that all too anxiously outsource their manufacturing or development activities not only lose the opportunity to develop their own 'seamless' approach to learning and commercialization, but also unwittingly give their partner significant insight into the firm's operations elsewhere in the value chain. Competence, discipline and skill enhancement depend upon a corporate perspective of learning that is deeply entrenched throughout the firm's many activities. This shared view of what skills the company must learn provides a vital guidepost to choosing both alliance partners as well as what technologies and skills are needed to plant the seeds of future competitive advantage.

CHOOSE PARTNERS WITH COMPLEMENTARY SKILLS AND MARKETS

A second step managers must take to understand the relationship between alliances and competitive advantage is to realize that most alliances represent a temporary coalignment of interests. Many alliances have been designed to last only for a few years, or until the alliance partner masters the skills it seeks. As an alliance partner succeeds in learning and developing its own set of distinctive skills from both internal and external efforts, there is little rationale for the alliance to continue. Over time, senior management should be able to sense and detect the partner's willingness and efforts to learn. For example, a partner's willingness to continue supplying high-quality components at a deep discount suggests it is bent on even faster learning of additional manufacturing, design or cost-improvement skills. Similarly, a partner's entrance into a new market with products of its own design strongly suggests that the alliance's usefulness is becoming more limited as the partner's confidence in its indigenous skills grows.

To avoid addictive dependence on alliance partners, it is often better to choose a partner whose skills and markets are complementary to those of the firm. Firms with complementary skills may make better partners because of the reduced potential for direct competition in end products and markets. In addition, firms bringing complementary skills to the alliance may find that the venture generates numerous opportunities to blend and mix technologies from different existing competence and skill sets to create entirely new skills. For example, DuPont's alliance with ICI in automotive coatings and paints combines the two firm's complementary skills in chemicals to produce new products to serve an entirely unrelated industry. Moreover, alliances whose partners offer complementary skills are less likely to view each other as latent threats, as the AT&T and Corning cases exemplify. Both companies have sought to find partners in which the skills they contribute to the venture are not only distinctive, but also separate enough so that the alliance begins its life in a balanced, symmetric relationship. Corning's relationship with a wide array of other glass, enzyme, high-technology and consumer products firms is designed to minimize potential conflict over end markets, while offering both firms a unique way of helping each other to learn new skills. AT&T's choice of NEC, Intel, Go Corporation, and other firms in the semiconductor and computer industries help the U.S. company to learn a wide array of skills necessary to transform its internal operations, while posing little risk that the partner will directly invade its core tele-communications business.

One of the more enduring alliances that combine complementary skills from two firms to form new technologies is that of Fuji-Xerox, whose operations and activities are managed independently of both parents—Fuji Photo Film and Rank Xerox Ltd. Fuji–Xerox designs and produces low-cost small photocopying machines to serve the Far East and other countries. In turn, however, the manufacturing skills that this highly autonomous joint venture de-veloped and tested has helped revitalize Xerox's own manufacturing operations in the United States, while helping Fuji's imaging operations in Japan. Some observers note that many of Xerox's dramatic im-provements in designing large-capacity photocopiers and accelerating time-to-market new products were the result of knowledge and learning acquired from its venture/subsidiary.

MATCH EXTERNAL ALLIANCES WITH INTERNAL STRATEGIC INTENT

In their search for lower costs and to avoid investing in their own manufacturing skills, many U.S. and European firms have wantonly entered into alliances with Japanese partners, only to feel that somehow they 'gave away too much' or lost control over their technology and knowledge flows. Alliance forma-tion demands a systematic analysis of both the risks of co-operation as well as a solidly grounded under-standing of the firm's own strategic intent of how alliances will interrelate with both the firm's skill evolution and future direction of the industry. Enter-ing into partnerships solely to round out the com-pany's product line or to bypass difficulties in manu-facturing often results in the firm's loss of long-term initiative and ability to control what knowledge or skills flow to its partner.

One firm that has been noted by many researchers as knowing how to design its alliances according to long-term strategic intent is IBM.[9] Table 4 shows the

Table 4. IBM's Alliance Strategy

Personal Computers	IBM	Software and Processing
Matsushita		Microsoft
(Low-end PCs)	Memory Chip Technology	Lotus
Ricoh (Hand-held PCs)	Micron Technology	Silicon Graphics
	Motorola (X-ray lithography)	Metaphor
Computer Hardware/Screens	Motorola (Microprocessor designs)	Wang
Toshiba (Display tech)	Sematech (U.S. Consortium)	Sun Microsystems
Mitsubishi (Mainframes)	Intel (Microprocessor designs)	Hewlett Packard
Canon (Printers)	Siemens (16 and 64 Megabit chips)	
Hitachi (Large Printers)	Perkin-Elmer (20% stake)	Customer Linkages
	Apple Computer (Operating systems	MCI/Rolm
Factory Automation	and multimedia technology)	Prodigy
Texas Instruments	SGS-Thomson (Graphics technology)	Sears
Sumitomo Metal	Eteq (Electron beam technology)	Mitsubishi Bank
Nippon Kokan	Toshiba & Siemens (256 Megabit	Eastman Kodak
Nissan Motor	chips)	Baxter Healthcare
	Toshiba (Flash memory)	Hogan Systems
Telecommunications		
NTT (Value-added networks)		Supercomputers
Motorola (Mobile data nets)		SSI
		Thinking Machines

wide array of some of the more notable alliances that IBM has consummated in recent years to assist the firm to simultaneously defend its core technologies and skills and enter the Japanese market. These alliances are organized along both offensive and defensive lines. In the United States and Europe, its wide array of alliances has been structured to prevent severe Japanese encroachment or take-over of many other capital-starved firms that possess promising new technologies to improve semiconductor and component manufacturing, such as X-ray lithography, advanced logic devices and new chip-making processes. Within the U.S., linkages with highly innovative, smaller firms such as SSI, Thinking Machines, Eteq, Micron Technology, and others give IBM access to superior software design, while keeping such valuable technologies as parallel processing, supercomputers, and electron-beam etching away from foreign competitors. Its 20 percent acquisition of Perkin–Elmer's semiconductor equipment manufacturing business was an attempt to protect its core 'flank' from Japanese buyers who then would be able to control the kinds of equipment that both IBM and other U.S. makers would have had to use in the future. The three-way alliance with Apple Computer and Motorola serves two purposes. First, IBM gains access to Apple's popular and user-friendly software in exchange for Apple's access to IBM's superior distribution power. This step helps IBM remain on the forefront of both industry consolidation and the movement to open systems architecture. Second, the deal with Motorola further reinforces the company's relationship to jointly develop and manufacture new masking and etching techniques to make even denser memory chips. In turn, Motorola benefits because its microprocessors and memory chips complement those of IBM and lead to reduced costs for both. In effect, IBM secures a call option, or 'mobile reserve' of capacity in Motorola's production facilities. In Europe, IBM's relationship with Siemens helps buttress both companies' flanks and operations from the outflanking alliances of Fujitsu throughout the continent. Two separate deals to co-develop and co-produce 16 and 64 M chips help keep both partners away from relying on Japanese partners for future supplies of more powerful memory devices. IBM's relationship with Siemens also ripostes Fujitsu's attempted strategic encirclement and 'proxy alliance war' against IBM, as shown in Table 5.[10]

In Japan, IBM works with an array of different domestic firms to encircle Fujitsu, Hitachi and NEC in their home markets. Working with multiple partners in applications of computers and software to

Table 5. Encircling IBM: Fujitsu's Alliance Strategy

Partner	Technology	Intent
Amdahl	Mainframe computers	OEM linkage helps Fujitsu set beachhead in U.S.
Siemens	Mainframe computers	OEM agreement gives Fujitsu exposure to continental Europe
ICL	Mainframe computers and software	Helps encircle IBM in U.K. and Europe
Nokia Oy	Computers and operating systems	Gives Fujitsu solid grasp of Scandinavia
Advanced Micro Devices	Flash memory chips	Technology sharing agreement
Poqet Computer	Hand-held and note pad computers	30% interest allows Fujitsu to learn new designs for growing market niche
Intellistor	Software and computer architecture	Small U.S. company gets capital infusion in exchange for technology sharing arrangement
Sun Microsystems	RISC Technology	Technology sharing and co-production agreement in new realm of microprocessors

such activities as factory automation (Nissan Motor and Nippon Steel), high-temperature controls in steel-making (Nippon Kokan), low-end computers (Ricoh and Matsushita), and printers (Canon and Hitachi) gives IBM a platform for experimenting and learning new applications of its current and future product line, while keeping key Japanese computer firms from monopolizing their home base. IBM also obtains a window on learning new manufacturing technologies and processes from a wide variety of firms from different industries. Perhaps the most important linchpin of IBM's alliance strategy in Japan is its growing relationship with Toshiba, which is believed to have manufacturing skills and expertise that is better than that of IBM Japan. One venture is based on co-designing and producing laptop computers using the most advanced flat-panel display technologies available. By working together with Toshiba in their jointly-owned plant in Hemiji, Japan, IBM gains a valuable central position to begin learning and absorbing some of the highly tacit manufacturing skills that are vital to both flat-panel displays and other applications. A separate deal with Toshiba involves co-development of flash memory chips, a new device which retains memory after power shut-off. These memory chips are believed to be superior and will supplant current DRAM devices.

Most recently, IBM in June 1992 consummated a three-way venture with both Toshiba and Siemens to co-develop and co-produce 256-megabit chips at its East Fishkill, New York facility. The rationale for this three-way alliance is that the manufacturing technology required for making this product is so untested and unknown that it is beyond the learning capability of any one firm alone. On the one hand, IBM's allowing Toshiba and Siemens engineers to work at its facility gives both partners additional insight into the pace of IBM's own manufacturing development. However, IBM is in a superior position to control what technologies and skills both partners will be able to 'take home' with them.

KEEP ALLIANCE PERSONNEL LONG-TERM

Another potential reason why Western firms are unable to learn as much as their Japanese counterparts is that technicians and managers are not kept in the alliance or joint venture for extended periods. Japanese firms often expect their key personnel to work within the alliance as long as necessary to observe and learn key skills from their partners. In contrast, U.S. managers are assigned to an alliance with little forethought or understanding of how the alliance can contribute to the firm's learning efforts through viewing its partner's skills and activities. Consequently, no base for sustained learning is created. Each time managers and technicians are replaced, the alliance loses an opportunity to form a critical mass of knowledge and the alliance's day-to-day operations effectively becomes renegotiated to the benefit of the partner. Because alliance implementation depends upon frequent day-to-day contact between the employees and managers involved, it is difficult to seal off the many unforeseen gateways and opportunities for a partner to learn about a firm's technologies. Topics of negotiation, such as the division of labour, development of new technology, capital financing, plant site location and human resource issues, cannot broadly incorporate the specific type, rate and flow of information that occurs once the partners implement the alliance. Ironically, one-time transfer of technology as blueprints and design sketches, are not nearly as effective learning mechanisms (or dangerous) as the partner's working with a host's skilled engineers and development people who are able to essentially 'de-bug' and bypass potential technological problems simultaneously. Therefore, it is critical that firms support managers and technicians involved in the alliance to ensure that uninterrupted learning and observation continue. Tacit information and knowledge that cannot be easily transmitted is often the information most valuable (and thus sought after) in day-to-day contact. Reshuffling the alliance's staff makes it easier for the partner to probe and learn, while complicating the firm's own efforts to maintain a steady watch. It is often at the plant or design site where the two firms' employees interact daily that the greatest potential for fast learning, encroachment and co-optation of core competences and skills occurs. Knowledge of the partner's implicit communication patterns and learning rates is vital to prevent unintended knowledge leaks. Skilled personnel associated with the venture over an extended period will come to know and feel which technologies and skills should be kept off-limits to the partner. Short-term managers and technical specialists working with their alliance counterparts are often apt to divulge important technical or design information in incremental amounts that do not seem to matter much at any one time, but which cumulatively represent a rich body of information.

'PRE-NUPTIAL' PLANNING

Working with another company informally on an un-related product or uncontested market before entering a formal alliance is one of the best ways a firm can gauge the compatibility and likely behaviour of a prospective partner. Many of Corning's alliances depicted in Table 3 resulted from long courtship, extended negotiations and close involvement between the two CEOs to ensure a trustworthy relationship can be established. Prior to alliance formation, companies may wish to engage in such limited steps as combining sales forces activities in an undeveloped region, or undertaking small-scale co-production of an existing or mature product for a new market with little capital involved. These steps can help both firms gain a rough assessment of their learning propensities, skill priorities and day-to-day operational habits that may be important in shaping future alliance activities.

MEASURING THE ALLIANCE'S WORTH

Conventional financial analysis tools and organizational frameworks often undervalue the potential contribution of the alliance in helping the firm to learn new technologies and skills. Allocating resources along strict profit and loss criteria means that alliances must constantly spend prodigious amounts of time justifying expenditures and efforts because skill acquisition and learning do not fit within established accounting measures. Part of the problem is that the expense of learning new skills today will not translate into new products until well into the future. Furthermore, this problem encourages managers to

flee alliance assignments because they will be evaluated negatively for external factors beyond their immediate control. The internal workings of the alliance will exhibit a high level of interdependence with the partner's efforts, thus making it even more difficult to capture how well the alliance is performing. If the strategic intention of the alliance is to observe and learn new skills from a partner, then it will be a long time before consistent profits are sent back home. Alliances between Hewlett-Packard and Yokogawa Electric, as well as Motorola and Toshiba, required considerable persistence before new products were developed and commercialized successfully.

UNDERSTANDING THE DUAL ROLE OF ALLIANCES

Perhaps the single greatest impediment managers face when seeking to learn or renew sources of competitive advantage is to realize that co-operation can represent another form of unintended competition, particularly to shape and apply new skills to future products and businesses. Companies are not destined to become 'hollowed out' once they understand the duality of alliances. The rise and convergence of new technologies, breakthroughs and applications from many different industries make it imperative for managers to learn from a variety of internal and external sources to refine skills and knowledge. Continuous and sustained learning is the only mechanism that firms can utilize to revitalize their operations and position themselves to develop new products faster. Figure 1 attempts to capture some of the most significant dimensions of the duality underlying co-operation and competition within an alliance mechanism. Along each dimension, the benefit gained from co-operation often exacts a potentially dangerous cost if the partner is unaware of it.

Rushing into an alliance without understanding how the alliance contributes to renewing competitive advantage is a mistake all too many Western firms have made, particularly with Japanese and other

Co-operative	Competitive
☆ Economies of scale in tangible assets (e.g., plant and equipment).	☆ Opportunity to learn new intangible skills from partner, often tacit or organization-embedded.
☆ Upstream/downstream division of labour among partners.	☆ Accelerate diffusion of industry standards and new technologies to erect barriers to entry.
☆ Fill out product line with components or end products provided by supplier.	☆ Deny technological and learning initiative to partner via outsourcing and long-term supply arrangements.
☆ Limit investment risk when entering new markets or uncertain technological fields via shared resources.	☆ Encircle existing competitors and preempt the rise of new competitors with alliance partners in 'proxy wars' to control market access, distribution and access to new technologies.
☆ Create a 'critical mass' to learn and develop new technologies to protect domestic, strategic industries.	☆ Form clusters of learning among suppliers and related firms to avoid or reduce foreign dependence for critical inputs and skills.
☆ Assist short-term corporate restructurings by lowering exit barriers in mature or declining industries.	☆ Alliances serve as experiential platforms to 'demature' and transform existing mature industries via new components, technologies or skills to enhance the value of future growth options.

Figure 1. The Dual Role of Strategic Alliances

Asian partners. The lure of long-term supply arrangements, an inexpensive source of components and end products, and the short-term need to avoid costly investments in training and new facilities all contribute to making an alliance that much more appealing, especially for those firms facing high costs of capital. In many cases, alliances are designed with the intention of disarming a potential competitor without the latter's cognizance. Alliances work best to develop competitive advantage when they supplement and are combined with internal development efforts driven by focused learning and a clear strategy.

NOTES

1. C.K. Prahalad and G. Hamel, The core competence of the corporation, *Harvard Business Review,* May/June, pp. 79–93 (1990). Also see G. Hamel and C.K. Prahalad, Strategic intent, *Harvard Business Review,* May/June, pp. 63–76 (1989). These authors' landmark work on core competences is forcing senior management in much of the West to question their basic assumptions on how to formulate corporate strategy and efforts to organize global operations, including alliances.

2. See H. Itami, *Mobilizing Invisible Assets.* Harvard University Press, Cambridge, Massachusetts (1987). Also see G. Hamel, Y. Doz and C.K. Prahalad, Collaborate with your competitors and win, *Harvard Business Review,* January/February, pp. 133–139 (1989).

3. M. Porter, *Competitive Advantage.* The Free Press, New York (1985).

4. C.H. Ferguson, Computers and the coming of the U.S. Keiretsu, *Harvard Business Review,* July/August, pp. 55–71 (1990).

5. An excellent study that focuses on how alliances can help a company redefine its operations is Joseph L. Badaracco's *The Knowledge Link,* Harvard University Press, Boston, Massachusetts (1991).

6. Prahalad and Hamel, op. cit.

7. Hamel, Doz and Prahalad, op. cit.

8. Ibid. See also Itami, op. cit.

9. Badaracco, op. cit. Also see Ferguson, op. cit., and Breaking Up Big Blue, *Fortune,* 27 July, pp. 44–60 (1992).

10. Hamel, Doz and Prahalad, op. cit.

18

INTERFIRM DIVERSITY, ORGANIZATIONAL LEARNING, AND LONGEVITY IN GLOBAL STRATEGIC ALLIANCES

ARVIND PARKHE*
Indiana University

ABSTRACT   Organizational theorists have correctly argued that the emergence and maintenance of robust cooperation between global strategic alliance partners is related to the diversity in the partners' characteristics. Yet previous research has failed to systematically delineate the important dimensions of interfirm diversity and integrate the dimensions into a unified framework of analysis. This paper develops a multilevel typology of interfirm diversity and focuses on organizational learning and adaptation as critical processes that dynamically moderate diversity's impact on alliance longevity and effectiveness.

On March 6, 1990, West Germany's Daimler Benz ($48 billion in sales) and Japan's Mitsubishi Group ($200 billion in sales) revealed that they had held 'a secret meeting in Singapore to work out a plan for intensive cooperation among their auto, aerospace, electronics, and other lines of business. However, combining operations of the two companies seems remote: Daimler's orderly German corporate structure doesn't mesh well with Mitsubishi's leaderless group management approach' [Business Week 1990b].

This research has been supported by a grant from the School of Business at Indiana University, Bloomington. The author gratefully acknowledges the helpful comments of Charles Schwenk, Janet Near, and the anonymous *JIBS* reviewers.
* Arvind Parkhe (Ph.D., Temple University) is an Assistant Professor of International Business in the Department of Management, Graduate School of Business, Indiana University (Bloomington). Following an undergraduate degree in chemical engineering, he held corporate management positions with a German company in the United States and Germany. His research focuses on the formation, structuring, and management of interfirm cooperative arrangements, and the impact of national security export control regimes on the global competitiveness of high-technology firms.

This example illustrates an important paradox in international business today. On one hand, global strategic alliances (GSAs) are being used with increasing frequency in order to, inter alia, keep abreast of rapidly changing technologies, gain access to specific foreign markets and distribution channels, create new products, and ease problems of worldwide excess productive capacity. Indeed, GSAs are becoming an essential feature of companies' overall organizational structure, and competitive advantage increasingly depends not only on a company's internal capabilities, but also on the types of its alliances and the scope of its relationships with other companies. On the other hand, GSAs bring together partners from different national origins, with often sharp differences in the collaborating firms' cultural and political bases. As in the above illustration, there may also exist considerable diversity in *firm-specific* characteristics that may be tied to each firm's national heritage. Interfirm diversity can severely impede the ability of companies to work jointly and effectively [Adler and Graham 1989; Harrigan 1988; Perlmutter and Heenan 1986], since many GSA partners—relative newcomers to voluntary cooperative relationships with foreign firms—have yet to acquire the necessary skills to cope with their differences. Not surprisingly, the rapid growth of GSAs is accompanied by high failure rates (Hergert and Morris 1988; Porter 1986].[1]

Before probing the nexus between diversity and alliance performance, however, it is fruitful to begin with the recognition that (1) in GSAs, significant interfirm diversity is to be expected, and (2) this diversity can be analytically separated into two types. Type I includes the familiar interfirm differences (interdependencies) that GSAs are specifically created to exploit. These differences form the underlying strategic motivations for entering into alliances; an inventory of such motivations is provided, for instance, by Contractor and Lorange [1988: 10]. Thus, Type I diversity deals with the reciprocal strengths and complementary resources furnished by the alliance partners, differences that actually facilitate the formulation, development, and collaborative effectiveness of GSAs.

Type II diversity, the major focus of this paper, refers to the differences in partner characteristics that often negatively affect the longevity and effective functioning of GSAs. Over the life of the partnership, the dynamics of Types I and II are very different, since the two types are differentially impacted by the processes of organizational learning and adaptation. In the case of Type I, learning through the GSA may enable one partner to acquire the skills and technologies it lacked at the time of alliance formation, and eventually rewrite the partnership terms or even discard the other partner. Thus, the GSA becomes a race to learn, with the company that learns fastest dominating the relationship and becoming, through cooperation, a more formidable competitor. Conversely, organizational learning and adaptation can progressively mitigate the impact of Type II differences, thereby promoting longevity and effectiveness. To summarize, a minimum level of Type I differences are essential to the formation and maintenance (raison d'être) of an alliance, and their erosion destabilizes the partnership. Type II differences, though inevitably present at the initiation of an alliance, may be overcome by iterative cycles of learning that strengthen the partnership.

A large number of previous studies have examined how Type II interfirm differences can play a major role in frustrating the joint efforts of GSA partners. For example, Adler and Graham [1989] found that cross-cultural negotiations are more difficult than intra-cultural negotiations. Several other studies have also established that negotiations between businesspeople of different cultures often fail because of problems related to cross-cultural differences [Adler 1986; Black 1987; Graham 1985; Tung 1984]. Harrigan [1988] studied the influence of sponsoring-firm asymmetries in terms of strategic directions (horizontal, vertical, and relatedness linkages with the venture) on performance. Hall [1984] analyzed the effects of differing management procedures on alliances. Still other researchers have examined the influence of variations in corporate culture [Killing 1982] and national setting [Turner 1987] on successful collaboration. This brief overview, while not exhaustive, conveys the basic directions in which research to date has progressed.

Unfortunately, the usefulness of these important studies in an overview assessment of international interfirm interactions is limited, since they examine the impact of selected aspects of interfirm diversity on cooperative ventures in a piecemeal fashion. The academic literature thus remains fragmented at different levels of analysis, with no overarching theme cohesively pulling together the various dimensions of interfirm diversity in systematic theory-building. Therefore, the main contributions of this paper will be to extend current theory (1) by developing and justifying a typology of the major dimensions of interfirm diversity in the context of GSAs; and, (2) by examining diversity's impact on alliance outcomes through a dynamic model rooted in organizational learning theory. For this purpose, the following questions will be addressed: What are the theoretical dimensions of diversity between GSA partners? In what ways and under what circumstances does each dimension, individually or collectively, translate into reduced collaborative effectiveness? To what extent can deliberate learning/adaptation actions by firms deter expensive alliance failures and promote longevity?

A PREFATORY NOTE ON TERMINOLOGY

It is important at the outset to define terminology. Interfirm cooperative relationships have previously been defined by Borys and Jemison [1989], Schermerhorn [1975], Nielsen [1988], and Oliver [1990]. However, the conceptual domain of GSAs must include the additional properties of being international in scope, mixed-motive (competitive + cooperative) in nature, and of strategic significance to each partner, i.e., tied to the firms' current and anticipated core businesses, markets, and technologies (commonly referred to as the corporate mission). Thus, GSAs are the relatively enduring interfirm cooperative arrangements, involving cross-border flows and linkages that utilize resources and/or governance structures from autonomous organizations headquartered in two or more countries, for the joint accomplishment of individual goals linked to the corporate mission of each sponsoring firm. This definition delineates GSAs from single-transaction market relationships, as well as from unrelated diversification moves, while accommodating the variety of strategic motives and organizational forms that accompany global partnerships. For example, GSAs can be used as transitional modes of organizational structure [Gomes-Casseres 1989] in response to current challenges as firms grope to find more permanent structures including, sometimes, whole ownership after the GSA has achieved its purpose. Often, however, longevity is an important yardstick of performance measurement by each parent company [Harrigan 1985; Lewis 1990].

It must be clearly noted that longevity is an imperfect proxy for ''alliance success.'' Longevity can be associated, for instance, with the presence of high exit barriers. And in some alliances, success can also be operationalized in terms of other measures such as profitability, market share, and synergistic contribution toward parent companies' competitiveness (cf. Venkatraman and Ramanujam [1986]). Yet, achievement of these latter objectives can be thwarted by premature, unintended dissolution of the GSA. Furthermore, objective performance measures (e.g., GSA survival and duration) are significantly

and positively correlated with parent firms' reported (that is, subjective) satisfaction with GSA performance and with perceptions of the extent to which a GSA performed relative to its initial objectives [Geringer and Hebert 1991], so that for many research purposes the use of longevity as a surrogate for a favorable GSA outcome is probably not too restrictive. With the above limitations acknowledged, we focus mainly on the subset of GSAs where longevity (not planned termination) is sought by each partner, but is threatened by problems stemming from Type II interfirm diversity; however, inasmuch as planned termination represents an important potential alliance outcome involving the deliberate erosion of Type I diversity, it is treated as a special case of a more general diversity/longevity dynamic model later in the paper.

Interfirm diversity refers to the comparative interorganizational differences on certain attributes or dimensions [Molnar and Rogers 1979] that continually shape the pattern of interaction between them [Van de Ven 1976]. In sum, this paper examines the interorganizational interface at which inherent interfirm diversity between GSA partners often makes effective management of pooled resource contributions problematic.

THE PROBLEM OF DIVERSITY

Just as modern business organizations are complex *social* entities (and therefore studied in the ambit of the social sciences), GSAs represent an emerging *social institution.* As researchers in sociology, marketing, and interorganizational relations theory have long noted, dissimilarities between social actors can render effective pairwise interactions difficult, and vice versa.

Evans' [1963] ''similarity hypothesis,'' for example, maintains that ''the more similar the parties in a dyad are, the more likely a favorable outcome.'' The proposed mechanism is: Similarity leads to attraction (sharing of common needs and goals), which causes attitudes to become positive, thus leading to favorable outcomes [McGuire 1968]. Likewise, Lazarsfeld and Merton [1954] identify the tendency for similar values and statuses to serve as bases for social relationships, as a basic mechanism of social interaction. These same principles may explain the characteristics of linkages between organizations [Paulson 1976]. And Whetten [1981: 17] argues that "potential partners are screened to reduce the costs of coordination that increase as a function of differences between the collaborating organizations."

Although the above literatures primarily focus on problems of surmounting communication difficulties and establishing a common set of working assumptions, a broader set of dimensions is crucial in understanding GSA interactions, given the nature of GSAs as defined above. These dimensions are developed next.

DIMENSIONS OF INTERFIRM DIVERSITY IN GSAs

The major dimensions of Type II interfirm diversity in global strategic alliances are described below; Table 1 summarizes this discussion.[2] In a departure from previous studies that have focused on limited aspects of interfirm diversity, Table 1 spans multiple, critical levels of analysis that are indispensable in providing a fuller understanding of the factors that may lead to friction and eventual collapse of the GSA. In addition, the following discussion also includes an analysis of how each diversity dimension can influence ongoing reciprocal *learning* within the partnership, an important consideration in the study of alliance longevity and effectiveness. Table 1 distinguishes between levels of conceptualization and levels of phenomena. Levels of phenomena refer to dimensions of interfirm diversity that can, with arguable intersubjectivity, be observed and measured. (Hofstede [1983], for example, operationalized culture in four dimensions.) Conceptual levels deal with ideas and theories about phenomena. Thus, the social behavior of interfacing managers from each GSA partner firm is an output of the managers' respective societal (meta), national (macro), corporate-level (meso), and operating-level (micro) influences. While the actual behaviors can be observed, appreciating the often significant differences between them

Table 1. Interfirm Diversity in GSAs: A Summary

Conceptual Level	Phenomenological Level	Dimension of Diversity	Sources of Tension	Coping Mechanisms	Proposition
Meta	Supranational	Societal culture	Differences in perception and interpretation of phenomena, analytical processes	Promote formal training programs, informal contact, behavior transparency	1a, 1b
Macro	National	National context	Differences in home government policies, national industry structure and institutions	Emphasize "rational" (i.e., technological and economic) factors	2
Meso	Top management	Corporate culture	Differences in ideologies and values guiding companies	Encourage organizational learning to facilitate "intermediate" corporate culture	3
Meso	Policy group	Strategic direction	Differences in strategic interests of partners from dynamic external and internal environments	Devise flexible partnership structure	4
Micro	Functional management	Management practices and organization	Differences in management styles, organizational structures of parent firms	Set up unitary management processes and structures	5

requires an abstraction to the underlying conceptual level of analysis. Finally, it is noted that the dimensions in the typology are often interrelated, and therefore cannot be treated as mutually exclusive.

SOCIETAL CULTURE

The influence of a society's culture permeates all aspects of life within the society, including the norms, values, and behaviors of managers in its national companies. The cross-cultural interactions found in GSAs bring together people who may have different patterns of behaving and believing, and different cognitive blueprints for interpreting the world [Kluckhohn and Kroeberg 1952; Black and Mendenhall 1990]. Indeed, Maruyama [1984] argues that cultural differences are at the epistemologic level, that is, in the very structure of perceiving, thinking, and reasoning.

Excellent examples of the deep impact of culture on GSA management can be found in the partners' approaches to problem solving and conflict resolution. In some cultures, problems are to be actively solved; managers must take deliberate actions to influence their environment and affect the course of the future. This is the basis for strategic planning. In contrast, in other cultures, life is seen as a series of preordained situations that are to be fatalistically accepted [Moran and Harris 1982]. Similarly, GSA partners must routinely deal with conflicts in such areas as technology development, production and sourcing, market strategy and implementation, and so on [Lynch 1989]. In some cultures, conflict is viewed as a healthy, natural, and inevitable part of relationships and organizations. In fact, programmed or structured conflict (e.g., the devil's advocate and dialectical inquiry methods) has been suggested as a way to enhance the effectiveness of strategic decision-making (cf. Cosier and Dalton [1990]). But in other cultures, vigorous conflict and open confrontation are deemed distasteful. Embarrassment and loss of face to either party is sought to be avoided at all costs by talking indirectly and ambiguously about areas of difference until common ground can be found, by the use of mediators, and other techniques. Effective handling of such cultural differences

must begin with developing an understanding of the other's modes of thinking and behaving. For example, reflecting on the failed AT&T-Olivetti alliance, AT&T group executive Robert Kavner regretted, ''I don't think that we or Olivetti spent enough time understanding behavior patterns'' [Wysocki 1990]. Avoidance of such preventable mistakes may become increasingly essential, and investments in sophisticated programs to promote intercultural awareness may become increasingly cost-effective, given the accelerating trend of GSA formation and the often enormous losses stemming from failed GSAs.[3] Ethnocentric arrogance (or cultural naivete) and GSAs simply do not mix well.

Nonetheless, Black and Mendenhall [1990] report from their survey of twenty-nine empirical studies that the use of cross-cultural training (CCT) in U.S. multinationals is very limited. Essentially, American top managers believe that a good manager in New York or Los Angeles will be effective in Hong Kong or Tokyo, and that a candidate's domestic track record can serve as the primary criterion for overseas assignment selection. Such a culturally insensitive approach is particularly unfortunate in light of CCT's proven success in terms of enhancing each of its three indicators of effectiveness: cross-cultural skill development, adjustment, and performance [Black and Mendenhall 1990: 115–20]. Clearly, CCT can be a powerful catalyst not only in enhancing intrafirm foreign operations, but also toward overcoming cultural diversity between GSA partners and facilitating ongoing mutual learning that promotes alliance longevity. More formally:

Proposition 1a: Societal culture differences will be negatively related to GSA longevity. However, this relationship will be moderated by formal training programs that enhance intercultural understanding.

Furthermore, bridging the culture gap between GSA partners may be facilitated by effective communication at all interfacing levels. This suggests the need to improve behavior transparency at each level, including effective recognition, verification, and signaling systems between the partners.

> Proposition 1b: The relationship between differences in societal culture and longevity of the alliance will be further moderated by structured mechanisms that improve behavior transparency.

NATIONAL CONTEXT

A company's national context primarily includes surrounding industry structure and institutions, and government laws and regulations. The great diversity that exists in the national contexts of global companies can hamper effective collaboration. For instance, disparities in the national context differentially impact global companies' ability to enter and operate GSAs. Of central relevance to this paper are national attitudes about simultaneous competition and cooperation. As noted below, however, national differences notwithstanding, important common patterns may be emerging internationally.

Japanese Context In Japan, companies have a long history of cooperating in some areas while competing in others, a practice that can be traced primarily to two factors: direction from the Ministry of International Trade and Industry (MITI), and *keiretsu,* or large industrial groups of firms representing diverse industries and skills. However, driven by recent trends in the competitive and political environments, Japanese companies are increasingly entering into GSAs, in the process forsaking their traditionally close *keiretsu* ties. In the context of this paper, the significant implications can be summed up as follows: (1) traditional Japanese industrial associations are in a state of flux; (2) a gradually diminishing role of the *keiretsu* in the future and a greater focus on the individual company; and (3) greater opportunities to enter into GSAs with Japanese firms.[4]

U.S. Context In the U.S., the federal government has traditionally viewed cooperation between companies with suspicion, particularly if they competed in the same markets. The environment of strict antitrust regulations spawned companies with little experience in successfully managing interfirm cooperation. More recently, however, in an attempt to help correct structural problems in mature industries and to promote international competitiveness in high-tech industries, the U.S. government has adopted more favorable attitudes toward interfirm cooperation, as reflected in its patent, procurement, and antitrust policies. For example, the National Cooperative Research Act of 1984 holds that cooperative ventures between companies are permissible when such arrangements add to the companies' overall efficiency and benefit society at large.

Though intended primarily to benefit U.S. firms, these changes in American national attitudes and policies regarding interfirm cooperation may also have spillover benefits for non-U.S. firms, in that the latter may have greater opportunities to enter into GSAs with U.S. companies.[5] Recent developments in the U.S. may also mean that the ability of U.S. companies to spot, structure, and manage interfirm cooperative relationships will improve over time.

European Context In Europe, interfirm cooperation historically has been hampered by fragmented European markets, cultural and linguistic differences, diverse equipment standards and business regulations, and nationalist and protectionist government policies. Only in the past several years has the impending threat of a European technology gap against U.S. and Japanese competition compelled European governments to promote the integration of European firms, such as the European Strategic Programme in Information Technologies (ESPRIT). However, such efforts to build a more dynamic, technologically independent Europe do not diminish the fact that Europe is too small to support the risky, multibillion dollar commitments required in many new industries.[6] As Ohmae [1985] argues, companies also need to establish a strong presence in U.S. and Japanese markets to survive.

Three major points emerge from the preceding discussion. First, firms from the Triad regions are heavily influenced by their unique national contexts. Second, cooperating in GSAs may be rendered difficult by the significant differences in national contexts. And third, while these differences are likely to persist, as seen above, they may be progressively overwhelmed by powerful technological and economic factors.

> Proposition 2: Differences in partner firms' national contexts and GSA longevity will be negatively related. The effects of these differences on longevity will be moderated by the technological and economic imperatives facing global firms.

Before concluding this discussion of national contexts, it is essential to broach one question that may have a significant bearing on global firms' future partnering abilities and success patterns: Will experience in managing linkages within a firms' home base provide an advantage in building linkages with foreign organizations (cf. Westney [1988])? As just seen, Japanese firms have greater domestic experience in interfirm cooperation than U.S. and European firms, though the latter are also accumulating more local experience. But is this experience transferable to GSAs, where partners typically have more widely varying characteristics? Insufficient evidence currently exists to answer this question; however, systematic research may yield important insights into the differential organizational learning patterns of companies weaned in different domestic contexts.

CORPORATE CULTURE

Corporate culture includes those ideologies and values that characterize particular organizations [Beyer 1981; Peters and Waterman 1982]. The notion that differences in corporate culture matter, familiar to researchers of international mergers and acquisitions [BenDaniel and Rosenbloom 1990], is also crucially important in GSAs. Such firm-specific differences are often interwoven with the fabric of the partners' societal cultures and national contexts, as reflected in the phrases: European family capitalism, American managerial capitalism, and Japanese group capitalism.

Harrigan [1988] argues that corporate culture homogeneity among partners is even more important to GSA success than symmetry in their national origins.

(She maintains, for example, that GM's values may be more similar to those of its GSA partner, Toyota, than to those of Ford.) However, studies have shown that a corporation's overall organizational culture is not able fully to homogenize values of employees originating in national cultures [Laurent 1983], indicating the transcending importance of meta- and macro-level variables relative to corporate culture. Although the relative importance of these dimensions must be determined empirically, it is clear that each dimension can be instrumental in erecting significant barriers to effective cooperation.

For example, strikingly different temporal orientations often exist in U.S. versus Japanese corporations. The former, pressed by investors and analysts, may tend to focus on quarterly earnings reports, while the latter focus on establishing their brand names and international marketing channels, a sine qua non of higher order advantage leading to greater world market shares over a period of several years. Thus, Japanese partners may give GSAs more time to take root, whereas their U.S. counterparts may be more impatient.

Significant differences may also exist on the issues of power and control. As Perlmutter and Heenan [1986] assert, Americans have historically harbored the belief that power, not parity, should govern collaborative ventures. In contrast, the Europeans and Japanese often consider partners as equals, subscribe to management by consensus, and rely on lengthy discussion to secure stronger commitment to shared enterprises.

For effective meshing of such diverse corporate cultures, each GSA partner must make the effort to learn the ideologies and values of its counterpart. For managers socialized into their own corporate cultures [Terpstra and David 1990], openness to very different corporate orientations may be difficult. Yet, new forms of business often necessitate the acquisition of new core skills. Among some U.S. firms, for instance, this may mean a reduced emphasis on equity control and an acceptance of slower payback periods on GSA investments in the interest of future benefits over longer time horizons. Among Japanese firms, this may mean a keener recognition of the demands on U.S. managers to show quicker results, with possible modifications in the goals of the GSA and the means used to achieve those goals. Turner [1987] found some support for the emergence of "intermediate" corporate cultures—those characterized by priorities and values between those of the sponsoring firms—as GSA partners made mutual adjustments. However, he did not relate his findings to alliance longevity, and his study was limited to U.K.-Japanese alliances. More empirical work is needed to test the following proposition:

Proposition 3: Corporate culture differences will be negatively related to alliance longevity. This relationship will be moderated by the development of an intermediate corporate culture to guide the GSA.

Finally, corporate culture has a circular relationship with learning in that it creates and reinforces learning and is created by learning; as such, it influences ongoing learning and adaptation within and between GSA partners. Miles and Snow [1978] demonstrate, for example, that a firm's posture (defender, prospector, etc.) is tied closely to its culture, and that shared norms and beliefs help shape strategy and the direction of organizational change. These broad norms and belief systems clearly influence the behavioral and cognitive development that each GSA partner can undergo; in turn, learning and adaptation in organizations often involves a restructuring of these norms and belief systems [Argyris and Schon 1978].

STRATEGIC DIRECTIONS

As Harrigan [1985] observes, "asymmetries in the speed with which parent firms want to exploit an opportunity, the direction in which they want to move, or in other strategic matters are destabilizing to GSAs" (p. 14). Partner screening at the alliance planning stage tests for strategic compatibility by analyzing a potential partner's motivation and ability to live up to its commitments, by assessing whether there may exist probable areas of conflict due to overlapping interests in present markets or future geographic and product market expansion plans. Yet, a revised analysis may become necessary as

the partners' evolving internal capabilities, strategic choices, and market developments pull them in separate directions, diminishing the strategic fit of a once-perfect match. Strategic divergence is particularly likely in environments characterized by high volatility, rapid advances in technology, and a blurring and dissolution of traditional boundaries between industries.[7]

One key to managing diverging partner interests may be to build flexibility into the partnership structure, which allows companies to adjust to changes in their internal and external environments. Flexible structures may be attained, for example, by initiating alliances on a small scale with specific, short-term agreements (such as cross-licensing or second sourcing), instead of huge deals that can pose "lock-in" problems with shifting strategic priorities. In a gradually developed relationship, areas of cooperation can be expanded to a broader base to the extent that continuing strategic fit exists. Alternatively, flexibility can be attained by entering into a general (or blanket) cooperative agreement which is activated on an as-needed basis. For example, RCA and Sharp have a long-established cooperative agreement within which they have worked on a series of specific ventures over the years, including a recent $200 million joint venture to manufacture complementary metal oxide semiconductor (CMOS) integrated circuits.

Proposition 4: Divergence in the parents' strategic directions will be negatively related to GSA longevity. The relationship between divergence and longevity will be moderated by structural flexibility that permits adaptation to shifting environments.

Strategy can affect organizational learning, and through learning alliance longevity, in various ways. Since strategy determines the goals and objectives and the breadth of actions available to a firm, it influences learning by providing a boundary to decisionmaking and a context for the perception and interpretation of the environment [Daft and Weick 1984]. In addition, as Miller and Friesen [1980] show, a firm's strategic direction creates a momentum for organizational learning, a momentum that is pervasive and highly resistant to small adjustments.

MANAGEMENT PRACTICES AND ORGANIZATION

The wide interfirm diversity in management styles, organizational structures, and other operational-level variables that exists across firms from different parts of the world can largely be traced to diversity along the first four dimensions discussed above. In turn, these differences, illustrated by the Daimler Benz versus Mitsubishi contrast at the outset of this paper, can heighten operating difficulties and trigger premature dissolution of the GSA. An important issue in this regard is the problem of effectively combining the diverse systems of *autonomous* international firms, each accustomed to operating in a certain manner.

Many researchers in international cooperative strategies have tended, perhaps unwittingly, to focus solely on this final dimension of interfirm diversity (e.g., Dobkin [1988]; Hall [1984]; Pucik [1988]). Among the major differences that have been noted are the style of management (participatory or authoritarian), delegation of responsibility (high or low), decisionmaking (centralized or decentralized), and reliance on formal planning and control systems (high or low). To prevent problems of unclear lines of authority, poor communicaton, and slow decisionmaking, GSAs may need to set up *unitary* management processes and structures, where one decision point has the authority and independence to commit both partners. Implementation of this recommendation is difficult in cases where both partners are evenly matched in terms of company size and resource contributions to the GSA (cf. Killing [1982]).[8] Yet, agreement on the streamlining of tough operational-level issues must be reached *prior* to commencement of the GSA.

> Proposition 5: Diversity in the sponsoring firms' operating characteristics will be negatively related to longevity of the GSA. This relationship will be moderated by the establishment of unitary management processes and structures.

Though structure is often seen as an outcome of organizational learning, it plays a crucial role in determining the learning process itself [Fiol and Lyles 1985]. This observation can be important in the context of GSAs, where one firm's centralized, mechanistic structure that tends to reinforce past behaviors can collide with another firm's organic, decentralized structure that tends to allow shifts of beliefs and actions. More broadly, different management practices and organizational structures can enhance or retard learning, depending upon their degree of formalization, complexity, and diffusion of decision influence.

Theory and practice are linked in Table 2, which illustrates how significant Type II differences between GSA partners can impact the entire spectrum of alliance activities. For the sake of brevity, Table 2 outlines only a select number of characteristics that are derived from the typological dimensions of Table 1. Yet, a review of Table 2 clearly indicates that: (1) the extent of interfirm diversity in global strategic alliances may be high; and (2) as stressed earlier, the various dimensions of diversity are not distinct and unrelated, but rather share a common core that touches GSAs.

Furthermore, Type I and Type II diversity can undergo distinctly different patterns over time, generating different alliance outcomes. The dynamic model of longevity presented in the next section suggests that a pivotal factor in the interfirm diversity/alliance outcome link is organizational learning and adaptation to diversity by the GSA partners.

LONGEVITY IN GSAs: A LEARNING-BASED DYNAMIC MODEL

Organizational theorists [Lyles 1988; Fiol and Lyles 1985] define learning as "the development of insights, knowledge, and associations between past actions, the effectiveness of those actions, and future actions," and adaptation as "the ability to make incremental adjustments." Learning can be minor, moderate, or major. In stimulus-response terms, in minor learning, an organization's worldview (tied to

Table 2.   Selected International Differences and Impacted Areas of GSA Management

Characteristic	Value	Country Examples	Description	Impacted Areas of GSA Management
Ownership of Assets	Private	"Free World" Countries	Factors of production predominantly privately owned.	Sourcing strategy, pricing flexibility, quality control, technology transfer, profit repatriation
	Public	East Bloc Countries,[1] Communist China[2]	Factors of production predominantly publicly owned.	
Coordination of National Economic Activity	Market	"Free World" Countries	Consumer sovereignty, freedom of enterprise, equilibration of supply and demand of resources and products by market forces.	Sourcing strategy, pricing flexibility, quality control, technology transfer, profit repatriation
	Command	East Block Countries,[1] Communist China[2]	Centralized planning of production quotas, prices, and distribution. Pyramidal hierarchy of control.	
Perceived Ability to Influence Future	Self-determination	USA	Individuals and firms can take actions to influence their environment and improve prospects for the future.	Long-range planning, production scheduling
	Fatalistic	Islamic Countries	People must adjust to their environment. Life follows a preordained course.	
Time Orientation	Abstract, Lineal	USA	The clock serves to harmonize activities of group members. Punctuality is important. Time is money.	Productivity, joint project deadlines
	Concrete, Circular	Argentina, Brazil	Activities are timed by recurring rhythmic natural events such as day and night, seasons of the year.	
Communication	Low Context	USA	Most information is contained in explicit codes, such as spoken or written words. Articulation ("spelling it out") is important.	Initial negotiations, ongoing communications
	High Context	Saudi Arabia	Sending and receiving messages is highly contingent upon the physical context and non-verbal communication.	
Information Evaluation	Pragmatic	U.K.	Emphasis on practical applications of specific details in light of particular goals.	Structure of the GSA management
	Idealistic	Soviet Union	Utilization of abstract frameworks for structuring thinking processes which are molded by a dominant ideology.	
Conflict Management Style	Confrontation	USA	Openness and directness in work relations is promoted. Conflict resolution is preferred over conflict suppression.	Conflict management
	Harmony	Japan	Wa (maintaining harmony in Japanese) is important. Saving face is preferred over direct confrontation and disharmony.	
Decisionmaking[3]	Autocratic	South Korea	Decisions fully formulated before being announced, either individually or with input from experts.	Negotiation and bargaining
	Group	Japan	Information is shared with subordinates, whose input is sought before decisions are made.	
Leadership Style	Task Oriented	West Germany	Enforcement of rules and procedures. Focus on technological aspects.	Decisionmaking, leadership
	People Oriented	Japan	Greater attention to human factors, including morale and motivation. Utilization of group dynamics to reach organizational goals.	
Problem Solving	Scientific	Most Occidental Countries	Logic and scientific method are the means of solving new problems. Accurate data are more important than intuition.	Decisionmaking process
	Traditional	Most Oriental Countries	Solutions to new problems are derived by sifting through past experiences.	
Employment Duration	Variable	USA	Employees can quit to accept better jobs. Employers can terminate low-performing employees.	Human resources management
	Lifetime	Japan	Employees are a "family" which cannot be abandoned. Termination causes enormous loss of prestige and must be avoided.	
Power Distance[4]	Low	Austria	Relative equality of superiors and subordinates. Greater participation of subordinates in decisionmaking.	GSA structure and communication
	High	Mexico	Distinct hierarchical layers with formal and restricted interactions. Emphasis on ranks. Top-down communication.	

Table 2. (Continued)

Characteristic	Value	Country Examples	Description	Impacted Areas of GSA Management
Uncertainty Avoidance[4]	Low	Denmark	Uncertainties are a normal part of life. Business risks are judged against potential rewards. Flexibility and innovation are emphasized.	Choice of projects tackled, information and control systems
	High	South Korea	Business risks lead to high anxiety, leading to mechanisms that offer a hedge against uncertainty: written rules and procedures, plans, complex information systems.	
Individualism[4]	Individualistic	Canada	Reliance on individual initiative, self-assertion, and personal achievement and responsibility.	Accountability, performance evaluation systems
	Collectivistic	Singapore	Emphasis on belonging to groups and organizations, acceptance of collective decisions, values, and duties.	
Masculinity[4]	Masculine	Italy	Machismo attitudes. Valued ideals are wealth, power, decisiveness, growth, bigness, and profits. Compensation in monetary rewards, status, recognition, and promotion is expected in proportion to achievement of ideals.	Organizational design, reward systems
	Feminine	Netherlands	Nurturing attitudes. Care of people, interpersonal relations, quality of life, service, and social welfare are valued ideals. Members seek cooperative work climate, security, and overall job satisfaction.	

[1] The situation in the East Bloc countries is in a state of flux, with political reform toward democratization and economic reform embracing free markets and private property. However, Western companies rushing to enter into cooperative ventures with these countries are likely to encounter considerable inertia from past practices (see *Business Week* [1990a]); as such, managers must remain aware of fundamental differences and their implications for alliances.

[2] The international business environment in Communist China has deteriorated considerably following the Tiananmen Square Massacre, forcing corporate strategists to reassess their commitments in the PRC and Hong Kong (see *New York Times* [1990]).

[3] From Kolde [1985].

[4] From Hofstede [1983].

its national and corporate identity) remains the same, and choice of responses occurs from the existing behavioral repertoire. In moderate learning, partial modification of the interpretative system and/or development of new responses is involved. And in major learning, substantial and irreversible restructuring of one or both of the stimulus and response systems takes place [Hedberg 1981]. This conceptualization parallels Argyris and Schon's [1978] single-loop (or low-level) learning that serves merely to adjust the parameters in a fixed structure to varying demands, versus double-loop (or high-level) learning that changes norms, values, and worldviews, and redefines the rules for low-level learning.

Using a contingency theory perspective, we may expect the extent of learning (minor, moderate, or major) necessary for a given level of GSA longevity to be commensurate with the extent of interfirm diversity. Highly similar partners would require relatively little mutual adjustment for sustained collaborative effectiveness. Highly dissimilar partners

would need to expend greater (double-loop) efforts and resources toward learning, absent which longevity may be expected to suffer.

Moreover, Type I and Type II diversity may shift dynamically along different phases of alliance development. Regarding the former, Porter [1986] observes that:

Coalitions involving access to knowledge or ability are the most likely to dissolve as the party gaining access acquires its own internal skills through the coalition. Coalitions designed to gain the benefits of scale or learning in performing an activity have a more enduring purpose. If they dissolve, they will tend to dissolve into merger or into an arm's-length transaction. The stability of risk-reducing coalitions depends on the sources of risk they seek to control. Coalitions hedging against the risk of a single exogenous event will tend to dissolve, while coalitions involving an ongoing risk (e.g., exploration risk for oil) will be more durable. [p. 329]

Thus, Type I strategic motivations and organizational learning interact to shape alliance stability and outcome. Similarly, the impact of Type II diversity on alliances can be dynamically altered by organizational learning that itself is an outcome of certain types of deliberate management investments during different phases of alliance development. The pattern of these investments may be a function of the configuration of Type II diversity, i.e., the *degree* and *type* of interfirm differences. If the relatively stable dimensions of societal culture, national context, or corporate culture constitute salient interfirm differences, then organizational learning becomes a threshold condition for alliance success, and management attention must be targeted at the relevant dimensions during the earliest phases of alliance development (such as partner screening and precontractual negotiations). In cases where significant diversity arises from the relatively more volatile dimensions of strategic direction and management practices and organization, later adaptive learning under new partner circumstances is a necessary precondition for GSA longevity.

It is evident, then, that the magnitude and timing of Type I and Type II diversity shifts contribute to different alliance outcomes. Specifically, when Type I diversity (mutual interdependency) is larger than Type II diversity, ceteris paribus, longevity will be high. In this situation, additional alliances between the GSA partners become more likely, and ongoing organizational learning in repeated successful collaborative experiences may further reduce Type II diversity, reinforcing the alliancing process.

But when Type II diversity is larger than Type I diversity, ceteris paribus, longevity will be low. This situation can arise in one of two ways: shrinkage of Type I diversity, or escalation of Type II diversity. The first way represents the stepping-stone strategy (planned termination), in which one partner rapidly internalizes the skills and technologies of the other; after the process is completed, that is, when Type I diversity vanishes, little incentive remains for the internalizer firm to remain in the partnership. The second way represents untimely dissolution of the GSA, as a lack of learning and adaptation exacerbates problems of social interaction among managers from the alliance partners. Such unplanned termination is more likely when the partner firms are working together for the first time and have yet to establish a history of prior successful collaborative experiences; differ sharply on one or more of the Type II dimensions; and the efforts and resources committed to learning and adaptation are not commensurate with this diversity.

Thus, the relationship between diversity and longevity is dynamic, and is strongly influenced by the amount of learning and adaptation occurring between the GSA partners. The greater the amount of learning, the greater the negative impact of Type I diversity on longevity, but the smaller the negative impact of Type II diversity on longevity.

IMPLICATIONS AND CONCLUSIONS

The process model of longevity proposed in this paper, drawing upon learning-based management of differences in the properties of the partners, offers rich and exciting opportunities for improved research and practice in GSAs. Only a few of these are touched upon below.

First, there is a need for inductive theory-building (following covariance structure modeling and empirical research) on the relative importance, patterns of interconnectedness, and tension-inducing capacity of the typological dimensions of diversity in a variety of partnering situations, especially in longitudinal studies focusing on the phases of alliance development. Such research will be timely and useful for developing ex post alliance performance generalizations as well as ex ante partner selection criteria. Although preliminary work has been done in both of these areas, as noted above, the research has been fragmented and theory-building in GSAs has been slow, reflecting the lack of systematic conceptualization of a typology of interfirm diversity, much less a dynamic link between diversity and longevity.

The propositions and model developed here draw attention to the crucial aspect of *learning* among interfacing managers of GSA partners; important corollary implications flow from this emphasis. For example, faced with rapid internationalization and even faster growth of interfirm cooperation, how best can global firms quickly enlarge the severely limited cadre of culturally sophisticated, internationally experienced managers (cf. Strom [1990]; Hagerty [1991])? Since coping with interfirm diversity (e.g., formal training programs) is not costless, how are (or methodologically should be) the costs and benefits of such coping efforts assessed by managers or researchers? Fledgling attempts toward institutionalizing learning within the company and enhancing the cumulativeness of cooperative experiences with other companies are already evident, such as General Electric Company's establishment of GE International in 1988. Created as a special mechanism to efficiently handle the swift growth of GSAs and facilitate organizational learning, GE International's primary roles are to identify and implement GSAs, to promote enhanced international awareness within GE, and to permit the sharing of international partnership expertise throughout the company.

In conclusion, as global firms' technological, financial, and marketing prowess increasingly becomes tied to the excellence of their external organizational relations, "GSA sophistication"—the ability to diagnose important differences between partners and fashion a productive partnership by devising novel solutions to accommodate the differences—is likely to become an imperative. GSAs represent a type of competitive weapon, in that they involve interorganizational *cooperation* in the pursuit of global *competitive* advantage. Sharpening the edge of this competitive weapon may require the adoption of multifirm, multicultural perspectives in joint decisionmaking, a process rendered difficult by the perceptual blinders imposed by culture-bound and corporate-bound thinking (e.g., respectively, the "ugly foreigner" mentality and the NIH, or not invented here, syndrome).[9] Thus, future research on GSA longevity and performance must take into account the partners' cognition of, and adaptation to, the important dimensions of diversity that is an integral, inescapable part of such alliances.

NOTES

1. Although other factors, such as hidden agendas and conceptually flawed logic of the GSA may also account for a portion of these failures, interfirm diversity remains a prime culprit. More-

over, as noted shortly, dissolution of a GSA does not necessarily constitute failure. When GSAs are used as "stepping stones," their termination may be viewed by the parents as a success, not a failure.

2. This typology is suggested as a parsimonious framework to be built upon in future research on GSAs, not as the comprehensive final word. For instance, differences in industry-specific considerations and firm sizes can be significant factors in some cases; these factors are not explicitly considered here.

3. GSAs typically involve commitment of substantial resources on both sides, in cash and/or in kind. Failure can result in a loss of competitive position far beyond merely the opportunity cost of the resources deployed in the GSA itself; synergistic gains and expected positive spillover effects for the parent firm may not be realized.

4. However, the speed with which these changes may occur should not be overestimated, in light of the deeply embedded industry structure and institutions in Japan.

5. One example is the GM-Toyota alliance called New United Motor Manufacturing, Inc. (NUMMI). NUMMI was approved despite strenuous objections from Chrysler and others, whose traditional (antitrust-based) arguments were rejected by the U.S. Department of Justice.

6. This is likely to remain true even after taking into account (a) the move toward a more genuine Common Market in 1992, which creates an integrated economy of 320 million consumers, and (b) the increase in the size of the market arising from East Block upheavals.

7. For example, the growing inseparability of data transmission and data processing has created hybrid businesses among companies in computers, telecommunications, office products, modular switchgears, and semiconductors. Similarly, auto firms, driven by cost, quality, and efficiency considerations, increasingly invest in electronics, new materials, aerodynamics, computers, robotics, and artificial intelligence.

8. GSAs must ultimately be guided by careful consideration of the respective management practices and organization of the parents, as well as the operational needs of the venture, such as response time to market developments and management information systems that accurately reflect the magnitude and scope of the alliance.

9. This problem may be particularly severe for Japanese companies, whose overseas activities until recently strongly emphasized exports and direct investments in wholly owned subsidiaries. The historically closed nature of Japan's society and corporations makes integrating outsiders—even other Japanese—difficult.

REFERENCES

Adler, Nancy, J. 1986. *International dimensions of organizational behavior.* Boston, MA: Kent.

———— & John L. Graham. 1989. Cross-cultural interaction: The international comparison fallacy? *Journal of International Business Studies,* Fall: 515–37.

Argyris, Chris & Donald A. Schon. 1978. *Organizational learning.* Reading, MA: Addison-Wesley.

BenDaniel, David J. & Arthur H. Rosenbloom. 1990. *The handbook of international mergers and acquisitions.* Englewood Cliffs, NJ: Prentice-Hall.

Beyer, Janice M. 1981. Ideologies, values, and decision making in organizations. In P.C. Nystrom & W.H. Starbuck, editors, *Handbook of organization design.* New York: Oxford University Press.

Black, J. Stewart. 1987. Japanese/American negotiation: The Japanese perspective. *Business and Economic Review,* 6: 27–30.

———— & Mark Mendenhall. 1990. Cross-cultural training effectiveness: A review and a theoretical framework for future research. *Academy of Management Review,* 15: 113–36.

Borys, Bryan & David B. Jemison. 1989. Hybrid arrangements as strategic alliances: Theoretical issues in organizational combinations. *Academy of Management Review,* 14: 234–49.

Business Week. 1990a. Big deals run into big trouble in the Soviet Union. March 19: 58–59.

————. 1990b. A waltz of giants sends shock waves worldwide. March 19: 59–60.

Contractor, Farok J. & Peter Lorange (editors). 1988. *Cooperative strategies in international business.* Lexington, MA: Lexington Books.

Cosier, Richard A. & Dan R. Dalton. 1990. Positive effects of conflict: A field assessment. *International Journal of Conflict Management,* January: 81–92.

Daft, Richard L. & Karl E. Weick. 1984. Toward a model of organizations as interpretation systems. *Academy of Management Review,* 9: 284–95.

Dobkin, James A. 1988. *International technology joint ventures.* Stoneham, MA: Butterworth Legal Publishers.

Evans, F.B. 1963. Selling as a dyadic relationship—a new approach. *American Behavioral Scientist,* 6 (May): 76–79.

Fiol, C. Marlene & Marjorie A. Lyles. 1985. Organizational learning. *Academy of Management Review,* 10: 803–13.

Geringer, J. Michael & Louis Hebert. 1991. Measuring performance of international joint ventures. *Journal of International Business Studies,* 22: 249–64.

Gomes-Casseres, Benjamin. 1989. Joint ventures in the face of global competition. *Sloan Management Review,* Spring: 17–26.

Graham, John L. 1985. The influence of culture on the process of business negotiations: An exploratory study. *Journal of International Business Studies,* 16:81–95.

Hagerty, Bob. 1991. Firms in Europe try to find executives who can cross borders in a single bound. *The Wall Street Journal,* January 25: B1, B3.

Hall, R. Duane. 1984. *The international joint venture.* New York: Praeger.

Harrigan, Kathryn R. 1985. *Strategies for joint ventures.* Lexington, MA: Lexington Books.

————. 1988. Strategic alliances and partner asymmetries. In F.J. Contractor & P. Lorange, editors, *Cooperative strategies in international business.* Lexington, MA: Lexington Books.

Hedberg, Bo. 1981. How organizations learn and unlearn. In P.C. Nystrom & W.H. Starbuck, editors, *Handbook of organizational design.* New York: Oxford University Press.

Hergert, Michael & Deigan Morris. 1988. Trends in international collaborative agreements. In F.J. Contractor & P. Lorange, editors, *Cooperative strategies in international business.* Lexington, MA: Lexington Books.

Hofstede, Geert. 1983. National cultures in four dimensions. *International Studies of Management and Organization,* 13: 46–74.

Killing, J. Peter. 1982. How to make a global joint venture work. *Harvard Business Review,* May–June.

Kluckhohn, C. & A.L. Kroeberg. 1952. *Culture: A critical review of concepts and definitions.* New York: Vintage Books.

Kolde, Endel-Jakob. 1985. *Environment of international business.* Boston: PWS-Kent Publishing Co.

Laurent, Andre. 1983. The cultural diversity of management conceptions. *International Studies of Management and Organization,* Spring.

Lazarsfeld, Paul M. & Robert K. Merton. 1954. Friendship as a social process. In Monroe Berger, Theodore Abel & Charles Page, editors, *Freedom and control in modern society.* New York: Octagon Books.

Lewis, Jordan D. 1990. *Partnerships for profit: Structuring and managing strategic alliances.* New York: The Free Press.

Lyles, Marjorie A. 1988. Learning among joint venture-sophisticated firms. In F.J. Contractor & P. Lorange, editors, *Cooperative strategies in international business.* Lexington, MA: Lexington Books.

Lynch, Robert P. 1989. *The practical guide to joint ventures and alliances.* New York: Wiley.

Maruyama, Magoroh. 1984. Alternative concepts of management: Insights from Asia and Africa. *Asia Pacific Journal of Management,* 1(2): 100–11.

McGuire, W.J. 1968. The nature of attitudes and attitude change. In L. Gardner & G. Aronson, editors, *The handbook of social psychology.* Reading, MA: Addison-Wesley.

Miles, Robert E. & Charles C. Snow. 1978. *Organizational strategy, structure and process.* New York: McGraw-Hill.

Miller, D. & P.H. Friesen. 1980. Momentum and revolution in organization adaption. *Academy of Management Journal,* 23: 591–614.

Molnar, Joseph J. & David L. Rogers. 1979. A comparative model of interorganizational conflict. *Administrative Science Quarterly,* 24: 405–24.

Moran, Robert T. & Phillip R. Harris. 1982. *Managing cultural synergy.* Houston: Gulf Publishing Co.

New York Times. 1990. Bush distressed as policy fails to move China. March 11: 1, 11.

Nielsen, Richard P. 1988. Cooperative strategy. *Strategic Management Journal,* 9: 475–92.

Ohmae, Kenichi. 1985. *Triad power.* New York: The Free Press.

Oliver, Christine. 1990. Determinants of interorganizational relationships: Integration and future directions. *Academy of Management Review,* 15: 241–65.

Paulson, Steven. 1976. A theory and comparative analysis of interorganizational dyads. *Rural Sociology,* 41: 311–29.

Perlmutter, Howard V. & David A. Heenan. 1986. Cooperate to compete globally. *Harvard Business Review,* March–April: 136–52.

Peters, Thomas J. & Robert H. Waterman. 1982. *In search of excellence.* New York: Warner Books.

Porter, Michael E., editor. 1986. *Competition in global industries.* Boston: Harvard Business School Press.

Pucik, Vladimir. 1988. Strategic alliances with the Japanese: Implications for human resource management. In Farok Contractor & Peter Lorange, editors, *Cooperative strategies in international business.* Lexington, MA: Lexington Books.

Schermerhorn, John R., Jr. 1975. Determinants of interorganizational cooperation. *Academy of Management Journal,* 18: 846–56.

Strom, Stephanie. 1990. The art of luring Japanese executives to American firms. *New York Times,* March 25: F12.

Terpstra, Vern & Kenneth David. 1990. *The cultural environment of international business.* Cincinnati: Southwestern-Publishing Co.

Tung, Rosalie. 1984. *Key to Japan's economic strength: Human power.* Lexington, MA: Lexington Books.

Turner, L. 1987. *Industrial collaboration with Japan.* London: Routledge and Keegan Paul.

Van de Ven, Andrew H. 1976. On the nature, formation, and maintenance of relations among organizations. *Academy of Management Review,* 2: 24–36.

Venkatraman, N. & W. Ramanujam. 1986. Measurement of business performance in strategy research: A comparison of approaches. *Academy of Management Review,* 11: 801–14.

Westney, D. Eleanor. 1988. Domestic and foreign learning curves in managing international cooperative strategies. In F.J. Contractor & P. Lorange, editors, *Cooperative strategies in international business.* Lexington, MA: Lexington Books.

Whetten, David A. 1981. Interorganizational relations: A review of the field. *Journal of Higher Education,* 52: 1–28.

Wysocki, Bernard. 1990. Cross-border alliances become favorite way to crack new markets. *Wall Street Journal,* March 26: A1, A12.

19

UNILATERAL COMMITMENTS AND THE IMPORTANCE OF PROCESS IN ALLIANCES

RANJAY GULATI, TARUN KHANNA, AND NITIN NOHRIA

ABSTRACT   How the partners in an alliance view their joint venture can have much to do with its success or failure. Do they fear that the other partner will get a larger payoff, while they operate in good faith? Or do they make seemingly counterintuitive unilateral commitments that involve acts of faith by one or both companies? Here the authors present a framework, derived from field interviews and viewed in game theory terms, for securing partners' cooperation, managing an alliance, and ensuring its success.

The rapid proliferation of strategic alliances during the past decade has captured the interest of both the business press and the academic literature. A number of empirical studies have documented the unprecedented growth of joint ventures in a variety of industries, and much has been made of the beginning of a new era of cooperation in which firms seek partnerships in several facets of their operations. Many see the growth of alliances as a key to sustained competitive advantage for U.S. industry.

Yet despite the popularity and presumed strategic importance of alliances, the fact that they often fail suggests that our understanding of the appropriate ways for managing different kinds of alliances is quite limited. There are numerous cases of firms that have become disenchanted with alliances. Several studies have reported failure rates as high as 80 percent, failure that usually leads to their dissolution or acquisition by one of the partners.[1] Prominent failures in the automobile industry alone include, for example, alliances between General Motors and Daewoo Corporation, General Motors and Isuzu Motors, Chrysler and Mitsubishi Motors, Chrysler and Maserati, Fiat and Nissan.

We believe that part of the reason contemporary alliances fail so often is because many partners view them, in game theory terms, as prisoner's dilemma situations. Each partner fears that the other will get the larger payoff by acting opportunistically while it cooperates in good faith. The result is that both partners choose not to cooperate and are worse off than if they had cooperated. Conceptualizing alliances in this way, while appropriate in some instances, is restrictive, leading to the false belief that one management style fits all alliances and all stages of a particular alliance. In fact, as we will show in this paper, alliances vary considerably and, depending on their structure and how they evolve, they may need to be managed very differently from the recommendations that result from seeing them in a prisoner's dilemma context.

One shortcoming of the prisoner's dilemma framework is that it underestimates the importance of each partner acting unilaterally to enhance the possibility that all partners will cooperate. Our fieldwork has shown how vital unilateral commitments can be to the success of alliances. In this paper, we present a view of alliances that helps us understand why unilateral commitments can be so helpful.

We also argue that process is important. When unexpected changes (technological, political, regulatory, or industry changes that are beyond the alliance partners' control) alter the economics and underlying incentives of the participants, different formulations and, hence, different management styles become appropriate. The management process for the day-to-day running of the alliance matters because institutionalizing methods to ensure that all parties appreciate such changes is important to the alliance's continued success. That managers and academics underappreciate this is fairly clear. A Coopers & Ly-

brand study suggests that, while executives spent 23 percent of their time on developing alliance plans and 19 percent on drafting legal documents, they spent only 8 percent actually managing the alliance.[2] Even if different stages of the alliance do require different time commitments by managers, the little time spent on managing its day-to-day affairs is startling.

For this study, we interviewed 143 managers in seventeen organizations in the United States and abroad that are engaged in alliances. The interviews were open-ended, with a focus on understanding some of the factors critical to the alliances' success. The analytical framework we present here is derived from our observations during these field interviews. We base our discussion on the following observations and illustrate it with examples from our fieldwork. We observed firms that made unilateral commitments with the professed intent of somehow trying to influence the outcome of the alliance. These commitments, which appeared in a variety of guises, are difficult to rationalize if, indeed, the prisoner's dilemma formulation is not appropriate for all alliances at all times. We also observed that unexpected disruptions, completely outside the control of any of the alliance participants (individually or collectively), were commonplace in virtually every alliance we studied. Further, the way managers dealt with these disruptions differed widely across organizations, suggesting the importance of process issues in managing alliances.

We first review one approach to analyzing alliances—the prisoner's dilemma—that has received the greatest attention. We then offer an alternative way of thinking about alliances, also couched in the language of game theory, and suggest the major differences.

THE LIMITATIONS OF THE PRISONER'S DILEMMA

The payoff that a firm gets from participating in an alliance depends not only on its own actions, but also on its partner's. The tools of simple game theory are ideally suited to suggest conceptual frameworks that

Table 1. Payoffs in a Prisoner's
Dilemma Situation

		Prisoner B	
		Cooperate	Not Cooperate
	Cooperate	7,7	3,9
Prisoner A			
	Not Cooperate	9,3	5,5

capture this interdependence. For our purposes, game theory also provides a way to explain the counterintuitive findings from our research and give us a solid basis for our normative recommendations.

The most frequently used game, the prisoner's dilemma in its simplest form, involves two players, A and B, who can either cooperate or not cooperate with each other. Table 1 shows their payoffs, depending on their choice of action. If prisoners A and B cooperate with each other, they have a greater payoff than if neither cooperate. However, if one does not cooperate, while the other does, then the noncooperative prisoner receives the highest possible payoff, while the cooperative prisoner loses out. The only equilibrium is if each prisoner does not cooperate.[3] Thus, despite the existence of an alternative that is better for each prisoner (the 7,7 payoff that is obtained if both parties cooperate), this formulation for alliances suggests that the only thing that each prisoner will do is not cooperate. On the face of it, the much discussed failure of alliances is not surprising (if failure is equated with disappointment that the best outcome is not realized).

Of course, if alliances based on the prisoner's dilemma theory are bound to fail, then each participant should rationally anticipate this and not enter the alliance in the first place. The reason alliances are formed at all is that most participants expect to get better payoffs than they would without the alliance. Thus, even if neither cooperate, they still expect to get more than if they did nothing. A manager at a firm with many alliances commented:

The benefits we obtain from our alliances are manifold. There are, of course, the direct benefits from the partnership itself. But above and beyond that, even if there are no positive payoffs from the alliance, there are other benefits that make it worth our while. Some alliances allow us to signal our interest in a particular area that might deter entry by our competitors, and others serve as important stimuli for our own internal engineering staff to redouble efforts in particular areas. Generally, the more alliances we do, the better we get at doing them.

To understand what we mean by cooperating or not, let us assume that any alliance requires something from each partner. Typically this investment is the sum of some tangible investment plus some unobservable effort. Noncooperation can arise if either partner reneges on its tangible investment commitments or shirks on its unobservable investments. In either case, in the payoff structure of the game, we would expect one partner to benefit and the other to lose.

As a conceptual framework for thinking about alliances, the prisoner's dilemma is limited to particular types of situations. It assumes that each company's best response to its partner's choice of action is the same, regardless of what its partner chooses. Thus, it always pays for me not to cooperate with my partner, even if my partner is cooperating. In this framework, it is this dominance of one alternative ("not cooperate") over the other ("cooperate") that results in only one equilibrium outcome.

This conceptual framework gets more complicated if firms engage in a series of alliances over time. In repeated situations, an equilibrium may arise if firms are able to sustain mutual cooperation by threatening to punish the rival by not cooperating in the future if the latter does not cooperate now. Experimental game theory confirms that such "tit-for-tat" strategies outperform the strategy of not cooperating in every episode of a prisoner's dilemma game. In recent years, management scholars have argued that alliances can be seen as having the same structure as repeated prisoner's dilemma games and have recommended that firms adopt a tit-for-tat strategy in their ongoing governance of alliances.[4]

The literature on alliances suggests several additional modifications of this repeated prisoner's dilemma game. A mechanism such as building a reputation might be used so that both players cooperate in each iteration of the game. Hamel, Doz, and Prahalad view the benefits of not cooperating in repeated games as increasing over time, and argue that this is especially true for the firm that learns more quickly from the alliance during the period of cooperation.[5] Their recommendation, therefore, is that firms view alliances as learning races: the key is to learn fastest so that one can later back out of the alliance at an advantage.

Our fieldwork also suggests that many firms use a similar framework for their alliances and adopt tit-for-tat strategies. But we observed that such strategies were often unsuccessful. For instance, in an alliance between a U.S.-based office automation equipment manufacturer and an Indian engineering firm to manufacture and distribute office automation equipment in India, each partner agreed to provide twenty employees to the alliance. At the outset, the Indian firm had an internal crisis, compounded by a slow hiring and training process; as a result, it sent only fifteen employees to the alliance, promising that five more would follow. The U.S. partner immediately withdrew five of its own employees and insisted that they would return only when the Indian partner provided its share of employees. Shortly thereafter, the alliance was terminated. Further interviews with managers in the U.S. firm suggested that they had not had much success with alliances. Their behavior in this example was consistent with their behavior in others; they followed reactive tit-for-tat strategies. One manager remarked, ''We are very careful in our alliances and monitor our partner's behavior very carefully. Our experience suggests that we must look for early indicators of the integrity of our alliance partner . . . It doesn't take much for our warning bells to go off.''

This example illustrates how blind adherence to the recommendations of the prisoner's dilemma concept may not always be the best approach. This is particularly true for alliances formed in the past decade, since their character has become quite different. Alliances are increasingly strategic, moving closer to the core of a firm's activities than to its periphery. Today, alliances encompass traditionally protected areas such as R&D, and there is a greater parity between the partners' relative size and contribution to the alliance.[6] In contrast, alliances in the past usually had one dominant partner that contributed much of the technology and manufacturing prowess, and another that made smaller contributions such as providing personnel, financial resources, or specific market knowledge.

Because of their changing scope, contemporary alliances tend to be more interdependent, requiring crucial inputs from all partners involved to be successful. In such alliances, cooperating and not cooperating are abstractions for, say, ''invest properly'' and ''withhold quality resources from the alliance,'' respectively. The prisoner's dilemma framework is unlikely to be the right one for such alliances since it is difficult to see how a partner can gain the most by withholding its crucial input. *It is precisely in alliances where each partner is crucial to its success that is advisable for each to make unilateral commitments to ensure the venture's success.* Thus, it is important to broaden our understanding of different kinds of alliances and the appropriate managerial strategies. We now turn to some alternative game theory views of alliances that coincide more closely with our field research observations.

THE IMPORTANCE OF UNILATERAL COMMITMENTS

Other simple models highlight ways in which alliance participants can attain the best possible payoffs. Here we present one alternative, akin to many alliances in our research, and detail how the behavior patterns it suggests are considerably different from those of the prisoner's dilemma formulation.

The feature that distinguishes the game shown in Table 2 from the prisoner's dilemma game is that there are two possible equilibriums. No longer is a company's best response to its rival's strategy the same, regardless of what the rival does. Thus, Company A's cooperation is best responded to by cooperation from Company B; Company A's failure to cooperate is best answered by a similar failure to

Table 2. Payoffs If Both Companies Cooperate

		Company B	
		Cooperate	Not Cooperate
	Cooperate	9,9	4,7
Company A			
	Not Cooperate	7,4	5,5

cooperate by Company B. The outcome under which both companies get a higher payoff (9,9) is now a possible equilibrium. The other possible equilibrium, however, is one in which both players do not cooperate. The question remains: How can we influence which equilibrium will arise in practice? Making unilateral commitments emerges as one way to influence the outcome.

COMMITMENT TO SACRIFICE

There are two kinds of unilateral commitments. The first refers to actions that a particular company can take to alter only its own payoffs under particular outcomes. What is such a unilateral commitment? It could be something like signing a long-term contract with a supplier (not the partner in the alliance, but a third-party supplier) for material needed for the alliance. Then, if the company signing the contract chose not to cooperate, it would still be saddled with the contract's implications and could lose heavily as a result. Or it could be emphasizing the importance of the alliance and commiting the firm's reputation to its success. Then failure sends a bad message to the market about the firm's ability to implement its strategy.

Examples from our fieldwork illustrate such unilateral commitments more concretely. One of the goals of an alliance between a U.S.-based software firm and a hardware manufacturer was to combine the latter's superfast chip technology with the former's new PC operating system. To demonstrate its commitment to the alliance, the hardware manufacturer decided to disband unilaterally its own internal PC software development group. By amputating a

crucial part of the overall strategy's success, the hardware manufacturer set itself up to be a big loser if it did not cooperate with its software development partner by providing it with information to take advantage of the chip's capabilities. In making this unilateral commitment, the hardware manufacturer indicated that it had every intention of cooperating with its partner, hoping that the partner would also cooperate.

If the software firm lived up to its side of the bargain, the hardware manufacturer felt that it had a good chance of making its chip the leader in the PC market. But the software firm made no such commitment in turn: it could continue to develop its new operating system, so it did not rely as heavily on the advantages of the hardware manufacturer's new chip. But since the new operating system could be superior if designed to take advantage of the new chip's capabilities, the hardware manufacturer believed that, by making a unilateral commitment, it had created a situation in which it was more likely that both firms would cooperate fully.

In another example, a startup U.S.-based firm that designed computer disk drives and a large Japanese disk drive manufacturer agreed to an alliance in which the Japanese firm would manufacture computer disk drives for the U.S. firm in exchange for the rights to market them in Asia. The Japanese firm agreed up front to pay any costs that arose from design changes. Just after the Japanese firm had spent $6 million tooling up for production, a technology shift forced the U.S. firm to modify its designs. This, in turn, required the Japanese firm to spend an additional $600,000 adjusting its manufacturing processes. The Japanese firm kept its commitment and chose to absorb the costs and respond promptly to the changes. The Japanese manufacturer's unilateral decision to pay any subsequent additional costs arising from technology shifts was an important signal to the U.S. startup of the Japanese manufacturer's commitment to the partnership.

In a game theory context, the unilateral commitment mechanism does not work according to the prisoner's dilemma scenario. In that situation, nothing that, say, prisoner A does to alter his own situation changes the fact that it is better for prisoner B

Table 3. Payoffs If One Company Makes a Sacrifice

		Company B	
		Cooperate	Not Cooperate
	Cooperate	9,9	4,7
Company A			
	Not Cooperate	7,4	4-e,5

to choose not to cooperate, regardless of prisoner A's choice. The dominant strategy for each is always to choose not to cooperate, regardless of what the partner does.

In the situation illustrated by Table 2, Company A is best off choosing not to cooperate if Company B does the same. Now suppose that Company A undertook a unilateral commitment beforehand so that, rather than getting 5 when both companies chose not to cooperate, it got something less than 4, say 4-e. Then Company B will realize that if it chooses not to cooperate, Company A will no longer respond by not cooperating. In this new situation, both partners not cooperating is no longer an equilibrium. Thus, it is possible for one company to act first to change the payoff structure and cause the more desirable outcome (see Table 3).

Unilateral commitments can be thought of as analogous to posting a bond: Company A goes to its lawyer and says it will pay $1 million to charity if the alliance fails. By doing so, it convinces its partner, Company B, that it really does not want the alliance to fail. Convinced of Company A's intentions, Company B also cooperates. The result is that Company A does not lose the $1 million and both firms derive the full benefits of cooperation. Thus, *the commitment to sacrifice something in the event that a less desirable outcome emerges can be sufficient to ensure that this outcome does not emerge in the first place.*

SEQUENTIAL, IRREVERSIBLE COMMITMENTS

A second kind of unilateral commitment is conceptually distinct from the one discussed above. Rather than acting to alter its payoffs, a firm irreversibly commits to one of the choices already available to it. Then the other company takes this into account in making its decision. Sequential commitments can take a variety of forms. As the following examples illustrate, one form is to commit resources unilaterally. For instance, in one alliance we studied, one partner gave the other the résumés of all fifty of its development engineers and let the partner choose ten engineers that it considered best suited to the alliance. The same firm also let its partner decide how to deploy the engineers and who would supervise their work. By making this commitment, this firm clearly demonstrated its intention to cooperate fully toward the success of the alliance, removing the partner's doubt about sharing its technology. The partner responded with equal cooperation, and the alliance led to the development of a successful telecommunications switch that exceeded both companies' initial expectations.

Sequential actions can also take the form of unilateral technology commitments. For instance, in a joint venture between a Japanese automobile manufacturer and an Indian firm, the Japanese firm made its car designs available well in advance of the Indian firm's investments. Thus, the Japanese firm signaled to its partner that it had every intention of transferring auto manufacturing technologies to the Indian firm and was not simply taking advantage of the low labor costs in India. Impressed with its counterpart's gestures, the Indian partner did everything it could to make the venture succeed, ensuring the joint venture's runaway success.

To further explain sequential commitments in terms of game theory, let us reconsider the game in Table 2. Suppose Company A is able to make its choice first (rather than both companies moving simultaneously). Company A knows that if it chooses to cooperate, B will respond by cooperating; conversely, a choice of noncooperation will result in Company B choosing not to cooperate. But Company A prefers the payoff resulting when both cooperate, so it will choose to cooperate, and so will Company B.

If an alliance is structured so that choices are made sequentially rather than simultaneously, a better outcome can result. What does it mean in practice for moves to occur simultaneously or sequentially? Sequential moves imply that the first company's choice is already known when the second makes its move. Then the second company simply chooses the best response to the first company's move. The first company considers this fact when initially making its choice.

In contrast, in moving simultaneously, neither company can simply respond to its rival's move because the latter's actions are contingent on its own choices that have not yet been made. Thus simultaneous moves are an abstraction for saying that one does not know the other player's choice, in the sense that one's own choice will actively influence the other's choice in real time. So an alliance that is structured so that one company moves first and is able to demonstrate its choice to the other company should be analyzed as a game with sequential rather than simultaneous moves.

Another form of sequential unilateral commitments is the promise of exclusivity. In our research, there were many instances in which one company in an alliance made an offer to work exclusively with the partner, even when it could have chosen others with comparable capabilities. For instance, some firms agreed to offer an exclusive license to their partners, when they could easily have kept open the option of licensing their technology to others. In another case, a firm committed to tendering all bids for local telecommunications contracts in collaboration with its foreign partner, even though that was not a stipulation in their agreement. In all these cases, the managers explained their actions as an attempt to demonstrate to the partner that they were fully committed to the alliance and hoped for a reciprocal commitment. We found no examples in which the partner took advantage of this unilateral gesture; in all cases, the partner responded by cooperating.

It appears as though the game theoretic framework suggested here is valid in a number of situations. In each of these examples, the firm making the unilateral commitment was always able to credibly convey the choice it had made. Thus the firm that made its engineers available to its partner first relieved them of their existing responsibilities. Similarly, the Japanese company's release of automobile design plans was an irreversible move. However, such credible commitments may not always be feasible. For example, if by cooperating a company invests heavily in research and if by not cooperating a company does not invest in research, it may be hard to convincingly demonstrate to one's partner that one has in fact chosen to cooperate.

There is something counterintuitive in one company allowing its rival to move first and thus influence the final outcome. Yet this results in a payoff that is better for both parties. Certainly, not all formulations will result in this outcome. The crucial feature is the coincidence of both companies' interests; Company B is best off exactly when Company A is best off. To clarify this, consider an example in which there is a coordination problem similar to that in Table 2, but where the coincidence of interests does not arise (see Table 4).

Sequentially, if Company A moves first, cooperation by both will result, since Company A will choose the action giving the highest payoff. However, Company B would have preferred that neither cooperate, because it would get more in that situation. This example illustrates that structuring the alliance so that sequential moves provide the appropriate analytical measure need not result in a choice that both partners favor.

The prisoner's dilemma formulation completely misses how important the distinction is between the sequential and the simultaneous dynamic. In the prisoner's dilemma context, regardless of the nature of the moves, the only possible outcome is for both

Table 4. Payoffs If Companies Move Sequentially

		Company B	
		Cooperate	Not Cooperate
	Cooperate	20,10	4,7
Company A			
	Not Cooperate	7,4	8,5

partners to not cooperate. One partner's unilateral commitments are of no consequence. Again, this points to the restrictive nature of the prisoner's dilemma formulation.

THE IMPORTANCE OF PROCESS

Managers must understand the economics of an alliance. Their recommendations for appropriate actions depend crucially on the nature of the alliance. An alliance in which the economics are better represented by one game versus another can lead to different avenues to ensure the participants' cooperation. For example, unilateral commitments play a much greater role in the formulation shown in Table 2 and play no role in the prisoner's dilemma formulation.

If we think of the two actions available to each party as "cooperate" and "don't cooperate" (which are abstractions for different degrees of cooperation by the parties), then the first question that a manager should ask is: *What does cooperation mean in the context of my particular alliance?* The next issue to ponder is *the size of the pie* that the alliance hopes to get. The pie could exist for two broadly different reasons: the alliance could be pursuing a new market opportunity that has become feasible due to, say, new technologies developed in the alliance, or the alliance could be targeted at product or process improvements that result in delivering a higher quality per unit cost. It is important to ask if the alliance is of any value if neither party cooperates. Is there some benefit to be had simply by being exposed to the partner's environment? These are indicative of the kinds of questions needed to get a sense of the payoffs in an alliance. Such questions also provide guidance in the event that there are environmental changes and the payoff structures need to be reassessed. Though the exact payoffs are important to properly value the alliance as one of several investment options, it is the structure of the payoffs that determines whether the alliance is viable in the first instance, and how it should be managed to get the most value out of it.

In addition to understanding the payoff structure of any alliance, managers must also remember that

the payoffs may change over time due to a whole host of unexpected factors. For example, when the alliance between Digital Equipment Corporation and Tandy was first formed, Tandy was to be the sole source of low-cost PCs for DEC's entry into this market, whereas DEC's installed customer base would allow Tandy to increase its production volume and achieve greater sale economies. The alliance worked well while low-cost production was the dominant strategy in the industry. However, the benefits of the alliance changed when Compaq forced the market toward a performance, rather than price, orientation. Increasingly, DEC felt it had to offer higher-performance PCs to remain competitive in the industry, and the value of its alliance with Tandy suddenly diminished as DEC now needed a partner with more sophisticated design and engineering capabilities than Tandy had to offer.

DEC sought an alliance with Intel to develop its high-performance PCs, reducing the scope of its venture with Tandy. But, in the rapidly changing PC industry, DEC was shortly forced to reassess its situation because the success of Dell changed the competitive dynamics of the industry yet again. Price again became the competitive imperative, as Dell was able to match Compaq on performance and yet offer much lower prices due to its innovative use of a direct marketing and sales strategy. To respond to this new competitive challenge, DEC created its own direct sales and mail-order organization, terminated its alliance with Tandy, started manufacturing its own low-cost PCs in Taiwan, and even moved away from its alliance with Intel to develop its own high-performance machine based on a new alpha chip.

Moreover, after Robert Palmer replaced Kenneth Olsen as DEC's CEO, there was a marked shift in DEC's strategy in the PC market. Under Olsen, the PC business had always been the orphan child; he had repeatedly called PCs mere toys. Soon after his appointment, Palmer declared his intention to make DEC a major competitor in the PC market, bringing in outside leadership. This strategic change further altered the way DEC viewed the payoffs from its alliances.

While the DEC story illustrates how unforeseen

events lead to reduced expectations of payoffs from alliances, there are times when events can increase the payoffs. In the case of the joint venture between the Japanese and Indian automobile firms described earlier, changes in the Indian government's economic policies more favorable to foreign investors and international trade, coupled with a stronger Japanese yen, led to significant changes in the benefits that both partners thought they could derive from the alliance. Their reassessment led to changes in the scope of the venture; the Japanese partner increased its investment and is now planning to manufacture cars for export to the European market instead of only for domestic consumption in India. For the Japanese firm, the venture provides a low-cost platform, whereas, for the Indian partner, the venture is now a way to earn much-needed foreign exchange.

The general lesson of these examples is that a series of circumstances, technological and otherwise, can cause payoffs to be altered. Coupled with our earlier discussion of how different payoff situations need to be managed differently, this leads us to recommend that alliances be managed quite actively.[7] It is extremely important for an alliance and its parents to adapt to changes in roles and relationships as circumstances demand. Even more so than typical organizations, an alliance is particularly likely to change significantly over time. Not only is it subject to changes in its own environments, which is usually highly risky and volatile, it is also subject to derivative changes that come from shifts in one or more of its parent firms. In a game theory context, this translates to the fact that the payoffs associated with the partnership may alter over time, thus altering the incentive structure for each participant.

Operating in such a dynamic context, alliances' very survival may hinge on adapting rapidly to any internal or external changes. Cooperation of the parent firms in such a relationship may actually be contingent on their ability to modify the alliance to meet their changing needs, since an alliance that was once important can soon become obsolete. In such situations, the alliance must be flexible enough to adapt itself to changing demands. A McKinsey & Company study suggests that such flexibility is a significant element of many successful alliances.[8]

Many of the successful alliances we studied had contractual clauses whereby the relationship was assessed and renegotiated every few years. Such opportunities were not mere legal formalities but were used at distinct junctures to reformulate the relationship and further the understanding between the parent firms. CFM International, a fifty-fifty joint venture between General Electric and Snecma, the French jet engine manufacturer, is an example of a successfully open relationship that may be terminated once it has outlived its usefulness to its partners. The seventeen-year-old alliance has taken orders for 10,300 engines totaling $38 billion. Despite this obvious success, the alliance is neither permanent nor monogamous. Each partner exercises its right to enter into alliances with other competitors and reserves the right to exit from the alliance when its usefulness runs out.

Parent firms can ensure their alliances' adaptability by conducting periodic reassessments with alliance managers. Frequent meetings between the parents' top managers ascertain the alliance's proper functioning, further mutual understanding between the partners, and realign and reorganize the alliance in response to changing parental needs.

An important element in managing the process dynamics of alliances is ensuring the open and free flow of information between the partners and the alliance. Many firms rely extensively on their assigned liaison managers or teams to manage the information interface between the firm and the alliance. In addition to gathering information, such boundary-spanning teams or individuals are also responsible for overseeing the inflow and outflow of resources, as well as managing any conflicts that may arise. These individuals must possess considerable diplomatic skills to keep the alliance together. DEC has designated ''relationship managers'' who are responsible for all aspects of the firm's relationship with specific partners. Ford relies heavily on its top management to establish concrete communication channels with the partner's top management. For instance, in Ford's successful alliance with Mazda, the top managers of both companies meet with the alliance managers three to four times a year to discuss the general and specific developments in the relationship. Such individual connections can build close personal ties and trust across organizations and provide a useful hands-on assessment of the alliance.

In addition to informal or personal links among parent firms and their alliance, partnering firms can establish formal systems to provide useful performance information, such as detailed reports and frequent presentations by alliance managers to parent firm representatives. The information must be broader than simple performance reports and should encompass the alliance's strategic decisions, current activities, and future concerns and agenda.

Information flows between the parent firms and the alliance provide the partners with an early warning system to indicate if the partnership is going askew. The alliance can provide partners with estimates of performance; simple accounting results are usually not appropriate, and the parent firms may need to rely on more creative measures. Unfortunately, our research confirmed that many firms use standardized measures of output to assess the performance of their alliances. In most cases, we found that at least one of the parent firms had standard accounting and measurement systems for evaluating the alliance. Furthermore, many parent firms made no distinctions between the alliance and their other wholly owned divisions. In such instances, the alliance managers expressed frustration at being unable to convince their parent firms of the alliance's effectiveness. Not only were such standard measures misaligned with the alliance's goals, they led parent firms to become so discouraged that they imposed stringent financial controls or, even worse, withdrew prematurely from the alliance.

There are many alternative measures of performance more appropriate for alliances. One solution that some firms in our research used was the subjective assessment of their partners, at least in the early stages of the venture. Another, less frequent, solution was to rely more on input measures such as morale, learning, and level of harmony, as opposed to simplistic output measures. In seeking appropriate measures for alliance performance, successful firms also took into account the evolving character of alliances and modified the measures accordingly. Some even used straightforward output measures once the alli-

ance had matured into a stable business. On this issue, managers within many alliances have taken the initiative and developed appropriate measures that coincide with the parent company's needs. The crucial point here is that, for the alliance to be successful, parent firms need a regular, comprehensible stream of information about its progress.

CONCLUSION

Each partner's understanding of the alliance's economics is crucial for understanding the incentives to cooperate and for realizing the possible ways each can unilaterally influence the alliance's outcome. Indeed, one of our main points in this paper is that the payoff structure matters.

We have used two contrasting payoff structures to show their fundamentally different implications for how alliances should be managed. Our framework emphasizes how various unilateral commitments, observed in the field, played an important role in ensuring alliances' success. The popular prisoner's dilemma framework that is traditionally used to conceptualize alliances does not recognize a role for these commitments.

Further, we have drawn attention to the fact that the payoff structure in any alliance changes over time. Circumstances, technological or otherwise, can cause the payoff structure to be altered. Since different payoff situations have different managerial implications, we suggest that companies structure and manage alliances to recognize changes in the payoff structure and build in explicit mechanisms to acquire an appropriate managerial style.

Most important, we have provided a rich framework for thinking and talking about alliances. In the past decade, alliances have become a ubiquitous aspect of the corporate landscape. Yet many have failed to live up to the partnering firms' expectations. While some of their disappointing results may be due to the partners' unrealistic expectations, we think some of the failures may have been the result of the very restrictive models and frameworks used for thinking about alliances. By using different frameworks for securing cooperation between partners, managers will get more out of their alliances.

REFERENCES

1. For a discussion of the many pitfalls associated with alliances and some examples of prominent failures, see: J.B. Levine and J.A. Byrne, "Corporate Odd Couples: Joint Ventures Are the Rage, But the Matches Often Don't Work Out," *Business Week*, 21 July 1986, pp. 100–105; and R.B. Reich and E.D. Mankin, "Joint Ventures with Japan Give Our Future Away," *Harvard Business Review*, March–April 1986, pp. 78–86.

2. Coopers & Lybrand study, reported in Levine and Byrne (1986), p. 101.

3. An equilibrium in the game theory sense is an outcome where none of the participants can do better by choosing a different action, given that their rivals' choices are as specified in the equilibrium. Thus, in the prisoner's dilemma example, prisoner A cannot do better than to "not cooperate," given that prisoner B has also chosen to "not cooperate." The same is true for prisoner B, given prisoner A's choice.

4. For experimenal approaches to the prisoner's dilemma, see: R. Axelrod, *The Evaluation of Cooperation* (New York: Basic Books, 1984). For applications of the prisoner's dilemma to interfirm alliances, see: R. Johnston and P.R. Lawrence, "Beyond Vertical Integration: The Rise of Value-Added Partnerships," *Harvard Business Review*, July–August 1988, pp. 94–101.

5. G. Hamel, Y. Doz, and C.K. Prahalad, "Collaborate with Your Competitors and Win," *Harvard Business Review*, January–February 1989, pp. 133–139.

6. For a discussion of changes in the character of recent alliances, see: K.J. Hladik, *International Joint Ventures: An Economic Analysis of U.S. Foreign Business Partnerships* (New York: Lexington Books, 1988); D.C. Mowery, *International Collaborative Ventures in U.S. Manufacturing* (Cambridge, Massachusetts: Ballinger Books, 1988); and H.V. Perlmutter and D.A. Heenan, "Cooperate to Compete Globally," *Harvard Business Review*, March–April 1986, pp. 136–152.

7. For general discussions on how to manage alliances, see: J. Main and W. Woods, "Making Global Alliances Work," *Fortune*, 17 December 1990, pp. 121–126; J.M. Geringer and L. Herbert, "Control and Performance of International Joint Ventures," *Journal of International Business Studies* 19 (1988): 235–254; R. Gulati and N. Nohria, "Mutually Assured Alliances," *Proceedings of the Academy of Management*, 1992, pp. 17–21. K.R. Harrigan, *Managing for Joint Venture Success* (New York: Lexington Books, 1986); J.P. Killing, "How to Make a Global Joint Venture Work," *Harvard Business Review*, May–June 1982, pp. 120–127; Perlmutter and Heenan (1986); and T.W. Roehl and J.F. Truitt, "Stormy Open Marriages Are Better: Evidence from U.S., Japanese, and French Cooperative Ventures in Commercial Aircraft," *Columbia Journal of World Business*, Summer 1987, pp. 87–95.

8. For a summary of the McKinsey study findings, see: J. Bleeke and D. Ernst, "The Way to Win in Cross-Border Alliances," *Harvard Business Review*, November–December 1991, pp. 127–136.

SECTION 5

MARKETING

Marketing and strategic planning are closely related activities in any successful firm regardless of whether it is domestic or global. Marketing helps to identify the best product/market foci for the firm and plays a key role in implementing strategic plans. In contrast to the purely domestic marketer, the marketer in a multinational or global firm must deal with a much larger, more diverse set of competitors, market conditions, and decision alternatives.

The multinational or global marketer's decisions include selecting products, country/markets within which to compete with those products, and marketing strategies for the chosen countries. Entering a new country/market means dealing with environments that can be very different from those already experienced. Even in a world that may be moving toward increasing similarities in consumer tastes, differences are likely to persist in marketing methods, production processes, and business practices. Some of these differences will be subtle and some will not.

There are many examples of global products, such as Coca Cola and Levis jeans, made possible by convergence in consumer taste. But consumers across the world are still different. In Japan, sales of rice still lead bread sales. In the United States the situation is reversed. As a result, electric rice cookers show a higher level of market penetration in Japan than in the United States. Many more households in the United States have toasters as compared to Japanese households.

In many European countries per-capita beer consumption is higher and soft drink consumption lower than in the United States. But the Japanese *do* eat bread, people in the United States *do* eat rice, and both Europeans and Americans drink beer and soft drinks. Although everyone seems to like Coca Cola, consumer differences persist. Japanese and American consumers prefer different textures and grains in bread. Many Europeans and Americans prefer different tastes, strengths, and brews of beer.

The examples above, and a multitude of others, lead to a question that has occupied marketers for many years. Should companies standardize worldwide or customize on a market-by-market basis? There are three components of marketing that managers must decide to standardize or customize. They are the marketing mix used, the process, and the activities that implement the program. We addressed this problem briefly in the strategy section of this book. We return to it now and explore it in more depth.

READING SELECTIONS

Kenichi Ohmae makes a case for considering the boundaries of regions rather than national boundaries when defining markets. He bases his case on the argument that the nation state no longer represents a shared community of economic interests or activity. The real boundaries that define markets may be regions within countries or they may be regions that encompass parts of two or more countries. For example, in many industrializing countries, economic activity and, consequently, both the consumer and business-to-business markets are concentrated in a few areas. A cross-border example might be Hong Kong and the contiguous areas in the southern part of Guangdong province in China. The Guangdong Chinese are more similar in consumption habits to the Hong Kong Chinese than to Chinese in the interior of the country.

Observing some evident decline in national and regional differences in product preference, some marketers have advocated global standardization as the product policy of the future. Susan Douglas and Yoram Wind strongly disagree. In ''The Myth of Globalization,'' they label the strategy of global standardization ''naive and oversimplistic.'' They critically examine the assumptions behind the global standardization argument. They look at program and process as well as product. Douglas and Wind conclude there are certain situations that favor global standardization and present a framework for identifying them.

Subhash Jain presents a framework for determining the appropriate degree of product and marketing mix standardization. (His definition of *program* encompasses products as well). He goes on to present and discuss specific propositions about the degree of standardization appropriate in different circumstances. They are grounded in an extensive review of the literature. While Jain formulates his hypotheses as proposals for research, they are also useful starting points for managerial decision making. It is worthwhile to compare and integrate Jain's perspective with that of Douglas and Wind. The views and framework presented in these two articles may be useful in deciding what strategy to use in a specific country as well as what to do worldwide.

Saeed Samiee observes that, while consumers usually think they shop locally where they live, they actually shop globally because products and brands from around the world are increasingly available to them. In his article, he analyzes a large body of studies that have examined the effect of a product's country of origin on consumers' perceptions of the product. He shows how consumers use country of origin information in different situations and develops a conceptual framework for assessing its influence on purchaser behavior. If, in standardizing a product, the marketer must give consumers information about the product's origin, should this consideration affect the decision to standardize? If so, under what conditions?

Gabriel Benito and Lawrence Welch remind us there is more to marketing in a foreign country than deciding what to standardize. The marketer must also devise and implement a strategy for entering and subsequently servicing the market. The authors emphasize the dynamic nature of markets and the consequent need that a firm may experience to change its market servicing arrangements over time. They present some ways of thinking that will assist a firm in identifying and managing the changes that may be indicated. Implicit in Benito and Welch's work is that a firm entering a market should choose an entry strategy that is consonant with potential changes in servicing mode. The entering firm must also therefore anticipate the requirements for change that may become evident as it progresses.

20

THE RISE OF THE REGION STATE

KENICHI OHMAE*

THE NATION STATE IS DYSFUNCTIONAL

The nation state has become an unnatural, even dysfunctional, unit for organizing human activity and managing economic endeavor in a borderless world. It represents no genuine, shared community of economic interests; it defines no meaningful flows of economic activity. In fact, it overlooks the true linkages and synergies that exist among often disparate populations by combining important measures of human activity at the wrong level of analysis.

For example, to think of Italy as a single economic entity ignores the reality of an industrial north and a rural south, each vastly different in its ability to contribute and in its need to receive. Treating Italy as a single economic unit forces one—as a private sector manager or a public sector official—to operate on the basis of false, implausible and nonexistent averages. Italy is a country with great disparities in industry and income across regions.

On the global economic map the lines that now matter are those defining what may be called "region states." The boundaries of the region state are not imposed by political fiat. They are drawn by the deft but invisible hand of the global market for goods and services. They follow, rather than precede, real flows

of human activity, creating nothing new but ratifying existing patterns manifest in countless individual decisions. They represent no threat to the political borders of any nation, and they have no call on any taxpayer's money to finance military forces to defend such borders.

Region states are natural economic zones. They may or may not fall within the geographic limits of a particular nation—whether they do is an accident of history. Sometimes these distinct economic units are formed by parts of states, such as those in northern Italy, Wales, Catalonia, Alsace-Lorraine or Baden-Württemberg. At other times they may be formed by economic patterns that overlap existing national boundaries, such as those between San Diego and Tijuana, Hong Kong and southern China, or the "growth triangle" of Singapore and its neighboring Indonesian islands. In today's borderless world these are natural economic zones and what matters is that each possesses, in one or another combination, the key ingredients for successful participation in the global economy.

Look, for example, at what is happening in Southeast Asia. The Hong Kong economy has gradually extended its influence throughout the Pearl River Delta. The radiating effect of these linkages has made Hong Kong, where GNP per capita is $12,000,

---

* Kenichi Ohmae is Chairman of the offices of McKinsey & Company in Japan.

the driving force of economic life in Shenzhen, boosting the per capita GNP of that city's residents to $5,695, as compared to $317 for China as a whole. These links extend to Zhuhai, Amoy and Guangzhou as well. By the year 2000 this cross-border region state will have raised the living standard of more than 11 million people over the $5,000 level. Meanwhile, Guangdong province, with a population of more than 65 million and its capital at Hong Kong, will emerge as a newly industrialized economy in its own right, even though China's per capita GNP may still hover at about $1,000. Unlike in Eastern Europe, where nations try to convert entire socialist economies over to the market, the Asian model is first to convert limited economic zones—the region states—into free enterprise havens. So far the results have been reassuring.

These developments and others like them are coming just in time for Asia. As Europe perfects its single market and as the United States, Canada and Mexico begin to explore the benefits of the North American Free Trade Agreement (NAFTA), the combined economies of Asia and Japan lag behind those of the other parts of the globe's economic triad by about $2 trillion—roughly the aggregate size of some 20 additional region states. In other words, for Asia to keep pace existing regions must continue to grow at current rates throughout the next decade, giving birth to 20 additional Singapores.

Many of these new region states are already beginning to emerge. China has expanded to 14 other areas—many of them inland—the special economic zones that have worked so well for Shenzhen and Shanghai. One such project at Yunnan will become a cross-border economic zone encompassing parts of Laos and Vietnam. In Vietnam itself Ho Chi Minh City (Saigon) has launched a similar ''sepzone'' to attract foreign capital. Inspired in part by Singapore's ''growth triangle,'' the governments of Indonesia, Malaysia and Thailand in 1992 unveiled a larger triangle across the Strait of Malacca to link Medan, Penang and Phuket. These developments are not, of course, limited to the developing economies in Asia. In economic terms the United States has never been a single nation. It is a collection of region states: northern and southern California, the ''power corridor'' along the East Coast between Boston and Washington, the Northeast, the Midwest, the Sun Belt, and so on.

WHAT MAKES A REGION STATE

The primary linkages of region states tend to be with the global economy and not with their host nations. Region states make such effective points of entry into the global economy because the very characteristics that define them are shaped by the demands of that economy. Region states tend to have between five million and 20 million people. The range is broad, but the extremes are clear: not half a million, not 50 or 100 million. A region state must be small enough for its citizens to share certain economic and consumer interests but of adequate size to justify the infrastructure—communication and transportation links and quality professional services—necessary to participate economically on a global scale.

It must, for example, have at least one international airport and, more than likely, one good harbor with international-class freight-handling facilities. A region state must also be large enough to provide an attractive market for the brand development of leading consumer products. In other words, region states are not defined by their economies of scale in production (which, after all, can be leveraged from a base of any size through exports to the rest of the world) but rather by their having reached efficient economies of scale in their consumption, infrastructure and professional services.

For example, as the reach of television networks expands, advertising becomes more efficient. Although trying to introduce a consumer brand throughout all of Japan or Indonesia may still prove prohibitively expensive, establishing it firmly in the Osaka or Jakarta region is far more affordable—and far more likely to generate handsome returns. Much the same is true with sales and service networks, customer satisfaction programs, market surveys and management information systems: efficient scale is at the regional, not national, level. This fact matters because, on balance, modern marketing techniques and technologies shape the economies of region states.

Where true economies of service exist, religious, ethnic and racial distinctions are not important—or, at least, only as important as human nature requires. Singapore is 70 percent ethnic Chinese, but its 30 percent minority is not much of a problem because commercial prosperity creates sufficient affluence for all. Nor are ethnic differences a source of concern for potential investors looking for consumers.

Indonesia—an archipelago with 500 or so different tribal groups, 18,000 islands and 170 million people—would logically seem to defy effective organization within a single mode of political government. Yet Jakarta has traditionally attempted to impose just such a central control by applying fictional averages to the entire nation. They do not work. If, however, economies of service allowed two or three Singapore-sized region states to be created within Indonesia, they could be managed. And they would ameliorate, rather than exacerbate, the country's internal social divisions. This holds as well for India and Brazil.

THE NEW MULTINATIONAL CORPORATION

When viewing the globe through the lens of the region state, senior corporate managers think differently about the geographical expansion of their businesses. In the past the primary aspiration of multinational corporations was to create, in effect, clones of the parent organization in each of the dozens of countries in which they operated. The goal of this system was to stick yet another pin in the global map to mark an increasing number of subsidiaries around the world.

More recently, however, when Nestlé and Procter & Gamble wanted to expand their business in Japan from an already strong position, they did not view the effort as just another pin-sticking exercise. Nor did they treat the country as a single coherent market to be gained at once, or try as most Western companies do to establish a foothold first in the

Tokyo area, Japan's most tumultuous and overcrowded market. Instead, they wisely focused on the Kansai region around Osaka and Kobe, whose 22 million residents are nearly as affluent as those in Tokyo but where competition is far less intense. Once they had on-the-ground experience on how best to reach the Japanese consumer, they branched out into other regions of the country.

Much of the difficulty Western companies face in trying to enter Japan stems directly from trying to shoulder their way in through Tokyo. This instinct often proves difficult and costly. Even if it works, it may also prove a trap: it is hard to "see" Japan once one is bottled up in the particular dynamics of the Tokyo marketplace. Moreover, entering the country through a different regional doorway has great economic appeal. Measured by aggregate GNP the Kansai region is the seventh-largest economy in the world, just behind the United Kingdom.

Given the variations among local markets and the value of learning through real-world experimentation, an incremental region-based approach to market entry makes excellent sense. And not just in Japan. Building an effective presence across a landmass the size of China is of course a daunting prospect. Serving the people in and around Nagoya City, however, is not.

If one wants a presence in Thailand, why start by building a network over the entire extended landmass? Instead focus, at least initially, on the region around Bangkok, which represents the lion's share of the total potential market. The same strategy applies to the United States. To introduce a new top-of-the-line car into the U.S. market, why replicate up front an exhaustive coast-to-coast dealership network? Of the country's 3,000 statistical metropolitan areas, 80 percent of luxury car buyers can be reached by establishing a presence in only 125 of these.

THE CHALLENGES FOR GOVERNMENT

Traditional issues of foreign policy, security and defense remain the province of nation states. So, too, are macroeconomic and monetary policies—the taxation and public investment needed to provide the necessary infrastructure and incentives for region-based activities. The government will also remain responsible for the broad requirements of educating and training citizens so that they can participate fully in the global economy.

Governments are likely to resist giving up the power to intervene in the economic realm or to relinquish their impulses for protectionism. The illusion of control is soothing. Yet hard evidence proves the contrary. No manipulation of exchange rates by central bankers or political appointees has ever "corrected" the trade imbalances between the United States and Japan. Nor has any trade talk between the two governments. Whatever cosmetic actions these negotiations may have prompted, they rescued no industry and revived no economic sector. Textiles, semiconductors, autos, consumer electronics—the competitive situation in these industries did not develop according to the whims of policymakers but only in response to the deeper logic of the competitive marketplace. If U.S. market share has dwindled, it is not because government policy failed but because individual consumers decided to buy elsewhere. If U.S. capacity has migrated to Mexico or Asia, it is only because individual managers made decisions about cost and efficiency.

The implications of region states are not welcome news to established seats of political power, be they politicians or lobbyists. Nation states by definition require a domestic political focus, while region states are ensconced in the global economy. Region states that sit within the frontiers of a particular nation share its political goals and aspirations. However, region states welcome foreign investment and ownership—whatever allows them to employ people productively or to improve the quality of life. They want their people to have access to the best and cheapest products. And they want whatever surplus accrues from these activities to ratchet up the local quality of life still further and not to support distant regions or to prop up distressed industries elsewhere in the name of national interest or sovereignty.

When a region prospers, that prosperity spills over into the adjacent regions within the same political confederation. Industry in the area immediately in and around Bangkok has prompted investors to explore options elsewhere in Thailand. Much the same is true of Kuala Lumpur in Malaysia, Jakarta in Indonesia, or Singapore, which is rapidly becoming the unofficial capital of the Association of Southeast Asian Nations. São Paulo, too, could well emerge as a genuine region state, someday entering the ranks of the Organization of Economic Cooperation and Development. Yet if Brazil's central government does not allow the São Paulo region state finally to enter the global economy, the country as a whole may soon fall off the roster of the newly industrialized economies.

Unlike those at the political center, the leaders of region states—interested chief executive officers, heads of local unions, politicians at city and state levels—often welcome and encourage foreign capital investment. They do not go abroad to attract new plants and factories only to appear back home on television vowing to protect local companies at any cost. These leaders tend to possess an international outlook that can help defuse many of the usual kinds of social tensions arising over issues of "foreign" versus "domestic" inputs to production.

In the United States, for example, the Japanese have already established about 120 "transplant" auto factories throughout the Mississippi Valley. More are on the way. As their share of the U.S. auto industry's production grows, people in that region who look to these plants for their livelihoods and for the tax revenues needed to support local communities will stop caring whether the plants belong to U.S.- or Japanese-based companies. All they will care about are the regional economic benefits of having them there. In effect, as members of the Mississippi Valley region state, they will have leveraged the contribution of these plants to help their region become an active participant in the global economy.

Region states need not be the enemies of central governments. Handled gently, region states can provide the opportunity for eventual prosperity for all areas within a nation's traditional political control. When political and industrial leaders accept and act on these realities, they help build prosperity. When they do not—falling back under the spell of the nationalist economic illusion—they may actually destroy it.

Consider the fate of Silicon Valley, that great early engine of much of America's microelectronics industry. In the beginning it was an extremely open and entrepreneurial environment. Of late, however, it has become notably protectionist—creating industry associations, establishing a polished lobbying presence in Washington and turning to "competitiveness" studies as a way to get more federal funding for research and development. It has also begun to discourage, and even to bar, foreign investment, let alone foreign takeovers. The result is that Boise and Denver now prosper in electronics; Japan is developing a Silicon Island on Kyushu; Taiwan is trying to create a Silicon Island of its own; and Korea is nurturing a Silicon Peninsula. This is the worst of all possible worlds: no new money in California and a host of newly energized and well-funded competitors.

Elsewhere in California, not far from Silicon Valley, the story is quite different. When Hollywood recognized that it faced a severe capital shortage, it did not throw up protectionist barriers against foreign money. Instead, it invited Rupert Murdoch into 20th Century Fox, C. Itoh and Toshiba into Time-Warner, Sony into Columbia, and Matsushita into MCA. The result: a $10 billion infusion of new capital and, equally important, $10 billion less for Japan or anyone else to set up a new Hollywood of their own.

Political leaders, however reluctantly, must adjust to the reality of economic regional entities if they are to nurture real economic flows. Resistant governments will be left to reign over traditional political territories as all meaningful participation in the global economy migrates beyond their well-preserved frontiers.

Canada, as an example, is wrongly focusing on Quebec and national language tensions as its core economic and even political issue. It does so to the point of still wrestling with the teaching of French and English in British Columbia, when that province's economic future is tied to Asia. Furthermore, as NAFTA takes shape the "vertical" relationships between Canadian and U.S. regions—Vancouver and Seattle (the Pacific Northwest region state); Toronto, Detroit and Cleveland (the Great Lakes region state)—will become increasingly important. How Canadian leaders deal with these new entities will be critical to the continuance of Canada as a political nation.

In developing economies, history suggests that when GNP per capita reaches about $5,000, discretionary income crosses an invisible threshold. Above that level people begin wondering whether they have reasonable access to the best and cheapest available products and whether they have an adequate quality of life. More troubling for those in political control, citizens also begin to consider whether their government is doing as well by them as it might.

Such a performance review is likely to be unpleasant. When governments control information—and in large measure because they do—it is all too easy for them to believe that they "own" their people. Governments begin restricting access to certain kinds of goods or services or pricing them far higher than pure economic logic would dictate. If market-driven levels of consumption conflict with a government's pet policy or general desire for control, the obvious response is to restrict consumption. So what if the people would choose otherwise if given the opportunity? Not only does the government withhold that opportunity but it also does not even let the people know that it is being withheld.

Regimes that exercise strong central control either fall on hard times or begin to decompose. In a borderless world the deck is stacked against them. The irony, of course, is that in the name of safeguarding the integrity and identity of the center, they often prove unwilling or unable to give up the illusion of power in order to seek a better quality of life for their people. There is at the center an understandable fear of letting go and losing control. As a result, the center often ends up protecting weak and unproductive industries and then passing along the high costs to its people—precisely the opposite of what a government should do.

THE GOAL IS TO RAISE LIVING STANDARDS

The Clinton administration faces a stark choice as it organizes itself to address the country's economic issues. It can develop policy within the framework of the badly dated assumption that success in the global economy means pitting one nation's industries against another's. Or it can define policy with the awareness that the economic dynamics of a borderless world do not flow from such contrived head-to-head confrontations, but rather from the participation of specific regions in a global nexus of information, skill, trade and investment.

If the goal is to raise living standards by promoting regional participation in the borderless economy, then the less Washington constrains these regions, the better off they will be. By contrast, the more Washington intervenes, the more citizens will pay for automobiles, steel, semiconductors, white wine, textiles or consumer electronics—all in the name of ''protecting'' America. Aggregating economic policy at the national level—or worse, at the continent-wide level as in Europe—inevitably results in special interest groups and vote-conscious governments putting their own interests first.

The less Washington interacts with specific regions, however, the less it perceives itself as ''representing'' them. It does not feel right. When learning to ski, one of the toughest and most counterintuitive principles to accept is that one gains better control by leaning down toward the valley, not back against

the hill. Letting go is difficult. For governments, region-based participation in the borderless economy is fine, except where it threatens current jobs, industries or interests. In Japan, a nation with plenty of farmers, food is far more expensive than in Hong Kong or Singapore, where there are no farmers. That is because Hong Kong and Singapore are open to what Australia and China can produce far more cheaply than they could themselves. They have opened themselves to the global economy, thrown their weight forward, as it were, and their people have reaped the benefits.

For the Clinton administration, the irony is that Washington today finds itself in the same relation to those region states that lie entirely or partially within its borders as was London with its North American colonies centuries ago. Neither central power could genuinely understand the shape or magnitude of the new flows of information, people and economic activity in the regions nominally under its control. Nor could it understand how counterproductive it would be to try to arrest or distort these flows in the service of nation-defined interests. Now as then, only relaxed central control can allow the flexibility needed to maintain the links to regions gripped by an inexorable drive for prosperity.

21

STANDARDIZATION OF INTERNATIONAL MARKETING STRATEGY: SOME RESEARCH HYPOTHESES

SUBHASH C. JAIN

ABSTRACT   Two aspects of international marketing strategy standardization are process and program standardization. A framework for determining marketing program standardization is introduced. Factors affecting program standardization are examined critically. In an attempt to establish a research agenda on the standardization issue, the author develops research propositions for each factor.

Global marketing is much on the minds of academicians and practitioners today. It has been argued that the worldwide marketplace has become so homogenized that multinational corporations can market standardized products and services all over the world, by identical strategies, with resultant lower costs and higher margins. Interestingly, the standardization issue is not new. Whether to standardize or to customize has been a vexing question with which international marketers have wrestled since the 1960s. The world went on without the issue being fully resolved. Recent resurgence of interest in the international standardization issue is attributed to such global influences as TV, films, widespread travel, telecommunications, and the computer.

Though much has been said and written lately on globalization of marketing, we are nowhere close to any conclusive theory or practice. This situation is not surprising, as empirical studies in the area of international marketing are limited. Because empirical detection requires a theoretical base, this article is an attempt to provide a conceptual framework for gaining insights into the standardization issue. Hypotheses are presented in the form of propositions. Ideas for testing these hypotheses are given. In brief, an attempt is made to establish a research agenda on the standardization issue.

LITERATURE REVIEW

As used here, standardization of international marketing strategy refers to using a common product, price, distribution, and promotion program on a worldwide basis. The issue of standardization first was raised by Elinder (1961) with reference to advertising. He stressed that emerging similarities among European consumers make uniform advertising both desirable and feasible. Interestingly, advertising continues to be the leading standardization concern (Killough, 1978; Miracle, 1968; Peebles, Ryans, and Vernon, 1977, 1978). In the last 25 years, of the 34 major studies on the subject, 14 have been on adver-

tising. In addition, almost 55% of these studies have been conceptual. Though the subject of standardization has not been researched conclusively, an examination of these writings leads to the following conclusions.

- There are two aspects of standardization, process and program (e.g., Sorenson and Wiechmann, 1975).
- Across-the-board standardization is inconceivable (e.g., Killough, 1978).
- The decision on standardization is not a dichotomous one between complete standardization and customization. Rather, there can be degrees of standardization (e.g., Quelch and Hoff, 1986).
- A variety of internal and external factors impinge on the standardization decision. Among these, product/industry characteristics are paramount (e.g., Wind and Douglas, 1986).
- Generally standardization is most feasible in settings where marketing infrastructure is well developed (e.g., Peebles, Ryans, and Vernon, 1978).

The preceding observations, taken as a whole, seem to suggest that standardization at best is difficult and impractical. However, we do know that the marketplace is becoming increasingly global and indeed there are global products. Among consumer durable goods, the Mercedes car is a universal product. Among nondurable goods, Coca-Cola is ubiquitous. Among industrial goods, Boeing jets are sold worldwide as a global product. How do we explain this phenomenon conceptually?

This article is an attempt to establish a research agenda on the standardization issue. The article is organized into four sections. In the first section a framework for determining marketing program standardization is introduced. The next section critically examines various factors that affect standardization. Research propositions for establishing a research agenda on the standardization issue are developed around these factors. The degree of standardization feasible in a particular case and its impact on performance in program markets are discussed in the third section. In the last section, managerial implications are provided.

Source: Journal of Marketing, Vol. 53 (January 1989), pp. 70–79.

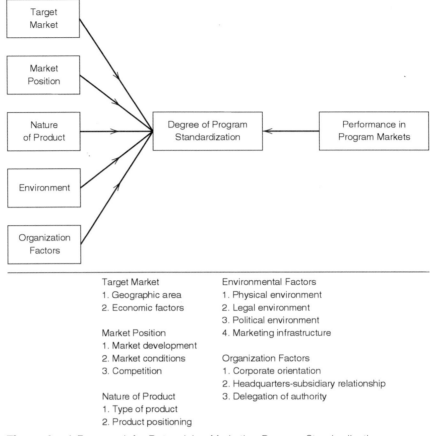

Figure 1. A Framework for Determining Marketing Program Standardization

STANDARDIZATION FRAMEWORK

As noted before, standardization has two aspects: marketing *program* and marketing *process.* The term ''program'' refers to various aspects of the marketing mix and ''process'' implies tools that aid in program development and implementation. A company may standardize one or both of these aspects. Inasmuch as the current controversy pertains to program standardization, this article addresses only that aspect.

Figure 1 is a framework for determining the degree of standardization feasible in a particular case. The following key concepts underlie the rationale for this framework.

● Likelihood of program standardization depends on a variety of factors identified as target market, market posi-

tion, nature of product, and environment. Explanation of these factors is given in Figure 1.

● Effective implementation of standardization strategy is influenced by organization perspectives.

● Total standardization is unthinkable.

● The degree of standardization in a product/market situation should be examined in terms of its long-term advantage.

MARKETING PROGRAM STANDARDIZATION

With few exceptions, most of the literature on standardization, especially the earlier studies, addresses globalization/standardization of marketing program (Walters, 1986). The term ''program'' comprises various facets of marketing mix, which can be classified as product design, product positioning, brand name, packaging, retail price, basic advertising message, creative expression, sales promotion, media allocation, role of salesforce, management of salesforce, role of middlemen, type of retail outlets, and customer service (Quelch and Hoff, 1986; Sorenson and Wiechmann, 1975; Wind and Douglas, 1986).

Advertising (ad message and creative expression) and, to a lesser extent, product design are two aspects of the marketing program that have been examined more often than others, in both conceptual and empirical studies. Future research should explore globalization of other aspects of the marketing program as well.

Conceptually, standardization of one or more parts of the marketing program is a function of five factors identified in Figure 1. Individually and collectively these factors affect standardization differently in different decision areas.

TARGET MARKET

The standardization decision is situation-specific, requiring reference to a particular target market for a particular product. Researchers have examined the globalization issue, either explicitly or implicitly, with reference to advanced countries, especially Western Europe. Elinder (1961), Fatt (1964), and Roostal (1963) considered globalization feasible because of the increasing similarity and international mobility of the European consumers. According to Ohmae (1985), the United States, Western Europe, and Japan, which constitute the major world markets accounting for the bulk of product, appear to be becoming fairly homogeneous and hence fit for globalization.

Opponents of globalization also use advanced countries as their reference point. Fournis (1962) notes that customs and traditions tend to persist and therefore the concept of the ''European consumer'' is a misnomer. Scholars observe that as people around the globe become better educated and more affluent, their tastes actually diverge (Fisher, 1984). Boddewyn (1981) found sharp income and behavior

differences between European consumers to be discouraging for globalization.

The studies cited raise an important research question: Does economic similarity (referring to per capita GNP, disposable income, quality of life) among nations foster market homogeneity in terms of specific product needs, opening the door for globalization? The following proposition is advanced.

> Proposition 1: In general, standardization is more practical in markets that are economically alike.

The point can be illustrated with reference to the Organization for Economic Cooperation and Development (OECD) countries. OECD nations, which make up only 15% of the total number of countries in the world, account for as much as 55% of the global GNP. Markets in these countries have similarities in consumer demand and commonalities in lifestyle patterns that are explained by several factors (Nissan Motor Company, 1984). First, the purchasing power of OECD residents, as expressed in discretionary income per individual, is more than eight to 15 times greater than that of residents of less developed countries (LDCs) and newly industrialized countries (NICs). Second, in OECD countries the penetration of television into households is greater than 75% whereas in NICs it is about 25% and in LDCs it is less than 10%. Third, more than one-third of the OECD consumers graduate from high school or higher educational institutions, but a comparable level of education still is offered to less than 15% of the population in NICs and to an even lower percentage in LDCs. Briefly, it is their education level (what they read and see), their television watching (their level of awareness), and their purchasing power that make the OECD residents similar to each other in behavior and that distinguish them from the rest of the world. Thus standardization may be feasible among the OECD nations.

Rather than looking at the target market in terms of rich/poor nations, it may be possible to identify segments, in both developed and developing countries, that are similar and represent a homogeneous market. Several scholars have explicitly endorsed this type of approach (Kale and Sudharshan, 1987; Levitt, 1983; Sheth, 1986; Simmonds, 1985). Levitt states (p. 92, 94),

The multinational corporation operates in a number of countries, and adjusts its products and practices in each at high relative costs . . . [companies should] know that success in a world of homogenized demand requires a search for sales opportunities in similar segments across the globe in order to achieve the economies of scale necessary to compete. Such a segment in one country is seldom unique—it has close cousins everywhere precisely because technology has homogenized the globe.

Empirical evidence on the *intermarket segment concept* is provided by Hill and Still (1984), who found that greater product adaptation was required in rural areas than in urban areas in the LDCs. This finding can be interpreted to mean that the urban areas in developing countries may have segments that are similar in character to those in industrialized nations.

As a research idea, country markets can be segmented, say on the basis of occupation, and the needs and shopping traits of a particular segment can be examined on a worldwide basis. This suggestion leads to the following proposition.

> Proposition 2: Standardization strategy is more effective if worldwide customers, not countries, are the basis of identifying the segment(s) to serve.

The significance of the intermarket segmentation concept can be illustrated with reference to India and Kuwait. Kuwait's per capita GNP in 1983 was $18,000 and India's $260. On the basis of these figures, Kuwait is about 70 times more attractive than India. However, India's total GNP in 1983 was eight times greater than Kuwait's and its population was 400 times as large. If we assume that only 5% of the Indians would have the purchasing power of a Kuwaiti, the Indian market would be 20 times as attractive as the Kuwaiti market. Thus segments for

standardization may be present in both rich and poor countries.

MARKET POSITION

Segmenting world markets in isolation of market-specific contexts is insufficient. *Market development, market conditions,* and *competitive factors* must be considered.

Different national markets for a given product are in different stages of development. A convenient way of explaining this phenomenon is through the product life cycle concept. If a product's foreign market is in a different stage of market development than its United States market, appropriate changes in the product design are desirable in order to make an adequate product/market match (Jain, 1984; Kirpalani and MacIntosh, 1980). Polaroid's Swinger camera is claimed to have failed in France because the company pursued the same strategy there as in the United States when the two markets were in different stages of development. The United States market was in the mature stage, whereas the French market was in the introductory stage (de la Torre, 1975).

The three market conditions that influence the standardization decision are cultural differences (Arndt and Helgesen, 1981; Hall, 1959; Lee, 1966; Ricks, 1983, 1986; Terpstra and David, 1985), economic differences (Douglas, Craig, and Keegan, 1986; Henzler, 1981; Luqmani, Quraeshi, and Delene, 1980; Terpstra 1986), and differences in customer perceptions (Bilkey and Nes, 1982; Cattin, Jolibert, and Lohnes, 1982; Kaynak and Cavusgil, 1983; Nagashima, 1977; Narayana, 1981) in foreign markets.

Culture influences every aspect of marketing. The products people buy, the attributes they value, and the principals whose opinions they accept are all culture-based choices (Lipman, 1988). For example, different levels of awareness, knowledge, familiarity, and affect with people, products in general, and specific brands may result in differential attitudes toward similar products (Parameswaran and Yaprak, 1987). Cultural differences influence consumer acculturation which, in turn, affects acceptance of standardized products (Schiffman, Dillon, and Ngumah,

1981). Hence, where a product is culturally compatible with the society, it is likely to be more suitable for standardization (Britt, 1974; Keegan, 1969).

Poor economic means may prevent masses in LDCs from buying the variety of products that U.S. consumers consider essential. To bring such products as automobiles and appliances within the reach of the middle class in developing countries, for example, the products must be appropriately modified to cut costs without reducing functional quality. Finally, the decision on product standardization should be based on the psychological meaning of the product in different markets (Friedman, 1986). Foreign products in many cultures are perceived as high quality products. In such cases, standardization would be desirable (Aydin and Terpstra, 1981). In contrast, if the image of a country's products is weak, it would be strategically desirable to adapt a product so that it could be promoted as different from, rather than typical of, that country's products.

From the preceding discussion, the following propositions are presented as a research agenda.

Proposition 3: The greater the similarity in the markets in terms of customer behavior and lifestyle, the higher the degree of standardization.

Proposition 4: The higher the cultural compatibility of the product across the host countries, the greater the degree of standardization.

In the absence of current and potential competition, a company may continue to do well in a market overseas with a standard product. However, the presence of competition may necessitate customization to gain an advantage over rivals by providing a product that ultimately matches local conditions precisely. Similarly, if the competitive position of the firm does not vary among markets, pursuing a global strategy may be worthwhile (Henzler and Rall, 1986; Porter, 1986). For example, if a company has a "leadership" position (in terms of market share) in both the U.S. and select overseas markets, other things being equal, it can successfully standardize its marketing strategy in all those countries.

In addition, if the firm competes with the same rivals, with similar share position, in different markets, standardization would be more likely (Copeland and Griggs, 1985; Quelch and Hoff, 1986). Therefore:

Proposition 5: The greater the degree of similarity in a firm's competitive position in different markets, the higher degree of standardization.

Proposition 6: Competing against the same adversaries, with similar share positions, in different countries leads to greater standardization than competing against purely local companies.

NATURE OF PRODUCT

Studies on the subject show that standardization varies with the nature of the product. Two product aspects are relevant, *type of product* (i.e., industrial vs. consumer product) and *product positioning*.

Standardization is more feasible for industrial goods than for consumer goods (Bakker, 1977; Boddewyn, Soehl, and Picard, 1986). Among consumer goods, durables offer greater opportunity for standardization than nondurables because the latter appeal to tastes, habits, and customs, which are unique to each society (Douglas and Urban, 1977; Hovell and Walters, 1972).

Empirical evidence in this matter comes from a recent study showing that industrial and high technology products (e.g., computer hardware, airliners, photographic equipment, heavy equipment, and machine tools) are considered most appropriate for global brand strategies. Confections, clothing, food, toiletries, and household cleaners are considered much less appropriate (Peterson Blyth Cato Associates, Inc., and Cheskin & Masten, 1985). Briefly, if a product meets a universal need, it requires little adaptation across national markets and standardization is facilitated (Bartlett, 1979; Levitt, 1988). Corning Glass Works, for example, considered its electronic and medical products to be universal products that did not vary by country. They tended toward standardization in product policy, product development, and pricing. Corningware, in contrast, is not a universal product. It must be adapted to suit various market needs. For example, the ''oven-to-freezer'' feature has been very popular in the United States but was not appropriate in France; a souffle dish was popular in France but did not have a big market in the U.S. (Yoshino and Bartlett, 1981).

''Positioning'' refers to designing the product to fit a given place in the consumer's mind (Kotler, 1984). If a product is positioned overseas by the same approach as at home, standardization would be feasible (Sorenson and Wiechmann, 1975). Tang has been positioned in the United States markets as an orange drink substitute, but not in France (where orange drink is not a breakfast staple), making standardization inappropriate (Grey Advertising, Inc., 1984). Phillip Morris, Inc., has been able to standardize Marlboro's marketing program because it has positioned the brand everywhere with the same emphasis, the Marlboro Country concept.

Future research can be planned around two propositions:

Proposition 7: Industrial and high technology products are more suitable for standardization than consumer products.

Proposition 8: Standardization is more appropriate when the home market positioning strategy is meaningful in the host market.

ENVIRONMENT

Global marketing decisions about product, price, promotion, and distribution are no different from those made in the domestic context. However, the environment within which these decisions are made is unique to each country. Hence differences in environment are an important concern affecting the feasibility of standardization (Britt, 1974; Buzzell, 1968; Cavusgil and Yavas, 1984; Donnelly, 1970; Donnelly and Ryans, 1969; Dunn, 1976; Green, Cunningham, and Cunningham, 1975). Operationally, four types of environments can be identified: *physical, legal, political,* and *marketing infrastructure.* (A

fifth factor, culture, is also important, but it is examined under Market Position).

The *physical conditions* of a country (i.e., climate, topography, and resources) may affect standardization in various ways. In a hot climate, as in the Middle East, such products as cars and air conditioners require additional features for satisfactory performance (*World Business Weekly,* 1981). Differences in the size and configuration of homes affect product design for appliances and home furnishings.

Different countries have different *laws* about product standards, patents, tariffs and taxes, and other aspects (Buzzel, 1968; Hill and Still, 1984; Kacker, 1972; Rutenberg, 1982). These laws may necessitate program adaptation. Pricing decisions commonly involve localization because pricing elements such as taxes vary among countries (Sorenson and Wiechmann, 1975). Kacker's (1972, 1975) research showed that legal requirements forced a substantial proportion (45%) of the responding American firms operating in India to localize their products to meet pricing restrictions.

The perspectives of the *political environment* of a country may result in intervention in the affairs of foreign businesses. Political interference can be defined as a decision on the part of the host country government that forces a change in the operations, policies, and strategies of a foreign firm (Poynter, 1980). Political intervention may invalidate standardization even in carefully chosen overseas markets (Vernon, 1971). Doz and Prahalad's (1980) research showed that fear of political interference led many MNC affiliates to diversify into areas in which neither the parent nor the affiliate had core capabilities. Price guidelines in overseas markets may be based on political considerations rather than economic realities (Henley, 1976).

The *marketing infrastructure* consists of the institutions and functions necessary to create, develop, and service demand, including retailers, wholesalers, sales agents, warehousing, transportation, credit, media, and more. The availability, performance, and cost of the infrastructure profoundly affect standardization (Bello and Dahringer, 1985; Ricks, Arpan, and Fu, 1979; Shimaguchi and Rosenberg, 1979; Tajima, 1973; Thorelli and Sentell, 1982).

In terms of environmental factors, no two markets are exactly alike. However, the research question is, "What is the tolerable level of difference in physical, legal, and political environments and the infrastructure to permit standardization?" This question leads to the following propositions.

Proposition 9: The greater the difference in physical, political, and legal environments between home and host countries, the lower the degree of standardization.

Proposition 10: The more similar the marketing infrastructure in the home and host countries, the higher the degree of standardization.

ORGANIZATION FACTORS

The preceding discussion explores the external imperatives that affect standardization. Examined in this section are the organizational aspects that create conditions for successful implementation of standardization strategy.

Effective standardization is accomplished through a tight linkage of the subsidiaries with the headquarters. The relevant factors are *corporate orientation, headquarters-subsidiary relationship,* and *delegation of authority.* The orientation of a company's managers toward the various aspects of doing business overseas includes such considerations as managers' attitudes toward foreigners and overseas environments, their willingness to take risks and seek growth in unfamiliar circumstances, and their ability to make compromises to accommodate foreign perspectives. Perlmutter (1969) has identified among international executives three primary orientations toward building multinational enterprises: ethnocentric (home-country-oriented), polycentric (host-country-oriented), or geocentric (world-oriented).

An organization having either an ethnocentric or a geocentric orientation is likely to standardize its program. However, in the former case the subsidiary managers may resist any sudden move toward increased standardization, considering it to be an imposition from headquarters. If the orientation is truly geocentric, however, a standardized program can be recommended without affecting the decision-making authority of the local managers. Geocentric perspectives provide flexibility sufficient to exploit standardization opportunities as they emerge and to react to unanticipated problems within the context of the overall corporate interest (Simmonds, 1985). If country managers consider headquarters' approaches to be mutually beneficial, they are least likely to resist accepting them (Quelch and Hoff, 1986).

The second organizational factor that influences standardization of marketing strategy is the headquarters-subsidiary relationship. In any organization, conflicts may arise between parent corporation and overseas subsidiaries because of their different points of view (Das, 1981; Nowakoski, 1982; Reynolds, 1978; Sim, 1977). If the conflict is excessive, it is likely to discourage program transfer. Opel, the German subsidiary of General Motors, is an example. Opel had developed into an independent organization that did things its own way. It developed its own product line and set its own policies. On every issue, Opel had an approach different from the parent's, making it difficult for General Motors to develop a *world car* using Opel as the base (Prahalad and Doz, 1987).

An interesting research question that can be raised here is whether the conflict is likely to be within tolerable limits if the organization is geocentrically oriented. Indirect evidence shows that these factors may not be related. For example, Wind, Douglas, and Perlmutter (1973) concluded that international orientation alone does not appear to provide sufficient guidelines for developing international marketing policies.

The final organizational factor that influences the standardization of marketing strategy is the extent to which decision-making authority is delegated to the foreign subsidiaries (D'Antin, 1971; Doz, 1980). Marketing is a polycentric function that is deeply affected by local factors. Primary authority for international marketing decisions therefore is decentralized in favor of host country managers. Aylmer (1970) found that local managers were responsible for 86% of the advertising decisions, 74% of the pricing decisions, and 61% of the channel decisions, but product design decisions were made primarily by the parent organization. A similar study by Brandt and Hulbert (1977) substantiates Aylmer's findings. Thus, the product decision seems to offer the most opportunity for standardization.

Effective implementation of strategy suggests the following propositions.

Proposition 11: Companies in which key managers share a common world view, as well as a common view of the critical tasks flowing from the strategy, are more effective in implementing a standardization strategy.

Proposition 12: The greater the strategic consensus among parent-subsidiary managers on key standardization issues, the more effective the implementation of standardization strategy.

Proposition 13: The greater the centralization of authority for setting policies and allocating resources, the more effective the implementation of standardization strategy.

STANDARDIZATION AND PERFORMANCE

In the final analysis, the decision on standardization should be based on economic payoff, which includes financial performance, competitive advantage, and other aspects. Concern for financial performance, in the context of standardization, has been expressed for a long time (Buzzell, 1968; Keegan, 1969). In recent years, Hout, Porter, and Rudden (1982), Rutenberg (1982), Levitt (1983), and Henzler and Rall (1986) have emphasized the scale effects that transcend national boundaries and provide cost advantages to companies selling to the world market. As a matter of fact, it is the concern for financial performance that has led researchers to stress one marketing decision area over others for standardization (Hovell and Walters, 1972; Walters, 1986). Though concern for financial performance implications has been commonly expressed, few researchers have supported their viewpoint with hard data. Hence the topic affords an opportunity for future research.

The decision on standardization also should be examined for its impact on competition, measured in terms of competitive advantage that it may provide (Hamel and Prahalad, 1985; Porter, 1986; Robinson, 1984). In addition to financial performance and competitive advantage, Walters (1986) recommends standardization for coherent international image, rapid diffusion of products and ideas internationally, and greater central coordination and control. Clearly, the topic of performance criteria in the realm of marketing program standardization has not been thoroughly examined and warrants new investigation (Buzzell, 1968; Chase, 1984; Hamel and Prahalad, 1985; Hout, Porter, and Rudden, 1982; Huszagh, Fox, and Day, 1986; Keegan, 1969; Levitt, 1983; Rutenberg, 1982).

IMPLICATIONS AND CONCLUSIONS

A model for making the standardization decision is developed by synthesizing both theoretical and empirical works in marketing, international business, and strategic planning. A distinction is made between process and program standardization. Program standardization is proposed to be a function of several factors and can be reviewed with reference to product, price, promotion, and distribution decisions. The ultimate relevance of standardization depends on its real economic payoff. Previous research has focused primarily on program standardization; with emphasis on the product and advertising areas. A comprehensive framework such as the one proposed here has been lacking. This framework is likely to be useful in future studies in directing research attention to key variables and relationships.

The framework developed in this article has implications for domestic marketing decisions, as well as the actors involved in the standardization process— international corporate managers and subsidiary managers.

DOMESTIC MARKETING DECISION IMPLICATIONS

What type of headquarters marketing perspective will help foster globalization? The framework discussed here can be used to seek answers to this question. For example, the propositions stated can be tested to determine whether a higher degree of similarity in competitive market shares offers greater opportunity for standardization. Likewise, one can test whether the similarity between markets (in development and conditions) is likely to lead to greater globalization.

An important aspect of standardization is the combination of common segments in different country markets to designate the target market. How a firm should go about recognizing identical segments throughout the world, coalescing them, and then serving them as one market is an interesting research question.

CORPORATE MANAGEMENT IMPLICATIONS

The framework implies that corporate managers can influence certain variables to create a climate in which a greater degree of standardization would be feasible. These variables include (1) establishing a geocentric orientation in the organization (which is conducive to achieving standardization), (2) balancing the objectives of the headquarters and large affiliates (because the presence of the latter affords greater opportunity for standardization), (3) providing opportunities for an ongoing parent-subsidiary dialogue for greater harmony (to avoid conflict between the two groups), and (4) encouraging an international outlook in general.

On a different level, corporate managers can reduce the detrimental effects of cultural differences between corporate and subsidiary marketing managers through a proper staffing/training system. For example, marketing managers with international background can be hired at headquarters. Similarly, a common marketing program can be organized for managers from all over the world.

IMPLICATIONS FOR SUBSIDIARY MANAGERS

By conceptualizing standardization in terms of degree of involvement and information sharing in various stages of marketing decision making at headquarters, subsidiary managers can better understand their own role *vis-à-vis* the corporate managers. The proposed framework can be used to answer such questions as ''Which group is most capable of providing authoritative information on what topics?'' and ''Which group should undertake what tasks?'' Once respective areas of strength are established, the degree of standardization feasible in a particular case can be explored.

Instead of simply implying that multinational companies should aim at standardization, the framework helps in identifying the specific problem areas. Hence it should aid in resolving the controversy on the subject and provide a much-needed base for empirical research.

REFERENCES

Arndt, J., and T. Helgesen. (1981). ''Marketing and Productivity: Conceptual and Measurement Issues.'' In *Educators' Conference Proceedings,* Series 47, Kenneth Bernhardt et al., eds. Chicago: American Marketing Association, 81–84.

Aydin, N., and Vern Terpstra. (1981). ''Marketing Know-How Transfers by MNCs: A Case Study in Turkey,'' *Journal of International Business Studies,* 12 (Winter), 35–48.

Aylmer, R.J. (1970). ''Who Makes Marketing Decisions in the Multinational Firm?'' *Journal of Marketing,* 34 (October), 25–30.

Bakker, B.A. (1977). ''International Marketing Standardization,'' presentation to European International Business Administration Annual Meeting (December), 1–21.

Bartlett, Christopher. (1979). ''Multinational Structural Evolution: The Changing Decision Environment in International Divisions,'' doctoral dissertation, Harvard Business School.

Bello, Daniel C., and Lee D. Dahringer. (1985). ''The Influence of Country and Product on Retailer Operating Practices: A Cross National Comparison,'' *International Marketing Review,* 2 (Summer), 42–52.

Bilkey, Warren J., and Eric Nes. (1982). ''Country of Origin Effects on Product Evaluations,'' *Journal of International Business Studies,* 13 (Spring–Summer), 89–99.

Boddewyn, J.J. (1981). ''Comparative Marketing: The First Twenty-Five Years,'' *Journal of International Business Studies,* 12 (Spring–Summer), 61–79.

Boddewyn, J.J., Robin Soehl, and Jacques Picard. (1986). ''Standardization in International Marketing: Is Ted Levitt in Fact Right?'' *Business Horizons,* 29 (November–December), 69–75.

Brandt, William K., and James M. Hulbert. (1977). ''Headquarters Guidance in Marketing Strategy in the Multinational Subsidiary,'' *Columbia Journal of World Business,* 12 (Winter), 7–14.

Britt, Stuart H. (1974). ''Standardizing Marketing for the International Market,'' *Columbia Journal of World Business,* 9 (Winter), 39–45.

Buzzell, Robert. (1968). "Can You Standardize Multinational Marketing?" *Harvard Business Review,* 46 (November–December), 102–113.

Cattin, Philippe, Alain Jolibert, and Colleen Lohnes. (1982). "A Cross-Cultural Study of 'Made In' Concepts," *Journal of International Business Studies,* 13 (Winter), 131–141.

Cavusgil, S. Tamer, and Ugur Yavas. (1984). "Transfer of Management Knowledge to Developing Countries: An Empirical Investigation," *Journal of Business Research,* 12 (January), 35–50.

Chase, Dennis. (1984). "Global Marketing: The New Wave," *Advertising Age* (June 25), 49.

Copeland, Lennie, and Lewis Griggs. (1985). *Going International.* New York: Random House, Ch. 3.

D'Antin, P. (1971). "The Nestle Product Manager as Demigod," *European Business,* 6 (Spring), 41, 49.

Das, Ranjan. (1981). "Impact of Host Government Regulations on MNC Operations: Learning from Third World Countries," *Columbia Journal of World Business,* 16 (Spring), 85–90.

de la Torre, Jose. (1975). "Product Life Cycle as a Determinant of Global Marketing Strategies," *Atlantic Economic Review,* 9 (September–October), 9–14.

Donnelly, James H., Jr. (1970). "Attitudes Toward Culture and Approach to International Advertising," *Journal of Marketing,* 34 (July), 60–63.

Donnelly, James H., Jr., and John K. Ryans, Jr. (1969). "Standardized Global Advertising, a Call as Yet Unanswered," *Journal of Marketing,* 33 (April), 57–60.

Douglas, Susan P., Samuel C. Craig, and Warren J. Keegan. (1986). "Approaches to Assessing International Marketing Opportunities for Small and Medium-Sized Companies." In *International Marketing: Managerial Perspectives,* Subhash C. Jain and Lewis R. Tucker, Jr., eds. Boston: Kent, 157–169.

Douglas, Susan P., and Christine D. Urban. (1977). "Life-Style Analysis to Profile Women in International Markets," *Journal of Marketing,* 41 (July), 46–54.

Doz, Yves L. (1980). "Strategic Management in Multinational Companies," *Sloan Management Review,* 22 (Winter), 27–46.

Doz, Yves L., and C.K. Prahalad. (1980). "How MNCs Cope with Host Government Intervention," *Harvard Business Review,* 58 (March–April), 147–157.

Dunn, S. Watson. (1976). "Effect of National Identity on Multinational Promotional Strategy in Europe," *Journal of Marketing,* 40 (October), 50–57.

Elinder, Erik. (1961). "How International Can Advertising Be?" *International Advertiser* (December), 12–16.

Fatt, Arthur C. (1964). "A Multinational Approach to International Advertising," *International Advertiser* (September), 17–20.

Fisher, Anne B. (1984). "The Ad Biz Gloms onto 'Global'," *Fortune* (November 12), 77–80.

Fournis, Y. (1962). "The Markets of Europe or the European Market?" *Business Horizons,* 5 (Winter), 77–83.

Friedman, Roberto. (1986). "The Psychological Meaning of Products: A Simplification of the Standardization vs. Adaptation Debate," *Columbia Journal of World Business,* 21 (Summer), 97–104.

Green, Robert T., William H. Cunningham, and Isabel C. Cunningham. (1975). "The Effectiveness of Standardized Global Advertising," *Journal of Advertising,* 4 (Summer), 25–30.

Grey Advertising, Inc. (1984). "Global Vision with Local Touch." New York: Gray Advertising, Inc. (report).

Hall, Edward T. (1959). *The Silent Language.* Garden City, N.Y.: Doubleday, pp. 61–81.

Hamel, Gary, and C.K. Prahalad. (1985). "Do You Really Have a Global Strategy?" *Harvard Business Review,* 63 (July–August), 139–148.

Henley, Donald S. (1976). "Evaluating International Product Line Performance: A Conceptual Approach." In *Multinational Product Management.* Cambridge, MA: Marketing Science Institute.

Henzler, Herbert. (1981). "Shaping an International Investment Strategy," *McKinsey Quarterly* (Spring), 69–81.

Henzler, Herbert, and Wilhelm Rall. (1986). "Facing Up to the Globalization Challenge," *McKinsey Quarterly* (Winter), 52–68.

Hill, J.S., and R.R. Still. (1984). "Effects of Urbanization on Multinational Product Planning: Markets in LDCs," *Columbia Journal of World Business,* 19 (Summer), 62–67.

Hout, Thomas, Michael E. Porter, and Eileen Rudden. (1982). "How Global Companies Win Out," *Harvard Business Review,* 60 (September–October), 98–105.

Hovell, P.J., and P.G. Walters. (1972). "International Marketing Presentations: Some Options," *European Journal of Marketing,* 6 (Summer), 69–79.

Huszagh, Sandra, Richard J. Fox, and Ellen Day. (1986). "Global Marketing: An Empirical Investigation," *Columbia Journal of World Business,* 21 (Twentieth Anniversary Issue), 31–44.

Jain, Subhash C. (1984). *International Marketing Management.* Boston: Kent, 351.

Kacker, M.P. (1972). "Patterns of Marketing Adaptation in International Business," *Management International Review,* 12(4–5), 111–118.

Kacker, M.P. (1975). "Export-Oriented Product Adaptation," *Management International Review,* 15(6), 61–70.

Kale, Sudhir, H., and D. Sudharshan. (1987). "A Strategic Approach to International Segmentation," *International Marketing Review,* 4 (Summer), 60–71.

Kaynak, Erdener, and S. Tamar Cavusgil. (1983). "Consumer Attitudes Toward Products of Foreign Origin: Do They Vary Across Product Classes?" *International Journal of Advertising,* 2(3), 147–157.

Keegan, Warren J. (1969). "Multinational Product Planning: Strategic Alternatives," *Journal of Marketing,* 33 (January), 58–62.

Killough, James. (1978). "Improved Payoffs from Transnational Advertising," *Harvard Business Review,* 56 (July–August), 102–110.

Kirpalani, Vishnu H., and N.B. MacIntosh. (1980). "International Marketing Effectiveness of Technology-Oriented Small Firms," *Journal of International Business Studies,* 11 (Winter), 81–90.

Kotler, Philip. (1984). *Marketing Management,* 5th ed. Englewood Cliffs, N.J.: Prentice-Hall.

Lee, James A. (1966). "Cultural Analysis in Overseas Operations," *Harvard Business Review,* 44 (March–April), 108–116.

Levitt, Theodore. (1983). "The Globalization of Markets," *Harvard Business Review,* 61 (May–June), 92–102.

Levitt, Theodore. (1988). "The Pluralization of Consumption," *Harvard Business Review,* 66 (May–June), 7–8.

Lipman, Joanne. (1988). "Marketers Turn Sour on Global Sales Pitch Harvard Guru Makes," *The Wall Street Journal* (May 12), 1.

Luqmani, Mushtaq, Zahir A. Quraeshi, and Linda Delene. (1980). "Marketing in Islamic Countries: A Viewpoint," *MSU Business Topics,* 28 (Summer), 16–26.

Miracle, Gordon E. (1968). "International Advertising Principles and Strategies," *MSU Business Topics,* 16 (Autumn), 29–36.

Nagashima, Akira. (1977). "A Comparative 'Made In' Product Image Survey Among Japanese Businessmen," *Journal of Marketing,* 41 (July), 95–100.

Narayana, Chem L. (1981). "Aggregate Images of American and Japanese Products: Implications on International Marketing," *Columbia Journal of World Business,* 16 (Summer), 31–34.

Nissan Motor Company. (1984). *Automobile Industry Handbook.* Tokyo: Nissan Motor Company.

Nowakoski, Christopher A. (1982). "International Performance Measurement," *Columbia Journal of World Business,* 17 (Summer), 53–57.

Ohmae, Kenichi. (1985). *Triad Power: The Coming Shape of Global Competition.* New York: The Free Press.

Parameswaran, Ravi, and Attila Yaprak. (1987). A Cross-National Comparison of Consumer Research Measures." *Journal of International Business Studies,* 18 (Spring), 35–50.

Peebles, Dean M., Jr., John K. Ryans, and Ivan R. Vernon. (1977). "A New Perspective on Advertising Standardization," *European Journal of Marketing,* 11(8), 569–576.

Peebles, Dean M., Jr., John K. Ryans, and Ivan R. Vernon. (1978). "Coordinating International Advertising," *Journal of Marketing,* 42 (January), 28–34.

Perlmutter, Howard V. (1969). "The Tortuous Evolution of the Multinational Corporation," *Columbia Journal of World Business,* 4 (January–February), 9–18.

Peterson Blyth Cato Associates, Inc., and Cheskin & Masten. (1985). "Survey on Global Brands and Global Marketing," empirical report, New York.

Porter, Michael E. (1986). *Competition in Global Industries.* Boston: Harvard Business School Press.

Poynter, Thomas A. (1980). "Government Intervention in Less-Developed Countries: The Experience of Multinational Companies," Working Paper Series, No. 238, School of Business Administration, University of Western Ontario.

Prahalad, C.K., and Yves L. Doz. (1987). *The Multinational Mission.* New York: The Free Press, 157–168.

Quelch, J.A., and E.J. Hoff. (1986). "Customizing Global Marketing," *Harvard Business Review,* 64 (May–June), 59–68.

Reynolds, John I. (1978). "Developing Policy Responses to Cultural Differences," *Business Horizons,* 21 (August), 30–34.

Ricks, David A. (1983). *Big Business Blunders: Mistakes in Multinational Marketing.* Homewood, Ill.: Dow Jones–Irwin.

Ricks, David A. (1986). "How to Avoid Business Blunders Abroad." In *International Marketing: Managerial Perspectives,* Subhash C. Jain and Lewis R. Tucker, Jr., eds. Boston: Kent, 107–121.

Ricks, David A., Jeffrey S. Arpan, and Marilyn Y. Fu. (1979). "Pitfalls in Overseas Advertising." In *International Advertising and Marketing,* S. Watson Dunn and E.S. Lorimer, eds. Columbus, Ohio: Grid, 87–93.

Robinson, Richard D. (1984). "New Factors in International Competition for Markets," paper presented at American Marketing Association International Conference, Singapore (March).

Roostal, I. (1963). "Standardization of Advertising for Western Europe," *Journal of Marketing,* 27 (October), 15–20.

Rutenberg, D.P. (1982). *Multinational Management.* Boston: Little, Brown.

Schiffman, Leon G., William R. Dillon, and Festus E. Ngumah. (1981). "The Influence of Subcultural and Personality Factors on Consumer Acculturation," *Journal of International Business Studies,* 12 (Fall), 137–143.

Sheth, Jagdish N. (1986). "Global Markets or Global Competition?" *Journal of Consumer Marketing,* 3 (Spring), 9–11.

Shimaguchi, Mitsuaki, and Larry J. Rosenberg. (1979). "Demystifying Japanese Distribution," *Columbia Journal of World Business,* 14 (Spring), 32–41.

Sim, A.B. (1977). "Decentralized Management of Subsidiaries and Their Performance," *Management International Review,* 17(2), 45–51.

Simmonds, Kenneth. (1985). "Global Strategy: Achieving the Geocentric Ideal," *International Marketing Review,* 2 (Spring), 8–17.

Sorenson, Ralph Z., and Ulrich E. Wiechmann. (1975). "How Multinationals View Marketing Standardization," *Harvard Business Review,* 53 (May–June), 38.

Tajima, Yoshihiro. (1973). *Outline of Japanese Distribution Structures.* Tokyo: Distribution Economics Institute of Japan.

Terpstra, Vern. (1986). "Critical Mass and International Marketing Strategy." In *International Marketing: Managerial Perspectives,* Subhash C. Jain and Lewis R. Tucker, Jr., eds. Boston: Kent, 93–106.

Terpstra, Vern, and Kenneth David. (1985). *The Cultural Environment of International Business,* 2nd ed. Cincinnati, Ohio: South-Western.

Thorelli, Hans B., and Gerald D. Sentell. (1982). "The Ecology of Consumer Markets in Less and More Developed Countries," *European Journal of Marketing,* 16(6), 53–62.

Vernon, Raymond. (1971). *Sovereignty at Bay: The Multinational Spread of U.S. Enterprises.* New York: Basic Books, 192–201.

Walters, Peter G. (1986). "International Marketing Policy: A Discussion of the Standardization Construct and Its Relevance for Corporate Policy,'' *Journal of International Business Studies,* 17 (Summer), 55–69.

Wind, Yoram, and Susan P. Douglas. (1986). ''The Myth of Globalization,'' *Journal of Consumer Marketing,* 3 (Spring), 23–26.

Wind, Yoram, Susan P. Douglas, and Howard V. Perlmutter.

(1973). ''Guidelines for Developing International Marketing Strategies,'' *Journal of Marketing,* 37 (April), 14–23.

World Business Weekly. (1981). ''Rolls-Royce Beaten by Canada's Winters'' (April 6), 41.

Yoshino, Michael Y., and Christopher A. Bartlett. (1981). ''Corning Glass Works International (B),'' Case 9-381–161, Harvard Business School.

22

CUSTOMER EVALUATION OF PRODUCTS IN A GLOBAL MARKET

SAEED SAMIEE*

The University of Tulsa

ABSTRACT   Marketing scholars' interest in the influence of source countries on product evaluations has intensified during the past twenty-five years. As this research tradition has evolved, the literature has gradually gained more depth and sophistication. Nevertheless, research in this area lacks a common conceptual framework. Furthermore, research priorities with regard to the role of this area of inquiry within the broader field of consumer behavior, marketing and general business decisions have not been made clear. This article rationalizes the buying decision processes within the context of source-country influences and offers a conceptual framework for further development. In addition, it links country-level considerations to firm-level decisionmaking, thus providing a foundation for meaningful managerial decisions.

In a global marketplace, the competitive position of firms is determined by many factors. One critical consideration that influences this position is the number of competing brands and their acceptance by customers. The developed nations constitute the biggest markets in the world, which annually import hundreds of billions of dollars worth of foreign products. In addition, there has been a proliferation of foreign brands that are manufactured or assembled and marketed in these nations by local and foreign-based firms. Customers everywhere can choose from a set of brands that includes foreign-manufactured or licensed products covering every conceivable product category, from foods, toys, and apparel to automobiles, computers, and industrial robots. Quite understandably, many such brands have achieved an enviable market position. Nevertheless, the marketing of such a large number of foreign brands leads to the issue of whether customers are sensitive to and concerned about where products and/or brands are manufactured or originate.

The literature in this area, generically labeled as ''country-of-origin,'' has almost invariably revealed some source-country-related bias toward non-domestic products [Bilkey and Nes 1982]. The

The author gratefully acknowledges the contribution of Terence A. Shimp in the development of this manuscript and the helpful comments of William O. Bearden and Subhash Sharma, University of South Carolina, and Steven Brown, Southern Methodist University.

* Saeed Samiee is Professor of Marketing and Director of the International Management Center in the College of Business Administration at The University of Tulsa.

implied rationale behind the close scrutiny of the country-of-origin issue is its utility as a predictor of customer attitudes and subsequent choice behavior. Researchers have examined this phenomenon for over twenty-five years. Not surprisingly, with so many studies and research designs, some have produced conflicting results (see Table 1). Marketing scholars remain intensely interested in studying this phenomenon and, as this line of research has matured, the depth and quality of projects have also improved (e.g., Johansson, Douglas and Nonaka [1985]; Han and Terpstra [1988]).

A systematic investigation of country-of-origin studies is of importance in three respects. First, much of the research in this area has been criticized for its oversimplification of the subject matter and limited or lack of scientific rigor [Bilkey and Nes 1982]. Second, only a handful of studies have been theory or conceptual framework-driven and/or linked to buyer behavior models. The great majority of empirical investigations are atheoretic, and typically consist of simple opinion surveys of students [Obermiller and Spangenberg 1989]. Nevertheless, the studies of country-of-origin to date provide a base of knowledge upon which further advances can be made. Although the great majority of the research effort to date has been empirical and has identified some key constructs and influences in this area, findings have not always been consistent. Third, if customers are indeed influenced by the country-of-origin phenomenon, then a firm's sourcing, manufacturing, and marketing plans and strategies may need to be reappraised. The globalization of markets has created complex and intertwined sourcing and marketing strategies. If any bias resulting from these strategies is present in the buying decision, then manufacturers, exporters, importers, distributors, and other channel intermediaries must pay close attention to how this affects their businesses and use proper strategies to respond to this phenomenon. Nevertheless, managerial implications of the literature are not entirely clear, and a closer scrutiny of managerial implications is unlikely in the absence of a more cohesive body of knowledge.

The purpose of this review is to delineate the domain of the country-of-origin construct. First, the concept is rationalized within the context of buying situations. Second, a literature-based conceptual framework is offered. Finally, the issues of marketing program standardization and corporate performance are discussed within the context of the country stereotyping effect.

RATIONALIZING BUYER DECISION PROCESS AND CHOICE BEHAVIOR

Consumer research has shown that individuals base their purchasing decisions on information cues. For this reason, information processing is central to all comprehensive consumer behavior models. Information cues can be intrinsic (e.g., product design) and extrinsic (e.g., brand name, price) [Olson and Jacoby 1972]. Although consumers use both intrinsic and extrinsic cues in evaluating products, the latter are likely to be used in the absence of intrinsic cues [Jacoby, Olson and Haddock 1971; Olson and Jacoby 1972; Jacoby, Szybillo and Busato-Schach 1977; Gerstner 1985], or when their assessment is not possible. For example, price may be used as a surrogate for performance. To complicate matters, it has also been shown that information search by consumers prior to making purchase decisions is limited [Newman and Staelin 1972].

The importance of the country stereotyping effect in marketing stems from its potential use by consumers as an extrinsic cue in purchase decisions. It is evident from the literature that evaluations based on extrinsic cues are more common when intrinsic cues are not readily available [Olson and Jacoby 1972; Olson 1977; Huber and McCann 1982; Johansson et al. 1985]. Clearly, the most serious consideration of this phenomenon is in situations where consumers reject a product outright solely on the basis of its country-of-origin. However, such occurrences are likely to be rare, and it is expected that consumers use a form of trade-off between known intrinsic and extrinsic cues regarding the product.

DEFINITION OF CONSTRUCTS

Since an intertwined transnational network of exchanges (e.g., ideas, R&D, product design, sourcing

Table 1. Findings of the Country-of-Origin Literature

Finding	Supported	Refuted
In general, consumers display a preference for products made in some countries more than others.	The great majority of CO studies: e.g., Schooler 1965; 1971; Hampton 1977; Baumgartner & Jolibert 1978; Bannister & Saunders 1978; Schooler & Sunoo 1979; White 1979; Cattin et al. 1982; Papadopoulos et al. 1987	Gaedeke 1973;[1] Johansson et al. 1985; Ettenson et al. 1988
This preference tends to be related to the level of economic development of nations.	Gaedeke 1973; Kaynak & Cavusgil 1983; Wang & Lamb 1980, 1983; Hallén & Johanson 1985; Lumpkin and Crawford 1985	Schooler & Sunoo 1969;[2] Schooler 1971; Bannister & Saunders 1978
Consumers from different countries respond differently to the CO cue.	Stephens et al. 1985; Papadopoulos et al. 1987	None
There tends to be a preference for domestically produced products.	Reierson 1966; Gaedeke 1973; Lillis & Narayana 1974; Krishnakumar 1974; Baumgartner & Jolibert 1978; Narayana 1981; Cattin et al. 1982; Morello 1984; Lumpkin et al. 1985	Nagashima 1977; Hester & Yuen 1987; Daser & Meric 1987
Preference for domestic products displayed by the ethnocentric group; the nonethnocentric group exhibits characteristics similar to those of "innovators": younger, educated, higher income, etc.	Wang 1978; Shimp & Sharma 1987; Han & Terpstra 1988	None
Patriotic sentiments typically increase CO awareness but not the brand choice.	Daser & Meric 1987; Hester & Yuen 1987	Han 1988
CSE varies by product type.	Reierson 1966; Nagashima 1970, 1977; Gaedeke 1973; Bannister & Saunders 1978; Chasin & Jaffe 1979; Dornoff et al. 1979; Niffenegger et al. 1980; Festervand et al. 1985; Lumpkin et al. 1985; Wall & Heslop 1986	None
The influence of CO increases with increased product familiarity.	Johansson et al. 1985; Heimbach et al. 1989	Erickson et al. 1984;[3] Hong & Toner 1989; Cordell 1992; Tse & Gorn 1993
Consumer perceptions of product quality vary for uninational and binational products.	Han & Terpstra 1988	None
Appropriate marketing strategy can change CSE.	Reierson 1967; Schooler et al. 1987	None
CO assessments are dynamic in nature.	Nagashima 1970, 1977; Darling 1987; Darling & Wood 1990	None
A large proportion of consumers are not aware of nor do they take CO into consideration.	Hugstad & Durr 1986; Hester & Yuen 1987	The majority of studies support the presence of CSE.

[1] CO information does not influence opinions regarding the quality of branded products.

[2] Areas rather than countries were tested.

[3] Although a relationship between product familiarity and attitude is shown, no relationship between attitude and CO was established; rather, CO was shown to be related to beliefs.

of raw materials and subassemblies, manufacture, and distribution) that results in the final product is inherent in global markets, distinctions must be made among the country-of-origin, country-of-manufacture, and country stereotyping effects:

Country-of-Origin (CO)	CO denotes the country with which a firm is associated. Typically, this is the home country for a company. CO is inherent in certain brands. IBM and Sony, for example, imply U.S. and Japanese origins, respectively.
Country-of-Manufacture (COM)	COM denotes the location of manufacture or assembly of a product. Although many products include parts and components from several countries, COM refers to the final point of manufacture which can be the same as CO. Using this definition, COM pertains to firms that maintain a relatively large global network of operations or do business with a variety of suppliers, e.g., contract manufacturing.
Country Stereotyping Effect (CSE)	CSE denotes any influence or bias resulting from CO and/or COM. The origin of CSE for consumers may be varied, some based on experience with a product(s) from the country in question, others from personal experience (e.g., study and travel), knowledge regarding the country, political beliefs, ethnocentric tendencies, fear of the unknown, etc.

The first two constructs, CO and COM, are factual information (though not always available to consumers) and, hence, not subject to change based on consumers' attitudes, sentiments, or biases. With minor exceptions (e.g., Tse and Gorn [1993]), the literature makes no distinction between CO and COM. The third construct, CSE, is central in the majority of CO studies and reflects customers' attitudes and emotions and is a direct result of their knowledge of, or beliefs regarding, the true or perceived CO and COM.

THE COUNTRY STEREOTYPING EFFECT

The earliest CO study was published by Schooler [1965] in which he examined the CSE among the Central American Common Market nations which might have led to an advantage for some member countries. The results demonstrated that products identical in every respect except for their CO were evaluated differently. Since then, over sixty empirical studies have been published. However, as shown in Table 1, their findings do not always converge and raise questions or refute the findings of others. About one-half of the findings are refuted by one or more studies, though typically more studies support each area than refute it.

The conflicting nature of some of these findings suggests that whether or not CSE is present depends on how the buying situation and, hence, the research design, are conceptualized. Furthermore, it is evident that at least a segment of customers might discount or ignore CO/M as salient attributes in their decision processes. In a product category such as television, for example, Sony might primarily denote a high quality product as opposed to a Japanese product. In the case of an anglicized brand such as Goldstar, the name might denote inexpensive instead of Korean. That is, inferential belief [Fishbein and Ajzen 1975] might be limited to experience with brand image and remain independent of CO/M.

The use of CO to form inferential beliefs has not been investigated. Nevertheless, some studies (e.g., Erickson, Johansson and Chao [1984]) suggest that CO/M is used to form inferential beliefs (e.g., German cars are durable, hence Opel is a durable car). In cases where the identity of a brand is associated with its CO, as with cars, it would be impossible to separate the brand image effect from the CSE. There is no empirical support, however, that this is necessarily the case with low-involvement products. For example, it does not follow that the high quality of German products is necessarily "carried-over" to German frozen dinner entrees [Obermiller and Spangenberg 1989].

It is also possible to envision circumstances where customers' opinions about a country's products are based entirely on limited, and often indirect, information from a few products. Furthermore, a negative product experience or publicity is likely to create a more powerful perception than a positive one (i.e., ''bad news travels fast'' and ''lingers on''). A bad experience with a British car, for example, may affect one's perception of cars from Britain and could possibly ''carry over'' to other products made there. The introduction and failure of Yugo cars from the former Yugoslavia, a country that was not known for any other major brand of merchandise, provides a good example in this regard. Empirical research has demonstrated that respondents are generally hardpressed to recall specific products and/or brands from various countries [Samiee, Shimp and Snyder 1990]. Out of 1,045 thoughts expressed by respondents regarding products from 11 countries, 376 (36%) were product-category related but only 55 (5%) were brand-related. Thus, CSE appears to be present even though customers' opinions regarding products made in various nations are generally inconsistent with their knowledge of products from these nations.

Unlike buyer behavior studies, which have had the benefit of drawing from a relatively well-developed, interdisciplinary body of knowledge, CO studies are still relatively new and require further development. The limited development in the CO literature is particularly evident in CO studies in which an a priori assumption was made that customers were typically knowledgeable or sought to acquire CO/M information, and that CO is a salient attribute in their decisions. This assumption clearly biases the effect size. The literature has clearly paid insufficient attention to customer awareness and saliency of CO. The findings by Hugstad and Durr [1986] and Hester and Yuen [1987] provide some empirical evidence that awareness and saliency are quite limited or nonexistent for some segments. Nevertheless, in the majority of CO studies, all subjects, in one way or another, are exposed to CO, whereas in reality they may have little or no interest in it.

The literature has not examined the influence of CO/M from the perspective of how multinational firms operate. MNCs seek to manufacture and/or source their raw materials, components, and finished products from multiple countries. Intuitively, one might take the position that the location of corporate headquarters (or a manufacturing subsidiary) is the relevant independent variable in assessing CSE. On the other hand, there is no empirical evidence for the presence of a market segment that, aside from the saliency issue, distinguishes between COs and products with single and/or multiple COMs.

A CONCEPTUAL FRAMEWORK

The findings of the CO literature (see Table 1) appear to center around three main factors. First, the presence of a set of antecedent conditions that lead to knowledge of, and sensitivity to, CO as a purchase cue. Customer and market-level considerations represent a second set of determinants and are comprised of (1) customer factors consisting of (a) product familiarity and experience, (b) level of involvement in purchase decisions, and (c) ethnocentrism and patriotic tendencies; (2) market factors, including (a) product type, characteristics and attributes, (b) brand image, (c) the reputation of channel intermediaries, and (d) market demand (i.e., sellers' vs. buyers' markets); and (3) the environmental conditions of nations including their (a) presence and influence in global markets, (b) levels of economic development, and (c) political, social and cultural standing. In particular, the level of competition and the number of competing brands in the market are likely to influence the presence and the level of CSE; however, they have not been previously examined. The outcome of these three groups of factors determines the level of CO/M bias and, when combined with other customer influences, should result in purchase decisions. Third, there are a series of managerial decisions that are generally independent of the customer choice process. These decisions include (a) marketing program standardization, (b) product image and positioning decisions, and (c) manufacturing site selection decisions. Production rationalization and site selection decisions are inherently intertwined with marketing program standardization and product image and positioning decisions. Yet from all indications in the literature, these decisions are made independently of CO considerations. In addition, CSE influences purchase decisions that, in turn, affect corporate performance. It is ultimately in this light that management must make a decision to counteract negative attitudes toward CO/M of its products. Thus, brand/product profitability is the final consideration in the framework. The CO literature has yet to be extended to firm-level considerations and these issues are discussed within the context of future directions for CO research. These components are central to the conceptual framework shown in Figure 1 and are explored in the following sections.

SEGMENT IDENTIFICATION

KNOWLEDGE AND SALIENCY OF CO

If CO knowledge does not exist, or an individual is not sensitive to CO information, then choice will be independent of CO factors, and the buying process can be viewed as a conventional one. In much of the writing to date, either implicitly or explicitly, it has been assumed that customers seek or are necessarily exposed to the CO cue. Thus, subjects are exposed to CO information and their resultant [modified] attitudes toward products (i.e., CSE) are measured and purchase intentions and final choices predicted. Furthermore, other important considerations such as product familiarity, ownership and usage pattern, and the number of competing brands that play a role in the decision process are frequently not investigated.

Available evidence, though scant, seems to contradict the key assumption underlying much of the CO literature. For example, two studies have shown that consumers are typically uninformed about the CO of products and their choice behavior is not influenced by it. In the first study, Hugstad and Durr [1986] reported that 70% of those under thirty-five years of age have little or no interest in determining the CO of their purchases. This finding is consistent with that of Shimp and Sharma [1987] who found that ethnocentric tendencies are less common among younger subjects. Later, Hester and Yuen [1987] demonstrated that 65% of Canadian subjects and 52% of U.S. subjects neither knew nor cared about the CO of garments they had purchased. If so, then there is a substantial market segment that neither seeks nor uses CO information.[1]

It would appear that once CO information has been made available to respondents, as in the case of most CO studies, their evaluation of products does change. Branded products [Gaedeke 1973] and unbranded products [Lumpkin, Crawford and Kim 1985] are viewed more or less favorably by consumers when they become aware of the origins of the products. It is also noteworthy that customer impressions of CO are often generated by indirect sources [Heald 1979; Shimp, Samiee and Madden 1993]. Further validation of these findings should lead to very different treatments of CO cues in future studies.

Accordingly, the first and the most important consideration in future CO studies should center on investigating the presence of the relevant market segment, its characteristics, knowledge of CO, and the relative importance it associates with CO cues. Therefore, the influence of CO and COM upon purchase decisions as expressed in the discussion that follow pertains only to the segment that seeks or uses these cues.

CO AND COM DISTINCTION

The global nature of businesses, the presence of multinational, multi-product corporations, and the intertwined nature of commercial transactions complicate the assessment of CSE in product evaluations. As noted earlier, CO studies have typically made no distinction between CO and COM. Han and Terpstra [1988] have made some advances by making a distinction between home- versus host-country brands and production and Tse and Gorn [1993][2] found that famous brand stereo equipment (Sony) made in its CO (Japan) was rated higher than that made in a developing nation (Indonesia). A distinction between CO and COM is critical as firms attempt to become global suppliers via central or regional manufacturing, using standardized marketing programs that include global brands and universal appeals for their products.

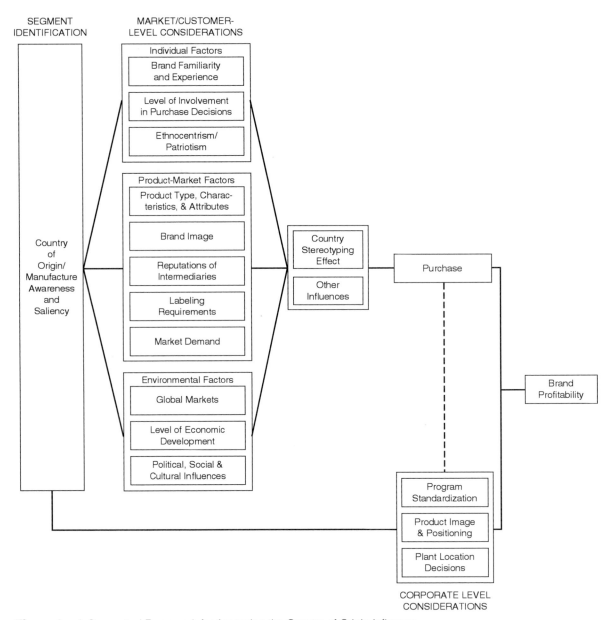

SEGMENT
IDENTIFICATION

MARKET/CUSTOMER-
LEVEL CONSIDERATIONS

Individual Factors

Brand Familiarity
and Experience

Level of Involvement
in Purchase Decisions

Ethnocentrism/
Patriotism

Product-Market Factors

Product Type, Charac-
teristics, & Attributes

Brand Image

Reputations of
Intermediaries

Labeling
Requirements

Market Demand

Environmental Factors

Global Markets

Level of Economic
Development

Political, Social &
Cultural Influences

Country
of
Origin/
Manufacture
Awareness
and
Saliency

Country
Stereotyping
Effect

Other
Influences

Purchase

Brand
Profitability

Program
Standardization

Product Image
& Positioning

Plant Location
Decisions

CORPORATE LEVEL
CONSIDERATIONS

Figure 1. A Conceptual Framework for Assessing the Country-of-Origin Influence

Virtually no effort has been made to assess the influence of the global sourcing of parts and components. The importance of CO in global sourcing is voiced by Khanna [1986] who cites an incident in India whereby consumers, in evaluating color television sets assembled in India, would open them to make certain that their subassemblies were imported from some countries but not others. Some American cars are being sourced from Canada, Korea and Mexico, and Japanese firms are producing cars in Europe, the U.S., and other parts of the world. Though this is probably known to many buyers, they may not be aware that the local content of both foreign and domestic brands can be as little as 30%. Samiee et al. [1990] found that the majority of respondents were aware of the global and intertwined network of supply sources in manufacturing. Yet, no distinction between the CO and the COM of products was made.

Since CO and COM are to some extent matters of customer perception, research must determine the nature of this perception. If a distinction between the two constructs is not made, then the location of COM becomes inconsequential as a decision criterion and the firm's job is to focus, improve and capitalize upon its CO equity, rather than to carefully select future COMs.

GLOBAL SOURCING

Although CO and COM constitute factual information, it is the customer perception of the CO/M and his/her reaction to this perception that are crucial. As the literature in this field has matured, a distinction is made between uninational and multinational products. In cases where the CO and the COM of a product are different, higher ratings for products made in the home country have been reported. Tse and Gorn [1993] and Han and Terpstra [1988] reported the presence of a more positive CSE for uninational versus binational products. The authors reported higher ratings for products made in the home country (i.e., CO) as compared to those imported from the source country (i.e., COM). Presumably this finding is not universal in that research has shown that products from developed nations are typically preferred.

CUSTOMER-RELATED INFLUENCES

BRAND FAMILIARITY

The subject of brand familiarity has not been directly addressed. However, Johansson et al. [1985] reported that familiarity with brands of different national origins affects evaluations, but does not necessarily influence perceptions of brands. It is reasonable to expect increased product familiarity to be a function of the cumulative knowledge, including CO, of brands and to expect greater use of non-CO information with greater product familiarity. However, brand knowledge by itself does not necessarily

convey product familiarity. For example, one may be quite familiar with Sony, yet not know much about its optical disk information retrieval system or medical equipment products. Thus, from the CSE viewpoint, CO information may not be as important when other information is available. Respondents' self-reported importance of CO versus brand familiarity supports this notion [Cordell 1992] and Erickson et al. [1984] did not find a link between product familiarity and CO, though CO was shown to be related to beliefs. It is thus reasonable to expect product familiarity to result from brand familiarity, which plays a greater role in purchase decisions. For this reason, firms typically extend their successful brands to other products. Thus, CO should influence entire product lines that are marketed under identical brands, including brand extensions.

It is also reasonable to expect customers to pay closer attention to COM with lower levels of brand familiarity. For example, Han and Qualls [1985] found that consumer perceptions of product quality for German-made Gründig television sets (a brand with which respondents were not familiar) were favorably influenced by their COM. When brand familiarity is high, e.g., IBM, brand image is likely to be more closely associated with the CO and, hence, it plays a more important role in the purchase decision than COM. An individual considering the purchase of a Honda may be more concerned about the fact that it is ''Japanese'' quality and workmanship and less concerned about the final point of assembly, i.e., its COM. However, when brand familiarity is low or nonexistent, as in the case of Gründig, other informational cues, including COM, will play a greater role in assessing products.[3] As noted earlier, it has been shown that the perception of product quality is affected by source country (i.e., COM) [Tse and Gorn 1993] as well as brand name [Han and Terpstra 1988].

LEVEL OF INVOLVEMENT IN PURCHASE DECISIONS

As noted earlier, in high-involvement purchase decisions, as in the case of automobiles, it is impossible to decouple brand image (and all that it might imply) from CSE.[4] Cross-cultural studies of CSE are further hindered by the lack of equivalence of the chosen product(s) (familiarity, ownership, importance, role, level of involvement, etc.) in countries being considered for investigation. Equivalence of salient attributes needs to be established across stimuli as well as across countries being tested. Consider, for example, the use of cars as stimuli for a cross-cultural study involving Japan and the U.S. Compared to the U.S., Japan has a much lower level of automobile ownership (.529 cars per capita versus .224 cars per capita) and foreign cars have a very low market penetration (about 4% of total new car registrations).

Many CO studies have experimented with well-known brands and/or high-priced products that are typically classified in the high-involvement category. Johansson et al. [1985], however, suggest that for low-involvement subjective evaluations, CO may play a more significant role, albeit no evidence is offered to support this conclusion. On the other hand, one can argue that because of the relative unimportance of many low-involvement purchase situations, the buyer may be just as likely to discount the influence of CO. Hugstad and Durr [1986] found that of those seeking CO information, nearly four times as many subjects sought CO information for cars (typically a high-involvement product) than for a product category such as shirts (typically a low-involvement product). It is, therefore, reasonable to expect CSE to vary with the level of involvement in purchase decisions, though further research is needed to establish the direction of the relationship.

PREFERENCE FOR DOMESTIC PRODUCTS

CSE has been shown to be a function of socio-demographic characteristics [Schooler 1965]. A high level of education and low levels of conservatism and dogmatism, for example, are related to a preference for foreign products. As noted in Table 1, preference for domestically produced products appears to have considerable support. Preference for domestic products is in part due to ethnocentrism and patriotism [Shimp and Sharma 1987; Han 1988] and partly due to a perceived risk in products of foreign origin. In particular, CO bias can be strong enough for a given segment that price reductions would not

affect the final choice behavior [Schooler and Wildt 1968]. Likewise, Lumpkin et al. [1985] found that perceived risk associated with CO did not depend on price. There is also evidence that industrial buyers and consumers alike view domestic products more favorably than foreign products [Nagashima 1977; Baumgartner and Jolibert 1978; Cattin et al. 1982]. However, choice behavior was not a consideration in studies examining preference for domestic products.

A study by Landor Associates [1988] provides further support for ethnocentric tendencies. The unaided brand recall survey of 3,000 European, Japanese and U.S. consumers revealed that the top ten brands for the U.S. group were entirely domestic brands. With the exception of Coca-Cola, which was shared by all three groups, the European and the Japanese groups also stuck to their own brands. On the other hand, research by Daser and Meric [1987] and Hester and Yuen [1987] suggests that patriotic advertising and CO cues do not generally influence the final choice. Thus, a preference for domestic products does not necessarily result in the purchase of such products.

PRODUCT- AND MARKET-LEVEL INFLUENCES

PRODUCT TYPE

CSE has been shown to vary by product type [Reierson 1966; Nagashima 1970, 1977; Dornoff, Tankersley and White 1979; Niffenegger, White and Marmet 1980; Festervand, Lumpkin and Lundstrom 1985; Roth and Romeo 1992]. Also, Hugstad and Durr [1986] found that the respondents' search for CO information varied by product type. The emphasis on CO/M by product type is understandable. Some nations are famous for their expertise in producing certain types of goods, such as French wines and perfumes, and hence, there tends to be a preference for some products from a nation but not others.

An important consideration in CO studies is the use of branded products. Some of the product-type findings in the CO literature are based on the use of branded products. Since some brands and their COs are inseparable, it is essential to separate the influence of product category from brand image in order to obtain unbiased estimates of CSE. When CO studies employ well-known brands, the findings are likely to be brand specific. In an interesting design used by Johansson et al. [1985], the authors bypassed CO as a cue and let the brand names of their stimuli be indicative of the origins of their products. Although this approach is quite useful for assessing CSE for well-known global brands, no information regarding the subjects' knowledge of CO of cars used in the study was furnished. The downside of using this approach is that CO cannot be decoupled from the brand itself and, from this perspective, the external validity of the findings is open to question. Nevertheless, a linkage of products and brands to CSE in future CO research effort is critical.

INDUSTRIAL PRODUCTS

Industrial buyers tend to be better informed about their purchases than consumers and their decision processes are typically policy-driven and rationalized. Furthermore, they exhibit repeat purchase patterns that lead to a more accurate and broader information base about manufacturers and greater product familiarity and experience than is the case for consumers. Thus, industrial buyers' use of CO/M cues is likely to be linked to their more frequent experience with manufacturers and their sourcing countries. In other words, industrial buyers possess a richer cognitive structure regarding CO/M based on a wealth of experience and information and, as compared to consumers, their use of CO/M cues is more likely to be rational than emotional. It is then expected that the use of CO/M is moderated by buyer role, with industrial buyers using these cues more rationally than consumers, so a comparison between industrial buyers and consumers with regard to their knowledge base should be critical consideration in future research efforts.

Despite the rational nature of industrial purchasing patterns, empirical evidence has demonstrated the presence of CO bias among industrial buyers [Greer 1971; White and Cundiff 1978; Cattin et al.

1979; Niffenegger 1980; Crawford and Lamb 1981]. Thus, there may be two opposing forces at work in industrial purchasing decisions. On the one hand, the greater information base possessed by industrial buyers coupled with their policy-driven purchasing practice could lead to greater sensitivity to the attributes of various products and, hence, their association with their respective COMs (e.g., the precision of German machine tools or the accuracy of Swiss measurement devices). On the other hand, industrial buyers have been shown to exhibit CO bias in evaluating industrial products. If so, then industrial buyers are expected to use CO cues less than consumers. Conversely, because of industrial buyers' greater knowledge regarding products and their source countries (i.e., COMs), they are more likely to associate intrinsic product cues with their COMs. Thus, it is reasonable to expect industrial buyers to use COM more (or use CO less) than consumers.

PRODUCT ATTRIBUTES

Empirical evidence suggests that it might be more relevant to emphasize product attributes instead of general national product attitudes in assessing CSE and predicting choice behavior [Etzel and Walker 1974; Johansson et al. 1985]. CSE is likely to be multidimensional in nature and its influence is likely to span the range of all salient product-attributes to varying degrees. CO and COM can potentially influence the customer's perception of quality, performance, design, aesthetics, prestige, price, etc., differently. A Swiss watch or a German camera made in the Far East may not be rated as high along some product attributes (e.g., quality) as those made in Switzerland and Germany; whereas, it might receive the same rating for an attribute like design. If CSE toward cars is the subject of investigation, German brands may conceivably have a higher rating for quality but a lower score for design than Italian and British cars. There is only scant evidence regarding the multidimensionality of CO [Lawrence, Marr and Prendergast 1992]. Thus, the appropriateness of the use of CSE measures for countries or product classes as a whole is open to question. To the extent that CSE is multidimensional in nature, separate product attribute weights might have to be developed for each CO/M under consideration.

THE INFLUENCE OF BRAND IMAGE

An important consideration in investigating the influence of CO is the process through which customers become familiar with or form an opinion regarding the CO of products. As with other intrinsic and extrinsic cues, customer groups who seek CO information are likely to be getting these data from several sources. Brand name, for example, is sometimes used to infer a CO. That is, the reputation of some countries appears to enhance the credibility of product groups for which the country is known. Also, the use of a brand name that implies a CO, e.g., Sony, will strengthen the desired image or source association. France and Italy, for example, have positive country-images for their fashion and food products [Lumpkin et al. 1985; Samiee et al. 1990], and The Limited, Inc., has used Forenza and Paul et Duffier brands to capitalize on these images. LeSeur brand frozen vegetables and Prego spaghetti sauce are among many foreign-sounding brands intended to develop specific CO images.

Some mature and well-known brands, such as IBM, Mercedes, or Sony, inherently contain CO information and the two cannot be decoupled from one another. In general, large-ticket items fall into this category, yet much of the research dealing with brands has used such branded products which, in turn, has made it virtually impossible to assure that a residual CO effect has not spilled over in the experimental setting (e.g., Johansson and Nebenzahl [1986]; Han and Terpstra [1988]; Tse and Gorn [1993]). On the other hand, some brands have had the benefit of being considered ''domestic'' in more than one country. For decades, Singer was considered a German enterprise by Germans, a U.K.-based firm in the U.K., and an American firm in the U.S. Thus, considerable forethought should precede the use of well-known brands in CO research.

The presence of many powerful domestic and foreign brands is likely to influence and possibly diminish the significance of CO. Gaedeke [1973] suggests that the informational value of brand name out-weighs the impact of CO. Within the context of their research design, Tse and Gorn [1993], however, have refuted the notion that a strong global brand can overcome a negative CO bias. Likewise, Hampton [1977] reported a lower level of perceived risk for some products manufactured abroad, even though he found a general increase in risk associated with imported products, and Gaedeke [1973] found that CO information did not significantly affect opinions regarding the quality of branded products. Therefore, it is conceivable that brand reputation and penetration may be more important than CO [Bilkey and Nes 1982].

REPUTATION OF INTERMEDIARIES

The customer satisfaction policies of distributors and retailers are aimed at reducing perceived risk associated with purchases. Sears, Kmart, JC Penney, Bloomingdale's, and many other retailers and distributors use their acceptance, reach, and/or prestige to market a variety of domestic and imported products, often under private brands. Reierson [1967] found that the use of a prestigious retailer (Neiman-Marcus) positively influenced attitudes toward Italian, but not Japanese, products. Other scant evidence [Chao 1989] suggests that the retailer's name improves sales of products from countries with negative CO bias. Thus, it would be reasonable to expect an inverse relationship between the reputation of retailers and CSE.

LABELING REQUIREMENT

An important and accurate source of CO/M information for the majority of brands in the market is the label on the product. Country-of-manufacture labeling is not required by all countries and for all products. Where nations possess a positive CO image with regard to one or more product attributes, such as product quality in Germany, firms may label their products with the CO to take advantage of this image as a part of their marketing strategy.[5]

It is apparent that countries develop an image over time based on the reputation of the products they export. The use of country-labels to take advantage of a positive country-image is analogous to the brand extension strategy whereby successful brand names are extended to new products. In much the same way as firms capitalize on their brand equity, they can also exploit their "country equity" [Shimp et al. 1993]. CO labeling is thus used as a strategic tool to profit from country-equity and enhance one or more product attributes.

Even when COM labeling is required, as in the U.K. and the U.S., it is quite possible that the local content which is attributable to the country stated on the label is very small. A small New Jersey importer of surgical scissors, for example, sources its scissors from Pakistan and sends them through a polishing process in the U.S. to improve their quality and appearance. The scissors are subsequently labeled "Made in U.S.A.," a practice which apparently is within the law.[6] Major Swiss watches and German cameras are also put together in such places as Mauritius and Macau. For this reason, some manufacturers go to great lengths to emphasize the CO of their products. Some point out that it is "assembled in . . . ," others go so far as indicating "assembled in . . ." from "U.S. made . . . (components/raw materials)." Thus, the roles of CO and COM labeling in decision processes need to be clarified.

The influence of labeling laws on CSE is likely to become more complicated in integrated markets. The EC Commission, for example, is working to remove CO/M labeling requirements so as to minimize any CSE that might influence purchase decisions within the EC. If this ruling is accepted and enforced by the Parliament, the role of COM in purchase decisions will be reduced and, when CSE is present, CO will influence choice behavior only to the extent that it is reflected in brand names.

MARKET DEMAND

The influence of CSE is likely to vary from country to country depending on the level of competition and the supply level in local markets. Two possible scenarios are conceivable. First, in a sellers' market, particularly for basic staples and necessities, CO and COM may not be relevant considerations since demand exceeds the available supply. This is especially true if free market entry has been curtailed by the government. The majority of developing countries maintain at least some import and foreign exchange restrictions that significantly affect the availability of foreign products. Although it can be argued that some degree of CSE might exist everywhere, CO/M may only be of greater concern in the developed markets where an abundant supply of domestic and imported merchandise is offered. Second, it can be argued that the limited availability of foreign products, particularly in developing nations, may actually enhance their perceived value, i.e., there is a greater influence of CO/M in these sellers' markets. Neither of these scenarios has been investigated in the literature.

ENVIRONMENTAL INFLUENCES

THE INFLUENCE OF GLOBAL MARKETS

To the extent that markets are global, the CO may be less important in the choice process and behavior than other considerations. In an era of global sourcing, manufacturing and marketing, coupled with a better informed audience influenced with increased levels of global communications, it is increasingly difficult to precisely define the CO of products and measure its impact on the choice processes of various customer segments. Nowadays, multinational collaboration for product research, design, sourcing, and manufacturing is the norm. In the case of well-known brands such as IBM, customers are not likely to care about the COM of their products. Less known industrial and consumer brands manufactured and sold in second or third countries, however, are more likely to be scrutinized with regard to the COM of their products [Kaynak and Cavusgil 1983; Khanna 1986].

THE LEVEL OF ECONOMIC DEVELOPMENT

Several studies have concluded that consumers typically view foreign products from developed countries more favorably [Schooler 1971; Tongberg 1972; Gaedeke 1973; Krishnakumar 1974; Hampton

1977; Wang and Lamb 1983; Cordell 1992]. Two other studies using macro-measures of economic and political systems of nations conclude that both variables significantly affect consumers' choice [Wang 1978; Wang and Lamb 1980, 1983]. Other evidence suggests a strong bias towards products from Eastern European nations, even though their level of development might have suggested otherwise [Schooler 1971; Bannister and Saunders 1978]. In addition, Schooler and Sunoo [1969] found no bias towards imports from the four ''areas'' studied. Also, Lumpkin and Crawford [1985] found that the respondents actually favored apparel made in the cluster of nations comprised of Hong Kong, Mexico, Singapore, South Korea, and Taiwan.

POLITICAL, CULTURAL AND SOCIAL INFLUENCES

A country's image is likely to be a function of many influences. Although some measures (e.g., GNP per capita, level and types of exports and imports, the presence of a convertible currency) are related to the level of economic development, many are not. Political and military hostility, nationalistic attitudes, local customs, music, food, costumes, and tourist attractions have nothing to do with the level of development, yet they all influence a country's image and equity [Shimp et al. 1993]. In general, environmental traits have been shown to be related to a preference for foreign products [Wang and Lamb 1983].

Political events combined with the varying levels of economic and technological development further complicate the CSE issue. For example, Hallén and Johanson [1985] demonstrated a preference for products from affluent nations. The authors found German and Swedish products to be more desirable than those originating in Great Britain or Italy.

A negative country image can affect buyers' perceptions toward products made in a given country for at least some segments of potential markets. Such perceptions, however, are not always influenced by the level of economic development of nations. Rather, they are caused by differences in cultural and political ideologies, history, military action, etc. Samiee et al. [1990], for example, indicate that out

of a total of 1,369 unaided country-thoughts expressed by their sample of respondents, only 44 (3%) were related to products or their attributes. When products from a specific country are ruled out by one or more market segments because of their level of development, political system, humanitarian, or philosophical reasons, other attributes of the products may not matter much. That is, the choice process may work in a conjunctive fashion. For these groups of customers, CO is consequential only when a product is made by a specific country(ies) that they hold in contempt, thus CO is not being used to infer belief. In addition, nationalism and protectionist attitudes in many parts of the developed world, as in Europe and Japan, still hinder free trade and acceptance of foreign manufactured products [Ball 1983; Samiee and Mayo 1990].

Since political, cultural, social, and, in particular, economic conditions change over time, the relative influence of CO is also likely to change. Although CO is typically treated as a static construct, even over relatively short periods its influence can change significantly. The shift in the reputation of Japan as a supplier of cheap and low-quality products to that of a supplier of high-quality products as noted by Nakanishi [1981] and Nagashima [1977] provides an excellent example of this change. These findings point to the dynamic nature of product attributes as well as the influences of CO and COM. A significant drop in the price of gas, for example, can change the attitude of car buyers toward bigger cars, since the efficiency factor as measured by miles-per-gallon will be a less important consideration. Customer preference for products from Russia and Iran changes with the political climate in these nations. In fact, public opinion towards these nations changed almost overnight.

The dynamic nature of CO/M is evident from the findings of three studies. Nagashima [1977] reported that the Japanese respondents' perception of attributes of Japanese and German products had changed significantly, implying a relative decline for the position of U.S.-made goods in an eight-year period between his two data collection periods. Also two longitudinal studies by Darling [1987] and Darling and Wood [1990] indicate that Finnish perceptions of

Japanese products improved significantly over ten years. Furthermore, this improvement was significantly greater than that achieved by U.S. products.

CSE AND CORPORATE-LEVEL CONSIDERATIONS

STANDARDIZATION OF MARKETING PROGRAMS

An important consideration, particularly for multinational firms, is the influence of CO/M upon their ability to standardize their marketing programs. This issue too has not been raised in the CO literature, but warrants close scrutiny. A large body of literature on marketing standardization has evolved over the years. Though many critical issues pertaining to standardization remain largely unresolved, there is a general belief that greater efficiencies might be achieved through the standardization of global marketing activities [Sorenson and Wiechmann 1975; Levitt 1983; Jain 1989]. Global firms typically rationalize their manufacturing, warehousing and marketing activities on a global (or, at the very least, regional) basis to meet market demand and to optimize coordination and control of various functions [Samiee and Carapellotti 1984]. Increased consolidation of global manufacturing and standardization of marketing activities result in products being sourced from fewer (but presumably larger) manufacturing facilities located in fewer countries, thus exposing the firm to a greater risk of facing CSE.

Successful standardization of marketing activities is dependent on a high level of rationalization, coordination, and control of various sourcing, manufacturing and marketing activities. Well-managed global firms source from fewer manufacturing facilities than multidomestic firms, which rely on more regional or localized manufacturing and can therefore modify or even customize to local market preferences.[7] IBM, for example, sources its personal systems for all of Europe, the Middle East and Africa from Scotland. If some markets preferred a system from one country and a second and a third market

favored the same product made in a second and a third country, production and distribution would become a corporate nightmare.

PRODUCT IMAGE AND POSITIONING

Research seems to indicate that consumers from different countries respond differently to CO cues [Papadopoulos et al. 1987]. If firms were to establish manufacturing facilities in more markets to evade or reduce CSE risk, the benefits and the economies offered by marketing program standardization would erode. Naturally, the marketing variable most affected by standardization is the product, but changes in the product may necessitate modifications in other aspects of the marketing program, notably the promotion aspects. An increasing number of firms are developing standardized positioning and communications for their global markets. If the foreign sourced product and/or the global position envisioned for it include elements that heighten CSE, then different strategies must be developed for various markets. In part, this might explain why some firms acquire and retain local brands (e.g., Magnavox by Philips, Quasar by Matsushita).[8]

The presence of these conditions implies that when significant negative CSE is present, other variables of the marketing plan, most notably the promotional elements, should be used to respond to existing conditions in given markets. Country managers generally use some localized promotional programs even when a standardized program is implemented. Tailor-made promotional programs involve additional expenditures and are typically the antithesis of a standardized marketing program, but such cost increases will be nominal compared to the competitive disadvantages that might result from selecting suboptimal sites.

PLANT LOCATION DECISIONS

The location of assembly or manufacturing facilities in foreign direct investment (FDI) decisions is generally made without explicit consideration of the CO issue. There is no evidence in the FDI literature that the CO of products is an explicit factor in site selection decisions. Interestingly, it has been suggested that firms should assess the presence of CSE and circumvent it by avoiding FDI in areas for which there is a strong bias (e.g., Johansson and Nebenzahl [1986]; Han and Terpstra [1988]). Yet, some important FDI considerations are likely to lead to increased levels of CSE. Low-cost labor, for example, is typically available in less developed or industrializing nations for which there is greater likelihood of encountering negative CSE than in industrialized nations (e.g., Gaedeke [1973]; Kaynak and Cavusgil [1983]; Wang and Lamb [1980, 1983]; Hallén and Johanson [1985]; Lumpkin and Crawford [1985]).

CORPORATE PERFORMANCE

From a corporate perspective, the most important consideration is whether CSE is strong enough to affect its performance in its various markets. Naturally, when CSE is positive, it provides the firm with a strategic advantage in its marketing plan. However, it is not entirely clear what level of negative CSE has negligible influence on performance and how high levels of negative CSE might be planned for or treated. The influence of CSE upon performance has not been examined in the literature. It would appear that the performance of some firms is not affected by CSE. Large apparel retailers, such as The Limited and The Gap, concurrently contract identical private-label designs to suppliers in several countries and their performance is among the best in the industry. Thus, meaningful analyses of the impact of CSE on performance should have to account for both industry- and firm-related influences.

DIRECTIONS FOR FUTURE RESEARCH

Bilkey and Nes [1982] have enumerated three short-comings in the CO literature (the use of a single cue, the verbal descriptions of products, and the validity and reliability of measurement scales used) which should be avoided in future research. Four additional observations in the CO literature can assist in the fine-tuning of future investigations. First, much of the past research has relied on nonrepresentative,

nonrandom samples, often using student subjects. Thus, the external validity of their findings is open to question. Second, some cross-cultural comparisons have relied on foreign students in the U.S. from one or more nations who responded to the questions in the same English version of the questionnaire. The assumption that foreign students in the U.S. necessarily act in the same manner as the broader populations of their respective countries is weak and unsubstantiated. Also, the use of a single research instrument for all subjects is likely to violate one or more tests of equivalence in cross-cultural studies [Green and White 1976; Mayer 1978]. Third, some studies have involved the assessment of attitudes toward products made in many countries. Wall and Heslop [1986], for example, examined attitudes toward nineteen nations. The validity of using such a wide range of countries, particularly nations that typically do not export consumer products (e.g., Romania) may be open to question as respondents have little or no knowledge regarding the countries or their products [Samiee et al. 1990]. Fourth, it is imperative that future research integrate CO in the broader perspectives of buyer behavior and managerial decisionmaking with the realization that the marketing manager has little say with regards to the location of the manufacturing or sourcing of products. The model in Figure 1 provides a good basis upon which future studies might be based.

IMPLICATIONS AND CONCLUSIONS

The developed markets consume a very large share of the world's total exports. In 1990, for example, the U.S. alone imported more than any other nation; i.e., 18% of the world's total non-U.S. exports. This figure is about twice as much as for other countries except West Germany and Japan. In relative terms, however, imports represent a smaller percentage of the GNP in the U.S. than in most other industrial countries. That is, customers in other developed countries are faced with a much larger pool of imported brands and products. Concurrently, most other developed nations are in closer proximity to each other and are more exposed to cultures, languages and the media of other countries. Therefore, empirical results of CSE studies obtained in one country are not necessarily applicable elsewhere. A whole host of variables such as education, travel, abundant supply of multiple brands in every product category, labeling laws, general predisposition of the population towards foreign manufactured goods, and many others must be considered in order to achieve universal validity.

Furthermore, the majority of the empirical research assessing CSE has been conducted in the United States where COM labeling is required and it is a buyers' market with an abundance of alternative brands from which to choose. Thus, the identification of CO/M by customers has not been a problem. On the other hand, the U.S. is a relatively high-income nation with well-established distribution and retailing structures that emphasize customer satisfaction. These conditions influence the perceived risk associated with CSE differently in the U.S. compared to other nations [Lumpkin et al. 1985]. There are simply too many intervening considerations that are yet to be accounted for. In this article, an attempt has been made to address these considerations by using the findings in the literature and by developing a framework to assess more accurately the presence of CSE and its relationship to other relevant variables.

Unquestionably, priority in CO research should be given to establishing its importance and saliency in customer evaluations and subsequent choice. In addition, CO has frequently been studied independently of information acquisition and buyer behavior models. The integration of CSE into the existing body of literature will significantly enhance its validity and practical utility. An equally important consideration is the influence of CSE on performance. If CSE cannot be shown to influence corporate performance, the issue becomes inconsequential. Once these requirements are met, research findings must enter the planning and decisionmaking phases. Thus, a critical consideration for future research is the integration of CSE findings in business and marketing plans in a management-oriented fashion.

NOTES

1.   There is no mention in the literature of the relevance and the role of CSE in segmenting a firm's market. However, given the state of the art in CO research, it would be inappropriate to use CSE as a primary construct for delineating market segments. The use of CSE as one of the variables for segmenting the market requires (a) a proof of its presence and (b) that the target markets meet the theoretical and managerial underpinning required of any segmentation strategy.

2.   This study did not control for the country's level of development, which has been shown to influence CO bias.

3.   Within the context of global manufacturing and marketing of products, as brand familiarity decreases, the distinction between CO and COM becomes increasingly difficult. In part, this results from the great majority of national labeling laws that require only the made-in information to be displayed on the products, and in part due to a proclivity to rely more on COM when less information about CO and the brand is made available. Thus, it is the examination of the relative roles of COM (i.e., goods produced in host or third nations) and CO in low brand familiarity situations that is of interest.

4.   Though the level of involvement in purchase decisions is not always a function of the product under consideration, many CO studies have focussed on product categories such as cars that, at least in the U.S., are high-involvement. Naturally, levels of involvement in purchase decisions for products vary across countries. Thus, the choice of product categories to be tested is critical in developing accurate assessments of CSE.

5.   It is noteworthy that the labeling requirements for Germany became a requirement following its defeat in World War I in 1918. Thereafter, German products were required to carry the ''Made in Germany'' labeling, in English, as a punishment but also to warn European consumers [Morello 1984]. However, Germany does not require labeling of imported products.

6.   CO labeling requirements in the U.S. originate with the Tariff Act of 1890. For a discussion of legal issues and definitional problems associated with ''made-in'' labeling see Samter [1986].

7.   Global and multidomestic firms pursue strategies that differ in both philosophy and organization, such that the former view makes no distinction between home and host markets, whereas firms in the latter view the world in a more fragmented manner, but consider foreign markets to be as important as the domestic market. Global firms possess a high degree of coordination and control of global activities, whereas foreign affiliates of multidomestic firms are relatively autonomous in their decisionmaking.

8.   The contribution of an anonymous reviewer regarding the possible corporate use of this strategy is gratefully acknowledged.

REFERENCES

Ball, Robert. 1983. The Common Market's failure. *Fortune,* 108 (November): 188–98.

Bannister, J.P. & J.A. Saunders. 1978. U.K. consumers' attitudes towards imports: The measurement of national stereotype image. *European Journal of Marketing,* 12(8): 562–70.

Baumgartner, Gary & Alain Jolibert. 1978. The perception of foreign products in France. In H. Keith Hunt, editor, *Advances in consumer research,* Vol. 5, 603–605. Provo, Utah: Association for Consumer Research.

Bilkey, Warren J. & Erik Nes. 1982. Country-of-origin effects on product evaluations. *Journal of International Business Studies,* 13(1): 89–99.

Cattin, Philippe, Alain Jolibert & Colleen Lohnes. 1982. A cross-cultural study of ''made in'' concepts. *Journal of International Business Studies,* 13(3): 131–41.

Chao, Paul. 1989. The impact of country affiliation on the credibility of product attribute claims. *Journal of Advertising Research,* 29(2): 35–41.

Chasin, Joseph B. & Eugene D. Jaffe. 1979. Industrial buyer attitudes toward goods made in Eastern Europe. *Columbia Journal of World Business,* 14 (Summer): 74–81.

Cordell, Victor V. 1992. Effects of consumer preferences for foreign sourced products. *Journal of International Business Studies,* 23(2): 251–69.

Crawford, John C. & Charles W. Lamb. 1981. Source preference for imported products. *Journal of Purchasing and Materials Management,* 17 (Winter): 28–33.

Darling, John R. 1987. A longitudinal analysis of the competitive profile of products and associated marketing practices of selected European and non-European countries. *European Journal of Marketing,* 21(3): 17–29.

——— & Van R. Wood. 1990. A longitudinal study comparing perceptions of U.S. and Japanese consumer products in a third/neutral country: Finland 1975–1985. *Journal of International Business Studies,* 21(3): 427–50.

Daser, Sayeste & Haava J. Meric. 1987. Does patriotism have any marketing value: Exploratory findings for the 'crafted with pride in the U.S.A.' campaign. In Melanie Wallendorf & Paul Anderson, editors, *Advances in consumer research,* 14: 536–37. Provo, Utah: Association for Consumer Research.

Dornoff, Ronald J., Clint B. Tankersley & Gregory P. White. 1974. Consumers' perceptions of imports. *Akron Business and Economic Review,* 5 (Summer): 26–29.

Erickson, Gary M., Johny K. Johansson & Paul Chao. 1984. Image variables in multi-attribute product evaluations: Country-of-origin effects. *Journal of Consumer Research,* 11 (September): 694–99.

Ettenson, Richard, Janet Wagner & Gary Gaeth. 1988. Evaluating the effect of country of origin and the 'made in U.S.A.' campaign: A conjoint approach. *Journal of Retailing,* 64 (Spring): 85–100.

Etzel, Michael J. & Bruce J. Walker. 1974. Advertising strategy for foreign products. *Journal of Advertising Research,* 14 (June): 41–44.

Festervand, Troy A., James R. Lumpkin & William J. Lundstrom. 1985. Consumers' perceptions of imports: An update and extension. *Akron Business and Economic Review,* 16 (Spring): 31–36.

Fishbein, Martin & Icek Ajzen. 1975. *Belief, attitude, intention, and behavior: An introduction to theory and research.* Reading, Mass.: Addison-Wesley.

Gaedeke, Ralph. 1973. Consumer attitudes toward products 'made in' developing countries. *Journal of Retailing,* 49 (Summer): 13–24.

Gerstner, Eitan. 1985. Do higher prices signal higher quality? *Journal of Marketing Research,* 22 (May): 209–15.

Green, Robert T. & Phillip D. White. 1976. Methodological considerations in cross-national consumer research. *Journal of International Business Studies,* 7 (Fall-Winter): 81–87.

Greer, Thomas V. 1971. British purchasing agents and the European Economic Community: Some empirical evidence on internal industrial perceptions. *Journal of Purchasing,* 7 (May): 57–63.

Hallén, Lars & Jan Johanson. 1985. Industrial marketing strategies and different national environments. *Journal of Business Research,* 13: 495–509.

Hampton, Gerald M. 1977. Perceived risk in buying products made abroad by American firms. *Baylor Business Studies,* 113 (August): 53–64.

Han, C. Min & William J. Qualls. 1985. Country-of-origin effects and their impact upon consumers' perception of quality. In Andrew A. Mitchell, editor, *Advances in consumer research,* Vol. 9, 162–67. Ann Arbor, Mich.: Association for Consumer Research.

Han, C. Min & Vern Terpstra. 1988. Country-of-origin effects for uni-national and bi-national products. *Journal of International Business Studies,* 19(2): 235–56.

———. 1988. The role of consumer patriotism in the choice of domestic versus foreign products. *Journal of Advertising Research,* 28 (June–July): 25–32.

———. 1989. Country image: Halo or summary construct? *Journal of Marketing Research,* 26 (May): 222–29.

Heald, G. 1979. *European perceptions of competition and economic relationships between Japan, Europe, and the U.S.A.* London, U.K.: Gallup Poll Ltd.

Heimbach, Arthur E., Johny K. Johansson & Douglas McLachlan. 1989. Product familiarity, information processing, and country-of-origin cues. In Thomas K. Srull, editor, *Advances in consumer research,* Vol. 16, 460–67. Provo, Utah: Association for Consumer Research.

Hester, Susan B. & Mary Yuen. 1987. The influence of country of origin on consumer attitude and buying behavior in the United States and Canada. In Melanie Wallendorf & Paul Anderson, editors, *Advances in consumer research,* Vol. 14, 538–42. Provo, Utah: Association for Consumer Research.

Hong, Sung-Tai & Robert S. Wyer, Jr. 1989. Effects of country-of-origin and product-attribute information on product evaluation: An information processing perspective. *Journal of Consumer Research,* 16 (September): 175–87.

——— & Julie F. Toner. 1989. Are there gender differences in the use of country-of-origin information in the evaluation of products? In Thomas K. Srull, editor, *Advances in consumer research,* Vol. 16, 468–72. Provo, Utah: Association for Consumer Research.

Huber, J. & J. McCann. 1982. The impact of inferential beliefs on product evaluations. *Journal of Marketing Research,* 19 (August): 324–33.

Hugstad, Paul S. & Michael Durr. 1986. A study of country of manufacturer impact on consumer perceptions: In Naresh Malhotra & Jon Hawes, editors, *Developments in marketing science,* Vol. 9, 115–19. Coral Gables, Fl.: Academy of Marketing Science.

Jacoby, Jacob, Jerry C. Olson & R.A. Haddock, 1971. Price, brand name, and product composition characteristics as determinants of perceived quality. *Journal of Applied Psychology,* 55: 570–79.

Jacoby, Jacob, George Szybillo & Jacqueline Busato-Schach. 1977. Information acquisition behavior in brand choice situations. *Journal of Consumer Research,* 3 (March): 209–16.

Jain, Subhash. 1989. Standardization of international marketing strategy: Some research hypotheses. *Journal of Marketing,* 53 (January): 70–79.

Johansson, Johny K., Susan P. Douglas & Ikujiro Nonaka. 1985. Assessing the impact of country of origin on product evaluations: A new methodological perspective. *Journal of Marketing Research,* 22 (November): 388–96.

Johansson, Johny K. & Israel D. Nebenzahl. 1986. Multinational production: Effect on brand value. *Journal of International Business Studies,* 17 (Fall): 101–26.

———. 1987. Country-of-origin, social norms and behavioral intentions. In S. Tamer Cavusgil, editor, *Advances in international marketing,* Vol. 2. Greenwich, Conn.: JAI Press.

Kaynak, Erdener & S. Tamer Cavusgil. 1983. Consumer attitudes toward products of foreign origin: Do they vary across product classes? *International Journal of Advertising,* 2 (April–June): 147–57.

Khanna, Sri Ram. 1986. Asian companies and the country stereotyping paradox: An empirical study. *Columbia Journal of World Business,* 21 (Summer): 29–38.

Krishnakumar, Parameswar. 1974. An exploratory study of the influence of country of origin on the product images of persons from selected countries. Ph.D. dissertation, The University of Florida.

Landor Associates. 1988. It is the real thing. *Economist,* 309 (November): 80.

Lawrence, C., N.E. Marr & G.P. Prendergast. 1992. Country-of-origin stereotyping: A case study in the New Zealand motor vehicle industry. *European Journal of Marketing,* 26(3): 37–51.

Levitt, Theodore. 1983. The globalization of markets. *Harvard Business Review,* 61 (May–June): 92–102.

Lillis, Charles M. & Chem Narayana. 1974. Analysis of 'made-in' product image: An exploratory study. *Journal of International Business Studies,* 5 (Spring): 119–27.

Lumpkin, James R. & John C. Crawford. 1985. Consumer perceptions of developing countries. In Naresh K. Malhotra, editor, *Developments in marketing science,* Vol. 8, 95–97. Coral Gables, Fl.: Academy of Marketing Science.

——— & Gap Kim. 1985. Perceived risk as a factor in buying foreign clothes. *International Journal of Advertising,* 4(2): 157–71.

Mayer, Charles S. 1978. Multinational marketing research: The magnifying glass of methodological problems. *European Research,* 6 (March): 77–83.

Morello, Gabriele. 1984. The 'made in' issue: A comparative research on the image of domestic and foreign products. *European Research,* 12 (January), 5–21.

Nagashima, Akira. 1970. A comparison of Japanese and U.S. attitudes toward foreign products. *Journal of Marketing,* 34 (January): 68–74.

———. 1977. A comparative product 'made in' image survey among Japanese businessmen. *Journal of Marketing,* 41 (July): 95–100.

Nakanishi, Masao. 1981. Marketing developments in Japan. *Journal of Marketing,* 45 (Summer): 206–208.

Narayana, Chem L. 1981. Aggregate images of American and Japanese products: Implications on international marketing. *Columbia Journal of World Business,* 16 (Summer): 31–35.

Newman, Joseph W. & Richard Staelin. 1972. Purchase information seeking for new cars and major household appliances. *Journal of Marketing Research,* 9 (August): 249–57.

Niffenegger, Phillip B. 1980. How imports rate in comparison to domestic products: A retailer study. In John H. Summey & Ronald D. Taylor, editors, *Evolving marketing thought for 1980,* 369–73. Carbondale, Ill.: Southern Marketing Association.

———, J. White & G. Marmet. 1980. How British retail managers view French and American products. *European Journal of Marketing,* 14(8): 493–98.

Obermiller, Carl & Eric Spangenberg. 1989. Exploring the effects of country of origin labels: An information processing framework. In Thomas K. Srull, editor, *Advances in consumer research,* Vol. 16, 454–59. Provo, Utah: Association for Consumer Research.

Olson, Jerry C. 1977. Price as an informational cue: Effects on product evaluations. In A.G. Woodside et al., editors, *Consumer and industrial buying behavior.* Amsterdam: North Holland.

——— & Jacob Jacoby. 1972. Cue utilization in the quality perception process. In M. Venkatesan, editor, *Advances in consumer research,* Vol. 1, 169–79. Provo, Utah: Association for Consumer Research.

Papadopoulos, Nicolas G., Louise A. Heslop, Françoise Garby & George Avlonitis. 1987. Does 'country of origin' matter? Some findings from a cross-cultural study of consumer views about foreign products. Report No. 87–104. Cambridge, Mass.: Marketing Science Institute.

Parameswaran, Ravi & Attila Yaprak. 1987. A cross-national comparison of consumer research measures. *Journal of International Business Studies,* 18(1): 35–49.

Reierson, Curtis. 1966. Are foreign products seen as national stereotypes? *Journal of Retailing,* 42 (Fall): 33–40.

———. 1967. Attitude changes toward foreign products. *Journal of Marketing Research,* 4 (November): 385–87.

Roth, Martin S. & Jean B. Romeo. 1992. Matching product category and country image perceptions: A framework for managing country-of-origin effects. *Journal of International Business Studies,* 23(3): 477–97.

Samiee, Saeed & Larry Carapellotti. 1984. The use of portfolio models for production rationalization in multinational firms. *International Marketing Review,* 1(3): 5–13.

———— & Adam Mayo. 1990. Barriers to trade with Japan: A socio-cultural perspective. *European Journal of Marketing,* 24(12): 48–66.

————, Terence Shimp & David Snyder. 1990. Consumers' cognitive structures for countries and their products. *Enhancing knowledge development in marketing.* In William Bearden et al., editors, *Enhancing knowledge development in marketing,* Vol. 1 (Summer): 43. Chicago: American Marketing Association (Summer).

Samter, N.S. 1986. National Juice Products Association vs. United States: A narrower approach to substantial transformation determination for country-of-origin marking. *Law & Policy in International Business,* 18: 671–94.

Scholar, Y.D. 1984. Labeling regulation poses problems for distributors. *Industrial Distribution,* 74 (January): 63.

Schooler, Robert D. 1965. Product bias in Central American common market. *Journal of Marketing Research,* 3 (November): 394–7.

———— & Albert R. Wildt. 1968. Elasticity of product bias. *Journal of Marketing Research,* 6 (February): 78–81.

Schooler, Robert D. & Don H. Sunoo. 1969. Consumer perception of international products: Regional vs. national labeling. *Social Science Quarterly,* 50 (March): 886–90.

Schooler, Robert D. & Don H. Sunoo. 1971. Bias phenomena attendant to the marketing of foreign goods in the U.S. *Journal of International Business Studies,* 2 (Spring): 71–80.

————, Albert R. Wildt & Joseph M. Jones. 1987. Strategy development for manufactured exports of third world countries. *Journal of Global Marketing,* 1 (Fall/Winter): 53–68.

Shimp, Terence A. & Subhash Sharma. 1987. Consumer ethnocentrism: Construction and validation of the CETscale. *Journal of Marketing Research,* 24 (August): 280–89.

Shimp, Terence A., Saeed Samiee & Thomas Madden. 1993. Countries and their products: A cognitive structure perspective. *Journal of the Academy of Marketing Science,* 21 (Fall): 323–30.

Sorenson, Ralph Z. & Ulrich E. Wiechmann. 1975. How multinationals view marketing standardization. *Harvard Business Review,* 53 (May–June): 38.

Stephens, Keith T., Harold W. Fox & Myron J. Leonard. 1985. A comparison of preferences concerning the purchase of domestic vs. imports. In Naresh K. Malhotra, editor, *Developments in marketing science,* Vol. 8, 100–104. Coral Gables, Fl.: Academy of Marketing Science.

Tongberg, Richard C. 1972. An empirical study of relationships between dogmatism and consumer attitudes towards foreign products. Ph.D. dissertation, Pennsylvania State University.

Tse, David K. & Gerald J. Gorn. 1993. An experiment on the salience of country-of-origin in an era of global brands. *Journal of International Marketing,* 1(1): 57–76.

Wall, Marjorie & Louise A. Heslop. 1986. Consumer attitudes toward Canadian made-in versus imported products. *Journal of the Academy of Marketing Science,* 14 (Summer): 27–36.

Wang, Chih-Kang. 1978. The effect of foreign economic, political and cultural environment on consumers' willingness to buy foreign products. Ph.D. dissertation, Texas A&M University.

———— & Charles W. Lamb, Jr. 1980. Foreign environmental factors influencing American consumers' predisposition toward European products. *Journal of the Academy of Marketing Science,* 8 (Fall): 345–56.

————. 1983. The impact of selected environmental forces upon consumers' willingness to buy foreign product. *Journal of the Academy of Marketing Science,* 11 (Winter): 71–84.

White, Phillip D. & Edward W. Cundiff. 1978. Assessing the quality of industrial products. *Journal of Marketing,* 42 (January): 80–85.

————. 1979. Attitudes of U.S. purchasing managers toward industrial products manufactured in selected western European nations. *Journal of International Business Studies,* 10 (Spring/Summer): 81–90.

23

FOREIGN MARKET SERVICING: BEYOND CHOICE OF ENTRY MODE

GABRIEL R.G. BENITO
LAWRENCE S. WELCH

ABSTRACT   This article focuses on the operation method (or entry mode) that a company utilizes in developing its involvement in a foreign market. An overview and critique of 'economics' and 'process' approaches to this issue is undertaken. It is argued that both approaches use relatively constrained frameworks of influences on mode choice, and have yet to come to terms with the frequent reality of operation modes in combination. Methodological and conceptual issues arising out of the analysis are considered as a basis for moving forward the research in this area.

The foreign market servicing decision has been the subject of considerable attention by researchers recently—even being described as a "frontier issue" in international marketing (Anderson and Gatignon 1986; Kogut and Singh 1988; Welch and Luostarinen 1988; Hill, Hwang, and Kim 1990). What appears to be emerging from the many strands of research is a recognition that foreign operation mode (or entry mode) decisions are critical in establishing the basis of a firm's foreign market penetration capacity and that effective internationalization may well require the use of a broader array of operation modes (Luostarinen and Welch 1990). For example, research into the activities of U.S. "cutting edge" and "Fortune 500" firms indicated a trend toward "more flexibility and imagination in overseas operations," including greater use of contract manufacturing, joint ventures, and licensing (Ryans 1987, p. 153). Since the mid-1980s there has been a noticeable rise in the use of international strategic alliances and other cooperative modes in international business operations (Ohmae 1989). Likewise, the growth of franchising activities in many countries, beyond the United States, has begun to filter through into increased global use of franchising as a means of internationalization (Welch 1990).

In this article the foreign market servicing decision is examined first by reviewing the two main approaches to this issue: a so-called "economics" stream, and a behavioral/process stream that could be loosely termed "internationalization theory" (Johanson and Vahlne 1977, 1990). While considerable progress has been made in both streams, substantial deficiencies still exist, for example, in dealing with foreign market servicing as a choice of modes in combination rather than on a singular basis. The methodological and conceptual issues raised by this analysis are then considered as a basis for moving forward the depiction and explanation of the choice of foreign market servicing modes.

CHOICE OF OPERATION MODE: AN ECONOMICS PERSPECTIVE

Internationalization exposes companies to an array of new challenges, including deciding on appropriate arrangements for organizing their business activities in foreign markets. The alternatives are, at least in principle, numerous. Apart from the location effect differentiating exports from other servicing methods (Buckley 1989), foreign market servicing methods have been characterized along several dimensions: degree of control (Anderson and Gatignon 1986; Root 1987), level of risk and resource commitment

(Hill, Hwang, and Kim 1990), and skill requirements (Grønhaug and Kvitastein 1993). Also, from the viewpoint of the individual company, the various market servicing methods represent different levels of involvement and organizational commitment to a foreign market (Johanson and Vahlne 1977; Welch and Luostarinen 1988).

Several frameworks of the choice of foreign market servicing method have been advanced in the literature—a recent overview is provided by Young et al. (1989). Much of the reasoning has been rooted in economics. Anderson and Gatignon (1986) developed a model of choice of mode based on transaction cost theory. Focusing mainly on control considerations, they suggested that the degree of control inherent in a given operation method is a function of ownership structure. Thus, licensing and various other contractual arrangements are low-control modes, while a fully owned subsidiary would allow the internationalizing firm to enjoy a high degree of control over a foreign operation. Anderson and Gatignon (1986) then proposed that factors likely to cause high transaction costs—asset specificity, external and internal uncertainty and free-riding potential—should be positively associated with the level of control offered by the market servicing method chosen by a company. Hill, Hwang, and Kim (1990) introduced some additional explanatory factors. They argued that modes differ not only in their level of control, but also with regard to resource commitments and dissemination risk; that is, the risk that firm-specific advantages in knowledge will be expropriated by a foreign partner. In their model, the market servicing decision is treated as a function of three broad groups of variables: strategic variables, environmental variables, and transaction cost variables. Strategic variables, such as the extent of scale economies and global concentration, influence the mode decision primarily through control requirements. For example, firms that pursue global strategies are, *ceteris paribus,* likely to prefer a high-control mode— i.e., fully owned subsidiaries. The resource commitment aspect of mode choice is influenced by environmental variables. For instance, when country risk is high and/or when cultural distance is large, firms are likely to select low-resource commitment methods

in order to retain strategic flexibility. Finally, the dissemination-risk aspect of operation methods is mainly influenced by transaction cost variables such as the value of firm-specific knowledge assets and the nature of this know-how. Thus, the more valuable and/or tacit the know-how, the greater the probability that the firm will choose a mode involving low dissemination risk, such as a fully owned subsidiary.

The above economics approach indicates an attempt to build a more comprehensive model of operation mode choice, although still within a highly constrained decision-making framework.[1] Despite this widening, perhaps inevitably, concerns have still been raised about the limitations of the assumptions underlying the frameworks, such as their rather simplistic view of organizational decision-making behavior and the degree of rationality assumed (Macharzina and Engelhard 1991; Calof 1993). For example, one simplifying assumption is the notion that different modes entail different (objective) relative levels of control, resource commitments, risk, etc., which again are regarded as largely a function of ownership. Control, however, can also be gained by means other than ownership. A joint venture may feature different levels of control—high, medium or even low control—depending on other characteristics of the actual arrangement (Schaan 1988). A licensing agreement in association with a joint venture may be an important means of raising the effective level of control (Luostarinen and Welch 1990). Such combinations have rarely been dealt with in the literature as the frameworks do not encompass bundles or packages of methods for servicing a foreign market as viable alternatives. Moreover, the *perceived* levels of control, risk, etc., offered by a given operation method, may vary considerably across different firms.

In addition, there has been a lack of attention to the dynamics of foreign market servicing in the economics approach because of a primary focus on how firms, as rational economic actors, arrive at a more or less "optimal" mode of *entry* into a particular foreign market at a given point in time. Less attention has been paid to *changes* to the initial entry decisions, to how relationships between entities *evolve* over time and influence the decision-making process, and to how market servicing decisions *interact* with other aspects of the internationalization of the firm. In a review of foreign market servicing theories, Buckley (1989, p. 83) has noted: "The preceding theoretical frameworks have a limited dynamic content and it is in this direction which theory must develop to encompass the complexities of market servicing strategies." This echoes a much earlier concern about the lack of dynamic considerations in foreign direct investment theory—one that still remains to be adequately addressed (Horst 1972; Hirsch and Meshulach 1991). A similar concern has been evident in the strategic change field; and in a review of research, Johnson (1988, p. 58) has argued that "we no longer need to demonstrate that the rational models are inadequate descriptions of process."

CHOICE OF OPERATION MODE: A PROCESS PERSPECTIVE

The alternative main approach to foreign operation mode decision making involves a process perspective. Here there is a strong emphasis on behavioral factors as driving forces over time in internationalization, of which any given step is seen as an integral part of the overall process. While the operation (or entry) mode dimension is only one aspect of internationalization, it has been the subject of considerable research because it is one of the most overt signposts of the unfolding pattern for individual companies—as compared to, say, the human resources dimension (Welch and Luostarinen 1988). Various patterns of operation mode development over time—"establishment chains"—have been revealed by diverse empirical studies. The most consistent pattern is one of "evolution rather than revolution"—i.e., from low-commitment to high-commitment modes gradually over time (Johanson and Vahlne 1990; Buckley and Ghauri 1993). More recently, though, there is evidence of firms leapfrogging some steps used in past establishment chains, and a general speeding up in the whole process (Nordström 1991).

The more holistic research on internationalization and its various component steps has not been specifically focused on each foreign market servicing decision but rather on determinants of the overall process. Of course, if such overall process influences are of significance, they must therefore be important factors at particular points when operation mode decisions are in prospect, in combination with any distinctive situational influences. Nordic researchers, particularly, have been responsible for much of the early research on internationalization as a process, and for exploring the impact of such variables as learning activities, which provide a feedback link from past to current international operations (Johanson and Vahlne 1977, 1990; Johanson and Wiedersheim-Paul 1975).

EXPERIENCE, KNOWLEDGE, CONTROL, AND RISK FACTORS

The Nordic explanation of internationalization has placed particular stress on the contribution of knowledge and experience. The greater the depth of knowledge and experience in a foreign market, it is argued, the more confident a firm tends to be about making commitments, and about its judgment of the degree of risk exposure. Relevant knowledge and experience is, however, acquired preeminently through actual foreign marketing activities, providing an important feedback loop in the process. Without appropriate experience and knowledge, from the decision maker's perspective, there tends to be a stronger sense of risk and uncertainty, which is likely to constrain the market servicing decision. At the same time though, perceived risk exposure can be altered by the choice of foreign operation mode: for example, high risk might be counterbalanced by the use of a low-commitment mode such as licensing. As an illustration of these factors, in a study of small exporting and nonexporting U.S. firms, Yaprak (1985, p. 81) concluded: "The primary implication of these findings is that the export behavior of smaller firms follows a learning curve with competence, knowledge, and confidence increments accumulated marginally in successive phases."

Nordic research also indicated how control concerns could affect the choice of operation form and were connected with risk, knowledge, and experience factors. Without knowledge of and experience in a foreign market it is clearly difficult to achieve effective control of operations. Therefore, the firm tends to be less prepared to operate in ways that require stronger involvement and control, instead depending more on locals with the requisite local knowledge and networks. Deeper experience can of course shift the balance and allow deeper commitment. For example, the Australian multinational Brambles, which specializes in the security and materials handling area, has stressed the role of experience in modifying its approach to European operations, shifting from "lower risk" joint ventures initially to wholly owned subsidiaries over time (Thomas 1988, p. 127).

However, research by Erramilli (1991), on U.S. service companies, has shown that such connections are not necessarily straightforward, having found that the desire for control of foreign operations was relatively high for firms with little experience, low for firms with moderate experience, but rose to a high level again for firms with extensive international experience. It might be argued that the drop in desire for control is explained partly by the nature of service companies' international operations whereby it is easier and cheaper in many cases to establish an entry point in a foreign market than to set up, say, a full manufacturing facility. Initially, in culturally similar markets, companies are probably more able and prepared to assume control, but as they move into less familiar locations, there tends to be less confidence and a stronger feeling of needing local partners in order to successfully adapt. This was the case when McDonald's took on a joint venture partner for its Japanese operations (Erramilli 1991; Love 1986).

In a similar vein, earlier research indicated that some firms perceive higher levels of risk and uncertainty as internationalization proceeds, in response to increased information and knowledge (Welch and Wiedersheim-Paul 1980). Decision makers with an entrepreneurial orientation and a strong focus on international market opportunities may have limited awareness at the outset of the more practical demands or "problems" of foreign market penetration.

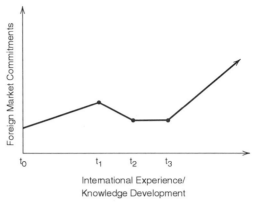

Figure 1. International Experience and Foreign Market Commitments: A Hypothetical Example

Such ignorance may also flow from the fortuitous, unplanned way in which so many firms achieve a start in foreign operations (Bilkey and Tesar 1977). As companies gain experience and seek external information and advice, they may become more conscious of and concerned about the problems and risks of international involvement; in general, the tendency may well be to induce greater care and caution in subsequent foreign moves. In some cases this will lead to reversals of foreign market involvement or even total withdrawal (Welch and Wiedersheim-Paul 1980; Smith and Zeithaml 1993).

Figure 1 illustrates an example of reversal in foreign market involvement. In the initial stages (t_0 to t_1) the company expands its foreign market commitments and, through related activities, increases its international experience and knowledge. However, at t_1, because of what it has learned about the requirements of international operations, it decides to reduce its commitments—perhaps withdrawing from some markets. From t_2 to t_3 its reduced foreign market position is maintained, although knowledge and experience continue to develop. After t_3, the company feels assured enough to resume expansion of its foreign market commitments. Clearly, many pattern variations on this example are likely to be found in actual cases. In general they illustrate that although greater international experience and knowledge normally empower a company to expand its international activities, it may also act in seemingly perverse ways to constrain forward steps at some stages of the overall process.

NETWORKING

An integral part of the process of internationalization is the establishment, maintenance, and expansion of networks of relationships in foreign markets. In fact, much of what is involved in international operations could be characterized as networking activity. Relationships have to be built with a wide range of organizations and individuals—foreign customers, intermediaries, banks, government officials, and the like. Extensive European research has demonstrated just how widespread and long-standing the resulting networks may become (Håkansson 1982; Ford 1990; Forsgren and Johanson 1992). Much of the critical information and knowledge about foreign markets is contained in the networks that a company is able to develop—anchored by key actors within them. Contacts between people, both formally and informally, in social and work situations, form the heart of networking activity (Cunningham and Homse 1986). As such, people can add or remove network connections and knowledge as they move to new positions. Overall then, network development, in its many facets, emerges as an additional explanatory factor in the ability and preparedness of a company to expand its foreign market servicing commitments.

RESOURCES

While resource availability has not been a particular focus of much of the research on internationalization, it has nevertheless been shown to be an important issue facing companies at various stages when operation mode decisions are being contemplated. For example, smaller firms, given their limited financial resources, can be expected to face a narrower set of viable foreign market servicing options than larger firms (Bonaccorsi 1992). Numerous studies also report, as expected, that the likelihood of using daughter-companies in order to service particular foreign markets increases with the resource base of the firm (Horst 1972; Grubaugh 1987; Terpstra and Yu 1988; Agarwal and Ramaswami 1992).

The *human resources* dimension is one element of the broader resources question that has been increasingly drawn into the analysis of foreign market servicing. One study even concluded that human resources policy ought to be leading rather than following overall international strategy (Luostarinen and Svärd 1982). A shortage of persons with appropriate skills, knowledge, and international orientation can be a brake on internationalization—while appointing the wrong person to manage operations in a given foreign market can have disastrous consequences for some time in that market (Tung 1982; Dowling and Welch 1988). Research has also shown that managerial succession can be a key factor in explaining major new steps in a company's internationalization process—including ''leapfrogging'' over intermediate steps directly to the more advanced entry form of a foreign direct investment (Björkman 1989, 1990; Björkman and Eklund 1991).

The examples noted above illustrate that resource development, in its many forms, can have a significant impact on whether and how a company takes on foreign market commitments. Resource availability to carry on international operations, though, is affected not just by specific decisions to support development but also by the ongoing process of internationalization and its outcomes.

THE PROCESS PERSPECTIVE AND SITUATIONAL INFLUENCES

The research on internationalization has focused on better understanding the process by which a company builds its international operations, with an emphasis on the key variables driving forward momentum. A number of variables are active in the process—typically interconnected—and act at times to constrain additional steps forward, but over time may change in ways that make a company better able and more willing to extend international involvement. Such factors not only influence internationalization and its component parts, including foreign operation modes, but are also affected by the process, thereby providing a mechanism for positive (and negative) feedback loops through time, as shown in Figure 2.

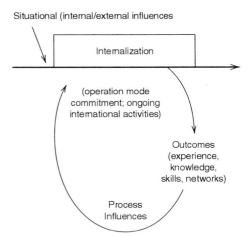

Figure 2. Process and Situational Influences on Internationalization

When considering the operation mode step as part of internationalization, process variables, however important in any particular case, are unlikely to provide a full explanation of any decision undertaken. Many other influences may be operative; in general, they can be labeled as situational (see Figure 2), deriving from the company's internal and external context (Pettigrew 1988). Internal situational variables that could be important are the financial state of the company, decision-maker attitudes, and the degree of utilization of production facilities. Because of internal problems, a company may opt for a low commitment mode in response to a foreign market opportunity.

External context or environmental variables can also be important in mode choice. Pettigrew (1988, p. 6) argues that in the strategy change field process researchers have tended to ''de-emphasize the explanatory role of outer context variables,'' whereas they require more complete incorporation into models of change. It could similarly be argued that process models of internationalization need to take greater account of external variables—despite recognition of their influence. The sometimes erratic character of internationalization for individual firms appears to be related to the seeming randomness with which opportunities and threats relevant to international activity arise in a company's external environ-

ment. This is often due to the action of external change agents, as indicated by research into licensing (Lowe and Crawford 1982), exporting (Bilkey and Tesar 1977) and franchising (Welch 1990). Required on such occasions is a rapid response to an opportunity that arises in a very specific form (Cullen 1986). As a result, it may not be a question of considering the alternatives available—of operation modes, locations, and so on. Rather, it could well be that the critical issue is how a specific option fits the current and future objectives of the company, judged from the perspective of its current situation and past international operations. Research into the foreign direct investment move by Finnish companies indicated a restricted choice range (Larimo 1987). Likewise, in a study of a sample of Canadian companies, it was found that only 18 percent had considered alternative modes in the decision-making process when changing foreign operation modes (Calof 1993).

In attempting to understand and explain the decision process itself, there is a danger of overfocusing on the particular stimulus or stimuli that started consideration of a particular project, as this may obscure the underlying reasons for the interest and ultimate go-ahead if it occurs (Macharzina and Engelhard 1991). For example, a common triggering cause of companies shifting from the use of agents to setting up sales subsidiaries in foreign markets is difficulties encountered with particular agents. The preparedness to make this move is often explained by emerging control concerns, but this will be typically linked to better knowledge of and accumulated experience and skills in the foreign market. In general, therefore, the decision represents a response to a conjunction of emerging process influences and triggering events—often external to the firm.

Some models of operation mode choice incorporating process elements as well as internal and external context influences have been developed, although they have tended to focus on specific steps in internationalization—for example, exporting and franchising (Wiedersheim-Paul, Olson, and Welch 1978; Welch 1990). Even at the initial international step, important process influences were evident, although closely linked to external and, even more so, internal behavioral factors.

PATTERN CHANGE— IMPACT ON EXPLANATION?

One direction of empirical research on internationalization has been further study of patterns of foreign market servicing over time in different foreign environments. While earlier research in other countries indicated similarities to the Nordic pattern (Johanson and Vahlne 1990), increasingly this has been challenged, even from within the Nordic countries, as different studies reveal many exceptions to the incremental path (Hedlund and Kverneland 1985; Björkman and Eklund 1991; Nordström 1991; Benito and Gripsrud 1992). To some extent the research in this area has taken on a ''straw man'' quality, with departures from the ''typical'' establishment chain of operation modes—i.e., from no exports to exporting via an agent, then a sales subsidiary, then a production subsidiary, being taken as disproving the ''Nordic internationalization model'' (see for example Turnbull 1987). Clearly though, the notion of what is an incremental international step in one context may vary considerably in another—yet the same internal driving forces may have been in operation. Much depends on individual decision-maker perception.

As a general impression, companies in the 1980s seem to have been more prepared to utilize experience and knowledge gained from one foreign environment and apply it to other environments in a way that has enabled more widespread leapfrogging of the establishment chain shown in Nordic research, but with incrementalism still apparent (Nordström 1991). Better understanding of the process, though, probably requires a move away from simplistic pattern measures, from which wide-ranging inferences about process are sometimes drawn. For example, the categories of agent and sales subsidiary are relatively broad, masking a wide range of feasible variation in types of operation within them (Bonaccorsi and Dalli 1990). Also, more account needs to be taken of other forms of operation that may comple-

ment or sometimes replace the traditional steps used in measuring the establishment chain.

Clearly then the measuring sticks of internationalization, typically focused as they are on major operation mode steps, need both broadening and deepening if further light is to be shed on the debate about this topic. What is probably required is not just a charting of the main steps in the process, but the measurement of smaller steps in between, such as the appointment of additional staff, which may be less apparent but nevertheless important in advancing the process, and in understanding more substantial and obvious changes in foreign market servicing.

OPERATION MODES IN COMBINATION

In modeling the entry mode or foreign market servicing decision, from both economics and process perspectives, there has been a focus on the choice of individual modes rather than the prospect of using a combination of modes in a foreign market at a point in time. For example, in a recent review of earlier studies, Kim and Hwang (1992, p. 29) noted: ''Common to existing studies . . . is their assumption that each entry decision is made in isolation.'' While this reduction of the decision-making situation has simplified model building and eventual testing, it has been at the expense of reflecting the reality of the situation that companies frequently face—of not simply choosing one method versus another, but rather of putting together the most appropriate *package* of methods for penetrating a foreign market.

Figure 3 presents an illustrative example of the range of foreign market servicing methods that a company might use in different foreign markets at a given point in time (t_2), in response to the type of internal and external influences noted previously. While in some markets a single mode may be used (markets 2, 3, and 4), in others a combination or package of modes might be employed (markets 1 and 5). The firm's foreign market servicing pattern shown at time t_2 could be the outcome of a number of package alterations during preceding periods, as illustrated for Foreign Market 4. In this market, the

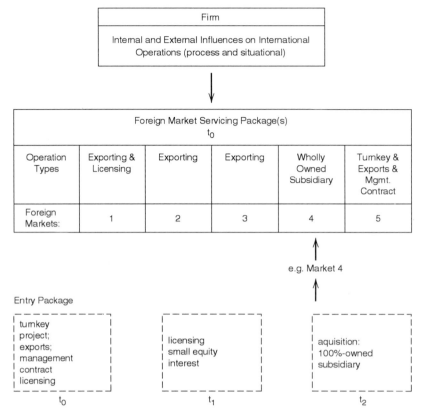

Figure 3. Foreign Market Service Packages

company is shown as using a broad package at its entry point (t_0), which led to an altered package at time t_1, then full acquisition of the operation at time t_2.

Research into the use of management contracts in international operations, for example, has shown that most management contracts are used in connection with other modes of operation (Brooke 1985). In one case a Swedish company entered a Middle Eastern market via a turnkey operation at the outset, but also took a small equity position in the foreign venture, along with a management contract involving management of the continuing operation (a dairy farm and milk processing unit). As a result of its insider position, the Swedish company was not only able to maintain its place as principal supplier to the venture of spare parts, equipment, and the like, but later won the contract for a new turnkey project that repre-

sented an extension of the earlier one (Sharma 1984). The management contract's full role and significance in this case, from the perspective of foreign market penetration, were developed within the context of the total package of foreign market servicing activity by the Swedish company. Likewise, the contribution of different parts in the overall package differed over time—although ultimately fitting into a cohesive whole. However, only in the longitudinal perspective is it fully clear what roles the different parts of the foreign operation package play.

In general, therefore, from a company's perspective, an important question is not only the fit and contribution of the different parts of an operation package at a particular point in time, but also the fit and contribution *over* time. The longer term potential of a given market and, more particularly, of different combinations of operation packages to exploit it may not be foreseen or even considered in decision making at the outset; therefore, alterations over time will often take on the character of emergent strategies (Mintzberg and McHugh 1985). In his study of foreign licensing activity by Swedish companies, Svensson (1984, p. 223) found that where a stepping stone strategy from licensing to other operation modes was used it "was seldom intended from the beginning but emerged as the firm's financial resources and management, production and marketing skills increased." However, the ability of a company to respond to any possibilities that emerge may be affected by the form in which the initial foreign entry package is constructed—as the case of the Swedish company in the Middle East noted above demonstrates. A licensing and/or joint venture arrangement might of itself restrict the ability of a firm to switch to other operation forms.

If the choice of any particular foreign operation mode is undertaken in a package context, the decision to actually use it may have little to do with its normally assumed foreign marketing role, but rather could be explained by the way in which it contributes to the functioning of a broader package. An illustration is the way in which licensing activity is often linked to foreign direct investment. Despite its potential as an independent contributor to foreign market penetration, its primary purpose in this context may be as a means of achieving more effective control over a joint venture partner, to transfer funds from the subsidiary, and/or to reduce taxation payments in the country concerned (Luostarinen and Welch 1990). In such situations, the choice setting commonly employed in studies of entry mode choice noted previously becomes highly inappropriate.

Accepting the broadened choice situation poses a significant problem for economics-based models of entry mode choice because of its attack on the assumption of isolated choice between single modes (Kim and Hwang 1992). Additionally, the issue has not been accounted for in process-oriented studies, which are typically based on relatively restricted measures of internationalization, as noted previously. In fact, tracing the influence of process-related variables through time becomes much more difficult when packages of modes are involved, as their impact may be more diffused (and less obvious) through parts of the package. For both economics and process approaches though, an extended range of questions associated with the packages themselves becomes important in the mode choice context; for example, why do companies use single versus multiple modes of operation and why do they move into and out of these formats over time (see Figure 3)?

A WAY FORWARD? METHODOLOGICAL ISSUES

The preceding analysis of the two main approaches to foreign operation mode choice has exposed a number of issues that need to be confronted in order to advance models of the decision-making process, and in general to enhance understanding of an important question in effective international business operations. The issues can be broadly classified as methodological and conceptual, although there are some connections between them. Both economics and process-oriented approaches have been criticized for their lack of dynamics—perhaps surprisingly so in the latter case. It can be argued that not only is the time factor poorly integrated into explanations (Andersen 1993), but the process of moving from lower to higher commitment modes in international operations is not adequately developed. To some extent, such problems have been accentuated by the type of empirical methodology used in this area, i.e., typically cross-sectional studies that are not very well designed to pick up the longitudinal processes at work (Macharzina and Engelhard 1991; Melin 1992). In commenting on their survey of Finnish foreign direct investment in Germany, Björkman and Eklund (1991) observed that "so far little in-depth case research has been conducted on the internationalization process of the firm." They added that there was a need for case studies to be conducted "preferably carried out on-time as the processes evolve" (Björkman and Eklund 1991, p. 818). In a recent study of the internationalization process of Swedish companies, Nordström (1991) also called for a return to exploratory research and in-depth longitudinal studies as a way of building new descriptions and understanding of the process.

Such an approach does, of course, become more difficult as the complexity of a firm's international operations increases—especially when it involves a number of subsidiaries in diverse locations. Staff at headquarters do not necessarily have a complete picture of what is driving the company's global developments as some subsidiaries may be able to build operations, even in third countries, independently from headquarters direction (Forsgren 1990; Forsgren and Holm 1991). As a result, tracing decision-making processes through time in large international companies, even on an individual-case basis, is bound to be a very demanding exercise.

An emphasis on "in-process" investigations appears to be particularly appropriate when analyzing the operation method decision given the importance of timing of events. Foreign market servicing decisions seem to require a coalition of forces (Calof 1993), interacting over time in ways that make it difficult to pin down primary determinants, and are often sparked by outsiders and outside events. Reconstructing patterns and influences after the event is always difficult. The subtleties of processes and interactions can be easily missed. Key individuals may not be able to recall all aspects of past events, and might even have a vested interest in 'rewriting' history (Mintzberg and McHugh 1985). Commenting on studies of strategy change, Van de Ven (1992, p. 181) has argued that it is "widely recognized that prior knowledge of the success or failure of a strategic change effort invariably biases a study's findings"—thus the strength of in-process investigations in actual settings. In the end this is the only way to understand the dynamic processes facing managers.

The issue of choice between packages of operation modes, rather than choice among individual modes, has already been noted as a significant problem at both conceptual and methodological levels, which is yet to be adequately addressed. Research indicates that as companies become internationalized they tend to use a wider array of operation modes, thereby developing a facility to operate with mode combinations (Welch and Luostarinen 1988). Once mode packages are accepted in a decision-making context, complexity is inevitably increased; in empirical research there are a variety of new questions to be confronted connected with the role and linkages *within* packages as well as *between* packages through time. While the same package is used during a given period, the roles played by the parts may well change. In this context, obtaining reliable longitudinal data becomes particularly difficult, providing a further argument for in-process empirical investigations, and in general for qualitative methodologies more appropriate for building new conceptualizations (Patton 1990; Yin 1989).

A WAY FORWARD? CONCEPTUAL ISSUES

While there is perhaps a clear-cut message on the methodological front, the path to improved conceptualization of foreign operation mode choice appears to be much more uncertain with many, although interrelated, lines of development being suggested by the preceding analysis. Further development of the conceptual framework will depend on the outcome of future, extended qualitative research.

CHANGE FACTORS

In both economics and process approaches, there has been a call for the introduction of a stronger dynamics emphasis in operation mode choice models. In general this reflects a concern to deal more effectively with the change process in which the mode decision is embedded. Clearly the process-oriented approaches start with this perspective, but, as has been noted, while considerable progress has been made, with some broad process influences identified, much remains to be accomplished. The mechanisms of change, through time, have yet to be fully explained—particularly while a given mode is being used (Bonaccorsi and Dalli 1990). The broad influences noted, especially in the Nordic research (Johanson and Vahlne 1990), have yet to be taken down to a more operative level, specifying the type of changes that develop within the firm as a result of, for example, the learning process. To some extent the problem is about the linkages between the broadly identified process factors and other influences, internal and external to the firm, as noted in Figure 2, which are also important in foreign market servicing decisions. Because of the behavioral orientation of process approaches, it is important to establish the extent to which the perception of other influences is tied to process variables. The timing of developments becomes particularly important once it is accepted that operation mode decisions require a conjunction of forces.

INTERNAL CONTEXT

The linkage between process variables and the company's internal context (Pettigrew 1988) has been surprisingly poorly developed, considering that the process emphasis is on the effect of internationalization within the firm. Examination of the process effects almost stops at the outer edge of the firm, leaving many of the internal pathways and influences unexplored. As an illustration, although we know a great deal about the types of information that companies use in exporting activities, and what types are considered most useful (Benito, Solberg, and Welch 1993), many internal process-oriented questions remain, for example:

- exactly how do individuals within the firm acquire appropriate information?
- how does information penetrate the firm and which individuals are involved?
- what are the connecting paths (networks) for information transfer—from outside and within the firm?
- how is information translated into management decisions regarding foreign market servicing?
- how does knowledge build within the firm over time (individuals, routines, etc.) and in response to changes such as staff transfers and departures?

In tracing the pathways of international information flow and influence, considerable groundwork has been laid in the networks field, which has been concerned with both inter-company and related intra-company linkages (Forsgren and Johanson 1992). Although research has not been applied to internationalization theory and the operation mode decision as such, the networks field provides an avenue for exploring not only process and internal context connections, but also internal/external connections, given that international business activity inevitably involves networking in one form or another. In general, there is considerable scope for extending the study of organizational behavior in its relation to decision-making for internationalization.

EXTERNAL CONTEXT

One of the strengths of the Nordic approach to internationalization has been its focus on a set of process-related variables, with feedback loops, which help to explain how a company is moved forward in international operations, without being tied to specific external events or broad industry considerations. However, external factors may have a bearing on foreign market servicing decisions, not just in independent ways but also in connection with the ongoing process influences. In models of particular operation mode decisions (Welch 1990) the external role is frequently represented as a factor in sparking a change in thinking about foreign operations—for example, a change in government policy, action by a competitor, or an unsolicited foreign order. Especially in behaviorally oriented models the external impact typically ends there, with other factors, such as decision-maker influence, taking over and determining the response by a company. Essentially the external role is disconnected, but there are situations where it can act in a more involved way, and be linked to process influences. For example, it has been argued that ''a highly internationalized context may to a greater degree pull a purely domestic firm into an internationalization process'' (Mattsson, Kjellberg, and Ulfsdotter 1993, p. 19. See also Johanson and Mattsson 1988; and Welch and Luostarinen 1993). Research on small Italian companies has revealed that a critical context for internationalization is the industrial district to which a company belongs, with export commitment being affected by the group experience of exporting (Bonaccorsi 1992). In such cases the external context not only affects the likelihood of international contacts, but also affects the thinking of decision makers about foreign market possibilities. A challenge therefore is to include the external context in models of operation mode decision making in a more meaningful way, and particularly to link it with process factors.

OPERATION MODE PACKAGES

The process dimension has perhaps proven to be the most difficult issue to grapple with in conceptual frameworks, yet the most ignored has been that of operation mode packages.

While the focus of the economics approach has been upon how a choice is made, under certain conditions, on efficiency grounds between different entry (or operation) modes, there has been limited discussion of what constitutes an ''entry'' mode. Once the concept of operation mode packages is accepted, it poses a significant challenge to both economics and process approaches to mode choice, requiring a basic reformulation of conceptual frameworks and of the research object under study.

OVERVIEW

Taken together, the preceding concerns with existing approaches to conceptualization of foreign operation mode choice indicate that much is yet to be achieved, although clearly the boundaries are continually being stretched, as in Kim and Hwang's (1992) introduction of some strategic variables into the economics approach. Process issues, while demonstrably important, have yet to be adequately linked to the company's internal and external context (Pettigrew 1988) and it would appear that considerable scope exists in this direction for developing a more comprehensive approach. In the end, however, it may be questioned as to whether it is feasible to aim for some all-encompassing model, covering all stages of internationalization (from initial exporter to large multinational), the various types of foreign market servicing packages, and the full array of often subtle process factors. In addition, instead of an overall, comprehensive model a more reasonable aim could

be a series of connected sub-models covering different stages and dimensions of internationalization. Rather than limited extensions of existing models, with early testing, the greater need would appear to be a return to exploratory research as a basis for more far-reaching conceptualizations.

NOTES

Gabriel R.G. Benito is assistant professor in the Department of Economics and Business Administration, Østfold College, Norway.

Lawrence S. Welch is a member of the faculty of economics, commerce, and management at Monash University, Melbourne, Australia.

1. A number of empirical studies, typically using a cross sectional design, provide corroborative support for several of the propositions advanced in the various economic frameworks (see for example Davidson and McFetridge 1985; Anderson and Coughlan 1987; Agarwal and Ramaswami 1992; Kim and Hwang 1992).

REFERENCES

Agarwal, S., and S.N. Ramaswami. ''Choice of Foreign Market Entry Mode: Impact of Ownership, Location and Internalization Factors.'' *Journal of International Business Studies* 23, no. 1 (1992): 1–27.

Andersen, O. ''On the Internationalization Process of Firms: A Critical Analysis.'' *Journal of International Business Studies* 24, no. 2 (1993): 209–32.

Anderson, E., and H. Gatignon. ''Modes of Foreign Entry: A Transaction Cost Analysis and Propositions.'' *Journal of International Business Studies* 17, no. 3 (1986): 1–26.

Anderson, E., and A.T. Coughlan. ''International Market Entry and Expansion via Independent or Integrated Channels of Distribution.'' *Journal of Marketing* 51, no. 1 (1987): 71–82.

Benito, G.R.G., and G. Gripsrud. ''The Expansion of Foreign Direct Investments: Discrete Rational Location Choices or a Cultural Learning Process?'' *Journal of International Business Studies* 23, no. 3 (1992): 461–76.

Benito, G.R.G., C.-A. Solberg, and L.S. Welch. ''An Exploration of the Information Behavior of Norwegian Exporters.'' *International Journal of Information Management* 13, August (1993): 274–86.

Bilkey, W.J., and G. Tesar. ''The Export Behavior of Smaller-sized Wisconsin Firms.'' *Journal of International Business Studies* 8, no. 1 (1977): 93–98.

Björkman, I. *Foreign Direct Investments: An Empirical Analysis of Decision Making in Seven Finnish Firms.* Helsinki: The

Swedish School of Economics and Business Administration, 1989.

———. ''Foreign Direct Investments: An Organizational Learning Perspective.'' *Finnish Journal of Business Economics* 39, no. 4 (1990): 271–94.

Björkman, I., and M. Eklund. ''Entering Foreign Markets: An Analysis of the Market Entry Modes Used by Finnish Direct Investors in Germany.'' In *An Enlarged Europe in the Global Economy,* vol. 2, edited by H. Vestergaard, 791–820. Copenhagen: European International Business Association (EIBA), 1991.

Bonaccorsi, A. ''On the Relationship between Firm Size and Export Intensity.'' *Journal of International Business Studies* 23, no. 4 (1992): 605–35.

Bonaccorsi, A., and D. Dalli. ''Internationalization Process and Entry Channels: Evidence from Small Italian Exporters.'' In *Advanced Research in Marketing,* vol. 1, edited by H. Mühlbacher and C. Jochum, 509–26. Innsbruck: European Marketing Academy, 1990.

Brooke, M.Z. *Selling Management Services Contracts in International Business.* London: Holt, Rinehart and Winston, 1985.

Buckley, P.J. ''Foreign Market Servicing Strategies and Competitiveness: A Theoretical Framework.'' In *International Strategic Management,* edited by A.R. Negandhi and A. Sevara, 69–88. Lexington, MA: D.C. Heath, 1989.

Buckley, P.J., and P.N. Ghauri, eds. *The Internationalization of the Firm: A Reader.* London: Academic Press, 1993.

Calof, J. ''The Mode Choice and Change Decision Process and its Impact on International Performance.'' *International Business Review* 2, no. 1 (1993): 97–120.

Cullen, J. ''Case Study: International Collaboration.'' *Les Nouvelles* 21, no. 3 (1986): 117–21.

Cunningham, M.T., and E. Homse. ''Controlling the Marketing-purchasing Interface: Resource Development and Organisational Implications.'' *Industrial Marketing and Purchasing* 1, no. 2 (1986): 3–27.

Davidson, W.H., and D.G. McFetridge. ''Key Characteristics in the Choice of International Transfer Mode.'' *Journal of International Business Studies* 16, no. 2 (1985): 5–22.

Dowling, P.J., and D.E. Welch. ''International Human Resource Management: An Australian Perspective.'' *Asia Pacific Journal of Management* 6, no. 1 (1988): 39–65.

Erramilli, K. ''The Experience Factor in Foreign Market Entry Behavior of Service Firms.'' *Journal of International Business Studies* 22, no. 3 (1991): 479–501.

Ford, D., ed. *Understanding Business Markets: Interaction, Relationships, Networks.* London: Academic Press, 1990.

Forsgren, M., and J. Johanson, eds. *Managing Networks in International Business.* Philadelphia: Gordon and Breach, 1992.

Forsgren, M. ''Managing the International Multi-centre Firm: Case Studies from Sweden.'' *European Management Journal* 8, no. 2 (1990): 261–67.

Forsgren, M., and U. Holm. ''Multi-centre Structure and Location of Divisional Management in Swedish Multinational Firms.'' In *An Enlarged Europe in the Global Economy,* vol. 1, edited by H. Vestergaard, 185–205. Copenhagen: European International Business Association (EIBA), 1991.

Grubaugh, S.G. ''Determinants of Foreign Direct Investment.'' *The Review of Economics and Statistics* 69, no. 1 (1987): 149–52.

Grønhaug, K., and O. Kvitastein. ''Distributional Involvement in International Strategic Business Units.'' *International Business Review* 2, no. 1 (1993): 1–14.

Håkansson, H., ed. *International Marketing and Purchasing of Industrial Goods.* Chichester: Wiley, 1982.

Hedlund, G., and Å. Kverneland. ''Are Strategies for Foreign Markets Changing? The Case of Swedish Investment in Japan.'' *International Studies of Management and Organization* 15, no. 2 (1985): 41–59.

Hill, C.W.L., P. Hwang, and W.C. Kim. ''An Eclectic Theory of the Choice of International Entry Mode.'' *Strategic Management Journal* 11, no. 2 (1990): 117–28.

Hirsch, S., and A. Meshulach. ''Towards a Unified Theory of Internationalization.'' In *An Enlarged Europe in the Global Economy,* vol. 1, edited by H. Vestergaard, 577–601. Copenhagen: European International Business Association (EIBA), 1991.

Horst, T. ''Firm and Industry Determinants of the Decision to Invest Abroad: A Study of Direct Investment.'' *The Review of Economics and Statistics* 54, no. 3 (1972): 258–66.

Johanson, J., and L.G. Mattsson. ''Internationalization in Industrial Systems—A Network Approach.'' In *Strategies in Global Competition,* edited by N. Hood and J.-E. Vahlne, 287–314. New York: Croom Helm, 1988.

Johanson, J., and J.-E. Vahlne. ''The Internationalization Process of the Firm: A Model of Knowledge Development and Increasing Foreign Market Commitments.'' *Journal of International Business Studies* 8, no. 1 (1977): 23–32.

———. ''The Mechanism of Internationalization.'' *International Marketing Review* 7, no. 4 (1990): 11–24.

Johanson, J., and F. Wiedersheim-Paul. ''The Internationalization of the Firm: Four Swedish Cases.'' *Journal of Management Studies* 12, no. 3 (1975): 305–22.

Johnson, G. Commentary on ''Understanding Strategic Change Processes: Some Preliminary British Findings.'' In *The Management of Strategic Change,* edited by A.M. Pettigrew, 56–62. Oxford: Basil Blackwell, 1988.

Kim, W.C., and P. Hwang. ''Global Strategy and Multinationals Entry Mode Choice.'' *Journal of International Business Studies* 23, no. 1 (1992): 29–53.

Kogut, B., and H. Singh. ''The Effect of National Culture on the Choice of Entry Mode.'' *Journal of International Business Studies* 19, no. 3 (1988): 411–32.

Larimo, J. ''The Foreign Direct Investment Decision Process: An Empirical Study of the Foreign Direct Investment Decision Behavior of Finnish Firms.'' Research Paper 124. Vaasa: Vaasa School of Economics, 1987.

Love, J.F. *McDonald's: Behind the Arches.* Toronto: Bantam, 1986.

Lowe, J., and N. Crawford. ''Technology Licensing and the

Small/Medium Sized Firm.'' Interim Report (July). Bath: School of Management, University of Bath, 1982.

Luostarinen, R., and M. Svärd. ''Yritysten henkilöstön kansain-välistämistarve'' (Personnel needs in internationalizing firms). FIBO-publications 19. Helsinki: Vientikoulutussäätö, 1982.

Luostarinen, R., and L.S. Welch. *International Business Operations.* Helsinki: Export Consulting KY, 1990.

Macharzina, K., and J. Engelhard. ''Paradigm Shift in International Business Research: From Partist and Eclectic Approaches to the GAINS Paradigm.'' *Management International Review* 31 (1991): 23–43.

Mattsson, L.-G., H. Kjellberg, and F. Ulfsdotter. ''Internationalization Process in the European Food Production—A Network Approach.'' Paper presented at the 9th IMP Conference, Bath, 23–25 September 1993.

Melin, L. ''Internationalization as a Strategy Process.'' *Strategic Management Journal* 13 (1992): 99–118.

Mintzberg, H., and A. McHugh. ''Strategy Formation in an Adhocracy.'' *Administrative Science Quarterly* 30, no. 2 (1985): 160–97.

Nordström, K. *The Internationalization Process of the Firm: Searching for New Patterns and Explanations.* Stockholm: Institute of International Business, The Stockholm School of Economics, 1991.

Ohmae, K. ''The Global Logic of Strategic Alliances.'' *Harvard Business Review* 67, no. 2 (1989): 143–54.

Patton, M.Q. *Qualitative Evaluation and Research Methods.* Newbury Park: Sage, 1990.

Pettigrew, A. ''Introduction: Researching Strategic Change.'' In *The Management of Strategic Change,* edited by A.M. Pettigrew, 1–13. Oxford: Basil Blackwell, 1988.

Root, F.R. *Entry Strategies for International Markets.* Lexington, MA: D. C. Heath, 1987.

Ryans, J.K. ''Maintaining and Improving Competitiveness in Overseas Markets: The Corporate Perspective.'' In *Improving U.S. Competitiveness.* Washington, D.C.: U.S. Department of Commerce, 1987.

Schaan, J.-J. ''How to Control a Joint Venture Even as a Minority Partner.'' *Journal of General Management* 14, no. 1 (1988): 4–16.

Sharma, D.D. ''Management Contract and International Marketing in Industrial Goods.'' In *International Marketing Management,* edited by E. Kaynak. New York: Praeger, 1984.

Smith, A., and C.P. Zeithaml. ''The International Expansion Process: A Model and Empirical Evidence.'' In *Academy of Management Best Papers Proceedings,* edited by D.P. Moore, 152–56. Atlanta: Academy of Management, 1993.

Svensson, B. *Acquisition of Technology through Licensing in Small Firms.* Linköping: Department of Management and Economics, Linköping University, 1984.

Terpstra, V., and C.-M. Yu. ''Determinants of Foreign Direct Investment of U.S. Advertising Agencies.'' *Journal of International Business Studies* 19, no. 1 (1988): 33–46.

Thomas, T. ''Brambles' Golden Return-on-assets Rule.'' *Business Review Weekly* (29 July 1988): 125–28.

Tung, R. ''Selection and Training Procedures of U.S., European and Japanese Multinationals.'' *California Management Review* 7, no. 2 (1982): 57–71.

Turnbull, P.W. ''A Challenge to the Stages Theory of the Internationalization Process.'' In *Managing Export Entry and Expansion,* edited by P.J. Rosson and S.D. Reid, 21–40. New York: Praeger Publishers, 1987.

Van de Ven, A.H. ''Suggestions for Studying Strategy Process: A Research Note.'' *Strategic Management Journal* 13 (1992): 169–88.

Welch, L.S. ''Internationalization by Australian Franchisors.'' *Asia Pacific Journal of Management* 7, no. 2 (1990): 101–21.

Welch, L.S., and R. Luostarinen. ''Internationalization: Evolution of a Concept.'' *Journal of General Management* 14, no. 2 (1988): 34–55.

———. ''Inward-outward Connections in Internationalization.'' *Journal of International Marketing* 1, no. 1 (1993): 46–58.

Welch, L.S., and F. Wiedersheim-Paul. ''Initial Exports—A Marketing Failure?'' *Journal of Management Studies* 17, no. 3 (1980): 333–44.

Wiedersheim-Paul, F., H.C. Olson, and L.S. Welch. ''Pre-Export Activity: The First Step in Internationalization.'' *Journal of International Business Studies* 9, no. 1 (1978): 47–58.

Yaprak, A. ''An Empirical Study of the Differences Between Small Exporting and Non-exporting U.S. Firms.'' *International Marketing Review* 2, no. 2 (1985): 72–83.

Yin, R.K., *Case Study Research.* Rev. ed. Newbury Park, CA: Sage Publications, 1989.

Young, S., J. Hamill, C. Wheeler, and J.R. Davies. *International Market Entry and Development: Strategies and Management.* Hemel Hempstead, England: Harvester Wheatsheaf, 1989.

PRODUCTION

The diligent student might want to reread John Dunning's article in Section 3B before studying the articles in this section. He or she should relate the following question to issues of manufacturing site selection or sources of purchased raw materials and/or components. Do the points Dunning makes about country competitiveness suggest that his analysis might help to identify or confirm a particular country as a good site?

READING SELECTIONS

Alan MacCormack, Lawrence Newman, and Donald Rosenfield examine manufacturing site location decisions in light of important trends in the global economy and in manufacturing technology and management. They point out the disadvantages of making these decisions based only on comparative costs. They emphasize the importance of following strategies that give them a manufacturing presence where their markets are located and where trade restrictions dictate.

The authors propose a four-phase framework for making production location decisions. They begin with an analysis of the business and the role of manufacturing and progress to a quantitative analysis conducted among acceptable sites. Their framework points out the importance of understanding one's business and one's present and anticipated competitive environment in selecting manufacturing locations.

William Johnston reminds us that, just as production has moved across national boundaries, so has both skilled and unskilled labor. He sees this trend as accelerating, driven by a growing gap between labor supply and demand in many areas of the world. His article presents some rather interesting data on work force growth in the developing and the industrialized countries and on women's participation in the work force.

Johnston envisions a world in which labor moves to where the jobs are, while the previous article assumes that manufacturing will move to where the labor is. What will actually happen is worth some speculation. Is it possible, for example, that labor movement goes in two directions? For years, large cohorts of Korean, Taiwanese, and Indian students came to the U.S. for graduate work in science and engineering. Many stayed on after finishing school because there were few opportunities at home. Since the late 1980s, these engineers and scientists have been returning home in increasing numbers as excellent opportunities opened up in their home countries.

Tamer Cavusgil, Attila Yaprak and Poh-Lin Yeoh recognized the growing importance of outsourcing as an alternative to in-house manufacture. They show that firms' decisions to outsource may be motivated by different considerations; they may be proactive or reactive and may be aimed either at gaining competitive advantage or at capitalizing on comparative advantage peculiar to a specific location.

The authors emphasize the importance of sourcing, or at least investigating sourcing alternatives globally. They present a decision-making framework to organize and implement a global sourcing program. In common with the conclusions of the MacCormack, Newman, and Rosenfield article, they point to the importance of understanding the business as a prelude to effective outsourcing. It is worth comparing the MacCormack et al. framework for selecting a production site with the outsourcing framework in this article. How do the two decisions fit together? Do plant site decisions affect where one outsources? Should the ready availability of outsourced needs influence manufacturing site locations?

24

THE NEW DYNAMICS OF GLOBAL MANUFACTURING SITE LOCATION

ALAN DAVID MacCORMACK, LAWRENCE JAMES NEWMAN III, AND DONALD B. ROSENFIELD*

ABSTRACT   Manufacturing site location has received limited exposure in strategic planning literature. Approaches often emphasize quantitative data such as transport costs, exchange rates, taxes, labor rates, and other cost-based variables. Yet location decisions based primarily on cost underestimate the importance of qualitative factors that are more likely to provide long-term advantages. This article examines the impact on location of recent trends in the global trading environment, new production systems, and new technologies. These suggest that global corporations of the future will develop a manufacturing network of decentralized plants based in large, sophisticated, regional markets. Each plant will be smaller and more flexible than is typical today. The location of such plants will be based more on regional infrastructure and local skill levels than on purely cost-based factors.

The past twenty years have seen the development of a global marketplace in almost all major industries. Since 1962, worldwide exports have increased from 12 percent to more than 30 percent of world GNP,[1]

* Alan David MacCormack is an associate at Booz-Allen & Hamilton's London office. Lawrence James Newman III is a senior engineer at Analog Devices, Inc. Donald B. Rosenfield is a senior lecturer and director of the Leaders for Manufacturing Fellows Program, MIT Sloan School of Management.

totaling $3.5 trillion in 1992.[2] If one considers the potential exposure to import penetration, more than 70 percent of goods now operate in an international marketplace.[3] Every organization must now formulate strategies within a global context.

Global competition affects a firm's manufacturing strategy by dramatically increasing the complexity of decision making. Worldwide markets can be served in many ways; for example, by export, local assembly, or fully integrated production. Underpinning these factors is the optimal configuration of the organization's production resources. Location is an important part of that picture, but one that is usually given only limited attention. Decisions are often based purely on quantitative analyses that trade off transport costs, scale economies, and other cost-based variables. This practice, however, can lead to suboptimal results, as decision makers tend to focus only on factors that are *easily* quantifiable. Important qualitative issues are frequently neglected or used only to temper results. These factors are often central to supporting or creating a competitive advantage. For example, location dictates the level of knowledge embedded in the workforce; as such, it can affect the ability of firms to implement skill-based process technologies, or it can limit the effectiveness of quality programs.

Another disadvantage of strictly cost-based methods is that they tend to focus on factor cost advantages, which are all too often transitory. Government regulations, tax systems, and exchange rates can quickly change. Strategies based on such parameters may eventually be rendered obsolete by the very factors that first created advantage.

When formulating a site location strategy, companies should therefore emphasize the qualitative factors required to ensure that it supports the business strategy. Only after establishing a set of desirable location options should companies refine choices using cost-based algorithms.

In this paper, we examine how recent macroeconomic- and business-level trends have affected site location decisions. We describe how the dynamics in production systems, technologies, and management philosophies have changed location requirements. Finally, we propose a new framework for assisting in site location decisions and a model of the future global manufacturing firm.

MACROECONOMIC-LEVEL TRENDS AND IMPLICATIONS

The presence of large overseas markets suggests that there are benefits of scope for firms that sell globally. However, trends in trade and investment patterns indicate that the most effective way to serve global markets is with a regional approach, which reduces cost, provides better customer feedback, and minimizes risk resulting from exchange rate fluctuations and other political factors.

OVERSEAS MARKETS

The development of large and sophisticated overseas markets dictates a global presence for leading manufacturers.

The global company cannot ignore the large potential markets that have emerged overseas. Many countries once regarded as less developed or developing now constitute large markets for leading-edge, quality products. U.S. companies no longer possess the world's largest, most sophisticated market. The collective income of Europe has now surpassed that of North America.[4] Japanese consumers have the largest per capita income of any large industrialized nation.[5] In addition, the fastest growing economies are not the existing industrial giants but are in the emerging and developing markets and, in particular, those areas of Southeast Asia that have historically been the base for low-cost exporters.

As global firms expand their presence to these markets, the economies of scope they can generate will provide a significant source of advantage against local players. Global giants can sink large sums into product development, which are recouped across multiple markets. They have deep pockets to fight local market share wars. For the national player with no niche to hide in, the choice can be stark. Get global, get eaten, or get out.

Firms cannot compete in these global markets, however, by pushing mature products to overseas subsidiaries. Vernon's ''product cycle'' approach to overseas markets became antiquated long ago.[6] Product innovations introduced in the United States will be rapidly copied, improved on, and introduced to other markets within months if the producer doesn't quickly exploit worldwide opportunities.

The development of such sophisticated markets means that lead users are no longer in one place but have to be sought out in the most demanding market (for example, in consumer electronics, Japan; in sophisticated computers, the United States). Locating production within such markets will facilitate quicker customer feedback, giving the firm a product development edge and enabling it to capture spillover benefits from the local industry base. It also allows tailoring to local tastes.

TRADE AND INVESTMENT PATTERNS

Increasing levels of nontariff barriers (NTBs) are forcing firms to localize production resources.

NTBs are trading requirements that circumvent the General Agreement on Tariffs and Trade (GATT) legislation. By placing restrictions on local content, sales volumes, or market share, NTBs interfere with a firm's ability to serve a market through an export-based strategy. The 1980s saw a trend of increased protectionism in developed economies through such mechanisms. During this decade, the percentage of U.S. imports subject to NTBs doubled to 25 percent.[7] For major industrialized countries, over 22 percent of imports are affected.[8] More important, such practices are increasingly directed at imports from less developed, low labor-cost countries. The European Community (EC), for example, restricts only 13 percent of imports from advanced economies, but almost 25 percent of imports from less developed countries.[9]

Particularly in Europe, there has been an increase in restrictive rules of origin and local content requirements, forcing firms to localize more parts of their manufacturing value chain. Products sourced within the EC qualify for national origin status and its compensating benefits. Voluntary Export Restraints (VERs) have also found favor as a trade-restrictive tool. The value of trade affected by VERs increased by 60 percent during the 1980s, representing half the growth in government intervention. Currently some 250 agreements are in force, most directed at Japan and other Asian companies.[10]

These policies penalize an export-based strategy; they force a shift toward foreign investment and therefore promote a decentralized manufacturing strategy. For companies that have established facilities within a region, these policies shape the nature of the operation, expanding the scope of local activities. More components are sourced from local suppliers, or the firm increases the local value-added within its manufacturing process. This trend is illustrated by a recent study of Japanese companies operating in Europe: more than 40 percent had increased local content during the preceding twelve months.[11]

Regionalization of trading economies is increasing the benefits to decentralized manufacturing structures.

The past decade has seen a shift from an economic world dominated by the United States to a world with three relatively equal economies: The United States, Europe, and Japan. These economic powers and others are now moving toward a system of regionalized trading blocs, each characterized by relatively free internal movement of goods and production resources, common standards, and coordinated macroeconomic policies.

The EC constitutes one focus of regional trade; it encompasses twelve member nations and special arrangements with most European states. The United States, Canada, and Mexico, through the North American Free Trade Agreement (NAFTA), are also linking their economies. The Pacific Basin, centered principally in Japan, but including the newly industrialized countries (NICs) and Association of South-East Asian nations (ASEAN), although not technically a free trade area, has become the fastest growing and foremost trading region of the world. Finally, no fewer than four free-trade blocs have been created or proposed in Latin America.[12]

This shift toward regionalization can be detected from the trends in trade and investment flows. The levels of intraregional trade have been growing faster than interregional trade. For example, the percentage of total EC exports flowing between member countries increased from 53 percent to 61 percent between 1975 and 1990.[13] Similar patterns occurred in the Americas and in the Pacific Rim.

The evolution of a world trade system based on regional blocs creates incentives for firms to follow direct investment strategies that give them a manufacturing presence in each region of significant demand and unrestricted trade. The more formally managed nature of trade between blocs will mean that firms using export-based strategies will face additional administrative hurdles and potentially damaging regulatory barriers.

RISK MANAGEMENT AND EXCHANGE RATES

Exchange rates and other aspects of risk are forcing firms to be flexible in terms of capacity and locations and to view their global networks in a coherent way.

Exposure to risk becomes critical as firms develop global networks with multiple facilities serving many markets. If a company sells in a particular market, not producing in that market exposes it to a risk of currency depreciation, thus lowering revenues. Conversely, having a large production site in a country exposes the firm to the risk of currency appreciation. In addition, the firm may face a range of political risks from political instability to increased barriers to trade.

Clearly, the trend to global operations has heightened the impact of these economic risks. From a financial and operational point of view, increased flexibility reduces risk and can even reduce average costs.[14] From a production viewpoint, such flexibility can be gained by having a number of plants serving demand, with the ability to vary plant loadings according to exchange rate trends.

While it is clear that a firm does not want to shift production cavalierly around the world, chasing every fluctuation in exchange rate, moving *marginal* production can be useful. That is, a firm can set up extra capacity so that it can execute relatively small volume shifts easily. In fact, evidence indicates that companies value such flexibility. In a recent survey, 63 percent of foreign exchange managers cited having locations ''to increase flexibility by shifting plant loading when exchange rates changed'' as a factor in international siting.[15] In general, a company needs to examine the complexities of multiple markets, sources, and production stages through sophisticated modeling approaches that consider the entire supply chain.

BUSINESS-LEVEL TRENDS AND IMPLICATIONS

The macroeconomic trends discussed above suggest that a sound strategy for the global firm is to have a manufacturing presence in each region of significant demand. Business-level trends suggest that, while declining economies of scale facilitate this approach, the need for highly skilled labor and developed communication, transportation, and institutional infrastructures has increased. Organizational trends suggest that there are benefits to locating close to major customer markets.

CHANGES IN PRODUCTION SYSTEMS

The emergence of manufacturing technologies and methodologies such as flexible manufacturing systems, just-in-time manufacturing, and total quality management have reduced scale, increased the importance of worker education and skill, and placed demands on local infrastructure.

A flexible manufacturing system (FMS) integrates computer-controlled tools and material handling systems with a centralized monitoring and scheduling function. Such systems are most efficient when numerous different parts need to be manufactured in relatively small batches. They offer significant advantages over other manufacturing methods when the nature of product demand requires differentiation. Penetration of FMSs has been rapid. In Europe, the established base has grown at around 33 percent annually.[16] In the United States and Japan, diffusion has been even faster; the number of installed FMSs appears to be doubling every two years.[17]

Two dynamics explain the increasing attractiveness of FMSs. First, product life cycles are rapidly declining, and customers increasingly prefer customized rather than generic products. The implication is that, over time manufacturers will be forced to produce greater product variety within shorter lead times. Second, technical advances in FMSs are making them increasingly attractive to low-volume producers and more competitive with hard automation for high-volume production.

Just-in-time (JIT) manufacturing is a demand-pull production system first adopted by Japanese manufacturers and now used in many industries and countries. Based on a daily demand schedule, parts are pulled through each of the manufacturing steps, each process producing only to the demand of the succeeding process. In essence, the production process is better synchronized with customer demand, wasteful in-process inventories are avoided, and cycle times are subsequently reduced. One of the many benefits of JIT manufacturing is that these advantages can be realized with very little investment—and with wider applicability to a more diversified industry base.

The automotive and electronics industries were the torchbearers of non-Japanese JIT implementation. In 1986, a survey established that 71 percent of automotive products manufacturers had already instituted JIT, or at least a pilot program, and that 87.5 percent intended to do so within a year.[18] Similarly, in 1988, a survey of top electronics manufacturers showed that 71 percent used JIT to some degree.[19] This trend is not limited to the auto and electronics industries. A 1990 survey of 260 high-tech firms found that one-half had established JIT programs.[20] JIT is also applicable to smaller businesses, suggesting that scale is not necessarily a prerequisite.

Total quality management (TQM) is a philosophy that changes the nature of an organization. Its principles differ from classic quality control in that it takes a proactive rather than a reactive approach to improving quality. At the heart of TQM methodology is the concept of continuous improvement. By constantly looping through the "plan, do check, act" steps, improvements can be made to a process. Additionally, heavy emphasis is placed on understanding and incorporating customer requirements into daily job routines at every level. In 1989, roughly 26 percent of Japanese firms had adopted TQM.[21] Similarly, a 1990 survey of senior managers in 260 U.S.

high-tech firms indicated that 22 percent had TQM programs in all manufacturing areas.[22]

All three approaches tend to change the optimal configuration of production resources: they reduce the benefits to scale; they require well-educated, highly skilled workers; and they depend on sophisticated, well-maintained local infrastructures.

Reductions in Scale Studies of FMSs show dramatic increases in equipment utilization, thereby decreasing plant scale.[23] In one study, a comparison of a U.S. and a Japanese automotive component supplier showed that the Japanese producer manufactured a similar product in a factory with one-third the scale and three times the variety at half the cost of the U.S. producer.[24] In the days of U.S. supremacy in car production, a conventional automation system required annual volumes of a million units, relatively little year-to-year variation in demand, and a market of at least three years duration.[25] FMS scale, on the other hand, corresponds to annual sales of roughly 24,000 units.[26]

Although FMSs are the most prominent hard technology for reducing scale, the general trend is toward a range of scale-reducing technologies and methodologies, which allow smaller facilities to be constructed without the cost penalty of operation at lower volumes. However, technology *by itself* does not provide the most significant advantages. For automation to be fully leveraged, it must be accompanied by improvements in production methodologies such as JIT and TQM.[27]

A survey of firms that have implemented JIT production shows 33 percent to 40 percent reductions in setup time, scrap, and downtime.[28] Combined, these improvements increased utilization rates 26 percent and reduced the amount of workspace by 34 percent. TQM activities share similar results. When NEC IC Microcomputer Systems (NIMS) introduced TQM, productivity increased between 2.4 and 2.9 times every two years.[29]

A study quantified the benefits gained from production automation with simultaneous implementation of JIT and TQM.[30] Focusing on mature industries, the study showed that savings, depending on the country in which they were implemented, ranged from approximately 10 percent to 20 percent. Interestingly, automation alone accounted for only 2 percent to 4 percent of overall savings, while improved manufacturing methodologies like JIT and TQM had created most of the improvement.

Through the productivity increases common to these new management philosophies and improved production techniques, a plant is able to produce to the same demand with less overhead. Plant scale is thus reduced, which implies that smaller, more focused plants can satisfy given levels of demand. In addition, overhead reductions decrease labor costs as a percentage of overall product costs. The cost structure of products is therefore primarily determined by material cost, equipment depreciation, capital charges, and overhead support costs. Many of these costs are not location specific, but rather are embedded in the product through both the technologies used within it and the processes used to manufacture it. Low-cost labor therefore becomes less of a consideration in location decisions.

These benefits do not come with concessions. All these methodologies rely heavily on workforce quality and skill. Thus, while the total number of production employees may decrease, the remaining workforce must be highly qualified.

Increases in Worker Education and Skill Levels The benefits of FMSs can be obtained only through a dramatic change in the nature of the workforce. FMSs are highly automated and thus reduce direct labor, relying instead on qualified engineers. In a typical system, engineers outnumber production workers three to one.[31] In considering a location for an FMS or other highly automated manufacturing facility, the company must therefore consider the local engineering labor pool.

The success of FMS, JIT, or TQM also depends on the quality of direct labor. All employees must be highly flexible and multiskilled. For FMS, an ability to understand complex machinery and computers is essential. Successful JIT manufacturing requires that employers perform preventive maintenance, repairs, and complex planning activities. TQM also requires a highly skilled workforce, since the improvement tools make extensive use of mathematics and

statistics. Softer skills such as team dynamics and proactive problem-solving techniques are also important.

Some companies have assumed responsibility for educating employees through internal training programs. Motorola, a company committed to TQM and JIT, spends approximately $60 million annually for internal training. As a percentage of payroll, this exceeds that of the average company by a factor of two.[32] Nevertheless, Motorola recognizes that the workforce must have a knowledge base to enhance the internal training program's effectiveness. All new employees are required to pass entrance tests and must have at least a high school diploma.[33]

While these methodologies may emphasize different skills, employees must be more highly skilled than the factory worker of a generation ago. When considering potential sites, firms must regard local employee skills as a key decision variable. Plant locations should be supported by an educational infrastructure that provides workers with basic science, math, and communication skills. Preferably they should also have some exposure to modern technology and manufacturing practices. Such factors suggest that progressive manufacturing practices will be more effective in developed regions, close to relatively sophisticated markets, rather than in less developed, low labor-cost regions.

The importance of labor skill and effective management philosophies has been corroborated in a recent empirical study comparing select mature industries in less developed countries (LDCs) to those in NICs.[34] The authors demonstrated that the overall costs saved from locating in NICs exceeded the labor cost savings from locating in LDCs. In effect, the authors showed that NICs are more competitive than LDCs even though they have higher factor costs.

Trends in foreign direct investment parallel the conclusions of this study. In the 1970s, one-third of foreign direct investment went to less developed countries. In the 1980s, this proportion declined substantially; less than one-fifth of foreign direct investment went to less developed countries. Instead, investment flowed between the sophisticated markets of the EC, the United States, and Japan. The proportion of direct investment flowing between these regions increased from 30 percent to 39 percent during the 1980s.[35]

Importance of Institutional and Transportation Infrastructures The adoption of JIT policies increases a manufacturer's dependence on its supplier network and support services. Complete production shutdowns can result if raw materials, components, or assemblies are delivered late. Therefore, a reliable institutional infrastructure is critical. In major industries like automobile production, it is possible to develop such an infrastructure, as Japanese automobile transplants in the United States demonstrated when they attracted component suppliers to the "transplant corridor" from Ontario to Tennessee. However, most companies possess neither the scale nor the leverage to create their own supplier network where they choose to locate. It is generally easier to choose a manufacturing location where an infrastructure already exists. Whether existing or attracted after the fact, such infrastructure is critical.

These considerations have influenced Motorola's manufacturing site location decisions in the cellular telephone industry. Currently, 80 percent to 90 percent of Motorola's vendors deliver directly to the line. In considering the location of manufacturing facilities, the presence of a sophisticated supplier infrastructure was of primary importance. Not all global manufacturing locations meet this criterion. A previous attempt to take advantage of cost-based manufacturing, through location in Puerto Rico, was unsuccessful.[36] When faced with the decision of how to serve the European market, Motorola chose to produce cellular phones in Easter Inch, Scotland. Located in the "Silicon Glen" region of Scotland, vendor proximity and a well-educated labor pool were readily available.[37]

That JIT manufacturing requires constant contact with suppliers also places demand on the local infrastructure. Companies frequently request suppliers to make deliveries several times a day. This consideration tends to favor locating JIT-based manufacturing facilities in industrialized regions with developed transport and communications systems.

ORGANIZATIONAL PHILOSOPHIES

The need for organizational learning has increased the benefits of being close to all major, sophisticated markets.

During the 1980s, U.S. corporations awoke to the fact that technical superiority alone does not provide a sustainable source of advantage. Management approaches can have even more dramatic impact on performance, as the Japanese automakers demonstrated. Product innovations did not initially drive their success, but rather a new managerial philosophy that overcame scale disadvantages by reducing time to market, improving quality, reducing inventories, and increasing productivity.[38]

In the 1990s, however, both product and management advantages are no longer sustainable. For example, technical positions can easily be copied and even built upon, as demonstrated by PC clone manufacturers like Dell. As globalization increases, firms will increasingly find that static advantages based on traditional competitive positions are no longer enough. Those firms that are capable of learning and disseminating knowledge faster than their competitors will achieve superior performance.

A proponent of this view, Ray Stata, CEO of Analog Devices, argues that "the rate at which individuals and organizations learn may become the only sustainable competitive advantage, especially in knowledge-intensive industries."[39] Research in the shoe, bike, PCB, and steel industries supports the view that the key to establishing manufacturing excellence is to create a learning organization capable, for example, of assimilating new production methodologies.[40] Companies that succeed not only will harbor the cost advantages noted earlier but, since knowledge is cumulative, will also be better poised for further incremental improvement.

Pivotal in establishing a learning organization is an awareness of global developments, suggesting that international information networks or linkages are a key factor in organizational and technical learning. The importance of creating "global feelers" is often underestimated. It could be argued, for example, that if U.S. firms had had a stronger presence in the Japanese market, the value of JIT and TQM philosophies would have been recognized and adopted sooner.

The importance of building a learning organization suggests that decentralization can benefit the firm. Such companies will have a network of feelers that can recognize new technological, market, and management trends. Although disseminating this knowledge through a far-flung, decentralized organization is difficult, firms that have experienced such difficulties and reembraced more centralized control are missing an opportunity. Those that harness the advantages of decentralization to create a dynamic learning organization will possess a formidable and sustainable source of advantage.

TOWARD A NEW FRAMEWORK

Traditional approaches to production location no longer apply. Large, centralized manufacturing facilities in low-cost countries with poorly skilled workers are not sustainable. The trends we have discussed lead to a more decentralized manufacturing structure with smaller, lower-scale plants serving demand in regional markets. Location will depend increasingly on educational and institutional infrastructure.

These trends must be set in the context of the overall environment, with both internal and external constraints. Internally, the corporate strategy, the availability of capital, the characteristics of the existing site network, and the company's growth strategy will influence its decisions. Externally the location strategies of competitors will also have impact.

These factors can be synthesized into a new framework for setting location policy. We propose a four-phase procedure to aid decision makers.

PHASE 1

Establish the critical success factors of the business, the degree of global orientation necessary, and the required manufacturing support role.

The first step in formulating a site location strategy is to examine how the firm competes. Managers should assess the degree to which the business strategy requires leading performance in each of four areas: cost, quality, innovation (time-to-market), and flexibility. The differences in emphasis between each of these factors will have significant impact on aspects of the location strategy.

For businesses where cost leadership is the sole driver of competition, location is important only as a driver for reducing transportation, labor, and inventory costs. For markets with a stronger emphasis on other factors, however, location has an expanded role: leadership in quality places higher demands on both the workforce and the suppliers. Competing through innovation and time-to-market requires customer proximity, a coordinated design-manufacturing link, and, potentially, local development resources. Achieving best-in-class flexibility may again require customer proximity and, potentially, a different set of production techniques and skills. Such requirements must be fully understood at the outset to help define many features evaluated in subsequent phases.

The second step is to forecast the likely evolution of the industry in terms of global market requirements. That is, can companies survive by serving only localized markets, or will they eventually submit to larger, financially strong companies, operating globally? In addressing this question, it is useful to examine three outcomes for an industry's evolution: scale-driven consolidation, scope-driven consolidation, and niche/local market-driven fragmentation. The factors that determine this evolution are the underlying basis of competition, strategies of competitors, and the industry cost structure.

To develop a forecast of evolution, managers need to evaluate the drivers most likely to affect the industry's development, and to what degree. For example, the presence of high economies of scale is often a key factor in the need to leverage greater product volumes. This tends to take effect at the plant level, suggesting ever-bigger plants serving multiple markets. Economies of scope also drive consolidation, but in a different manner; these are gained through scale in market access or capital resources. Large pharmaceutical companies, for example, have escalated research expenditures to levels that smaller companies cannot sustain. Those levels can be achieved only by serving many markets, across which investments are recouped.

The third step is a review of the internal constraints that may limit a firm's ability to implement the optimal location strategy—primarily, the availability of investment capital and managerial resources. These limitations should be fully understood and defined at the outset. For example, while industry dynamics may suggest that global scale is a necessity for success, financial and managerial limitations may restrict the options available for expansion. In such cases, firms may be better served by seeking alliances to increase product volumes.

The nature of a firm's growth strategy may also have substantial impact on location decisions. Building a coherent network of plants serving local markets can take more than ten years. Any company that generates growth primarily through acquisition is likely to become a significantly different organization over such time frames. Location is unlikely to be a strategic priority for firms that rely on frequent asset trading to increase shareholder value.

The final step in this phase is to synthesize the impact of all these factors on the overall manufacturing strategy. The business strategy, for example, will dictate to a great extent the type of production processes and technologies to employ: at one extreme, cost-sensitive markets may require large transfer line systems; at the other, locally responsive markets may require more flexible operations, located within markets, and with the ability to customize products for individual customers.

The output of phase one is a comprehensive assessment of the company's basis of competition and the manufacturing capabilities for supporting it. These factors will be the primary determinants of whether a global manufacturing network is appropriate, and to what degree such a network can generate and sustain competitive advantage.

PHASE 2

Assess options for regional manufacturing configuration, considering market access, risk management, *customer demand characteristics, and the impact of production technologies on plant scale.*

The first step is to assess political and market access requirements. To avoid tariffs and other nontariff trading restrictions, firms should locate within trading blocks. They should understand the nature and composition of the blocks, as well as their likely development. In addition, market requirements for exempt status, such as local content stipulations, should be well defined. Firms should assess other political issues, such as incentives for local investment in facilities or contract offset agreements, for an overview of the political imperatives. Obviously, the level of long-term political stability is also critical.

The second step is to assess the degree of risk inherent in serving the regional market. Assessing risk and the options for managing it encompasses both the forecasting of exchange rate movements and development of scenarios on product sourcing. Rapid fluctuations in rates can be hedged in the short term with financial instruments, but the value of production flexibility should be evaluated for longer-term changes, within and between given regions of demand.[41] The value of flexible production capacity will influence the assessment of optimal site numbers and their specific locations.

Step three defines the characteristics of regional demand: the level of homogeneity in customer requirements across a region, the size of demand in each country, and the forecast for future development. The objective is to elaborate on the firm's ability to serve demand from one point within a region versus the benefits of multiple sources. For example, in industries with a premium for local differentiation, markets may be better served by multiple plants, each with a high degree of production flexibility. When combined with the basis of competition, such characteristics will define priority areas of demand, potential plant numbers, and those areas most likely to be considered potential location choices.

The final step is to establish the effect of production technologies on plant scale in order to define a range of production parameters, such as the potential number of sites in each region, the ranges of product volumes, and the capacities for each stage of production. As we discussed earlier, developments in production process technologies have significantly reduced the benefits to scale at the plant level, thus enabling smaller plants to serve markets effectively. For a company competing on, say, innovation and time-to-market, maximizing the number of plants subject to minimum scale may be appropriate. Companies adopting such a dispersed strategy, however, must weigh the costs of complexity against forecast market benefits.

All these factors must be set in the context of competitors' strategies. Many competitors will likely be attempting to establish a global presence simultaneously. First movers often have advantages, for example, in tying up local joint-venture partners, or establishing a "blue chip" distribution network. In fast-growing regions, such dynamics can lead to preemptive capacity expansion, committing investments to markets with less volume than appears economically viable.

PHASE 3

Define a set of potential sites, primarily based on infrastructure, that adequately supports the business and manufacturing strategies.

The first step in this phase is to assess the production methodologies for each location. This assessment will dictate demands on the workforce, the supplier base needed, and the requirements of transport/communication networks. As discussed, new techniques such as JIT, FMS, and TQM give more responsibility to line workers than traditional systems do. They also make more stringent demands on local suppliers and physical infrastructure.

The components of site infrastructure should be separated into "hard" and "soft" requirements. Hard or tangible factors relate to the physical availability of supplier, communication, and transport systems. These factors are influenced by the nature of the manufacturing system and the degree of vertical integration. Softer factors relate to organizational and educational infrastructure, for example, inherent workforce education levels, or suppliers with specific technical know-how. These factors, often overlooked in traditional location algorithms, are among

the most important for future sources of competitive advantage.

The second step is to examine, on a pro forma basis, the levels of infrastructural development for each broad location option defined in previous phases. For example, the need for trained technical staff might suggest a location near specific institutions or science parks. On this basis, the range of potential sites can be narrowed to specific areas in a region. In practice, there will be many other such factors to integrate in the analysis. The resulting options are those that best meet a range of infrastructural parameters, yet do not fail to meet any that are critical.

The output of this phase is a detailed evaluation of specific sites that have sufficient infrastructure to maintain the firm's basis of competition.

PHASE 4

Rank the most cost-effective solutions, using a quantitative analysis of remaining location options, and define the manner of operation.

After defining a range of sites with suitable infrastructure, as well as the potential ranges of activity for each site, the company should establish the size of the facilities, the specific locations, the product flow from source to market, and the sourcing and location of specific products and processes. Computer-based models should be used to detail the manufacturing network. The company should decide which facilities to use and which production and distribution activities for each time period to handle at that location. Specifically, it should define a decision level for each combination of plant, market, and production stage for a given product, as well as a distribution path. For a given scenario of exchange rates and facility options, a numerical algorithm would identify activity levels. The company should then iteratively evaluate currency scenarios and major strategy options. While the details of such an approach are beyond this paper's scope, an example can give a sense of the nature of the decision variables.

A pharmaceutical manufacturer had already selected sites, but it needed to determine product sourcing and material flow. It had a mixture of plants in the United States, Europe, Asia, and Latin America and made syrups all over the world, pills and capsules in two U.S. plants, Puerto Rico, and Ireland, and animal-based products at a different U.S. plant. The plants were each a jumble of different products and processes, and detailed costs and levels of scale were little understood. While scale was important for some products, others could be made efficiently in different markets. A decision support system, based on the classification of products into twenty-five groups, showed the ideal locations and volumes for each of the products and processes. As a result, the U.S. plants were better focused on different types of products and process steps for some products (the latter when different scale and technology needs characterized the process steps for a given set of products). The two tax havens of Puerto Rico and Ireland were focused on their most appropriate products.

TOWARD A MODEL OF THE GLOBAL MANUFACTURING COMPANY

Three basic principles will direct global decision makers' thinking as they reconsider how to make manufacturing location decisions: increasingly, companies will serve all major markets; manufacturing will be based on regional presence; and infrastructure will be more important than pure ''cost'' factors.

ESTABLISHING GLOBAL PRODUCT VOLUMES

Global companies of the future will serve all major markets, leveraging economies of scope to undermine the competitive strength of domestic players. These dynamics are being brought about through the evolution of fixed costs as the primary determinant of a firm's cost structure. Although manufacturing scale is decreasing, other effects are playing out in areas such as technology and marketing.

In high-tech products, scale in technology has become more relevant than scale in manufacturing. In-

vestment levels have risen in the drive for rapid innovation, so industry players have sought more markets across which to recoup R&D expenditures. In pharmaceuticals, this evolution has already occurred. Industry giants such as Merck have raised the stakes through massive R&D investment. During a short time, the industry underwent substantial transformation through mergers, acquisitions, and divestments. Now there are few, if any, purely national players.

In consumer products, financial scale is playing a transformative role. Global competitors use financial scale to their advantage by managing cash flows between different product segments or national markets. A giant like Procter & Gamble can gain entry into a local market by undercutting domestic competitors and investing heavily in promotion. Local players cannot compete with P&G's deep pockets without significant profit penalty.

Establishing global product volumes does not mean that products have to be homogeneous across markets. Scale in technology can be spread across locally tailored products, differentiated products, or, indeed, different product families. Honda, for example, has unique capabilities in the design and manufacture of engines. It uses this to great advantage across a line of businesses, from automobile to power boats to lawn mowers. Honda's competitive advantage now lies in fast-cycle innovation and in the scope of its operations. In essence, economies of scope rather than scale are now the driving force in global competition.

ESTABLISHING A DECENTRALIZED MANUFACTURING NETWORK

The global company of the future will establish a manufacturing presence in each region of significant market demand. These facilities will be smaller and more flexible. Trends in trade and investment incentives are exerting powerful pressures in this direction, and new production methods and management techniques facilitate it through reduced economies of scale and increased flexibility. Regional manufacturing plants will benefit from rapid customer feedback on product performance and will help efforts to build a learning organization through exposure to multiple markets.

Once a manufacturing presence is established in a market, the number of sites for serving the region becomes a function of the classical trade-off between scale benefits and transport costs. Where scale benefits are reduced significantly, there is potential for multiple plants to serve a single region. Currently, the major world markets are North America, Europe, and Asia-Pacific. Competing in these regions is essential for the global player. As developing economies grow to significant size, however, other regions of critical scale will emerge.

EMPHASIZING INFRASTRUCTURE OVER COST

Increasingly, the location of manufacturing sites will be based less on the classic measure of labor cost and more on manufacturing infrastructure. Companies will locate facilities closer to final markets, where the workforce has the necessary skill and knowledge base.

The labor requirements of new systems and techniques are driving the need for a better educated direct-labor workforce. FMS, JIT, and TQM systems place greater importance on the flexibility of the workers and their ability to operate under growing autonomy. The increasing sophistication of product and process technologies has also increased skill requirements.

As new production systems have reduced the amount of direct labor in product cost, capital has become proportionately more important. Capital costs are essentially the same the world over, and therefore increasing the capital intensity of the production process decreases the sensitivity to site location. Companies continuing to focus on direct labor cost savings may find transitory advantages, but eventually, as has happened in Korea, cost pressures will wipe out such advantages. Given these factors, locating facilities closer to final markets, with less emphasis on labor cost, is a natural progression.

The final factor in site infrastructure as the key determinant of production location is the need for a sophisticated vendor network. JIT systems require a supplier base that is capable, reliable, and physically close (around two hours or 100 miles). Such requirements dictate that existing industrialized regions will increasingly attract the investment of global manufacturing firms. Deploying manufacturing resources in larger, sophisticated regions will allow leverage of existing suppliers' capabilities. This will aid entry strategies that rely on significant outsourcing during initial production while higher value-added capabilities are developed.

SOME CAVEATS

Although the trends affecting production location are pushing all firms toward globally dispersed manufacturing, their effects will not be felt equally by all industries, and not in any one industry at all stages.

Young Industries Industries still in the early stages of their life cycle will tend to adopt more centralized manufacturing networks than industries in more mature stages because of the rate of change in product and process technology and the nature of product demand.

Early on, the technology involved in a product fluctuates as firms are still making design innovations. At the same time, the process technology for manufacturing evolves through a flexible, general purpose form toward a more efficient, capital-intensive process.[42] The control of this evolutionary process provides many challenges to the firm, such as maintaining a strong link between manufacturing and development. The firm's manufacturing systems must be flexible enough to incorporate the changes, and the workforce must be able to understand and adapt to different technologies.

In industries characterized by this fluidity, managing a dispersed manufacturing network is particularly complex. As each innovation occurs, it has to be rolled out coherently. Possible major changes in product and process technology could render existing investments inefficient or obsolete. In such an environment, therefore, there is a tendency to limit the amount of decentralized manufacturing to a level below that expected in the long term.

Although these dynamics also occur in life cycles at the individual product level, the manufacturing location decision is usually concerned only with the dynamics at the industry level. In a mature industry, even new products should have relatively stable technologies, and the product rollout decision is driven by the need to access all global markets quickly. Thus a decentralized strategy makes sense.

Products with High Unskilled Labor Content

For products with unavoidably high levels of direct labor, the tendency will be to choose lower-cost locations near final markets rather than the final market itself. In this way, advantages of proximity are not diminished significantly. In Europe, for example, assembly operations would conceivably be located in Portugal, rather than in a more developed country.

A high labor content, however, should not immediately be viewed as sufficient grounds for a low-cost country strategy. New production technologies are getting cheaper and provide many other advantages in terms of flexibility, quality, and consistency. Successful companies will drive changes in production technologies, rather than tacitly accepting the existing way of doing business.

Production Systems with High Minimum Efficient Scale

Industries with large scale-intensive elements will tend to consolidate these operations and, potentially, split the supply chain. Where these operations constitute the major part of the manufacturing process, large, scale-driven plants may still exist. In the semiconductor industry, for example, wafer fabrication is tremendously scale intensive because of the immense investments in equipment—between $500 million and $1 billion. Most manufacturers, therefore, consolidate all such processing to a few major facilities, while relying on local assembly and tests to satisfy local content regulations.

Although a significant minimum efficient scale in a process makes a strong case for the breakup of the value chain, firms should be careful not to take these economics as given. A thorough investigation of all production methods is needed. For example, the advent of FMSs substantially changed the economics of transfer line systems. Decades ago, U.S. automobile firms setting their facilities strategy developed large-scale myopia. The Japanese have since shown that economies of scale are not static; they tend to move in one direction—down.

CONCLUSION

In this paper, we have examined recent trends in global competition that affect the location of international manufacturing sites. Advances in technology, changes in management philosophies, and shifting market requirements are the new dynamics that shape a firm's facility network. These trends suggest that global corporations of the future will move to a manufacturing network of decentralized plants, based in large, sophisticated regional markets. Specific locations will be based more on local infrastructure, such as workforce capabilities, than on cost-based considerations. Each plant will, in general, be smaller than current ones, yet have significantly more flexibility to produce multiple products.

REFERENCES

1. *Statistical Abstract of the United States* (Washington, D.C.: U.S. Bureau of the Census).
2. *The Economist Yearbook 1993* (London: Economist Books, Ltd., 1993).
3. M.C. Bogue and E.S. Buffa, *Corporate Strategic Analysis* (New York: The Free Press, 1986), chapter 4.
4. *The Economist Yearbook 1992* (London: Economist Books, Ltd., 1992).
5. Ibid.
6. R. Vernon, "International Investment and International Trade in the Product Cycle," *Quarterly Journal of Economics,* May 1966, pp. 190–207.
7. "Mercantilists in Houston," *The Economist,* 7 July 1990, pp. 14–15.
8. Japan External Trade Organization, "White Paper on International Trade" (Tokyo, Japan, 1989).
9. *World Development Report* (New York: Oxford University Press, 1991).
10. *OECD Observer* (Paris, France: Organization for Economic Cooperation and Development, 1991).
11. Coopers and Lybrand on-line publication, "EC Commentaries on Trade Relations, EC-Japan" (Brussels, Belgium: European Union Office, section 3.2, 24 February 1994).
12. "Free Trade Free-For-All," *The Economist,* 4 January 1992, p. 63.

13. *Handbook of International Development Statistics* (New York: U.N. Conference on Trade and Development, 1991), p. 39.

14. A. Huchzermeier, "Global Manufacturing Strategy Planning under Exchange Rate Uncertainty" (Philadelphia, Pennsylvania: University of Pennsylvania, Wharton School, working paper 91-02-01 and PhD dissertation, 1991).

15. D.B. Lessard, "Survey on Corporate Responses to Volatile Exchange Rates" (Cambridge, Massachusetts: MIT Sloan School of Management, working paper, 1990).

16. Frost & Sullivan, Inc., "Flexible Manufacturing Systems in Europe" (New York: Frost & Sullivan Report E953, 1987).

17. "Factory of the Future," *The Economist,* 30 May 1987, pp. 1–18 (survey).

18. "Just in Time Inventories Put Australian Firms on Stronger Footing," *Business Asia,* 9 November 1987, p. 360.

19. "Issues in Manufacturing: The View from the Top; Poll of 100 VPs for Manufacturing," *Electronic Business,* 1 November 1988, p. 106.

20. "High-Tech Vendors Lack Desire to Boost Productivity, Quality; American Electronics Association Survey," *PC Week,* 19 November 1990, p. 189.

21. "Managers of Quality," *Look Japan,* April 1989, pp. 30–31.

22. PC Week (1990).

23. R. Jaikumar, "Postindustrial Manufacturing," *Harvard Business Review,* November–December 1986, pp. 69–76; and "A Competitive Assessment of the U.S. Flexible Manufacturing Systems Industry" (Washington, D.C.: International Trade Administration, U.S. Department of Commerce, July 1985).

24. G. Stalk, Jr., "Time—The Next Source of Competitive Advantage," *Harvard Business Review,* July–August 1988, pp. 41–51.

25. D. Luria, "Automation, Markets, and Scale: Can Flexible Niching Modernize U.S. Manufacturing?" *International Review of Applied Economics,* June 1990, pp. 127–165.

26. Jaikumar (1986).

27. A. Mody, R. Suri, and J. Sanders, "Keeping Pace with Change: Organizational and Technological Imperatives," *World Development* 20 (1992): 1797–1816.

28. A.R. Inman and S. Mehra, "The Transferability of Just-in-Time Concepts to American Small Businesses," *Interfaces,* March–April 1990, pp. 30–37.

29. "Quality, From Top to Bottom," *Look Japan,* September 1989, pp. 36–37.

30. Mody et al. (1992).

31. Jaikumar (1986).

32. "Motorola Sends Its Work Force Back to School," *Business Week,* 6 June 1988, pp. 80–81.

33. Interview with Motorola managers, 14 April 1992.

34. Mody et al. (1992).

35. "Foreign Investment and the Triad," *The Economist,* 24 August 1991, p. 57.

36. Interview with Motorola managers, 14 April 1992.

37. Ibid.

38. M.A. Cusumano, "Manufacturing Innovation: Lessons from the Japanese Auto Industry," *Sloan Management Review,* Fall 1988, pp. 29–39.

39. R. Stata, "Organizational Learning—The Key to Management Innovation," *Sloan Management Review,* Spring 1989, pp. 63–74.

40. Mody et al. (1992).

41. D.B. Lessard and J.B. Lightstone, "Volatile Exchange Rates Can Put Operations at Risk," *Harvard Business Review,* July–August 1986. pp. 107–114.

42. W. Abernathy and J. Utterback, "Patterns of Industrial Innovation," in *Readings in the Management of Innovation,* ed. M.C. Tushman and W.C. Moore (New York: HarperBusiness, 1988), pp. 25–36.

25

GLOBAL WORK FORCE 2000:
THE NEW WORLD LABOR MARKET

WILLIAM B. JOHNSTON

ABSTRACT Today we talk about world markets for cars, computers, and capital. Tomorrow we will talk about a world market for labor.

For more than a century, companies have moved manufacturing operations to take advantage of cheap labor. Now human capital, once considered to be the most stationary factor in production, increasingly flows across national borders as easily as cars, computer chips, and corporate bonds. Just as managers speak of world markets for products, technology, and capital, they must now think in terms of a world market for labor.

The movement of people from one country to another is, of course, not new. In previous centuries, Irish stonemasons helped build U.S. canals, and Chinese laborers constructed North America's transcontinental railroads. In the 1970s and 1980s, it was common to find Indian engineers writing software in Silicon Valley, Turks cleaning hotel rooms in Berlin, and Algerians assembling cars in France.

During the 1990s, the world's work force will become even more mobile, and employers will increasingly reach across borders to find the skills they need. These movements of workers will be driven by the growing gap between the world's supplies of labor and the demands for it. While much of the world's skilled and unskilled human resources are being produced in the developing world, most of the well-paid jobs are being generated in the cities of

the industrialized world. This mismatch has several important implications for the 1990s:

- It will trigger massive relocations of people, including immigrants, temporary workers, retirees, and visitors. The greatest relocations will involve young, well-educated workers flocking to the cities of the developed world.

- It will lead some industrialized nations to reconsider their protectionist immigration policies, as they come to rely on and compete for foreign-born workers.

- It may boost the fortunes of nations with ''surplus'' human capital. Specifically, it could help well-educated but economically underdeveloped countries such as the Philippines, Egypt, Cuba, Poland, and Hungary.

- It will compel labor-short, immigrant-poor nations like Japan to improve labor productivity dramatically to avoid slower economic growth.

- It will lead to a gradual standardization of labor practices among industrialized countries. By the end of the century, European standards of vacation time (five weeks) will be common in the United States. The 40-hour work week will have been accepted in Japan. And world standards governing workplace safety and employee rights will emerge.

Several factors will cause the flows of workers across international borders to accelerate in the coming decade. First, jet airplanes have yet to make their greatest impact. Between 1960 and 1988, the real cost of international travel dropped nearly 60%; during the same period, the number of foreigners entering the United States on business rose by 2,800%. Just as the automobile triggered suburbanization,

William B. Johnston, author of *Workforce 2000* (Hudson Institute, 1987), is a senior research fellow at the Hudson Institute. This article is based on a study of world work force trends prepared under a grant from the U.S. Department of Labor.

which took decades to play out, so will jumbo jets shape the labor markets over many years. Second, the barriers that governments place on immigration and emigration are breaking down. By the end of the 1980s, the nations of Eastern Europe had abandoned the restrictions on the rights of their citizens to leave. At the same time, most Western European nations were negotiating the abolition of *all* limits on people's movements within the boundaries of the European Community, and the United States, Canada, and even Japan began to liberalize their immigration policies. Third, these disappearing barriers come at a time when employers in the aging, slow-growing, industrialized nations are hungry for talent, while the developing world is educating more workers than it can productively employ.

These factors make it almost inevitable that more workers will cross national borders during the 1990s. Exactly where workers move to and from will greatly influence the fates of countries and companies. And even though those movements of people are not entirely predictable, the patterns already being established send strong signals about what is to come.

THE CHANGING WORLD LABOR FORCE

The developments of the next decade are rooted in today's demographics, particularly those having to do with the size and character of various countries' work forces. In some areas of the world, for instance, women have not yet been absorbed in large numbers and represent a huge untapped resource; elsewhere the absorption process is nearly complete. Such national differences are a good starting point for understanding what the globalization of labor will look like and how it will affect individual nations and companies.

Although looming labor shortages have dominated discussion in many industrialized nations, the world work force is growing fast. From 1985 to 2000, the work force is expected to grow by some 600 million people, or 27% (that compares with 36% growth between 1970 and 1985). The growth will take place unevenly. The vast majority of the new workers—570 million of the 600 million workers—will join the work forces of the developing countries. In countries like Pakistan and Mexico, for example, the work force will grow at about 3% a year. In contrast, growth rates in the United States, Canada, and Spain will be close to 1% a year, Japan's work force will grow just .5%, and Germany's work force (including the Eastern sector) will actually decline.

The much greater growth in the developing world stems primarily from historically higher birth rates. But in many nations, the effects of higher fertility are magnified by the entrance of women into the work force. Not only will more young people who were born in the 1970s enter the work force in the 1990s but also millions of women in industrializing nations are beginning to leave home for paid jobs. Moreover, the work force in the developing world is also better and better educated. The developing countries are producing a growing share of the world's high school and college graduates.

When these demographic differences are combined with different rates of economic growth, they are likely to lead to major redefinitions of labor markets. Nations that have slow-growing work forces but rapid growth in service sector jobs (namely Japan, Germany, and the United States) will become magnets for immigrants, even if their public policies seek to discourage them. Nations whose educational systems produce prospective workers faster than their economies can absorb them (Argentina, Poland, or the Philippines) will export people.

Beyond these differences in growth rates, the work forces of various nations differ enormously in makeup and capabilities. It is precisely differences like these in age, gender, and education that give us the best clues about what to expect in the 1990s.

Women will enter the work force in great numbers, especially in the developing countries, where relatively few women have been absorbed to date. The trend toward women leaving home-based employment and entering the paid work force is an often overlooked demographic reality of industrialization. As cooking and cleaning technologies ease the burden at home, agricultural jobs disappear, and other jobs (especially in services) proliferate, women tend to be employed in the economy. Their output

The World Work Force Is Growing Rapidly (in millions)

Country or Region	Labor Force 1970	Labor Force 1985	Labor Force 2000	Labor Force Annual Growth Rate 1985–2000
World*	1,596.8	2,163.6	2,752.5	1.6%
OECD*	307.0	372.4	401.3	0.5%
United States	84.9	122.1	141.1	1.0
Japan	51.5	59.6	64.3	0.5
Germany	35.5	38.9	37.2	−0.3
United Kingdom	25.3	28.2	29.1	0.2
France	21.4	23.9	25.8	0.5
Italy	20.9	23.5	24.2	0.2
Spain	13.0	14.0	15.7	0.8
Canada	8.5	12.7	14.6	0.9
Australia	5.6	7.5	8.9	1.3
Sweden	3.9	4.4	4.6	0.3
Developing Regions*	1,119.9	1,595.8	2,137.7	2.1%
China	428.3	617.9	761.2	1.4
India	223.9	293.2	383.2	1.8
Indonesia	45.6	63.4	87.7	2.2
Brazil	31.5	49.6	67.8	2.1
Pakistan	19.3	29.8	45.2	2.8
Thailand	17.9	26.7	34.5	1.7
Mexico	14.5	26.1	40.6	3.0
Turkey	16.1	21.4	28.8	2.0
Philippines	13.7	19.9	28.6	2.4
South Korea	11.4	16.8	22.3	1.9
USSR	117.2	143.3	155.0	0.5%

* Totals include some countries not listed in table.
Sources: For OECD nations except Germany: OECD, Department of Economics and Statistics, *Labor Force Statistics, 1967–1987;* U.S. Bureau of Labor Statistics; The World Bank, *World Development Report, 1987.* For developing nations and Germany: International Labour Office, *Economically Active Population, 1950–2025;* The World Bank, *World Development Reports, 1987.*

is suddenly counted in government statistics, causing GNP to rise.

More than half of all women between the ages of 15 and 64 now work outside the home, and women comprise one-third of the world's work force. But the shift from home-based employment has occurred unevenly around the world. The developed nations have absorbed many more women into the labor force than the developing regions: 59% for the former, 49% for the latter.

More telling than the distinction between the developed and developing worlds, though, are the differences in female labor force participation by country. Largely because of religious customs and social expectations, some developed countries have relatively few women in the work force, and a small number of developing nations have high rates of female participation. The fact that women are entering

the work force is old news in Sweden, for instance, where four-fifths of working-age women hold jobs, or in the United States, where two-thirds are employed. Even in Japan, which is sometimes characterized as a nation in which most women stay home to help educate their children, about 58% of women hold paid jobs. Yet highly industrialized countries like Spain, Italy, and Germany have fairly low rates of female participation. And for ideological reasons, China, with one of the lowest GNPs per capita of any nation, has female participation rates that are among the world's highest.

The degree of female labor force participation has tremendous implications for the economy. Although a large expansion of the work force cannot guarantee economic growth (Ethiopia and Bangladesh both expanded their work forces rapidly in the 1970s and 1980s but barely increased their GNP per capita), in

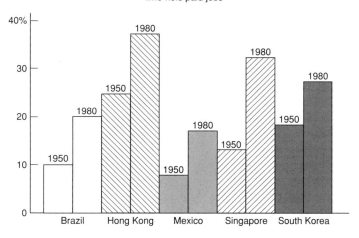

Women Join the Work Force
as Nations Industrialize

percentage of women age 15 to 64
who hold paid jobs

Source: International Labour Organization, Economically Active Population, 1950-2025, Table 2.

many cases, rapid work force growth stimulates and reinforces economic growth. If other conditions are favorable, countries with many women ready to join the work force can look forward to rapid economic expansion.

Among the developed nations, Spain, Italy, and Germany could show great gains. If their economies become constrained by scarce labor, economic pressures may well overpower social forces that have so far kept women from working. In developing countries where religious customs and social expectations are subject to change, there is the potential for rapid expansion of the work force with parallel surges in the economy.

Women are unlikely to have much effect in many other countries—Sweden, the United States, Canada, the United Kingdom, and Japan, all of which have few women left to add to their work forces. They may be able to redeploy women to more productive jobs, but the economic gains will likely be modest. Also, countries that maintain their current low utilization of women will have a hard time progressing rapidly. It is hard to imagine Pakistan, for example, a largely Moslem country where 11% of

women work, joining the ranks of the industrialized nations without absorbing more of its women into the paid work force.

As more women enter the work force worldwide, their presence will change working conditions and industrial patterns in predictable ways. The demand for services like fast food, day care, home cleaners, and nursing homes will boom, following the now-familiar pattern in the United States and parts of Europe. Child rearing and care for the disabled will be increasingly institutionalized. And because women who work tend to have more demands on them at home than men do, they are likely to demand more time away from their jobs. It is plausible, for example, that some industrialized nations will adopt a work week of 35 hours or less by the end of the 1990s in response to these time pressures.

The average age of the world's work force will rise, especially in the developed countries. As a result of slower birth rates and longer life spans, the world population and labor force are aging. The average age of the world's workers will climb by more than a year, to about 35, during the 1990s.

But here again it is important to distinguish between the developed and the developing countries. The population of the industrialized nations is much older. Young people represent a small and shrinking fraction of the labor force, while the proportion of retirees over 65 is climbing. By 2000, fewer than 40% of workers in countries like the United States, Japan, Germany, and the United Kingdom will be under age 34, compared with 59% in Pakistan, 55% in Thailand, and 53% in China.

The age distribution of a country's work force affects its mobility, flexibility, and energy. Older workers are less likely to relocate or to learn new skills than are younger people. Countries and companies that are staffed with older workers may have greater difficulty adapting to new technologies or changes in markets compared with those staffed with younger workers.

By 2000, workers in most developing nations will be young, relatively recently educated, and arguably more adaptable compared with those in the industrialized world. Very young nations that are rapidly industrializing, like Mexico and China, may find that the youth and flexibility of their work forces give them an advantage relative to their industrialized competitors with older work forces, particularly over those in heavy manufacturing industries, where shrinkage has left factories staffed mostly with workers who are in their forties and fifties.

Most industrialized nations will have 15% or more of their populations over age 65 by the year 2000, compared with less than 5% for most developing nations. The challenge that industrialized nations may face in preserving their competitive positions as their work forces age may be stiffened by the high costs of older workers and older societies. Older workers typically have higher wages because of seniority sys-

Women Hold More Than One-Third of the World's Jobs

Country or Region	Working Women 1985 or 1987* (in millions)	Female Share of Work Force (percentage of total work force)	Female Labor Force Participation (percentage of all females age 15 to 64)
World†	790.1	36.5%	51.3%
Developed Regions‡	156.5	40.9%	58.6%
United States	53.9	44.1	66.0
Japan	24.3	39.9	57.8
Germany	11.1	39.3	51.3
United Kingdom	11.7	41.4	62.6
France	10.2	42.5	55.2
Italy	8.9	36.9	43.4
Spain	4.8	32.6	37.5
Canada	5.7	43.2	65.4
Australia	3.1	39.7	54.1
Sweden	2.1	48.0	79.4
Developing Regions‡	554.2	34.7%	48.6%
China	267.2	43.2	75.5
India	76.8	26.2	32.3
Indonesia	19.8	31.3	38.0
Brazil	13.5	27.2	32.2
Pakistan	3.4	11.4	12.1
Thailand	12.2	45.9	74.8
Mexico	7.1	27.0	31.1
Turkey	7.3	34.0	47.4
Philippines	6.4	32.1	39.2
South Korea	5.7	34.0	42.2
USSR (1985)	69.2	48.3%	72.6%

* For developed regions, 1987 figures were used; for developing regions, 1985 figures.
† Totals include some countries not listed in table.
‡ Developed and developing regions as defined by the International Labour Office.
Source: International Labour Office, *Economically Active Population, 1950–2025,* Table 2.

The World's Work Force and Population Are Aging

Country or Region	Share of Work Force Under Age 34		Share of Population Over Age 65		Labor Force Participation of Workers Over Age 65
	1985	2000	1985	2000	1985
World*	57.1%	51.7%	5.9%	6.8%	32.8%
Developed Regions†	46.9%	40.7%	11.2%	13.3%	9.0%
United States	50.4	39.5	12.3	12.9	10.3
Japan	33.8	33.9	11.1	15.8	26.0
Germany	45.7	37.4	14.2	16.0	3.2
United Kingdom	43.6	38.8	15.5	15.4	4.6
France	47.0	41.5	13.6	15.6	3.0
Italy	48.0	44.6	14.0	16.7	3.9
Spain	49.9	49.0	9.1	11.5	3.8
Canada	50.9	39.7	11.1	13.1	7.1
Australia	50.7	44.4	10.7	11.6	5.1
Sweden	38.7	36.3	16.9	17.2	5.4
Developing Regions†	60.7%	54.9%	4.2%	5.1%	26.3%
China	63.7	53.3	5.5	7.3	16.0
India	55.6	52.0	3.4	4.1	40.1
Indonesia	55.7	52.7	2.8	4.2	38.3
Brazil	62.5	42.1	4.0	4.9	17.7
Pakistan	63.3	59.2	4.1	3.9	33.7
Thailand	62.8	55.2	3.9	5.2	27.2
Mexico	61.4	51.9	4.1	4.9	42.1
Turkey	59.6	54.4	4.3	5.2	10.9
Philippines	59.2	54.8	3.3	3.8	44.8
South Korea	54.7	44.2	4.5	5.9	26.5
USSR	50.2%	42.9%	9.3%	11.9%	4.4%

* Totals include some countries not listed in table.

† Developed and developing regions as defined by the International Labour Office.

Sources: International Labour Office, *Economically Active Population, 1950–2025* and *Yearbook of Labour Statistics, 1988.*

tems, and their pension and health care costs escalate sharply during the later years of their work lives. As more workers in industrialized nations retire toward the close of the century, national health and pension taxes in these nations may rise as well. Unless these rising costs are offset by productivity gains, employers and nations that have older work forces may lose their competitive leadership in industries with standardized production technologies. This could be especially challenging for Japan, where the aging of the population is proceeding even more rapidly than in other industrialized nations.

One silver lining to this cloud of higher costs may be the higher rates of personal saving that come with older populations. As workers age, they tend to save a bigger chunk of their paychecks. This could increase the capital available for investment in industrialized countries and give them more money to buy productivity-enhancing equipment. (Of course, in a world of mobile capital, these funds could just as easily flow to the developing nations if economic conditions were more promising there.)

Wealth could be redistributed in another way too. As the number of retirees in industrialized countries rises, more of them are likely to cross national borders as tourists or immigrants. Traditionally, few retirees have settled outside their home countries. But cross-border retirements and travel are likely to burgeon in the 1990s: Japanese retiring to Hawaii, Americans receiving Social Security checks in Mexico, and English pensioners sunning themselves on the coast of Spain. As Algerians, Turks, and Mexicans return home bringing retirement checks with them, these flows could mirror the movements of young workers.

People worldwide will be increasingly well edu-

Developed Countries Send More of Their Young to School

Country or Region	Percentage of Age Group in High School* 1986	Percentage of Age Group in College* 1986
OECD†	93.0%	39.0%
United States	95.0	59.0
Japan	96.0	29.0
Germany	72.0	30.0
United Kingdom	85.0	22.0
France	95.0	30.0
Italy	76.0	25.0
Spain	98.0	32.0
Canada	103.0	55.0
Australia	96.0	29.0
Sweden	83.0	37.0
Developing Regions†	40.0%	7.0%
China	42.0	2.0
India	35.0	9.0
Indonesia	41.0	7.0
Brazil	36.0	11.0
Pakistan	18.0	5.0
Thailand	29.0	20.0
Mexico	55.0	16.0
Egypt	66.0	21.0
Turkey	44.0	10.0
Philippines	68.0	38.0
South Korea	95.0	33.0
USSR	99.0%	22.0%

* Ratio of those enrolled to total school-age population. For high school, population base is typically age 13 to 17. For college population, age 20 to 24 is used. Gross enrollment level can exceed 100% if people from outside these ages are enrolled.
† Totals include some countries not listed in table.
Sources: United Nations Educational, Scientific, and Cultural Organization (UNESCO), *Statistical Yearbook, 1988;* U.S. Department of Education, National Center for Education Statistics, *Digest of Education Statistics, 1989.*

cated. The developing countries will produce a growing share of the world's high school and college graduates. Educational trends are hard to track because school and college systems differ so much from country to country and because the linkage between years of school and work skills is indirect and hard to document. Even the national data on years of education are often incomplete.

Still, the data reveal important developments. Based on the numbers of high school and college graduates, the world's work force is becoming better educated. In the decade and a half between 1970 and 1986, world high school enrollments grew by some 120 million students, or more than 76%. College enrollments more than doubled during the period—from 26 million to 58 million. This trend is likely to continue, as nations and individuals increasingly

recognize the economic value of education. By the year 2000, it is likely that high school enrollment could grow by another 60%, reaching nearly 450 million, while college attendance could double again to top 115 million.

Today, higher percentages of children in industrialized nations attend high school and college. Most of them educate nearly all children through high school and typically further educate about one-third of college-age youths. (Germany and Italy are notable exceptions; only three-quarters of children between ages 12 and 17 go to secondary school.) Most of the developing nations have less than half their young people in high school, and they seldom place more than one-fifth in college (although South Korea, Argentina, and the Philippines enroll more than one-third in college).

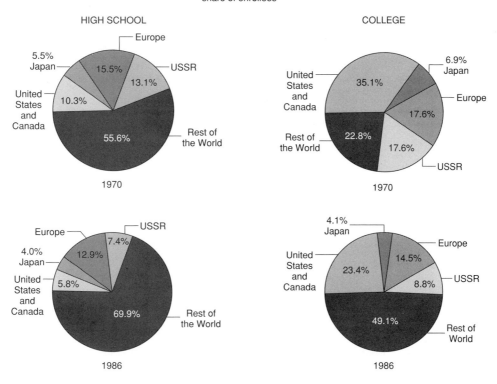

The Developing Countries Supply a Growing Share
of the World's Educated People

share of enrollees

Source: U.S. Department of Education, National Center for Education Statistics,
Digest of Education Statistics, 1989, Table 341, pp. 386-387.

But an important shift is underway: the developing world is producing a rapidly increasing share of the world's skilled human capital. This trend has been underway for some time and will accelerate through the turn of the century. In the decade and a half between 1970 and 1986, the United States, Canada, Europe, the Soviet Union, and Japan saw their share of world high school enrollees shrink from 44% to 30%. If current trends continue, their share is expected to drop to only 21% by the year 2000.

U.S. high school students made up 9% of world enrollees in 1970 but only 5% in 1986. Not only is their relative number shrinking but also U.S. students are performing worse relative to the rest of the world. International standardized tests suggest that high school students from many other nations are now better pre-

pared, at least in mathematics and science. In tests given to high school students worldwide during the mid-1980s, for instance, U.S. seniors ranked thirteenth among 13 nations in biology, twelfth in chemistry, and tenth in physics. The U.S. performance looks even weaker considering that only small fractions of American students took the tests, while greater percentages of non-U.S. students did.

The developed world is also losing ground when it comes to higher education. Between 1970 and 1985, the share of the world's college students from the United States, Canada, Europe, the Soviet Union, and Japan dropped from 77% to 51%. The share of college students in the developing world leaped from 23% to 49%, and these figures may be understatements because many students in Western universities are citizens of other countries and will return home when they graduate. By the year 2000, students from developing nations will make up three-fifths of all students.

It's true that in absolute numbers, the United States, the Soviet Union, and Japan are still the leading producers of college graduates of all kinds, but a growing number of the world's college graduates originate outside the traditionally highly educated countries. Four of the next six greatest sources of college graduates are developing countries: Brazil, China, the Philippines, and South Korea. Differences in the numbers of graduates are especially intriguing when sorted by discipline. China and Brazil rank third and fifth in numbers of science graduates, followed by Japan. For engineering graduates, Brazil, China, Mexico, Korea, and the Philippines all place ahead of France and the United Kingdom.

What makes the rising levels of education in developing countries especially significant is the link between education and economic growth. Those developing nations that educate large proportions of their young have achieved above average rates of growth and higher standards of living. Among the 42 nations labeled by the World Bank as ''low income,'' only one, Sri Lanka, sends more than half of its high school-age children to school. Among those labeled ''upper middle'' or ''high income'' (excluding the oil producers), all but two send more than 60% of teenagers to school. Only Brazil and Portugal send less.

THE PRESSURES TO EMIGRATE

The link between the education levels of the work force and economic performance argues that some well-educated, middle-income nations may be poised for rapid growth in the 1990s. In Eastern Europe, for example, Poland, Hungary, and Czechoslovakia are especially well positioned for development because of their relatively well-educated work forces coupled with their relationships with other European countries. The Philippines, Egypt, Argentina, Peru, Cuba, and Mexico also have huge growth potential because they too have relatively well-educated work forces. But their fragile political and economic infra-

structures and sometimes foolish economic policies make their development far less certain.

The tentative economic prospects of these well-educated nations illustrate the risks and opportunities facing countries whose educational systems outperform their economies. During the 1990s, workers who have acquired skills in school will be extremely valuable in the world labor markets. And if job opportunities are lacking in their native lands, better jobs will probably be only a plane ride away. Countries that fail to find a formula for growth can expect to become exporters of people. In Eastern Europe, for example, if the post-Communist rebuilding process stretches on for many years, hundreds of thousands—if not millions—of Poles, Czechs, and Hungarians will seek better opportunities in Western Europe or the United States. Similarly, if South America cannot find ways to restore investor confidence, the northward flow of economic refugees will accelerate.

Although most governments in industrial nations will resist these movements of people for social and political reasons, employers in the developed world are likely to find ways around government barriers. The combination of slow work force growth, fewer women left to enter the work force, earlier retirements, and a shrinking share of high school and college graduates virtually guarantees that many industrialized nations will face labor shortages at various points during the economic cycles of the 1990s. When they do, a growing array of occupations and labor markets will become internationalized.

Not all workers are equally likely to emigrate—or equally likely to be welcomed elsewhere. The image of the labor force as a large pool of similar workers competing for jobs is inexact. There are actually many smaller labor pools, each defined by occupational skills. Patterns of immigration will vary, depending on the conditions of markets that are defined by specific skills.

Typically, unskilled workers—janitors, dishwashers, or laborers—are recruited locally. At higher skill levels, companies often search across states or regions. Among college graduates, national labor markets are more common: New York banks interview MBAs from San Francisco; Midwestern manufactur-

Many Developing Countries Send More Than Two-Thirds
of Teenagers to High School

percentage of students age 12 to 17
enrolled in secondary school in 1989

South Korea	95%		Romania	79%		Hungary	70%	
Greece	88%		Trinidad and Tobago	76%		Chile	70%	
Yugoslavia	82%		Argentina	74%		Philippines	68%	
Poland	80%		Uruguay	71%		Egypt	66%	

Source: The World Bank, World Development Report, 1989, Table 29, p. 221.

ers hire engineers from both coasts. At the highest skill levels, the labor market has been international for many years. Bell Laboratories physicists, for example, come from universities in England or India as well as from Princeton or MIT. At Schering-Plough's research labs, the first language of biochemists is as likely to be Hindi, Japanese, or German as it is English.

When labor markets tighten and become even more specialized, however, many employers will expand the geography of their recruitment efforts. Recent trends in nursing and software design suggest the emerging patterns of the 1990s. As the shortage of nurses at U.S. hospitals became acute during the 1970s and 1980s, health care providers began to recruit in ever-widening circles. What was once a local labor market became regional, then national, and finally international. By the end of the 1980s, it was routine for New York hospitals to advertise in Dublin and Manila for skilled nurses. Similarly, in systems development, the shortage of engineers led rapidly growing companies to look to universities in England, India, and China to fill some of their U.S. job openings.

Government policies and corporate needs are likely to focus most on the immigration of younger, higher skilled workers filling specific occupational shortages. But while such flows of higher skilled workers will predominate, even unskilled jobs may become more internationalized in the 1990s. Indeed,

during the 1970s and 1980s, some of the largest international movements of workers were relatively low-skilled workers immigrating to take jobs natives didn't want: Turks to Germany, Algerians to France, Mexicans to the United States. Although these movements of low-skilled workers generate explosive social and political tensions, the economic realities of the 1990s argue that the numbers will grow.

GAINS FROM TRADE IN PEOPLE

The globalization of labor is good for the world. It allows human capital to be deployed where it can be used more productively. Countries that recognize it as a positive trend and facilitate the flow of people will benefit most.

When workers move to a developed country, they become more productive because an established economic infrastructure can make better use of their time. A street corner vendor of tacos in Mexico City would be lucky to gross $50 for a day's work, while the same worker at a Taco Bell in Los Angeles might sell 10 to 50 times as much in a day. The higher output translates into higher wages. Even at minimum wage, the new Taco Bell employee will earn 10 times his or her former daily income.

For highly skilled workers, the effects are magnified. An engineer once relegated to clerical work in Bangkok may design a new computer system when

Much of the World's Scientific Brain Power Comes from Developing Countries
(thousands of college graduates in 1986)

Country or Region	Total College Graduates	Scientists	Engineers	Ph.D.s
United States	979.5	180.7	77.1	394.3
USSR	839.5	61.7	352.3	na*
Japan	378.7	33.5	74.5	23.5
Brazil	**244.6**	**34.1**	**20.0**	**8.9**
China	**227.7**	**44.7**	**72.7**	**14.2**
Philippines†	**212.0**	**26.3**	**23.4**	**na***
Germany	172.5	35.4	30.2	22.3
France	164.4	30.6	15.0	53.9
South Korea	**155.0**	**16.9**	**21.9**	**20.7**
United Kingdom	132.7	31.4	17.0	37.4
Canada	118.9	21.1	8.4	19.8
Mexico	**112.8**	**20.4**	**25.3**	**8.0**
Egypt	**101.0**	**11.4**	**9.3**	**10.4**

* Not available.   ■ Developing countries.
† Estimated.
Source: United Nations Educational, Scientific, and Cultural Organization (UNESCO), *Statistical Yearbook, 1988,* Tables 3–10; pp. 3–306.

employed by a Boston electronics company. A Filipino nurse can go from poverty to middle class by taking a job at a hospital in Atlanta. The positive impacts of immigration are visible in robust economies of Southern California and South Florida.

Immigration will be especially good for advanced nations with high levels of capital per worker but constrained labor. In particular, immigration may boost the economies of the United States, Canada, Germany, and other European nations.

The United States is likely to fare particularly well for a number of reasons. For one thing, its wages are among the world's highest, so they attract top talent. Also, political barriers have always been low, and opportunities for immigrants to advance are great. Further, its higher education system draws a large number of students from around the world. In 1987, U.S. universities granted to foreigners some 51% of doctorates in engineering, 48% in mathematics, 32% in business, and 29% in physical sciences. Many of these graduates return home, but many stay. Either way, they stimulate the U.S. economy—by enhancing trade relationships or by increasing the U.S. supply of human capital.

Australia, New Zealand, and some European nations—notably, Germany—are also likely to gain from the international flow of people. Historically, political and cultural obstacles have constrained emigration to Europe. But language and political barriers are weakening (English and German are becoming the languages of business), and the integration of formerly Communist states in Eastern Europe into the OECD trading regime suggests that Europe will increasingly welcome people who want to cross its borders. During the summer of 1990, for example, five nations in Western Europe agreed that they would eliminate all restrictions on the rights of their citizens to live and work anywhere within their five borders. In Germany, there has been a sharp political backlash against the guest worker program that allowed many Turkish workers into the country during the 1970s. Germany remains committed to preserving its ethnic identity and plans to tighten restrictions on immigration by non-Germans, but it continues to accept thousands of German-speaking people from Russia, Poland, and other East European countries. These workers are likely to strengthen the German economy during the 1990s.

While the politics of accepting more foreigners are unfavorable in virtually every industrialized nation (and may grow worse during the coming recession), the demographic and economic trends will create pressures in most nations to accept greater flows of people. Only Japan is likely to reject increased immigration, regardless of its looming labor shortages. Japan's enormous language and cultural barriers and

High School Students in Other Countries Outperform Americans in Science (science test scores*)

Country or Region	Biology	Chemistry	Physics
Singapore	**66.8**	**66.1**	**54.9**
England	63.4	69.5	58.3
Hungary	**59.7**	**47.7**	**56.5**
Poland	**56.9**	**44.6**	**51.5**
Norway	54.8	41.9	52.8
Finland	51.9	33.3	37.9
Hong Kong	**50.8**	**64.4**	**59.3**
Sweden	48.5	40.0	44.6
Australia	48.2	46.6	48.5
Japan	46.2	51.9	56.1
Canada	45.9	46.6	48.5
Italy	42.3	38.0	28.0
United States	37.9	37.7	45.5

* Scores normalized to a mean of 50, with a standard deviation of 10.
■ Developing countries.
Source: U.S. Department of Education, *Digest of Education Statistics, 1989,* Table 348, p. 391.

its commitment to preserving its racial homogeneity virtually rule out the acceptance of many foreign workers. For the foreseeable future, Japanese economic growth will depend on native Japanese human resources. This may pose a stiff challenge for Japan because its work force is among the oldest in the world and its work force growth rate is among the lowest. One opportunity for Japan to pursue may lie in its female labor force: although a high proportion of Japanese women have paid jobs, many are underemployed and therefore not as productive as they could be. This may also be true for many—if not all—developed economies, but it seems to be especially true of Japan.

Leaders of developing nations often express concern that mass migration of their young people will harm their economies, but there is little evidence to support these fears. The large numbers of Korean, Taiwanese, and Chinese scientists and engineers who have emigrated to the United States do not seem to have had any appreciable impact on the economies at home. Indeed, many immigrants have returned home at some point in their careers, and the cross-fertilization seems to have boosted both economies. Nor have larger movements of less skilled workers harmed the economies left behind. Actually, the earnings sent home from Mexicans in the United States, Turkish guest workers in Germany, Algerians in France, and Egyptians throughout the Middle East have stimulated growth in labor-exporting countries.

A demonstration of the gains from trade in people occurred in Kuwait in 1990, when the gains were suddenly extinguished. When Iraq invaded, Kuwait's economy ground to an immediate and almost complete halt. Kuwait could no longer export oil, the occupying military force looted many businesses, but most important, the Asian and Middle Eastern workers who had made up two-thirds of the work force left for home. Hospitals lacked doctors and nurses, buses had no drivers, stores had no clerks. In the space of a few weeks, most of Kuwait's economy disappeared. Kuwait is not the only country to suffer. The huge repatriation of hundreds of thousands of Pakistani, Filipino, and Egyptian workers was equally traumatic for those nations. Not only did these workers and their families return to economies with few jobs available but their foreign earnings (a great part of which had been sent home from Kuwait) were also suddenly missing from the local economy. The gains from trade in people had been lost, and both the sending and the receiving nations were poorer because of it.

The developing countries can thrive despite massive emigration. The real test of whether they will realize their economic potential is how well they can combine their human capital with financial backing,

Developed Countries Use Labor More Productively

output per worker

Country or Region	Gross Domestic Production Value Per Worker, 1987 (in dollars)		Country or Region	Gross Domestic Production Value Per Worker, 1987 (in dollars)
World*	$6,755			

Developed Regions

United States	37,821
Japan	39,143
West Germany	38,066
United Kingdom	20,900
France	35,004
Italy	32,579
Spain	20,557
Canada	28,758
Australia	24,110
Sweden	32,318

Developing Regions

China	457
India	724
Indonesia	1,048
Brazil	5,783
Pakistan	780
Thailand	1,736
Mexico	5,112
Turkey	2,729
Philippines	1,657
South Korea	6,927

| USSR | 14,244 |

*Total includes some countries not listed in table

Sources: World Bank, World Development Report, 1989, table 3, pp. 168-169; International Labour Office, World Labour Report, 1989, Table A-1, pp. 152-155.

sensible economic policies, and a sound business infrastructure. As always, they must win investors' confidence if they are to make any real progress.

FROM GLOBALIZATION TO STANDARDIZATION

The globalization of labor is inevitable. The economic benefits from applying human resources most productively are too great to be resisted. At least some countries will lower the barriers to immigration, and at least some workers will be drawn by the opportunity to apply their training and improve their lives. But more likely, many countries will make immigration easier, and many workers will travel the globe. By the turn of the century, developing countries that have educated their young and adopted market-oriented policies will have advanced faster than those that have not. Developed countries that have accepted or sought foreign workers will be

stronger for having done so. As the benefits become more obvious, the movement of workers will become freer.

The world will be changed as a result. As labor gradually becomes international, some national differences will fade. Needs and concerns will become more universal, and personnel policies and practices will standardize. As developing nations absorb women into the work force, for example, they are likely to share the industrialized world's concern about child care and demand for conveniences.

Two forces will drive workplace standardization: companies responding to global labor markets and governments negotiating trade agreements. For a global corporation, the notion of a single set of workplace standards will eventually become as irresistible as the idea of a single language for conducting business. Vacation policies that are established in Germany to attract top scientists will be hard to rescind when the employees are relocated to New Jersey; flexible hours of work that make sense in California will sooner or later become the norm in Madrid; health care deductibles and pension contributions designed for one nation will be modified so that workers in all nations enjoy the same treatment. Typical of most innovations in corporate personnel practices, the benefits of most importance to high-wage, highly valued employees (who will be the most often recruited internationally) will be standardized first.

Government efforts to harmonize workplace standards will accelerate these market-based responses. Currently, for example, officials from most EC countries are seeking to draft a single set of rules to govern workplaces throughout Europe, beginning in 1992. These will cover such things as wage and hour standards, employment rights, and worker safety. While the comprehensive European process is not likely to be repeated elsewhere, standardized working conditions and reciprocal work rules may become an element in many trade negotiations in the 1990s, particularly those relating to services. If Mex-

ican and U.S. truck drivers were to be freely employed by companies on both sides of the border, for example, a U.S.-Mexico free trade agreement would need to cover driver licensing standards, hours of work, and fringe benefits.

Like the process of globalization of product and financial markets, the globalization of labor will be uneven and uncertain. Governments will play a greater role in the world labor markets than in other markets, and governments often will be motivated by factors other than economic gain.

But for companies and countries that accept the trends, the 1990s and beyond can be a time of great opportunity. For countries seeking to maximize economic growth, strategies that develop and attract human capital can become powerful policy tools. For companies prepared to operate globally, willingness to compete for human resources on a worldwide basis can be a source of competitive advantage.

26

A DECISION-MAKING FRAMEWORK FOR GLOBAL SOURCING

S. TAMER CAVUSGIL,* ATTILA YAPRAK†‡ AND POH-LIN YEOH§

*International Business Center, Michigan State University, USA
†Marketing and International Business, Wayne State University, USA
§International Business, University of South Carolina, USA

‡ To whom correspondence should be addressed at: Marketing and International Business, Centre for International Business Education and Research, School of Business Administration, Wayne State University, Detroit, MI 48202, USA.

    S. Tamer Cavusgil is Professor of Marketing and International Business and Director, International Business Centers at Michigan State University. Attila Yaprak, Associate Professor of Marketing and International Business at Wayne State University is also the Executive Secretary of the Academy of International Business. Poh-Lin Yeoh is an Assistant Professor of International Marketing at University of South Carolina. The authors contributed equally to the article; their names appear in alphabetical order.

INTRODUCTION

Global sourcing has become a key strategic competitive tool in firms' global marketing strategy (Allio, 1989; Kotabe and Omura, 1989). In the computer industry, US manufacturers have been advised to stop making, and start buying the computers they sell because "there is no correlation between manufacturing prowess and market share" (Parraport and Halevi, 1991). A 1986 survey of manufacturers in the machinery and allied products industry found that the dollar amounts spent on offshore purchases grew from 11% in the early 1980s to more than 15% in 1986 (*MAPI*, 1986). Similarly, in the automobile industry, during the 1980s, General Motors externalized about $4 billion worth of parts and components from its 89 plants to outside suppliers. GM's share of parts and components manufactured in-house, subsequently, declined from 60% to 45% by the end of the decade. Today, manufacturing competency means "learning not to make things—how not to make the parts that divert a company from cultivating its skills and outsourcing components to suppliers that could make them more efficiently" (Venkatesan, 1992, p. 98).

This hollowing-out manufacturing strategy among US firms (*Business Week*, 1986) is used as an alternative to investing in new automated facilities. According to a study by Giffi *et al.* (1991), "an increasing number of US companies have discovered that it is cheaper to outsource than to own all stages of the production process . . . outsourcing can provide immediate cost reductions without the usual capital investments." While offshore sourcing has been frequently used as a reactive response to global competitive pressures, that is, as a means to gain access to raw materials, components, or finished materials to remain competitive in the marketplace, the offshore procurement strategies of firms today are different—global sourcing is increasingly used as a proactive strategy to gain competitive advantages.

As more and more firms recognize the strategic impact of offshore purchasing on overall corporate strategy, formulating outsourcing strategies that are consistent with the firm's other functional strategies have become critical decisions. Production decisions pertaining to the optimal size and number of foreign manufacturing facilities, their missions and locations around the world, and the types of technological processes each will employ are also important considerations in the firm's integrated global procurement strategy. Finally, choices about the use of internal versus external suppliers will also influence the way inventories are managed, how technologies are shared, and the way product quality is maintained.

In summary, as a firm moves toward an integrated global sourcing strategy, effective coordination of the sourcing function vertically with the firm's policy objectives as well as horizontally with its other functional activities is critical for the efficient utilization of worldwide material resources. Therefore, the purpose of this article is to present a decision-making process model which describes the wide array of decision variables involved in global sourcing and how they are interrelated with each other. To accomplish this objective, several issues are addressed: motivation for global sourcing activity; selection of locations and products for offshore sourcing; and designing an optimal sourcing configuration for the firm's global operations. A decision-making framework is presented to highlight critical sourcing decisions. Managerial guidelines are also offered to assist companies in offshore sourcing activities.

WHY SOURCE OFFSHORE

Kotabe (1989, 1992) argued that outsourcing is being increasingly used to acquire and sustain cost competitiveness. Several studies (e.g. *MAPI*, 1986; Fagan, 1991; Monczka and Trent, 1991; Dobler *et al.*, 1990) also found that foreign suppliers can significantly affect four critical areas of a firm: (i) cost reduction; (ii) quality improvement; (iii) increased exposure to worldwide technology; and (iv) delivery and reliability improvements. Figure 1 displays the wide range of reasons which motivate firms toward global sourcing.

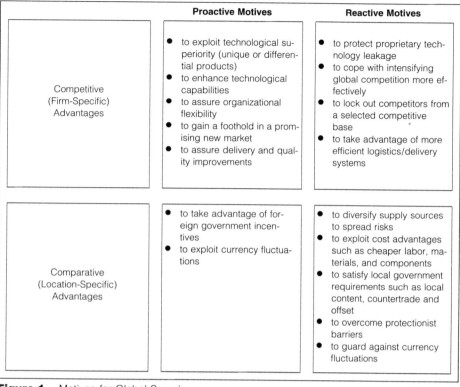

Figure 1. Motives for Global Sourcing

REACTIVE MOTIVES

Reactive motives are exemplified by the firm's response to intensified global competition. This happened in the 1980s when US companies went abroad to secure foreign markets to take advantage of the cheaper factors of production. However, many of the low-cost countries (e.g. Hong Kong, Taiwan, and Singapore) have lost their labor cost advantages and this has led apparel manufacturers such as Nicole Miller to move its garment making operations from the Pacific back to the United States (*Fortune*, 1991).

Geographical diversification of the firm's supply sources to spread risks (Kogut, 1985) is also an important reactive motive. Other reactive motives include satisfying foreign governments' countertrade and offset requirements, as well as local content specifications (Norquist, 1987). Firms are also motivated to source offshore due to their domestic suppliers' reluctance to manufacture private label brands, or to overcome protectionist measures. A 1988 survey of American apparel manufacturers showed that they were forced to source from abroad because their domestic suppliers were reluctant to produce certain brands (*Daily News Record,* 1988).

PROACTIVE MOTIVES

Clearly, the strongest *proactive* motive is the need to secure or exploit manufacturing cost differentials which are sufficiently favorable to overcome the additional overhead costs associated with foreign sourcing such as shipping and inventory costs, concerns over engineering control, quality assurance, and customer service. Exploitation of a firm-specific (competitive) advantage such as a unique, differentiated product or technologically superior process is another strong proactive motive.

Increasingly, firms are also discovering that outsourcing allows them greater exposure to worldwide technology; specifically, technical competencies of their foreign suppliers. A survey conducted by Monczka (1989) found that there was a growing need among U.S. manufacturers to acquire process and product technology from suppliers. For example, Volkswagen has been quite successful in using its sourcing strategy as a "know-how turntable" where research and development ideas, acquired from some sourcing locations, are transferred to other sourcing locations (including the headquarters). This process has helped Volkswagen internationalize and appropriate throughout its manufacturing networks invaluable quality assurance competencies.

Another example of a company that has successfully exploited technological transfer from its foreign manufacturing plants is the Ford Motor Company that owns about 25% of Mazda and has had a long standing relationship of product co-development with the Japanese automobile manufacturer. Ford builds the Escort and Tracer models in two different plants: Hermosillo, Mexico and Wayne, Michigan. The Hermosillo plant is an exact replica of Mazda's plant in Japan in terms of plant design and managerial practices. Even with lower wages and higher labor turnover than any U.S. plant, Hermosillo generates the highest quality of Ford assembly plant in North America. Subsequently, the operations at the Michigan plant were patterned closely after Hermosillo's plant experience (Welch and Nayak, 1992).

With intensified global competition and rapid diffusion of technology, the quality of components and subassemblies produced in offshore locations has improved significantly. Delivery of products from offshore locations has also improved while lead times have become shorter. Tapping into this market to exploit quality and/or delivery advantages has become another proactive motive for offshore sourcing.

Hedging against currency rate fluctuations is also an important proactive motive. Exchange rates affect the price paid for imported materials or components when payment is in the supplier's currency, and there is a lag between the time the contract is signed and payment is made. Depending on the countries of buyers and sellers, and the direction of the exchange rate movement, buyers can end up paying substantially much more than the original contract price. To neutralize the impact of the strong yen in the late 1980s, Minibea Ltd, a Japanese manufacturer of miniature bearings, sought suppliers from Singapore and Malaysia rather than domestically from Japan (*American Metal Market,* 1987).

In summary, whatever their motives, firms that source globally should view sourcing as a powerful determinant of global strategic leverage and not a tool to achieve immediate supply goals (Monczka and Guinipero, 1984). To be effective, global sourcing has to be integrated into the corporate philosophy of the firm—an essential ingredient of the firm's global competitive strategy.

WHERE TO SOURCE OFFSHORE?

In deciding where to source offshore, focus is on the benefits that are expected to be derived from offshore procurement compared to those derived from sourcing domestically. Outsourcing from offshore locations increases both the number and complexity of costs to be evaluated; while certain costs such as taxes, transportation, and insurance are relatively easy to evaluate, others are more difficult to evaluate. For example, Applied Digital Data Services (ADDS), a subsidiary of NCR, began sourcing in the Far East during the late 1980s, primarily to gain material cost advantages. While product cost dramatically reduced by 23% the company faced other qualitative concerns such as long lead times, lack of flexibility, and higher inventory costs (Sheridan, 1991). Another US company, American Tourister, a luggage manufacturer, transferred its manufacturing operations from the Pacific Rim to the Dominican Republic to reduce the long lead times. Before American Tourister sourced from the Dominican Republic, the wait from order to delivery from its Asian suppliers took about seven months. In addition, suppliers in Taiwan and Korea began to manufacture in Thailand, the Philippines, and China to counter the rising wages in their own countries—this only added to longer lead times (*Fortune,* 1991).

Other qualitative concerns that should be considered are different countries' economic and political risks, overhead costs, and intangibles. Economic risks such as fluctuations in inflation and interest rates, and deteriorating balance of payment accounts as well as political risks arising from exchange controls, currency transfer restrictions, and government requirements may help favor certain offshore locations over others (Strauss, 1985). In contrast, overhead costs such as availability and the relative effectiveness of communications, transportation infrastructures, and public services may direct focus away from certain locations. Other locations may have to be eliminated because of perceived difficulties associated with engineering and differentiation coordination, lack of commonality of components and production processes, misfit with the firm's profit center and profit route objectives, and concerns over worker dislocation (Strauss, 1985). In sum, offshore sourcing locations which offer differential procurement benefits over other sourcing locations in both qualitative and quantitative terms are preferred.

WHAT TO SOURCE OFFSHORE?

Decisions about which components/materials/parts to outsource will differ by industry, technology, and specific inputs. Casson (1985) and Williamson (1985) found greater offshore sourcing interest in vertically integrated process industries, knowledge-intensive industries, and quality assurance-dependent products.

Other studies have developed profiles of products which are good candidates for offshore sourcing. Using the economic order quantity (EQS) model, Srinivasan (1988) demonstrated, for example, that overseas sourcing can be economically attractive if: (i) the item is replenished in lots or batches and is not replenished continuously, and (ii) usage rates are

uniform and low compared to the rate at which the item is replenished.

In a similar vein, Moxon (1982) described products appropriate for offshore production as those which (i) are labor intensive (e.g. textiles); (ii) are standardized in specifications and manufacturing technology (e.g. auto components); (iii) show predictable sales patterns (e.g. electronics); (iv) have a high ratio of value to weight (e.g. precision instruments; semiconductors); and (v) are not subjected to high duties (e.g. scientific instruments).

In this context, Kotabe and Omura (1989) showed that firms opt for internal sourcing in their production of proprietary products to protect monopolistic advantages in know-how while preferring to license out patents for the manufacturing of standardized products to external suppliers. For example, Honda's core competencies are internalized in combustion engines and power trains, and the company does not outsource these critical items because its ability to design and build them is critical to the firm's competitive advantage (Prahalad and Hamel, 1990). In sharp contrast, Chrysler has outsourced the manufacture of many components of its automobile to foreign suppliers. In the process, Chrysler has become more dependent upon its suppliers, some of whom are major competitors such as Mitsubishi.

A DECISION-MAKING FRAMEWORK FOR GLOBAL SOURCING

Once the firm decides to source globally, it has to think and act globally. This means it must marshall the necessary resources, commit management time and strategic focus, and learn to make decisions about production and supply locations, phases of manufacturing and assembly, and prudent use of internal versus external suppliers. Welch and Nayak (1992) cautioned firms to think of their offshore sourcing decision in terms of strategic imperatives rather than purely in classical cost-oriented terms. Figure 2 presents a comprehensive decision-making framework for global sourcing which incorporates

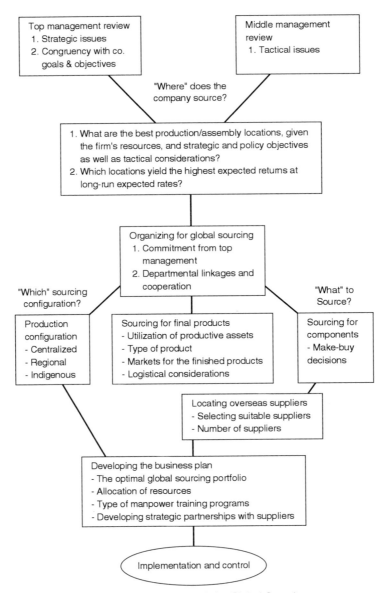

Figure 2. Decision-Making Framework for Global Sourcing

these strategic issues. The following discussion highlights the significant features of this framework.

SENIOR MANAGEMENT INPUT

The key ingredient to achieving effective global sourcing is securing management involvement at both the strategic (top), and the tactical (middle) levels. While top management may be primarily concerned with optimal product configurations in light of corporate policy variables, middle management may be more involved in the basic economic determinants of sourcing decisions such as determining the optimal set of sourcing locations that will yield the highest expected returns in light of an array of constraints.

When management has established the firm's global sourcing needs, policies and procedures which will guide the company's international purchasing task need to be developed. Fundamental at this stage are commitment of top management and coordination among departments. Monczka and Trent (1991) argue that it is the responsibility of top management to drive key functional departments to pursue opportunities from global sourcing. If organizational systems do not exist that encourage using a particular world source, then the firm needs to move toward a system of performance rewards so that its worldwide business unit managers have a strong incentive to make global sourcing strategy work. Japanese firms tend to exhibit a total investment approach to their offshore purchasing in which their top management is fully committed and involved. Purchasing, engineering, design, and manufacturing cooperate closely and link themselves with the vendor to produce a stable operating environment that will produce parts at strategic prices, at the right quality, delivered on time, all the time (*Pacific Purchaser,* 1986).

SOURCING CONFIGURATION

Whether for final products or for components, the most significant global sourcing decisions center around the sourcing configuration (Fig. 2). This decision involves a choice between adopting a centralized or decentralized (distributed) approach to global sourcing. Porter (1986) has viewed sourcing configuration as a key determinant of strategic mobility of resources along the value added chain, a function that allows each participant in the global network to capitalize on its particular strategic competency. For example, in centralized sourcing, the company produces everything in a single worldwide manufacturing location and supplies all its markets from that location. The Ford Motor Company is an excellent example of a firm that utilizes this approach. Since Ford of Europe is recognized as having a major competitive advantage over the rest of the firm in the small car market, it is responsible for the design and building of cars that will be sold in Europe and the United States. Additionally, Ford Europe is also re-

sponsible for the sourcing of required component materials (Daniels and Radebaugh, 1989).

The spread of global competition has also led many firms to adopt a decentralized sourcing approach which involves an integrate network of plants situated strategically around the globe. This type of sourcing strategy can take one (or a combination) of forms.

In integrated sourcing, each plant specializes in the production of products at which it has a comparative advantage (e.g. technology, manufacturing) and exports them to other markets. This form of sourcing exhibits a high degree of rationalization because it streamlines the number of products manufactured at each site. It also leads to greater efficiency as it allows for longer production runs, and therefore, lower unit costs. Interdependence of operations in these systems require extensive coordination and planning which may lead to economically inefficient flows between affiliates.

In regional sourcing, each manufacturing plant which specializes in the production of one or more components, are positioned strategically around the globe to serve the needs of a larger network of assembly plants. For example, Wortzel and Wortzel (1985) describe a two stage process in the pharmaceutical industry whereby active ingredients are manufactured at various specialist plants and then shipped to a larger number of assembly plants where inert ingredients are added and dosage forms fabricated. In similar fashion, auto plants often ship some of their output as completely knocked down (CKD) which are then assembled in the country of destination.

In indigenous sourcing, the simplest of the three decentralized forms, production plants serve particular markets. These systems form collections of domestic firms which produce more than one product for a single market and are usually smaller than integrated or regional networks. They are, thus, costlier to operate when compared to regional and integrated networks.

Differences in production capabilities, labor skills, and government requirements at different locations sometimes result in sourcing configurations where some plants end up more capital intensive or labor intensive than local factors would suggest as the optimum. Wortzel and Wortzel (1985) contend that such compromises often lead to mixed sourcing systems. In addition, effective sourcing configuration also depends upon the firm's internationalization stage. As a firm matures into a dynamic network of affiliates, subsidiaries, and joint ventures, it seems to favor more complex configurations which provide more effective use of resources in multiple locations rather than accumulating and maintaining them in single (or a few) locations (Kotabe, 1992).

SOURCING FOR FINAL PRODUCTS

In sourcing for finished products, the most important consideration is the efficient utilization of productive assets around the globe. Where such assets are underutilized, final product sourcing can take place when scale economies can permeate the firm's entire value-added chain. This, of course, can only be possible when component suppliers are highly interdependent and are located in close proximity to final assembly points.

A second consideration relates to the type of product involved in final production or assembly. Products of high intrinsic value with sophisticated or special processing requirements and relatively short product lives which are subjected to frequent technological upgrading are generally sourced internally enroute to final assembly. On the other hand, external sourcing of old, and lower-technology products can free-up the firm's manufacturing capacity for newer, high-technology and high-margin products.

A third consideration relates to the nature of industry in which the firm competes, global or multidomestic. Global industry competitors exploit similarities across countries while multidomestic competitors exploit differences among countries. In multidomestic industries, firms may favor an indigenous sourcing system to meet heterogeneous market demands. Low-technology, consumer-product firms such as Unilever, Colgate-Palmolive, and Proctor and Gamble exemplify this type of sourcing approach to global markets. In global industries, sourcing is managed in an integrated manner to take advantage of scale economies in sourcing, distribution, and product development. High-technology, industrial-product firms in the automotive (GM, Ford), construction equipment (Kotmatsu, Caterpillar) and electronics (GE, Mitsubishi) industries exemplify this approach. Characteristics of sourcing patterns in both types of industries are contrasted in Table 1.

SOURCING FOR COMPONENTS

When sourcing for components, the critical decision variable centers around whether and to what extent the firm should outsource components. The decision is usually a function of two key determinants: the nature of technology, and the product/process specification requirements of the product in question. Technologies that promise future advantages and are still emerging should be nurtured in-house. In general, labor-intensive, low-technology components

Table 1. Sourcing Patterns in Different Types of Industries

	Multidomestic Industries	**Global Industries**
Scope of competition	Local	Global
Scale of efficient manufacturing	Small	Large
Incentives to use local inputs	High	Low
Customer needs	Diverse	Uniform
Extent of standardization	Low	High
Predominant sourcing system	Indigenous	Integrated
Examples of industries	Personal care products	Automobiles
	Clothing	Chemicals
	Publishing	Construction equipment
	Retail business	Telecommunications

Table 2. Conditions Favoring Greater Sourcing Emphasis

Internal Sourcing		External Sourcing
Early	Product's stage in the technological life cycle	Advanced
Low	Scope of firm's international activities	Extensive
High	Degree of product differentiation	Low
Low	Consumer price sensitivity	High
Low	Level of price competition	High
Low	Manufacturing costs as a percentage of total costs	High
Low	International production costs differentials	High

are routinely outsourced to external suppliers, while patented, high-technology production inputs are internally sourced (Kotabe and Omura, 1989). Table 2 summarizes the conditions that favor greater external sourcing emphasis.

SUPPLIER RELATIONSHIPS

Traditionally, manufacturers have preferred to work with multiple suppliers in a wide array of arrangements. Recently, however, many firms have chosen to work with a narrow range of supply sources that willingly enter into long-term cooperative relationships with them. This has become necessary as Just-in-Time (JIT) manufacturing has become a norm in many industries (*Business International,* 1987).

Harmonious, long-lasting relationships between a firm and its supplier network depends upon reliability and timeliness of delivery, managerial competency and the fit between the supplier's component inputs or processes and the firm's value-added chain. Additionally, since currency exchange factors can have a tremendous impact on sourcing costs, a study by McKinsey (Hertzell and Caspar, 1988) suggests that companies should consider suppliers on the basis of their contribution to balancing currency flows, rather than relying on price and performance alone.

It is also important to note that supplier relationships that involve high value inputs and operations carry higher risk because supplier failure can lead to deficient performance of the firm. For example, numerous Asian companies from newly industrializing countries such as Malaysia, Singapore, Taiwan, and Thailand developed competency in core prod-

ucts through their OEM-supply contracts with US manufacturers. This eventually led to the "hollowing-out" of their competitors. Through such subcontracting, Asian companies built up advantages in component markets first and then leveraged off their superior products downstream to gain market share. To minimize the possibility of creating competitors from one's supplier, the firm may vertically integrate the supplier into its operations to reduce transaction costs.

DEVELOPING THE BUSINESS PLAN

Porter (1986) argues that many forms of competitive advantage for the global firm derive less from where the firm performs activities than from how it performs them on a worldwide basis. The evaluation of available alternatives to ensure global competitiveness under changing monetary and economic conditions are always important strategic considerations. It is, therefore, critical that the firm develops alternative sourcing portfolios given its budgetary, manpower, and technology resources.

Two requirements are necessary for effective global sourcing: preparation of manpower training and allocation of resources. Whether internal or external to the firm's value-added chain, component suppliers, purchasers, transshippers, and agents in the sourcing network need continuous acculturation into the firm's corporate philosophy and competitive strategy portfolios. An important part of this task involves the planning and installation of a data communications network which facilitates the exchange of up-to-date information on each other's purchasing and sales activities. Resource commitment, special managerial skills, logistical knowledge, and investment capital are also needed for effective management of global sourcing.

IMPLEMENTATION AND CONTROL

The final components of the sourcing decision involve implementation and control of the sourcing system. This phase calls for organizational structure and style adjustments as well as the development of the evaluation methods with which to implement a smoothly functioning global sourcing system.

An important question relates to the firm's resource base and the flexibility with which the firm can gear-up, launch, and control its global sourcing system. Those firms which are resource-rich and possess strategic flexibility are likely to be more adept at the modification of strategies mandated by environmental constraints. Resource-poor firms, on the other hand, can engage in cooperative arrangements to tap other suppliers' resources or establish international purchasing offices (IPOs). A survey conducted by Michigan State University (Monczka and Trent, 1991) found that almost half the firms surveyed have international purchasing offices. IPOs serve specific tasks such as (i) identifying foreign suppliers; (ii) expediting and tracing shipments; (iii) negotiating supply contracts; (iv) obtaining samples; (v) managing technical problems; and (vi) obtaining design and engineering support.

Clearly, the overriding dilemma permeating the entire decision-making process outlined here is the choice between internal and external sourcing. This decision is a function of the interplay among various factors. The nature of the cost structure and manufacturing processes of the firm's industry are important determinants. The relative size and bargaining power of buyers and sellers are also factors to consider. In the automobile industry, for example, the sheer size of the users assures continuous supply of key inputs. Heavily concentrated user industries such as auto-

mobiles which have a wide range of input requirements are more likely to source externally. On the other hand, concerns over assured supply in vertically-integrated industries stimulate firms to nurture captive suppliers through long-term harmonious relationships. If the supply source market for a key input is highly concentrated, the need for internal sourcing becomes attractive.

Other factors also favor external sourcing. For example, frequent technological changes in the input sector of an industry can discourage the user sector from relying on internal sources due to the high investment that accompanies R&D efforts and the uncertainty associated with future sourcing needs. In these industries, where the manufacturing process is capital-intensive with continuous process technology, external sourcing is preferred.

It is clear that, to be effective, global sourcing needs to become an integrated component of the formal strategy of the firm so that it is: (i) vertically coordinated with the company's overall corporate policy with worldwide information systems, sophisticated personnel capabilities, coordination mechanisms, an effective organizational structure; and highest level of executive management support; and (ii) horizontally coordinated with other functional divisions of the firm; that is, procurement, manufacturing, and technology groups working together to establish the best worldwide offshore sourcing network and develop more productive supplier capabilities.

CONCLUSIONS

The sourcing dilemma—to buy or not to buy overseas—is an important strategic decision facing firms. Firms that continually outsource on the basis of capital expenditure approval (Johnson and Mankin, 1991) will lose out in the long-run as they are "generally biased toward importing rather than developing their own manufacturing capabilities." This article has argued that while cost considerations will be important in firms' offshore sourcing decisions, firms should also consider strategic and technological issues in conjunction with cost decisions. For example, if quick response time is desired by a company, sourcing from a distant country will not allow the company to respond quickly to such short notices. As explained by the CEO of GE Fanuc, ''the labor content is down to 5%, . . . it's important to look not only at labor and material costs, but also at the ''total cost'' of getting a product to a customer, including the time value of fast services''. In addition, for industries faced with shortening technological life cycles, close coupling between design and manufacturing is critical for speedy new product development. And this close interaction is only possible when the two departments are located in close proximity to each other.

For other industries, global sourcing will become a requisite for competing. This is in response to the increased integration of North America, Europe, and the Pacific Rim as well as other developments such as standardization of products and production processes at increasingly faster rates, material shortages, and adjustments to the international monetary framework. More importantly, the urgent need to generate and to transfer product and process innovations in global networks which are becoming increasingly dynamic should propel global sourcing to the forefront of global competitive activity. Finally, firms that are able to create a system that emphasizes the pursuit of a coordinated and integrated sourcing strategy will be positioned to exploit greater sustained competitive advantages to meet the global challenges of the 1990s, over firms that are not.

REFERENCES

Allio, R.J. (1989) Formulating Global Strategy. *Planning Review,* Vol. 2, March–April, pp. 22–8.

American Metal Market (1987) Offshore Manufacturing Pays Off for Minebea. November 17, p. 30.

Business International (1987) Offshore sourcing: Expanding Options Mean More Coordination. March 12.

Business Week (1986) The Hollow Corporation. March 3, pp. 56–62.

Casson, M. (1985) The Theory of Foreign Investment, in Buckley, P.J. and Casson, M. (Eds) *The Economic Theory of the Multinational Enterprise.* Macmillan, London.

Daily News Record (1988) Source Works. October 31, pp. 24–27.

Daniels, J.P. and Radebaugh, L.H. (1989) Ford in Europe—The Early Years, in *International Business.* Addison Wessley, Reading, MA.

Dobler, D.W., Burt, D.N. and Lee, L. Jr (1990) *Purchasing and Materials Management: Text and Cases.* McGraw-Hill, New York.

Fagan, M.L. (1991) A Guide to Global Sourcing. *The Journal of Business Strategy,* March–April, pp. 21–75.

Fortune (1991) US Companies Come Back Home. December, pp. 106–112.

Giffi, C., Roth, A.V. and Seal, G.M. (1991) *Competing in World Class Manufacturing: America's 21 Century Challenge.* Irwin, Homewood, IL.

Hertzell, S. and Caspar, C. (1988) Rethinking Financial Strategies: Coping With Unpredictable Currencies. *The McKinsey Quarterly,* Summer, pp. 12–24.

Johnson, D. and Mankin, E. (1991) Manufacturing Capabilities: Make-or-Buy Decisions Affect Your Company's Future. *Industry Forum,* April, pp. 1–3.

Kogut, B. (1985) Designing Global Strategies: Comparative and Competitive Value-added Chains. *Sloan Management Review,* Vol. 26, Summer, pp. 15–28.

Kotabe, M. (1989) Hollowing-out of U.S. Multinationals and Their Global Competitiveness. *Journal of International Business Studies,* Vol. 19, August, pp. 1–15.

Kotabe, M. (1992) Patterns and Technological Implications of Global Sourcing Strategies: a Study of European and Japanese Multinational Firms. *Journal of International Marketing,* Vol. 1, No. 1, pp. 26–43.

Kotabe, M. and Omura, G. (1989) Sourcing Strategies of European and Japanese Multinationals: A Comparison. *Journal of International Business Studies,* Vol. 20, No. 1, pp. 133–130.

MAPI (1986) MAPI Survey of Global Sourcing as a Corporate Strategy—An Update. *Machinery and Allied Products Institute,* February, p. 8.

Monczka, R.M. (1989) *Integrated Procurement Strategies.* Graduate School of Business Administration, Michigan State University (unpublished study).

Monczka, R.M. and Giunipero, P. (1984) International Purchasing: Characteristics and Implementations. *Journal of Purchasing and Materials Management,* Vol. 20, pp. 2–9.

Monczka, R.M. and Trent, R.J. (1991) Global Sourcing: A Development Approach. *International Journal of Purchasing and Materials Management,* Spring, pp. 2–8.

Moxon, R.W. (1982) Offshore Sourcing, Subcontracting, and Manufacturing, in Walter, I. (Ed.), *Handbook of International Business.* John Wiley and Sons, New York.

Norquist, W. (1987) Countertrade: Another Horizon for Purchasing. *Journal of Purchasing and Materials Management,* Summer, pp. 2–6.

Pacific Purchaser (1986) Far East Procurement—The Myths and Realities, Part 1, August.

Parraport, A.S. and Halevi, S. (1991) The Computerless Computer Industry. *Harvard Business Review,* July–August, pp. 69–80.

Porter, M. (1986) *Competition in Global Industries.* Harvard Business School Press, Boston.

Prahalad, C.K. and Hamel, G. (1990) The Core Competence of the Corporation. *Harvard Business Review,* May–June, pp. 79–91.

Sheridan, J.H. (1991) ADDS Finds There's No Place Like Home. *Industry Week,* June 7, pp. 40–43.

Srinivisan, K. (1988) Source of Supply: Overseas or Domestic. *Production and Inventory Management,* Vol. 29, No. 1, pp. 65–68.

Strauss, H. (1985) *Foreign Sourcing: Donaldson Company.* Case Development Center, University of Minnesota, School of Management, Minneapolis, Minnesota.

Venkatesan, R. (1992) To Make or Not to Make. *Harvard Business Review,* November–December, pp. 98–107.

Welch, J.A. and Nayak, P.R. (1992) Strategic Sourcing: A Progressive Approach to the Make-or-Buy Decision. *Academy of Management Executive,* Vol. 6, No. 1, pp. 23–31.

Williamson, O.E. (1985) *The Economic Institutions of Capitalism: Firms, Markets, Relational Contracting.* The Free Press, New York.

Wortzel, H. and Wortzel, L. (1985) *Strategic Multinational Management: The Essentials.* John Wiley and Sons, New York.

R&D AND TECHNOLOGY MANAGEMENT

Technology has become an ever more important component of competitive advantage. It is difficult to think of many products that do not either embody sophisticated technology or use it in manufacture of that product. Firms have become technology dependent. To stay competitive, they must not only develop technology in their own R&D labs; they must also acquire it from outside. Regardless of the sources of firms' technology, the firms must have a strategy for technological planning, development, and management. As firms have grown and spread globally, problems of diffusing technology within the firm as well as developing or acquiring it have grown in importance.

The emerging view, in fact, is that a firm's technology strategy should guide its R&D efforts; the technology strategy should set the research agenda. This view ties R&D more tightly to the firm's overall competitive strategy.

READING SELECTIONS

Farok Contractor and V.K. Narayanan present and explain a framework for planning and managing technology within the firm. Their framework takes into account several important concerns about technology development and management. The authors assert it should be synchronous rather than sequential; it should consider external as well as internal sources; it should provide for internal diffusion; and it should fully use the firm's technological assets no matter where they are located.

Contractor and Narayanan go on to present a technology planning methodology that encompasses three stages. The first, and perhaps the most critical stage, is an audit designed to determine what are the technologies in which the firm ought to be. The purpose of Stage 2 is to lay out a development strategy for each technology identified for development in Stage 1. Stage 3 is the implementation and audit stage. One important goal of this stage is to see that the technology is diffused as broadly as possible given the geographic reach of the firm. The audit component of this stage recognizes that technology is iterative and endeavors to ensure that results and information from using the technology are fed back to a new Stage 1.

Alphonso O. Ogbuehi and Ralph A. Bellas, Jr. note, as others have done in earlier sections, the ongoing debate over centralization versus decentralization of activities in

MNCs. They suggest that globally, the successful development and introduction of new products may require a decentralized orientation for R&D. They point to advantages of decentralization: ease of incorporating local market requirements; reduced product development time; accelerated new product acceptance; and reduced trade frictions.

Ogbuehi and Bellas focus on decentralization through strategic global alliances. The alliances take the form of international licensing, cooperative research, mergers, acquisitions, and equity control in R&D firms. They further point to corporate commitment, careful planning, and corporate coordination as prerequisites for decentralized R&D. They caution that new product development is a precarious venture that requires a firm's total commitment of resources and conviction that change is necessary.

Arnoud De Meyer's central proposition is that technical learning has become one of the core reasons underpinning the decision to internationalize R&D. He goes on to examine how this proposition helps improve the management of geographically dispersed R&D.

De Meyer stresses the importance of credibility in managing the international R&D network for technical learning. If an R&D manager wants to integrate a new R&D center in the technical learning system, the new center needs visible success fairly quickly. Giving the R&D laboratory a clear strategic role within the company seems to help it obtain some quick and easy success.

Diffusion of know-how throughout the company depends on the firm's communication network. Geographical distance and cultural differences sometimes impede communication. However, the identification of an individual as a cultural ''boundary spanner'' and the use of technological innovations such as fax, teleconferencing, e-mail, and videoconferencing help improve communication. De Meyer argues that a powerful formal and informal communication system and a well-organized network organization are requirements for effective R&D diffusion.

27

TECHNOLOGY DEVELOPMENT IN THE MULTINATIONAL FIRM: A FRAMEWORK FOR PLANNING AND STRATEGY

FAROK J. CONTRACTOR AND V.K. NARAYANAN

Graduate School of Management, Rutgers University, 92 New Street, Newark, NJ 07102-1895, USA

ABSTRACT   The authors' purpose is to improve the coupling between technology development and corporate strategic planning in multinational firms by providing a much needed technology planning framework.

The framework, which is developed in some detail, divides the planning process into three stages: technology scanning, strategy development (product level) and implementation (country level). In the first stage an answer is sought to the question, "What technologies (as distinct from businesses) are we, or should we be in?"; in the second, the aim is to develop a strategy for each of the products from the chosen technologies; in the third stage, details of implementation on a country-by-country basis are worked out. Although presented as a sequence of three stages, the framework is to be applied iteratively.

The authors argue that technology for all its vital importance to a global company, cannot be treated as a profit centre. This is part of the difficulty in implementing the technology management function, especially in multidivisional and global firms. They believe that use of this framework will make it easier to integrate technology development into the strategic planning process. In addition it will serve to integrate managers from different parts of the company into a formalized technology planning exercise.

INTRODUCTION

The need to incorporate the technological dimension in the strategic planning function of the firm has long been recognized as crucial in a globally competitive environment. But company practice and the scholarly literature have lacked a standard paradigm. Many companies feel that there is a poor coupling between technology development and strategic planning, possibly due to a lack of adequate planning frameworks for technology.

According to a Booz-Allen and Hamilton survey of 800 U.S. executives, two-thirds felt their companies were making inadequate use of their technologies in the strategic development of the firm (Ford, 1988). Among the reasons was the divisionalization of companies which tends to compartmentalize and fragment technology strategy. Some product divisions may not be aware of valuable technologies available from other divisions; the problem is often acute when units of a transnational firm are geographically and administratively scattered in distinct regional or national profit centres. The management of technology—that is to say, its development, transfer and optimal utilization in the multinational firm—is a function that cuts across the product as well as the geographic dimensions of the company. Increasingly, technology needs to be developed and used by more than one product group or nation for maximum efficiency and exploitation. Moreover, a typical technology cycle from research to commercialization takes about ten years whereas a normal corporate planning cycle is three to five years; finally, the R&D function may be overly centralized.

A planning framework should address the following concerns. First, the Research and Development process can no longer be considered sequential, but rather synchronous with global manufacturing and global marketing decisions (Takeuchi and Nonaka, 1986). This calls for an enlarged role for the R&D manager. But most firms are organized with regions or global product divisions as profit centres (Chandler, 1986; Porter, 1986). How to harness the apparently different technology strategies and capabilities of various divisions into an overall global strategy direction for the firm is a key issue tackled by this paper. Second, the environment in many industries has undergone such a rapid transformation that technology acquisition from other firms sometimes has as great a strategic importance as internal development or the sale of technology beyond the firm's boundaries. Third, multi-product and multinational companies have begun to focus on the critical issue of inter-divisional transfer of technology and coordination between different R&D facilities (De-Meyer and Mizushima, 1989). Finally, the effective utilization of the company's technical assets across the many country markets the firm may operate in, is an issue growing in importance.

MANAGING TECHNOLOGY IN THE MULTINATIONAL AND MULTI-PRODUCT COMPANY

Managements used to product divisions or countries as profit centres often neglect the development of a

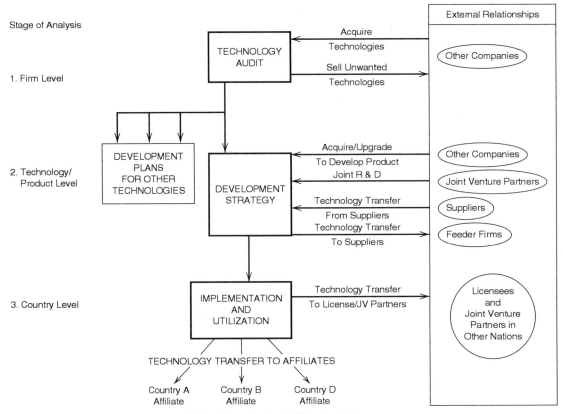

Figure 1. A Technology Planning Methodology for the Multinational Firm

technology strategy. It is difficult to think in terms of a technology as a profit centre or as a unit of measure since its boundaries are often fuzzy and spill over into several product areas. A company that has developed a technology has to know whether to use it in-house and/or how to transfer it to other industries, and in several nations for a full return on its investment. In doing so it must decide which end-applications it will exploit internally, by itself manufacturing and marketing products, and which industries it will serve by contractual transfers such as licensing or joint ventures. When the end-applications are very diverse such as the use of information systems, no computer firm these days can claim to have fully exploited its commercial opportunities without partners and licensees internationally (Wiseman, 1988).

The second reason it is difficult to think of tech-

nology as a profit centre is because the lifecycle of a technology may be longer or shorter than that of a product depending on how narrowly we define each.

Third, ordinary capital budgeting and manager evaluation methods break down when a technology is the unit of measurement (Leonard-Barton and Kraus, 1985). Ordinary ROI criteria may not correctly measure the true strategic benefits and costs of a technology program because its externalities are not well measured (Morone, 1989). For instance, investments in Computer-Aided Manufacturing and Robotics often appear to generate a poor ROI because their benefits (external to the manufacturing division) such as superior service and delivery to customers are not incorporated into the analysis (Goldhar and Jelinek, 1982). Using another example, the ROI from a transfer of technology under licensing or joint venture may appear to be superior to that from a fully-owned subsidiary—until, that is, the negative externality of subsequent competition from the licensee or partner is factored in (Contractor, 1985). This is especially true when transferring technology to capable partners in Japan.

On the input side, technology transcends the product and country dimensions since research, development and manufacturing involve numerous techniques, all of which may not be possessed by the firm. This requires a worldwide search followed by an internal development versus external acquisition decision.

Globalization presents the manager with two additional strategy decisions at the manufacturing level. First, the configuration of pieces of the manufacturing and distribution chain must be optimized geographically. The cost of internal technology transfer and coordination of foreign affiliates are two determining variables (Bartlett and Ghoshal, 1987). Second, the costs of internal development and manufacture are weighted against the alternative of an intermediate product simply being bought in. There can be strikingly different strategy solutions in the same industry. Toyota and Nissan for instance, have 18 employees per thousand vehicles produced, compared to over 100 employees for General Motors (Eckard, 1984). The bulk of the difference is not productivity but the vastly greater level of subcontracted parts and component purchases in the Japanese firms.

Such differences are not just technological, but cultural and organizational. A useful planning framework would link these issues and provide criteria for evaluating questions such as the optimal degree of integration with suppliers, the optimal level of global standardization, and the degree to which the firm will utilize its technical assets by establishing fully-owned foreign subsidiaries versus sharing its technologies with corporate partners and licensees.

This paper proposes that such decisions need to be made at the same time as the R&D function and feed back into it. In today's environment, technology development and international strategy can no longer be separate or sequential decisions. They have to be synchronous (Takeuchi and Nonaka, 1986).

The analytical framework presented in this paper

is intended to initiate a common thinking process in a company, between the technologists and business managers who frequently have very different assumptions, approaches to risk, time values and ''rules of evidence'' (Gold, 1988). This framework is an important first step in initiating a systematic analysis of technology policy by different personnel in a global company. However, there is an equally important set of process, behavioural and organizational learning issues, relating to the interaction of diverse personnel from various parts of the firm (Maidique and Zirger, 1985). For want of space these are not covered in this paper and may be the subject of a future article. Here we present the framework.

THE OBJECTIVE OF THIS PAPER: A TECHNOLOGY PLANNING FRAMEWORK

This paper presents a three stage planning process, 1. Technology Scanning and Audit (Firm level), 2. Development Strategy (Technology/Product level) and, 3. Implementation and Utilization (Country level).

The *first* stage is a company-wide inventory, categorization and selection of technologies and an assessment of the firm's overall competitive position. It asks questions such as 'What technologies are, or ought we to be in?'

The *second* stage occurs at the technology-specific or product level. For those technologies chosen to be developed, the second level treats questions such as the allocation of costs over various aspects of the development process, the optimal configuration of global suppliers and co-development partners, speed/cost tradeoffs, the optimal level of global standardization and the degree of vertical integration. Here the focus is on formulating a development and commercialization strategy for a particular product type.

The *third* stage called Implementation and Utilization treats the optimum utilization of a developed technology at the country level, incorporating criteria such as the characteristics of the technology, its codifiability, transferability to other nations, the appropriability of profits from the fully-owned subsidiary mode versus a joint venture or a licensing arrangement, and other external factors such as diffusion of technology to potential competitors.

We now describe each stage in some detail.

STAGE 1: TECHNOLOGY AUDIT

During the first stage the firm strives to answer the question 'What technologies should we be in?' Operationally, this means identifying actual and potential technologies inside and outside the firm, assessing the product applications that might emerge, categorizing technologies that define the distinctive competence of the company and deciding how to fill the gaps in the technology portfolio by either internal development, joint research with another firm or external acquisition. As part of planning stage 1 two subordinate issues are also tackled, namely technology progression and an intellectual property strategy in a global arena.

TECHNOLOGY INVENTORY

Technology inventory refers to the process of identifying all technologies strewn throughout the multinational and multidivisional firm. It may appear surprising, but many companies do not know what is

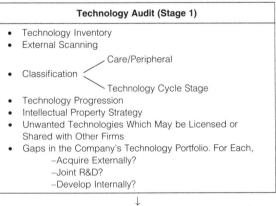

Technology Audit (Stage 1)
• Technology Inventory
• External Scanning
• Classification — Care/Peripheral — Technology Cycle Stage
• Technology Progression
• Intellectual Property Strategy
• Unwanted Technologies Which May be Licensed or Shared with Other Firms
• Gaps in the Company's Technology Portfolio. For Each, —Acquire Externally? —Joint R&D? —Develop Internally?

↓
Go to Stage 2
Development Plan

Figure 2. Steps in the Technology Audit Process

in their technology portfolio. To be meaningful, identification should be specific, not general. For example, a general identification as 'biotechnology' is valueless since biotechnology is a cluster of widely differing technologies from genetic engineering to bio-gas.

Entirely new strategic directions are sometimes revealed by changing the unit of measurement or analysis from a product or nation to a technology. For instance, Martin Marietta's portfolio of *businesses* or divisions includes aerospace, as well as construction aggregates obtained from quarrying operations (Westwood, 1984). Quarrying cost and efficiency depend on the proper placement of explosive charges so as to produce fragments of optimal size, detonated and placed optimally for easy collection. For defence applications the aerospace division had developed ultra-high-speed imaging techniques to track missiles and projectiles. By defining the *technology* rather than the business as the unit of analysis the company spotted the applicability of this new technique to the construction aggregates division. The new technology which can record images of a millionth of a second or less in (literally) explosive environments, was put to use in improving rock fragmentation efficiency through an optimum distribution and timing of charges in a quarry face, improving productivity in quarries by '15–30 percent' (Westwood, 1984). The technology can also be sold or licensed externally.

Levitt's famous question ''What Business Are We Really In?'' may thus be restated to read 'What Technologies Are We Really In?' (Levitt, 1960). Otherwise, opportunities are missed for want of asking the right question.

A technology inventory process thus identifies and enables the application of a proprietary technology to other divisions of the firm. It also identifies external technology transfer opportunities (whose competitive impact may first be assessed by members of the planning team called 'Gatekeepers,' Goldstein, 1987).

TECHNOLOGY SCANNING

This is the process of identifying technologies external to the firm that may affect its technology profile.

A considerable literature on scanning the technological environment is currently available (see Fahey and Narayanan, 1986). Scanning complements the inventory process to determine the firm's desired technology portfolio and because critical 'make or buy' decisions hinge on an awareness of external developments.

Besides an investigative element, scanning requires maintaining interpersonal and organizational linkages with relevant actors. For example, W.R. Grace's laboratory in Japan is partly motivated to serve as a window on developments in Japan. Similarly, Rockwell established an office of external technology development to ensure a continuing exchange of information, in their case from Europe.

CLASSIFICATION OF COMPANY TECHNOLOGIES

The next step would be to classify each technology as Base, Core or Peripheral. Since base technologies are known to most competitors, transferring these to other firms outside the industry need not have competitive implications. An example would be ovens and furnaces which are basic to the steel industry but find applications in several others. Core technologies, on which competitive advantage is based may not be easily shared outside the firm even in the mature stage. An example of a peripheral technology is the rather complex art of galvanizing a car body which requires precise application of currents and control over bath chemistry. This kind of technology is peripheral to a large auto company, but it is a very desirable technology to other industries. Some firms have established 'Technology Marketing Groups' to fully exploit the potential of peripheral but valuable technical assets.

Each technology may also be classified according to its stage in its technology cycle. This forces focus on the time element, on how the firm is doing vis-à-vis competitors, and on the technology progression issue.

TECHNOLOGY PROGRESSION

Technology Progression refers to managing a technology portfolio so that it contains products and technologies at various stages of development and maturity. This is important for balanced long term growth and strategic direction, as well as to ensure that the 'cash cows' will finance new developments—and conversely that the company will in fact have new developments to be financed in the future. Technology progression is an especially crucial aspect for start-up firms to manage. Smith and Fleck (1988) report that new high-technology firms exhibit a high dependence on technology transfer to and from external companies in the early years. Technology acquisitions are for rapid starts. Technology sales are to raise crucially-needed cash. In a later stage there is a greater use of in-house development and commercialization. The firm's business may make a corresponding progression. A biotechnology firm may move from contract research and testing for others, to manufacture of diagnostic kits, and finally to the mass marketing of drugs. In pharmaceuticals and computers the marketing function increasingly presents a formidable, capital-consuming obstacle to be tackled last. Technology progression is therefore a joint technology and financial planning exercise. The entire technology planning exercise has to be multidisciplinary, drawing personnel from several parts of the company.

INTELLECTUAL PROPERTY STRATEGY

As part of the overall Technology Audit procedure a firm should formulate a patent and intellectual property strategy. The environment now is quite different from a decade ago.

For the majority of industries in the past, patents were seen as having symbolic value, applied for on defensive grounds, rather than as valuable cash-generating assets in their own right. The company's technology was judged to reside in unpatented 'know-how' rather than in the patent, *per se*, in most industries. Worse, in the 1970s two-thirds of judgments in U.S. courts were made against the patent holder (Kerr, 1988). And a vastly greater number of patents were, and to a considerable extent continue to be, 'worked around' by competitors without legal challenge. Worst of all, the very act of filing in some nations could reveal proprietary secrets, while an underdeveloped legal system provided no effective protection there.

In the 1980s the environment has changed considerably for the computer, semiconductor, pharmaceutical, chemical, and other industries that depend on patents. For these industries, intellectual property protection has become an important strategy and marketing consideration. As the number of technologically proficient firms has increased globally, as competitors are better able to assimilate and reproduce technology, the importance of patent protection is more keenly felt. At the same time, in the U.S. under the Reagan administration, executive and judicial attitudes towards patent rights and anti-trust issues underwent a change. A special federal court for patent appeals was set up in 1982. Appeals heard there have doubled from the 1983 total of 172 (Kerr, 1988), and the rights of patent holders are upheld more frequently than in the 1970s. Enforcement and recourse are also tighter overseas. In 1987, Texas Instruments was said to have collected $191 million in settlements from Asian chip makers. Suits, such as Polaroid's multi-billion dollar claim on Kodak, pepper the headlines.

Today patents have a far more important competitive strategy implication than cash settlements. They are used to stake out a market, to negotiate cross-licensing arrangements, and for technology and territorial swaps rather than for cash value. The strategy lesson has not been lost on foreign firms which, since the mid-1980s, have registered half the patents in the U.S. In 1986 Hitachi topped the list for patents awarded in the U.S.

OUTCOME OF THE TECHNOLOGY AUDIT

The Technology Audit process results in identification and categorization of technologies to be abandoned, developed further and those which may be exchanged, licensed or shared with joint venture partners. The latter may be handed over to a Technology Marketing department for external exploitation. The rest are intended for internal development, and a Development Plan is drawn up for each (in Stage 2 of the Technology Planning Methodology). At the same time, gaps in the company's technology portfolio are identified, with a recommendation to fill the gap by either external acquisition, joint R&D, or via internal development.

STAGE 2: THE DEVELOPMENT STRATEGY FOR EACH TECHNOLOGY IMPACT OF INTERNATIONAL FACTORS

Stage 2 of the planning process is concerned with the development of *one* technology at a time. This may lead to one, or a multiplicity of products, applications and manufacturing processes. Nevertheless, it is important, during the development stage, to keep the manufacturing and tooling aspects in mind from the very start for the most important expected products. In Japanese firms there are often two teams set up simultaneously. While the development venture team is working on the technical aspects, a manufacturing process team is already formulating design and manufacturing specifications. For many industries, we are no longer in Utterback and Abernathy's (1975) comfortable, sequential world where production and manufacturing innovation became crucial only in the later stages of the technology cycle (as they themselves later recognized).

Development Strategy for a Technology (Stage 2)

- Company's Position Relative to Competitors
  - Development Times
  - Level of Integration
- Distribution of Costs in Development Stage
- Acquisition of Technology
  - From Licensing
  - Joint Venture R&D
  - From Suppliers
- Globalization Issues
  - Standardization of Design/Manufacturing
  - Minimum Economic Scale
  - Degree of Vertical Integration
  - Tariff/Transport/Other Barriers
  - International Product Cycle
  - Variations Across Nations in
    - Consumer Behaviour
    - Distribution
    - Advertising Practices

↓
Go to Stage 3
Utilization Audit

Figure 3. Considerations in Formulating the Development Plan

At the technology development stage itself, the firm has to plan for

—Development time vs. cost tradeoffs

—The anticipated level of integration (or quasi-integration with joint venture partners, suppliers, etc.). This affects development costs and time, as well as later manufacturing decisions.

—Allocation of total development costs over various sub-activities such as tooling, pilot plant, startup, and market studies.

—Anticipated speed of imitators and the expected dominant design standards in the industry

—Optimal degree of globalization

DEVELOPMENT COSTS AND TIME

Recently, there has been a burgeoning of ideas about the value of speed as a competitive tool, not only in production (Schmenner, 1988) but also in development of new products (Takeuchi and Nonaka, 1986). We discuss here the development cost vs. time trade-off. In general, development costs are spread over the sub-categories of (a) Product or process specifications, (b) Pilot plant, (c) Tooling and equipment, (d) Startup including training of personnel and, (e) Market studies.

Two planning decisions are needed:

1. Overall level of expenditure versus development time.
2. Allocation of budgeted expenditures over the above sub-categories.

In a world of accelerating product cycles the company that can develop an item faster has a survival edge. Recent work suggests that the Japanese outperform some U.S. industries in terms of shorter development times and/or development costs. Mansfield's (1988) work with SO matched pairs of American and Japanese firms showed that, in part, Japanese companies have a faster development and commercialization time because of their greater expenditures to consciously shorten the development stage. For all industries Mansfield found the Japanese operating on the time-cost tradeoff function at a point where their costs would show a nine percentage points increase in order to reduce time by one percent; by comparison the U.S. all-industry mean elasticity was about four. That is to say, Japanese firms appear willing to expend on average twice the funds to achieve equivalent reductions in development and commercialization time. Why? Apparently, some of them place a far higher premium on being first (or early) to market as a strategic imperative.

Many Japanese firms on the other hand have lower development costs than comparable American firms in the same industry. There are two explanations. The first has to do with the allocation of development costs within the sub-categories shown in Table 1. The Japanese allocate a far higher percentage of expenditures to tooling and equipment compared to U.S. firms which spend more than double the Japanese level on market studies. Second, the Japanese place a far greater reliance on external technical relationships with suppliers and sub-contractors. The

Table 1. Percentage Distribution of Innovation Costs, 100 Firms, Japan and the United States, 1985

	Percent of Innovation Cost Going For:						
	Applied Research	Preparation of Product Specifications	Prototype or Pilot Plant	Tooling and Manufacturing Equipment and Facilities	Manufacturing Startup	Marketing Startup	Total
All industries combined							
Japan	14	7	16	44	10	8	100
United States	18	8	17	23	17	17	100

Source: Mansfield, E., 'The Speed and Cost of Industrial Innovation in Japan and the United States: External vs. Internal Technology,' *Management Science,* October 1988.

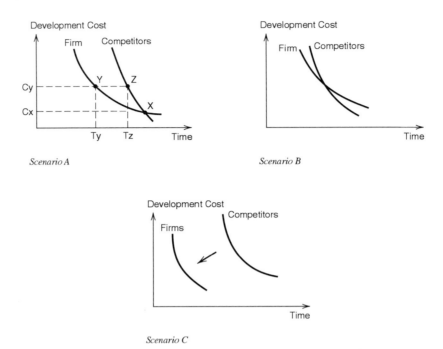

Figure 4. Alternative Scenarios for Development Cost-Time Tradeoffs

value-added to sales ratio in Toyota or Nissan's factories was about 15 to 20 percent compared to 48 percent for GM in the first half of the 1980s (Eckard, 1984). But the term sub-contracting or outsourcing has a different connotation in Japan. The relationship is not merely contractual. Interlocking equity ownership, intense transfers of technology both ways, and non-adversarial, cooperative behaviour make for what is really a co-development and co-manufacturing relationship. Mansfield's (1988) all-industry comparison from a sample of 30 matched pairs of Japanese and American companies, concludes that the speed and lower cost of development in Japanese industry is partially explained by their external relationships.

Figure 4 depicts three alternative scenarios which the planning group should consider. Scenario A shows our firm having a shallower slope than competitors on the development cost-time tradeoff. If so, it may consider moving from a point such as X to point Y. Even if competitors matched the higher level of expenditures to point Z, our firm would still enjoy time advantage T_Z–T_Y. The increase in expen-

diture C_Y–C_X is justified only if the consequent lead time over competitors T_Y–T_X enables the firm to descend the experience and scale curve first and capture a larger market share—or by having the company's standards adopted as the industry norm. In scenario B our firm and competitors have fairly similar time-cost tradeoff curves. Increased development expenditures are not justified as they may set off negative-sum, oligopolistic countermoves. In Scenario C our firm is able to move to an entirely new, and lower, curve by using external relationships such as co-development joint ventures and help from suppliers as in the case of the Japanese auto industry.

The above diagrams are not entirely theoretical abstractions. Some firms calculate alternative budgets for the development expenditure on a particular technology and assess times for each. At the very least, the above figures provide the basis for an informed discussion within the planning group. The Japanese, as well as several American and European companies appear very conscious of the strategic value of such an exercise.

With global competition, it is becoming imperative for a firm to examine each technology in the development stage for (a) The time-cost tradeoff, (b) Competitors' time-cost functions, (c) Determining at what point on the function the firm chooses to be—that is to say, what it will spend, and (d) Relationships with suppliers and partners which may lower development times and cost.

ACQUISITION OF TECHNOLOGY

The alternative of acquiring the technology (or pieces of it) externally, should form part of the planning process at this stage. There are various arrangements such as R&D partnerships, development joint ventures, licensing, and contracted research. While we will not examine the benefits and costs of each, we can state some general criteria for evaluating them against each other and the in-house development alternative.

We begin with an overall criterion, useful not only during negotiations, but also useful in identifying acquisition targets. A technology sale between companies may occur when the value of a technology is perceived to be considerably higher by the purchaser than by the company that developed it—so much so, that the incremental profitability to the acquiring firm less the transaction and adaptation cost to the acquirer must be greater than the technology's perceived profitability to the developer, with the final purchase price lying somewhere in between. Otherwise there would be no sale.

Why would the buyer and seller place unequal values on a technology? The reasons are both structural and perceptual.

Among structural reasons are (i) Capital constraints in the developer firm, (ii) Diversification advantages to the acquiring firm, not enjoyed by the present technology owner. These could be geographical, as well as diversification in a product line sense, (iii) Incremental costs of commercialization and launch greater in the developer firm than in the acquiring company, (iv) Pre-emption of a third competitor from acquiring a significant technology, and (v) Other complementarities or externalities eventually accruing to the purchaser, which the seller cannot enjoy.

In regard to the last point, it is still worth reiterating an assertion made by several authors (Maidique and Zirger, 1985; Gold, 1988; Morone, 1989) that the long term strategy implications and complementarities are often far more important than the narrow calculations of capital budgeting and profit estimates can capture—especially if the time values and perceptions embedded in the calculation do not incorporate the viewpoints of the technology/R&D personnel, as well as executives in different parts of the global firm.

Among perceptual reasons (Why a technology's value is rated differently across companies, as well as across departments in the same firm) are (i) Variations in perceptions of the speed vs. cost tradeoffs shown in Figure 4, (ii) Sensitivity to the competitive ramifications of linking the firm to a technology developed by others, (iii) questions of whose designs will dominate the industry, (iv) the perceived maturity of the technology, and (v) the possible atrophying of internal technical capability. Stopford and Baden-Fuller (1987) report that it is not so much the economics of production, as perceptions of the 'strategic future' of the European appliance industry, that explains the variations in technology, scale and productivity between European companies. Italian firms were described as believing in European integration, and as having a longer-term orientation than their British counterparts who are said to pursue a policy of defending their 'national niche.'

Later in the paper, we discuss the third alternative of co-developing a technology via contracted or cooperative relationships. There are benefits and costs. For instance, joint ventures and co-development partnerships are often quicker and entail lower overall development costs; but the market has to be shared, and today's partners may become tomorrow's enemies.

'GLOBALIZATION' AND ITS LINK TO TECHNOLOGY PLANNING

'Globalization' involves, in part, international plant location and product design decisions. These are determined by minimum economic scale, transport cost, protectionist barriers, after-sales service, flexi-

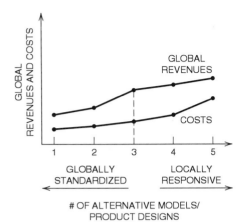

Figure 5. The Optimum Level of Globalization

ble manufacturing and other design and production technology questions best considered at the development stage and not after manufacturing methods and specifications are finalized.

Consider two alternative strategies depicted in Figure 5. A 'global' approach strives to cut costs and realize efficiencies by reducing the differences in models of a product sold in different nations. In the development and engineering stages, economies of scale and rationalization are planned from a few large, low-cost plants to serve the world market.

A 'local responsiveness' strategy on the other hand tries to introduce variations, from one country to another, in product design, after-sales service and other technical parameters, in order to suit local customers and governments better. The scale of production is necessarily smaller and the number of plants worldwide is larger compared with a global strategy. The multinational firm can afford to be more decentralized, enabling local managers to be more responsive to local country conditions. Many designs of the product are needed, preferably with easy adaptability to different customer tastes or technical standards. (Also, the overall strategy of the firm can more easily include joint venture and licensing arrangements in certain nations, a theme we will return to in Stage 3, the Utilization Audit).

Which of the two strategies is best? As Figure 5 suggests, 'neither' is the likely answer for the majority of industries. The optimum lies somewhere in between. A local responsiveness strategy is rewarded

by worldwide total sales revenue increasing with a larger number of models adapted to conditions in each national market. But costs would then increase as well, with a larger number of smaller scale plants and duplication of facilities and staff. Hence the optimum level of local responsiveness versus globalization is likely to be found in an intermediate position.

At the development stage we need to consider technical as well as managerial variables, which will affect the optimal degree of globalization of a product. Some are shown in Figure 6, such as Minimum Efficient Scale (MES) of manufacture. Consider the evolution of the television receiver industry. MES has gone from 50,000 receivers per year in the early 1960s, to 500,000 sets in the late 1970s, to 2.5 million in the 1980s (Bartlett and Ghoshal, 1987). This is more than one maker can hope to sell in many countries. Globalizing firms have therefore to assess the ratio of MES over the mean size of the market in the countries they serve. By comparison, pharmaceutical manufacture is amenable to very small scale of efficient manufacture, enabling formulations to be easily varied to suit local medical practice and regulations, without a large cost penalty.

Such strategy questions should be considered at the development stage and not after engineering and specifications are finalized. If considered early enough, it may be possible to develop manufacturing processes that are efficient at smaller scales of operation. This is especially true with computer-aided design and manufacturing, and with the flexible use of corporate partners overseas. An alternative approach is to design the product so as to build in easy, or relatively low cost adaptability to local tastes and conditions.

Consider the large appliance industry (refrigerators, washers, dryers, etc.). Baden-Fuller and Stopford (1988) report that "the market for domestic appliances in Europe is not united" because of persistent "cultural distinctions," brand loyalty and high national entry barriers in the distribution end of the business. Some companies, however, believe that globalization is setting in and that there is a convergence in buyer preferences. In these companies appliances are being redesigned with substantially fewer parts and flexible manufacturing systems which enable variations in output types despite pro-

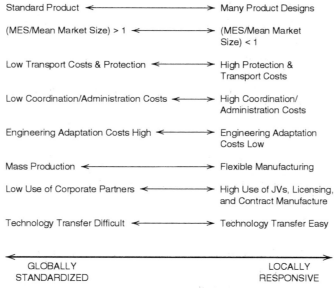

Standard Product ⟷ Many Product Designs

(MES/Mean Market Size) > 1 ⟷ (MES/Mean Market Size) < 1

Low Transport Costs & Protection ⟷ High Protection & Transport Costs

Low Coordination/Administration Costs ⟷ High Coordination/Administration Costs

Engineering Adaptation Costs High ⟷ Engineering Adaptation Costs Low

Mass Production ⟷ Flexible Manufacturing

Low Use of Corporate Partners ⟷ High Use of JVs, Licensing, and Contract Manufacture

Technology Transfer Difficult ⟷ Technology Transfer Easy

GLOBALLY STANDARDIZED ⟷ LOCALLY RESPONSIVE

Figure 6. Variables Affecting the Optimal Degree of Globalization

duction on a larger scale. In such a case the engineering adaptation costs for switching from one model to another are dramatically reduced. For the large appliance industry in general, Baden-Fuller and Stopford's empirical study presents a mixed picture, with entrenched national firms and considerable impediments to the further concentration of manufacture in fewer and larger plants.

Compared to one factory in each nation, a multinational firm which attempts to serve many markets from a few plants has significantly higher coordination and administrative costs, and risks arising from supply interruptions, currency and political fluctuations. These act counter to the tendency to entirely centralize global operations. These risks may also be perceived by customers who do not wish to be so dependent on a foreign supplier. In the telecommunications and other 'strategic' industries customers, who are often governments, mandate local value-added and joint ventures with local firms to reduce such perceived risks. Despite pouring billions into R&D on state-of-the-art switching equipment, the two leading firms of the early 1980s, AT&T and ITT, failed in their globalization drive; ITT sold off its business entirely.

Today alert companies make the search for the op-

timum number of models part of their development planning. While some industries such as large appliances move towards fewer variations; others such as automobiles and consumer electronics may be moving towards more choice. Between 1980 and 1985 Matsushita doubled their worldwide models of tape recorders and portable audio equipment (Bartlett and Ghoshal, 1987). In the context of Figure 5 above, Matsushita's incremental development and production costs of introducing an additional model was more than recouped by the incremental global revenue resulting from offering customers a larger choice responsive to local tastes.

Thus each firm hunts for its optimum between the extremes of complete global standardization and producing a different model for each country market—an engineering and strategy exercise that begins at the development stage.

STAGE 3: IMPLEMENTATION AND UTILIZATION AUDIT

The focus at this level of the technology planning exercise is on maximizing the international utiliza-

---

Implementation and Utilization Audit (Stage 3)

- Create a Technology/Country Matrix
- Assess Market Potential for Each Cell of the Matrix
- For Surviving Combinations Choose Business Model Based on
    - Appropriability of Revenues
    - Global Strategy Fit
    - Cost/Ease of Technology Transfer
    - Reduction in Risk and Cost by accepting JV partners/licensees
    - Opportunity Costs
    - Danger of Creating Competitors

Figure 7. Steps in the Utilization Audit

---

tion of the developed product. One country at a time is examined to determine the optimal mode of business. In the broadest sense the firm needs to decide whether to extend its own organization into the foreign nation by means of a fully-owned subsidiary (5), or whether to go in for a contractual mode such as contract manufacture (C), or licensing (L) the pro-cess and/or product design to an independent firm which learns the technology and manufactures the item in the country. In the middle of the spectrum are various quasi-contractual or quasi-integrated modes such as minority-owned joint ventures (JVM), and majority-owned joint ventures (JVS) which function like a subsidiary despite some shareholding by another firm.

Overall, the company ends up with a global pattern of business shown in Figure 8, a planning matrix of products versus countries. In the majority of product/country combinations the markets would simply be served by imports; or no business at all is feasible because of impediments to investment and trade such as protectionist barriers, transportation costs, restriction on foreign investment in certain sectors, and political or currency convertability risks.

For a newly developed product how does a firm decide on which mode is best for a country? Choosing between a firm's own controlled and integrated

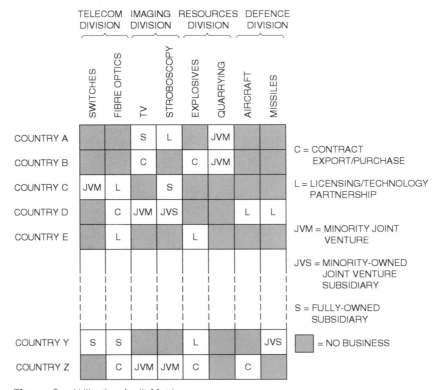

	TELECOM DIVISION		IMAGING DIVISION		RESOURCES DIVISION		DEFENCE DIVISION	
	SWITCHES	FIBRE OPTICS	TV	STROBOSCOPY	EXPLOSIVES	QUARRYING	AIRCRAFT	MISSILES
COUNTRY A			S	L		JVM		
COUNTRY B			C		C	JVM		
COUNTRY C	JVM	L		S				
COUNTRY D		C	JVM	JVS			L	L
COUNTRY E		L			L			
COUNTRY Y	S	S			L			JVS
COUNTRY Z		C	JVM	JVM	C		C	

C = CONTRACT EXPORT/PURCHASE

L = LICENSING/TECHNOLOGY PARTNERSHIP

JVM = MINORITY JOINT VENTURE

JVS = MINORITY-OWNED JOINT VENTURE SUBSIDIARY

S = FULLY-OWNED SUBSIDIARY

▨ = NO BUSINESS

Figure 8. Utilization Audit Matrix

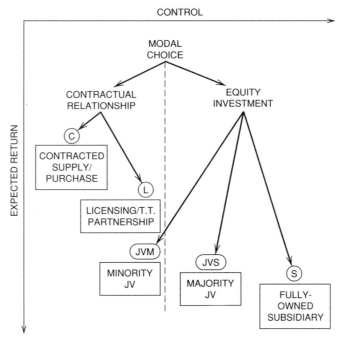

Figure 9. Control vs. Return Mapping of Modal Choices

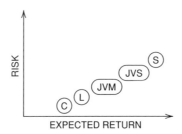

Figure 10. Risk vs. Return Map of Alternatives

subsidiary, or a contractual transfer of technology, or quasi-integration with another partner firm is a complex exercise. For each option not only do market revenues and production costs vary, but with joint venture partners and licensees the share of revenues and costs allocated to each firm is also subject to negotiation. Other strategic implications such as creating a potential competitor also need to be considered. Figures 9 and 10 provide some strategic guidance.

Figure 9 shows a decision tree of major options, and it plots them on a return versus 'degree of control' map. In general, a fully-owned subsidiary provides the highest potential return as well as control

over strategy and operations. But as Figure 10 indicates it also carries the highest level of risk since the largest invested assets are at stake. Contracted modes carry the lowest degree of control in a long-run strategic sense, especially if a significant technology is transferred to an independent licensee who could eventually become a competitor. But such a risk can be contained by agreement provisions, a strong patent position, or most effectively, by remaining technologically one step ahead of licensees and joint venture partners. Moreover licensing bears the lowest level of commercial risk, most of which is borne by the licensee company.

A fully-owned foreign investment affords the firm

the opportunity to appropriate the entire return on the investment and make its investment congruent with global strategy, unhindered by the possibly divergent and parochial objectives of partners. Fully-owned investments are preferred by firms which dominate the designs of products and have a strong patent position (Teece, 1988).

Figures 9 and 10 depict joint ventures as occupying the middle ground on the (1) Return, (2) Risk, (3) Control, and (4) Competitor Risk dimensions. However, we should remember that in recent years companies have found that joint ventures in some cases offer the best overall mix on these four dimensions—to the extent that firms often prefer them over the fully-owned subsidiary alternative. For instance a company that enters a foreign market alone bears all the investment risk, and its unfamiliarity with the local market may carry a heavy penalty in reduced sales. This penalty can be mitigated by taking a local partner who also shares in the investment risk of a joint venture. Moreover, the local partner can significantly reduce investment costs if they have an existing manufacturing and distribution establishment in the nation. In such cases joint ventures are preferred over fully-owned investments.

In the case of a license, the risk is shifted even further away; the licensee makes the investment and bears the investment risk, allocating the technology supplying company a relatively safe, fixed percentage of revenues. This option is chosen when a company possesses a desirable technology but is unwilling to muster the managerial or financial investment, or face the perceived high risk in the nation, contenting itself with receiving a fixed royalty in return for very little or no incremental investment (over and above the sunk cost of development).

We should not make the mistake of assuming that licensing is undertaken mainly by small technology firms which lack the financial or management personnel resources to make their own investments. Larger, multidivisional and multinational companies have a much larger potential for a profitable licensing and joint venture program for their non-core technologies. The largest of companies such as a GM or a General Electric will typically have about a hundred or fewer majority or fully-controlled foreign in-

vestments for its core businesses. It is administratively and financially undesirable to have more. That still leaves hundreds or thousands of possible technology–country combinations unexploited on the matrix in Figure 8. Recall our earlier example of the auto company which had developed a new metal galvanizing technology with better rust protection of its cars in mind. Instead of neglecting the utilization of this technology with applications in other industries in virtually every nation, it can be licensed, or joint ventures set up to greatly increase the return on the R&D investment. And this may be done without the fear that there will be an adverse competitive impact on its main business of selling automobiles.

Medium and large companies have dozens to hundreds of such valuable but underutilized technologies strewn throughout the firm. It takes a technology inventory (Stage 1) plus a Utilization Audit (such as the one recommended in Stage 3) to maximize the return on a company's R&D investment.

SUMMARY

The paper has presented a methodology for technology planning in the multinational and multidivisional firm. Since a technology cannot be operationalized as a profit centre, nor easily regarded as a unit of administrative measurement, the role of technology in formulating strategy is often *ad hoc,* or neglected in many larger, multidivisional companies. This is not for lack of awareness. It is because corporate planning procedures have not fully integrated the technology management aspect.

This paper presents a three-stage technology planning framework. The first stage, called Technology Audit, is a company and worldwide identification of technologies within and outside the firm. At this stage of the planning exercise the planning group examines the technology progression issue and intellectual property strategy, and makes a broad assessment of technologies which may be shared with other firms and those to be reserved for the company's exclusive development. At the same time, gaps in the company's strategy are identified, with a recommendation for how they may be filled by internal development, external purchase of the technology, or by means of a joint venture partnership.

The second stage of the planning exercise called the Development Strategy focusses on one technology at a time. It treats issues such as development cost and time *vis-à-vis* competitors, time-cost trade-offs in the development budget, allocation of the budget over sub-categories, acquisition of pieces of the technology from partners and suppliers, and the anticipated degree of globalization versus local responsiveness which in turn feeds back into product design and manufacturing technology decisions.

The third stage of the planning exercise is called the Implementation and Utilization Audit. A technology/country matrix is created; each cell is then assessed for market potential. For large, and even medium-sized firms, the matrix can have hundreds of cells. Many of these will be eliminated as having little potential. For a new technology or product the analysis next recommends the mode of business, ranging from fully-owned direct investments to arms-length licensing, with varieties of quasi-integrative or quasi-contractual options such as joint ventures, in between.

While the methodology is presented in three steps, in practice it is iterative. In essence, the exercise integrates the national and functional diversity of the firm into a formalized consideration of the most critical component of its long run strategic success—technology.

REFERENCES

Baden-Fuller, C. & Stopford, J.M. (1988) 'Why Global Manufacturing?' *Multinational Business,* Spring, pp. 15–25.

Bartlett, C. & Ghoshal, S. (1987) 'Managing Across Borders: New Strategic Requirements,' *Sloan Management Review,* pp. 7–17.

Chandler, A. (1986) 'The Evolution of Modern Global Enterprise,' in Porter, M., *Competition in Global Industries* (Boston: Harvard Business School Press).

Contractor, F. (1985) *Licensing in International Strategy: A Guide for Planning and Negotiations* (Westport, CT: Quorum Books).

De Meyer, A. & Mizushima, A. (1989) 'Global R&D Management,' *R&D Management,* Vol. 19, No. 2, pp. 135–145.

Eckard, E. (1984) 'Alternative Vertical Structures: The Case of the Japanese Auto Industry,' *Business Economics,* October, pp. 57–61.

Fahey, L. & Narayanan, V. (1986) *Macroenvironmental Analysis for Strategic Management* (St. Paul: West Publishing Co.).

Ford, D. (1988) 'Develop Your Technology Strategy,' *Long Range Planning.* Vol. 21, No. 5, pp. 85–95.

Gold, B. (1988) 'Charting a Course to Superior Technology Evaluation,' *Sloan Management Review,* pp. 19–27.

Goldhar, J. & Jelinek, M. (1982) 'CAM Sets New Rules for Production,' *Harvard Business Review,* pp. 85–91.

Goldstein, M. (1987) 'Gatekeepers Fit the Key into New Technology,' *Industry Week,* November 16, pp. 75–77.

Kennedy, C. (1988) 'Planning Global Strategies for 3M,' *Long Range Planning,* Vol. 21, No. 1, pp. 9–17.

Kerr, J. (1988) 'Management's New Cry: Fight for Your Technology Rights.' *Electronic Business,* August 15, pp. 44–48.

Lenz, R. & Engledow, J. (1986) 'Environmental Analysis Units And Strategic Decision Making: A Field Study of Selected Leading Edge Corporations,' *Strategic Management Journal,* Vol. 7, No. 1, pp. 69–83.

Leonard-Barton, D. & Kraus, W. (1985) 'Implementing New Technology,' *Harvard Business Review,* pp. 102–110.

Levitt, T. (1960) 'Marketing Myopia,' *Harvard Business Review.*

Maidique, M. & Zirger, B. (1985) 'The New Product Learning Cycle,' *Research Policy.* December.

Mansfield, E. (1988) 'The Speed and Cost of Industrial Innovation in Japan and the United States: External vs. Internal Technology,' *Management Science,* pp. 1157–1168.

Morone, J. (1989) 'Strategic Use of Technology,' *California Management Review,* Summer, pp. 91–112.

Porter, M. (1986) 'Competition in Global Industries: A Conceptual Framework,' in Porter, M., *Competition in Global Industries* (Boston: Harvard Business School Press).

Schon, D. (1967) 'Forecasting and Technological Change,' *Daedalus,* pp. 759–770.

Schmenner, R. (1988) 'The Merit of Making Things Fast,' *Sloan Management Review,* Fall, pp. 11–17.

Smith, J. & Fleck, V. (1988) 'Strategies of New Biotechnology Firms,' *Long Range Planning,* Vol. 21, No. 3, pp. 51–58.

Stopford, J. & Baden-Fuller, C. (1987) 'Regional-Level Competition in a Mature Industry: The Case of European Domestic Appliances,' *Journal of Common Market Studies,* December, pp. 173–192.

Takeuchi, H. & Nonaka, I. (1986) 'The New, New Product Development Game,' *Harvard Business Review,* Jan–Feb., pp. 137–146.

Teece, D. (1988) 'Capturing Value from Technological Innovation: Integration, Strategic Partnering and Licensing Decisions,' *Interfaces,* May–June, pp. 46–61.

Thomas, L. (1984) 'Technology and Business Strategy—The R&D Link,' *Research Management,* May–June, pp. 15–19.

Utterback, J. & Abernathy, W. (1975) 'A Dynamic Model of Process and Product Innovation,' *Omega,* Vol. 3, No. 6, pp. 639–656.

Westwood, A. (1984) 'R&D Linkages in a Multi-Industry Corporation,' *Research Management,* May–June, pp. 23–26.

Wiseman, C. (1988) 'Strategic Information Systems: Trends and Challenges over the Next Decade,' *Information Management Review,* Summer, pp. 9–16.

28

DECENTRALIZED R&D FOR GLOBAL PRODUCT DEVELOPMENT: STRATEGIC IMPLICATIONS FOR THE MULTINATIONAL CORPORATION

ALPHONSO O. OGBUEHI AND
RALPH A. BELLAS, JR
Illinois State University, USA

INTRODUCTION

In 1975 Donald Frey, former chief executive of Bell and Howell, decentralized the corporate research and development (R&D) function in his company. The rationale behind this action was that a centralized R&D function was ''too far from the marketplace to avoid failures of new products ill-suited for that market, too removed from customer ideas or influence, and too slow to explore new technologies'' (Frey, 1989). The Bell and Howell CEO took this action after enduring a decade in which there were no major innovations from the centralized R&D function. As a result of his action, a number of successful major innovations were developed over the next decade.

The timely relationship needed between marketing and technology has received some attention in the literature (Capon and Glazer, 1987; Ford and Ryan, 1981). As posited by Ford and Ryan (1981), understanding the technology life cycle enables the multinational firm to introduce new products in a timely fashion. In recognizing the strategic coalignment between marketing and technology, Capon and Glazer (1987) argue that corporate success in a rapidly changing world order depends on the ability of firms to integrate technology and marketing strategy. The extent to which such a relationship between marketing and technology are integrated in a centralized or decentralized manner remains an issue to be resolved.

There is an ongoing debate in the strategic management domain over the centralization versus decentralization of activities in the multinational corporation (MNC). For most firms, centralization and decentralization differ in *degree* rather than in kind. The dilemma facing the globally-oriented MNC is how to organize authority centrally so that it operates as a vast interlocking system that achieves synergy and, at the same time, decentralize authority so that local managers can make the decisions necessary to meet the demands of the local market (Stobaugh and Wells, 1984; Wheelen and Hunger, 1990).

Research and development, historically, has evolved from a geocentric view with development and production intended for local markets. However, a decentralized process may bring about benefits in such areas as product adaptability and production (Ronkainen, 1983). The successful development and introduction of new products in worldwide markets may require an orientation that significantly deviates from the traditional geocentric viewpoint. A decentralized orientation for R&D may be defined as one in which a multinational corporation seeks to distribute worldwide R&D activities and responsibilities among local subsidiaries. In other words, it is an orientation to withdraw from the historical tendency to concentrate R&D efforts at one particular location. Indeed, there is adequate evidence in the literature to support such a reorientation.

Davidson and Harrigan (1977), in considering problems associated with new product introductions in overseas markets, observed that most innovations by US firms seem keyed to the domestic market. Although products may be adapted to local market requirements little significant product innovation is carried out with foreign markets in mind. They recommend that the next phase of corporate evolution should focus upon the product-development *process.* One can make the point that a decentralized R&D will be a logical first step in this process.

Ronstadt and Kramer (1982) argue that firms need to employ overseas-based resources to enhance their ability to compete globally. Their recommendations were based on acquiring international contacts and having R&D investments overseas as ways to add new items to the firm's existing product line. The outcome of this may be R&D decentralization where various units autonomously define their optimal strategies.

In studying how firms adapt products for export, Yorio (1983) observes that firms dependent on international sales are concerned about issues of product adaptation at the design or product-development stage. Findings from this study advocate a "worldwide" marketing orientation to avoid future adaptation problems. This approach partially implies a de-emphasis of centralized R&D operations, so that new products would be brought online to serve domestic and overseas markets concurrently.

The purpose of this article is to examine the effect of the strategic dispersion of R&D facilities and product innovation in the MNC. Specifically, the article focuses on the problems associated with a centralized R&D function as they are expressed in Frey's (1989) statement given earlier. Conversely, it also focuses on the advantages for a dispersed R&D function. Furthermore, it outlines how the decentralized R&D function might be organized so it can meet the firm's strategic goals in the most efficient manner. Finally, it discusses various disadvantages to decentralizing the R&D function and offers suggestions for minimizing potential problems.

ADVANTAGES OF DECENTRALIZED R&D

The decentralization of R&D within the MNC has several possible advantages. Some of these include:

ease of incorporating local market requirements into the product; reduced product development time; accelerated new product acceptance; and reduced trade frictions. As stated by one executive: "Our thesis on the international conduct of R&D is simple: new product development is best undertaken closest to the market user" (Ronstadt and Kramer, 1982). By developing a new product in the vicinity of the target markets, it is possible to incorporate local market flavours and uniqueness into the new product. In addition, a company is able to respond more quickly to changing market requirements by developing new prototypes to suit current and future local needs.

Shortening the development time of new products is crucial to beating competitors to the markets and thus establishing brand awareness. Honda Motor Company found that putting designers and factory experts closer to customers gave them an extra edge. Honda executives figure that their new Accord wagon will reach US customers two months sooner than if it had been produced 6,600 miles away (Taylor, 1990).

Customizing the production process and features available on a product allows for quicker introduction of the product. An example of a product which took advantage of customization is the 1988 Toyota Corolla. In this model year, the Corolla was available in 289 basic model variations to reflect different market needs and different use conditions. The car was also produced in 11 different countries. Another illustration of satisfying particular market needs is the Kijang utility vehicle designed for an exclusive market. This vehicle was designed and manufactured exclusively for drivers and driving conditions in Indonesia. Because of this, it has become the best-selling commercial vehicle in that market.

Another advantage of dispersing R&D facilities among strategic global locations is that it reduces trade frictions between the countries involved. Dispersed R&D limits exposure to currency fluctuations and can have the effect of quieting "Buy Home Country Products" movements. Finally, having R&D facilities located in international markets can offset the impact of economic downturns that may occur in other countries. If business in one continent becomes economically unfavourable, production can be switched to another. Also, these extra facilities allow a company to spread its R&D costs over worldwide production.

Multinational companies can also capitalize on economies of scale by expanding their R&D facilities abroad. Companies can achieve these economies mainly through the human resources and equipment components of the R&D department. Additionally, a higher level of research will be achieved by incorporating elements of technical centres of excellence that are globally dispersed. To experience fully the rewards associated with dispersed R&D, several issues must be recognized and understood by the multinational corporation. Some of these issues relate to the various sources of R&D information, the nature and scope of R&D alliances in the global marketplace, the degree and magnitude of corporate commitment required for international R&D, and to the organization of a successful dispersion of corporate R&D programmes. Other pertinent issues include ways of coping with inherent problems of dispersed R&D, as well as considerations in devising a strategy for a dispersed R&D effort. The rest of the article is devoted to addressing each of these relevant issues as they affect MNCs. Whenever appropriate, illustrations are provided to clarify the issues.

SOURCES OF INFORMATION FOR DISPERSED R&D

Multinational companies of all sizes need to be continually informed about the changing technologies around the world. One relatively inexpensive method of staying informed is to monitor and adapt to external factors that affect success or failure of a company. This environmental scanning can include reading R&D journals, perusing patent reports, having face-to-face contact with other R&D personnel, and maintaining contacts with academic researchers. It has been demonstrated that R&D managers stress the value of face-to-face contact with foreign scientists and technical experts through scientific-technical conferences or through in-house seminars (Ronstadt and Kramer, 1982). Multinational companies would

do well to increase their involvement in international research by creating advisory panels with outside technical experts. These advisory panels would supply the companies with information regarding any significant emerging technologies. Companies can also include R&D specialists, as well as marketing managers, production personnel, and customer service representatives, on project teams that are assigned the task of seeking new product-related projects in international markets. This will allow companies associated with these markets to take advantage of team members' understanding of the unique characteristics of their respective foreign businesses. Companies could also encourage their R&D experts to undertake overseas assignments so they will be exposed to the different technologies that are available.

IBM has successfully used a strategy of tapping the engineering manpower of less developed nations to carry out competitive research and development (Liu, 1989). What impressed IBM was the pool of talented, eager engineers, the low costs, governmental support, and good credit terms available in less developed countries. They successfuly rode the crest of emerging technical development expertise by assigning specific design projects to teams in Taiwan. This benefited local engineers by giving them valuable experience and enabled the country to upgrade its industry. IBM benefited by receiving good, solid products for its peripheral product line. In addition to such benefits, by locating R&D facilities in foreign countries, companies could employ local nationals in the R&D process to provide insight to the local market's unique product and market requirements.

FORMS OF STRATEGIC R&D ALLIANCES

Decentralization of R&D can be carried out through strategic global alliances, which can be achieved in various ways. Some of these include international licensing, cooperative research, mergers and acquisitions, or equity control in R&D firms. Each of these methods offers unique benefits to the MNC and, at the same time, poses different constraints. Each strategic R&D alliance requires varying amounts of commitment, resources, control, risk and flexibility (Jain, 1987; Peet and Hladik, 1989; Rudolph, 1989).

INTERNATIONAL LICENSING

Multinational corporations can also obtain external technology through international licensing. The corporation could ''license-in'' the technological innovation it wants from another international company or from a company in the host country. Smith-Kline Beecham, a major international pharmaceutical company, utilizes its R&D resources as a means of attracting licenses from other firms to develop and market new products (Liu, 1989). By doing this, Smith-Kline Beecham has been able to enhance its product line.

A corporation might also choose to become involved in cross-licensing, in which firms exchange technological innovations with each other. Some companies are forced to do reciprocal licensing to gain access to the technology they want. As a Hoffman-Laroche executive noted: ''We found we had to enter negotiations with something to trade rather than just with dollars'' (Ronstadt and Kramer, 1982, p. 97). The licensing could be done on a corporate basis and the technology spread to the company's R&D facilities on an as-needed justification.

COOPERATIVE RESEARCH

Some multinational corporations will enter into cooperative research projects with each other. They do so in order to reduce R&D expenses and to reduce the risk associated with new research projects. Also, by combining their knowledge, multinational corporations can gain access to each other's technology (Perlmutter and Heenan, 1986). For example, Nissan Motor Co. Ltd entered into a research project with Ford Motor Co. to develop a new multipurpose vehicle (Liu, 1989). An R&D unit, Nissan Research and Development Inc., was established to develop the vehicle, as well as other vehicles, from the design stage through manufacturing. This co-operative research project will allow both Nissan and Ford to increase

significantly their new product development capabilities.

MERGERS AND ACQUISITIONS

To further improve their R&D capabilities, multinational enterprises may acquire or merge with foreign companies that have extensive innovative capabilities. By adding the newly acquired capabilities to their existing facilities, the multinational enterprise can increase its ability to innovate abroad (Hamel *et al.,* 1989). For example, when CPC International acquired Knorr Foods of Switzerland, CPC received new technological capability to help it innovate in the ''processed food'' industry.

EQUITY CONTROL

Multinational corporations can also gain access to outside technology by establishing an equity position in a company with innovative technology. By controlling the ownership of an innovative company, the parent company will be able to ''import'' the essential technology back to its facilities at little or no cost (Modic, 1988). In the case of Bieri Pumpenbau AG Biral International, which owns a majority share of RCB Electroapparate (RCB), it was able to use RCB's technology of producing efficient electric motors almost exclusively for its own product lines. Biral International was able to expand its product capabilities by making RCB part of its portfolio of businesses.

When and why firms choose a certain mode of strategic R&D alliance rather than another is a function of several factors, including the required level of capital investment and the level of risk. For example, licensing is an acceptable strategy for low risk and minimal commitment that provides an entry point into developing international R&D exposure for the firm. International licensing may have intuitive appeal for firms that neither possess capital investment nor the technological know-how. Thus, it may eliminate the risk of R&D failures and the cost of trying to design around the licensor's patents, or the fear of patent infringement litigation. In addition, most licensing agreements have provisions for continuous cooperation and support, and thereby enabling the licensee to gain from new technological developments.

Overall, however, a significant level of commitment is required if a firm wishes to implement a decentralized R&D structure successfully. The next section of this article addresses some of these commitment issues.

CORPORATE COMMITMENT AS A PREREQUISITE FOR DECENTRALIZED R&D

Although commitment is a nebulous term, often lacking precise definition, its use here is in reference to the level of importance attached to a firm's market presence and the willingness to pledge the necessary resources in support of that presence. Few empirical studies exist in which commitment has been isolated as a causal factor in the performance of MNCs in the global marketplace. The operation of a local subsidiary business in a foreign country is a visible demonstration of commitment to that particular country. It follows, therefore, that the sizeable outlay of cash to develop a productive R&D facility indicates that multinational companies recognize the strategic consequences and importance of their regional image. Japanese automakers provide recent examples of the commitment required to be successful in international markets. Toyota, for example, is spending $400 million on a 12,000-acre test track in Arizona, and on new engineering and design studies in three other United States locations. Honda is building a 7.5 mile test track in California, and doubling the size of its research staff to 500 professionals. Similarly, Nissan is assembling a 500-person R&D staff of its own to supplement the staff at a ten-year-old California design centre (Taylor, 1990). The financial commitment of each of these companies indicates the effort required for success in foreign markets. Perhaps it is also an indication of why these three companies have been so successful in the United States market. In any case, these examples illustrate financial commitment as a function of the large company. Indeed, companies venturing into

R&D abroad need to invest sizeable resources into foreign facilities.

A company needs to be fully committed to the advancement and continuity of its R&D facilities abroad to reap the best possible results from the venture. Management must realize that new product development is a precarious venture that requires total commitment of resources and an unrestrained devotion to change. Such commitment is illustrated in the following amusing anecdote:

A chicken and a pig were strolling by a diner one morning and the chicken smiled and said, "Isn't that nice . . . doesn't that make you feel proud, that we are responsible, you and I, for enabling those humans to enjoy their breakfast?" The pig replied, "That's easy for you to say. For you it's merely a contribution, for me it's total commitment" (Buggie, 1982, p. 27).

Total commitment is required to foster changes and promote new product developments. To ensure that adherence to the R&D commitment is maintained, the company needs to assign the responsibility to someone who will emphasize product development above all else. R&D managers should be selected to oversee their own facilities. This will increase their commitment and responsibility, and encourage efficient new product development activities.

ORGANIZING FOR DISPERSED R&D

To organize effectively for a dispersed R&D, three issues need to be fully addressed:

1. The need to recognize R&D as a multifunctional activity.
2. The need for more flexibility in the degree of permanence for R&D units.
3. The extent to which the firm can harness external resources into the R&D process.

The extent to which the firm can involve representatives from the engineering, marketing and manufacturing departments gives the R&D organization a multifunctional design. Given the market-driven character of most new innovations, it follows then that marketing will play an integral role from the beginning, as would engineering and manufacturing, to achieve timely, competitive, cost and quality advantages (Frey, 1989). Although the findings of a recent study show that virtually all major international product breakthroughs were the result of technological push rather than market pull, co-ordination between all the operating departments was considered essential (Humble and Jones, 1989). The implication is that firms interested in dispersing R&D programmes should seek a higher degree of collaboration between existing functional units to ensure an effective R&D dispersion.

Flexibility in the degree of permanence is also essential for the effective organizing of dispersed R&D. Committees or teams composed of representatives from engineering, marketing, and manufacture need to be created for a specific innovation. If successful, the team will become the core of the new business or product line. However, if unsuccessful, the team could be dissolved and its members freed to join new teams. This method of coordinating R&D functions keeps the team members fresh and allows them to get intimately involved with each new innovative team they join. Furthermore, it makes it possible for firms to mobilize an R&D team quickly whenever such a need arises in any part of the globe.

To organize an MNC for overseas R&D property, the company may also need to incorporate outside resources into the process. Enterprises that desire to be active in overseas R&D may have to pursue projects with foreign academics because they can provide the scientific and technological knowledge important for innovative success. Other MNCs may want to form consulting agreements with foreign faculty members to tap into the local academic stream. Foreign education establishments may also have separate agreements to perform certain tasks for the enterprise. Instead of actually building R&D facilities, some companies have signed contracts with research institutes which conduct paid research and experimental projects for the firms. For example, organizations such as the Battelle Memorial Institute and the Illinois Institute of Technical Research have signed agreements to perform research for various companies. Since the dispersion of R&D can be complex, and sometimes cumbersome, strategic issues of importance to the firm deserve to be considered in the process of implementing a decentralized R&D system. Some of these issues are discussed in the next section.

STRATEGIC CONSIDERATIONS FOR DISPERSED R&D

Careful planning is needed to prevent haphazard acquisition or location of R&D facilities. There is the danger of duplication skills and capabilities when a company has several R&D facilities around the world. Overhead-support functions could also increase and be duplicated across the facilities, thus increasing the overall cost of R&D. In addition, by having R&D facilities spread worldwide, a company may lose control over the activities that the R&D facilities conduct. Consequently, the home office may be unable to maintain senior management's commitment to R&D and strategic objectives in the dispersed facilities.

In some situations, dispersed research and development is neither applicable nor advisable. These occur when the enterprise is such that innovation is not significant, being the first product in a market is not important, and benefits of economies of scale are minimal. When these situations exist dispersed research and development provides little strategic advantage.

However, if dispersed research and development are applicable, then several issues of strategic relevance deserve further consideration, Ronstadt and Kramer (1982) have identified three important areas of consideration in devising an effective strategy that will determine the ultimate success of dispersed R&D activities. These areas include:

1. Corporate planning.
2. Corporate control.
3. Corporate coordination.

Each of these is considered individually.

CORPORATE PLANNING

Prior to the full implementation of a decentralized R&D system, perhaps the first strategic issue to which a company needs to pay careful attention is the area of corporate planning. The corporate planning process has to include the nature of planned global R&D activities in determining the company's overall strategic plans. Decentralized R&D corporate planning involves defining the strategic objectives of all the proposed R&D facilities, deciding on the overall R&D expenses and budgets, according to specific product development and strategic innovation needs, and estimating the proper amount of resources (human, raw materials, etc.) to be allotted to each R&D facility. The plans should also include decisions regarding the level of local adaptation for the new products that will be developed. The home office needs to decide on the magnitude of adaptation or standardization of the new product that is necessary to meet local needs. In addition, the corporate strategic plans should include the appropriate time horizon for each foreign R&D laboratory to generate a stipulated number of new product developments.

CORPORATE CONTROL ISSUES

It is important to consider the balance of power and control over decentralized R&D facilities between the home office and the local subsidiary. One corporate R&D manager succinctly described the balancing act as follows: ''The local R&D unit cannot have unbounded discretion over its performance . . . We must help them succeed by making certain they do not try to do considerably more than they are capable of doing'' (Ronstadt and Kramer, 1982, p. 99). The home office may consider setting restraining limits on the amount and type of R&D activities carried out at the overseas facilities, depending on the available resources. The division of power and control needs to be satisfactory to both sides to minimize unproductive friction between the home office and various R&D units, scattered around the world as a result of the decentralized R&D framework.

Proper reward systems have to be designed according to the needs of the overseas R&D facility's employees. Different nationals working in foreign laboratories have different levels of needs. For example, some nationals may value monetary rewards for excellence in R&D performance, while others may prefer personal recognition. The home office may need to develop and establish an overall standard of performance for each of its foreign R&D laboratories, but allow each subsidiary to design the reward system that it feels is most appropriate for its local R&D personnel.

CORPORATE COORDINATION

A third area to which the home office needs to pay attention, in implementing a decentralized R&D system, is the coordination of all R&D activities at each overseas R&D laboratory. The home office must have the ability to coordinate the activities of all the facilities to ensure that activities are authorized and conducted properly. This could be accomplished by utilizing modern communications tools such as telephone, FAX machines and computer satellite linkups. Occasionally, however, it may be necessary to send managers from the home office to various R&D subsidiary locations for observation purposes. The home office could also ensure proper coordination by appointing on-site coordinators for each R&D facility to assure that the activities performed are as specified in the corporate plans. The on-site coordinator should have extensive powers that would allow him or her to carry out the home office's plans effectively. Furthermore, the coordinator should also maintain good contacts and communications with the appropriate home office counterpart and superior.

Attempts by MNCs to coordinate decentralized R&D activities across countries may result in the consolidation of several local R&D activities. This could cause problems with local R&D personnel involved because they may resent losing control over their own R&D activities. Host governments may also express their displeasure in losing access to the available technologies when companies attempt to move their dispersed R&D facilities.

Since the stage of a product life cycle in the home country market does not parallel the life-cycle stage in other international markets, increased communication between different R&D facilities is required. This communication will allow company personnel in the international market to learn from and improve on the actions taken in the home country. In this way, different product sophistication levels can be designed to match local requirements. This coordination must be considered in relation to each stage of the product development process, from idea generation all the way to product testing and eventual commercialization. This is crucial because, at any stage of this process, a decision could be made to drop a product concept or to discontinue further product testing. Failure in this downstream coupling mechanism may mean that the product idea would not emerge or, if it did emerge, may not match market needs.

It is apparent from the preceding discussion that the adoption of a dispersed R&D operation requires careful deliberation. Some firms clearly are not in a position to embrace fully a dispersed R&D structure. Others stand to enhance their global competitive position if R&D activities are decentralized. For such firms, it is prudent to consider carefully planning, control and coordination issues associated with a global decentralization of R&D programmes.

SUMMARY AND CONCLUSIONS

Multinational corporations have invested tremendous resources in establishing extensive operations abroad. Foreign operations are important sources of technological innovations for new product developments that improve the chances for global success. The potential increase in new product development capabilities may offset the cost of establishing dispersed R&D facilities, depending on the nature of market opportunities and the level of risk involved.

Companies do not always have to rely on internal R&D facilities. Development capabilities for new products can be obtained in a variety of ways. These include mergers or acquisitions of technologically competent companies, co-operative research projects with other companies, licensing rights to innovative technologies, and partnerships with academia. As

yet, there is no evidence in the literature to suggest the presence of any prevailing pattern in the type or size of organizations that are active in dispersed R&D. However, organizations must be large enough to afford the seemingly high, initial cost of implementing a decentralized R&D structure. A company that is capable of employing any of the methods of acquiring technological innovation may benefit from such an alliance. A small company can enter into co-operative arrangements with similar companies to exchange technology. Innovative success in new product development will help to ensure continued competitiveness in the business environment.

Multinational corporations must be aware of the difficulties that might arise from the dispersion of their development facilities. For instance, there are potential problems arising from increases in overall operating costs through duplication of functions and activities in the dispersed laboratories. To avoid any unnecessary problems, careful planning and the appropriate organizational structures have to exist. These will allow for a conducive environment and the successful interrelated existence of all the operating R&D facilities. Suitable co-ordinating devices have to be utilized to ensure that the R&D activities will benefit the whole organization.

Corporations should also avoid haphazard placement of their research laboratories. Research and development facilities are best located where the corporations intend to market their products. Local, regional and national markets can be served by the products developed at the research laboratories. However, some research facilities can be, and often are, located away from the intended target markets and nearer to scientific and technological pools. Various surveys have shown that corporations prefer to locate their foreign laboratories in industrialized countries, such as Canada, the United States, Japan, the United Kingdom, Germany, Italy and Australia.

There are many uses for foreign R&D facilities. They can be responsible for adapting the home country's technology and products to the local markets. They can generate new products and processes expressly for local uses. They can develop products and technology for commercialization in other countries. Corporations have to determine beforehand how they intend to use their foreign research and development facilities, to avoid any misunderstanding regarding the status of R&D operations within the organization. As was noted throughout this article, establishing overseas R&D functions is a risky proposition for many companies. However, if a company is totally committed to establishing an international R&D effort, history has shown that the benefits will far outweigh the risks.

REFERENCES

Buggie, F. (1982). "Strategies for New Product Development," *Long Range Planning,* Vol. 15, No. 2, April, pp. 22–31.

Capon, N. and Glazer, R. (1987). "Marketing and Technology: A Strategic Coalignment," *Journal of Marketing,* Vol. 51, July, pp. 1–14.

Davidson, W.H. and Harrigan, R. (1977). "Key Decisions in International Marketing: Introducing New Products Abroad," *Columbia Journal of World Business,* Vol. 12, Winter, pp. 15–23.

Ford, D. and Ryan, C. (1981). "Taking Technology to Market," *Harvard Business Review,* March–April, pp. 117–26.

Frey, D.M. (1989). "Junk Your Linear R&D!" *Research Technology Management,* May–June, pp. 7–8.

Hamel, G., Doz, Y.L. and Prahalad, C.K. (1989). "Collaborate With Your Competitors—And Win," *Harvard Business Review,* January–February, pp. 133–9.

Humble, J. and Jones, G. (1989). "Creating a Climate for Innovation," *Long Range Planning,* Vol. 22, No. 4, August, pp. 46–51.

Jain, S.C. (1987). "Perspectives on International Strategic Alliances," *Advances in International Marketing,* Vol. 2, pp. 103–52.

Krubasik, E.G. (1988). "Customize Your Product Development," *Harvard Business Review,* November–December, pp. 46–52.

Liu, P. (1989). "Big Blue Benefits from Funding R&D in Taiwan," *Electronic Business,* May, pp. 105–6.

Modic, S.J. (1988). "Strategic Alliances: A Global Economy Demands Global Partnerships," *Industry Week,* October, pp. 46–52.

Peet, J. and Hladik, K.J. (1989). "Organizing for Global Product Development," *Electronic Business,* 6 March, pp. 62–4.

Perlmutter, H.V. and Heenan, D.A. (1986). "Cooperate to Compete Globally," *Harvard Business Review,* March–April, pp. 136–52.

Ronkainen, I.A. (1983). "Product-Development Process in the Multinational Firm," *International Marketing Review,* Winter, pp. 57–65.

Ronstadt, R. and Kramer, R.J. (1982). "Getting the Most Out of Innovation Abroad," *Harvard Business Review,* March–April, pp. 94–9.

Rudolph, S. (1989). "Sometimes the Best Solution is in Someone Else's Lab," *Business Month,* October, p. 91.

Stobaugh, R. and Wells, R.T. Jr (1984). *Technology Crossing Borders,* Harvard Business School Press, Boston, MA.

Taylor, A. (1990). "Japan's New US Car Strategy," *Fortune,* 10 September, pp. 65–80.

Wheelen, T.L. and Hunger, J.D. (1990). *Strategic Management,* (3rd ed.), Addison-Wesley Publishing Company, New York, NY.

Yorio, V. (1983). *Adopting Products for Export,* The Conference Board, New York, NY.

29

MANAGEMENT OF INTERNATIONAL R&D OPERATIONS

ARNOUD DE MEYER

INTRODUCTION

In the latter half of the 1980s the globalization of the company has become a widely studied issue in management. Different terms such as the transnational company (Bartlett & Ghoshal, 1989) or the internationally operating company have been used. As part of that globalization we have observed an increased interest in global technology development. This is a result of the growing interdependence of technological development in industrialized countries and the increasing importance of global firms to participate in the technological development networks of countries other than their home country.

To participate in an international network of technology development, a company can obviously follow different tracks. The simplest one consists of technology scanning or the creation of technological antennae with the aim of monitoring the development in other countries. Though such an approach may have its merits, it limits the company to the position of a bystander. In the case of technologies with a low analyzability and a high degree of complexity, this is usually insufficient to understand and transfer the technology developed abroad.

A second approach consists of technology-based joint ventures. The difficulty of managing such joint ventures, and the risk of losing out in such a joint venture have been described elsewhere (Doz, Hamel, & Prahalad, 1991).

A third possibility is the internationalization of the R&D function. This is the topic of this paper. Firms have traditionally been reluctant to internationalize this function. The reason for this are easy to see. Emotions may play a role: the physical distance created between the headquarters and the research function may be seen as a risk for the long-term strategy of the firm, or a source of the lack of relevance of the results of the R&D efforts. Fear that internationalization of R&D entails risk for the protection of proprietary information may equally lead to a hesitation to go abroad with laboratories. Furthermore, the difficulties in communication created by geographical decentralization may lead to a productivity decrease in development (Allen, 1977). Creating a series of laboratories abroad may lead to a frittering away of resources, and individual laboratories may run the risk of not reaching the critical mass needed for effective development work.

Yet, offshore spending on R&D is on the rise. A survey of the National Science Foundation indicates that R&D spending abroad by U.S. companies jumped 33% in 1986 and 1987, while spending in the United States went up by only 6% during that same period. In a study of 20 Swedish multinationals, it was found that the share of foreign R&D as a percentage of total R&D expenditures had risen from 1980 to 1987 from 20.6 to 22.8% (Hakanson & Nobel, 1989). In spite of the rapid escalation of domestic expenditures from 1980 to 1987 (214% in current prices), these Swedish multinationals, had increased their expenditures in foreign R&D locations even more (252%). Though there are, with some exceptions, no ambiguous data available for Japan, casual observation of what large Japanese companies state in their yearly reports seems to point in the same direction: carrying out R&D abroad or overseas is on the rise.

This increase in offshore spending on R&D is a challenge both for theory and management practice. Few theories have been formulated on the creation of an international R&D function, and even less empirical or theoretical work has been published on how one can manage the dispersion of the R&D function. In fact, the reason why companies internationalize is a topic more for economical than managerial study. We could limit ourselves to a position whereby we accept the existence of an international network of laboratories, and study how the network is managed. But we need to explain why we see a change in the long entrenched behavior of centralized R&D since it has an important impact on how the process of internationalization can be managed. The central proposition of this paper is that technical learning has become one of the core reasons underpinning the decision to internationalize R&D. If one accepts this proposition, the next step is to examine how this proposition can help us to improve the management of geographically dispersed R&D.

THE RESEARCH BASIS

Our observations are based on in-depth interviews in 15 internationally operating companies. Data about the why and the how of international R&D operations were gathered through interviews with research managers, laboratory directors, and in some cases customers or users of the results of the R&D department. Interview time per company ranged, depending on the complexity of the situation, from several hours to several days. A checklist of topics was used as basis for the interviews, but given the diversity of the firms which were studied, the interview format was kept fairly open.

The fifteen companies do not form a homogeneous sample. They are not representative of a specific industry. Four companies belong to the electronics industry, one to the food industry, three to the pharmaceutical industry, five to the chemicals industry and two to the automobile industry. Ten of them have European headquarters, three have North American headquarters, and two have Japanese headquarters. The number of overseas or foreign lab-

oratories ranged from 1 to 17. In each of the cases the companies employed several hundreds of professionals in research and/or development. At the time of the interviews, each of the companies was considered to be successful by the specialized business press, as well as by judging from the financial performance over the last five years. This is obviously not an indication of success in R&D, or of the internationalization process of R&D. In fact, in more than one company we were granted interview time since the managers concerned had some doubts about the performance of their international R&D performance, and they hoped to get through the interviews a sort of benchmark for their international R&D operations. In two of the companies we interviewed, a major restructuring of the international R&D operations followed quite soon after our visit. We can consider these companies consequently to be below standard performers. With respect to the performance of the other companies' international R&D operations we cannot make any judgment. It would be impossible to do so since in some cases we studied, international R&D networks had been in existence for less than ten years, a time horizon which was often considered by research managers to be the minimum necessary to evaluate the performance of a research laboratory.

The activities of the set of laboratories we have studied ranged from very basic industrial research to applied development. We excluded from the analysis simple process engineering or technical customer support activities.

WHY INTERNATIONALIZATION OF R&D

A review of the literature (De Meyer, 1989b) reveals three categories of reasons why companies have created geographically decentralized networks of R&D laboratories. The oldest approach is in fact an elaboration of the international product life cycle theory (Vernon, 1966), and was described by Ronstadt (1977) and Behrman and Fischer (1980). In this model, technology transfer units are first created to transfer products and processes from central head-quarters to the international sales and production operations. These technology transfer units appear to have an almost unstoppable momentum to evolve into indigenous technology units developing new and improved products expressly for the local foreign market. Some of these technology units could develop such a degree of expertise that they would be allocated responsibility for worldwide product and process developments. In theory, some of these laboratories in our sample suggested that many foreign laboratories had an origin and evolution which was very different from this evolutionary path. Laboratories were often results of acquisitions, or created as a corporate research lab with worldwide responsibility straight away. Rondstadt (1977) indicated already that more than half of the overseas laboratories he studied originated in fact in a way different to that which would have been ''prescribed'' by the international product life cycle.

A second model is a variation on the neoclassical approaches to location of production sites: companies will invest abroad to take advantage of cost differences between countries (Roman & Puett, 1983). One can consider R&D as a production operation of ideas for new processes and products. Companies can locate them where they find the cheapest resources available for the production of these new ideas. Since the human resources are often the critical production factor in the development of new products and processes, the availability of engineers, the quality of the educational system of a country, the sheer number of engineers and scientists graduating per year, and the quality of the network of research institutes and universities may determine the location of a laboratory.

The third category of reasons for internationalizing R&D is the one which is most often quoted by the pure technologists: access to technology. This approach is based on the observation that the development of technology is unevenly distributed across the world (Perrino & Tipping, 1989), and that there has been a growing interrelatedness between formerly separate technologies (Cantwell, 1989). The results of the research carried out in the concentrations of technology development usually get diffused either through the classical scientific process of conference presentations and publications, or through salesmen of the component suppliers. The argument has been made that this distribution system is too slow for a company which wants to be at the forefront of technological improvements (De Meyer & Mizushima, 1989). To be informed at a very early stage of the new developments, one has to become part of the local network of technology production. To be part of such a network, one may be obliged to broaden its technological activity and to create a laboratory in the immediate neighborhood of these concentrations of technology development (Herbert, 1989; Westney & Sakakibara, 1986).

The transaction cost literature (Teece, 1981) provides some theoretical basis for this foreign investment in R&D triggered by the desire to get access to technology. The market for knowledge does not work in a perfectly frictionless way. The transactional difficulties which make contractual agreements about know-how almost impossible, are usually summarized in recognition, disclosure and team organization problems. Creating laboratories overseas may often be the only solution to overcome these difficulties.

Three major categories of reasons exist for internationalizing R&D, and each of them to some extent are supported by theoretical consideration. Originally, it was our intention to use this categorization to classify each of the nearly 100 laboratories described in the interviews in one of the three categories. After this classification exercise, we hoped to be able to describe how to manage laboratories of each category, by studying the common characteristics of the laboratories in each category.

After classification, and though we tried to limit the laboratory activity to its main task, it turned out that most of the laboratories in the sample had to be classified in each of the three categories. In fact, the decision to go and remain abroad with a laboratory was with a few exceptions a complex decision, the result of a complex interaction of different motives, rather than one single motive explaining the existence of the laboratory (Dixon, 1990). A categorization which does not separate the laboratories in group with limited overlap is not very useful. So we had to look for different reasons for internationalization, if we wanted to use these reasons to look for guidelines of how the laboratories had to be managed.

This brings us back to the ultimate objective of R&D, and its function in the company. R&D has two main contributions to make to the company. The first one is technical problem solving, that is, tackling the technical problems related to the current development of products and processes. This problem solving requires a high integration with both marketing and manufacturing. The need for close integration may bring part of the development team close to the geographical location of the marketing team and/or the manufacturing team responsible for the project. This does not, however, warrant the creation of a permanent development laboratory abroad. It suggests rather that on an ad hoc basis teams of marketing, manufacturing and development people can be created in those locations where the core of the innovative action goes on. Creation of a permanent laboratory has in those cases the purpose of making technical resources and capital equipment available in a given location, in the expectation that location will become a continuing focal point of product and process development.

But R&D has a second function. It also has the responsibility of building a know-how base for the company, which will enable the company in the future to react to new competitive challenges, or to explore new markets. Cohen and Lewinthal (1989) corroborate with this view: They assert that the role of R&D is not only to solve problems, but also to enhance the firm's ability to generate, assimilate, and exploit existing information. This technical learning is thus a core activity of the R&D process (Imai, Nonoka, Takeuchi, 1985; Myers, 1990). The central hypothesis of this paper is that technical learning in a globalizing world requires the creation of an international network of R&D outlets. In principle, this network will contain technological antennae, R&D joint ventures, and laboratories. Internationalization of the R&D operations contributes to faster and qualitatively improved technical learning.

When analyzing the interview reports from this angle, it was almost as if the pieces of a jigsaw puzzle fell into place. In the description of how laboratories were created or in arguing why a particular laboratory was kept in place, the preservation of the existing technical know-how base and the further technical learning about markets, technologies, and competitive environment were very often used.

One should be careful with learning. Recent management literature has abundantly stressed the need for improved organizational learning. Simplistically said, this refers to how the firm can improve its organizational and managerial processes through some form of single and double loop learning (Argyris & Schon, 1978). This is not the learning we refer to. Though organizational learning should be a part of the management of the R&D function, it cannot be the primary purpose of the internationalization process. It is the extension, improvement, and maintenance of the technical know-how base of the firm which is referred to here.

INTERNATIONAL R&D AS TECHNICAL LEARNING

Learning can be defined as the process within the organization by which knowledge about action-outcome relationships and the effects of the environment on these relationships is developed (Duncan & Weiss, 1978). Unlike individual learning which involves relatively permanent changes in an individual's behavior, technical learning by an organization involves the development of a know-how base owned by an organization, which would make such change possible. The outcome of the learning process is knowledge that is distributed across the organization, is communicable among members, has consensual validity, and is integrated into the working procedures of the organization.

If one applies this to the technical learning process, it appears that exposure to sources of knowledge in different countries is important, but that to be effective, one has to create mechanisms on an international scale to diffuse, validate and integrate the new knowledge across the whole network of laboratories. Validation of the information has often to do with the *credibility* of the laboratory vis-à-vis its partners. To produce unique information (i.e., information which could not have been produced in the central R&D laboratory), the foreign laboratory must be able to take advantage of the local circumstances. A certain degree of *diversity* among the laboratories is thus needed. Diffusion, validation and integration are heavily determined by the quality of the formal and informal *communication* system. The informal communication system is highly dependent on the organizational *network* which exists in the firm.

Furthermore, from a management point of view, we are interested in learning systems which can be managed, where conscious efforts by research managers can improve the effectiveness of the international R&D network. The creation of laboratories in locations far away from the headquarters indicates that the firm wants to learn through an organization, and not through an individual. If the learning would be dependent on a single individual, the firm would probably be better off by paying the individual enough so that he moves to the central R&D laboratory, or by guilding a monitoring device around that person. Thus the technical learning must become part of the procedures. The focal part of these procedures is often the planning process.

Precisely these five focal points could be observed in the description of the management of an international R&D network: enhancing the credibility, preserving the diversity, stimulating the communication, managing the networks, and using the planning procedures for learning purposes.

MANAGING THE INTERNATIONAL R&D NETWORK FOR TECHNICAL LEARNING

CREDIBILITY

To be accepted as a source of technical know-how, a newly created laboratory or a recently acquired laboratory has to gain credibility. In the European laboratory of a North American specialty chemicals producer, the laboratory director told us that it had then taken seven years to gain acceptance by his American colleagues. The final "credibility" breakthrough came when the European laboratory developed a product which became an immediate commercial success. Up to that point, the European laboratory had been greatly appreciated by the local manufacturing and marketing groups. But, the commercial success of one of their brainchildren gave the European laboratory visibility within the whole group, and made non-European divisions and departments interested in interacting with the European laboratory. Only from that point onwards this laboratory could make a contribution to the learning of the whole group.

Similar credibility breakthroughs, or the existence of credibility hurdles were observed with some laboratories recently created in Japan. Often these laboratories were created as the result of a strategic choice to be present in Japan, and a recognition of the technological capabilities in Japan. Some of these ventures did not receive a clear objective, or the necessary resources to fulfil their task, or the patience to penetrate the local R&D networks. These laboratories seem to be doomed to fail to contribute to the technical learning of the company. Indeed, after initial enthusiasm for the creation of the Japanese laboratory, the other laboratories and the rest of the company base their willingness to learn from the newly created laboratory upon the evaluation of the results.

Consequently, to speed up the contribution of the newly created or recently acquired laboratories, it seems important to the managers of the R&D function to create the circumstances which will help the laboratory gain lasting credibility. Time and again it was repeated during the interviews that the real credibility is based on technical results which have a significant impact on the economic performance of the firm.

Successful, applied technical work can contribute in the short run to the effectiveness of a foreign R&D center. In the case of a food company, the Singaporean centre acted not only as a technological development centre, but also as the coordinator for Quality Assurance activities (De Meyer, 1989a). Somewhat unexpectedly, this activity provided a lot of useful information on product performance and market needs. And some successes in quality improvement gave the needed credibility to the development centre to create good links to production and marketing.

There is an important managerial message in all this. If the R&D manager wants to integrate a new R&D centre in the technical learning system, it seems to be important to create fairly quickly some visible successes in the new center. Assigning them a meaningful task within the organization, providing them with some short-term goals, and the resources with which to reach them, seem to be necessary conditions to create the long-term contribution of the center to the technical learning system.

The contribution to the learning determined by this image of credibility was not only for newly established centers. In one particular case, the comment was made that a particular well-established laboratory was just no longer responsive to the market. Though the laboratory was generally recognized to be competent in its specific field and to have contributed in the past to the development of important patent positions, its lack of adaptation to new requirements had created a credibility gap which seriously decreased the laboratory's contribution to the know-how base of the firm. One should notice that the technical credibility of the scientists had not disappeared. The researchers in this laboratory were still considered to be very competent, but they were also considered to have become irrelevant. They had not lost their individual technical credibility, but rather their credibility to contribute to the relevant know-how base of the firm. In some way the laboratory had lost its strategic role within the company.

To conclude, it seems that a way to increase the credibility of a newly established lab or an existing lab is to give it a clear strategic role within the company, and give it a portfolio of projects which can help it obtain some quick and easy successes.

DIVERSITY IN APPROACH

A recurrent comment was that there was no standard R&D laboratory within the company. Of course, the work done by the different laboratories is different, but diversity existed also in culture, or hierarchical organization.

No "hard and fast" model existed within the R&D organizations. Diversity was actively pursued and stimulated. The rationale for this can be easily understood from the learning point of view. The literature on learning strongly emphasizes the need for diversity of the existing knowledge base to improve the learning. Bower and Hilgard (1981) suggest that the breadth of categories into which prior knowledge is organized and the linkages across those categories permit individuals to make sense of and, in turn, acquire new knowledge. Morgan and Ramirez (1983) contend that one of the three prior conditions for self-organizing learning systems is requisite variety. Breadth and variety of learning and problem-solving approaches consequently enrich the learning system. Discussions of learning all indicate that it is a cumulative process. The variety of the stock of existing knowledge increases the capability of an individual, and mutatis mutandis the organization as a collection of individuals, to place new information, which does not extend the existing knowledge in a linear way. The variety in organization and hierarchical structure contributes to the diversity of the existing knowledge base in the firm, and will enhance the technical learning process in fields which do not belong to the core competence of the firm.

IMPROVED COMMUNICATION

The communication network is of high importance for the diffusion, consensual validation and integration of newly acquired know-how. Communication is, of course, not a new issue in the context of management of R&D.

The most interesting aspect of communication in an international context is the added difficulty of geographical distances and cultural differences. Indeed, it makes the core element of communication in R&D, the informal personal contact (Allen, 1977), much more difficult. We identified several elements that we expect to figure prominently in the companies' communication efforts (De Meyer, 1991): organizational structure, "boundary spanning" individuals, and communications technology.

The literature on R&D communication has often stressed that communication patterns are highly influenced by project structure, organizational structure, and by change-over time in the project structure (Utterback, 1975). And since open, person-to-person communication is often a result of having people working together, reallocating personnel to different project teams can create links between teams. But altering organizational structure, the technical assignment, or project groups can also destroy communication. In addition, the style of project management can have an important influence on the creation of links between project teams. Consequently, one could expect multinational companies to take organizational measures and use career planning to manage communication patterns.

Second, a constant element in the research on communication patterns is the important role played by ''boundary-spanning'' individuals or ''gatekeepers'' (Allen, 1977). Information often comes from outside into a group by a two-step process. Particular individuals seem to have the capability of monitoring what is going on in the outside environment and translating that external information into messages comprehensible to the group to which they belong. They are different from the integrators or liaisons described in the literature on integration and differentiation. Indeed, gatekeepers do not integrate tasks and actions, but only improve the flow of information. A boundary-spanning person, an international gatekeeper, might be able to manage the flow of information between international laboratories.

Third, recent technological innovations such as fax machines, teleconferencing, and videoconferencing have considerably improved the tool kit for complementing individual, face-to-face communication. As with telephone calls, one wonders to what extent these technological means can support or even replace face-to-face communication. The images in videoconferencing and the pictures, graphs, and tables available with fax machines, electronic mail, and computer conferencing provide a quantum improvement over the simple telephone call.

In our study we saw a bit of everything. The companies were all strongly aware of the need to improve communications and often admitted that breakdown of the communication lines was the biggest recurring problem in their organization. We sorted the solutions they were pursuing into five broad categories:

1. *efforts to increase socialization in order to enhance communication and information exchange:* temporary assignments, constant travelling, implicit rules and procedures which are part of the company culture and international training programs were all part of the portfolio of socialization efforts;

2. *implementation of rules and procedures in order to increase formal communication:* much more attention was paid to careful reporting and documentation and to the communication flows related to the planning cycle, than one would normally observe in a laboratory in one site;

3. *creation of boundary-spanning roles—assigning individuals to facilitate communication flows:* in every organization we studied, we observed the use of individuals in transferring technology, but their role seemed preeminent when major structural changes in the R&D network were ongoing;

4. *creation of a centralized office responsible for managing communication or the development of a network organization;* and

5. *replacement of face-to-face communication by electronic systems:* in particular it was observed that electronic communication could lengthen the time between two face-to-face contacts, but could never replace completely the face-to-face communication. Electronic communication can never be the sole means of information exchange between people. This seems obvious, but the relative convenience of electronic data communications as opposed to travel, direct contact, or even telephone calls between different time zones gives researchers enough reason to fool themselves. Moreover, to be able to work together, people need to trust each other. In case of geographical separation, there is almost a certainty that this trust will decrease over time. Misunderstandings, slow feedback of information, and so on will all contribute to deterioration of the climate. We observed that electronic communication can lengthen the ''half-life time'' of trust, but cannot completely prevent trust between collaborating researchers from breaking down.

This categorization of communication mechanisms is, of course, somewhat artificial. Companies do not think in these categories: they made efforts in nearly all categories, but attributed a different weight to the different categories in their portfolio of efforts.

MANAGING THE NETWORKS

Scholars of international business and technology management have also shown considerable interest in the concept of networks in recent times. Hakanson and Zander (1986) 'put it in this way: ''Increasingly Swedish firms are now moving towards an 'integrated network model', characterized by tight and complex controls and high subsidiary involvement in the formulation and implementation of strategies. In consequence . . . heavy flows of technology, finance, flows and materials tie subsidiaries to each other and the parent.'' Bartlett and Ghoshal (1989) say that precisely the integrated network is the structural framework of the transnational company. Perrino and Tipping (1989) propose a global network model of technology management. This model consists of a network of technology core groups in each of the major markets, managed in a coordinated way for maximum impact. In the limited field of R&D as a learning process, Meyers and Wilemon (1989) indicate that informal networks are by far the most efficient tool for intergroup learning. Imai and Baba (1989) propose that in the case of systemic innovations, a network organization within the company and across the company's boundaries is a necessary condition for innovation success.

What seemed most important throughout the interviews was the recognition that these several interdependent networks each require a different approach and attention. We observed four types of networks: local and international networks, both internal to the firm and external to the firm. The local internal and external network is the main mechanism through which the local laboratory can fulfil its role of local learning. The density and quality of the communication with local partners is a measure of the laboratory's effectiveness to tap in the local network of research institutions, consumers, producers, and so on.

The information and knowledge learned locally has to be diffused in the company. A local external network can only be effective if it is linked to a strong internal but international network. This is par-

tially an issue of interlaboratory communication. But it is also related to how well the laboratory is embedded in the network inside the company, but outside R&D. In one company the senior management had taken two successful actions to strengthen the intracompany network. First, they had chosen persons with a high visibility in the headquarters to act as laboratory directors or as senior researchers in the laboratory. These people had the explicit role of being the ambassadors of the laboratory at the headquarters and the other functions in the company. Second, realizing there was a gap between decentralized laboratories and centralized marketing, some of the marketing functions were decentralized to the same locations as the laboratories. One sees here two complementary actions: a strengthening of the local intracompany network (decentralizing marketing) and a strengthening of the international intracompany network (the ambassador role).

Apart from the local external and the intracompany networks, we were several times confronted with the existence and importance of the external international network. The external local networks of the different laboratories are also connected among themselves. Careful management of this international network external to the company can provide a boost to the effectiveness of the learning and diffusion process in the company, stabilize the information flow, and reduce the distortion of information due to internal filters. In the most extreme case, the external network can be a more efficient diffusion mechanism than the internal communication network. This does not necessarily have to be the result of a breakdown of the internal networks. It simply can be that two laboratories work on very different projects, but work with a common technology provided by an outsider. Let us take an example.

Most laboratories have local external contacts with suppliers or research organizations. These suppliers or research organizations with which two laboratories of the firm located in different countries have contact, may actually have a link between them. In one case we observed that a supplier of mechanical components had actually a better insight in the portfolio of the projects executed in the different laboratories of the firm, than the individual laboratory managers. In this extreme case, it seemed that the external international network was actually more performing in transferring information than the internal international network.

Another widespread example is that of academic researchers which are part of the international invisible college in their field. Two researchers in very different academic institutions may actually be in contact with different subsidiary laboratories of the same firm.

In one of the case studies, the R&D management had consciously attempted to nurture these international links between academics by organizing so-called private conferences to whom all the academics who worked for the company were invited to make presentations. The R&D management of this company told us explicitly that the main goal of these conferences was to create an international invisible network of academics working for their company.

PLANNING IN R&D AS LEARNING

Behrman and Fischer (1980) focus on how planning and control is exercised in international R&D. Following a taxonomy of managerial styles proposed by De Bodinat (1975), they assign these styles of the companies in their sample to four discrete points on a continuum from absolute centralization of the decision making to total freedom. As one could expect, they find neither many successful examples of absolute freedom, nor of absolute centralization, and the majority of the cases in their sample of 50 companies is characterized by either participative centralization or supervised freedom. In an earlier study we found a similar result (De Meyer & Mizushima, 1989). However, the categorization in discrete points on this continuum is somewhat artificial, and we have observed that planning and control and managerial style of decision making can move on the continuum over time, and depends on the technological characteristics of the specific foreign laboratory involved. The position on this continuum is dynamic rather than static. It does not depend in the first place on the characteristics of the parent company, but rather on the characteristics of the individual laboratory.

The parent company's culture plays a role here, but only in second order.

A second observation is that in most of the companies we studied, the planning and related activities had a strong learning component. This has been observed in other studies.

Meyers and Wilemon (1989) come to the conclusion on the basis of an exploratory survey on learning in new product development teams that the strongest inhibitors for learning have to do with not establishing and maintaining clear project objectives. This is clearly an element of the planning process. De Geus (1988) gives a description of Shell's planning process and asserts that planning should be a learning process, and that one of the objectives for improving planning systems should be the acceleration of the learning process. Consequently, common scenario building, common preparation of the strategy formulation, and projects common to different laboratories can contribute to the better linking of R&D and strategy through improved learning. In the trade-off between planning efficiency and learning of the organization, the choices should favor the learning side.

How did this learning component find its expression? In many of our cases the managerial decision making on planning issues was closer to participative centralization than to supervised freedom. Each time, there was, however, an enormous effort to involve local laboratory personnel and local laboratory management in the formulation of objectives, and the means to reach those objectives. One company had a biennial planning cycle with internal scientific conferences which were not only used to determine research targets but also to exchange information between strategic planning, the business units, and the scientists. In one of the specialty chemical companies, the description of the process showed that the whole planning cycle was used more for purposes of educating each other and for diffusing information than for planning itself. A yearly budget cycle was even said to make no sense in this company, since development cycles were from five years upward. But the educational value to the company of the planning process seemed very important. The same company also had a central data base for general access.

All data generated by the different development centres are entered in the database in a uniform format. The database, which is accessible to all researchers and product managers is considered to be an excellent means of diffusion of information as well as control of the ongoing activities.

CONCLUSION

Internationalization of R&D decorations is a decision which is the result of a complex trade-off of different factors. The traditional discussions of R&D management have attempted to categorize the reasons for internationalizing R&D in three broad theoretical categories: the international product life cycle, the neoclassical economic theory, and the transaction cost approach to the diffusion of information. In the analysis of the interviews, we did not find this categorization very helpful. Many of the foreign laboratories were created for a complex set of reasons which fell into each of the three categories. Moreover, this categorization in three groups does not provide the manager with a clear set of tools to manage the geographically dispersed network of laboratories.

Analyzing the data from a different angle, we understood that the internationalization of R&D was actually a tool to improve the technical learning capability of the firm. We propose on the basis of the firms' experience that at least five elements contribute to this learning system.

In order to be able to contribute to technical learning, a laboratory must first obtain technical credibility with its partners. Creating a clear strategic role for the laboratory and giving the laboratory a portfolio of short-term projects through which it can prove its credibility are of utmost importance for the creation of a new laboratory or for the integration of an acquired laboratory. In the process of creating this credibility, one must be careful not to destroy the specific strength of a particular laboratory. Credibility does not require homogeneity. The diversity between the different laboratories must be preserved. A credible laboratory, with its own characteristics must be able to diffuse its contribution of the company's know-how. A powerful formal and informal communication system, and a well organized network organization will contribute to this. Finally, it seems that many companies attempt to use the planning and control system to organize the diffusion of knowledge and the technical learning of the organization.

REFERENCES

Allen T.J. (1977). *Managing the flow of technology*. Cambridge, MA: MIT Press.

Argyris, C., & Schon, D. (1978). *Organizational learning: A theory of action perspective*. Reading, MA: Addison-Wesley.

Bartlett C.A., & Ghoshal, S. (1989). *Managing across borders, the transnational solution*. Boston, MA: Harvard Business School Press.

Behrman J.N., & Fischer W.A. (1980). *Overseas activities of transnational companies*. Cambridge, MA: Oelgeschlager, Gunn, & Hain.

Bower G.H., & Hilgard E.R. (1981). *Theories of learning*. Englewood Cliffs, NJ: Prentice-Hall.

Cantwell, J. (1989). *Technological innovation and multinational corporations*. Oxford, UK: Basil Blackwell.

Cohen, W.M., & Lewinthal, D.A. (1989). Innovation and learning: The two faces of R&D. *The Economic Journal, 99,* 569–596.

De Bodinat, H. (1975). *Influence in the multinational enterprise: The case of manufacturing*. Unpublished doctoral dissertation, Harvard Business School.

De Geus, A.P. (1988). Planning as learning. *Harvard Business Review, 66*(2), 70–74.

De Meyer, A. (1989a). *Nestlè S.A*. In W.H. Davidson & J. de la Torre (Eds.), *Managing the global corporation* (pp. 463–477). New York: McGraw-Hill.

De Meyer, A., & Mizushima, A. (1989). *Global R&D management, R&D management, 19*(2), 135–146.

De Meyer, A. (1991, Spring). *Tech talk: How managers are stimulating global R&D communication. Sloan Management Review,* 49–58.

Dixon, L.M. (1990). The motivation to go international with research and development. In M.W. Lawless & L.R. Gomez-Mejia (Eds.), *Proceedings of the Conference on Strategic Leadership in High Technology Organization*. Boulder, CO: University of Colorado Press.

Doz, Y., Hamel, G., & Prahalad, C.K. (1991). The competitive logics of strategic alliances. New York: The Free Press.

Duncan, R., & Weiss, A. (1978). Organizational learning: Implications for organizational design. In B. Staw (Ed.), *Research in Organizational Behavior* (pp. 75–123). Greenwich, CT.: JAI Press.

Hakanson, L., & Nobel, R. (1989, December). *Overseas research and development in Swedish multinationals.* Paper presented at the Academy of International Business Meeting, Singapore.

Hakanson, L., & Zander, U. (1986). *Managing international R&D.* Stockholm School of Economics, Stockholm, Sweden.

Herbert E. (1989). Japanese R&D in the United States. *Research and Technology Management, 32*(6), 11–20.

Imai, K., & Baba, Y. (1989). *Systemic innovation and cross-border networks.* Discussion Paper no. 135, Institute of Business Research, Hitotsubashi University, Kunitachi, Tokyo, Japan.

Imai, K., Nonoka, I., & Takeuchi, H. (1985). Managing the new product development. In K.B. Clark & R.H. Hayes (Eds.), *The uneasy alliance* (pp. 337–375). Boston, MA: Harvard Business School Press.

Meyers, P.W. (1990). Non-linear learning in large technological firms: Period four implies chaos. *Research Policy, 19*(2), 97–115.

Meyers, P.W., & Wilemon, D. (1989). Learning in new technology development teams. *Journal of product innovation management, 6,* 79–88.

Morgan, G., & Ramirez, R. (1983). Action learning: A holographic metaphor for guiding change. *Human Relations, 37*(1), 1–28.

Perrino, A.C., & Tipping, J.W. (1989). Global management of technology. *Research and Technology Management, 32*(3), 12–19.

Roman, D.D., & Puett, J.F. (1983). *International business and technological innovation.* New York: North Holland.

Ronstadt, R. (1977). *Research and development abroad by U.S. multinationals.* New York: Praeger.

Teece, D. (1981). The multinational enterprise: Market failure and market power considerations. *Sloan Management Review, 22*(3), 3–17.

Utterback, J.L. (1975). Innovation in industry and the diffusion of technology. *Science, 183,* 620–626.

Vernon, R. (1966). International investment and international trade in the product cycle. *Quarterly Journal of Economics, 80,* 190–207.

Westney, E., & Sakakibara, K. (1986). The role of Japan-based R&D in global technology strategy. In M. Horwitch (Ed.), *Technology in the modern corporation, a strategic perspective* (pp. 223–228). New York: Pergamon.

FINANCE

Finance is concerned with allocating and investing funds and with measuring and evaluating financial performance. These activities are much more complex in a multinational or global firm than for a firm that deals only with a domestic currency. Global financial managers must deal with multiple investments or holdings denominated in foreign currencies that can appreciate or depreciate against the currency in which the firm keeps its accounts and reports its results.

A finance manager in a global firm will have alternatives in borrowing. For example, a parent might borrow in one currency and relend the proceeds to a subsidiary. The foreign subsidiary might, itself, borrow in its local currency. Because of currency fluctuations, different borrowing choices carry different risks, even if interest rates are the same. In choosing a borrowing alternative, the firm must balance several factors including currency convertibility, relative interest rates, and expected future currency relationships.

Raising equity as well as debt capital is now a global possibility. Industrialized-country firms now float equity issues simultaneously in New York, London, and Tokyo, for example. As firms from the industrializing countries have become multinational in scope, their need to raise capital has increased significantly. In the past, their principal source has been bank debt rather than equity, in part because their home countries did not have capital markets in which it was possible to float equity issues.

Once developing-country firms reach a very large size, as for example the Korean *chaebol,* they can float equity offerings almost anywhere in the world. Industrializing-country firms of smaller size have had more difficulty raising equity. Capital markets providing a source of equity for their own domestic firms have grown in many industrializing countries. In addition, it is becoming common for multinationals from the industrialized countries to sell shares of their industrializing-country subsidiaries in the capital markets in which the subsidiaries are located. This trend further complicates the CFO's job.

READING SELECTIONS

Donald Lessard explores the many facets of the financial function in the global corporation and describes how it has evolved. Two major trends, globalization of competition for both customers and production factors, coupled with deregulation and integration of financial markets around the world, are changing the financial management function. Financial officers must, of course, manage their traditional relationships with external financial institutions such as banks and investment bankers that provide their financing. They must also participate in setting corporate strategy and interact with many of the firm's operating functions.

Lessard discusses how and why the two major trends he cites affect several of the important facets of the financial function. The evaluation of investment opportunities has become more complex, wider search is required to find "financial bargains," and managing risks and minimizing taxes requires a considerably wider scope of investigation before making decisions. Financial management includes a wide variety of tasks encompassing both short-term considerations, such as managing foreign exchange, and long-term functions, such as minimizing cost of capital.

Foreign exchange risks are inevitable in a firm that does business across borders. Michael Moffett and Jan Karl Karlsen examine these foreign exchange risks from two perspectives. One perspective is *strategic exposure,* using financial hedges to mitigate the potential effects of unfavorable changes in currency relationships. *Economic exposure,* on the other hand, looks at changes in the value of a firm that come from changes in future operating cash flows that are caused by unexpected changes in exchange rates. The two kinds of exposure are, of course, quite different. Moffett and Karlsen explain their ramifications and effects.

Jack Glen and Brian Pinto analyze emerging capital markets and discuss their growing role in providing financing for firms in industrializing countries. Capitalization in these markets has increased over 25 percent per year since the 1980s. It has outstripped, by almost two to one, growth in industrialized countries' capital markets. Equity markets have been growing considerably more rapidly than debt markets, they note, because of the lack of institutions such as insurance companies and pension funds that customarily make term loans. The authors go on to explain the reasons for industrializing-country firms' financing decisions. The bias of industrializing-company firms toward debt may be diminishing with the increasing availability of equity funds.

John Holland presents a framework for making capital budgeting decisions in international firms. He recommends a model using adjusted present value so that the decision maker can adjust individual components of the problem for differences in risk. He recommends the decision maker separate cash flows into those that are specific to the product and can be separately estimated and those that depend on corporate cash flows. He points out that financial theory, as applied to the typical domestic situation, is not fully applicable to international capital budgeting situations. Holland discusses the modifications required for effectiveness and concludes with a discussion of capital budgeting as applied to strategic planning.

30

GLOBAL COMPETITION AND CORPORATE FINANCE IN THE 1990s

DONALD R. LESSARD
Massachusetts Institute of Technology*

Financial management is undergoing fundamental change as the result of two major sets of external forces—the globalization of competition in product and factor markets and the deregulation and integration of world financial markets. These two forces, together with major advances in the analytical and information technologies underlying financial transactions, are broadening the role of finance in corporate management well beyond its traditional tasks of raising and managing funds.

For example, financial managers increasingly participate in corporate strategic issues—matters that were once almost exclusively the province of corporate planning departments—such as: Which businesses should the company be in? How should these businesses be linked together? And how should the company's participation in these activities be structured?

Donald Lessard is Professor of International Finance at MIT's Sloan School of Management. He has published extensively in leading professional journals on topics of international corporate finance, finance for developing countries, and international portfolio management. His current research centers on strategic and tactical responses to shifting exchange rates and the implications of the globalization of product and factor markets for the boundaries, strategies, and management structures of multinational companies.

* This article draws liberally from two of my earlier published articles: "Finance and Global Competition: Exploiting Financial Scope and Coping with Volatile Exchange Rates," *Midland Corporate Finance Journal,* Vol. 4 No. 3 (Fall 1986); and "Corporate Finance in the 1990s: Implications of a Changing Competitive and Financial Context," *Journal of International Financial Management and Accounting,* Vol. 1 No. 3 (1989).

Global competition also requires greater interaction between finance and a number of operating functions. This is particularly the case in the management of macroeconomic risks, such as those arising from changes in interest rates, currencies, and key commodity prices. In managing such risks, not only should financial hedges be based on knowledge of the companies' expected operating responses to price shifts, but financial perspectives should be used to guide those responses. Finally, corporate finance is also in the process of expanding to become a business in its own right as well as an "expert function" contributing to business decisions outside of the financial domain.

The new competitive and financial environment is thus creating two often opposing pulls on financial management. On the one hand, it calls for a deepening of financial technology and, hence, an increase in the specialist nature of financial management.[1] At the same time, it calls for greater *integration* of financial perspectives into overall strategic and operating management decisions. This is especially

[1] Among the most promising technical advances in finance now underway are the following: (1) the extension of current risk management methods to the hedging of long-term *economic* exposures based on simulations of multi-period cash flows; (2) the use of derivative asset valuation techniques (most notably, option pricing models) in the evaluation of corporate strategic investments; and (3) securities innovations designed (in many cases, by corporate issuers themselves) to take advantage of tax and investor clientele effects or unusual asset exposures. Corporate applications of this new finance technology typically involve teams of specialists, more like the R&D function than the prototypical finance function of only a few years ago, when knowledge of NPV and the ability to manipulate a spreadsheet was sufficient.

clear in the task of coping with volatile exchange rates. Under global competition, exchange rate fluctuations not only change the dollar value of the firm's foreign profits, but they affect its competitive position. As such, currency shifts often call for changes in operating variables such as pricing, output, and sourcing. These operating decisions are complicated by the fact that volatile exchange rates distort traditional measures of current and long-term profitability, creating illusions that depend on the currency in which strategic alternatives are weighed and operating managers' performance evaluated.

Finance also increasingly plays a strategic role in the evaluation of corporate investments—if only because of the presence of capital market outsiders who are prepared to intervene if they see ways to increase a firm's value. To the extent a given investor clientele is willing to pay more for a company's assets when separated from the corporate form or otherwise "repackaged," management can increase stockholder value by exploring alternatives to ownership such as project financing or limited partnerships that still provide them with adequate control.

Because of this greatly increased scope for interaction between finance and strategy, the finance function must seek to integrate itself more fully into other corporate functions even as it becomes more technically advanced and specialized. This set of demands calls for a group of "expert managers"—that is, neither isolated technical specialists nor "thin veneer" generalists, but managers who can operate effectively in both domains.

In this article, I discuss the changing role of finance in the context of global competition and increasingly integrated financial markets. I focus special attention on two areas: (1) exchange risk management and (2) the growing linkage between global finance and strategy. In exploring the management problem caused by shifting exchange rates, I argue that adoption of a global perspective critically affects a company's ability to maintain or strengthen its competitive position. Global perspective is also important in evaluating the firm's strategic options—both in the funding and structuring of overseas projects—in order to achieve the highest value for shareholders.

THE CHANGING COMPETITIVE AND FINANCIAL CONTEXT

Multinational corporations (MNCs) today not only participate in most major national markets, but are also increasingly coordinating their activities across these markets to gain advantages of scale, scope, and learning on a global basis. The emergence of global competition represents a major threat, as well as an opportunity, to those European and American companies that gained competitive advantage under an older mode of multinational competition. Labeled "multi-domestic" competition by Michael Porter, this now passing phase in the development of international business was characterized by large MNCs with overseas operations that operated for the most part independently of one another. What centralization existed in this stage of the evolution of the MNC was typically restricted to areas such as R&D and finance. With global competition, a much larger proportion of corporate activities is coordinated globally, including aspects of manufacturing, marketing, and virtually all R&D.

The emergence of global competition reflects the merging of previously segmented national markets caused by a variety of forces, including reductions in trade barriers, a convergence of tastes, and significant advances in product and process technologies. New global strategies also take advantage of changes in information technology and increased organizational sophistication to improve coordination among geographically dispersed operations.

The emergence of global competition has coincided with and, to some extent, given rise to major changes in the financial environment. The world economy continues to display a high degree of turbulence that has plagued it since the early 1970s. Divergences in macroeconomic policies among countries and massive structural pressures have led to violent shifts of interest rates, exchange rates, and relative prices of commodities. While such turbulence presents a challenge to any business organization, it is particularly troubling for those companies that face global competitors with differing geographic configurations and, thus, different exposures to these key market variables. National financial markets have become increasingly linked into a single global market, as a result of both deregulation and an increase in the market power, global reach, and financial skills of both corporate and institutional users of financial services. At the same time, as mentioned earlier, a significant deepening of financial technology has taken place not only in terms of the information, trading, and document-processing systems, but also in the refinement of analytical techniques that have given rise to new financial instruments, more precise pricing of assets, and new economic risk management approaches.

A major feature of the new international financial environment, especially in Europe, is the emergence for the first time of an *international market for corporate control*.[2] Cross-border mergers and acquisitions are increasing rapidly, to the point where differences among nations in openness to foreign takeovers are likely to become an important source of conflict among national and corporate interests. At the corporate level, such changes mean that companies based in different countries competing in a single European or global market must match their competitors in terms of the cost and access to capital, especially in periods of corporate reorganization and integration. In this sense, industrial companies have a major stake in how financial institutions evolve in the coming years.

The trend toward greater integration of financial markets is not universal, though. Many less-developed countries, in response to foreign exchange crises brought about by their own external borrowing coupled with the world recession, have seen their financial systems cut off from the world system by debt ''overhang.'' Thus, the financial map of the world includes an increasingly integrated core, with pockets of local differences due to domestic intervention, and a large periphery of LDCs which, while dependent upon the core international market, are only loosely linked to it. In this article, we restrict

our attention to the integrated core, primarily the OECD countries.[3]

THE EVOLUTION OF THE CORPORATE FINANCE FUNCTION

Notwithstanding periodic attempts of conglomerateurs and asset strippers to create value by repackaging financial claims, finance derives most of its value from the real business operations it makes possible. In an idealized world characterized by complete information, perfect enforceability of all contracts, and neutral taxation, the principal roles of the finance function would be to provide a yardstick for judging business options to ensure that they meet the ''market test'' for the use of resources, to raise sufficient funds to enable the firm to undertake all projects with positive net present values, and to return funds to shareholders when they cannot be reinvested profitably.

Of course, the world does not match this idealization. Managers often possess information that they cannot or will not disclose to investors, and investors often disagree among themselves as well as with managers regarding future prospects. As a result, defining and monitoring contractual relationships between managers and various classes of claimants is extremely complex and imperfect. Further, taxes are not neutral and access to particular capital markets is often restricted. As a result, financial contracts at times are not fairly priced.

In such an environment, finance can contribute to the firm's value in several ways in addition to its basic role of evaluating and funding investment opportunities. Finance can add value, for example, by allowing the firm to (1) exploit pricing distortions in financial markets, (2) reduce taxes, and (3) mitigate risks, in part by allocating them among different par-

[2] See the article by Mike Wright et al. and the interviews of European executives that appear later in this issue. See also Ingo Walter, ''Competitive Positioning in International Financial Services,'' *Journal of International Financial Management and Accounting,* Spring 1989.

[3] For a journalistic account of promising solutions to the LDC funding problem, see the article by Greg Millman later in this issue. See also my own article, ''Recapitalizing the Third World: Toward A New Vision of Finance for Lesser-Developed Countries,'' *Midland Corporate Finance Journal* (Fall 1987).

ties in order to take advantage of diversification benefits, create appropriate managerial incentives, and reduce costs of financial distress. The nature and potential contribution to value of each of these functions will differ according to the type of international strategy pursued by the firm. For the sake of simplicity, I will here view all MNCs as falling into three categories: (1) international opportunists—firms that focus primarily on their domestic markets but engage in some international sales or sourcing from time to time; (2) multi-domestic competitors—firms committed to a number of national markets with substantial value added in each country, but with little cross-border integration or coordination of activities; and (3) global competitors—firms that focus on a series of national and supranational markets with substantial cross-border integration and coordination of activities.

To what extent, then, does the finance function differ in these three different contexts?

The nature and potential contribution of some aspects of finance would appear to depend on the firm's multinationality—that is, the extent to which it spans different currency areas or tax jurisdictions—rather than on the degree of integration or coordination of the firm's primary activities such as manufacturing or marketing. Other aspects, however, especially those related to exchange rate risk, will differ dramatically depending on the pattern of competition. For this reason, an MNC may have a global orientation in finance but not in other activities. On the other hand, merely the fact of having multinational operations does not guarantee that it will realize the benefits of global scope in finance. Nevertheless, there are many reasons why the finance function will differ in the context of global competition.

Table 1 provides an overview of the changing nature of the finance function and its linkages to the firm's overall competitive position under international, multi-domestic, and global competition. It classifies firms into these three categories according to their method of dealing with a number of tasks typically assigned to the corporate treasury and planning staffs: evaluation of new investment, funding, performance measurement, and exchange risk management. I also include tactical pricing and output changes to exchange rate changes—not typically thought of as finance functions—because they are closely linked to exchange risk management and strongly influenced by a firm's currency perspective.

In the rest of this section I review the implications of increased global competition together with the increased integration of financial markets for each of the major finance functions identified in Table 1.

EVALUATING INVESTMENT OPPORTUNITIES

A clear implication of the current competitive environment is an increase in the complexity of investment opportunities, and a corresponding increase in the potential for management error. The estimation of incremental benefits from resource outlays must take into account increased international interdependence among the various activities of the firm in terms of the benefits of scale, scope, learning, and, hence, future opportunities.

In analyzing alternative plant locations, for example, management must evaluate not only differences in the direct costs of operating in each location, but also the impact of different choices on other strategic factors such as access to particular markets and the scale and experience "platforms" that each alternative provides for future operations. Choices among alternative product and marketing programs are even more complex, since gains in some product market segments will result in erosion in others, while in other cases there may be positive carryover.

Because of differences in government tax and financing subsidies among nations, choices among strategic alternatives are further complicated by the need to trade these direct and indirect benefits off against alternative packages of investment incentives and performance requirements. While similar complications existed prior to the rise of global competition, in general they were much easier to sort out since they influenced only whether a firm should enter a particular national market, rather than which (mutually exclusive) way they should serve a world market.

Table 1. Implications of Global Competition for Finance Function

Function	Nature of Competition		
	International Opportunist	Multi-domestic	Global
Investment Evaluation	Domestic perspective, few "foreign" considerations	Yes/no decision to enter market or change mode to serve local market	Mutually exclusive global choices, currency and tax issues central
Funding Operations*	Meet domestic norms	Meet local norms	Match global competitors' cost of capital
Exchange Risk Management	Focus on exposure of foreign currency contracts	Focus on exposure converting foreign profits into dollars	Focus on exposure of home and foreign profits to competitive effects of exchange rate shifts
Output/Pricing Responses to Exchange Rate Movements	No change in home currency price	No change in local currency price	Change in home and local price to reflect global competitive position
Performance Measurement	Measure all operations in dollars at actual rates	Measure foreign operations in local currency	Measure all operations relative to standard that reflects competitive effects of exchange rate

* The entries in this row reflect typical behaviors of firms. Clearly, firms can and some do pursue global cost-minimizing financing strategies regardless of degree of global linkage of operations.

Given the volatility of the world economy, the strategic investment alternatives facing MNCs will increasingly include option-like elements. With the approach of Europe 1992, for example, much of the value of overseas investments by U.S. firms today can be thought of as deriving from the "platforms" they will provide for other, future growth opportunities. Besides opportunities for "learning" and future expansion, such investments may also derive considerable value from operating options that give management the flexibility to shift production geographically and to defer add-on investments until the most opportune moment.[4] Valuing such complex operating options clearly requires the supplementing of single discount rate DCF approaches with "option pricing" or "contingent claims" approaches that allow for explicit treatment of operating flexibility.[5]

And, finally, to the extent financial markets and tax regimes are not yet fully integrated, the appropriate risk premiums used in evaluating projects could be affected not only by the location of the activity, but also by the nationality of the investing cor-

[4] For a telling indictment of the failure of U.S. corporate capital budgeting practices to capture such effects, see James Hodder and Henry Riggs, "Pitfalls in Evaluating Risky Projects," *Harvard Business Review* (January–February, 1985).

[5] In cases where there is only one or a small number of state variables that determine a project's value, such as commodity prices for extractive ventures, derivative valuation techniques can be applied directly. See, for example, Michael Brennan and Eduardo Schwartz, "A New Approach to Evaluating Natural Resource Investments," *Midland Corporate Finance Journal*, Vol. 3 No. 1 (Spring 1985). However, in cases where the range of state variables is more complex, some combination of valuation by components with discrete modelling of key options will probably have to suffice.

poration and its shareholders. If companies with different fiscal and financial bases have different costs of capital for the same activities, they should attempt wherever possible to shift ownership of assets—or at least the readily separable components of the returns from those assets—to those investor clienteles with the lowest required rates of return. (At the end of this article, I will return to this emerging—and, at least among finance scholars, highly controversial—area of potential interaction between finance and competitive strategy.)

EXPLOITING FINANCING BARGAINS

To the extent that financial markets are not fully integrated or that financing concessions differ among countries, MNCs' ability to span these markets will increase not only their ability to fund global operations, but also the likelihood that they can identify and exploit financing bargains. If a firm can identify financial investment or borrowing opportunities that are mispriced, it can add value by engaging in arbitrage or speculation. In general, opportunities for such gains should be far more scarce than opportunities for gains from real market advantages. Nevertheless, such opportunities do exist from time to time, especially in capital markets that are distorted and isolated by controls on credit and exchange market transactions. Exxon, for example, was able to issue zero-coupon bonds at a rate lower than the U.S. Treasury yield on the comparable maturity, defease the issue by buying an offsetting portfolio of Treasuries, and pocket a profit of nearly $20 million—largely because of differences in the Japanese tax code and restrictions on Japanese foreign investment.

The Industrial Company as Investment Banker This Exxon example also illustrates an important new development in financial markets. The deregulation of financial transactions and the deepening and diffusion of financial technology have had two major effects on the relationship between traditional *suppliers* of financial services—that is, commercial and investment banks and other financial institutions—and the *users* of these services such as industrial companies and institutional investors.

The first of these is *disintermediation.* Corporations are increasingly issuing securities directly to the ultimate holders, bypassing intermediaries and, in some cases, even market agents. Such disintermediation is taking place not only in "normal," recurring finance such as commercial paper and asset-backed financings, but also increasingly in strategic finance involving takeovers, repurchases, and other restructurings. Further, when intermediaries are involved in such fundings, they increasingly compete on the basis of expertise in specific activities and in distribution capability rather than according to their ability to use their own balance sheet.

The second major development is *internalization,* whereby non-financial or industrial firms increasingly perform many of the analytical and trading functions for which they previously relied on outside specialists. Many companies with active treasury philosophies, for example, maintain their own "in-house" trading operations in foreign exchange and money markets as well as in those commodities that traditionally have been shared between financial and non-financial players. Further, non-financial firms often equal or surpass the depth of expertise of outside financial institutions in questions of financial structure and securities issues.

As industrial companies develop their own capabilities in financial transactions, many of them have begun to treat the finance function as a business in its own right. British Petroleum, for example, has organized BP Finance as a separate entity with the objective of not only providing financial services for BP at large, but also functioning as a *transactional treasury* that seeks to profit from its trading activities. A number of such companies extend this business role beyond trading and other recurring functions to include design, packaging, and even issuing of new securities and other forms of participation in the companies' underlying activities. BP, for example, has pioneered the issue of commodity-linked securities, having made several oil-option- or gold-option-linked issues. Marriott has a project finance function that exists primarily to package its own hotel properties for sale to investors, generally in the form of limited partnerships with various forms of credit and business risk enhancement by the corporation.

REDUCING TAXES

By appropriately "packaging" the cash flows generated by business operations, moreover, companies often can substantially reduce the present value of governments' tax take. The simplest example in a single country setting is the use of debt as a way to reduce corporate income taxes. Firms operating internationally may be in a position to shift income into jurisdictions with relatively low rates and/or relatively favorable definitions of income.

While some of these profit shifts occur through transfer prices of real inputs and outputs, the pricing of interaffiliate financial transactions often provides the greatest flexibility. In the current global competitive environment, though, a new factor is coming into play. As governments seek actively to manipulate their fiscal systems for nationalistic or distributional gains, companies shop fiscal regimes and actively bargain over the distribution of rents resulting from a given activity. This is especially true of facilities on a world scale which, by definition, are not premised on access to any single market. In these cases, tax system arbitrage becomes an area of active bargaining as well as gaming of passive fiscal systems.

Yet another way that an international firm can reduce (the present value of expected) taxes is to structure interaffiliate commercial and financial dealings, as well as hedging the risks of individual units through external transactions, so as to minimize the chance that any of its corporate components will experience losses on its tax accounts and, as a result, have to carry forward some of its tax shields. Virtually all corporate income tax regimes are "asymmetric" in that they collect a share of profits but rebate shares of losses only up to taxes paid in the prior, say, three years.

As with financing costs, an environment of increasingly global competition puts companies under much greater pressure to match the lowest tax burden obtainable by any firm in the industry while increasing their flexibility in locating and coordinating activities.

MANAGING RISKS

An important insight of modern financial theory is that in an idealized capital market, the allocation of risk among firms, as well as the form in which it is passed on to investors, does not affect the value of the firm's securities. The reasoning is that sophisticated investors, simply by holding diversified portfolios, can manage most risks just as efficiently as corporate management. Under these circumstances, hedging by the corporation does not add to the value of a company's shares.

In practice, however, firms devote a great deal of effort to risk allocation in the form of hedging and risk sharing. While much of this behavior can be traced to attempts by managers to "look good" within imperfect control systems, several recent analyses provide a rigorous basis, consistent with shareholder value maximization, for hedging under some circumstances. In brief, currency fluctuations can accentuate the volatility of earnings and cash flows. Such volatility can in turn distort management information systems and incentives, hinder access to capital markets, jeopardize the continuity of supplier and customer relationships, and, in the extreme, put the firm into bankruptcy.[6]

For such reasons, companies facing large exposures to exchange rates (or, for that matter, interest rates or commodity prices) may benefit by laying off these risks to other firms or investors that have smaller or perhaps even opposite exposures. As the earlier BP example illustrates, companies with large price exposures can also lower their cost of funding by issuing securities that reduce those exposures.

Unfortunately, current corporate methods of managing exchange rate risk are unlikely to help firms

---

[6] For various reviews regarding the economic rationale for hedging, see Alan Shapiro and Sheridan Titman, "An Integrated Approach to Corporate Risk Management," *Midland Corporate Finance Journal* (Summer 1985); and Clifford Smith and Rene Stulz, "The Determinants of Firms' Hedging Policies," *Journal of Financial and Quantitative Analysis* (December 1985).

compete effectively and, indeed, are likely to provide misleading signals. As practiced by many if not most companies, corporate foreign exchange risk management has focused primarily on hedging exposures that lead to identifiable foreign exchange gains or losses. Under global competition, however, exchange rate fluctuations affect not only the dollar value of the firm's foreign profits, but indeed its overall position relative to its global competitors. As such, managing foreign exchange risks often calls for changes in operating variables such as pricing, output, and sourcing. It may even involve strategic changes such as shifting ownership of assets to other investors, relocating plants, and changing the internal organizational structure to improve the corporate-wide ability to respond to exchange rate shifts. And, as I discuss in some detail later in this article, such strategic and tactical responses to exchange rate shifts will require far greater integration of finance into the once largely separate strategic and operating domains of MNCs.

ORGANIZATIONAL IMPLICATIONS

In sum, global competition is bringing about a blurring of the boundaries between finance and operations. This in turn has created the demand for what I call the *operational treasury*—in effect, a group of financial managers that will perform an "expert function" in strategic and tactical business decisions. Investment analysis, to be sure, has long been part of the finance function through its role in capital allocation. Today, however, the greater complexities of risk-return assessment, cross-border taxation, and multiple risk exposures of various business activities imply a greater interaction between finance and real corporate activities. At the highest level, these interactions also suggest that an advantageous financial or project structure could even become the decisive factor in a firm's decision to participate in a given operating activity.

A similar interaction between financial and business perspectives takes place on a day-to-day tactical level, most visibly in the case of responding to shifts in exchange rates, interest rates, and other market variables. While the financial manager is active in these domains, possessing both analytical frameworks and critical current information, appropriate corporate responses often involve adjustments in marketing or production—adjustments that require knowledge of and responsibility for non-financial processes. The task of the *operational treasury* is to bring these financial perspectives to bear on business decisions, thereby enhancing overall corporate performance.

COPING WITH EXCHANGE RATE VOLATILITY

Global competition has dramatically changed the problem of managing foreign exchange risk. In the past, when markets were primarily national in scope, exchange rate shifts did not significantly change the relative costs of firms operating in a particular market. In such cases, corporate revenues and costs moved together in response to shifts in exchange rates, and profits from foreign operations, when converted into dollars (or other reference currency), moved roughly proportionally with exchange rates. Therefore, operating decisions regarding pricing and output were largely unaffected by these changes.

Under global competition, by contrast, prices in various national markets are more closely linked and larger proportions of firms' value added are likely to be concentrated in particular countries as they seek to exploit economies of scale. Therefore, unless all companies have the same global patterns of value added across different countries, which is highly unlikely, shifts in exchange rates will change their relative costs and profit margins. With the increased importance of Japanese and European firms in many industries, exchange rate effects on operating profits are becoming the rule rather than the exception.[7]

---

[7] It is useful to think of the responsiveness of operating profits to shifts in exchange rates as comprising two effects: a conversion effect and a competitive effect. The *conversion* effect, the proportional adjustment of foreign currency operating profits into the reference currency (dollars for U.S.-based firms), exists for all firms with foreign operations, but applies only to those foreign operations. The *competitive* ef-

IMPLICATIONS FOR FINANCIAL MANAGEMENT OF EXCHANGE RISK

The presence of operating exposures to exchange risks creates several challenges for financial management given its specialist role not only in hedging exposures, but also in monitoring exchange rate developments and assessing their likely effect on the company's competitive position. These challenges include: (1) defining the problem to be managed; (2) accurately assessing these exposures so that they can be incorporated into the assessment of the firm's overall exposure; (3) hedging these exposures as part of an overall risk management program; (4) interpreting for top management the impact of this exposure on current and long-run corporate profitability, as well as on the performance of specific profit centers; and (5) advising operating management in identifying and executing the appropriate strategic and tactical responses to exchange rate volatility.

Defining the Problem The recognition of operating exposures in many cases calls for a reassessment of the firm's objectives in managing foreign exchange risks. As discussed earlier, the benefits to shareholders from corporate hedging are less than obvious. Since these exposures do not lead to identifiable foreign exchange gains or losses, they don't matter if the sole objective is treasury's attempt to avoid exchange rate embarrassments. But they will be very important if the firm is trying to stabilize cash flows, or at least limit the probability that they will fall below some critical level.

In my view, the most compelling arguments for hedging lie in ensuring the firm's ability to meet two critical sets of cash flow commitments: (1) the exercise prices of their operating options reflected in their growth opportunities (for example, the R&D or promotion budgets) and (2) their dividends. The importance of both of these commitments derives from

specific information "imperfections" in capital markets. The growth options argument hinges on the observation that, in the case of a funding shortfall relative to investment opportunities, raising external capital will be costly. Investors unable to tell if the firm really faces profitable investment opportunities or a continuing operational cash deficit are likely to reduce their estimate of a company's value, especially in anticipation of a new equity issue.[8] The importance of meeting the dividend commitment relies on similarly negative information released by a dividend cut.

Assessing Exposures Assessing operating exposures requires a substantial blurring of the boundaries between the traditional treasury and operating functions. This is because estimates of such exposures cannot be based solely on the firm's current financial information. Instead they must be based on a combination of historical analysis of the sensitivity of operating cash flows to currency shifts and an evaluation of the range and effectiveness of possible operating responses to such shifts. Typically, the formulation of such scenarios cuts across the economics and planning functions of the firm, and the competitive aspects of the sensitivity analysis require inputs from planning and operating management. Further, the resulting estimates inevitably lack the specificity possible with transactions exposures, where virtually all commitments are known.

This organizational and analytical complexity historically has led a number of firms to exclude operating exposure from their definitions of exposure to be managed—or to limit it to, say, one year's projected revenues. The resulting narrow definition of exposure, however, is likely to be misleading and undermines virtually any logical basis for exposure management.

Hedging Exposures While the hedging of operating exposures does not involve many cross-functional complexities, it presents a series of techni-

---

fect, which is the sensitivity of local currency operating profits to exchange rate shifts resulting from the interaction of the various competitors' supply and price responses, applies only to companies facing some degree of cross-border competition. Moreover, it applies to purely domestic as well as overseas activities.

---

[8] This argument was first articulated by Stewart Myers and Nicholas Majluf, "Corporate Financing and Investment Decisions when Firms Have Information that Investors Do Not Have," *Journal of Financial Economics* (June 1984).

cal complexities for at least four reasons: (1) operating exposures are of longer term than the typical foreign exchange transactions; (2) they arise from movements in real exchange rates (relative prices) as distinguished from nominal exchange rates (and the two can diverge substantially over the medium term); (3) they cannot be estimated with certainty, especially since the volume of future transactions will to some extent depend on the exchange rate; and (4) they are not based on explicit commitments, and therefore hedges of these exposures may be subject to speculative rather than hedge accounting under FAS 52. The most prevalent foreign exchange hedges, short-dated forwards (or equivalently, redenomination of short-term borrowing) and options do not offset the effect of long-run cumulative exchange rate movements on operating profits. If this problem is addressed by lengthening the term and using long-dated or forwards options, the firm is then exposed to differential movements in real and nominal exchange rates, a phenomenon which we only now are beginning to understand.[9] The uncertainty about future revenues would appear to suggest the use of options rather than forwards, but appropriate strategies in general will involve a mix of forwards and options at varying strike prices.[10]

Benchmarking Performance Currency fluctuations clearly have an impact on measured performance, and these measures presumably feed back to a host of operating choices. While there are many technical issues in measuring performance in the face of fluctuating exchange rates, the debate among practitioners appears to be centered on whether performance should be measured in local currency or parent currency terms. Under conditions of global competition, neither is appropriate.

An ideal performance measurement system would hold managers responsible for those aspects of performance over which they have substantial control, but would limit responsibility for performance shifts due to factors largely beyond their control. Of course, this ideal is seldom met because, for example, fluctuations in aggregate demand are inextricably linked with managerial success in producing and selling a product. The emphasis of many firms on market share, however, is an attempt to separate these two effects. In the case of currency fluctuations, some aspects of the problem are easily separable while others are not. Gains or losses on accounts receivable due to currency surprises, for example, are outside the control of operating managers and can be split out by transferring these claims to treasury at forward rates. If this is done, treasury's contribution through "selective hedging" (that is, speculation in the form of market timing) can be measured fairly as well.

In contrast, with the competitive component of operating exposures, such a clear separation is not possible because managers can and should react to exchange rate shifts by altering prices, output, and sourcing. However, so long as there is some degree of global competition it should be recognized that profits in either local or parent currency should fluctuate in line with real exchange rates. In "benchmarking" their costs relative to their competitors', for example, management should use exchange rates that represent best estimates of purchasing power parity as well as the least favorable rates that might prevail in a particular period. When the yen began rising in 1985, for example, Japanese firms were benchmarking their cost competitiveness at rates that were roughly 25 percent less favorable than the then current rates. Similar adjustments must be made in assessing the contribution of specific business units.

A failure to incorporate such adjustments into the control system is likely to lead managers to "leave money on the table" when they are favored by exchange rates, and to sacrifice too much market share by attempting to hold constant dollar margins when exchange rates work against them. Many top managers assume that they are being tough by insisting on a particular level of dollar returns on foreign as well

---

[9] There is substantial new research regarding the existence of mean reversion in real exchange rates. See, for example, Bernard Dumas, "Pricing Physical Assets Internationally," (Unpublished paper, Wharton, March 1988); and Niso Abuaf and Philippe Jorion, "Purchasing Power Parity in the Long Run," *The Journal of Finance* (March 1990).

[10] Proper treatment of this issue requires better models of the stochastic processes of the underlying variables than is typical in current practice.

as domestic operators regardless of exchange rates. In fact, they are being tough only under unfavorable circumstances. Under favorable circumstances for U.S. companies, such as those that obtained in 1978–79, 1986–88, and again in 1990, they should have been doing considerably better than normal.

What is required, then, is a budgetary standard that adjusts for exchange rate impacts. The process of developing such a budget should involve a joint exploration by corporate and business unit managers of the impacts of and appropriate responses to exchange rate movements, thus providing a dress rehearsal of future tactics as well as a standard against which future performance can be judged.

Role of Financial Expertise in Operating Responses   As we have seen, shifts in exchange rates require decisions about pricing, output, and sourcing. Such decisions will typically involve a balancing act between vaguely understood limits to sustainable price differentials across countries and the impact of local currency price shifts on demand and operating profits. Further, given the emergence of global oligopolies in many industries, pricing decisions must reflect anticipations of competitor actions or reactions. Estimating these reactions is likely to be complicated by the fact that competitors differ significantly in the currency composition of their costs and, perhaps more importantly, in the currency "eyeglasses" they wear.

Currency fluctuations also introduce noise into measures of current performance, reducing the firm's ability to monitor its evolving competitive position and distorting its results-based managerial incentives. If these distortions are significant, and if many key decisions are made on a decentralized basis, the firm's choices are likely to be distorted as well. Finally, the impact of currency fluctuations on the accounting-based performance of current operations is likely to distort management's perception of the long-term profitability of strategic choices.

Because of this intermingling of financial, strategic, and operating factors, coping effectively with exchange rate volatility necessarily involves information, expertise, and action that span multiple corporate functions and timeframes. For this reason, the traditional financial steps of assessing exposures and determining technically efficient hedges, while important, are not sufficient.

Based on interviews with a number of firms, Nitin Nohria and I identified three elements that we believe hold the key to effective management in the face of exchange rate volatility. First, the overall framing of the problem—coupled with an understanding of the limits to various responses built into the companies' overall strategies, structures, and systems—is a critical factor in successful responses. Second, an expert group explicitly charged with helping line managers cope with exchange rates is an important element in success. Finally, we found that the most successful firms also create incentives for these experts to support line managers in their decisions, and not just to be successful transactional profit centers.[11]

Framing. Three principles are important in formulating the problem. The first is the recognition that coping with volatile exchange rates requires an options-like perspective, and that the problem cannot be ''structured away'' by any amount of prior analysis or planning. The second is that ''finance cannot do it all.'' No matter how sophisticated, the treasury function can at best serve to reduce fluctuations in profits resulting from exchange rate swings. Treasury expertise cannot substitute for the business judgment required as circumstances change, nor can it be expected through astute trading to earn back losses incurred in operations (attempting to do so, moreover, is a prescription for disaster). The third is that appropriate responses often involve the linking of normally differentiated functions and thus require ''going out of the ordinary channels'' with special structures and systems.

While some experts in the firm may develop this understanding through their own experience, reliance on consultants, external seminars, or discus-

---

[11] For a more complete discussion of these results, see Donald Lessard and Nitin Nohria, ''Rediscovering Functions in the MNC: The Role of Expertise in Firms' Response to Shifting Exchange Rates'' in Christopher Bartlett, Yve Doz and Gunnar Hedlund eds., *Managing the Global Firm* (London: Routledge, 1989).

sions with peers in other firms, extending that expertise to a larger constituency requires special efforts. We observed several promising approaches, including (1) the "rehearsal" of exchange rate impacts and responses within ongoing management processes, (2) attempts to classify various activities in terms of their sensitivity and response potential, and (3) efforts to make managers vary their "currency frame."

Rehearsing responses to exchange rate shifts differs from conventional contingency planning in that it involves those who must take actions as well as the expert group framing the problem. As one finance staffer put it, "Our job is not to tell (operations) how to respond, but to ask the right questions and so make sure that these considerations are taken into account."

The practice of classifying different activities—for example, pricing in particular market segments or stages in the production process—according to their sensitivity to exchange rate shifts and to the latitude of operating managers in responding to such shifts serves two purposes. First, it reduces complexity by allowing managers to ignore exchange rate responses in a large number of activities where shifts might "cause you to smile or cry but not change what you are doing." Second, it provides experts and line managers with "templates" that allow them to recognize similarities and, hence, to better learn from experience and link reactions.

Varying the currency frame helps managers identify biases arising from their own money illusion, the fact that business measurements implicitly assume that the numeraire or currency yardstick being used is constant over time. Managers in a dollar-based firm, for example, will typically perceive currency impacts as something that primarily affect foreign operations even if competitive effects are substantial in the home market. As a result, they often overlook home responses such as raising dollar prices when the dollar is relatively weak. In several firms the currency group reported raising questions such as "What would we do differently if we were a German firm or if we used the SDR as a unit of account?" One firm had even gone so far as to consider shifting the organization's currency reference point to SDRs

in order to place U.S. operations in the same currency context as all others.

Organizing. In organizing for foreign exchange risk management, it is unrealistic either to centralize operational foreign exchange management in one unit or diffuse it throughout the organization. None of the firms we studied (with the exception of one where all critical pricing and production decisions were made by a small group at the top) succeeded in having a complete framing of operational responses to shifting exchange rates permeate the full range of managerial levels and functions involved in the response. Therefore, they had to rely on an expert cadre for this purpose. In some cases, this cadre sought to act as a catalyst, incorporating itself into the relevant areas of activity. More often, though, it sought to maintain its own isolated expert function.

The most successful firms in our sample established separate units to deal with operational exchange rate impacts and responses other than the traditional forex group in treasury. In several cases, this was a task force that cut across functional lines, in another it was a planning group, and in yet another a special purpose unit in treasury separate from the transactional foreign exchange group. Those firms that left the coordination of operational exposure to a transaction-oriented foreign exchange group at best appeared to do a good job in hedging these *financial* exposures, but they provided little support for operating responses. At worst such groups' interactions with the rest of the firm amounted to little more than reconciling actual with budgeted hedging results.

Aligning incentives. As a general rule, organizational changes alone are not sufficient, and corporate information and compensation *systems* must be aligned with the organization for success. This certainly appears to be the case with the management of operational exposure. Those successful firms with special purpose structures also provided strong incentives for experts to support line managers, in several cases going so far as to set profit targets that had to be met from "identified improvements" in line units attested to by line managers. In other firms, these incentives were more informal, with the task force receiving top-level sponsorship and having its impact observed by senior management. By contrast, those units with transactions-based financial goals (gains on foreign exchange trading) did little other than trade.

LINKING FINANCE AND GLOBAL STRATEGY

Finance plays an increasingly strategic role in the evaluation of corporate investments, whether in specific capital or in technology or product programs. To some extent, this increasingly strategic focus of finance reflects the sense that how (and even perhaps where) an investment is financed may significantly affect its value.

This growing interaction between a company's business and financial strategy is perhaps most visible in the case of corporate takeovers and restructurings in the 1980s. There has, of course, been a foreign investment and takeover boom in the United States—one that has been attributed in large part to changes in tax regimes and exchange rates as well as expected economies from globalization.[12] With the approach of Europe 1992, moreover, this takeover phenomenon is spreading rapidly from the U.S. to Europe (and to Asia as well) and, increasingly, involves cross-border commercial and financial elements.

The movement toward a single European commercial and financial market is particularly interesting in this regard since a large number of firms will face a *simultaneous* choice of the form of commercial integration and financial structure, including

---

[12] The tax argument is best elaborated by Myron Scholes and Mark Wolfson, ''The Effects of Changes in Tax Laws on Corporate Reorganization Activity,'' (Unpublished paper. Stanford University, 1988). For the most sophisticated exchange rate argument, see Kenneth Froot, ''Multinational Corporations, Exchange Rates and Direct Investment,'' in W. Branson, J. Frenkel, and M. Goldstein eds., *International Policy Coordination and Exchange Rate Determination* (Chicago: University of Chicago Press, 1989). For an excellent review of the evidence and the various arguments for foreign investment in the U.S., see Edward Graham and Paul Krugman, *Foreign Direct Investment in the United States,* (Washington, D.C., Institute of International Economics, 1989).

their country of domicile. The rise of active investors and shareholder-value perspectives, once viewed as an American aberration by European corporations, are now becoming a consideration in their strategies as well. At the same time, however, the much larger corporate governance role played by banks and other financial institutions in Japan and Europe may constitute a significant advantage to firms in those countries, effectively increasing their optimal leverage ratios and lowering investors' required rates of return. To the extent particular national financial systems provide advantages in the form of reduced taxes, lower capital costs, or a superior corporate governance system from the viewpoint of shareholders, managers, and employees, control of the new Pan-European organizations will shift—as will the basis of competitive advantage—among European, American, and Japanese firms.

In the rest of this section, I will briefly explore two dimensions in which global competition is bringing about further integration of corporate finance and strategy: (1) cost of capital as a competitive variable and (2) alternative investment structures to equity ownership.

THE COST OF CAPITAL AS A COMPETITIVE VARIABLE

It has become commonplace for observers of competition between U.S. and Japanese industry to cite differences in the cost of capital as a major factor favoring Japan. With its higher savings rates, Japan is seen by many as having lower interest rates as well as greater advantages from financial leverage and other aspects of corporate financial structure. This is reinforced by the observation that Japanese equities command much higher multiples than U.S. equities.

The results of studies of this issue vary widely, with some researchers contending that although differences in capital costs exist, they do not consistently favor one country or the other (for example, Kester and Luehrman [1989]); some conclude that they favor Japan, but by a relatively small margin (French and Poterba [1989]); others conclude that they consistently favor Japan by a substantial margin (McCauley and Zimmer [1989]); while still others point out that Japanese investors have earned, if anything, considerably higher risk-adjusted returns than their U.S. counterparts (Baldwin [1986] and Ibbotson [1989]).[13]

While some of these conflicting findings can be traced to questionable assumptions or methods, most result from different definitions of required returns and different time periods over which the rates are measured.[14] If one focuses on the period after 1981, when virtually all formal capital controls were abolished, it appears that firms based in Japan have a cost of capital advantage, but that this advantage is at most on the order of 1 to $1\frac{1}{2}$ percent.[15] But even apparently small differences can make a big difference in international competitiveness.

While more research is required to establish these differences, they do suggest that the fiscal and financial context of multinationals should be expanded to explicitly take these into account. The two major domains for managing these fiscal/financial advantages are in the area of funding, discussed earlier, and investment structuring, to which subject we now turn.

INVESTMENT STRUCTURING

With deregulation, financial innovation, and increasing investor sophistication, companies face a much broader range of ways of structuring their participation in particular commercial activities. Alternatives to full equity ownership include joint ventures, strategic alliances, and project finance. Some such alternative structures are motivated primarily by the need to create compatible incentives for the various participants (including, in some cases, governments) that significantly influence outcomes. Others, however, are motivated largely by purely financial considerations.

In resource-based industries, for example, companies with operating expertise may choose among the following structures: full ownership through a variety of ownership chains, joint ventures with other active partners, joint ventures with passive partners, and narrower forms of financial participation such as incentive management contracts or partnerships in a revenue trust (where the bulk of the returns flow directly to passive investors). Further, they are increasingly engaging in sales or exchanges of assets that are driven as much by tax considerations as by operating synergies or differences in views about the prospects of particular properties. Technology-based firms similarly can choose among ownership, joint ventures, or licensing. Union Carbide, for example, has largely retrenched to North America as an operating firm, but has increased its global reach as a licensor of technology. Even service firms face these options. Walt Disney participates in its European and Japanese "Fantasylands" by means of creative vehicles for capturing royalties, thereby maintaining its operating links but choosing more financially effective routes for extracting profits.

Traditionally, strategic choices have been dictated almost entirely by the firm's operating advantage—that is, the extent to which it is uniquely good at some activity based on its cumulative experience or

---

[13] Full citations for the studies cited in this paragraph are as follows: Carl Kester and Timothy Luehrman, "Real Interest Rates and the Cost of Capital: A Comparison of the United States and Japan," *Japan and The World Economy* (1989); Kenneth French and James Poterba, "Are Japanese Stock Prices Too High?" (unpublished paper, NBER, 1989); Robert N. McCauley and Steven A. Zimmer, "Explaining International Cost of Capital Differences," *Federal Reserve Board of New York Quarterly Review* (Summer 1989); Carliss Baldwin, "Competing for Capital in a Global Market," *Midland Corporate Finance Journal,* Vol. 5 No. 1 (Spring 1987).

[14] Some studies focus on the *supply cost of capital*—pre- (personal) tax required returns to investors, or returns realized by investors as proxies for these *ex ante* required returns. Of these, some limit their comparisons to real (risk free) interest rates, while others incorporate risk premia on equities and still others seek to determine the weighted average faced by industry at large. Others focus on the *rental cost of capital*— pre- (corporate) tax returns required on real investments, either in the aggregate or for particular projects, necessary to ultimately meet the supply cost of capital. Still others focus on differences of risk of doing business or coping with various forms of distress in the U.S. versus Japan, which may affect both the rental and supply costs of capital.

[15] This figure is also obtained by French and Poterba, cited in note 13, when examining cost of capital differences implied by differences in price-earnings ratios between the U.S. and Japan.

possession of complementary assets. But, to the extent financial markets are not completely integrated and major differences in cost of capital persist among nations (or among different ownership forms within a single tax jurisdiction), strategic choices may also be influenced by financial advantages— that is, the extent to which its shareholders or other investors will place a higher value on a given stream of operating cash flows. For example, if the firm is operationally advantaged, but fiscally disadvantaged, management will increase the value of the firm by restricting its participation to those activities where its expertise and involvement are most valuable, while stripping out more passive components for investment by tax-advantaged players. The decision of Marriott, mentioned earlier, to sell its hotels to private investors in limited partnerships—and to restrict its activities solely to the management of those hotels—is a good example of such creative asset restructuring. So are the oil and gas royalty trusts formed in the early 1980s.

The choice of structure may also increase value by improving management incentives to serve shareholders. For example, managers in the exploration and development arms of oil companies have strong incentives to expand operations whenever they ''are good at it,'' regardless of whether the expected returns on investment meet shareholder requirements. Managers in such cases are likely to resist value-increasing asset trades or sales, and perhaps even conceal important information that might argue for such sales. By structuring the investment so as to give operating managers a significant stake in the profitability or value of their operation, the natural incentive of managers to overinvest in their own activities can be corrected.

CONCLUSIONS

Global competition among corporations together with an increasingly integrated world financial system, continued macroeconomic volatility, and a rapid deepening of financial technology, increases not only the competitive impact of corporate financing choices, but also the potential value added by financial input to strategic choices and operating decisions. Further, in many cases, the finance function can be expected to operate as a business in its own right, employing innovative instruments and risk management frameworks. This simultaneous broadening and deepening of financial management will require further improvements in and wider dissemination of financial technology, but also greater sensitivity to the role of financial management as a *supportive, complementary* function in addition to its traditional control and oversight function. This means paying greater attention to the driving forces of strategy and to opportunities to improve management incentives and organizational structure.

The fact that the financial environment is moving toward, but has not yet become, a fully integrated system means that multinationals can continue to gain from spanning systems to take advantage of ''bargains'' created by financial and fiscal distortions. Moreover, the existence of a less than perfectly integrated financial market also implies that valuation comparisons across countries will continue to be difficult—because value to a certain extent will continue to depend on the nationality (and tax position) of the beholding investor.

As global financial markets become increasingly integrated, the very different corporate governance systems among countries also appear to be moving toward integration, spurred in part by the European movement toward a single market. That is, the Japanese and European reliance on concentrated institutional ownership seems to be lessening with the rise and expansion of their relatively new capital markets while institutions in the U.S. and the U.K. appear to be preparing for a larger role in corporate governance. One of the most interesting matters for speculation is whether a single homogeneous governance system will emerge—one which incorporates both aspects of the Japanese and the American systems— or whether different countries will continue to preserve their pronounced differences in the role of capital markets in exercising corporate control. At present we lack a clear understanding of the competitive advantage of different systems, and which elements of particular systems are most vulnerable as integration proceeds.

31

MANAGING FOREIGN EXCHANGE RATE ECONOMIC EXPOSURE

MICHAEL H. MOFFETT

Thunderbird—The American Graduate School of International Management, Glendale, Arizona, USA

JAN KARL KARLSEN

Corporate Strategy Group, Statoil, Stavanger, Norway

ABSTRACT   The foreign exchange (FX) economic exposure of the firm is now receiving the attention once showered on the other two traditional FX exposures, transaction and translation. This economic exposure, recently referred to as *competitive* or *strategic,* is now seen by many financial managers as the primary exposure. Our preliminary opinion is that what is commonly referred to as competitive exposure management is a simplified economic exposure which, although potentially useful, is generally not applicable to most multinational firms and their own economic exposure profiles.

INTRODUCTION

The volatility of exchange rates, interest rates, and commodity prices, combined with the increasing internationalization of firms, has resulted in a greater interest in the evaluation of firm exposure to financial price risk. A number of major multinational firms have undertaken large hedging programs to manage what they refer to as *strategic exposure.* Strategic exposure management is frequently defined as the use of financial hedges or contracts (value replacements), for losses in firm value resulting from long-term financial price movements. The question at hand is whether strategic exposure management is fundamentally different from the traditional concept of *economic exposure,* and whether the contrac-

tual hedging programs being utilized by some firms are potentially effective management methods.

The first section of the paper is our view of organizational structure of price risks and exposure management for the multinational firm. The second section recounts the current literature and areas of debate on economic and strategic exposure management. The third part develops a categorization of economic exposure types, which in turn allows us to identify the efficacy of individual firms actually managing their economic/strategic exposure. The following part outlines the two primary hedging approaches available for economic exposure management, which we refer to as *green hedging* and *LEGO® hedging.* This section also highlights the practical constraints of using these hedge techniques, discusses the appropriateness and applicability of these techniques under different forms of economic exposure, and presents analyses of several of the most prominent examples of economic exposure management currently in use. The final section of the paper returns to the question of whether the hedg-

The authors would like to thank the Danish Summer Research Institute (DSRI) in Gilleleje, Denmark, sponsored by the Kingdom of Denmark and the Copenhagen Business School, for providing initial research support. The paper has benefited greatly from the comments of John Dunning, Arthur Stonehill, and Heather Hazard. All remaining errors are of course the sole responsibility of the authors.

ing of such risk is either desired or practical for the specific subject firm.

THE STRATEGIC EXPOSURE LITERATURE

The literature on competitive and strategic exposure is relatively narrow, but has been presented to date as if totally differentiated from classic economic exposure. Rawls and Smithson (1990) serves as the central piece of the academic literature to date, with that of Lewent and Kearney (1990) being the primary industrial source of applied use. Both articles seek to differentiate the strategic exposure of the firm as being much wider in scope than the traditional definitions of corporate foreign currency exposure. Rawls and Smithson define strategic exposure as a type of umbrella-term:

A company has a strategic exposure to the extent that changes in foreign exchange rates, interest rates, or commodity prices affect its market value—that is, the present value of the expected future cash flows.[1]

This is also often labeled the firm's financial price-risk profile. The approach pursued by Rawls and Smithson is to estimate the sensitivity of firm value to exchange rate, interest rate, and commodity price changes through the use of econometric techniques, using historical financial data on the firm's performance. The most recent and ambitious example is that of Nance, Smith, and Smithson (1993); Lewent and Kearney (1990) explain Merck's use of similar statistical and econometric techniques to determine the firm's future exchange rate exposures. Bilson (1994) also demonstrates how easy this approach is in analyzing an individual airline's exchange rate exposure.

A second literature has taken a more competitive markets approach, and is represented by the work of Leuhrman (1990), Glaum (1990), and Grant and Soenen (1991). These articles have sought to emphasize the nature of medium to long-term currency ex-

posure as arising from the changing competitiveness of firms internationally by business lines and market structures. The latter two articles have taken a qualitative approach, emphasizing the integration of financially-based risks from exchange rates impacting decision-making in production, marketing, planning, and strategy. To quote Grant and Soenen (1991):

Measuring the long-term exposure requires an understanding of the structure of the markets in which the company and its competitors operate. We should examine for all market players their flexibility to change sales markets, product mix, sourcing and technology.[2]

Luehrman (1990) provides a more theoretical approach, developing an oligopolistic model of a multinational firm's operating cash flows, which is used to analyze theoretical competitor responses in such oligopolist markets.

Finally, possibly the most insightful literature is that series of industry publications and interviews which provide some indication as to how some multinational firms are now viewing these exposures and sometimes managing them. This is represented by Dickins (1988), Millar (1989), Kohn (1990), and Millar and Asher (1990).

STRATEGIC RISKS AND EXPOSURE DEFINITION

The first and foremost problem is terminology. The sensitivity of the value of the firm to the three major price-risks, foreign exchange rates (FX), interest rates (I/R), and commodity prices (CP), is termed Strategic Exposure following the lead of Rawls and Smithson (1990). A number of firms actively measure and manage all three price-risks, although foreign exchange is the one which has traditionally been considered a 'risk,' and therefore requiring active management. This article will focus solely on foreign exchange (FX) risk.

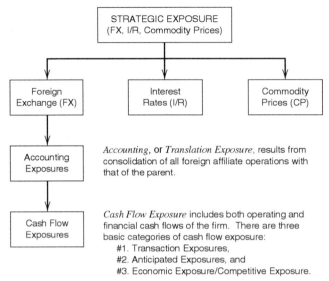

Exhibit 1. Categorization of Price Risks to the Firm

As illustrated in Exhibit 1, the FX exposure of the firm can in turn be sub-divided into Accounting Exposure and Cash Flow Exposures. *Accounting-based exposure,* or Translation as it has traditionally been termed, results from the restatement of financial statements of foreign affiliates into the single currency of the parent firm. This is a necessary evil for all firms worldwide for consolidated reporting purposes. The exposure is the potential for such accounting-based activities to result in changes in owners' equity, and in some cases income, resulting from exchange rate changes.[3]

Cash Flow Exposure includes three different forms of price-risk: Transaction Exposures, Anticipated Exposures, and finally Economic Exposure. Transaction Exposures are traditionally defined as those contractual commitments which combine a fixed amount of foreign currency to be exchanged at a future date, and therefore at an uncertain future exchange rate.[4]

Transaction Exposure: $E[CF_{t+1}^\$] = \overline{CF_{t+1}^{fc}} \times E(S_{t+1})$,

where the cash flow to occur at time t + 1 (CF_{t+1}), denominated in foreign currency (fc), is known with perfect certainty. The value of the foreign currency cash flow in domestic currency terms (U.S. dollars

in this case) is dependent only on the expected value of the spot exchange rate (U.S. dollars per unit of foreign currency) at time t + 1 (S_{t+1}).

Anticipated Exposures are those expected future cash flows of the firm which are expected to give rise to transaction exposures. These are foreign currency-denominated cash flows which are 'firmly anticipated,' an expression used in industry to portray an exposure which is thought highly probable. The source of the uncertainty is that it does not yet exist as a line item on a financial statement (off balance sheet asset or liability). Operationally, the uncertainty can be the specific quantity of foreign currency or the timing of the cash flow. Since all FX exposures addressed here are future payments with an inherent time-element, we will assume the uncertainty of the anticipated exposure is of the quantity variety.

Anticipated Exposure: $E[CF_{t+1}^\$] = E(CF_{t+1}^{fc}) \times E(S_{t+1})$,

where the expected domestic currency value of the future cash flow is the product of two expected values, the expected quantity of foreign currency, $E(CF_{t+1}^{fc})$, and the expected spot exchange rate in effect on the date of settlement, $E(S_{t+1})$. This anticipated exposure is inherently subjective, and it is up to the individual firm to determine with what degree of certainty the expected value of the foreign currency cash flow exists.[5] Many of the FX instruments which have been developed in the past decade, primarily option-based, have focused their applications on these anticipated exposures.

The Economic Exposure of the firm is the final extension of operating cash flows into the (uncertain) future. Economic exposure measures

the change in the present value of the firm that results from changes in future operating cash flows caused by an unexpected *change in exchange rates. The change in value depends on the effect of the exchange rate change on future sales volume, prices, and costs.*[6]

The firm's economic exposure is derived from the competitiveness of its line of business as impacted by future unexpected exchange rate movements, and not simply from the settlement of existing or probable transactions. Starting with the work of Dufey (1972), a large and well-developed literature on economic exposure has developed.[7]

Economic exposure is profoundly and fundamentally different in concept from the two preceding categories of cash flow exposure. Where the previous transaction and anticipated exposures are essentially risks arising from the translation of foreign currency cash flows to home currency, true economic exposure also includes the consideration of the firm's long-term ability to *generate* those foreign currency cash flows. The ability to generate foreign currency cash flows over the long-term will in turn depend on the competitiveness of the firm and the competitive responses of others in the industry. It would therefore be rare that an individual multinational firm would be able to separate one from the other. Traditional economic exposure management focuses on passive diversification; because exchange rate changes are unexpected and their impacts relatively unpredictable, simple diversification of operations and financing are normally prescribed.[8]

What is now occasionally referred to as *strategic currency exposure* or *competitive currency exposure* is a theoretical subset of economic exposure. *Competitive exposure* has taken on a quite different—and

narrower—meaning than that of economic exposure: the risk arising to the firm from long-term exchange rate movements which may hinder the firm's ability to maintain and achieve its strategic business plan. It is basically the extension of transaction/contingent exposure analysis to the longer-time span in which inadequate domestic currency earnings from predicted future foreign currency cash flows threaten the firm's ability to compete.

Competitive exposure analysis relies on the predictability of two critical elements to the firm's financial future: 1. the predictability of the firm's cash flows, both operating and financing; and 2. the predictability of competitor response in a future world of altered exchange rates. In the following section we explain what we think this requires of the firm and its markets in order for competitive exposure analysis to work.

SUGGESTED TAXONOMY OF ECONOMIC FX EXPOSURE

As illustrated in Exhibit 2, the economic exposure of any individual firm is composed of two parts: 1. the firm's *functional structure,* and 2. the firm's *competitive environment.* The *functional structure* is how the firm is organized and therefore operates internationally. The simplest interpretation is the primary currency of production (currencies of sourcing) versus the currencies of sales (product markets). This is the firm's currency structure geographically and functionally. Does the firm buy, sell, manufacture, finance, or compete internationally? The structure reaches increasing levels of complexity as the firm internationalizes, competing with other firms for inputs and output sales in markets worldwide. The multitude of cash flow transfers within the multinational firm, profits, fees, intra-firm debt and capital flows, also increases the complexity of the structure internationally.

It is the *competitive environment* which has led many in international finance to refer to economic exposure as 'competitive' or 'strategic'. The competitive environment element of economic exposure

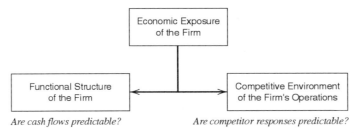

Are cash flows predictable?   *Are competitor responses predictable?*

Exhibit 2. The Components of Economic Exposure

consists of two parts: 1. the nature of the product and market; 2. the responses of competitors to FX movements. This second part is simply how competitors react to the same exchange rate changes given their views of their own functional structure and competitive environment.

If the firm is operating within an industry which has significant international competition, the actual structure and strategies of competitors may prove extremely important in whether the firm has any managerial discretion in its pricing (exchange rate pass-through) policies, or whether market conditions will dictate response (for both the subject firm and possibly competing firms). The subject firm's exposure is as much an *exposure to competitors* as it is an exposure to the market.

The primary point at this stage of the definition of economic exposure is that the actual exposure of any individual firm is dependent not only on its own structure and operations, but on the competitive response of competing firms to these same unexpected exchange rate changes. And their response is in turn dictated by their functional structure.

TAXONOMY OF ECONOMIC FX EXPOSURE

Exhibit 3 provides a taxonomy of firm competitive exposure as described by the firm's functional structure and competitive environment. We measure the functional structure of the firm's competitive exposure by the degree to which the firm is internationally diversified in its operations. If the firm is a multinational firm which operates manufacturing and/or sales offices abroad, it is easily classified by sourcing and products.

The *competitive environment* of the firm's competitive exposure is defined by the nature of competi-

Firm's Competitive Environment	Firm's Functional Structure (degree of international diversification)		
	Domestic	Sourcing or Products	Sourcing and Products
Fixed-Share Markets (regulated goods, fixed-pricing)	Indirect Economic Exposure*	Anticipated Exposure	Anticipated Exposure
Non-Differentiated Good Markets (homogenous goods, cost-based pricing)	Indirect Economic Exposure*	Direct Economic Exposure	Direct Economic Exposure
Differentiated or Niche Good Markets (niche-goods, tactical pricing)	Indirect Economic Exposure*	Competitive Exposure	Competitive Exposure

* Indirect economic exposure exists for all firms in all markets. We define indirect competitive exposure as those changes in firm cash flows resulting from altered market or demand conditions.

Exhibit 3. Taxonomy of Economic Exposure

tion. Competition is based on the firm's actual effectiveness in securing market shares and revenues/costs in local currency markets. We have defined three categories of markets: fixed-share markets, non-differentiated good markets, differentiated or niche-good markets. The categories are defined on the basis of the firm's ability and incentives to alter price as a result of exchange rate movements.

Fixed-share markets are most frequently seen in regulated markets in which firms are assured sales levels and market shares, yet prices are regulated to protect resident consumers. If exchange rates move adversely to the producer of the good, requiring additional price increases in local currency markets, approval must be obtained from local governmental authorities. Large adverse exchange rate movements combined with inadequate regulatory adjustments may eventually result in the exit of the firm from the market.

Non-differentiated goods markets are typical of products which are homogenous, where a high degree of competition among producers dictates narrow margins and a cost-leadership competitive positioning (Porter, 1980). In the event of an adverse exchange rate movement, due to the highly competitive nature of the industry and the cost-based pricing structure with initially low margins, the firm either accepts unit losses or raises prices in order to prevent losses. If the exchange rate changes are large enough, and the price changes therefore significant in size, the firm may lose substantial market share, or at the extreme, exit.

The third and final category is the differentiated or niche-good market. Firms operating in these markets do have the ability to selectively alter product price in response to a number of tactical (short term market share strategies) or environmental factors (e.g., exchange rate movements). Their products are sufficiently differentiated to provide them with price-making ability.

The resulting forms of competitive exposure aid in determining *which firms* have the ability to manage their exposure to exchange rate movements, and therefore mitigate the impacts of exchange rates on the value of the firm. We therefore identify the following three forms of competitive exposure:

1. ANTICIPATED EXPOSURE

The parent firm perceives foreign currency market share to be assured for all practical purposes. Sales volume and sales price vary over narrow ranges, resulting in highly predictable foreign currency net earnings net expenses). Exchange rate changes are only reflected in market prices as allowed by official authorities, and the differentiation of products—along with normally high degrees of own price elasticity—result in stable sales volumes. The final exposure is then the home currency value of a known future foreign currency cash flow.

2. DIRECT ECONOMIC EXPOSURE

The parent firm is participating in a market in which the high degree of competition allows it little in the way of revenue assurances (in foreign market sales volume or price) and little in the choice of the proportion of exchange rate changes to pass-through to final market prices (homogeneous goods). Although there is little in the way of managerial discretion involved—at least in the short to medium-term given the firm's existing international structure—competitive exposure is extremely important. The competitive environment of the competitive exposure is dominated in this case not by competitor response (that is known with a high degree of certainty given the nature of high price-based competition) but by similarity or dissimilarity of competitor international diversification and structure. For example, a firm with a competitor possessing the identical—but inverse—functional structure of competitive exposure, can rest assured that the competitor will respond as predicted (cut or maintain prices) and gain sales lost by the firm which raises prices because of adverse exchange rate movements.

3. COMPETITIVE EXPOSURE

The parent firm's foreign currency market share and earnings are in considerable competitive doubt. The ability of the firm to pass-through exchange rate changes is limited: 1. limited by the degree of differentiation between the firm's products and close competitive substitutes; 2. limited by the anticipated response of competitor's pricing practices. It is within these lower-right cells in Exhibit 3 that the analysis of competitive behavior is critical. Competitive exposure is a proper term for the firms operating in these markets.

Note that we do not use or identify a form entitled 'strategic exposure'. We believe that *competitive exposure* encompasses the concepts most relevant to what has recently been termed strategic (although we recognize this is not as fashionable).

COMPETITOR ANALYSIS

The only firms which need analyze competitor response to exchange rate-induced changes are those firms which possess Direct Economic Exposure or Competitive Exposure.[9] Firms in all other categories (Exhibit 3 cells) will hedge or not hedge their exposures on the basis of other non-competitive concerns. Although firms with Direct Economic Exposure have essentially no choice as to whether exchange rate changes are passed-through into final foreign currency prices, it may be in the firm's interest to manage/hedge the inevitable foreign currency earnings changes. Those firms possessing Competitive Exposure have not only the difficulty in anticipating competitor response, but must also establish whether they have sufficient knowledge regarding their competitive exposure in order for hedging to be beneficial and not inherently speculative. In the following section detailing the practical aspects of hedging competitive exposure we will return to the discussion of the appropriateness of hedging for firms with either Direct Economic Exposure or Competitive Exposure.

HEDGING ECONOMIC EXPOSURE

Although commonly omitted, any discussion of foreign exchange hedging by the firm should initially address the motivation for such hedging.[10] The 'why hedge?' literature has come to a relatively short but widely accepted list of defensible reasons for foreign exchange management by the firm:[11]

1. Agency issues of firm management motivation and performance evaluation;
2. Direct costs associated with financial distress;
3. Contingent investments or implementation of long-term strategic plans requiring increased certainty or assurance of future cash flows.

ALTERNATIVE HEDGING TECHNIQUES

Assuming the firm then wishes to reduce the variance of future (medium to long-term) cash flows, what are the primary channels or techniques by which the firm may achieve this goal? We see two major categories of FX hedging for these longer-term cash flows and exposures, *green (natural) hedging* and what we term *LEGO® (financial) hedging*.[12]

Green or natural hedging is the deliberate construction of the firm's cash flows to diversify across currencies. It is achieved by internationally diversifying (manufacturing, distribution, and sales—operational cash flows) and diversifying financing (financial cash flows). The international diversification of the operational structure of the firm will simplistically hedge the firm's competitive exposure. Diversification of production across countries has long been a strategy employed for a number of competitive reasons, only one of which would be exchange rate-related.[13] Although multinational firms may include this element in their corporate diversification strategy, the question of stable exchange rate correlations over the long-term remains.

LEGO® or financial hedging is the use of financial instruments and derivatives to offset exchange rate-induced changes in firm cash flow values. The hedging of competitive exposure with financial hedges (forwards, futures, and options), has generally been considered impractical. Because the cash flows of the firm beyond known transactions are uncertain, and the exchange rate movements and their impacts on firm cash flows—as well as competitor response uncertain—the use of financial hedges for hedging this exposure has been generally considered ill-conceived. In fact, there is a strong possibility that the firm may actually introduce more—not less—cash flow volatility through the use of these instruments.

IMPLEMENTATION OF GREEN HEDGING

Of all techniques considered, green hedging requires more planning, time, and resources than any other technique. Although it also possesses the highest long-run quality of exposure minimization, diversification of operations requires all major managerial areas of the multinational firm, far beyond international treasury. The more commonly utilized green hedge is the matching of financial and operational cash flows in combination; for example the acquisition of currency debt which can then be serviced by positive currency cash flows generated by the line of business (operational cash flows) of the firm. DuPont (U.S.) is an example of a firm which determined in the early 1970s that diversification of production worldwide was necessary in order to service worldwide markets and preserve competitiveness. Through a massive capital-intensive construction plan, DuPont was able to achieve the desired international diversification of its overall competitive exposure by the early 1980s.

IMPLEMENTATION OF LEGO® HEDGING

The steps necessary for the implementation of a LEGO® hedging program are the following:

1. Identification of the foreign currency amounts, at specific future dates, which are at risk.
2. The actual hedging of the competitive exposure is achieved with FX instruments such as forwards, options, and futures, whose value changes will offset identified foreign currency exposures. The hedge is constructed so that whatever cash flows or earnings which are lost by the firm as a whole as a result of adverse exchange rate movements (ΔS) is replaced by an equal but opposite movement in the direction of the hedge position (ΔF).

$$\Delta V = \Delta S - \Delta F.$$

The goal is to formulate an effective hedge which will result in no change in market value, $\Delta V = 0$, following an adverse exchange rate movement.

3. On the specific dates of maturity the LEGO® hedge values will be realized. If the feared exchange rate movements have not materialized, the LEGO® hedge values are either net zero or net negative. If the feared exchange rate movements did occur, the LEGO® hedge values replace those lost by the underlying exposure.

Although this appears relatively straightforward in principle, in practice the problem is exceedingly complex. First the identification of which cash flows in which amounts of what points in time is difficult to determine, even for firms with highly predictable long-term foreign currency cash flows (for example those in the upper left cells of Exhibit 3). If the firm is hedging to replace profits arising from foreign currency export sales, the actual exposure is the net profit amounts before tax which theoretically would have been earned. However, many firms would view the loss as consisting of the gross sales and associated costs of fulfilling the sales. In the process of producing and delivering the greater level of sales the firm may well achieve other scale and scope benefits which are not really captured by simple losses in the 'bottom line.' In this case, the total exposure will be much greater in foreign currency amount.

Secondly, to provide insurance against adverse FX movements without creating enormous FX liabilities, the instrument of choice for practical purposes will be the foreign currency option.[14] This is obvious given that the use of forward contracts would require the firm to honor the value of the forward contract at the specific future date, essentially eliminating the profits if the adverse exchange rate movements do not occur. The foreign currency option, however, would expire worthless if the adverse FX movements did not occur. The difficulty with the FX option, however, would be the magnitude of the up-front premium payment for option purchase. Given the extreme length of time and the magnitude of the values being hedged, this may require enormous capital outlays for option purchases.

Third, under generally accepted accounting principles and tax laws in many countries the firm would be required to mark-to-market the financial instrument (option) at the end of the fiscal year. This would result in the realization of additional profits/losses and related tax liabilities of relatively large amounts over the period prior to the maturation of the hedge.[15] Once again, the impacts on the firm's cash flows and management of such large values is not trivial.

Fourth, the original LEGO® hedge program must be monitored over its life-span, possibly requiring continual revision and reconstruction for the same future time span. The actual amount of FX exposure of the firm will likely be changing over time as the nature of the market and the firm's competitors change.

Finally, it should be pointed out that although the firm may be able to replace earnings or profits lost by medium to long-term adverse exchange rate movements, it is not replacing actual business sales (market share). Although the financial hedge replaces the cash flows, it is not a direct investment in the ability of the firm to recapture lost sales. The resource use of the LEGO® hedging program must be evaluated with this opportunity cost to the firm in mind.

CONTEMPORARY ECONOMIC EXPOSURE MANAGEMENT

The two multinational firms which have gained the most notoriety for their economic exposure management programs using financial hedging to date are Merck and Eastman Kodak.

Merck has been one of the true leaders in not only the implementation of what they term their strategic exposure management program, but also in the publication of it. Following the publication in 1990 of 'Identifying, Measuring, and Hedging Currency Risk

at Merck,' by Judy C. Lewent and A. John Kearney, Treasurers at Merck, the firm has been cited as an innovator in this area.[16] However, it is interesting to note that Merck, as explained by its own treasury staff, views its foreign currency earnings abroad as extremely stable and predictable. Merck views its pharmaceutical markets as highly regulated (price controlled) while product differentiation effectively separates and preserves market shares. Merck would therefore fall into the upper middle cell of Exhibit 3, Anticipated Transaction Exposure, given its domestic sourcing and export sales. The hedging of this series of anticipated future cash flows is straightforward, with no significant consideration given to competitor response in order to estimate future currency exposure. Also, Merck's primary motivation according to treasury for hedging these future cash flows is the ability to pursue the implementation of the firm's long run strategic plan.

Eastman Kodak, another U.S.-based multinational, has also been very public in its admissions of what it terms its 'competitive risk.'[17] Kodak, however, does face significant competitor response in its markets as a result of medium to long-term FX movements. Kodak, like Merck, is primarily domestically-sourced (U.S.), with sales concentrated in major export markets in Europe and Japan. If, however, the U.S. dollar were to appreciate versus the Japanese yen for example, Kodak would have little choice over the medium-term to pass-through the exchange rate change into higher prices in Japanese yen. Kodak faces a significant Japanese-based competitor in Fuji (Japan). Fuji's economic exposure, both in its functional structure and competitive environment, is essentially identical to Kodak's, but *inverse*. Fuji would therefore gain what Kodak lost. As shown in Exhibit 4, we believe this is a typical example of a firm operating with Direct Economic Exposure in a Non-Differentiated Good Market.[18] Because competitor response is highly predictable, resulting in direct market share gains lost by Kodak, Kodak need not debate competitor response in order to approximate currency exposure.

If one were to consider candidates for economic exposure management, large multinational firms

Competitive Environment of the Firm	Functional Structure of the Firm (degree of international diversification)		
	Domestic	Sourcing or Products	Sourcing and Products
Fixed-Share Markets (regulated goods, fixed-pricing)	Indirect Economic Exposure	Anticipated Exposure Merck	Anticipated Exposure
Non-Differentiated Good Markets (homogenous goods, cost-based pricing)	Indirect Economic Exposure	Direct Economic Exposure Kodak	Direct Economic Exposure
Differentiated or Niche Good Markets (niche-goods, tactical pricing)	Indirect Economic Exposure	Competitive Exposure	Competitive Exposure GM, BMW, Honda

Exhibit 4. Examples of Economic Exposure

such as the world's major auto-makers could prove an interesting subject. As suggested by Exhibit 4, firms such as General Motors of the United States, BMW of Germany, or Honda of Japan, may find the active management of economic exposure extremely complex. The problems once again are easily identified by the two basic elements of economic exposure (functional structure and competitive environment); all three major automobile manufacturers not only source and sell internationally, they must determine over what product lines and price ranges their competitors exist, and how their competitors may respond to medium to long-term exchange rate movements. This is obviously a task that is inherently combined with that of corporate strategy on the corporate level.

These final auto examples also serve to highlight a last, yet important feature of the taxonomy of economic exposure which we have constructed in Exhibits 3 and 4. As one moves from upper-left to lower-right across the spectrum of economic exposures, the complexity of the economic exposure of the firm increases significantly, and subsequently the ability to effectively manage that economic exposure also comes increasingly into question. Those firms which are highly internationally diversified in their operations and financing, who also face substantial international competition, may still find the area of economic exposure management by any name (economic exposure, competitive exposure, strategic ex-

posure, super-hedging, etc.) purely an academic exercise.

SUMMARY

At present we know little of the magnitude of active economic exposure management. Few firms are willing to either publicize or discuss their economic exposure or competitive exposure management programs, either because of their unwillingness to divulge information which they believe is inherently competitive, or to provide details of financial contracts and derivatives which could result in heavy criticism from investors or financial analysts.

The number of firms actively managing economic exposure is unknown, though it has been estimated in the United States at between 50 and 100, while 20 to 30 major European multinationals are thought to be active at a minimum. Whether this reflects differences in corporate governance, goals and methods of financial management, or even the incentives and performance evaluation methods of management and management's effectiveness, are questions for future research.[19]

This paper is a first attempt at systematizing the analysis of economic exposure management. We have attempted to clarify old and new terminology in order that the subject may be linked to the previous and contemporary literatures of international financial management in specific, and international business in general. Our suggested taxonomy of what we prefer to simply call economic exposure is helpful in understanding which firms may or may not find economic exposure management beyond diversification of production and financing (natural hedging) useful or practical. We have also provided some basic principles which firms must address if they are to truly consider the hedging of economic exposure, and be cognizant of contractual hedging's effectiveness. Although little data exists at present regarding the degree of current corporate activity in economic exposure management, it is believed that continued exchange rate volatility on world markets combined with increasing degrees of direct international activity by firms will only serve to increase the level of interest.

NOTES

1. Rawls and Smithson, *Journal of Applied Corporate Finance*, 1990, p. 6.

2. Grant and Soenen, 1991, p. 3.

3. The debate continues between those who believe that translation exposure is a non-cash expense to the firm and should therefore not be managed or hedged, and those who believe that accounting conventions and practices do have real cash flow impacts. Regardless of the academic literature on this point, a number of studies such as Belk and Glaum (1990) find many firms who continue to actively manage their translation exposure.

4. We should note that we differ here with Rawls and Smithson (1990) in the classification of transaction exposure as a cash flow exposure rather than an accounting exposure. We prefer to maintain the traditional distinction between exposures arising from pure accounting issues (i.e., consolidated reporting) versus financial and operating cash flow issues (receivables and payables, debt service, divided payments, etc.).

5. The contingent exposure covers a wide range of cash flows within international business. A firm with a continuing series of foreign currency earnings (expenses) from foreign customers (suppliers) may believe the sales are quite firm for the next year, although they have not yet been shipped and booked, or even if a sales contract has not been signed. At the other extreme, the contingent exposure may be a foreign currency bid placed on a contract for proposal, the probability of success being extremely difficult to estimate.

6. Eiteman, Stonehill, and Moffett, 1992, p. 185. Economic exposure is also commonly referred to as *operating exposure*.

7. A sampling of this rich academic literature would include Dufey (1972), Logue and Oldfield (1977), Dufey and Srinivasulu (1983), Flood and Lessard (1986), and Lessard (1990).

8. We will assume throughout this paper that future exchange rate movements are *unexpected* by definition. Although all business decisions, whether primarily domestic or international, financial or non-financial, require the manager to form expectations, we believe that although many firms may diversify their operational or financial structures in order to be prepared for future exchange rate movements, these passive diversification strategies are long run in scope and therefore are still relatively blind strategies for management of foreign exchange exposure.

9. We note once more that we address competitive response to exchange rate-induced competitive factors only here; the multitude of other competitive factors and forces which firms must address in competitive markets are a completely different matter.

10. We assume that purchasing power parity does not hold in the short to medium term in which managerial decision-making must occur. For a detailed discussion of the meaning of purchasing power parity and economic exposure see Dufey and Srinivasulu (1983).

11. This literature is best represented by Smith, Smithson, and Wilford (1989), and Levi and Sercu (1991). There are of course a number of other potential arguments which support the management and hedging of foreign exchange exposure in the firm including differential tax rates and policies and the desire to decrease income volatility.

12. The Term LEGO® has been popularized in this area by Charles W. Smithson, most notably in his article entitled 'A LEGO® Approach to Financial Engineering,' *Midland Corporate Finance Journal,* vol. 4, no. 4, 1987, 16–28. The term is used to characterize the creation of financial instruments and techniques using basic building blocks (LEGO®s) available from a few traditional financial instruments.

13. This diversification of operations is akin to the financial practice of Markowitz portfolio diversification, in which a portfolio is constructed by combining assets, whose future returns are expected to be weakly or negatively correlated (usually on the basis of historical correlations).

14. If, for example, a U.S.-based firm with domestic sourcing and export earnings believed that there was the possibility of an adverse movement in the U.S. dollar versus major export earnings in French francs, the firm would purchase a series of long-maturity put options on French francs.

15. Any firm wishing to avoid marking-to-market a financial hedge instrument in the United States must qualify for what is termed *hedge accounting. Hedge accounting* means that the instrument and the underlying exposure are integrated and treated as if they were one single account, the recognition of both values not being required until both are realized (simultaneous expiration or maturity). However, in most cases, in order to qualify for hedge accounting the exposure must be firm (although a firm anticipation may qualify) and must be a single identifiable cash flow. Unfortunately, income derived from foreign subsidiaries, for example, does not qualify because it is the compilation of many different

cost and revenue cash flows. For a more complete description of hedge accounting see Bierman, et al., 1991.

16. *Continental Bank Journal of Applied Corporate Finance,* 1990, 19–28.

17. See Dickins, *Corporate Finance,* 1988, p. 11, and *Intermarket* Supplement, November 1986, 26, 28.

18. Many would of course legitimately argue that Kodak and Fuji do not produce homogeneous products. We assume here that the FX movement over the medium to long-term would be large enough to force relative price differences which would cause consumers to eventually substitute the products of one (cheaper) for the products of the other (expensive).

19. The DM1.5 billion in losses reported in 1994 by Metallgesellschaft of Germany stemming from commodity futures trading (purportedly as hedges) may prove an informative case study in the examination of this question.

REFERENCES

Belk, P.A. and M. Glaum, "The Management of Foreign Exchange Risk in UK Multinationals: An Empirical Investigation," *Accounting and Business Research,* vol. 21, no. 81, 1990, 3–13.

Bierman, Harold J., L. Todd Johnson and D. Scott Peterson, *Hedge Accounting: An Exploratory Study of the Underlying Issues,* Financial Accounting Standards Board, Norfolk, Connecticut, September 1991.

Bilson, John, "Managing Economic Exposure to Foreign Exchange Risk: A Case Study of American Airlines," in Y. Amibud and R. Levich, editors, *Exchange Rates and Corporate Performance,* Irwin Professional Publishing, 1994.

Dickins, Paul. "Daring to Hedge the Unhedgeable," *Corporate Finance,* August 1988, 11–13.

Dufey, Gunter, "Corporate Finance and Exchange Rate Variations," *Financial Management,* Summer 1972, 51–57.

Eiteman, David K., Arthur I. Stonehill and Michael H. Moffett, *Multinational Business Finance,* Sixth Edition, Addison-Wesley, Boston, 1992.

Flood, Eugene and Donald Lessard, "On the Measurement of Operating Exposure to Exchange Rates: A Conceptual Approach," *Financial Management,* Spring 1986, 25–36.

Glaum, Martin, "Strategic Management of Exchange Rate Risks," *Long Range Planning,* vol. 23, no. 4, 1990, 65–72.

Grant, Robert and Luc A. Soenen, "Conventional Hedging: An Inadequate Response to Long-Term Foreign Exchange Exposure." *Managerial Finance,* Vol. 17, No. 4, 1991.

Hekman, Christine R., "Foreign Exchange Management: New Opportunities and a New Perspective," *Managerial Finance,* vol. 17, No. 4, 1991, 5–9.

Kohn, Ken, "Futures and Options: Are You Ready for Economic-Risk Management?" *Institutional Investor,* September 1990, 203–204, 207.

Lessard, Donald R., "Global Competition and Corporate Finance in the 1990s," *Continental Bank Journal of Applied Corporate Finance,* 1990, 59–72.

Levi, Maurice D. and Piet Sercu, "Erroneous and Valid Reasons for Hedging Foreign Exchange Rate Exposure," *Journal of Multinational Financial Management,* vol. 1(2), 1991, 25–37.

Lewent, Judy C. and A. John Kearney, "Identifying, Measuring, and Hedging Currency Risk at Merck," *Continental Bank Journal of Applied Corporate Finance,* 1990, 19–28.

Luehrman, Timothy A., "The Exchange Rate Exposure of a Global Competitor," *Journal of International Business Studies,* Second Quarter, 1990, 225–242.

Millar, Bill, "Exposure Management at the Crossroads," *Business International Money Report,* Special FX Issue, December 18, 1989, 401–411.

Millar, William and Brad Asher, *Strategic Risk Management,* Business International, New York, January 1990.

Nance, Deana R., Clifford W. Smith Jr. and Charles W. Smithson, "On the Determinants of Corporate Hedging," *Journal of Finance,* March 1993, 267–284.

Porter, Michael E., *Competitive Strategy: Techniques for Analyzing Industries and Competitors,* Macmillan Publishing, New York, 1980.

Pringle, John J., Managing Foreign Exchange, *Continental Bank Journal of Applied Corporate Finance,* 1990, 73–82.

Rawls, S. Waite III and Charles W. Smithson, "Strategic Risk Management," *Continental Bank Journal of Applied Corporate Finance,* Winter 1990, 6–18.

Smith, Clifford W. Jr., Charles W. Smithson and D. Sykes Wilford, "Why Hedge?" *Intermarket,* July 1989, 12–16 (excerpted from *Managing Financial Risk,* Harper & Row, New York, NY, September 1989).

32

EMERGING CAPITAL MARKETS AND CORPORATE FINANCE

JACK D. GLEN AND BRIAN PINTO

ABSTRACT   The new pattern of foreign finance emphasizes direct funding of developing country firms rather than sovereign borrowing, which was the dominant theme for many years. The shift away from bank sources of finance to direct use of emerging capital markets has been precipitated by the pervasive atmosphere of economic liberalization and privatizations throughout these markets. This article analyzes the unique situations accompanying this shift and the role emerging capital markets play.

How do developing country firms decide between debt and equity? And what role do domestic and international capital markets play in this decision? These are topical questions given the tremendous interest in emerging markets in recent years and the observation that new patterns of foreign and domestic finance are emerging for developing countries.[1] The new pattern of foreign finance emphasizes direct

Jack D. Glen is a Senior Economist at the International Finance Corporation. He conducts research on issues related to IFC investment activities, including analysis of country risk and review of project proposals. Glen is also involved in research projects investigating capital markets and corporate finance in the emerging markets.

Brian Pinto is Lead Economist in the IFC's economics department. He is responsible for managing an economics team that does country risk assessments, reviews investment proposals and engages in applied research on topics of business interest to the IFC.

This paper is based on conversations with numerous company managers and investment bankers in many developing countries, to whom we are extremely grateful. We acknowledge the support and guidance of Guy Pfeffermann, and especially thank N. Balasubramanian, Pedro Batalla, Eugene Galbraith, Don Hanna, Brett Hutton, Kent Lupberger, Vijay Sood, Darius Lilaoonwala, N. Vaghul, Samuel Otoo, Lester Seigel, Uma Sridharan, and Ravi Vish for helpful comments and/ or discussion. Mariusz Sumlinski provided superb research assistance. Errors and omissions are solely our responsibility. The views herein are not necessarily shared by the World Bank Group or affiliated institutions.

funding of developing country firms rather than sovereign borrowing, which was the dominant theme for many years. This switch is being facilitated by the trade and financial liberalization under way in many developing countries. Led by actual or potential balance of payments crises and the belief that globalization is inevitable, many developing country governments are jumping on to the free-market bandwagon to ensure that their firms can compete on the same terms as their less constrained foreign competitors.[2] An exciting outcome partly attributed to such liberalization and accompanying privatization is that developing country firms have continued to grow in the 1990s in spite of recession in the west.

The reforms are also influencing domestic financing patterns by revitalizing capital markets at home. Developing country finance has traditionally been equated with state banks and development finance companies (DFCs) with an emphasis on project, rather than corporate, finance. Leverage ratios and financing requirements have been norm-driven, with guidelines for lending based on project technology, capital intensity, the applicant's track record, perceived importance of the project within national priorities, average payback periods and the like. This is an apt characterization of the 1980s; but applies less so to the 1990s, with domestic markets for corporate debt and equity undergoing substantial transformation. At the margin, there is a shift away from bank sources of finance to direct use of the capital markets. As a result, the role of banks and DFCs is also undergoing basic change.

Firms have three main sources of capital: internally-generated funds, bank loans and financing raised in capital markets, (i.e., corporate bonds and equity). The breakdown among these sources is not well documented for developing countries. One study for a set of developing countries covering the last decade found that internally-generated finance represented between 12% and 58% of total financing needs, leaving substantial portions to be financed by external sources;[3] but the available information does not permit a breakdown among bank loans on the one hand and corporate bonds and equity on the other. By comparison, internally-generated finance represented between 52% and 100% of the financing needs for the G7 nations.[4] Evidently, external financing is more important in developing countries than in some of the developed countries.

In the 1990s, the use of capital markets as a source of external financing in developing countries has soared. In a sample of seven developing countries, new issues of equity and corporate debt in the domestic capital market were 19% and 41% higher in 1992 compared to 1990.[5] Further increases are expected. In the international markets, investor interest in emerging market instruments has reached headline-making proportions. For 1992 alone, international portfolio investment in emerging markets was more than $19 billion, which exceeds net loans from international commercial banks, and is more than three times the level achieved in 1990.[6] Again, increases are expected. These shifts in the nature of corporate finance in developing countries leads to the questions—How do firms arrive at a given debt/equity mix and how do they view the cost and risk of different instruments?

CAPITAL MARKETS AND CORPORATE FINANCE

In principle, firms have available to them a range of debt and equity instruments which can be used to meet the needs of even the most discriminating is-

suer. In practice, firms in many emerging markets have only a limited menu of instruments, owing both to regulatory constraints that close some markets and economic instability that limit investor interest in others. But the liberal economic programs adopted by so many emerging market governments in recent years are fostering the development of vibrant domestic capital markets. In many cases, firms have, often for the first time, access to medium- and even long-term domestic-currency debt capital, not to mention equity and quasi-equity. Equally impressive is the rapid increase in international access that emerging market firms have to debt and equity capital. As a result, many emerging market firms are finding more and cheaper equity and debt capital than ever before.

EMERGING EQUITY MARKETS

Emerging equity markets have grown in importance in recent years. Growth in stock market prices has been dramatic, especially in those countries where governments have embarked on liberalization measures, as well as in countries that have experienced rapid economic growth. This is apparent when one looks at either the market capitalization of the emerging markets, or at the number of firms listed in these markets. Both are presented in Chart 1.[7]

Except for the downturn in 1990, which can be attributed almost entirely to a significant decline in the Taiwanese market, the emerging equity markets have been extremely buoyant over the last decade, with total market capitalization increasing an average of 28% per annum in U.S. dollar terms compared with only 13.5% in the developed equity markets. Such high emerging market growth arises from three sources: the number of firms listed; new issues by listed firms; and price increases. As shown in the graph, the number of firms listed has grown from less than 7,000 in 1983 to more than 13,000 in 1992, an average growth rate of nearly 8%. As this is significantly below the total increase in market capitalization, the difference must be due to price increases and new equity issues by already listed firms. Information on new issues by listed firms is not readily

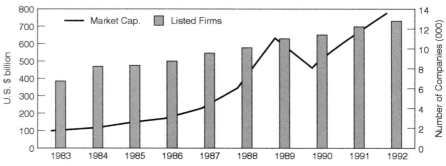

Chart 1. Emerging Equity Markets

available, but the IFC emerging market price index increased an average of 13% per annum in U.S. dollar terms over the period 1984–92, an indication of how significant price increases have been in recent years. Given the inverse relationship between stock price and cost of equity, it is not surprising that the number of firms choosing to go public in the emerging markets has been so high.

Despite rapid improvement in the emerging equity markets, however, they are still dwarfed in size by those of the developed countries. For example, the market capitalization of all of the emerging markets combined is only 92% of the U.K. equity market. And emerging market capitalization as a percentage of emerging market GDP was only 19% in 1992, compared with 60% in the developed economies.

Obtaining information on the primary markets for corporate debt and equity securities in emerging markets is not easy. Some information is available, however, and annual primary market activity for both equity and medium- and long-term corporate debt markets for a group of emerging market countries is presented in Chart 2.[8] As the chart shows, both debt and equity markets have grown in importance over the years. Particularly striking is the relative growth in equity issues in the 1990s following two years in which debt dominated. One source for this divergence is the privatization programs that have taken place, especially in some of the Latin American countries in the sample. Argentina, for example, privatized a number of state-owned enterprises over the period 1989–93, which contributed significantly to the equity issues in those years.

Those privatizations may have offsetting effects in future years, however, as the privatized companies in Argentina were typically sold stripped of much of their debt, which the government assumed. To the extent that there are cost and control advantages to leverage, one should see debt being issued by these firms as they undergo their future investment programs. In fact, one is already seeing this happening. There have been substantial increases in international issues of debt by Argentine firms, some of which are coming from the recently privatized firms.

Country-specific information provides additional insight into the debt/equity choice. Chart 3 presents primary equity market activity over the last decade for India and Venezuela. The chart illustrates at least two points. First, the relative importance of equity can differ significantly across countries. India's GNP of more than $280 billion far exceeds Venezuela's $54 billion, but primary market activity in Venezuela was roughly comparable to India's during several of the years presented. Evidently, different countries

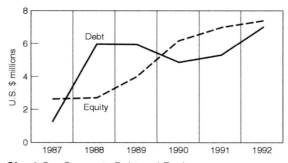

Chart 2. Corporate Debt and Equity

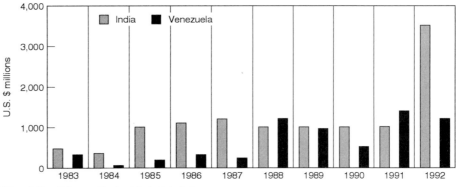

Chart 3. Primary Equity Market Activity

have more or less preference for equity, but that preference is obviously affected by cost factors, which introduces the second point. New issues of equity jumped in both countries, but at different times: 1991 for Venezuela and 1992 for India. Both jumps represent relative cost shifts, but for different reasons. In India, the desire to issue new equity was tempered over the years by governmental insistence on pricing new equity according to a formula which apparently did not reward firms much for large movements in market prices; the Bombay market moved up significantly in 1985, as well as in 1988–1991 without any large increase in new equity issues. In 1992, however, as part of the government's liberalization measures, new issues were priced according to the market, not by bureaucratic formulae. The result was a substantial decrease in the cost of new equity and a surge in new issues. The Venezuelan story is simpler. Market prices were high in 1986–88 and in 1990–92, and issuers responded by issuing more equity, albeit with somewhat of a lag. What remains to be seen is if the Indian market in 1992 represents a new equilibrium level of equity issues, or if it was a one-time affair and if the relative importance of equity in the two countries will go back to its 1980s level.

INTERNATIONAL EQUITY MARKETS

Firms in need of equity are not limited to their domestic markets. By issuing equity (or debt) in for-

eign markets, especially the most developed markets of Europe and the United States, emerging market firms gain access to a much larger group of investors than they have in their local markets. In many cases a move into these international markets provides firms with much more capital than they would have access to in their domestic markets, and, to the extent that international investors are better diversified and demand less return for risk, often at a lower cost. Moreover, the competitive pressure of an international issue can reduce the cost of capital at home as well.

For equity issues the most popular instrument among emerging market firms these days is the American Depository Receipt (ADR) or Global Depository Receipt (GDR).[9] Firms choose to list their shares abroad through depository receipts in order to facilitate access to international investors. Listing of shares directly on foreign exchanges and attracting foreign investors to the firm's domestic market are other options, but depository receipts have advantages both for the issuer and for the investor that sometimes make them preferable. With a depository receipt, the depository is responsible for conversion of dividends into foreign exchange and for the distribution of dividends and financial statements to investors. In addition, unlike foreign investment in a firm's domestic equity market, because the depository receipts are registered securities in the market in which they trade, settlement is facilitated and restrictions that some institutional investors face on holdings of foreign securities can be avoided. Thus,

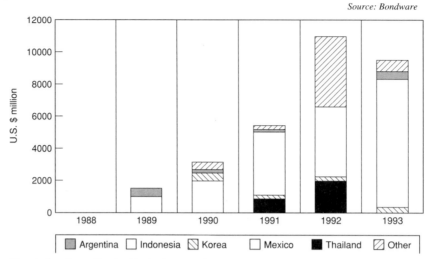

Source: Bondware

Chart 4. Cross-Border Equity Issues: Emerging Market Firms

depository receipts provide a convenient means for increasing a firm's shareholder base.

Furthermore, depository receipts can legally be created without the sponsorship of the firm whose shares are being traded. Unsponsored ADRs exist for a number of emerging market firms, but they are a distinct minority. Sponsored ADRs require that the sponsor pay fees to the depository, but in return the depository provides services that contribute to the success of the ADR.

The importance of the cross-border market, which comprises both types of depository receipts, has increased dramatically in recent years. Chart 4 presents aggregate annual statistics for the market, and also identifies the major issuing countries for each year. The entry of different countries into the market corresponds to changing market conditions, especially the implications of government economic programs and, in the case of Argentina and Mexico, resolution of international debt problems which allowed those countries renewed access to the markets.[10] The growth in the cross-border market has been especially significant for Mexico, which dominated the market in each of the last three years.

In the U.S. market, all publicly-traded shares must be registered with the U.S. Securities and Exchange Commission (SEC), which requires issuers to report financial information compiled according to U.S. accounting standards periodically, something that adds to the cost of any foreign equity issue. Shares listed on exchanges must also meet exchange listing requirements, but some firms elect to have their shares traded in the over-the-counter market (OTC), which reduces reporting requirements somewhat. The OTC market, however, has a major drawback as well: few of its shares receive the public notice that is offered by listing on a major exchange. For this reason, firms sometimes consider the OTC market as a first step into the U.S. market before undergoing the more formal process of listing on an exchange.

In a 1990 move that further increased the options available to foreign issuers, the U.S. relaxed requirements on issues traded exclusively among qualified institutional buyers. Under the assumption that institutions are better able to assess risk than private investors, firms whose shares are traded in the 144A market, named after the regulation that created it, are not required to disclose as much information to the SEC (and hence to shareholders) as do publicly-traded firms. These reduced disclosure requirements are appealing to many emerging market issuers who find the costs associated with disclosure onerous or who are reluctant to make some information public.

Both the over-the-counter and 144A markets have

been attractive to emerging market issuers. In Mexico, for example, of 36 cross-border issues traded in 1992, 42% were traded in the OTC market and one third were traded in the 144A market, leaving just 25% of the issues listed on exchanges. By year-end 1993 the situation had changed in total number of issues, but not in the relative importance of the exchanges; similar patterns are evident in other emerging market countries. One hypothesis is that the number of listed shares will increase over time as the issuers become more sophisticated, but at this time it still appears that the marginal cost of listing on a major exchange outweighs the advantage that it generates for a majority of Mexican (and most emerging market) firms.

The decision to issue a depository receipt is not necessarily equivalent to raising new equity capital. Firms can choose to list existing shares in the foreign market. In this way, they gain access to a larger body of investors, which may increase the value of their equity. Ultimately, of course, most firms that choose this route expect to raise new equity in the foreign market at a future date, but decide to wait for some time in order to gain the attention of international investors before issuing new capital. In some cases, however, governments have intervened in order to prevent this seemingly logical progression. Chilean firms, for example, can go to the international markets only with new issues of equity; the trading of existing shares is prohibited.

EMERGING CORPORATE DEBT MARKETS

While domestic equity markets have long been important in many developing countries, the development of medium- and long-term corporate debt markets is much more recent. One reason for this may be the lack of a network of institutional investors in such countries. Retail investors are willing to buy equities, which offer significant upside potential, but corporate debt often offers little advantage over government debt. Without well established institutional investors, such as pension funds, an active medium- or long-term corporate debt market might be difficult to establish.

Information on the primary market for corporate debt in the emerging markets is limited. Chart 2 showed that the market has grown in recent years, but has fallen behind the equity market in importance. This trend most likely reflects the relative cost of debt and equity. As noted, increases in equity prices have reduced the cost, while real interest rates are up in many countries. The rise in equity prices partly reflects the interest of international investors in emerging market equity.

Chart 5 shows primary debt issues for India and Venezuela, for which equity market activity was depicted earlier in Chart 3. Unlike equity, the debt market was substantially larger in India than in Venezuela over most of the period. There was a significant increase in Indian market activity beginning in 1986,

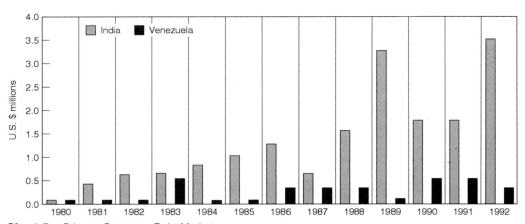

Chart 5. Primary Corporate Debt Market

ascribed to a more lenient attitude toward corporate fund raising by the government. Further, much of the debt issued was in the form of partially convertible debentures, which were designed to enable firms to recoup part of the loss from equity price controls by issuing the pure debt component at substantially below markets interest rates. Interestingly, the surge in debt coincided with the rise in the stock market noted earlier. In Venezuela the ups and downs in the market reflect a number of factors, including the current level of interest rates and the overall demand for investment capital by firms.

INTERNATIONAL CORPORATE DEBT MARKETS

Parallel with development of the international market for emerging market equity, an international market for emerging market corporate debt developed both for debentures and convertibles. For the most part, this market is a part of the larger Euromarket. Some issuers have participated in the debt side of the U.S. 144A market, and for firms from countries that are investment grade, access to the U.S. Yankee bond market, with its lower rates and longer maturities, is a possibility. As with the equity market, international issues of corporate bonds from the emerging markets have surged in recent years, as presented in Chart 6. The attraction for the international debt markets are the lower interest rates and longer maturities

available there compared to the domestic markets of most emerging market countries. As with the equity market, growth in the debt market has followed international debt restructuring programs with the major debtor nations. Also like the equity markets, Mexico and Argentina have come to play significant roles in the debt market. Unlike cross-border equity issues, however, Brazil has also tapped the debt market for large amounts, reflecting both the conservative nature of the capital structures of Brazilian firms, as well as the relatively low price level of the domestic Brazilian equity market.

CASE STUDY: EUROCONVERTIBLE BONDS AND GDRs IN INDIA

Indian companies were first permitted to tap the Euromarket in 1992. Between May 1992 and November 1993, nine companies raised close to $1 billion in this market. Companies have been drawn overseas because the volumes that can be raised are higher while issuance costs at 2% to 3% are substantially lower than comparable rupee issues. Achieving name recognition overseas is another important benefit. And the prevalent view is that Indian real interest rates are too high. Foreign investors are drawn to these issues attracted by high yields compared to alternatives in the West and the expectation of significant capital gains.

Potential instruments include syndicated bank

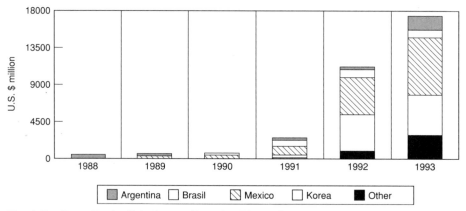

Chart 6. Cross-Border Debt Issues: Emerging Market Firms

loans; Yankee or high-yield bonds; and GDRs and Euroconvertible bonds. Bank loans are ruled out over concern about exposure to India. India not yet being investment grade, Yankee bonds are infeasible, while high-yield bonds are considered too expensive. The strategy with GDRs and Euroconvertibles is to place these with groups that are chasing high yields and have low exposure to India, such as emerging market funds and various foreign institutional investors. Compared to Western issues, the size of these issues is small enough to allow them to be placed during the roadshow. This also lowers issuance costs. The job of signalling that the companies have a better grade than the sovereign rating is left to the lead manager, who not only complies with the due diligence requirements (disclosure, conformity with U.K. accounting principles, listing requirements in Luxembourg—the place of choice), but also promotes the issue. How do companies and lead managers signal that a given company is a better-than-sovereign risk? This is a tricky issue because of the trade liberalization that is in progress and lack of clarity about how corporate fortunes will look when the dust settles. The response is that lead managers market the issue by drawing comparisons from similar situations in other countries and by concentrating on the big firms, which they believe will be bailed out in case of difficulty.

The choice between GDRs, which amount to a new equity issue, and Euroconvertible bonds, a quasi equity instrument, is left to the company. The following are the main considerations: 1) GDRs are often issued at a substantial discount to existing quoted prices to compensate for risk and the settlement delay in case GDRs are redeemed. The first two GDRs, by Reliance and Grasim, were both issued at a discount of 18%; but the conversion price for Euroconvertibles is much closer to the quoted price; 2) Euroconvertibles avoid immediate dilution and carry low nominal coupons because of the conversion option. As a result, companies like them; 3) foreign investors like Euroconvertibles because there is limited downside risk through put options that guarantee a minimum rate of return.

Companies must obtain permission from the Ministry of Finance (MOF) and the Reserve Bank of India. Being the first, the Reliance GDR took some four months from conceptualization to the realization of proceeds. Subsequent issues have been much faster. The money raised is typically for the foreign exchange component of expansion projects, although Reliance went overseas to pay off foreign debt with its GDR issue proceeds. MOF recently indicated that it might put restrictions on overseas transactions designed purely for treasury purposes (hedging or raising funds and keeping these offshore).

A number of different lead managers have been used by the various companies. For the first nine Euroissues, no fewer than five different lead managers were used.

GLOBAL DEPOSITARY RECEIPTS (GDRs)

Following the pioneering issue of GDRs by the Reliance group in May 1992 for $150 million, five subsequent issues have been done up to November 1993 for a total of close to $500 million. GDRs are basically an instrument for issuing equity overseas. The following parties are typically involved: issuing company; overseas depositary bank; a local agent of the depositary bank; investors; and a lead manager.

EUROCONVERTIBLE BONDS

Essar Gujarat, a steel company, was the first to issue a Euroconvertible bond, for $75 million. The liberalization affected Essar in two basic ways: first, with steel delicensed, the company decided to increase its investment outlay; second, with the free pricing of equity introduced, it decided to go for a debt/equity ratio of 0.65 compared to an original target of 2.5! Further, the Euroconvertible bond itself was chosen (after the option became feasible) to lower borrowing from the term-lending institutions, because their interest rates were regarded as high.

The bond has a 5-year maturity, a coupon of 5.5% and involved issuance costs of 3.5%. The conversion price was at a premium of about 1.5% over the market price of the share at the time the bond was issued in July 1993. The conversion option commences one month after issue. The bond can be called at any time after two years if the rupee price of the share exceeds the conversion price by 40% and the closing share price in dollars exceeds the dollar conversion price by 30%. The bondholders have a one-time put option (at par) at the end of the third year.

Companies are generally pleased with the pricing they have obtained on Euroconvertibles. A few months after Essar issued its bond, SCICI (a company financing ship purchases, but rapidly diversifying into other activities as well) issued its Euroconvertible with a conversion price premium of close to 7.5%. This is a $100 million issue with maturity of 10 years and five months, and a coupon of 3.5%. Conversion can take place anytime three months after issue. The bond can be called anytime after 5 years and five months if the share price exceeds the conversion price by 40% (in rupees and dollars). There is also a one-time put option after 5 years and five months whereby the investor can obtain a yield-to-put of 5.65%.

The SCICI issue was oversubscribed 10 times compared to 4–5 times for Essar, attesting to the growing popularity of this instrument among investors and the potential volume of funds that can be raised. It is difficult to directly compare the pricing of the bonds and conclude which one is ''better,'' because the value of the conversion option is very different (depending upon the prospects of the company) and the call and put options may be structured differently.

Pricing of Euroconvertible bonds is based on market demand rather than mathematical models. The basic intuition is that in return for the lower interest rate, the investor would like a conversion option, which is a gamble on share price appreciation. Further, put options, which are typically part of the package, minimize downside risk for investors. Similarly, companies that issue Euroconvertible bonds are banking on eventual conversion.

Lastly, there are indications that even medium-sized companies can approach the Euro-market. Bharat Forge, not large by international standards, was able to do a Euro-issue for only SFR 20 million (about $14 million). Indications are that second-tier companies are already being approached for Euro-issues, a major attraction being low issuance costs compared to rupee issues.

A PECKING ORDER

All companies actively seek financing instruments that will minimize the cost of capital, thereby enhancing returns to shareholders. The notion of optimality in capital structure is related to the choice of a financing mix that makes the weighted average cost of capital as low as possible. In the theoretical world of corporate finance, this choice is made in an environment where capital markets work perfectly and interest rates and share prices are freely determined, a description that applies in large part to many western economies. In such circumstances, how do companies choose between internal and external funds on the one hand and between debt and equity on the other? The so-called ''pecking order'' theory posits that firms choose the following sequence: first, rely on retained earnings, then issue debt and lastly, issue new equity.[11] The reasons given for this sequencing stem from differences in information between company insiders and outsiders and transactions costs. For example, if existing shareholders believe that the market is going to undervalue new equity, then they would be reluctant to issue new shares. Likewise, if the transaction costs of securing debt are lower than those associated with issuing shares, then this would also be a deterrent to equity financing.

Interestingly enough, the pecking order theory may work quite well with developing country firms in that debt may be preferred to equity, even though markets may not function freely. There are four reasons for expecting this. First, with interest rates administratively set, the after-tax real cost of debt may be negative, creating a bias toward debt. Second, there may be restrictions on the issue price of new equity that function effectively as a tax on issuing shares. Third, with limited competition among investment banks, issuance costs may be very high, making bank loans a far cheaper alternative. Fourth, with the government directing credit through DFCs, there may be a pre-disposition toward debt.[12]

With the financial liberalizations that have been underway in the late 1980s and 1990s, however, companies may begin re-examining their financial structure. They now have a richer and less constrained menu of instruments to choose from (in terms of pricing), as the example below illustrates.

CASE STUDY: *AN INDONESIAN PECKING ORDER*

Indonesian companies first rely on internal funds and state bank loans, then private and foreign banks, then list on the Jakarta Stock Exchange (JSE) and lastly, go overseas. The pressure to list and go public is growing as the role of state banks goes down in tandem with declining oil revenues. At the margin, non-state bank sources, including private and foreign banks, equity and direct access to foreign capital markets are becoming more important; but the role of state banks is still large in absolute terms. In particular, for small companies, the major sources of funding continue to be existing shareholder funds, retained earnings and bank loans.

The impression picked up from interviews is that the focus is much more on the volume than the cost of funds. Companies are expanding rapidly and rates of return are very high. The concern is much more with profit potential and market share. Beyond a point, however, companies may be forced to list to both expand the sources and lower the cost of funding. There is a tendency to regard existing equity as ''free'' and to measure its cost by the dividend yield alone. As companies get established, if becomes easier to borrow a foreign currency, which is stimulated by the belief that rupiah interest rates have always been too high (in comparison to dollar interest rates plus expected depreciation). If companies wish to gain direct access to the international capital markets, then they have to go through a rigorous process of disclosure to satisfy listing requirements abroad. At this point, it will usually be the case that compa-

nies have already been through the listing process on the JSE. Once companies go public, they will be increasingly subject to the scrutiny of banks, foreign investors and brokers. At this stage, business intrinsics and the debt-equity ratio become extremely important.

AN EXAMPLE

This company, belonging to a well-known business group, has had its own ''pecking order'' in sourcing funds. It started in classical fashion with internal funds and state bank loans. It went public during the 1990 stock market boom, doing a 100% listing. The initial public offering (IPO) proceeds were partly used to pay off state bank loans. The rest was kept for use in connection with the company's long-term business plan, which involves a new rayon plant and an expansion in its existing markets pulp business. After the expansion is complete, the pulp/rayon mix is expected to be 60/40. The total expansion cost is $250 million, of which $100 million will come from the balance of the IPO proceeds and retained earnings. The remainder has come from issuing new long-term debt.

The company has made a calculated decision to go for long maturity U.S. dollar and Swiss franc convertible bonds to raise the $150 million. The desire for long-term debt was motivated by the observation that the pulp business is cyclical. And convertible bonds gave the company the best pricing. The company is betting that inflation will remain low and that there will be no maxi-devaluation, the last one having occurred in 1986. Fixed rate rupiah funding for the same maturities is simply not available.

The typical structure of the convertible bonds is illustrated by the U.S. dollar bond, which was issued in late 1992 with a maturity of 10 years. It carries a coupon of 5.5%. The investor can convert to shares at any time at a pre-determined price. The price used for determining the number of shares for conversion was set at the time of issue at a premium of 9% over the prevailing quoted price.[13] At the end of 5 years, the investors have a one-month window to put the bond back to the company with a yield-to-put of 9%.

The company expects market pulp prices to peak in five years' time and is betting that stock prices will have risen sufficiently that conversion will take place.

The company also recently did a high-yield U.S. dollar bond issue of 7 year maturity of amount $110 million, with an option to call the bond at a small premium between years 5 and 6 and at par thereafter. Including underwriting fees of 2.5%, the all-in-cost is about 10%. In order to issue this bond, the company went through a rating process and secured a BB, which places it below investment grade. This ruled out a private placement of a "Yankee" bond, both of which require investment grade. The company therefore chose a high-yield, noninvestment grade bond, which is U.S. SEC registered and requires maximum disclosure (as compared to a private placement or 144A). Anyone can buy this bond. The company plans to use this issue as a stepping stone to a NYSE-listed ADR. It already has an ADR traded in the OTC market.

CONCLUSIONS

Developing country firms have the same objective as their advanced country counterparts; to minimize the cost of capital given the financial instruments available. But the environment in which these firms operate often differs dramatically from what is found in most developed countries.

The capital markets of most developing countries are only now emerging to fully serve the needs of issuers. State banks and development finance companies have traditionally been the prominent lenders, often not operating on commercial principles. Government controls have in the past limited, and in many cases continue to limit, the potential list and pricing of capital market instruments. And access to international markets has been constrained both by controls and by sovereign credit ratings that may be below investment grade, overshadowing the true potential of the private sector. As a result, developing country firms have faced much more constrained choices than their developed country counterparts. Thus, the observed "pecking order" in the funding

decisions of firms in developing countries is likely to reflect the extent of financial liberalization chosen by the government.

But financing decisions go beyond cost considerations. Risk, control and disclosure also have an impact. While family-owned businesses have played a dominant role in the past, as markets develop and stock prices increase, more and more firms are going public, despite the potential control problems and disclosure that this entails. The alternative, issuing corporate debt, is also popular, but only for firms with healthy balance sheets that can absorb the risk involved.

The 1990s are fast becoming a watershed in corporate finance, with significant financial liberalization under way in several emerging markets.

First, in many instances, financial liberalization has been spurred by actual or anticipated foreign debt and balance of payments crises, and/or a realization that traditional funding sources may not be sustainable in the long run.

Second, governments have consciously begun limiting the role of state banks and DFCs either by phasing out special guarantees that enable cheap acquisition of funds, or curtailing their operations in various ways. Freeing corporate finance has meant that the larger, more credit-worthy companies, the traditional clients of the banking system, will increasingly be self-reliant. This is likely to lead DFCs to direct their financial expertise toward small and medium-sized enterprises and more risky companies.

Third, in many cases, large spreads in the banking system as a result of inefficiency or bad loans are spurring companies to issue commercial paper for working capital and bonds for long-term finance.

Fourth, financial liberalization is being accompanied by trade liberalization, which is bound to affect the competitiveness, and hence the risk class, of many established companies. Such liberalization is also affecting corporate business strategy (e.g., a focus on scale economies and the core business in India in contrast to haphazard, license-driven diversification).

Fifth, foreign institutional investors and private mutual funds have arrived, inevitably implying greater pressure for more disclosure, improved accounting standards and rational financial regulation.

And lastly, the interest in emerging markets poses an interesting question. To what extent is this a temporary ''flavor-of-the-month'' phenomenon in response to low yields and recession in the West? What will happen when the economic slump in OECD countries is replaced by growth? Our hunch is that interest in emerging markets will continue for three reasons: first, growth rates in the emerging markets surpass those of most of the developed countries, giving emerging markets higher potential returns; second, low correlations between emerging markets and the rest of the world suggest that there are substantial diversification benefits from investing in these markets; and third, the percentage of assets invested by Western institutional investors in emerging markets is still relatively small. Total equity assets managed by U.S. institutional investors alone was $2018 billion in 1991 and has grown at the rate of 14.5% per annum over the last decade. Gross portfolio capital flows to the emerging markets on the other hand was equal to $34 billion in 1992, less than 2% of the U.S. portfolio.[14] Evidently, there is still some way to go before international investors have their fill of emerging market assets.

NOTES

1. See The World Bank, *Global Economic Prospects and Developing Countries,* 1993; and *The Economist,* ''Third-World Finance,'' September 25, 1993.

2. Two recent examples are Argentina and India.

3. We use the term ''external'' to refer to funding sources outside the firm, and the word ''foreign'' to denote non-domestic external sources.

4. Michael Atkin and Jack Glen, ''Comparing Capital Structures Around The Globe,'' *The International Executive* 34, 369–387.

5. Authors' calculations based on information provided by security market authorities in Argentina, Brazil, Chile, India, Indonesia, Turkey and Venezuela.

6. The World Bank, *World Debt Tables 1993–94,* 1993.

7. Chart 1 represents all countries included in the IFC Emerging Market Database.

8. The countries included in the graph are: Argentina, Brazil, Chile, India, Indonesia, Turkey and Venezuela.

9. ADR and GDR are often used interchangeably. Indeed, many issues are done simultaneously in the U.S. and global markets. In other cases, however, only one of the two instruments may exist.

10. The graph includes only equity issued by private companies; no issues by state-owned enterprises are included. Thus, Argentina's state oil company, YPF, which was privatized in 1993 through a combination of a local market offer and an ADR offering earning $3 billion in the process, is not included.

11. See Steward Myers, ''The Capital Structure Puzzle,'' *Journal of Finance* 39, 575–597; and Stewart Myers and Nicholas Majluf, ''Corporate Financing and Investment Decisions when Firms Have Information That Investors Do Not Have,'' *Journal of Finance* 13, 187–221.

12. India is a good example.

13. For example, if the face value of a bond is $1000, the rupiah/dollar rate is 2000 and the price of the company's share at the time of issue is 5000 rupiah, each bond will be convertible into $(1000 \times 2000)/5000 \times 1.09 = 367$ shares if a 9% premium applies.

14. The World Bank *Global Economic Prospects;* and Sudarshan Gooptu, ''Portfolio Investment Flows to Emerging Markets,'' IECED Working Paper, World Bank.

33

CAPITAL BUDGETING FOR INTERNATIONAL BUSINESS: A FRAMEWORK FOR ANALYSIS

JOHN HOLLAND

Department of Accountancy and Finance, Glasgow Business School

ABSTRACT   This article focuses on three related themes. Firstly, normative decision rules for the international capital budgeting decision are outlined. Secondly, the strengths and limitations of finance theory in guiding the capital budgeting plan within the MNC are discussed. Thirdly, strategic views are introduced to complement financial analysis in the area of international capital budgeting.

The increased internationalisation of the domestic firm and the rise of the multinational firm has accentuated the need for decision models to help managers cope with the attendant increased complexity in the overseas Capital Budgeting decision.

These complexities arise because the international manufacturing and trading firm operates within a range of different political, legal, taxation and cultural systems. They manufacture and trade within a wide range of product and factor markets, each with differing levels of competition, and efficiency. This inevitably leads to transactions taking place in a wide range of currencies and as a result the multinational company (MNC) has frequent resort to foreign exchange markets and exploits a wide variety of funding sources. All of these activities and associated cash flows arise in a variety of political systems each with a differing propensity to interfere in corporate operations.

The additional complexities mean that the conventional capital budgeting model must be adapted to this international context. This is done by expanding the model to cope with novel issues and by placing capital budgeting within the broader set of strategic problems facing the multinational enterprise. We begin, in section 1, by looking at adaptions to the conventional Net Present Value decision model.

1. THE ANALYSIS OF THE CAPITAL BUDGETING DECISION

The two primary tasks in a capital budgeting exercise are:

The development of a decision model or rules to value the risky cash flows emanating from a project.

The prediction of the size and risk of the incremental after tax cash flows of the project.

The first task, concerning the appropriate decision model, has long been the focus of financial theory. This task involves answering two questions. Firstly, what is the appropriate opportunity cost of capital for the project cash flows? Secondly, how can value dependencies between the investment decision, the financing decision and foreign exchange risk management decisions be analysed? The first question is considered in this section, and the value dependency question is discussed in section 3.

The second major capital budgeting task is concerned with how to create high quality information on the project's expected cash flow stream. In this case the finance director has to clarify what is meant by incremental cash flows. In particular, whether the project cash flows should be incremental to the parent, subsidiary, or both. He must also classify the cash flows so that the effects or otherwise of the parity relationships can be isolated. This should allow identification of those parts of the cash flow stream affected by deviations from parity and those parts unaffected.

The choice of a decision model and the creation of cash flow information are central to the international (and domestic) capital budgeting decision. In the following pages an attempt is made to answer some of the above questions concerning the decision model and cash flow information issues.

AN INTERNATIONAL CAPITAL BUDGETING DECISION MODEL

The international treasurer or financial manager's choice of a capital budgeting decision model is restricted to various forms of the net present value rule. This model is generally considered to be conceptually superior to both the internal rate of return model, and the payback model (Holland 1986, pp. 106–108).

Myers (1974) suggests that many of the problems of complexity in capital budgeting can be solved by a return to the fundamental principle of value additivity. This states that the whole value of a project is equal to the sum of the values of the parts (Brealey and Myers 1981, p. 400). This method can be widened to include all important side effects of accepting a project. The idea behind this 'adjusted present value' (APV) rule is to 'divide and conquer' complex capital budgeting problems. No attempt is made to try and capture all effects in one calculation, especially when interactions between investment and financing decisions are expected to occur (Brealey and Myers 1981, p. 406). The APV rule therefore divides up the present value terms and focuses on each present value term to maximise the development and use of information. Each present value term employs a unique discount rate for its level of systematic risk.

Lessard (1981) has extended this approach to deal with the problems of evaluating foreign investment projects. The APV equation now contains additional terms that explicitly deal with the following factors.

DISCOUNT RATES FOR INTERNATIONAL CAPITAL BUDGETING

In the above model each of the terms is discounted at an appropriate rate to reflect its unique systematic riskiness. Some version of the capital asset pricing model is used to calculate discount rates for foreign risks that are considered systematic in nature. At the present state of knowledge, management will have to decide which view of international capital markets (integrated or segmented) corresponds to the systematic relationship (if any exists) between the project returns and those of an economy (world or domestic). For example, if the project has input and output prices dependent on the world economy then a world capital market factor seems most appropriate.

Managers estimating discount rates for overseas projects may initially assume that projects arising in politically unstable regimes require larger risk premiums than those recommended for comparable domestic projects. However, if capital markets are segmented the foreign project may be providing otherwise unattainable diversification benefits to home based shareholders. These are valuable to shareholders and as a result discount rates can be lowered to reflect the diversification benefits. Alternatively, if capital markets are assumed to be integrated, the foreign project's Beta measured relative to a world portfolio may be relatively low. This is more likely if the project is located in a less developed country (LDC) where greater political risks can provide larger diversification benefits. Such benefits should however not be exaggerated, because the economies of most LDCs and the internationally attractive projects that arise within them are likely to be linked to the world economy in a significant way. Again, in this case, discount rates may be much lower than initially assumed by managers.

In a further development of the international capital budgeting method of analysis, Shapiro (p. 11, 1978), has argued that the expected cash flows can be adjusted for unsystematic risk. Those political and economic risks that are deemed unsystematic in na-

		PV of		PV of Tax		PV of		PV of project		PV of		PV of		PV of
		PV of		PV of										
APV	=	Capital	+	Remittable	+	saving	+	Financial	+	contribution	+	other	+	extra	+	residual
		Outlays		After tax		from		subsidies		to corporate		tax		remit-		plant &
				Operating		depreciation				debt		savings		tances		equipment
				Cash flows						capacity						

ture (relative to say a world or domestic portfolio surrogate) are identified and expected cash flows are adjusted to reflect managerial views on these risks. As long as these adjustments do not alter the systematic risks of the project, then there is no reason (from the CAPM view) to change the discount rates to reflect these risks.

The APV approach is considered by many authors to be suitable for the international capital budgeting decision because it is relatively easy to acquire information on discount rates for the riskless or low risk cash flow streams, even though it may still be fairly difficult to identify the pure equity rate for the operating cash flows. The use of the APV version of the NPV rule does not solve the problem of whether systematic risk should be measured relative to the firm's home country market portfolio, or relative to a world portfolio. However, by separating out the financing effects it may simplify the search for information on market discount rates for the various cash flow terms.

Finally, it should be noted that it is possible to employ many features of the APV approach with the more conventional form of the NPV rule. Furthermore, Booth (1982) points out that the APV method needs all of the complicated adjustments required for the conventional NPV method and that the APV approach should be adopted only with the full understanding of its limitations.

IMPROVING THE QUALITY OF CASH FLOW INFORMATION

The quality of the project cash flow information can be further improved by classifying the cash flows terms into two categories. Firstly, cash flows that can be estimated independently for a project and those that depend upon the corporate wide tax and cash flow position. Secondly, contractual and non-contractual foreign currency cash flows can be considered separately.

In the first case, local subsidiary managers and parent MNC managers are likely to have relative advantages in developing information about particular sources of cash flows. Thus project specific cash flows generated within the subsidiary's economic sphere of influence and activity may best be esti-

mated from the subsidiary's viewpoint. In the same way, additional cash flows generated in the corporate system may best be estimated by senior head office managers with a broad view of the overall activities and position of the MNC.

Once this basic information on cash flows has been generated the firm needs to identify precisely which project and system dependent cash flows are incremental to the parent. The incremental funds to the parent are the funds ultimately available to the shareholders of the MNC and therefore form the basis for evaluating the project. This approach identifying the incremental benefits and costs of the project blends in well with the APV equation and can ensure that a corporate as opposed to a subsidiary view dominates the evaluation process.

In the case of contractual and non-contractual cash flows we can consider the effects of parity relationships on these cash flows. For example, in the case of non-contractual foreign currency cash flows if purchasing power parity and the international fisher effect hold then the problem of cash flows in different currencies and their appropriate discount rates can be much simplified. In equilibrium, discounting nominal cash flows using nominal discount rates is identical to discounting real cash flows using a real rate. Since many companies develop real data first, and then adjust for exchange rate and inflation rate changes, a real analysis seems simplest (Lessard 1981 p. 123). The current spot rate can then be used to convert the (real rate) discounted (real) foreign cash flows to a single currency base.

This analysis can be extended to cope with deviations from parity conditions. For example, purchasing power parity (PP) may hold generally between economies, but there may be significant changes expected in project specific (relative) prices. These relative prices can have a large impact on the value of the project compared with deviations from PP and they will therefore need to be considered in the (real) analysis of non-contractual cash flows above.

2. FINANCIAL THEORY AND INTERNATIONAL CAPITAL BUDGETING

In the ideal world of orthodox finance in which capital and foreign exchange markets are efficient and international trade in goods is subject to a common pricing mechanism, a variety of market imperfections are ignored. These include taxes, capital market segmentation and various governmental actions. In this 'first best' situation only the investment decision determines the value of the firm. Capital structure and foreign exchange exposure decisions are irrelevant. Managers should therefore expend their energies in seeking suitable investment opportunities in the pursuit of maximising shareholder wealth. The source of funds is considered irrelevant as it does not affect shareholder wealth. Such funds will be immediately available for positive NPV projects. Capital budgeting is restricted to the identification, acquisition and evaluation of investment opportunities. There are no problems of value interactions between the financing, foreign exchange risk and capital budgeting decision areas. Firms that do not obey the very limited normative rules for the evaluation of international capital budgeting projects will be rapidly penalised by an omniscient world capital market.

It is clear that if these ideal conditions hold then coping with the problems of international capital budgeting becomes a question of using existing domestic corporate finance theory to see through these apparent complexities to the fundamental evaluation problems common to all firms. In this situation the domestic and international environments coalesce into one and international capital budgeting problems are interesting but not significantly different to those of a wholly domestic firm. This idealised approach is generally seen in the literature as a valuable reference point, but in need of adaption according to circumstances, notably imperfections in markets for international capital, foreign exchange and goods and services.

ASSESSING VALUE INTERACTIONS BETWEEN CAPITAL BUDGETING, FINANCING, AND FOREIGN EXCHANGE RISK MANAGEMENT DECISIONS

In a world in which there are imperfections in some domestic capital markets and in international goods markets we are now dealing with 'second best' circumstances relative to the ideal of orthodox finance.

There are now presumed to be value dependencies or interactions between investment, financing, and foreign exchange exposure decisions. The major task for senior financial management is to identify these sources of value for each decision area and for each major interaction.

For example, in capital budgeting, positive net present values (NPV) stem both from corporate specific advantages such as unique firm knowledge, technology, market power and from location specific advantages (see section 3). In the exposure decision, potential losses of NPV may exist in situations where exchange rates fully adjust to expected inflation differences between countries (purchasing parity holds) but where a firm's specific input/output prices are expected to deviate from parity. In the financing decision, additional sources of NPV may stem from government subsidised funds, tax asymmetries between countries and through internal transfers of funds.

Once the sources of NPV gain and loss have been identified the task is to analyse the tradeoffs between these decision areas so that progress towards shareholder wealth maximisation is achieved. Interactions and desirable tradeoffs between these decision areas can be partially assessed by employing the APV variant of the NPV rule. For example, the decision to match assets and liabilities to minimise foreign exchange exposure and risk may affect project APVs and financing costs. The explicit trade-off here is between loss of APV versus reduced foreign exchange risk. The reduced effect or influence of unanticipated exchange rate events on corporate value may therefore be offset by a decreased set of valuable financing opportunities. These possibilities can be incorporated in the terms identified in the expanded APV equation and the interactions assessed.

Orthodox finance theory suggests that interactions between the major financial decision areas should be dealt with in a simultaneous manner. However, McInnes and Carleton (1982), show in their detailed study of the use of financial theory and financial models in mainly large international companies, that there was often considerable separation between financing and investment decisions. The common logical pattern was to proceed from a plan for operations, to a plan for new investment, and finally to a plan to finance these investments. Some information was recycled back through the planning process but the sequential process seemed to restrict a full consideration of the joint set of opportunities and constraints (p. 968).

An analysis of the interactions between capital budgeting and other major financial decisions is crucial both for the evaluation and management of projects. In the latter case, this information can help the Board and project managers to assess project responsiveness to unanticipated events. If, at this stage, managers feel that the project cannot respond flexibly to a wide range of uncertain and risky contingencies then this may colour the way in which they evaluate the project. Specifically, they may adjust this data to reflect the expected project risk management problem or choose decision models which allow them to control the choice of risky projects. Such a focus on the total risk of the project and managerial capacity to deal with total risk is inconsistent with the precepts of financial theory. Wilson (1988) provides some recent UK insight into such managerial behaviour. In his sample he showed how many UK MNCs separated out risk and return decisions and in some cases pursued risk minimisation as the primary goal of international capital budgeting.

It is clear from McInnes and Carleton's and Wilson's empirical research that international financial managers are adopting crude 'rules of thumb' in their capital budgeting planning exercises. These are their managerial solutions to the limitations of financial theory in dealing with the interactions between international capital budgeting, financing and foreign exchange risk management decisions and with potential problems of managing many risky projects.

It is also apparent from the above that international corporate finance scholars are advocating second best solutions for second best (imperfections) financial policy decision situations. However, as Myers (1984) asserts, if finance theory is applied correctly it provides the best 'state of the art' decision rules for financial planners and strategic analysts. If it can be extended to include time series relationships amongst investment projects (via option theory) then its role in strategic analysis will be much enhanced. However, it still suffers from the

problems outlined above, and clarifying a comprehensive capital budgeting planning framework under these conditions is a very complex task. Factors such as tax and intermittent government interference in markets means that financial scholars have yet to make explicit a framework for analysing the trade-offs over time between the international capital budgeting, financing and foreign exchange risk management decisions.

In order to compensate for some of these problems, capital budgeting can draw on developments elsewhere in economics and strategic analysis. From these perspectives firms are no longer seen solely as imperfections in markets. These sources will now be used to develop an alternative but complementary view of capital budgeting.

3. STRATEGIC PLANNING AND INTERNATIONAL CAPITAL BUDGETING

The establishment of a rational and integrated capital budgeting plan is a central task for the manager of the international enterprise. As we have seen from section 2, current financial theory only provides broad guidelines for doing this. The specific trade-offs established in the plan and the achievement of the shareholder wealth maximisation goal depend upon the unique circumstances of the firm, the knowledge and experience of the treasures of such MNCs, as well as correct implementation of existing finance theory.

However, a strategic analysis can be used to give greater direction and clarity to capital budgeting plans. Specifically, it will be used in the following section to guide the search for positive APV projects, to differentiate between different, often competing, forms of project and to incorporate political risk assessments in the evaluation of projects. Strategic analysis, focussing on long term investment overseas decisions can also be used to enrich the supply of information concerning cash flows, riskiness of the project, interactions between major financial decision areas, and risk responsiveness characteristics of projects. These benefits, in turn, may encourage the use of normative decision criteria such as the APV rule.

THE DECISION TO INVEST OVERSEAS

In this section two additional policy sources for international capital budgeting are considered. These are the eclectic theory of international production and the political risk literature. In the first case the financial manager is viewed as a member of an enterprise which is able to internalise, enhance and maintain market imperfections. This view in which the firm exercises considerable economic power, is in sharp contrast to the market perspective adopted in section 2. In the second case an analysis is made of the impact of 'political risk' on corporate financial decision making. In this analysis the effects of political constraints on strategic options are discussed. Particular stress is laid on the role of political events in limiting the perceived set of strategic opportunities open to international firms. Both of these views can provide an alternative, if fragmented source of additional policy guidelines for international capital budgeting.

Dunning (1979) has integrated related theories of direct foreign investment and other forms of international corporate involvement into an eclectic theory of international production based around ownership, locational, and internalisation advantages, i.e. The OLI theory of international production. Ownership specific advantages may derive from unique corporate attributes such as heavy investment in research and development and in the general marketing function. They may also be attributed to industry and country characteristics. Circumstances such as home market size and extent of product differentiation in an industry may contribute to ownership specific advantages held by a firm. It is essential that a firm understands its unique ownership specific advantages and that this knowledge plays a key role in the investment opportunity search process. Without such advantages, the firm cannot consider any form of international involvement. Current location specific advantages may stem from comparative cost advantages, they may arise from multiplant economies or they may flow from industry characteristics such as

industry specific tariffs in a particular location. Emerging location specific advantages could include new tax benefits, expansion of the higher education system, and the availability of new 'soft' loans. Internalisation advantages may be created if the firm is able to reorganise and achieve internal transaction cost economies. This may be done through the introduction of new organisational structures which reduce internal search, contracting and monitoring (hierarchical control) costs. One example of such reorganisation was the change from a divisionalised structure to a global matrix structure in some MNCs. This was designed to capture the benefits of centralisation and local knowledge at the same time. Unfortunately, there are some well publicised cases, such as Dow Chemical, in which this kind of reorganisation has not achieved its promised benefits. Bartlett (1983) argues that the central issue is to build and maintain a complex decision process rather than finding the right formal organisation structure. This may be particularly relevant to the capital budgeting decision process in a MNC.

In this latter respect, much empirical work has confirmed that capital budgeting decision making (both national and international) is a complex organisational decision process (Pinches 1982). Pinches when reviewing this literature notes that many phases could be identified in this decision making process. He employs a simple four stage model which consists of identification of areas of investment opportunity, development of various projects, selection or choosing of one or more of the projects, and finally control or evaluation of the performance of the approved projects. Such phases typically occur sequentially but there is no reason to believe they always do so. The first three stages of Pinches phase model are relevant to the choice of the overseas expansion mode and these are adopted in the rest of this article to guide the global strategic analysis of overseas expansion opportunities.

IDENTIFICATION OF OVERSEAS CAPITAL BUDGETING PROJECTS

The identification of areas for overseas expansion and the assessment of the strength and persistence of the factors underlying them is the essential first step in capital budgeting. From a finance perspective this first step is concerned with pinpointing positive APV overseas projects which maximise shareholder wealth (SWM). Unfortunately, finance theory is less than clear on how managers might identify positive APV projects (Brealey and Myers 1981, p. 736). Recent work by Shapiro (1985) and Martin and Kensinger (1988) provide some insight on how this might be done. However, Dunning's (1979) work on the eclectic theory of international production is particularly valuable in identifying how combinations of ownership specific, location specific and internalisation advantages create valuable overseas investment opportunities. It can therefore be used to give detailed guidance to the above search.

The key strategic questions to be asked of OLI theory can be simply stated as follows.

At the Industry Level:

What are the specific OLI advantages held by, or accessible to, most firms in the industry? Thus firms in the world banking industry are expected to have different OLI advantages to firms in say the global car industry.

What are the OLI advantages necessary for an overseas presence in specific market sectors or niches? In the banking industry the OLI advantages may differ between the corporate banking market and the retail banking market. In a similar fashion, differences may exist for global car firms in ownership, locational, and internalisation advantages between their truck and car markets.

At the Level of the Firm:

What specific OLI advantages are held by the firm (or more specifically, its strategic business units) or are only obtainable by the firm?

What specific OLI advantages are held by the firm's major competitors or are only obtainable by these competitors? In particular, how are these likely to contribute to the erection or maintenance of entry or exit barriers for the firm in specific markets?

Answers to the above questions can provide considerable guidance to a global search for positive APV overseas investment projects. Such a systematic global search would include the identification of all major markets in which demand for the company's products are expected to grow. This could be followed by an assessment of the strength and persistence of growth in these markets. Finally forecasting the likely actions of competitors in these markets and the analysis of barriers to entry and exit in specific markets is crucial to a global capital budgeting plan and corporate strategy.

DISTINGUISHING BETWEEN TYPES OF PROJECT

The major categories of overseas involvement are direct foreign investment, licensing and exporting opportunities. Step two of the global investment strategy is concerned with distinguishing between these various forms of capital budgeting project. The eclectic theory is helpful here in that it shows that the absence or presence of certain advantages changes the strategic options open to the firm. If internalisation and location advantages do not exist, but ownership specific advantages are present then licensing or other forms of contractual resource transfer are the only feasible means to expand abroad. If locational advantages are absent, but ownership and internalisation advantages are present, then exporting is a feasible route for servicing the overseas market. If all three advantages are available to the MNC, then direct foreign investment is a feasible strategic option. If one of the ownership, locational, or internalisation advantages is expected to be eroded or completely lost, then disinvestment may be necessary. Licensing or exporting may therefore replace direct foreign investment as the current mode of economic involvement in a country.

EVALUATION OF PROJECTS— THE ROLE OF THE APV MODEL

Once the direct foreign investment, disinvestment, licencing, and exporting options have been identified, they can be defined as different capital budgeting projects and their unique cash flows identified. This, the third step in the global strategy involves evaluating each overseas expansion choice using the adjusted present value rule to assess whether the opportunities uncovered are expected to increase shareholder wealth. The most satisfactory set of projects can therefore form the basis of a tentative financial plan. The basic data for the APV analysis can be generated by analysing the impact of ownership, locational and internalisation factors on the incremental cash flows expected by the parent for licencing, exporting and foreign direct investment projects and for other hybrid forms of overseas involvement.

INCORPORATING POLITICAL RISK ANALYSIS

The simple strategic procedure outlined above can be extended to include corporate assessments of political risk in each step of the above analysis. The major difficulty in this approach lies in the poor conceptual link between analysis of political changes and the identification of events likely to impinge upon the firm and its investment projects (Kobrin 1979). Despite this problem, an attempt to explicitly identify the possible impact of political events on the firm, is a superior strategy to one in which political events are assumed away or only partially incorporated in the decision process. In the first step of the capital budgeting decision procedure, involving search for overseas opportunities, political risk analysis can help identify both the origin of certain market imperfections, and the role of governments in their maintenance. In step 2, information on governmental attitudes concerning certain kinds of MNC involvement can be crucial in the assessment of the political feasibility of direct foreign investment, licencing, or exporting options. International banking is a classic example of such political interference changing the strategic options open to the multinational bank. Most barriers to entry and exit in domestic banking systems are government created. It may not be possible to chose any of the above forms of overseas expansion when dealing with certain domestic banking markets. The multinational bank may therefore prefer to offer banking services to customers in these segmented markets via offshore facilities. Finally, political risks considered to be unsystematic in nature can be identified, and adjustments made in step 3 to expected cash flows to reflect the risks. No changes are made to the discount rate, be-

cause these events are not expected to alter the systematic risks of the project.

The capital budgeting procedure outlined above can be used to co-ordinate direct foreign investment, licencing and exporting aspects of capital budgeting planning in the MNC. It is based upon the 'best state of the art' theories concerning the economic behaviour of MNCs and it explicitly incorporates political risk analysis throughout the complete strategic analysis. It also uses well established concepts of finance in the form of the APV rule for the evaluation of projects, and the major output of the procedure is a tentative schedule of planned investment projects. This is a major portion of the capital budgeting planning exercise and a key source of data for planning foreign exchange exposure and financial decisions. Given the increased globalisation of world markets MNCs will inevitably move towards such a global strategy and devote scarce resources to the overseas investment decision. A decision to organise the capital budgeting decision area employing the best elements of theory and practice is therefore essential for the MNC.

SUMMARY

This article has been primarily concerned with the unique international aspects of capital budgeting planning. The basic framework employed in this article has drawn from domestic finance theory adapted to the international context of the MNC. The limitations of orthodox finance theory has been recognised and strategic analysis has been used to provide an alternative, complementary source of guidance for international capital budgeting. This intended to stimulate an iterative interchange of information and ideas between the capital budgeting and strategic planning. It may release finance from its relative isolation from other developments in corporate decision theory and allow the unique insights of finance to be exploited on a wider stage.

REFERENCES

Bartlett, C.A., ''MNCs: get off the reorganization merry-go-round,'' *Harvard Business Review,* March/April, 1983, pp. 138–146.

Booth, L.D., ''Capital Budgeting frameworks for the Multinational corporation,'' *Journal of International Business Studies,* Fall 1982, p. 11.

Brealey, R., Myers, S., *Principles of Corporate Finance,* McGraw Hill, 1981.

Dunning, J.H., ''Explaining Changing Patterns of International Production: In Defence of the Eclectic Theory,'' *Oxford Bulletin of Economics and Statistics,* Nov. 1979, pp. 269–295.

Holland, J.B., *International Financial Management,* Basil Blackwell, 1986, Oxford and London.

Kobrin, S.J., ''Political Risk: A Review and Reconsideration,'' *Journal of International Business Studies,* Spring/Summer, 1979, pp. 67–80.

Lessard, D., ''Evaluating international projects: An adjusted present value approach,'' Chapter 6 *Capital Budgeting under conditions of uncertainty,* Ed. R.L. Crum, F.G. Derkinderen, Martinus Nijhof Publishing, 1981.

Martin, J., Kensinger, J., ''The evolving role of strategy-considerations in the theory and practice of finance,'' *Managerial Finance,* Vol. 14, No. 2/3 1988, pp. 9–15.

Myers, S.C., ''Interactions of corporate financing and investment decisions—Implications for capital budgeting,'' *Journal of Finance,* Vol. 29, March 1974, pp. 1–25.

Myers, S.C., ''Reply,'' *Journal of Finance,* Vol. 32, March 1977, pp. 218–220.

Myers, S.C., ''Finance theory and Financial Strategy,'' pp. 177–188, Chapter in *Readings in Strategic Management,* edited by Arnoldo Hax, Ballinger Publishing Co., Cambridge, Mass., 1984.

McInnes, J.M., Carleton, W.J., ''Theory, Models and Implementation on Financial Management,'' *Management Science,* Vol. 28, No. 9, Sept. 1982, pp. 957–978.

Pinches, G.E., ''Myopia, Capital Budgeting and Decision Making,'' *Financial Management,* Autumn 1982, pp. 6–19.

Shapiro, A., *Multinational Financial Management,* Allyn and Bacon, Boston, 3rd edition, 1989.

Shapiro, A., ''Capital Budgeting for the Multinational Corporation,'' *Financial Management,* Spring 1978, pp. 7–16.

Shapiro, A., ''Corporate Strategy and the Capital Budgeting decision,'' *Midland Corporate Finance Journal,* Spring 1985.

Wilson, M., ''An empirical investigation of the use of a conceptual framework of risk and return in international capital budgeting by United Kingdom based Multinationals.'' Paper present at September 1988 meeting of the British Accounting Association Group Northern Accounting Group Conference.

SECTION 9

ORGANIZATION AND HUMAN RESOURCES MANAGEMENT

As global corporations shed the cultural perspective of headquarters and become more homogeneous, they are adopting global management cultures that more fully encompass their subsidiaries. We might expect managers of these companies to feel equally at home in their Japanese, French, Indonesian, or U.S. operations. We might also expect them increasingly to adopt culture-free human resource policies.

In fact, one's own national culture is an astonishingly powerful factor in multinational and even global management. No matter how large a company becomes or in how many national environments it operates, cultural factors will have a profound impact. Culture can be defined as "that complex whole which includes knowledge, belief, art, morals, law, customs and any capabilities and habits acquired by man [and woman] as a member of society."[1] Some components of culture are attitudes, religion, education, norms, social organization, language, and community organization. Geert Hofstede calls culture "a selective programming of the mind."[2]

People in a particular culture think, feel, and react in patterned ways and have a collective personality. Global managers must understand the critical elements of headquarters' culture, their own home-country culture, and the culture of the host-country in which they and their subsidiary managers operate. Headquarters' strategy still determines how and to what extent home and host-country managers interact. The nature of products, difference in customer preferences, employee relations, legal requirements, and financial arrangements are all part of strategy. Headquarters' national and corporate culture may profoundly affect the management of one subsidiary firm but may have little relevance to another.

Managers of global firms should seek to maximize the positive interaction of national and corporate cultural elements. Managerial skills, attitudes, and commitments must fit the firm's global strategy. Even when managers try to treat the firm as a single unit with overall planning, objective setting, and goal implementation, they cannot ignore

---

[1] Edward B. Taylor, "Primitive Culture," in Vern Terpstra, *The Cultural Environment of International Business* (Cincinnati, OH: Southwestern, 1978), p. xii.

[2] Geert Hofstede, *Culture's Consequences* (Beverly Hills, CA: Sage Publications, 1980), p. 13.

481

cultural differences. Most firms work out their own combination of host and home policies and use them to foster the most effective use of their resources.

The four articles in this section cover important aspects of making a global organization function effectively. The articles' usefulness, however, is not by any means limited to managing global organizations. Any firm with a foreign subsidiary, or even with a foreign independent subsidiary, can benefit from the material in this section. In fact, any firm with foreign customers or suppliers will find the information in this section enlightening.

READING SELECTIONS

Geert Hofstede reminds us of the important role national cultures play in determining the way organizations from different countries function. Drawing upon extensive empirical work in over 50 countries, he identifies five dimensions of national culture: power distance; individualism versus collectivism; masculinity versus femininity; uncertainty avoidance; and long-term versus short-term orientation. He then presents examples of how national cultural differences can affect some popular management theories.

Hofstede also presents findings from a two-country study of organizational, rather than national, culture. That study identifies six independent dimensions of organizational culture that can be used to describe most of the variety in organizational practices. Two important questions arise from these two studies. The first, of course, is how do national cultures interact with, influence, or determine organizational cultures? A second, perhaps more intriguing, question may be whether observed differences in national cultures are as pervasive or as important as they might have been in the past, especially within organizations.

Many more managers have had experiences with national cultures other than their own than was the case several years ago. Around the world, growing numbers of managers are being exposed to a North American model of business education using teaching materials written in English. Business education is a process of socialization as well as a process of teaching principles and techniques. Are universities and business schools educating a generation of managers from different national cultures who are becoming homogenized as the result of exposure to a common perspective?

Christopher Bartlett and Sumantra Ghoshal ask what is a global manager. They conclude that a global manager is a network of specialists rather than a single individual. They describe the jobs of four types of specialists: business managers, country managers, functional managers, and corporate managers. Each of these specialist types can be found in many global corporations, and each must perform his or her work effectively for the corporation to be effectively managed as a whole. In the course of a career with a global corporation, the aspiring corporate manager will most likely have to pass through a series of different specialist jobs. This article, in addition to providing insights into the management of global firms, is also useful as a tool for career planning.

Ran Lachman, Albert Nedd, and Bob Hinings present a framework for analyzing cross-national management and organizations. Their framework considers the effect of cultural values on the behavior of individuals in the firm. The reader may want to think about the interplay of national cultural values and business culture values (derived from a business education).

The Lachman, Nedd, and Hinings framework goes beyond culture and includes economic as well as human resource availability as a determinant of organization effectiveness. The authors view cultural values as influencing role perception and behavior, and view economic resource availability as influencing organizational structure and process. In their model, the effective organization will have integrated role perceptions and behavior with organizational structure and process.

Y.L. Doz and C.K. Prahalad review several theories that have been promulgated to increase our understanding of and ability to practice management in multinational firms. Among the theories they examine are economic organization, environmental adaptation, power relationships and organizational adaptation, and organizational learning. They point out the strengths and weaknesses of each approach and conclude, not surprisingly, that none is wholly adequate.

Doz and Prahalad lay out a series of conditions that a workable theory must meet. Their key propositions are that we must look at both the substance and process of satisfying conflicting demands as a whole rather than examining each element separately. They also assert that the unit of analysis we should use is the individual manager rather than aggregates of managers. If we look at the totality of each of the specialist jobs outlined in the Bartlett and Ghoshal article, would it help us better understand the *gestalt* of managing a multinational firm?

34

THE BUSINESS OF INTERNATIONAL BUSINESS IS CULTURE

GEERT HOFSTEDE

Organizational Anthropology and International Management,
University of Limburg and Maastricht, The Netherlands

ABSTRACT   National cultures are distinguished from organizational cultures. The first have been studied from over 50 countries, and described with the help of five dimensions. The differences shown set limits to the validity of management theories across borders. Special attention is paid to characteristics of East Asian cultures that help explain the recent economic success of these countries. Organizational cultures were studied across 20 organizational units in Denmark and the Netherlands; this research identified six dimensions of organizational cultures. The findings lead to a number of suggestions for the management of organizational cultures. Managing international business means handling both national and organizational culture differences at the same time. Organizational cultures are somewhat manageable while national cultures are given facts for management; common organizational cultures across borders are what keeps multinationals together.

CULTURE DEFINED

Management is getting things done through (other) people. This is true the world over. In order to achieve this, one has to know the "things" to be done, and one has to know the people who have to do them. Understanding people means understanding their background, from which present and future behavior can be predicted. Their background has provided them with a certain culture. The word "culture" is used here in the sense of "the collective programming of the mind which distinguishes the members of one category of people from another." The "category of people" can be a nation, region, or ethnic group (national etc. culture), women versus men (gender culture), old versus young (age group and generation culture), a social class, a profession or occupation (occupational culture), a type of business, a work organization or part of it (organizational culture), or even a family.

NATIONAL CULTURE DIFFERENCES

In three different research projects, one among subsidiaries of a multinational corporation (IBM) in 64 countries and the other two among students in 10 and 23 countries, respectively, altogether five dimensions of national culture differences were identified (Hofstede, 1980, 1983, 1986, 1991; Hofstede and Bond, 1984, 1988; The Chinese Culture Connection, 1987):

(1) POWER DISTANCE

This is the extent to which the less powerful members of organizations and institutions (like the fam-

ily) accept and expect that power is distributed unequally. This represents inequality (more versus less), but defined from below, not from above. It suggests that a society's level of inequality is endorsed by the followers as much as by the leaders. Power and inequality, of course, are extremely fundamental facts of any society and anybody with some international experience will be aware that "all societies are unequal, but some are more unequal than others."

Table 1 lists some of the differences in the family, the school, and the work situation between small and large power distance cultures. The statements refer to extremes; actual situations may be found anywhere in between the extremes. People's behavior in the work situation is strongly affected by their previous experiences in the family and in the school: the expectations and fears about the boss are projections of the experiences with the father—or mother—and the teachers. In order to understand superiors, colleagues and subordinates in another country we have to know something about families and schools in that country.

(2) INDIVIDUALISM VERSUS COLLECTIVISM

Individualism on the one side versus its opposite, collectivism, is the degree to which individuals are integrated into groups. On the individualist side, we find societies in which the ties between individuals are loose: everyone is expected to look after him/herself and his/her immediate family. On the collectivist side, we find societies in which people from birth onwards are integrated into strong, cohesive in-groups, often extended families (with uncles, aunts and grandparents) which continue protecting them in exchange for unquestioning loyalty. The word "collectivism" in this sense has no political meaning: it refers to the group, not to the state. Again, the issue addressed by this dimension is an extremely fundamental one, regarding all societies in the world.

Table 2 lists some of the differences between collectivist and individualist cultures; most real cultures will be somewhere in between these extremes. The words "particularism" and "universalism" in Table 2 are common sociological categories (Parsons and Shils, 1951, 1977). Particularism is a way of thinking

The author is emeritus professor of Organizational Anthropology and International Management, University of Limburg at Maastricht and also Senior Research Associate, IRIC (Institute for Research of Intercultural Cooperation). This article is a summary of Geert Hofstede's book *Cultures and Organizations: Software of the Mind* (1991, McGraw-Hill, London).
Key Words—National Cultures, Organizational Cultures.

TABLE 1. Distances According to Power Distance

Small Power Distance Societies	Large Power Distance Societies
In the family:	
Children encouraged to have a will of their own	Children educated towards obedience to parents
Parents treated as equals	Parents treated as superiors
At school:	
Student-centered education (initiative)	Teacher-centered education (order)
Learning represents impersonal "truth"	Learning represents personal "wisdom" from teacher (guru)
At the work place:	
Hierarchy means an inequality of roles, established for convenience	Hierarchy means existential inequality
Subordinates expect to be consulted	Subordinates expect to be told what to do
Ideal boss is resourceful democrat	Ideal boss is benevolent autocrat (good father)

in which the standards for the way a person should be treated depend on the group or category to which this person belongs. Universalism is a way of thinking in which the standards for the way a person should be treated are the same for everybody.

(3) MASCULINITY VERSUS FEMININITY

Masculinity versus its opposite, femininity, refers to the distribution of roles between the sexes which is another fundamental issue for any society to which a range of solutions are found. The IBM studies revealed that: (a) women's values differ less among societies than men's values: (b) men's values from one country to another contain a dimension from very assertive and competitive and maximally different from women's values on the one side, to modest and caring and similar to women's values on the other. The assertive pole has been called "masculine" and the modest, caring pole "feminine." The

TABLE 2. Differences According to Collectivism/Individualism

Collectivist Societies	Individualist Societies
In the family:	
Education towards "we" consciousness	Education towards "I" consciousness
Opinions pre-determined by group	Private opinion expected
Obligations to family or in-group:	Obligations to self:
—harmony	—self-interest
—respect	—self-actualization
—shame	—guilt
At school:	
Learning is for the young only	Permanent education
Learn how to do	Learn how to learn
At the work place:	
Value standards differ for in-group and out-groups: particularism	Same value standards apply to all: universalism
Other people are seen as members of their group	Other people seen as potential resources
Relationship prevails over task	Task prevails over relationship
Moral model of employer–employee relationship	Calculative model employer–employee relationship

TABLE 3. Differences According to Femininity/Masculinity

Feminine Societies	Masculine Societies
In the family:	
Stress on relationships	Stress on achievement
Solidarity	Competition
Resolution of conflicts by compromise and negotiation	Resolution of conflicts by fighting them out
At school:	
Average student is norm	Best students are norm
System rewards students' social adaptation	System rewards students' academic performance
Student's failure at school is relatively minor accident	Student's failure at school is disaster—may lead to suicide
At the work place:	
Assertiveness ridiculed	Assertiveness appreciated
Undersell yourself	Oversell yourself
Stress on life quality	Stress on careers
Intuition	Decisiveness

women in feminine countries have the same modest, caring values as the men; in the masculine countries they are somewhat assertive and competitive, but not as much as the men, so that these countries show a gap between men's values and women's values.

Table 3 lists some of the differences in the family, the school, and the work place, between the most feminine versus the most masculine cultures, in analogy to Tables 1 and 2.

(4) UNCERTAINTY AVOIDANCE

Uncertainty avoidance as a fourth dimension was found in the IBM studies and in one of the two student studies. It deals with a society's tolerance for uncertainty and ambiguity: it ultimately refers to man's search for truth. It indicates to what extent a culture programs its members to feel either uncomfortable or comfortable in unstructured situations. Unstructured situations are novel, unknown, surprising and different from usual. Uncertainty avoiding cultures try to minimize the possibility of such situations by strict laws and rules, safety and security measures, and on the philosophical and religious level by a belief in absolute truth; "there can only be one truth and we have it." People in uncertainty avoiding countries are also more emotional, and mo-

tivated by inner nervous energy. The opposite type, uncertainty accepting cultures, are more tolerant of opinions different from what they are used to; they try to have as few rules as possible, and on the philosophical and religious level they are relativist and allow many currents to flow side by side. People within these cultures are more phlegmatic and contemplative, and not expected by their environment to express emotions.

Table 4 lists some of the differences in the family, the school, and the workplace, between weak and strong uncertainty avoidance cultures.

(5) LONG TERM VERSUS SHORT TERM ORIENTATION

This fifth dimension was found in a study among students in 23 countries around the world, using a questionnaire designed by Chinese scholars (The Chinese Culture Connection, 1987). It can be said to deal with Virtue regardless of Truth. Values associated with long term orientation are thrift and perseverance; values associated with short term orientation are respect for tradition, fulfilling social obligations, and protecting one's "face." Both the positively and the negatively rated values of this dimension remind us of the teachings of Confucius

TABLE 4. Differences According to Uncertainty Avoidance

Weak Uncertainty Avoidance Societies	Strong Uncertainty Avoidance Societies
In the family:	
What is different, is ridiculous or curious	What is different, is dangerous
Ease, indolence, low stress	Higher anxiety and stress
Aggression and emotions not shown	Showing of aggression and emotions accepted
At school:	
Students comfortable with:	Students comfortable with:
—Unstructured learning situations	—Structured learning situations
—Vague objectives	—Precise objectives
—Broad assignments	—Detailed assignments
—No time tables	—Strict time tables
Teachers may say ''I don't know''	Teachers should have all the answers
At the work place:	
Dislike of rules—written or unwritten	Emotional need for rules—written or unwritten
Less formalization and standardization	More formalization and standardization

(King and Bond, 1985). It was originally called ''Confucian dynamism;'' however, the dimension also applies to countries without a Confucian heritage.

There has been insufficient research as yet on the implications of differences along this dimension to allow the composition of a table of differences in the family, the school and the work place similar to those for the other four dimensions (Tables 1–4).

Scores on the first four dimensions were obtained for 50 countries and three regions on the basis of the IBM study, and on the fifth dimension for 23 countries on the basis of the student data collected by Bond *et al*. All scores have been transformed to a scale from approximately 0 for the lowest scoring country to approximately 100 for the highest. Table 5 shows the scores for twelve countries. For the full list the reader is referred to Hofstede (1991).

Power distance scores tend to be high for Latin, Asian and African countries and smaller for Germanic countries. Individualism prevails in developed and Western countries, while collectivism prevails in less developed and Eastern countries; Japan takes a middle position on this dimension. Masculinity is high in Japan, in some European countries like Germany, Austria and Switzerland, and moderately high in Anglo countries; it is low in Nordic countries and in The Netherlands and moderately low in some

Latin and Asian countries like France, Spain and Thailand. Uncertainty avoidance scores are higher in Latin countries, in Japan, and in German speaking countries, lower in Anglo, Nordic, and Chinese culture countries. A long term orientation is mostly found in East Asian countries, in particular in China, Hong Kong, Taiwan, Japan, and South Korea.

The grouping of country scores points to some of the roots of cultural differences. These should be sought in the common history of similarly scoring countries. All Latin countries, for example, score relatively high on both power distance and uncertainty avoidance. Latin countries (those today speaking a Romance language, i.e. Spanish, Portuguese, French or Italian) have inherited at least part of their civilization from the Roman empire. The Roman empire in its days was characterized by the existence of a central authority in Rome, and a system of law applicable to citizens anywhere. This established in its citizens' minds the value complex which we still recognize today: centralization fostered large power distance and a stress on laws fostered strong uncertainty avoidance. The Chinese empire also knew centralization, but it lacked a fixed system of laws: it was governed by men rather than by laws. In the present-day countries once under Chinese rule, the mindset fostered by the empire is reflected in large power distance but medium to weak uncertainty

TABLE 5. Scores of 12 Countries on Five Dimensions of National Cultures

Country	Power Distance		Individualism		Masculinity		Uncertainty Avoidance		Long Term Orientation	
	Index	Rank	Index	Rank	Index	Rank	Index	Rank	Index	Rank
Brazil	69	14	38	26–27	49	27	76	21–22	65	6
France	68	15–16	71	10–11	43	35–36	86	10–15	no data	
Germany	35	42–44	67	15	66	9–10	65	29	31	14–15
Great Britain	35	42–44	89	3	66	9–10	35	47–48	25	18–19
Hong Kong	68	15–16	25	37	57	18–19	29	49–50	96	2
India	77	10–11	48	21	56	20–21	40	45	61	7
Japan	54	33	46	22–23	95	1	92	7	80	4
The Netherlands	38	40	80	4–5	14	51	53	35	44	10
Sweden	31	47–48	71	10–11	5	53	29	49–50	33	12
Thailand	64	21–23	20	39–41	34	44	64	30	56	8
USA	40	38	91	1	62	15	46	43	29	17
Venezuela	81	5–6	12	50	73	3	76	21–22	no data	

Ranks: 1 = highest, 53 = lowest (for long term orientation, 23 = lowest).

avoidance. The Germanic part of Europe, including Great Britain, never succeeded in establishing an enduring common central authority and countries which inherited its civilizations show smaller power distance. Assumptions about historical roots of cultural differences always remain speculative but in the given examples they are quite plausible. In other cases they remain hidden in the course of history (Hofstede, 1980, pp. 127, 179, 235, 294).

The country scores on the five dimensions are statistically correlated with a multitude of other data about the countries. For example, power distance is correlated with the use of violence in domestic politics and with income inequality in a country. Individualism is correlated with national wealth (per capita gross national product) and with mobility between social classes from one generation to the next. Masculinity is correlated negatively with the share of gross national product that governments of wealthy countries spend on development assistance to the Third World. Uncertainty avoidance is associated with Roman Catholicism and with the legal obligation in developed countries for citizens to carry identity cards. Long term orientation is correlated with national economic growth during the past 25 years, showing that what led to the economic success of the East Asian economies in this period is their populations' cultural stress on the future-oriented values of thrift and perseverance.

THE CULTURAL LIMITS OF MANAGEMENT THEORIES

The culture of a country affects its parents and its children, teachers and students, labour union leaders and members, politicians and citizens, journalists and readers, managers and subordinates. Therefore management practices in a country are culturally dependent, and what works in one country does not necessarily work in another. However not only the managers are human and children of their culture; the management teachers, the people who wrote and still write theories and create management concepts, are also human and constrained by the cultural environment in which they grew up and which they know. Such theories and concepts cannot be applied in another country without further proof; if applicable at all, it is often only after considerable adaptation. Four examples follow.

(1) PERFORMANCE APPRAISAL SYSTEMS

These are recommended in the Western management literature. They assume that employees' performance will be improved if they receive direct feedback about what their superior thinks of them, which may well be the case in individualist cultures. However, in collectivist countries such direct feedback destroys the harmony which is expected to govern interpersonal relationships. It may cause irreparable damage to the employee's ''face'' and ruin his or her loyalty to the organization. In such cultures, including all East Asian and Third World countries, feedback should rather be given indirectly, for example through the withdrawing of a favor, or via an intermediary person trusted by both superior and employee.

(2) MANAGEMENT BY OBJECTIVES

Management by Objectives (MBO) is a management concept developed in the USA. Under a system of MBO, subordinates have to negotiate about their objectives with their superiors. The system therefore assumes a cultural environment in which issues can be settled by negotiation rather than rules, which means a medium to low power distance and a not too high uncertainty avoidance. In the German environment it had to be adapted to the more structured culture of a stronger uncertainty avoidance; it became ''Führung durch Zielvereinbarung'' which is much more formal than the US model (Ferguson, 1973).

(3) STRATEGIC MANAGEMENT

This is a concept also developed in the USA. It assumes a weak uncertainty avoidance environment, in which deviant strategic ideas are encouraged. Although it is taught in countries with a stronger uncertainty avoidance, like Germany or France, its recommendations are rarely followed there, because in these cultures it is seen as the top managers' role to remain involved in daily operations (Horovitz, 1980).

(4) HUMANIZATION OF WORK

This is a general term for a number of approaches in different countries trying to make work more interesting and rewarding for the people who do it. In the USA, which is a masculine and individualist society, the prevailing form of humanization of work has been ''job enrichment:'' giving individual tasks more intrinsic content. In Sweden which is feminine and less individualist, the prevailing form has been

the development of semi-autonomous work groups, in which members exchange tasks and help each other (Gohl, 1977). In Germany and German-speaking Switzerland the introduction of flexible working hours has been a very popular way of adapting the job to the worker. Flexible working hours have never become as popular in other countries; their popularity in German-speaking countries can be understood by the combination of a small power distance (acceptance of responsibility by the worker) with a relatively large uncertainty avoidance (internalization of rules).

EASTERN VERSUS WESTERN CATEGORIES OF THINKING

A study of students' values in 23 countries using a questionnaire designed by Chinese scholars (the Chinese Value Survey, CVS) produced partly similar, but partly different results from the two other studies (among 64 IBM subsidiaries and among students in 10 countries) which used questionnaires designed by Western (European and American, respectively) minds. The CVS study did not identify a dimension like uncertainty avoidance, which deals with the search for truth. It seems that to the Chinese minds who designed the questions the search for truth is not an essential issue, so the questions necessary to identify this dimension were not included in their questionnaire.

One of the basic differences between Eastern thinking (represented by, for example Confucianism, Buddhism, and Hinduism) and Western thinking (dominant in the Judaeo-Christian-Muslim intellectual tradition) is that in the East, a qualification does not exclude its opposite, which is an essential element of Western logic (Kapp, 1983). Thus in the East the search for truth is irrelevant, because there is no need for a single and absolute truth and the assumption that a person can possess an objective truth is absent. Instead, the Eastern instrument includes the questions necessary to detect the dimension of long versus short term orientation expressing a concern for virtue: for proper ways of living (like, practising perseverance and thrift, or respecting tradition and social obligations) which is less obvious in the West where virtue tends to be derived from truth.

These findings show that not only practices, values and theories, but even the categories available to build theories from are products of culture. This has far-reaching consequences for management training in a multicultural organization. Not only our tools, but even the categories in which we think, may be unfit for the other environment.

ORGANIZATIONAL CULTURES

The use of the term ''culture'' in the management literature is not limited to the national level: attributing a distinct culture to a company or organization has become extremely popular. However, organizational cultures are a phenomenon of a different order from national cultures, if only because membership of an organization is usually partial and voluntary, while the ''membership'' of a nation is permanent and involuntary. Our field research to be described below showed that national cultures differ mostly at the level of basic values while organizational cultures differ mostly at the level of the more superficial practices: symbols, heroes, and rituals.

In the popular management literature, organization cultures have often been presented as a matter of values (e.g., Peters and Waterman, 1982). The confusion arises because this literature does not distinguish between the values of the founders and leaders and those of the ordinary employees. Founders and leaders create the symbols, the heroes and the rituals that constitute the daily practices of the organization's members. However, members have to adapt their personal values to the organization's needs, to a limited extent only. A work organization, as a rule, is not a ''total institution'' like a prison or a mental hospital. Precisely because organizational cultures are composed of practices rather than values, they are somewhat manageable: they can be managed by changing the practices. The values of employees cannot be changed by an employer, because they were acquired when the employers were children. However, sometimes an employer can activate latent values which employees were not allowed

to show earlier: like a desire for initiative and creativity, by allowing practices which before were forbidden.

DIMENSIONS OF ORGANIZATIONAL CULTURES

A research project similar to the IBM studies but focusing on organizational rather than national cultures was carried out by the Institute for Research on Intercultural Cooperation (IRIC) in The Netherlands. Data were collected in twenty work organizations or parts of organizations in The Netherlands and Denmark. The units studied varied from a toy manufacturing company to two municipal police corps. As mentioned above the study found large differences among units in practices (symbols, heroes, rituals) but only modest differences in values, beyond those due to such basic facts as nationality, education, gender and age group.

Six independent dimensions can be used to describe most of the variety in organizational practices. These six dimensions can be used as a framework to describe organizational cultures, but their research base in 20 units from two countries is too narrow to consider them as universally valid. For describing organizational cultures in other countries and in other types of organizations, additional dimensions may be necessary or some of the six may be less useful (see also Pümpin, 1984). The dimensions of organizational cultures found are:

(1) PROCESS-ORIENTED VERSUS RESULTS-ORIENTED CULTURES

The former are dominated by technical and bureaucratic routines, the latter by a common concern for outcomes. This dimension was associated with the culture's degree of homogeneity: in results-oriented units, everybody perceived their practices in about the same way; in process-oriented units, there were vast differences in perception among different levels and parts of the unit. The degree of homogeneity of a culture is a measure of its ''strength:'' the study confirmed that strong cultures are more results-oriented than weak ones, and vice versa (Peters and Waterman, 1982).

(2) JOB-ORIENTED VERSUS EMPLOYER-ORIENTED CULTURES

The former assume responsibility for the employees' job performance only, and nothing more; employee-oriented cultures assume a broad responsibility for their members' well-being. At the level of individual managers, the distinction between job orientation and employee orientation has been popularized by Blake and Mouton's Managerial Grid (1964). The IRIC study shows that job versus employee orientation is part of a culture and not (only) a choice for an individual manager. A unit's position on this dimension seems to be largely the result of historical factors, like the philosophy of its founder(s) and the presence or absence in its recent history of economic crises with collective layoffs.

(3) PROFESSIONAL VERSUS PAROCHIAL CULTURES

In the former, the usually highly educated members identify primarily with their profession; in the latter, the members derive their identity from the organization for which they work. Sociology has long known this dimension as local versus cosmopolitan, the contrast between an internal and an external frame of reference, first suggested by Tönnies (1887).

(4) OPEN SYSTEM VERSUS CLOSED SYSTEM CULTURES

This dimension refers to the common style of internal and external communication, and to the ease with which outsiders and newcomers are admitted. This dimension is the only one of the six for which there is a systematic difference between Danish and Dutch units. It seems that organizational openness is a societal characteristic of Denmark, much more so than of The Netherlands. This shows that organizational cultures also reflect national culture differences.

(5) TIGHTLY VERSUS LOOSELY CONTROLLED CULTURES

This dimension deals with the degree of formality and punctuality within the organization; it is partly a function of the unit's technology: banks and pharmaceutical companies can be expected to show tight control, research laboratories and advertising agencies loose control; but even with the same technology, units still differ on this dimension.

(6) PRAGMATIC VERSUS NORMATIVE CULTURES

The last dimension describes the prevailing way (flexible or rigid) of dealing with the environment, in particular with customers. Units selling services are likely to be found towards the pragmatic (flexible) side, units involved in the application of legal rules towards the normative (rigid) side. This dimension measures the degree of "customer orientation," which is a highly popular topic in the management literature.

MANAGING ORGANIZATIONAL CULTURES

In spite of their relatively superficial nature organizational cultures are hard to change because they have developed into collective habits. Changing them is a top management task which cannot be delegated. Some kind of culture assessment by an independent party is usually necessary, which includes the identification of different subcultures which may need quite different approaches. The top management's major strategic choice is either to accept and optimally use the existing culture or to try to change it. If an attempt at change is made it should be preceded by a cost–benefit analysis. A particular concern is whether the manpower necessary for a culture change is available.

Turning around an organizational culture demands visible leadership which appeals to the employees' feelings as much as to their intellect. The leader or leaders should assure themselves of sufficient support from key persons at different levels in the organization. Subsequently, they can change the practices by adapting the organization's structure—its functions, departments, locations, and tasks—matching tasks with employee talents. After the structure, the controls may have to be changed, based on a decision on which aspects of the work have to be co-ordinated how and by whom at what level. At the same time it is usually necessary to change certain personnel policies related to recruitment, training and promotion. Finally, turning around a culture is not a one-shot process. It takes sustained attention from top management, persistence for several years, and usually a second culture assessment to see whether the intended changes have, indeed, been attained.

MANAGING CULTURE DIFFERENCES IN MULTINATIONALS

Many multinational corporations do not only operate in different countries but also in different lines of business or at least in different product/market divisions. Different business lines and/or divisions often have different organizational cultures. Strong cross-national organizational cultures within a business line or division, by offering common practices, can bridge national differences in values among organization members. Common practices, not common values, keep multinationals together.

Structure should follow culture: the purpose of an organization structure is the coordination of activities. For the design of the structure of a multinational, multibusiness corporation, three questions have to be answered for each business unit (a business unit represents one business line in one country). The three questions are: (a) which of the unit's in- and outputs should be coordinated from elsewhere in the corporation? (b) where and at what level should the coordination take place? and (c) how tight or loose should the co-ordination be? In every case there is a basic choice between coordination along geographical lines and along business lines. The decisive factor is whether business know-how or na-

tional cultural know-how is more crucial for the success of the operation.

Matrix structures are a possible solution but they are costly, often meaning a doubling of the management ranks, and their actual functioning may raise more problems than they resolve. A single structural principle (geographic or business) is unlikely to fit for an entire corporation. Joint ventures further complicate the structuring problem. The optimal solution is nearly always a patchwork structure that in some cases follows business and in others geographical lines. This may lack beauty, but it follows the needs of markets and business unit cultures. Variety within the environment in which a corporation operates should be matched with appropriate internal variety. Optimal solutions will also change over time, so that the periodic reshufflings which any large organization undergoes, should be seen as functional.

Like all organizations, multinationals are held together by people. The best structure at a given moment depends primarily on the availability of suitable people. Two roles are particularly crucial: (a) country business unit managers who form the link between the culture of the business unit, and the corporate culture which is usually heavily affected by the nationality of origin of the corporation, and (b) "corporate diplomats," i.e., home country or other nationals who are impregnated with the corporate culture, multilingual, from various occupational backgrounds, and experienced in living and functioning in various foreign cultures. They are essential to make multinational structures work, as liaison persons in the various head offices or as temporary managers for new ventures.

The availability of suitable people at the right moment is the main task of multinational personnel management. This means timely recruiting of future managerial talent from different nationalities, and career moves through planned transfers where these people will absorb the corporate culture. Multinational personnel departments have to find their way between uniformity and diversity in personnel policies. Too much uniformity is unwarranted because people's mental programmes are not uniform. It leads to corporate-wide policies being imposed on subsidiaries where they will not work—or only receive lip service from obedient but puzzled locals. On the other side, the assumption that everybody is different and that people in subsidiaries therefore always should know best and be allowed to go their own ways, is unwarranted too. In this case an opportunity is lost to build a corporate culture with unique features which keep the organization together and provide it with a distinctive and competitive psychological advantage.

Increasing integration of organizations across national borders demands that managers have an insight in the extent to which familiar aspects of organizational life like organization structures, leadership styles, motivation patterns, and training and development models are culturally relative and need to be reconsidered when borders are crossed. It also calls for self-insight on the part of the managers involved, who have to be able to compare their ways of thinking, feeling and acting to those of others, without immediately passing judgment. This ability to see the relativity of one's own cultural framework does not come naturally to most managers, who often got to their present position precisely because they held strong convictions. Intercultural management skills can be improved by specific training; this should focus on working rather than on living in other countries. The stress in such courses is on recognizing one's own cultural programmes and where these may differ from those of people in other countries.

REFERENCES

Blake, R.R. and Mouton, J.S. (1964) *The Managerial Grid.* Gulf Publishing, Houston.

Ferguson, I.R.G. (1973) *Management By Objectives in Deutschland.* Herder and Herder, Frankfurt/Main.

Gohl, J. (Ed.) (1977) *Probleme der Humanisierungsdebatte.* Goldmann, München.

Hofstede, G. (1980) *Culture's Consequences: International Differences in Work-Related Values.* Sage Publications, Beverly Hills.

Hofstede, G. (1983) Dimensions of National Culture in Fifty Countries and Three Regions, in Deregowski, J.B., Dziurawiec, S. and Annis, R.C. (Eds), *Expiscations in Cross-Cultural Psychology,* pp. 335–355. Swets & Zeitlinger, Lisse, The Netherlands.

Hofstede, G. (1986) Cultural Differences in Teaching and Learning. *International Journal of Intercultural Relations,* Vol. 10, pp. 301–320.

Hofstede, G. (1991) *Cultures and Organizations: Software of the Mind.* McGraw Hill, London.

Hofstede, G. and Bond, M.H. (1984) Hofstede's Culture Dimensions: an Independent Validation Using Bokeach's Value Survey. *Journal of Cross-Cultural Psychology,* Vol. 15. pp. 417–433.

Hofstede, G. and Bond, M.H. (1988) The Confucius Connection: From Cultural Roots to Economic Growth. *Organizational Dynamics,* Vol. 16, No. 4, pp. 4–21.

Hofstede, G., Neuijen, B., Ohayv, D.D. and Sanders, G. (1990) Measuring Organizational Cultures. *Administrative Science Quarterly,* Vol. 35, pp. 286–316.

Horovitz, J.H. (1980) *Top Management Control in Europe.* Macmillan, London.

Kapp, R.A. (Ed.) (1983) *Communicating with China.* Intercultural Press, Chicago.

King, A.Y.C. and Bond, M.H. (1985) The Confucian Paradigm of Man: a Sociological View, in Tseng, W. and Wu, D. (Eds). *Chinese Culture and Mental Health,* pp. 29–45. Columbia University Press, New York.

Parsons, T. and Shils, E.A. (1951) *Toward a General Theory of Action.* Harvard University Press, Cambridge, Massachusetts.

Peters, T.J. and Waterman, R.H. (1982) *In Search of Excellence: Lessons from America's Best-Run Companies,* Harper & Row, New York.

Pümpin, C. (1984) Unternehmenskultur, Unternehmensstrategie und Unternehmenserfolg. *GDI Impuls,* Vol. 2, pp. 19–30.

The Chinese Culture Connection (1987) Chinese Values and the Search for Culture-free Dimensions of Culture. *Journal of Cross-Cultural Psychology,* Vol. 18, pp. 143–164.

Tönnies, F. [1963 (1887)] *Community and Society.* Harper & Row, New York.

35

WHAT IS A GLOBAL MANAGER?

CHRISTOPHER A. BARTLETT AND SUMANTRA GHOSHAL

In the early stages of its drive overseas, Corning Glass hired an American ex-ambassador to head up its international division. He had excellent contacts in the governments of many nations and could converse in several languages, but he was less familiar with Corning and its businesses. In contrast, ITT decided to set up a massive educational program to ''globalize'' all managers responsible for its worldwide telecommunications business—in essence, to replace its national specialists with global generalists.

Corning and ITT eventually realized they had taken wrong turns. Like many other companies organizing for worldwide operations in recent years, they found that an elite of jet-setters was often difficult to integrate into the corporate mainstream; nor did they need an international team of big-picture overseers to the exclusion of focused experts.

Success in today's international climate—a far cry from only a decade ago—demands highly specialized yet closely linked groups of global business managers, country or regional managers, and worldwide functional managers. This kind of organization characterizes a *transnational* rather than an old-line multinational, international, or global company. Transnationals integrate assets, resources, and diverse people in operating units around the world.

Christopher A. Bartlett is a professor at the Harvard Business School and chairman of the International Senior Management Program there. Sumantra Ghoshal is a professor and Digital Equipment Research Fellow at INSEAD in Fontainebleau, France. Recent books by Bartlett and Ghoshal include *Managing Across Borders: The Transnational Solution* (Harvard Business School Press, 1989) and *Transnational Management: Text, Cases, and Readings in Cross-Border Management* (Irwin, 1992).

Through a flexible management process, in which business, country, and functional managers form a triad of different perspectives that balance one another, transnational companies can build three strategic capabilities:

- global-scale efficiency and competitiveness;
- national-level responsiveness and flexibility, and
- cross-market capacity to leverage learning on a worldwide basis.

While traditional organizations, structured along product or geographic lines, can hone one or another of these capabilities, they cannot cope with the challenge of all three at once. But an emerging group of transnational companies has begun to transform the classic hierarchy of headquarters-subsidiary relationships into an integrated network of specialized yet interdependent units. For many, the greatest constraint in creating such an organization is a severe shortage of executives with the skills, knowledge, and sophistication to operate in a more tightly linked and less classically hierarchical network.

In fact, in the volatile world of transnational corporations, there is no such thing as a universal global manager. Rather, there are three groups of specialists: business managers, country managers, and functional managers. And there are the top executives at corporate headquarters, the leaders who manage the complex interactions between the three—and can identify and develop the talented executives a successful transnational requires.

To build such talent, top management must understand the strategic importance of each specialist. The careers of Leif Johansson of Electrolux, Howard Gottlieb of NEC, and Wahib Zaki of Procter & Gamble vividly exemplify the specialized yet interdependent roles the three types of global managers play.

THE BUSINESS MANAGER: STRATEGIST + ARCHITECT + COORDINATOR

Global business or product-division managers have one overriding responsibility: to further the company's global-scale efficiency and competitiveness. This task requires not only the perspective to recognize opportunities and risks across national and functional boundaries but also the skill to coordinate activities and link capabilities across those barriers. The global business manager's overall goal is to capture the full benefit of integrated worldwide operations.

To be effective, the three roles at the core of a business manager's job are to serve as the strategist for his or her organization, the architect of its worldwide asset and resource configuration, and the coordinator of transactions across national borders. Leif Johansson, now president of Electrolux, the Swedish-based company, played all three roles successfully in his earlier position as head of the household appliance division.

In 1983, when 32-year-old Johansson assumed responsibility for the division, he took over a business that had been built up through more than 100 acquisitions over the previous eight years. By the late 1980s, Electrolux's portfolio included more than 20 brands sold in some 40 countries, with acquistions continuing throughout the decade. Zanussi, for example, the big Italian manufacturer acquired by Electrolux in 1984, had built a strong market presence based on its reputation for innovation in household and commercial appliances. In addition, Arthur Martin in France and Zoppas in Norway had strong local brand positions but limited innovative capability.

As a result of these acquisitions, Electrolux had accumulated a patchwork quilt of companies, each with a different product portfolio, market position, and competitive situation. Johansson soon recognized the need for an overall strategy to coordinate and integrate his dispersed operations.

Talks with national marketing managers quickly convinced him that dropping local brands and standardizing around a few high-volume regional and global products would be unwise. He agreed with the local managers that their national brands were vital to maintaining consumer loyalty, distribution leverage, and competitive flexibility in markets that they saw fragmenting into more and more segments. But Johansson also understood the views of his division staffmembers, who pointed to the many similarities in product characteristics and consumer needs in the various markets. The division staff was certain Electrolux could use this advantage to cut across markets and increase competitiveness.

Johansson led a strategy review with a task force of product-division staff and national marketing managers. While the task force confirmed the marketing managers' notion of growing segmentation, its broader perspective enabled Johansson to see a convergence of segments across national markets. Their closer analysis also refined management's understanding of local market needs, concluding that consumers perceived ''localness'' mainly in terms of how a product was sold (distribution through local channels, promotion in local media, use of local brand names) instead of how it was designed or what features it offered.

From this analysis, Johansson fashioned a product-market strategy that identified two full-line regional brands to be promoted and supported in all European markets. He positioned the Electrolux brand to respond to the cross-market segment for high prestige (customers characterized as ''conservatives''), while the Zanussi brand would fill the segment where innovative products were key (for ''trendsetters'').

The local brands were clustered in the other two market segments pinpointed in the analysis: ''yuppies'' (''young and aggressive'' urban professionals) and ''environmentalists'' (''warm and friendly'' people interested in basic-value products). The new strategy provided Electrolux with localized brands that responded to the needs of these consumer groups. At the same time, the company captured the efficiencies possible by standardizing the basic chassis and components of these local-brand products, turning them out in high volume in specialized regional plants.

So, by tracking product and market trends across borders, Leif Johansson captured valuable global-scale efficiencies while reaping the benefits of a flexible response to national market fragmentation. What's more, though he took on the leadership role as a strategist, Johansson never assumed he alone had the understanding or the ability to form a global appliance strategy; he relied heavily on both corporate and local managers. Indeed, Johansson continued to solicit guidance on strategy through a council of country managers called the 1992 Group and through a set of product councils made up of functional managers.

In fact, the global business manager's responsibility for the distribution of crucial assets and resources is closely tied to shaping an integrated strategy. While he or she often relies on the input of regional and functional heads, the business manager is still the architect who usually initiates and leads the debate on where major plants, technical centers, and sales offices should be located—and which facilities should be closed.

The obvious political delicacy of such debates is not the only factor that makes simple economic analysis inadequate. Within every operating unit there exists a pool of skills and capabilities that may have taken a lot of time and investment to build up. The global business manager has to achieve the most efficient distribution of assets and resources while protecting and leveraging the competence at hand. Electrolux's household appliance division had more than 200 plants and a bewildering array of technical centers and development groups in many countries. It was clear to Johansson that he had to rationalize this infrastructure.

He began by setting a policy for the household appliance division that would avoid concentration of facilities in one country or region, even in its Scandinavian home base. At the same time, Johansson wanted to specialize the division's development and manufacturing infrastructure on a ''one product, one facility'' basis. He was determined to allocate important development and manufacturing tasks to each of the company's major markets. In trying to optimize robustness and flexibility in the long term rather than minimize short-term costs, Johansson recognized that a specialized yet dispersed system would be less vulnerable to exchange-rate fluctuations and political uncertainties. This setup also tapped local managerial and technical resources, thereby reducing dependence on the small pool of skilled labor and management in Sweden.

Instead of closing old plants, Johansson insisted on upgrading and tailoring existing facilities, whenever possible. In addition to averting political fallout and organizational trauma, Electrolux would then retain valuable know-how and bypass the startup problems of building from scratch. An outstanding example of this approach is Zanussi's Porcia plant in Italy, which Electrolux turned into the world's largest washing machine plant. After a massive $150-million investment, the Porcia plant now produces 1.5 million units a year.

Although acquisition-fueled growth often leads to redundancy and overcapacity, it can also bring new resources and strengths. Instead of wiping out the division's diversity through homogenization or centralization, Johansson decided to leverage it by matching each unit's responsibilities with its particular competence. Because of the Scandinavian flair for modular design, he assigned the integrated kitchen-system business to Electrolux's Swedish and Finnish units. He acknowledged Porcia's experience in component production by consolidating design and production of compressors there. Johansson's reshaping of assets and resources not only enhanced scale economies and operational flexibility but also boosted morale by giving operating units the opportunity to leverage their distinctive competences beyond their local markets.

Newly developed business strategies obviously need coordination. In practice, the specialization of assets and resources swells the flow of products and components among national units, requiring a firm hand to synchronize and control that flow. For organizations whose operations have become more dispersed and specialized at the same time that their strategies have become more connected and integrated, coordination across borders is a tough challenge. Business managers must fashion a repertoire of approaches and tools, from simple centralized control to management of exceptions identified through formal policies to indirect management via informal communication channels.

Leif Johansson coordinated product flow—across his 35 national sales units and 29 regional sourcing facilities—by establishing broad sourcing policies and transfer-pricing ranges that set limits but left negotiations to internal suppliers and customers. For instance, each sales unit could negotiate a transfer price with its internal source for a certain product in a set range that was usually valid for a year. If the negotiations moved outside that range, the companies had to check with headquarters. As a coordinator, Johansson led the deliberations that defined the logic and philosophy of the parameters; but he stepped back and let individual unit managers run their own organizations, except when a matter went beyond policy limits.

In contrast, coordination of business strategy in Johansson's division was managed through teams that cut across the formal hierarchy. Instead of centralizing, he relied on managers to share the responsibility for monitoring implementation and resolving problems through teams. To protect the image and positioning of his regional brands—Electrolux and Zanussi—he set up a brand-coordination group for each. Group members came from the sales companies in key countries, and the chairperson was a corporate marketing executive. Both groups were responsible for building a coherent, pan-European strategy for the brand they represented.

To rationalize the various product strategies across Europe, Johansson created product-line boards to oversee these strategies and to exploit any synergies. Each product line had its own board made up of the corporate product-line manager, who was chair, and his or her product managers. The Quattro 500 refrigerator-freezer, which was designed in Italy, built in Finland, and marketed in Sweden, was one example of how these boards could successfully integrate product strategy.

In addition, the 1992 Group periodically reviewed the division's overall results, kept an eye on its manufacturing and marketing infrastructure, and supervised major development programs and investment projects. Capturing the symbolic value of 1992 in its name, the group was chaired by Johansson himself and included business managers from Italy, the United Kingdom, Spain, the United States, France, Switzerland, and Sweden.

Indeed, coordination probably takes up more of the global business manager's time than any other aspect of the job. This role requires that a manager have great administrative and interpersonal skills to ensure that coordination and integration don't deteriorate into heavy-handed control.

Many traditional multinational companies have made the mistake of automatically anointing their home country product-division managers with the title of global business manager. Sophisticated transnational companies, however, have long since separated the notions of coordination and centralization, looking for business leadership from their best units, wherever they may be located. For example, Asea Brown Boveri, the Swiss-headquartered electrical engineering corporation, has tried to leverage the strengths of its operating companies and exploit their location in critical markets by putting its business managers wherever strategic and organizational dimensions coincide. In Asea Brown Boveri's power-transmission business, the manager for switchgear is located in Sweden, the manager for power transformers is in Germany, the manager for distribution transformers is in Norway, and the manager for electric metering is in the United States.

Even well-established multinationals with a tradition of tight central control are changing their tack. The head of IBM's telecommunications business recently moved her division headquarters to London, not only to situate the command center closer to the booming European market for computer networking but also ''to give us a different perspective on all our markets.''

THE COUNTRY MANAGER: SENSOR + BUILDER + CONTRIBUTOR

The building blocks for most worldwide companies are their national subsidiaries. If the global business manager's main objective is to achieve global-scale efficiency and competitiveness, the national subsidiary manager's is to be sensitive and responsive to the local market. Country managers play the pivotal role not only in meeting local customer needs but also in satisfying the host government's requirements and defending their company's market positions against local and external competitors.

The need for local flexibility often puts the country manager in conflict with the global business manager. But in a successful transnational like Electrolux, negotiations can resolve these differences. In this era of intense competition around the world, companies cannot afford to permit a subsidiary manager to define parochial interests as ''king of the country.''

Nor should headquarters allow national subsidiaries to become the battleground for corporate holy wars fought in the name of globalization. In many companies, their national subsidiaries are hothouses of entrepreneurship and innovation—homes for valuable resources and capabilities that must be nurtured, not constrained or cut off. The subsidiaries of Philips, for one, have consistently led product development: in television, the company's first color TV was developed in Canada, the first stereo model in Australia, and the first teletext in the United Kingdom. Unilever's national subsidiaries have also been innovative in product-marketing strategy: Germany created the campaign for Snuggle (a fabric softener); Finland developed Timotei (an herbal shampoo); and South Africa launched Impulse (a body perfume).

In fact, effective country managers play three vital roles: the sensor and interpreter of local opportunities and threats, the builder of local resources and capabilities, and the contributor to and active participant in global strategy. Howard Gottlieb's experience as general manager of NEC's switching-systems subsidiary in the United States illustrates the importance of all three tasks.

As a sensor, the country manager must be good at gathering and sifting information, interpreting the implications, and predicting a range of feasible outcomes. More important, this manager has the difficult task of conveying the importance of such intelligence to people higher up, especially those whose perceptions may be dimmed by distance or even ethnocentric bias. Today, when information gathered locally increasingly applies to other regions or even globally, communicating effectively is crucial. Consumer trends in one country often spread to another; technologies developed in a leading-edge environment can have global significance; a competitor's local market testing may signal a wider strategy; and national legislative initiatives in areas like deregulation and environmental protection tend to spill across borders.

Gottlieb's contribution to NEC's understanding of changes in the telecommunications market demonstrates how a good sensor can connect local intelligence with global strategy. In the late 1980s, Gottlieb was assigned to build the U.S. market for NEAX 61, a widely acclaimed digital telecom switch designed by the parent company in Japan. Although it was technologically sophisticated, early sales didn't meet expectations.

His local-market background and contacts led Gottlieb to a quick diagnosis of the problem. NEC had designed the switch to meet the needs of NTT, the Japanese telephone monopoly, and it lacked many features U.S. customers wanted. For one thing, its software didn't incorporate the protocol conversions necessary for distributing revenues among the many U.S. companies that might handle a single long-distance phone call. Nor could the switch handle revenue-enhancing features like ''call waiting'' and ''call forwarding,'' which were vital high-margin items in the conmpetitive, deregulated American market.

In translating the needs of his U.S. division to the parent company NEC, Gottlieb had a formidable task. To convince his superiors in Japan that redesigning NEAX 61 was necessary, he had to bridge two cultures and penetrate the subtleties of the parent company's Japanese-dominated management processes. And he had to instill a sense of urgency in several corporate management groups, varying his pitches to appeal to the interests of each. For instance, Gottlieb convinced the engineering department that the NEAX 61 switch had been underdesigned for the U.S. market and the marketing department that time was short because the Bell operating companies were calling for quotes.

A transnational's greater access to the scarcest of all corporate resources, human capability, is a definite advantage when compared with strictly local companies—or old-line multinationals, for that matter. Scores of companies like IBM, Merck, and Procter & Gamble have recognized the value of harvesting advanced (and often less expensive) scientific expertise by upgrading local development labs into global centers of technical excellence.

Other companies have built up and leveraged their overseas human resources in different ways. Cummins Engine, for example, has set up its highly skilled but surprisingly low-cost Indian engineering group as a worldwide drafting resource; American Airlines's Barbados operation does much of the corporate clerical work; and Becton Dickinson, a large hospital supply company, has given its Belgian subsidiary pan-European responsibility for managing distribution and logistics.

Indeed, the burden of identifying, developing, and leveraging such national resources and capabilities falls on country managers. Howard Gottlieb, after convincing Tokyo that the United States would be an important market for NEC's global digital-switch design, persuaded headquarters to permit his new engineering group to take part early on in the product development of the next generation switch—the NEAX 61 E. He sent teams of engineers to Japan to work with the original designers; and, to verify his engineers' judgments, Gottlieb invited the designers to visit his customers in the United States. These exchanges not only raised the sensitivity of NEC's Japan-based engineers to U.S. market needs but also significantly increased their respect for their American colleagues. Equally important, the U.S. unit's morale rose.

As a builder, Gottlieb used this mutual confidence as the foundation for creating a software-development capability that would become a big corporate asset. Skilled software engineers, very scarce in Ja-

pan, were widely available in the United States. Gottlieb's first move was to put together a small software team to support local projects. Though its resources were limited, the group turned out a number of innovations, including a remote software-pitching capability that later became part of the 61 E switch design. The credibility he won at headquarters allowed Gottlieb to expand his design engineering group from 10 to more than 50 people within two years, supporting developments not only in North America but also eventually in Asia.

In many transnationals, access to strategically important information—and control over strategically important assets—has catapulted country managers into a much more central role. As links to local markets, they are no longer mere implementers of programs and policies shaped at headquarters; many have gained some influence over the way their organizations make important strategic and operational decisions. In most of today's truly transnational companies, country managers and their chief local subordinates often participate in new product-development committees, product-marketing task forces, and global-strategy conferences. Even at the once impenetrable annual top management meetings, national subsidiary managers may present their views and defend their interests before senior corporate and domestic executives—a scenario that would have been unthinkable even a decade ago.

Of course, the historic position of most national units of worldwide companies has been that of the implementer of strategy from headquarters. Because the parent company's accepted objectives are the outcome of discussion and negotiation involving numerous units, divisions, and national subsidiaries, sometimes a country manager must carry out a strategy that directly conflicts with what he or she has lobbied for in vain.

But a diverse and dispersed worldwide organization, with subsidiaries that control many of the vital development, production, and marketing resources, can no longer allow the time-honored ''king of the country'' to decide how, when, and even whether his or her national unit will implement a particular strategic initiative. The decision made by the North American subsidiary of Philips to outsource its

VCRs from a Japanese competitor rather than the parent company is one of the most notorious instances of how a local "king" can undermine global strategy.

At NEC, Howard Gottlieb spent about 60% of his time on customer relations and probing the market and about 30% managing the Tokyo interface. His ability to understand and interpret the global strategic implications of U.S. market needs—and the software-development group he built from scratch—allowed him to take part in NEC's ongoing strategy debate. As a result, Gottlieb changed his division's role from implementer of corporate strategy to active contributor in designing that strategy.

THE FUNCTIONAL MANAGER: SCANNER + CROSS-POLLINATOR + CHAMPION

While global business managers and country managers have come into their own, functional specialists have yet to gain the recognition due them in many traditional multinational companies. Relegated to support-staff roles, excluded from important meetings, and even dismissed as unnecessary overhead, functional managers are often given little chance to participate in, let alone contribute to, the corporate mainstream's global activity. In some cases, top management has allowed staff functions to become a warehouse for corporate misfits or a graveyard for managerial has-beens. Yet at a time when information, knowledge, and expertise have become more specialized, an organization can gain huge benefits by linking its technical, manufacturing, marketing, human resources, and financial experts worldwide.

Given that today's transnationals face the strategic challenge of resolving the conflicts implicit in achieving global competitiveness, national responsiveness, and worldwide learning, business and country managers must take primary responsibility for the first two capabilities. But the third is the functional manager's province.

Building an organization that can use learning to create and spread innovations requires the skill to transfer specialized knowledge while also connecting scarce resources and capabilities across national borders. To achieve this important objective, functional managers must scan for specialized information worldwide, "cross-pollinate" leading-edge knowledge and best practice, and champion innovations that may offer transnational opportunities and applications.

Most innovation starts, of course, when managers perceive a particular opportunity or market threat, such as an emerging consumer trend, a revolutionary technological development, a bold competitive move, or a pending government regulation. When any of these flags pops up around the world, it may seem unimportant to corporate headquarters if viewed in isolation. But when a functional manager acts as a scanner, with the expertise and perspective to detect trends and move knowledge across boundaries, he or she can transform piece-meal information into strategic intelligence.

In sophisticated transnationals, senior functional executives serve as linchpins, connecting their areas of specialization throughout the organization. Using informal networks, they create channels for communicating specialized information and repositories for proprietary knowledge. Through such links, Electrolux marketing managers first identified the emergence of cross-market segments and NEC's technical managers were alerted to the shift from analog to digital switching technology.

In the same manner, Wahib Zaki of Procter & Gamble's European operations disapproved of P&G's high-walled organizational structures, which isolated and insulated the technical development carried out in each subsidiary's lab. When Zaki became head of R&D in Europe, he decided to break down some walls. In his new job, he was ideally placed to become a scanner and cross-pollinator. He formed European technical teams and ran a series of conferences in which like-minded experts from various countries could exchange information and build informal communication networks.

Still, Zaki needed more ammunition to combat the isolation, defensiveness, and "not invented here" attitude in each research center. He distributed staff among the European technical center in Brussels and the development groups of P&G's subsidiaries. He used his staff teams to help clarify the particular role of each national technical manager and to specialize activities that had been duplicated on a country-by-country basis with little transfer of accumulated knowledge.

In response to competitive threats from rivals Unilever, Henkel, and Colgate-Palmolive—and to a perceived consumer trend—P&G's European headquarters asked the Brussels-based research center to develop a new liquid laundry detergent. By that time, Zaki had on hand a technical team that had built up relationships among its members so that it formed a close-knit network of intelligence and product expertise.

The team drew the product profile necessary for healthy sales in multiple markets with diverse needs. In several European markets, powdered detergents contained enzymes to break down protein-based stains, and the new liquid detergent would have to accomplish the same thing. In some markets, a bleach substitute was important; in others, hard water presented the toughest challenge; while in several countries, environmental concerns limited the use of phosphates. Moreover, the new detergent had to be effective in large-capacity, top-loading machines, as well as in the small front-loading machines common in Europe.

Zaki's team developed a method that made enzymes stable in liquid form (a new technique that was later patented), a bleach substitute effective at low temperatures, a fatty acid that yielded good water-softening performance without phosphates, and a suds-suppressant that worked in front-loading machines (so bubbles wouldn't ooze out the door). By integrating resources and expertise, Zaki cross-pollinated best practice for a new product.

The R&D group was so successful that the European headquarters adopted the use of teams for its management of the new brand launch. P&G's first European brand team pooled the knowledge and expertise of brand managers from seven subsidiaries to draft a launch program and marketing strategy for the new liquid detergent Vizir, which ensured its triumphant rollout in seven countries in six months. P&G's homework enabled it to come up with a product that responded to European needs, while

Colgate-Palmolive was forced to withdraw its liquid detergent brand, Axion—which had been designed in the United States and wasn't tailored for Europe—after an 18-month market test.

As a reward for his performance in Europe, Wahib Zaki was transferred to Procter & Gamble's Cincinnati corporate headquarters as a senior vice president of R&D. He found that researchers there were working on improved builders (the ingredients that break down dirt) for a new liquid laundry detergent to be launched in the United States. In addition, the international technology-coordination group was working with P&G's Japanese subsidiary to formulate a liquid detergent surfactant (the ingredient that removes greasy stains) that would be effective in the cold-water washes common in Japanese households, where laundry is often done in used bath water. Neither group had shared its findings or new ideas with the other, and neither had incorporated the numerous breakthroughs represented by Vizir—despite the evidence that consumer needs, market trends, competitive challenges, and regulatory requirements were all spreading across national borders.

Playing the role of champion, Zaki decided to use this development process to demonstrate the benefits of coordinating P&G's sensitivity and responsiveness to diverse consumer needs around the world. He formed a team drawn from three technical groups (one in Brussels and two in the United States) to turn out a world liquid laundry detergent. The team analyzed the trends, generated product specifications, and brought together dispersed technical knowledge and expertise, which culminated in one of Procter & Gamble's most successful product launches ever. Sold as Liquid Tide in the United States, Liquid Cheer in Japan, and Liquid Ariel in Europe, the product was P&G's first rollout on such a global scale.

As Zaki continued to strengthen cross-border technology links through other projects, Procter & Gamble gradually converted its far-flung sensing and response resources into an integrated learning organization. By scanning for new developments, cross-pollinating best practice, and championing innovations with transnational applications, Wahib Zaki, a superlative functional manager, helped create an organization that could both develop demonstrably better new products and roll them out at a rapid pace around the world.

THE CORPORATE MANAGER: LEADER + TALENT SCOUT + DEVELOPER

Clearly, there is no single model for the global manager. Neither the old-line international specialist nor the more recent global generalist can cope with the complexities of cross-border strategies. Indeed, the dynamism of today's marketplace calls for managers with diverse skills. Responsibility for worldwide operations belongs to senior business, country, and functional executives who focus on the intense interchanges and subtle negotiations required. In contrast, those in middle management and front-line jobs need well-defined responsibilities, a clear understanding of their organization's transnational mission, and a sense of accountability—but few of the distractions senior negotiators must shoulder.

Meanwhile, corporate managers integrate these many levels of responsibility, playing perhaps the most vital role in transnational management. The corporate manager not only leads in the broadest sense; he or she also identifies and develops talented business, country, and functional managers—and balances the negotiations among the three. It's up to corporate managers to promote strong managerial specialists like Johansson, Gottlieb, and Zaki, those individuals who can translate company strategy into effective operations around the world.

Successful corporate managers like Floris Maljers, co-chairman of Unilever, have made the recruitment, training, and development of promising executives a top priority. By the 1980s, with Maljers as chairman, Unilever had a clear policy of rotating managers through various jobs and moving them around the world, especially early in their careers. Unilever was one of the first transnationals to have a strong pool of specialized yet interdependent senior managers, drawn from throughout its diverse organization.

But while most companies require only a few truly transnational managers to implement cross-border strategies, the particular qualities necessary for such positions remain in short supply. According to Maljers, it is this limitation in human resources—*not* unreliable or inadequate sources of capital—that has become the biggest constraint in most globalization efforts.

Locating such individuals is difficult under any circumstances, but corporate managers greatly improve the odds when their search broadens from a focus on home-country managers to incorporate the worldwide pool of executives in their organization. Because transnationals operate in many countries, they have access to a wide range of managerial talent. Yet such access—like information on local market trends or consumer needs that should cross organizational boundaries—is often an underexploited asset.

As a first step, senior executives can identify those in the organization with the potential for developing the skills and perspectives demanded of global managers. Such individuals must have a broad, nonparochial view of the company and its operations yet a deep understanding of their own business, country, or functional tasks. Obviously, even many otherwise talented managers in an organization aren't capable of such a combination of flexibility and commitment to specific interests, especially when it comes to cross-border coordination and integration. Top management may have to track the careers of promising executives over a number of years before deciding whether to give them senior responsibilities. At Unilever, for example, the company maintains four development lists that indicate both the level of each manager and his or her potential. The progress of managers on the top ''A1'' list is tracked by Unilever's Special Committee, which includes the two chairmen.

Once corporate managers identify the talent, they have the duty to develop it. They must provide opportunities for achievement that allow business, country, and functional managers to handle negotiations in a worldwide context. A company's ability to identify individuals with potential, legitimize their diversity, and integrate them into the organization's corporate decisions is the single clearest indicator that the corporate leader is a true global manager—and that the company itself is a true transnational.

36

ANALYZING CROSS-NATIONAL MANAGEMENT AND ORGANIZATIONS: A THEORETICAL FRAMEWORK

RAN LACHMAN
Faculty of Management, Tel Aviv University, Tel Aviv 69978, Israel

ALBERT NEDD
University of Alberta, Edmonton, Alberta, Canada T6G 2R6

BOB HININGS
University of Alberta, Edmonton, Alberta, Canada T6G 2R6

ABSTRACT   The differential social control embedded in core and periphery values indigenous to a cultural setting, and the availability of resources in that setting, are discussed as critical factors for the effective adaptation of organizations and management practices transferred across cultural boundaries. The relationships between these factors and organizational structure, processes, and behavior, are analyzed and specified in a theoretical framework. The framework postulates the importance of congruent or, at least, accommodative relationships between the core values dominating the local setting, and those underlying transferred practices for the effectiveness of "imported" organizational practices. Four main contingencies of local-imported values' incongruence are described, and their implications for "entry" and "coping" strategies of cross-national organizations are discussed. The framework also offers a scheme for generating hypotheses regarding the effects of values on structures and behavior in cross-national organizations. The theoretical and managerial implications of the scheme are discussed and illustrated.

(*Contingency Theory; Culture; Resource; Availability; Organization Structure*)

Recent literature on cross-cultural organizations and management, has considerably advanced our awareness of the complexity of the impact indigenous cultural settings may have on organizational structures and processes (Ronen 1986, Nath 1988, Shin et al. 1990, Miller et al. 1990, Martinko and Fenzeng 1990). However, more major theoretical and methodological issues still require attention. An important issue is the use of culture as an explanatory variable in the study of cross-cultural and international organizations. Frequently, cross-national studies observing differences in management or organization practices in different countries, attribute them to cultural differences (e.g., Howard et al. 1983, Cavusgil and Yavas 1984, Vertinsky et al. 1990). However, they provide neither sufficient theoretical nor empirical indications of how culture causes such differences. Consequently, relevant theories were characterized as being scarce, pre-paradigmatic, and lacking sufficient specification of the role indigenous cultures may play in the transferability of management and organizational practices (Adler 1983, Kelly and Worthley 1981, Schein 1981, Roberts and Boya-cigiller 1984). It appears, therefore, that further attention ought to be devoted to key issues such as: (a) whether culture is a significant explanatory factor; (b) if so, what are the specific aspects of culture to which differences can be attributed; (c) how do these cultural elements cause the differences. A focus on these issues is important for cross-national theory building as it is for any theory development (Whetten 1989).

Recent attempts to develop theoretical frameworks have pointed at cultural values as the important elements of culture to impact organizations (Hofstede 1980). Efforts were made to identify and classify several cultural values, or patterns of values, on which different countries can be compared and contrasted in terms of commonality in values (e.g., Glenn 1981; Hofstede 1980; Triandis 1982, 1984; Ronen and Shenkar 1985). The focus on values as the relevant cultural dimensions, followed by the identification of specific values or groups of values, that are prevalent in one or a number of cultural settings, is undoubtedly an important contribution. However, we contend that theory development ought to take a further step by adding a dimension of values' centrality.

The impact cultural values have is determined by their centrality within the value system of a cultural setting more than by their prevalence in this setting. Therefore, values should be examined not only in terms of their prevalence, but also in terms of their centrality and importance within the relevant cultural setting. We argue that major problems faced by cross-cultural and international management may stem, not simply from value differences, but from incongruency between management's underlying core values and the values central to the host cultural setting. This is the focus of the paper. Proposed here is a framework that specifies the mechanisms through which culture exerts its influences, differentiates between core and periphery cultural values, and accounts for the differential impact and consequences these values have for organizations and management within and across cultural boundaries.

SPECIFYING THE EFFECTS OF CULTURE

The basic premise advocated in our proposed theoretical framework is that the social control exerted by values is the main factor in the impact of culture. The level of social control inherent in each value dif-

fers by the centrality of that value within the cultural system.

Culture is viewed here as a system of patterned meanings or the collective mental programming of a social group (Hofstede 1980). In order to appropriately articulate its effects on specific organizational structures and processes the concept of culture must be further specified. In specifying the effects of culture we propose that the focus be on the social control aspect of cultural values. Values are the bases for the choice, by a social group, of particular ends and of particular means by which these ends are to be accomplished. They determine and provide legitimacy for (or sanction) collective and individual preferences for certain states of affairs and modes of conduct over available alternatives (Kluckhohn and Strodtbeck 1961, Rokeach 1973, Schein 1985). Thus, values serve as mechanisms of social control by regulating behavior in accord with the requirements of the socio-cultural system for order and for selective, nonimpulsive behavior (Kluckhohn 1951). The value system legitimizes behavior by stipulating positive or negative sanctions for what is expected, desired, required, or forbidden behavior within a cultural setting. Cultural values have, therefore, an important role of controlling and directing social behavior, organizational behavior included.

However, not all values are equally important, or have the same impact in regulating behavior. Cultural values ought to be differentiated in terms of the impact they have in legitimizing and directing choices of modes of organizing and patterns of managerial behavior.

CENTRALITY OF VALUES

In the cross-cultural organizational literature most of the proposed classifications of cultural values identify certain sets of values or cultural dimensions and examine the extent to which countries vary in their commitment to and expression of these values (e.g., Hofstede 1980, Ronen and Shenkar 1985). We maintain that the effect of values on organizations in a cultural setting goes beyond their mere expression. To a large extent, this effect is determined by the relative importance of a value within the given culture: the more important and central the value, the stronger will be its impact and the more consequential it will be for differences in organizational and managerial practices.

In any given culture some values are regarded as more important than others, and in different cultures the relative importance attributed to particular values may differ (Kluckhohn and Strodtbeck 1961, Shils 1961, Rokeach 1973, Allport 1961). Within a culture, values are organized in a hierarchy or a relative order of priority. This hierarchy reflects the relative importance, endurance of values in the system, and their power to control social behavior. Values higher in the hierarchy are more important, more enduring and resistant to change, are highly accepted and agreed upon, and hence are more involved in social control than those lower in the hierarchy (Rokeach 1969, 1973; Shils 1961; Schein 1985). The terms ''core'' and ''periphery'' may be used to represent, respectively, the relatively high and the relatively low positioning of values in the values hierarchy and the extent to which they are involved in social control. For analytical clarity, only the two ends of the continuum are contrasted here. The middle range has been omitted from the analysis.

Parsons (1964) suggests that values, as the evaluative aspect of culture, constitute the core of the stabilizing mechanisms of the social system. However, not all values are completely stable, thus allowing for continuity and change within a cultural system. The core values tend to maintain continuity in the unique and distinct characteristics of a cultural system. They maintain continuity because they tend to be more stable and resistant to change, their social control effects are more enduring, and because consensus and acceptance of core values is higher relative to that of periphery values. Periphery values are less stable or enduring because members of society may manifest different levels of attachment to them, or may even disregard them. The divergence in acceptance of periphery values and their resulting susceptibility to change make them more accommodating to social change and innovation. This perspective suggests that culture is a relatively adaptive system that can change mostly through changes in periphery values. While core values too can change, or their relative priority in the hierarchy can shift, changes impinging on periphery values are more likely to occur.

Thus, core values are the high priority values that are central to a social, cultural, or an individual's value system, are important in regulating social behavior, and tend to be enduring. Periphery values refer to values of low priority, low consensus (high divergence and ambiguity), and less importance for social control. Consequently, they are relatively susceptible to change (Shils 1961).

The differential susceptibility of core and periphery values to contextual change influences can be illustrated. The Confucian value of hierarchical relations, still prevailing in China, has been described as one of the main tenets of that philosophy which underlies the Chinese cultural system (Eberhard 1971). Confucianism's emphasis on the differential hierarchical position of individuals in the social system was in conflict with the dominant egalitarian values of Maoist ideology (Liu 1964, Hsu 1981). During the Cultural Revolution this Confucian value was strongly attacked in the attempt to abolish organizational and other hierarchies. These attempts did not, however, have lasting effects on management and organizations, which have gradually returned to hierarchical systems (Laaksonen 1988). Indeed, the attempts to abolish them seem to have further strengthened the position of traditional Chinese values (Bond and Wang 1983).

However, while the value of hierarchy withstood the Maoist challenge, the Confucian value of the status of women did not. Laaksonen (1988) suggests that, under the pressure of Maoist ideology, women have been raised from their traditional subjugated status. This Confucian value was not as dominant in the overall cultural system as the value of hierarchy (Laaksonen 1988). It can be regarded as a periphery value and, therefore, was less resistant to change.

In another study the status of women relative to men was classified as a core value in four countries studied: Argentina, Chile, India, and Israel (Lachman 1983). Studying core and periphery values among factory workers it was found, however, that the values classified as core or periphery in one country were not necessarily classified in the same way in all the others. It was further found that organizational socialization influences had little or no effect on core values, but had some effect on change in employees' periphery values (Lachman 1983, 1988).

Thus, rather than searching for "common" cultural values on which cross-cultural comparisons of managerial practices and organizational forms may be made, efforts should be directed at identifying the core values of particular cultural settings, and examining their impact on organizational practices. This does not preclude the study of values' diffusion and transferability across countries, and the factors influencing their spread. However, it suggests that such diffusion be examined in terms of its congruence with local core/periphery values and local interpretations of the imported values.

THE THEORETICAL FRAMEWORK

The theoretical framework presented here describes the influences of cultural values on organizations and management, focusing on the social control functions of core and periphery cultural values. The basic arguments advocated in our framework are: (a) the general, all-inclusive construct of culture can be specified by focusing on the effects particular cultural values have in determining a range of legitimate modes of organizing and patterns of social interaction, out of which specific organizational forms and behavior are chosen; (b) a distinction ought to be made between core and periphery values in a cultural setting; (c) transferred, or contextually induced organizational adjustments that are incongruent with relevant core values of the cultural setting, will impact the effective functioning of the organization more negatively than adjustments incongruent with periphery values; (d) incongruence between the manifestations of core values at the organizational (structural) and the individual (role behavior) levels of the organization, will also impede organizational effectiveness. The processes through which cultural values influence individuals and organizations are discussed in more detail later on.

The main assertion underlying the framework is that congruence between core values governing modes of organizing in a cultural setting, and the value assumptions underlying the structure and processes of cross-national organizations operating within that setting, is of critical importance for organizational effectiveness. Another premise of the framework is that organizational adaptations to pressures and constraints posed by the environment are essential because organizations depend on their environment for necessary inputs and outputs. Many environmental dimensions such as the social, political and legal systems, the availability of resources and technology, may have important impacts on such adaptations. Undoubtedly, all these dimensions of the organization's host environment ought to be considered and incorporated into a comprehensive theory. However, since it would require a very complex framework to describe such an elaborate set of relationships, we have decided at this initial stage of theory building, to prefer parsimony and simplicity to complexity and comprehensiveness. Hence, in addition to the impact of values, the framework considers one additional dimension: the economic dimension of availability (scarcity or munificence) of resources in the organizations' environment.

There are several reasons for choosing the factor of resources out of the many relevant environmental or contextual elements affecting organizational structure and behavior. First, it has been persuasively argued in the literature that the economic aspects of any society and its cultural values are intricately bound together, and any comprehensive theory of cross-national organization and management should incorporate both (e.g., Smelser 1963, Jamieson 1982). Secondly, since economic conditions differ across nations, the conditions prevailing within a nation (or a region thereof) are of particular importance for cross-national organization theory and practice, especially when highly developed and less-developed nations are compared (Kiggundu et al. 1983). Finally, since cross-national management involves for the most part economic organizations and activities, the potential impact of the economic environment is of considerable importance.

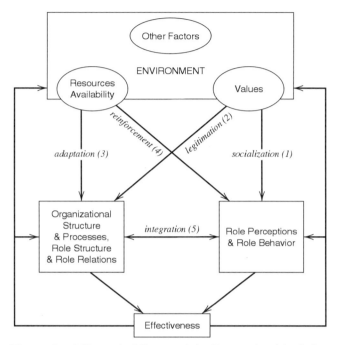

Figure 1. A Theoretical Framework for Cross-cultural Analysis

EFFECTS OF CULTURAL VALUES

Cultural values have an important role of legitimizing the organization's existence and its modes of functioning, as well as the patterns of behavior of its members. In addition, cultural values also filter the impact of other environmental factors on the organization through their role as managerial interpretive schema (Ranson et al. 1980, Ford and Baucus 1987). All these effects may vary with the centrality of the relevant values, because the more central a value, the stronger its social control effects and the lower the tolerance for deviations.

CULTURAL VALUES AND INDIVIDUAL BEHAVIOR

Link 1 in Figure 1 denotes that the behavior of individuals in the organization are influenced by the values, orientations, attitudes and beliefs individuals bring with them to their jobs. Acquisition of values

(particularly core ones) by individuals occurs, in the main, prior to their joining work organizations. Consequently, the values held by employees are not necessarily congruent with those required by their organizations. Organizations try to minimize incongruency through selection procedures, aiming at identifying and recruiting individuals who already have at least some of the required values (Brim 1968). To further decrease incongruency, organizational socialization processes are employed to assist recruits in acquiring the required organizational values (Van Maanen and Schein 1979). The question in this regard is whether or not organizational socialization can effectively override the influence of members' previously internalized values, and change them to conform to those required by the organization. If indeed they can, the effects of previously held values on individuals' behavior in organizations becomes irrelevant.

It is well recognized that early childhood socialization plays a primary role in personality development and the acquisition of basic values. The impact of adult socialization on personal values has, however, been debated. Some scholars suggest that both early and adult socialization may be equally important in determining personal values. They argue that late socialization influences can override the influences of early socialization and change employees' values that are incongruent with the organizations' requirements (Inkeles and Smith 1974). Other studies have suggested that organizational socialization serves mainly to reinforce, rather than change, values acquired prior to joining an organization (Frese 1982, Mortimer and Lorence 1979).

Lachman (1983, 1988) tried to reconcile these different perspectives by showing that early and late socialization induce changes in different categories of values. Early socialization affects core values, and late socialization affects only periphery values. Thus, employees' periphery values may change as a result of pressures to comply with organizational requirements and managerial policies, whereas their core values will not. When organizational role requirements are incongruent with core values, employees tend to modify these role requirements. If they fail to modify them, employees may change their jobs rather than their values (Holland 1976).

CULTURAL VALUES AND ORGANIZATIONAL STRUCTURE

At the most fundamental level, cultural legitimation may define the kinds of organizations that are allowable in a society, in terms of product or service, type of ownership and rules of competition (Child 1981, Maurice 1979). Since cultural values are embedded in the institutional arrangements of socio-political systems, they affect not only the broad nature of organizational possibilities but also the more specific structural factors such as differentiation and integration, degree of specialization, the form of hierarchies, the use of rules and procedures, and the locus of decision-making in organizations (Clark 1979, Gallie 1978, Hofstede 1980, Jamieson 1982). Thus cultural values permeate organizations by defining organizational processes, role structures, and role relations as culturally acceptable, relatively neutral, or

in conflict with culturally prescribed norms and, therefore, unacceptable (link 2, Figure 1).

Cultural values also have indirect effects on structure. Managerial activities directed toward organizational adaptation are determined by processes of social cognition and social perceptions (Weick 1979, Kiesler and Sproull 1982). The cultural values held by decision makers provide interpretations of which contextual influences are critical for the organization and require a response, and which can be ignored. Thus, cultural values also affect organizational structures and processes through their influences on the selectivity of management's perceptions.

Indeed, organizations in different countries show a wide variation in structural dimensions (Lammers and Hickson 1979, McMillan et al. 1973). However, there has been an ongoing debate on the utility of employing cultural factors in accounting for these variations. The contrasting perspectives in the debate are the ''culture free'' and ''culturalist'' perspectives. Advocates of the former maintain that variations in organizational forms are due to differences in economic environments or imperatives of technology but not culture (Hickson et al. 1974, 1979). Proponents of the latter maintain that much of the variation is due to cultural differences (Child 1981, Child and Tayeb 1982, Jamieson 1982).

It seems, though, that this debate is misplaced. Organizations are located in milieux comprising not only their technology and economic environment but a cultural one as well (Hickson et al. 1974, Hofstede 1980, Jamieson 1978, Triandis 1984). Hence, the issue of cross-national variations in organizational forms is not whether variations are due to one environmental effect or another, but centers around their relative impact (Hickson and McMillan 1981). The economic environment and the technologies employed by organizations impose constraints with respect to structural configurations. But cultural values determine range of organizational responses to such constraints; they serve to provide meaning (Ranson et al. 1980). In many studies the comparison of organizational adaptations has been restricted in range and incorporates only those adaptations that have already been culturally legitimized in the settings examined, or adaptations of a narrow technical nature.

Consequently, these adaptations do not impinge on the cultural environment (Kiggundu et al. 1983). In such research, adaptations conforming to the culturally approved range, may indeed appear to be "culture free" while in fact they are "culture congruent," not free.

The distinction between core and periphery values may help resolve this debate about the effects of culture. Since core values resist change in the face of contextual pressures, and peripheral values are apt to yield to these pressures, configurations of organizational structures and managerial approaches that impinge on core values will be culturally bound, while those impinging on periphery values may appear to be culture-free. It is the inconsistent results of previous research, where this distinction was not made, that gave rise to this debate. This is not to say that all organizations within a culture will be the same, but that existing variability would be confined to those approved by the relevant core values.

AVAILABILITY OF ECONOMIC RESOURCES

The framework proposes that the environmental dimension of relative scarcity of economic resources may affect organizations (link 3, Figure 1) as well as individual behavior (link 4) within given settings. Such possible effects are briefly discussed here.

ECONOMIC RESOURCES AND ORGANIZATIONAL STRUCTURE

Although the dimension of scarcity vs. munificence of resources has been regarded by organization theorists as an important component of the organizational environment (Katz and Kahn 1978, Pfeffer and Salancik 1978) it has not been given sufficient attention by researchers. The few studies that have examined the effects of resource munificence on organizations have indicated that choices of organizational structures and practices can vary with resource availability (Leff 1978, Robbins 1984, Staw and Szwajkowski 1975, Zussman 1983). In some developing nations, for example, a rather unique form of structuring organizational activities, the "economic group," has been developed as a basis of capital formation, industrial organization and entrepreneurship. The "economic group" is a multiorganizational entity comprising organizations which operate in synergy in a variety of economic sectors but share entrepreneurial, managerial and financial control. The capital and top managerial resources are mobilized from and remain within the group, which constitutes a combined economic unit. This enables the group to utilize its own resources to expand and diversify its investments, or to support organizations within it.

Leff (1978) argues that in developing nations this organizational form is a successful response to scarcity of resources. Because of conditions of market imperfections, mobilization of resources is otherwise difficult for organizations, even when resources are not really scarce. A similar organizational form that serves similar functions is the Kereitsu, which has developed in Japan as a post-war offspring of the more traditional form of Zaibatsu. One of its main characteristics is the synergy among the firms comprising it and the form of cross share holding among them (Abegglen and Stalk 1985).

Another example is the tendency of organizations in relatively munificent economic environments to develop considerable slack to buffer their operational core from environmental fluctuations, permitting a strategy concerned mainly with expansion and growth. On the other hand, in environments of relative scarcity, organizations generally have little slack and, consequently, management's main concern is organizational maintenance and survival. It is quite clear that the organizational processes and managerial approaches required by the latter organizations are very different from those required by the former (Whetten 1980, Zussman 1983).

A similar argument can be found in research on the organizational life cycle. It has been suggested that managing organizational growth is different from managing decline, particularly when organizational decline results from cutbacks (Levine 1979, Rudie-Harrigan 1980, Whetten 1980, Cameron et al. 1987). For example, the structure of such organizations tends to become centralized and controls are tightened. It has also been suggested that organizations with relatively abundant resources tend to use inter-organizational labor markets as sources of specialized and qualified personnel, as well as the vehicle for disposing of personnel. On the other hand, organizations faced with scarcity of resources tend to utilize their internal labor market as the source of needed personnel (Pfeffer and Cohen 1985).

Staw and Szwajkowski (1975) have shown that the congruence of organizational adaptation practices with prescribed norms is related to scarcity or munificence of resources. They studied the effect of scarcity in economic resources on the tendency of organizations to deviate from the legally prescribed range of activities in their coping attempts. The findings suggested that under conditions of scarcity, when organizations were forced to exert greater efforts to obtain needed resources, they were more likely to engage in legally questionable or clearly proscribed activities (e.g., price fixing, franchise violations, tax evasion).

Organizational adaptation is a vehicle for absorbing the effects of economic or other contextual constraints into organizational structures and practices (link 3, Figure 1). However, organizational choices of responses to these constraints are controlled and bound by cultural legitimation. While adoption of responses incongruent with peripheral values may be possible, adoption of responses incongruent with core values may have serious consequences for the effectiveness of organizational functioning.

ECONOMIC RESOURCES
AND INDIVIDUAL BEHAVIOR

Scarcity of economic resources influences individual adherence to certain values, by reinforcing specific choices within the legitimized range (link 4, Figure 1). This proposition is supported by Triandis (1984). He argues, for example, that in less-developed countries under conditions of meager economic resources, the high uncertainty about the economic pay-off of work efforts reinforces the low emphasis placed there on work and work values.

A study of managers' work-goals priority in four Chinese societies (PRC, Hong-Kong, Taiwan, Singapore) suggests that observed differences in rankings of earnings and benefits as work-goals, can be explained by the different economic conditions of these culturally similar societies (Shenkar and Ronen 1990). These findings suggest that it is probable that different levels of resource scarcity may engender individual differences in value emphasis even within the same cultural setting.

CONGRUENCY AND
ORGANIZATIONAL EFFECTIVENESS

Emphasized in the framework is the congruency between core value assumptions underlying specific organizational structures and processes, and the core values of the host cultural setting that govern and legitimize (or sanction) corresponding patterns of behavior. It is proposed that incongruencies among these elements may strongly impact organizational effectiveness. This is manifested not only at the interface of organization and culture (link 2) but also within the organization at the interface between role expectations and behavior, on the one hand, and prescribed structures and processes on the other (link 5). We acknowledge the importance of effective organizational adaptation to the economic and other context factors of its environment (link 3) which has frequently been argued by others (e.g., Lawrence and Lorsch 1969, Pfeffer and Salancik 1978, Kiggundu et al. 1983). However, we contend that not every adaptation will necessarily be effective. Those adaptations which are consistent with and legitimized by core values will be more effective than adaptations incongruent with core cultural values. Similarly, if management were to engage in activities that are negatively sanctioned by local cultural (particularly core) values, culturally based resistance may impede these activities or alienate important constituencies whose support is required for the effective organizational functioning.

Also proposed by the framework are feedback effects of organizations' effectiveness within as well as outside the organization. This suggests that the level of effectiveness may, in turn, influence role expectations and organizational structures and processes. Similarly, it can influence the availability of resources in the environment, or even some cultural values.

The effect of differential cultural congruency on effectiveness is illustrated in a study by Roniger (1987). It examines the organizational consequences of different cultural emphases on hierarchical relations in Brazil, Mexico and Japan. These cultural differences were found to affect the formulation of organizational patterns of mobilizing commitment to collective tasks. Roniger argues that the nature of the hierarchical trust particular to these societies resulted in divergent patterns of modernization: more effective in Japan than in the two Latin-American societies. Another example, on the level of managerial practices is Shenkar and Ronen's (1987) argument that many business negotiations conducted by Americans in China have failed because the former may have failed to accommodate for the negotiation patterns acceptable to the latter.

However, incongruencies of management activities with periphery values may be less consequential and more easily overlooked. While the Staw and Szwajkowski (1975) study did not deal directly with the effect of periphery values, such an effect can be suggested. It can be speculated that among American firms there is no strong and wide acceptance of the values governing the illegitimate activities examined in their study (e.g., price fixing, franchise violations), and the social sanctions for their violation are not very strong. Consequently, firms facing economic pressures choose to overlook, or ''bend,'' these values and engage in those questionable activities.

SPECIFYING CULTURAL EFFECTS ON ORGANIZATIONAL DIMENSIONS: ILLUSTRATIONS

By articulating the impact of cultural values on organizational structure and processes, the framework can serve as an hypotheses-generating schema

(Figure 2). The relationships proposed in the framework can be translated into testable hypotheses by presenting them as a set of separate or interrelated propositions. For example, linking its parts together, the schema proposes that values (core or periphery) influence individuals through different socialization influences (home, community, or workplace) exerted at different (early or adult) life cycle stages, and sanctioning (positively or negatively) patterns of action manifested in organizational structure and processes that correspond to resource availability (scarcity or munificence). This leads to (high or low) congruence, which results in (high or low) organizational effectiveness. Various combinations of all or some of these propositions can be generated from the schema and tested separately, or as path models (Lachman 1988).

As an illustration, it can be proposed that organizational socialization influences will have little effect on employees' core values inculcated at their early life stage. Consequently, when these values are concerned, employees' selection and differential retention may be more effective methods for obtaining congruence with organizational values than organizational efforts to socialize employees. Further, it can be proposed that the higher the incongruency between employees' core values and those of the transplanted organization, the lower the employees' satisfaction, the higher the turnover and the more difficult it will be for the organization to recruit employees. Similarly, it can be proposed that local values adopted by employees at the adult life stage, can be changed through organizational socialization since these will constitute periphery values of these employees. Other propositions can be formulated in a similar way.

In addition, by inserting particular values into the framework, specific hypotheses regarding their impact on organizational dimensions can be derived and tested. Four values, often studied, are used for illustration: values governing power relations, social relations, orientations to work and values pertaining to uncertainty. Table 1 summarizes several hypotheses illustrating some implications of these four values for the structure and processes of organizations, as well as for the behavioral styles of their members.

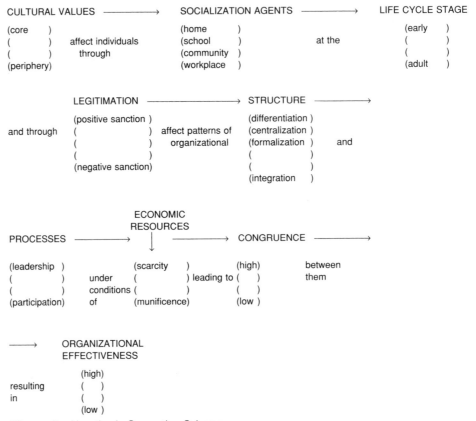

Figure 2. Hypothesis Generating Scheme

Power values are cultural values that specify appropriate forms of power relationships and authority in social organizations. They define the appropriate hierarchical arrangements and the power-compliance strategies that should be employed within organizations. Derived from these values are, for example, preferences for long as opposed to short power distances in social relations (Hofstede 1980). Thus, it can be hypothesized (link 2, Figure 1) that a cultural emphasis on high power distance will be associated with the choice of compatible patterns of structural configurations such as high hierarchical differentiation or high centralization. Similarly, it can be associated with the choice of corresponding organizational processes of nonparticipative decision making, hierarchical rather than collegial or "clan" control and coordination. Through the effects of cultural values on individual behavior (link

1, Figure 1) it can be hypothesized that preference for high power distance will be associated with preference for an authoritarian leadership style. It can be further hypothesized that congruence between the choice of a highly centralized organizational power structure and non-participative decision processes, on the one hand, and the preference for a style of high distance in interpersonal relations on the other, will enhance organizational effectiveness.

Some concrete examples can be suggested as illustrations. A study by Hinings and Badran (1981) describes how the high degree of participation required by the prescribed structure of public organizations in Egypt was difficult to implement, because the indigenous cultural values emphasized social and hierarchic distance in interpersonal relationships. The outcome of this incongruency were poor internal processes and low levels of participation in the real-

Table 1. The Effects of Cultural Values on Organizational Choices: An Illustration

Cultural Values	Structure	Processes	Behavioral Style
Power			
High/low power	Hierarchy: differentiation high/low Centralization: high/low	Decision making: participative/nonparticipative Communication: vertical/horizontal Control: tight/loose Coordination: vertical/horizontal	Leadership: authoritarian/democratic Subordinates' compliance strategies: high/low authoritarian, or coercive/permissive
Social Relations			
Individualistic/collectivistic orientation	Horizontal differentiation: specialization high/low Rewards: differential high/low	Rewards and incentives: individual/group emphasis Communication: specific/diffuse Decision making: contentious/consensus	Commitment: self/group goals Compliance strategies: calculative/moralistic Climate: competitive/cooperative
Work Orientation			
Work/nonwork centrality	Span of control: wide/short	Rewards and incentives: intrinsic/extrinsic	Climate: expressive/instrumental Commitment: internal/external
Uncertainty			
High/low avoidance	Formalization: high/low Centralization: high/low	Locus of decisions: hierarchical/diffuse	Climate: reserved/open

ized organizations, not the high levels required by the prescribed structure (Badran 1979, Hinings and Badran 1981).

Birnbaum and Wong (1985) suggested that in Hong Kong where the cultural emphasis was on high power distance, the structure of organizations will tend to be centralized, and local employees (Chinese) will be more satisfied working in a centralized rather than decentralized structure. This was supported by the results of their study on multinational banks in Hong Kong. However, similar hypotheses regarding satisfaction with organizational differentiation and formalization, were not supported. While Birnbaum and Wong do not use this interpretation, their findings can be explained by suggesting that the value governing hierarchical power relations is (as they do argue) core to the Chinese culture in Hong Kong, whereas those governing formalization and

differentiation are not. Consequently, when a core value is concerned, value incongruency can explain employees' dissatisfaction (i.e., lower effectiveness). But when variations in practices (differentiation or formalization) among the multinational organizations were incongruent with values that were not core, work satisfaction of local employees was not affected.

Social interaction values specify the particular forms of human bonds, determining cultural preferences for particular interaction patterns and role relationships. They may range from an individualistic to a collectivistic orientation. Illustrating the effect of such values is Schein's (1981) argument that it will be difficult to implement Japanese management approaches in an American context when the core cultural values underlying these approaches differ considerably from core American values. He points to individualism as a key value of U.S. culture which emphasizes the pursuit of self-interest and the individual's responsibility for his/her actions. The Japanese place a high value on collectivity and deliberately blur individual responsibility by adopting methods, like consensus decision making, that accommodate such blurring. This consensus method is incongruent with American individualism and in many ways irrelevant to management in the U.S. (Schein 1981).

From this, it can be hypothesized that in a cultural setting where individualism is a core value (e.g., the U.S.) contentious rather than consensual methods of decision making should be employed. Local employees will be more satisfied working in organizations employing a contentious decision process than in organizations employing consensual ones. This hypothesis is corroborated by findings that in Japanese organizations operating in the U.S., Japanese employees were the most satisfied with the organizational structure, Japanese-Americans were less satisfied and non-Japanese Americans were the least satisfied (Lincoln et al. 1981).

The effects of the other two values can be similarly analyzed and hypotheses generated (Table 1). The value placed on work itself governs the view of work as a distinct form of social activity, and the centrality of work in life. It specifies the importance of organized work activity to individuals and the preferred methods to motivate and direct the investment of human energy in this activity. In this respect, cultural preferences may range from a strong emphasis on work as a means for achieving nonwork goals and social status (instrumental orientation), to a strong emphasis on work as a highly valued activity in itself (expressive orientation). Values pertaining to uncertainty govern the culturally preferred reaction to it, which may range from high avoidance of uncertainty to its acceptance (Hofstede 1980). However, the framework here is by no means limited to these particular values or to an examination of the possible effects of a single value at a time. The core values or combinations of values particular to any cultural, or subcultural settings can be introduced to generate testable hypotheses about their effects on organiza-

tional forms and managerial practices. In either case, the basic approach underlying the framework is that of "cultural congruence" with core values.

COPING WITH INCONGRUENCIES

Our argument suggests that not every incongruency in organizational adaptation with local values is dysfunctional and should be avoided. It suggests differential effects of incongruencies with core or periphery values. Advocated here is a contingency approach of "cultural congruence" describing different incongruencies which may have different consequences for cross-cultural organizations and may require different managerial approaches or coping strategies. For analytical purposes the organization-culture value incongruencies can be presented as crude combinations on the core/periphery dimension. Four "types" of incongruencies or contingencies may be encountered by organizations: (a) between values core to the organizational system and values core to the cultural system; (b) between values core to the organization but peripheral to the cultural system; (c) between those peripheral to the organization but core to the culture; (d) between values peripheral to both systems. These contingencies call for different management approaches, involving different entry, and coping strategies (Table 2).

TYPE A: CONTENTION

This incongruency is potentially most problematic for the effectiveness of cross national organizations and management. Here the core organizational values contest the local core ones, attempting to radically change them. This contingency has high potential for severe conflicts and frictions that may alienate important constituencies whose cooperation may be essential for the organization. This may impair effectiveness, even if radical change is eventually obtained. Some forms of value coupling are, therefore, proposed as an overall strategy. The *entry strategy* to a host setting under this contingency should account for the equally dominant local val-

Table 2.   Contingencies of Value Incongruencies

	Values at the Local Cultural Level	
Values at the Organizational Level	**Core**	**Periphery**

Core	Contention
	
	Overall Strategy
	  Coupling
	Entry Strategy
	  Joint ventures
	Coping Strategy
	  Negotiation
	  Log-rolling
	  Coalition formation
	
	A
		Primacy
		
		Overall Strategy
		  Forcing change
		Entry Strategy
		  Transplantation
		Coping Strategy
		  Proactive
		  Change-oriented
		  Innovative
		
		B

Periphery	C
	Submission
	
	Overall Strategy
	  Yielding
	Entry Strategy
	  Operating through locals
	  Franchises
	  Mergers
	Coping Strategy
	  Compliance
	  Accommodation
	  Reorientation
		D
		Indifference
		
		Overall Strategy
		  Ignoring differences
		Entry Strategy
		Nonspecific
		
		Coping Strategy
		Nonspecific

ues. A joint venture with a local organization may be an entry form that allows the conjugation or loose coupling of core values from both the local and foreign parents, in a way that corresponds with the local setting. The *coping strategy* that may be advisable here is conflict avoidance. Negotiation, log-rolling, coalitions, or at times even co-optation, may be more effective than contention or confrontation as strategies for coping with the host culture. Given the incongruency in core values it can also be proposed that attempts to increase congruence between values required by the organization and those held by members (both at the top and at lower levels) will focus on human resources strategies of selection rather than on organizational socialization efforts.

The examples of Confucian values in China discussed earlier can serve as a case in point. The traditional Confucian value of obligation to kinship affiliation has maintained its centrality in the Chinese cultural system for many generations. Although the Maoist ideology officially opposed kinship affiliation it has preferred not to challenge this value, thus leaving intact a major basis of the traditional system. Moreover, kinship allegiances were utilized by the Maoist system for its own benefit (Parish and Whyte 1978). On the other hand, the traditional core value of hierarchical relations was contested by the Maoist system which also regarded this value as a core one. However, as indicated above, Maoist attempts to radically change hierarchical relations by abolishing them, have failed (Laaksonen 1988). These examples suggest that even a very powerful and culturally indigenous organization may find it more effective to accommodate core cultural values than to challenge them.

TYPE B: PRIMACY

This contingency is conducive to change and innovations introduced by the "imported" organization. The organization can adopt a general approach of increasing congruence with its host cultural environment by pressuring for change in local peripheral values to match the core organizational ones. The *entry approach* proposed for foreign organizations in this situation is of organizational "transplantation." Organizational structures and processes can be transplanted across the cultural boundaries into the host setting, mostly as is. Incongruencies will then be reduced through changes in the local periphery values. Unlike the previous contingency (A), efforts to attain congruence here imply a *coping strategy* of organizationally planned and controlled change for management. Under this type of incongruency an externally induced change may even be desired and encouraged by the host country. Similarly, since organizational core and host periphery values are concerned, a strategy of transferring expatriate management into the host setting can be proposed. Through this strategy organizational core values can be maintained, possible incongruency between the values of top managers and those of the organization can be reduced, and the required change in local values can be stimulated. Lower level employees can be recruited locally and their (periphery) values changed through organizational socialization practices.

TYPE C: SUBMISSION

In this contingency, periphery organizational values are incongruent with local core ones. Since the incongruent values are peripheral to the organization, efforts to change local core values may not be worthwhile. Organizational compliance with, or adoption of local core values may be a more effective *coping strategy* for achieving congruence or at least accommodation. The *entry strategy* that may be appropriate under this contingency is to operate through local organizations (e.g., mergers, franchises, or purchases), to reduce possible incongruency with local core values. Similarly, hiring local human resources at all levels of the organization may be a valid strategy.

TYPE D: INDIFFERENCE

This is perhaps the least disruptive incongruency for cross-cultural organizations. Incongruency between peripheral values may either be bridged, or left to coexist, with relatively low costs to the organization. Consequently, no specific coping and entry strategies are proposed. Strategic choices can be made based on other considerations.

Thus, the above approach to cultural congruence strongly suggests that when moving across cultural settings, management should carefully examine the type of incongruency they may encounter, as these may require different entry and coping strategies. Much like market, resources, and feasibility surveys conducted by organizations, values' congruency with a local setting ought also be surveyed and investigated as a major organizational consideration. Some methodological issues regarding value examination are discussed in Appendix A.

CONCLUSIONS

The framework presented here attempts to articulate the impact of cultural values on the structures and processes of cross national organizations. It proposes that: (1) core and periphery cultural values exert differential social control at both the individual and organizational levels by legitimizing certain ranges of behavior and patterns of organizing; (2) individual behavior is regulated by the values inculcated through early or late socialization processes; (3) organizations are shaped through the legitimation of certain choices of organizational structure and processes; (4) particular organization choices, within the legitimized ranges, are influenced by other contextual factors, one of which is availability of economic resources that pose constraints to which organizations have to adapt; (5) these contextual factors also influence individual choices by reinforcing certain values and behaviors; (6) incongruencies in integrating these influences affect organizational effectiveness and have to be contended with.

Thus, the framework offers a theory-based approach for crossnational as well as intranational (regional) comparisons, and contributes toward the development of a much-needed paradigmatic approach to crossnational organizations. As such, this framework has both theoretical and practical contributions. The importance of the effects of cultural values on transferred organizational and management practices has been stressed by previous research. The theoretical contribution in our framework goes beyond that. It points to the social control and social sanctions that values exert on behavior, as the specific value dimension to which differences in organizational practices ought to be attributed. Hence, the focus offered here is on the differentiation between core and periphery cultural values which reflect their differential social control. The framework goes further to describe and discuss the processes and mechanisms through which these differential social control effects, embedded in core and periphery values, are exerted at the organizational and individual levels. It argues for a cultural congruence approach to crossnational organizations not in terms of similarity in specific values but in terms of value centrality at both the organizational and the cultural levels. It is this congruency that may impact organizational effectiveness. Furthermore, proposed and discussed here were contingencies under which culture may have differential impact and consequences for organizations. Another important advantage of the framework is its capacity for generating specific testable hypotheses pertaining to the effects of values particular to a cultural setting.

The proposed framework also has a contribution in offering a uniform and coherent interpretation to different studies that previously were not tied together under a single conceptual scheme. For example, the framework may help resolve the debate between the ''culture free'' and ''culturalist'' approaches to cross-cultural analysis. We argue that the focus in the debate should be shifted from the question of the relative impact of cultural and noncultural influences, to the ''culture congruence'' perspective, and the impact of core relative to periphery

cultural values in determining the range of acceptable adjustments to contextual factors. We suggest that inconsistencies in results of previous research concerning this debate may have resulted from the comparison of ''unlikes''; while some studies examined organizational adaptations all governed by values of similar susceptibility to change (e.g., all peripheral values), giving the impression of ''culture-free'' adaptations, others focused on adaptations governed by values of different susceptibility to change (e.g., some governed by core and some by peripheral), thus giving rise to the ''culturalist'' interpretation. The comparison of organizational adaptations governed not by similar values but by values of similar susceptibility (e.g., all core) is an important issue that needs to be carefully addressed and considered by future research. A potentially fruitful line of research is to compare not only organizations in different settings but also organizations in settings of the same core values. Also, research may benefit most by focusing on longitudinal rather than crosssectional comparisons of such organizations. This design can help identify the factors facilitating and restraining change and innovation.

Of a more practical nature are the implications of the framework for the cross-national transferability of organizational arrangements and managerial practices. Managerial choices of structural adjustments should be in line with the relevant core values of the particular host setting and those held by its members. ''Imported'' practices may fail, or be ineffectively implemented, if they are inconsistent with the core values of local settings (e.g., Schein 1981, Sethi et al. 1984). However, if the underlying values of an imported organizational practice are incongruent with the peripheral values of the host setting, socialization efforts exerted by the organization can be directed at reducing incongruency, and a successful transfer of this practice may be achieved. We maintain that forcing change while challenging local core values may be very difficult to accomplish. The contingency approach to cultural congruency proposed here offers management of cross-cultural organizations a conceptual tool for analyzing and better understanding their interface with local cultural settings, and the implications this may have for effectiveness. Furthermore, considering these contingencies may be important for organizations in their choice of organizational adaptations, practices, and strategies for their operations in local settings.

The conformity to local values implied by the framework, raises some important ethical issues. These issues require theoretical and empirical attention which are beyond the scope of this paper. For example, an interesting question is to what extent should management compromise its own values to comply with those of local settings? Recent practices of multinational organizations have brought such ethical issues to the fore ground. Systematic study of these issues ought to follow.

In conclusion, the congruence of a given practice with local cultural values can be an important contingency to be considered in any decision to transfer across cultural settings. Careful preliminary assessment of compatibility between local core values and those underlying organizational structures and processes may prevent costly and sometimes irreversible mistakes of implementing structures and practices that are not suited to local environments.

APPENDIX

Measuring Core and Periphery Values The call for a close examination of core and periphery values of a cultural setting, raises the methodological issue of the identification of specific values as core or peripheral in given cultures. Although such methods require further development, few approaches can be proposed. One possible approach is qualitative methods for classifying values through analyses of contents, behaviors, or the implicit assumptions in social discourse. Such analyses can be performed by social scientists expert on a given culture (e.g., Eberhard 1971, Ouchi 1981, Pascale and Athos 1981, Schein 1981). A shortcoming of this approach is that the results obtained by different scientists may not always be consistent and it may be difficult to evaluate their validity and reliability.

Another approach is a systematic study of choices of actions or social goods within a cultural setting. For example, iterative interviewing methods can be used (Schein 1985), or individuals in a certain culture can be asked to rank values in terms of importance (Dawson et al. 1971, Rokeach 1973, Hofstede 1980). A high consensus or disagreement on the importance or unimportance of certain values can indicate their relative position as core or peripheral values, respectively. Lachman (1983) has shown that on the basis of consensus in ranking, a number of values previously measured by Inkeles and Smith (1974) in four countries, can be classified as core or periphery.

While each of these approaches can provide some indications as to the values' rank order, it appears that employing a multimethod approach may be a preferred way for tapping and classifying values in local settings. Since each of the above methods has its limitations, a multimethod approach is more likely to result in valid and reliable classifications than a single measure. Evidently, further research efforts are required in order to develop more adequate and reliable measures for differentiating core from periphery values in a cultural setting.

REFERENCES

Abegglen, J.C. and G. Stalk, Jr., *Kaisha, The Japanese Corporation,* Basic Books, New York, 1985.

Adler, N.J., ''Cross-cultural Management Research: The Ostrich and the Trend,'' *The Academy of Management Review,* 8 (1983), 226–232.

Allport, G.W., *Patterns and Growth in Personality,* Holt, Rinehart & Winston, New York, 1961.

Argyris, C., *Integrating The Individual and The Organization,* Wiley, New York, 1964.

Badran, M., *The Relationship Between Democratic Administration and Bureaucracy,* Ph.D. Thesis, University of Birmingham, England, 1979.

Birnbaum, P.H. and G.Y.Y. Wong, ''Organizational Structure of Multinational Banks in Hong Kong from a Culture-Free Perspective,'' *Administrative Sci. Quarterly,* 30 (1985), 262–277.

Bond, M.H. and S. Wang, ''China: Aggressive Behavior and the Problem of Maintaining Order and Harmony,'' In A.P. Goldstein and M.H. Segall (Eds.), *Aggression in Global Perspective,* Pergamon Press, New York, 1983.

Brim, O. Jr., ''Adult Socialization,'' *International Encyclopedia of Social Sciences,* 14 (1968), 555–562.

Cameron, K.S., ''The Effectiveness of Ineffectiveness,'' In B.M. Staw and L.L. Cummings (Eds.), *Research in Organizational Behavior,* 6, JAI Press, Greenwich, CT, 1984.

———, D.A. Whetten, and M.U. Kim, ''Dysfunctions of Organizational Decline,'' *Academy of Management J.,* 30 (1987), 126–138.

Cavusgil, T.S. and U. Yavas, "Transfer of Management Know-how to Developing Countries: An Empirical Investigation," *J. Business Research,* 12 (1984), 35–50.

Child, J., "Culture Contingency and Capitalism in Cross-cultural Study of Organizations," In L. Cummings and B. Staw (Eds.), *Research in Organizational Behavior,* 3 (1981), 303–356.

———— and M. Tayeb, "Theoretical Perspectives in Crossnational Organizational Research," *International Studies of Management and Organization,* 12, 4 (1982), 23–70.

Clark, P., "Cultural Context as a Determinant of Organizational Rationality: A Comparison of the Tobacco Industries in Britain and France," In C.G. Lammers and D.J. Hickson (Eds.), *Organizations Alike and Unlike,* Routledge & Kegan Paul, London; 1979.

Connolly, T., E.J. Conlon and S.J. Deutch, "Organizational Effectiveness: A Multiple-Constituency Approach," *Academy of Management Review,* 5 (1980), 211–217.

Dawson, J.L., M. Law, A. Leung and R.W. Whitney, "Scaling Chinese Traditional-Modern Attitudes and the GSR Measurement of Important vs. Unimportant Chinese Concepts," *J. Cross-Cultural Psychology,* 2 (1971), 1–29.

Downey, H.K., D.L. Hellriegel and J.W. Slocum, Jr., "Environmental Uncertainty: The Construct and Its Application," *Administrative Sci. Quarterly,* 20 (1975), 613–629.

Eberhard, W., *Moral and Social Values of the Chinese—Collected Essays,* Chinese Materials and Research Aids Service Center, Washington, DC, 1971.

Ford, J.D. and D.A. Baucus, "Organizational Adaptations to Performance Downturns: An Interpretation Based Perspective," *Academy of Management Review,* 12 (1987), 366–380.

Frese, M., "Occupational Socialization and Psychological Development," *J. Occupational Psychology,* 55 (1982), 209–224.

Gallie, D., *In Search of the New Working Class,* Cambridge University Press, Cambridge, England, 1978.

Glenn, E., *Man and Mankind: Conflict and Communication Between Culture,* Ablex, Horwood, NJ, 1981.

Hickson, D.J., C.R. Hinings, C.J. McMillan and J.P. Schwitter, "The Culture-Free Context of Organization Structure," *Sociology,* 8 (1974), 59–80.

———— and C.J. McMillan, *Organization and Nation,* Gower Press, London, England, 1981.

————, ————, K. Azumi, and J.P. Schwitter, "Grounds for Comparison of Organization Theory: Quicksands or Hard Core?" In C.J. Lammers and D. Hickson (Eds.), *Organizations Alike and Unlike,* Routledge and Kegan Paul, London, England, 1979.

Hinings, C.R. and M. Badran, "Strategies of Administrative Control and Contextual Constraints in a Less Developed Country," *Organization Studies,* 2 (1981), 3–22.

Hofstede, G., *Culture's Consequences,* Sage Publication Ltd., London, England, 1980.

Holland, J.L., "Vocational Preferences," In M.D. Dunnette (Ed.), *Handbook of Industrial and Organizational Psychology,* Rand McNally, Chicago, IL, 1976.

Howard, A., K. Shudo and M. Umeshima, "Motivation and Values Among Japanese and American Managers," *Personnel Psychology,* 36 (1983), 883–898.

Hsu, Francis L., *American and Chinese: Passage to Differences,* The University Press of Hawaii, Honolulu, HI, 1981.

Inkeles, A. and D.H. Smith, *Becoming Modern,* Harvard University Press, Cambridge, MA, 1974.

Jamieson, I.M., "Some Observations on Socio-Cultural Explanations of Economic Behavior," *Sociological Review,* 26 (1978), 777–805.

————, "The Concept of Culture and Its Relevance for an Analysis of Business Enterprise in Different Societies," *International Studies of Management and Organization,* 12, 4 (1982), 71–105.

Katz, D. and R. Kahn, *The Social Psychology of Organizations,* Wiley, New York, 1978.

Kelly, L. and R. Worthley, "The Role of Culture in Comparative Management: A Cross Cultural Perspective," *Academy of Management J.,* 24 (1981), 164–173.

Kiesler, S. and L. Sproull, "Managerial Response to Changing Environments: Perspectives on Problem Sensing from Social Cognition," *Administrative Sci. Quarterly,* 27 (1982), 548–570.

Kiggundu, M.N., J.J. Jorgensen and T. Hofsi, "Administration Theory and Practice in Developing Countries: A Synthesis," *Administrative Sci. Quarterly,* 28 (1983), 66–84.

Kluckhohn, C., "Values and Value Orientations in the Theory of Action: An Exploration in Definition and Classifications," In T. Parsons and E. Shils (Eds.), *Toward General Theory of Action,* Harvard University Press, Cambridge, MA, 1951.

Kluckhohn, F.R. and F.L. Strodtbeck, *Variations in Value Orientations,* Row, Peterson, New York, 1961.

Laaksonen, O., *Management in China,* Walter de Gruyter, Berlin, 1988.

Lachman, R., "Modernity Change of Core and Periphery Values of Factory Workers," *Human Relations,* 36, 6 (1983), 563–580.

————, "Factors Influencing Workers' Orientations: A Secondary Analysis of Israeli Data," *Organization Studies,* 99 (1988), 487–510.

Lammers, C.J. and D.J. Hickson (Eds.), *Organizations Alike and Unlike,* Routledge & Kegan Paul, London, 1979.

Lawrence, P.R. and J.W. Lorsch, *Organization and Environment,* Irwin, Homewood, IL, 1969.

Leff, N.H., "Industrial Organization and Entrepreneurship in the Developing Countries: The Economic Groups," *Economic Development and Cultural Change,* 26 (1978), 661–675.

Levine, C.H., "More on Cutback Management: Hard Questions for Hard Issues," *Public Administration Review,* (1979), 179–183.

Lincoln, J.R., M. Hanada, and J. Olsen, "Cultural Orientations and Individual Reactions to Organizations: A Study of Employees in Japanese Owned Firms," *Administration Sci. Quarterly,* 28 (1981), 93–115.

Liu, Hui-chen W., "An Analysis of Chinese Clan Rules: Confusian Theories in Action," In A.F. Wright (Ed.), *Confucianism and Chinese Civilization,* Stanford University Press, Stanford, CA, 1964.

Martinko, M.J. and Y. Fenzeng, ''A Comparison of Leadership Theory and Practice in the People's Republic of China and the United States,'' In *International Human Resource Management Review,* 1 (1990), 109–122.

Maurice, M., ''For a Study of 'The Societal Effect,''' In Lammers and Hickson (Eds.), *Organizations Alike and Unlike,* Routledge and Kegan Paul, London, 1979.

McMillan, C.J., D.J. Hickson, C.R. Hinings and R.E. Schneck, ''The Structure of Work Organizations Across Societies,'' *Academy of Management J.,* 16 (1973), 555–569.

Miller, Edwin L., Rosalie L. Tung, Robert W. Armstrong and Bruce W. Stening, ''A Comparison of Australian and United States Management Succession Systems,'' *International Human Resource Management Review,* 1 (1990), 123–140.

Mortimer, J.T. and J. Lorence, ''Work Experience and Occupational Value Socialization: A Longitudinal Study,'' *American J. of Sociology,* 84 (1979), 1361–1385.

Nath, Raghu, *Comparative Management: A Regional View,* Ballinger Publishing Company, Cambridge, MA, 1988.

Negandhi, A.R., ''Comparative Management and Organizational Theory: A Marriage Needed,'' *Academy of Management J.,* 18 (1975), 337.

Nivison, D.S. and F. Wright (Eds.), *Confucianism In Action,* Stanford University Press, Stanford, CA, 1959.

Ouchi, W., *Theory Z: How American Business Can Meet the Japanese Challenge,* Addison-Wesley, Reading, MA, 1981.

Parish, W.L. and M.K. Whyte, *Village and Family in Contemporary China,* Chicago University Press, Chicago, IL, 1978.

Parsons, T., *Social Structure and Personality,* The Free Press, New York, 1964.

Pascale, R.T. and A.G. Athos, *The Art of Japanese Management: Applications for American Executives,* Simon & Schuster, New York, 1981.

Peterson, K. and J.A. Dutton, ''Centrality, Extremity, Intensity,'' *Social Forces,* 54 (1975), 394–414.

Pfeffer, J. and Y. Cohen, ''Determinants of Internal Labor Markets in Organizations,'' *Administrative Sci. Quarterly,* 29, 4 (1985), 550–572.

———— and G.R. Salancik, *The External Control of Organizations: A Resource Dependence Perspective,* Harper and Row, New York, 1978.

Price, J.L., ''The Study of Organizational Effectiveness,'' *The Sociological Quarterly,* 13 (1972), 3–15.

Ranson, S., C.R. Hinings and R. Greenwood, ''The Structuring of Organizational Structures,'' *Administrative Sci. Quarterly,* 25 (1980), 1–17.

Robbins, S.P., *The New Management: Managing Declining Organizations,* Paper Presented at the Western Academy of Management Annual Meeting, Vancouver, B.C., Canada, 1984.

Roberts, K.H. and N.A. Boyacigiller, ''Cross-National Organizational Research: The Grasp of the Blind Men,'' In L. Cummings and B. Staw (Eds.), *Research in Organizational Behavior,* 6, JAI Press, Inc., Greenwich, CT, 1984.

Rokeach, M., *Beliefs, Attitudes and Values,* Jossey-Bass, Inc., San Francisco, 1969.

————, *The Nature of Human Values,* The Free Press, New York, 1973.

Ronen, S., *Comparative and Multinational Management,* John Wiley & Sons, New York, 1986.

———— and O. Shenkar, ''Clustering Countries on Attitudinal Dimensions: A Review and Synthesis,'' *Academy of Management Review,* 10 (1985), 435–454.

Roniger, L., ''Coronelismo, Caciquismo, and Oyabun-Kobun Bond: Divergent Implications of Hierarchical Trust in Brazil, Mexico and Japan,'' *The British J. Sociology,* 38 (1987), 310–329.

Rudie-Harrigan, K., ''Strategy Formulation in Declining Industries,'' *Academy of Management Review,* 5 (1980), 599–604.

Schein, E.H., ''Does Japanese Management Style Have a Message for American Managers?'' *Sloan Management Review,* 21, 1 (1981), 55–68.

————, *Organizational Culture and Leadership,* Jossey-Bass, San Francisco, 1985.

Sethi, S.P., N. Namiki and E.L. Saranson, *The False Promise of the Japanese Miracle,* Pitman, Boston, MA, 1984.

Shenkar, O. and S. Ronen, ''The Cultural Context of Negotiations: The Implications of Chinese Interpersonal Norms,'' *J. Applied Behavioral Science,* 23 (1987), 263–275.

———— and ————, ''Culture, Ideology or Economy: A Comparative Exploration of Work Goal Importance Among Managers in Chinese Societies,'' In S.B. Prasad (Ed.), *Advances in International Comparative Management,* 5 JAI Press, Inc., Greenwich, CT, 1990.

Shils, E., ''Center and Periphery,'' In M. Polany (Ed.), *The Logic of Personal Knowledge,* Routledge and Kegan Paul, London, 1961.

Shin, Y.K., R.M. Steers, G.R. Ungson and S. Nam, ''Work Environment and Management Practice in Korean Companies,'' *International Human Resource Management Review,* 1 (1990), 95–108.

Smelser, N., ''Mechanisms for Change and Adjustment to Change,'' In B.F. Hoselitz and W.F. Moore (Eds.), *Industrialization and Society,* UNESCO/Moimt, Paris, 1963, 32–48.

Staw, B.M. and E. Szwajkowski, ''The Scarcity-Munificence Component of Organizational Environment and the Commission of Illegal Acts,'' *Administrative Sci. Quarterly,* 20 (1975), 345–354.

Thompson, J.D., *Organizations in Action,* McGraw-Hill, New York, 1967.

Triandis, H.C., ''Dimensions of Cultural Variation as Parameters of Organizational Theories,'' *International Studies of Management and Organization,* 12 (1982), 139–169.

————, ''Toward a Psychological Theory of Economic Growth,'' *International J. Psychology,* 19 (1984), 79–95.

Van Maanen, J. and E.H. Schein, ''Toward a Theory of Organizational Socialization,'' In B. Staw (Ed.), *Research in Organizational Behavior,* 1 (1979), 209–264.

Vertinsky, I., K. Tse, D.A. Wehrung and K. Lee, "Organizational Design and Management Norms: A Comparative Study of Managers Perception in the People's Republic of China, Hong Kong and Canada," *J. Management,* 16 (1990), 853–867.

Weick, K.E., *The Social Psychology of Organizing,* Addison-Wesley, Reading, MA, 1979.

Whetten, D.A., "Sources, Responses and Effects of Organizational Decline," In J. Kimberly and R.H. Miles (Eds.), *The Or-* *ganization Life Cycle: Issues in the Creation, Transformation and Decline of Organizations,* Jossey-Bass, San Francisco, 1980.

———, "What Constitutes a Theoretical Contribution?" *Academy of Management Review,* 14 (1989), 490–495.

Zussman, Y.E., "Learning from the Japanese: Management in a Resource Scarce World," *Organizational Dynamics* 11, 3 (Winter 1983), 68–80.

37

MANAGING DMNCs: A SEARCH FOR A NEW PARADIGM

Y.L. DOZ
INSEAD, Fontainebleau, France

C.K. PRAHALAD
Graduate School of Business Administration, University of Michigan,
Ann Arbor, Michigan, U.S.A.

ABSTRACT This article reviews and assesses the contribution, explicit or implicit, of various schools of organization theory to the development of a stream of research on the management of multinational companies, and summarizes what is seen as the emerging paradigm of multinational management. While the contribution of some of the schools has been substantial, we conclude that opportunities for more cross-fertilization between organization theorists and scholars of multinational strategic management have been missed, mainly because the differences between theory development and phenomenological understanding have seldom been bridged.

The increasing intensity of global competition (Porter, 1986), the development of multinational companies (Dunning and Pearce, 1985; Stopford, Dunning and Haberich, 1980) and the attendant academic and managerial interest in the role of the diversified multinational firm (DMNC) (Bartlett and Ghoshal, 1989; Ghoshal, 1987; Prahalad and Doz, 1987) is too well documented in the literature to merit repetition. While there has been a lot of debate on the nature

Comments and suggestions by Sumantra Ghoshal, Mitchell Koza, Karl Weick, Harry Korine, and two anonymous *SMJ* reviewers are gratefully acknowledged.

of global competition and that of the DMNC, very little attention has been paid to the conceptual and theoretical frameworks used to analyze DMNCs and their management. Many attempts have been made to analyze aspects of the MNC starting from an established theoretical base. For example, Buckley and Casson (1986), and Hennart (1982) have attempted to seek a rationale for the MNC using a transaction cost perspective. Others (e.g., Dunning, 1973, 1980, 1981) have emphasized the need for an 'eclectic' theory explaining the DMNCs. We will argue, in this article, that on the whole, scholarly research in the area of the functioning of the MNC has suffered from a desire, among some scholars, to persist with existing paradigms, and among others from the ignorance of what existing theories could bring them. Since existing paradigms, by the very nature of their underlying simplifying assumptions, are not fully adequate to capture the complexity and richness of the DMNC, and since discipline-based researchers have seldom taken the DMNC as an object of research, this discrepancy is not surprising.

The development of a 'process school' of research on the DMNC over the past 15 years has led to the emergence of a new paradigm. This article positions this new paradigm and existing 'streams' of organization theory research *vis-à-vis* each other, in an attempt to resolve the observed discrepancy between organization theorists and scholars of the DMNC. The argument is developed in three main steps. First, we will describe the nature of the DMNC—its complexity and scope. We will derive some basic requirements that a paradigm used in the study of DMNCs must satisfy. Second, we will analyze the dominant paradigms that have been used by researchers studying organizations (not necessarily DMNCs) and evaluate the adequacy as well as the adaptability of specific paradigms to the study of DMNCs. Finally, we will outline the search for a new paradigm, and the contributions of a process school of research on multinational management.

THE NATURE OF THE DMNC AND THE 'SPECIFICATION' OF A PARADIGM FOR RESEARCH

In this section, based on the empirical and inductive analysis of management processes in DMNCs, we attempt to establish how the complexity of the DMNC, as an organizational form, sets some distinctive requirements for any theory to be useful in analyzing, conceptualizing and explaining management tasks in the DMNC.[1]

[1] Our purpose here is not to explain why the DMNC exists, as an organizational form. Various researchers, starting with Hymer (1960) and culminating in Dunning's 'eclectic theory,' have explained the logic for 'internalization' of transactions and firm-specific assets in the DMNC. Our purpose in this article is to analyze management processes in DMNCs, not to set the boundaries of DMNCs against other forms of organization of international investment and trade.

We see the essential difference between DMNCs and simpler organizations as stemming from the combined consequences of multidimensionality and heterogeneity.

Multidimensionality results from the very nature of DMNCs: they cover multiple geographical markets, with multiple product lines, in typically multifunction activities, such as sales, manufacturing, service, R&D, etc. DMNCs therefore face the problem of structuring the interfaces between these multiple dimensions that are intrinsic to their activities. In turn, multidimensionality means that no simple unidimensional hierarchical 'solution' to the issue of structuring the DMNC exists (Beer and Davis, 1976; Davis and Lawrence, 1977; Doz, 1976, 1979; Prahalad, 1975; Stopford and Wells, 1972). Beyond the *structural indeterminacy of DMNCs* lies the need to handle multiple stakeholders, externally, and by reflection internally, and multiple perspectives on choices and decisions. Simple concepts of centralized vs. decentralized organizations break down in the face of strategic, structural and political multidimensionality, calling for more complex 'multifocal' approaches which constantly reach trade-offs between priorities expressed in different dimensions (Doz, 1979, 1986) and embodied in different management subgroups.

Heterogeneity results from the differences between the optimal trade-offs for different businesses, countries, functions and tasks as a function of a whole range of economic and political characteristics which differ between countries and affect individual businesses and tasks in quite varied ways. DMNCs are therefore very heterogeneous organizations. Any theory of organization that one sets out to apply to DMNCs has to be able to incorporate this heterogeneity. In particular, some businesses and functions may be much more 'global' than others, which are more 'local.' The advantages of globalization vs. the needs for local responsiveness and adaptations are quite varied across businesses, countries and functions. To be applied to DMNC an organizational theory must therefore incorporate a *differentiated approach to businesses, countries and functions,* and provide enough flexibility for different trade-offs between multiple dimensions to be made.

The need for differentiation makes a structural

theory of DMNCs relatively difficult to develop. In fact, except in advocating a matrix organization, which is another way to acknowledge structural indeterminacy, a structural theory of DMNCs would have little to offer. One needs a theory that transcends the structural dimensions to focus on underlying processes. Issues of information and control become essential. More than the formal structure, the informal flow of information matters (Egelhoff, 1982). So do the processes of influence and power, of *how* the trade-offs between multiple stakeholders and multiple perspectives are made.

If one considers the evolution of sources of advantage in global competition, the perception of the importance of information flows is reinforced. As competitors increasingly achieve parity in access to resources (including technology) between various parts of the world, sources of competitiveness shift from location-specific factors to firm-specific factors, and to overall organizational capabilities to coordinate the use of resources to respond to short-lived opportunities that may arise in many different parts of the world. The traditional stable international oligopolies, with a handful of 'friendly' competitors are replaced by a quick succession of potential shorter-term monopolies, which only the more agile and discerning firms identify and exploit. While this shift takes place unevenly across global industries (with financial services and electronics leading the way, and more stable traditional products such as tires being less affected) it does suggest that researchers need to shift their emphasis from the physical infrastructure and the resource deployment of DMNCs to their information processing networks and to resource mobilization (Doz and Prahalad, 1988; Martinez and Jarillo, 1989).

Adopting an information network and organizational capability perspective, however, is not enough. The size and complexity of the typical DMNCs, often with hundreds of business units active in scores of countries, means that linkages and interdependencies cannot be planned, or centrally managed.

Which linkages are going to be useful at a particular point in time for a specific task between two or more subunits is unpredictable, and probably needs to be self-adjusting. Management in the DMNC thus calls for providing decentralized delegated decision contexts within which opportunities for linkages between subunits will arise at various points, levels in organization, and times. In that sense an interorganizational relation perspective may well be necessary to account for the polycentric MNCs (Ghoshal and Bartlett, 1990).

This raises an issue of 'fuzzy boundaries,' in which relational contracting within the DMNC and with external partners, customers, and suppliers is no longer always clear-cut and well delineated. A theory of DMNC management has to take this fuzziness of firm boundaries into consideration as well. Here again an interorganizational network perspective is appropriate.

The nature of this decentralized network management process creates a trade-off between repeatability and learning. For the DMNC organization to survive and keep its value to subunits, it must allow repeatability at a low cost, i.e., provide for routines and organizational memory that allow interaction patterns to be repeated. Yet at the same time it has to invent, select, and retain new interaction patterns when external conditions require an innovative response. This involves a delicate balance between institutional continuity and change capability.

In summary, considering the multidimensionality and the heterogeneity of the DMNC has led us to specify particular demands on the DMNC organization and on its management task that an organizational theory of the DMNC has to take into account.

1. *Structural undeterminacy:* no single stable unidimensional structure, or simple concepts of structure like centralization and decentralization, are likely to be useful.
2. *Internal differentiation:* management processes need to differentiate between various countries, products, and functions in the management process.
3. *Integrative optimization:* i.e., the need for management processes to foster varied decision trade-offs between multiple priorities expressed along different dimensions, and represented by diverse groups of managers.
4. *Information intensity:* the importance of information flows, both formal and informal, in DMNCs is such, as a source of competitive advantage and as an implicit

structure, that managing information becomes a central task of management.

5. *Latent linkages:* the fact that in a complex DMNC it is not possible to prespecify linkages and interdependencies, but only to facilitate the emergence of appropriate linkages as the need for them arises, in a decentralized self-structuring process.

6. *Networked organization and 'fuzzy boundaries':* this creates a need to explicitly incorporate partners, customers, and suppliers' relationships, as well as networked relationships in the management tasks.

7. *Learning and continuity:* the tension between the need for repeatability of interactions at a low cost and that for innovation and change.

These seven demands on DMNC organization and management derived from the multidimensionality, complexity, and heterogeneity of the DMNC provide a grid against which to review various strands of organizational theory, and to assess how, and to what extent, they may contribute to an understanding of DMNC management.

THE APPLICABILITY OF ORGANIZATION THEORY TO THE STUDY OF DMNCs

In the first section we have summarized the distinctive demands facing the management of DMNCs, from a phenomenological perspective, and outlined the conditions a theoretical paradigm of the management of DMNCs would have to meet. In this section we review what the major streams of organization theory contribute to the development of such a paradigm.

Organizational theorists have very seldom taken the DMNC as their focus of investigation. They have, however, dealt with many of the issues which are germane to the DMNC, and some which are conceptually similar. We will examine the contributions that theorists can make to the study of DMNCs from two standpoints: do contributions meet the seven criteria established above, and how useful are they to help conceptualize DMNC management processes?

The study of complex organizations has had a long

intellectual history. Illustrious scholars have contributed to this effort. Any attempt to summarize this field must therefore be approached with caution and humility. By its very nature such an effort is likely to cluster different streams of intellectual effort, attempt to distill the basic premises behind the lines of enquiry, and make generalizations. Also, the focus of our effort is *not* to review exhaustively many different theoretical and empirical streams of research, but merely to highlight how a few key contributions to these streams contribute to research on DMNCs, as key steps in the evolution of these research streams. Further, our brief review is made from a very particular perspective: to what extent do these theories contribute to an understanding of the tasks involved in meeting the specific demands of DMNC management, as outlined in the first section of this paper. We recognize the risks; but this attempt, with all its limitations, is an important part of building a new paradigm.

An implicit recognition of the complexity of the phenomenon under scrutiny—complex organizations—is the fact that there is no dominant paradigm that is used to study it. However, over the last 10 years, several streams have gained currency in the academic literature. We will examine them below.

ECONOMIC THEORIES OF ORGANIZATION

The application of institutional economics theories to DMNCs has grown from two distinct but increasingly intertwined theories: transaction cost analysis and principal-agent theory (Arrow, 1985; Williamson, 1975, 1985; Williamson and Ouchi, 1981). The former focuses on transaction costs in markets, and explains organizations as a consequence of market failure. The latter focuses on transaction costs within hierarchies and focuses on the cost of control and compliance in organizations (Fama and Jensen, 1983; Jensen and Meckling, 1976).

Transaction cost analysis provides a powerful departure point to analyze choices between institutional forms, and thus can be used to establish the efficient boundaries of a DMNC (Buckley and Casson, 1986; Dunning, 1980; Hennart, 1982; Teece, 1985). The usefulness of transaction cost analysis for research on management processes is limited by the simplifying assumptions inherent in the 'hierarchy' category, and by its primary focus on single transactions as units of analysis. Thus, although transaction cost analysis does not formally violate the seven criteria we have established, it is of limited usefulness for our purpose unless one adds to it reputational (Kreps, 1984) and relational contracting (Dore, 1983) dimensions.

Transaction cost analysis has proven useful in analyzing specific types of inter-organizational relationships in a North American context such as relationships between US firms and their suppliers, vertical integration (Monteverde and Teece, 1982; Stockey, 1983) and joint ventures with rigorous constraints on the nature of the joint venture (Hennart, 1982). Transaction cost analysis, however, does not explain relationships between Japanese firms and their suppliers, a relationship built on mutual trust and on a belief that the joint benefits (in contrast to self-interest) are worth pursuing in a 'win-win' framework, over the long term (Dore, 1983).

In fact one of the most challenging management tasks in the DMNC is to make the assumptions of transaction cost analysis 'untrue'; hence the emphasis on organizational culture, clan behavior and control (Ouchi, 1980) and normative integration of managers in MNCs (Hedlund, 1981). Transaction cost analysis, by its very assumptions about human beings and organizations, prohibits itself from addressing managerial issues.

Agency theory, on the other hand, aims itself at analyzing management control issues in various forms of contractual relationships between principals and agents, and makes a useful contribution to the study of DMNC management. Agency theory does raise relevant managerial issues by casting issues of control in 'outcome' or 'behavioral' terms (Eisenhardt, 1989). For example, the outcome-based model of control provides an interesting perspective in which to cast the problem of controlling subsidiaries; especially nationally responsive subsidiaries about which the headquarters may have very little information, whose behavior cannot be monitored easily and whose managers may not fully share headquarters goals. Conversely, control over globally integrated subsidiaries may be seen as a problem in behavior-based control, as the relationship between specialized and interdependent subsidiaries can be based on substantive understanding at the headquarters of the tasks to be performed. In fact, headquarters may provide the skills needed at the subsidiaries. The task is one of creating greater goal convergence between headquarters and subsidiaries which is often fostered by international mobility of managers, multidimensional measurement systems, and a desire to create a shared sense of purpose. In that sense agency theory provides but a departure point for the study of DMNC management issues. In fact the dichotomy between outcome-based and behavior-based control is not new, remains quite simplistic, and certainly underemphasizes the non-economic dimensions of control. The simplicity of the binary choice it posits prevents it from exploring the more subtle blends of control and management approaches used in companies (Lawrence and Dyers, 1983).

By emphasizing these non-economic dimensions the literature on organizational culture which stresses 'clan' behavior and control (Ouchi, 1980) and normative integration of MNCs (Hedlund, 1981) challenges the simplifying assumptions of the agency theory approach in a much-needed direction to include psychological affiliation models of control and goal congruence often ignored by the economic theories of organization—somewhat relaxing the assumptions of economic self interest and rationality.

Further, agency theory implies a hierarchical relationship between principal and agent, and assumes implicitly the centrality of headquarters. By treating the organization as a series of contracts, agency theory may not include the multitude of contingencies that arise in the management of DMNCs. As one tries to extend the agency theory framework to include a complex web of networked relationships, the researcher's task becomes extremely complex and difficult as the one-to-one nature of relationships, the simplicity of contracts and the clear identities of principals and agents tend to fade.

The increasingly related theories of transaction

costs and principal–agent relationships both suffer from too restrictive, and culturally bound, assumptions to allow them to do more than raise managerial issues. While they provide useful starting points to consider firm boundaries and control issues, their formulation of the working of an organization is excessively simplified to be useful for management research purposes.

ENVIRONMENTAL ADAPTATION THEORIES

The issue of whether, and how, organizations adapt to their environment to succeed—or at least survive within it—has been central to organization theory for decades. Out of the very rich and diverse literature on organizational adaptation, which we cannot review in whole, stand out the themes of proactive vs. reactive or even random adaptation, and that of the modes and processes of adaptation, which are studied at various levels of aggregation populations of organization, organizational fields, and individual organizations and their subunits. Since each of these levels is relevant to DMNC management research, as is the polarity between active and passive adaptation, we concentrate our analysis on three main streams of environmental adaptation theories: population ecology, institutional theory, and differentiation-integration models.

POPULATION ECOLOGY

Population ecology provides the 'null hypothesis' to strategic management of the DMNC: population ecology assumes that environmental resources are unequally distributed between 'niches' in the environment, and either an organization finds itself in a resource niche it can use or it does not, and succeeds or falters accordingly (Hannan and Freeman, 1977). Population ecology normally assumes strategic choices on the part of organizations to be unfeasible (Aldrich, 1979), although some more recent developments now distinguish 'core' unchanging features of organizations, and 'peripheral' ones which can be

changed, creating the possibility of proactive adaptation (Singh and Lumsden, 1990). From the standpoint of research on the management of DMNCs, population ecology is most useful when it stresses the difficulties that limit the feasibility of successful strategic redirection in MNCs (Hannan and Freeman, 1989). Population ecology reaches similar findings to those of some researchers of DMNC management processes when it stresses how over-adaptation to specific environmental condition makes reaction to changes in the environment particularly difficult (Aldrich, 1979; Doz, 1979; Prahalad and Doz, 1987). However, the level of aggregation of the theory of population ecology—populations of organizations—tells us little about why or how companies fail to adapt, as compared to the management process literature (Bartlett and Ghoshal, 1989; Doz, 1979; Doz and Prahalad, 1984).

The very fact that population ecology does not consider managerial issues, but questions their relevance, makes it a little unfair to apply our seven criteria of appropriateness to management issues to population ecology: population ecology fails on nearly all criteria (see Table 1), but population ecology never set out to analyze managerial behaviour!

Perhaps, however, the population ecology theory can be made useful by shifting the level of aggregation at which it is applied to the inside of large complex firms, where it can provide a logic to selection and adaptation of subunits within the DMNC network, the network itself being considered as the population (Hannan and Freeman, 1989; Delacroix and Freeman, forthcoming). Focusing on selection processes within the firm and on the relative success of various geographical affiliates and product lines in different environments, and over time under specified management processes and management system settings, can open an interesting avenue for research and use population ecology reasoning to study the adaptation of subunits to different environments under different management conditions.

INSTITUTIONAL THEORY

Considering subunit adaptations to differentiated 'local' environment and to corporate management systems is roughly where institutional theory is most useful for research on DMNCs. The concept of organizational field (Di Maggio and Powell, 1983) allows us to consider interactions, mutual awareness, information and patterns of competitive and coalitional behavior between organizations as determinants of their adaptation. This is clearly consistent, in spirit, with the early categorization work on MNC structures (Fayerweather, 1960; Perlmutter, 1969) and the more recent clinical studies of organizational adaptation to diverse types of mutational environments (Bartlett and Ghoshal, 1989; Doz, 1976, 1979; Prahalad, 1975). By showing that some of the most interesting institutionalization processes may occur in organizations that straggle several 'fields' (Zucker, 1987), institutional theory is also consistent with the observation on the part of DMNC scholars that 'multifocal' (Doz, 1979, 1986) or 'transnational' (Bartlett and Ghoshal, 1989) management processes both hold the most strategic promises and raise the most difficult managerial issues in the context of DMNCs.

At a second level of analysis, that of adaptation within firms rather than between institutions, institutional theory is also interesting. Both Meyer and Rowan (1977) and Zucker (1983) stress that organizations are powerful entities providing meaning and encouraging conformity in individual behavior. The fact that MNC managers are subject both to corporate and external influences (Westney, forthcoming) makes them a particularly rich territory to apply institutionalization theory.

Although the current development of institutional theory is not specific enough—in its analysis and conceptualization of institutionalization mechanisms—to make it directly applicable in the management of MNCs, it provides a most helpful theoretical base to researchers. For example, it allows formulation of problems of headquarters–subsidiaries relationships, and of the possible organizational implications of addressing national responsiveness and global integration demands at multiple levels of aggregation from the individual to the interorganizational level (Scott, 1987).

In summary, institutional theory is very consistent in its approach to organizational phenomena with the criteria established earlier. The dearth of explicit use of institutional theory in the study of DMNCs may reflect more the 'youth' of the theory, the lack of discipline base for many MNC scholars (more on that later) and the methodological and epistemological differences between institutional theory researchers and the clinical researchers working on the management of DMNCs. However, it seems that institutional theory holds many promises for the study of DMNC management issues, and processes, as institutional theory further develops.

CONTINGENCY THEORY

Contingency theories of organization developed mainly in the 1960s (Lawrence and Lorsch, 1967; Thompson, 1967; Woodward, 1965). Contingency theory clearly influenced research on MNCs. The early models of structural adaptation of MNCs to geographic and product diversity (Fouraker and Stopford, 1968; Stopford and Wells, 1972) are clearly examples of structural functionalist contingency theory applied to MNCs organizational forms. Research on patterns and modes of headquarter control over affiliates (Doz and Prahalad, 1984; Ghoshal and Nohria, 1989; Hedlund, 1981; Negandhi and Baliga, 1981; Negandhi *et al.,* 1980), has also been clearly cast in a contingency model, although it considered both the adjustment and subsidiaries to their environment and to the culture and style of the parent company, thus raising issues of institutional isomorphism which are closer to the institutional school of organization theory. Researchers who focused on information flows and information processing capabilities of MNCs also clearly adopted a contingency framework (e.g. Egelhoff, 1988), drawing largely on the work of Lawrence and Lorsch (1967) and on that of Galbraith (1973). Subsequent research by Bartlett and Ghoshal (1986, 1989) also clearly draws on the contingency framework, although the interpretation of their detailed analysis of nine MNCs draws on many strands of theory, and remains phenomenological in focus.

Although the contingency theory of organization, and its emphasis on differentiated responses to diverse environments and integration of action across environments, has had the most direct impact of all strands of organization theory on MNC management research, it leaves the issues of change and adaptation to new environmental demands, and thus part of the challenge to management research from population ecology, unanswered. Empirical research on contingency theory has been mostly static, seldom researching change process. The most notable exceptions are Doz (1976, 1979), Doz and Prahalad (1981, 1987) and Prahalad (1975). The primarily static and functionalist views taken by most contingency theory research do not easily allow the incorporation of change processes in their theory, except at the broadest level of assuming system dynamics applies to organizational change processes. Issues of empowerment decentralization, deliberate 'mismatch' between organization and environment to create a state of tension that facilitates adaptation are all recent additions, and often challenges, to contingency theory (e.g., Hamel and Prahalad, 1989; Normann, 1976). A functionalist top management-driven perspective, in which adaptation is primarily organization design and development, begs the issue of how top management perceives the need for adjusting the 'fit', or altogether for responding to new environmental conditions.

Further, an explicit use of contingency theory may lead one to simplistic dichotomous thinking in considering the management of DMNCs, in particular to polarizing one's understanding of MNC management into an opposition between responsiveness and integration categories when, in fact, a fusion is needed: i.e., to consider how to achieve integration and responsiveness together, and to build on the dualities that result (Evans and Doz, 1989).

Despite the possible criticisms towards contingency theory being static and encouraging dichotomous thinking, it does meet most of our criteria, at least to an extent. While contingency theory does not encompass structural indeterminacy (except in its extension to matrix organizations by Davis and Lawrence, 1977), it does provide for internal differentiation and multiple perspectives. It also stresses the importance of information flows (e.g., the interfunctional integration in Lawrence and Lorsch, 1967) and the possibility of new emergent linkages, in the management of interdependencies, rather than the presumption of linkages *a priori*.

Beyond the obvious applicability of a differentiation-integration framework to the managerial dilemmas of the DMNC, argued above, the language in which contingency theory was developed provided the intermediate levels/conceptual constructs that allowed us to bridge theory and the phenomenological approach to MNC management. The analysis of management processes and systems done by Lawrence and Lorsch (1967) provides a rich basis to study integration within complex organizations, and can be readily applied to DMNCs. In sum, contrary to the other more abstract streams of organization theory described above, which seldom develop intermediate level constructs, contingency theory went a good part of the way towards process research and provided a relatively firmer and easier framework for scholars of the DMNC. In fact, one wonders whether contingency theory has not had an excessive influence on subsequent research and thus limited progress in research on the DMNC.

POWER RELATIONSHIPS AND ORGANIZATIONAL ADAPTATION

Among other analyses of power in organizations, the work of Crozier (1964) and Crozier and Friedberg (1980) provides an insightful analysis of organizations as networks of relationships in which 'actors' play self-interested and individually rational strategies in collective 'games' mediated by collectively accepted 'rules' and driven by the resources and constraints of the individual 'actors'. In particular, control over uncertainties affecting the performance of other members of the organization was seen by Crozier as a critical resource.

The network of relationships is thus never totally integrated or disintegrated. Organizations maintain a degree of cohesion, and consistency *vis-à-vis* their environment through the regulation of internal antagonism (Astley and Van de Ven, 1983). The 'game' in the system of relationships balances tensions between integration and fragmentation. Its rules must be followed, for the mutually beneficial association to continue, but 'players' follow different personal strategies in the game depending on their own objectives and the resources they control.

In this perspective, adaptation to the environment takes place through the 'players' most directly able to mediate dependencies with the environment for other players becoming more influential in the network of power relationships. Uncertainty—brought by control over information—is a key dependency, but other sources of dependence are also important: for example, the ability to influence environment's munificence. Structural inertia does exist, as in the population ecology view, but adaptation to changes in the environment may take place through an evolution in the game that reflects the changing relative criticality of various dependencies with the environment and brings more power to players best able to face these dependencies successfully. The adaptive capability of the organization depends on the density of the network of relationships. Very hierarchical organizations, with star-and-spoke patterns of communication and dependence, are not adaptive because the 'games' they allow comprise relatively few strategies and cannot be changed easily. Organizations with more diverse linkages in their networks, in particular more lateral and diagonal rather than vertical linkages, are more adaptive. The network of relationships can reconfigure itself as new environmental contingencies become important. A system of relationships is, therefore, more or less 'blocked' or adaptive, depending on whether its structure is narrowly hierarchical or not (Crozier, 1964). This is congruent with earlier studies of the innovativeness and adaptativeness of organizations (e.g., Burns' and Stalker's (1961) contrast of 'mechanistic' and 'organic' organizations).

In this approach power flows to 'players' who control resources, irrespective of their hierarchical positions: the model thus posits no hierarchical system or collective goals, and thus escapes the criticisms levelled by population ecologists at the strategic choice and deliberate environment–organization adaptation models. Adaptation takes place, or not, as a function of the structure of the network of relationships, and of the external constraints in the environment (and presumably of how fast they change). While individual rationality is usually assumed, organizational rationality does not necessarily follow. Information asymmetry, misunderstanding of the strategies of other actors, and differences in goals among individuals allow for the 'loose coupling' and unstructured decision-making processes. Action can emerge, and generate random variation in the system, which in turn helps its adaptation. Events can thus unfold and be incorporated into the relational system which responds to them (March and Olsen, 1976; Weick, 1979).

By providing a very rich, yet simple, analytical theory of intraorganizational influence processes the power dependence 'school' addresses, albeit often implicitly, the seven criteria in this paper for a relevant theory of the management of DMNCs. Beyond these criteria the power and dependence model holds clear seduction to MNC management scholars, who usually originated from a phenomenological rather than disciplinary perspective, and had an applied rather than theoretical focus.

First, its assumptions about human beings, and the nature of organizations, seem more realistic than that of other models, including the strategic choice model. The assumptions about human beings as purposively rational and self-interested, but with differentiated personal goals, and operating in a boundedly rational fashion is realistic enough to those familiar with organizational life. The assumption of an organization as a network of relationships, between members of the organization, where uncertainty-reducing information is a resource, and a source of influence is also useful. In particular, it makes it possible to incorporate information processing theories of MNCs (Egelhoff, 1988) into a broader theory. The fact that the network of relationships may extend outside the organization, to key 'players' in its environment is also realistic.[2]

[2] For example, researchers on MNC management have observed that headquarter–subsidiary relationships in the MNC could not necessarily be understood without an explicit analysis of the relationship with major customers and the governmental authorities of countries in which the subsidiaries operate. Country managers may use their privileged relationships with the local subsidiary environment to limit the influence

Second, the power and dependence model is seductive to MNC management scholars because it clearly holds application potential. It is both a theoretical and an applied model, i.e., it can easily drive action. Analyzing and understanding the network of relationships that constitute the organization, and discovering the strategies followed by participants in the 'games' played along these relationships allow the researcher to start considering how the stakes and perceptions of the 'players' can be modified, and to simulate how changes in the 'rules' of the game, and in the active relationships in the network would affect outcomes, i.e., the overall behavior of the system of relationships. This is clearly a powerful set of tools for implementing actions in MNCs, in line with an applied perspective.

However, gains in realism and applicability offered by the power and dependency theory, as compared to the other strands of organization theory applied to MNCs, come at a loss of simplicity and theoretical power. The detailed analysis of internal relationships, and the careful categorization of 'players' (which do not easily match organizational lines) require a clinical research of a very detailed variety, not easily carried out by most organization researchers. Simpler models of power relationships in and between organizations (Dahl, 1957; Pfeffer, 1981), provide a less 'grounded' argument than Crozier's, but make its integration with other theories easier and more explicit. Pfeffer's work, for instance, introduces explicit contingency dimensions and can be seen as a detailed analytical approach to the solution of agency 'problems.'

The influence of the resource dependence and power approach on scholars of MNC management is rather obvious. Early work on the responsiveness-integration dilemma in MNC's conceptualized the issue as one of relative power (Prahalad, 1975) and discussed adaptation to contradictions in the environment as achieving a 'power balance' between geographic and product line executives (Doz, 1976, 1979). Work on matrix organizations in DMNCs used a rather similar set of premises (Davis, 1974; Davis and Lawrence, 1977). Thus, the research on MNC management process has drawn extensively on the power and dependence literature. Similarly, issues of strategic control of affiliates have been using the power and dependency model extensively (Doz and Prahalad, 1981; Negandhi *et al.*, 1980a,b).

Although less explicitly connected to process research on DMNCs, the research on external power and dependence (in particular Pfeffer and Salancik, 1978) is also quite relevant to research on DMNCs, models of external control and dependence being used, for example, by Prahalad and Doz (1980) in their study of different relational modes between headquarters and subsidiaries in DMNCs.

ORGANIZATIONAL LEARNING AND THE DMNC

Of the various major strands of organization theory, the organizational learning literature is the only one to focus primarily on change and development. Although they all discuss environment–organization adaptation, other strands of the literature usually start from a static perspective and do not empirically address learning, change and development processes, with the exception of some recent institutionalization theorists (Scott, 1987).

This may be partly because most scholars of organization learning take the view that learning and development are essentially individual, but in the context of an organization, while other theories have a more aggregate view of learning, and ignore the issue altogether. More recent work stresses that learning involves adaptive processes at all levels of the organization (Levitt and March, 1988) and that the institutionalization of learning takes place through organizational routines into which inferences about

---

headquarters, or other affiliates, may exert on their operations. Since the relationship is not transparent, such opportunities to leverage external relationships internally lead managers to 'seek out' their environment in ways that increase their own influence in the organization. In so doing, they contribute to making the organization more responsive to the constraints and opportunities in the environment. Strategic choice is not central, it results from individual strategic choices made by individual 'players' in selecting and adapting to their relevant environment.

past successes, and failures are embedded (Nelson and Winter, 1982). Organizational routines then guide behavior. Levitt and March (1988) also point out why and how the concept of organizational learning itself is fraught with problems. Learning along a wrong trajectory leads to 'competency traps.' Inductive learning from experience by individuals is far from always being accurate, largely because real causality linkages may be much more complex and interdependent than those inferred by observers and participants in an organization. Satisfying behavior leads to superstitious learning, i.e., the first plausible explanation of successful outcome is taken for true. Further, the assessment of outcomes as 'successful' or 'unsuccessful' may be very idiosyncratic and personal. Finally, the diffusion of results from learning in organizations is far from perfect, and learning results decay if they are not frequently used. Further, the process of 'deepening' the knowledge of an organization (from information to understanding) often conflicts with the process of sharing such knowledge within the organization (Chakravarthy and Kwun, 1989).

Although the organizational learning literature, as opposed to the individual learning literature, is still in its infancy, it holds tantalizing promises for the MNC management scholars. It has been loosely argued (e.g. Ghoshal, 1987) that a key asset of MNCs is their opportunity to learn from multiple markets and multiple environments, in particular as they build differentiated networks to achieve such learning (Ghoshal and Nohria, 1989), our limit of the applicability of the organizational learning literature is its content-free nature, i.e., what the object of learning is remains unspecified. In the context of the MNC the extent and process of learning may be quite different according to content. A lot of local autonomous learning may be vital to marketing success, while local experimentation and learning on safety of operations may be lethal if technical operators are invariant between countries. The blend of responsiveness and integration in various tasks drives the need for autonomous localized learning and for sharing such learning in those tasks. Processes for learning may need to be different for geography-based learning, for learning about management systems

and processes, which need to reflect both integration and responsiveness needs, and for rather invariant disciplines, such as safety procedures. More research is needed on both organizational learning processes in general and their application to MNCs.

OVERVIEW

In the first section of this paper we set out to specify the MNC-specific issues that organization theory needs to address to be relevant to strategic management in DMNCs. We then briefly discussed what we see as the major streams of research in organizational theory from the perspective of strategic management in DMNCs. A summary of that discussion is provided in Table 1, using the seven categories we have established.

With the exception of population ecology, where level of analysis makes our criteria less applicable unless one applies the theory to subunits within a DMNC (which was assumed in our treatment of population ecology in Table 1), most other streams of research do not contradict the criteria established earlier in this article. However, the managerial usefulness of these theories varies greatly.[3]

Although they differ deeply in their premises, as well as in the levels of analysis they cover (Figure 1, on the vertical axis), most streams of organization theory share a few key characteristics that make their application to the study of management in MNCs somewhat difficult.

First, with the exception of contingency theory and of some recent developments of institutional theory these theories fail to operationalize the theories into a model, or a framework, in terms other than statistical. As a result they are relatively weak at the operational construct level, i.e., the linkage between theory and empirical analysis, the horizontal axis on Figure 1. When the object of study is homogeneous groups of organizations that are relatively similar

---

[3] Obviously, most organization theorists would not consider managerial usefulness as relevant, since they did not set out to analyze, enlighten or improve managerial behavior, but rather to analyze the behavior of organizations.

Table 1. The Relevance of Organization Theories to DMNC Management Research

Criteria of relevance to DMNC management	Major streams of organization theory						
	Transaction cost	Agency	Population ecology	Institutional theory	Contingency theory	Power relationships and adaptation	Organizational learning
1. Structural indeterminacy	Yes	Implicitly hierarchical	No	Yes	No, structure 'fits' the environment, except for matrix management	Yes, self-adjusting network of power relationships	Yes
2. Internal differentiation	Yes	Simplistic: outcome vs. behavior control	No	Yes, depending on influences	Yes	Yes, depending on external uncertainties	Yes
3. Decision trade-offs between multiple priorities	Narrowly defined 'self-interest' not compatible, extension needed to include relational contracting	No, mainly dyadic principal–agent relationships	No	Not explicitly, but encompassed in multiple 'fields'	Yes, at least on the part of some researchers (Lawrence and Lorsch, 1967)	Yes, power 'games' embody multiple priorities	Yes, part of learning processes
4. Importance of information flows	Yes, but limited to uncertainty and asymmetry issues	Yes, but focused mainly on observability of behavior and measurability of results	No	Yes	Yes	Yes, information is a key determinant of influence	Yes
5. Emergent rather than prescribed linkages	Transaction patterns are not specified a priori. Hierarchies, however, are useful for interorganizational analysis	Yes, series of contracts but not encompassing multiplicity of linkages	No	Yes	Possible, but not specified clearly, although consistent with theory	Yes	Yes, result of learning processes
6. Fuzzy boundaries	Yes, well suited to the analysis of boundaries, but needs to be complemented to incorporate relational contracting	Yes	No	Yes, 'isomorphic' pressures to conform	Not explicitly	Yes, network of relationship in and out of the organization	Not explicitly, but not excluded
7. Repeatability vs. change			Change capabilities are very limited	Yes	No	Yes, depends on network structure	Yes, central to theory

(e.g., local administrative units and agencies in public administration) and not excessively complex, it is indeed quite feasible to move between variable specification and measurement and theory directly, using simple statistical tests. This is clearly less feasible when dealing with heterogeneous groups of complex organizations, or when focusing on their management. Mid-range constructs are needed to conceptualize and model the behavior (both strategic and organizational) of complex organizations and to be managerially relevant (Bourgeois, 1979). In summary, studying large numbers of relatively similar, relatively simple organizations leads one to very generalizable theories, but theories that treat the organizations as a 'black box' and do not develop detailed knowledge of how organizations work. What is needed from a managerial research standpoint is a robust conceptual 'model' of how the DMNC works, a model researchers and managers can play with to simulate reality.

Although we did not review it here, much of the literature on multinational management suffers from an opposite, but almost symmetrical problem. While it is long on descriptive analysis, it is short on theories, and even shorter on mid-range constructs. As a result, many clinical studies of MNCs amount to little more than compendia of descriptive case studies, and the few large sample studies focusing on the management of MNCs often suffer from lack of conceptual and theoretical integrity (e.g., Negandhi *et*

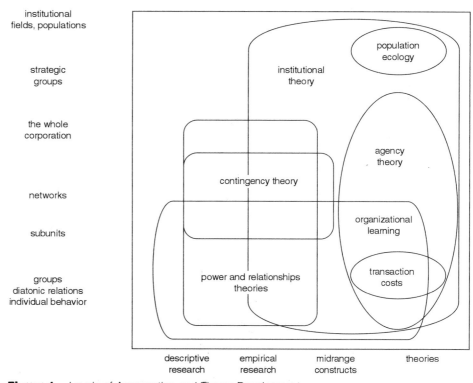

institutional
fields, populations

strategic
groups

the whole
corporation

networks

subunits

groups
diatonic relations
individual behavior

descriptive   empirical   midrange   theories
research   research   constructs

Figure 1. Levels of Aggregation and Theory Development

al., 1980a,b). What is required is a mid-range theory that bridges the gap between descriptive analysis and theories, and can span various levels of aggregation, from individuals and small groups within MNCs, to clusters of MNCs following conceptually similar strategies.

Second, the streams of organization theory, while all conceptually relevant, need a more detailed way to address process variables and process issues. Key managerial processes, such as resource allocation (both financial and human) or conflict resolution processes within organizations need to be captured by the theory. With the exception of the models based on power and relationship analysis, organization theories usually operate at too high a level of abstraction to capture such processes. Further, they do not, for the most part, focus on processes, with the exception of institutional, power, and learning theories.

Third, change and adaptation processes need more explicit attention. Organizational theories are mostly static, geared to cross-sectional analysis rather than

to longitudinal processes of change. While it is possible to use these theories to analyze and conceptualize change processes, such use requires many intermediate steps of conceptualization, with the exception of the organizational learning and power/relationship streams.

Fourth, most theories of organization do not accommodate substantive variables, i.e., do not overcome the false dichotomy between context and process observed in the strategy literature. Context variables are captured, if at all, by abstract proxies.

Lastly, although the tests have seldom been made systematically, some aspects of organization theory may well be culture-bound. For example, the assumption of self-interest and opportunism, key to transaction cost theory, may be deeply rooted in an economic and legal tradition quite specific to the professions in the United States.

In summary, the review of the main strands of the organization theory literature suggests the need for a mid-range theory of the working of DMNCs, emphasizing constructs and frameworks and linking a potentially very useful set of theories with the often insufficiently conceptual and theoretical descriptive analyses performed by the observers and analysts of DMNC. An effort at developing such a mid-range theory is summarized in the next section.

THE SEARCH FOR A PARADIGM

THE DEVELOPMENT OF MNC MANAGEMENT RESEARCH: TOWARD A NEW PARADIGM

While early scholars of the MNC phenomenon (e.g., Fayerweather, 1960; Perlmutter, 1969; Wilkins, 1970) had developed organizational process categories, and identified the essential tension between fragmentation and unity in managing MNCs, the bulk of researchers' attention was then focused on economic and competitive models of the MNC, building on the seminal works of Hymer (1960) and Vernon (1966). Only Stopford and Wells (1972) and Franko (1976) devoted their main attention to structural and managerial issues in the research stream originated by Vernon. It is only later, following the development of contingency theory and the emergence of a process school of policy research (e.g., Bower, 1970) that empirical research on the organization and management processes of MNCs started anew.

The line of research starting with the work of Prahalad (1975) is united on the common theme of organizational processes and organizational capabilities in DMNCs, but focuses on various aspects of the general management task in DMNCs (Bartlett and Ghoshal, 1989; Doz and Prahalad, 1988; Prahalad and Doz, 1987). While a full summary of the findings of this research is not the purpose of this article, a few words putting the various contributions to that line of research in perspective may be useful. In particular, understanding the stream of process research on the management of DMNCs is complicated by the lack of discipline among researchers in the choice of labels to describe the concepts and in the language systems used. Further, the language system used by individual researchers has also evolved over time as their understanding progressed. This can give the impression to a casual reader of a lack of conceptual unity to the whole line of research.

Prahalad's research (1975) focused on the processes by which the management of a single business, not subject to intense host government constraints, perceived changing environmental demands and responded to these by redirecting the attention of managers, refocusing the strategic direction, and realigning power and influence processes, consistent with the new environmental conditions. The work of Doz (1976, 1979) analyzed, on a comparative basis, the management processes used in several companies, and several businesses in each company, to manage the tension between economic and technological pressure for globalization and integration, and host government demands for responsiveness to national industrial policies. Doz (1979, 1980) then analyzed how differences in competitive positions between firms in the same industry affected their response to the tension outlined above. Bartlett (1979) then compared the management systems and processes used in a sample of companies in industries differently affected by global integration and national responsiveness demands, and also analyzed how different functions were affected by these pressures, and further extended the understanding of redirection processes initiated by Prahalad (1975) and Doz (1978). Mathias (1978) compared redirection processes initiated by top management, with processes emerging from tensions among middle managers in the organization without top management playing an active role in the initiation of change processes. Bartlett then considered how what he called 'institutional heritage' of a firm constrains the development of new capabilities, and constituted a form of 'organizational inertia' that top management has to take into consideration (Bartlett, 1981).

Ghoshal (1986) added a detailed analysis of innovation processes, stressing the existence of different patterns of interactions between affiliates and headquarters, and among affiliates in the innovation process. This led to a more general analysis of DMNCs as differentiated networks (Ghoshal and Nohria, 1989), and to the discussion of network theory applied to DMNCs (Ghoshal and Bartlett, 1990).

Finally, the research of Prahalad and Hamel (1990) led to reconceptualization of the basis for global competitiveness away from resource deployment to skill development and leverage, and both that work, and that of Doz and Prahalad (1988), stress the importance of organizational capabilities in this process.

Simultaneously, but largely independently, a rather similar line of process research developed in Sweden, based on the clinical analysis of the internationalization of major Swedish companies. Initially much of this work was concentrated on empirical tests of the validity of various propositions stemming from previous research (e.g., that a subsidiary's managerial autonomy would be inversely correlated to cross shipments of goods between that subsidiary and other parts of the organization) or of grounded propositions stemming from detailed case studies of Swedish MNCs (e.g. Hedlund, 1981). However, interesting theoretical developments followed from the empirical research, in particular the concept of 'heterarchic' DMNC (Hedlund, 1986; Hedlund and Rolander, 1990) emphasizing the geographic diffusion of corporate functions, a wide range of 'between market and hierarchy' governance modes and an emphasis on action learning and on variation selection and retention processes in organizational adaptation.

Although this enumeration of issues, authors, and research work may look somewhat disjointed, it is important to understand its cumulative nature and underlying logic. The process of research has been to start initially with relatively discrete, researchable 'building blocks,' bounding both the territory researched and the complexity of the concepts and constructs developed. *Each step then constitutes an attempt to challenge, extend, and enrich the preceding steps by taking their findings to a broader more complex set of issues, and adding to the existing concepts based on a richer understanding of their applicability.*

While each research piece illuminates only an aspect of the managerial task in DMNC, taken together the work of Prahalad, Doz, Bartlett, Ghoshal, Hedlund, Hamel, and others following the same research approach, provides us with a rich organizational theory of the DMNC, and with a detailed understanding of managerial tasks in DMNCs.

The emerging paradigm which results from this cumulative work has a few key characteristics:

1. *Substance and process in a DMNC are captured using the same underlying framework.* The underlying business characteristics can be mapped using the *'global integration–local responsiveness' (I–R) framework* (for a summary, see Prahalad and Doz, 1987). All the elements that contribute to the pressures for global integration (I) needs such as economies of scale, universal products, privileged access to raw materials, global customers, technology intensity, and presence of global competitors, are supported directly in the literature on competitive dynamics and strategy. *The framework considers all factors that contribute to the pressure for global integration simultaneously, rather than one element at a time, as is common in the literature.* Similarly, pressures for local responsiveness needs such as distribution differences, local customs, differences in customer needs, market structure, and host government demands, also find support in the literature, and are *considered simultaneously.* Further, the relative importance of the integration and responsiveness pressures can be used to *map industry characteristics.* The critical difference between this approach and traditional research approaches is that it explicitly recognizes the need for integrative optimization between multiple and often conflicting pressures in a business. *Studying the process of balance across apparently conflicting demands is seen as more important than studying the management demands created by one element of the business (e.g., technology intensity) at a time.*

2. The same framework can be used to chart the changing nature of a business—by evaluating the shifts in the relative balance between the forces that contribute to the integration and responsiveness needs, and their impact on various key functions within a business—such as R&D, manufacturing, or marketing.

Furthermore, one can analyze management systems in a DMNC, and in its various countries of operation, functions, and businesses, and assess whether these management systems form a context consistent with the external demands, given business conditions and competitive positions.

The causes of enduring mismatches between external demands, strategic choices, and management systems, and the refocusing and realignment processes used to adapt to, or to anticipate, new environmental demands have been part of the emerging paradigm throughout (Doz, 1978; Doz and Prahalad, 1981; Doz, Bartlett and Prahalad, 1981; Prahalad, 1976; etc.). In that sense *the emerging paradigm can be used both cross-sectionally, to compare industries, business strategies and management systems and processes at one point in time, and longitudinally to map out, analyze, and understand change and adaptation processes.*

3. *The basic unit of analysis of the paradigm is the individual manager, rather than an abstraction at a higher level of aggregation.* Thus, the primary purpose of organizational processes—formal structure, administrative tools, decision-making culture—can be conceptualized as (i) influencing the 'mind sets' or the *cognitive orientations of managers,* (ii) legitimating a currently dominant *coalition* of managers representing a certain 'strategy' that is pursued, and (iii) representing the authority structure and *power* to allocate resources. Organization can then be conceptualized as consisting of these three subprocesses. We can make the following generalizations.

(a) Formal structure in an organization (e.g., organization structure) is nothing more than a shorthand way of capturing the underlying subprocesses—manager's mindsets (and the attendant information infrastructure in the firm), a consensus on strategy, and power to allocate resources consistent with strategy. As a result, managers consistently desire to have 'pure organizations'—be it worldwide business or area organization—because they describe the three orientations of managers unambiguously (Prahalad and Doz, 1987).

(b) Managers believe that a matrix organization is complex, because in a matrix the three subprocesses—cognitive orientations, strategic consensus, and power—are not aligned with the lines in an organization chart. Managers must understand the subprocesses in the matrix, independent of the formal structure. Irrespective of the formal structure, as shown in the organization chart, these three subprocesses go on, and must be explicitly managed. Top managers must deal with the subprocesses and individual managers. This need to deal at the level of subprocesses in the organization makes a matrix 'complicated' for managers who are not skilled at operating at the level of subtlety and detail.

(c) Strategic change requires that managers change the cognitive orientations of a constellation of managers, gain a new consensus of strategy, and realign the relative power balance among the various groups involved in the interaction in the business.

(d) The management of the subprocesses in the organization can be effectively managed by the use of administrative tools such as planning, budgeting, MIS, rewards and punishments, training, career management and socialization (Doz and Prahalad, 1984). The implication is that major strategic redirection can take place without a formal structural change.

(e) The nature of interaction and the intensity of information flow between subsidiary and head office and across subsidiaries is a reflection of the strategic missions assigned to various units (Ghosal and Nohria, 1989). Even within a single business, all country organizations need not have the same strategic mission, and the differences will be manifest in the pattern and intensity of information flow. Patterns of information flow are a predictor of the cognitive orientation of managers (which depend on the information infrastructure that they have access to), the strategic consensus process (where are the sources of tension and who is involved in resolving the tensions), and the relative power balance to allocate resources.

4. *The whole paradigm is focused on mid-range constructs.* It does not pretend to develop a universally applicable all-encompassing theory of organization, but much more modestly to provide a set of integrative constructs allowing the observation, analysis, understanding, and normative assessment of interaction processes between managers in DMNCs. As such it provides a starting point toward the development of a mid-range theory, useful to link strategic issues with theoretical bases (Bourgeois, 1979).

5. It is not possible to ensure a theory is not culture-bound. It may be culture-bound in its observations or in its observers. *Scholars of DMNC management belong to a wide range of nationalities and cultures and have researched MNCs with a variety of home countries.* Several research contributions (e.g., Bartlett and Ghoshal 1989) have built cultural variety in their research design by systematically comparing US-, Europe- and Japan-based MNCs. While this does not offer over a full guarantee against cultural bias, at the very least it decreases the odds of cultural boundaries.

Finally, this line of research cumulatively addresses the seven specific demands on DMNC organization defined in this article. For example, Prahalad and Doz's early work clearly focuses on structural indeterminacy, the need for internal differentiation and the mechanisms and preconditions for integrative optimization. Most researchers have clearly recognized the high information-intensity required of the DMNC network and discussed how to provide for it, while Egelhoff (1982, 1988) adopts explicitly an information processing view. The core of Bartlett's and Ghoshal's research, as summarized in their 1989 book, clearly focuses on latent linkages, while their more recent work explicitly advocates the use of interinstitutional models for the study of relationships within DMNCs. Finally, while many authors identify the trade-off between learning and continuity. Hedlund's analysis of the DMNC as a 'heterarchy' represents a clear attempt at identifying how the trade-off may be managed in practice.

CONCLUSION—MNC MANAGEMENT RESEARCH AND ORGANIZATION THEORY: A MISSED OPPORTUNITY FOR CROSS-FERTILIZATION?

We stressed above that most organization theories were compatible with the characteristics that make the DMNC different from simpler organizations as laid out in this article. We stressed that it was not so much the features of the theories as the perspective adopted by the proponents of these theories which made their application to MNCs difficult. We also showed that researchers studying the management processes of MNCs had borrowed more from organization theories than they, or for that matter organization theorists, are likely to acknowledge. Why such a surreptitious rather than explicit convergence?

THEORETICAL DOGMA VS. ATHEORETICAL PHENOMENOLOGY

We believe that organization theorists have remained too involved with the development of their theories, while many, if not all, scholars of MNC management have underexploited the theories available to them. The former have typically studied much simpler organizations than DMNCs, while the latter have often been engrossed in the complexity of what they studied, and failed to develop, or borrow, a sufficiently

powerful conceptual network to shed light on the observed phenomenon. As a result the 'bridge' between the MNC phenomenon and organization theory was not built.

MANAGERIAL VS. INSTITUTIONAL CONCERNS

The difference in perspective between organizational theorists and scholars of the MNC also extends to the purpose of their theories: MNC scholars have usually undertaken to 'educate' practice, i.e., have put managerial relevance before theoretical elegance. The converse is true of most organizational theorists. This made the dialogue more difficult.

THEORY BUILDING VS. THEORY TESTING

By and large, scholars of MNC management have used data to develop their understanding of the phenomenon and then to illustrate their concepts to facilitate their presentation. There was essentially no attempt to test propositions and hypotheses. Theory development progressed by attempts at refutation, and by tentative extensions. Some researchers were not concerned with testing hypotheses (their priority being to provide a useful insightful perspective on the MNC phenomenon rather than to delimit its exact contours or specify all its characteristics). Most deemed the testing of hypotheses premature, or too complex given the complexity of MNCs and the large number of control variables. As a result, the line of research lacks rigor in measurement techniques. The work of Ghoshal (1987) constitutes a useful shift of emphasis toward measuring and testing. Overall, it is only very recently that researchers have undertaken to test systematically some of the key propositions from process research on DMNCs (Kim and Mauborgne, 1991). More of this work can be done now as the conceptual structure exists to understand the management processes in DMNCs.

RESEARCH COMPLEXITY VS. SIMPLICITY

Process research on the DMNC is complex and costly, not always consistent with the funding and reward processes in place at many academic institutions. It is also demanding for the researcher, involving numerous interviews and process observations in many parts of the world that only skilled field researchers can carry out effectively. As a result, management process research on MNCs has taken place only at a relatively few academic institutions with a tradition of field research, abundant funding, and a specific institutional interest in MNCs. The dearth of researchers has slowed down research progress.

A STATE OR AN ELUSIVE PHENOMENON?

Observers have noticed that both managerial cognitive maps and management tools in MNCs, and the focus of attention of MNC scholars, have shifted over time, without much clarity as to which influenced the other (or maybe they influenced each other over time). The underlying difficulty is the evolutionary nature of the MNC phenomenon itself. For example, the shift in MNCs from relatively long-term positions rooted in access to resources, or in economies of scale, to a succession of shorter-term positions built on intangible assets, puts very different demands on management. Or the evolution of communication and information technologies may, in turn, allow very different responses to existing problems, and change management approaches. It is therefore not even clear that the search for a stable organization theory of the MNC is warranted. Perhaps researchers ought to satisfy themselves with addressing an evolving agenda of managerial issues created by changes in success conditions for MNCs and in enabling technologies for their management?

REFERENCES

Aldrich, H.E. *Organizations and Environments,* Prentice-Hall, Englewood Cliffs, NJ, 1979.

Arrow, K.J. 'The economics of agency.' In J.W. Pratt and R.J. Zeckhauser (eds), *Principals and Agents: The Structure of Business,* HBS Press, Boston, MA, 1985, pp. 37–51.

Astley, W.G. and A.H. Van de Ven. 'Central perspectives and debates in organization theory,' *Administrative Science Quarterly,* **28**, 1983, pp. 265–73.

Bartlett, C.A. 'Multinational structural evolution: The changing decision environment in international divisions,' unpublished doctoral dissertation, Harvard Business School, 1979.

Bartlett, C.A. 'Multinational structural change: Evolution versus reorganization.' In L. Otterbeck (ed.) *The Management of Headquarters-Subsidiary Relationships in Multinational Corporations,* Gower, Aldershot, England, 1981, pp. 121–145.

Bartlett, C.A. and S. Ghoshal, 'Tap your subsidiaries for global reach.' *Harvard Business Review,* November–December 1986, pp. 87–94.

Bartlett, C.A. and S. Ghoshal, *Managing Across Borders,* HBS Press, Cambridge, MA, 1989.

Beer, M. and S.M. Davis, 'Creating a global organization, failures along the way,' *Columbia Journal of World Business,* Summer 1976, pp. 72–84.

Bourgeois, J. 'Toward a method of middle-range theorizing,' *Academy of Management Review,* **4**(3), 1979, pp. 443–447.

Bower, J.L. *Managing the Resource Allocation Process,* HBS Division of Research, Boston, MA, 1970.

Buckley, P.J. and M.C. Casson. *The Economic Theory of the Multinational Enterprise,* Macmillan Press, London, 1986.

Burns, T. and E. Stalker, *The Management of Innovation,* Tavistock, London, 1961.

Chakravarthy, B.S. and S. Kwun, 'The strategy-making process: An organizational learning perspective,' Strategic Management Research Center, University of Minnesota, Working Paper, 1989.

Crozier, M. *The Bureaucratic Phenomenon,* University of Chicago Press, Chicago, IL, 1964.

Crozier, M. and E. Friedberg, *Actors and Systems: The Politics of Collective Action,* University of Chicago Press, Chicago, IL, 1980.

Dahl, R. 'The concept of power,' *Behavioral Science,* **2**, 1957, pp. 201–215.

Davis, S. 'Two models of organization: Unity of command vs. balance of power,' *Sloan Management Review,* Fall 1984, pp. 29–40.

Davis, S. and P.R. Lawrence, *Matrix,* Addison Wesley, Reading, MA, 1977.

Delacroix, J. and J. Freeman, 'The organizational ecology of european subsidiaries of American multinational companies: An empirical exploration.' In S. Ghoshal and E. Westney (eds), *Organization Theory and the Multinational Corporation* (forthcoming), Macmillan Press, London.

DiMaggio, J. and W. Powell, 'The iron cage revisited: Institutional isomorphism and collective rationality in organizational fields,' *American Sociological Review,* **48**, 1983, pp. 147–160.

Dore, R.P. 'Goodwill and the spirit of market capitalism,' *British Journal of Sociology,* **34**(4), December 1983, pp. 459–482.

Doz, Y. 'National policies and multinational management,' unpublished doctoral dissertation, Harvard Business School, 1976.

Doz, Y. 'Managing manufacturing rationalization within multinational companies,' *Columbia Journal of World Business,* **13**(3), Fall 1978, pp. 82–94.

Doz, Y. *Government Control and Multinational Strategic Management,* Praeger, New York, 1979.

Doz, Y. 'Strategic management in multinational companies,' *Sloan Management Review,* **21**(2), Winter 1980, pp. 27–46.

Doz, Y. and C.K. Prahalad, 'Headquarter influence and strategic control in MNCs,' *Sloan Management Review,* **23**(1), Fall 1981, pp. 15–29.

Doz, Y. *Strategic Management in Multinational Companies,* Pergamon Press, Oxford, 1986.

Doz, Y. and C.K. Prahalad, 'Patterns of strategic control in multinational corporations,' *Journal of International Business Studies,* Fall 1984, pp. 55–72.

Doz, Y. and C.K. Prahalad, 'A process model of strategic redirection in large complex firms: The case of multinational corporations.' In A. Pettigrew (ed.), *The Management of Strategic Change,* Basil Blackwell, Oxford, 1987, pp. 63–83.

Doz, Y. and C.K. Prahalad, 'Quality of management: An emerging source of global competitive advantage?,' In N. Hood and J.E. Vahlne (eds), *Strategies in Global Competition,* Croom-Helm, London, 1988, pp. 345–369.

Doz, Y., C.A. Bartlett and C.K. Prahalad, 'Global competitive pressures vs. host country demands: Managing tensions in multinational corporations,' *California Management Review,* **23**(3), Spring 1981, pp. 63–74.

Dunning, J.H. 'The determinants of international production,' *Oxford Economic Papers,* November 1973, pp. 289–336.

Dunning, J.H. 'Toward an eclectic theory of international production: Some empirical tests,' *Journal of International Business Studies,* Spring/Summer 1980, pp. 9–30.

Dunning, J.H. *The Eclectic Theory of the MNC,* Allen & Unwin, London, 1981, Chapter 4.

Dunning, J.H. and R.A. Pearce, *Profitability and Performance of the World's Largest Industrial Companies,* The Financial Times, London, 1985.

Egelhoff, W.G. 'Strategy and structure in multinational corporations: An information processing approach,' *Administrative Science Quarterly,* **27**, 1982, pp. 435–458.

Egelhoff, W.G. 'Strategy and structure in multinational corporations: A revision of the Stopford and Wells model,' *Strategic Management Journal,* **9**(1), 1988, pp. 1–14.

Einsenhardt, K. 'Agency theory: An assessment and review,' *Academy of Management Review,* **14**(1), 1989, pp. 57–74.

Evans, P.E. and Y. Doz. 'The dualistic organisation'. In P. Evans, Y. Doz and A. Laurent (eds), *Human Resource Management in International Firms,* Macmillan Press, London, 1989, pp. 219–242.

Fama, E.F. and M.C. Jensen. 'Separation of ownership and control,' *Journal of Law and Economics,* **26**(2), 1983, pp. 301–325.

Fayerweather, J. *Management of International Operations: Text and Cases,* McGraw-Hill, New York, 1960.

Fouraker, L.E. and J. Stopford, 'Organization structure and multinational strategy,' *Administrative Science Quarterly,* **13**(1), 1968, pp. 47–64.

Franko, L.G. *The European Multinationals: A Renewed Challenge to American and British Big Business,* Greylock, Stamford, CT, 1976.

Galbraith, J. *Designing Complex Organizations,* Addison Wesley, Reading, MA, 1973.

Ghoshal, S. 'The innovative multinational: A differentiated network of organizational roles and management processes,' unpublished doctoral dissertation, Harvard Business School, 1986.

Ghoshal, S. 'Globe strategy: An organizing framework,' *Strategic Management Journal,* **8**, 1987, pp. 425–440.

Ghoshal, S. and C.A. Bartlett, 'The multinational corporation as an interorganizational network,' *Academy of Management Review,* **15**(4), 1990, pp. 603–625.

Ghoshal, S. and N. Nohria. 'Internal differentiation within multinational corporations,' *Strategic Management Journal,* **10**(4), 1989, pp. 323–338.

Hamel, G. and C.K. Prahalad. 'Strategic intent,' *Harvard Business Review,* **89**(3), 1989, pp. 63–76.

Hannan, M.T. and J. Freeman, 'The population ecology of organizations,' *American Journal of Sociology,* **82**, 1977, pp. 929–964.

Hanna, M.T. and J. Freeman, *Organizational Ecology,* Harvard University Press, Cambridge, MA, 1989.

Hedlund, G. 'Autonomy of subsidiaries and formalization of headquarters subsidiary relations in Swedish MNCs.' In L. Otterbeck (ed.), *The Management of Headquarter Subsidiary Relations in Multinational Corporations,* Gower, Aldershot, 1981, pp. 25–78.

Hedlund, G. 'The hypermodern MNC: A heterarchy?' *Human Resource Management,* Spring 1986, pp. 9–35.

Hedlund, G. and D. Rolander, 'Action in heterarchies: New approaches to managing the MNC.' In C. Bartlett, Y. Doz and G. Hedlund (eds), *Managing the Global Firm,* Routledge, London, 1990, pp. 15–46.

Hennart, J.F. *A Theory of Multinational Enterprise,* University of Michigan, Ann Arbor, MI, 1982.

Hennart, J.F. 'A model of the choice between firms and markets.' Working paper, Wharton School, 1989.

Hymer, S.H. 'The International operations of national firms: A study of direct foreign investment,' MIT, doctoral dissertation, 1960, published by MIT Press in 1976.

Jensen, M.C. and W.H. Meckling, 'Theory of the firm: Managerial behavior, agency costs and capital structure,' *Journal of Financial Economics,* **3**, 1976, pp. 305–360.

Kim, Chan W. and R.A. Mauborgne, 'Implementing global strategies: The role of procedural justice,' *Strategic Management Journal,* Special Issue, summer 1991, pp. 125–143.

Kreps, T. 'Corporate culture and economic theory,' Working Paper, Stanford Graduate School of Business, Stanford University, 1984.

Lawrence, P.R. and J. Lorsch. *Organization and Environment,* Harvard University Press, Cambridge, MA, 1967.

Lawrence, P.R. and D. Dyers. *Renewing American Industry,* Free Press, New York, 1983.

Levitt, B. and J.G. March. 'Organizational learning,' *Annual Review of Sociology,* **14**, 1988, pp. 319–340.

March, J.G. and J.P. Olsen. *Ambiguity and Choice in Organizations,* Univerisitetsforlaget, Bergen, Norway, 1976.

Martinez, J.I. and J.C. Jarillo. 'The evolution of research on coordination mechanisms in multinational corporations,' *Journal of International Business Studies,* **20**(3), Fall 1989, pp. 489–514.

Mathias, P. 'The role of the logistics system in strategic change', unpublished doctoral dissertation, Harvard Business School, 1978.

Meyer, J. and B. Rowan. 'Institutionalized organizations: formal structures as myth and ceremony,' *American Journal of Sociology,* **83**, 1977, pp. 340–363.

Monteverde, K. and D.J. Teece. 'Supplier switching costs and vertical integration in the automobile industry,' *Bell Journal of Economics,* **13**, 1982, pp. 206–213.

Negandhi, A.R. (ed.). *Functioning of the Multinational Corporation,* Pergamon Press, Oxford, 1980.

Negandhi, A.R. and R. Baliga. 'Internal functioning of American, German and Japanese multinational corporations,' In L. Otterbeck (ed.), *The Management of Headquarter Subsidiary Relationships in Multinational Corporations,* Gower, Aldershot, 1981, pp. 107–120.

Negandhi, A.R. *et al.* 'Multinationals in industrially developed countries: A comparative study of American, European and Japanese multinationals,' In A.R. Negandhi and B.R. Baliga (eds), *Functioning of the Multinational Corporations,* Pergamon, Oxford, 1980a, pp. 117–135.

Negandhi, A.R. *et al.* 'Adaptability of American, European and Japanese multinational corporations in developing countries,' In A.R. Negandhi and B.R. Baliga (eds), *Functioning of Multinational Corporation,* Pergamon, Oxford, 1980b, pp. 136–164.

Nelson, R.R. and S.G. Winter. *An Evolutionary Theory of Economic Change,* Harvard University Press, Cambridge, MA, 1982.

Normann, R. *Management and Statesmanship,* SIAR, Stockholm, 1976.

Ouchi, W.G. 'Markets, bureaucracies and clans,' *Administrative Science Quarterly,* **25**, 1980, pp. 120–142.

Perlmutter, H.V. 'The tortuous evolution of the multinational corporation,' *Columbia Journal of World Business,* 1969, pp. 9–18.

Pfeffer, J.R. *Power in Organizations,* Pitman, Marshfield, MA, 1981.

Pfeffer, J.R. and G.R. Salancik. *The External Control of Organizations: A Resource Dependence Perspective,* Harper & Row, New York, 1978.

Porter, M.E. *Competition in Global Industries,* HBS Press, Cambridge, MA, 1986.

Prahalad, C.K. 'The strategic process in a multinational corporation,' unpublished doctoral dissertation, School of Business Administration, Harvard University, 1975.

Prahalad, C.K. 'Strategic choices in diversified MNCs,' *Harvard Business Review,* July–August 1976, pp. 67–78.

Prahalad, C.K. and Y. Doz. 'Strategic management of diversified multinational companies,' In A. Negandhi (ed.) *Functioning of the Multinational Corporation,* Pergamon Press, Oxford, 1980, pp. 77–116.

Prahalad, C.K. and Y. Doz. *The Multinational Mission,* Free Press, New York, 1987.

Prahalad, C.K. and G. Hamel. 'The core competence of the corporation,' *Harvard Business Review,* **90**(3), 1990, pp. 79–93.

Scott, W.R. 'The adolescence of institutional theory,' *Administrative Science Quarterly,* **32**, 1987, pp. 493–511.

Singh, J.V. and C.J. Lumsden. 'Theory and research in organizational ecology,' *Annual Review of Sociology,* **16**, 1990, pp. 161–195.

Stockey, J. *Vertical Integration and Joint Ventures in the Aluminum Industry,* Harvard University Press, Cambridge, MA, 1983.

Stopford, J., J. Dunning and K.O. Haberich. *The World Directory of Multinational Enterprises,* Facts on File, New York, 1980.

Stopford, J.M. and L.T. Wells, Jr. *Managing the Multinational Enterprise,* Basic Books, New York, 1972.

Teece, D. ''Multinational enterprise, internal governance and economic organization,' *American Economic Review,* **75**, 1985, pp. 233–238.

Thompson, J.D. *Organizations in Action,* McGraw-Hill, New York, 1967.

Vernon, R. 'International investment and international trade in the product cycle,' *Quarterly Journal of Economics,* **80**(2), May 1966, pp. 190–207.

Weick, K.E. *The Social Psychology of Organizing,* Addison Wesley, Reading, MA, 1979.

Westney, E. 'Institutionalization theory and the multinational enterprise,' In S. Ghoshal and E. Westney (eds), *Organization Theory and the Multinational Corporation,* Macmillan Press, London, forthcoming.

Wilkins, M. *The Emergence of the Multinational Enterprise: American Business Abroad from Colonial Era to 1914,* Harvard University Press, Cambridge, MA, 1970.

Williamson, O.E. *Markets and Hierarchies: Analysis and Antitrust Implications,* Free Press, New York, 1975.

Williamson, O.E. *The Economic Institutions of Capitalism,* Free Press, New York, 1985.

Williamson, O.E. and W.G. Ouchi. 'The markets and hierarchies program of research: Origins, implications, prospects,' In W. Joyce and A. Van de Ven (eds), *Perspectives on Organizational Design and Behavior,* Wiley, New York, 1981, pp. 347–370.

Woodward, J. *Industrial Organization: Theory and Practice,* Oxford University Press, London, 1965.

Zucker, L.G. 'Organization as institutions,' In S. Bacharach (ed.), *Advances in Organizational Theory and Research,* vol. 2, JAI Press, Greenwich, CT, 1983, pp. 1–43.

Zucker, L.G. 'Institutional theories of organization,' *Annual Review of Sociology,* **13**, 1987, pp. 443–464.

SECTION 10

INFORMATION AND INFORMATION PROCESSING

We have entered the information age. Technology ranging from satellites to fax machines to computer networks has made communication of information around the world instantaneous. Computers have made possible the capture, storage, and manipulation of incredibly large amounts of information. Business firms have voracious appetites for information and communication among widely separated business units within the firm as well as with customers that may be geographically dispersed.

The ability to collect, process, analyze, and disseminate information within the firm has become an important component of competitive advantage. With competencies in manufacturing and marketing becoming more widespread, for example, the firm that acquires information first and uses it most effectively may be the winner. In the readings to follow, we examine three important dimensions of the multiple roles of information in the multinational firm.

READING SELECTIONS

Egelhoff proposes that it is useful to view organizations as information processing systems for gathering data, transforming that data into information, and storing and disseminating it within the organization. He presents frameworks for identifying, classifying, and dealing with the different kinds of information a transnational firm must collect and process. He organizes the frameworks around the idea that environmental conditions determine the information processing requirements an organization faces and that organizational design features determine the organization's information-handling capacity.

Egelhoff identifies four classes of information, organized around two subjects, either company and country or product. Each information subject can have either a tactical or a strategic purpose and perspective. His classification scheme identifies by function and location the specific units in the organization that should be the recipients and processors of each type of information. He goes on to explain how, using these and subsequent frameworks, managers can build a maximally effective information system for a transnational firm.

Sunil Babbar and Arun Rai deal with competitive intelligence, a specific type of information that is increasingly critical to domestic as well as global firms. Broadly, they define competitive intelligence as any information from external sources that can help improve performance. They believe that an environmental scanning system is the key to developing competitive intelligence. A properly designed system should focus the firm's intelligence collection efforts on increasing the firm's ability to lead rather than to follow competitors.

Babbar and Rai present a series of considerations for making such a system effective. It should be flexible since predefined strategic objectives may focus it so narrowly that the firm will miss opportunities. It should focus on consumers' unmet, as well as their presently met, needs. It must encourage learning within the organization. To make effective use of competitive information, the firm must create and maintain a culture that encourages the collection and use of such information. This requires top management commitment, incentives, and training, not to mention the ability to understand and interpret events and trends in countries foreign to the firm.

38

COMPETITIVE INTELLIGENCE FOR INTERNATIONAL BUSINESS

SUNIL BABBAR* AND ARUN RAI**

ABSTRACT   In an era of globalization, competitors need to incorporate new approaches in managing their intelligence processes. Globalization of markets, resulting from advances in communication and transportation, rapidly changing political climates and ideologies, and the reduction in trade barriers has opened doors to new international opportunities for business. With foreign competitors invading domestic markets, firms must aggressively identify 'windows of opportunity' and then institute programmes to achieve continuous improvement, creativity and innovation to enhance their competitive position. This article analyses the trends in the international business environment, and explores the strategic issues for management. The authors develop guidelines for the design and implementation of effective competitive intelligence systems and for the redesign of managerial processes for intelligence gathering and utilization. They also identify management approaches which can help to create a supportive corporate culture.

Businesses today compete in an increasingly dynamic environment. The effective scanning of the business environment permits better utilization of resources including information. It also enables timely identification and quick response to 'windows of opportunity.' Firms which cannot effectively scan and react to their business environment can expect to decline when faced by more capable competition. Chief executives in high-performance companies scan their environment more frequently and broadly in response to strategic uncertainty than their counterparts in low-performance companies.[1]

In today's global context, firms are increasingly operating internationally. Moreover, the business environment is being constantly redefined by global shifts. Now, more than ever, top managers must maintain a global perception of their competitive environment. Understanding and adapting to this environment demands continuous and intense scanning, and the collection and analysis of data into 'competitive intelligence.' Irregular or periodic scanning efforts aimed at generating corporate responses, to environmental crises or other specific problems limits the potential benefits that can be obtained through scanning. Continuous scanning systems are the ideal portrayed in planning literature.[2] However, our focus is on opportunity-finding and the realization that planning systems contribute to the growth and survival of the organization in a proactive way. Competitive intelligence gathered through continuous scanning should form the basis for strategic and operational changes that drive continuous improvement and ensure organizational adaptation to the ever-changing environment.

The term 'competitive intelligence,' as used, is defined as any information obtained from sources external to the firm, that can help improve the firm's performance. In keeping with the Continuous Improvement Systems (CIS) philosophy as expressed by Dingus and Golomski,[3] performance can always be improved further by putting proper organizational structure and processes in place.

Organizations then are faced with the challenge of identifying and monitoring a dynamic set of environmental factors that influence their performance. The

* Sunil Babbar is Assistant Professor at the Department of Management at Kansas State University. ** Arun Rai is Assistant Professor at the Department of Management at Southern Illinois University, Carbondale.

careful monitoring of these factors and adjusting of related organizational processes is critical for the attainment of corporate goals and objectives. The potential benefits from environmental scanning essentially become a function of the opportunity cost of unobtained and unacted upon intelligence. How should managers conceptualize and manage their business environment in order to ensure continuous improvement? As a first step, it seems pertinent to contrast the essential traits of the traditional view of dealing with one's environment with that of the proposed perspective. Then we will illustrate several ways in which the proposed approach can be applied.

THE TRADITIONAL VIEW AND A PROPOSED PERSPECTIVE

Today's global, multinational, and even domestic competitors need to approach environmental scanning from a perspective that is fundamentally different from traditional management thought. Duncan[4] defined the environment as the relevant physical and social factors outside the boundary of an organization that are taken into consideration during organizational decision-making. Such a view of the organization's external environment has led to limitations on the scope of the environmental scanning process, in many firms. It fails to recognize the environment as truly composed of all interacting factors that influence, or have the potential to influence the organization's performance—irrespective of whether they are presently considered, or their existence even recognized by the organization.

A firm's definition of its environment should encompass not only the business, but also the natural and social environments it operates in and influences. Environmental Impact Analysis[5] involves the identification, prediction, and analysis of environmental and social impacts, and the analysis of policy alternatives. Applied in conjunction with environmental scanning this further contributes to benefits derived from information gathered through the scanning effort. Most environmental scanning systems of business firms fall into one of the four phases: primi-

tive, *ad hoc*, reactive, and proactive.[6] Faced with intense competitive pressures of global competition, today's global managers must adopt a proactive stance in scanning the environment continuously for opportunities that can translate into competitive advantage.

How managers define their firm's business, its strategic goals and objectives, and view present and future markets and competition, are important determinants of the firm's ability to relate to its environment. Since the environment provides but data and cues, it is only the proper comprehension, analysis, synthesis and evaluation of such data that enables extraction of meaningful environmental intelligence. It is then the intelligent application of gathered intelligence that shapes an organization's chance of continued success.

Traditionally, due to the prevalence of protectionist policies and the constraints of sheer distance, businesses and even competition have been viewed as domestic or multi-national. Defining businesses as domestic or multi-national offers little more than a label based solely on geographic coverage of markets served. Such a view reflects only the perception of management which fails to recognize the global scope of existing markets, competition, and the business environment.

Today's global shrinkage is the result of advances in communication, transportation technologies and changing ideologies. While there are domestic markets, there are few industries that are comprised of only domestic competitors. Absence of foreign competitors at a given point in time does not limit the market arena to domestic competitors. Windows of opportunity left open by prevailing domestic providers will inevitably induce entry of foreign competitors.

It follows then, that the concept of 'market share' is relative rather than absolute. Approached traditionally, from a self-imposed and preconceived conceptualization of the industry and market, the concept precludes expansion through innovation, creativity and internally-driven self improvement. Moreover, it is an outcome; the consequence of business activities. As such, it is these activities, the means to an end, that need to be of primary concern rather than market share. If a firm adds to its competitive advantage through improved managerial decisions, an increase in market share should follow.

Competitor intelligence and analysis has been the focus of traditional scanning, but it, too, has maintained a predominantly tactical marketing thrust. It is often argued that through competitor intelligence, businesses are able to counter moves and preempt advantages competitors may attempt to gain. Market share is the driving force—call it the 'bottom line' in such a perspective. In this traditional view, competitor intelligence is seen as the tool for product positioning, technological awareness, strategy formulation and tactical manœuvres by managers. U.S. firms have in fact relied heavily on competitor analysis as the predominant mode of competitive intelligence.

The rapid pace of change in today's markets makes it increasingly difficult for firms to focus on particular product lines and competitors. Today, organizations that escalate competitive pressures on firms—sometimes driving them out of business—are those that are often not even recognized as competitors. Competition now involves anyone or anything that displaces demand for a firm's product by luring customers away. For example, the little juice boxes that many kids now carry with their lunch packs dealt a severe blow to the canning industry.[7] The post offices now compete against major carriers such as Federal Express and United Parcel Service, and they all compete in some segments against electronic mail, phone, fax and video conferencing technologies. Seeing the market as a given constant and competing for 'a larger slice of that fixed pie' offers at best a very limited view for business expansion.

Is there more to environmental scanning than competitor intelligence? Must competitor intelligence and actions based on such information be the primary basis for competitiveness? How should the business environment be viewed and scanned? What are the implications of a global context? And in this context, how feasible is it to collect comprehensive and useful intelligence? What stream of managerial thought and practice will it take to grow and prosper in today's global marketplace? These are all pressing issues that need to be carefully considered.

Competitor intelligence and analysis alone fail to meet the requirements for sustained competitive advantage and continued growth. For one, actions taken to counter competitor moves can only be reactive. Beating a major competitor in the introduction of a product through competitor intelligence is not what ensures a sustained competitive edge in today's global markets. Competitor intelligence is merely a necessary but not a sufficient condition for continued competitive vitality. Basking in the glory of existing competitive advantage spells eventual failure through a gradual erosion of competitive position. Success follows only a constant drive for continuous improvement through innovation and expansion of competitive advantage over time.

In analysing competitors, it is important to recognize that it is not just the tangible resources they possess that make them potent competitors. It is often the intangibles (ability to relate to consumers, management style, philosophies, conceptualization, innovation, corporate culture and commitment) that determine their potential. It is this potential for competitive advantage that demands careful consideration. Table 1 outlines underlying differences between the traditional and proposed approaches to environmental scanning.

Firms differ in the nature of their competitive environments. Their environment can be assessed along three primary dimensions—heterogeneity, dynamism, and hostility.[8] *Heterogeneity* indicates the number and diversity of external factors, such as government regulations, customers, suppliers and nature of technology. *Dynamism* represents the rate and unpredictability of change in these factors. *Hostility* (or lack of it—munificence) reflects the restrictiveness of the environmental factors. This includes the restraining effects of powerful customers and suppliers, new entrants, and government regulations on the organization.

Firms operating in environments where customers essentially want low prices rather than novelty may not recover costs of innovations.[9] Firms may adopt a multidomestic strategy with their new operations started in foreign countries having close resemblance to local organizations. In such cases, production resources are restricted to those available in the local environment and the output is largely targeted to the

Table 1. Alternative Environment Scanning Characteristics

System Characteristics	Traditional Approach	Proposed Approach
Purpose	Specific competitive position	Creative competitive advantage
Scope	Domestic Multi-domestic	Global
Intent	Tactical	Strategic
Orientation	Reactive	Proactive
Focus	Competitor intelligence	Competitive intelligence
Intelligence Sensitivity	Customer-based	Consumer-based
Action Mode	Response to competitor weaknesses	Control through leadership position
	Quick-fix	Continuous improvement
Centres of Gravity	Relatively stationary	Rapidly shifting

local market. The retail industry has been a typical example, though it may be argued that this is fast changing as well. In addition to other factors, such multidomestic conditions may be brought about by restrictive regulations of local governments. However, companies not affected by industries in other countries are becoming an exception rather than the rule.[10]

Product innovations have been found to be most significant in uncertain environments where competing products and preferences alter significantly.[11] This is increasingly true of firms that are competing for global markets and are under pressure to reduce cycle times for the introduction of new products due to aggressive moves of global competitors. Firms such as Intel and Motorola are clearly impacted by moves of ICL, Fujitsu, and NEC. In fact, such entrepreneurial firms are themselves responsible for making the environment dynamic. These firms maintain a perspective not delineated by traditional definitions of industry and geography. They are also distributing operations where they can be accomplished best. While one part of the value-chain may be accomplished in one country, the rest are accomplished in others. The focus is on distributing operations and using an effective information technology infrastructure that enables co-ordination and logical integration to far-flung business operations. Through co-ordination and logical integration, these firms are able to reduce cycle time for key processes, eliminate rework and waste, and capitalize on human resources globally. While co-ordinating their global

activities they maintain the necessary local capability needed to effectively operate in the local environment. Table 2 presents some key contextual environmental and organizational factors that can influence the firm's choice of the environmental scanning mode.

MAKING ENVIRONMENTAL SCANNING WORK FOR YOU

A STRONG COMMITMENT AT THE TOP

It is essential that upper management recognize the role of environmental scanning in building competitive advantage. A weak commitment at the top spells failure for most efforts at other levels. According to a 1988 survey, of the 300 marketing, sales and planning managers surveyed by the Conference Board—a New York business research organization—most felt it was important to monitor competitive activities, though they felt more strongly about the need to do so than the top executives of their companies.[12] In another recent study, 49 percent of the firms surveyed did not monitor public and international affairs, 55 percent did not monitor supplier and procurement practices or did so rarely, and 38 percent rarely monitored the human resource.[13] This was the case, even though 75 of the 95 firms surveyed had sales in excess of US$250m, and 65 of them had sales in excess of US$1bn. Management must ensure

Table 2. Contextual Factors Influencing Choice of Environmental Scanning Mode

Contextual Factors	Traditional Approach	Proposed Approach
Environmental		
Homogeneity	Homogeneous	Heterogeneous
Dynamism	Static	Dynamic
Hostility	Munificent	Hostile
Organizational		
Strategic mode	Defender	Prospector
Decision-making	Centralized	Decentralized
Differentiation	Similar markets	Dissimilar markets
	Few product/service lines	Many product/service lines
Risk propensity	Low	High

the scanning of such areas, as they can be among the most revealing ways in identifying opportunities.

The performance of many of today's business organizations hinges on how well they respond to their external macroenvironment.[14] Analysis of the social, economic, technological, political and regulatory components of the macroenvironment involves the study of current and potential changes and how such changes impact the organization.[15] Again, leadership that stimulates effective monitoring and enables prompt response to changes in the external macroenvironment can provide the firm with opportunities that others might well miss.

CONCEPTUALIZE YOUR ENVIRONMENT CAREFULLY

It is the proper conceptualization and consequent scanning of the environment that enables organizations to identify and exploit opportunities. Such conceptualization while *essential* at the top must be made to filter down through the levels of the organization. Inability to define one's environment correctly and monitor change is analogous to a 'battleship without a radar,' or one with a limited range. The consequence of either is inevitably a first strike by the enemy.

The traditional notion of domestic businesses is fast eroding with global competitors emerging in areas never contemplated. Today environmental factors such as changes in political climates, legal systems, technological capability, relative wage rates,

fluctuations in exchange and interest rates and shifts in the location of centres of gravity for resources and distribution have become critical. As such, they need to be carefully monitored. With recent changes in political climates—especially in Europe and Russia, the world seems to be moving in the direction of forming clusters of increasingly homogeneous communities. A single European Community internal market is likely to become a greater reality in 1993. In addition to economic and political factors, understanding demographic and cultural trends is a key ingredient in the recipe of success in such environments.

Although not all industries will exhibit continued growth, there are many growth opportunities that firms can continually pursue. Growth and expansion are a function of an organization's ability to relate to changing consumer needs. Innovation, positioning, adjustment, redefinition and improvement of both product and processes, in response to environmental conditions and consumer needs, should form the basis of growth in today's global economy. Growth for an organization can no longer be viewed as the predestined outcome of a perceived sequence of stages in the life cycles of its products.

OFFER A GLOBALLY COMPETITIVE VALUE

Business firms must strive to provide the best value globally for goods and services they offer. The assessment of value by consumers in foreign markets is based on exchange-rate-adjusted comparisons with competing domestic and other foreign substitutes for goods and services in question.

A global conceptualization coupled with an understanding of potential buyers is what results in global brands and leadership positions. Firms that deliver a globally competitive value, can if required, successfully tailor their products and services to the needs of individual nations. This task is more easily accomplished when the firm has value-based products to offer in foreign markets. However, the need for significant customization worldwide may diminish for some products as the world moves towards larger geographic or cultural clusters, but the converse may result for some goods and services where individuals can pay for unique attention.

Sony TVs and Panasonic VCRs offer good examples of global brands that are preferred for their value based on their technological superiority, and yet tailored to varied transmission systems and needs worldwide. Toyota has successfully tailored select models of its cars for appropriate competitive positioning in Asian and Western markets. Even with differences in construction of its cars offered in some Asian countries when compared to those offered in Western nations, Toyota remains a dominant competitor in both markets. Its 'Corolla' model, for example, is tailored (with a lower cost and quality of components for the Thai version than those used in the version sold in the U.S.) and positioned as an economical and yet reliable family car in the two markets. While accounting for a dominant share of the Thai taxi-cab market, it remains ever popular as an economical family car in both Thailand and America. The primary reason for Toyota's success is the global perception of Toyota quality and the excellent value it offers.

STRIVE TO LEAD, NOT TO IMITATE

Though it is important to know your competition—and know it well—most firms should not adopt imitation as a policy. Too many companies expend enormous energy simply reproducing the cost and quality advantages their global competitors already enjoy. While imitation may contribute to short-term benefits, including reduction in R&D outlays, it will not lead to competitive revitalization, let alone competitive advantage. Strategies based on imitation are short sighted, limited in scope, and, most importantly, transparent to competitors who have already mastered them.[16]

McDonald's spends huge sums of money on research aimed at identifying optimal location sites for its stores. Would competitors who choose to avoid the cost of such investigation by locating across the street from every McDonald's store gain a competitive advantage? Experience suggests 'no!' those who adopt the role of 'followers' view research dollars spent as expenses while failing to recognize the magnitude of advantage which might be gained through the compounding of benefits over time. On the contrary, those striving for leadership positions view such dollars as an *investment* for competitive advantage.

Recognizing the limitations of an imitation-driven policy contributes to a thrust for further expanding the scope of environmental scanning. To be successful, companies must constantly innovate in their use of technology, product design, and management practices by drawing from an astute understanding of their environment. Rather than benchmarking competitors' products to ensure competitive parity, benchmarking should be used only as an information tool for increased awareness. Improvement and innovation rather than imitation, result in leadership positions for others to try to mimic. A major ad campaign by Honda during the introduction of its new and much improved 1990 Accord showed the confidence of a competitor able to make significant headway in the U.S. car market. The theme of the campaign—while competitors were carefully benchmarking the 1989 Accord for its superior performance, Honda already had a further improved and expanded new model of the same car available as an option for buyers—effectively conveyed a leadership stance.

The best defence is often a strong offence. Innovation, search for competitive intelligence, the pursuit of opportunities and continuous improvement, are all effective weapons in a firm's arsenal. They are not only the strongest barriers for competition that a firm can erect, but they also contribute to pressures on competitors. Obsession for improvement, and commitment to a leadership position can help overcome the traditionally binding constraints of resource base, firm size, and narrow conceptualization of one's business domain.

BUILD IN STRATEGIC FLEXIBILITY

The design of environmental scanning systems has traditionally followed a rigid, structured and sequential approach with predefined strategic objectives determining their focus. As a result, firms using such systems often miss opportunities that fall outside their immediate goals and frame of reference. Environmental scanning should not be limited to information consistent with existing products, services, markets, competitors or even customers. It is essential that one look at the broader environment in identifying and exploiting market possibilities. Moving away from traditional systems, managers should use feedback from a broader environmental scanning effort to make necessary changes to an evolving and dynamic set of strategic objectives.

By evaluating its competitive position in the broader entertainment industry rather than just in the electronic audio and video components sector, Sony has further enhanced its competitive advantage through its recent acquisition of Columbia Pictures. Its initiative and farsightedness in recognizing and exploiting the complementarity of products coupled with its innovative managerial philosophies are what make it a dominant global competitor. Stopford and Baden-Fuller,[17] in describing the dynamics of changes in the knitwear industry, show how success during the 1980s came to those who changed their strategy to exploit changing conditions in the marketplace. Such manœuvring was not tactical, but strategic and required change in all parts of the firm including new mind sets for all managers from top to bottom. Globally competitive markets deny a sustained competitive edge to firms with static strategic objectives. Strategic manœuvring and adaptation to signals detected through the scanning effort are key to remaining globally competitive.

FOCUS ON CONSUMER-BASED SCANNING

In scanning their business environment, firms may choose a *competitor-based, resource-based,* or a *consumer-based* focus. While the limitations of competitor-based intelligence were noted earlier, management must also recognize that resource-based scanning is not necessarily the way to sustain competitive advantage over time. With lower transportation costs and the lifting of trade barriers, many global competitors are gravitating towards markets which now offer lower priced labour and other resources contributing to production economies. But such markets are destined for shared exploitation by an increasing number of global competitors. Advantages offered by cheaper resources soon evaporate, leaving individual firms to ponder the possible relocation costs to new centres of gravity. Though business firms can benefit from resource-based scanning, they must carefully rethink and reevaluate the strategic implications of committing primarily to such a scanning strategy. An essential ingredient for sustained competitive advantage lies in adopting a consumer-based scanning focus.

Consumers perform an essential part of competitor analysis through their very choice of goods and services. As the final users of products and services, they are the best source of information on competitiveness and relative value because their choices are driven by attempts to maximize personal utility. They are also the best consultants and are available to all firms irrespective of size, type, and location. A firm's customer base must be viewed as being comprised of both existing and *potential* customers. Traditionally, firms have focused on customer satisfaction as measured by feedback from already established customers. Competitive intelligence can often result from information gathered from competitors' customers. Such intelligence should provide important feedback and serve as an input for corporate competitive strategy.

To be effective, management must look beyond customer preferences to consumer needs. Preferences are a function of options available or known at a point in time. Needs may or may not be fulfilled through goods and services presently available to consumers. It is the inability to identify and meet the needs of people in their role as consumers that results in increased domestic and overseas competition. Better performance by the competition, in this regard, erodes a firm's competitive advantage and leadership position. The U.S. auto industry provides a striking example. While U.S. auto makers focused on gas-guzzling power machines, many consumers in the 1960s and 1970s were looking for reliable fuel-efficient cars, especially after the rapid oil price increases in 1973. Instead of attempting to identify customer preferences among products they were planning to offer in the market, they should have focused on establishing what consumers really wanted. Similarly, U.S. farm equipment manufacturers ignored the call for low horsepower tractors for smaller farms and non-farm or specialty users, only to lose this market to foreign competition. Technical-market research is one relatively new way to efficiently synthesize consumer interests with options feasibly available from a firm's R&D laboratories.[18] A better understanding of consumer needs and industry trends constitutes an important objective for environmental scanning systems. Mapping consumer needs against goods and services currently available to them can help reveal new opportunities for business firms.

LEARN TO LEARN

It is misleading to assume that Japan's progress and its present competitive superiority, are the result of their having been given advanced technology from the U.S. in the post-World War Two years. Even if domestic technology were transferred overseas, it should at best have brought foreign competitors to a position on par with the exporters. It must be recognized, though, that imports of advanced technology help establish a higher base to further build on and can often save millions of dollars in R&D. The Japanese have indeed taken this to heart. Yet, it is the cultural values and other intangible traits which they have learned, adopted, tailored and fine-tuned, that have made them dominant global competitors.

Identifying opportunities for joint ventures, alliances, collaboration and outsourcing is a frequent outcome of environmental scanning. Interestingly, Asian companies have been found to gain more from collaborations with U.S. firms than their counterparts.[19] The reason lies in the Asian partners' *desire to learn.* In collaborations with U.S. firms, the Japanese have, in many instances, shown how quality and

productivity can both be significantly enhanced. Such results have been achieved with the alliances manufacturing in the U.S. while using the American labour force—something the U.S. manufacturers have found difficult to accomplish on their own.

1984 saw the launching of New United Motors Manufacturing, Inc. (NUMMI)—a joint venture of Toyota and General Motors. A few years later, a carefully undertaken study of over fifty automobile assembly plants was conducted for the International Motor Vehicle Program at MIT.[20] In the study, productivity at NUMMI was found to be around 40 percent higher than at traditional GM plants in the U.S. and at par with Toyota's Japanese plants. NUMMI's success was attributed to 'sound management principles,' and to the use of the team concept. Interestingly, this success was possible even though the level of automation at NUMMI was considered mid-range when compared with GM's latest technology.

Western managers must learn and implement important principles, concepts and processes, just as the Japanese did when they incorporated the Deming[21] teachings on quality. Drawing from international exposure, they can use environmental scanning to incorporate and expand on the strengths of systems that have made global superiority possible for some competitors. Realizing that continuous learning is an essential prerequisite to continuous improvement can make this objective easier to accomplish.

ASSUME AN AGGRESSIVE POSTURE IN SEEKING OPPORTUNITIES

It helps to be optimistic—for opportunities are essentially a function of one's comprehension and understanding of the environmental context. Opportunities such as possible collaborations with foreign companies to target non-domestic markets should be under constant surveillance by the corporate environmental scanning system. Many Asian companies have successfully used the strategy of collaborating with U.S. companies and introducing their products under U.S. brand names. In doing so, they are able to test the foreign market, use established distribution channels and brand positions, gather intelligence, make adjustments, and when well positioned at a

Table 3. Managerial Traits of the Traditional and Proposed Approaches to Environmental Scanning

Managerial Trait	Traditional Approach	Proposed Approach
Leadership	Middle management	Upper management
Involvement	Designated	Institutional
Justification	Short payback	Deferred payback
Incentives	Insufficient	Abundant
Feedback	Minimal	Extensive
ES Personnel		
Composition	Homogeneous	Heterogeneous
	Domestic nationals	Domestic and foreign nationals
Training	Limited and rudimentary	Extensive and detailed
Evaluation	Short-term performance	Time-phased expectations

new market 'beach head' are able to launch the same products under their own names. Japanese companies selling colour TVs under J.C. Penney and Sears brand name and Korean tool makers collaborating similarly with U.S. machine tool manufacturers are just some examples where this strategy has been successfully employed.[22]

CREATING AN ENABLING CORPORATE CULTURE

Corporate culture is perhaps the most basic yet significant competitive asset an organization can possess. Discrete technologies and mechanical processes are relatively more easily transferred across corporate and national boundaries than are the intangible assets deeply entwined in the corporate culture. It is corporate management's responsibility to create a desirable culture. Table 3 outlines essential differences in many of the managerial traits comprising cultures surrounding the traditional and proposed approaches to environmental scanning.

INSTILL A CULTURE FOR CONTINUOUS IMPROVEMENT

Consumers continually expect a better value for their money. For global leadership positions, companies must maintain a consistent value advantage in delivering goods and services. Such advantage can only be assured by a persistent drive for continuous improvement and a race against competition—even phantom competitors if that is what it takes to maintain competitive superiority.

The corporate culture must challenge employees and engage them intellectually so as to optimize the use and development of the human resource. Managers can make this possible by providing the necessary infrastructure required to bring out the best in their employees and building in mechanisms for them to use in order to draw from the environment. This, in turn, should facilitate continuous improvement in basic processes and raise the productivity of individuals. Sponsorship by top management and their participation in designing and implementing such mechanisms is essential.

INSTITUTIONALIZE INVOLVEMENT AND OPEN CHANNELS FOR COMMUNICATION

Western managers often remain focused on day-to-day problems. As such, not having enough time on hand, they choose to pay little attention to the overall environment and the opportunities it might offer on an ongoing basis. In Japanese corporations, managers are trained to make competitive intelligence everyone's business. Today a formal consideration of the business environment should form a regular part of management practice.

Upper management must raise environment related questions and concerns in promoting and directing the scanning effort while soliciting and providing feedback on actions initiated. Insufficient feedback on the intelligence gathered through scanning and the effectiveness of intelligence activities not only deters effort in support of this cause but also impedes the very success of the environmental scanning process. Managers can further facilitate institutional involvement by regularly discussing environmental issues and information gathered through scanning. This could be done when holding business meetings or while interacting with personnel at various levels and across functional areas. Such steps would not only allow for better interpretation through brainstorming sessions, but even more importantly, would instill greater sensitivity towards the environment and the need for its constant surveillance.

Traditionally, environmental scanning has received greater attention only during times of crisis and at 'trigger points,' such as unexpected shifts in demand or when making investment and expansion decisions. Environmental scanning should be a continuous process. The information gathered herein should be integrated into the planning processes. As Fahey and King suggest, firms that fail to achieve such integration not only make the information gathered useless, but their very collection of environmental information may be short-lived.[23]

In scope, the environmental scanning effort should encompass much more than the identification of market niches. The scanning of the global environment provides market and operations related insights in both domestic and non-domestic contexts. This allows the firm to build a base of attack. Managers should shape response and initiate action to capitalize on opportunities the environment offers—for inaction is bound to erode competitive vitality by precipitating crises.

BUILD INCENTIVES

Reward systems should be carefully evaluated, keeping in mind their implications in promoting the cause of intelligence gathering and involvement. Strong incentives for intelligence gathering and sharing of information should be established. Tangible rewards are not the only means of providing incentives for employees. Recognition, consideration of contributions to corporate goals, advancement opportunities, resource support and training, close communication, building esteem and self worth, all go a long way in shaping effectiveness of intelligence gathering mechanisms.

APPOINT CULTURAL LIAISONS THEREBY INJECTING CULTURAL AWARENESS

With global markets and an increasing involvement in overseas operations, business firms have much to gain from the appointment of foreign nationals at key positions in the corporate hierarchy. Such positions should be carefully designated at both the firm's headquarters and its domestic and foreign subsidiaries. Foreign nationals bring with them a first-hand experience of a different culture, the people and their domestic environments. They not only act as liaisons between the organization and its interests abroad, but contribute to the organization's effectiveness in fulfilling these same interests.

Percy Barnevik, president and CEO of ABB Asea Brown Boveri, which employs over 240,000 people around the world and generates annual revenues in excess of US$25bn encourages people to work in mixed-nationality teams. Moreover, numerous foreign nationals serve as members on the firm's executive committee. In his words: 'When we sit together as Germans, Swiss, Americans, and Swedes, with many of us living, working, and travelling in different places, the insights can be remarkable.'[24] But upper management must shape such situations. Mixing nationalities does not just happen. A survey of 150 of the largest global competitors found that barely 1 percent of senior headquarter positions were filled by foreign nationals, despite the fact that the average income generated by overseas operations was at least 20 percent of the companies' total income.[25]

INSTITUTE VIGOROUS TRAINING AND COUPLE LONG OVERSEAS ASSIGNMENTS WITH STRONG 'HOME BACKING'

According to one survey of large U.S. and Japanese multinationals, 68 percent of American companies had no formal training programmes to prepare personnel for overseas work. Even the remaining 32 percent provided training that was essentially limited in briefing sessions that imparted rudimentary knowledge of the foreign country in question. Moreover, three-quarters of these U.S. multinational corporations had to dismiss or recall 10 to 40 percent of their personnel assigned overseas due to their poor performance. On the contrary, 86 percent of the similar Japanese corporations reported a failure rate of less than 10 percent.[26] Success of personnel assigned to scanning activities abroad is not an outcome of chance. It is largely dependent on the extent to which employees, particularly those assigned abroad, are prepared through training in culture, customs, and language.

The sharing of a common language removes barriers, builds trust, earns respect, reduces misunderstanding in communication and provides easier access to foreign sources. Most importantly, it facilitates the learning and understanding of different cultures, thereby enhancing one's ability to act on information gathered from foreign environments. The importance of 'learning a foreign language' and how it figures in the competitive equation must be appreciated by managers.

Management should make assignments for work overseas early so that those assigned can undergo careful training prior to departure. Short assignments and job switching are not conducive to the effectiveness of the scanning effort abroad because thoroughly adapting to new cultures and business environments takes time. It is only when contracts are established and familiarity gained that the greatest returns are attainable. A strong communication link should be maintained with the personnel abroad. It is common to find assigned personnel feel left out, ignored or insecure in a foreign environment. Recognizing the significance of their undertaking and *conveying* to them this recognition greatly increases their sense of security and commitment.

STRIVE TO BE DIFFERENT FROM YOUR COMPETITORS

Managers should continuously strive to gain competitive advantage for their firm by identifying and developing contrasting or new capabilities. In addition,

they must make the need to identify and develop such capabilities *understood* at all levels. Businesses can differentiate themselves through creativity, innovation, redefinition, repositioning and continuous improvement. Effective employment of competitive intelligence should drive this differentiation effort.

Hitachi, a \$62bn giant and dominant global competitor with 28 factories, 800 subsidiaries and 320,000 employees cranking out nearly 2 percent of Japan's yearly GNP[27] is an outstanding example of a firm that not only achieved but also maintains its leadership position by developing new product and process capabilities. Moreover, in part, its broader approach seems attuned to the proposed framework presented thus far. Hitachi holds the largest portfolio of Japanese patents and has topped America's list of patent earners for most of the last decade. As Japan's star technology innovator, the company has amassed a wealth of intellectual properties and has an obsession with R&D. It has carefully positioned its products from a diverse product line that includes computers, TVs, VCRs, consumer electronics, power plants, generators, elevators, robots and even trains. In fact, at Hitachi's Energy Research Lab they are conceptualizing a new train—if one can call it a train—that makes the sleek bullet train seem more like a steam engine. The company has further strengthened its position in world markets by building alliances, for example, with Texas Instruments, Hewlett-Packard, General Electric and IBM in the U.S. It has even spread its research network overseas to include applied math in Dublin, high speed chips at Britain's Cambridge, and American-style high-definition television in Princeton. The pursuit of a proactive strategy, innovation, creativity, relating to the consumer and global markets, and the value it offers through its products is essentially what makes Hitachi the global leader it is today.

RISK FACTORS

Globalization as a competitive strategy is inherently more vulnerable than a multi-domestic, an export/import or a domestic strategy due to the increased exposure created by operating in a multidimensional environment.[28] Nevertheless, often the benefits that can be derived from global operations more than justify the incremental risk incurred through the pursuit of such strategy. Starr[29] points to specific benefits that can be obtained through the pursuit of a global operations strategy.

Moving to new and advanced technologies in an attempt to offer a better value requires significant investment expenditures. Firms must expand their markets to include other nations so as to achieve sales that justify such investment. Operations abroad can be used to avert protectionist sentiment of nations and to facilitate entry into emerging unified economies such as that of the European Community– 1992. Japan has succeeded in effectively minimizing the impact of a rising U.S. protectionist sentiment during the 1990s through a proactive pursuit of plant installations in the United States during the 1980s.

The availability and price of relevant resources in other nations often attracts entry. Government support of export industries in most nations provides firms with further incentive to expand to international markets. In addition, ever-increasing volumes of shipments between nations has significantly lowered the costs of distribution for global firms. Through proper management, global firms that build strategies based on flexibility can benefit from fluctuations of interest rates, exchange rates, inflation and other volatile factors that provide advantages precisely because they do fluctuate. As an example, Glaum[30] shows how tactical and strategic approaches to managing exchange rate risks can complement one another.

Through environmental scanning, firms can identify opportunities for global operations and expansion while overcoming threats posed by competitive pressures. The issue today is not whether going global is good or bad, rather, it is more a question of how decisions related to global operations are made and implemented. Management's ability to comprehend the dynamics and to recognize what truly constitutes an 'opportunity' in a global context is a critical element in the consideration of risk. The perils of committing to multinational projects, be they joint ventures, outsourcing, plant locations, rationalization or marketing and distribution purely from a short-term perspective have been well documented.[31] Long-term and strategic implications must be carefully considered for actions based on competitive intelligence gathered.

Welch and Nayak provide one framework for a more strategic approach to the sourcing decisions. Ohmae provides a multitude of convincing arguments in support of multinational strategic alliances.[32] In addition, he suggests specific 'do's' and 'don'ts' for successful collaboration.

The approach to environmental scanning should be innovative. According to Vrakking,[33] innovation in essence is any renewal, designed and realized, that strengthens the organization's position against its competitors', and which allows a long-term competitive advantage to be maintained. Potential benefits that result from a broad-based scanning effort can be substantial. As in R&D, or investments in the human resource, management should not focus on immediate payback from the scanning effort. Rather, expectations should be deferred with contribution assessed over a longer term. The fact that many of the benefits derived are often difficult to measure in absolute terms and attribute to specific scanning effort must be recognized. Moreover, synergies that result from an institutional commitment to scanning provide the necessary thrust for continuous improvement and competitiveness.

CONCLUDING REMARKS

Corporate managers should recognize the growing importance and changing nature of environmental scanning systems. The design and nature of these systems depends on top management's understanding of the global business environment and their firm's strategic vision. It is important to develop an appropriate corporate culture context, as firms increasingly look overseas for improved opportunities. Environmental scanning can form a basis for effectively managing competitive intelligence and ensuring continuous improvement, and ultimately, increasing competitive vitality for business firms.

REFERENCES

1. R.L. Daft, J. Sormunen and D. Parks, Chief executives scanning environmental characteristics, and company performance: an empirical study, *Strategic Management Journal*, **9** (2), 123–139 (1988).

2. L. Fahey, W.R. King and V.K. Narayanan, Environmental scanning and forecasting in strategic planning—the state of the art. *Long Range Planning,* **14** (1), 32–39 (1981).

3. V.R. Dingus and W.A. Golomski, *A Quality Revolution in Manufacturing,* Industrial Engineering and Management Press, Norcross, Georgia (1988).

4. R.B. Duncan, Characteristics of organizational environments and perceived environmental uncertainty, *Administrative Sciences Quarterly,* **17** (3), 313–327 (1972).

5. K. Vizayakumar and P.K.J. Mohapatra, Environmental impact analysis: a synthetic approach, *Long Range Planning,* **24** (6), 102–106 (1991).

6. S.C. Jain, Environmental scanning in U.S. corporations, *Long Range Planning,* **17** (2), 117–128 (1984).

7. C. Mellow, The best source of competitive intelligence, *Sales & Marketing Management,* **141** (12), 24–29, December (1988).

8. D. Miller and P.H. Friesen, Innovation in conservative and entrepreneurial firms: two models of strategic momentum, *Strategic Management Journal,* **2** (1), 1–25 (1982).

9. D. Miller, Relating Porter's generic business strategies to environment and structure and performance implications, *Academy of Management Journal,* **31** (2), 280–308 (1988).

10. P.M. Rosenzweigh and J.V. Singh, Organizational environments and the multinational enterprise, *Academy of Management Review,* **16** (2), 340–361 (1991).

11. H. Mintzberg, *The Structuring of Organizations,* Prentice Hall, Englewood Cliffs, NJ (1979).

12. T. Eisenhart, Where to go when you need to know, *Business Marketing,* **74** (11), 38–50 (1989).

13. J.E. Prescott, and D.C. Smith, The largest survey of 'leading-edge' competitor intelligence managers, *Planning Review,* **17** (3), 6–13 (1989).

14. P.M. Ginter and W.J. Duncan, Macroenvironmental analysis for strategic management, *Long Range Planning,* **23** (6), 91–100 (1990).

15. L. Fahey and V.K. Narayanan, *Macroenvironmental Analysis for Strategic Management,* West Publishing, St. Paul, MN, p. 3 (1986).

16. G. Hamel and C.K. Prahalad, Strategic intent, *Harvard Business Review,* **67** (3), 63–76 (1989).

17. J.M. Stopford and C. Baden-Fuller, Flexible strategies—the key to success in knitwear, *Long Range Planning,* **23** (6), 56–62 (1990).

18. A.S. Lauglaug, Integrating customers and innovation through technical-market research, *Long Range Planning,* **26,** April (1993).

19. G. Hamel, Y.L. Doz and C.K. Prahalad, Collaborate with your competitors—and win. *Harvard Business Review,* **67** (1), 133–139 (1989).

20. J. Krafcik, Triumph of the lean production system, *Sloan Management Review,* **30** (1), 41–52 (1988).

21. M. Walton, *The Deming Management Method,* Dodd, Mead, & Company, New York (1986).

22. J.F. Mahon and S. Vachani, Establishing a beach-head in international markets. *Long Range Planning,* **25** (3), 60–69 (1992).

23. L. Fahey and W.R. King, Environmental scanning for corporate planning, *Business Horizons,* **20** (4), 61–71 (1977).

24. W. Taylor, The logic of global business: an interview with ABB's Percy Barnevik, *Harvard Business Review,* **69** (2), 91–105 (1991).

25. H.V. Perlmutter and D.A. Heenan, How multinational should your top managers be?, *Harvard Business Review,* **52** (6), 121–132 (1974).

26. R.L. Tung, *Key to Japan's Economic Strength: Human Power,* D.C. Heath, Lexington, MA (1984).

27. N. Gross, Inside Hitachi, *Business Week,* 92–100, 28 September (1992).

28. B. James, Reducing the risks of globalizations, *Long Range Planning,* **23** (1), 80–88 (1990).

29. M.K. Starr, Global production and operations strategy, *Columbia Journal of World Business,* **19** (4), 17–22 (1984).

30. M. Glaum, Strategic management of exchange rate risks, *Long Range Planning,* **23** (4), 65–72 (1990).

31. See, for example, R.B. Reich and E.D. Mankin, Joint ventures with Japan give away our future, *Harvard Business Review,* **64** (2), 78–86 (1986); N. Jonas, The hollow corporation, *Business Week,* 57–59, 3 March (1986); C.C. Markides and N. Berg, Manufacturing offshore is bad business, *Harvard Business Review,* **66** (5), 113–120 (1988).

32. J.A. Welch and P.R. Nayak, Strategic sourcing: a progressive approach to the make-or-buy decision, *Academy of Management Executive,* **6** (1), 23–31 (1992); and K. Ohmae, The global logic of strategic alliances, *Harvard Business Review,* **67** (2), 143–154 (1989).

33. W.J. Vrakking, The innovative organization, *Long Range Planning,* **23** (2), 94–102 (1990).

39

INFORMATION-PROCESSING THEORY AND THE MULTINATIONAL ENTERPRISE

WILLIAM G. EGELHOFF*

Fordham University

ABSTRACT   This paper attempts to extend information-processing theory so that it can be meaningfully applied to MNCs. A specific multidimensional framework is developed that can be used to measure the information-processing capacities of macro-level features of MNC organizational design. An applied example, transnationalism, is used to illustrate how to apply the framework and demonstrate that it can contribute meaningful new insight to this complex organizational problem.

The multinational corporation (MNC) is probably the most complex form of organization in widespread existence today. Operating across products and markets, nations and cultures, it faces problems and situations far more diverse than even the largest domestic firms. With the increasing globalization of business, a rapidly growing level of economic activity now depends upon this form of organization. Thus, the MNC is an important entity for scholarly study both because its influence is growing and it presents organizational problems that lie at the forefront of organization theory and challenge the capacities of existing organization theory.

MNC research of an organizational nature has focused on two primary topics:

- What kinds of organizational design contribute to ef-

fective MNC performance and under what strategic and environmental conditions is one form of design preferable to another.

- How have MNC organizational designs changed and evolved over time and what factors cause or explain this evolution.

The principle concept associated with the first type of research has been the concept of fit (between organizational design and strategy or environment). Work has centered around how to measure fit and how to relate such fit to performance [Stopford and Wells 1972; Franko 1976; Daniels, Pitts and Tretter 1984]. Regarding how to measure fit, most MNC research has used some form of correlation technique to relate organizational design to a variety of strategic and environmental variables. Generally, little attention has been given to developing an abstract theoretical framework that could explain or support hypothesizing the relationships. A noteworthy exception is Herbert's [1984] proposed set of relationships between four types of strategy and a variety of organizational characteristics, based on resource flow considerations. While research studies frequently discuss why certain fits might contribute to effective MNC performance, fit in MNC research has tended to be expressed more in empirical than in theoretical terms. That is, the primary reason for anticipating certain fits in MNCs is that they have

An earlier version of this paper was presented at the Workshop on Organizational Theory and the Multinational Corporation at INSEAD on September 1–2, 1989. The author wishes to thank David Whetten, John Daniels, Andrew Van de Ven, Michael Gerlach and Susan Schneider for their helpful comments. Three anonymous *JIBS* reviewers also provided new insights into the material.

* William G. Egelhoff is Associate Professor of Management Systems at Fordham University's Graduate School of Business. His current research primarily deals with strategy and strategy implementation in multinational corporations.

Received: March 1990; Revised: November 1990; Accepted: January 1991.

been found in the past, and not that any abstract theoretical framework can explain why and when they should exist. This paper will argue that information-processing theory is an attractive candidate for extending MNC research to include such a theoretical framework.

The second type of MNC research effort, how MNC organizational designs change and evolve, has largely produced a documentation, rather than a theory, of the evolution of MNC structure over time [Pavan 1972; Stopford and Wells 1972; Dyas and Thanheiser 1976]. Contingency relationships developed with cross-sectional data have not been tested longitudinally. Evolution has generally been measured only with a limited number of case studies. Existing notions about what has caused MNC structure to change and evolve over time are relatively simple and tend to lack empirical support. The basic evolution of international business form or strategy has generally been explained in economic terms [Vernon 1971; Kindleberger 1973; Stevens 1974; Hymer 1976]. As evidenced in the various stages of organizational growth models [Stopford and Wells 1972; Dyas and Thanheiser 1976], it is generally presumed that organizational structure has followed the evolution of MNC strategy and environment.

This brief overview of organizational research on the multinational enterprise has attempted to identify where the frontiers of such research might lie today. Throughout the present paper, which will develop and discuss an information-processing perspective of MNCs, we will attempt to evaluate how such a perspective might support future research on these issues.

THE CONCEPTUAL FOUNDATIONS FOR AN INFORMATION-PROCESSING PERSPECTIVE OF ORGANIZATIONS

The general idea that it would be useful to view organizations as information-processing systems seems to have several sources. Quite a few theorists have sought to understand organizations by describing them as communications systems, decisionmaking

systems, or systems that have to cope with uncertainty. Although definitions of these concepts vary and for certain purposes the distinctions may be important, they can all be subsumed under the broader notion of information processing. Information processing in organizations is generally defined as including the gathering of data, the transformation of data into information, and the communication and storage of information in the organization [Galbraith 1973; Tushman and Nadler 1978].

Theorists interested in viewing the organization from an information-processing perspective generally have focused on environmental uncertainty and how organizations absorb uncertainty as the important contingency concept. Thompson [1967:10,13] presents the conceptual argument for the importance of uncertainty:

we will conceive of complex organizations as open systems, hence, indeterminate and faced with uncertainty, but at the same time as subject to criteria of rationality and hence needing determinateness and certainty. . . .

With this conception the central problem for complex organizations is one of coping with uncertainty. As a point of departure, we suggest that organizations cope with uncertainty by creating certain parts specifically to deal with it, specializing other parts in operating under conditions of certainty or near certainty. In this case, articulation of these specialized parts becomes significant.

We also suggest that technologies and environments are major sources of uncertainty for organizations, and that differences in those dimensions will result in differences in organizations.

Thus, Thompson suggests that uncertainty arises from certain characteristics in the environment and technology facing an organization and that differences in uncertainty somehow lead to differences in the organization's design.

Galbraith [1969, 1973, 1977] added some additional conceptualization to Thompson's general framework and developed a much more operational framework and model that has generally been referred to as an information-processing approach to organizational design. He rigorously defined the concept of uncertainty in terms of information processing: "Uncertainty is the difference between the amount of information required to perform the task and the amount of information already possessed by the organization." Thus, there is a relationship between the amount of uncertainty faced by an organization and the amount of information processing that must go on in an organization. Effective organizations are those that fit their information-processing capacities (for gathering, transforming, storing, and communicating information) to the amount of uncertainty they face.

Galbraith also specified the relative information-processing capacities of different organizational design features. These features are listed below, in order of increasing information-processing capacity [Galbraith 1973:15]:

- Rules and programs
- Hierarchical referral
- Goal-setting
- Vertical information systems
- Lateral relations

Where conditions are routine and simple, rules and programs can be used to absorb the relatively small amount of uncertainty facing the organization. For example, how foreign subsidiaries will set up their accounting systems is usually specified in a set of rules from the parent HQ describing the chart of accounts and various closing and reporting dates. Such rules absorb a good deal of uncertainty and eliminate the need for other forms of parent-subsidiary information processing. Where uncertainty increases, exceptions must be referred up the hierarchical authority structure for decisionmaking. When information-processing requirements threaten to overload the management structure, goal-setting and planning allow more decisions to be made at lower levels in the organization as long as they are within the plan. This relieves the information-processing load on the hierarchical structure.

When this is no longer adequate, various vertical information-processing systems can be attached to the hierarchical structure, which increase the organization's information-processing capacity. These frequently include computer-based information systems and staff groups and tend to increase the capacity for centralized information processing. When uncertainty and information-processing requirements are very great, the use of lateral relations allows more information processing to be decentralized so that the more limited information-processing capacity at higher levels of the organization is not overloaded. Lateral relations mechanisms include direct contact between individuals, liaison roles, task forces, teams, and matrix designs. Thus, Galbraith's model suggests a more operational framework for linking quite a number of organizational design features to the level of uncertainty or information-processing requirements facing an organization.

Uncertainty and information-processing concepts have served as the basis for a substantial number of empirical studies [Burns and Stalker 1961; Lawrence and Lorsch 1967; Galbraith 1970; Duncan 1973; Van de Ven, Delbecq and Koening 1976; Tushman 1978; Egelhoff 1982; Kmetz 1984]. It will be helpful to summarize these views in what might be called "the general information-processing approach to organizational design." As shown in Figure 1, this general approach or model is a summary of the Galbraith [1973] and Tushman and Nadler [1978] models. It is also consistent with the conceptual approaches used in the empirical studies mentioned above.

On the one hand, the impact on an organization of its strategy and the environmental factors that it chooses to deal with can be expressed in terms of the information-processing requirements they create. On the other hand, the potential of the organization to cope with these requirements can be expressed in terms of the information-processing capacities furnished by its organizational design.

The strategic and environmental conditions include all those factors that are external to the organization's design and that influence the information-processing requirements of the organization. These include technology, size, environmental change, environmental complexity, subunit interdependency, and goals. Similarly, the different features of an

Figure 1. The General Information-Processing Approach to Organizational Design

organization's design (such as structure, degree of centralization, planning and control systems, interpersonal communication patterns) must also be measured or expressed in terms of the information-processing capacity they provide.

Measuring fit between such dissimilar phenomena as (1) strategic and environmental conditions and (2) features of organizational design has troubled organization theory ever since it became contingency oriented. Aldrich [1979:45] has stated, ''we know the physics of air, water, and light to which flying, swimming, and seeing creatures must conform. We need much better knowledge of organizational types and appropriate environments before we can do as well in understanding organizational change.'' Information-processing theory suggests that information processing may be the missing ''physics'' that can help us to understand better critical conformities between organizational types and environments and the impact of such conformities on organizational survival and change. The information-processing perspective calls for translating strategic and environmental conditions and organizational design features into their respective information-processing implications. Then it will be easier to measure fit between information-processing requirements and information-processing capacities, which are more comparable phenomena.

An important assumption underlying the information-processing perspective is that the quality of information-processing fit is constraining on organizational performance and survival. This assumption is more likely to be valid for large, complex organizations operating in difficult environments (competitive, heterogeneous, changing), than it is for small organizations operating in benign environments (low

competition, homogeneous, stable). If information-processing fit is not constraining on performance, it makes sense to organize around some other principle that might be. For example, how to fit or satisfy the desires of local governments (a political perspective), or how to best motivate employees (a motivation perspective). Obviously it is desirable that the basis for evaluating organizational fit be stable over an extended period of time. It seems reasonable to assume that for large, complex organizations such as MNCs, the limits of information-processing capacity are frequently reached or exceeded by information-processing requirements and that the difficulty in realizing information-processing fit consistently constrains performance in such organizations.

Before proceeding, it is useful to evaluate the proposed framework against more cognitive views of organizational information processing, which have recently become prominent in the literature. Cognitive theory views organizations as systems that learn [Fiol and Lyles 1985; Ginsberg 1990] and interpret their environments [Daft and Weick 1989]. Information processing is primarily represented in terms of the cognitive abilities of organizational members (either individually or collectively) to learn, make sense out of, and make decisions for an organization, when influenced by a variety of factors such as values, beliefs, culture, and differences in power [Wood and Bandura 1989]. Environmental conditions may still be the stimulus for information processing to occur, but the emphasis is on explaining how it is influenced by what goes on within the heads of individuals (psychological determinants) and between individuals (social-psychological determinants).

By contrast, the proposed perspective, which has sometimes been referred to as a logistical view of organizational information processing [Huber 1982], views organizations as systems that need to balance the organization's information-processing capacities against the information-processing requirements inherent in its strategy and environment. Fit is equated with good organizational performance and survival, and misfit with poor performance and failure. Information processing is largely represented in terms of the capacities of different kinds of organizational structures and processes to transfer information within an organization, to move it across the boundaries of an organization, and to access specific kinds of knowledge and decisionmaking capabilities needed to transform data or information. The focus of this view is primarily on how information processing is influenced by organizational characteristics, independent of the individual characteristics of organizational members. The focus of the cognitive view is primarily on how information processing is influenced by the psychological and social-psychological characteristics of organizational members.

The two perspectives should be viewed as complementary and not contradictory explanations of organizational information processing. The cognitive perspective largely addresses how strategic decisions are made. It argues that much of the input or influence is cognitive and that strategic decisions are not merely, even primarily, determined by organizational and environmental considerations. The unit of analysis tends to be the strategic decision or strategic issue [Dutton and Jackson 1987]. From a population ecology perspective, such strategic decisions become a source of variation and change in an organization and its position in its environment. The logistical perspective of information processing, on the other hand, does not attempt to explain the source of organizational or strategic variation or change. It tries to explain the information-processing capacities inherent in an organization's design and generally evaluates these against requirements for information processing inherent in an organization's strategy or environment.

This evaluation of fit and misfit between organizational characteristics and environmental conditions responds to the selection mechanism in a population ecology perspective and explains change not in terms of strategic decisions, but in terms of differential selection by competitive forces in firms' environments. Thus, the two perspectives have different arguments and a different purpose.

INFORMATION PROCESSING AS AN ABSTRACT INTERVENING CONCEPT

With the exception of some of Galbraith's case studies [1970, 1977], the information-processing perspective has primarily been used in more micro-level studies, where the units of analysis are either individuals or small groups. Such studies have managed to measure directly such aspects of information processing as the frequency of oral communications between work groups [Tushman 1978], the extent to which policies and procedures, work plans, personal contact, and meetings are used to coordinate members of work teams [Van de Ven, Delbecq and Koening 1976], and the structure of groups during decisionmaking [Duncan 1973]. For more macro-level studies, such as those focusing on the parent HQ-foreign subsidiary relationship in MNCs, the difficulty of directly measuring such detailed information-processing phenomena between very large subunits of an organization necessitates a different approach to operationalizing the information-processing perspective.

Instead of attempting to directly measure information processing, macro-level studies must use information processing more as an abstract intervening concept to aid in positing relationships between directly measured characteristics of an organization's design and its strategy and environment, both of which have identifiable information-processing implications. This approach is already reflected in the general information-processing approach to organizational design shown in Figure 1. The solid lines indicate that strategic and environmental conditions and organizational design features are directly measured variables, while the broken lines indicate that information-processing requirements and information-processing capacities are abstract variables that can only be derived from measured variables.

For the information-processing approach to advance, what is needed is a more precise translation of the measured contextual and design variables into the abstract information-processing concepts that are so useful for general theory-building. This should be easier to accomplish if one first identifies the dimensions of information processing that are important to the type and level of organization being modeled and then constructs decision rules for mapping measured contextual and design variables onto these dimensions.

MULTIDIMENSIONAL MEASURES OF INFORMATION PROCESSING

Most existing research that has sought to use an information-processing perspective to link organizational design to various strategic and environmental conditions does not rigorously specify the dimensions that are being used to measure and evaluate information-processing capacities and requirements. For example, consider the case of a bank that as a result of a growth strategy faces a sharp increase in the number of checks it must clear. Obviously such a strategy has led to increased requirements for information processing. Galbraith [1973] has indicated that increased information-processing requirements frequently need to be addressed by the addition of lateral information-processing systems, such as more face-to-face communications, cross-functional committees and task forces, and matrix structures, to an organization. Yet, it is doubtful that these information-processing mechanisms address the requirements associated with the increased load of check clearing. Instead, an expanded computer system, which Galbraith regards as a vertical information-processing system, seems better able to provide the kind of information-processing capacity needed to cope with the increased requirements for check-clearing.

The bank's growth strategy may also call for the development of new financial products and services. This also increases requirements for information processing within the organization, and this time the kind of information-processing capacity provided by cross-functional teams and matrix designs seems more appropriate than that provided by an expanded computer system. Both strategies lead to increased information-processing requirements for the bank, but somehow the kinds of information-processing capacity needed differ, and exactly what dimension or dimensions define this difference is not clear.

Empirical studies such as Galbraith's [1977] analysis of the information-processing requirements associated with Boeing's development of the 747, Van de Ven, Delbecq and Koenig's [1976] analysis of the differing task requirements found in an unemployment agency, or Tushman's [1978] analysis of the differing information-processing requirements facing development groups as opposed to research groups in an R&D laboratory generally match suitable information-processing mechanisms to the different information-processing requirements and discuss a number of reasons for the suitability of the match. While such discussion often hints at how one information-processing requirement differs from another, this difference is not rigorously defined by explicitly specifying what dimension or dimensions consistently differentiate one type of information processing from another.

In other words, whether one, two, three, or four dimensions are needed to distinguish one information-processing requirement from another (or the capacity of one information-processing mechanism from another) is not clear in most studies. Information-processing requirements and capacities are not mapped onto some prespecified multidimensional framework. Instead, information-processing is used in a looser, less rigid way that only implicitly, rather than explicitly, distinguishes one type of information processing from another.

An important exception to this complaint can be found in the work of Daft and Lengel [1986] and Daft and Macintosh [1981]. These studies distinguish between equivocality reduction and uncertainty reduction in information processing and attempt to define the relative capacities of a variety of information-processing mechanisms for handling both types of information-processing requirement.

Our view is that at the macro level of large, complex organizations, other dimensions of information processing may also be useful—perhaps even more useful than uncertainty and equivocality—for measuring and evaluating information-processing requirements and capacities. At the macro level, information processing can readily vary in terms of subject and in terms of organizational purpose and perspective [Egelhoff 1982]. It can also vary in terms of being relatively routine or nonroutine within an organization and in terms of the nature of the interdependency shared by organizational subunits involved in an information-processing event. Following this view, the next section will attempt to illustrate that existing organization theory and research in a number of areas provides useful guidance for constructing explicit multidimensional frameworks for measuring information processing.

DEVELOPING AN INFORMATION-PROCESSING PERSPECTIVE OF MNCs

This section will attempt to use the information-processing concepts already discussed to develop an explicit framework for analyzing and understanding organizational design in MNCs. Deciding which dimensions to measure information processing along requires some judgment, but the general criterion should be to select dimensions that best reflect the information-processing limitations of the various features of organizational design for the strategic and environmental context in which they must operate (in this case, the complex and dynamic environment faced by most large MNCs).

STRUCTURAL DIMENSIONS

The first set of dimensions reflects the purpose and perspective of information processing (whether it is strategic or tactical) and the subject or content of information processing (whether it deals with product matters or company and country matters). Both require some explanation and conceptual development. (The following discussion about the framework shown in Figure 2 is excerpted from Egelhoff [1982].)

The *purpose and perspective of information processing* can be defined in terms of whether it is primarily strategic or primarily tactical. The conceptual distinction between these two concepts comes from the strategic management literature. Ansoff [1965] refers to operating, administrative, and strategic decisions in organizations. Tactical information processing combines the first two categories and deals with the large volume of relatively routine day-to-day problems and situations confronting an organization. The decisionmaking perspective required to handle these situations tends to be relatively narrow, and it usually exists at the middle and lower levels of management. Strategic information processing attempts to deal with a much smaller volume of relatively nonroutine, and usually more important, problems and situations. These problems deal with the fundamental position of the organization in its environment and usually involve changing this position. Thus, strategic information processing has a different purpose and requires a different perspective than

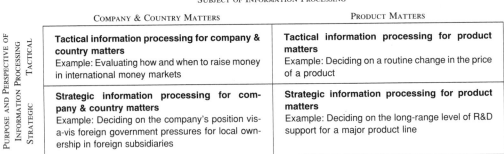

SUBJECT OF INFORMATION PROCESSING

	COMPANY & COUNTRY MATTERS	PRODUCT MATTERS
TACTICAL	**Tactical information processing for company & country matters** Example: Evaluating how and when to raise money in international money markets	**Tactical information processing for product matters** Example: Deciding on a routine change in the price of a product
STRATEGIC	**Strategic information processing for company & country matters** Example: Deciding on the company's position vis-a-vis foreign government pressures for local ownership in foreign subsidiaries	**Strategic information processing for product matters** Example: Deciding on the long-range level of R&D support for a major product line

(Row label at left: PURPOSE AND PERSPECTIVE OF INFORMATION PROCESSING)

Figure 2. The Structural Dimensions of Information Processing

tactical information processing. It addresses higher level organizational goals, is broader in scope, and usually has a longer time horizon.

Research suggests that different levels of an organization's hierarchy tend to process different kinds of information and have different purposes for processing information [Landsberger 1961; Thomason 1966]. Mintzberg [1979:54] states that "the issues each level addresses are fundamentally different," and notes that strategic decisions generally involve members of the "strategic apex" or top management of an organization. Since the majority of tactical decisions do not involve members of the strategic apex, tactical and strategic information processing tend to occur at different levels of an organization. The association of tactical and strategic perspectives with different levels of an organization presupposes that hierarchy exists in most MNCs. Recent literature suggests that MNCs may be becoming less hierarchical [Hedlund 1986; Bartlett and Ghoshal 1989]. To the extent that an MNC is less hierarchically organized, it becomes more difficult to generalize about where strategic and tactical perspectives exist in an organization.

The framework also reflects the *subject or content of information processing* and distinguishes between information processing for product matters (product and process technology, market information) and information processing for company and country matters (finance, tax, legal, government relations, human resources). Subject knowledge or specialization tends to vary horizontally across organizations. Different organizational structures tend to cluster it into different subunits. Using these distinctions, four types of information processing are developed, as shown in Figure 2. The four types are generally not substitutes for each other, since they tend to address different problem areas that require different types of knowledge and different perspectives of the organization and its goals.

The above set of information-processing dimensions works well to distinguish where in an organization different kinds of knowledge and different kinds of decisionmaking capability lie. It helps to identify which parts of an organization need to be linked to-gether in order to solve a given problem or address a specific decisionmaking situation. It other words, these dimensions are useful for measuring the structural aspects of organizations and understanding their implications for information processing.

PROCESS DIMENSIONS

Another set of dimensions is needed, however, to measure and distinguish differences in the process by which information processing occurs, how information is gathered, processed, stored and exchanged. Such information processing occurs within and between the organizational subunits and levels that have already been identified. This second set represents the process dimensions of information processing. Here we will distinguish between routine and nonroutine information processing and sequential and reciprocal information processing.

There is a substantial literature supporting and describing the distinction between *routine and nonroutine information processing* [Simon 1977; Daft and Macintosh 1981; Daft and Weick 1984]. Routine information processing deals with inputs that are frequent and homogeneous. It transforms them under conditions of high certainty and assumes that goals and means-ends relationships are well known. Information-processing mechanisms that most efficiently provide routine information-processing capacity are rules and programs (including organizational policies, SOPs, and standard methods), formal single-cycle planning systems (where there is no feedback from a later stage of the process to an earlier stage), post-action control systems (where feedback occurs after the controlled activity or time period is completed) [Newman 1975], and most computer-based information systems. Nonroutine information processing deals with inputs that are either unique or infrequent and heterogeneous. It transforms them under varying degrees of uncertainty about goals and/or means-ends relationships. Information-processing mechanisms that provide nonroutine information-processing capacity are hierarchical referral; some vertical information systems such as planning staffs; multi-cycle, interactive planning

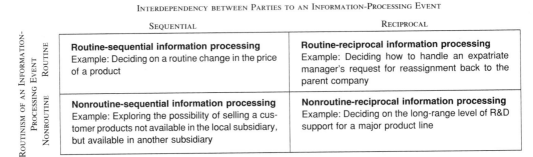

Figure 3. The Process Dimensions of MNC Information Processing

systems (where information developed in later stages of a planning process can feed back to earlier stages); steering control systems (where feedback occurs before an event is completed) [Newman 1975]; and most horizontal or lateral information systems (direct contact, task forces and teams, integrating roles, and matrix designs).

The distinction between *sequential and reciprocal information processing* reflects the kind of interdependency that exists between the parties to an information-processing event. This distinction is based on Thompson's [1967] typology of the three different forms of interdependence that can exist between organizational subunits (pooled, sequential, and reciprocal). Information processing is sequential to the extent that information flows in a predetermined direction across parties to an information-processing event. Information-processing is reciprocal to the extent that information flows back and forth between parties in a kind of give-and-take manner that has not been previously determined.

Figure 3 shows the four types of information processing that emerge when the routine-nonroutine and sequential-reciprocal axes are combined. A specific information-processing event is also provided to illustrate each type. In order to understand better the logic employed, we will further discuss one of these events.

Consider the event where it is necessary to decide on a routine change in the price of a subsidiary's product. Since this event occurs frequently and the kinds of things that need to be considered (e.g., effect on volume and gross profit, relationship to competitors' prices) are well known, information processing

is routine. And, since the information inputs of the various parties to this event (subsidiary marketing manager, subsidiary CEO, HQ marketing manager) can be combined in a sequential manner in order to arrive at an informed and responsible decision, information processing will tend to be sequential (probably represented by a flow of memos between the concerned parties). In process terms this is simple hierarchical referral (or information processing through the chain of command), which is a commonly used routine-sequential information-processing mechanism in organizations.

But, in order to describe this event more fully, we need also to consider its structural dimensions. Recalling the previous set of information-processing dimensions described in Figure 2, it is obvious that this event deals largely with product-related knowledge as opposed to company and country-related knowledge (if host government approval for the price increase were required, the latter might also be involved). In this case the subsidiary marketing manager provides information about the increase and its relationship to competitors' prices as well as the anticipated impact on margins and sales volume. The subsidiary CEO merely checks the proposal for broad consistency with his budgeted sales and profit targets and goals concerning competitive position. The proposal is approved at a relatively low level in the HQ marketing group, where it is again checked for consistency with broad goals for the product line and more specifically checked against the price in other subsidiaries whose markets might interact with the subsidiary. Since this kind of decision is not expected to alter significantly the position of the product line in its competitive environment, the perspective that these managers tend to apply is more tactical than strategic. Thus, this event largely requires tactical information processing for product matters.

This identification or measurement has largely structural implications. It pinpoints which subunits or individuals in the organization need to be involved in the information-processing event (i.e., which can contribute the right kinds of knowledge and capabilities). The previous identification or measurement has largely process implication. It helps to identify which information-processing mechanisms (processes) are most suitable for linking together the specific subunits or individuals that possess the necessary knowledge and capabilities.

THE INFORMATION-PROCESSING CAPACITIES OF STRUCTURE

Where specific kinds of knowledge and capabilities reside in an organization is strongly influenced by its formal structure. Research on MNC structure [Brooke and Remmers 1970; Stopford and Wells 1972; Franko 1976; Hulbert and Brandt 1980; Egelhoff 1982] has helped to identify where different kinds of knowledge and capabilities tend to be located in the four elementary structures used to organize international operations. Figure 4 attempts to summarize where each of the four previously identified types of information-processing capacity tends to be located within a specific structure.

A worldwide functional division structure means that the functional activities in a foreign subsidiary report directly to their respective functional divisions in the parent. Tactical information-processing capacity for company and country matters tends to lie in such functional divisions as finance, human resources, tax, and government affairs, both at the parent HQ and the foreign subsidiary levels. Similarly, tactical product-related information-processing capacity tends to lie in the R&D, manufacturing, and marketing divisions found at both levels. This structure should facilitate tactical information processing between the parent and foreign subsidiaries as long as the processing can take place within a functional

area. Tactical information-processing across functions, however, will be difficult (and require non-hierarchical processes) since the structure does not facilitate communication between divisions at either the subsidiary level or the tactical levels of the parent.

Since the formulation of business strategy requires a cross-functional perspective, strategic information processing cannot readily occur within a foreign subsidiary or even at lower levels of the parent HQ. Only at the CEO- and executive-committee level does a cross-functional or general management perspective exist, and only at this level does the structure facilitate multifunctional information coming together. While non-hierarchical information processes might be employed to bring such information together at lower levels of the organization, there is still a problem regarding the lack of a general management perspective at such levels in a functional division structure. Thus, subunits in foreign subsidiaries cannot generally participate in or make direct inputs to the strategy-formulation process. This centralization of strategic information processing means that processing capacity is limited (only a few people at one level of the parent are involved) and it is difficult for new information about the environment to enter the process.

With an international division structure, all foreign subsidiaries report to an international division that is separate from the domestic operations. Brooke and Remmers [1970] found that this structure tends to facilitate information processing between the parent and foreign subsidiaries, while at the same time it hinders information processing at the parent level between the international division and the domestic operations. Product knowledge tends to be centered in the domestic divisions, while knowledge about such company and country matters as international finance and foreign political conditions is centered in the international division. Consequently, parent-subsidiary information-processing capacity is relatively high for company and country matters and relatively low for product matters. There is a general management or strategic apex at both the subsidiary and international division levels. Thus, strategic as well as tactical information processing can take place

TYPES OF INFORMATION-PROCESSING CAPACITY

Type of Structure	Tactical Information-Processing Capacity for Company & Country Matters	Strategic Information-Processing Capacity for Company & Country Matters	Tactical Information-Processing Capacity for Product Matters	Strategic Information-Processing Capacity for Product Matters
Worldwide Functional Divisions	Company & country-related functional divisions of parent HQ (e.g., finance, human resources) Similar functional divisions of foreign subsidiaries	CEO & executive committee of parent HQ	Product-related functional divisions of parent (e.g., R&D, manufacturing, marketing) Similar functional divisions of foreign subsidiaries	CEO & executive committee of parent HQ
International Division	International division HQ Foreign subsidiary HQs	Higher management of international division HQ Higher management of foreign subsidiary HQs	Domestic product divisions (outside of international structure) Product divisions of foreign subsidiaries	Higher management of domestic product divisions (outside of international structure) Higher management of product divisions of foreign subsidiaries
Geographical Regions	Company & country-related management and staff of regional HQs Domestic & foreign subsidiary HQs	Higher management of parent corporate HQ Higher management of regional HQs Higher management of domestic & foreign subsidiaries	Product-related management & staff of regional HQs Product divisions of domestic & foreign subsidiaries	Higher product-related management of regional HQs Higher management of product divisions of domestic & foreign subsidiaries
Worldwide Product Divisions	Foreign subsidiary HQs	Higher management of foreign subsidiary HQs	Parent product division HQs & domestic product operations Product divisions of foreign subsidiaries	Higher management of parent product division HQs Higher management of product divisions of foreign subsidiaries

Figure 4. Location of Information-Processing Capacity in the Four Elementary MNC Structures

between a subsidiary and the international division, but it will center around company and country matters rather than product matters. In order to connect foreign subsidiaries to the centers of product knowledge in the domestic product divisions, non-hierarchical information processes must be used.

A geographical region structure divides the world into regions, each with its own HQ. Each HQ is responsible for all of the company's products and business within its geographical area. The regional HQ is the center of the company's knowledge about company and country matters within the region. Most regional HQs also contain either product or functional staffs to provide coordination for product matters across subsidiaries in the region [Williams 1967]. There is a general management or strategic

apex at both the subsidiary and regional HQ levels. As a result, this structure facilitates a high level of all four types of information processing between a subsidiary and its regional HQ. The information-processing capacity between a foreign subsidiary and domestic operations or a subsidiary in another region is low. The only structural mechanism for coordinating across regions is the corporate HQ, and most geographical region companies tend to have relatively small corporate managements and staffs [Egelhoff 1982]. Thus, largely non-structural or non-hierarchical information processing needs to be established if, for example, product technologies and strategies are to be coordinated between regions (the former requires largely tactical information processing, the latter, strategic information processing).

A worldwide product division structure extends the responsibilities of the domestic product divisions to cover their product lines on a worldwide basis. Under this structure, there is a tendency to centralize product-related knowledge and decisionmaking capability in the parent product groups and to decentralize nonproduct knowledge and decisionmaking to the foreign subsidiaries [Brooke and Remmers 1970]. Consequently, the capacity for processing information on company and country matters tends to be concentrated in the foreign subsidiaries, while the parent HQ tends to have a product orientation. Product-related tactical and strategic information-processing capacities, on the other hand, tend to be highly developed at both the foreign subsidiary and parent product division levels. The product divisions in the foreign subsidiaries are directly connected through the hierarchy to the centers of product knowledge in the parent. For each product line, there is a strategic apex at both the subsidiary and parent product division levels, which facilitates strategic information processing at both levels for product matters.

As can be seen in the above discussion and Figure 4, formal structure significantly influences where specific types of knowledge and decisionmaking capability reside in large organizations. The four dimensions of information processing employed in Figure 4 seem a useful framework for describing these differences in MNCs. The specific locations of knowledge and decisionmaking capability are consistent with previous research findings concerning the influence of formal structure on information flows in organizations. A framework similar to that expressed in Figure 4 was previously used to develop hypotheses about strategy-structure relationships in MNCs. These were empirically tested using a sample of thirty-four elementary structure MNCs and fifteen matrix and mixed structure MNCs, representing both U.S. and European firms [Egelhoff 1988: 61–128]. The testing tended to support the framework. Thus, research to date seems (1) strongly to support the assumption that formal organizational structure has a major influence on the location of knowledge and decisionmaking capability in organizations, and (2) to provide reasonable support for the logic used in developing the specific framework shown in Figure 4. Formal structure is not the only determinant of the location of knowledge and decisionmaking capability, however, and there can be significant variance between companies with the same structure.

THE CAPACITIES OF INFORMATION-PROCESSING MECHANISMS

Having created a kind of directory of where knowledge and capability tend to lie in an MNC, we need to produce an analogous directory of the kinds of information-processing mechanisms that can be used to access and connect the various sources of knowledge and capability. Figure 5 attempts to provide such a directory, by showing the different information-processing capacities of Galbraith's information-processing mechanisms plus others that are frequently used at the parent-foreign subsidiary level of analysis in MNCs.

It is important to realize that the routinism and interdependency axes are Gutman-like scales. Thus, mechanisms capable of providing nonroutine information processing can also provide routine information processing and mechanisms capable of providing reciprocal information processing can also provide sequential information processing, but usually at a lower volume and/or at a greater cost than mechanisms specifically designed to cope with more routine or sequential information-processing requirements.

Mechanisms that are specifically designed to provide routine-sequential information processing include rules and programs, single-cycle planning processes, post-action control systems, and stand-alone computer systems. As Figure 5 indicates, these mechanisms provide relatively high volumes of information processing and do this at relatively low cost when compared to other mechanisms. Other forms of vertical information systems such as assistants, clerical staffs, and planning staffs [Galbraith 1973] can usually handle more nonroutine information processing than the preceding mechanisms, but also tend to provide largely sequential information processing. Hierarchical referral, such as the referral of an exception or nonroutine event up the hierarchy

	SEQUENTIAL INFORMATION-PROCESSING CAPACITY		RECIPROCAL INFORMATION-PROCESSING CAPACITY
Routine Information-Processing Capacity	Rules & programs (H) Single-cycle planning (H) Post-action control (H) Stand-alone computer systems (H) Vertical information systems: assistants, clerical staff, & planning staff (M)	Steering control (M) Multi-cycle, interactive planning systems (M)	Integrated database computer systems (H)
Nonroutine Information-Processing Capacity	Hierarchical referral (L)		Horizontal information systems: Direct contact (L) Task forces (M) Teams (M) Integrating roles (L) Matrix designs (M)

Note: The letters in parentheses indicate relative volumes of information-processing capacity: H = High, M = Medium, L = Low.

Figure 5. The Capacities of Information-Processing Mechanisms

and the transmission of a decision back down, provides a two-way flow of information that also tends to be sequential. Since managerial hierarchies can easily become overloaded, this mechanism provides a relatively low volume of information-processing capacity and usually does so at a relatively high cost.

Computer systems with integrated databases (such as airline reservation systems) that can be simultaneously shared by many users provide more reciprocal information processing, but largely for predetermined routine events. Galbraith [1973] identified a number of mechanisms that tend to provide horizontal or lateral information processing across subunits or individuals: direct contact between individuals, task forces and teams, integrating roles, and matrix designs. These mechanisms facilitate information inputs being made in a flexible, give-and-take manner among all parties to the information-processing event, and, consequently, they are the primary providers of nonroutine-reciprocal information processing in organizations.

Several mechanisms are shown at the midway point of both axes in Figure 5, indicating that they fall between the two extremes already presented. Steering control systems (such as interim reviews by parent HQ of a foreign plant's startup), clearly provide more reciprocal information processing and can handle more nonroutine situations than post-action control systems (such as annual reviews of a subsidiary's sales and profits) [Newman 1975]. Multi-cycle, interactive planning systems also provide

more nonroutine and reciprocal information processing than single-cycle planning systems. Obviously, all locations in Figure 5 are approximations. Information-processing capacities can vary considerably depending on the exact design of a mechanism, how it is implemented, and how it interacts with other aspects of an organization. Yet, the generalizations expressed in Figure 5 are both useful and necessary if one wants to build a more systematic theory about information processing in organizations.

The reader will probably have noticed that there may be some positive correlation between the routine-nonroutine dimension and the sequential-reciprocal dimension when they are used to measure actual information-processing mechanisms. Thus, many mechanisms seem to fall along a single dimension (the 45 degree diagonal in Figure 5). Mechanisms that provide reciprocal information-processing capacity seem to be able to handle nonroutine situations and mechanisms that only provide sequential information-processing capacity seem to most frequently be confined to handling routine situations. It is useful here to recall that Galbraith [1973] originally ranked his information-processing mechanisms along a single dimension, in an order that is roughly similar to that which occurs along the diagonal in Figure 5. Galbraith did not explicitly identify the routine-nonroutine or the sequential-reciprocal dimensions as underlying his ordering, but simply referred to information-processing mechanisms as varying from low to high. At a minimum, Figure 5 helps one to better understand the differences that underlie Galbraith's general ordering of information-processing mechanisms. Daft and Lengel [1986] developed a similar ordering of information-processing mechanisms based upon the relative amounts of equivocality reduction and uncertainty reduction capacity a mechanism can provide.

It is the argument of this paper, however, that the multidimensional framework in Figure 5 represents a significant extension of Galbraith's unidimensional ordering and that both the routine-nonroutine and the sequential-reciprocal dimensions need to be retained as conceptually different, even if information processing in organizations frequently reveals some correlation between them. There are three reasons supporting this argument. First, some important mechanisms do seem to lie off of the diagonal and, thus, contradict a unidimensional ordering. Second, new information-processing mechanisms may be developed that will increasingly lie off of the diagonal. This seems especially likely in the computer-based information systems area [Huber 1990]. And third, many of the indicated mechanisms can be altered to vary along one dimension without necessarily varying along the other. For example, rules and programs can be altered to fit different contingencies or even turned into guidelines (which leaves the implementer with greater flexibility in responding to an information-processing event). Both alternatives increase the nonroutine information-processing capacity of this mechanism without changing the fact that it provides only sequential information processing between the creator and the implementers of the rule or guideline.

The conceptual framework developed in this section defines four structural dimensions and four process dimensions that are to be used to measure information processing in MNCs. The framework provides a more explicit way to measure and define information processing at the macro-level, where information processing is a useful intervening concept for evaluating an organization's fit with its strategy and environment. The following section will apply the framework to a currently important subject in international management—transnationalism. The purpose here is to illustrate how the framework can be applied and also to demonstrate that it can provide meaningful new insight into complex organizational issues.

APPLIED EXAMPLE—THE INFORMATION-PROCESSING IMPLICATIONS OF TRANSNATIONALISM

Recently there has been growing interest in new ways to organize and manage MNCs [Hedlund 1986; Perlmutter and Trist 1986; Prahalad and Doz 1987; Bartlett and Ghoshal 1989]. While details and terminology may vary, most of these proposals have at their core more multidimensional organizational designs and a wider variety of integrating and coordinating mechanisms than can usually be found in "traditional" designs. The new designs are responses to the need to compete with new strategies in an international business environment that is increasingly complex and competitive. Bartlett and Ghoshal [1989] call this new trend in strategy and organizational design "transnationalism."

Transnational strategies attempt simultaneously to realize (1) efficiency and economy through global-scale operations and global integration, (2) responsiveness to national and local differences through local differentiation, and (3) a high level of innovation worldwide through extensive learning and knowledge transfer. Traditional strategies primarily emphasize one of these. It is obvious that transnational strategies create much greater requirements for information processing between parent HQ and foreign subsidiaries and among foreign subsidiaries than is the case under more traditional strategies. Depending on the specifics of the strategy (e.g., where does product knowledge have to be locally differentiated? where does it need to be globally integrated?) and the company's organizational structure (which according to Figure 4 provides a directory as to where different types of knowledge and decision-making capabilities are located), a variety of information-processing mechanisms (taken from Figure 5) can be employed to link together the relevant sources of knowledge and capability with the appropriate information-processing capacity (e.g., nonroutine-reciprocal information processing). This is an information-processing picture of the flexible way that organizations will need to be designed in order to implement transnational strategies.

Bartlett and Ghoshal [1989] describe the key characteristics of transnational design, as revealed in their research on companies that are moving in this direction: (1) Assets and capabilities are dispersed, interdependent, and specialized. (2) There are differentiated contributions by national units to integrated worldwide operations. (3) Knowledge is developed jointly and shared worldwide. Other characteristics include: flexibility, dropping the need for symmetry and consistency in designing HQ-subsidiary relationships, self-regulating systems, and a heavy dependence on company culture and shared values in facilitating coordination.

The information-processing framework developed in the previous section seems uniquely suited to analyze the new transnational designs that are now emerging in firms and provide useful insight into them. Four information-processing implications are particularly important to the future of transnational design.

1. The role and function of formal organizational structure may be changed.

As discussed in the previous section, formal structure is important because it provides a basis for locating, maintaining, and accessing different kinds of knowledge and decisionmaking capabilities. This is especially important in large, complex organizations like MNCs, where the range of knowledge and decisionmaking capabilities is extremely wide. A key function of formal MNC structure is that managers across the company know where specific sources of knowledge and capability lie, the locations tend to be fairly stable, and managers are generally familiar with how to access them.

Compared to traditional designs, transnational designs will tend to locate knowledge and decisionmaking capability in a more eclectic manner that is at the same time more dynamic and subject to change. For example, the Australian subsidiary may replace the parent's R&D laboratory as the center of knowledge for a new generation of product technology. The company's foreign subsidiaries are familiar with monitoring and transferring new technology from the parent's R&D laboratory (several existing information-processing mechanisms already provide the necessary linkage), but not from the Australian subsidiary. New, non-hierarchical information-processing mechanisms will have to be developed. Several years later industry trends in some countries favor yet another version of product technology that has been developed in the company's German subsidiary for use in the local market. Again, sources of knowledge and information flows have to change. As the situation in this example becomes widespread, formal structure begins to lose its value as an accurate and stable directory of where knowledge and capability reside and how they can be accessed.

The design logic that underlies formal structure is hierarchy and symmetry. Transnational design gives up this logic in order to gain more flexibility. In the process, the organization loses some of its ability to locate and access knowledge and capability, due to the diminished role of formal structure. Thus, transnational designs need to provide new information-processing capabilities that address this loss.

2. The amount of strategic information-processing capacity for product matters must be greatly expanded.

Of the four types of information processing identified in Figure 2, strategic information processing for product matters is the type that should increase the most under a transnational strategy. Under traditional strategies and structures strategic knowledge and decisionmaking capability tends to be fairly centralized at the upper levels of product division HQs and geographical region HQs. Only with a multidomestic or polycentric strategy does the locus of this information-processing capacity move to the subsidiary level and become diffused. Thus, most strategic decisionmaking for product matters tends to take place either through hierarchical referral or within strategic planning processes that are also hierarchically structured. As a result, there is frequently a great deal of similarity in strategic product planning across product lines and subsidiaries within a company.

An important characteristic of transnationalism is that it disperses product knowledge across foreign subsidiaries and reduces the concentration of such knowledge at the parent HQ and in home country operations. This should result in a much more complex, heterogeneous, and less hierarchical strategic planning process in transnational firms. For some product matters, strategic information processing should occur directly between concerned foreign subsidiaries, with little or no involvement from parent HQ. Other matters will need to be coordinated globally through the parent HQ. And still other matters, which primarily respond to local conditions, will be left to each subsidiary. Since these three information-processing events tend to supplement rather than replace each other, the amount and variety of strategic information-processing capacity for product matters will need to be greatly expanded in transnational as opposed to traditional MNCs.

These first two implications primarily stem from the impact of transnationalism on the location of knowledge and decisionmaking capabilities in MNC structures. They are the structural implications of transnationalism for information processing. The next issue deals with the primary process implication of transnationalism for information processing.

3. The use of nonroutine-reciprocal information-processing mechanisms will need to be significantly expanded.

Transnational designs require high flexibility in the way they link different parts of the MNC organization together. Bartlett and Ghoshal [1989:12] state: "Companies see that they can gain competitive advantage by sensing needs in one country, responding with capabilities located in a second, and diffusing the resulting innovation to markets around the globe." Thus, a transnational firm seems to need unusually high amounts of nonroutine-reciprocal information-processing capacity in order to respond to the variety of changing opportunities this strategy seeks to exploit. Figure 5 shows the various horizon-

tal information-processing mechanisms that provide this kind of capacity. All are people-intensive, in the sense that they employ large amounts of managers' and key employees' time. They are costly and difficult to control when contrasted with more routine and sequential information-processing mechanisms. An important issue that MNCs will have to face is the extent to which they are prepared to provide large amounts of nonroutine-reciprocal information-processing capacity as they begin to embrace transnational strategies.

It is interesting to recall that matrix structure were once heralded as the inevitable design for coordinating more multidimensional international strategies [Stopford and Wells 1972; Davis and Lawrence 1977]. Yet, many MNCs were forced to abandon matrix structures when they could not successfully implement them [Bartlett and Ghoshal 1990]. Matrix structures (like transnational designs) also require large amounts of nonroutine-reciprocal information-processing capacity to coordinate and resolve conflict between the two formal hierarchies that comprise the matrix. Many MNCs adopted matrix structures without recognizing this fact or providing the required nonroutine-reciprocal information-processing capacity. As a result, conflict was frequently not resolved through lateral information processing at lower levels (as it was supposed to be), but pushed vertically up the hierarchies to be resolved at the top by hierarchical referral. In some firms that abandoned matrix structures, such as Dow Chemical, the costs of duplication and conflict resolution seem to have outweighed the benefits. In others, such as Texas Instruments, the matrix structure resulted in more severe problems: the breakdown of information processing, the overcentralization of decision-making due to the organization's inability to resolve conflict at lower levels, and serious delays in making critical decisions.

MNCs face a similar problem if they adopt transnational strategies and designs, but fail to develop the necessary nonroutine-reciprocal information-processing capacities to make them work. Here the problem is not conflict resolution between two formal hierarchies, as it was with matrix structures. Instead, it is (1) conflict resolution between some non-hierarchically organized transnational activity and the traditional hierarchy that still exists and interfaces with the transnational parts of a company, and (2) the need continually to redesign and alter transnational relationships within a company. Both of these activities will be commonplace in transnational firms and will require an increased use of such nonroutine-reciprocal information-processing mechanisms as direct contact and meetings, task forces and work teams, liaison and integrator roles.

Bartlett and Ghoshal [1989] state that transnational firms need to rely primarily upon informal matrixing accompanied by high levels of commitment and shared values to achieve the necessary coordination. These facilitate the kind of lateral, nonroutine-reciprocal information processing we have been discussing, but do not automatically insure it will occur. Many firms may require significant changes to their culture and large-scale OD (organizational development) interventions (team-building, survey feedback, process consultation, grid OD) in order to develop the potential for high levels of nonroutine-reciprocal information-processing capacity. The costs of this may be extremely high (in some cases even prohibitive) and clearly need to be weighed against the benefits of a transnational approach.

4. There will be a much greater need for design rules at all levels of the organization.

A fourth implication of transnationalism is that the process of design itself is going to be a major problem. It must be flexible, emergent from the individual situation, and fitted to the opportunities and problems posed by a firm's technology and environment. Instead of largely imitating a well-known prototype, managers at various levels will require some kind of guidance on how to design transnational relationships, how to interface them with more traditional, hierarchical, and symmetrical parts of the organization, and when to convert emergent and informal coordination to more formal and traditional coordinating mechanisms. In short, the transnational organization requires a widely understood set of design

rules that can be used to implement the various complexities of a transnational strategy by helping to create suitable flexible designs. Organizing itself becomes a new technology that almost all managers in a transnational firm must master. Such is not the case in a traditional firm, where organizing is done infrequently by relatively few people.

At present, implementing transnational designs in MNCs appears to rely too much on the simple notions of informal matrixing plus heavy doses of commitment and shared values among organizational members. More technical knowledge than is implied by this will be required to activate and maintain effective transnational designs. The information-processing model developed in the previous section provides both a design logic and a preliminary set of design rules that seem to address this problem. While other conceptual frameworks for design might also be useful, information processing seems to be one of the primary characteristics that differentiates a transnational approach from more traditional approaches to strategy and organizational design. More traditional approaches to change have typically called for structural change, which indirectly leads to information-processing change. Transnational design generally bypasses structural change, but calls for more direct changes in information-processing capacities both within and outside of the existing formal structure of a firm. Thus, there is a need within such firms for a more comprehensive design approach and model based on an information-processing perspective of the organization.

This attempt to apply the preceding information-processing framework and model to transnationalism seems to have produced some new insight and understanding. At the present time, transnational design exists largely as an illustrated but not a conceptual form. It is explained and illustrated by discussing examples of firms that are employing it. This section has attempted to demonstrate that the information-processing framework and model can provide a more conceptual and general understanding of transnationalism, that is both useful to practitioners and can serve as a base for further research and theory-building.

CONCLUSION

This paper has sought to develop an information-processing perspective of organizational design that can be used when studying large, complex organizations, such as MNCs. To date, most rigorous attempts to build theory with an information-processing perspective have taken place in micro-level studies, where the unit of analysis has been the individual or work group. By using information processing as an abstract intervening concept to relate organizational design to the strategic and environmental conditions facing an organization, researchers can better evaluate fit between these two dissimilar and hard-to-compare sets of variables. The use of more explicitly defined multidimensional frameworks (such as the one developed in this paper for MNCs) to measure both the information-processing capacities of organizational design and the information-processing requirements inherent in an organization's strategy and environment will add rigor to the measurement and evaluation of such fit.

Going back to the introduction of this paper and the two primary topics MNC research of an organizational nature has focused on, it is probable that the information-processing perspective will be of greater interest to researchers working on the first topic (the study of what kinds of organizational design contribute to effective MNC performance and under what strategic and environmental conditions one form is preferable to another). In order to further develop and extend the information-processing model presented in this paper, systematic empirical research is needed on the structural dimensions framework and the process dimensions framework, described respectively in Figures 4 and 5. As indicated, some empirical research has already been done in MNCs on the structural dimensions of information processing, while support for the process dimensions framework rests largely on conceptualization intended more for use at the micro levels of organizations and supported by research in settings quite different from the MNCs. Research in MNCs also needs to identify and understand the capacities of new information-processing mechanisms, which

Bartlett and Ghoshal [1989], Prahalad and Doz [1987], and others report are currently evolving in MNCs. It is probably reasonable to expect much more dynamism on the process side than on the structural side of MNCs. What is important for theory is that new forms of information processing be identified and understood in terms of some conceptual framework, such as the one suggested here.

Currently there is a danger that new international business strategies are being created with too little consideration for the high information-processing requirements that accompany them. Similarly, the costs of providing new forms and levels of information processing in complex organizations like MNCs need to be more explicitly understood. Finally, the risks and costs of information-processing misfit need to be taken very seriously in highly competitive environments.

The second type of MNC research described in the introduction, how MNC organizational designs change and evolve, may seem a less likely candidate for the information-processing perspective. While this paper has not explicitly explored the role such a perspective might play in theories of change and evolution, there appear to be possibilities. To the extent that evolutionary change involves the maintenance of organizational fit during transition, the framework developed above might be useful. At the other extreme, serious organizational (information-processing) misfit might be equally interesting. It should conceivably lead to failure and a more revolutionary pattern of change. Thus, the information processing perspective would appear to be potentially applicable to theories about change and evolution as well.

Theory and science are increasingly lagging the advancement of art when it comes to the management of MNCs. Recent books and articles report on many new trends and management approaches that seem to be currently developing within MNCs. Yet the identification as well as our understanding of these phenomena lie largely outside of existing theory. Consequently, there is a pressing need for theory-building to catch up to practice. Otherwise, practice will be increasingly operating without theory. Only theory and science—not practice and art—provide the kind of abstract and generalized understanding that can be moved, with some reliability, from one situation to another and integrated with other theories of understanding.

REFERENCES

Aldrich, Howard, E. 1979. *Organizations and environments.* Englewood Cliffs, NJ: Prentice-Hall.

Ansoff, H. Igor, 1965. *Corporate strategy, An analytic approach to business policy for growth and expansion.* New York: McGraw-Hill.

Bartlett, Christopher A. & Sumantra Ghoshal. 1989. *Managing across borders: The transnational solution.* Boston: Harvard Business School Press.

———. 1990. Matrix management: Not a structure, a frame of mind. *Harvard Business Review,* July–August: 138–45.

Brooke, Michael Z. & H. Lee Remmers. 1970. *The strategy of multinational enterprise.* New York: Elsevier.

Burns, Tom & G.M. Stalker. 1961. *The management of innovation.* London: Tavistock.

Daft, Richard L. & Norman B. Macintosh. 1981. A tentative exploration into the amount and equivocality of information processing in organizational work units. *Administrative Science Quarterly,* 26(2): 207–24.

Daft, Richard L. & Karl E. Weick. 1989. Toward a model of organizations as interpretation systems. *Academy of Management Review,* 9(3): 284–95.

Daft, Richard L. & Robert H. Lengel. 1986. Organizational information requirements, media richness and structural design. *Management Science,* 32(5): 554–71.

Daniels, John D., Robert A. Pitts & Marietta J. Tretter. 1984. Strategy and structure of U.S. multinationals: An exploratory study. *Academy of Management Journal,* 27(2): 292–307.

Davis, Stanley M. & Paul R. Lawrence. 1977. *Matrix.* Reading, MA: Addison-Wesley.

Duncan, Robert B. 1973. Multiple decision-making structures in adapting to environmental uncertainty: The impact of organizational effectiveness. *Human Relations,* 26: 273–91.

Dutton, Jane E. & Susan Jackson. 1987. Categorizing strategic issues: Links to organizational action. *Academy of Management Review,* 12: 76–90.

Dyas, Gareth P. & Heinz T. Thanheiser. 1976. *The emerging European enterprise: Strategy and structure in French and German industry.* London: Macmillan.

Egelhoff, William G. 1982. Strategy and structure in multinational corporations: An information-processing approach. *Administrative Science Quarterly,* 27(3): 435–58.

———. 1988. *Organizing the multinational enterprise: An information-processing perspective.* Cambridge, MA: Ballanger Publishing.

Fiol, C. Marlene & Marjorie A. Lyles. 1985. Organizational learning. *Academy of Management Review,* 10: 803–13.

Franko, Lawrence G. 1976. *The European multinationals: A renewed challenge to American and British big business.* Stamford, CT: Greylock Publishing.

Galbraith, Jay R. 1969. Organization design: An information processing view. Working paper #425-69, MIT, Sloan School of Management.

———. 1970. Environmental and technological determinants of organization design. In Jay W. Lorsch & Paul R. Lawrence, editors, *Studies in organization design.* Homewood, IL: Irwin.

———. 1973. *Designing complex organizations.* Reading, MA: Addison-Wesley.

———. 1977. *Organization design.* Reading, MA: Addison-Wesley.

Ginsberg, Ari. 1990. Connecting diversification to performance: A sociocognitive approach. *Academy of Management Review,* 15: 514–35.

Hedlund, Gunnar. 1986. The hypermodern MNC: A heterarchy? *Human Resource Management,* Spring: 9–35.

Herbert, Theodore T. 1984. Strategy and multinational organization structure: An interorganizational relationships perspective. *Academy of Management Review,* 9: 259–70.

Huber, George P. 1982. Organizational information systems: Determinants of their performance and behavior. *Management Science,* 28(2): 138–55.

———. 1990. A theory of the effects of advanced information technologies on organizational design, intelligence, and decision making. *Academy of Management Review,* 15: 47–71.

Hulbert, James M. & William K. Brandt. 1980. *Managing the multinational subsidiary.* New York: Holt, Rinehart and Winston.

Hymer, Stephen H. 1976. *The international operations of national firms: A study of direct investment.* Cambridge, MA: MIT Press.

Kindleberger, Charles P. 1973. *International economics* (fifth edition). Homewood, IL: Richard D. Irwin.

Kmetz, John L. 1984. An information-processing study of a complex workflow in aircraft electronics repair. *Administrative Science Quarterly,* 29: 255–80.

Landsberger, Henry A. 1961. The horizontal dimension in bureaucracy. *Administrative Science Quarterly,* 6: 299–332.

Lawrence, Paul R. & Jay W. Lorsch. 1967. *Organization and environment.* Homewood, IL: Irwin.

Mintzberg, Henry A. 1979. *The structuring of organizations.* Englewood Cliffs, NJ: Prentice-Hall.

Newman, William H. 1975. *Constructive control.* Englewood Cliffs, NJ: Prentice-Hall.

Pavan, Robert J. 1972. The strategy and structure of Italian enterprise. Doctoral dissertation, Harvard Graduate School of Business.

Perlmutter, Howard & Eric Trist. 1986. Paradigms for societal transition. *Human Relations,* 39(1): 1–27.

Prahalad, C.K. & Yves Doz. 1986. *The multinational mission: Balancing local demands and global vision.* New York: Free Press.

Simon, Herbert A. 1977. *The new science of management decision* (revised edition). Englewood Cliffs, NJ: Prentice-Hall.

Stevens, Guy V.G. 1974. The determinants of investments. In John H. Dunning, editor, *Economics analysis and the multinational enterprise,* 47–88. New York: Praeger Publishers.

Stopford, John M. & Louis T. Wells, Jr. 1972. *Managing the multinational enterprise.* New York: Basic Books.

Thomason, G.F. 1966. Managerial work roles and relationships, part I. *Journal of Management Studies,* 3: 270–84.

Thompson, James D. 1967. *Organizations in action.* New York: McGraw-Hill.

Tushman, Michael L. 1978. Technical communication in research and development laboratories: Impact of project work characteristics. *Academy of Management Journal,* 21: 624–45.

———— & David A. Nadler. 1978. Information processing as an integrating concept in organizational design. *Academy of Management Review,* 3: 613–24.

Van de Ven, Andrew H., Andre L. Delbecq & Richard Koenig, Jr. 1976. Determinants of coordination modes within organizations. *American Sociological Review,* 41: 322–38.

Vernon, Raymond. 1971. *Sovereignty at bay: The multinational spread of U.S. enterprise.* New York: Basic Books.

Williams, Charles R. 1967. Regional management overseas. *Harvard Business Review,* 45: 87–91.

Wood, Robert & Albert Bandura. 1989. Social cognitive theory of organizational management. *Academy of Management Review,* 14: 361–84.

INDEX

This is a subject index. Page locators followed by a lowercase f indicate illustrations, while locators followed by lowercase t indicate material in tables. Page numbers followed by an italic lowercase n indicate footnotes. References consisting of italic lowercase n followed by a number indicate end of chapter notes, with the number referring to note number.